The NEW International
Dictionary of
Biblical
Archaeology

The NEW International

Dictionary of Biblical Archaeology

Edward M. Blaiklock

R. K. Harrison
GENERAL EDITORS

David R. Douglass
MANAGING EDITOR

Regency
Reference Library
from Zondervan Publishing House
1415 Lake Drive, S.E., Grand Rapids, Michigan 49506

New International Dictionary of Biblical Archaeology
Copyright © 1983 by The Zondervan Corporation
Grand Rapids, Michigan

Library of Congress Cataloging in Publication Data
Main entry under title:

New international dictionary of biblical archaeology.

   Includes bibliogrphical references.
   1. Bible—Antiquities—Dictionaries.   I. Blaiklock,
E. M.   II. Harrison, R. K. (Roland Kenneth)
BS622.N48   1982   220.9'3'0321   82-13552
ISBN 0-310-21250-2

Printed in the United State of America

83 84 85 86 87 88 89 — 9 8 7 6 5 4 3 2 1

Contents

Editor's Preface

Since this book purports to survey biblical archaeology, the scope, nature, and provenance of the information from which the material is drawn is set forth in comparatively brief form. The field is daunting in extent, and the associated literature is vast. Any scheme of selection and compression will evoke questions and perhaps objections. It reminds one of a remark by Pericles in his famous funeral oration: "One who is familiar with all the facts of the story may think that some point has not been set forth with that fullness which he wishes, and knows it to deserve. On the other hand, he who is a stranger to the matter may be led to suspect exaggeration."

The scholars who have worked on this project have sought judiciously to select, arrange, and focus the material. On a thousand matters of biblical relevance and interest, archaeology is but one of many sources of information, and its special area of contribution should not be isolated from the rest.

Occasional inconsistencies of interpreation, and even of facts (such as in dating), are due sometimes to ambiguous or incomplete evidence, sometimes to differences of perspective, and sometimes to both. In deference to the contributors, each of whom has expertise in the fields in which he or she writes, no effort has been made to completely harmonize all material. The reader will find, however, that inconsistencies are infrequent and seldom involve areas of critical importance.

For a great many people, archaeology has a romantic aura. The modern archaeologist, however, is not a dilettante, treasure hunter, or adventurer, but a scientifically trained investigator who follows careful and proven methods. In excavating mounds, he does not attack them indiscriminately, but generally digs a trench across a selected area of a site to reveal the various levels built up over the centuries.

When a part of the mound, or tell, is exposed, the excavator works downward from the uppermost layer and continues to bedrock if possible, or to the level where the site apparently was first occupied. Numerous techniques have been devised to assist in assessing the significance of what is discovered. These techniques include carbon-14 dating, pollen analysis (*see* PALYNOLOGY), and many other sophisticated procedures that are discussed in this volume.

While archaeologists talk about "excavating a site," the fact is that only a small area of a given location generally can be unearthed to any significant degree. Only a very small percentage of Tell el-Areini (*see* TELL SHEIKH AHMED EL-AREINI) has been uncovered, and the same is true for Arad. At the thirty-hectare (90 a.) site of ancient Ashdod, perhaps 2 percent has been excavated. It is easily possible, therefore, to overlook areas of a site that would provide important information for archaeologists and other Near Eastern scholars. Accurate analysis is especially difficult when one level intrudes on another, whether such is the result of natural causes, such as an earthquake, or is due purely to human activity, such as the cutting of foundation trenches or the construction of storage silos by later residents of the site.

The purpose of biblical archaeology is to recover material remains of man's past, not to "prove" the accuracy or historicity of the Bible. Nevertheless it is important to note that Near Eastern archaeology has demonstrated the historical and geographical reliability of the Bible in many important areas. By clarifying the objectivity and factual accuracy of biblical authors, archaeology also helps correct the view that the Bible is avowedly partisan and subjective. It is now known, for instance, that, along with the Hittites, Hebrew scribes were the best historians in the entire Ancient Near East, despite contrary propaganda that emerged from Assyria, Egypt, and elsewhere.

Advances in the understanding of chronological sequences can be expected to result from the work being undertaken at new sites such as Tell Mardikh (Ebla), from which the first significant data goes back to about 3500 B.C. Once the history of Ebla has been integrated properly with that of other Ancient Near Eastern states, it may well be necessary to revise certain accepted dates.

This book has been designed to be as functional as possible. The readership in view is the growing number of informed, intelligent people who find the Bible vital to their way of life, as well as the student of biblical archaeology and the professional scholar. Our object has not been primarily polemical or evidential. We have sought, within prescribed limits, to present basic facts. Those who use the book must, for the most part, draw their own theological conclusions.

The scholars whose work is offered here hope that they have so written that the casual reader may find in these contributions the beginnings of a wider interest in this important field of study.

Archaeology, like other sciences, is an ever-expanding field. Discoveries of new sites, advances in technology and methodology, more complete correlation and interpretation of data—all these continually add to the body of knowledge. Again, therefore, as in other fields, absolute currency of published materials, especially in book form, is rarely, if ever, possible. But every effort has been made to make this volume as up to date as reasonably possible at the time of release.

E.M. Blaiklock

Acknowledgments

An immense amount of work went into this volume, from initial planning to the final production. It includes the labor of those who painstakingly sifted through the writings, effecting a uniformity of style and consistency of form without detracting from the varied and distinctive modes of expression of the individual authors. For this work two people deserve special thanks. Norma Camp provided much of the groundwork in the long editorial process, including the addition of measurements according to the metric system and the marking of words and names for cross-referencing. David R. Douglass, the managing editor for this project, had the expertise and the determined persistence required to pull everything together and present a well-prepared manuscript to the typesetter. To these, and to others who have labored to make this volume a reality, we express deep-felt gratitude.

The Publisher

List of Contributors

CEA   ARMERDING, Carl Edwin, B.D., Ph.D., Associate Professor of Old Testament, Regent College, Vancouver

EMB   BLAIKLOCK, Edward Musgrave, Litt. D., Emeritus Professor of Classics, University of Auckland

FFB   BRUCE, F. F., M.A., D.D., F.B.A., Rylands Professor of Biblical Criticism and Exegesis (Emeritus), University of Manchester

BCC   CHAPMAN, Benjamin C., Th.M., Ph.D., General Editor, Academic Books, Zondervan Publishing House

JJD   DAVIS, John J., Th.M., Th.D., Professor of Old Testament and Hebrew, Grace Theological Seminary

GGG   GARNER, Gordon G., B.D., Director and Editor, Australian Institute of Archaeology, Melbourne

BFH   HARRIS, Bruce F., B.D., M.A., Ph.D., Associate Professor of History, Macquarie University, Sydney

RKH   HARRISON, R. K., M.Th., Ph.D., Professor of Old Testament, Wycliffe College, University of Toronto

MHH   HEICKSEN, Martin H., M.A., Director of Near East Institute of Archaeology

JEJ   JENNINGS, James E., M.A., Associate Professor of Archaeology, Wheaton College, 1972–1980

KAK   KITCHEN, Kenneth A., Ph.D., Reader in Egyptian and Coptic, School of Archaeology and Oriental Studies, University of Liverpool

WHM   MARE, W. Harold, A.M., B.D., Ph.D., Professor of New Testament; Chairman, Department of New Testament, Covenant Theological Seminary

WJM   MARTIN, W. J., B.Th., Ph.D., former Professor in Old Testament Studies and Vice-Principal, Regent College. Deceased.

HWP   PERKIN, Hazel W., M.A., Headmistress, St. Clements School, Toronto

WFR   RICHARDSON, W. F., M.A., B.D., Senior Lecturer in the Department of Classics and Ancient History, University of Auckland

DBS   SADDINGTON, Denis B., M.A., Ph.D., Professor of Classics, University of Zimbabwe

DWS   SEARLE, David W., L.Th., Staff Lecturer, Australian Institute of Archaeology, Melbourne

JAT   THOMPSON, John Arthur, M.Sc., Ph.D., Senior Lecturer, Department of Middle Eastern Studies, University of Melbourne

WW   WHITE, William, Jr., Th.M., Ph.D., Editorial Director (Science), North American Publishing Co.; Managing Editor (Medical), Emergency Care Research Institute

EY   YAMAUCHI, Edwin, M.A., Ph.D., Professor of History Department, Miami University, Ohio

General Explanations

All the articles, except for brief definitions, are signed. (See List of Contributors, p. x.)

Articles are listed in strict letter, rather than word, order. For example, "Urartu" and "Urfa" are between "Ur" and "Ur, Lamentation over the Destruction of." Common alternate spellings are given in parentheses directly after the main entry word or phrase.

A few sites are discussed under two different headings—for example, Baalbek/Heliopolis and Philadelphia/Rabbah. Corresponding articles have distinctive emphases and generally focus on widely separated time periods.

The basic Bible version quoted in this volume is the New International Version (NIV), though other versions, as well as renderings by contributors, appear frequently. NIV forms and spellings are used in the entry headings, with a few exceptions—such as using the more common "Dead Sea" rather than the NIV "Salt Sea" and the Greek "bema" rather than the NIV "judge's seat," "court," or "judgment seat." Within articles, many forms, spellings, and equivalents of a name or term may be used.

Pronunciations, original language forms, and transliterations that appear directly after main entries relate to the first-listed spelling when there is more than one. Diacritics are not used in the main entries, though they frequently appear within articles. Pronunciations are not given for common English and many well-known biblical words. Since pronunciations of foreign and ancient words vary from region to region and from scholar to scholar—and are necessarily only proximate—the forms given here should be considered as general guides. Transliteration systems likewise vary, but the one followed here (see p. xxii) is commonly used and gives uniformity within the work.

Cross-references are given in a number of forms and locations in order to increase the book's usefulness. Closely related topics and variant names and spellings are listed alphabetically with the main entries and are cross-referenced to the appropriate article or articles. Cross-references within articles most often are indicated by an asterisk (*) directly after the first appearance of a word or phrase. In longer articles an important word or term may be cross-referenced more than once. When an asterisk is not appropriate, the reference is given in parentheses in capital and small capital letters, preceded by "*see*." References of special relevance that are not mentioned within an article are listed at its end, also in capital and small capital letters, and preceded by "*See also*."

For the sake of economy and simplicity, cross-referenced names and terms are not always in precisely the same form as that of the related article title. For example, an asterisk after "chronological" refers to the article "Chronology." Similarly, "Judea" refers to the article "Judah," "chariotry" to "Chariot," "Middle Bronze Age" or "MB II" to "Bronze Age," and so on.

Asterisks are generally placed after the final word of a multiword name or term (such as "Appian Way" or "spectrographic analysis"), in which case the referenced article is to be found under the key word of the name or term—which in the examples just given are "Appian" and "spectrographic," respectively.

Selected bibliographies are listed chronologically by publication dates at the ends of major articles. In some articles, bibliographic data is also given within the text when it has seemed important to note the special relevance of a title to a specific point or subject.

Use of non-English languages (especially the original biblical languages) is frequent, but within the body of articles such words are often only in transliterated form. For the sake of readers not acquainted with these languages, every effort has been made to indicate, by translation or context, essential meaning and significance.

Measurements are most often given in metrics, with English equivalents given in parentheses. Figures are sometimes approximate when exactness is not possible or significant. When ancient measurements, such as the cubit, are cited, the metric equivalent is given in parentheses.

Frequently used technical, bibliographic, and literary terms and titles are usually abbreviated, for which complete lists are given on pages xiii–xxi.

In a work of this size and complexity occasional errors are sure to slip by even the most careful editing and proofreading. The reader's bringing any such errors to the attention of the publisher will be appreciated.

Abbreviations

A. General Abbreviations

A	Codex Alexandrinus	et al.	*et alii*, and others
a.	acre	Ethio.	Ethiopian
abr.	abridged, abridgment	EV	English versions of the Bible
acc.	according	exp.	expedition
add.	addenda	ff.	following (verses, pages)
ad loc.	*ad locum*, at the place	fem.	feminine
Akkad.	Akkadian	fig.	figuratively
Aleph	Codex Sinaiticus	f.n.	footnote
anc.	ancient	ft.	foot, feet
Ap. Lit.	Apocalyptic Literature	gal.	gallon(s)
Apoc.	Apocrypha	gen.	genitive
app.	appendix	Ger.	German
Aq.	Aquila's Greek Translation of the OT	Gr.	Greek
		ha.	hectare
Arab.	Arabic	Heb.	Hebrew
Aram.	Aramaic	Hel.	Hellenistic
art.	article	hist.	history, historical
B	Codex Vaticanus	Hitt.	Hittite
b.	born	ibid.	*ibidem*, in the same place
bib.	biblical	id.	*idem*, the same
bk.	book	i.e.	*id est*, that is
BrM	British Museum	illus.	illustration
C	Codex Ephraemi Syri	impf.	imperfect
c.	*Circa*, about	in.	inch(es)
cent.	century	incl.	inclusive
cf.	*confer*, compare	infra	below
ch., chs.	chapter, chapters	in loc.	*in loco*, in the place cited
cm.	centimeter	inscr.	inscription
cod., codd.	codex, codices	introd.	introduction
col.	column	jour.	journal
comm., comms.	commentary, commentaries	kg.	kilogram
comp.	compiler	kl.	kiloliter
contra	in contrast to	km.	kilometer
cu.	cubic	l., ll.	line, lines
D	Codex Bezae	lang.	language
d.	died	Lat.	Latin
dict.	dictionary	LB	Late Bronze Age
div.	division	lex.	lexicon
DSS	Dead Sea Scrolls	lit.	literal, literally
dyn.	dynasty	LL	Late Latin
E	east	LXX	Septuagint
EB	Early Bronze Age	M	Mishna
ed., edd.	edition, editions; editor (*pl.*, eds.)	m.	meter
e.g.	*exempli gratia*, for example	marg.	margin, marginal
Egyp.	Egyptian	masc.	masculine
EI	Early Iron Age	MB	Middle Bronze Age
encyc.	encyclopedia	mg.	milligram
Eng.	English	mi.	mile
ep., epp.	epistle, epistles	misc.	miscellaneous
esp.	especially	mm.	millimeter

mod.	modern		qt.	quoted
MS, MSS	manuscript, manuscripts		rep.	reprinted
MT	Masoretic text		rev.	revised, reviser, revision
N	north		Rom.	Roman
n., nn.	note, notes		S	south
n.d.	no date		Samar.	Samaritan recension
NE	northeast		Sanh.	Sanhedrin
Nestle	Nestle, ed., *Novum Testamentum Graece*		SE	southeast
			sec.	section
no.	number		Sem.	Semitic
NovTest	*Novum Testamentum*		seq.	sequel, the following
NT	New Testament		ser.	series
NW	northwest		sing.	singular
OB	Old Babylonian		Sumer.	Sumerian
obs.	obsolete		supp., supps.	supplement, supplements
OL	Old Latin		s.v.	*sub verbo*, under the word
om.	omitted		SW	southwest
onom.	onomasticon, onomastic		Targ.	Targum
OP	Old Persian		text.	textual
OS	Old Syriac		Theod.	Theodotion
OT	Old Testament		theol.	theology
p., pp.	page, pages		TR	Textus Receptus
Pal.	Palestine		tr.	translation, translator
par.	paragraph		UBS	United Bible Societies' text
Pers.	Persian		Ugar.	Ugaritic
Pesh.	Peshitta		v., vv.	verse, verses
Phoen.	Phoenician		*VetTest*	*Vetus Testamentum*
pl.	plural		viz.	*videlicet*, namely
pref.	preface		vol.	volume
prob.	probably		vs.	versus
Pseudep.	Pseudepigrapha		VS(S)	Version(s)
pt.	part		Vul.	Vulgate
pub.	published, publisher		W	west
Q	Quelle ("Sayings" source of the Gospels)		wt	weight
			yd.	yard(s)

B. Abbreviations for Modern Translations and Paraphrases

AmT	Smith and Goodspeed, *The Complete Bible, An American Translation*		Mof	J. Moffatt, *A New Translation of the Bible*
			NAB	New American Bible
ASV	American Standard Version, American Revised Version (1901)		NASB	New American Standard Bible
			NEB	New English Bible
			NIV	New International Version
Beck	Beck, *The New Testament in the Language of Today*		Ph	J. B. Phillips, *The New Testament in Modern English*
BV	Berkeley Version (The Modern Language Bible)		Rieu	C.H. Rieu. The Book of Acts
			RSV	Revised Standard Version
GNB	Good News Bible		RV	Revised Version (English, 1881–1885)
JB	Jerusalem Bible			
JPS	Jewish Publication Society Version of the Old Testament		RVm	Revised Version margin
			TCNT	*Twentieth Century New Testament*
KJV	King James Version		TEV	Today's English Version
Knox	R. G. Knox, *The Holy Bible: A Translation from the Latin Vulgate in the Light of the Hebrew and Greek Originals*		Wey	*Weymouth's New Testament in Modern Speech*
			Wms	C. B. Williams, *The New Testament: A Translation in the Language of the People*
LB	Living Bible			

C. Abbreviations for Books of the Bible, the Apocrypha, and the Pseudepigrapha

OLD TESTAMENT

Gen	2 Chron	Dan
Exod	Ezra	Hos
Lev	Neh	Joel
Num	Esth	Amos
Deut	Job	Obad
Josh	Ps(Pss)	Jonah
Judg	Prov	Mic
Ruth	Eccl	Nah
1 Sam	Song of Songs	Hab
2 Sam	Isa	Zeph
1 Kings	Jer	Hag
2 Kings	Lam	Zech
1 Chron	Ezek	Mal

NEW TESTAMENT

Matt	1 Tim
Mark	2 Tim
Luke	Titus
John	Philem
Acts	Heb
Rom	James
1 Cor	1 Peter
2 Cor	2 Peter
Gal	1 John
Eph	2 John
Phil	3 John
Col	Jude
1 Thess	Rev
2 Thess	

APOCRYPHA

1 Esd	1 Esdras	Ep Jer	Epistle of Jeremy
2 Esd	2 Esdras	S Th Ch	Song of the Three Children (or Young Men)
Tobit	Tobit		
Jud	Judith	Sus	Susanna
Add Esth	Additions to Esther	Bel	Bel and the Dragon
Wisd Sol	Wisdom of Solomon	Pr Man	Prayer of Manasseh
Ecclus	Ecclesiasticus (Wisdom of Jesus the Son of Sirach)	1 Macc	1 Maccabees
		2 Macc	2 Maccabees
Baruch	Baruch		

PSEUDEPIGRAPHA

AsMoses	Assumption of Moses	Odes Sol	Odes of Solomon
2 Baruch	Syriac Apocalypse of Baruch	P Jer	Paralipomena of Jeremiah
3 Baruch	Greek Apocalypse of Baruch	Pirke Aboth	Pirke Aboth
1 Enoch	Ethiopic Book of Enoch	Ps 151	Psalm 151
2 Enoch	Slavonic Book of Enoch	Pss Sol	Psalms of Solomon
3 Enoch	Hebrew Book of Enoch	Sib Oracles	Sibylline Oracles
4 Ezra	4 Ezra	Story Ah	Story of Ahikar
JA	Joseph and Asenath	T Abram	Testament of Abraham
Jub	Book of Jubilees	T Adam	Testament of Adam
L Aristeas	Letter of Aristeas	T Benjamin	Testament of Benjamin
Life AE	Life of Adam and Eve	T Job	Testament of Job
Liv Proph	Lives of the Prophets	T Levi	Testament of Levi
MA Isa	Martyrdom and Ascension of Isaish	T 12 Pat	Testaments of the Twelve Patriarchs
3 Macc	3 Maccabees		
4 Macc	4 Maccabees	Zad Frag	Zadokite Fragments

D. Abbreviations of Names of Dead Sea Scrolls and Related Texts

CD	Cairo (Genizah text of the) Damascus (Document)	1Q,2Q, etc.	Numbered caves of Qumran, yielding written material; followed by abbreviation of biblical or apocryphal book.
DSS	Dead Sea Scrolls		
Hev	Nahal Hever texts		
Mas	Masada Texts	QL	Qumran Literature
Mird	Khirbet Mird texts	1QapGen	Genesis Apocryphon of Qumran Cave 1
Mur	Wadi Murabba'at texts		
P	Pesher (commentary)	1QH	*Hodayot* (Thanksgiving Hymns) from Qumran Cave 1
Q	Qumran		

1QIsa$_{a,b}$	First or second copy of Isaiah from Qumran Cave 1	4QNum$_b$	Numbers B text from Qumran Cave 4
1QpHab	Pesher on Habakkuk from Qumran Cave 1	4QPrNab	Prayer of Nabonidus from Qumran Cave 4
1QM	*Milhamah* (War Scroll)	4QSam$_a$	Samuel A text from Qumran Cave 4
1QS	*Serek Hayyahad* (Rule of the Community, Manual of Discipline)	4QSam$_b$	Samuel B text from Qumran Cave 4
		4QTest	Testimonia text from Qumran Cave 4
1QSa	Appendix A (Rule of the Congregation) to 1QS	4QTLevi	Testament of Levi from Qumran Cave 4
1QSb	Appendix B (Blessings) to 1QS	4QPhyl	Phylacteries from Qumran Cave 4
3Q15	Copper Scroll from Qumran Cave 3	11QMelch	Melchizedek text from Qumran Cave 11
4QFlor	Florilegium (or Eschatological Midrashim) from Qumran Cave 4	11QtgJob	Targum of Job from Qumran Cave 11
4Qmess ar	Aramaic "Messianic" text from Qumran Cave 4		

E. Abbreviations of Organizations and Institutions

AIA	Australian Institute of Archaeology	BBC	British Broadcasting Corporation
ASCSA	American School of Classical Studies at Athens	Br. M.	British Museum
		IES	Israel Exploration Society
ASOR	American Schools of Oriental Research	SPCK	Society for the Promoting of Christian Knowledge
ASSU	American Sunday School Union		

F. Abbreviations for Periodicals, Reference Works, and Classical Sources

AA	Alttestamentliche Abhandlungen	ANF	Roberts and Donaldson, *The Ante-Nicene Fathers*
AAA	*Annals of Archaeology and Anthropology*	AnSt	*Anatolian Studies*
AASOR	*Annual of the American Schools of Oriental Research*	ANT	M.R. James, *The Apocryphal New Testament*
AASy	*Les Annales archéologiques de Syrie*	AOTS	Thomas, *Archaeology and Old Testament Study*
AB	*Anchor Bible*	APAW.PH	*Abhandlungen der (k.) preussischen Akademie der Wissenschaften*
ABR	*Australian Biblical Review*		
ActAnt	*Acta Antiqua*	APEF	*Annual of the Palestine Exploration Fund*
AE	*L'Année épigraphique*		
Aen.	Vergil, *Aeneid*	Apol.	Tertullian, *Apologeticus*
AfO	*Archiv für Orientforschung*	APOT	R.H. Charles, *Apocrypha and Pseudepigrapha of the Old Testament*
AIs	R. de Vaux, *Ancient Israel*		
AJA	*American Journal of Archaeology*		
AJP	*American Journal of Philology*	ARAB	D.D. Luckenbill, *Ancient Records of Assyria and Babylonia*
AJS	*American Journal of Anthropology*		
AJSL	*American Journal of Semitic Languages and Literature*	ARC	*Archaeology*
		Arch.Anz.	*Archäologischer Anzeiger*
AJT	*American Journal of Theology*	ARE	J. H. Breasted, *Ancient Records of Egypt*
Alf	Alford, *Greek Testament Commentary*		
		ArOr	*Archiv Orientální*
AMI	*Archäologische Mitteilungen*	Arr.	Arrian
An.	Zenophon, *Anabasis*	AS	*Assyriological Studies*
Anab.	Arrian, *Anabasis*	A-S	Abbot-Smith, *Manual Greek Lexicon of the New Testament*
AncSoc	*Ancient Society*		
ANE	J.B. Pritchard, ed., *The Ancient Near East: Supplementary Text and Pictures*	ASAE	*Annales du service des antiquités de l'Egypte*
		AThR	*Anglican Theological Review*
ANEA	*Ancient Near Eastern Archaeology*	Att.	Cicero, *Epistulae ad Atticum*
ANEP	J.B. Pritchard, ed., *The Ancient Near East in Pictures*	Aug.	Suetonius, *Divus Augustus*
		August.	Augustine
ANET$_{2,3}$	J.B. Pritchard, ed., *Ancient Near Eastern Texts* (2nd ed., 3rd ed.)	AUSS	*Andrews University Seminary Studies*

AustBibArch	Australian Journal of Biblical Archaeology
AW	Aramco World
BA	Biblical Archaeologist
BAAE	Badawy, Architecture in Ancient Egypt and the Near East
BAB	Barton, Archaeology and the Bible
BAG	Bauer, Arndt, and Gingrich, Greek-English Lexicon of the New Testament
BAR	Biblical Archaeologist Reader
BASOR	Bulletin of the American Schools of Oriental Research
BBSAJ	Bulletin of the British School of Archaeology in Jerusalem
BC	Foakes-Jackson and Lake, The Beginnings of Christianity
BCH	Bulletin de correspondence hellénique
BDB	Brown, Driver, and Briggs, Hebrew-English Lexicon of the Old Testament
BDF	Blass, Debrunner, and Funk, A Greek Grammar of the New Testament and Other Early Christian Literature
BDT	Harrison, Baker's Dictionary of Theology
Beng.	Bengel's Gnomon
Ber.	Berytus
BETS	Bulletin of the Evangelical Theological Society
Bibl.Stud.	Biblische Studien
BJRL	Bulletin of the John Rylands Library
Blunt	Blunt, Dictionary of Doctrinal and Historical Theology
BMC	Catalogue of Greek Coins in the British Museum
BP	Berlin Papyri
BrAP	Brooklyn Museum Aramaic Papyri
BS	Bibliotheca Sacra
BT	Babylonian Talmud
BTh	Biblical Theology
BW	C. Pfeiffer, The Biblical World
BWANT	Beiträge zur Wissenschaft vom Alten und Neuen Testament
BWL	Babylonian Wisdom Literature
BZ	Biblische Zeitschrift
BZF	Biblische Zeitfragen
CA	Current Anthropology
CAH	Cambridge Ancient History
CAHrev	Cambridge Ancient History, revised
CanJTh	Canadian Journal of Theology
Cass. Dio	Cassius Dio
CBQ	Catholic Biblical Quarterly
CBSC	Cambridge Bible for Schools and Colleges
CCSL	Corpus Christianorum, Series Latina
CDC	Cairo Genizah Document of the Damascus Covenanters
CE	Catholic Encyclopedia
CGT	Cambridge Greek Testament
CH	Code of Hammurabi
CHS	Lange, Commentary on the Holy Scriptures
ChT	Christianity Today
Cic.	Cicero (Marcus Tullius)
CIG	Corpus inscriptionum graecarum
CIL	Corpus inscriptionum latinarum
Clem.Al.	Clement of Alexandria
CNFI	Christian News from Israel
CNT	E.M. Blaiklock, Cities of the New Testament
ContTM	Concordia Theological Monthly
Corp. Herm.	Corpus Hermeticum
Crem.	Cremer, Biblico-Theological Lexicon of New Testament Greek
CSCO	Corpus scriptorum christianorum orientalium
CSEG	Corpus scriptorum ecclesiasticorum graecorum
CSEL	Corpus scriptorum ecclesiasticorum latinorum
DDB	Davis' Dictionary of the Bible
De Arch.	Vitruvius, De Architectura
De cic. D.	Augustine, De civitate Dei
DeissBS	Deissmann, Bible Studies
DeissLAE	Deissmann, Light from the Ancient East
DeLegAgr	Cicero, De Lege Agraria
Ditt.Or.	W. Dittenberger, Orientis Graecae Inscriptiones Selectae
DJD	Discoveries in the Judean Desert
DMM	Drumm, Mammoths and Mastodons
DOTT	Documents from Old Testament Times
DWHG	Dunbar and Waage, Historical Geology
EA	Tell el-Amarna Tablets
EB	Etudes bibliques
EBC	Bowdie, ed., Ellicott's Bible Commentary, one vol. ed.
EBi	Encyclopedia Biblica
EBr	Encyclopedia Britannica
EDB	Encyclopedic Dictionary of the Bible
EEHL	Encyclopedia of Archaeological Excavations in the Holy Land
EGT	W.R. Nicoll, The Expositor's Greek Testament
ENC	Encounter
EncJud	Encyclopedia Judaica
Epiph.Adv.H.	Epiphanius, Adversus Haereses
EQ	Evangelical Quarterly
ERE	Encyclopedia of Religion and Ethics
ESAR	Economic Survey of Ancient Rome
ETh	Evangelische Theologie
Euseb.Hist.	Eusebius, History of the Christian Church (Historia Ecclesiastica)
Euseb.Onom.	Eusebius, Onomasticon
ExB	The Expositor's Bible
ExBC	The Expositor's Bible Commentary

Exp	*The Expositor*
Exped.	*Expedition*
ExpT	*The Expository Times*
Fam.	Cicero, *Epistulae ad Familiares*
FFR	Filby, *The Flood Reconsidered*
FLAP	Jack Finegan, *Light from the Ancient Past*
FLAPrev	Jack Finegan, *Light from the Ancient Past*, revised
GaR	*Greece and Rome*
Gordon	C.H. Gordon, *Ugaritic Manual*
GR	*Gordon Review*
GTT	J. Simons, *Geographical and Topographical Texts of the Old Testament*
HAT	*Handbuch zum Alten Testament*
HBD	*Harper's Bible Dictionary*
HBH	*Halley's Bible Handbook*
HDAC	*Hastings Dictionary of the Apostolic Church*
HDB	*Hastings Dictionary of the Bible*, 5 vols.
HDBrev.	*Hastings Dictionary of the Bible*, 1 vol, rev. by Grant and Rowley
HDCG	*Hastings Dictionary of Christ and the Gospels*
Hdt.	Herodotus
HE	A.S. Hunt and C.C. Edgar, Loeb Classical Library Collection of Papyri
HERE	*Hastings Encyclopedia of Religion and Ethics*
HGEOTP	Heidel, *The Gilgamesh Epic and Old Testament Parallels*
HGHL	G.A. Smith, *Historical Geography of the Holy Land*
HJ	*Hibbert Journal*
HJP	E. Schürer, *A History of the Jewish People in the Time of Jesus Christ*
HKAT	*Handkommentar zum Alten Testament*
HNT	H. Lietzmann, *Handbuch zum Neuen Testament*
Hom.	Homer
Hor.	Horace
HPN	Gray, *Studies in Hebrew Proper Names*
HR	Hatch and Redpath, *Concordance to the Septuagint*
HTR	*Harvard Theological Review*
HTS	*Harvard Theological Studies*
HUCA	*Hebrew Union College Annual*
IAE	*Iscrizioni Antico-Ebraici Palestinesi*
IB	*Interpreter's Bible*
IBA	D.J. Wiseman, *Illustrations from Biblical Archaeology*
ICC	*International Critical Commentary*
IDB	*Interpreter's Dictionary of the Bible*
IEJ	*Israel Exploration Journal*
IG	*Inscriptiones Graecae*

IG Rom.	*Inscriptiones Graecae, ad res Romanas pertinentes*
Il.	Homer, *Iliad*
ILN	*Illustrated London News*
ILOT	S.R. Driver, *Introduction to the Literature of the Old Testament*
ILS	*Inscriptiones Latinae Selectae*
In Flacc.	Philo, *In Flaccum*
Inscr.Br.Mus.	E.L. Hicks, *Ancient Greek Inscriptions in the British Museum*
INT	E. Harrison, *Introduction to the New Testament*
Int	*Interpretation*
IOT	R.K. Harrison, *Introduction to the Old Testament*
IPN	*Die israelitischen Persoanennamen im Rahmen der germein semitischen Namengehbung*
IrAnt	*Iranica Antiqua*
Iren.Her.	Irenaeus, *Against Heresies*
ISBE	*International Standard Bible Encyclopedia*
ISBErev.	*International Standard Bible Encyclopedia*, rev. ed., 1979–
ITQ	*Irish Theological Quarterly*
Iul.	Suetonius, *Divus Iulius*
JA	*Journal asiatique*
JAA	*Journal of the Archaeological Society of Athens*
JAAR	*Journal of the American Academy of Religion*
JAOS	*Journal of the American Oriental Society*
JASA	*Journal of the American Scientific Affiliation*
JBL	*Journal of Biblical Literature*
JBR	*Journal of Bible and Religion*
JCS	*Journal of Cuneiform Studies*
JE	*Jewish Encyclopedia*
JEA	*Journal of Egyptian Archaeology*
JESHO	*Journal of Economic and Social History of the Orient*
JETS	*Journal of the Evangelical Theological Society*
JFB	Jamieson, Fausset, and Brown, *A commentary on the Old and New Testaments*
JHS	*Journal of Hellenic Studies*
JNES	*Journal of Near Eastern Studies*
Jos.Antiq.	Josephus, *The Antiquities of the Jews*
Jos.Apion.	Josephus, *Against Apion*
Jos.LIfe	Josephus, *Life*
Jos.War	Josephus, *The Jewish War*
JPOS	*Journal of the Palestine Oriental Society*
JQR	*Jewish Quarterly Review*
JR	*Journal of Religion*
JRAI	*Journal of the Royal Anthropological Institute*
JRAS	*Journal of the Royal Anthropological Institute*

JRAS	*Journal of the Royal Asiatic Society*	NED	*New English Dictionary*
JRS	*Journal of Roman Studies*	Ner.	Suetonius, *Nero*
JSJ	*Journal for the Study of Judaism in the Persian, Hellenistic, and Roman Periods*	NHS	Nag Hammadi Studies
		NIC	*New International Commentary*
		NIDCC	J.D. Douglas, *The New International Dictionary of the Christian Church*
JSOR	*Journal of the Society of Oriental Research*		
JSS	*Journal of Semitic Studies*	NKZ	*Neue Kirchliche Zeitschrift*
JT	*Jerusalem Talmud*	NPNFSS	Nicene and Post-Nicene Fathers, Oathera, 2nd series
JTS	*Journal of Theological Studies*		
JTVI	*Journal of the Transactions of the Victoria Institute*	NSI	G.A. Cooke, *Handbook of North Semitic Inscriptions*
KAHL	Kenyon, *Archaeology in the Holy Land*	NTA	E. Hennecke, *New Testament Apocrypha*
KAT	E. Sellin, ed., *Kommentar zum Alten Testament*	NTS	*New Testament Studies*
		OCD	*Oxford Classical Dictionary*
KB	Koehler-Baumgartner, *Lexicon in Veteris Testamenti libros*	Od.	Homer, *Odyssey*
		ODCC	*Oxford Dictionary of the Christian Church*
KD	Keil and Delitzsch, *Commentary on the Old Testament*	ODCCrev.	*Oxford Dictionary of the Christian church, rev. ed.*
KHC	*Kurzer Hand-Kommentar zum Alten Testament*		
		ODEE	*Oxford Dictionary of English Etymology, rev. ed.*
Leg.	Philo, *Legatio ad Gaium*		
Loeb	Loeb Classical Library	OED	*Oxford English Dictionary*
LS	Lewis and Short, *Latin Dictionary*	Off.	Cicero, *De Officiis*
LSJ	Liddell, Scott, and Jones, *Greek-English Lexicon*	OGIS	*Orientis Graeci Inscriptiones Selectae*
LT	A. Edersheim, *The Life and Times of Jesus the Messiah*	OIC	Oriental Institute Communications
		OLZ	*Orientalische Literaturzeitung*
MA	*Monumentum Ancyranum*	OP	Oxyrhynchus Papyri
MCh	*Modern Churchman*	OrSuec	*Orientalia Suecana*
Met.	Ovid, *Metamorphoses*	P.Amh.	Grenfel and Hunt, eds., *The Amherst Papyri*
Meyer	Meyer, *Critical and Exegetical Commentary on the New Testament*		
		Paus.	Pausanias
		PBFIE	Patten, *The Biblical Flood and the Ice Epoc*
MGT	Moulton, *Grammar of New Testament Greek*		
MIOr	*Mitteilungen des Instituts für Orientforschung*	P.BM.	Greek Papyri in the British Museum
		PCDZ	Pennak, *Collegiate Dictionary of Zoology*
MM	Moulton and Milligen, *The Vocabulary of the Greek Testament*		
		Peake	Black and Rowley, ed., *Peake's Commentary on the Bible*
MNT	Moffatt, *New Testament Commentary*		
		PECS	*Princeton Encyclopedia of Classical Sites*
MPL	*Migne Patrologia Latina*		
MSt	McClintock and Strong, *Cyclopaedia of Biblical, Theological and Ecclesiastical Literature*	PEFA	*Palestine Exploration Fund Annual*
		PEFQSt	*Palestine Exploration Fund Quarterly Statement*
MUSJ	*Mélanges de l'université Saint-Joseph*	P.Eleph.	*Elephantine Papyri*, ed. O. Rubensohn
		PEQ	*Palestine Exploration Quarterly*
MWPE	Martin and Wright, *Pleistocene Extinction*	P.Fay.	*The Fayum Papyri*, ed. Grenfell and Hunt
NBC	F. Davidson, Kevin, and Stibbs, *New Bible Commentary*	P.Hib.	*The Hibeh Papyri*, ed. Grenfell and Hunt
		Philo	Philo Judaeus
NBCrev	Guthrie and Motyer, *New Bible Commentary, rev. ed.*	PlinyNH	Pliny (the Elder), *Natural History*
		PlinyEp.	Pliny (the Younger), *Epistulae*
NBD	J.D. Douglas, *New Bible Dictionary*	PNF 1	P. Schaff, *The Nicene and Post-Nicene Fathers*, 1st series
NCB	*New Century Bible*		
NCE	*New Catholic Encyclopedia*	PNF 2	P. Schaff and H. Wace, *The Nicene and Post-Nicene Fathers*, 2nd series
NDB	*Neue deutsche Biographie*		
NEASB	*Near East Archaeological Society Bulletin*		
		PRU	*Le Palais royal d'Ugarit*

P.Ryl.	Catalogue of Greek Papyri in the John Rylands Library	ST	Studia theologica
PSBA	Proceedings of the Society of Biblical Archaeology	Strom.	Clement of Alexandria, Stromateis
		Suet.	Suetonius
P.Tebt.	The Tebtunis Papyri	SWP	Survey of Western Palestine
PTR	Princeton Theological Review	Syll. Graec.	Corpusculum poesis epicae Graecae ludibundae, vol. 2, Syllographi Graeci
PW(PWRE)	Pauly-Wissowa, Real-Encyclopädie der classischen Altertumswissenschaft		
		Syr. D.	Lucian, De Syria Dea
PWsup.	Supplement to PW	Tac.Ann.	Tacitus, Annals (Annales)
QDAP	Quarterly of the Department of Antiquities of Palestine	Tac.Hist.	Tacitus, Histories (Historiae)
		TCERK	L.A. Loetscher, The Twentieth Century Encyclopedia of Religious Knowledge
QJAIA	Quarterly Journal of the Australian Institue of Archaeology		
RA	Revue d'assyriologie et d'archéologie orientale	TDNT	G. Kittel and G. Friedrich, eds., Theological Dictionary of the New Testament (Eng. ed. of TWNT)
RAI	Compt rendu de l'onzieme recontre assyriologique internationale		
		Ter.	Tertullian
RB	Revue Biblique	Theol.	Theology
RdQ	Revue de Qumran	ThLZ	Theologische Literaturzeitung
REJ	Revue des études juives	ThR	Theologische Rundschau
RGG	Die Religion in Geschichte und Gegenwart	ThT	Theology Today
		Thuc.	Thucydides, History
RHA	Revue Hittite et Asianique	TNTC	Tyndale New Testament Commentaries
RHD	Random House Dictionary of the English Language		
		Trench	Trench, Synonyms of the New Testament
RHG	Robertson, Grammar of the Greek New Testament		
		TSBA	Transactions of the Society of Biblical Archaeology
RHPR	Revue d'histoire et de philosophie religieuses		
		TWNT	G. Kittel and G. Friedrich, ed., Theologisches Wörterbuch zum Neuen Testament
RLA	Reallexikon der Assyriologie		
RS	Revue sémitique		
RSO	Revista degli studi orientali	UBD	Unger's Bible Dictionary
RTP	Revue de théologie et de philosophie	UGIOT	Unger, Introductory Guide to the Old Testament
		UT	Gordon, Ugaritic Textbook
RTWB	Richardson, A Theological Wordbook of the Bible	VB	Allmen, Vocabulary of the Bible
		VC	Vigiliae christianae
Sat.	Horace, Satirae	Verg.	Vergil
SBFLA	Studii biblici fransciscani liber annus	Verr.	Cicero, In Verrem
		Vincent	Vincent, Word-Pictures in the New Testament
SBK	Strack and Billerbeck, Kommentar zum neuen Testament aus Talmud und Midrash		
		Vitr.	Vitruvius
		VT	Vetus Testamentum
SBT	I. Epstein, ed., The Babylonian Talmud	VTSup	Vetus Testamentum, Supplements
		WBC	Wycliffe Bible Commentary
SHERK	The New Schaff-Herzog Encyclopedia of Religious Knowledge	WBE	Wycliffe Bible Encyclopedia
		WC	Westminster Commentaries
		WesBC	Wesleyan Bible Commentaries
SIG	Dittenberger, W., Sylloge inscriptionum graecarum, 3rd ed.	WH	Wescott and Hort, The New Testament in Greek
SJT	Scottish Journal of Theology	WO	Die Welt des Orients
Small.	E.M. Smallwood, Documents Illustrating the Principates of Gaius Claudius and Nero	WTJ	Westminster Theological Journal
		Xen.	Xenophon
		ZA	Zeitschrift für Assyrologie
SMS	Syro-Mesopotamian Studies	ZAS	Zeitschrift für Aegyptische Sprache und Altertumskunde
SOT	Girdlestone, Synonyms of the Old Testament		
SOTI	Archer, A Survey of Old Testament Introduction	ZAW	Zeitschrift für die alttestamentliche Wissenschaft
SPap	Studia papyrologica	ZDMG	Zeitschrift der deutschen morgenländischen Gesellschaft
SPEAK	Stanek, The Pictorial Encyclopedia of the Animal Kingdom		
		ZDPV	Zeitschrift des deutschen Palästina-Vereins
SSS	Semitic Study Series		

ZNW	*Zeitschrift für die neutesta-*	ZPEB	*Zondervan Pictorial Encyclopedia*
	mentliche Wissenschaft		*of the Bible*
ZPBA	*Zondervan Pictorial Bible Atlas*	ZST	*Zeitschrift für systematische*
ZPBD	*Zondervan Pictorial Bible Dic-*		*Theologie*
	tionary		
ZPE	*Zeitschrift für Papyrologie und*		
	Epigraphik		

Transliterations

Hebrew

א	=	ʾ	ד	=	$\underline{d}$	י	=	y	ס	=	s	ר	=	r
ב	=	b	ה	=	h	כ	=	k	ע	=	ʿ	שׂ	=	ś
ב	=	$\underline{b}$	ו	=	w	ך כ	=	$\underline{k}$	פ	=	p	שׁ	=	sh
ג	=	g	ז	=	z	ל	=	l	ף פ	=	$\underline{p}$	ת	=	t
ג	=	$\underline{g}$	ח	=	ḥ	ם מ	=	m	ץ צ	=	ṣ	ת	=	th
ד	=	d	ט	=	ṭ	ן נ	=	n	ק	=	q			

(ה)ָ	=	â (h)	ָ	=	ā	ַ	=	a	ֲ	=	^{a}
ֵי	=	ê	ֵ	=	ē	ֶ	=	e	ֱ	=	^{e}
ִי	=	î	ֹ	=	ō	ִ	=	i	ְ	=	^{e} (if vocal)
וֹ	=	ô				ֹ	=	o	ֳ	=	^{o}
וּ	=	û				ֻ	=	u			

Aramaic

ʾ b g d h w z ḥ ṭ y k l m n s ʿ p ṣ q r ś š t

Arabic

ʾ b t ṯ ǧ ḥ ḫ d ḏ r z s š ṣ ḍ ṭ ẓ ʿ ǵ f q k l m n h w y

Ugaritic

ʾ b g d ḏ h w z ḥ ḫ ṭ ẓ y k l m n s ṣ ʿ ǵ p ṣ q r š t ṯ

xxii

Greek

α	—	a	π	—	p	ai	— ai
β	—	b	ρ	—	r	αὐ	— au
γ	—	g	σ,ς	—	s	ϵι	— ei
δ	—	d	τ	—	t	ϵὐ	— eu
ϵ	—	e	υ	—	y	ηὐ	— ēu
ζ	—	z	φ	—	ph	oι	— oi
η	—	ē	χ	—	ch	οὐ	— ou
θ	—	th	ψ	—	ps	υι	— hui
ι	—	i	ω	—	ō		
κ	—	k				ῥ	— rh
λ	—	l	γγ	—	ng	‘	— h
μ	—	m	γκ	—	nk		
ν	—	n	γξ	—	nx	ᾳ	— ā
ξ	—	x	γχ	—	nch	ῃ	— ē
ο	—	o				ῳ	— ō

Vowel Pronunciation Key

a	land, map, Antioch	oi	soil, coin, Troy
ā	cave, spade, Babel	o͝o	brook, book, Uruk
ä	wadi, jar, Armageddon	ou	ground, tower, town
â(r)	square, denarius, Sharon	u	mud, mummy, Lud
e	trench, text, Ebla	ū	lute, tomb, Dumah
ē	street, meter, Nebo	û(r)	turf, urn, Ur
i	rift, dig, Kidron	ə	used for very short vowels:
ī	site, line, Cyprus		a as in distance, Jerusalem
o	sod, rock, Joppa		e as in oven, Colosse
			i as in rarity, Jericho
ō	stone, road, Antonia		o as in ivory, Decapolis
ô	coffin, form, Jordan*		u as in locust, Damascus

* When followed by r, the sound of this vowel is somewhere between ō and ô.

A Select, Annotated List of Current Archaeological Periodicals in English

Prepared by

Gordon G. Garner

Journals that provide up-to-date information relating to biblical archaeology fall broadly into two categories. First are those that deal directly with the subject, that is, with the explicit application of archaeological finds to the study of the Scriptures—background, cultural setting, linguistic data, textual information, and evidence bearing directly or indirectly on historical and exegetical questions.

Second are the periodicals that deal with the archaeology of a particular country or region, or with sites all over the world, with many articles relating to the lands of the Bible. These often provide valuable data for biblical studies but do not necessarily correlate the two. Writers, however, often note significant facts that impinge on biblical history or literature.

In both categories are technical as well as popular works. The technical publications deal with primary source material, excavations, and linguistic surveys or assessments, and are intended more for the specialist. The popular journals largely use secondary sources and are useful to the pastor, teacher, or general Bible student.

Following is a select list of periodicals taken from both these categories as well as from several other areas of related study.

I. General Biblical Archaeology

A. Technical or Semitechnical

Bulletin of the American Schools of Oriental Research (BASOR). Quarterly. Reviews and reports on the Schools' work in Israel, Jordan, Mesopotamia, and other areas. Articles on technical and linguistic subjects. Scholarly work more suited for the specialist. Illus. 80pp.

Annual of the American Schools of Oriental Research (AASOR). Hard cover, single volume. Usually devoted to detailed studies—excavation reports, language study, or topical reviews. For the specialist.

The Biblical Archaeologist (BA). A quarterly of the American Schools of Oriental Research. Reviews of archaeological data related to biblical studies. Reliable but generally less technical than *BASOR* or *AASOR*. A valuable resource for the minister and informed layman. Illus. 64pp.

Other publications. Some universities and societies publish journals that often include archaeological material relevant to the Bible. These include the *Andrews University Seminary Studies (AUSS)*, *The Tyndale Bulletin*, and *Journal for the Study of the Old Testament*. Contents vary considerably in subjects and in level.

B. Popular

Biblical Archaeology Review (BAR). Biblical Archaeological Society, Washington, D.C. Well illustrated, dealing with the archaeology of Bible lands, especially Israel. Quality varies but has generally reliable and popularly written articles, often by competent field workers. Six issues a year 60pp.

Bible and Spade. Quarterly. Word of Truth Productions, New York. Dedicated to "the authentification and illumination of the Holy Scriptures." Popular and strongly conservative.

Buried History. Quarterly review of biblical archaeology. Australian Institute of Archaeology, Melbourne. Reports on current archaeological work in Bible lands, especially that which bears on understanding the Bible. For the preacher and serious Bible student.

Foundations. A short news and reviews sheet. The Foundation for Biblical Research and Preservation of Primitive Christianity, New Hampshire, U.S.A. Focuses on New Testament and early church history.

II. Specific Countries or Areas

Since these works are too numerous to list exhaustively, only those that publish reports most relevant to biblical studies or that deal with Bible lands are included, with brief indications of contents. All are technical but are often helpful to the nonspecialist.

A. Israel

The Israel Exploration Journal (IEJ). Quarterly. Israel Exploration Society, Jerusalem. Good coverage of sites and studies on Israel.

The Palestine Exploration Quarterly (PEQ). Palestine Exploration Fund, London. Twice yearly. Mainly on Palestine but often includes wider coverage of Near East.

Levant. British School of Archaeology in Jerusalem. Annual. Covers Palestine, Syria, Phoenicia, and the Arabian Peninsula.

Tel Aviv. Tel Aviv University Institute of Archaeology. Quarterly. Excavation reports and technical studies, mainly on sites in Israel, but also touches Ancient Near East in general.

Other Israeli publications worth noting:

Atigot (English series).

Eretz Israel. English and Hebrew. For the specialist.

Christian News from Israel. Ministry of Religious Affairs, Jerusalem. Usually one article on archaeology. Popular.

B. Ancient Near East (for the specialist unless otherwise noted)

Journal of Egyptian Archaeology (JEA). Egypt Exploration Society, London. Annual. Specialized studies in Egyptology.

Iraq. British School of Archaeology in Iraq. Annual. General Mesopotamian area.

Sumer. Republic of Iraq Antiquities Department. English, French, and Arabic. Annual. General Mesopotamian area.

Iran. British School of Archaeology in Persia, London, Annual. Iran/Persia.

Iranica Antiqua (IrAnt). English, French, and German. Annual. Iran/Persia.

Anatolian Studies (AnSt). British School of Archaeology at Ankara, London, Annual. Turkey/Asia Minor.

Journal of Near Eastern Studies (JNES). University Chicago. Mainly English. Quarterly. General Mideast.

Archaeology (ARC). Archaeological Institute of America. Quarterly. Deals with any ancient culture. Reliable and popular.

III. Dead Sea Scrolls

Revue de Qumran (RdQ). Paris. English, French, and German. Current scholarly comment. Intended more for the specialist.

IV. New Testament

Bulletin of the John Rylands Library (BJRL). Wide range of subjects, with occasional significant articles on New Testament archaeology or manuscripts.

Journal for the Study of the New Testament. U.K. Occasional articles relating to archaeology.

V. The Classical World

The American Journal of Archaeology (AJA).

The Journal of Roman Studies (JRS).

The Journal of Hellenic Studies (JHS). Covers a wide range of topics, with limited references to New Testament sites and studies.

Chronological Chart of Archaeological and Historical Periods

Paleolithic (Old Stone Age/Pre-Cave)	before 10,000 B.C.
Mesolithic (Middle Stone Age/Cave)	10,000-8,000
Neolithic (New Stone Age)	
Prepottery	8000-5500
Pottery	5500-4000
Chalcolithic (Copper Age)	4000-3000
Bronze Age	
Early (EB)	
EB I	3000-2800
EB II	2800-2500
EB III	2500-2200
EB IV	2200-2000
Middle (MB)	
MB I	2000-1800
MB II	1800-1500
Late (LB)	
LB I	1500-1400
LB II	1400-1200
Iron Age	
Iron I	1200-1000
Iron II	1000-600
Babylonian and Persian periods	586-332
Hellenistic Period	332-37
Roman Period	37 B.C.-A.D. 325

The above divisions and dates reflect those generally accepted in biblical archaeology, though scholars, including the contributors to this volume, do not agree on all details.

The NEW International

Dictionary of Biblical Archaeology

A

AARON'S TOMB. The death and burial of Aaron is described in three biblical passages: Num 20:22–29; 33:37–39; and Deut 10:6 (cf. 32:50). His death was preannounced by Moses, and together with Eleazar, Aaron's son, they went up to the top of Mount Hor, where the latter was commissioned as the new high priest with ceremonial transfer of garments. Aaron died there at the age of 123 and was buried.

The identification of Mount Hor presents some difficulty by reason of (1) the differences in terminology (cf. "Moserah," Deut 10:6); and (2) the need for a topographic situation which would enable the events on the mount to be seen by all ("in the sight of the whole congregation"); as well as (3) the continuing uncertainties concerning the actual route followed in the Exodus. Two locations have valid reasons to be considered.

1. *Jebel Haroun*, just W of Petra* on the edge of the mountains of Edom,* has long been identified as Mount Hor. This tradition existed before the time of Josephus (Jos. Antiq. 4.4.7), and Eusebius said the tomb of Aaron was near Petra.* The peak, which is about 1336 m. (4382 ft.) in height has on its top a Muslim *weli*, or shrine, built on or forming part of an early Christian church from the time of Justinian (A.D. 527–65), all in memory of Aaron's burial. Eusebius's *Onomasticon** also agrees with the Jebel Haroun identification and its location "on the border of Edom" (Num 33:37). Though it is evident from Deut 2:5 that not the slightest part of Mount Seir (Edom) was to be given Israel, this exclusion need not be classified as a territorial concession. Certainly Jebel Haroun was not "in the midst of Edom," as frequently suggested.

2. *Moserah* (Deut 10:6), about 12–15 km. (7.5–9.3 mi.) NE of Kadesh Barnea,* is usually identified with Jebel el-Medhra (Har ha-Har), on the route toward Arad.* It is a high, steep-sided hill with a flat top that stands up from the surrounding terrain on every side. On its summit is evidence of occupation during antiquity, but its identification with Mount Hor is uncertain, though subscribed to by such eminent authorities as Aharoni and Glueck.

It may be noted that the passage in Num 33 records the death of Aaron immediately following the list of encampments on the way to Mount Hor, and Deut 10:6 may refer to the place from which the people turned eastward in their journey, or to the place from which the funeral procession traveled to the mountain on which the described events occurred. Substance to this interpretation may be derived from the etymology of the name Moserah used

in the accusative sense: "(to the) place of affliction."

Further archaeological exploration of both sites will be necessary before anything approaching proper identification is possible.

BIBLIOGRAPHY: *Map of Israel*, 1:250,000, Sheet 3, Israel Ministry of Labor, Survey Department (1958), Coordinates 030 N., 150 E.; N. Glueck, *Rivers in the Desert* (1959), 205–6; Y. Aharoni, *The Land of the Bible* (1967), 184–85.

MHH

ABEL-SHITTIM. *See* SHITTIM.

ABILA (ab'i lə; Gr. Ἀβίλα, *Abila*). The city, modern Tell Abil, was a center connected with Abilene,* a region of Anti-Lebanon 29 km. (18 mi.) NW of Damascus.* The remains of the ancient site are near the village of Es-Suk. Eusebius lists it as a city of the Decapolis,* an assertion supported epigraphically by an inscription of Hadrian* from the vicinity of Palmyra.* Pliny omits Abila from his catalog of the Ten Towns, but the full list is far from certain, and the exact number, whatever the nature of their federation, need not be pressed. Coinage remains from the time of Pompey to that of Caracalla and suggests a place of some importance.

See ABILENE.

BIBLIOGRAPHY: E. G. Kraeling, *Bible Atlas* (1956), index ref. A5 XIV, XV, XVI; H. H. Rowley, *The Teach Yourself Bible Atlas* (1960), 12:C4, 26:C4.

EMB

ABILENE (ab i lēn'ə; Gr. Ἀβιληνή, *Abilēnē*). A small territory with its city, Abila,* in the Anti-Lebanon mountains NE of Mount Hermon,* and NW of Damascus;* ruled by Lysanias* the tetrarch according to Luke 3:1.

Archaeological evidence for Abilene includes two Greek and two Latin inscriptions and some Greco-Roman ruins. The Greek inscriptions, similar in wording, both speak of Lysanias the tetrarch and were found in the area of ancient Abilene. One (*CIG*, 4521) was found by Pococke at Nebi-Abil, the word *Abil* no doubt being derived from the name of the ancient city, Abila. The other was discovered by P. R. Savignac in the same area near the village of Suk Wadi Barada. This location of Abila accords with the *Itinerarium Antonini* and the Peutinger Tables, which place it about 30 km. (18 mi.) from Damascus on the road to ancient Heliopolis.* *See* also Jos. Antiq. 18.237 and 19.275 for references to this tetrarchy of Abila.

The Greek inscriptions indicate that this tetrarchy

Pottery figurine of woman in bath from ez-Zib cemetery excavation. Iron Age II. Courtesy Israel Dept. of Antiquities and Museums.

was ruled by a Lysanias before Tiberius's death as shown by the occurrence in both of the title Sebastoi, the plural form not occurring before it was applied to Tiberius (A.D. 14–37) and his mother, Livia.

The two Latin inscriptions found on a rock wall near Abila are from c. A.D. 165 and speak of the Abilenians. All this agrees with Luke 3:1.

BIBLIOGRAPHY: E. Robinson, *Biblical Researches in Palestine*, III (1857), 478–84; E. Schürer, *History of the Jewish People*, I, ii (1891), 335–39; H. Leclercq, "Lysanias d'Abilene," *Dictionnaire d'Archaeologie*, X (1931), 406–11; E. G. Kraeling, *Bible Atlas* (1956), index ref. A5 XIV; B4 XV, XVI; Emilio Gabba, *Iscrizioni Greche e Latine per lo Studio della Bibbia* (1958), 47–49; F. F. Bruce, *The New Testament Documents*, 2d ed., rev. (1960), 87–88; T. C. Mitchell, *ZPEB*, 1 (1975), 14f.

WHM

ABLUTIONS. A technical designation for ceremonial lustrations, referring to the washing of the human body rather than to the cleansing of other objects, such as clothes.* Ritual ablutions with water were required of priests and Levites before certain ceremonial occasions (Exod 30:20; Lev 8:6; Num 8:21) and were also prescribed for a variety of impure and unclean conditions (Lev 14:9; 15:13; Num 19:10). In Isa 1:16 and 4:4, water is used figuratively to describe

cleansing from sin, a usage found in the NT with special reference to baptism* (Eph 5:26, Titus 3:5). In Heb 6:2 the author alludes to pointless arguments about the relative merits of Christian and other ablutions, while in 9:9–10 he notes that the ritual washings of Leviticus have been outmoded by the work of Christ.

In the OT, the most familiar objects connected with ceremonial ablutions were the lavers (basins*) of the Solomonic temple (1 Kings 7:38). These vessels consisted of round bronze* bowls fitted into a square framework (cf. 2 Chron 6:12–13) and contained water for cleansing for the sacrificial offerings (2 Chron 4:6). An analogous tripod base that originally held a metal laver has been recovered from Ras Shamra (Ugarit*).

At Qumran* a number of cisterns* were unearthed, one of which had fourteen stone steps leading down into it, suggesting that it had been used for ritual ablutions by the religious community there. According to their literature, the sectaries believed that, by indulging in ceremonial washings, they received sanctification of the spirit and the power to live blamelessly in the precepts of the Torah.

From the er-Ras cemetery at ez-Zib, a striking pottery* figurine of a woman taking a bath in a shallow container was recovered. Dated about 800 B.C., it is reminiscent of 2 Sam 11:2.

BIBLIOGRAPHY: J. M. Allegro, *The Dead Sea Scrolls* (1956), 85, 87, 89–90, 170; plates 27, 30.

RKH

ABU GHOSH (ab'ū gōsh). An Arab village 14 km. (8½ mi.) W of Jerusalem,* bearing the name of a chieftain famous for exacting tribute from pilgrims in the nineteenth century. It is also called Qariet el Enab ("Village of the Grapes") or El Qarie. Nearby is the modern Kibbutz Kiryat 'Anavim ("Village of Grapes"), founded in 1920. The height dominating Abu Ghosh is Tell el-Azhar, or Deir el Azhar ("The Mound, or Monastery, of Eleazar"), originally the site of Kiriath Jearim* ("Town of Forests"). Kiriath Jearim is mentioned in Josh 15:9, Judg 18:12, 1 Sam 7:1, and 2 Sam 6:2 (where it is called Baalah of Judah; Baalah = "possessor"). It had apparently been named Kiriath Baal at first (cf. Josh 15:60; 18:14). The ark* of the covenant* was kept here for twenty years in the care of Eleazar, at the house of his father, Abinadab, before being brought up to Jerusalem by David (1 Sam 7:1; 1 Chron 13:5; cf. Ps 132:6).

Excavations were carried out by the Abbé Moreau in 1901 and at the Crusader church below the village during the 1930s by the École Biblique et Archéologique Française. A cistern* and inscription of the Tenth Roman Legion was found. On Tell el-Azhar itself the French Sisters of St. Joseph of the Apparition built, in 1924, the Monastery of the Ark and erected a huge statue* of the Virgin, which is now the principal landmark of the area. Tiles of the Tenth Legion indicate that the Roman camp was located on the hill. The monastery was built on the ruins of a fifth century Byzantine* church, beneath which parts of a still earlier synagogue* mosaic have been found.

Jean Perrot, in excavations for the Centre de recherches préhistoriques français (1967–68, 1970), discovered a prehistoric square building of the Tahunian (prepottery Neolithic*) culture at Abu Ghosh.

BIBLIOGRAPHY: *ISBE*, 3:1811–12; J. Perrot, *Syria*, 29 (1952), 119ff; R. de Vaux and A. M. Steve, *Fouilles a Qaryet el-enab (Abu Gosh) Palestine* (1950); F. T. Cooke, "The Site of Kirjath-jearim," *AASOR*, 5 (1923-24), 105-20, *EEHL*, 1 (1975), 3–8; *IEJ* 17 (1967), 266–67; 19 (1969), 115–16; 20 (1970), 222–23; 21 (1971), 226.   JEJ

ABU HABBA. See SIPPAR.

ABU MATAR (a'bū ma'tär). A Bronze Age tell near Beersheba* excavated from 1952 to 1954 by J. Perrot. It is noted for its underground houses and traces of copper smelting (*see* METALLURGY) operations and contains a considerable number of pottery* and art relics. The two or three centuries of activity in the locality during the second half of the fourth millennium B.C. have put the term "Beersheba culture" into Palestinian archaeology.

BIBLIOGRAPHY: R. de Vaux, *CAH*, 1, Part 1 (1970), 524–25, 527, 530.

EMB

ABU SIMBEL (á bū sim'bəl). A large rock-cut temple on the Nile in Nubia.* It was built by Ramses II,* the most powerful pharaoh of the Nineteenth Dynasty (c. 1290–1224 B.C.). The temple, well known for its four immense statues* of the king, is located between the first and second cataracts of the Nile. It is well situated, so that the rising sun will penetrate its deepest halls and cause the figures of the gods to blaze with sunlight. Two important inscriptions are known from Abu Simbel*—the hieroglyphic* version of the Asiatic campaigns of Ramses II, including the invasion of Palestine, and the battle of Kadesh, which ended inconclusively and forced Ramses to sign a peace treaty with the Hittites.* The text of the treaty was carved on the walls of the temple at Karnak (*see* THEBES) and on the wall of Ramses's tomb, the Ramesseum. A parallel and somewhat more objective version in Hittite has been excavated at Boghazköy,* ancient Hatti. The other important inscription in the temple of Abu Simbel is a long graffito* carved on the leg of one of the colossal statues on the front of the temple. It was scratched there by a Greek mercenary of Pharaoh Psammetichus II (594–588 B.C.) and is one of the earliest Greek inscriptions known from Egypt.* In recent decades the form and substance of Hittite treaties have become important in understanding the form of Deuteronomy and other books. The building of the Aswan* Dam by Russian and Egyptian engineers threatened the Abu Simbel temple with flooding. A worldwide concern for the great archaeological sites led to the raising of the temple in an engineering feat rivaling that of the original builders.

BIBLIOGRAPHY: J. Vandier, *Manuel D'Archeologie Egyptienne* T.II (1955), 944–71; A. Gardiner, *The Kadesh Inscriptions of Ramesses II* (1960); M. G. Kline, *Treaty of the Great King* (1963); W. MacQuitty, *Abu Simbel* (1965).   WW

ABYDOS (ə bi'dəs; Gr. 'Aβύδος, *Abydos*). An Egyptian city located on the W bank of the Nile, between Asyut and Luxor.* One of the most famous and important ancient cities of Egypt,* Abydos was a religious center second only to Thebes.* The area figured as a royal necropolis* from the time of the First Dynasty and reached its zenith of influence during the Ramesside period. Multitudes of Egyptians made pilgrimage to the shrines of Abydos, considered to be the holiest of all sanctuaries. For generations it was customary to include ritual barks in tombs or to symbolically depict a journey by boat on tomb stelae,* the journey representing the deceased person's actual or intended pilgrimage to Abydos.

The importance of the city lay in its religious history. At first sacred to the jackal-god Wepwawet, and later to Khenti-Amentiu, the city soon came to be identified in mythology with Osiris,* god of vegetation, resurrection, and the underworld. Osiris had been murdered by the god Seth and cut into numerous pieces, each buried in a different place. Abydos claimed to possess his head, and by the Fifth Dynasty it seems that the tomb of the First Dynasty King Zer was associated, though wrongly, in popular consciousness with this sacred location. Nothing else in Egyptian religion equaled the public enthusiasm generated by the Osiris cult. Ceremonies reenacting the passion of Osiris were held, and vast quantities of pottery* and other votive offerings were brought to the shrine, where the triad of Osiris, Isis, and the younger Horus were venerated.

The capital of the first two dynasties was located at Thinis, a few km. S of Abydos. For some reason unknown to us, the site was chosen for the royal tombs. Abydos became a favorite building site by later pharaohs. Khufu, builder of the great pyramid,* presumably erected the Fourth Dynasty temple of Khenti-Amentiu. Senusert III of the Twelfth Dynasty sent his chief treasurer, Ikhernofre, to provide the temple of Osiris with furniture inlaid with gold,* silver,* and lapis lazuli.* The grandest temples on the site, and still among the most outstanding tourist attractions in Egypt, were those built by Seti I and his successor, Ramses II,* between 1309 and 1224 B.C. Characterized by massive pylons, open courts, and colonnades, these temples and their associated chapels contain, in addition to the usual adulatory inscriptions, splendid reliefs depicting various stages of the Osiris ceremony and important king lists that provide historical information.

In terms of modern research it is natural that Abydos should have received considerable attention. Mariette excavated extensively at the great temples of Seti I and Ramses II, as well as in the necropolis,* but he discovered no tombs earlier than the Sixth Dynasty. E. Amélineau, a French scholar of Coptic with no archaeological experience, began digging at Abydos in 1895. On a low spur of sand about 1.5 km. (1 mi.) W of the cultivated valley, he dug into an area called Umm el Ka'ab ("mother of pots") by the natives because of the vast quantities of potsherds (*see* SHARD) strewn on the surface. He found a group of crude brick tombs in pit form, of which the mastaba* superstructure had been robbed. Large central chambers, surrounded by numerous smaller rooms, proved to be the royal tombs of the kings of the First and Second Dynasties.

Fortunately for Egyptology, this unscientific and devastating work was salvaged by Sir Flinders Petrie, who meticulously reexcavated the site in 1899 and published the findings rapidly in memoirs of the Egypt Exploration Fund. Later campaigns were conducted by Eduard Naville and T. E. Peet. The inscriptions and jar sealings recovered by Amélineau and Petrie allowed Egyptologists Griffith and Sethe (working independently) to reconstruct much of Manetho's* First and Second Dynasties.

See OSIRIS; RAMSES II.

BIBLIOGRAPHY: E. Amélineau, *Les Nouvelles fouilles d'Abydos*, 4 vols. (1899–1905); W. M. F. Petrie, *Royal Tombs of the Earliest Dynasties*, 2 vols. (1900–1901); W. M. F. Petrie and others, *Abydos*, 3 vols. (1902–4). JEJ

ABYSSINIA. See ETHIOPIA.

ACCA. See ACCO.

ACCAD. See AKKAD.

ACCO (ACCHO; ACRE) (ak'o; Heb. עַכּוֹ, *'akkô*; Gr. Ἀχχω, *akchō*). NT Ptolemais. The ancient city is identified with modern Tell el Fukhkhâr, a town 14½ miles N of Haifa on the Bay of Acre. In Judg 1 it is included in the territory of Asher. Paul landed at

Ptolemais in A.D. 58 when he returned from his third missionary journey. He greeted the Christians and spent a day with them (Acts 21:7). Egyptian Execration Texts* refer to the town c. 1900 B.C. under the designation *'ky*, and the Amarna Letters* mention the city as Acca. Because of its strategic geographical position at the intersection of principal land and sea routes (the Via Maris and the Esdraelon–Jezreel highway), Acco was repeatedly brought under the control of competing powers. Thutmose III, Seti I, and Ramses II* successively subdued the town, as did Sennacherib* and Ashurbanipal* at a later period (cf. ANET, 287, 300). The latter's rigorous measures decimated and enslaved the population, and were a vivid foretaste of the city's later history. It was fortified by Ptolemy* II Philadelphus in 261 B.C. and renamed Ptolemais in his honor, only to be lost by his grandson, Ptolemy IV, to Antiochus III of Syria in 219 B.C. After a checkered political history in the days of the Maccabees (cf. 1 Macc 5:15; 10:51–66; 11:21–74; 12:39–48), it became an important Roman city* with a considerable Jewish population. Its most flourishing period was from the First Crusade onward, when, under the name St. Jean d'Acre, it became the chief Crusader seaport in the Holy Land. Nearly 100,000 Crusaders died in the fierce struggle for the fortress between 1189 and 1191. Other famous battles occurred in 1291, when the Mamelukes finally expelled the Crusaders from the Holy Land; in 1801, when Napoleon failed to capture it; and in 1948, when the city fell to the Israelis.

Archaeological exploration at Acco has been lim-

Aerial view of Acre from north to southwest. *(See also photo under* MIRROR.*)* Courtesy Israel Government Press Office.

ited. Tell el Fukhkhâr (Mound of Potsherds), 1.5 km. (1 mi.) outside the Crusader walls, is presumed to be the site of the Canaanite city. Because Asher failed to take Acco for the Israelites, it remained an important Phoenician* city. The town of the third and second millennia B.C. was confined to the area of the mound, but in the Persian period the inhabitants spread along the seacoast. In the Persian and Hellenistic periods the population may have reached 100,000, but Caesarea* in the Roman period supplanted Acco as the major Palestinian* seaport.

The classical ruins are extensive but scattered, and very little remains to be seen. The refectory of the Hospice of the Knights of St. John was cleared by the Israel Department of Public Works and the National Parks Authority, beginning in 1955 under a grant from the American Embassy. The Israel Department of Antiquities supervised the work and conducted excavations in 1956 and again in 1960. Additional excavations from 1959 to 1962 under a nearby Arab school uncovered the Crusader infirmary.

Underwater explorations (see ARCHAEOLOGY, UNDERWATER) in 1966 and cemetery excavations in 1967 were both carried out by the Israel Antiquities Department.

Major excavations in the ancient Canaanite and Israelite city began in 1973 under Dr. Moshe Dothan, with sponsorship by Haifa University, the Hebrew University, and the Israel Department of Antiquities.

In area B on the slope, an MB II rampart was discovered, with subsequent LB I occupation and Iron I fill of the twelfth to tenth centuries B.C. Area A stratification reveals evidence of an Iron II destruction (attributed to Ashurbanipal) in level 6. Level 5 represents late Phoenician and neo-Babylonian materials. Level 4 is Persian, with two later levels of Hellenistic occupation, ending with the latest settlement on the mound in the last half of the second century B.C. Some Crusader and Mameluke remains were also found (level 1).

In area E, 400 m. (1300 ft.) W of the tell, a late Persian stratum was followed by a round tower of Hellenistic date and what may be an early Roman foundry. Late Roman and Byzantine materials represent the latest occupation in this section of the excavation.

BIBLIOGRAPHY: M. Dothan, *IEJ* 23 (1973), 257–58; *IEJ* 24 (1974), 44–49; 276–79; *IEJ* 25 (1975), 163–66; *IEJ* 26 (1976), 207–8; *IEJ* 27 (1977), 241–42; Zeev Goldman, "The Hospice of the Knights of St. John in Akko," *Archaeological Discoveries in the Holy Land*, *AIA* (1967), 199–206; Y. H. Landau, "A Greek Inscription from Acre," *IEJ* 11 (1961), 118–26; E. T. Hall, A. Flinder, E. Lindner, "Acre," *RB* 75 (1968), 421–22; A. F. Rainey, *ZPEB*, 1 (1975), 33–34.

JEJ

ACHOR, VALLEY OF (ā'kôr; Heb. עֵמֶק עָכוֹר, *'emeq 'ākôr*, "valley of trouble"). A valley on the border between Benjamin and Judah, notable as the place of the stoning of Achan and his family after Israel's initial defeat at Ai* (Josh 7:1–26). Its exact location is unknown and a considerable range of scholarly opinion has developed from the facts that the biblical references are vague, and that there are few definitely established geographic indicators. It is clear from the text that the valley is somewhere between Jericho* and Jerusalem.* The word *achor* means "trouble" and could refer to any of the valleys leading up into the central hill country from the Jordan Valley, or even to parts of the valley itself. One group of experts places Achor in the Buqeiah, a broad valley within the Judean Desert, paralleling the Dead Sea.*

A review of the biblical evidence gives some clues that may be helpful in fixing the probable location. First of all, some renderings (NASB, RSV) of Josh 7:24 describe Achor as "up" from Gilgal. Josh 15:1–7 has the fullest description of the valley's location, inasmuch as Achor is included in the list of landmarks or sites that delineate the N border of Judah.* Many of these places are unknown, but the N shore of the Dead Sea and the Pass of Adummim are both easily fixed. Achor is somewhere between them. If it is the valley just N of Adummim, as verse 7 implies, then it could logically be identified with the Wadi Qelt. It is interesting that the parallel description of Benjamin's S border (Josh 18:15–19) fails to mention either Debir* or the Valley of Achor and refers to Beth Gilgal as Geliloth (cf. Neh 12:29). The Stone of Bohan the Son of Reuben, formerly identified with Hajar el Asbah, may be one of the large landmarks on either side of the highway at the point of entering the hill country—Rujm el Qibliyeh or Rujm esh-Sherqiyeh, according to a suggestion by Noth. Aharoni's identification of Beth Hoglah with Deir Hajla and of Beth Arabah with Ain Gharbeh should be accepted; both are in an approximate line running from the shore of the Dead Sea to the opening of the Wadi Qelt. The text seems to require Beth Arabah to be near or at the base of the hills.

J. Simons associates the Debir of Josh 15:7 with the Wadi Debr and a place near its head, Tughret ed-Debr. The "Waters of En Shemesh" correspond to the Apostle's Fountain on the old Roman road.* Using the following fixed points as a basis for identification, the Wadi Qelt is again indicated: En-Shemesh (Apostle's Fountain), Debir (Tughret ed-Debr), Pass of Adummim (Tal'at ed-Damm), Stone of Bohan (possibly Rujm esh-Sherqiyeh), Beth Hoglah (Deir Hajla), mouth of Jordan (N end of Dead Sea). This process yields a line roughly E-W from the mouth of the Jordan to Jerusalem and points to the Wadi Qelt (just N of Adummim) as being the Valley of Achor. Achor can hardly be very far N of the Wadi Qelt in any case, since it forms the S border of Benjamin, and the tribe's N border is just N of Jericho.* Wadi Qelt fits the data better than either of the adjacent wadis,* Wadi Maquq on the N or Wadi Og on the S. It is difficult to *see* how the area around Nebi Musa can fit into the border description at all.

Two other references add credibility to the identification. Sharon is paralleled with Achor in Isa 65:10, apparently as eastern and western antipodes of the land, and Achor as a "door of hope" in Hos 2:15 recalls the route of the invading Israelites. The prophet declares that "There [Israel] will sing as in the days of her youth, as in the day she came up out of Egypt."

BIBLIOGRAPHY: J. Simons, *The Geographical and Topographical Texts of the Old Testament* (1959), 271; Y. Aharoni, *The Land of the Bible* (1967), 235–36; L. E. Stager, "Farming in the Judean Desert During the Iron Age," *BASOR*, 221 (1976), 145–58.   JEJ

ACRE. *See* ACCO.

ACROPOLIS (ə krop'ə lis; Gr. ἀκρόπολις, *akropolis*). Acropolis is simply the Greek for "upper, or higher, city," a citadel, like the Capitol Hill of Rome* or the Polynesian *pa* sites on the volcanic cones of Auckland. In Attic writers and in general modern parlance it is preeminently the Acropolis of Athens,* a vast rocky outcrop, precipitous on its northern and eastern flanks, steeply sloping to the S, but more accessible from the W. The top forms an oval of about 300 by 150 m. (1000 by 500 ft.).

From earliest times the Athenian acropolis was a sanctuary, particularly dedicated to Athena. Cimon built great retaining walls on the S and E in the fifth century before Christ, and it was there that Athena's temple, the Hecatompedon, was located. After its complete destruction in the Persian Wars, the whole complex was made magnificent by Pericles with the buildings whose amazing fragments and ruins still remain as monuments to the golden age of Attic culture—the Parthenon, the Erechtheum, and the small temple of the Wingless Victory. The colossal statue of the Athena Promachus stood between the Propylaea,* the magnificent staired and columned approach to the Acropolis, and the Parthenon.

For the Bible student, the interest of the Parthenon and its astonishing relics of Attic culture lies in the fact that all the structures mentioned, already then five hundred years old, were in full view of the Areopagus* ("Hill of Ares," or Mars Hill) an adjacent and smaller outcrop of stone, when Paul spoke there (Acts 17). At least for some of its functions the court met on this eminence, and the verses quoted below seem to be evidence that the apostle's apologia for his preaching in Athens was made here.

It was therefore against a background of surpassing pagan magnificence, much of which distressed him, that Paul uttered the words of Acts 17:24, 29–30. His audacity, prompted by his Jewish horror of idolatry (vs. 16), is no more remarkable than the tolerance of those who, in a city of such proud antiquity so artistically adorned, permitted, without adverse comment, such freedom of speech.

BIBLIOGRAPHY: W. A. McDonald, "Archaeology and St. Paul's Journeys in Greek Lands: Part II, Athens," *BA*, 4 (1941), 1–10; I. T. Hill, *The Ancient City of Athens* (1953); The American School of Classical Studies at Athens, *The Athenian Agora, A Guide to the Excavations* (1954); O. Broneer, "Athens, City of Idol Worship," *BA*, 21 (1958), 2–28; J. Finegan, *IDB*, 1 (1962), 307–9; A. Rupprecht, *ZPEB*, 1 (1975), 403–9.   EMB

ACROSTIC. An acrostic is a poem or other artificial composition in which the first or other selected let-

ters of lines or phrases form a word, phrase, or sentence. The Greek word for "fish" (*ichthus*) can be built out of the initial letters of the Greek words for "Jesus Christ, God's Son, Savior." Hence the secret sign of the fish found in the catacombs* frequented by the early Christians. This symbol is found in conjunction with the first dated inscription (A.D. 234) to be accompanied by an emblem of any sort, and at least a hundred examples go back to the third century. Later, no doubt with the end of persecution and of need to communicate in cryptic (*see* CRYPTOGRAM) forms, the symbol disappeared. Both Eusebius and Augustine quote early Christian writings containing the word "fish" used acrostically (e.g., August. *De civ. D.* 18.23). The symbol also occurs in an Alexandrian catacomb. Indeed, since the symbol is first mentioned by Clement of Alexandria, it could have had its origin in the allegorizing school of interpretation that sprang up there. Jewish Christians of that city would have been familiar enough with such acrostic coinage, for it was claimed in some quarters that the title of the apocryphal Book of Maccabees* was built out of the initial Hebrew letters of their battle cry: "Who is like unto Thee, O Lord, among the gods?"

See CATACOMBS; FISHING, FISHERMAN.

BIBLIOGRAPHY: F. Dornseiff, *Das Alphabet in Mystik Und Magie* (1922); J. B. Payne, *ZPEB*, 1 (1975), 38.   EMB

ACZIB (ACHZIB) (ak'zib; Heb. אַכְזִיב, *'ăkzîb*, "a deception"). 1. A town identified with ez-Zib, 18 km. (11 mi.) N of modern Acre (Acco*). The site was excavated in 1959 and 1960, and again in 1963, under the joint auspices of the University of Rome* and the Israel Department of Antiquities. During this time levels of culture from the Phoenician* period to Persian times were studied. During the Hebrew settlement, the Asherites, to whom the coastal city had been given (Josh 19:29–31) were unable to dispossess the Canaanite* inhabitants and were compelled to live in association with them (Judg 1:31). During the

Clay figure kneading dough in trough; Iron Age II. From Aczib. Courtesy Israel Dept. of Antiquities and Museums.

Hellenistic period the site became known as Ekdippa and was important as a trading center because of its position on the road between Tyre* and Acco (Ptolemais). References in Josh 11:1; 12:20; 19:25, which speak of Acshaph are sometimes thought to be connected with Aczib. Though both sites have Bronze Age foundations, only Acshaph is mentioned in the nineteenth-century B.C. Egyptian Execration Texts,* the Karnak inscription of Thutmose III (c. 1490–1436 B.C.), the fourteenth-century B.C. Amarna Letters,* and the thirteenth-century B.C. Papyrus Anastasi.* Acshaph was perhaps the modern Tell Kisan, some 11 km. (7 mi.) SE of Acco.

2. A town in the Judean Shephelah,* probably the Kezib of Gen 38:5 and the Cozeba of 1 Chron 4:22. Perhaps the site was that of the modern Tell el-Beida.

BIBLIOGRAPHY: E. G. Kraeling, *Bible Atlas* (1956), 149; index refs. D2 III; B3 VI, VII, VIII, IX, X, XIV, XV, XVI; C4 XI; E. S. Kalland, *ZPEB*, 1 (1975), 38.

EMB

ADANA (ə dā′nə). A town in Turkey on the Seyhan River at the extreme NE of the Mediterranean, the site of an ancient kingdom, called Adaniya in Hittite* and Hurrian inscriptions. A city, Adanat, which may be a variant form of the name is mentioned in a cuneiform* tablet from Alalakh* (c. 1650 B.C.). For centuries this area of Asia Minor* was under mixed Mitannian–Egyptian rule and influence. About 1365 B.C. it was conquered by the Hittites* and subsequently overrun by the "Sea Peoples"* about 1200 B.C. In the tenth century B.C. Adana and its neighboring towns thrived under a coalition of Neo-Hittite and Phoenician* rulers. The plain of Adan is mentioned in the inscription of Azitawadda (c. 720 B.C.), discovered at Karatepe.* Since the area and some of the place names have interesting parallels in classical Greek literature, there has been a great deal of speculation about the relationship this small kingdom had to the Semites to the E and S and to the Indo-Europeans to the W and N. Since many of the inscriptions are bilingual Phoenician and hieroglyphic* Hittite, there is evidence that both populations were represented in the area. Ahimelech, mentioned in 1 Sam 26:6, and Uriah, mentioned in 2 Sam 11–12, were Hittites from this Neo-Hittite confederacy.

See ALALAKH; HITTITES; KARATEPE.

BIBLIOGRAPHY. H. Th. Bossert, A. U. Bahadir, and other Turkish scholars have written extensively on the Hittite kingdoms of Anatolia in various numbers of the *Türk Tarih Kurumu Yayını*, Istanbul; M. C. Astour, *Hellenosemitica* (1965), 38ff.; *CAH*, 1, Part II, 504.

ww

ADAPA LEGEND. Adapa is the hero of a story preserved in four cuneiform* fragments from collections as diverse as Ashurbanipal's* library and the Tell el-Amarna* archives (Amarna Letters*). The latter copy was probably a cuneiform text brought to Egypt* to teach scribes how to write Babylonian cuneiform. The legend is not complete in these accounts but must have been widely current. Adapa was not immortal but a man of standing and intelligence, and was priest of the god Ea at Eridu.* His boat was

capsized by a blast of the South Wind, as he pursued his occupation of fishing* in the Persian Gulf to provide food for Ea's sanctuary at Eridu. In anger Adapa broke the wings of the wind, with disastrous results on the climate. Anu, the great god, was distressed and arraigned Adapa before their fellow deities. Ea warned the culprit not to eat or drink during the trial, lest he be fed the fruit of death, and to try to win the favor of Tammuz (cf. Ezek 8:14) and Gizzida, the two keepers of the gate. In fact, Adapa was offered the fruit of life but, because of Ea's misguided warning, refused it and failed to win immortality. With its polytheistic setting and the gods' mistaken or mendacious advice, the Adapa Legend has little in common with the Genesis story. There is no note of personal responsibility or choice, which is the point of the biblical account of the Fall. The legend has no moral significance and no elevated concept of deity.

BIBLIOGRAPHY: *ANET*, 101–2; J. B. Pritchard, *Archaeology and the OT* (1958), 193–200.

EMB

ADOPTION. The term as such does not occur in the OT, nor are any laws of adoption formulated there. In Semitic society it was not necessary for blood relationship to be established before family privileges could be obtained and rights transferred from one member to another (cf. Gen 48:5; 49:4, 26; Deut 21:15–17, et. al.). However, adoption was legislated for in Babylonian society by the Code of Hammurabi* (Sections 185ff.), and by the fifteenth-century B.C. social traditions at Nuzi,* which are also represented at Alalakh* in Syria. At Nuzi, adoption frequently marked the sale of land but was also common among childless couples as a means of obtaining an heir and providing for old age. The relationship of Abraham and Eliezer* (Gen 15:2–3) can be assessed against this background of social custom. At both Nuzi and Alalakh it was possible for a man to adopt another as "father." Thus a certain citizen of Alalakh named Tulpuri adopted King Ilimilimma as father in return for lifelong support. At Ras Shamra (Ugarit*) deeds of adoption have been attested, one of which probably related to the disposal of property. Something like legal adoption occurred in the case of Moses (Exod 2:10) and Esther (Esth 2:7, 15). In Ruth 4:16, while it might appear that Naomi adopted the son of Ruth and Boaz, the child was already her descendant by levirate marriage. In the Near East a poor landless man was sometimes allowed to marry into a family and be adopted. Such OT marriages probably included those of Moses (Exod 2:21; cf. 2:16; 3:1), Jarha (1 Chron 2:34–35), and Barzillai (Ezra 2:61; Neh 7:63). Jacob's marriages to Leah and Rachel (Gen 29:18–30) were probably similar in character. In the OT, Israel was God's son by divine choice rather than by physical relationship (Deut 14:2), a concept stressed by Paul (Rom 8:15, 23; 9:4; Gal 4:5; Eph 1:5) to emphasize divine graciousness in His adoption of Israel.

BIBLIOGRAPHY: C. H. Gordon, "Biblical Customs and the Nuzu Tablets," *BA*, 3 (1940), 1–12; W. H. Rossell, *JBL*, 71 (1952), 233–34; C. H. Gordon, *Introduction to Old Testament Times* (1953), 100–105.

RKH

ADRAMYTTIUM (ad rə mit′ē um; Gr. Ἀδ-ραμύττιον, *Adramyttion*). A port at the head of the gulf by that name in Mysia,* northern Asia Minor.* The actual site is at modern Karatash, but the name is preserved in nearby Edremid. The "ship from Adramyttium" in which Paul traveled from Caesarea* to Myra* (Acts 27:2–5) was presumably sailing back to its home port. Rendel Harris proposed that the Greek name Adramyttium represents the original Semitic "Hadramaut," the spice-bearing area of S Arabia* that exported frankincense and myrrh to Mediterranean countries, and that Myra and Smyrna* were variations of the Semitic word for myrrh. He identified the people of Hadramaut with the Atramitae mentioned by the Elder Pliny (NH 6.36) and claimed that the cowrie shell (*Cypraea*) was provided by the S Arabians as a Mediterranean currency, their name still surviving in "atramatiri" (a head of cowrie strings). The theory thus pictures the Arabians not only as traders but as colonists who founded this center in Mysia (also a station on the island off Lycia called Adramyttis by Stephanus of Byzantium) and others in N Africa. These arguments are largely etymological and have not been confirmed by archaeological evidence from Asia Minor. Confirmation is needed, perhaps on the basis of numismatic (*see* COINS) or papyrological (*see* PAPYROLOGY) evidence, of the seaward and westward extensions of the incense* routes from S Arabia, whose land paths were marked by Freya Stark in her *Southern Gates of Arabia*.

BIBLIOGRAPHY: W. Leaf, *Strabo on the Troad* (1923), 318ff.; Rendel Harris, *Contemporary Review*, 128 (1925), 194–202; Freya Stark, *Southern Gates of Arabia* (1936).

BFH

ADULLAM (ə dul′ləm; Heb. עֲדֻלָּם, "*dullam*, "refuge"). A city of the Shephelah,* Adullam is mentioned five times in OT lists. In each of these (Josh 12:15; 15:35; 2 Chron 11:7; Mic 1:15; Neh 11:30) it is apparent that Adullam is a lowland site, rendering impossible the traditional identification of the cave of Adullam (1 Sam 22:1ff.; 2 Sam 23:13; 1 Chron 11:15) with the cave of Khareitun, SE of Bethlehem* in the central hill country. The ancient name was, early in the nineteenth century, recognized in the Arabic (*Id el-Ma*), the name given to a ruin in the Wadi es-Sur about 4 km. (2.5 mi.) WSW of Socoh and the junction of the wadi with the Valley of Elah. Although the site was identified by the French orientalist Clermont-Ganneau and others as ancient Adullam, it is now widely accepted, following surface pottery* analysis by W. F. Albright et al., that the ancient city itself is represented by Tell esh-Sheikh Madhkur, immediately above and to the S of the ruin known as Khirbet 'Id el-Ma. Although the city figured prominently in the history of Israel from the days of Joshua, when it was a Canaanite* royal city-state, to at least the time of Judas Maccabeus, who retired to the city in 163 B.C. after fighting Gorgias, (2 Macc 12:38ff.), the site remains unexcavated. The city was fortified by Rehoboam, perhaps as an auxiliary to Socoh and Adoraim for protecting the passes

between Judah and Philistia. It was destroyed by Sennacherib* III and was later inhabited by returnees from the Exile.*

BIBLIOGRAPHY: G. A. Smith, *HGHL* (1910), 229ff.; W. F. Albright, "Researches of the School in Western Judea," *BASOR*, 15 (1924), 3–4.

CEA

ADULTERY. Joseph's expression in his rejection of the advances of Potiphar's wife (Gen 39:1,7–9) recalls a similar phrase in Abimelech's rebuke to Abraham (Gen 20:9). The expression "great sin" occurs in four Egyptian marriage* contracts where it can only mean adultery. It is interesting to find the same phrase used in OT attacks on idolatry, which is metaphorically described as spiritual adultery (e.g., Exod 32:21,30–31; 2 Kings 17:21). Texts from Ugarit* are further illustration. They concern the wife of King Ammistamru, who was guilty of some fault which made her escape to her native land of Amurru. Sausgamuwa, the king of Amurru, refused a request from the angry husband to surrender the refugee. Ammistamru then appealed to the Hittite* monarch Tudhaliya IV, who was in a position to order Sausgamuwa to return the offender. A compensation, which looks like a bribe or a *solatium* of some sort, was paid to the Amurru king. In the correspondence the phrase "great sin" recurs several times.

The popular Egyptian "Story of Two Brothers" (*see* TWO BROTHERS) has no connection with the story of Joseph.

BIBLIOGRAPHY: J. J. Rabinowitz, *JNES*, 17 (1959), 73; J. Nougayrol, *Le Palais Royal d'Ugarit*, 4 (1956), 129–42.

EMB

ADUMMATU. *See* DUMAH.

ADYTUM. The inner sanctuary of a temple where only priests officiated, as with the Hebrew Most Holy Place (Holy of Holies).

AEGEAN CIVILIZATION. *See* MINOA.

AELIA CAPITOLINA (ē′lē ə kap ə tə lē′nə). After the destruction of Jerusalem* in A.D. 70, the city became the camp of the famous Roman Tenth Legion. It must, of course, be presumed that much of it was still habitable, and in that case it would have remained, in Jewish minds, the symbol of their nation and its destiny. Hadrian* (A.D. 117–38), in his vast and careful reorganization of the frontiers of the Roman Empire, found the Jews, whose presence on the eastern edge of the Roman world was a security problem, an incomprehensible people. It was a lamentable mistake on the part of the cultured and able emperor to reconstitute Jerusalem under his own name (Publius Aelius Hadrianus) and that of Capitoline Jupiter. In Jewish eyes the loss of Jerusalem involved (cf. John 11:48) a calculated insult that could only be answered by rebellion, hence the Second Revolt (A.D. 132–33).

In the large archaeological projects round the SW corner of the old city many Roman remains have

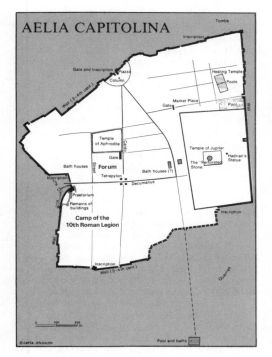

AELIA CAPITOLINA

been found. To the E of this section was a garden area. Many significant finds were uncovered here including a Latin inscription from the days of Emperor Septimius Severus (A.D. 193–211). Many bricks and tiles bear the stamp *Colonia Aelia Capitolina*, and many coins,* fragments of marble sculptures, bronze figures, and large quantities of pottery and glass* have also been found.

Beneath the Roman levels lay the Herodian remains. A Herodian street was discovered along the edge of the great temple* wall, littered with huge fragments of stone thrown from the top of the wall during the destruction of A.D. 70. The latest coin found was from the fourth year of the First Jewish Revolt, A.D. 69. The Herodian street was bordered on its southern side by a wall beyond which was a plaza some 12 m. (40 ft.) wide, probably a gathering place for pilgrims going into the temple.

It seems clear that Aelia Capitolina never advanced far enough in its construction to have had its debris cleared from the destruction of Titus's* siege over sixty years earlier.

BIBLIOGRAPHY: K. M. Kenyon, "Excavating in Jerusalem," *BA*, 27 (1964), 34–52; id., *Jerusalem: Excavating 3000 Years of History* (1967).

EMB

AENON (ē'non; Gr. Αἰνών, *Ainōn*, from Heb. עֵינַיִם, עֵינוֹן, עֵינָן, "double spring," LXX Ἀινών, *Ainón*). A place not located accurately, mentioned in John 3:23, and said to be near Salim, where John the Baptist was baptizing.*

Basically there are two principal sites with which

Aenon may be identified. The one, according to Eusebius (Euseb. *Onom.* 40.1) lay 13 km. (8 mi.) S of Scythopolis* in the Jordan Valley in N Samaria,* and is the location argued for by Lagrange and Abel. The other is a site with the current name Salim, about 5.5 km. (3.5 mi.) E of Shechem.* It is mentioned by Epiphanius (Epiph. *Adv. Haeres.* 55.2) and is the one preferred by W. F. Albright. Various archaeological surveys seem to support the latter view. There is an excellent spring on the N face of the wadi,* and, as the text says, "there was plenty of water" (or "many streams") there. A third view places Aenon on the E side of the Jordan and N of the Dead Sea.*

The Medeba Mosaic Map* (from c. A.D. 560), found on a church floor at Medeba,* in Jordan, shows two sites for ancient Aenon. One Aenon is placed on the E side of the Jordan, N of the Dead Sea, near what probably was understood to be the hill of Elijah. To the description is added: "There now Sapsaphas." Since Aenon means "springs," and since the context of John 3:22-23 suggests that the place may have been close to Judea (Judah*) (cf. *en de kai* introducing v. 23), this site fits the area with its hill and spring, where Elijah was supposed to have ascended. John the Baptist may have used this spring for baptizing, it being the spring 3 km. (2 mi.) from the Jordan, as reported by the Anonymous of Piacenza (CCSL 175, 134).

The Medeba mapmaker shows another Aenon farther N and on the W side of the Jordan River, which he identifies as "near Salim." This location is so vaguely placed that it could fit in with the church tradition of Eusebius (Euseb. *Onom.* 40.1-4) noted above, who says it is a spot near Salim and Jordan. Aetheria (c. A.D. 385) describes the site as in a garden with a spring or pool, and the bluish-green row of cubes in the Medeba map may indicate the spring in question. Some travelers in the area have noted the local name, Sheikh Salim.

The Aenon located on the Medeba map W of the Jordan will also, however, fit the site argued for by Albright—that the Aenon of John 3:23 was the ancient town of that name, modern Salim, located 5.5 km. (3.5 mi.) E of Nablus. This town (Salim) is referred to in Gen 14:18 (*see* NIV footnote and LXX) and in Jer 41:5 (Jer 48:5, LXX) and was known in the time of Judith. The ancient Aenon was nearer than the modern Salim to the wadi Far'ah, a perennial stream with five springs at its source.

BIBLIOGRAPHY: F. M. Abel, "Exploration de la vallee du Jourdain," *RB*, 22 (1913), 222–23; W. F. Albright, "Some Observations Favoring the Palestinian Origin of the Gospel of John," *HTR*, 17 (1924), 193–94; F. M. Abel, "La Laure de Sapsaphus," *RB*, 41 (1941), 248–52; M. Avi-Yonah, *The Madaba Mosaic Map* (1954); J. Finegan, *The Archaeology of the NT* (1969), 11–13.

WHM

AERIAL PHOTOGRAPHY. The practice of taking photographs from an aircraft or satellite to determine features of the earth's surface not easily distinguished from the ground. Aerial photography was a surveillance technique employed for military purposes as

Early aerial photograph ca. 1917. Jerusalem from the southeast.

early as the Franco-Prussian War (1870). Since that time it has been used only intermittently in the politically troubled Middle East, where large areas are classified as military zones. The introduction of high-speed electronic shutters and of film sensitive to restricted spectral characteristics of light have made it possible to trace, from the air, the courses of ancient walls,* ditches, and roads. With continual perfecting of zoom lenses and computer-enhanced images, it is now possible to trace features of the subsurface of the earth undetectable by other means.

In Israel, work has been done on Roman walls, roads (see ROMAN ROADS), and farms by the employment of these techniques, which were pioneered in England by O. G. S. Crawford. Satellite photographs, telecast to earth, are astoundingly informative, but the critical nature of their military data is such that little satellite-gained material has been available to archaeologists. Of special importance is the possibility of remote sensing for the long-term ecological study and development of a given area of the earth's surface, as has been done in the southwestern United States. Used in the Middle East, such techniques could lead to startling new conclusions about ancient migration routes and agricultural zones.

One outcome of aerial investigation has been a new appreciation of the astrological* arrangement of many ancient buildings. The astral and solar orientation of long lines of stones, pillars, and other features becomes immediately obvious from the air.

In the 1890s the Germans and French used balloons for aerial surveys of Iraq and Iran, and after World War I British and American expeditions made such surveys of Palestine and Egypt.* Modern equipment and improved techniques, however, have made aerial photography a new science since World War II. Israeli military photographers have aided in the surveys and excavations of such sites as Masada* and the waterways of Nabataean* farms. The most recent techniques—infrared sensing devices and laser holography—promise to open whole new vistas for archaeology.

BIBLIOGRAPHY: H. E. Ives, *Airplane Photography* (1927); D. R. Lueder, *Aerial Photographic Interpretation* (1959); V. C. and C. F. Miller, *Photogeology* (1961); L. Deuel, *Flights into Yesterday* (1969); H. C. Simmons, *Archaeological Photography* (1969).

WW

AFFULEH (AFULA) (af' fu le; Heb. עֲפֻל, *'ōpĕl*, "citadel"). This ancient mound, set within the limits of the modern town of the same name, has been largely destroyed but is interesting as the possible site of Gideon's Ophrah (Judg 6:1–12, 24), and for the archaeological activity of Israeli investigators at various dates between 1926 and 1952. Considerable finds of Bronze Age pottery* have been made. There are other rivals for the site of Ophrah, including et-Taiyibeh, NW of Beth Shan;* Silet ed-Dahr, N of Shechem;* and a location to the NW of Megiddo.* Gideon's town must not be confused with the Ophrah of Benjamin (Josh 18:23; 1 Sam 13:17), which was located to the NE of Jerusalem.*

BIBLIOGRAPHY: F.-M. Abel, *Géographie de la Palestine*, 2 (1956), 154; E. G. Kraeling, *Bible Atlas* (1956), index ref. D2 XXI.

EMB

AGADE. *See* AKKAD.

AGORA (ag' or ə; Gr. ἀγορά, *agora*, "forum," "marketplace"). The agora was the community center of a Greek city.* The term appears twice in the Greek NT, in Acts 16:19 and 17:17, where it is translated "marketplace"; but this gives a very inadequate idea of its function, for which there is no single word in English. Similar references in the Gospels are to the marketplaces of Jewish towns. Basically the agora was a large open area near the center of the city, and played at least three roles. As the commercial center of the city it contained the shops and booths of a wide variety of merchants and tradesmen, from bankers to barbers. These buildings were often of a temporary nature and could be removed, if desired, to clear all or part of the area. For this role the translation "marketplace" is a reasonable equivalent. The agora, however, was also surrounded by the public buildings of the city, including temples, the town hall, and law courts. It was therefore the civic center of the city, the role reflected in Acts 16:19. Its third function, arising naturally from the other two, was simply that of a meeting place for the citizens (Matt 23:7). In Athens* official provision had been made for this by the construction of buildings called stoas,* which were porticoes where citizens could meet and converse. Paul's choice of the agora at Athens as the place to talk with people about the new faith (Acts 17:17) shows his familiarity with the agora in this third role.

Those seeking employment congregated in the agora (Matt 20:3), and because of the proverbial readiness for evil of idle hands, it proved to be the haunters of the agora who often provided the raw material for riot and demonstration (Acts 17:5). Children, too, found the open place of the agora a convenient playground in the cramped ancient towns (cf. Matt 11:16; Luke 7:32).

The Roman equivalent of the agora was the forum,* the word that occurs in the place-name "Forum of Appius" in Acts 28:15. The massive archaeological history of the Roman forum lies outside the scope of biblical archaeology. Excavations at Gerasa* have revealed a magnificent forum surrounded by fifty-six huge columns, many of which are still standing. The best known forum is that of Rome* itself; but although this was originally a marketplace, its shops were removed at an early date. It functioned primarily as the political center of the city, though it played a part in commercial and religious life as well.

The agora of Athens, extensively excavated since World War II, lies under the N side of the Acropolis,* and although little more than the ground plan survives, it has been possible to identify certain major structures. The Corinthian agora was a splendid city center to which access was gained by a fine propylaeum* at the end of the road to the port of Lechaion. It was a rectangle divided into two parts surrounded by colonnades, basilicas,* and shops, and was well-supplied with water from the finely engineered Peirene spring. A road to Corinth's* port of Cenchrea (E on the Saronic Gulf) emerged from the S end. Various trades, shopping facilities, taverns, and religious structures are identifiable, but of special biblical interest is the bema* in the center where Paul stood before Gallio. An inscription from Corinth states that a certain proclamation "was read from the rostrum." The reference is to the bema, or "judgment seat," and strikingly aligns the Greek concept of the agora with that of the Roman forum.

BIBLIOGRAPHY: *Ancient Corinth: A Guide to the Excavations*, American School of Classical Studies at Athens (1954).

WFR and EMB

AGRAPHA (ag′rə fə; Gr. ἄγραφα, *agrapha*). The word literally means "unwritten things" and was a term invented by Clement of Alexandria (c. 155-c. 220) and revived two centuries ago by J. G. Korner to represent sayings of Jesus not recorded in the canonical Gospels. It was not a good description, for it assumed that such sayings were part of a reliable oral tradition not committed to writing—a quite gratuitous assumption.

It has always been known that much of what Christ said and did found no place in the brief records of the Gospels. In the Codex Bezae version of Luke's Gospel, one supposed "lost saying," a striking remark about the Sabbath, seriously intrudes into the narrative. Who slipped it into the text is not known, but it runs thus: "On the same day, seeing someone

working on the Sabbath, He said to him: Man, if you know what you are doing, blessed you are. If you do not know you are accursed, and a transgressor of the law." It is amazing that more sayings of this kind did not find their way into the text, for John himself remarked, "I suppose that even the whole world would not have room for the books" if the whole story were told (John 21:25). Paul quotes Jesus: "It is more blessed to give than to receive" (Acts 20:35), an aphorism not contained in the record of the evangelists. Luke says that "many have undertaken to draw up an account" (Luke 1:1), and tradition has it that Matthew, before he wrote his Gospel, made a collection of sayings of Christ.

There is further evidence of such sayings from the records of the Third Crusade by the French chronicler De Joinville, who describes how an envoy of King Louis discovered a book in the possession of the Lebanese Sheikh of the Assassins purporting to be "the words of the Lord to Peter."

Archaeology has made a few contributions to the subject. Toward the end of the nineteenth century a fragmentary* papyrus* was recovered from Oxyrhynchus,* in N Egypt,* which contains sayings, or *logia*, of Jesus written in Greek. It was dated about A.D. 200 by its discoverers, B. P. Grenfell and A. S. Hunt. In one of the aphorisms the Lord says, "Thou hearest with one ear, but the other thou hast closed."

In 1903 another papyrus roll was recovered from the same area and was found to contain additional sayings of a rather late date. One of these reports Jesus as saying, "Let him who seeks cease not till he finds, and when he finds he shall be astonished; astonished he shall reach the Kingdom, and having reached the Kingdom he shall rest." An ancient tradition retains another saying of Christ that similarly links wonder and spiritual progress: "Wonder at the things before you. This is the first step to the knowledge that lies beyond." This saying seems to link Jesus with Plato, who said, "The mark of a philosopher is this—wonder."

In 1946 a large collection of sayings called the *Gospel of Thomas** was discovered. It is discussed in detail under this heading.

See OXYRHYNCHUS; THOMAS, GOSPEL OF.

BIBLIOGRAPHY: B. P. Grenfell and A. S. Hunt, *Oxyrhynchus Papyri* (1897–1924); J. G. Korner, *De sermonibus Christi agraphois* (1776); H. G. E. White, *The Sayings of Jesus from Oxyrhynchus* (1920); J. Jeremias, *Unbekannte Jesusworte* (1948); M. S. Enslin, *IDB*, 3 (1962), 614–16.

EMB

AGRICULTURE. Even before the end of the Mesolithic* period (c. 7000 B.C.) the Natufians* of Palestine were occupied with farming, as implements such as sickles with flint (*see* FLINT KNIVES) edges recovered from the Wadi* el-Mugharah* in the Carmel* range indicate clearly. At the same time, at Tell Es-Sultan* (OT Jericho*), the people there were also engaged in cultivating the land, and they too left behind recognizable agricultural tools.* Two millennia later, Neolithic* sites at Nineveh,* at Tell ej-Judeideh in Syria, and in Upper Egypt* retained

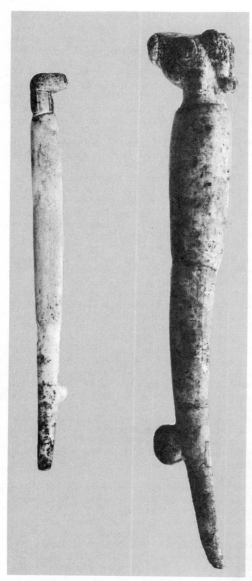

any rain, and even after October the rainfall was often irregular. Added to these natural difficulties were the amazingly stony terrain, the devastation that often followed hot desert winds from the E, and crop losses from such eventualities as locust* plagues.

Agricultural implements in biblical times were primitive, the plow being little more than a heavy wooden stick with a metal tip (cf. 1 Kings 19:19). During the Bronze Age, plow tips were made of copper or bronze,* but after the tenth century B.C. iron* came into use for this purpose. Excavations at Gibeah,* the home of Saul, uncovered the remains of a plow, and an iron plow point dated about 1010 B.C. is one of the earliest datable iron implements recovered to the present from the Palestinian uplands. A small hand sickle, made either of flints set in a curved handle, such as has been recovered from Gerar* and elsewhere, or manufactured from iron, was used by farmers to cut grain close to the ground. When harvested, cereals were threshed with sticks (Ruth 2:17) or the hoofs of cattle (Deut 25:4) and were winnowed by means of primitive shovels (Isa 30:24; Jer 15:7). Then it was stored in underground silos or in the kind of pottery* jars recovered in great numbers from Palestinian sites by excavators. The Gezer Calendar, a small limestone tablet found at Gezer and dated to the tenth century B.C., describes the work farmers did at different times of the year, including planting, hoeing, and harvesting. While the growing of grain was obviously important for Palestinian agriculture, the cultivation of grapes was also widespread in the Mediterranean area, furnishing the populace with fresh and dried fruit as well as wine.* A relief from a tomb at Saqqara (Memphis*) dated about 2200 B.C. depicts men in a wine vat, treading out the grapes. The olive* tree, well-suited to the Palestinian terrain, was also a valuable source

Sickle hafts with carved animal heads from Mount Carmel, belonging to Natufian Culture of Mesolithic Age. Courtesy Israel Dept. of Antiquities and Museums.

deposits that have demonstrated the nature of contemporary agriculture by revealing ancient flint implements, basalt mortars* and pestles, saddle querns* for grinding cereals to flour, and actual grains of barley and emmer wheat.

From earliest times farming has been difficult in Palestine. Water is seldom available in ample quantities, making necessary the construction of cisterns* (cf. 2 Chron 26:10; Neh 9:25) or the use of streams such as the Jabbok for irrigation. During the five-month summer season a farmer could expect little if

Mortar and pestle (right), Upper Palaeolithic, En Gev. Mortar (left), basalt, Late Mesolithic (Natufian Culture), Eynan excavations (See also photo under ECOLOGY AND ARCHAEOLOGY.) Courtesy Israel Dept. of Antiquities and Museums. Exhibited at the Israel Museum, Jerusalem. Photo David Harris.

of food as well as of oil, while the sycamore-fig (cf. Amos 7:14), along with honey, was the chief source of sugar in biblical times. Although farming was an exacting, year-round task for Palestinians, its labors were interrupted by periodic feasts as the various crops were harvested (cf. Judg 9:27; 21:19–21), beginning with the olive gathering. Bunches of grapes, ears of grain, and other familiar agricultural symbols were regularly incorporated into decorative motifs. One of these, from the city of Akhenaton* (c. 1340 B.C.) in Egypt, consists of a painted wall sculpture in limestone and depicts a popular Armana*-age theme of festooned grapes and flowers. Another outstanding representation occurs on the stele of Esarhaddon* (681–669 B.C.), which depicts a plow, a seed drill, a date palm, and heaps of grain. Agricultural imagery is used throughout Scripture in a variety of ways to express the relationship between God and man (cf. Isa 5:1–7; Zech 12:6; Mark 4:1–20; Luke 6:43–44, et al.).

BIBLIOGRAPHY: W. F. Albright, *BASOR*, 92 (1943), 16–26; A. E. Wright, *BA* (1957), 180–84; R. Braidwood, *Courses Toward Urban Life* (1962), 132–64; G. J. Jennings, *ZPEB*, 1 (1975), 71–78.

RKH

AHAB (ā'hab; Heb. אַחְאָב, *'aḥāb*, "uncle" or "the [divine] brother is father [?]"). In 1 Kings 16:28–22:40, some five chapters are devoted to Ahab's life, the understanding of which has been enlarged by archaeological activity at Samaria.* Excavations at that ancient site have revealed the original city founded by Omri* (1 Kings 16:23–24) and extended by Ahab. Large quantities of ivory* in the palace area illustrate 1 Kings 22:39, which mentions the "ivory* house" constructed by Ahab. Fine masonry bears witness to skillful artisans, who executed outstanding workmanship (*see* CRAFTS).

Assyrian records also testify to the virility of Israelite political life in the time of Ahab. An inscription of Shalmaneser III (854–824 B.C.) refers to Ahab as one member of a coalition of twelve kings involved in the battle of Qarqar* in 853 B.C. At that time Ahab reportedly provided two thousand chariots* and ten thousand foot soldiers as mentioned in the cuneiform* account (cf. ANET, 278–81).

Canaanite texts from ancient Ugarit* have furnished a picture of the gods Baal* and Asherah* (1 Kings 18:19) and help to explain Jezebel's* behavior as one who herself was a royal personage and a priestess of the Tyrian Baal deities Melcart and Asherah.* Canaanite cult worship was particularly lewd and orgiastic, and Jezebel's vigorous promotion of such practices among the Israelites provoked stern opposition from Elijah and Elisha.

See IVORY; JEZEBEL; MELCART STELE; SAMARIA; SHALMANESER, BLACK OBELISK OF.

BIBLIOGRAPHY: J. W. Crowfoot, K. M. Kenyon et al., *Samaria I: the Buildings of Samaria* (1943); id., *Samaria II: Early Ivories at Samaria* (1938); id., *Samaria-Sebaste III, The Objects from Samaria* (1957); *ANE* (1954), 227, 718; D J. Wiseman, *NBD* (1962), 20–21; R. D. Culver, *ZPEB*, 1 (1975), 78–81.

JAT

AHASUERUS. *See* XERXES.

AHIRAM (ə hī'rəm; Heb. אֲחִירָם, *'aḥîrām*, "my brother is exalted"). A biblical name (Num 26:38) but best known as that of a Phoenician* king of Byblos (Gebal*) whose sarcophagus* carries an important inscription on the edge of the lid. The sarcophagus was discovered in 1923 by Pierre Montet. Prepared by the son of Ahiram about 1000 B.C., it shows the king seated on a throne resembling a winged sphinx. The inscription reads: "Itobaal, son of Ahiram, king of Gebal, has made this sarcophagus for Ahiram his father as a resting place for eternity." Written in the Phoenician alphabet,* it is one of the earliest examples of Phoenician script. Byblos also provided stonemasons for King Solomon* (1 Kings 5:18).

BIBLIOGRAPHY; J. McKee Adams, *Ancient Records and the Bible* (1946), 94; *ANET* (1955), 504.

JAT

AHMAR, TELL. *See* TIL-BARSIP.

AHMED EL-AREINI. *See* TELL SHEIKH AHMED EL-AREINI.

House-shaped incense burner from Ai, Early Bronze Age III. Courtesy Israel Dept. of Antiquities and Museums. Exhibited and photographed at Israel Museum, Jerusalem.

AI (ī, ā'ī; Heb. **עַי**, **עַיָּא**, *'ay*, *'ayya'*, "ruin"). The name is usually accompanied by the article in Hebrew (*ha 'ay*, "the ruin"). Relevant topographical references seem to locate the site E of Bethel,* near Bethaven and N of Micmash (Gen 12:8, 13:3; Josh 7:2; Isa 10:28). Josh 7 and 8 contain useful details along with the account of the Israelite repulse and subsequent victory. It was a small settlement (Josh 10:2); a valley lay to the N (Josh 8:10) and an adjacent plain fell away toward Jericho.*

W. F. Albright was the first to suggest Et Tell as the site, following J. Marquet-Krause's and S. Yeivin's work there in 1933–35 (*BASOR*, 74 [1939], 11–23; J. Marquet-Krause, *Les Fouilles d'Ay* [1949]). Albright's identification was consequent of his own identification of Beitin, about 3 km. (2 mi.) NW of Et Tell (*AASOR*, 39 [1968]). Archaeological evidence reveals a flourishing community in the third millennium B.C. This community was destroyed, perhaps by Amorite* invaders, about 2200 B.C. and left unoccupied and ruined for a thousand years. Marquet-Krause uncovered a triple wall and a temple with stone bowls and ivory* objects of Egyptian origin. The long period of dereliction, if the evidence is read correctly (it is apparently confirmed by J. A. Callaway's 1964 excavations), would seem to imply no great strength of occupation at Et Tell at the time of the Israelite invasion. There is complete lack of Late Bronze Age material.

Writing more recently on the subject, David Livingston reexamines the evidence and rejects Beitin as the site of Bethel, claiming that Bireh is the more likely site. He consequently suggests that some ruins between 1.5 and 3 km. (1 and 2 mi.) to the SE on the far side of a high hill called Et-Tawil are likely to be the true relics of Ai (*WTJ*, 33 [1970], 20–44).

Further archaeological work is clearly necessary before the problem can be resolved.

BIBLIOGRAPHY: D. J. Wiseman, *AIA* (1971), 4–6; E. Yamauchi, *The Stones and the Scriptures* (1972), 54–57, with refs.; 1 (1975), 36–52.   EMB

AIALUNA. *See* AIJALON.

AIJALON (AJALON) (ā'jə lon; Heb. **אַיָּלוֹן**, *'ayyālôn*, "deer location"). A city assigned to Dan* (Josh 19:42). It was also set apart as a Levitical city (Josh 21:24; 1 Chron 6:69–70), being assigned to the sons of Kohath. It overlooked the Vale of Aijalon near Jericho* and has been identified with Tell el-Qoq'a, the modern Yalo, some 22 km. (14 mi.) NE of Jerusalem.* Remains going as far back as the beginning of the Middle Bronze Age have been recovered from the site, which is mentioned in the Amarna Letters* under the name Aialuna. During the settlement period the site was occupied successively by Ephraimites (1 Chron 6:69) and Benjamites (1 Chron 8:13). In the monarchy it was in Judean territory and in the days of King Ahaz was the object of a Philistine* raid (2 Chron 28:18).

BIBLIOGRAPHY: F.-M. Abel, *Géographie de la Palestine*, II (1938), 241; E. G. Kraeling, *Bible Atlas* (1956), 270; index refs. E2 III; E3 VI, VII, VIII, IX, X; H. G. Andersen, *ZPEB*, 1 (1975), 92.   EMB

AIJUL (ā'jəl). The tell* of Aijul lies at the mouth of the Wadi Ghazzeh, 9.5 km. (6 mi.) S of Gaza.* Excavations date back to Flinders Petrie (1930 and 1934), who worked for the British School of Archaeology. Petrie made important discoveries, but his results were marred by inaccurate dating* (rectified, fortunately by W. F. Albright). Copper weapons, for example, dated by Petrie 3300 to 3100 B.C., proved to belong to the date of the earliest stratum of Beit Mirsim (RABÛD), a full millennium later (Early Bronze Age). The site provided rich evidence of burial customs through the Bronze Age. In the Middle Bronze Age Aijul was a powerful Canaanite city heavily fortified with walls, glacis* and ditch, and covered some 2 ha. (5 a.). Ornaments in gold* and silver* and sophisticated jewelry testify to the wealth of the community. Its only biblical significance lies in the fact that trade routes of the Fertile Crescent* narrowed at this point, converging on the Nile and its delta. This was the commerce reflected in the Genesis picture of patriarchal Palestine. A few pottery* artifacts* mark the beginnings of Philistine* intrusion and indicate that in the Middle Bronze Age these European colonists were beginning to form an influential group on the coast.

BIBLIOGRAPHY; E. G. Kraeling, *Bible Atlas* (1956), index ref. E2 XXI.

EMB

AILA. *See* ELATH.

AIN EL QUDEIRAT (QUEDERAT) (äyn' el Qū' də rat). A spring located about 100 km. (60 mi.) SW of the S end of the Dead Sea* and about 8 km. (5 mi.) NW of another small desert spring, 'Ain Qudeis (Kadeis). Being NE of the inhospitable SINAI* peninsula, 'Ain el Qudeirat (Quederat) was particularly important because of its good supply of water and vegetation. The region was watered by a group of springs of which Qudeirat was the principal one. Some authorities have located Kadesh Barnea* here, since it served as a base during much of the Israelite wilderness wanderings (Num 33:36–37; cf. Num 14:32–35). The site would readily provide necessary water and grazing facilities for a wilderness sojourn, especially so if the Israelites moved periodically across the whole area between 'Ain el Qudeirat and 'Ain Qudeis. Certainly the topographical requirements of such wilderness happenings as the bringing of water from the rock by Moses (Num 20:8–11) would be met properly by this identification.

See KADESH BARNEA.

BIBLIOGRAPHY: D. Baly, *Geography of the Bible* (1957), 265–66.

RKH

AIN FESHKA (AIN FESHKHA) (äyn fesh'kə). The Arabic name for an oasis on the shore of the Dead Sea,* 3 km. (2 mi.) S of Qumran.* The site served as a center for excavations of the caves* used by followers of Simeon ben Kosiba (Bar Kochba*) in the Jewish uprising of A.D. 132–35. It is visible from the Qumran observation post as a green flat filled with rough sedge and scrub and fed by the spring that gives the oasis its name. Small traces remain of the farming activities of the Qumran community.

BIBLIOGRAPHY: G. L. Harding, "Khirbet Qumran and Wadi Muraba'at," *PEQ*, 84 (1952), 104–9; F. M. Cross, Jr., "The Manuscripts of the Dead Sea Caves," *BA*, 17 (1954), 8–12; Y. Yadin, *Bar-Kokhba: The rediscovery of the legendary hero of the Second Jewish Revolt against Rome* (1971); R. DeVaux, "Qumran, Khirbet 'Ein Feshka," *EEHL*, 4 (1978), 978-86.

CEA

AIN KAREM. See BETH HACCEREM.

AIN JIDI. See EN GEDI.

AIN SHEMS. See BETH SHEMESH.

AIN SILWAN. See SILOAM.

AIN SITTI MARGAM. See GIHON, SPRING OF.

AITUM. See ETAM.

AJALON. See AIJALON.

AKHENATON (a'kən a'tən; Egyp. *'ḫ-n-itn*; either "it is well with Aton," or "one serviceable to Aton"). A pharaoh of Egypt,* in the fourteenth century B.C.

1. *History.* Son of Amenophis III and Queen Tiy when the Egyptian Empire reached a peak of outward splendor. He may have been coruler with his father for up to eleven years of his sixteen-year reign (c. 1374–1358 B.C., or up to eleven years later), but this is still disputed. By his sixth year, he had changed his name from Amenophis (IV) to Akhenaton, marking publicly his allegiance to the sun-god Aton instead of to the state-god Amun, and moved his capital to the new city of Akhetaton ("Horizon of Aton"), now Amarna,* halfway between the earlier capitals of Memphis* and Thebes.* The old gods, especially Amun, were banished and replaced by Aton. Meantime, unrest among Egypt's vassals in Syria–Palestine went almost unchecked, some defecting to the Hittite* Empire. Having no son, Akhenaton associated his brother Smenkhkare in the kingship; when they died within a short time of each other, Tutankhaton (later Tutankhamen*) became king.

2. *Religion and Literature.* Akhenaton's "new" religion was essentially worship of the sun-god as manifest in the solar disk, in particular as creator and sustainer of all life (hence the disk shown with descending rays ending in hands that present the life symbol to the king). The main source of this religion is the great "Hymn to the Aton*" (cf. tr., *ANET*, 369–71), a lesser hymn, and assorted religious formulas—all found in tombs of the nobles at Akhetaton (Amarna). These sources show Aton as caring for all mankind (not just Egyptians) and even animals. But in formal worship only the king (Akhenaton) worshiped Aton directly. By contrast, the people were to worship Akhenaton as the son and incarnation of Aton. Notwithstanding the creation and sustainment

concepts, there was no moral teaching given; "truth" consisted of what was seen by Akhenaton and was not absolute.

3. *Akhenaton and the OT.* There is no proven link between Akhenaton and biblical literature. Some have suggested that Ps 104 was inspired by the "Hymn to the Aton"; but a separation in time of some centuries makes this highly unlikely. Also both hymns belong squarely within their respective literary traditions, and the concepts they share are common to much Egyptian, OT, and other Near Eastern literature. Differences are striking—as for example in the case of Akhenaton, for whom the sun is creator, and moral teaching is totally lacking. By contrast, in Ps 104 the sun is but one creation of the supreme God along with others, and that psalm ends with a sharp reminder of the primacy of righteousness over wrongdoing. There is no warrant, either, for deriving Mosaic (or later) monotheism from the inherently different solar religion of Akhenaton.

The Aton hymn is a witness to the early existence of the concept of a universal divine providence for all men and other creatures.

BIBLIOGRAPHY: K. A. Kitchen, *Ancient Orient and OT* (1966), 127 ("universalism"); C. Aldred, *Akhenaten, Pharaoh of Egypt: a New Study* (1968); K.-H. Bernhardt, "Amenophis IV and Psalm 104," *MIOr*, 15 (1969), 193–206, esp. 201ff.; C. Aldred, *CAH*, 2, Part 2 (1975), 49–97; R. W. Smith, D. E. Redford et al., *The Akhenaton Temple Project*, 1 (1976).

KAK

AKHETATON (AKEHET-ATON; AKHETATEN). See AMARNA.

AKIR. See EKRON.

AKKAD (ak'kad; Heb. אַכַּד, *'Akkād*; Gr. Ἀρχαδ, *Archād*). A city of ancient Mesopotamia,* mentioned in Gen 10:10 along with Babylon,* Erech* and Calneh.* All are grouped under the domain of the shadowy King Nimrod, who was probably the conqueror Šarrukin (Sargon of Akkad*), founder of the dynasty of Akkad and first ruler of a large sector of the Mesopotamian alluvium (2371–2316 B.C.). Sargon appears to have been the first East Semite ruler to ascend to the throne long held by Sumerians. In the inscriptions, the term for the city and state is *Akkadî*; the Sumerian equivalent is *Agade*. The city-state and its inhabitants are distinguished from Sumer* and the Sumerians by the term *Akkad*, and the language is called *Akkadu*.

All the evidence for this culture is archaeological. In later ages the texts and tales of the Akkad period were treasured, and the rulers revered. Texts as late as 600 B.C. make mention of the ruins of Akkad, but no trace of them has ever been located. Some scholars, pointing to its great antiquity, argue that it could well have been one of the many poorly identified or totally unidentified mounds still to be seen in Iraq. Others have theorized that it was another more ancient name of Babylon, which, however, would contradict the evidence both of Genesis and of the large

number of cuneiform* texts that list the sites separately. Texts of the Akkad period, usually designated
Sargonic or Pre-Sargonic, after the name of the first
ruler, have been studied extensively, as they are the
earliest known specimens of a Semitic language of
which linguistic and stylistic aspects are seen in the
Hebrew Bible. Such phrases as "king of the whole
world," "king of kings," "servant of god," and "shepherd of———" appear in these royal inscriptions.
The dialect is exceedingly difficult and filled with
Sumerian words and constructions. The writing system is almost identical to the Sumerian cuneiform
syllabary of the time. The signs are large, linear, and
graphic. There are a number of Akkadian-Sumerian
bilingual inscriptions from this period, and many of
these yield important historical data about the early
period of Mesopotamian political and economic development. The texts reveal a complicated society of
mixed Sumerian and Semitic population, engaged in
agriculture* and trade, with the temple and the city-
cult as the central force in society. An involved hierarchy, half-religious and half-mercantile, controlled every aspect of life in the name of the deity
whose image and temple they maintained. Many of
the texts deal with the building and restoring of temples and shrines. The religious beliefs of Akkad are
very difficult to assess, as there is nothing in the way
of philosophical or theological dialogue presented in
the texts. It is apparent, however, that there were
local cults of fertility gods and goddesses centered in
each little farming community by the late fourth
millennium B.C. For a ruler to gain legality and authority he had to be a priest and devotee of the cultic
god. Consequently, migration, succession, and conquest produced a whirlpool of polytheism. In time,
the older gods and shrines were elevated to seniority
in the religious hierarchy. The presentation of this
elaborate scheme and its promulgation is found in
mythology. However, the only insight into early Akkadian mythology is through the Sumerian epics and
tales of later ages. The vast preponderance of extant
tablets are economic documents. They record sales,
leases, and inventories of goods. Although the temple and the gods owned the land in some religious
sense, a great deal of private business is in evidence.
Trade and travel over great distance was carried on
as a state monopoly through private caravaneers.
Sargonic period sites containing Mesopotamian minerals, ornaments, and pottery* have been excavated
in N Iraq, Iran, Pakistan, and the Mediterranean Sea
Coast. There is evidence that the two great campaigns of Sargon's kingship—his conquest of Elam*
with its capital, Susa,* and his march through Northern Syria-Lebanon—were the high points of his career and brought Akkad to eminence. The effects of
Akkadian supremacy extended considerably beyond
the few hundred years of Akkad's political power.
The political and cultural force welded together from
Sumer and Akkad, using the extremely precise cuneiform script, was to dominate the Ancient Near
East until the rise of Alexander the Great, over two
thousand years later. The grandson of Sargon, Naram-
Sin, became one of the most famous rulers of Mesopotamian history. The unequaled stability of the

Stele of Naram-Sin of Agade, depicting king standing before stylized mountain as victor over the Lullu(bians). The
stele was found at Susa and dates from the first half of the
23rd century. Courtesy of Musées Nationaux, Paris.

Akkadian tradition can be seen in the fact that Nebuchadnezzar* of Babylon (605–552 B.C.) could read
the inscriptions of the Sargonic kings, admire their
images, and worship their gods, although he was further removed from them in time than we are from
Constantine. The Akkadians introduced into world
culture many notions of politics, laws, trade, and social organization, along with a graphic representation
of Semite speech and a new realism in art. The mention of Sargon and his realm as a high point of hu-
manism in the early days of human history is well
justified in the context of the Genesis catalog of un-
believers. Recent evidence from the excavations of
ancient I/Ebla (Tell Mardikh*), a site of N Syria,
shows the large extent and importance of Akkad,
which held all of the area of the Middle Euphrates
in the time of I/Ebla's prime—about 2000 B.C. Preliminary reports of the vast collection of cuneiform
tablets at I/Ebla indicate that Akkad and its dynasty
of rulers were frequently mentioned.

BIBLIOGRAPHY: The texts and language of Akkad
have been thoroughly discussed in I. J. Gelb, *Ma-*

terials for the Assyrian Dictionary, nos. 1–3 (1952–57); for the history and archaeology cf. E. Unger, "Akkad," RLA (1928), 62–123; A. Scharff and A. Moortgat, Ägypten und Vorderasien im Altertum (1950), 256–71; C. J. Gadd, "The Dynasty of Agade and the Gutian Invasion," CAH, 1 part 2 (1971), 417ff.

ww

ALABASTER (al'ə bas'tər; Heb. שַׁיִשׁ, šēš; may be translated "white marble"; Gr. ἀλάβαστρον, alábastron). A mineral used for making vases or other containers and for ornamentation. It is a soft material well suited for fine detailed carving and capable of taking a polish. In Palestine, two kinds of alabaster are found in the excavations.

1. A hard, compact calcium carbonate or variety of fine-grained gypsum, somewhat translucent, and sometimes beautifully banded. Most of the objects made from this were imported from Egypt,* especially perfume flasks. Some of this material was used for the facings on parts of buildings or other structures. The mines at Hat-nub (Egypt*) date to the Third Dynasty. Other mines were located in Sinai,* Helwân, and Wadi Asyûti. The Egyptian objects were worked (bored) with drills, but those made in Palestine were cut with chisels (see CRAFTS).

2. The material in Palestine was a lower grade hydrous calcium sulphate, which occurred principally in the Jordan Valley. Objects were made of it from the Middle Canaanite period to the beginning of the Israelite period, but especially during Middle Bronze II. A quarry used for making vases for Beth Shan* during the Late Bronze Age is still producing gypsum near Gesher. The large deposits in the Ramon Crater in the Negev* seem not to have been used in antiquity.

Alabaster vases or boxes were highly regarded. Pliny the Elder (Plin. 13.4) said "perfumes are best kept in alabaster vases." This concept of value is seen in the outcry made when the woman at Bethany* broke the vase to anoint Jesus (Matt 26:7-8; Mark 14:3-4; Luke 7:37). The classic form of the alabaster vase or flask for storing perfume had a long neck, which was broken to release the contents.

The word alabaster was also used in the generic sense for flasks of this shape made of any material. The Greek word alabastron designates a standard or basic vase form—a small, elongated shape. In Esth 1:6 the relevant Hebrew term is usually translated "marble" בַּהַט though BDB translates "porphyry." The word may also be used in an adjectival sense, i.e., of or resembling alabaster, specifically having a nearly white color and a diffusing surface.

Numerous specimens of alabaster ware have been found in Palestinian excavations. Usually the shapes of local products were influenced by Egyptian imports but in time began to acquire the forms of the domestic pottery.* Since the native material (sulphates) tended to deteriorate more rapidly than the foreign (calcites), specimens found of the latter are generally better preserved.

BIBLIOGRAPHY: I. Ben-Dor, "Palestinian Alabaster Vases," QDAP, 11 (1944), 93–112; O. C. Smith, Identification and Qualitative Chemical Analysis of

Minerals (1953), 306–7, 336–37; G. W. van Beek, "Frankincense and Myrrh," BA, 23 (1960), 89; E. F. Campbell, "Excavations at Shechem," BA, 23 (1960), 119; J. B. Pritchard, "A Bronze Age Necropolis at Gibeon," BA, 24 (1961), 22; E. Orni and E. Efrat, Geography of Israel (1964), 286–87; R. W. Fairbridge, ed., The Encyclopedia of Geomorphology (1968), 652–53; R. D. Bowes, ZPEB, I (1975), 95–96.

MHH

ALALAKH (al'ə lak). When Woolley was excavating Tell 'Atshana in N Syria, near the Orontes River, in 1937–39 and 1946–49, he uncovered two principal levels (VII and IV) in which tablets were found, out of a total of sixteen occupational levels, dating from c. 3100 to c. 1200 B.C. These two strata contained archive material from the palace of Yarimlim in level VII (c. 1720–1650 B.C.) and of Niqmepa in level IV (c. 1483–1370 B.C.). The latter palace had been sacked, and someone hurriedly trying to save the archives dropped a trail of tablets, some 250, all the way from the archive office to the courtyard. Yarimlim's office was a room similar to that of his predecessor and contained the rest of the tablets. The 457 texts from the two sites are roughly contemporary with the groups of tablets recovered from Mari* and Ras Shamra (Ugarit*).

Probably at the close of the Old Babylonian period Alalakh came under the control of a W Semitic family and continued in this way until the palace was sacked and burned, probably by the Hittite* ruler Mursilis I, c. 1650 B.C. During a period of Mitanni* dominance Alalakh became a vassal state, but after the time of King Niqmepa was compelled to pay tribute to Thutmose III of Egypt.* Under the Hittite Suppiluliumas* the city was subjected to Anatolian control until the twelfth century B.C., when it was destroyed by the Aegean "Sea People."*

Treaties discovered at Alalakh include agreements between sovereign states and follow the pattern of Hittite international treaties. As at Nuzi* and Ugarit, the father of a family could disregard the law of primogeniture and choose the son who was to be designated "firstborn." This illumines Abraham's annulment of Ishmael's position when Isaac was born (Gen 21:10–12), Jacob's choice of Joseph* in the place of Reuben (Gen 49:3–4), and the elevation of Ephraim over Manasseh (Gen 48:13–14). One Alalakh Treaty included extradition rights similar to those indicated in 1 Kings 2:39–40 (cf. Deut 23:15–16). The practice of the exchange of villages may reflect the activities of Solomon* and Hiram* (1 Kings 9:10–14). A law whereby one who committed wrongdoing or rebelled against the king could be executed and his property confiscated, may have prompted Ahab's* action against Naboth (1 Kings 21:15).

Little is known of religion at Alalakh, but the mention of Hittite, Hurrian,* and Babylonian deities in the texts suggests a syncretism similar to that of Hittite religion.

Alalakh was an important trading post for traffic moving from the port of Al Mina southward along the Orontes Valley route and eastward along the Euphrates Valley. Elephant tusks in Yarimlim's palace suggest a considerable luxury trade. The king may have had a monopoly control of this, along with large interests in the Lebanon cedar* trade.

A number of tablets from the eighteenth century B.C. in the possession of the Australian Institute of Archaeology are a good illustration of the mundane but enlightening contents:

Tablet 21: Ammitaku (governor subordinate to King Yarimlim) loans Wanti-Ishara one-half mana (one shekel) of silver.* As surety, Wanti-Ishara must enter the palace as a slave,* but he is to be freed on payment.

Tablet 243: Monthly distribution of rations from the palace. Mainly grains to feed oxen* and horses.* Some grain for beer making.

Tablet 262: Monthly distribution of grain rations to persons. Six personal names.

Tablet 379: Receipt for fifty shekels of silver for plot of land.

Tablet 413: List of gold,* silver, bronze,* and copper objects, possibly in treasury of god Nergal. Many Hurrian names occur in the list.

The ideogram* SA.GAZ on Tablet 181 recurs several times. It denotes seminomad people, some of them apparently wealthy, who were capable of fielding considerable war parties. Tablet 181 mentions 20 men from different areas who made up the armed men of the SA.GAZ. Tablet 183 mentions 1436 men of SA.GAZ of whom 80 are charioteers. Tablet 350 lists sheep belonging to the men of SA.GAZ.

A note from the Australian Institute of Archaeology runs: "In keeping with other references to SA.GAZ—in such places as Nuzi (15th cent.), Mari (18th cent.), Boghazköy* (14th cent.), Cappadocia (19th cent.), Ras Shamra (14th cent.), and elsewhere—the Alalakh tablets refer to these people usually in the context of armed forces and raiding parties. Also in keeping with these other texts, the Alalakh tablets show that the SA.GAZ did not belong to a particular ethnic group, but rather that they were frequently one stratum in a society. They seem to have been foreign semi-nomads who owned no land and did not rate as citizens in any society. They usually lived at peace with the people amongst whom they dwelt but could when necessary summon raiding bands for specific needs.

"Generally, it is agreed that SA.GAZ can be translated by the word *Hapiru* [Habiru*]—a term used with a similar significance in other ancient Near Eastern documents. It is a similar word, *Hebrew*, which is used of Abraham in Gen. 14:13. Here, too, the word does not signify race, but social status. Genesis makes it quite clear that Abraham had no land of his own—he even had to buy a burial-place for his wife, Sarah. Further, he did not settle in a particular place permanently but was often on the move. He was a man who had flocks. He well fits the picture of the Hapiru.

"Further in the reference in Gen. 14 Abraham is described as leading a raiding-party of 318 men to rescue his nephew, Lot, from the kings of the East, paralleling exactly the raiding role of the SA.GAZ/ Hapiru in the Alalakh tablets." [In the Tell el Amarna

Letters* 318 men constituted the usual size of raiding parties.]

"W. F. Albright has suggested that *Hapiru* originally referred to donkey* caravaneers who plied the great trade routes of the ancient world. He believes that the word later changed slightly, as the donkey caravaneers were forced into other occupations, to *Habiru*, meaning 'One from beyond,' i.e., the stateless semi-nomads. It is clear that Abraham, who owned donkeys and flocks, fits well into this class of people.

"Incidentally, Tablet 58 is dated in 'The Year Irkebtum the king made peace with Semuma and the ha-'a-bi-ru warriors.' It is quite interesting to compare this with Gen. 14:21–24, where the king of Sodom negotiates with Abraham and his men."

BIBLIOGRAPHY: C. L. Woolley, *A Forgotten Kingdom* (1953); D. J. Wiseman, *The Alalakh Tablets* (1953); M. Greenberg, *The Hab/piru* (1955), 3 passim; G. G. Garner, *Buried History*, AIA, 7.1 (1971), 8–12.   RKH and EMB

ALASEHIR. See PHILADELPHIA.

ALEPPO (ə lep′ ō; W Sem. חלב *ḥlb*; Akkad. *Ḥalab*). An ancient city-kingdom and the second city of modern Syria. In the second millennium B.C., it was the seat of a powerful monarchy (land of Yamkhad), whose rulers, as early as the time of Abraham, rivaled in power those of Mari* and Babylon* down the Euphrates Valley. A Hammurabi of Yamkhad was the equal of the Hammurabi* of Babylon. The Hittite* kings sought to supplant the power of Aleppo. In the fourteenth century B.C. they succeeded when Suppiluliumas I* conquered Aleppo, and installed his son Telepinus as its priest-king. Thereafter Aleppo ceased to be capital of a kingdom, belonging to other states, and retained fame mainly as a sacred city of the weather/storm god—Teshub or Tarhuns to Hurrians* or Hittites, Hadad or Baal* to the Aramaeans* (the equivalent of the baals* of Canaan). A satellite-city of Aleppo in the second millennium was Alalakh,* where valuable clay tablet archives in cuneiform* script were excavated. These tablets afford background for the times of the patriarchs.

BIBLIOGRAPHY: H. Klengel, *Geschichte Syriens im 2. Jahrtausend v.u.Z.*, I (1965), 102ff.; id., 3 (1970), passim; *CAH*, 1, part 2 (1971), 547, 550, 558.

                                                        KAK

ALEXANDRIA. A city* founded by Alexander the Great c. 331 B.C. and located on a narrow piece of land between the Mediterranean Sea and Lake Mareotis, about 22 km. (14 mi.) from the most W part of the mouth of the Nile. Its magnificent lighthouse, Pharos (one of the Seven Wonders of the ancient world), was located on a parallel strip of land on the Mediterranean side and stood 120 to 150 m. (400 to 500 ft.) high at the entrance of the eastern or Great Harbor. Opposite the other end of Pharos Island lay the Eunostos Harbor (the harbor of "happy return"). Pharos Island was connected to the main part of Alexandria by an embankment causeway 1,300 m. (4,200 ft.) long, called the Heptastadion ("seven stadia"),

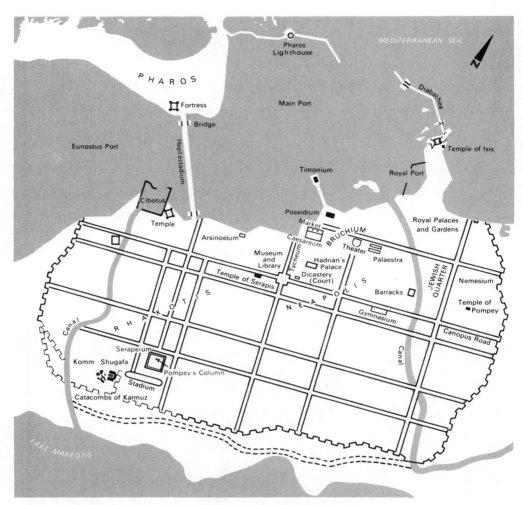

Alexandria in early Christian times. Courtesy Encyclopaedia Judaica, Jerusalem.

which was cut at either end for water passage from the one harbor to the other and bridged over for land travel to and from Pharos Island. On the Lake Mareotis (S) side of Alexandria was another inner harbor (the Cibotos, or the Ark) to which was brought the produce of Egypt.*

Biblical references to Alexandria are found only in Acts: Stephen disputed with members of the synagogue of the Alexandrians (6:9); the preacher Apollos is said to have come from this city (18:24); and Paul traveled to Rome* on two ships of Alexandria (27:6; 28:11).

In NT times the ancient city was divided into the following sections: (1) the Jewish quarter (near the royal palace), with its many synagogues, located on the E; (2) the Regia Brucheion (or Royal Area) in the center, this section containing the theater;* the famous library and museum; the Soma (in which were the tombs of the Ptolemaic kings of Egypt, built

around the Mausoleum containing the alabaster* sarcophagus* with the bones of Alexander the Great); the agora, or forum (to the N); the temple of Neptune at the Eastern Harbor; and, toward the S, the Panium (temple of Pan), gymnasium, and Hall of Justice; (3) the western quarter, which was Egyptian and was called Rhakotis, behind which on a rocky hill stood the magnificent Serapeum (temple of Serapis, or Osiris-Apis); and (4) farther west, the necropolis.*

Most of the ancient city was destroyed, is under the sea, or is under later buildings. Pompey's Pillar, however, is still visible, as are some sphinxes. The Pillar, dating from the time of Emperor Diocletian, is a monolithic shaft with a Corinthian capital* and is located near the site of the ancient Serapeum.

Excavations at Alexandria were carried out by the English in 1895 and by the Germans in 1898–99, but few things were found except remains of the Serapeum, some large catacombs,* and later (1907) some fine sphinxes.

Of further archaeological interest are important Greek manuscripts that have come from Alexandria, including the Septuagint (c. 250 B.C.,) and the uncial codices Alexandrinus (fifth century A.D.), Sinaiticus (fourth century A.D.), and Vaticanus (fourth century A.D.).

BIBLIOGRAPHY: E. Schürer, *A History of the Jewish People in the Time of Jesus Christ*, 2d rev. ed., div. 2, vol. 2 (1891), 226–30; A. Weigall, "The Alexandria of Antony and Cleopatra," in J. Hammerton, ed., *Wonders of the Past*, 2 (1924), 477–90; C. M. Cobern, "Alexandria," *ISBE*, I (1925), 93–96; H. I. Bell, "Alexandria," *JEA*, 13 (1927), 171–84; V. Tcherikover, *Hellenistic Civilization and the Jews* (1961), 320–28, 409–15; E. Badian, *Studies in Greek and Roman History* (1964), 179–91; E. M. Blaiklock, *ZPEB*, I (1975), 100–103; S. Shenouda, "Alexandria," in R. Stillwell, ed., *PECS* (1976), 36–38.

WHM

ALEXANDRIA TROAS. See TROAS.

AL-HIBA (AL HIBBEH) (al hib′ bə). A mound in S Mesopotamia,* slightly E of the present channel of the Shaṭṭ el-Hayy, a river that connects the Tigris and the Euphrates before they meet to form the Shaṭṭ el-Arab. Now generally identified as the center of the Sumerian city of Lagash,* which in its totality included the neighboring site of Tello.*　　CEA

AL JIB. See GIBEON.

ALPHABET. From very ancient times men sought to find a way of providing a visual record for speech in order to communicate with others separated either by space or time. Early attempts were in the form of crude pictographs*—miniature pictures of familiar objects, in which a part was often used to represent the whole. This practice was very widespread, and examples have been found from 4000 B.C. down to recent times, and among peoples as far apart as the Sumerians* and the Indians of N America. Pictographic writing, of course, has severe limitations. It can communicate only what can be illustrated; hence nonmaterial things and abstract ideas defy representation.

Many devices were introduced in attempts to create a fully representative script. It was only with the invention of the alphabet that this was finally achieved.

Four main stages preceded the appearance of the

Painted hieroglyphs on end board of small coffin of Dehuti Nekht (XII Dynasty 1990-1780 B.C.) found at el-Bersheh. Courtesy Museum of Fine Arts, Boston.

alphabet, the first of which was picture writing. All scripts—Sumerian, Babylonian cuneiform,* Egyptian, Cretan, and Chinese—had their origin in picture writing. The purpose of picture writing is to transmit a message through the eye of the recipient. The second stage was the development of the ideograph,* which, by a process of association of ideas or transference, greatly enlarged the field of representation of the pictograph. Thus the pictograph of a star was also adopted as the sign for a divinity; that of the sun represented day; that of two human legs could express the action of running; etc. Methods were also devised to represent abstract concepts; for instance, in Egyptian hieroglyphics* a pictograph of hair was used to denote mourning.

The third step was the pictorial representation of sound, the introduction of the "phonograph." Hitherto no attempt had been made to indicate the name of a thing, and so signs could have been used interlingually, very much as, say, the plus sign (+) is used. It was a revolution, therefore, when an appeal was made to the ear through the eye. The representation now had phonetic as well as pictorial value. The principle of rebus was employed and is still used in children's picture puzzles. In English, for instance, a picture of a bee can be used to signify "be" or "to be."

A fourth step was taken when the initial syllables of the names of several objects were used to construct the visualized name of an abstract word. Thus in English, *charity* might have been expressed by pictographs for chalice, river, and tiara—pronunciation being determined by the initial syllable of each pictograph.

The final and greatest advance was to a type of alphabet, and was a refinement of the previous stage. Someone hit on the idea of using only the initial sound, rather than the whole first syllable, of the name of each pictograph or sign. It was the application of what is now called the principle of acrophony. To illustrate it from English, *bat* would have been spelled by means of a pictograph of a box, an apple, and a tree (though in the original system only consonants were used). This was the most momentous step of all and doubtless the greatest invention of all time. The effect it had on all subsequent civilization is incalculable. The genius who made the discovery may have been familiar with the systems used by the Babylonians and the Egyptians. But the ingenious Egyptians had not been able to reduce the number of their signs to below six hundred, although they had apparently the necessary alphabetic signs already embedded in their script. The Babylonian cuneiform consisted of many hundreds of simple syllabic signs in addition to innumerable sign groupings. Apparently no one considered the possibility that the number of signs could be drastically reduced.

The new system contained twenty-two signs. The signs were simplified pictures of familiar things: the ox;* camel;* serpent* (or fish); water; parts of the human body, such as the head, back of the head, hand, palm of the hand, eye, mouth, and tooth; house;* door; and tent-peg. The Semitic name of the first pictograph, the face of an ox, was *aleph*. The

Semitic name of the second, a house, was *beth*. When the Greeks took over this alphabet, these forms were adapted by adding a terminal "a" (these may, however, be Aramaic* forms), thus: *alpha*, *beta*. Our word *alphabet* itself, derived through the Greek, from the two Semitic words above, is unmistakable

Bronze dagger Lachish (Tell ed-Duweir) with Proto-Canaanite inscription 18th-17th century, B.C. Courtesy Israel Dept. of Antiquities and Museums.

proof of the Semitic origin of our present system of writing.

The time of origin of the alphabet cannot be determined with certainty. Already in the fourteenth century B.C. at Ugarit* in Syria a type of alphabet in the form of simplified cuneiform signs was in use. The most ancient examples are from Sinai* and Tell ed-Duweir,* probably from eighteenth and seventeenth centuries, respectively. The alphabet reached the Greeks through Phoenician traders or Arameans* as early as the ninth or eighth century. The oldest known Latin* example is found on the Praeneste brooch, dated in the sixth century. There is no reason why the Hebrews could not have been using what we may call N Semitic script from as early as the fifteenth century B.C..

See PICTOGRAPHY; WRITING, GENERAL and PICTORIAL.

BIBLIOGRAPHY: G. R. Driver, *Semitic Writing From Pictograph to Alphabet* (1948); J. G. Février, *Histoire de L'Ecriture* (1959); D. Diringer, *The Alphabet* (1968 ed.).   WJM

AL-TABIYA. See TOB.

ALTAKU. See ELTEKEH.

ALTAR. The Bible makes numerous references to altars. The patriarchs built altars (Gen 12:6–8; 13:18; 22:9; 26:25; 33:20; 35:1–7). Moses gave a command that Israel should build altars of hewn stone or earth without steps (Exod 20:24–26). The tabernacle, Solomon's temple,* and the second temple all had altars both for burnt offerings and for incense.* Ezekiel's vision refers to an altar of burnt offering (Ezek 43:13–18).

Archaeological work has produced a wide variety of evidence about temples and altars in Palestine, both from pre-Israelite and Israelite times. Pre-Israelite altars date from Neolithic,* Chalcolithic,* and Early Bronze ages and come from Jericho,* En Gedi,* Megiddo,* and Ai.* Early Bronze Ai contains an altar of plastered stones built against a wall, where animal and food offerings had been made. Excavations in Megiddo of the Middle Bronze Age, which was the patriarchal age, produced two temples with rectangular altars, one of mud bricks and one of limeplastered stones. Late Bronze Age temples from Lachish,* Beth Shan,* and Tell el-Far'ah have revealed a number of Canaanite* altars with associated sacred pillars, cult vessels, benches for offerings, and sometimes actual bones from the sacrifices. A variety of small, hewn limestone altars with four horns at the upper corners, probably incense altars, have been uncovered at such places as Megiddo, Beth Shan and Lachish from Late Bronze and Iron Age levels.

One of the most remarkable temples built in Solomon's time and which stood till the days of Josiah was found at Arad.* The outer room contained a large square altar for burnt offerings. This altar was made of earth and small fieldstones and was covered by a large flint slab surrounded by two plastered grooves. On steps leading to an inner room rested two small stone altars, on the surface of which were

Small limestone four-horned altar from Iron Age, found at Megiddo *(See also photo under* HIGH PLACE.) Courtesy Israel Dept. of Antiquities and Museums.

the charred remains of burnt offerings of some kind. In the inner room was a small elevated platform, presumed to be a bamah or high place,* which suggests the unauthorized altars condemned by the prophets (Amos 3:14; Hos 8:11; cf. 1 Kings 12:28–33).

As excavations proceed, increasing amounts of information will become available about the religious environment, including sacrificial customs, against which Israel had to contend.

BIBLIOGRAPHY: G. R. H. Wright, "Pre-Israelite Temples in the Land of Canaan," *PEQ* (1971), 17–32; Y. Aharoni, "Arad: Its Inscriptions and Temple," BA, 31 (1968), 2–32; O. Tufnell, *Lachish II* (1940); R. de Vaux, *AIs* (1962), 274–330; E. M. Blaiklock, *ZPEB*, 1 (1975), 118–22; E. M. Lerner, "Altar," *EncJud*, 2 (1971), cols. 760–71.   JAT

AL UBAID. See TELL AL-UBAID.

AMARNA (ə mär'nə). A city on the right bank of the Nile, about 305 km. (190 mi.) S of Cairo, so called from the Beni 'Amrān who settled there about A.D. 1737. The form Tell el-Amarna was artificially coined by John Gardner Wilkinson about 1830, when he combined the name of the district with that of the village et-Till (corrupted to Et Tell). The coinage is inappropriate, since et-Till is not a tell* ("mound") in the normal sense. In the first half of the nineteenth century archaeologists paid some attention to rock tombs in the area, but Amarna did not become one of the great archaeological sites of the Near East until 1887 when a peasant woman came upon tablets (Amarna Letters*) of baked clay bearing cuneiform* inscriptions. The site proved to be Akhetaton ("horizon of Aton"), the capital city of Akhenaton,* the so-called "heretic king" of Egypt* in the fourteenth century B.C. It was excavated by the Egypt Exploration Fund (1891) and the German *Orientgesellschaft* (1911–14).

BIBLIOGRAPHY: T. E. Peet, H. Frankfort, and J. D. S. Pendlebury, *City of Akhenaten*, 1–3 (1923–51); C. F. Pfeiffer, *Tell el Amarna and the Bible* (1963); A. Bowling, *ZPEB*, 5 (1975), 614–21.

FFB

AMARNA LETTERS. The cuneiform* tablets found in 1887, and subsequently, at Tell el-Amarna, ancient Akhetaton, which Pharaoh Akhenaton* founded as his capital c. 1372 B.C. They form part of the archives of his reign (1379–1362 B.C.) and of the last eight years of the reign of his father Amenophis III. Thus far 378 Amarna tablets have been published. They include epic and mythological texts and lists of signs and words that probably were used for practice in writing cuneiform.* But most (356) of them are diplomatic letters which passed between the Egyptian king and Asian rulers. Over forty letters were correspondence with peers of the Pharaoh (e.g., the kings of Babylon,* Assyria, Mitanni,* and the Hittites*); the rest passed between him and his vassals. Of the latter, fifty-three were sent to him by Ribadda, king of Byblos (Gebal*); these contain several references to a powerful official named Yanhamu, a Semite who acted as viceroy of Egypt* in Syria. One of the letters ends with the unsolicited testimonial: "There is no servant like Yanhamu, a faithful servant to the king!" (Perhaps the writer thought that Yanhamu would see the letter and appreciate these words.)

Six vassal letters are addressed to the king by Abdi-hiba, ruler of Jerusalem.* He declares his loyalty vehemently: "At the feet of my lord seven times and seven times I fall. . . . Behold, this land of Jerusalem, neither my father nor my mother gave it to me; the king's mighty arm gave it to me." He felt himself menaced by people called the Habiru,* who were encroaching on the Pharaoh's territory in Palestine, and begs for modest military reinforcements to repulse them; even fifty men would suffice, he says. But no reinforcements came, and the Habiru seized more territory; even the town of Beth-ninib, in the Jerusalem region itself, fell to them. Abdi-hiba complains that his neighbors have slandered him to the king, but that he maintained his allegiance faithfully all the while they were acting hand-in-glove with the Habiru. Lab'ayu, ruler of Shechem,* he says, is particularly guilty in this regard; he surrendered the king's possessions to the Habiru; or if not he, then his son.

But Abdi-hiba's neighbors avow their own loyalty and accuse him of betraying the king's interests. Shuwardata, a ruler in the Hebron* district of whom Abdi-hiba complains, charges Abdi-hiba with trying to deprive him of his territory; Abdi-hiba, he says, is another Lab'ayu. Lab'ayu himself, when he writes to the king, claims to be second to none in loyalty and defends himself against his neighbors' slanders. It is his son, not he, he affirms, that has sided with the king's enemies, and Lab'ayu has handed the son over to an Egyptian commissioner. Lab'ayu does not call the king's enemies Habiru but SA.GAZ (*see* Alalakh*); it is plain, however, that SA.GAZ (an ideographic* sign) is identical in meaning with Habiru. In the Amarna letters Abdi-hiba is the only correspondent who calls them Habiru. Ribadda of Byblos says that the SA.GAZ have been threatening the Egyptian Empire in Asia for a generation; he complains of an Amorite ruler Abdi-ashirta who has SA.GAZ under his command and has been taking city after city in the Pharaoh's sphere of influence in Phoenicia, even threatening Ribadda himself. Abdi-ashirta, for his part, writes to complain that he is being slandered and is vigilantly protecting Egyptian interests.

The ideograph SA.GAZ, in the Amarna texts and elsewhere, seems to mean "marauder." Now and then the SA.GAZ appear in the Amarna texts as allies of a loyal vassal, like Biryawaza, the Pharaoh's lieutenant governor at Ube in Syria, who has a contingent of them under his command. But inevitably a neighbor of Biryawaza represents him as working with the SA.GAZ against the Pharaoh's interests.

It is plain that, whatever the reason might be, Egypt's grip on Syria was weakening during Akhenaton's reign. Instead of strong, unified control over the area, we have the spectacle of each vassal playing his own hand—a situation ready-made for freebooters like the Habiru to exploit to their own advantage.

The Habiru (SA.GAZ) are mentioned in cuneiform texts from various parts of W Asia between the twentieth and twelfth centuries B.C. and appear to have been represented in many Near Eastern lands. Wherever they are referred to, it is as foreigners; only rarely did they have a settled home of their own. Sometimes they hired themselves out as domestic servants or as mercenary soldiers; at other times they organized into marauding bands. They have been equated with the *'pr.w* mentioned as foreign laborers in inscriptions in the Egyptian language between 1450 and 1150 B.C.; this equation is probably correct. More problematic is their equation with the biblical Hebrews. Linguistically this equation is possible; it is also supported by the fact that in the OT, from Abraham's time to Jeremiah's, the word is chiefly used either of Israelites by non-Israelites or by Israelites when speaking of themselves to non-Israelites. In one place (1 Sam 14:21) reference is made to Hebrews as distinct from Israelites. All Israelites were probably Hebrews to their neighbors, but all Hebrews were not Israelites. The marauding activities of the Habiru recorded in the Amarna Letters cannot be identified with the Israelite invasion of Canaan under Joshua; the names and other details are different, and the Amarna Age antedates Joshua by a century or more. But the letters throw welcome light on movements in the Israelites' homeland while they themselves were sojourning in Egypt.

See AKHENATON; ALALAKH; AMARNA; HABIRU.

BIBLIOGRAPHY: J. A. Knudtzon and O. Weber, *Die El-Amarna-Tafeln* (1915); F. Thureau-Dangin, *Revue d'Assyriologie*, 19 (1922), 91–108; S. A. B. Mercer, *The Tell el-Amarna Tablets* (1939); *ANET* (1955 ed.), 482–90; M. Greenberg, *The Hab/piru* (1955).

FFB

AMBER. A fossilized pine resin highly prized in antiquity for its color and beauty, as well as for its ability to attract particles when rubbed.

AMENEMOPET, THE INSTRUCTION OF (ä mə nem'ō pet). An Egyptian* wisdom text in hieratic* script dating from the seventh century B.C. (British Museum Papyrus 10474) and a later copy of a text now in Turin, Italy. About thirty paragraphs are still extant, each divided into a dozen or so poetic statements. The general tone is subdued, humble, and reflects resignation to fate. The striking parallels between the Amenemopet text and Prov 22:17–24:22 have rendered the papyrus* one of the most important for biblical study. The order of the sayings is different, and the Egyptian text is longer. The problem of priority has never been solved, but the Egyptian proverb seems to be earlier than the Hebrew. Both are nonmaterialistic and laud wisdom. The papyrus yields valuable insights into the state of Egyptian affairs in the New Kingdom and describes the loss of imperialism. The passive resignation to the god's design is characteristic of later literature of the declining archaic religious-states.

BIBLIOGRAPHY; *ANET*, 421–25. The most complete edition and translation is still that of E. W. Wallis Budge (1912).

WW

AMMAN. *See* RABBAH.

AMMON, AMMONITES (am'ən; Heb. עַמּוֹן, 'ām-môn, "people"[?]). A country and people that had an independent existence in central Trans-Jordan from 1300 to 580 B.C., along the fertile strip of land bordering the N-S arm of the Jabbok River. Their origins are obscure (Gen 19:38). The Israelites did not conquer Ammon at the time of the Exodus (Deut 2:19,37; Judg 11:15), but from the days of the judges onward there were numerous military contacts (Judg 11:27–33; 1 Sam 11:11; 2 Sam 10; 2 Chron 20; 2 Kings 24:2; Jer 49:1–6; Ezek 21:20; 25:1–7; Amos 1:13–15).

Archaeologically, Ammon is not well known because extensive excavation has not been undertaken. Surface surveys show that many sites were occupied from the beginning of Iron Age I onward. The capital was Rabbah* Ammon, the modern Amman (Josh 13:25; 2 Sam 11:1; 12:27,29; Jer 49:3; Ezek 25:5; Amos 1:14). The ancient town has disappeared, but pottery* found on Citadel Hill indicates a long occupation, covering even the Middle and Late Bronze ages (c. 1900–1200 B.C.). An important Late Bronze Age tomb (*see* GRAVE) was found near the modern airport. Most of the tombs, however, come from the Iron II (*see* IRON AGE) period. These have yielded large quantities of Ammonite pottery,* mostly from

the seventh century B.C.; numerous inscribed seals;* some statues,* including small pottery horse*-and-rider figurines; utensils of iron,* limestone, and alabaster;* beads and other ornaments. A broken stone slab carrying eight lines of writing from the middle of the ninth century B.C. and referring to a temple of Molech* (1 Kings 11:5), the god of Ammon, was found in 1961 near the Iron Age fortifications on Citadel Hill. It is the third longest Palestinian inscription known at present.

Yet another inscription in the form of an inscribed bronze* bottle that carried eight lines of writing was found in 1972. It refers to the works of Amminadab, king of Ammon, c. 600 B.C.. Another important structure, a Late Bronze Age temple, has come to light near the airport. A vigorous program of excavation in Jordan will fill out the picture considerably.

See MOABITE STONE; SILOAM INSCRIPTION.

BIBLIOGRAPHY: F. M. Cross, "Notes on the Ammonite Inscription from Tell Siran," *BASOR*, 212 (Dec. 1973), 12–15; N. Glueck, *The Other Side of the Jordan* (1940); id., "Explorations in Eastern Palestine, III," *AASOR*, 18–19 (1937–39); ibid., IV, *AASOR*, 25–28 (1945–49), passim; H. O. Thompson and F. Zaydine, "The Tell Siran Inscription," *BASOR*, 212 (Dec. 1973), pp. 5–11; G. M. Landes, "The Material Civilization of the Ammonites," *BA*, 24 (1961), 66–95; S. H. Horn, "The Amman Citadel Inscription," *BASOR*, 193 (1969), 2–13; F. M. Cross, Jr., "Epigraphic notes on the Amman Citadel Inscription," *BASOR*, 193 (1969), 13–19; B. Oded, "Ammon, Ammonites," *EncJud*, 2 (1971), col. 853–60.

JAT

AMORITES (am'ə rīts; Heb. אֱמֹרִי, 'emôrî). The OT 'emôrî, thought to be an E Semitic loan word, was the equivalent of the Akkad. *amurrū* ("west"), which occurs as the designation of a land W of Mesopotamia.* Its inhabitants were known to the Babylonians (*see* BABYLON) and Assyrians (*see* ASSYRIOLOGY) as *amurrum*, but the precise nature of the connection between this name and the location known as "west" is uncertain. Some scholars have assumed that the whole area from the Euphrates westward to the Mediterranean was Amorite territory, while others have regarded either Syria or the Arabian* peninsula as the land of the Amorites. The last of these can now be eliminated as a possibility, since personal names once thought to be Arabic are now known to be W Semitic of the Amorite variety.

Amorites began to appear in Sumer* somewhat before 2600 B.C., being mentioned in cuneiform* texts by the name *mar.tus*, and in the last few centuries of the third millennium B.C. Amorite culture in northern Mesopotamia became characterized by well-developed urban centers represented by such sites as Tell Hariri (Mari*) and Hama, the economy of which was chiefly agricultural.* These early Amorite settlements maintained political and diplomatic contacts with other cities in Mesopotamia. Intertwined with their agricultural and urban-centered way of life was a specifically nomadic existence which was also characteristically Amorite and which dated from the Early Bronze Age. The myth of the god

Martu and his marriage reflects the nomadic pattern of living, typifying the Amorite mountaineer as one unfamiliar either with agricultural or urban life.

The first major Amorite incursions into Mesopotamia occurred about 2600 B.C., and these increased in number and influence as time progressed. In the Old Akkadian period (c. 2400–2150 B.C.) the Amorites were a commercial as well as a cultural and military power, and by about 2350 B.C. Sargon of Akkad* (Agade) was engaged in trade with them, having sent an expedition to the land of Amurru in order to obtain some much-needed building materials. That the people of S Mesopotamia continued trading with the Amorites is seen in the purchase of a quantity of marble by King Gudea* of Lagash,* about 2000 B.C. The capital of Amurru at that period was Mari (Tell Hariri) on the Euphrates River, and it was apparently from this center that the Amorites had been attacking Sumer for some time, making it necessary for the Sumerians to construct fortifications between the Tigris and Euphrates. A major assault against Ur* occurred under its last king, Ibbi-Sin (c. 2030–2004 B.C.), and this combined with internal economic trouble to weaken Sumer and increase Amorite influence in the S, where aggressive individuals obtained considerable power. The Amorites had by this time intermingled with the native Mesopotamians and founded a number of city-states including Babylon, the first dynasty of which was Amorite. This development, however, led to the undoing of the Amorites as an imperial power, and they passed into eclipse with the conquest of Mari by Hammurabi* (c. 1792–1750 B.C.). Some of the Amurru settled down in one area of Syria and were mentioned as such in texts from Mari and Alalakh.* During the Amarna Age a number of Amorite centers existed in Syria, one of which was Kadesh, but even these came to an end when the marauding Sea Peoples* brought about the destruction of the Hittite* Empire, about 1200 B.C. The early mar.tus who went to Sumer and nearby countries were traders in various commodities and, from certain Sumerian texts, appear also to have been metallurgists (see METALLURGY) and leather* workers. The Amorites were noted as goldsmiths (see GOLD) and silversmiths (see SILVER), and, because of third-millennium B.C. smelting activity in the Ararat* region, it seems highly probable that they manufactured bronze* as well. From an early period of its history the city-state of Isin was well known for the production of leather, and some Sumerian texts seem to imply that the Amorites were involved in the processing as well as in the purchasing of leather articles. The mar.tus seem also to have taken a prominent part in the lapis lazuli* trade between Afghanistan and Mesopotamia.

Amorite culture has been exposed most fully in modern times by the excavations of Parrot at Mari. From the many diplomatic and commercial documents recovered, it is evident that Amorite was one of the NW Semitic dialects, and thus closely related linguistically to Canaanite and the language spoken at Ebla (Tell Mardikh*). Some texts from Mari were also written in Hurrian.* As with other Mesopotamian peoples, magic and divination occupied an im-

portant place in life at Mari, with hepatoscopy (liver* divination) being in common usage. Some place-names associated with the Hebrew patriarchs occur in the Mari tablets—the city of Nahor (Nakhur), home of Rebekah, being mentioned frequently. Some Habiru* lived in the area, but references to them in the Mari texts are indeterminate in nature. In Amorite society administrative efficiency was high, as illustrated by two large tablets which listed nearly one thousand names of craftsmen and the guilds to which they belonged. Other texts recorded the great care expended on the vitally important irrigation canal system.

Some tablets referred to a warlike nomadic Amorite group known as the Banu-Yamina, who may have originated in the desert areas of the Euphrates. The activities of the Banu-Yamina have elements in common with the character of the Benjamites as described in the blessing of Jacob (Gen 49:27; cf. Judg. 20:17; 1 Chron 12:2), but to what extent the two groups were related is uncertain. At Mari an important means of ratifying a treaty between groups or individuals was the sacrificing of a donkey. This tradition survived among the Canaanite descendants of Shechem* (Gen 34:2ff.), who were also known as Bene Hamor or "sons of the ass" (Josh 24:32).

The term *Amorite* appears in some lists of pre-Israelite inhabitants of Palestine (cf. Gen 10:16; Exod 3:8; Deut 1:19ff; Num 13:29; Josh 10:5ff.), along with the mention of two Amorite kingdoms, Heshbon* and Bashan* (Num 21:13; Josh 2:10 et al.). The "Amorite border" of Josh 13:4f. corresponds to the general Late Amarna Age location of Amurru as an area N of Byblos (Gebal*) and Canaan.* The Amorite mountain dwellers of Deut 1:19ff. and Josh 10:5ff. may have preserved the ancient pastoral traditions of the *mar.tus* as found in Sumerian literature.

See ALALAKH; BABYLON; BASHAN; HESHBON; LAGASH; MARI; MESOPOTAMIA; SARGON OF AKKAD; SEA PEOPLES; SHECHEM; SUMER.

BIBLIOGRAPHY: A. Haldar, *Who Were the Amorites?* (1971); *CAH*, I, Part 2 (1971), 237, 321, passim; K. A. Kitchen. *The Bible in Its World* (1977), 24, passim.

RKH

AMPHIPOLIS (am fip'ə ləs; Gr. Ἀμφίπολις, *amphipolis*, "surrounding city"). Capital city of the first district of Macedonia, through which Paul passed on his journey along the Egnatian Way* from Philippi* to Thessalonica* (Acts 17:1). It was surrounded on three sides by the Strymon River (hence the name: literally, "around-city") and was settled by the Athenian colonizer Hagnon in 424 B.C., who built a wall on the exposed E side (Thuc. 4.102). From the gold* and silver* of the mines* at Mount Pangaeus the Macedonian kings minted coins* at Amphipolis of superb quality, especially the tetradrachms featuring Apollo and the flaming torch symbol. On the site (modern Neochori) the base of an early Christian basilica* has been excavated.

BIBLIOGRAPHY: B. V. Head, *Historia Numorum*, 2d ed. (1911), 214ff.; S. Pelekides, *Proceeds of the Athenian Arch. Soc.* (1920), 86–87; S. Casson, *Mac-

edonia, Trace and Illyria (1926), 214ff.; C. Seltman, *Greek Coins* (1955), 115–16; W. K. Pritchett, *Studies in Ancient Greek Topography* (1965), 30ff.; D. I. Lazaridis and E. Stikas, *Proceeds of the Athenian Arch. Soc.* (1971), 43–49, 50–62.

BFH

AMPHITHEATER. A Roman oval or circular structure in which games* or contests were held. Examples include the Colosseum* at Rome* and the amphitheater at Puteoli.*

AMPHORA (am'fər ə; Gr. ἀμφορεύς, *amphoreus*, "jar"). A type of large two-handled, narrow-necked pot made of stone or clay* and used for storing wine,* oil, or grain. The term is Greek and may be traced to the Minoan* or Mycenaean* Age (c. 2000 B.C.). Large amphorae* have been located by underwater archaeologists (*see* UNDERWATER ARCHAEOLOGY) in the wrecks of ancient trading vessels in the Aegean Sea and the Mediterranean. The standard amphorae are about 1 m. (c. 3 ft.) high and narrow-necked, with two very large handles. Most were wheel*-made, and many were brilliantly decorated. Some special types had a pointed or rounded base that fitted into receptacles on shipboard for safer storage during voyages. In time the use of amphorae for storage and transport of wine and olive oil* spread over most of the classical world and became commonplace during the Roman era.

The amphora was not the same as the large vessels used in Palestine—the "stone water jars" (John 2:6) or the "jars of clay" (2 Cor 4:7) sometimes employed for the safekeeping of fragile materials, such as the scrolls* hidden in the Qumran* caves.* The common water pitcher (Jer 19:1,10; 35:5) was the nearest in shape to the typical amphora, having a narrow neck with one handle attached.

See QUMRAN.

BIBLIOGRAPHY: J. L. Kelso, *The Ceramic Vocabulary of the Old Testament* (1948); W. F. Albright, *The Archaeology of Palestine* (1960 ed.), 148, figs. 1, 2, 6, 7, 16.

WW

AMPLIATUS (AMPLIAS) (am'plēa'təs; Gr. Ἀμπλιατος, *Ampliatos*). The name is found in Rom 16:8 and in inscriptions listing "Caesar's household*" (cf. Phil 4:22). In the first century most of the imperial household staff came from the East and were persons of some standing, especially under Claudius* and Nero. A tomb inscription of the late first century in the Catacomb* of Domitilla reads "Ampliati"—doubtless a genitive—i.e., "of Ampliatus." It is an ornate tomb and could be that of Paul's friend.

BIBLIOGRAPHY: R. Lanciani, *Pagan and Christian Rome* (1895), 342ff.; J. B. Lightfoot, *St. Paul's Epistle to the Philippians* (1913), 174.

EMB

AMRAPHEL (am'rə fĕl; Heb. אַמְרָפֶל, *'amrāpel*; LXX Gr. Ἀμαρφαλ, *amarphal*, meaning unknown). King of Shinar* (Babylonia?) and member of the coalition of kings defeated by Abram (Gen 14).

Group of Phoenician faience amulets from Beth Shemesh and Lachish, ninth to seventh centuries B.C. The amulets represent Egyptian deities, demons, and religious symbols: 1. Hathor, 2. Uzzat eye, 3. Baboon, 4. Bes, 5. Isis, 6. Bastet, 7. Sekhmet. Courtesy Israel Dept. of Antiquities and Museums. Exhibited and photographed at Israel Museum, Jerusalem.

No record of such a king is preserved in extrabiblical records, though at one time an identification with Hammurabi,* king of Babylon, was proposed. This is now largely abandoned, and neither archaeology nor philology has been able to identify this king.

BIBLIOGRAPHY: R. K. Harrison, *Introduction to the OT* (1969), 159–60.

CEA

AMULET (am'yə lət). A small object worn on the body as a charm, frequently around the neck, intended to ward off evil and harm. Amulets were often inscribed with a magical incantation* and usually had a symbolic meaning. These small ornaments, gems, stones, seals,* beads, earrings, plaques, and emblems included figurines of animals, birds, reptiles, fish, and humans. In addition, geometric figures, representations of various deities, parts of human anatomy, and other items of unknown significance are found. As well as being fashioned from gem stones, they were sometimes made of wood,* fired clay,* ivory,* faience,* lapis lazuli,* metal, and so on.

In early prehistoric times there is evidence that teeth, bones, and nails from the dead were worn as amulets. Rings were widely worn and thought to prevent the entrance of evil spirits. Predynastic Egyptian burials contain a variety of diverse animal, bird, fish, and human figurines—especially of apes, cats,* beetles (*see* SCARAB), and bulls. Knotted cords and tied bundles appear in Egyptian art, and it may be assumed that these are from a very early date. In later periods appeared great numbers of religious fig-urines—of the goddesses Hathor and Isis, of the god Horus, of the backbone of the god Osiris,* and of Life (ankh). There was also a very large class of oval-shaped objects, modified with asymmetrical projec-tions and worn about the neck, the meaning of which is obscure. Variations in the neck string and its bead-work seem also to have conveyed special significance.

A great many small objects, probably amulets, ap-pear in Palestinian excavations. They are predomi-nantly of Egyptian style, such as the ujat or eye amulet from Lachish.* However, the inverted crescent-shaped earrings found at various places (e.g., Tell el-'Ajjul, fourteenth to thirteenth century B.C.) are symbolic of the Astarte-Ishtar* goddess complex of Phoenician* and Mesopotamian* origin. Repre-sentations of human arms, legs, and other body parts evidently were for protection or healing and proba-bly reflect Aegean influence. Fruits such as pome-granates and grapes were popular, as was, in a special sense, the obese Egyptian god Bes.

The Bible does not use the term amulet, but it is certain that Isa 3:20 refers to them.

BIBLIOGRAPHY: W. M. F. Petrie, ed., Ancient Egypt, Part II (1917), 49–56; A. Deissman, Light From the Ancient East (1922), 59, 240, 254, 284; J. Frazer, The Golden Bough, abridged ed. (1948), 109, 242–43, 679–80; H. Smith, Man and His Gods (1953), 12, 31; E. Budge, Amulets and Talismans (1961); T. Schrine, Hebrew Amulets: Their Deci-pherment and Interpretation (1966).

MHH

AMWAS. See EMMAUS.

ANAK (ā'nak; Heb. עֲנָק, ʿⁿāq, "neck," "necklace"). The eponymous* ancestor of a race of pre-Israelite inhabitants of Palestine called Anakim. Three rulers

of Iy-anaq, all with Semitic names, are mentioned in the Egyptian Execration Texts* from the Middle Kingdom (c. 2000 B.C.), but whether this tribe is the same as that mentioned in the biblical account of the conquest is not certain.

According to Num 13:22, the chiefs of Hebron* claimed descent from Anak and occupied Hebron until they were driven into Philistine* territory by Caleb (Josh 11:22). Like the Rephaim, the Anakim were tall and forbidding in appearance (Deut 9:2).

BIBLIOGRAPHY: W. F. Albright, "The Egyptian Empire in Asia in the Twenty-first Century B.C.," JPOS, 8 (1928), 223–56; J. B. Pritchard, ANET, 328.

CEA

ANANIA. See BETHANY.

ANATA. See ANATHOTH.

ANATH (ANAT) (ā'nath; Heb. עֲנָת, ʿⁿāṯ; Ugar ʿnt). This Canaanite goddess is claimed by Philo to have been the daughter of El. In the literature of Ugarit,* modern Ras Shamra (fifteenth–fourteenth centuries B.C.), and in the writings of Egypt* of the thirteenth century B.C., she appears as the consort of Baal.* The etymology of the name is uncertain. It has been suggested that it originally meant "destiny" or "prov-idence" (AJSL, 41 [1925], 94ff.). The name, how-ever, may also be associated with the Akkadian* word ettu, meaning "sign" or "omen." According to Al-bright, the name ʿAnat probably meant originally "sign," "indication of purpose," or "act of will" and was applied to the personified or hypostatized will of Baal (BASOR, 84 [1941], 15). She, like Asherah* and Astarte (Ashtaroth), was a goddess of sex and of war. In Ugaritic literature she is often called btlt ʿnt ("the virgin ʿAnat"). She also bears the appellation

Lower part of Egyptian stele from XIX Dynasty (1350-1200 B.C.) depicting goddess Anath seated on her throne receiving offerings from three figures. Reproduced by courtesy of the Trustees of the British Museum.

"progenitress of the peoples." Besides the concepts of fertility associated with this goddess was that of her extreme brutality. In Ugaritic literature she is depicted as wading in the blood of her human victims (cf. *ANET*, 136). Like many of the other gods of Canaan,* she was attributed with the powers of procreation and fertility. Sacred prostitution* was invariably a concomitant of the cult. In Ugaritic mythology she was closely associated with Baal and on occasion came to his defense. In many respects she was like the goddess Astarte.

The name 'Anat to date has never appeared in materials discovered as a human name in either Israel or Ugarit. One of the predynastic judges in Israel, however, was described as being "the son of Anath" (Judg 3:31; 5:6). Some scholars have suggested that the reading here should not be Šamgar ben 'ᵃnāṯ, but should read Šamgar bēṯ 'ᵃnāṯ ("Shamgar [of] the house of Anat"), thus indicating that he was from the Canaanite city of Beth-Anath. The expression *ben* 'ᵃnāṯ ("Son of Anath") could well be an idiom referring to a warrior. Since 'Anat was a goddess of war, it is not impossible that the expression became idiomatic for a person known for superiority as a warrior. It is interesting that two men in Ugarit were also called "Son of Anat."

BIBLIOGRAPHY: C. H. Gordon, *The Common Backgrounds of Greek and Hebrew Civilizations*, 186ff.; W. F. Albright, "The Evolution of West-Semitic Divinity An-Anat-Atta," *AJSL*, 41 (1925), 73–101; id., *Archaeology and the Religion of Israel*, 3d ed. (1953), 74ff; Virolleaud, *Palais royal d'Ugarit* 2 (1957), text 43:12; 61:6.   JJD

ANATHOTH (an'ə thoth; Heb. עֲנָתוֹת, 'ᵃnāṯôṯ, meaning probably "great Anath"). A city of Benjamin.

The present-day village of 'Anata, 5 km. (c. 3 mi.) NE of Jerusalem,* preserves the name of Jeremiah's native town. One km. (c. ½ mi.) SW of the town lies Tell Ras el-Kharrubeh identified since 1936 (though not unanimously) with the ancient city of Anathoth. Investigations in that year by two students of the American Schools of Oriental Research showed occupation from the time of the Israelite Monarchy through the period of the Muslim conquest. The site is well situated on a ridge overlooking both the Jordan Valley to the E and Jerusalem to the SW. Various biblical references, as well as its location near important centers, indicate that Tell Ras el-Kharrubeh may preserve important historical and archaeological data.

BIBLIOGRAPHY: E. P. Blair, "Soundings at 'Anata," *BASOR*, 62 (1936), 18–21; A. Bergman, "Soundings at the Supposed Site of OT Anathoth," *BASOR*, 62 (1936), 22–25; A. Bergman, "Anathoth?" *BASOR*, 63 (1936), 22.   CEA

ANCHOR. Anchors are mentioned twice in the NT: in the account of Paul's shipwreck on Malta* (Acts 27:29–30,40) and in a vivid metaphor in Heb 6:19. In both cases the device is the bidens, or double-toothed, anchor, exactly like its common modern equivalent. Stones, no doubt grooved or pierced to give grip or attachment to the rope,* were the first

type of anchor (Hom. *Il.* 1.436). No Mediterranean examples seem to survive, either of this or of the later metal type, though underwater archaeology* on the many located wrecks, especially on the Syrtes* off the N African coast, may in time produce examples.

Anacharsis, one of the so-called Seven Sages, who lived around 600 B.C., invented the bidens, or at least the hooked anchor (cf. Plin. *NH* 7. 56. 209). A perfect example, no different from a modern anchor, may be seen in a wall graffito* accompanying the Christian symbol of the fish (*see* ACROSTIC) in the Catacomb of Hermes. A beautiful double-fluked anchor also occurs on the undated Christian patera and on a ring from Pompeii* in the Naples Museum, significantly accompanied by the Greek word *elpis*, "hope."

See SHIPS.

BIBLIOGRAPHY: *ANEP* (1954), 42.

EMB

ANCYRA (an kī'rə; Gr. Ἄγκυρα, *Ankyra*). This Galatian-populated city (mod. Ankara) of Phrygia* was an important strongpoint in the first-century imperial defense system. It became the chief city of Galatia* and is the capital of modern Turkey. It has no direct place in biblical archaeology except that, in a bilingual (Latin* and Greek) inscription on a surviving temple wall, Augustus* recorded what he considered the achievements of his principate: his founding of the Pax Romana ("Roman peace") and his establishment of the frontiers. His census system, mentioned in connection with the Nativity (Luke 2:1–2), was part of his world-wide organization. This *Monumentum Ancyranum*, therefore, is a document of importance in connection with the time of tranquillity in which the Christian church took root.

BIBLIOGRAPHY: E. G. Kraeling, *Bible Atlas* (1956), index refs. A3 XI, XIII; B5 XII; D12 XIX; A5 XX.

EMB

ANCYRANUM MONUMENTUM. *See* ANCYRA.

ANI, INSTRUCTION OF. A collection of Egyptian sayings credited to a scribe, Ani. It was written during the later Imperial period (c. 1700 B.C.) and survives in a copy of the tenth century B.C., Papyrus* Boulaq No. 4 in the Cairo Museum; in a fragment Musée Guimet No. 16969; and in a writing tablet, Berlin Museum No. 8934. The scribe exhorts his son to passive obedience and to the keeping of the prescribed rituals according to contemporary usage. It is instructive to biblical scholars as an early example of paternal instruction such as is found in the more profound sections of Proverbs. It is also interesting as showing an advance beyond earlier Egyptian wisdom literature as represented by Ptah-hotep.* Filial obedience to a mother is an illustration of such development. Ani instructs his son: "Double the food which you give to your mother, and carry her as she carried you. . . . She had a heavy load in you. . . . You were born in due time, but she was still yoked with you. . . . She put you into school . . . and continued on your behalf every day with bread and beer in your house. When you are a young man and take a wife and settle in your house, set your eye on how your mother gave birth to you and all her bringing up. Do not let her blame you nor raise her hands to the god to hear her cries." This is reminiscent of the commandment "Honor your father and your mother" (Exod 20:12).

BIBLIOGRAPHY: *ANET*, 420–21; J. B. Pritchard, *Archaeology and the OT* (1958), 236–37.

ww and EMB

ANIMALS. See CAMEL; CAT; CROCODILE; DOG; DONKEY; EAGLE; GOAT; HORNET; HORSE; LEVIATHAN; LOCUST; OX; OX, WILD; RABBIT; SCARAB; SERPENT.

ANI, PAPYRUS OF. This document, now Papyrus* British Museum No. 10470, is a fine copy of the so-called Egyptian Book of the Dead*—an anthology of magical spells intended to aid the deceased in the afterlife. This copy belonged to the "real, beloved King's Scribe Ani" (*see* ANI, INSTRUCTION OF) who flourished in the New Kingdom, c. fourteenth century B.C.. Often reproduced is its representation of chapter (or, spell) 125—the last judgment in Egyptian terms, with weighing of the heart against the plume of "truth" in relation to a person's conduct in this life. This chapter, with its denial to the gods of a series of sins, presupposes in Egypt* of the second millennium B.C. a clear consciousness of right and wrong, responsibility for one's deeds in this life, accountability to deity, and the effect of individual behavior on one's afterlife. But dependence on magical spells to steer the deceased safely through the final tribunal, regardless of sins, shows also how right-wrong concepts could easily be ignored in practice, because of a weakened moral imperative.

BIBLIOGRAPHY: E. A. W. Budge, ed., *The Papyrus of Ani* (1913). KAK

ANKARA. See ANCYRA.

ANKLETS. See BANGLES.

ANSHAN. See ELAM.

ANTAKYA. See ANTIOCH, SYRIAN.

ANTIOCH, CHALICE OF. This large silver cup, standing 19 cm. (7½ in.) high and embossed with twelve portraits, was first described in 1916 by G. A. Eisen (*AJA*, 20 [1916], 426–37). It consists of a plain inner cup, a highly decorated and gilded open-work shell, and a base—all of solid silver. Eisen claimed that the cup bore a first-century representation of Christ with eight apostles and two evangelists. There was some support for the contention that the cup was actually the Holy Grail, the vessel used at the Last Supper, and as such it was exhibited at the Chicago World's Fair in 1933. That the figure of Christ is represented seems beyond doubt, but on the other details doubt has formed. Details of the discovery are disappointingly obscure, and considerable argument about the style of the portraiture seems to lead to the conclusion that the chalice perhaps dates to the end of the fourth century. G. A. Eisen's further contention that this elaborately ornamented vessel could have been a container for the actual Grail is beyond proof. The matter can be pursued no further. The chalice is in the Cloisters Collection of the Metropolitan Museum of Arts in New York.

BIBLIOGRAPHY: G. A. Eisen, *AJA*, 20 (1916), 426–37; id., *The Great Chalice of Antioch*, 2 vols. (1923); A. B. Cook, *Cambridge Review*, 45 (1924), 213–16.

EMB

ANTIOCH, PISIDIAN (an'tē ok, pə sid'ē ən; Gr. Ἀντιοχεια Πισιδίας, *Antiocheia Pisidias*). More correctly, to distinguish it from the other Phrygian* foundation of the same name on the Maeander River, "Antioch toward Pisidia."

Strabo's statement, in his geographical survey, that Antioch was in Phrygia is confirmed by various inscriptions. One, for example, from Rome* is found in an epitaph of an Antiochian: "A Magnesian of Phrygian and Appe, devoted as a virgin to Artemis, . . . nursed me in the olive-clad Anthian plain." The city was a strong bastion for many centuries against the unruly mountaineers of central Asia Minor* and occupied a stategic plateau above the Anthios River. The first period of its history was from 300 to 25 B.C., at which latter date it passed to Roman control as part of the Kingdom of Amyntas. As an obvious site for a colony (a *propugnaculum imperii*, or "bulwark of the Empire," as Cicero called such bastions), Antioch thus passed into the province of Galatia* as Colonia Caeasareia Antiocheia. It was linked by firm military roads to other colonies (such as Lystra*) as part of Augustus's* efforts to stabilize the frontiers. It is significant that fragments of Augustus's monumental inscription describing his life's enterprises (the *Res Gestae*, of which a fairly full version was found at Ancyra of Galatia in 1555—the so-called "*Monumentum Ancyranum*" [*see* ANCYRA]), was discovered at Antioch. These fragments are called the *Monumentum Antiochenum*. A few fragments, no doubt also from the temple of Augustus, came from neighboring Apollonia. The inscription emphasizes the determined Roman imperial penetration of the area, which is of interest as a possible motive in Paul's strategic evangelization of this part of Galatia.

It may also be noted that Antiochene inscriptions, both Greek and Latin,* show no trace of other than Roman citizens. Every free inhabitant of whom such a record has survived bears the full Roman name that denotes citizenship. It seems that the whole city, though not as early as NT times, ultimately acquired the coveted status. The pride of the city in its colonial and Roman character is also demonstrated in its coinage (*see* COINS). The citizens who formed the original core of the colony (the first, it would seem, in central Asia Minor) were veterans of the Skylark Legion (Alauda), a Gallic legion formed by Julius Caesar and named for its helmet decoration.

Ramsay's contention that Antioch was included in the province of Galatia in the first and second centuries A.D. (*A Historical Commentary on Galatians*, 177f., 209f.), was confirmed by the discovery in 1905 of milestones E of nearby Apollonia. They were dated A.D. 198 and bore the name of the governor of Galatia, who at that time was Atticius Strabo.

The presence of an ancient Jewish element in the population is demonstrated by an inscription from neighboring Apollonia belonging to the first or second century after Christ. It runs: "An Antiochian, sprung from ancestors who held many offices of state in the fatherland, by name Debbora, given in marriage to a famous man Pamphylus, and receiving this monument as a return of gratitude from him for my virgin marriage." Note the Septuagint spelling of the name Deborah, which marks the Hellenistic Jew.* It is highly probable that the husband, Pamphylus, was a citizen of Apollonia, and that, in consequence, some right of intermarriage between the two cities existed. Deborra's reference to the positions of dignity held by her forbears refers to the higher magistracies of the free cities. Since the existence of a solitary Jew in a Greek city was impossible (W. M. Ramsay, *The Letters to the Seven Churches*, 148–50), there must have been a legally constituted "tribe" for Jews. For a Jew to be a magistrate in a Greek city involved a large measure of compromise with pagan practice, and this may throw some light on the mixed marriage of Timothy's parents, as well as on the nature and constitution of the group of social liberals who gave to the early church the problem of Nicolaitanism (probably a heresy promoting idolatry and immorality; see Rev 2:6, 15). They could have been Hellenistic Jews who had learned the art of adapting too well to a pagan environment. The apparent influence of the synagogue* with the authorities, evident at the time of Paul's visit, may also find explanation in the same context.

Antioch was a fine city. The walls* are prominent around the three exposed sides. The Anthios River protected the fourth and provided water, which made the city independent of the aqueduct*—of which arches* survive and which brought the main water supply from the Sultan-Dagh several km. away. A Corinthian-columned temple to the Anatolian god Mên and to Augustus has left some of its sculptured features, and some of the other fine public places of the city are also visible—including a theater in a ruined state.

BIBLIOGRAPHY: W. M. Ramsay, *A Historical Commentary on St. Paul's Epistles to the Galatians* (1900), 177–78, 209–10; id., *The Letters to the Seven Churches* (1905), 148–50; id., *Cities of St. Paul* (1907), 245–314; Strabo, *The Geography of Strabo*, 8 vol. (1917–32 ed.); D. Magie, *Roman Rule in Asia Minor* (1950), 457–63; E. M. Blaiklock, *Cities of the NT* (1965); B. Levick, *Roman Colonies in Southern Asia Minor* (1967); A. H. M. Jones, *The Cities of the Eastern Roman Provinces*, 2d ed. (1971).   EMB

ANTIOCH, SYRIAN (an'tē ok; Gr. Ἀντιόχεια, *Antiocheia*). Syrian Antioch, second city of the Early Church and third city of the Roman Empire, is modern Antakya, which lies inland from the Mediterranean by a few km., at the limit of ancient navigation up the Orontes River. It was a foundation city of Seleucus, one of Alexander's "successors," in 300 B.C.

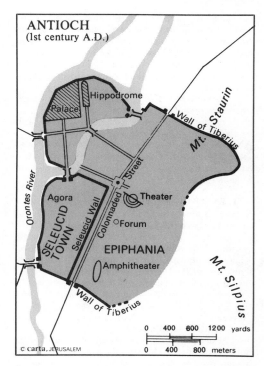

ANTIOCH
(1st century A.D.)

Hippodrome
Palace
Wall of Staurin
Mt. Tiberius
Orontes River
Agora
Seleucid Wall
Colonnaded Street
Theater
Forum
SELEUCID TOWN
EPIPHANIA
Amphitheater
Mt. Silpius
Wall of Tiberius

0   400   800   1200 yards
0   400   800 meters

© carta, JERUSALEM

and represented part of the Greek and Macedonian penetration of Syria. Like Tarsus,* it was one of the fruitful points of contact between E and W and became the recipient of notable enlargements and benefactions from the early Roman emperors.

As with many centers of ancient life whose sites are still under active occupation, less archaeological exploration has been possible at Antioch than on such comparatively deserted areas as the site of its Pisidian namesake. The street plan of a considerable portion of the ancient city has, however, been established, and since modern Antakya occupies a smaller area than the ancient city, more digging may produce rewarding results. The work of the seven most active years (1932–39, when World War II interrupted exploration) has not been actively extended at the time of this writing.

A controversial object of Christian art known as the Chalice of Antioch* was discovered in 1910 by well-diggers and must have been extremely valuable. It was hidden in a basilica,* in the ruins of which it was found, either when Julian repressed the church in A.D. 362 or at the time of Chosroe's inroad in 1611.

See ANTIOCH, CHALICE OF; ANTIOCH, PISIDIAN; BASILICA; TARSUS.

BIBLIOGRAPHY: B. M. Metzger, "Antioch on the Orontes," *BA*, 11 (1948), 69–88; H. H. Arnason, "The History of the Chalice of Antioch," *BA*, 4 (1941), 49–64; id., 5 (1942), 10–16. (There is an earlier description and discussion in G. A. Barton's still valuable *Archaeology of the Bible* [1916–17], 513–19.)

            EMB

ANTIPATRIS (an tip′ə tris; Gr. Ἀντιπατρίς, *Antipatris*). A city on the Plain of Sharon at Ras el-'Ain at the headwaters of the Aujeh River (the biblical Yarkon; the Greek Pegai; the medieval Nahr Abu Furtus; and also known as the Jaffa or Antipatris River), rebuilt in 9 B.C. on the site of Caphar Saba (cf. Jos. Antiq. 16.142–3) by Herod* the Great and named for his father, who was procurator of Judea under Julius Caesar. In the Bible it is mentioned only in Acts 23:31 as the stopover place when Paul was taken from Jerusalem* to Caesarea.*

The ancient site was excavated in 1946 by the Palestine Department of Antiquities and was shown to be, as Alt and Albright had claimed, that of OT Aphek (cf. Josh 12:18; Judg 1:31; 1 Sam 4:1; 1 Sam 29:1), which was in existence as early as 2000 B.C.

Ancient Antipatris, a Roman military relay station and point on the border between Samaria* and Judah,* was on the Antipatris–Gophnah route, which in Roman times lay on the important road leading up SE to Bethel.* Antipatris was seen by the Bordeaux Pilgrim* (c. A.D. 333), and at Ras el-'Ain ruins of the medieval castle* of Mirabel are still visible.

At Antipatris is a Roman-period mausoleum with an open court, a vestibule, and a single burial chamber—in which was found an ornamented sarcophagus* and Late Roman–Early Byzantine* multicolored mosaic* floors with geometric patterns.

Recent excavations have been conducted at Aphek-Antipatris by the Israelis under M. Kochavi, with American archaeologists cooperating. Evidence of what seems to be an ancient Roman road* and possibly a Roman-period plaza have been found at the site.

BIBLIOGRAPHY: E. Smith, "A Visit to Antipatris," *BS*, 1 (1843), 478–98; C. R. Condor and H. H. Kitchener, *The Survey of Western Palestine* (1881–83); W. F. Albright, "A Philistine Military Base," *BASOR*, 11 (1923), 6–7; Y. Aharoni, *The Land of the Bible* (1967), 56; J. L. Kelso, *ZPEB*, 1 (1975), 196; M. Kochavi, "The First Two Seasons of Excavations at Aphek-Antipatris, Preliminary Report," *Tel Aviv*, 2, no. 1 (1975), 17ff.; A. Negev, "Antipatris," in R. Stillwell, ed., *PECS* (1976), 64.

WHM

ANTONIA, TOWER OF. A structure not mentioned by name in the NT but referred to in Acts 21:34ff.; 22:24 et al. as the barracks (KJV "castle"*) in which some of the Jerusalem guard lived. It was a defensive fortress erected by Herod* the Great at the NW corner of the temple* area in Jerusalem* and named in honor of Mark Antony. It stood on a precipice and had four strong towers at its corners. According to Josephus it was furnished elegantly so as to serve on occasion as a royal residence. Its commanding location may possibly have been dominated by a tower* as far back as the monarchy period, though whether such a structure can be identified with the Millo (*see* Solomon*), an uncertain project of King David, is uncertain. It seems probable, however, that the stronghold mentioned in Neh 2:8 was the precursor of the structure rebuilt by Herod which served as one of the official residences of the Roman

procurators. In Herod's time a stairway led directly from the Tower of Antonia to the inner porches in the Court of the Gentiles.* Excavations in the center of the Antonia Tower have uncovered a pavement which antedates the time of Herod Agrippa I (A.D. 41–44). This structure is composed of large stone slabs 9 m. (3 ft.) square and about .3 m. (1 ft.) thick. Assuming that Pontius Pilate was living in the Antonia Tower at the time of Christ's trial, the tower would thus be the Praetorium ("palace" NIV, John 18:28,33; 19:9; cf. Acts 23:35) to which Christ was taken, while the paved area would be the Gabbatha* of John 19:13. Paul also found himself in the Tower of Antonia during his dispute with the Jews (Acts 21:37ff.). Standing on the steps of the highest tower, which faced the temple courts, Paul described his conversion in a manner that almost precipitated a riot. While his case was under scrutiny, the apostle was lodged in the tower for his own protection (Acts 22:24ff.; 23:10,16ff.). The tower was destroyed in A.D. 70 by Titus* during the final assault on the temple mount.

See HEROD, FAMILY OF; TITUS.

BIBLIOGRAPHY: L. H. Vincent, *Jérusalem de l'Ancien Testament*, 1 (1954), 193ff.; J. L. Kelso, *ZPEB*, 1 (1975), 197–98.

RKH

APHEK. *See* ANTIPATRIS.

APHRODISIAS (af′rə diz′ē əs; Gr. Ἀφροδίσιος, *Aphrodisios*, "belonging to the goddess of love"). A city of the province of Asia some 220 km. (135 mi.) SE of Smyrna.* A notable archaeological project is under way there, and a small well-equipped city is emerging from the tell* that covered it. A temple to Aphrodite and a theater* are already uncovered, and although the place seems to be unmentioned in any ancient text, it appears clear that Aphrodisias was opulent. A copy of Diocletian's decree on prices and wages, promulgated in A.D. 301, came to light there in 1973.

The city is mentioned in this volume not because of any immediate significance to the Bible student, but because Aphrodisias will probably soon be added to the list of Ten Towns of Asia known to have been first-century centers of Christian witness. It is known that a bishop (*see* EPISKOPOS) of Aphrodisias attended the Council of Nicaea in A.D. 325.

BIBLIOGRAPHY: F. van der Meer, *Atlas of the Early Christian World* (1958), maps 1,4.

EMB

APOCRYPHA. *See* PSEUDEPIGRAPHA.

APOCRYPHON, GENESIS. *See* GENESIS APOCRYPHON.

APPIAN WAY (VIA APPIA). The final stage of Paul's journey to Rome,* possibly from Capua N, followed the Appian Way (Via Appia). From Forum* Appii, a place, according to Horace, "full of bargees and rascally innkeepers" (Hor. *Sat.* 1.5), Paul moved on through the village of Three Taverns* (Lat., *Tres Ta-*

bernae) to the capital. The polygonal blocks of stone— polished, cut, and fitted without cement—which excited the admiration of Procopius when he followed the Byzantine* general Belisarius to Rome in A.D. 536—are still visible. Paul would have passed many funereal monuments. In Rome, as in most ancient cities, burial was not permitted within the city (*see* NECROPOLIS). The dead were interred outside the walls,* in fields on either side of the roads. Patrician Romans (members of the original senatorial aristocracy) preferred to build their tombs beside the Appian Way. Walled enclosures were constructed so that families, clans, or members of burial societies could be buried together.

For a great distance outside the Roman Wall the Appian Way was lined with ornate monuments to the dead and adorned with soaring columns, colorful frescoes, rich carvings, and beautifully chiseled statuary. The marble statues* are soon to be replaced with plaster copies, and the originals moved to the protection of museums.

See ROADS, ROMAN.

BIBLIOGRAPHY: V. W. Von Hagen, *The Roads That Led to Rome* (1967). EMB

APSE. A recess of polygonal or semicircular shape with a domed ceiling, found usually in churches at one end of an aisle, or in a chapel.

AQAR QUF (ä' kär kūf). The modern Arabic name for the archaeological site of ancient Mesopotamian* Dur-Kurigalzu, located a few miles west of Baghdad in Iraq. It was a residential city of the Kassite* kings from the fourteenth to the twelfth centuries B.C. and boasts a well-preserved ziggurat.*

Excavations were begun by the Directorate General of Antiquities under Taha Bakir and Seton Lloyd during the years 1942–1945, and have since been continued intermittently.

The extensive ruins include the ziggurat (staged temple-tower) and a number of other structures. One of these, on hill A, is another artificial mound surmounted by some type of presumably cultic building. SE of the ziggurat is a huge "temple" complex unlike the traditional Mesopotamian temples. It consists of square courtyards surrounded by rooms. These were dedicated to the gods Ninlil and Ninurta, and to Enlil as Lord of the great Whole (E-U-gal). A central tower in this complex compares favorably with that on Mound A, and with the *Edublalmah* at Ur,* forming a kind of foundation platform for the sacred precinct. Tell Abiad, the most westerly part of the ruins, contains a palace with large barrel-vaulted* storerooms. The Kassite King Kurigalzu I (early fourteenth century B.C.) was the founder of Dur-Kurigalzu. Toward the end of the Kassite period, king Marduk-apal-iddina I (1176–64 B.C.) contributed to the buildings of stratum I. The latest part of the palace was the so-called annex H, which contained some important wall paintings from the very end of the Kassite period.

BIBLIOGRAPHY: Anton Moortgat, *The Art of Ancient Mesopotamia* (1969), 93–98; *Iraq* 8; *Iraq Suppl.* (1944/45). JEJ

ALASHIA. *See* CYPRUS.

ANATOLIA. *See* KIRIATH JEARIM.

APIS. *See* CALF, GOLDEN.

AQUEDUCT. Any channel or conduit for conveying water, especially one for a large quantity of flowing water such as is needed for human settlements. It could take nearly any form—as a flume, tunnel, shaft, pipe, or siphon, in addition to the classical channel supported on masonry arches.*

Aqueducts were invented in very ancient times. A large aqueduct was built by King Sennacherib* of Assyria in 691 B.C. that conveyed water 80 km. (50 mi.) from a tributary of the Greater Zab to Nineveh.* This was said to be as wide as a major highway and paved with masonry. Remains of it may be seen at Jerwal. It had a dam with sluice gates for control. Sennacherib boasted that it was constructed in only fifteen months, although it was built from large limestone blocks, quarried* at a minimum of 16 km. (10 mi.) from any point of use. This king also built a large underground water system to supply the city of Erbil.

The Achaemenid kings in Persia (sixth century B.C. to 331 B.C.) built many underground systems, including those in the remote oases of Kharga and Dakhla. Throughout N Africa, along the edge of the Sahara, vaulted conduits are found, generally attributed to the Romans, but more likely built by Persians. Palmyra* was served by large aqueducts, ruins of which are still visible. In S Arabia's* Hadhramaut, near the moon temple in the Wadi 'Amd, archaeologists found a network of channels dating from the sixth to the fourth centuries B.C.

Underground installations are of particular interest, since they solved several problems inherent to hot arid regions by preventing evaporation, by keeping water cool, by eliminating much pollution, and, perhaps most importantly, by collecting minuscule flows and seepage of water from the ground. This Near Eastern invention also provided the proper grade for water movement, while at the same time possibly tapping a natural aquifer,* as it conveyed water from hilly slopes to valleys where settlements were located. The qanaat, as it was called, was essentially a long sloping tunnel that carried the collected water to a place of emergence, which might be on the surface or underground in the form of a cistern* or well.* About every 15 m. (50 ft.) a vertical shaft was made for construction and maintenance purposes, for providing air, and for removal of debris. In archaeological reconnaissance, the qanaat may be identified by a series of somewhat cone-shaped depressions occurring in relatively straight lines. Such are a large installation at Aleppo* in Syria and several in the E side of the lower Jordan Valley.

The qanaat was essentially the same as the adit, driven horizontally into a hillside by miners and may owe its origin to them. Armenia—one of the oldest mining and metallurgical* centers in the Near East— was probably the source of the qanaat. The water tunnels of the Greco-Roman world were often very similar to these. Greek water transport used the qanaat, as well as pipelines supported by stones in valleys and carried through hills in tunnels (as, e.g., the aqueduct of Samos, sixth century B.C.). Inverted siphons were a Greek innovation. At Pergamum* (c. 180 B.C.) the pipeline went *over* hills and *down* across valleys. Since great pressures resulted, the Romans seldom used the siphon, partly because of problems in preventing leakage, and partly because of the costly materials required for construction.

The Romans attached great importance to adequate water supply, as demonstrated by the remains of aqueducts seen throughout the Empire. Immense quantities of water were required for the great thermae (hot baths), the public fountains, and the domestic use of large populations. For example, the city of Rome* itself was said by Frontinus, water commissioner of Rome in A.D. 97–104, to require about 1,010,600 cubic m. (c. 267 million gal.) of water per day, which was provided by eight aqueducts entering the city. This seems reasonable when we realize that fourth-century A.D. Rome had 11 public baths, 856 private smaller baths, and 1,352 fountains and cisterns.

Irrigation* was not widely practiced by the Romans, but occasionally aqueducts were needed for industry, as at the gold* mines in Spain. Because of the abundance of cheap labor and stone, tunnels and masonry supports, usually carried on arches, were most often used. The conduits they carried might vary in number from one to three, and in size from .5 to 1.2 m. (1.5 to 4 ft.) wide by .6 to 2.5 m. (2 to 8 ft.) high. They were lined with a special stucco cement, *opus signinium*, of ground terra cotta and lime.* Sometimes the channel was cut into the face of a cliff, as in Mount Silpius at Antioch, but frequently they were merely open channels or canals, especially in the provinces where they generally followed the contours of the land.

The earliest major Roman aqueduct was the Aqua Appia (c. 300 B.C.), which was an underground conduit. This was followed by the Anio Vetus, built with spoils taken from King Pyrrhus (d. 272 B.C.); and the

Aqua Marcia (146–44 B.C.), also financed by victories in Corinth* and Carthage. As it entered the city by the Porta San Lorenzo, it became a triple aqueduct, also carrying the conduits of the Aqua Tepula (127 B.C.) and the Aqua Julia. One of the most impressive of the aqueducts, whose remains may be seen in the Campagna, is the Aqua Claudia (A.D. 138). It brought water from the Sabine Hills, 72 km. (45 mi.) distant. Part of its length was solid masonry, and for 15 km. (9½ mi.) it was raised on arches as much as 30.5 m. (100 ft.) in height. Five km. (3 mi.) from the city it was joined by the Anio Novus (A.D. 38), which was 100 km. (62 mi.) in length.

The Romans built aqueducts throughout the Empire, notably in the European provinces, but only those in the biblical world will be noted here. They built aqueducts in Asia Minor* at Ephesus,* Sardis,* Pergamum, Smyrna,* Miletus,* Nyssa, and Pisidian Antioch (*see* ANTIOCH, PISIDIAN). The latter was built as a garrison city in Seleucid times and later became an important center of the Roman province of Galatia,* where the water supply was brought by an impressive aqueduct. In Palestine proper, several aqueducts may still be seen. NT Jericho* had water brought in great quantities from large springs in the Wadi Qelt. Channels still in use date in part back to Herod the Great (*see* HEROD, FAMILY OF) who built a winter palace there (Tell Abu el-'Alayiq). These aqueducts run along the steep sides of the gorge, being cut out of the rock and built of plastered masonry and rubble. Some make precipitous descents and cross to the other side on arched masonry supports.

At Sebaste Herod built another aqueduct to bring water into the city. It was carried on an exceptionally high 49 m. (c. 160 ft.) classical arched construction across a valley. At Caesarea,* another Herodian city, water was brought in an aqueduct across the coastal plains from the Carmel* range. This is still well preserved in part. Lastly, Herod the Great brought water in aqueducts to the Masada* fortress, and from the Pools of Solomon* to the Herodium.* Numerous other water conduits in Palestine deserve notice— such as that at the Qumran* settlement with its cis-

Section of Roman aqueduct at outskirts of Caesarea (to the left [south]). This aqueduct brought water to the city from the Carmel range to the north. Courtesy Israel Government Press Office.

tern complex, an installation at Tekoa, and a lengthy aqueduct N of Acre (Acco*), reconstructed by the Ottoman Turks and presently in excellent condition.

Aqueducts serving Jerusalem are of prime interest. The early Jebusite* settlers, as well as the Israelites during their first occupation, secured their water supply from the Spring of Gihon.* A system of tunnels and shafts was developed for security. An early aqueduct carried water from the spring along the side of the Kidron* Valley into the reservoir called the Old Pool (Isa 22:11), which is evidently the same as the Lower Pool (22:9), and also into the Upper Pool (7:3). Another channel carried water to irrigate the gardens of Siloam.* One of these was built up, and the other was cut out of the rock, the latter serving the Old Pool. Both of these began at an enlarged and deepened reservoir in the cavern where Gihon's waters collect, which is doubtless the Upper Pool.

In improving the fortifications of Jerusalem to withstand siege, King Hezekiah built a conduit to contain the waters of Gihon within the city walls. This is the well-known Hezekiah's or Siloam Tunnel* (2 Kings 20:20). The Pool of Siloam (see SILOAM) received the water through a tunnel some 550 m. (1,800 ft.) in length, laboriously cut through the Hill of Ophel. The outlet from Gihon to the Kidron Valley was then blocked and concealed. An inscription describing the work was carved into the wall of the tunnel near the Pool of Siloam and has been taken to a museum in Istanbul.

At some early time water was brought to Jerusalem from collection basins in the hills some distance S of Bethlehem.* These basins were commonly known as Solomon's Pools.* The total distance is about 24 km. (15 mi.) tb the three large reservoirs. Water was brought in aqueducts known as contour ducts, which followed the terrain to the temple reservoirs. Two of these aqueducts may still be traced, at differing levels. The construction included rock-hewn, built-up masonry, rubble concrete, and stone pipes made of sections of limestone blocks with round holes through them and connected with rabbeted flanges. In one place an inverted siphon was made from these pipes. Herod the Great and Pontius Pilate built these aqueducts, and Josephus informs us (Jos. Antiq. 18.3. 2) that temple* funds were used for this purpose and caused a great uproar.

Further work was done during the period of Aelia Capitolina* by the Tenth Roman Legion (Fretensis), as shown by inscriptions. Recent excavations around the SW corner of the temple platform, by the Israel Department of Antiquities under the direction of B. Mazar, have produced much information concerning the arrangement of these aqueducts and water channels at their receiving end.

BIBLIOGRAPHY: Pliny, NH, 36. 24 (Aqua Claudia); F. Bliss and A. Dickie, Excavations at Jerusalem (1894–97; 1898), 53–56, 115–16, 331–33; G. Weber, Archaelogische Jahrbuch (1904), 96ff.; W. Ramsay, The Cities of St. Paul (1907), 249; Sextus Julius Frontinus, Aqueducts of Rome, M. B. McElwain, ed. (1925); T. Jacobsen and S. Lloyd, Sennacherib's Aqueduct of Jerwan (1935); J. Simons, Jerusalem in the OT (1952), 157–94; C. Singer et al., A History of Technology, 1 (1954), 531–35; id., 2 (1956), 666–71; M. Bieber, "Aqua Marcia in Coins and in Ruins," Archaeology, 20 (1967), 194–96; B. Mazar, The Excavations in the Old City of Jerusalem, Preliminary Report of the 1968 Season, (1969), 1–24.

MHH

AQUIFER. A system or structure that produces or conveys water. See also AQUEDUCT.

AQIR. See EKRON.

ARABIA. Jaziret el-Arab, "The island of the Arabs," as it is termed by the Arabic-speaking inhabitants of the Near East, is an arid peninsula some 2,100 km. (1,300 mi.) in length, comprising the modern states of Saudi Arabia, Yemen, South Yemen, Muscat and Oman, and seven small sheikhdoms now called the Federation of Arab Emirates (Dubai, Ahu Dhabi; Ras al-Kheimeh, Fujaira, esh-Sharja, Umm al-Khawain, and Ajman). Also included is the island group of Bahrain and the peninsula of Qatar, which, with Kuwait, completes the roster of modern governments. Geologically, Arabia forms a part of the African–Arabian shield of horizontal masses of resistant sandstone, disturbed on the W by the Red Sea* fissure and adjacent mountains rising to an average height of 1,524 m. (5,000 ft.) and tilting gradually toward the E and the Persian Gulf. The climate is the typical subtropical dry variety of N Africa and the Sahara. The ancient Romans subdivided Arabia into three areas, Arabia Petraea (the Edomite* and Nabataean* mountainous region extending from the latitude of Medeba* to Mada'in Salih), Arabia Deserta (Central Arabia), and Arabia Felix (the highlands of Yemen and coasts of S Arabia). Various sectional topographical names are applied to the deserts, depending on their character. The Dahna is the narrow band of wasteland in the center of the eastern region. Nafud refers to the expanse of sandy desert in N-central Arabia. The most famous is the largest expanse of pure sand desert in the world, the Rub' al-Khali ("Empty Quarter"). The mountainous Hijaz on the W-central coast is the heartland of Islam, with Mecca situated about 64 km. (40 mi.) from the sea.

Historically, the most important pre-Islamic areas were the city-states of S Arabia, but the Neo-Babylonians* and Nabataeans* also had noteworthy caravan centers in the N. E Arabia, and particularly the Persian Gulf Coast and Oman, figured largely in trade connections from the earliest times.

The archaeological exploration of Arabia has lagged far behind that of other Near Eastern countries, and the region was virtually unknown until very recently. Prior to 1900, fewer than fifteen Europeans had entered the interior of Arabia. Since that time, excavations have taken place in the S and E, especially since 1950, when Wendell Phillips initiated a new era in Arabian archaeology.

The three areas which have received most attention correspond to the historically significant regions.

N Arabia has been explored extensively but not excavated. The inscriptional evidence, however, together with the standing ruins which have been described by travelers, has provided a synopsis of the area's archaeological history. Burckhardt discovered Petra* and visited Mecca in 1812. The first European scholar to visit the important ruins of Tayma was Wallin (1848), but it remained for the indomitable Charles Doughty to give the first description after a visit in 1877. Jaussen and Savignac, French Dominican scholars, made three expeditions to N Arabia between 1907–10 and carefully examined Tabuk, Mada' in Salih, and al-Ula', also visiting Tayma. Their notable contribution was the two-volume *Mission Archéologique en Arabie* (Paris, 1909 and 1914), basic to all modern research into Arabian antiquities. The explorer H. St. J. B. Philby and a party of scholars conducted an epigraphic (*see* EPIGRAPHY) expedition between Jiddah and Riyadh in 1951–52. They collected more than 10,000 inscriptions (cf. Philip Lippens, *Expedition en Arabie Centrale* [Paris, 1956]). F. V. Winnett and W. L. Reed led a month-long ASOR expedition into N Arabia in 1962 which was successful in recording a large number of inscriptions in the Old Arabian scripts called Taymanite, Dedanite, Thamudic, and Lihyanite—ranging in date from the eighth century B.C. to the fourth century A.D. Minaean, Nabataean, Palmyrene, and Hebrew inscriptions were also found. In addition, the expedition described the monuments of the region as far S as al-Ula. Winnett has refined the classification of the scripts, but the pottery* sequences remain to be established.

In eastern Saudi Arabia, Aramco archaeologists have performed some clearing operations at Jawan and near Qatif. But the Danish expedition, under Geoffrey Bibby and Peter Glob, made the most significant contribution to E Arabian archaeology by virtue of a series of excavations undertaken since 1954 on the Persian Gulf Coast of Saudi Arabia—in Qatar, Bahrain, Kuwait, and Ahu Dhabi. Several Ubaid period (c. 4000 B.C.) sites have been located, and the ceramic chronology* has been established for the later periods based on the stratification (*see* STRATIGRAPHY) at Qala'at al-Bahrain. The famous and extensive grave*-mounds on Bahrain have been dated c. 2000 B.C. An outstanding votive shrine is the Barbar Temple, apparently dedicated to Enshag/Inzak, the god which Rawlinson equated with Nabu in identifying Bahrain as the fabulous land of Dilmun* in the Sumerian legends. The Danes have likewise argued for the same geographical identification of the island, although without conclusive proof. The chronology of the Barbar temple and the second phases of city I to the end of city II at Qala'at al-Bahrain closely parallels the literary references to Dilmun in the Akkadian, Neo-Sumerian, and Isin-Larsa periods (2300–1800 B.C.). The expedition's claim that Oman is ancient Babylonian Magan (Makan) and that the Indus Valley represents Meluhha is far less

The probability that the distinctive culture unearthed at Bahrain and Failaka island (Kuwait) does represent Dilmun is enhanced by the scores of button-like stamp seals from those sites which are native to neither Sumer* nor the Indus Valley, but which have occasionally been found in both places.

certain and still unresolved.

S Arabia has attracted the attention of a small but select group of scholars who have at least partially filled in the archaeological history of the area.

The region is mentioned in ancient biblical literature (cf. 1 Kings 10:1–13; 2 Chron 9:1–12). Herodotus also mentions S Arabia as did Strabo, Pliny, and Claudius Ptolemy.* The *Periplus of the Erythraean Sea*, whose author is unknown, is an important source for knowledge of Arabia Felix in Roman times. Carsten Niebuhr accompanied an ill-fated expedition to Yemen in 1761, but credit for the earliest decipherment of S Arabian inscriptions belongs to Emil Rodiger (1837) and Wilhelm Gesenius (1841). The Frenchman, Thomas Arnaud, visited Marib in 1843, and was followed by Joseph Halevy in 1870. Each had copied inscriptions, but it remained for Eduard Glaser in 1888 to collect 391 inscriptions there.

Field archaeology had its beginnings in 1932, when H. Von Wissmann and C. Rathjens excavated N of San'a in Yemen. Gertrude Caton-Thompson worked in the Hadhramaut in 1937, finding the moon temple of Sin at Hureidha. The American Foundation for the Study of Man excavated in 1950–52 at Timna and at Marib, where the spectacular Mahram Bilquis was found. This temple, called Awwam, was dedicated to the god Ilumquh, the Sabean* version of the moon god. An immense ovoid temenos* wall, 4.1 m. (13½ ft.) thick and 8.2 m. (27 ft.) high ran nearly 300 m. (1,000 ft.) around the temple. Its diameter was 114.3 by 76.2 m. (375 by 250 ft.). The enclosure wall contained eight monumental inscriptions in the Sabean script. On the N side was an elaborate peristyle entrance hall measuring 17.5 by 22 m. (57 by 72 ft.) with thirty-two monolithic rectangular pillars arranged around a court. The original wall of the enclosure was believed by the excavators to be perhaps as early as the eighth century B.C., but the peristyle structure was no earlier than the fifth century B.C. Numerous votive statues* and inscriptions were found in proximity to the temple. Albert Jamme, the epigrapher for the expedition, has published the inscriptions.

G. Lankester Harding carried out an archaeological survey of the former Aden protectorate in 1959–60. Unfortunately the chronology for the area is not well developed, especially for the earlier periods, but W. F. Albright has worked out the Minaean chronology and dated the earliest known dynasty at Ma'in to about 400 B.C.

Gus W. Van Beek has also provided an indispensable tool for S Arabian archaeology by establishing the pottery* chronology from the eleventh century B.C. to the fourth century A.D. based on the 1950–51 excavations at Hajar Bin Humeid in the Wadi Beihan. The dates assigned are not exact, since S Arabian archaeology is in its infancy, but imports from the N have provided parallels which fix the relative positions of the strata at this site within a century or two. Hajar Bin Humeid has the longest occupational history of any excavated site in S Arabia and contains the oldest datable ceramic material so far found. Eighteen strata were differentiated in the

15 meters (nearly 45 ft.) of occupational debris, and the prescience of W. F. Albright and Wendell Phillips in choosing this particular tell* as a S Arabian type site has been amply confirmed by Van Beek's landmark publication.

Various development and modernization programs undertaken by the Saudi Arabian government have tended to open more opportunities for archaeological exploration. Aramco employs archaeologists as well as geologists, and the expatriate community at Dhahran sponsors a vigorous amateur archaeology club.

American engineers have investigated remains of mining installations at Mahd ed-Dahab between Mecca and Medina. The work of Peter Parr and the British in northeastern Arabia has been particularly significant in conducting several minor excavations. A number of surveys have also been commissioned by the government.

Most promising of all for the future of Arabian archaeology are the facts that antiquity departments have been established by most governments (including Yemen and Oman), annual reports are being published, and university professorships in history, archaeology, and epigraphy have been created in a number of cities, notably at Riyadh and Sanaa.

BIBLIOGRAPHY: G. Caton-Thompson, *The Tombs and Moon Temple of Hureidha (Hadhramaut)* (1944); W. F. Albright, "The Chronology of Ancient S Arabia in the Light of the First Campaign of the Expedition of Qataban," *BASOR*, 119 (1950), 5–15; R. L. Bowen, Jr., "The Early Arabian Necropolis of Ain Jawan," *BASOR*, Supplementary Studies, nos. 7–9 (1950); A. Fakhry, *An Archaeological Journey to Yemen*, parts I–III (1951–52); F. P. Albright, "The Excavations of the Temple of the Moon at Marib (Yemen)," *BASOR*, 128 (1952), 35–38; G. W. Van Beek, "Recovering the Ancient Civilization of Arabia," *BA* 15 (1952); W. F. Albright, "The Chronology of the Minean Kings of

Arabia," *BASOR*, 129 (1953); W. L. Brown and A. F. L. Beeston, "Sculptures and Inscriptions in Shabwa," *JRAS*, 1–2 (1954), 43–62; W. Phillips, *Qataban and Sheba* (1955); R. L. Bowen, Jr. and F. P. Albright, *Archaeological Discoveries in S Arabia* (1958); R. L. Cleveland, *An Ancient S Arabian Necropolis* (1958); G. W. Van Beek, "Frankincense and Myrrh in S Arabia," *JAOS* 78, no. 3 (1958), 141–52; id., "Frankincense and Myrrh," *BA*, 23 (1960); A. Jamme, *Sabean Inscriptions from Mahram Bilquis (Marib)* (1962); G. L. Harding, *Archaeology in the Aden Protectorates* (1964); G. W. Van Beek, *Hajar Bin Humeid* (1969); G. Bibby, *Looking for Dilmun* (1969); F. V. Winnett and W. L. Reed, *Ancient Records from N. Arabia* (1970); B. Doe,. *Southern Arabia* (1971).

JEJ

ARAD (âr'ad; Heb. עֲרָד, *ʿarāḏ*). A site in the Negev* of uncertain identification. A "king of Arad . . . lived in the Negev" and attacked Israel in the days of the Exodus (Num 21:1). Later reference is made to the "Negev near Arad" (Judg 1:16) and still later to an Arad conquered by Joshua (Josh 12:14). Possibly the first of these is Tell el Milh where trial excavations produced evidence of a fine Middle Bronze Age fortress. Tell Meshash, 6.5 km. (4 mi.) to the W, may have been Hormah. The modern site of Tell Arad, 11 km. (7 mi.) NE of Tell el Milh, was thoroughly excavated during 1962–67. Pharaoh Shishak* refers to the capture of Arad Rabbat (the great Arad), evidently one of Solomon's* fortresses that may well be the modern Tell Arad.

Excavation has shown that Tell Arad was a city surrounded by a wall 2.5 m. (8.25 ft.) thick in the Early Bronze Age, but it was destroyed c. 2700 B.C. and not rebuilt for 1,500 years. In the eleventh century an open village was built here, perhaps by the

Model of area K in Early Bronze Age lower city at Arad, showing part of city wall with three of its semicircular towers, houses, and streets. Courtesy Israel Museum, Jerusalem.

Kenites of Judg 1:16 (Stratum XII). In the tenth century B.C. a strong fortress was erected, probably by Solomon (Stratum XI). Thereafter Strata X to VI were Israelite; V to III Persian, Hellenistic, and Roman, respectively; II Islamic; and I Medieval. The Early Israelite period (Strata X and IX) is distinguished by a remarkable temple some 20 m. long and 14 m. broad (65 ft. by 45 ft.) with an altar* for burnt offerings and a Holy Place with its "high place*" and stone pillar. In the seventh century B.C. (Stratum VII), in the days of Hezekiah, the altar and high place were removed, but the structure remained. In the next city (VI), during the days of Josiah, the temple disappeared. This city was destroyed by Nebuchadnezzar* in 586 B.C.

Tell Arad has produced over two hundred ostraca,* some in Aramaic from Persian times but many in Hebrew from the time of the monarchy, some from each stratum giving a palaeogeographic series from the late tenth to the sixth century B.C. The series from Stratum VI includes seventeen from official archives. One refers to an Edomite* attack (cf. 2 Kings 24:2, with an emendation of Aram* [Syria] to Edom).

BIBLIOGRAPHY: Y. Aharoni and R. Amiran, "Excavations at Tel Arad: Preliminary report on the first season, 1962," *IEJ*, 14, no. 3 (1964), 131–47; Y. Aharoni, "Hebrew Ostraca from Tel Arad," *IEJ*, 16, no. 1 (1966), 1–7; Y. Aharoni, "Excavations at Tel Arad: Preliminary report on the Second Season, 1963," *IEJ*, 17, no. 4 (1967), 233–49; Y. Aharoni, "Arad: Its Inscriptions and Temple," *BA*, 31 (1968), 2–32; H. G. Andersen, *ZPEB*, 1 (1975), 245; Y. Aharoni, *Arael Inscriptions*, Jerusalem, 1975.

JAT

ARAD RABBAT. *See* ARAD.

ARAIR. *See* AROER.

ARAM, ARAMEANS (âr′əm; Heb. אֲרָם, *'ᵃrām*). An ancient country and people of undefined extent in the general area of modern Syria. Aram was never a political or geographical entity but was a collection of city-states, several of which are mentioned in the OT—such as Damascus,* Bit-Adini, Beth Rehob, Maacah, and Zobah. The origin of the Arameans is unknown, but a personal name *Aramu* is attested at Ur* about 2000 B.C. and at Mari* and Alalakh* in the eighteenth century B.C. The biblical patriarchs were associated with NW Mesopotamia,* in Aram Naharaim. Leaving Ur, they settled at Haran* (Gen 11:28–32). The wives of Isaac and Jacob were Arameans (Gen 24, 28), and Jacob is called a "wandering Aramean" (Deut 26:5).

In the chaos that fell on Asia just after 1200 B.C. when the "Sea Peoples*" destroyed the Hittite* Empire and swept into Syria–Palestine, Cushan-Rishathaim from Aram invaded Palestine (Judg 3:7–11). From the twelfth century B.C. onward the city-states of the Arameans are attested in the inscriptions of the Assyrians. Tiglath-Pileser* I of Assyria (c. 1100 B.C.) sought to stem the advance of the Akhlamu-Aramean people in the Euphrates region. During the period 1000 B.C. to 700 B.C., Israel had frequent

Basalt stele from ninth century B.C. of god Melcart erected by Ben-Hadad, king of Aram, and mentioned in Aramaic inscription at base of stele. Courtesy James B. Pritchard, The University Museum, University of Pennsylvania.

contact with the Arameans under Saul (1 Sam 14:47), David (2 Sam 3:3, 5; 8:1–12; 13:37–39), Solomon* (1 Kings 11:23–25), and throughout the period of the kings, when rulers like Ben-Hadad, Hazael, and Rezin of Damascus caused Israel much trouble.

The Arameans are most familiar from numerous Assyrian inscriptions. Shalmaneser III (c. 858–824 B.C.) describes his battle at Qarqar* in 853 B.C., against a S Aramean coalition of twelve kings which included Hadadezer of Damascus, the king of Hamath,* and Ahab* the Israelite. On another monument this ruler refers to Hazael, the usurper, as a "son of nobody" (cf. 2 Kings 8:7–15). Tiglath-Pileser III (747–727) lists Jehoahaz of Judah along with the king of Hamath* and others from Phoenicia,* Philistia,* Moab,* et al. Eventually this ruler captured Damascus in 732 B.C. Other references to Aramean kings on Assyrian monuments are too numerous to mention here.

A number of cultic inscriptions have been found. One is the famous Melcart Stele,* set up by Ben-Hadad, son of Tabrimmon the son of Hezion king of Aram, for his god Melcart (cf. 1 Kings 15:18). Another stele found near Aleppo* was set up by Zakir, king of Hamath, to commemorate his victory over Ben-Hadad, son of Hazael king of Aram, and his allies early in the eighth century B.C. This conflict enabled Israel to recapture areas lost in Trans-Jordan (2 Kings 12:17–18; 13:3–7, 22–24).

Another group of three stelae records a treaty between two Aramean kings in the seventh century B.C.

Culturally the Arameans inherited much from their neighbors, as excavations in strata from c. 2000–700 B.C. have shown. Among other things they made great use of Phoenician inlay work, some of which carries inscriptions. The most notable cultural contribution of the Arameans to the Ancient Near East was their script and language. By Persian times Aramaic was the language of diplomacy. The script was taken up and modified to write Hebrew (see EPIGRAPHY, HEBREW), Nabataean,* Palmyrene (see PALMYRA), Mandaic, Parthian, and Syriac.

BIBLIOGRAPHY: A. Dupont-Sommer, *Les Arameens* (1949); *ANET* (1955), 278–81, 283, 501, 503–4; M. F. Unger, *Israel and the Arameans of Damascus* (1957); B. Mazar, "The Aramean Empire and Its Relations With Israel," *BA*, 25 (1962), 98–120; S. Moscati, *JSS*, 4 (1959), 303–7; L. L. Walker, *ZPEB*, 1 (1975), 246–49; D. J. Wiseman, ed., "The Arameans" by A. Malamat, *Peoples of Old Testament Times* (1973), 134–155. JAT

ARAMAIC (âr ə mā′ ik; Heb. אֲרָמִית, *'arāmît*). A NW Semitic language originally of the Arameans (*see* ARAM), which became widespread throughout the Near East as an international language during the Persian Empire.

I. *Dialects*. The various dialects of Aramaic may be chronologically classified as follows: A. *Old Aramaic* (925–700 B.C.) includes important treaties and royal inscriptions from N Syria. B. *Imperial Aramaic* (700–200 B.C.). Because its alphabet* was more efficient than cuneiform* scripts, Aramaic became the international language, first under the Assyrians then under the Babylonians (*see* CHALDEA) and the Persians (*see* SUSA). This phase includes inscriptions from Anatolia to Afghanistan and passages in Ezra and in Daniel. C. *Middle Aramaic* (200 B.C.–A.D. 200). After Alexander's conquest of the Near East, various local dialects of Aramaic developed. From this period come NT Aramaic, some of the Dead Sea Scrolls,* the Bar Kochba* texts, and the Nabataean* and Palmyrenean (*see* PALMYRA) languages. D. *Late Aramaic* (A.D. 200–700). In this era the W branch included Samaritan (*see* SAMARIA) and Christian Palestinian Aramaic, the eastern branch Syriac, Babylonian Talmudic Aramaic, and Mandaic. E. *Modern Aramaic*. Isolated populations in Syria, Turkey, and Iran still speak Aramaic dialects today.

II. *The Scripts*. Aramaic was written in an alphabet borrowed from the Phoenicians. This became a distinct script in the eighth century B.C. which remained quite uniform until after Alexander's conquests, when a variety of scripts were developed for such dialects as Nabataean, Palmyrenean, Syriac, and Mandaic. Occasionally Aramaic texts were written in non-Aramaic scripts—as was an Egyptian text of the Persian period in Demotic and an incantation from Uruk* (c. 300 B.C.) in cuneiform.

III. *Old Aramaic*. The oldest Aramaic text, inscribed on an altar at Tell Halaf, is dated to 925 B.C. An inscription dedicated by Bir Hadad, king of Damascus,* is dated to c. 850 B.C. From the same period comes an ivory plaque from Arslan Tash and graffiti* of the ninth–eighth centuries from Hamath.* An inscription on the Zakir Stele* (early eighth century) mentions a usurper of Hamath whose victory over Damascus gave relief to Israel. The Hadad stele, the Bir-Rakib stele, and three stelae* from Sefire vividly illuminate the Assyrian expansion into Syria in the eighth century B.C. (*see* TIGLATH-PILESER). Short inscriptions from the ninth–seventh centuries have been found in Israel at Dan,* Hazor,* Ein Gev, and Tel Zeror, and in Jordan at Amman and Deir 'Alla.

IV. *Imperial Aramaic*. A. *Mesopotamia*. As early as the late ninth century B.C. we have a reference to an Aramaic letter in an Akkadian* document. As Aramaic was useful for writing dockets on cuneiform tablets for quick inspection, the use of Aramaic by scribes became widespread by the seventh century. According to 2 Kings 18:26 (cf. Isa 36:11), in 701 B.C. the Assyrian officials of Sennacherib* were requested by Hezekiah's officers to converse in Aramaic (KJV, "the Syrian language"). From Ashurbanipal's* reign comes a letter inscribed on an ostracon (*see* OSTRACA). At Nimrud (*see* CALAH) an ostracon was found which lists Israelite exiles in Assyria. B. *Persia*. The earliest Aramaic texts from the Iranian plateau are on a jug and two bowls from Luristan, dated to the eighth–seventh centuries. The largest group of Aramaic texts from Persia are the 203 inscribed stone mortars* and pestles found in the Great Hall of Hundred Columns at Persepolis.* Though discovered in 1936–38, these inscriptions were only published in 1970 by Bowman. He interprets these texts as references to the haoma ceremony, but Levine believes that they are merely records of the donors.

C. *Egypt.* The most important texts from Egypt* are the fifth-century B.C. papyri recovered from the island of Elephantine* from 1893 to 1908. Most of these documents, which belonged to a Jewish mercenary garrison under the Persians, were published between 1903 and 1911 by Cowley, Sayce, and Sachau. A collection of twelve documents and five fragments acquired by Charles Wilbour in 1893 was donated to the Brooklyn Museum in 1947 and published by Kraeling in 1953.

The oldest Elephantine papyrus is dated to 495 B.C. and the latest to 399 B.C. The texts include letters, bills, marriage contracts, a manumission document, an adoption* document, the story of Ahikar, and a version of King Darius's* Behistun Inscription.* They shed important light on the era of Ezra and Nehemiah. They reveal that the Jews* of Elephantine* had admitted syncretistic elements into their religion and that they had a temple which had been destroyed by the Egyptians.

Also from the fifth century are thirteen letters on leather,* acquired by the Bodleian Library in 1943–44 and published by Driver in 1954. They are letters issued by Arsames, the Persian satrap of Egypt,* to his subordinates.

A group of eight letters, dated to the fifth century, was found in 1945 at Hermopolis. These letters from Syrians stationed in Egypt* were sent from Memphis* and intended for Thebes* or Syene.

An important papyrus found at Saqqara (*see* MEMPHIS) is a letter from Adon, a king of Philistia,* asking for aid on the eve of Nebuchadnezzar's* invasion c. 600 B.C From Sheik Fadl come seventeen ostraca which mention Tirhakah, Necho,* and Psamtik. Inscribed silver* bowls from Tell el-Maskhuta refer to Gashmu, who is possibly Geshem, the Arab opponent of Nehemiah. D. *Jordan and Israel.* In Jordan an Aramaic inscription of the sixth–fifth centuries B.C. identifies 'Araq el-Emir* as the home of the Tobiads. Numerous short inscriptions on ostraca dated from the seventh century to the Persian period have been found in Israel. In 1962–63 papyri dated to 375–335 B.C. were found in a cave in Samaria.* E. *Anatolia.* After Cyrus's* conquest of Lydia* in 546 B.C., Aramaic was spread to Anatolia. An Aramaic-Lydian bilingual document from Sardis,* dated to the fifth–fourth centuries B.C., is important for the decipherment of Lydian. F. *Arabia.* Inscriptions from Tema,* the city where Nabonidus* lodged for ten years, have been variously dated between the sixth to the fourth centuries B.C. G. *Pakistan and Afghanistan.* We have important texts in Aramaic, Greek, and Indic inscribed by Ashoka, the "Constantine" of Buddhism, c. 250 B.C. The first Aramaic text was discovered at Taxila in Pakistan in 1915. Then later discoveries were made in Afghanistan at Laghman in 1932 and at Qandahar in 1957. The king, who sent missionaries to the W, details how he stopped the killing of men and animals after his conversion to Buddhism.

V. *OT Aramaic.* Apart from two words in Gen 31:47 and a sentence in Jer 10:11, the main Aramaic sections in the OT are Dan 2:4–7:28 and Ezra 4:8–6:18;

7:12–26. The KJV translates *'arāmît* in Dan 2:4 as "Syriack" and in Ezra 4:7 as "Syrian" after the LXX.

Though some critics have claimed that the Aramaic of Ezra and especially of Dan is late, biblical Aramaic is essentially the same kind of Imperial Aramaic as that of the Elephantine documents. The use of *d* instead of *z* may represent either a true phonetic spelling or the result of a later spelling revision. The Aramaic of Daniel and Ezra reveals the strong influence of Akkadian and of Persian in numerous loan words. In view of many early contacts between the Aegean and the Near East, the three Greek words in Daniel's Aramaic hardly require a date later than Alexander's conquests.

Some scholars have used so-called Aramaisms, that is, the use of certain Aramaic roots, idioms, noun patterns, or syntax to detect late elements in Ezek, Ps, Prov, Eccl, and S of Sol. But many of these are not indisputable Aramaisms, and others may reflect northern rather than later influences.

VI. *NT Aramaic.* Though some have argued from the use of *Hebrais* in Acts 21:40, 22:2, 26:14, and *Hebraisti* in John 5:2, 19:13, 17, 20 and Rev 9:11, 16:16 that the language used by Jesus and his disciples was Hebrew, these terms simply mean the language used by the Hebrews or Jews. Though Jesus may have known not only Hebrew but also Greek, it is quite clear from the Gospels that his main language was Aramaic.

When Jesus cried out on the cross (Mark 15:34) *Eloi, Eloi, lama sabachthani?* he was uttering the Aramaic *Elahî, Elahî, l^ema sh^ebaqtanî*, rather than the Hebrew, *Elî, Elî, lamā 'azavtanî*. Many words in the NT are transliterations from the Aramaic: Peter's name "Cephas" is from *kēphā* "rock"; Thomas is from *tōmā* "twin"; the epithet for Simon misleadingly translated "Canaanite" in the KJV (Mark 3:18) is the Aramaic *qannāyā* or "Zealot" (cf. Luke 6:15). *Bar*, the Aramaic word for "son," occurs in such names as Bartholomew, Bar-Jonas (NIV "son of Jonah" [Matt 16:17]), Barabbas, and Bartimaeus. Gabbatha* is from *gabb^etā*, "raised place"; Golgotha* from *golgoltā*, "skull"; and Akeldama from *haqēl demā*, "bloody ground." Maranatha (1 Cor 16:22) comes from *māran*, "our Lord," and *etā*, "come" (NIV "Come, O Lord!").

Kutscher has argued that there was a distinctive Galilean* dialect, which involved the confusion of gutturals (cf. Mark 14:70), and that this dialect can be recovered from the early Midrashim, the Palestinian Talmud and Targums. Kahle, however, believes that the same Aramaic was used in Judea* and Galilee.*

There have been various ingenious but unconvincing attempts to reconstruct hypothetical Aramaic originals of the Gospels—by C. F. Burney in 1922 and C. C. Torrey in 1933. Their arguments were based on Semitisms and alleged mistranslations of the Aramaic. Recently M. Black has attempted to reconstruct parts of the Gospels and Acts by using materials from the Palestinian Targums and Christian-Palestinian Aramaic. G. M. Lamsa has even made a misguided attempt to recover the Aramaic of the NT from the Syriac Peshitta.

VII. *Middle Aramaic.* A. *Jewish Texts.* 1. *Qumran.* The most important Aramaic texts of the NT period are some of the Dead Sea Scrolls* from Qumran* which are written in a literary Aramaic. The most important of these is the Genesis Apocryphon* from Cave I, published by Avigad and Yadin in 1956. This has been dated between the first century B.C. and the first century A.D. Other Aramaic texts include a description of the New Jerusalem, fragments of Tobit, of Enoch, of Pseudo-Daniel, of the Testament of Levi, a Prayer of Nabonidus,* Visions of Amram, etc. (For Targum fragments *see* under VIII, below.) 2. *Bar Kochba Texts.* Numerous documents, mainly on papyri, dating from the Bar Kochba* revolt of A.D. 132–35, have been recovered from Murabba'at in 1951–52 and from Nahal* Hever in 1960–61. These letters and legal documents were written in Aramaic, Nabataean, Hebrew, and Greek. 3. *Other Texts.* Apart from the *Megillat Ta'anit,* "The Scroll of Fasting," and the plaque commemorating the transference of the bones of Uzziah, the main corpus of other Aramaic texts from the NT period from Israel comprises short inscriptions on ossuaries (100 B.C.–A.D. 70). Of the twenty-nine inscribed ossuaries* recovered by Bagatti in 1953–55 from the Mount of Olives,* eleven were in Aramaic, seven in Hebrew, and eleven in Greek. B. *Nabataean.* Texts of the Nabataean Arabs, dating from 100 B.C. to the second–third centuries A.D., have been found not only in their capital, Petra,* but in Arabia,* the Sinai,* Egypt,* Jordan, Israel, Anatolia, and Italy. C. *Palmyrenean.* The distinctive texts of the oasis city of Palmyra (Tadmor*) in Syria date from 33 B.C. to A.D. 274. They have been found not only in Baalbek,* Jerusalem,* and Dura Europos,* but also in Egypt, N Africa, the Ukraine, Italy, Hungary, and in England on the tombs of legionary soldiers. D. *Hatra.* Some two hundred Aramaic inscriptions have been published from Hatra,* a Parthian city NW of Ashur,* which flourished from the first to the third century A.D.

VIII. *Targums.* At some uncertain date after the Exile,* which Jewish tradition places as early as the time of Ezra (cf. Neh 8:8), Aramaic translations and paraphrases of the Scriptures called targums were made for those who understood Aramaic better than Hebrew. We have targums for all the OT books except Dan, Ezra, and Neh. A. *Qumran.* The earliest extant Targums are from Qumran, including a targum of Lev 16:12–15, 18–21 and one of Job 3:4–5; 4:16–5:4, both from Cave 4. An extensive targum of Job 37:10–42:11 and fragments of 17:14–36:33 comes from Cave 11. This targum, which is dated to 150–100 B.C., may possibly be the Job Targum which Gamaliel, Paul's teacher, ordered hidden (*BT,* Sabbath 115a). B. *Onkelos, Jonathan, Pseudo-Jonathan.* The major targum of the Pentateuch is known as Onkelos. A rather literal translation of the Hebrew, it seems to have originated in Palestine but was later edited in Babylonia between the second and fifth centuries A.D.

The major targum of the Prophets is known as Jonathan and was modeled after Onkelos but is less literal. It also originated in Palestine but was re-

edited in Babylonia before the fifth century A.D.

A later, more periphrastic targum of the Pentateuch is known as Pseudo-Jonathan. Its final form is quite late, but it preserves some early materials. C. *Cairo Genizah.* In 1930 P. Kahle published six manuscripts of a Palestinian targum of the Pentateuch that had been discovered in the genizah,* or storeroom, of a synagogue* in Cairo. He dated these fragments to the seventh to eleventh centuries A.D., and their origin to pre-Mishnaic times. D. *Neofiti.* The most important development in targum studies has been the discovery by A. Diez Macho in the Vatican Library in 1956 that a Neofiti codex* of about 450 parchment* pages is a complete ancient Palestinian Targum on the Pentateuch. The folio pages, transcribed in A.D. 1504, are inscribed without vocalization but with marginal notes. Diez Macho believes that the targum may even be pre-Christian in origin. Others believe that in its present form the targum dates no earlier than the third century A.D.

IX. *Late Aramaic.* A. *Samaritan.* The Samaritans used a literary Aramaic for their liturgy and their targum of the Pentateuch from the fifth century A.D. Aramaic was spoken by the Samaritans until the tenth century A.D. B. *Christian Palestinian.* Christian Jews in the sixth century A.D. translated Greek works into Aramaic. Their manuscripts had been preserved by monks in Sinai and in 1952 were discovered for the first time in Palestine at Khirbet Mird, S of Jerusalem. C. *Babylonian Jewish.* Parts of the Babylonian Talmud are in Aramaic. Magic bowls from Nippur,* dated c. A.D. 600, are in a related dialect. D. *Syriac.* Syriac is an eastern dialect of Aramaic that developed around Edessa in the second–third century A.D. In addition to important biblical translations such as the Peshitta and the Old Syriac Gospels, there is a wealth of Christian literature in Syriac, including the Odes of Solomon as well as numerous apocrypha (*see* PSEUDEPIGRAPHA) and apocalypses. Nestorian Christians carried the Syrian script into Central Asia and China. E. *Mandaic.* Mandaic is the dialect used by the Gnostic Mandaeans of Iraq and Iran. Their oldest texts are lead amulets* of the third–fourth centuries A.D. and magic bowls dated c. A.D. 600. Their extensive religious compositions, preserved in manuscripts from the sixteenth–nineteenth centuries A.D., have been used by Bultmann and others as a basis for a pre-Christian Gnosticism.

X. *Modern Aramaic.* In the Qalamon Valley about 50 km. (30 mi.) N of Damascus* are three small villages—Ma'lula, Yubb'adin, and Bah'a. Their inhabitants, who are 80 percent Melchite and 20 percent Greek Orthodox, speak a dialect of Aramaic. From the Turkish vilayets of Van and from adjacent Iranian Azerbaijan some 5000 Jewish inhabitants, most of whom have emigrated to Israel, speak a neo-Aramaic dialect, heavily influenced by Turkish and Kurdish.

BIBLIOGRAPHY: *General.* F. Rosenthal, *Die aramaistische Forschung* . . . (1939); J. J. Koopmans, ed., *Aramäische Chrestomathie* (1962); F. Rosenthal, ed., *An Aramaic Handbook* (1967); H. Donner and

W. Röllig, eds., *Kanaanäische und aramäische Inschriften*, 1–3, rev. ed. (1968–71); E. Y. Kutscher, "Aramaic," in T. Sebeok, ed., *Current Trends in Linguistics*, 6 (1970), 374–412; E. Y. Kutscher, "Aramaic," *EncJud*, 3 (1971), cols. 259–87, 266–68; W. E. Aufrecht and J. C. Hurd, *A Synoptic Concordance of Aramaic Inscriptions* (1975); J. C. L. Gibson, *Textbook of Syrian Semitic Inscriptions II: Aramaic Inscriptions* (1975); E. Lipinski, *Studies in Aramaic Inscriptions and Onomastics* (1975); J. A. Fitzmyer, *A Wandering Aramean* (1979).

The Scripts. C. H. Gordon, "The Cuneiform Aramaic Incantation," *Orientalia*, 9 (1940), 29–44; R. A. Bowman, "An Aramaic Religious Text in Demotic Script," *JNES*, 3 (1944), 219–31; J. Naveh, *The Development of the Aramaic Script* (1970).

Old Aramaic. J. A. Fitzmyer, *The Aramaic Inscriptions of Sefire* (1967); R. Degen, *Altaramäische Grammatik* (1969); S. Segert, *Altaramäische Grammatik* (1975).

Imperial Aramaic. A. E. Cowley, *Aramaic Papyri of the Fifth Century* B.C. (1923); E. G. Kraeling, *The Brooklyn Museum Aramaic Papyri* (1953); G. R. Driver, *Aramaic Documents of the Fifth Century* B.C. (1954); P. Eggermont and J. Hoftijzer, *The Moral Edicts of King Aśoka* (1962); F. Altheim and R. Stiehl, *Die aramäische Sprache unter den Achämeniden* (1963); F. M. Cross, "The Discovery of the Samaria Papyri," *BA*, 26 (1963), 110–20; J. A. Fitzmyer, "The Aramaic Letter of King Adon . . . ," *Biblica*, 46 (1965), 41–55; R. Bowman, *Aramaic Ritual Texts from Persepolis* (1968); E. Y. Kutscher, "The Hermopolis Papyri," *Israel Oriental Studies*, 1 (1971), 103–19; B. Levine, "Aramaic Texts from Persepolis," *JAOS*, 92 (1972), 70–79; A. R. Millard, "Some Aramaic Epigraphs," *Iraq*, 34 (1972), 131–37; P. Grelot, *Documents araméens d'Égypte* (1972); B. Porten, *Jews of Elephantine and Arameans of Syene* (1974); B. Porten, "Aramaic Papyri and Parchments: A New Look," *BA*, 42 (1979), 74–104; J. Naveh, "The Aramaic Ostraca from Tel Beersheba (Seasons 1971–1976)," *Tel Aviv*, 6 (1979), 182–98.

OT Aramaic. F. Rosenthal, *A Grammar of Biblical Aramaic* (1961); K. Kitchen, "The Aramaic of Daniel," in D. J. Wiseman et al., *Notes on Some Problems in the Book of Daniel* (1965), 31–79; M. Wagner, *Die lexikalischen und grammatikalischen Aramaismen im Alttestamentlichen Hebräisch* (1966); A. Hurvitz, "The Chronological Significance of 'Aramaisms' in Biblical Hebrew," *IEJ*, 18 (1968), 234–40; E. Vogt, *Lexicon Linguae Aramaicae Veteris Testamenti* (1971).

NT Aramaic. G. Dalman, *Jesus-Jeshua* (1929); E. Y. Kutscher, "Das zur Zeit Jesu gesprochene Aramäisch," *ZNW*, 51 (1960), 46–54; A. Diez Macho, "La Lengua hablada por Jesucristo," *Oriens Antiquus*, 2 (1963), 95–132; S. Brown, "From Burney to Black: The Fourth Gospel and the Aramaic Question," *CBQ*, 26 (1964), 323–39; M. Black, *An Aramaic Approach to the Gospels and Acts*, 3d ed. (1967); J. A. Fitzmyer, "The Languages of Palestine in the First Century A.D.," *CBQ*, 32 (1970), 501–31; W. C. van Unnik, "Aramaisms in Paul," *Sparsa Collecta I* (1973), 129–43; P. Lapide, "Insights from Qumran

into the Languages of Jesus," *RdQ*, 8 (1975), 483–502; J. A. Fitzmyer, "The Aramaic Language and the Study of the New Testament," *JBL*, 99 (1980), 5–21.

Middle Aramaic. P. Benoit, J. T. Milik, and R. de Vaux, *Les grottes de Murabba'at* (1961); J. A. Fitzmyer, *The Genesis Apocryphon of Qumran Cave I* (1966); J. P. van der Ploeg and A. S. van der Woude, *Le Targum de Job de la Grotte XI de Qumrân* (1971); J. A. Fitzmyer, "The Contribution of Qumran Aramaic to the Study of the NT," *NTS*, 20 (1974), 382–407; B. Jongeling, C. J. Labauschagne, and A. S. van der Woude, *Aramaic Texts from Qumran* (1976); E. Y. Kutscher, *Studies in Galilean Aramaic* (1976); M. Sokoloff, *The Targum to Job from Qumran Cave XI* (1974).

Targums. A. Sperber, *The Bible in Aramaic*, 1–4 (1959, 1962, 1968); R. le Déaut, *Introduction à la littérature targumique* (1966); P. Nickels, *Targum and NT* (1967); J. Bowker, *The Targums and Rabbinic Literature* (1969); A. Diez Macho, ed., *Neophyti*, 1–3 (1968, 1970, 1971); B. Grossfeld, *A Bibliography of Targum Literature* (1972); M. McNamara, *Targum and Testament* (1972); R. le Déaut, "The Current Status of Targumic Studies," *Biblical Theology Bulletin*, 4 (1974), 3–32; S. H. Levey, *The Messiah . . . The Messianic Exegesis of the Targum* (1974); A. Tal, "The Samaritan Targum to the Pentateuch," *JSS*, 21 (1976), 26–38; S. Lund and J. A. Foster, *Variant Versions of Targumic Traditions within Codex Neofiti I* (1977); B. Grossfeld, *Bibliography of Targum Literature*, 2 (1978); B. Grossfeld and L. H. Schiffman, *A Critical Commentary on Targum Neofiti I to Genesis* (1978); L. Smolar, M. Aberbach, and P. Churgin, *Studies in Targum Jonathan to the Prophets* (1978).

Late Aramaic. J. Montgomery, *Aramaic Incantation Texts from Nippur* (1913); R. Macuch, *Handbook of Classical and Modern Mandaic* (1965); E. Yamauchi, "Aramaic Magic Bowls," *JAOS*, 85 (1965), 511–23; E. Yamauchi, *Mandaic Incantation Texts* (1967); R. Macuch, *Geschichte der spät- und neusyrischen Literatur* (1976); R. Macuch, ed., *Zur Sprache und Literatur der Mandäer* (1976).

Modern Aramaic. I. Garbell, *The Jewish Neo-Aramaic Dialect of Persian Azerbaijan* (1965).

EY

ARAM NAHARAIM. See MESOPOTAMIA.

ARAQ EL-EMIR (âr'ək el ə mēr'). The "Caverns of the Prince" is situated W of Amman (*see* RABBAH), Jordan, in a valley called Wadi Syr, about two-fifths of the distance from Amman to Jericho.* In the vicinity are several settlements: the town of Wadi es-Syr (c. 4,500 pop.); a small village called El Bassa (pop. 200) located at a large spring; and 'Araq el-Emir, a town of nearly one thousand inhabitants. It is noted for a series of large caves* or tombs (*see* GRAVE) on two levels, cut into the limestone cliff. The caves have many rooms and long corridors, with a gallery in front of part of the upper level. While the local people presently use the chambers for storage, they originally served as tombs. One of these is

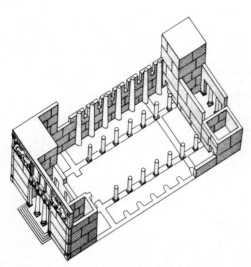

Plan of the temple at Tyros. Courtesy Carta, Jerusalem.

distinguished by the name "Tobiah" in third century B.C. Aramaic* letters, deeply cut into the rock.

The Tobiad family was evidently already established in Trans-Jordan as the leader of the Ammonites* by the end of the fifth century B.C. and was representative of the Seleucid period of control in this region. 'Araq el-Emir seems to have been founded by them in 260 B.C. as the Birtha of the Ammonites (Zeno papyri*). During the time of Nehemiah its head was allied with the governor of Samaria,* and with the Arabs. He was related to the high priest Eliashib of Judah,* and his wife, as well as the wife of his son, Jehohanan, were Jewish women of high estate (Neh 6:17, 18). Many of his friends in Jerusalem* corresponded with him, and he had a special room in the temple by arrangement with Eliashib. Nehemiah took measures to cleanse the temple,* and in so doing he threw out the belongings of Tobiah (13:4–9). The name Tobiah is also found in the Zeno papyri from Gerza in the Egyptian Fayum. Xeno was finance minister of Ptolemy* II. Among the papyri are two letters from Tobias dated in May, 259 B.C., requesting certain animals and slaves.* This Tobias married a sister of Onias the high priest and was the father of Joseph and grandfather of Hyrcanus.

The principal monument at the site is the building standing separate from the caves, known as Qsar el-'Abd ("Castle of the Slave"). It was constructed of huge, cut-stone slabs standing on edge in early Hellenistic style. The portico was adorned with Corinthian columns (four facing the front), which stylistically give a date later than third-century construction, providing identification with the last Tobiad, Hyrcanus (c. 190–175 B.C.). Josephus (Jos. Antiq. 12.4.2) gives a lengthy description of the withdrawal of Hyrcanus from Jerusalem to the E side of the Jordan and of this place in the Wadi Syr. He tells how Hyrcanus built there in the time of Seleucus IV (187–175 B.C.) a castle* of white stone, surrounded by a park and

lake (moat?), having on its walls representations of "animals of a prodigious magnitude." The previously mentioned portico had above its entablature* two smaller columns that were flanked by lions* on either side, facing inward. Reconstructions of the building are to be seen in the Albright and *Scientific American* references given in the bibliography to this article. The huge stones of the building proper were as large as 6 m. (20 ft.) in length, 3.5 m. (10 ft.) high, and had a thickness of 45 cm. (18 in.). They were set up as slab walls and have since collapsed. There appear to have been as many as three entrances.

The site was discovered during the explorations in Palestine and Trans-Jordan by two English scholars, C. L. Irby and James Mangles (1817–18), who made useful archaeological observations.

The American Schools of Oriental Research carried out excavations at 'Araq el-Emir from April 10 to May 15, 1961, under the direction of Paul W. Lapp. The objectives were to determine the stratigraphical* history of the place and to date the construction and subsequent history of the monumental building of Qsar el'Abd. Two trenches were cut, and findings indicate that the site was occupied in the eleventh century B.C. Subsequently there was a gap in occupation until the Hellenistic period in the second century B.C., when the building was erected. It further appeared that the ancient village arose around A.D. 200 and that, soon after, the site was again abandoned, as it has remained until modern times.

Recent scholarly investigations tend to view the building as one of the many Jewish temples apart from Jerusalem in use during its period. Of interest in corroborating this is the further description by Josephus (Jos. Antiq.), of a temple built in Egypt* shortly after Hyrcanus's time. The high priest of the temple in Jerusalem, Onias III, was deposed from office and fled to Egypt. There, with the permission of the authorities, he built a temple at a place called Leontopolis,* which remained in use until it was closed by the Romans soon after the destruction of the Jerusalem temple in A.D. 70.

According to Josephus the name given to the fortress was Tyros (Greek form of Tyre*). Tyros is a transliteration of the Aramaic *tûrā'* and Hebrew *sûr*, a rock or fortress. The Arab pronunciation is *sîr*. And so the fortress or castle gave its name to Wadi Syr.

BIBLIOGRAPHY: B. Mazar, "The Tobiads," *IEJ* (1957), 137–45, 229–38; C. C. McCown, "The 'Araq el-Emir and the Tobiads," *BA*, 20 (1957), 63–76; M. I. Rostovtzeff, *Social and Economic History of the Hellenic World*, 1 (1950), 426 (cf. 1959 ed.); W. F. Albright, *The Archaeology of Palestine*, rev. ed. (1960), 149–50; P. W. Lapp, "Soundings at 'Araq el-Emir (Jordan)," *BASOR*, 165 (1962), 16–34.   MHH

AR ARAH. See AROER.

ARARAT (âr'ə rat; Heb. אֲרָרָט, *'ᵃrārāṭ*). The ancient name of the mountainous region of central Western Asia surrounding Lake Van. The Hebrew form of the name, given above, is derived from the Assyrian *Urartu**/ *Uraṛtu*, and the Old Persian form, *Arminija* is used today for the whole area. Mount Ararat is the highest of the group of ridges around Lake Van. It has two peaks; the higher reaches 5,166 m. (16,948 ft.) and is volcanic, its last eruption having occurred in 1840. The biblical narrative of the deluge states that the ark landed on the "mountains of Ararat" (Gen 8:4) and that it was from there that postdiluvial civilization spread across the earth. The Scripture is not precise in describing the exact mountain or peak. The same area is cited in the story of the flood* in the Babylonian Gilgamesh Epic,* in the eleventh tablet. Only in that reference is Mount Nisir named. Numerous attempts have been made over the centuries to climb the mountains of the Van region and recover a piece of the supposed ark from the eternal snows of the higher elevations. Such expeditions have been unsuccessful. The time and the situation of the Flood narrative are such that it would be virtually impossible to demonstrate scientifically the verity of the account by recovering a fragment of wood from the area. It was considered the nether end of the known world in the most ancient E. The final resting place of the ark demonstrates the vast extent of the flood and the violent alteration of natural phenomena that occurred. If the deluge had been a normal Mesopotamian* flood the ark would have been swept to the deep sea not to the mountainous North. Ararat is a region of little villages and narrow valleys, and much is yet to be discovered about the area. The severity of the terrain and the lack of modern roads has held extensive archaeology to a minimum. The only areas well studied have been those immediately adjoining Lake Van, Lake Urmia, and the small rivers which flow into them. The major site thus discovered has been the remains of ancient Urartu. This central Asian state gained limited prominence in the ninth to eighth centuries B.C. The biblical references to Ararat in connection with the Assyrian King Sennacherib* (2 Kings 19:36; Isa 37:8) belong to this city which arose long after the deluge. The last reference (Jer 51:27) is against the confederation of peoples who, with the Medes* and Scythians,* brought about the downfall of Babylon* and the judgment of God upon Israel's captor. Considerable numbers of Babylonian artifacts* have been recovered from Persian and Armenian sites showing that trade and booty* from Mesopotamia were distributed over the whole area of W Asia.

See FLOOD; GILGAMESH EPIC.

BIBLIOGRAPHY: T. Beran, in *Kulturgeschichte des alten Orient*, ed., H. Schmokel (1971), 606ff.; H. A. Hoffner, Jr., *ZPEB*, 1 (1975), 255–57.

ww

ARCH. Used in the construction of buildings, it is usually curved and made of separate wedge-shaped blocks, sometimes cast or laminated. Beginning with the Hellenistic occupation, the arch was widely used in the Bible lands, being especially prominent in Roman and Crusader architecture.

No arches seem to have been built in the Bronze Age, though the architectural principle was evidently known both in Egypt* and Western Asia. The Greeks experimented briefly with the arch and barrel vault at an early period but did not use it for design so

much as for a variant of an opening or passage. Aesthetic reasons were at least partially responsible for their limited use of the arch, since they relied on the flat lintel. An arched form was permissible to span city gates,* probably because it would support a wider opening. However, some of the oldest (dating to the fifth century B.C.) were not true arches but were of corbeled design, borrowed from Mycenae.* This arch form, coming from the Bronze Age, consisted of overlapping straight courses of masonry, each extending from both sides farther than the one below, until the opening they spanned was closed. While it may seem to be universal, the true arch was never developed in the New World, the corbeled type alone being used.

Perhaps the earliest Greek example of the segmental arch occurs in the entrance to the agora* at Priene, added in 166 B.C. A flat-profiled arch was used for cisterns* (which, though weaker, was still adequate), and barrel-vaulting,* either semicircular or pointed, was commonly restricted to basements. Cross-vaulting appears in a Hellenistic tomb at Pergamum.* The temple of Concord at Agrigentum is distinguished by an ogival arch in the gable above the lintel or entablature,* reducing the weight of the masonry and giving access to the roof timbers. It may be that slow Greek development of the arch was the result of considering it to be aesthetically less desirable as a substitute for the flat lintel, which to them contributed to an epitome of beauty in architecture.

Roman excellence in masonry was accompanied by structural, if not so much aesthetic, progress. They seized on the arch as a formal substitute for post and lintel and the vault as a solution to covered space-design problems. The Roman temple continued the basic Greek design configuration, but incorporated vaults and arches, along with another borrowed feature—the colonnade, which appeared in the basilica.* Hellenistic Rome produced many archetypes of buildings that would follow—such as the theater,* amphitheater, and monumental avenue with its crossing cardo and decumanus.

The Roman city developed into a system of discrete, functional space, connected by arterials (streets and avenues) which were spanned at appropriate dividing points by monumental archways and articulated by lateral archways. Aqueducts,* crossing the countryside, were carried on arches, structurally appropriate and visually pleasing. The description of the temple and city in the closing chapters of Ezekiel (40–46) evokes feelings of the contribution made by functional mass, space, and ornamental detail to public spectacle, dignity and importance, achieved in their time by the Roman architects.

Very early Roman usage appears in the Porticus Aemilia, a vaulted porch carried on tiers of arches, along the banks of the Tiber River. The Pantheon at Rome* is a classic example of the use of built-in brick arches to distribute the loads and thrusts of enormous concrete buildings. The ubiquitous triumphal arch, an intended permanent signboard of achievement, is of considerable historical importance. The oldest known in the city of Rome is the fornix Fabianus, built in the year 633 of the city, to commemorate Fabius Maximus Allobrogicus, conqueror of Savoy. It was discovered and excavated in 1882. Most of its stone had been carried off for use in building the new Basilica* of St. Peter during 1541–45. The triumphal arch in honor of Augustus,* erected after the battle of Actium, suffered the same fate. The Arch of Constantine was restored by Clement XII with large blocks of marble from the temple of Neptune, near the Pantheon, while the latter itself was restored by Alexander VII, using in part the marble from a triumphal arch called in medieval times the Arch of Piety. One monument provided materials for another, and this cannibalizing of buildings and reuse of stones points up a major problem in archaeological interpretation. Fallen arches recovered by excavation, however, provide key units in the reasonable reconstruction of buildings because of their stones' unique shapes and type of fitting together.

See AQUEDUCTS; ECCE HOMO, ARCH OF.

BIBLIOGRAPHY: H. Frankfort, *The Art and Architecture of the Ancient Orient* (1954); S. Giedion, *The Beginnings of Architecture* (1964), 515.

MHH

ARCHAEOLOGICAL METHODS AND TECHNIQUES. See AERIAL PHOTOGRAPHY; ARCHAEOLOGY, UNDERWATER; ARCHAEOMETRY; BALK; CARTOGRAPHY; CHRONOLOGY; DATING, ARCHAEOLOGICAL; DEMOGRAPHY; DENDROCHRONOLOGY; GRID LAYOUT; PALAEOBOTANY; PALAEOGRAPHY, GENERAL; PALAEOGRAPHY, HEBREW; PALAEOPATHOLOGY; PALAEOSEROLOGY; PALYNOLOGY; PAPYROLOGY; PEDOLOGY; PHOSPHATE ANALYSIS; POPULATION ESTIMATION; QUADRANT METHOD; RADIOMETRIC ASSAY; SERIATION; SPECTROGRAPHIC ANALYSIS; STRATIGRAPHY; STRIP METHOD; TYPOLOGY; X-RAYS AND ARCHAEOLOGY; X-RAY FLUORESCENCE.

ARCHAEOLOGY. I. *Definition.* Satisfactory definition often requires description. This is notably the case with archaeology, which has developed as a science over little more than a century. It began as exciting treasure hunts, in which man ravaged the ancient lands for spectacular and financially valuable memorials of human culture. Layard's writings (recently republished in the "Travellers and Explorers" series by Routledge and Kegan Paul), Schliemann's amazing account of Troy* and Mycenae,* and all the stories of such digging before the momentous days when Flinders Petrie and Arthur Evans brought order and a measure of scientific methodology into the subject, illustrate this predatory period in archaeology.

Today the objects of investigation are much more comprehensive and widespread. To observe the care with which the very chalk marks on a street wall of Pompeii* are preserved, in vivid contrast to the heavy-handed and calamitous looting of that famous ruined town two centuries and less ago; to watch a New Zealand team sifting the dust of a moa hunters' camp and working on the evidence that has thrust back the date of the first Polynesian occupation of the South Pacific by many centuries; to see the

Roman-British archaeologist identifying bone fragments, and classifying remnants of coal from a milecastle on Hadrian's Wall* and so establishing dates of siege and invasion; or to note the care with which fragments from a Qumran* cave are measured in an effort to add even infinitesimal detail to the knowledge brought by the Dead Sea Scrolls*—all this marks the widening scope and the advancing method of the archaeologist, making definition in some ways simpler and in others more difficult.

Consider a definition from the *Century Dictionary*, now eighty years old: "Archaeology is that branch of knowledge which takes cognizance of past civilizations, and investigates their history in all fields, by means of the remains of art, architecture, monuments, inscriptions, literature, language, customs, and all other examples which have survived." This definition is quite inadequate today. R. A. S. Macalister's definition is half a century old and is much too circumscribed: "Archaeology is the branch of knowledge which has to do with the discovery and classification of the common objects of life."

Perhaps some such definition as the following might be risked: "Archaeology is that branch of historical research that draws its evidence from surviving material traces and remains of past human presence and activity." Such a statement allows room for the increasing scope of archaeological investigation, if only because modern techniques continually render significant hitherto neglected evidence. From aerial photography* to Carbon 14 dating (*see* DATING), the archaeologist has multiplied and improved his tools and methods in a hundred ways. Nor has the refinement of both theory and practice begun to reach the end of its development.

The vast increase in historical knowledge thus achieved is one of the wonders of this century. When Samuel Johnson remarked in his pontifical fashion some two centuries ago, saying that "all that is really known of the ancient state of Britain is contained in a few pages, and we can know no more than the old writers have told us," he was but representing the attitudes of his day. To be sure, when he talked in the George Inn of Fleet Street, Roman London lay beneath his feet, with part of its surviving wall within five minutes' walk of his house, up the narrow lane across the street; but the eighteenth century had not learned to read the record in the soil. We know far more of early Italy than Vergil knew, for all the acuteness of archaeological awareness that he displays in Book 8 of the *Aeneid* (337–57). We know incomparably more of prehistoric Greece than did Thucydides, in spite of the insight into the unrecorded past that he displays in the first chapters of his remarkable history of Peloponnesian War (Thuc. 1.1–23).

Our knowledge of the Bible, the preoccupation of this volume, has been transformed. Before archaeological research remedied the situation, supplementary sources for the history contained in the Old and New Testaments, and the only non-biblical sources for the early history of the lands concerned, were four in number. Herodotus, the "father of history," the brilliant and widely traveled Greek who lived from 484 to 420 B.C., is easily the most important of the four.

He introduced his story of the Persian assault on Greece, which was finally repulsed a few years after his birth, with two or three informative books on Babylon,* Egypt,* and the Middle East, lands which he visited and summarily investigated. Second is the fragmentary history of Berossus, a Babylonian priest who lived between 330 and 250 B.C. and who wrote a history of Babylon in Greek. Third is Manetho, an Egyptian priest of the same period, who wrote in Greek for Ptolemy* II a history of Egypt of which some portions survive. Finally is Flavius Josephus, the Jewish priest and guerrilla leader who became secretary to Vespasian,* and who wrote in the last decades of the first century two large volumes on the history of the Jews* up to his own time. This work is an extremely valuable source, uncritical and turgid in style though it sometimes is. This is the sum total of extraneous aid to understanding prior to the rise of archaeology and its intelligent and ordered use of existing evidence.

II. *Raw Material of Archaeology.* A. *Occupation Debris.* Modern investigation by microscopic analysis can produce masses of information on diet, with its changing patterns, using material from middens (refuse heaps) and the household debris from ancient sites. From early Polynesian camps in New Zealand, to the lake-dwellings of the first Europeans in Switzerland, and the garrison quarters and Mithraic shrines on Britain's Roman Wall, this work could be illustrated time and again. The nature of the pottery* used, whether or not a group felt a need to repair damaged utensils, piled oyster shells, bone needles,* fishhooks, fragments of writing materials (*see* WRITING BOARD), charred wood* (*see* CHARCOAL) and the nature of the wood—all these are evidence and are the source of important conclusions. B. *Human Remains.* Mummified remains of Egyptian royal persons; Norse skeletons from Greenland with their pathological evidence of deficiency diseases; frozen bodies discovered by Russian archaeologists in the Arctic latitudes of Siberia, which have yielded recognizable corpses for medical investigation; bodies preserved in peat bogs with evidence of the manner of death and style of clothing*—all tell their story. The crushed skeletons in a fallen house and the mutilated human remains in a well at Gezer,* reveal eloquently significant facets of Canaanite* life. More important are the contents of tombs (*see* GRAVE). Urn burials, Saxon and Norse ship burials, mound burial pits of Ur* discovered by Woolley, are archaeological finds of first importance. C. *Objects of Art.* On stone, bronze,* silver,* gold* or gems, cut crudely or with refinement, man has left the record of his love of beauty. The goldsmith's work, found from Ireland to the Crimea; the filigree art of the Sumerians; bronze mirrors* from Corinth* obliquely referred to in 1 Cor 13:12; carved gems from Crete— these and their like reveal features of the mind of man and not infrequently depict his activities. From the cave* drawings of Neolithic* men to the exquisite Vaphio Cups in the Athens* Archaeological Museum, and on to modern times, man has left records in his art of all that he has loved and done. Lost,

preserved, buried, or hidden artifacts* of this order constitute important archaeological material. Greek vase painting* has thrown notable light on Greek drama. The murals of Egypt,* Crete, and Assyria are priceless both for their material worth and for their history. D. *Pottery.* The study of pottery,* an almost universal object of human manufacture, and one which commonly can be dated (*see* DATING) with a large measure of accuracy, is an important feature of archaeology. Pottery is the ceramic expert's chief key to chronology. The merest fragment (*see* SHARD) of broken earthenware is of significance, and the archaeologist is at great pains to record and classify the exact level, place, and relationship of his finds. Pottery varies from the crude, round vessels of the "beaker people" (the first recognizable inhabitants of Britain) to the beautiful vases of the Athenians and the Chinese. In all its forms it has something to tell. E. *Buildings.* From the traces of the wattle huts, where the slave* gangs lived round the Gizeh* pyramid* to the pyramid itself, which was built to house the royal dead; from the brown stains of Roman post holes in the Cripplegate legionary camp to the fluted columns of the Parthenon; from the chariot* stables* of Megiddo* and Hazor* to the synagogue* of Capernaum;* from Roman-British villas, the forerunners of the manor houses, to Stone Age huts below the successive strata of Phoenician,* Greek, Roman, and Crusader occupation from Byblos (Gebal*) and Baalbek* to Tyre,* structures humble and magnificent, sacred and secular, the architectural memorials of man reveal his beliefs, problems, preoccupations, techniques, and industry. F. *Inscriptions.* Inscriptions—on stone, metal, or pottery—form part of the human record. They are infinitely varied, and from the marked jar-seals of the Aegean civilization (*see* MINOA) to the Nestorian Monument* of China, from the Rosetta Stone* to the Nazareth Decree,* from the Behistun inscription* to Augustus's* autobiographical Monumentum Ancyranum from the Ancyra* temple wall, the record of epigraphy* is contemporary history, brief and unadorned because of the physical limitations of such recording. The reading of such abbreviated and allusive material, together with its decipherment, forms an ancillary expertise. The study of graffiti*—on the wall scratchings, for example, of Pompeii*—is a difficult branch of this study. G. *Written Documents.* Papyrus* documents from Egypt* range from Pharaonic to Islamic times. Unearthed from tombs, crocodile* cemeteries, and the occupational debris of Nile Valley towns, the papyri* have provided data of the utmost variety. In particular they have illuminated the language and background of the NT, though papyri of biblical relevance go back, in fact, to the Elephantine papyri.* These latter throw light on the Persian period in Egyptian history and on the Book of Nehemiah.

Other writing materials fall under this head. The cuneiform* tablets of Babylonia and Assyria have preserved a wide range of literary traditions, and all that they reveal of human life and thought.

Inscribed potsherds also come into this category. Broken pieces of pottery (*see* OSTRACA; SHARD), which abounded in every ancient town, were used for brief letters. The Lachish ostraca (*see* LACHISH LETTERS), found by J. L. Starkey in 1934, are documents of this order. Leather* was also used for writing,* and the mass of documents from the Qumran caves, which astonished the world in 1947, were written on prepared leather. H. *Tools* and Weapons*. From antler picks found in Neolithic* flint (*see* FLINT KNIFE) mines, to weapons of bronze* and iron,* which reveal the transitions of the eras to which these metals have given their names, the record of man's activity, belligerent and peaceful, is written in his implements of war (*see* WARFARE) and peace. I. *Coins.* Whole tracts of Roman history depend on the records of coinage. Coinage, in its own unique fashion, provides vital information on the easternmost kingdom of Alexander's successor-states. It also traces the progress of Mediterranean trade with India. Numismatics (*see* COINS) is another expert branch of knowledge for which the activities of the archaeologist—collecting coins, medals, and the like—provide abundant raw material. As with ceramic studies, it is of prime importance in dating.* J. *Botanical Remains*. Great significance is also attached to pollen grains recovered from occupation debris (*see* PALYNOLOGY). Wood,* even in the form of charred remnants (*see* CHARCOAL), provides, in the growth rings of such long-lived trees as the redwoods of California, a dendrochronological* record of occupation and of climatic change. From the corn fragments in the Pueblo caves of America's Southwest to the traces of pine cones used as aromatic altar-fuel in the Carrawburgh Mithraeum of England's Northumberland, the fragile remains of flora, identifiable and datable by modern techniques, furnish a message for the investigator. K. *Cult Objects*. Much of this material might possibly be classified under art. The earliest recognizable piece of human sculpture, for example, is of a bear, molded in mud, found in a Pyrenaean cave,* and marked by the ritual thrusts of the hunters' stone spears. Fertility rituals, which may be traced from the Stone Age to the very end of the pagan centuries, have left such figurines as those found commonly in Canaanite* sites, and phallic emblems, crude or sophisticated, like those of which mutilated pieces are to be seen on Delos. It is sometimes difficult to distinguish cult figurines from children's toys, of which examples are found in Egypt and elsewhere. The Ram in a Thicket,* now in the British Museum, is a striking example of Sumerian* art and is doubtless a cult object. So, in fact, are the major surviving or recorded triumphs of Greek sculpture, such as the idols of anthropomorphic worship about which Paul comments in Acts 17:16, 23. Little, in fact, may be listed here that is not also art, unless it be such objects as the meteoric stone, if that is what the object was, which passed for Artemis's* image in Ephesus,* which supposedly had "fallen from heaven" (cf. Acts 19:35). L. *Earthworks*. Fortifications are distinctive types of walls* built for defensive purposes, as, for example, those of the Hyksos,* and provide a key to historical understanding. The manifold stratification of the defenses of Jericho* throws light on the continued but changing occupation of that ancient site. The traces of ancient land holdings from Celtic to

Anglo-Saxon times, the sites of Roman legionary camps and, above all, the line of Roman roads (*see* APPIAN WAY), have been revealed by shadow photography and especially by aerial photography.* In the realm of biblical archaeology, for example, the plane-borne camera has picked out the ancient irrigation works of the Negev* farmers, and sharpened the pattern of the Roman siege works at Masada.* The late A. Reifenberg, a Hebrew University soil scientist who served in World War II as a photographic interpreter for the Royal Air Force, announced interesting results from aerial photographs of Dothan,* Caesarea, the Samaritan shrine of Mount Gerizim,* the Jewish stronghold of Beth-Ter near Jerusalem* where two Roman camps were detected, and the hitherto unknown Philistine* harbor of Ashdod.* It is all grist for the archaeologist's mill.

III. *Relevance of Archaeology.* Many matters touched on briefly in this article are given fuller treatment and illustration under special headings in this volume. It will be observed how archaeology has illuminated history, literature, and language; how it has provided relevant and illustrative background; presented the interpreter and expositor with the missing detail or key that eliminates a difficulty, removes an incongruity, or reconciles a seeming contradiction. Archaeology has lifted man's past from the remoteness, the irrelevance, or the insignificance that sometimes invests ancient history when it is committed to a difficult language and cast in forms of thought alien to the patterns of today. Without the aid of the archaeologist, the historian is gravely limited. Without both the archaeologist and the historian the expositor lacks much relevant material.

BIBLIOGRAPHY: This is not intended to be exhaustive nor to contain the highly technical works of scientific archaeologists, their field reports, and the academic publications that properly preserve the finer and often the undigested details of archaeological investigation. Books at the moment out of print have not all been omitted, since most if not all of them are obtainable in libraries.
1. *General Archaeology and Description*.
S. L. Caiger, *Bible and Spade* (1936); J. P. Free, *Archaeology and Bible History* (1950); W. H. Boulton, *Archaeology Explains* (1952); S. G. Brade Birks, *Teach Yourself Archaeology* (1953); W. F. Albright, *The Archaeology of Palestine* (1956); F. E. Zeuner, *Dating the Past* (1958); L. Cottrell, *Wonders of Antiquity* (1960); L. Deuel, *The Treasures of Time* (1961); J. A. Thompson, *The Bible and Archaeology* (1962); D. J. Wiseman, *Illustrations in Biblical Archaeology* (1962); D. Brothwell and E. Higgs, eds., *Science in Archaeology* (1963); A. Eisenberg and D. P. Elkins, *Worlds Lost and Found* (1964); R. W. Ehrich, ed., *Relative Chronologies in Old World Archaeology*, 2d ed. (1965); C. W. Ceram, *Gods, Graves and Scholars*, rev. ed. (1967); D. N. Freeman and J. Greenfield, eds., *New Directions in Biblical Archaeology* (1969); R. K. Harrison, *Introduction to the OT*, Part Two (1969), 85–134; F. Hole and R. F. Heizer, *Introduction to Prehistoric Archaeology*, 2d

ed. (1969); D. H. K. Amiran, J. Elster, M. Gilead, N. Rosenan, N. Kadmon, U. Paran, *Atlas of Israel* (1970); L. Deuel, *Flights into Yesterday* (1971); E. Yamauchi, *The Stones and the Scriptures* (1972); M. Magnusson, *Archaeology of the Bible* (1977).

2. *The Old Testament.*

R. W. Rogers, *A History of Babylonia and Assyria*, 1 (1912, 1916, 1924); R. A. S. Macalister, *The Philistines* (1913); R. Koldewey, *The Excavations at Babylon* (1914); G. A. Barton, *Archaeology and the Bible* (1916); E. A. T. W. Budge, *The Rise and Progress of Assyriology* (1925); J. Baikie, *The Amarna Age* (1926); R. A. S. Macalister, *A Century of Excavation in Palestine* (1930); J. Garstang, *Joshua-Judges* (1931); A. S. Yahuda, *The Accuracy of the Bible* (1934); G. G. Cameron, *History of Early Iran* (1936); C. L. Woolley, *Digging Up the Past* (1937); E. Chiera, *They Wrote on Clay* (1938); P. Carleton, *Buried Empires* (1939); J. Garstang, *The Story of Jericho* (1940); C. L. Woolley, *Ur of the Chaldees* (1940); N. Glueck, *The River Jordan* (1946); H. R. H. Hall, *The Ancient History of the Near East* (1947); R. T. O'Callaghan and P. E. Dumont, "Aram Naharaim," *Analecta Orientalia*, v. 26 (1948); A. L. Perkins, *The Comparative Archaeology of Early Mesopotamia* (1949); H. H. Rowley, *From Joseph to Joshua* (1950); H. Frankfort, J. A. Wilson, and T. Jacobsen, *Before Philosophy* (1951); R. J. Braidwood, *The Near East and the Foundations for Civilization* (1952); R. Redfield, *The Primitive World and Its Transformations* (1953); G. Childe, *What Happened in History*, rev. ed. (1954); R. Ghirshman, *Iran from the Earliest Times to the Islamic Conquest* (1954); M. F. Unger, *Archaeology and the OT* (1954); C. L. Woolley, *Excavations at Ur* (1954); S. Lloyd, *Foundations in the Dust* (1955); P. van der Meer, *The Chronology of Ancient Western Asia and Egypt*, 2d rev. ed. (1955); A. Parrott, *Discovering Buried Worlds* (1955); id., *The Flood and Noah's Ark* (1955); id., *Nineveh in the OT* (1955); id., *Samaria* (1955); W. Phillips, *Qataban and Sheba* (1955); J. B. Pritchard, ed., *Ancient Near Eastern Texts Relating to the OT* (1955); C. W. Ceram [K. W. Marek], *Narrow Pass, Black Mountain* (Brit. ed., 1956); C. W. Ceram, [K. W. Marek], *The Secret of the Hittites* (Am. ed., 1956); L. Cottrell, *Life Under the Pharaohs* (1956); S. Lloyd, *Early Anatolia* (1956); J. A. Wilson, *The Culture of Ancient Egypt* (1956); W. F. Albright, *From the Stone Age to Christianity*, 2d ed. (1957); G. R. Driver, *Aramaic Documents of the Fifth Century* B.C. (1957); J. Friedrich, *Extinct Languages* (1957); K. M. Kenyon, *Digging Up Jericho* (1957); A. Parrot, *The Temple of Jerusalem* (1957); G. E. Wright, *Biblical Archaeology* (1957); N. M. Diakonoff, *Sumer* (1959); H. Frankfort, *The Birth of Civilization in the Near East* (1959); N. Glueck, *Rivers in the Desert* (1959); J. J. Simons, *The Geographical and Topographical Texts of the OT* (1959); M. E. L. Mallowan and D. J. Wiseman, *Ur in Retrospect*, vol. xxii (1960); S. Moscati, *The Face of the Ancient Orient* (1960); S. N. Kramer, *History Begins at Sumer*, 2d ed. rev. (1961); id., *Sumerian Mythology*, rev. ed. (1961); S. Lloyd, *The Art of the Ancient Near East* (1961); C. F. Pfeiffer, *The Patriarchal Age* (1961); S. Piggott,

ed., *The Dawn of Civilization* (1961); G. E. Wright, ed., *The Bible and the Ancient Near East* (1961); M. A. Beek, *Atlas of Mesopotamia* (1962); W. F. Saggs, *The Greatness That Was Babylon* (1962); E. Anati, *Palestine Before the Hebrews* (1963); *FLAP* (1963); J. H. Franken and C. A. Franken-Battershill, *Primer of OT Archaeology* (1963); S. N. Kramer, *The Sumerians* (1963); J. Laessoe, *The People of Ancient Assyria* (1963); T. Jacobsen, *The Sumerian King List*, no. 11, Assyriological Studies (1964); E. Strommenger, *The Art of Mesopotamia* (1964); H. Frankfort, *Cylinder Seals* (1965); A. H. Gardiner, *The Egypt of the Pharaohs* (1966); G. Roux, *Ancient Iraq* (1966); Y. Aharoni, *The Land of the Bible* (1967); J. Kelso, *Archaeology and Our OT Contemporaries* (1968); H. Frankfort, *The Art and Architecture of the Ancient Orient*, 4th rev. ed. (1969); *CAH*, 3 vols., rev. 3d ed. (1970).

3. *The New Testament.*

J. Baikie, *Egyptian Papyri and Papyrus Hunting* (1925); G. A. Deissman, *Light from the Ancient East* (1927); W. H. Davis, *Greek Papyri of the First Century* (1933); F. A. Banks, *Coins of Bible Days* (1955); C. K. Barrett, *The NT Background* (1956); F. F. Bruce, *Second Thoughts on the Dead Sea Scrolls* (1956); A. Guillaumont and G. Quispel, *The Gospel According to Thomas* (1959); F. F. Bruce, *The NT Documents* (1960); E. M. Blaiklock, *The Cities of the NT* (1965); id., *Archaeology and the NT* (1970).

EMB

ARCHAEOLOGY, HISTORICAL SURVEY OF.

This survey of two centuries of archaeology covers in broad outline the major events in the widening history and scope of biblical archaeology.

1717 The Society of Antiquaries was set up in London and may be regarded as the beginning of archaeology. The society received a royal charter in 1751 and issued its first volume of *Archaeologia* in 1770.

1798 A side effect of Napoleon Bonaparte's occupation of Egypt* was an awakening of interest in the land. A band of competent savants accompanied the army, and Vivant Deoon's vast *Description de l'Egypte* was a direct result of the brief Napoleonic occupation.

1799 The Rosetta Stone,* with the trilingual inscription that provided the key to the decipherment of Egyptian hieroglyphics,* was discovered in August 1799, while the French were repairing fortifications N of the town of Rosetta. The name of a certain Boussard is associated with the find, but whether he was an officer of the engineers who died in 1812, General Baron A. J. Boussard, or a sapper of the same name who actually unearthed the stone, is not clear. Napoleon had it copied, and it ultimately reached the British Museum as a trophy of war (E. A. Wallis Budge, *The Rosetta Stone, and the Decipherment of Egyptian Hieroglyphics*, [1929]).

1805 Ulrich Jasper Seetzen discovered Caesarea* Philippi* (Banias), Ammon* and Gerasa* (Jerash).

1811   Arab geographers knew where Babylon* was, and Benjamin of Tudela, a Jewish rabbi, visited and identified the site in 1173. Other Europeans mentioned it in the sixteenth, seventeenth, and eighteenth centuries. In 1811 C. S. Rich, the first British consul at Bagdad, excavated and mapped part of the ruins, thus beginning Babylonian archaeology.

1812   Johan Ludwig (or Louis) Burckhardt (1784–1817), the Swiss explorer, discovered Petra,* the "rose-red city half as old as time" of Dean Burgon's famous sonnet. No important monuments in Petra antedate the middle of the first century B.C., and no pottery* is older than Hellenistic. Many well-known travelers and writers (listed in G. L. Robinson's *Sarcophagus of an Ancient Civilization* [1930]; Katherine Sim, *Desert Dweller, The Life of Jean Louis Burckhardt*, [1969]) have invested the strange place with an aura of romance.

1815   Lady Hester Stanhope (1776–1839), who, after the death of her uncle, William Pitt, lived in eccentric exile in a Druse village near Sidon,* attempted with General Sir John Moore to unearth statuary at Ashkelon,* one of the five cities of the Philistines.*

1817   Giovanni Baptista Belzoni paid his second visit to Egypt, with which the modern search for the tombs of the pharaohs may be said to have begun. Belzoni was the first to enter the great temple of Ramses I at Abu-Simbel* in this year (Colin Clair, *Strong Man Egyptologist* [1957]).

1822   Jean Francois Champollion, working on material supplied by the Rosetta Stone and the Philae obelisk,* finally succeeded in deciphering the hieroglyphic inscriptions. In 1828 came the second general survey of the monuments under Rosellina and Champollion.

1833   Sir Henry Creswicke Rawlinson (1810–95) went to Persia as a young officer to organize the shah's army. He became interested in the cuneiform* texts already competently studied by Niebuhr (1778), De Sacy (1788), and Grotefend (1802). In 1837 Rawlinson, now a colonel, deciphered part of the trilingual inscription of Darius* I on the Rock of Behistun (*see* BEHISTUN INSCRIPTION). In 1842 he copied the whole inscription, an enterprise accompanied by some danger. Rawlinson's accounts (1846, 1850, 1854, 1861–84) are the foundation of our knowledge of cuneiform on which the study of the history of Babylonia and Assyria depends.

1838   The historical exploration of Palestine began in this year, when Edward Robinson, a Massachusetts teacher of Hebrew, and Eli Smith, a missionary to Syria, traveled through the country describing it geographically and identifying many biblical sites. Robinson was followed by Titus Tobler. The German was succeeded by a Frenchman, Victor Guérin, who began a great mapping project in 1852. Such work was basic for future archaeology (*see* R. A. S. Macalister, *A Century of Excavations in Palestine* [1925], 23ff.). Robinson's work extended to 1852.

1842   Paul Emile Botta (1802–70) was appointed French Consul at Mosul. He began exploration in December of that year on the mound of Koujunjik, opposite Mosul. Local tradition had identified the two tells of Koujunjik and Nebi Yanus on the E of the Tigris with Nineveh.* Travelers, from the twelfth-century Benjamin of Tudela to Carsten Niebuhr in 1766, had recorded the tradition. In the first quarter of the century, Claudius James Rich began measurements in the area. Deflected from this task in March 1843, Botta turned to another promising site and so discovered Khorsabad* and the palace of Sargon II.* Joined by M. E. Flandin in May 1844, Botta was able to demonstrate the worth of his discoveries by sculptures sent to Paris in 1846. In 1849/50 the two explorers published their results in five massive volumes. In 1851 Victor Place continued the work and made a competent plan of the site. Botta had opened the way to Nineveh and found Khorsabad. Assyriology* proper began as a result of this work.

1845   Austen Henry Layard (1817–94) began excavations at the tell of Nimrud (ancient Calah*) on November 8, 1845. He discovered the palaces of Ashurnasirpal,* Shalmaneser II (rebuilt by Tiglath-Pileser II*), of Adadnirari, and Esarhaddon.* The Black Obelisk of Shalmaneser* was found in the palace. Layard's shipment of the vast statuary of the Assyrian palaces to the British Museum was a feat of transportation rivaling the removal of Cleopatra's Needle to London. At Koujunjik in 1849 Layard discovered Sennacherib's* palace. Masses of material relevant to biblical studies were recovered, notably the slabs depicting the siege of Lachish* and innumerable clay tablets. Layard had unearthed the S palace and its library, and his achievements were matched in the N palace area by Hormuzd Rassam, Layard's assistant. Since Ashurbanipal, an assiduous collector of ancient artifacts* and documents, had also stored Babylonian records, these finds laid the basis for the study of the history of two empires. Layard finished his work in April 1851. Rassam made his discoveries in the next two years, during which (in December 1853) he discovered the palace of Ashurbanipal. Layard's *Nineveh and Its Remains*, first published in 1849, has been recently republished by H. W. F. Saggs (1970). Layard belongs, however, to the prescientific era and was preoccupied with the collecting of museum exhibits rather than with exact study of ancient history.

1848   F. de Saulcy cleared a site at Jerusalem known as the Tombs of the Kings, which later proved to be the tombs of the kings of Adiabene.

1849   Karl Richard Lepsius (1810–84) published the results of Prussian expeditions to Egypt (1842–45)—twelve volumes of *Denkmäler aus Aegypten und Aethiopien.*

1850   August Ferdinand Francois Mariette (1821–81) went to Egypt in search of Coptic manuscripts. He discovered the Serapeum (burial-ground of the sacred bulls of Apis, or Osiris*) at Saqqara. Mariette

1. Sir Austen Henry Layard. Painting by L. Passeni. Courtesy National Portrait Gallery, London. 2. Sir Arthur Evans. Sketch by Francis Dodd. Courtesy National Portrait Gallery, London. 3. Sir W. M. Flinders Petrie. Painting by P. A. de Laszlo. Courtesy National Portrait Gallery, London. 4. Heinrich Schliemann presenting paper on Troy before members of Paris Observatoire. Courtesy Camera Press Ltd., London.

established the Bulaq Archaeological Museum, later to become the National Museum at Cairo. He was the virtual founder and director of Egypt's Antiquities Department from 1858–81. In thirty years Mariette excavated and found fifteen thousand monuments, from Memphis* to Karnak, in thirty-seven sites. He excavated the temple of Edfu* in 1860, the temple of Hatshepsut at Deir el-Bahri in 1858, and partially cleared the temple of Abu-Simbel* in 1869.

In the same year (1850) W. F. Loftus, who succeeded Rassam at Nineveh,* visited the biblical Erech* (modern Warka, ancient Uruk) and other sites in the Euphrates Valley. Excavations at Erech had to await three German expeditions (1912–13, 1928–39, 1954–59). Loftus wrote of his work in 1857 in *Travels and Researches in Chaldaea and Susiana.*

1859 Constantin Tischendorf discovered the Codex* Sinaiticus, an early (first half of the fourth century A.D.) manuscript written in capitals, and the only one of its kind to contain the entire New Testament.

1863 J. T. Wood began his exploration of Ephesus* for the British Museum on May 2, 1863, and on May 2, six years later, discovered the temple of Artemis,* following the clue provided by an inscription from the time of Trajan. Wood's work was concluded

in 1874 and was recommenced thirty years later under the same auspices by David G. Hogarth. The Austrian Archaeological Institute conducted excavations in 1898–1913, 1926–35, and in 1954.

1864 Giovanni Battista De Rossi (1822–94) began his study of the Roman catacombs* in 1841. He was the first to recognize the necessity for a thorough knowledge of literary sources for the interpretation of the archaeological data. His three-volume *Roma Sotteranea Cristiana* was published 1864–77.

1865 The foundation of the Palestine Exploration Fund (PEF) in this year had as its major aim the survey of ancient Jerusalem. Between 1871 and 1878 the workers of the PEF surveyed most of western Palestine, with results which were basic for future archaeology.

1867 Lieutenant (later, Sir) Charles Warren, a young British artillery officer, was sent, amply financed by the PEF, to investigate Jerusalem. Warren's work was done in largely prescientific days, but he made much valuable progress, and his faulty datings* have been rectified. Warren, and his successor, Captain Charles Wilson, laid strong foundations for the archaeology of Palestine, especially for the topography

1. F. J. Bliss. Courtesy Palestine Exploration Fund, England. 2. Sir Charles Wilson. Courtesy Palestine Exploration Fund, England. 3. Charles Clermont-Ganneau. Photo: L'Academie des Inscriptions et Belles Lettres. Courtesy Institut de France. 4. Jean François Champollion. Courtesy Musées Nationaux, Paris. 5. Sir Charles Warren. Courtesy National Portrait Gallery, London.

and history of Jerusalem.* He was also the first to look at Jericho.* (*See* R. A. S. Macalister, *A Century of Excavation in Palestine* [1925], 30–40, 97, 128, 177, 185; W. F. Albright, *The Archaeology of Palestine* [1960], 26–27.)

1870 Charles Clermont-Ganneau (1846–1923), an orientalist of genius, joined the French consular service in Palestine in 1867, and in 1870 he sent the Mesha Stele* to the Louvre. In 1871 he discovered the notice prohibiting Gentiles from entering the temple court. He identified Gezer,* which was not to be excavated for another thirty years. In 1870 the American Palestine Exploration Society was founded to promote the survey of Trans-Jordan, a project subsequently abandoned for lack of money. Also during 1870 Heinrich Schliemann discovered Troy*—a lesson for historians on the folly of not taking recorded tradition seriously. Schliemann repeated his triumph at Mycenae.* (*See* Macalister, *Century of Excavation*.)

1872 The PEF sent a British party to make detailed survey of Western Palestine under Claude Rignier Conder (1848–1910) and Horatio Herbert Kitchener (1850–1916), who would become Lord Kitchener of Khartoum and British War Minister. Very few significant ruins were overlooked in this competent survey. Conder's *Memoirs* were published in 1880. His archaeological publications include *Tent Work in Pal-*

estine (1878); *Syrian Stone Law* (1886); *Altaic Hieroglyphs and Syrian Inscriptions* (1887); *The Tell el Amarna Tablets* (1902); *The City of Jerusalem* (1909).

1873 In 1872, among the 25,000 inscribed tablets from the libraries of Ashurbanipal and the temple of Nabu, a Babylonian account of the Deluge (Gilgamesh Epic*) had been identified, and the British Museum reopened excavations under George Smith, Rawlinson's one-time assistant, originally an engraver who became an Assyriologist of extraordinary talent. Smith discovered almost immediately the missing portion of the Deluge story, with the result that the sponsoring *Daily Telegraph* declared that the mission was accomplished and withdrew support. He returned to London, but in 1874, financed by the museum, he was back at Koujunjik. In April, after dogged local obstruction, he closed his trenches after recovering three thousand tablets. His *Assyrian Discoveries* and *The Chaldean Account of Genesis* stirred interest, and in 1876 he led a third expedition. It was again a time of frustration, which ultimately cost him his life.

1877 Ernest de Sarzec, French vice-consul at Basrah, worked at Lagash.* Among his discoveries were statues of the early governors and the Victory Stele of Eannatum (*see* Stele of Vultures*). De Sarzec sold the material from Tello (AL-HIBA) to the Louvre. Rassam (of Nineveh fame) also plundered the tell, and other clandestine diggers joined in, scattering the antiquities of Lagash all over the world. The Louvre purchases, however, awakened the world to Sumerian* archaeology. De Sarzec continued his work in 1880–81, 1889, 1893–95, and 1900. He died in 1901 but was succeeded by Captain Gaston Cros.

1878   Rassam resumed work for the British Museum at Nineveh. He recovered a clay* prism containing the annals of Ashurbanipal* and four barrel-shaped cylinders with accounts of the campaigns of Sennacherib.*

1879   Hormuzd Rassam, working at Babylon, discovered important tablets and possibly identified the Babylon Hanging Gardens.*

1881   Sir Gaston Camille Charles Maspero (1846–1916), lecturer on Egyptian archaeology at the École des Hautes Études from 1869, and later professor at the Collège de France, discovered many royal sarcophagi* at Deir el Bahari and continued clearing the temple of Karnak (see THEBES), scene of some important biblical wall paintings (*Histoire Ancienne des Peuples de l'Orient Classique* [1853–1900]).
Sir William Matthew Flinders Petrie (1853–1942) began his career as an Egyptologist and scientific archaeologist at this time, with work on the Giza* pyramids* and at Tanis* for the Egypt Exploration Fund.

1882   Edouard Naville commenced his long career as an Egyptian archaeologist. Dörpfeld joined Schliemann at Troy.*

1884   M. Dieulafoy—following W. K. Loftus and succeeded by J. de Morgan, R. de Mequehem, and R. Ghirshman—excavated the royal buildings of Susa* ("Shushan, the palace").

1887   A peasant woman, working in the ruins of Akhenaton's* town at Tell el-Amarna,* unearthed the Amarna letters.* Many were destroyed in transit but enough remained in the British and Berlin Museums to throw light on Egypt's foreign and Palestinian policy during the reign of the pacifist Pharaoh, Akhenaton. (*See* W. F. Albright, *ANET* [1969], 483–90; *BASOR*, 86ff.; C. J. Mullo Weir, *DOTT* [1958], 38–45; for a popular account, J. Baikie, *The Life of the Ancient East* [1923], 20–49.)

1888   John P. Peters, leading an American expedition along with Haynes and Hilprecht, discovered twenty thousand tablets at Nippur,* greatly expanding the knowledge of that day concerning Babylonian sacred literature. American expeditions, sponsored by the University of Pennsylvania, worked there in 1880–90, 1893–96, 1899–1900, 1948–49, and every other year to 1958, with remarkable results for Sumerian* history. (*See* H. V. Hilprecht, *The Excavations in Assyria and Babylonia* [1904], 289–577, and various University of Pennsylvania publications.)

1890   Flinders Petrie (*see above,* 1881) appeared on the scene in Palestine. Petrie spent six weeks on the mound of Tell el-Hesy* in SW Palestine, making vertical sections and noting the level at which every potsherd (*see* SHARD) was found. He thus established the principles of stratigraphy* and the use of pottery* to distinguish levels of occupation. F. J. Bliss, who spent the next three years on the Tell el-Hesy site, confirmed Petrie's principles. The Petrie-Bliss chronology* of 1894 proved correct as far back as 1500 B.C. The French School of Biblical and Archaeological Studies was founded in this year. (*See* W. F. Albright, *The Archaeology of Palestine* [1960], 29–30 passim.)

1894   Sir Arthur Evans (1851–1941), for ten years the keeper of Oxford's Ashmolean Museum, began work in Crete, excavated Knossos and found the Cretan script (not deciphered until 1953). He discovered the Minoan civilization,* not without importance in the history of the Philistines. From 1894–97, F. J. Bliss and his architect, A. C. Dickie, made important archaeological advances at Jerusalem. This was followed (1898–1900) by work on sites in the Shephelah* (Tell es-Safi, Tell ez-Zackariyeh, Tell el-Judeideh, Tell Sandahanna, the Hellenistic Marissa). R. A. S. Macalister, a brilliant Irish archaeologist, began work in Palestine at this time. The report of Bliss and Dickie in 1902 was notable for its scientific competence.

1895   This year marked the highest point in the work of Sir William Mitchell Ramsay, Professor of Humanity at Aberdeen, Scotland, from 1886 to 1911 (1851–1939). Ramsay was an epigraphist (*see* EPIGRAPHY, GREEK and HEBREW), a geographer, and classical historian. His archaeological work in Asia Minor* established the reputation of Luke as a historian and made vital contributions to the understanding of the Acts of the Apostles and Revelation. His books, published during the last decade of the nineteenth century, include *The Historical Geography of Asia Minor* (1921 rep.), *The Church in the Roman Empire* (1893), *The Cities and Bishoprics of Phrygia* (1895), *The Letters to the Seven Churches* (1963 rep.), *Saint Paul the Traveller and Roman Citizen* (1896), *Was Christ Born at Bethlehem?* (1898). His work leaned heavily on archaeological discovery. (*See* E. M. Blaiklock, *The Archaeology of the NT* [1974], 93 seq.)
Also Bernard Pyne Grenfell (1869–1926), with his colleague, Arthur S. Hunt, began their search in the Fayum for Greek papyri. In 1895 Grenfell and Hunt began at Oxyrhynchus,* 193 km. (120 mi.) S of Cairo, and discovered the first page of the logia (*see* AGRAPHA) of Christ. With Grenfell and Hunt, papyrology* was born, the term being first used in 1898. In 1889–90 Flinders Petrie had discovered papyri, some of them literary, at Gurob in the Fayum, and about the same time the British Museum acquired a parcel of papyri from Sir Ernest Wallis Budge. Sir Fredrick Kenyon (1863–1952) had written about the papyri in 1890–91, but it was Grenfell and Hunt who made the most momentous finds. They opened the way to

over a half century of discoveries, which have added vastly to the classicist's comprehension of ancient Greek literature, to the NT scholar's knowledge of the Common Greek* dialect, and to the ancient historian's information about the Middle East, especially Egypt—over three thousand years of history. Adolf Deissmann (1866–1937) was the first to make philological use of the new material from the papyri (*Bibel Studien* [1895], in English as *Bible Studies* [1901]; and his notable *Licht vom Osten*, in English as *Light from the Ancient East* [1910]). James Hope Moulton (1863–1917), a disciple of Deissmann, produced the two monumental volumes of his *Grammar of NT Greek* in 1906. The brilliant *Prolegomena* (vol. 1) was a landmark. Popular early studies that are still of value are Camden M. Cobern's *New Archaeological Discoveries* (1921) and James Baikie's *Egyptian Papyri and Papyrus Hunting* (1925), as well as A. S. Hunt and C. C. Edgar, *Select Papyri* (1923).

1896 G. M. Legrain began his notable work on the Karnak (*see* THEBES) temple. (*See* James Baikie, *A Century of Excavation in the Land of the Pharaohs* [1924], 123 seq.)

1897 J. de Morgan's work at Susa* (*see* under 1884). These excavations continued until 1912, and in 1902 unearthed the stele* bearing the Code of Hammurabi.* The year 1897 saw the publication of Sir George Adam Smith's *Historical Geography of the Holy Land.*

1898 M. Loret discovered in the Valley of the Kings (*see* THEBES, modern Luxor*) the tomb of Amenhotep II, son of Thutmose III. This was unique because it was the first tomb containing intact the body of a pharaoh, providing a foreshadowing of Tutankhamen's* tomb of later fame.

1899 Robert Koldewey, working for the *Deutsche Orient Gesellschaft*, began his years of systematic excavation at Babylon.* When Koldewey began his work in March, nothing serious, apart from some preliminary work by Rassam, had been attempted. In 1912, when he published a preliminary account of his investigations, he estimated that he was halfway through the task. The English edition, *The Excavations at Babylon*, appeared in 1914. Further digging continued at Lagash* (AL-HIBA) in this and succeeding years by Stephen Langdon.

1900 George L. Robinson discovered the "high place" of Petra (G. L. Robinson, *The Sarcophagus of an Ancient Civilization* [1930]).

1901 Captain Gaston Cros continued work at Lagash.

1902 R. A. S. Macalister began his excavation of Gezer.* Warren had first investigated the site, originally located by Clermont-Ganneau in 1871–74. The Gezer excavation covered seven years, until Macalister's appointment to a chair of archaeology in Dublin. The work was, says W. F. Albright (*The Archaeology of Palestine* [1949], 31), "a model of

economy . . . but stratigraphy* and photography were neglected; surveying and levelling were utterly inadequate; the architectural aspects of the dig were dealt with only sketchily." When the three volumes of Macalister's report appeared in 1912, "a monument of bee-like industry," they were hailed justly, Albright continues, "as a monumental achievement. . . . But almost everything in them had to be redated and reinterpreted. . . ." Macalister was under heavy disadvantages. To comply with Turkish law he was compelled to employ the strip method,* in which a site is cut strip by strip, the rubble from each successive strip being dumped into the preceding one, thus precluding further research.

Hammurabi's Code was discovered in this year by the French, and the Austrian scholar Ernst Sellin began a three-year survey of Taanach* with small results, due partly to neglecting the stratigraphy. This, however, was the first excavation to be carried out in the ancient kingdom of Israel.

1903 G. Schumacher, an architect long resident in Palestine who had received his initial training under Sellin, was placed in charge of a two-year investigation of Megiddo* by the *Deutscher Palästina Verein* and the *Orient Gesellschaft*. The well-known Jeroboam Seal was discovered at this time.

1904 David G. Hogarth worked at Ephesus for the BrM., studying the sanctuary of Artemis.*

1905 James Henry Breasted's *Ancient Records of Egypt* appeared in Chicago in September; also his *History of Egypt*, of which the second edition (1945) showed the striking advances in Egyptology.

1906 Hugo Winckler (1863–1913), a German Assyriologist who had worked at Sidon in 1903–4, won a Turkish firman (administrative order) to dig at Boghazköy.* A British archaeologist had identified Texier as this site, but the Germans were on good terms with the Turks at this time, thanks to the undertaking in 1899 of the Deutsche Bank to build the Berlin-Baghdad railway. A. H. Sayce had identified the area of Hittitology (*see* HITTITES) a generation before, but it was left to the German archaeologist to work seriously on it. The literature discovered at Boghazköy was in a language not deciphered until a decade later by F. Hrozny, the Czech (C. W. Ceram [K. W. Marek], *Narrow Pass, Black Mountain* [Brit. ed., 1956]; *The Secret of the Hittites* [Am. ed., 1956]).

In 1906 important fifth-century Aramaic papyri from the island of Elephantine,* opposite Aswan* in the Nile, were published. The first body of documents, mainly legal, was acquired from dealers and published by Archibald H. Sayce and Arthur Cowley (*Aramaic Papyri Discovered at Assuan*). The second, a more important batch, was recovered by a British Museum expedition on the site of the Jewish temple on the island and published by Eduard Schau in 1911 (*Aramaische Papyrus und Ostraka*). A third lot, much like the first, was actually known in 1893 and came to light in the Brooklyn Museum. It was published by Emil G. Kraeling in 1953 (*The Brooklyn Museum Aramaic Papyri*).

1. William Foxwell Albright. Courtesy Encyclopaedia Judaica Photo Archives.
2. Sir Charles Woolley. Courtesy National Portrait Gallery, London. 3. John Garstang standing by the Hellenistic round tower at Samaria. Courtesy Palestine Exploration Fund, England.

1907 Hermann Thiersch, Hermann Köhl, Carl Watzinger, and Ernst Sellin concluded a survey of the synagogues of Galilee.* Köhl and Watzinger had been engaged in clearing the temple complex of Baalbek,* one of the consequences of the Kaiser's spectacular visit to Palestine in 1898. The synagogues* had attracted Kitchener's attention during the Survey of Palestine, but this was the first investigation down to foundation level. Köhl and Watzinger published their *Antike Synanogen in Galilaea* in 1916.

In 1907 a joint German-Austrian expedition began two years' major work on Jericho* under Ernst Sellin and Carl Watzinger. The report, published in 1913, was full, accurate, and properly illustrated. The stratigraphy* was well handled, though dating was not perfect.

1908 A turning point in Palestinian archaeology was marked by the excavation of Samaria* this year and in 1910–11 by D. G. Lyon, C. S. Fisher, and G. A. Reisner. Thanks to the millionaire Jacob Shiff, this Harvard expedition was superbly conducted. Reisner, an archaeological genius worthy of comparison with Robinson, Clermont-Ganneau, and Petrie, had worked for a decade in Egypt and had combined the expertise of Petrie, Dörpfeld, and Koldewey, along with what Albright describes as "his native Middle-Western practicality and knack for large-scale or-

ganization" (*The Archaeology of Palestine* [1949], 34). The two large volumes of the report appeared in 1924.

1909 Duncan Mackenzie, invited by the Palestine Exploration Fund to direct the excavation of Beth Shemesh,* brought to the task an admirable knowledge of Aegean pottery.* He was able to identify the significant masses of Philistine* pottery, first noted by Hermann Thiersch in the previous year, which were found on the site. World War I interrupted Mackenzie's work.

1910 From 1910–14 Howard C. Butler led a magnificently equipped expedition to Sardis,* the ancient capital of Lydia.*

1913 The site of Shechem* was investigated in the two years before World War I by Sellin and Watzinger for the German Society for Scientific Research. Work was resumed in 1926–28, 1932, and 1934. It was demonstrated that Shechem was Balatah and was occupied until A.D. 67, when it was probably destroyed by Vespasian,* who razed the adjacent Samaritan temple on Mount Gerizim* (*see* W. F. Albright, *Archaeology of Palestine*, 247–48).

1917 The conquest of Palestine by the British in World War I opened a golden age of archaeology.

The Palestine Department of Antiquities was founded, headed by John Garstang of Liverpool University, and W. F. Albright began his work. He was in Palestine from 1920 to 1935, when civil disorders began.

1918 The distinguished Assyriologist, R. Campbell Thompson, then on the Intelligence Staff of the British Expeditionary Force in Iraq, began to dig at Eridu* (Tell Abu Shahrain) for the British Museum (Patrick Carleton, *Buried Empires* [1939], passim).

1919 Promptly with the end of hostilities, the archaeologists were at work again, especially in lands which remained under British control.
H. R. Hall, now nearing the end of his active career, was working on Sumerian archaeology at Tell Al Ubaid.* On the fringes of biblical archaeology, Clarence Fisher was following up Petrie's work at Memphis,* the old capital of Egypt.

1920 J. H. Breasted this year published the Edwin Smith Surgical Papyrus, and Pierre Montet in the French-mandated territory of Syria discovered at Byblos (Gebal*), the ancient Phoenician* cedar* port, the tomb of King Ahiram.*

1921 T. E. Peet was working at Tell el Amarna (*see* AMARNA) with Woolley. C. S. Fisher, A. Rowe, and G. M. Fitzgerald were excavating the tell of Beth Shan* on behalf of the Oriental Institute of the University of Chicago. Three periods of three seasons each (1921–23, 1925–28, 1930–33) were devoted to this Israeli Decapolis* town. The exploration penetrated five millennia of history.

1922 W. F. Albright began a two-season dig at Gibeah* (Tell el-Ful*) and Kiriath Sepher (Debir*). Large contributions were made to the knowledge of Iron Age* pottery.* The abiding lesson of Albright's work was that reliable results depend largely on meticulous care in digging and recording.
The year 1922 was also remarkable for two events that brought archaeology vividly to the attention of the world. The tomb of Tutankhamen* was discovered by Howard Carter in the Valley of the Kings (*see* THEBES) and the Indus Valley Culture of Harappa and Mohenjo-Daro was revealed by John Marshall (P. Carleton, *Buried Empires* [1939], 141 seq.).
In Palestine, A. Schmidt and H. Kaer worked at Shiloh.* The year 1922 saw the beginning of Sir Charles Leonard Woolley's excavations at Ur.* The ruins of Abraham's city, known as Al-Muqayyer, were first surveyed by the archaeologists Loftus and Taylor in 1854 and by Hall immediately after World War I. This latter work opened Mesopotamia* to archaeological exploration. Woolley's systematic exploration was carried on competently from 1922 to 1934 under the auspices of the British Museum and the University of Pennsylvania. Woolley's *Ur of the Chaldees* was published in 1929, and progressive reports appeared annually over the fourteen years of the excavations in *The Antiquaries Journal*. Woolley had been in charge of the British Museum's exploration of Carchemish* till the outbreak of hostilities in 1914.

1923 Excavations at Kish* (Tell El-Uheimir) 13 km. (8 mi.) E of Babylon unraveled much Sumerian history. Professor Stephen Langdon's report (*Excavations at Kish*) was published in the following year— the same year Langdon's historical account of Sumeria appeared in the first volume of *CAH*. (*See* also P. Carleton, *Buried Empires* [1939], passim.)
W. J. Pythian-Adams and John Garstang worked at Ashkelon,* and five years' work on the Ophel hill at Jerusalem was undertaken by Macalister, J. Garrow Duncan, and J. W. Crowfoot.

1924 David M. Robinson was working on Antioch of Pisidia. A monograph on the Roman sculptures of this imperial bastion in Asia appeared two years later (*The Art Bulletin* [1926–27], 5–69). The publication of the early volumes of *Cambridge Ancient History* in this year was a milestone. The discovery of Tutankhamen's tomb (1922), and particularly the beginning of the archaeological section of the *London Illustrated News*, awakened the world to the emergence of the new historical science.

1925 The Nuzi* documents with the light they shed on the patriarchal age attracted notice at this time. Nuzi is Yorghan Tepe, a tell* 240 km. (150 mi.) N of Baghdad, near the hill country of S Kurdistan, excavated in 1925–31 by a joint expedition of the American School of Oriental research in Baghdad and Harvard University. E. Chiera and E. A. Speiser wrote first about the site in *AASOR*, 6 (1926), 49–50, and R. F. Starr in *Nuzi* (1939).
E. L. Sukenik gave some preliminary attention to the problem of the walls* of Jerusalem in this year.
Remarkable advances in Palestinian prehistory marked the middle twenties. In 1925 a young Englishman, F. Turville-Petre, examining two caves above the Sea of Galilee, found the first traces of prehistoric Palestinian man. Dorothy Garrod followed up this work in 1928 to 1934 and established the outlines of what came to be known as the Natufian* Culture.
Also in 1925, Fisher joined the staff of the Oriental Institute of the University of Chicago. His first task was the Megiddo* excavations. Over fourteen years and at immense cost, until poor health forced Fisher's retirement, this fruitful site, till then only cursorily examined by the German expedition, was competently investigated. P. L. O. Guy and Gordon Loud succeeded Fisher, and to this day only a part of Megiddo's immense tell has been thoroughly examined. In 1925 Horsfield and Crowfoot began a nine-year clearance of Gerasa* (modern Jerash), a Jordan Decapolis town.

1926 The American School of Oriental Research in Jerusalem (founded in 1900) began the excavation of Tell en-Nasbeh (Mizpah*). The work was directed by Fisher's disciple, W. F. Badè, and a thorough excavation was completed. The two-volume report of the nine-years' digging, a model piece of writing, came out over the name of C. C. McCown in 1947. Simultaneously, a second project under M. G. Kyle and W. F. Albright examined Tell Beit Mirsim, SW of Hebron, the ancient Kiriath Sepher, or Debir*

(1926–32). An important result of this dig was the establishment of a clear pottery sequence. Palestinian chronology, in confusion when Albright began digging at Gibeah (Tell el-Ful*) in 1922, was greatly clarified by Pythian-Adams's work at Ashkelon, by the continued digging of Albright at Gibeah* and Tell Beit Mirsim (1926) and Bethel* (1934), by Reisner's work at Samaria* (published in 1924), and by Shipton at Megiddo.

1927 J. W. Crowfoot continued his work on the Ophel hill of Jerusalem in succession to Macalister and J. Garrow Duncan, finishing in 1928. The same archaeologist did important work at Samaria, one result of which, along with Kathleen Kenyon's activities, was to stabilize the chronology* of Palestine.

1928 Elihu Grant began a series of five campaigns at Beth Shemesh,* aided by Fisher. The work covered chiefly the period of Israelite occupation from the twelfth to the ninth centuries. With the assistance of G. E. Wright, the chronology was clarified in time for the report. E. Chiera, working at Nuzi* (also between 1930 and 1932) identified the Hurrians.* Chiera also worked at Khorsabad* in 1928 and 1929. From 1928 to 1937 M. Rostovtzeff and others continued the work at Dura Europos,* first begun six years earlier by F. Cumont for the French Academy. From 1928 to 1934 J. D. S. Pendlebury, Director of the Egyptian Exploration Society excavations, was engaged at Tell el-Amarna, and in 1928 T. Wiegand worked on the Pergamum* Asklepeion, a task which occupied three years. P. L. O. Guy, in the third season at Megiddo, discovered what he believed to be the royal stables.

1929 In 1929 Dorothy Garrod, a Cambridge prehistorian, began her six-years' work on Palestinian caves,* notably on Carmel.* She worked under the auspices of the British School of Archaeology at Jerusalem and the American School of Prehistoric Research. From her studies came further information about the Natufian culture (see W. F. Albright, The Archaeology of Palestine, 52ff.). Horsfield was at work at Petra, C. F. Schaeffer was making his remarkable finds at Ras Shamra (Ugarit*) (Albright, op. cit., 187), and the Jesuits* were beginning on Teleilat Ghassul* in the Jordan Valley in the same year. The Jesuits conducted eight campaigns up to 1938 (Albright, Archaeology of Palestine, 45).

1930 Theodore D. McCown, with C. S. Fisher, continued working at Gerasa* and on the Carmel caves with Dorothy Garrod (see Albright, op. cit., 169–70). John Garstang, Director of the Palestine Department of Antiquities, began six years' activity at Jericho.* The work had been initiated by the Germans Sellin and Watzinger in 1913 and was continued (1952–58) by Kathleen Kenyon. Garstang discovered the first Neolithic* urban culture (see J. B. Garstang, The Story of Jericho, [1948]).

1931 Ernest Herzfeld was at work at Persepolis* and A. Maiui at Pompeii* and Herculaneum.* O. R.

Sellers with W. F. Albright was working at Beth Zur,* a site of Maccabaean remains, commanding the road from Jerusalem to Hebron.* The British-American-Hebrew University project at Samaria, a four-year dig, began in 1931, and was to continue under J. W. Crowfoot, who began where Reisner left off, and with much more exact chronology. M. E. L. Mallowan commenced his work at Nineveh* and worked in this area for more than thirty years. The excavation of the agora* at Athens* began in this year and extended to 1939. It was directed for the American School of Classical Studies by Oscar Broneer. The Chester-Beatty Papyri* were discovered at this time.

1932 G. E. Ederkin worked on the site of Syrian Antioch.* Excavations continued there until 1939, without producing significant evidence from the apostolic period. On behalf of the Wellcome Expedition, J. L. Starkey, one of Petrie's pupils, began excavations at Lachish.* The work went on for four years until the death of the archaeologist at the hands of an Arab bandit in 1938. The major find was the Lachish Letters,* with their light on the period of Jeremiah. The Dura (see DURA EUROPOS) synagogue* (A.D. 244) was found almost intact by the French-American expedition in this year (Albright, Archaeology of Palestine, 175–76). In 1932 and 1933, R. W. Hamilton, of the Palestine Department of Antiquities, worked on a Bronze Age II site, at Tell Abu Huwam, at the foot of Carmel* on the coastal plain. The importance of the Nazareth Decree,* in the Louvre since 1789, was recognized in an article in JHS by M. I. Rostovtzeff in this year.

1933 Roman Ghirshman began five years' work on Tepe Sialk,* and P. Dikaias was excavating in Cyprus.* Mme. Judith Marquet-Krause began an important excavation at Ai,* which was interrupted in 1935 by her death. Charles Morey continued work at the Syrian Antioch, aided by Richard Stillwell. In this year, André Parrot, excavating Tell Hariri, near the Euphrates in SE Syria, began uncovering Mari.* This project extended to 1960. In 1933 the rabbi archaeologist Nelson Glueck began his thirteen-year survey of Trans-Jordan from Aqaba to the Syrian border, patiently identifying and dating the sites in an almost untouched area (see Albright, Archaeology of Palestine, 44, 76–78). Glueck's remarkable book The Jordan was first published in London in 1946.

1934 Hetty Goldman began four-years' work at Gozlu Kule (ancient Tarsus*). Two volumes of her report appeared in 1950 and 1960 (Excavations at Gozlu Kule). Excavations at Bethel were conducted by J. L. Kelso and W. F. Albright in this year. J. H. Steckweh brought the German project at Shechem* (Balatah) to a close. (This work was initiated by E. Sellin in 1913 and resumed by him in 1926.) In a brief season Steckweh cleared up much detail and produced valuable results (Albright, Archaeology of Palestine, 45–46; also an article in Avraham Negev's Archaeological Encyclopedia of the Holy Land [1972], 257).

1. Kathleen Kenyon. Courtesy Camera Press Ltd., London. Photo: Werner Braun. 2. Nelson Glueck. Courtesy Israel Government Press Office. 3. E. L. Sukenik. Courtesy The Hebrew University of Jerusalem.

1935 J. W. Jack was working at Samaria; Erich Schmidt, at Persepolis;* and Gordon Loud, at Megiddo,* having succeeded P. L. O. Guy. Two seasons later he found the famous Megiddo ivories.* The archaeological reports cover a generation. A further season of the joint expedition at Samaria* (1931–33) was undertaken this year. C. H. Roberts published papyrus fragments of John's Gospel, now in the John Rylands Library at Manchester, England.

1936 The large Jewish town of Bethshearim saw begun a four-year project under B. Mazar for the Hebrew University and Israel Exploration Society. Here B. Maisler and his colleagues found an important Jewish cemetery.

1937 Nelson Glueck excavated a Nabataean cemetery (*see* NABATEANS) on Jebel-et-Tannur, SE of the Dead Sea* (Albright, *Archaeology of Palestine*, 165).

1938 J. L. Starkey was murdered early in the year, a tragedy symptomatic of the gathering darkness. Lankester Harding and Charles H. Inge carried on briefly at Lachish,* but the troubles of seven years were lamentably bringing to a close the greatest decade of archaeology yet known.

1939 Just before World War II broke out, the Megiddo* exploration was terminated, though in 1941 Yigael Yadin, a new great name now appearing on the scene, did some work on the site and also in the area of Hazor.* Yadin was the son of E. L. Sukenik, who had already done much work in Palestine, especially on ancient Jewish tombs (see GRAVES) and synagogues.* At intervals between 1925 and 1940 he had investigated, along with L. A. Mayer, the location of the third wall of Jerusalem, which had been discovered by Robinson a century earlier. The troubled years preceding the formation of the State of Israel in 1948 delayed the launching of postwar projects in Palestine, except that, in 1946, French excavation began on a modest scale at Tell el-Farah, NE of Nablus.

1947 On November 23 of this year, E. L. Sukenik, of the Hebrew University of Jerusalem, received the first information about the famous Dead Sea Scrolls.* The acquisition of these documents, accidentally discovered during the preceding winter (1946/47) by Bedouins, is dramatically described in John C. Trevers, *The Untold Story of Qumran* (1965). The scrolls* have evoked a vast mass of learned writing. The discoveries from the Qumran* caves* included, by 1947, some Greek fragments (see QUMRAN NT FRAGMENTS). Also in 1947 John Cook was working at Smyrna.*

1948 Robert Braidwood worked at Qalat Jarmo in NE Iraq on a number of prehistoric villages. Anthropologists may find them relevant in the outline account of human prehistory in the first four chapters of Genesis. Braidwood's work continued at intervals until 1958. Excavations in Israel were undertaken at Tell Qasile* near Tel Aviv* (1948–49), directed by B. Mazar on behalf of the Israel Exploration Society and the Tel Aviv Museum. Excavations at Joppa* began and continued in 1950, 1952, and 1955, under J. Kaplan for the Jaffa Museum.

1949 Taking up Layard's work of the previous century, the British School of Archaeology in Iraq spent twelve years (1949 to 1961) tracing Calah's* history from prehistoric to Hellenistic times (see M. E. L. Mallowan, *Nimrud and Its Remains* [1962]; *Iraq*, 13–21 [1952–59]). R. de Vaux began his digging on the Essene* sites of Qumran and the community's farm, the nearby seaside oasis of 'Ain Feshka.*

1950 The seven-year investigation of the cemetery (see NECROPOLIS) under St. Peter's in Rome* began under the direction of Ludwig Kaas. The excavations at Dibon,* in Moab,* by William Merton for the American Schools at Jerusalem also were begun in 1950 and covered seven seasons. In this and the following years, J. L. Kelso and J. B. Pritchard worked on Roman Jericho.* Explorations by the American Foundation for the Study of Man (1950–53), followed by those of the University of Louvain (1951, 1952), brought to light much Sabean* art and the eighth century B.C. Temple of the Moon Goddess at Marib.

1951 G. L. Harding and Ronald de Vaux came into possession of the first Bar Kochba* documents.

1952 A copper scroll from the Dead Sea caves, sent

to Manchester College of Technology, NW England, for unrolling, describes the location of treasure owned by the Qumran community. Work that was to continue until 1958 was begun at Jericho, sponsored by the British School of Archaeology in Jerusalem, by the Palestine Exploration Fund, in collaboration with the American Schools of Oriental Research in Jerusalem, and by the Royal Ontario Museum. Under Kathleen Kenyon, this was to prove the most complete exploration of the ancient site yet undertaken. Nelson Glueck's work in the Negev* began in 1952. Roman Ghirshman, who had worked at Tepe Sialk from 1933 to 1937 and at Susa* from 1946, began, in 1952, his eight-year task of clearing the elaborate ziggurat* of the Elamite city of Chaga-Zambil, in Iran.

1953 Joseph P. Free, sponsored by Wheaton College, Illinois, began a series of campaigns at Dothan. Excavation reports are to be found in *BA* and *BASOR*.

1954 Kurt Bittel did notable work at Boghazköy.* This scholar had been at work for twenty years on the Hittite* Empire, its language and script. His work lies on the periphery of biblical archaeology, but a popular account of both Bittel's and Bossert's work, and the decipherment of Hittite, is to be found in C. W. Ceram [K. W. Marek] *Narrow Pass, Black Mountain* (Brit. ed., 1956), *The Secret of the Hittites* (Am. ed., 1956). This was a year of some activity, with Zakarie Goneiun busy at Saqqara (see MEMPHIS), André Godard at Persepolis, Richard Haines at Nippur (where he discovered the Inanna temple; see ISHTAR, DESCENT OF), Philip Hammond at Petra,* Kamal el Mallakh at Gizeh, Jean Perrot at Tell Abu Matar,* near Beersheba,* Heinrich Lenzen, for the German Archaeological Society, at Warka (ancient Erech*), Seton Lloyd at Beycesultan, and J. A. Puglish at Rome. Y. Aharoni opened the first of his four digs at Ramat Rahel (1954, 1959, 1960, 1963) on behalf of the University of Rome and associated Israel institutions.

1955 Emil Kunze was at work at Olympia. The Greek games* (Pythian at Delphi, Isthmian at Corinth,* and Olympic at Olympia in the western Peloponnese) are relevant to biblical archaeology only for the imagery they supplied for Paul and the writer of Hebrews. S. Yeivin continued the vigorous Israeli work at Caesarea,* where Antonio Frova, an Italian, uncovered the theater* in which, in 1960, a stone bearing a fragmented inscription of Pontius Pilate was found. The excavation of Hazor* by Y. Yadin began this year, continued until 1958, and was taken up again in 1968. Undertaken on behalf of the Hebrew University, it revealed the ability of a locally trained generation of Israeli archaeologists. The Jordan Department of Antiquities commissioned P. J. Parr to restore monuments at Petra. A Roman villa, uncovered in 1955 in Kent, at Lullingstone, contained evidence of Christianity in third-century Britain (G. W. Meates, *Lullingstone Roman Villa* [1958]).

1956 In this year, as well as in 1957, 1962, 1964,

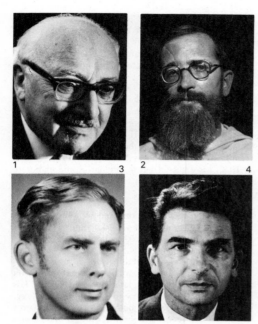

1. Michael Avi-Yonah. Courtesy The Hebrew University of Jerusalem. Photo: Schwerin. 2. Roland de Vaux. Courtesy École Biblique et Archéologique Française. 3. Paul Lapp. Courtesy Pittsburgh Theological Seminary, Pennsylvania. 4. Jean Perrot. Courtesy Centre de Recherches Prehistoriques Français de Jerusalem.

and 1968, Shechem* was excavated by G. E. Wright on behalf of the McCormick Archaeological Expedition, and J. B. Pritchard began work at Gibeon.* It was carried on in 1957, 1959, 1960, and 1962 by the same archaeologist on behalf of the Museum of the University of Pennsylvania. At Caesarea, M. Avi-Yonah, for the Hebrew University, excavated synagogue* ruins. Unfortunately, the troubles of Israel following the Suez crisis held up many projects, especially those under the widening sponsorship of Israeli institutions of learning.

1957   B. Ravani worked at Tiberias.* He excavated the baths of the ancient spa, S of the modern town.

1958   Harvard and Cornell universities, in cooperation with the American Schools of Oriental Research, began new excavations at Sardis* (*BASOR*, 154 [1959], 1–35). Franz Mittner was working at Ephesus,* and N. Zori at Beth Shan.*

1959   A four-year dig resumed work at Caesarea. Saul S. Weinberg was at work in Corinth. In 1959 UNESCO first promoted an international effort to lift the great temples of Abu Simbel* from the inundation of the Aswan* High Dam. This was accomplished at great expense (*see* A. S. McQuitty, *Abu Simbel* [1965]).

1960   A three-year underwater archaeology* en-

deavor at Caesarea was begun at the Roman port. A. Negev, on behalf of the National Parks Authority, mapped the Crusader town. In the third season of excavations at Shechem by the Drew-McCormick Expedition, the Bronze Age beginnings of the town were revealed. In this year the Israel Exploration Society made a thorough investigation of the Dead Sea caves, and Y. Yadin, in charge of one of the four teams, made a significant discovery behind En Gedi.* Using a helicopter to photograph the area, he located a Roman camp that in turn led to the discovery of the Bar Kochba* relics in the caves below (see, for a readily accessible account, Ronald Harker, *Digging up Bible Lands* [1972], 96–108). The exploration was resumed in March 1961.

1961   Paul Lapp excavated at 'Araq el-Emir* (1961 to 1963) and at Taanach* in 1964. He was Director of the Jerusalem School of the American Society for Oriental Research (1961–64). In a cave N of Jericho he found, in 1963, important papyri from Samaria* (722 B.C.). James Mellaart worked at Iconium* (modern Konya) from 1961 to 1963.

1962   H. F. Squarciapino was engaged at Ostia, the Tiber port of Rome, in 1962. He discovered a fourth-century-A.D. synagogue,* the oldest found in W Europe. In 1962 and 1963 the Roman theater* was excavated at Petra* by the Princeton Theological Seminary expedition, under the direction of P. Hammond, Jr. From 1962 to 1967 Yohanan Aharoni, Professor of Biblical Archaeology at Tel Aviv University, along with R. Amiram, excavated on behalf of the Hebrew University and the Israel Exploration Society at Arad;* and, for the Department of Antiquities and Museums, M. Dothan worked at Ashdod.* Both seasons extended until 1967. Simultaneously, until 1968, Kathleen Kenyon continued working at Jericho for the British School of Archaeology at Jerusalem, and W. G. Dever worked for the Hebrew Union College.

1963   In this and the two succeeding seasons, Y. Yadin organized and completed his massive archaeological assault on Masada,* whose story he tells in his fine book on the fortress (*Masada* [1966]).

1964   J. Callaway worked at Ai, and K. Schoonover at Et Tell.

1965   Mampsis, the easternmost town of the central Negev, 40 km. (25 mi.) E of Beersheba,* was excavated by A. Negev for the Hebrew University and Parks Administration. The work covered three seasons. (The site had been visited by E. Robinson in 1838 and E. H. Palmer in 1871. C. L. Woolley and T. E. Lawrence had drawn a plan of the ruins in 1914. A survey was made in 1937 by G. G. Kirk and P. L. O. Guy.)

1967   The Six Days' War brought many historic sites into Israeli control—first Old Jerusalem and then the whole of the Sinai Peninsula. In Sinai* during the period of earlier Israeli occupation from 1956 to 1957, a survey of sites was conducted and published in a magnificent book called *God's Wilderness*, by Beno Rothenberg (1961). A fine scroll from the Dead Sea caves 8.6 m. (28 ft.) long was bought by Y. Yadin from an Arab dealer. The scroll was located only after the occupation of Jordanian Jerusalem. It was a manual containing religious rules, architectural notes on how the temple* at Jerusalem should be built, and a mass of other directions. A plan for mobilization was oddly similar to that put into operation exactly two thousand years after the concealment of the writings in the caves.

1968 In this year, B. Mazar began the excavation of the S wall of the Temple Mount on behalf of three Israeli institutions. (The decade's work on this difficult site is detailed in Kathleen Kenyon's *Royal Cities of the OT* [1971], 39, 43, 45, 61, 110–11, 114.) In this year, during building operations at Giv'at ha-Mivtar, NE of Jerusalem, the ossuary* of Yehohanan Ha-Gaqol, a man who had been crucified, was discovered (*see* CRUCIFIXION). Other ossuaries discovered around the same time provided examples of names mentioned in John's Gospel and in Acts.

1969 N. Avigad began excavations in the Jewish Quarter of the Old City of Jerusalem, where remains of a magnificent Hellenistic villa have been revealed. S. Weinberg, on behalf of the Museum of Art and Archaeology of the University of Missouri, began work at Tell Anafah in the Hula Valley.

1970–72 Excavations in the Jewish Quarter of the Old City of Jerusalem in 1970 revealed traces of a preexilic city wall,* a Herodian residence, a bath house, and a Byzantine* church. Two years later another section of the city walls was discovered, along with the remains of buildings and some ceramic fragments. Glass* waste was also found under a section of Herodian street* pavement.

The 1970 and 1971 campaigns at Tell el-Hesy* uncovered forty burials from the Persian period in the SE slope of the tell.* Twelve of the burials were accompanied by such articles as seals,* iron* rings, and anklets (*see* BANGLES). Excavators at Tell Hesban in 1971 were unable to recover any remains prior to the seventh century B.C., leading them to think that the tell was probably not the site of Sihon's capital after all. They recovered 186 coins,* but even these were only first-century B.C. or later. The fourteenth campaign at Sardis* in 1971 continued work begun when the acropolis* wall was exposed in 1960. The reconstruction of the synagogue* mosaics* was continued, and extended to the marble court and the palestra.*

From 1971–72 a reexamination of Judith Marquet-Krause's work at Ai* (Et Tell) in 1933–35 was undertaken. One result was the discovery of an additional phase of the city walls in two of the areas studied. Work at that site has tended to support the identification of Et Tell with Ai. Also in 1971–72 a Philistine* temple was excavated at Tell Qasile* and is the only one to have survived from Philistia. The remains of two wooden pillars suggested the authenticity of the description of a Philistine temple in Judg 16:26.

1. Nahman Avigad. 2. Benjamin Mazar. 3. Yigael Yadin. (2 and 3) Courtesy The Hebrew University of Jerusalem. Photo: Werner Braun. 4. Yohanan Aharoni. Courtesy Tel Aviv University, Institute of Archaeology.

The area occupied by this temple was enlarged by subsequent excavations. In 1972 Israelite remains from the seventh century B.C. were recovered as a result of excavations in the court of an Armenian church on Mount Zion. Artifacts* at the site included figurines of animals and human beings, as well as pottery* fragments.

1973–75 During this period, excavators at Tell el-Hesy uncovered the remains of a complex series of fortifications that suggest a more sophisticated level of urban development than had been imagined previously. In 1973 excavators at Dan* discovered an Israelite horned altar* on the floor of the courtyard that was surrounded by the ninth-century-B.C. high place.* The artifact was almost a sixteen-inch cube that had been cut from a single block of limestone.

A reexamination of Tell Lachish* from 1973 resulted during the following two seasons in discoveries that included storage jars, a few of which bore a royal stamp with a four-winged scarab.* In 1974 at Tell Hesban excavators found some skeletal remains that on examination suggested a high level of infant mortality. Animal bones present at the site indicated that more than 160 wild-animal species, excluding fish and mollusks, had served as food during the occupational history of the site, which began about 1200 B.C. In Jerusalem in 1975, some Iron Age* tombs from the eighth and seventh centuries B.C. were discovered north of the Damascus Gate. The area proved to have been a large burial site (*see* NECROPOLIS) that extended to the slopes of the Kidron* Valley.

1976–79 In 1976, excavators working at Tell Lachish showed conclusively that Level III had been destroyed by Sennacherib* in 701 B.C., and Level II by Nebuchadnezzar* over a century later. In 1978 an Egyptian inscription was recovered from the debris of the Canaanite* city that dated the destruction to the twelfth century B.C. This artifact has obvious implications for the date of the Exodus and the Israelite conquest of Palestine. The 1977 season at Tell el-Hesy exposed more of the Early Bronze city. The results indicated that the inhabitants had enjoyed an expanding agricultural economy that probably included trade with neighboring city-states.

In 1979 President Anwar Sadat of Egypt announced the discovery near Cairo of the ancient city of Iyon, which had once been the home of Joseph, Moses, and Plato. The houses of the priestly families had already been located, and other areas of the site were under examination, with the cooperation of Israeli archaeologists.

Conclusion

Chronological recording has become difficult in recent years. Peace is elusive in the Middle East, and projects of importance frequently are deferred and interrupted. However, in Jerusalem the Place of the Trumpet and some Herodian streets have been found. Many discovered ossuaries* have authenticated biblical names. Evidence of early Christianity has accumulated from Jerusalem to Herculaneum,* with its Christian house-chapel. We await new discoveries with excitement.   EMB

ARCHAEOLOGY IN ISRAEL AND JORDAN SINCE 1948.

S. Yeivin, *A Decade of Archaeology in Israel, 1948–1958* (1960), and G. L. Harding, *The Antiquities of Jordan* (1959) describe the archaeological activities in Israel and in Jordan in the decade after Israel's independence. In the subsequent fifteen-year period, 1958–73, numerous excavations in Israel have been sponsored by the Department of Antiquities, the Hebrew University, the British School of Archaeology, the American Schools of Oriental Research, the Hebrew Union College, and various consortiums of American colleges and universities. In Jordan, excavations have been conducted chiefly by the Jordanian Department of Antiquities, the British School of Archaeology, and the American Schools of Oriental Research.

Some of the outstanding discoveries made during 1958–73 will be summarized according to chronological periods.

1. *Surveys.* In 1963 P. Lapp estimated that there had been scientific excavations at about one hundred fifty sites, including 26 major excavations, out of about five thousand known sites. Since 1967 Israeli surveys have uncovered thousands of new sites. Of twenty-five hundred sites surveyed in the Golan* Heights and Judah* in 1967 and 1968, one thousand were hitherto unknown. In a 1971 survey of the areas around Dor,* Atlit,* and Haifa,* half of the 800 sites were new. In a recent survey of the Negev,* 280 of 368 sites were previously unrecorded.

2. *The Middle Bronze Age.* There is disagreement among archaeologists with regard to the earliest phase of the Middle Bronze (MB) Age. W. Dever begins the MB I period at 2100 B.C.; Albright considers 2000–1800 as MB I, and K. Kenyon prefers to speak of an intermediate age, between Early Bronze (EB) and MB, with MB I beginning at 1900. This age was characterized by destructions caused by incursions of nomads, who set out large cemeteries (*see* NECROPOLIS). Kenyon and Dever believe that the invaders were Amorites* from Syria.

Lapp in 1965 excavated an enormous early MB I cemetery of twenty thousand tombs at Bab edh-Dhra'* on the Lisan of the Dead Sea.* Lapp in 1963 investigated three hundred shaft tombs at Dhahr Mirzbaneh 11 km. (7 mi.) NE of Bethel,* and at the nearby 'Ain Samiya, Yeivin in 1970 examined forty-four tombs and found a silver* cup bearing Mesopotamian mythological motifs. Between 1967 and 1971 Dever excavated a major MB I necropolis* at Jebel Qa'aqir, 13 km. (8 mi.) W of Hebron.* In addition to the shaft tombs carved in the limestone hills, the nomadic MB I tribes also set up some of the dolmens* in the basaltic Golan* area.

Albright, who dates Abraham c. 1800, associates the patriarchal movements with caravan sites in Trans-Jordan and the Negev* which flourished in the MB I period. Abraham's descendants lived in the eighteenth century (MB IIA), which was the period of King Hammurabi* of Babylon.* References to Hazor* in the Mari* letters (*see* MARI) illustrate the contacts between Mesopotamia* and Canaan* in this century. In 1972 Biran uncovered an MB IIA rampart at the northern site of Dan.*

The MB IIB–C (seventeenth–sixteenth century B.C.) period is the age of the Hyksos* domination of Egypt,* associated with Joseph and his descendants. At Dan* excavations since 1966 by A. Biran have revealed a typical "Hyksos" glacis* (sloped rampart). G. E. Wright, who excavated Shechem* from 1957 to 1966, uncovered from this period a large fortress-temple, 21 by 26 m. (68 by 84 ft.).

Dothan,* where Joseph sought his brothers, was excavated from 1953 to 1962 by J. Free. A massive city gate of the sixteenth century has been uncovered at Gezer,* which was reexcavated by Wright, Dever, Lance, and Seger from 1964 to 1972. The fortified city of Ashdod* was probably begun by the Hyksos to control the Via Maris.

Religious structures of the Canaanites during the MB II period include a spectacular row of masseboth (*see* MASSEBAH) or stone pillars, some over 3 m. (10 ft.) high, at Gezer. Discovered by Macalister in 1903, they were restudied in 1968 and dated to the MB IIC period. An MB II bamah or high place* with rows of cyclopean stones was discovered in 1971 by Epstein at Turbo Mecha just S of Beth Shemesh.* Kelso, who reexcavated Bethel* from 1954 to 1960, found beneath a gate destroyed in the sixteenth century traces of blood (*see* BLOOD GROUPING) which he interpreted as evidence of Canaanite sacrifices.

3. *The Late Bronze Age (LB).* The LB I (c. 1525–1400) was a period dominated by the imperialistic

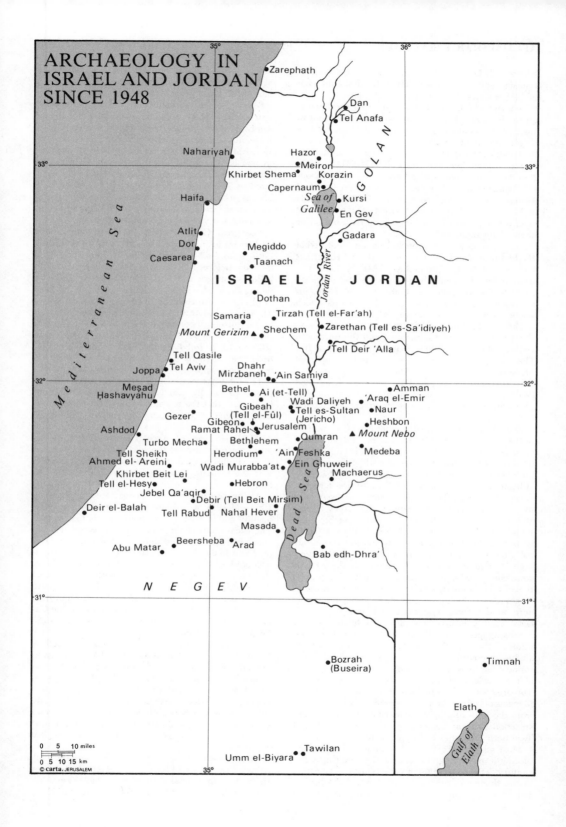

ARCHAEOLOGY IN ISRAEL AND JORDAN SINCE 1948

35° 36°

Zarephath

Dan
Tel Anafa

GOLAN

Nahariyah Hazor

33° Meiron 33°

Khirbet Shema Korazin
Capernaum
Sea of Galilee Kursi
Haifa En Gev

Atlit
Dor Gadara
Caesarea

Megiddo
Taanach

I S R A E L **J O R D A N**

Dothan

Samaria Tirzah (Tell el-Far'ah)
Mount Gerizim ▲ Shechem Zarethan (Tell es-Sa'idiyeh)

Tell Deir 'Alla

Tell Qasile Dhahr
Joppa Tel Aviv Mirzbaneh 'Ain Samiya

32° Bethel Amman 32°
Meṣad Ai (et-Tell)
Hashavyahu Wadi Daliyeh 'Araq el-Emir
Gezer Gibeah Tell es-Sultan Naur
(Tell el-Fûl) (Jericho)
Gibeon Heshbon
Ashdod Ramat Rahel Jerusalem
Turbo Mecha Bethlehem Qumran ▲ *Mount Nebo*
Tell Sheikh Herodium Medeba
Ahmed el- Areini 'Ain Feshka
Khirbet Beit Lei Wadi Murabba'at Ein Ghuweir
Tell el-Hesy Machaerus
Jebel Qa'aqir Hebron
Deir el-Balah Debir (Tell Beit Mirsim)
Tell Rabud Nahal Hever
Masada

Abu Matar Beersheba
Arad Bab edh-Dhra'

N E G E V

31° 31°

Bozrah Timnah
(Buseira)

Elath

Gulf of Elath

0 5 10 miles
0 5 10 15 km
© carta, JERUSALEM 35°

Tawilan
Umm el-Biyara

Mediterranean Sea

Jordan River

Dead Sea

Eighteenth Dynasty. Vivid evidence of the devastation wrought by Thutmose III in his first campaign of 1468 B.C. has been uncovered at Gezer.

Scholars who favor an "early" date for the Exodus on the basis of 1 Kings 6:1 would place this event in the fifteenth century. An argument used against this date is the demonstration by the surface surveys of N. Glueck of an apparent hiatus of settled habitations in Trans-Jordan between 1800–1300 (MB IIA–LB II). Recent discoveries in Jordan have raised doubts about this conclusion. MB materials have been found at Mount Nebo,* Naur, and Amman, and LB materials at Medeba* and Heshbon.* Outstanding is an LB square temple which was uncovered by a bulldozer at the Amman airport in 1955.

Similar square sanctuaries have been identified at the foot of Mount Gerizim* and at Hazor. Hazor has yielded outstanding examples of MB II–LB I Canaanite temples, including one with stelae* dedicated to the moon-god, a double temple analogous to Mesopotamian prototypes, and a long temple which was identified as such only in 1968.

The LB II period includes the fourteenth century, the Amarna* Age of Akhenaton,* and the thirteenth century, dominated by the long reign of Ramses II.* The dating of this era can be ascertained by imported Mycenaean* pottery* from the Aegean.

In 1970 excavators found a cave of the LB period at Gezer which contained an unusual ceramic sarcophagus,* analogous to types found on Cyprus* and Crete.

Recent discoveries illustrate the Egyptian interest in the Negev and the Via Maris along the Palestinian coast. A cemetery with forty anthropoid clay* coffins, used by an Egyptian garrison from the fourteenth to the eleventh century, was excavated in 1972 at Deir el Balah, 15 km. (9 mi.) SW of Gaza.* Important evidence of the Egyptians in the Negev was discovered by Benno Rothenberg in 1969 at "Solomon's Pillars" at Timnah* N of Elath.* He uncovered an Egyptian temple with inscriptions from Seti I (1318–1304) to Ramses V (1160–1156). In opposition to Glueck's attributing copper mining to Solomon,* Rothenberg suggests that the mining operations on the Arabah were conducted at an earlier date by the Egyptians. In 1974 Rothenberg followed up his work in the S Negev desert by uncovering one of the oldest underground mining* systems ever found. From artifacts* such as bronze* chisels, stone hammers, and a cooking pot found there, Rothenberg dated the mine in the Late Bronze Age, about 1400 B.C. A sophisticated system of nearly two hundred shafts, tunnels, and passages dug out on several levels was able to accommodate about one thousand workers. The area was rich in malachite, which was reduced to ingots of copper ore in furnaces about 1 km. (.6 mi.) from the mine. Rothenberg ascribed the initial construction work at the mine to the Nineteenth and Twentieth Dynasties of Egyptian rule.

Most scholars accept the late date of the Exodus, placing it in the reign of Ramses II in the thirteenth century. The destruction of various sites in Palestine in the thirteenth century is attributed by Albright, Lapp, Kelso, and Yadin to the conquest of the Israelites. Such an interpretation has been thoroughly criticized by Bimson (1978), an advocate of the early date of the Exodus.

Because of the ambiguity or lack of evidence at certain sites, some scholars such as Franken are skeptical about citing archaeological evidence for a thirteenth–century Israelite invasion. Kenyon, who reexcavated Jericho* from 1952 to 1958, found that erosion had removed all but the merest traces of a LB stratum. The site of Gibeon,* which was excavated by Pritchard from 1956 to 1962, yielded little LB materials except from tombs. Current excavations since 1964 by Callaway at et-Tell, identified as Ai,* have not yielded a LB settlement.

The great Canaanite city of Hazor, which was burned by Joshua (Josh 11:1–11), was excavated by Yadin from 1955–58 and 1968–69. The burning of the city before 1230 B.C. is assigned by Yadin to Joshua's campaign. The thirteenth-century devastation of Bethel,* which left debris 1.5 m. (5 ft.) thick in places, is also credited to the Israelites by Kelso. Albright had identified with Debir* a site destroyed in the thirteenth century—Tell Beit Mirsim, 19 km. (12 mi.) SW of Hebron, which he excavated from 1926 to 1932. Tell Rabud, 15 km. (9 mi.) S of Hebron, excavated by Kochavi in 1968 and 1969, has now been proposed as a better location for Debir.

The biblical record which indicates that Shechem* passed peacefully into Israelite hands is confirmed by the fact that the transition from LB to Iron I was accomplished without major destruction of the city.

4. *The Early Iron (EI) Age.* * The twelfth to the eleventh centuries B.C. is the period of the settlement of the Philistines* along the coast and their conflict with the Israelites during the days of the judges and Saul.

At the site of Taanach,* reexcavated by Lapp in 1963 and 1968, a mold for making figurines of a Canaanite goddess with a tambourine was discovered. The excavations confirm the biblical record that Taanach was not captured under Joshua but only later (c. 1125) under Deborah* (Judg 5:19). The devastation of Shechem in the twelfth century is thought by the excavators to be consistent with the work of Abimelech (Judg 9). At the northern city of Dan (also known as Leshem in Josh 19:47, and as Laish in Judg 18:29) Biran believes that the destruction of the Canaanite city in the twelfth century was due to the invasion of the tribe of Dan.

The famous port of Joppa* has been excavated by Kaplan since 1955. The 4 m.-wide (14-ft.) city gate, embellished with an inscription of Ramses II,* was probably destroyed by the Sea Peoples,* who invaded the Levant and Egypt in the reigns of Merneptah (*see* ISRAEL STELE) and Ramses III (late thirteenth and early twelfth centuries). The newcomers may be responsible for the shrine with a lion's* skull discovered in the thirteenth-century level at Joppa.

The most famous of the Sea Peoples were the Philistines.* Impressive Philistine objects, which betray their Aegean origins (Amos 9:7), have been recovered from Ashdod,* excavated since 1962 by

M. Dothan. A unique Philistine temple with two-column bases, reminiscent of the temple destroyed by Samson* (Judg 16:29), has been uncovered by A. Mazar in 1971–72 at Tell Qasile* on the outskirts of Tel Aviv.* The penetration of the Philistines into the interior has been illustrated by extensive Philistine remains at Gezer* and Philistine objects as far N as Dan.

Objects and peoples from the Aegean penetrated even into Trans-Jordan, e.g. to Tell es-Sa'idiyeh (Zarethan*), excavated from 1964 to 1967 by Pritchard. Tell Deir 'Alla, excavated by Franken from 1960 to 1964, has yielded tablets in a script which resembles the Aegean linear.

The mastery of iron* smelting which gave the Philistines an upper hand until the reign of Saul is vividly illustrated by the discovery of an iron plow in Saul's palace at Gibeah* (Tell el-Ful*), reexcavated by Lapp in 1964.

5. *The United Monarchy* (tenth century). David's capture of Jerusalem* from the Jebusites* to make it his capital has been illuminated by the important excavations of K. Kenyon from 1961 to 1967 in the area of Ophel, the southeastern hill of about 4 ha. (10 a.) which was OT Jerusalem. On the slope above the Gihon Spring* she found a massive corner of the wall of the Jebusite city.

Unfortunately almost all of Solomon's* extensive activities in Jerusalem have been obliterated. One possible Solomonic structure is a fragmentary casemate wall.* Kenyon believes that the enigmatic Millo ("filling") which was repaired by David (2 Sam 5:9) and by Solomon (1 Kings 9:15) referred to the massive platforms on the eastern edge of Ophel which were in constant need of repair.

Striking evidence to illustrate the statement that Solomon built "Hazor, Megiddo,* and Gezer" (1 Kings 9:15) has come from the discovery of nearly identical gates* at these sites. Yadin, recalling the fact that the earlier excavation at Megiddo had uncovered a Solomonic gate with three chambers on each side, anticipated the discovery of a similar gate at Hazor. His reexamination of Macalister's report on Gezer led to the discovery of an identical gate there.

The Solomonic gate at Gezer, which the Hebrew Union College excavation began reinvestigating in 1967, contains stone benches on the sides of the gate rooms and a large water trough for animals. This gateway was destroyed late in the tenth century probably by the Pharaoh Shishak,* who invaded Palestine five years after Solomon's death (1 Kings 14:25).

Shishak's raid also damaged Megiddo where Yadin and Usisshkin have recently identified two Bit-Hilani type palaces. The northern palace, 26 by 19 m. (84 by 63 ft.), seems to have been a ceremonial palace, whereas the S palace, 21 by 19.5 m. (69 by 64 ft.), was probably the residential palace of Solomon's governor (1 Kings 4:12).

Recent excavations at both extremes of Israel have uncovered additional gates from the tenth century. Biran uncovered a gate at Dan with a threshold about 4 m. (13 ft.) wide, benches, and a pedestal perhaps

for a throne. At Beersheba* excavations by Aharoni since 1969 have uncovered one of the largest and strongest gates of the Israelite period. The Solomonic city at Beersheba seems also to have been destroyed by Shishak.

Aharoni's earlier excavations from 1962 to 1967 at Arad,* halfway between Beersheba and the Dead Sea,* uncovered an unexpected Israelite Sanctuary dating from the Solomonic period.

6. *The Divided Kingdoms* (ninth–seventh centuries). Omri,* the sixth king of Israel, decided to transfer his capital from Tirzah* to Samaria* (1 Kings 16:23–24). This change has been confirmed by the excavations from 1946 to 1960 by R. de Vaux at Tell el-Far'ah, identified with Tirzah. The finds included an unfinished building dated to Omri's time.

Omri's son, Ahab,* who married the notorious Phoenician princess, Jezebel,* has been credited with considerable construction. At Hazor a large pillared hall is now identified by Yadin as a storage building of Ahab's time. The water system discovered by Yadin in 1968–69 at Hazor is attributed to Ahab's engineers. The shaft and tunnel, which descended 40 m. (130 ft.) to a spring, have stairs that were broad enough to accommodate two columns of donkeys,* one ascending and the other descending. A similar water system was discovered at Megiddo and one more recently at Beersheba.

The so-called "Solomonic" stables* at Megiddo were redated by Yadin to Ahab's age. Pritchard has now questioned whether these are stables; Aharoni believes that they are storerooms similar to the magazines he has uncovered at Beersheba.

The fine masonry at Samaria and other royal sites was no doubt the work of Phoenician artisans. Until recently we had very little from Iron Age* sites of Phoenicia proper. This lacuna has now been filled by excavations since 1969 by Pritchard at Zarephath,* a site between Tyre* and Sidon.*

In the eighth century Judah was threatened and Israel was destroyed by the Assyrian expansion to the W. Hazor was destroyed by Tiglath-Pileser* III in 732 during the reign of Pekah (2 Kings 15:29). In the burnt debris of the acropolis* the excavators of Hazor found an ostracon* with Pekah's name. The invasion of the Philistine coast in 712 by Sargon's general (Isa 20:1) is attested by the discovery of a fragment of an Assyrian stele* in 1963 at Ashdod.

The presence of paganism in Judah* has been illustrated vividly by the excavations at Jerusalem and Beersheba. Along the E slopes of Ophel, Kenyon discovered a ritual complex including two stone masseboth (*see* MASSEBAH) and a cave dated c. 800 (cf. 2 Kings 12:3, 14:4). In 1967 she discovered a rich cave deposit, dated c. 700, with thirteen thousand pottery vessels and numerous human and animal figurines. At Beersheba an ensemble of pagan cultic objects with strong Egyptian influence was found.

The Iron Age* settlement in Jerusalem has been clarified by recent finds. B. Mazar, excavating near the SW corner of the temple* platform, uncovered Iron Age tombs (c. eighth century), which he thought might represent a royal cemetery. In excavations to the W since 1969, Avigad has uncovered a massive city wall* which was probably built by Hezekiah c. 700. He suggests that the newly enclosed section is the mishneh or "second quarter" (2 Kings 22:14; Zeph 1:10) and that the wall is the "broad wall" mentioned in Neh 3:8.

In Jordan key discoveries have been made for the Iron Age. In 1961 a stone slab with eight lines in Ammonite* was discovered on the citadel mound at Amman (see RABBAH). The rare inscription, which includes a reference to Milcom* (1 Kings 11:5), is dated by Horn to the eighth century and by Cross to the ninth century. Horn's excavations at Heshbon* since 1968 have uncovered the first stratified seventh–sixth centuries Ammonite pottery.*

Since 1960 Crystal Bennett has conducted an examination of Edomite* sites. At Umm el-Biyara the mountain above Petra,* she found a seal* containing the name of Qos Gabar, an Edomite king mentioned in the seventh-century Assyrian annals. In 1968–70 she conducted excavations at Tawilan, E of Petra, and discovered a large Edomite settlement which flourished from the eighth to the sixth century. From 1971 to 1972 she conducted excavations 40 km. (25 mi.) S of the Dead Sea at Buseira, which is to be identified with biblical Bozrah* (Isa 34:6, Amos 1:12). A massive cache of Edomite pottery (eighth–seventh centuries) and a building which may be a palace-temple complex have been uncovered.

7. *The Babylonian Conquest* (sixth century). The sixth century witnessed the conquest of Judah by Nebuchadnezzar,* the return of the exiles from Babylonia, and the rebuilding of the temple.

At Ramat Rahel, just S of Jerusalem, excavated from 1954 to 1962, Aharoni believes that he has found the palace built by Jehoiakim, one of the last kings of Judah (Jer 22:13–19).

The presence of Greek words in Daniel may be better understood in the light of new evidence for the use of Greek mercenaries on Judean soil. In 1960 at Meṣad Ḥashavyahu on the coast a fortress, which was established by Greek mercenaries employed by Neco* (610–594), was discovered. From Arad have come ostraca* from the fort which was destroyed by Nebuchadnezzar in 598. They include instructions for the distribution of supplies to the Kittim, who according to Aharoni were Greek mercenaries.

A vivid memorial of Nebuchadnezzar's invasion are graffiti* from a tomb at Khirbet Beit Lei, 8 km. (5 mi.) E of Lachish,* published in 1963 by Naveh. Cross interprets the graffiti* as an expression of a refugee's trust in God's faithfulness in spite of the desolation of the Holy City (Lam 3:22–24).

The Israeli surveys of Judah* in 1967–68 uncovered many new sites which are small and nameless. As these have yielded sixth-century sherds,* the excavation of such places can probably give us a better picture of post-Exilic Palestine.

From the second temple of Zerubbabel* the only visible remains are found at a straight joint about 30 m. (100 ft.) N of the SE corner of the temple platform, examined in 1966. Dunand suggested to Kenyon that masonry with heavy bosses at this joint

is similar to masonry from the Persian period found in Lebanon.

8. *The Persian and Hellenistic Periods* (fifth–second centuries). Kenyon's excavations of the SE hill of Jerusalem have revealed that the perimeter wall was reduced to c. 2,600 m. (2,800 yd.) under Nehemiah, and this explains how the walls could be repaired within fifty-two days (Neh 6:15).

In Jordan the site of ʿAraq el-Emir,* 16 km. (10 mi.) W of Amman, associated with the Tobiad family (Neh 2:19), was reexcavated by Lapp in 1961–62. In 1973 Worrell began the reexcavation of the earliest site excavated in Palestine, Tell el-Hesy,* and uncovered phases of the fifth–fourth centuries occupation.

At Wadi Daliyeh NW of Jericho, Bedouins discovered a cave in 1962 and removed rare fourth-century papyri which contain the name of a Sanballat, perhaps the grandson of the governor of Samaria in Nehemiah's day. Lapp, who explored the cave in 1963, discovered grim remains of about two hundred men, women, and children who tried unsuccessfully to flee from the troops of Alexander the Great.

Since 1968 an important Hellenistic site in Upper Galilee, Tel Anafa, has been excavated by S. Weinberg. The settlement, which was founded before 200 B.C. and destroyed c. 80 B.C., perhaps by Alexander Jannaeus, has yielded an unparalleled amount of molded glass* and striking architectural ornaments.

9. *The Herodian Period* (first century B.C.). Several sites built by Herod* the Great (37–4 B.C.) have been examined by recent excavations, the most important of which is that directed by B. Mazar since 1968 in the area of the SW corner of the temple* platform in Jerusalem. Mazar has uncovered magnificent Herodian ashlars,* some 9 m. (30 ft.) long (cf. Mark 13:1), a 6 m. (20 ft.) street with a series of steps, and a 12 m. (40 ft.) plaza built later by Agrippa I or II. He has determined that Robinson's Arch supported a monumental staircase rather than a bridge. A Herodian aqueduct* has been traced underground for over 183 m. (600 ft.).

Among significant objects recovered are a small portion of a sundial, a limestone object inscribed *qrbn* "offering" (cf. Mark 7:11), and a fragment with the inscription *le-beit hat-teqiʿah* "for the house of the blowing (of the trumpet)." A cornerstone of the parapet of the Royal Stoa and fragments with gold* leaf help us to visualize the grandeur of the temple. Evidence for the destruction of the temple in A.D. 70 comes from 2 m. (6 ft.) of debris and ash, and an inscription of Vespasian* and Titus* discovered in 1970.

To the W in the Jewish quarter of the walled city, Avigad uncovered in 1969 a Herodian building with frescoes and a depiction of a menorah.* Another house contained mortars,* weights,* and a mold for coins.* Also uncovered was a sewage canal which may have served as a refuge for the Jews in A.D. 70.

At the W edge of the walled city of Jerusalem in the Citadel* area, Bahat and Broshi in 1970–71 found Herodian remains which they consider to be extensions of earlier structures discovered by Tushingham in 1967 in the Armenian Gardens to the S. They interpret this huge platform, which would have been c. 300–500 m. long, to be the foundation for Herod's palace (see HEROD, BUILDING ACTIVITIES OF).

At Caesarea* an underwater (see ARCHAEOLOGY, UNDERWATER) expedition under Fritsch and Ben-Dor in 1960 recovered a coin marked with the design of the ancient port. From 1959–61 Frova excavated the theater,* which was the scene of Agrippa I's fatal illness (Acts 12:23). The most important discovery was the first known inscription of Pontius Pilate. In 1962 Avi-Yonah found from a fourth-century A.D. synagogue* an inscription which is the first epigraphic attestation of Nazareth.* Since 1971 a new expedition under Bull has been clearing some of the buildings buried under the sand dunes.

Masada,* the spectacular Herodian fortress on the western shore of the Dead Sea,* was excavated under Yadin from 1963 to 1965. Among the discoveries were huge cisterns,* a Roman bathhouse, a pool,* and two palaces. Masada was reoccupied by the Zealots and was the last Jewish fortress to fall to the Romans (A.D. 73). Among important religious artifacts* are a unique first-century A.D. synagogue,* a ritual bath, shekels minted by the Jewish rebels, and biblical and sectarian scrolls.* Yadin found skeletons of some of the defenders and ostraca* inscribed with the name of their commander. The Roman siege ramp, the circumvallation wall, and camps are still visible.

Machaerus, the corresponding Herodian fortress on the eastern shore of the Dead Sea, was investigated by Vardaman in 1968. The site, which was the prison of John the Baptist, yielded aqueducts, a Roman bath, and evidences of the Roman siege.

Herodium,* just S of Bethlehem,* was the final resting place of Herod the Great (see HEROD, FAMILY OF). The conical hill with a double concentric wall and four towers* was excavated from 1962 to 1967 by Corbo and since 1969 by Foerster and Netzer. The Zealots converted Herod's banquet hall into a synagogue. Recent work at the base of the hill has uncovered a large reservoir-pool, c. 46 by 70 m. (150 by 230 ft.) and what may be a hippodrome (see CIRCUS).

10. The New Testament Era (first century A.D.). In Bethlehem at Beit Sahur, the Greek Orthodox site of the shepherds' fields (Luke 2:8–18), Tzaferis discovered a well-preserved fourth-century A.D. chapel in 1972. This is the earliest Christian monument in the Holy Land to survive in such a good state of preservation.

Jesus' exorcism of the so-called Gadarene (see GADARA) demoniac has been a problem because of the textual variants of the name of the site (Matt 8:28, Mark 5:1, Luke 8:26). Some MSS read Gerasene and others Gergesene. Origen's comment that there was a village on the shore of the Sea of Galilee* called Gergesa was confirmed in the course of road-building operations on the E shore in 1970. Urman has excavated a first-century A.D. fishing* village, called Kursi in Jewish sources, and a fifth-century church that commemorated the site of the miracle.

The synagogue* at Capernaum,* which may rest upon the site of the synagogue attended by Jesus, had been dated to the second century A.D. Corbo and Loffreda, who have been reexcavating the site since 1968, now date the building to the fourth century on the basis of coins.* The synagogue at Korazin,* reexcavated in 1969, and the synagogue at Khirbet Shema, excavated by Meyers since 1970, have also been dated to the fourth century.

About 9 m. (30 ft.) from the Capernaum synagogue the Franciscan excavators have dug under an octagonal structure. They have uncovered the remains of a house church, which they suggest was built over the home of Peter on the basis of graffiti* at the site and references by pilgrims (fourth–sixth centuries A.D.).

In 1968 the first physical evidence of crucifixion* was found in ossuaries* with redeposited bones found at Giv'at ha-Mivtar in NE Jerusalem. An ossuary, which dates between A.D. 6 and 66, contained the huge bones of a certain Yehohanan, with his heel bones still transfixed by an iron nail. His calf bones had also been shattered.

Excavations in and around the Church of the Holy Sepulcher have helped to demonstrate that it lay outside the wall in Jesus' day and was probably the site of the crucifixion. Shafts dug in the church in 1960–61 showed that the area was used as a quarry,* a conclusion which was also confirmed by Kenyon's excavation in the adjoining Muristan area.

11. Qumran and Nahal Hever (second century B.C.–second century A.D.). The outstanding development for biblical studies in the twentieth century was the discovery of the Dead Sea Scrolls* in the caves of Qumran.* From 1951 to 1956 R. de Vaux excavated the khirbeh* or ruins of the monastery which flourished from c. 130 B.C. to A.D. 68. In 1958 he excavated the farm buildings at 'Ain Feshka,* 3 km. (2 mi.) S of Qumran. He investigated 43 of the more than 1,100 tombs in the cemeteries (see NECROPOLIS). In 1966–67 Steckoll uncovered 10 skeletons, including some of women from the main cemetery. In 1969 Bar-Adon discovered a site at Ein Ghuweir, 14.5 km. (9 mi.) S of Qumran, where he uncovered what may be a banquet hall; the burial of 12 men, 7 women, and a child; and a jar with the same script as that used in the Scrolls.

In 1952 G. L. Harding and R. de Vaux investigated caves at Wadi Murabba'at, 18 km. (11 mi.) S of Qumran, where Bedouins had discovered letters* and contracts from Bar Kochba's* revolt in A.D. 132–35. In 1960–61 at Nahal Hever, just N of Masada, the Israelis found additional materials from this period. These include letters and documents in Aramaic,* Hebrew, and Greek (see EPIGRAPHY, GENERAL and HEBREW); inscribed wooden tablets; and the oldest Roman toga ever found.

BIBLIOGRAPHY: W. F. Albright, The Archaeology of Palestine, rev. ed. (1960); K. Kenyon, Archaeology in the Holy Land (1960); S. Yeivin, A Decade of Archaeology in Israel 1948–1958 (1960); J. Gray, Archaeology and the OT World (1962); M. F. Unger,

Archaeology and the NT (1962); J. A. Thompson, *The Bible and Archaeology* (1962); G. E. Wright, *Biblical Archaeology*, rev. ed. (1962); H. J. Franken and C. A. Franken-Battershill, *A Primer of OT Archaeology* (1963); R. K. Harrison, *The Archaeology of the OT* (1963); P. W. Lapp, "Palestine: Known But Mostly Unknown," *BA*, 26 (1963), 121–34; R. K. Harrison, *The Archaeology of the NT* (1964); M. Pearlman and Y. Yaacov, *Historical Sites in Israel* (1965); W. Williams, *Archaeology in Biblical Research* (1965); G. E. Wright, *Shechem* (1965); K. Kenyon, *Amorites and Canaanites* (1966); K. Kitchen, *Ancient Orient and OT* (1966); Y. Yadin, *Masada* (1966); Archaeological Institute of America, *Archaeological Discoveries in the Holy Land* (1967); G. L. Harding, *The Antiquities of Jordan*, rev. ed. (1967); K. Kenyon, *Jerusalem* (1967); P. W. Lapp, "The Conquest of Palestine in the Light of Archaeology," *ConTM*, 38 (1967), 283–300; D. Thomas, ed., *Archaeology and OT Study* (1967); N. Glueck, *Rivers in the Desert*, rev. ed. (1968); J. L. Kelso, *The Excavation of Bethel* (1968); J. Finegan, *The Archaeology of the NT* (1969); D. Freedman and J. Greenfield, eds., *New Directions in Biblical Archaeology* (1969); P. W. Lapp, *Biblical Archaeology and History* (1969); B. Mazar, *The Excavations in the Old City of Jerusalem* (1969); S. Weinberg, "Post-Exilic Palestine: An Archaeological Report," *Proceedings of the Israel Academy of Sciences and Humanities*, IV.5 (1969), 78–97; E. M. Blaiklock, *The Archaeology of the NT* (1970); N. Glueck, *The Other Side of the Jordan*, rev. ed. (1970); J. Sanders, ed., *Near Eastern Archaeology in the Twentieth Century* (1970); K. Kenyon, *Royal Cities of the OT* (1971); B. Mazar, *The Excavations in the Old City of Jerusalem* (1971); E. Vogel, "Bibliography of Holy Land Sites," *HUCA*, 42 (1971), 1–96; Y. Yadin, *Bar Kokhba* (1971); B. Rothenberg, *Were These King Solomon's Mines?* (1972); Y. Yadin, *Hazor* (1972); E. Yamauchi, *The Stones and the Scriptures* (1972); D. J. Wiseman, ed., *Peoples of OT Times* (1973); W. G. Dever, *Archaeology and Biblical Studies* (1974); K. Kenyon, *Digging Up Jerusalem* (1974); S. M. Paul and W. G. Dever, *Biblical Archaeology* (1974); E. Yamauchi, "A Decade and a Half of Archaeology in Israel and in Jordan," *JAAR*, 42 (1974), 710–26; H. T. Frank, *Discovering the Biblical World* (1975); J. E. Huesman, "Archaeology and Early Israel," *CBQ*, 37 (1975), 1–16; P. Lapp, *Tale of the Tell* (1975); B. Mazar, *The Mountain of the Lord* (1975); G. E. Wright, "The 'New' Archaeology," *BA*, 38 (1975), 104–15; Y. Yadin, *Hazor* (1975); Y. Yadin, ed., *Jerusalem Revealed* (1975); K. A. Kitchen, *The Bible in Its World* (1977); M. Magnusson, *Archaeology of the Bible* (1977); H. F. Vos, *Archaeology in Bible Lands* (1977); M. Avi-Yonah and E. Stern, ed., *EEHL*, 1–4 (1975–78); K. Schoville, *Biblical Archaeology in Focus* (1978); J. Bimson, *Redating the Exodus and Conquest* (1978); D. J. Wiseman and E. Yamauchi, *Archaeology and the Bible* (1979). For current reports *see AASOR, ARC, BA, BASOR, Bible et Terre Sainte: Christian News from Israel, Biblical Archaeology Review, IEJ, PEQ*, and *RB*.

EY

ARCHAEOLOGY, UNDERWATER. The investigation of archaeological remains submerged by sea or lake water had to await the invention of sophisticated diving apparatus. Many ancient wrecks—especially in shallow waters like the Syrtes* off the N coast of Libya (Acts 27:17)—have been investigated, and there are some promising sites in areas where habitable land has been submerged by subsidence or by the rising of the level of the sea. In biblical archaeology, probable sites could be listed along the coast of Palestine, where considerable harbor building took place, in such Phoenician* sites as Tyre,* in the Galilee* lake and at the southern end of the Dead Sea,* reputed site of Sodom* and Gomorrah.*

BIBLIOGRAPHY: *Underwater Archaeology, A Nascent Discipline* (1972); P. E. Cleator, *Underwater Archaeology* (1973); *The Courier* (May 1972).

EMB

ARCHAEOMAGNETISM. *See* DATING, ARCHAEOLOGICAL.

ARCHAEOMETRY. The term describes the application of specific advanced scientific techniques to the dating* of archaeological artifacts.* This approach, still in its infancy, could be of immense importance in vital dating* procedures. The process employs electronic devices designed for studying nuclear structure in order to make a chemical "fingerprint" of a piece of pottery.* The equipment, automated to permit around-the-clock operation, measures accurately the many trace elements of the pottery. It is now being installed in a suite of laboratories at the Institute of Archaeology on the Hebrew University of Jerusalem's Mount Scopus campus.

Small pottery samples are taken for irradiation in the reactor, where their various chemical elements are made radioactive. The gamma rays emitted are measured very precisely, and from the data supplied the computer can calculate chemical composition.

Once a shard* has been "fingerprinted," the task of identifying the origin of the fragment begins. Professor I. Perlman, late of Berkeley, California, and now of the Hebrew University, explains this process: "Although archaeologists draw their inferences about ancient history from all possible clues, pottery is still the largest single source of information. Pottery styles are distinctive with respect to different cultures and time periods, and from typological examinations, archaeologists can draw conclusions as to which ancient peoples were in contact with each other. But the general absence of detailed discrimination, where a particular style may have been made in many places, is a problem. The objective of the 'fingerprinting' is to provide just such detailed information."

There are frequent surprises. Instances have occurred where an entire category of pottery had been wrongly classified, obviously calling for reassessment of archaeological inferences.

"Even in Berkeley," adds Professor J. Yellin, also lately of the Hebrew University there, "much of our work was concentrated on the eastern Mediterranean. In Israel, work has been published or is under way on pottery from Tel Ashdod,* Tel el Ajjul, Deir el Balah, Megiddo,* Tel Magadim and Tel Dan.*"

As a footnote, it might be added that the appropriation of the term "fingerprinting" for this highly scientific process, might lead to confusion, for Professor Paul Aström of Göteborg University has suggested that actual fingerprints on ancient pottery and clay* tablets may provide valuable dating clues. Aström believes that individual races, nations, and tribes display distinctive patterns in the distribution of arches, loops, and whorls of their fingerprints.

Archaeologists have collected some two hundred impressions from ancient pottery found in Greece and Cyprus.* The Mycenaen* fingerprints had a distribution of 20 percent arches, 65 percent loops, and 15 percent whorls, while those from Minoan* Crete, some one thousand years older, show a distribution of 4 percent, 42 percent, and 54 percent, respectively. Such a sampling is admittedly too small to suggest a major conclusion, but might indicate that fingerprints someday can be used in defining a population and its movements.

EMB

ARCHELAUS (är kə lā'əs; Gr. Ἀρχέλαος, *archélaos*). A son of Herod the Great, who after his father's death was ethnarch of Judea (Judah*) from 4 B.C. to A.D. 6, when he was deposed by the Emperor Augustus* for misgovernment and banished to Vienne in Gaul. Like Herod the Great, he was a great builder but was violent and tyrannical. The one reference to Archelaus in Scripture is found in Matthew 2:22, where his cruelty is implied when it is said that Joseph* was afraid to have his family live in Judea while Archelaus ruled there.

Archelaus's title of ethnarch seemingly referred to a rank slightly above that of tetrarch, but both of these titles describe the position of subordinate prince. Evidence shows that, at an earlier time, Hyrcanus had also received the title "ethnarch," but otherwise references to it are rare. Matthew 2:22 simply says Archelaus ruled over Judea, a rule that was under the authority of Rome. Josephus (Jos. *Antiq.* 18.93) speaks of Archelaus as being *basileus* or "king."

On coins* Archelaus used the family name of Herod, as did his brother Antipas; the bronze* coins resembling those of his father, Herod the Great, and bearing the inscription ΗΡΩΔΟΥ ΕΘΝΑΡΧΟΥ (*ĒRŌDOU ETHNARCHOU*) undoubtedly refer to Archelaus. Evidence for this is, first, that Cassius Dio (*Roman History* 45.27.6) calls Archelaus ὁ Ἡρώδης ὁ Παλαιστῖνος (*ho Herōdēs ho Palaistinos*, "Herod the Palestinian"), thus showing that Archelaus bore the name Herod in common with other members of the Herodian family; and, second, that Archelaus was the only Herod to bear the title ethnarch.

BIBLIOGRAPHY: E. Schürer, *A History of the Jewish People*, div. I, vol. II (1891), 38–43; T. Reinach, *Jewish Coins* (1966), 33–34, appendix, Greek Legends; F. W. Madden, *History of Jewish Coinage* (1967), 38, 91–95, 295.

WHM

ARCHERY. See ARMS AND WEAPONS.

ARCHITECTURE. See AMPHITHEATER; APSE; ARCH; ARCHITRAVE; ASHLAR MASONRY; ATRIUM; BARREL VAULT; BASILICA; BUILDING MATERIALS; CAPITAL; CAPSTONE; CASEMATE WALLS; CELLA; CITADEL; CORNICE; CYCLOPEAN MASONRY; DOLMEN; ENGINEERING; ENTABLATURE; EXEDRA; GLACIS; HYPOCAUST; HYPOSTYLE; MASTABA; MOLE; MORTAR; PEDIMENT; PLASTER; PLINTH; PROPYLAEUM; PYRAMIDS; RECONSTRUCTION; STOA; THEATER; TILE; TOWERS; TRIGLYPH; VALLUM; WALLS, CITY; ZIGGURAT.

ARCHITRAVE. In architecture, the lowest section of the structure that rests upon the capital* of a column. The term also describes the wooden surroundings and moldings of windows and doors, as well as the decorative molding of an arch.*

AREOPAGUS (ar ē op'ə gəs). The official title was ἡ βουλὴ ἡ ἐξ Ἀρείου πάγου, *hē boulē hē ex Areiou pagou*—"the court of Ares" (or Mars) Hill.* This judicial body had its origin in the advisory council of the Athenian kings. It had jurisdiction in the more serious criminal cases. Aristotle described its functions in his *Constitution of Athens*, and his description, which can hardly be rejected, suggests its importance and dominance in Athens,* of which history provides few other indications. It would appear, however, to have been oligarchic in trend and, in consequence, to have blocked the advance toward complete democracy in Athens. In 462–461 B.C. a group of democrats led by Ephialtes stripped the court of some of its legal functions, but they left it operating in homicide and religious affairs. Hence the summons to Paul to appear and explain himself before the custodians of morals and religion in Athens. It seems likely that, in pursuing its various tasks, the court met in the Stoa* Basilikê or Royal Porch and for some tasks within its jurisdiction on the rocky outcrop NW of the Acropolis,* where cut foundations for seating are to be seen. Authorities are not unanimous on the question as to whether the religious inquisition of the apostle was designated for a sitting in the Royal Porch (which stands restored at the end of the now excavated agora* in Athens) or on the rocky knoll. A commonsense view might suggest that the weather sometimes determined the meeting place. Certainly, from either perspective, the temples and statuary of the Acropolis were magnificently in view, lending point to Paul's remarks.

BIBLIOGRAPHY: I. T. Hill, *The Ancient City of Athens* (1953); D. P. Stonehouse, *Paul Before the Areopagus* (1957); A. Rupprecht, *ZPEB*, 1 (1975), 298–99.

EMB

AREPO SQUARE (ə rep'ō). A twenty-five-word inscription scratched on a column of the palaestra* in Pompeii,* that could be evidence of a Christian group in the town who used the cross as a symbol was found by the excavator Matteo Della Corte. The words form a square that reads the same up and down, from left to right and from right to left. The sentence runs, ROTAS OPERA TENET AREPO SATOR. However, even taking AREPO as a name for the sower (SA-TOR), this does not yield a very satisfactory sense. On the other hand, if the square is read as the Hittite* hieroglyphics* are read—"boustrophedon," i.e., reading from right to left and left to right on alternate lines, a good sense, chiastically arranged is secured: SATOR OPERA TENET : TENET OPERA SATOR—"The Sower holds [His] works : [His] works the Sower holds." Of possible Christian interest is not only the reference to the sower but also the fact that TENET, horizontal and vertical, forms a cross (the cruciform lines are added).

EMB

ARES, HILL OF. See AREOPAGUS.

ARETAS (ar'ə təs). Paul's mention of Aretas IV (9 B.C.–A.D. 40) in the story of his escape from Damascus* (2 Cor 11:32–33) raises a small historical problem, on which archaeology may have more to say with the assembling of further numismatic (see COINS) and epigraphical (see EPIGRAPHY, GREEK and HEBREW) evidence.

The outstanding question is what authority the Nabataeans* had in Damascus, ostensibly part of the province of Syria, at the time of Paul's escape. The probable situation is that some remnant of Nabataean control was permitted under the Roman provincial administration (see ROMAN GOVERNMENT, ADMINISTRATION OF PROVINCES), and Damascene coins, as early as 85 B.C., show that the city was held by the Nabataeans in the early years of their two centuries of greatness, before Trajan annexed their territory in A.D. 105.

Caligula succeeded to the principate on March 16, A.D. 37. Aretas's old foe, Herod Antipas, father of the princess displaced by Herodias, was deposed by Caligula, and his kindgom was given to Herod Agrippa I, who had already received Philip's tetrarchy (Jos. Antiq. 18.6, 10). Aretas reigned until A.D. 40, and he may have been granted some authority in traditional spheres of Nabataean influence, of which Damascus was certainly one. There are no extant coins with the imperial superscription from A.D. 32–62, when coins with Nero's image began, and none bears the heads of Nero's two predecessors, Caligula and Claudius. This leaves Paul's statement unchallenged.

BIBLIOGRAPHY: HGHL (1899), 619–21; EGT, 2 (1897–1910), 240.2.

EMB

ARK, NOAH'S. See ARARAT; URARTU.

ARK OF THE COVENANT. The Hebrew term 'ārôn 'chest,' 'box' (Akkad. arānu), when associated with the word for covenant* (berît), described a rectangular container of acacia wood plated with gold,* in which were placed the tablets of the Sinai covenant, a container of manna, and Aaron's rod. In the preexilic sanctuary the ark was the central object, being particularly associated with the presence of God. Its dimensions were 1.2 m. (3¾ ft.) in length, while the width and height were .7 m. (2¼ ft.) each.

In addition to the gold leaf covering inside and outside, the ark had a gold border along each upper edge to keep the lid in position. This cover or "mercy seat" was of the same length and width as the ark and was also covered in pure gold plate. At each end were figures of cherubim,* facing each other and overshadowing the surface of the lid with their wings. Two gold-plated poles, placed through gold rings fixed on each side of the ark, were used to transport the structure when occasion required.

Parallels to the tabernacle have been drawn from archaeological and other sources to demonstrate that prefabricated shrines existed long before the time of Moses. Gold-plated wooden containers or portable shrines also boast a comparable degree of antiquity. A box from Tutankhamen's* tomb was equipped with carrying poles which slid into sockets located beneath the base. It had a gabled lid and contained some of the pharaoh's treasures. The concept was very close indeed to that of the Hebrew ark of the covenant, except that the latter was the most sacred object in preexilic Hebrew ritual and worship.

BIBLIOGRAPHY: J. Morgenstern, The Ark, the Ephod, and the "Tent of Meeting" (1945); F. M. Cross, BA, 10 (1947), 45–68; N. H. Tur-Sinai, VT, 1 (1951), 275–86; T. Worden, Scripture, 5 (1952), 82–90; K. A. Kitchen, The Tyndale House Bulletin, 5–6 (1960), 4–11; id., NBD (1962), 82, 1231; M. H. Woudstra, The Ark of the Covenant from Conquest to Kingship (1965); R. K. Harrison, Introduction to the OT (1969), 586–87; J. B. Payne, ZPEB, 1 (1975), 305–10.

EMB

ARMAGEDDON (är mə gĕd'ən; Gr. Ἁρμαγεδών, Harmagedōn, probably from the Hebrew הַר מְגִדּוֹן, har megiddôn, "Mount Megiddo"). No place by the name of Mount Megiddo* or Armageddon (see Rev 16:16) is known to geographers. Various suggestions have been suggested, most of which identify Armageddon with Jerusalem* or emend the text in a variety of ways.

CEA

ARMED FORCES IN THE NEW TESTAMENT. I. Non-Roman. Herod the Great is known to have had a large army and a strong bodyguard. His descendants who reigned for two brief intervals in Judea* (Archelaus* and Agrippa I) and for most of the NT period in the small territories surrounding Judea (e.g., Herod Antipas, Agrippa II) also had armed forces of their own but on a smaller scale. Soldiers from such armies (cf. the term strateumata, "armies," in Matt 22:7) appear at the Slaughter of the Innocents (Matt 2:16) or at the arrest of John the Baptist (Mark 6:17ff.). It is interesting to note that the terminology used, though not specifically Roman except in the case of the speculator, certainly suggests that the armies of the kings and tetrarchs were organized under Roman influence. We hear of a centurion (hekatontarchos, Matt 8:5), tribunes (chiliarchos, Mark 6:21), and a guard, a member of the secret police (spekoulatōr, Mark 6:27, a pure transliteration of a Latin* term into Greek).

An inscription from Syria mentions an officer of

the army of Agrippa II who described himself as follows: *stratēgēsas basilei megalō Agrippa kuriō Agrippas huios*, "commander of the great king lord Agrippa, the son Agrippa" (*OGIS*, 425).

II. *Roman*. The Roman army of the first century A.D. was composed of various categories, in addition to the imperial fleets. Of these, three may be noticed. 1. *The Praetorian Guard*. This was an elite body stationed in Rome* and specifically concerned with the defense of the emperor's person.

In the Western Text of Acts (28:16) Paul is turned over to a *stratopedarchēs* by the centurion who had brought him to Rome for trial. The import of this term has long been disputed, but the theory of Sherwin-White (*Roman Society and Roman Law in the NT* [1963], 108ff.) that the *princeps castrorum* is meant seems plausible. This officer is first attested in the epigraphical record at the beginning of the second century A.D. (ILS, 9189). He was one of the two senior centurions of the Praetorian Guard and administered the camp headquarters. As such, he would have been a suitable custodian of a prisoner awaiting trial before the emperor. 2. *The Legions*. The core of the Roman army consisted of legions, battalions some 5,500 to 6,000 strong and recruited exclusively from Roman citizens. There were no legions in Judea before the Jewish Revolt of A.D. 66–70, but the four stationed in Syria could always be called upon to intervene should the need arise. 3. *The Auxiliaries*. Troops of lesser status but numerically equal to the legionaries formed the next major division of the Roman army. These were known as auxiliaries and were recruited from the noncitizen population of the Empire. As time went on they were increasingly rewarded with Roman citizenship on being discharged from active service. They were drafted into two types of regiments, the *ala*, or cavalry, unit and the *cohort*, or infantry unit. Some cohorts were *equitatae*—that is, part-mounted. Cohort appears in Greek as *speira* (Matt 27:27). The units had commanders known as prefects or tribunes, and subordinate officers such as centurions (*see* Mark 15:39). The term *chiliarchos* represents *tribunus* or tribune, *hekatontarchos* represents centurion. Units were normally five hundred strong, though some were one thousand. In the latter case they were usually commanded by tribunes rather than prefects. The military headquarters of Judea in NT times was Caesarea,* not Jerusalem.* Most of the auxiliaries in the Judean units were of Syrian origin.

The archaeological record helps to illuminate Acts 10:1 and 27:2. The first passage records the conversion of Cornelius, described as *hekatontarchēs ek speirēs tēs kaloumenēs Italikēs*, centurion of a *cohors Italica*. Several Italian cohorts are known, but the inscription *Proculus Rabili f. Col. Philadel. mil. optio coh. II Italic. c. R. 7. Faustini ex uexil. sagit. exer. Syriaci* (Proculus, the son of Rabilus, of the Colline voting district, from Philadelphia* [Amman]), soldier, then adjutant of the Cohort II Italica of Roman citizens whose centurion was Faustinus, from the detachment of archers of the Syrian army (*ILS*, 9168), is of most interest. Proculus had a Roman

name, but he originated from Philadelphia, one of the cities in the Decapolis* in Arabia:* his father's name is one common in Nabataean* Arabia. As such he would have fitted well into a detachment of archers. The inscription was found at Carnuntum on the River Danube near Vienna. The likely occasion for this Proculus to have died there was A.D. 69, when soldiers from the E went to Italy to fight for Vespasian* as emperor. If this can be accepted, the inscription may be regarded as referring to the unit of Cornelius some twenty-five to thirty years after his conversion. The second passage names Julius, the centurion who took Paul to Rome for trial, and gives his regiment as a *speira Sebastē*. The most probable translation is *cohors Augusta*, a cohort at one stage honored with the emperor's name. An inscription from Batanea records a *speira Augousta* (*OGIS*, 421) in the time of Agrippa II—probably the same regiment. The Cohors Augusta I known from the famous stone recording the census under Sulpicius Quirinius* in Syria (ILS, 2683) is also possibly relevant. Even if these equations do not hold, they illustrate the presence of similar regiments in the same army command area as that of the cohorts of Cornelius and Julius.

BIBLIOGRAPHY: G. Webster, *The Roman Imperial Army* (1969); for the army in Judea, T. R. S. Broughton in F. J. Foakes Jackson and K. Lake, *Beginning of Christianity*, 5 (1932; rev. 1966); for the auxiliaries, G. L. Cheesman, *The Roman Auxilia* (1914; rep. 1971); D. B. Saddington, "The Development of the Roman Auxiliary Forces from Augustus to Trajan," in *Aufstieg und Niedergang der römischen Welt*, 2.3 (1975), 176ff.; for the terminology of auxiliaries in the NT, D. B. Saddington, *Acta Classica*, 13 (1970), 121f.

DBS

ARMENIA. *See* URARTU.

ARMS AND WEAPONS. Perhaps the most primitive of personal Near Eastern weapons was the sling,* used originally by shepherds to ward off predatory animals, and later developed as a means of attacking opposing forces or of harrassing the defenders of a besieged city.* Slingers, who are depicted on the Beni Hasan Tableau* and elsewhere in Near Eastern art, always complemented archery units, such as the Roman auxiliaries. Another ancient weapon was the spear, designed primarily for thrusting. It consisted of a metal head with a socket, or a tang, that was fixed to a stout staff. The javelin was a smaller version of the spear and, because of its shorter range, was sometimes given extra torque by a cord wound around the handle. As the javelin was thrown, the warrior momentarily held a loop at the end of the cord to spin and steady the weapon in flight.

The two main types of sword were those for stabbing and for striking, both being used in close combat. As illustrated from monuments and actual artifacts, the former had a handle, a hilt, and a long, straight tapering blade sharpened on both edges as well as at the point. The latter had only one sharp edge, the opposite one being rather thicker to add

Assyrians attacking Ekron with soldiers using large round shields for protection. Drawing of relief from palace of Sargon II at Khorsabad. Courtesy Carta, Jerusalem.

Curved copper knife and three copper axeheads from Early Bronze Age copper hoard of tools and weapons found in 1962 at Kfar Monash. *(See also first photo under* ALPHABET.) Courtesy Israel Dept. of Antiquities and Museums. Exhibited and photographed at Israel Museum, Jerusalem.

weight to the blow. Sometimes this sword had a curved blade, as illustrated from discoveries at fourteenth century B.C. Gezer* and elsewhere. The sword was seldom a decisive weapon in Near Eastern warfare, since its length made it less effective in close fighting than daggers (cf. Judg 3:16) or axes. The sword was one of the earliest iron* objects made in the Hittite* Empire, and some excellent specimens have been recovered from Anatolia. The sword of Rev 2:12 may be seen in many Roman monuments, from Rome's* Arch of Titus* to the crude votive monuments of centurions of the N British garrisons. It was the sharp-pointed, double-edged, short cut-and-thrust weapon of the Roman armies that, in the hands of the legions, conquered the world. It was quite distinct from the Oriental scimitar, or curved cutting sword.

The mace had a short handle and a metal or stone head, shaped like a pear, an apple, or a saucer—as depicted on Egyptian monuments. It was designed to beat or crush, as opposed to the axe, which was used primarily for piercing and cutting. With both these weapons the problem was to fit the head to the handle securely (cf. Deut 19:5), and this proved more difficult for the axe than for the mace. Whereas the latter declined in importance when troops became armored, the former enjoyed prominence at all periods. Archaeologists classify axes either as socketed, in which the handle fits into a blade-socket, or as tanged, in which the rear of the blade is fitted into the handle. Both types exhibit variations from the Early Bronze Age (twenty-sixth to twenty-third centuries B.C.), as successive periods demanded improvements in design to meet new tactical situations.

The shield was a prominent defensive weapon, designed to protect the warrior and allow him to use weapons at the same time. Third millennium B.C. shields at Lagash* were heavy rectangular objects which covered most of the body. In early Mesopotamian* battles they were often carried by a special shield bearer who accompanied each warrior. Late Predynastic Egyptian* shields were made from animal hides stretched on a wooden frame, which by the New Kingdom had been reinforced by metal studs or disks. In the Middle Bronze Age the cumbersome hide shields were supplemented by medium-sized ones having a rounded or pointed head and a broad base. The round shield that protected the uncovered head appeared in the fourteenth century B.C., being used by the Sea Peoples.* By contrast, a popular Hittite shield was in the shape of a figure eight and was a lighter form of the long shield. The Assyrians favored a shorter rectangular shield, but they also used convex ones, which protected the side of the body more effectively and deflected arrows quite well.

By the Late Bronze Age the coat of mail had been developed as defensive armor. It was used mainly by archers and charioteers, who needed both hands free for their tasks and therefore were unable to protect themselves by carrying a shield. A relief from Thutmose IV illustrated the use of such personal armor by Canaanite* charioteers. The coat was made from hundreds of small metal plates arranged like fish scales and sewn to a cloth or leather* cloak.* While affording considerable mobility, it had certain vulnerable areas such as the armpit (cf. 1 Kings 22:34). Portions of such coats of mail have been recovered from Nuzi,* Thebes,* and sites in Syro-Palestine, as well as being represented on a panel from the Ishtar temple at Mari* (c. 2500 B.C.) and on the Standard of Ur* (c. 2600 B.C.).

The metal helmet, first devised by the Sumerians,* covered the ears and nape of the neck, as illustrated by the celebrated golden helmet from Ur.* Helmets were in extensive use by the Late Bronze period and carried various forms of decoration, as illustrated by the relief on the gate-jamb at Boghazköy,* on many Assyrian bas-reliefs,* and Egyptian murals. Helmets were generally expensive, and Egyptian paintings often showed them in the hands of Semites bearing gifts. Up to the early monarchy period only kings, army commanders, and nobility wore them, but the effectiveness of the piercing axe made it especially necessary for archers and charioteers to be protected in this way. Special styles of helmets were adopted by different nations to facilitate identification in battle, as well as to reflect local, nonmilitary tradition.

There remains the bow and arrow, a devastating combination that has more than once changed history—from the Akkadians* to the battlefields of medieval Crecy and Poitiers.

Professor Yigael Yadin's sumptuous book on warfare in the lands of the Bible is full of illustrations. They go back to the vicinity of 3000 B.C., at which date an unknown king was shown on a Mesopotamian stele* armed with a semicircular bow. The second type of bow known to that millennium, the beautifully made double-convex weapon, appears in several Egyptian pictures.

Somewhere in the early years of the second millennium B.C. the composite bow was invented. Perhaps this new weapon accounted for the military ascendancy of the Akkadians. The upper and lower flexible portions were held together at the handgrip, and the bow had tremendous driving power. Both the Egyptians and the Assyrians seem to have adopted it. A granite block from the days of Amenhotep II shows the Pharaoh at firing practice from a moving chariot.* The target—a plaque of copper, in all probability—is shown shot through with four heavy arrows. A cylinder seal* similarly shows Ramses II* at archery with two prisoners tied sadistically just beneath the arrow-studded target.

The war-minded Assyrians could be trusted to have adopted this powerful bow, and their mural art shows two men exerting their strength to string the bow of Ashurbanipal.* Hunting* scenes depict great lions* shot through and broken-backed by the royal arrows. Crowded reliefs of siege and storming depict mass arrow barrages hardly to be paralleled till Agincourt and usually figuring the strong double bow. The flat, triangular cases and ornamented quivers are everywhere in Egyptian and Assyrian military art, and both peoples loved to depict the stricken field with arrow-pierced Asiatic dead piled on the ground. One Egyptian painting shows an armored charioteer dying as Jehoshaphat died (1 Kings 22:34–35), struck where

Assyrians attacking town with siege-engine and bowmen protected by reed shields. Drawing of stone relief from Nimrud (Tiglath-pileser III, 744-727 B.C.). *(See also photo under* MACHINES, WAR.) Courtesy Carta, Jerusalem.

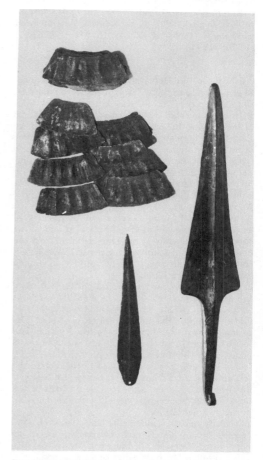

Two copper spearheads and small copper plaques, possibly armor scales from Early Bronze Age copper hoard of tools and weapons found in 1962 at Kfar Monash. Courtesy Israel Dept. of Antiquities and Museums. Exhibited and photographed at Israel Museum, Jerusalem.

the coat of mail was joined to the sleeve of the garment.

In all the ancient works of art the vigor and tension of the archer at work is plain, for the arms were flung wide and the body braced. This does not seem to be the case in one Egyptian representation of an archery school. It comes from a Theban tomb and shows the instructor placing the learner's hands in position, the left arm at full length, and the right, with the fingers gripping the feathered arrow end, pulling back to the ear.

There are numerous illustrations of quivers from the old empires. Some art was expended on this equipment, which was slung from the shoulder or hung beside the chariot. The arrow was as important as the bow—a weapon of individuality that the archer learned to understand and that he sought to accommodate and adapt to his bow.

See ARMED FORCES IN THE NT; BENI HASAN; WARFARE.

BIBLIOGRAPHY: Y. Yadin, *The Art of Warfare in Biblical Lands* (1963); K. M. Kenyon, *Amorites and Canaanites* (1966), 12–55; W. H. Mare, *ZPEB*, 1 (1975), 312–20.

RKH and EMB

AROER (ərō'ər; Heb. עֲרֹועֵר, *'ărô'ēr*; Gr. Ἀροήρ, *Aroēr*, "shrub, bare"?). Three towns were known by this name in the OT. 1. A place located on the border between Israel and Ammon,* described in Josh 13:25 as being "near Rabbah" in Gilead. Precisely where the site was in relation to Rabbah,* the ancient name of modern Amman, is unknown, not least because there are obvious difficulties in establishing the border of Gad at that period. The general area of es-Sweiwina, south of Amman, has been suggested as a possible location rather than any site due E of the Ammonite capital.

2. A settlement in the Negev about 12 miles SE of Beersheba,* known today as Khirbet 'Ar'arah. King David returned some of the plunder taken from the Negev* by an Amalekite raiding party (1 Sam 30:28), and also from this area came two of David's mighty warriors (1 Chron 11:44).

3. A city E of the Jordan, located on the N bank of the Arnon gorge (Deut 2:36; 3:12; 4:48). The site was about 22 km. (14 mi.) from the Dead Sea* and is still inhabited under the modern name of 'Arâ'ir. The Arnon formed the border between Ammon and Moab* (Num 21:13; Josh 12:2) and was also the S boundary of the land allotted to Reuben (Deut 3:12; Josh 13:15–16). The sons of Gad fortified it in the settlement period (Num 32:34) before the Reuben-ites occupied it. The census taken by Joab in the time of David began appropriately at the border point of Aroer (2 Sam 24:5).

The city remained in Israelite hands until the ninth century B.C., when Hazael of Syria (*see* ARAM) occupied it (2 Kings 10:33), but when Mesha (*see* ME-SHA STELE) of Moab defeated Israel it passed under Moabite control and apparently remained in their possession thereafter. It was mentioned on the Moabite Stone,* which stated that Mesha built Aroer and constructed, or repaired, the road by the Arnon

gorge. Aroer was last mentioned in Jer 48:19, where it is condemned along with Damascus* and Ephraim. The modern site is 'Ar'arah, about three miles SE of Dibhan, and close to the ancient road crossing the Arnon from N to S. The ruins at Aroer have been attributed to the Iron Age* and the Nabataean* period, and may well be the remains of forts guarding the crossings of the Arnon.

BIBLIOGRAPHY: N. Glueck, *AASOR* 14 (1934), 3, 36, 49–51; W. H. Morton, *IDB*, 1, 230–31; F. E. Young, *ISBE*, 1, 298.

RKH

ARPACHIYAH. *See* TELL ARPACHIYAH.

ARROW. *See* ARMS AND WEAPONS.

ARSLAN TASH. *See* HADATU.

ART. *See* BAS-RELIEF; FRIEZE; GLAZE; IVORY; KILN; MOSAICS; PAINT; PICTOGRAPHY; POTTERY.

ARTAS. *See* EMMAUS.

ARTEMIS (är'tə məs; Gr. Ἀρτεμις, *Artemis*). At Ephesus* the worship of Artemis, which was known in varied form all through the Greek world, had become grafted to some pre-Hellenic fertility cult. Corresponding to the Roman Diana, Artemis yields no Greek meaning, and it is impossible to speculate on the original form of the deity. In historical times her sphere was the uncultivated earth, the forests, and the hills. She was the virgin huntress, armed with bow and arrows and was somewhat analogous to Anat* of the Ugaritic* epics.

Most of the evidence is literary, but the search for the vast temple at Ephesus, one of the Seven Wonders of the World, forms one of the romantic stories of archaeology. Some of its polished green columns may still be seen in Istanbul, since Justinian looted the already ruined temple to aid in the building of Saint Sophia. The quest for the site began as long ago as 1699, when Edmund Chishall, chaplain to the Factory of the Turkey Company in Smyrna,* thought he had found its masonry. But a generation later, Richard Chandler could discover no trace of it.

The pertinacious J. T. Wood finally made the discovery in 1869. After six years of probing in the tobacco fields of Ephesus, or, in Turkish nomenclature, Ayasoluk, Wood found the pavement of a later shrine and, after encountering great difficulties for more than a decade, cleared and demonstrated the site. Rose Macaulay tells the story well in her book *The Pleasure of Ruins* (1953), 320–23.

The cult was served by priestess courtesans whose dress suggested some ancient link with the warrior-maids of Asia Minor.* Such sacred prostitution,* a common feature of fertility cults, centered on some cult-object, perhaps a meteoric stone (cf. Acts 19:35). Charles Seltman, in his *Riot in Ephesus* (1958), makes an odd suggestion concerning this *diopet* or "thing fallen from heaven," which, could it be proved, might be regarded as one of the strangest of archaeological discoveries. He mentions an inscription of A.D. 406

in which an iconoclast named Demeas boasts that he had torn "the demon Artemis from her base." He pictures a hunted girl-priestess carrying off the *diopet* and burying it. "Today," he concludes, "in the Liverpool City Museum, there is a 16-cm. (6¼-inch) stone pounder, adorned with rare metal and cherished in ancient times, and said, on very good authority, to have been found at Ephesus, near the ancient site. The thing is an unmistakable *Diopet*, and there can hardly have been more than one at Ephesus."

Acts 19:24 speaks of the preoccupation of the silversmiths of Ephesus with the manufacture of silver* shrines of Artemis for the pilgrim and tourist trade. In the old temple ruins of Ephesus some terra cotta images were found, archaic in style, representing the goddess sitting and holding an infant in her arms. Numbers of marble and terra cotta shrines still exist where the goddess is seen seated in a niche, sometimes alone, sometimes accompanied. Ordinarily she holds in one hand a tambourine, in the other a cup, while beside her are one or two lions;* occasionally a lion serves her as a footstool. There is just one silver statuette of Artemis in the British Museum, but it did not come from Ephesus.

See EPHESUS.

BIBLIOGRAPHY: W. M. Ramsay, *The Letters to the Seven Churches* (1904), ch. 17; C. Seltman, *The Twelve Olympians and Their Guests* (1960); E. M. Blaiklock, *ZPEB*, 1 (1975), 341–42.

EMB

ARTIFACT. An object produced by human action and for a designed purpose—such as a tool,* weapon, utensil, or the like. The term is usually restricted to the man-made relics of cultures which have historic or archæological significance. Artifacts, when grouped together, form what may be called "assemblages," or, when many of a single sort are found in some quantity, they may suggest an "industry." They may be treated as objects in themselves, or as features of the culture which produced them. Artifacts are handled by archaeologists in three ways: (1) by graphic representation, by which the artifact is drawn or photographed *in situ* and with proper scales to show relative morphology and size; (2) by statistical distribution, in which the number of the artifacts are recorded and the position of each is set down—which may be easily reduced to sets of x, y, z coordinates and assigned ordinals which may be further reduced to data processing symbols; and (3) by abstract analytical description, in which the basic parameters are set in coded symbols which may then be cross referenced in a multiple form convenient for data processing.

Artifacts have generally been classified within the recent geologic era called the Lower to Middle Pleistocene. The earliest natural stone artifacts, demonstrating the least working, are called "eoliths," flaked stones "paleoliths," and so on, into the traditional ages of bronze,* iron,* and then of steel.

It is in the realm of technical analysis that the artifact is most important. Traces of working, wear, stress, composition, and physical structure, can all be ascertained from artifacts. If they are of organic origin, Carbon 14 dating* (*see* DATING) can be profitably applied; if of ferrous clay,* archeo-magnetic measurements can be taken. Artifacts with designs, ownership marks (as in some Middle Mediterranean pottery*), or writing are of extreme importance. Rarely, however, if at all, do common household objects have their applied names written upon them. Artifacts have appeared which have helped to date a king or a culture, but more important than the object itself are always the data concerning its location and depth of discovery. It is the lack of such data from many excavations made in the last century that has rendered meaningless so many of the discoveries of the early archaeologists.

The artifacts of ancient Israel and other lands and peoples related to the Bible have been excavated in abundance since the middle of the nineteenth century. From these thousands of shards,* tools,* weapons (*see* ARMS AND WEAPONS), and the like, a very broad and detailed picture of daily life has emerged. They have led, in fact, to one definition of archaeology as "the discovery and classification of the common objects of life"—admittedly too narrow a definition, but reflecting the importance to the historian of the archaeologist's most common and mundane finds. Large and informative collections of such biblical material are located in Jerusalem, Tel Aviv, London, Leiden, Berlin, Rome, Paris, Dublin, Philadelphia, New York, and many other museums. The task of correlating the masses of minute fragments excavated by the archaeologists with a text of Scripture is enormous and continuing.

See DATING.

WW

ASCLEPIOS (ASKLEPIOS). See IMHOTEP.

ASHARA, TELL. See TERQA.

ASHDOD (ash'dod; Heb. אַשְׁדּוֹד, *'asdôd*). A city of the Philistine* pentapolis, located on the S coast of Palestine near the Nahal* Lachish* between Gaza* and Joppa.* The identity of the site has been known since ancient times, and the name was, until recently, preserved in the Arabic village of Isdud, now in ruins. The tell* itself consists of a lower city of possibly 36 ha. (90 a.) and an upper city of about 7 ha. (17 a.) rising to 22 m. (70 ft.) above a strip of sand dunes that border the Mediterranean. A number of nearby commercial and military centers formed a network of interconnected trading ports, all related to Ashdod at various periods of its history. These include Ashdod-Yam, Tell Mor, Tell Abu Haraza, Mesad Hashavyahu, and Yavneh-Yam.

In the fourteenth and thirteenth centuries B.C., Ashdod was an entrepôt equivalent to Acco* and Ashkelon,* according to the Ras Shamra (*see* UGARIT) tablets. These documents cite the production and export of textiles as being the primary mercantile activity of the city. The eleventh-century B.C. Onomasticon* of Amenope also mentions Ashdod, as do numerous biblical references. Allotted to the tribe of Judah* (Josh 15:45–47), but apparently never con-

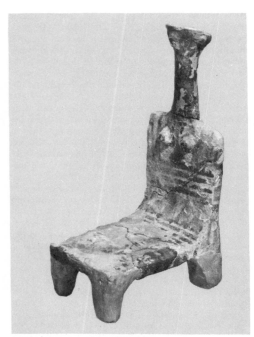

Philistine clay goddess figurine in shape of a throne, found at Ashdod; early 12th century B.C. Courtesy Israel Dept. of Antiquities and Museums.

quered until the time of Uzziah (2 Chron 26:6), Ashdod was one of the Philistine cities that suffered from a plague because of the presence of the Israelite Ark of the Covenant* (1 Sam 5:1ff.). In the reign of Hezekiah, Ashdod withheld its annual tribute from Sargon II* of Assyria (Isa 20:1) with the result that the city and its territories became an Assyrian province. The last OT reference to Ashdod is a sarcastic remark by Nehemiah about the inhabitants' intermarriages with Jews* and their descendants' Ashdodite dialect (Neh 13:23–24). Classical sources reflect a center of some importance at Ashdod during the Persian period, and it continued as a flourishing city during the Hellenistic era under the name Azotus. It appears in the NT under this latter name in the story of Philip and the Ethiopian* (Acts 8:40).

Archaeological exploration of the site was undertaken jointly in 1962–63, 1965, 1968, 1969, and 1970 by American and Israeli institutions. D. N. Freedman, J. L. Swauger, and M. Dothan represented the Pittsburgh Theological Seminary, the Carnegie Museum, and the Department of Antiquities of Israel in directing the work.

Some Chalcolithic* and Early Bronze Age evidences were found, but the first walled city was built on bedrock during the MB II-C period about 1625 B.C.

Ashdod was extensively occupied during the Late Bronze Age, with correlative information coming from the excavations and the Ugaritic documents. These serve to show that one of the principal activities of the city and its environs was the production of cloth*

dyed with the famous Canaanite* purple dye.* One text mentions two thousand shekels (weight) of purple wool. The archaeological evidence from nearby Tell Mor includes numerous murex shells from which the purple dye was obtained.

The worst catastrophe in all of Ashdod's history seems to be represented by a layer of ash and burned debris 90 cm. (3 ft.) thick at the end of LB II, or about 1250 B.C.

Important evidence for the Philistine occupation of the site was derived from two levels, dating from the twelfth and eleventh centuries B.C. In one area, a square Philistine fortress with brick walls 1.25 m. (4 ft.) thick was found. A twelfth-century group of cultic objects included a clay* goddess figurine in the shape of a throne.

From the tenth to the sixth centuries the city expanded greatly and flourished alongside the Judean kingdom. A small temple of the Iron II (see IRON AGE) stratum produced other cult vessels, including kernoi (a ceramic piece usually in the shape of a ring with cups or vases attached), animal figurines, and votive altars.* A group of pottery* kilns* of the same period was found. The level ended with a violent destruction, probably attributable to Sargon II,* rather than to Uzziah.

See PHILISTINES.

BIBLIOGRAPHY: A. H. Gardiner, *Ancient Egyptian Onomastica*, 3 vol. (1947); M. Dothan, "Ashdod," *IEJ*, 12 (1962), 147–48; id., *IEJ*, 13 (1963), 340–42; D. N. Freedman, "The Second Season at Ancient Ashdod," *BA*, 26 (1963), 134–39; M. Dothan, "Ashdod: Preliminary Report of the Excavations in Seasons 1962–63," *IEJ*, 14 (1964), 79–95; M. Dothan and D. N. Freedman, "Ashdod I," *'Atiqot*, 7 (1967), 1–171; M. Dothan, "Ashdod II–III: The Second and Third Seasons of Excavations 1963, 1965," *'Atiqot*, 9–10 (1971), 1–222; M. Dothan, "Ashdod: A City of the Philistine Pentapolis," *ARC*, 20 (1967), 178–86; W. H. Mare, *ZPEB*, 1 (1975), 352–54.

JEJ

ASHERAH (ə shē'rə; Heb. אֲשֵׁרָה, *'ăšērāh*, *'šyrh*; Ugar. *'ṯrt*). Both a Semitic goddess and a cult object by which she was represented. Both the masculine plural and feminine plural forms in Hebrew are translated by the word "groves" in the KJV. Translation of this word by the English "groves" is based on the LXX and the Vul. This translation, however, appears to be incorrect in the light of the specific usage of the term in various contexts. The authors of the Mishna explain the Asherah as a tree that was worshiped, including grapevines and pomegranate, walnut, myrtle, and willow trees. That Asherah was the chief goddess of the Canaanite* pantheon is now known from the rich mythical material unearthed a few decades ago at Ugarit* (modern Ras Shamra). In Ugarit she was regarded as the wife of El, the chief god. The name "lady Asherah of the sea" was given to her in a number of documents. In one Ugaritic text she is referred to as *'ṯrt ym* ("Asherah of the sea"). Apparently her domain proper was the sea, just as that of her husband El was the heavens. She is also described as the "progenitress of the gods."

Seventy of the gods were her children, including the well-known Baal,* Anath,* and Mot. Her relationship to her husband El was much like that of a typical oriental queen to her master or king. When she would enter the presence of El she would prostrate herself in humility, at which time she would be granted a hearing before her husband. Baal also came to her as an intercessor between himself and El.

Asherah as a goddess was not only known to the people of Ugarit, but her name appears in one form or another in the Amarna Letters* from Tell el-Amarna. She is mentioned in N Arabian* inscriptions, in which the Nabataeans* worshiped her as one of a triad of deities, and in early Babylonian literature. There she is referred to as Ashratum.

In the OT her name occurs both in the singular and the plural. The plural form of the name probably indicates that there was a localized form of worship for both this goddess and Baal. It is possible that wherever Baal was worshiped or venerated locally, Asherah was represented there as well (cf. Judg 6:25–30). The fact that the Asherahs of the OT are said to have been "made" indicates that they were objects made by human hands and not merely sacred trees as has been supposed (cf. 1 Kings 16:33; 2 Kings 17:26; 21:3; 2 Chron 33:3). In Isa 27:9; 2 Kings 17:10; and 2 Chron 33:19 an Asherah is described as being "set up" or "built." That this goddess was represented by a humanly formed wooden cult-object is further supported by other expressions which are used in the OT, such as "cut down" (Judg 6:25–26, 28, 30; 2 Kings 18:4; 23:14; Exod 34:13; 2 Chron 14:3; 31:1; Deut 7:5), "cut to pieces" (2 Chron 34:4, 7), "burned" (2 Kings 23:15; Deut 12:3), "rid the land" (2 Chron 19:3), "removed" (2 Chron 17:6), and "uproot" (Mic 5:14). Judging from the above expressions it is fair to conclude that the Asherah was some type of carved wooden image which was set on a base probably next to the altars* that were dedicated to Baal (Judg 6:25, 28). The exact form of the cult-object, however, and its particular method of worship are not described in the OT. Up to the present time no object has been found in excavations which can be identified unquestionably with Asherah. Some earlier investigators claimed that charred pieces of wood discovered at Qatna* and Megiddo* were related to the Asherah object. This, however, has been challenged by most scholars as being nothing more than the remains of charred wooden beams. A number of Palestinian temples have been uncovered, but in no case, however, has an Asherah survived—understandably in light of its perishability.

The etymology of the word itself is disputed among scholars. Prior to the discovery of the name in a Ugaritic text it was proposed that the name was derived from the Hebrew 'šr ("happiness, good fortune") or yšr ("to be upright") or even the Akkadian* aširtu ("temple, sanctuary"). The use of the term in Ugaritic literature points to the fact that it is probably derived from a form of the verb 'ṭr, meaning "to walk" or "to tread." Since the name 'ṭrt ym ("Asherah of the sea") is used, the idea would be that she is a goddess who treads or walks upon the sea.

BIBLIOGRAPHY: W. H. Ward, "The Asherah," AJSL, 19 (1902), 33–44; W. L. Reed, The Asherah in the OT (1949), 1–116; W. F. Albright, Archaeology and the Religion of Israel (1956), 73–76; W. L. Reed, IDB, 1 (1961), 250–52; C. H. Gordon, Ugaritic Textbook: Glossary (1965), 428; R. Patai, "The Goddess Asherah," JNES, 24 (1965), 37–52; L. L. Walker, ZPEB, 1 (1975), 355.

JJD

ASHGUZAI. See SCYTHIANS.

ASHKELON (ASKELON) (ash' kə lon; Heb. אַשְׁקְלוֹן, 'ašqelôn). One of five principal Philistine* centers in Canaan*—also called Askelon and Eshkalon, modern Asqalon—located on the Mediterranean coast

Greek goddess of victory, Nike, found in the bouleuterion (council chamber) at Ashkelon. Courtesy Israel Government Press Office.

about 20 km. (12 mi.) N of Gaza.* The site was first settled in Neolithic* times. It was mentioned in the nineteenth-century B.C. Egyptian Execration Texts* in conjunction with Jerusalem's* rebellion against the Middle Kingdom Pharaohs. But by the Amarna* Age, some four hundred years later, it was once more loyal to Egypt,* being mentioned in the el-Amarna tablets (see AMARNA LETTERS; Letters 287, 320, from c. 1370–50 B.C.). Rebellion against Egypt occurred once more under Ramses II,* who sacked Ashkelon in 1280 B.C., an episode recorded in a dramatic battle scene on the temple wall at Karnak (see THEBES). The tribe of Judah captured the city (Judg 1:18), and it was also described as a conquered Palestinian stronghold on the Israel (Merneptah) Stele* (c. 1220 B.C.). A half-century later, Egyptian religious influence was evident at Ashkelon, as attested by the Megiddo* Ivories. Asqalluna was made a vassal of Assyria by Tiglath-Pileser* III in 734 B.C. but revolted shortly after and was finally sacked by Sennacherib* (705–681 B.C.) in 701 B.C. The city was still paying tribute in 667 B.C. to Assyria but regained its independence in 630 B.C. The Babylonian Chronicle* recorded its fall to Nebuchadnezzar* in 604 B.C. (cf. Jer 47:5ff.; Zeph 2:4ff.). In the Persian period Ashkelon was controlled by Tyre* but in 104 B.C. became an independent Hellenistic city. From this period there remains part of the beautifully columned forum, or bouleuterion, a characteristic feature of a Hellenistic town. It was Herod the Great's (see HEROD, FAMILY OF) birthplace, and remains of this period were excavated in diggings from 1920 onward. Evidence of the Philistine incursion was also recovered, as were traces of Ashkelon's Middle Bronze Age origin. Unfortunately, the heavy-handed occupation of the Crusaders ravaged the site. The characteristic fortress walls which surround the site reveal the ends of looted columns, statuary, and other evidence of Crusader vandalism. Curiously enough, it was the eccentric Lady Hester Stanhope, expatriate niece of the great William Pitt, who first excavated at Ashkelon, early in the nineteenth century.

BIBLIOGRAPHY: J. Garstang and W. J. Phythian-Adams, PEQ (1920–24); W. F. Stinespring, IDB, 1 (1961), 252–54; W. White, Jr., ZPEB, 1 (1975), 356.

RKH and EMB

ASHKENAZ. See SCYTHIANS.

ASHLAR (ASHLER) MASONRY. Square, dressed stone used for buildings or for laying pavements.

ASHTARTU. See ISHTAR, DESCENT OF.

ASHTORETH. See ISHTAR, DESCENT OF.

ASHUR (ash'ər; Heb. אַשּׁוּר, 'aššûr). A city on the Tigris river in N Mesopotamia* and first capital of Assyria. The modern name of the site is Qala'at Sherqat.* In the cuneiform* literature, Ashur is the name of a city, a god, and a territory. These are differentiated by signs called determinatives. Sometimes scholars use different English spellings for each, for purposes of distinction. The name Assyria derives

from this city. Ashur was situated on a hill overlooking the river on the E with a canal on the W. Thus strongly fortified, it dominated the trade route which passed up the Tigris from Sumer* into the Kurdistan hills and thence to Urartu,* biblical Ararat* or Armenia. A certain amount of E-W traffic passed by the city as well, coming either from the Zagros or the Mediterranean, via the upper Euphrates.

The Ebla (Tell Mardikh*) tablets have dramatically illuminated the historical reality of the early history of the city. The Assyrian king list, once thought to be fictional, is now recognized to be substantially reliable. A treaty was in existence between the cities of Ebla and Ashur before 2400 B.C.

Archaeological excavations at the site began in the nineteenth century under A. H. Layard (1847) and continued under Hormuzd Rassam and Victor Place (1853). Prior to WW I, the German scholars Walter Andrae and Robert Koldewey worked at Ashur from 1903–1914. The nature of the discoveries confirmed the importance of the city. A courtyard-type temple identified as the archaic Ishtar temple was found beginning in the Jemdet Nasr*—Early Dynastic II period. Level G in this temple (Akkadian* period) yielded a gypsum head of the high priestess of Ishtar in fine style. It is now in Berlin, along with many of the other finds from Qala'at Sherqat.

A building termed the "old palace" at Ashur dates from the Akkadian period also. It has a square exterior wall with numerous internal courtyards surrounded by rooms, and is similar in plan to the palace of Naram-Sin at Tell Brak. An Akkadian period tablet in the foundation trench at Ashur and a spearhead inscribed with the name of Manishtushu, also from the same site, help to date the structure. Several sculptural fragments, also probably of Manishtushu, demonstrate the powerful musculature typical of the superb artistic style of that period.

The neo-Sumerian renaissance saw Ashur, like most of the important Mesopotamian cities, flourish anew with extensive building projects, including temples and large sacred precincts. Discoveries of the Old Assyrian period from Kanesh (Kultepe*) in Cappadocia (see CAPPADOCIAN TABLETS) reveal how far reaching was the commercial network of the city of Ashur, with corresponding artistic and cultural impact.

The kings of Ashur in the OB period exercised authority over a wide area as is shown by the paintings of Shamsi-Adad's son Ismah-Adad on the walls of court 106 and of court 34 in the palace of Mari.* In the OB period the god Ashur's temple at Ashur occupied the highest point of the city. Several forecourts led to a courtyard complex, but the original shape of the cella* cannot be determined because of the erosion of walls on the restricted space of the hill. Shamshi-Adad I also built a palace in this period.

Following the collapse of the Hammurabi* Dynasty, Ashur-Nirari I built at Ashur a Sin-Shamash temple which is perhaps the earliest prototype of the authentic Assyrian temple. It contains a rectangular center court, reached directly through a wide gatehouse built on a stepped façade. The antecella is broad, while the cella is long and narrow. Hurrian* influence is thought to be responsible for a Mitannian style stele* from the Ashur temple dating from about the fifteenth century B.C.

A palace was built by Adad-Nirari I at the beginning of the thirteenth century. Its architecture differed from the earlier palace on the site in being irregularly arranged around two courtyards, the court of the gate and the residential court.

The smaller objects found both in the Ishtar temple and in the tombs during this time reflect a new and genuinely native Assyrian artistic expression. Included are alabaster* jars, ivory* combs, and pyxides and painted pottery.*

The middle Assyrian period is illuminated by finds both at Ashur (the Ishtar temple built by Tukulti-Ninurta I) and at Kar-Tukulti-Ninurta a few kilometers N of Ashur, where an Ashur temple and ziggurat* were built by the same king.

See QALA'AT SHERQAT.

JEJ

ASHURBANIPAL (ash ər ban'i pal). The last great ruler (KJV Asnappar) of Assyria, son of Esar-Haddon,* ruled from his capital at Nineveh* from 668 to 629 B.C. Probably under the pressure of Greek and W Semite literature, which was flourishing at this time, Ashurbanipal encouraged literacy and left behind the finest cuneiform* library of antiquity. He was the appointed heir of the kingdom of Assyria at its height and fought numerous campaigns to keep and extend his realm. Many of his battles are documented fully in the surviving records. He inherited a revolt in Assyria's Egyptian territories led by the pharaoh, Taharqa of Ethiopia* (2 Kings 19:8, 9; Isa 37:9). This pharaoh, or a successor of the same name, was defeated by Ashurbanipal's army and driven into S Egypt and Nubia.* Ashurbanipal appointed twenty puppet officials whom he had to depose later when they joined Neco I,* founder of the Twenty-sixth Dynasty at Saïs in the Nile Delta. Ashurbanipal carried on campaigns against Tyre,* Arvad, and other towns of the Syrian coast. He declined a plea from Gyges, the king of Lydia,* to war upon the Cimmerians of Central Asia. Another series of wars were waged from about 660 onward against the Mannai and the Elamites,* which weakened Assyria to the point where Babylon, under Ashurbanipal's brother, Shamashshumukin, revolted and led a vast conspiracy that included Egypt,* Philistia,* Judah,* Syria, and the tribes of the S desert, along with the Elamites and distant Lydians. From 651 to 648 B.C. Assyria warred against Babylon and finally overran and destroyed it. The barbarism and vicious cruelty of Assyria, documented in realistic frescoes, not only carried her by force of terror to world leadership, but gained for her the undying enmity of the many peoples involved. The prophet Nahum spoke passionately of God's judgment against Assyrian sin. The last years of Ashurbanipal's reign are obscure, and his kingdom was obviously doomed in his own lifetime. In 1853 the archaeologist H. Rassam uncovered the magnificent remains of Ashurbanipal's palace at Nineveh. The extensive reliefs were some of the finest specimens of naturalistic art recovered from ancient times. However, the greatest find was the library which Ashurbanipal had collected. Much of it was taken from the older collection of tablets collected by the Assyrian king Tiglath-Pileser I* at Calah* (1115–1077 B.C.). This collection has provided scholars with one of the very few complete libraries from antiquity, and the catalogues of many other texts not recovered, but known by Ashurbanipal's scribes, have yielded a very fair picture of the wide range of cuneiform literature. The hideous character of Ashurbanipal, though so cultured in his attitude to literature, is presented in his annals, which glorify the horrors of war as do no other ancient texts. Ashurbanipal, whose name means "[The god] Assur has created an heir," was known to the Greeks as Sardanapalus and in the OT as Asnappar (Ezra 4:10), the Aramaic form being Asenappar.

See CALAH; LYDIA; NECO; NUBIA; TIGLATH-PILESER; TYRE.

BIBLIOGRAPHY: N. Streck, "Assurbanipal und die letzten assyrischen Könige bis zum Untergang Ninevehs," *Vorderasiatische Bibliothek*, 7 (1916); T. Bauer, "Das Inschriftenwerk Assurbanipals . . . ," *Assyriologische Bibliothek*, 1–2 (1933); A. C. Piepkorn, *Historical Prism Inscriptions of Ashurbanipal* (1933); *ANET*, 294–300; J. Oates, *Iraq* 27 (1965), 135–259; D. J. Wiseman, *ZPEB* 1 (1975), 361–63.

ww

ASHURNASIRPAL II (ash ər nas'ər pal; Akkad. *Aššur-naṣir-apli*, "Assur is the preserver of the heir/son"). A powerful and ruthless Assyrian monarch who ruled from 883–859 B.C. His reign was generally one of peace and stability, though his own records of military conquest seem to revel in barbaric practices. His western forays took him to Carchemish* and the Mediterranean, but there is no evidence that he reached Israel.

Most of the notable archaeological remains of this king have come from the great palaces built as part of his new capital city Kalhu (biblical Calah;* modern Nimrud), which was opened in 879 B.C. This amazing complex was first discovered by a British expedition (1845–47) under A. H. Layard and Sir Stratford Canning. From the earlier digs have come some of the finest examples of first millennium Assyrian sculpture in the round, especially a statue* of the king himself (2.3 m. [c. 7½ ft.] high) in sandstone and the colossal winged limestone figures (over 3 m. [10 ft.] high) that flanked the doorway to the palace (ANEP, 439, 646f.). Of special interest to Bible students is the composite character of these beasts, both of which incorporate the head of a man with the wings of an eagle,* and a body that is, respectively, that of a bull or a lion.* Although the sculpture is considered impressive, the figures seem lifeless and wooden, and it is in the field of relief-carving that art of this period finds its highest expression. Ashurnasirpal's reign saw the beginning of a revival of this art (ANEP, 350, 441, 617) which was to come to fuller development in the time of his son, Shalmaneser III.

Literary remains of Ashurnasirpal's reign are abundant, describing his campaigns (ANET, 275f.), his vast irrigation projects, the various animal and flower parks built during his time, and many other

Sandstone statue of King Ashurnasirpal II. Eight lines of text are carved on his chest, recording his name, titles, and exploits. Reproduced by courtesy of the Trustees of the British Museum.

details of his period. His annals are the last to be written in the neo-Assyrian of the time, and later kings seem to have been more influenced by Babylonian literary canons.

Comprehensive new excavations undertaken by M. E. L. Mallowan, et. al., from 1949–61 at Nimrud have provided much fresh knowledge of the times and projects of this king. Most revealing is a record from the throne room describing in detail the peoples imported into Kalhu when it was opened and the great ten-day banquet, complete with a list of foodstuffs, celebrating the event (*ANET*, 558ff.).

Ashurnasirpal was also possibly the builder of a palace in Nineveh* excavated in 1927–32 by R. C. Thompson and others of the British Museum.

See CARCHEMISH; NINEVEH.

BIBLIOGRAPHY: A. H. Layard, *Nineveh and Its Remains*, 2 vols. (1848–49); R. C. Thompson and R. W. Hamilton, "The Site of the Palace of Ashurnasirpal at Nineveh," *AAA*, 18 (1931), 79–112; M. E. L. Mallowan, "Excavations at Nimrud (Kalhu), 1949–50," 1951; 1952; 1953," *Iraq*, 12–16 (1950–54); S. A. Pallis, *The Antiquity of Iraq* (1956), 342–48; R. D. Barnett and M. Falkner, "The Sculptures of Assur-nasir-apli II . . . from the Central and SW Palaces at Nimrud," *Revista degli studi orientali* 40 (1965), 322–26; M. E. L. Mallowan, *Nimrud and Its Remains*, vol. 1 (esp. Sect. VI–VIII), and vol. 2 (1966); R. D. Barnett, "The Bronze Gates of Ashur-Nasir-Pal," Proceedings of the Twenty-Sixth International Congress of Orientalists, 2 (1968); J. D. Hawkins, "The Babil Stele of Assurnasirpal," *AnSt*, 9 (1969), 111–20.

CEA

ASHUR-UTIR-ASBAT. *See* PETHOR.

ASIA MINOR. A nonbiblical term describing the W portion of modern Turkey. The region was known in the NT as Asia, which really describes a Roman administrative province (*see* ROMAN GOVERNMENT, ADMINISTRATION OF PROVINCES) equivalent only to the W and SW end of Asia Minor, and not the entire peninsula as such. Mountain ranges fringed the Black Sea and the Mediterranean to protect the central plateau, while to the W more mountain ranges stretched to the Aegean. The central elevated plateau rose to a maximum of 4000 ft. (1200 m.) and extended E across Lycaonia* and Cappadocia. The rivers of the peninsula flowed mostly N and S, although at the W end a series of rivers flowed W through fertile valleys to the Aegean. The W portion of the peninsula enjoyed a Mediterranean type of climate, whereas the interior plateau was dry and the highlands were subjected to long, rigorous winters.

Asia Minor was an early land bridge between Mesopotamia* and Europe. One of the very oldest town sites in existence was excavated at Catal Hüyük, SE of the NT Iconium.* Shrine wall paintings* that go back to the seventh millennium B.C. were recovered, along with skulls, skeletons, and pottery.* The site was an estimated 13 ha. (32 a.) in the Neolithic* period, about four times larger than contemporary Jericho.* In the third millennium B.C. Early Bronze cultures flourished at Alaca Hüyük in the W central bend of the Halys River, where the indigenous Hatti lived about 2500–2000 B.C. and also at the site known subsequently as Troy,* on the NW coast.

SW of Alaca Hüyük was Hattusas (see BOGHAZKÖY), which became the capital of the Hittites* when they occupied the S central area somewhat after 2000 B.C. A millennium later the Assyrians had established an important trading colony at Kultepe,* a site later known as Kanesh, where the earliest examples of cuneiform* writing in Asia Minor were discovered. The excavation of the palace archives at Hattusas by Winckler in 1906 confirms the biblical representation of the Hittites as a powerful nation, and reveals the complexity and magnificence of their culture in the Bronze Age. That several languages were in use at that time became evident when Karatepe* and other sites in E Cilicia* were excavated.

The destruction of the Hittite empire by the Sea Peoples* about 1200 B.C. profoundly affected the cultural picture. Migrant groups occupied the area at the end of the second millennium B.C. and gradually Greek settlements spread from the W coast northward to the Black Sea. The kingdom of Phrygia* was founded in the eighth century B.C., but in the following century it declined in favor of Lydia,* under its powerful king Gyges. The Persians (see SUSA) brought Lydian influence to an end in 546 B.C., when Cyrus* conquered Sardis.* Thereafter the area was under Persian control until Xerxes* was defeated in battle in 480 B.C. Persia enjoyed a brief renewal of control over Greece after 386 B.C., but Alexander's conquests not merely united his divided homeland but made him master of the largest NE empire the world had known. After Alexander's death, Asia Minor ultimately came under the sway of the Seleucids, whose power was finally broken by Rome in 190 B.C. at Magnesia.

In NT times Asia was a political rather than a cultural unit. While Greek predominated, native languages were also spoken. Jewish settlements were encouraged by Rome,* and third-century A.D. synagogue remains at Sardis testify to the prominence of Jewish people there. Paul's birthplace was Tarsus,* capital of Cilicia, and much of his missionary work was directed at cities in Asia Minor. His first visit to the province of Galatia* occurred during his first missionary journey, and the same general area was revisited on his second. His ministry at Ephesus* (c. A.D. 52–55) made that city the center of Christian work in Asia Minor. His last recorded connection with the province of Asia was on his journey to Rome (Acts 27:5).

See also DERBE; EPHESUS; GALATIA; ICONIUM; LYSTRA.

BIBLIOGRAPHY: W. M. Calder, et. al. *Monumenta Asiae Minoris Antiqua* (1923–62); O. R. Gurney, *The Hittites* (1952); E. Akurgal, *Ancient Civilizations and Ruins of Turkey* (1973 ed.).

RKH

ASITIWATAYYA. See KARATEPE.

ASKAR. See SYCHAR.

ASMAR, TELL. See ESHNUNNA.

ASNAPPER. See ASHURBANIPAL.

ASPHALT. See BITUMEN.

ASPHALT SEA. See DEAD SEA.

ASS. See DONKEY.

ASSAR. See TEL ASSAR.

ASSHUR; ASSUR. See ASHUR.

ASSOS (as'os). This Mysian* seaport (cf. Acts 20:13–14) has been the scene of sporadic archaeological excavation since the work of the American Archaeological Institute at this site and at the modern Bahram Kol, began ninety years ago. There is a good Greek agora,* a Doric temple, dedicated to Athena Polias, and a Christian church built on the site of the first–century Roman bath. An inscription records a civic oath of allegiance dating from Caligula's accession in A.D. 37. It runs: "We swear by the Savior and God, Caesar Augustus,* and by the pure Virgin (i.e., Athena Polias), whom our fathers worshiped, that we will be faithful to Gaius Caesar Augustus and all his house."

BIBLIOGRAPHY: E. M. Blaiklock, *ZPEB*, 1 (1975), 370–71.

EMB

ASSYRIOLOGY. The science dealing with the recovery and study of the civilization of the Mesopotamian* Valley. Limits of the science are generally determined by linguistic criteria, and scholars studying peoples whose language is Akkadian* (the original Semitic language of the area) or one of its dialects, Assyrian or Babylonian, are considered Assyriologists.* The specialized study of one of the pre-Semitic peoples who wrote and spoke Sumerian* is called Sumerology.

Modern Assyriology began on two fronts. Linguistically it became a science when the Behistun Rock tri-lingual inscription (see BEHISTUN INSCRIPTION) was deciphered by various specialists after the heroic copying work of Henry Rawlinson in the years 1843–47. At the same time both French and British excavators were uncovering the ruins of the great palaces at Nineveh,* Khorsabad,* and Kalhu (biblical Calah*), providing archaeological support and material for the linguistic specialists who were now able to read Assyrian and Babylonian texts.

Today Assyriology is a developed branch of ancient history, and within the field are those who specialize in its various periods of history, its varied dialects, and its many geographical and cultural subgroupings.

BIBLIOGRAPHY: Various histories of Mesopotamia, plus S. A. Pallis, *The Antiquity of Iran* (1956); M. E. L. Mallowan, *Twenty-five Years of Mesopotamian Discovery* (1956); A. L. Oppenheim, "Assyriology, Why and How," *CA*, 1 (1960), 409–23; J. Laessøe, *People of Ancient Assyria* (1963).   CEA

ASTARTE. *See* ISHTAR, DESCENT OF.

ASTROLOGY; ASTRONOMY. Both of these developed to a high degree of proficiency in antiquity. The former dealt with observation of the heavenly bodies for purposes of attempting to establish the direction and character of coming events, while the latter was concerned with the movements of the celestial bodies as a means of calculating calendrical time and charting other related phenomena such as eclipses. Most of the megalithic* constructions of the Mediterranean and Atlantic coasts appear to have been built for astrological rites, the Tower of Babel* (Gen 11:1–9) perhaps being such a monument. The need to measure time, and to lay out the calendar* and its attendant cults more and more accurately, led to certain notably practical successes in calculation. True astronomy did not arise until the Greeks, under the drive of the natural philosophy of the Milesians and their followers. Ancient astrological calculation developed chiefly in Egypt* and Mesopotamia.* Reports on the movements of the heavenly bodies were made to the Assyrian kings. Rock paintings* and carvings of great antiquity, possibly as old as the tenth millennium B.C., are thought to record astronomical phenomena. In the Middle Kingdom period of Egypt (c. 2000 B.C.) star calendars were used as designs in tombs. Egyptian astronomical efforts, however, always suffered from the debilitating effects of the astrological state cult. By 1700 B.C. Babylonian astrologers were observing Venus, and under the Kassite* domination notations were made of the fixed stars in their heliacal rise. In the eighth century B.C. remarkable progress was made in the time of the Chaldean* era (c. 625 B.C.), and "Chaldean" became synonymous with "astrologer" in first-century Latin literature. Astrology was forbidden in Israel, and Isaiah predicted doom for its devotees (47:13–15). The Hebrews believed that the stars were the "work of His fingers" (Ps 8:3) and, as such, merited no worship.

The Magi of Matt 2 were no doubt astrologers who had an earnest desire for truth.

BIBLIOGRAPHY: E. Weidner, *Handbuch der babylonischen Astronomie* (1915); O. Neugebauer, *The Exact Sciences in Antiquity* (1957 ed.), 97–138; M. J. Dresden, *IDB*, 4 (1962), 241–44; W. L. Liefeld, *ZPEB*, 1 (1975), 393–94; D. C. Morton, *ZPEB*, 1 (1975), 394–99.

WW

ASWAN (äs'wän; Heb. סְוֵנֵה, *sĕwēnē*; LXX, συήνη, *syēnē*; from Egyp. *swnw*, "fortress" or "market"[?]). This was the mainland settlement on the E bank of the Nile just opposite the island of Elephantine,* about 1.6 km. (1 mi.) N (below) the first cataract. Either interpretation of its name suits its role, with Elephantine, as a place of trade with Nubia* to the S and of defense against incursions. The quarries of Aswan supplied the granite from which the Egyptians fashioned countless statues,* stelae,* obelisks,* etc., for their tombs and temples. Many graffiti* on the rocks commemorate the visits of pharaohs and their high officials to Nubia or to Aswan for the gran-

ite. As the S boundary of Egypt* in the first millennium B.C., Aswan ("Seveneh," etc.) is so cited by Ezekiel ("syēnē" KJV, 29:10; 30:6) with Migdol to sum up the N and S limits of Egypt. Isa 49:12 ("Sinim") probably refers to this town.

BIBLIOGRAPHY: B. Porter and R. L. B. Moss, *Topographical Bibliography of Ancient Egypt . . . Texts . . .*, 5 (1937), 221ff. (monuments); L. Habachi and H. Riad, *Aswan* (1959), a general outline.

KAK

ATAROTH ADDAR. *See* RADDANA.

ATHENS. In antiquity Athens was the principal city* of Attica and was first settled in the Neolithic* period. The Late Bronze Age Dorian invasions apparently bypassed the site, and in the Iron Age* an increase in population caused the city to expand toward the NW of the Acropolis.* Temples dedicated to Apollo and Athena were constructed here in the sixth century B.C. Thereafter Athens became increasingly prominent, reaching the peak of its political and cultural influence in the fifth century B.C. under Pericles. After a period of decline the city experienced some resurgence under Philip of Macedon but by the second century B.C. had succumbed to Roman imperial expansion.

The archaeology of Athens goes back in rich abundance from Imperial, to Classical, to Mycenaean* times, but most of it lies outside the scope and compass of this dictionary. The city is mentioned in Scripture only in the account of Paul's visit recorded in Acts 17:15–34. Of the agora*—where, adapting himself characteristically to the Athenian situation, Paul argued, like Socrates, with all who would listen—little more than foundations remain. The ruined temples of the Acropolis give some idea of what Paul saw—and swept away magisterially with a gesture as he spoke to the Areopagites.

See ACROPOLIS; AGORA; AREOPAGUS; UNKNOWN GOD, ALTAR TO THE.

BIBLIOGRAPHY: I. T. Hill, *The Ancient City of Athens* (1953); The American School of Classical Studies, *The Athenian Agora, A Guide to the Excavations* (1954); E. M. Blaiklock, *The Cities of the NT* (1965), 50–56; A. Rupprecht, *ZPEB*, 1 (1975), 403–6.

EMB

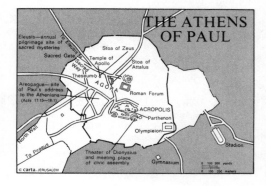

THE ATHENS OF PAUL

Eleusis—annual pilgrimage site of sacred mysteries

Stoa of Zeus

Sacred Gate
Sacred Way
Temple of Apollo
Theseumo
Stoa of Attalus

Areopagus—site of Paul's address to the Athenian (Acts 17:15—18:1)

AGORA
Roman Forum

ACROPOLIS
Parthenon

Olympieion

North Wall

To Piraeus

Theater of Dionysius and meeting place of civic assembly

Gymnasium

Stadion

C. carta. JERUSALEM

ATON, HYMN TO THE. Pharaoh Akhenaton,* "the heretic," who sought to establish a form of monotheistic sun-worship in fourteenth-century B.C. Egypt,* has left a psalm of adoration that bears some similarity to Ps 104. In the city that he built—the City of the Horizon of Aton—which was to be the purified capital (Akhetaton; see AMARNA) of a new Egypt, it was the custom, during the brief years of the pharaoh's reformation, to adorn the walls with hymns sung in the temple of the Aton. In the tomb of Ay, father of Queen Nefertiti, the elaborate hymn to the sun is found.

Akhenaton must have composed the hymn in his early twenties. In the remote event that it was known and adapted to the worship of Jehovah by the author of the Hebrew Psalm, that in no way diminishes the authority of the OT poem. See the remarks of K. A. Kitchen under AKHENATON.*

BIBLIOGRAPHY: A. Weigall, *The Life and Times of Akhenaton* (1910, 1922); J. Breasted, *A History of Egypt* (1946), 364–66, 392–93, 402; T. E. Peet, *Kings and Queens of Ancient Egypt* (1925), 81–116; *ANET* (1950), 369ff.; R. J. Williams in *OTT*, (1958), D. Winton Thomas, ed. (1961), 142–50.

EMB

ATRA-HASIS EPIC (a trə has'is). This epic reflects one literary form of the traditions emerging from Sumeria* and Babylonia (see CHALDEA) about the creation and the early history of mankind. George Smith first published it in 1876 under the title "The Story of Atarpi," along with translated excerpts from other Babylonian literary texts. His rendering was rather inadequate, due to difficulties involving the correct order of the damaged tablet material, and only in 1956 was the correct sequence obtained.

This anonymous work, whose title means "when the gods like man," exhibits certain Assyrian dialect forms, though the underlying text most probably comes from the Old Babylonian period. The epic began with a description of the way in which the ancient Mesopotamian* gods were supposed to have created the earth, and how junior deities objected to the hard work involved. Man was subsequently created to ease the gods of this burden, but the clamor of human activity irritated Enlil, who attempted to reduce the population by various methods. When these failed he sent a flood to wipe mankind out. The god Enki warned Atra-Hasis, who constructed a boat and escaped with his family and some animals, afterward offering sacrifice to the god. The theme has much in common with the Gilgamesh Epic* and other Mesopotamian creation and flood epics.

BIBLIOGRAPHY: W. G. Lambert and A. R. Millard, *Atra-Hasis: The Babylonian Story of the Flood* (1969).

RKH

ATRIUM. In Roman houses, the main hall or room. In churches, a porch or narthex in front of the main doors.

AUGUSTUS. The honorific title given by the Roman Senate in 27 B.C. to Gaius Julius Caesar Octavianus who, in the hindsight of history, is marked as the first of the emperors. In Luke 2:1 his decree to enroll the world is recorded. The Monumentum Ancyranum (see ANCYRA) gives the details of this remarkable man's own account of his career. Archaeology has other details to add. His statues*— such as the remarkable toga-clad figure in the Louvre—show a handsome and dignified figure, perhaps in his thirties. Coins show somewhat less idealized portraiture but maintain the impression of dignity and keen regard.

An inscription celebrating Augustus's fifty-sixth birthday supports the abundant literary evidence for the popularity of the man who brought peace to a war-ridden world—a popularity which was the main spur to the worship of the emperor, which was, in turn, the primary cause of Rome's clash with the church. The inscription is dated 7 B.C. and runs: "It is difficult to say whether the birthday of the most divine Caesar is more joyful or more advantageous. We may rightly regard it as like the beginning of all things. Everything was deteriorating and changing into misfortune but he set it right and gave the whole world another appearance. The birthday of the god was the beginning of the good news to the world on his account." Had Mark (1:1) this phrase in mind?

BIBLIOGRAPHY: Suetonius, 1.2, *Augustus* (Loeb, 1944), 123–287. BMC Catalog 1 (1923); *CAH, The Augustan Empire 44 B.C.–A.D. 70*, vol. 10 (1934); R. Syme, *The Roman Revolution* (1939).

EMB

AUROCHS. See OX, WILD.

AVARIS. See RAMSES, CITY OF.

AVDAT (äv′dat). Also called Eboda and Oboda, the name was probably taken from that of Obodas II, king of the Nabataeans,* who was buried in the city. The Nabataean and later Roman-Byzantine city dominated the trade route from Petra* to Gaza.*

Avdat was apparently founded in the third century B.C., together with Petra, when the Nabataean civilization pushed out to the Mediterranean. Like Elusa and Nessana, Avdat functioned as a way station on an important trade route. Its earliest period of glory closed when the Hasmonean Alexander Jannaeus (103–76 B.C.) conquered Gaza and rendered obsolete the city's chief function. It was rebuilt, together with Kurnub (Mampsis*) in the reign of Aretas* III (87–62 B.C.) and flourished until the general collapse of the region in the days of Malichus II (A.D. 40–71). The city was again rebuilt under Rabel II (A.D. 71–106) and terminated its last Nabataean phase with the annexation of the Nabataean realm by the Roman Emperor Trajan. Evidence for a destruction at that time is ambiguous, and a recent excavator (A. Negev) argues that it was not destroyed until c. A.D. 126 by Arab tribesmen.

No further activity is recorded until the third century when the city was revived with a strengthened acropolis* and a new large retaining wall. Later Roman history is obscure, and no datable materials have been found either for the fourth or fifth centuries,

Aerial view of Avdat showing acropolis with Nabataean, Late Roman, and Byzantine remains. Courtesy Israel Government Press Office.

although the city did rise perhaps to its greatest prominence under the Byzantine* rule of the sixth century, during which period the fortress at the top of the hill was built, along with two magnificent churches, a monastery, a baptistry, and many new dwellings. The final decline began with the Muslim conquest of the Negev* in A.D. 634, after which the site became chiefly used for its bathhouse along the roadside. Avdat was finally abandoned in the tenth century and remained largely forgotten until discovered by the English traveler Palmer in 1871.

Minor excavations were undertaken by the Dunscombe Colt expedition in 1935, but it remained for Israeli archaeologists M. Avi-Yonah, A. Negev, and Y. Cohen to do the major work of digging and restoration in 1958–60. In addition to the building activity already mentioned, Avdat has produced some of our finest Nabataean and Byzantine art inscriptions. A pottery* kiln* from the earlier period is accompanied by large quantities of fine thin Nabataean ware. From the same ruins have come several bronze* figurines, notably a small leopard and a diminutive siren-like creature. A charming little dolphin relief is still observable on a tiny Nabataean altar,* accompanied by an inscription ending with the consonants "s l m." Byzantine art, although dominated by Christian motifs, continues to display certain characteristics of the Nabataean period. Such an abundance of material makes Avdat an important source for any

study of the Negev in its two highest periods of civilization.

BIBLIOGRAPHY: A. Negev, "Abdah," *IEJ*, 9 (1959), 274–75; M. Avi-Yonah, "Abdah," *RB*, 47 (1960), 378–81; A. Negev, "Avdat, a Caravan Halt in the Negev," *ARC*, 14 (1961), 122–30; N. Glueck, *Deities and Dolphins* (1965), 6–7, 332–33, 520, 525–26; A. Negev, "Oboda, Mampsis, and Provinca Arabia," *IEJ*, 17 (1967), 187ff.; N. Glueck, *Rivers in the Desert* (1968), 271–76; E. D. Vogel, "Bibliography of Holy Land Sites," *HUCA*, 42 (1971), 3; A. Negev, "Eboda," *EEHL*, 2:345–55.

CEA

AXE. *See* ARMS AND WEAPONS.

AZARIYEH. *See* BETHANY.

AZEKAH (ə zē'kə; Heb. עֲזֵקָה, *ʿazēqâh*, "place dug up with a hoe"). A town in the Shephelah,* identified with Tell ez-Zakariyeh.

An important biblical city, Azekah is first mentioned as the place to which the kings of the Amorites* were pursued by Joshua (Josh 10:10). In the distribution of territory to Judah, Azekah is mentioned between Socoh and Shaaraim (Josh 15:35). Rehoboam fortified the site along with other cities facing Egypt* (2 Chron 11:9), and at the close of the Judean monarchy, both biblical (Jer 34:7) and extra-

biblical (Lachish letters,* #4) evidence testify to its
continued strength. After the exile, Azekah and its
suburbs (Heb. "daughters") were reoccupied by the
returnees (Neh 11:30).

Tell ez-Zakariyeh is a massive mound on the NE
end of the Valley of Elah (Wadi es Sunt), about 4.8 km.
(3 mi.) from Socoh to the SW and 14.5 km. (9 mi.)
due N of Beit Jibrin. The tell,* which occupies almost 3.5 ha. (9 a.), is larger than Tell Beit Mirsim
(see DEBIR) or Tell el-Hesy,* although not as large
as such ancient cities as Lachish* (Tell Ed-Duweir*)
or Megiddo.* It falls off sharply to the W (toward
the Valley of Elah) but is joined to another smaller
summit by a neck of land on the S. Excavations by
F. J. Bliss and R. A. S. Macalister for the Palestine
Exploration Fund in 1898–99 showed that there was
occupation from Canaanite* times, although the most
impressive remains were of an Israelite fortress with
towers at each corner. Foundation pottery* was used
to date the beginning of the fortress to the early monarchy (perhaps under Rehoboam), although the top
levels show affinities with Herodian buildings in other
parts of Palestine. During the monarchy the fort was
both enlarged and repaired, prior to its destruction
as one of the last strongholds against Nebuchadnezzar.* The post-Exilic settlement was followed by a
short Roman occupation. In Byzantine times there
was also a village named Azekah, but it was located
near the present tell at a site known as Khirbet el-
'Alami.

BIBLIOGRAPHY: F. J. Bliss and R. A. S. Macalister, *Excavations in Palestine* (1898–1900), 12–27; id.,
"First, Second, Third and Fourth Report on the Ex-

Lachish Letter No. IV (reverse side). One of twenty-one
inscribed sherds found at Lachish dating from just before
its destruction by Nebuchadnezzar in 588 B.C. This ostracon ends: "We are watching for the fire signals of Lachish,
according to all the signs my lord gave, because we do
not see Azekah." Courtesy Israel Dept. of Antiquities and
Museums.

cavations at Tell Zakariya," *PEFQS (PEQ)*, (1899),
10–25, 89–111, 170–87; id., *PEFQS (PEQ)*, (1900),
7–16; E. K. Vogel, "Bibliography of Holy Land Sites,"
HUCA, 42 (1971), 89; A. K. Helmbold, *ZPEB*, 1
(1975), 427–28; E. Stern, "Azekah," *EEHL*, 1:141–
43.

CEA

AZOTUS. *See* ASHDOD.

AZZA (AZATTI). *See* GAZA.

B

BAAL (bā'əl; Heb. בַּעַל, ba'al). Baal was the storm deity of the Canaanites, the equivalent of the Amorite* "Hadad." The name (meaning "lord," "master," or "husband") applied to men (1 Chron 5:5; 8:30) as well as to gods, and also denoted locality (Num 25:3; Deut 4:3) or special divine function (Judg 8:33). The title "Baal" was applied specifically to Hadad from the beginning of the second millennium B.C. The Late Bronze Age texts from Ugarit* (c. 1400 B.C.) contain many myths dealing with Baal, who by then had displaced El as the head of the Canaanite* pantheon to become the most vigorous deity in the cult. The texts depict him as principally operative in nature, being the god of storms and controller of earth's fertility. A relief on a stele* found at Ras Shamra (Ugarit) in 1942 shows Baal almost in the posture of the Zeus* at Olympia, with right hand uplifted. He bears, however, a club, not Zeus's characteristic thunderbolt. In the left hand is a lance with a top stylized as forked lightning. Baal was known as "Lord of heaven and earth" (cf. Ps 2:4; 103:19) and "rider of the clouds" (cf. Ps 68:4; 104:3). Other sculptures and figurines recovered from Ugarit, Megiddo,* and Lachish* depict Baal as a powerful warrior whose cult-animal was the bull, typifying the power of fertility. By the Eighteenth Dynasty Baal worship had penetrated to Egypt,* occurring primarily at Baal Saphon near Pelusium. The sensuous Baal cult challenged Israelite worship seriously in the pre-Exilic period, as shown in the Mount Carmel* incident (1 Kings 18), and was uniformly condemned by the prophets for its lasciviousness and child-sacrifice (cf. Jer 19:5). Baal worship was associated with that of the goddess Ashtoreth.

BIBLIOGRAPHY: J. Gray, *The Legacy of Canaan* (1957), 120–23; E. O. James, *The Ancient Gods* (1960), 87–90; J. Gray, *The Canaanites* (1964); A. S. Kapelrud, *The Ras Shamra Discoveries and the OT* (1965); A. E. Cundall, *ZPEB*, 1 (1975), 431–33.

RKH

BAALAH. *See* KIRIATH JEARIM.

BAALBEK (bäl'bek). A Lebanese town situated near the source of the Orontes River. Its name may refer to the particular Baal* worshiped there. The Greek designation was Heliopolis* (City of the Sun), from the identification in the Seleucid period of Baal with the sun deity. Baalbek is now famous for its ruined temples, the earliest of which belonged to the Amorite* weather-deity Hadad, being later rededicated to the sun-god and Jupiter. Other outstanding ruined shrines were dedicated to Dionysius and Venus and date from the second century A.D. They constitute excellent examples of Greek architectural achievement. Baalbek was captured by the Arabs in A.D. 637 and sacked by Mongol hordes in 1410, heavily damaged by earthquake in 1759, and first excavated by German teams in 1902.

BIBLIOGRAPHY: M. I. Aluf, *History of Baalbek*, 21st. ed. (1953).

RKH

BAAL GAD (bā'əl gad). This place was the N limit of the Israelite thrust into Palestine (Josh 11:17; 12:7; 13:5). Archaeological evidence, without complete certainty, places it at Tell Haush about 12 km. (7½ mi.) N of the modern town of Hasbeiya.

BAB EDH-DRHA (bab ed' drə). A major Early Bronze Age archaeological site in Trans-Jordan, just E of the Dead Sea* at the edge of the Lisan, or large tongue of land, extending into the sea from the E shore.

It was discovered by W. F. Albright in 1924. The fortified site consists of a great open-air enclosure, surrounded by walls of uncut stone. A distance away are some fallen menhirs* (masseboth; *see* MASSEBAH) which may originally have numbered seven. To the S of the occupational area was an extensive cemetery (*see* NECROPOLIS). The pottery* listing from Albright's soundings was not published until 1944, but the date he assigned for the age of the cemetery has been confirmed by subsequent excavations. Materials from the tombs cover the entire chronological range of the Early Bronze Age from c. 3100 B.C. down to the twenty-first century. Following reports of truckloads of EB pottery being illicitly excavated by grave robbers in the Kerak area from 1958–64, Paul Lapp of the American Schools of Oriental Research in Jerusalem discovered that the material was coming from Bab edh-Dhra' and initiated three campaigns in 1965 and 1967 to excavate the area scientifically. The occupational evidence in the town was extremely slight compared with the enormous cemetery, which measures 1 by .5 km. (.6 by .3 mi.) in size and is estimated by Lapp to contain twenty thousand tombs, several hundred thousand burials, and about two million pots. These estimates, the excavator claims, seem "overly conservative." The enigma presented by a vast cemetery adjoining an insignificant settlement has been explained by the hypothesis that Bab edh-Dhra' was a cultic center and burial ground for a wide area. The excavator faced the inescapable conclusion that the cemetery, because of its proximity and chronological synchronization with the "cities of the plain" (cf. Gen 13–14; 18–19) was in all likelihood connected with Sodom,* Gomorrah,* Admah, Zeboim, and Zoar, these being the only known population centers in the region at that time. He believes Bab edh-Dhra' was ". . . a cemetery for the Cities of the Plain,* which seem to have thrived in the Dead Sea basin south of the Lisan before it was inundated" (*BASOR*, 189 [1968], 14).

The graves were of three types: cairn burials, charnel houses, and shaft tombs. The shaft tombs were the earliest, and these are dated from the beginning of EB/IA (Kenyon's Proto-Urban and De Vaux's Middle and Upper Chalcolithic*) through the second quarter of the third millennium B.C. The charnel houses were later, covering the period of the fortified town. Latest were the cairns, which were shallow pits containing articulated burials with pots and sometimes a dagger. These had then been filled with stones forming a small tumulus over the grave, and apparently this represents an intrusive culture which probably destroyed the town. The charnel houses had cobbled floors, a door on the broad side, as in EB houses and temples, and in one case a wooden door frame and wooden nails* were found. The buildings contained piles of dolichocephalic (long-headed) newcomers who may have been related to the Kurgan invaders from the E steppes.

The ethnic and cultural identity of the successive Proto-Urban and Early Urban phases in Palestine is still under vigorous debate, but the earliest burials at Bab edh-Dhra' were presumably Indo-European in origin, while those at the end of the third millennium may possibly be connected with the Semitic Amorites* of the Bible, the Amurru/Martu of the Babylonian and Sumerian* texts. The close association of the patriarchs with the Amorites (e.g., Gen 14:13), and their predilection for masseboth (Gen 28:16–18; 31:45–46), emphasizes the importance of sites of this and subsequent periods for interpreting the background of the patriarchal narratives.

Survey work by Americans Walter Rast and Thomas Schaub since 1973 has brought new attention to the region of the Lisan and the SE coast of the Dead Sea. Surface pottery finds reveal a N-S line of EB city sites near major watercourses or perennial springs. The suggestion has been made that these represent the five Cities of the Plain mentioned in Gen 14. The southernmost site, Zoar, was already known through historical sources from the Byzantine* period.

Bab edh-Dhra' is the most northern and the largest of these sites, strengthening the possibility that it represents biblical Sodom.

Excavations undertaken by the American Schools of Oriental Research have revealed houses and part of the city wall of the *khirbe'*. The finds have generally paralleled the chronological range of the necropolis.

The Ebla (*see* TELL MARDIKH) tablets have been cited as mentioning the city of Sodom, a claim which has generated controversy. The emerging picture of a large and important third millennium population

center on the SE shore of the Dead Sea illuminates the cultural history of Palestine and has major implications for the interpretation of the patriarchal story.

BIBLIOGRAPHY: W. F. Albright, J. L. Kelso, and J. P. Thorley, "Early Bronze Age Pottery from Bab ed-Dra' in Moab," *BASOR*, 95 (1944), 3–11; P. W. Lapp, "The Cemetery at Bab edh-Dhra', Jordan," *Archaeology* 19 (1966), 104–11; *RB*, 73 (1966), 556ff.; *RB*, 75 (1968), 86ff.; P. W. Lapp, "Bab Edh-Dhra' Tomb A76 and Early Bronze I in Palestine," *BASOR*, 189 (1968), 12–41. Cf. Emmanuel Anati, *Palestine Before the Hebrews* (1963), 346, 364–68.

JEJ

BABEL, TOWER OF (bā′bəl). A place and structure mentioned in Gen 11:1–9. It was a tower* and shrine built by mankind after the Deluge (*see* FLOOD), in the Plain of Shinar. The Mesopotamian* river plain had many such structures that must have been notable for their engineering and beauty. The one excavated by Woolley at Ur* in 1924 is the best known. Babel is named with Erech* and Akkad* as a city of Nimrod (Gen 10:10). The name is a play upon the Hebrew בלל, *bālāl* ("to confuse," "to mix") as the place where the tongues of mankind were confused. Older scholars assumed that this tower was a ziggurat,* probably Esagila in Babylon.* Some have identified the vitrified remains of the tower at Borsippa* (Birs Nimrud some 11 km. [7 mi.] SW of Babylon) with the abortive structure of Genesis 11, but this suggestion lacks all proof. It is more likely that the actual Babel lies so far back in the Neolithic* Age as to be unidentifiable. So far there is no archaeological identification of the city of Babel. The use of burnt clay* bricks bound by bitumen* (or "tar," Gen 11:3) is attested from the earliest periods of Mesopotamian history.

Babel, as also with Babylon the metropolis, became a symbol of human arrogance and the divine judgment that falls on it. It was obviously a ziggurat or temple tower of unusual or peculiarly sinister significance.

BIBLIOGRAPHY: A. Parrot, *The Tower of Babel* (1955); D. J. Wiseman, *Illustrations from Biblical Archaeology* (1958), 20–21.

WW and EMB

BABYLON, CITY OF. An ancient city* on the Euphrates River, one of the capital cities of Mesopotamia.* The founding of the city is lost in antiquity, but it is now known that the name was a Semitic pronunciation of the Proto-Euphratean or Hurrian* *Papil/Papal*. The commonly-accepted "gate-of-god" interpretation of the Sumerians and Akkadians* is thus incorrect. The name first appears on the Sargonic text of Šar-kalī-šarri (2217–2193 B.C.). From that time until the rise of the Amorites* it was a provincial center and cult city. It was the grand capital of Hammurabi* (1792–1750 B.C.) and became thereafter one of the great centers of culture and religion. The Hittites* partially sacked the city in 1595 B.C., and a Kassite* dynasty ascended the throne. After 1300 B.C. it again lost political power, and during the last seven years of its independence it was ruled by Assyrians. In 1171 B.C. the Elamites overthrew the Kassite puppets of Assyria, and the rulers of a sister-city in S Mesopotamia, Isin, began the Fourth Babylonian Dynasty. In 689 B.C. Sennacherib* sacked Babylon and destroyed much of it. Later rulers allied themselves with the Medes* and overthrew Assyria in 612 B.C. The final dynasty of Babylonian kings were Chaldeans,* and they were dedicated to rebuilding the ancient temples and walls.* The short-lived but illustrious Neo-Babylonian Empire* was the result. The last truly formidable ruler was Nebuchadnezzar* II (605–562 B.C.). Cyrus* the Persian (see SUSA) took Babylon in 539 B.C. and ended forever her dominance in Near Eastern affairs. Subsequently, the Persian Empire fell to Alexander and then had its place in the long wars between the Parthians and the Romans. The archaeologist Robert Koldewey began to excavate the site for the Deutsche Orient Gesellschaft in 1899. In eighteen years he and his colleagues were able to clear much of the mound, but actually excavated in only a few areas. Because of the Babylonian habit of keeping precise records, many hundreds of texts are extant. Among these are plans for buildings, surveys of land, descriptions of festivals, and accounts of expenditure for refurbishing public buildings.

In the time of Alexander (330 B.C.) the great temples of Babylon, Esagila, and Etemenanki were still wonders. Babylon was very large, covering more than 1,200 ha. (3,000 a.), and was in the shape of a slightly bent rectangle, with its main axis from NE to SW. Competent surveys have mapped the place. The Euphrates flowed through the city from N to S, and on its E bank were situated the great temples and palaces. On their far side ran the great processional street,* Ai-ibur-sabu, "may the enemy not cross over." There were eight gates* through the massive walls, the most famous of which was the Ishtar gate covered with bright blue tiles and decorated with animal figures in color and high relief.

The external appearance of Babylon is unknown, except that the many kilometers of heavy walls, crenelated towers, and multistoried temples, must have been very impressive to travelers such as the Jews when they were taken there in captivity, and to Greek wanderers such as Herodotus, who expressed great wonder at the sight. The streets were narrow, with many alleys and dead ends, and private houses were only one-story high with no windows on the street side. Brick and mud-wall construction occurred everywhere, and the various social classes jostled in the narrow, twisting spaces between the house walls on either side. The true wealth of the city, aside from the booty of centuries laid up in the temples, was in the many irrigated fields that stretched on every side over the flat alluvium of the Euphrates. Canals, waterways, sluices, and bridges were continually being built and rebuilt. The memorials of Babylon are predominantly archaeological, and the spirit of the place lives in them. Babylon and its cruel and powerful rulers were the target of some of the strongest imprecations of the OT prophets. They saw clearly its evil and inhumanity. Given the relative poverty

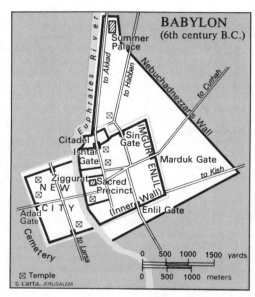

of S Mesopotamia in natural resources, and the lack of power and communication in antiquity, a city the size of Babylon could have been built and maintained only at the cost of immense human deprivation and suffering. Assyriologists have often noted that while the mood of Egyptian civilization seems to have been optimistic and benign, that of Babylon was pessimistic, dour, and filled with foreboding and fear. This gives Babylonian art and literature an intense quality that transcends time. It is for this reason that later ages employed the name of the great city to represent evil, the exemplar of moral corruption. Evidence that survives bears out that judgment. The vast size and depth of the excavations, the mass of cuneiform* material, and the hosts of later writers have not yet been indexed or studied adequately.

See CYRUS; NEBUCHADNEZZAR.

BIBLIOGRAPHY: R. Koldewey, *Das wieder erstehende Babylon* (1925); E. Unger, *Babylon, die heilige Stadt* (1931); specifics of the many excavations were published in various volumes of: *Wissenschaftliche Veröffenlichungen der Deutsche Orient-Gesellschaft*; O. E. Ravn, *Herodotus' Description of Babylon* (1942); H. W. F. Saggs, *The Greatness That Was Babylon* (1962); the best photographic plates published are in: A. Parrot, *Nineveh and Babylon* (1961); E. Strommenger, *The Art of Mesopotamia* (1964); H. W. F. Saggs and D. W. Thomas, eds., *Archaeology and OT Study* (1967), 39–56; D. J. Wiseman, *ZPEB*, 1 (1974), 439–48.

ww

BABYLON (BABYLONIA), COUNTRY OF. See CHALDEA; SHINAR.

BABYLON, HANGING GARDENS OF. As described by the Greek historian Herodotus in 460 B.C. during his visit to Babylon* (cf. *Hist.* 1, 178–88), the gardens* were regarded as one of the Seven Wonders of the World. Located by Koldewey at the NE corner of Nebuchadnezzar's* palace near the Ishtar Gate, the gardens were probably developed on a zigguratlike (see ZIGGURAT) foundation and built in the form of elevated terraces. Among Koldewey's discoveries at the site were vaults and massive arches,* which may have formed the base of the structure. He also uncovered spaces that were consistent with the functioning of an ancient hydraulic system similar to a chain pump. It has been estimated that the gardens, which were laid out at different levels, grew within or on top of a building that itself was about 23 m. (75 ft.) high. Such an elevated terrace would form a prominent landmark, visible from a considerable distance in a city set on a flat plain. Built by Nebuchadnezzar, the gardens are thought to have been designed for his wife Amytis, daughter of King Astyages, who was homesick for the mountains and vegetation of Media,* her native land.

BIBLIOGRAPHY: R. Koldewey, Das wieder erstehende Babylon (1925), 96–98; E. Unger, Babylon (1931), pl. 30, fig. 49; A. Parrot, Babylon and the OT (1958), 40–42, pls. XV, XVI; G. A. Larue, Babylon and the Bible (1969), 59–62; R. C. Thompson, CAH, 3 (1970 ed.), 216.

HWP

BABYLONIAN CHRONICLES. A name given to a collection of tablets covering events in the S part of Mesopotamia* from the time of Sargon of Akkad* (c. 2350 B.C.) up to the advent of Persian suzerainty in the area in the late sixth century B.C. The first of these texts was published in 1887 from tablets collected and held in the British Museum, from which all subsequent materials have also come. D. J. Wiseman, who has published several of the texts, speculates that the majority of them were compiled to inform the Achaemenid kings of the prior history of Babylon following their conquest of the area in 539 B.C.

The Chronicles are generally divided into three groups based largely on the type of tablet and the style of writing. Tablets with special relevance for students of the OT include a Babylonian account of the events referred to in 2 Kings 19:36 and Isa 37:37; backgrounds to the period of Manasseh and Josiah; exact information concerning the date of the demise of Nineveh;* a text that makes clear the translation of 2 Kings 23:29 ("The king of Egypt went up on behalf of the king of Assyria . . ."); some clarification of the putative but elusive 605 B.C. attack of Nebuchadnezzar* on Jerusalem* (Dan 1:1–2); the details of Jerusalem's fall in 597 B.C. and the captivity of Jehoiachin;* and finally an elaboration of the circumstances surrounding the fall of Babylon,* the role of Belshazzar,* and the advent of Cyrus* (cf. Isa and Dan).

BIBLIOGRAPHY: S. Smith, Babylonian Historical Texts Relating to the Capture and Downfall of Babylon (1924); D. J. Wiseman, Chronicles of Chaldaean Kings (626–556 B.C.) (1956); id., in DOTT (1956), 73–83; id., "Babylonian Chronicles," in C. F. Pfeiffer, ed., The Biblical World (1966), 133–37; G. Morawe, "Studien zum Aufbau der neubabylon-

ischen Chroniken in ihrer Beziehung zu den chronologischen Notizen der Koenigsbuecher," ETh, 26 (1966), 308–20; S. H. Horn, "Babylonian Chronicle and the ancient calendar of . . . Judah," AUSS, 5 (1967), 12–27; A. L. Oppenheim in ANET with supplement (1969), 266, 303, 305, 308, 560ff., 563; D. J. Wiseman, "Archaeology and Scripture," WTJ, 33 (1971), 133–52.

CEA

BABYLONIAN EMPIRE, NEO-. See NEO-BABYLONIAN EMPIRE.

BACTRIA (bak'tri ə; Old Pers. Bākhtrish; Elamite Bakshish; Avesta Bakhdhi; Pahlavi Bakhli). A region in northern Afghanistan which flourished as an independent Hellenistic kingdom from c. 250 to 100 B.C. It has been characterized as "at once a frontier, a trade corridor, and a granary."

I. The Site. Bactria proper, as defined by Strabo, is the area S of the Oxus River (the Amu Darya) and N of the Paropamisus Mountains (the Hindu Kush, a westward extension of the Himalayas), some of whose peaks tower over 6 km. (20,000 ft.). Bactria occupies the upper and middle reaches of the Oxus, which flows from the Pamirs and empties into the Aral Sea; classical writers mistakenly believed that it emptied into the Caspian Sea.

The region today includes barren clay* flats and soils impregnated with salts. It seems to have been more fertile in antiquity, when it was served by extensive irrigation.

From the Achaemenid period on, Bactria was associated with, or in control of, a number of adjoining regions: (1) Badakhshan is the mountainous area to the E that was the prime source of lapis lazuli,* a blue stone that was exported as far away as Egypt* and as early as the third millennium B.C. (2) Sogdiana is the area N of the Oxus today in SW Tadzhik USSR and SE Uzbek USSR. S Sogdiana, including the Zarafshan Valley with its famous oases of Bukhara and Samarcand, was closely linked with Bactria. N Sogdiana, centered on the Jaxartes River (the Syr Darya), is connected with the Ferghana Valley to the E, which provided access to Chinese Turkestan. (3) Margiana is the sandy area to the W with its oasis of Merv. It was controlled by Bactria from Achaemenid times until it was taken by the Parthians. (4) Paropamisadae is the strategic area of the Hindu Kush, its passes, and of the Valley of Kabul, modern capital of Afghanistan. It gives access to NW India through the famous Khyber Pass and was therefore open to Indian influence. It was under Bactrian control in the Hellenistic period.

II. Economy and Society. Bactria became wealthy as a central node in the most important trade routes to the W, both from India and from China. Trade from the NE brought Bactria gold from Siberia and, from 106 B.C., silk from China. The route from the SE ran from Taxila to Alexandria of the Caucasus—Bactria—Hecatompylos—Ecbatana*—Seleucia.*

There are three passes that lead over the Hindu

Kush to Bactria: (1) The E or Khawak Pass taken by Alexander leads primarily to Badakhshan. (2) The Central or Salang Pass, through which runs the modern road from Kabul to Baghlan. (3) The W or Bamian Pass, which descends to the Darrah River S of Balkh, was the most frequently used pass in antiquity.

According to Curtius, Bactria was a fertile land of extensive orchards, vineyards, and pastures. Much of the once intensely irrigated areas are but steppes today. Bactria provided some of the best cavalry horses; ten thousand were used by Euthydemus against Antiochus III. A thousand of the two-humped Bactrian camels* were used at the battle of Gaugamela in 331 B.C.

Society in Bactria was largely feudal, with the landed aristocracy dwelling in fortified strongholds in view of the danger of marauding nomads from the N. After Alexander, the descendants of the Greek soldiers formed a ruling class over the native Iranian population.

III. Sources Regarding. 1. Classical. Apart from the accounts of Alexander's invasion (Arrian, Curtius, etc.) and short references in Polybius, Pliny, and Strabo our extant sources are very limited. A major source of Bactrian history is the abridgment by Justin (second century A.D.) of the work of Trogus, a historian of the Augustan period. 2. Numismatic. Apart from the recently discovered "Bactrian" inscription at Surkh Kotal, our only contemporary evidence consists of the numerous coins* of the Bactrian rulers. Their portraits are acknowledged to be among the finest masterpieces of Greek numismatic art. 3. Oriental. Chinese records as preserved by Ssu-ma Ch'ien (99 B.C.) and Pan-Ku (A.D. 92) give us an invaluable record of the visit to Bactria by an intrepid diplomat named Chang K'ien from the court of the Han emperor Wu Ti. Chang K'ien set out in 138 B.C. but was detained for ten years in Chinese Turkestan. He reached Bactria (Ta-hsia) in 128, just after nomads battered the area. His return to China in 126 opened up the way for the silk trade.

A fascinating but apologetic work is the Buddhist Milindapañha, a dialogue between the Bactrian general Menander (Milinda), who invaded India c. 180 B.C., and Buddhist teachers. The work, which is extant in Pali and in Chinese fragments, is dated to the first century B.C. by Buddhist scholars and by Tarn, but to the second century A.D. by Derrett and Garbe. In actuality, Menander may or may not have become a Buddhist, though many of his successors did become converts.

IV. History 1. Pre-Achaemenid Age. Legends speak of the conquest of Semiramis in Bactria, and Ctesias suggests that there was an independent Bactrian kingdom c. 700 B.C. Iron Age* pottery* of the eighth–sixth centuries B.C. at Balkh and Khulm may suggest the incursion of an E Iranian people into the area of Bactria. 2. Achaemenid Period. Bactria was the most important satrapy of the Achaemenids in the E. Cyrus* seems to have subdued it between his conquest of Lydia* and of Babylon.* Darius* had to suppress a revolt in Bactria; he later banished some

Libyans to Bactria (Herodotus 4.204). Bactria was again the center of revolts under Xerxes* and under Artaxerxes I. Traditions hold that Zoroaster, the religious teacher, was born in the city of Bactra and that he was killed by invading Turanians.

Reliefs at Persepolis* depict the Bactrians as wearing their hair bunched at the back, short tunics, long baggy trousers, carrying bows and short spears, and leading two-humped camels. 3. Alexander. Before Alexander could overtake Darius III, who had fled from Ecbatana, the latter was killed by Bessus, viceroy of Bactria. In the spring of 328, Alexander surprised Bessus by crossing over the 3.5-km. (11,600-ft.) high Khawak Pass and wading through deep snow for a great distance both S and N of the pass. In Bactria Alexander put a stop to the practice of giving up the aged and the infirm to be eaten by dogs (Strabo 11. 11.3). Alexander fell in love with and married Roxane, the daughter of the Bactrian Oxyartes, whom he established as the satrap of Paropamisadae.

Bactria was the richest of Alexander's conquests E of Babylon. He founded about ten cities in Bactria and Sogdiana. Diodorus tells us that at his death twenty-three thousand Greek soldiers in Bactria revolted; Rostovtzeff believes that the true number was closer to three thousand. 4. Seleucids. After Alexander's death Bactria was ruled as a satrapy under Seleucus I (312–280) and Antiochus I (280–262). We are not certain as to when Bactria gained its independence. Parthia revolted c. 250 B.C. and tradition also suggests that Diodotus, satrap of Bactria, also revolted against Antiochus II (262–246) about the same time. The continued circulation of Seleucid coins inclines Tarn to believe that independence was achieved more gradually. 5. Euthydemids. All agree that the most brilliant period of Bactrian independence came in the reigns of Euthydemus I (230–189), a Greek from Magnesia, and his son Demetrios I (189–166). Antiochus III attacked Euthydemus in 208 and tried in vain to besiege Bactra for two years. In the settlement of 206 the Bactrian king gave Antiochus a number of elephants. Euthydemus was able to extend his rule to Sogdiana and probably to Ferghana.

Demetrius extended Bactrian rule to Paropamisadae, Aria, Arachosia, and Seistan. In 183—leaving behind in Bactria his son, Euthydemus II, and taking with him his general, Menander—Demetrius invaded India and thereby ushered in a century and a half of Greek rule in this area. At its height Demetrius's empire included the whole of Afghanistan and parts of what are now Soviet Turkestan, Iran, Pakistan, and India. 6. Eucratids. Demetrius was slain by Eucratides I (166–159), who is depicted as an independent rebel by the traditions. Tarn has made the plausible suggestion that Eucratides was acting for Antiochus IV. Eucratides himself invaded India c. 165 but was then attacked and killed by the Parthians in 159. His gold* stater is the largest extant gold coin.

Heliocles (159–c. 130), the son of Eucratides, is the last known Greek ruler of Bactria. The invading nomads made crude imitations of his coins. On the basis of the Kunduz Hoard of coins Narain believes that some Greeks may have been able to maintain a limited independence in the area of Badakhshan as late as 100 B.C. The outpost of Greco-Bactrian rule in India lasted until 80 B.C. 7. *The Yüeh-chih*. The end of the Bactrian kingdom is attributed by Justin to an invasion of Asiani and Sacaraucae and by Strabo to the Asii, Pasiani, Tochari, and Sacarauli. Chinese sources speak of the Yüeh-chih, who may have included Iranian elements such as the Tocharians. We learn that the Hsiung-nu, against whom the Ch'in Dynasty (255–206 B.C.) had built the Great Wall, pushed the Yüeh-chih westwards, so that in 160 B.C. they are found in the Lake Issyk Kul area in Kirgiz USSR. The Yüeh-chih then first propelled the Sacae (Scythians*) into Bactria c. 130 and then themselves occupied that area and NW India. 8. *The Kushans*. One group of the Yüeh-chih known as the Kushans established a powerful dynasty over these areas from 100 B.C. to c. A.D. 400. The silk trade, which reached its height from A.D. 90 to 130, made the Kushans rich.

The later Kushans, most notably Kanishka (second century A.D.), became converts to Buddhism and sponsored the striking Gandharan sculptures. Kushans translated Buddhist Scriptures into Chinese in the third century A.D. and were responsible for the spread of Buddhism into Central Asia and to China. 9. *The Sassanian Period*. In A.D. 225 the Kushans were conquered by Ardashir, the first Sassanid ruler of Iran. The culture of the Kushans of Bactria under the Sassanids declined in the third and fourth centuries. Their holdings in India were lost to the Guptas.

Turko-Mongol tribes from the Altai known to Byzantine writers as Ephthalites, or White Huns, occupied Bactria in the mid-fifth century and forced the Kushans S over the Hindu Kush. In the sixth century, soon after the Sassanian Khusro I had defeated the Ephthalites, a Turkish tribe occupied Bactria. 10. *The Islamic and Modern Periods*. The Muslims invaded Bactria in A.D. 647. By the tenth century the country was almost entirely Muslim. In Islamic times the area was called Tukharistan after the Tocharians.

In the nineteenth century the British attempted to establish control over the Khyber Pass in the face of opposition from the tribes in the area. Afghanistan's independence was recognized in 1919.

V. *Excavations and Discoveries* 1. *The Oxus Treasure*. The largest and most diversified lot of Achaemenid treasures was discovered at a ferry point N of Kunduz on the Oxus River in 1877. After many vicissitudes the lot was acquired by the British Museum. Among other objects, the hoard contains a scabbard believed to be Median and gold plaques depicting Scythians. Ghirshman suggests that the treasure may have belonged to the temple of Anahita at Bactra and may have been hidden before Alexander's arrival. On the other hand if the lot of 1500 coins acquired at the same time was an integral part of the hoard, it was probably buried c. 130 B.C. 2. *Balkh*. The capital of Bactria was the city of Bactra which, E of Babylon, was unequaled in reputation

for magnificence. Also known by its Iranian name, Zariaspa, it was the home of Zoroaster. It has been identified with the enormous mound with a circuit of 11.27 km. (7 mi.) located at the village of Balkh (modern Wazirabad). The acropolis* mound of Bala Hisar is an oval 1,500 by 1,000 m. (4,900 by 3,300 ft.). In spite of soundings by A. Foucher in 1923–25, by D. Schlumberger in 1947, and by R. Young in 1953, only two Hellenistic shards* have ever been found. 3. *Aï Khanum*. It is quite remarkable that until about a decade ago, apart from the coins, we had not a single object or building from Hellenistic Bactria. In 1961 the King of Afghanistan found some Corinthian column fragments at Aï Khanum on the Oxus about 40 km. (25 mi.) NE of Kunduz, which makes this the eastern-most Hellenistic settlement to be recovered. The excavations by P. Bernard in 1965–66 have brought to light purely Hellenistic buildings—an agora,* a gymnasium, and a temple. Most striking are a Greek inscription reflecting Delphic precepts and the first Greco-Bactrian sculpture—a herm (four-sided monument) of an old man. The site seems to have been established c. 300 B.C.; it was destroyed by flames c. the first century B.C.

The discovery of Bactrian art resolves the controversy surrounding the origins of the Greek elements in Buddhist Gandharan art in favor of Schlumberger's position. In 1960 Schlumberger suggested that the Kushans transmitted the Hellenistic elements from Bactria to Gandhara; he also predicted that one day Greco-Bactrian art objects would be discovered. Others had suggested a source in Roman objects of trade. 4. *The Kunduz Hoard*. The hoard of over six hundred coins called the Kunduz Hoard was actually found in 1946 at the frontier outpost of Khisht Tepe. They were displayed in a publication by A. Bivar in 1953. Buried between 140 and 100 B.C., the collection includes coins of Alexander that were still in circulation and some new Attic standard tetradrachms of several Bactrian kings. The latest possible date of their burial may indicate the survival of limited Greek authority in NE Bactria after the nomadic incursions of 130 B.C. 5. *Begram*. The ancient settlement at Begram, some 48.28 km. by air (30 air mi.) N of Kabul, was a strategic site where roads from the three passes over the Hindu Kush converged. It has been identified with Alexandria-Kapisa. Excavations by the French under J. Hackin in 1937–40 and R. Ghirshman in 1941–42 have yielded the coins of Bactrian kings—including thousands of Eucratides— Roman objects imported from Syria from the first century B.C. on, and Chinese textiles. 6. *Surkh Kotal*. The cutting of a section of the road from Kabul to Mazar-i-Sharif at Surkh Kotal, "The Red Pass," about 80 km. (50 mi.) S of Kunduz in 1951 revealed an important Kushan structure built on three terraces. Excavations by D. Schlumberger from 1952 to 1960 brought to light a fire temple built under Kanishka (second century A.D.), which was later restored under Nokonzoko. Inasmuch as the structure revealed no Buddhist elements, except for the symbol of a turban, the temple seems to have been built before Kanishka's conversion to Buddhism. An inscription in Greek letters is ascribed to Kanishka by Bivar but to Nokonzoko by Henning. It is the first text of the Iranian dialect spoken in Bactria. Its language has been called Tocharian by Maricq and Bactrian by Henning. 7. *Bamian*. In an isolated valley NW of Kabul at Bamian are two of the largest Buddhist structures in the world. Two statues of Buddha have been carved from red sandstone, the higher about 50 m. (170 ft.) high. These were made c. fourth century A.D. when Bamian was a Buddhist center with a thousand monks dwelling in its caves.* 8. *Tillya-tepe*. West of Balkh Soviet archaeologists have excavated since 1969 a Kushan capital called Yemshi-tepe. The royal family evidently buried their dead on an abandoned mound nearby called Tillya-tepe, "The Golden Mound." This had been the site of a fire temple during the first half of the first millennium B.C.

Though a highway had cut through the small mound of Tillya-tepe, the Soviets were able to uncover there in 1978 six burials with a spectacular collection of 20,000 objects, many in gold. Parthian and Roman coins date the find to the first century B.C. and first century A.D., an otherwise obscure period when the invading Yüeh-chih were proceeding to establish the Kushan dynasty.

Many of the exquisite masterpieces preserve the Greek heritage of the Bactrians, such as figures of Ares and Aphrodite, and the name of Athena in Greek. The faces portrayed have slanted eyes, reflecting the Mongoloid character of the Yüeh-chih; other faces have caste marks, an Indian feature. Some of the imported works bear Chinese ideographs.

BIBLIOGRAPHY: Several volumes of the *Mémoires de la délégation archéologique française en Afghanistan* published between 1928 and 1965 deal with sites such as Balkh, Begram, and Bamian. H. Rawlinson, *Bactria, the History of a Forgotten Empire* (1912); O. Dalton, *The Treasure of the Oxus* (1926, rep. 1964); D. Schlumberger, "La prospection archéologique de Bactres," *Syria*, 26 (1949), 175–90; W. Tarn, *The Greeks in Bactria and India* (1951); R. Curiel and D. Schlumberger, *Trésors monétaires d'Afghanistan* (1953); A. Bivar, "The Bactrian Treasure of Qunduz," *JNSI*, 17 (1955), 37–52; R. Young, "South Wall, Balkh-Bactra," AJA, 59 (1955), 267–76; F. Allchin, "The Culture Sequence of Bactria," *Antiquity*, 31 (1957), 131–41; A. Narain, *The Indo-Greeks* (1957); M. Rostovtzeff, *The Social and Economic History of the Hellenistic World* (1959), 542–51; W. Henning, "The Bactrian Inscription," *BSOAS*, 23 (1960), 45–55; D. Schlumberger, "Descendants non-Méditerranéens de l'art grec," *Syria*, 37 (1960), 131–66, 252–318; id., "The Excavations at Surkh Kotal and the Problem of Hellenism in Bactria," *Proceedings of the British Academy*, 47 (1961), 77–95; R. Frye, *The Heritage of Persia* (1963); P. Bernard and D. Schlumberger, "Aï Khanoum," *BCH* (1965), 590–657; T. Rice, *Ancient Arts of Central Asia* (1965), 123–72; H. Humbach, *Baktrische Sprachdenkmäler*, 2 vols. (1966, 1967); J. Derrett, "Greece and India: the Milindapañ . . . ," *ZRGG*, 19 (1967), 33–64; T. Abercrombie, "Afghanistan, Crossroad of Conquerors," *National Geographic*, 134 (1968), 297–

345; R. Barnett, "The Art of Bactria and the Treasure of the Oxus," *Iranica Antiqua*, 8 (1968), 34–49; M. Wheeler, *Flames over Persepolis* (1968); R. Grousset, *The Empire of the Steppes* (1970); F. Peters, *The Harvest of Hellenism* (1970), 276–81; J. Thorley, "The Silk Trade between China and the Roman Empire . . . ," *GAR*, 18 (1971), 71–79; P. Levi, *The Light Garden of the Angel King* (1972); P. Bernard, *Fouilles d'Aï Khanoum I, Campagnes 1965–1968* (1973); P. Leriche, "Aï Khanoum," *Revue archéologique*, 2 (1974), 231–70; M. Norton, "The Bright Thread," *Aramco World Magazine*, 28.5 (1977), 2–11; F. R. Allchin and N. Hammond, *The Archaeology of Afghanistan* (1978); V. Sarianidi, "The Treasure of Golden Hill," *AJA*, 84 (1980), 125–32; V. Sarianidi, "The Treasure of the Golden Mound," *Archaeology*, 33.3 (1980), 31–41; B. Brentjes, "Archäologie Afghanistans," *Das Altertum*, 27 (1981), 133–46.   EY

BAFFO. *See* PAPHOS.

BAG. *See* PURSE.

BAHRAIN. *See* DILMUN.

BAKHDHI. *See* BACTRIA.

BAKHTRISH. *See* BACTRIA.

BAKING. *See* OVEN.

BAKSHISH. *See* BACTRIA.

BALATA (BALATAH), TELL. *See* SHECHEM.

BALK (BAULK) (bälk). The smoothly excavated side of a trench or portion of a mound, enabling whatever occupational levels that are present to be studied in perspective.

BALLASAR. *See* BELSHAZZAR.

BALTHASER. *See* BELSHAZZAR.

BANGLES. The Hebrew term עֶכֶס (*'ekes*) in Isa 3:18 describes the bracelets, or metal rings, that upper-class Ancient Near Eastern women wore above the ankles. The same word occurs in Prov 7:22, where the RV reads "fetters." The MT is difficult to understand at this point, but if the RV sense is correct, the allusion would be to the bronze* fetters used for confining prisoners. The anklets were obviously much lighter in weight and were an ornamental type of ring. In the mind of Isaiah they were associated with eighth-century B.C. luxurious living in Judah.* Excavations in Palestine have uncovered many examples of this type of bangle. From graves at Lachish* have come some excellent specimens, consisting of narrow bracelets of heavy bronze measuring between 6.5 and 11.5 cm. (2.5 and 4.5 in.) across. Anklets were but one of many forms of personal ornamentation favored by women in antiquity.

RKH

Khirbet Qumran: One of the rock-hewn, plastered cisterns with steps for access to water at various levels. Courtesy Israel Dept. of Antiquities and Museums.

BAPTISM. The Greek term *baptizō* describes an act of washing or immersion in water. The origin of baptism has been traced variously to OT rites of purification, the lustrations of Jewish sects, and even to analagous initiation or cleansing ceremonies in pagan religions. Early Christians regarded baptism as a sacrament of initiation to be performed once only, as distinct from the more frequent formal lustrations of other sects or religions. Somewhat before the Christian era the Jews employed baptism as a symbolic initiatory act for converts from paganism to the Jewish religion.

1. *Jewish*. Baptism, as John the Baptist practiced it, had its origin in Jewish purification rites that took final shape in the first century after Christ. One of the most interesting discoveries on Masada* was a system of rock-cut cisterns designed to ensure a storage of rain water for the ritual bath. Pure rain water was the ideal, but Jewish regulation allowed an effusion of rain water into the tank as fulfilling the legal requirements. The storage containers above it illustrated a system whereby the bath itself could fulfill the requirements of a mingling of rain water. The bath (*mikve*) is described and photographed in Y. Yadin, *Masada* (1966).

The Jewish separatist movement whose relics have been recovered from Qumran* placed considerable emphasis on periodic cleansing in water as a means of receiving spiritual sanctification (1QS, III, 4 seq.; IV, 20 seq.). At Khirbet Qumran two rock-hewn cisterns* lined with a plaster coating were uncovered

during excavations. One of these was long and deep, having fourteen stone steps at one end that gave access to the water at various levels. Another large cistern near the S wall of the main building had a similar grouping of steps and suggested that these structures were used periodically as baptistries.

2. *Christian*. The catacombs* preserve several epitaphs of neophytes, a term which seems to have been applied especially to the newly baptized. They leave some major problems unresolved. For example, was age in these inscriptions determined from the date of physical birth or from the date of spiritual regeneration? It is almost certainly the latter.

The following are examples of this class: TEG.CANDIDIS NEOF Q.VXT.M.XXI—"The tile of Candidus, a neophyte, who lives twenty-one months;" FL. IOVINA. QVAE. VIX. ANNIS.TRIBVS. D. XXX. NEOFITA. IN   PACE—"Flavia Jovina, who lives three years and thirty days, a neophyte, in   peace"; MIRAE   INDVSTRIAE   ADQVE BONITATIS   . . .   INNOCENTIA   PREDITVS FL. AVR. LEONI. NEOFITO QVI VIXIT ANN VI. MENS. VIII DIES XI . . .—"Innocentia Preditus to Flavius Aurelius Leo, a neophyte of wonderful industry and goodness, who lived six years, eight months, eleven days"; ROMANO NEOFITO BENE   MERENTI QVI VIXIT.ANNOS. VIII. D. XV. REQVIESCIT IN PACE—"To the well-deserving neophyte Romanus, who lived eight years and fifteen days, he rests in peace." In some cases the phrase of John 3 "born again of water . . ." is used in figures.

The following is a characteristic example of this usage: . . . CAELESTE RENATVS AQVA (*sic*) . . .—"Born again of heavenly water" (A.D. 377). We read also of a certain Mercurius, who is described as a boy born and dying in the same year, aged twenty-four. The allusion is to the spiritual regeneration symbolized by baptism. With reference to this he was but a boy—*puer*—at the time of his death. This rite was also called illumination, and from the catacombs come epitaphs of persons said to be thus "newly illuminated."

On the mode of baptism archaeological evidence is similarly vague. It would be most difficult, in the tufa rock galleries, either to obtain or to store a large supply of water. From patristic evidence, immersion, aspersion, or affusion would all seem to have been acceptable. The catacombs seem to have contained no baptistries, no doubt for the practical reason mentioned above.

The nearest approach to a baptistry is a hewn container in the catacombs of Pontianus, 1.45 m. (4.8 ft.) long, .92 m. (3 ft.) wide, and 1.11 m. (3.5 ft.) deep. Obviously it was too small for immersion, but it indicates a ritual illustrated in a fresco above it. It is a late fresco, as the nimbus (halo) round the head of the figures shows. It depicts the Lord standing in the Jordan River, while John appears to pour water on his head, and the Holy Spirit descends in the form of a dove. An angel stands by as witness of the rite, and in the foreground a stag, the emblem of a fervent Christian, is drinking at the pure stream.

There is a similar, badly defaced fresco in the crypt

of Saint Lucina. Archaeology, therefore, supports the mass of patristic evidence which indicates that, from quite early times, the rite of baptism was variously administered, with manifold varieties of symbolism.

See also ABLUTIONS.

EMB

BARAK (bā' rək). W. F. Albright points out that a "dovetailing between archaeological and literary evidence" gives precise support to the presumed date of the conflict of Barak and Sisera (Judg 4–5). Barak was the son of Abinoam, from Kedesh in Naphtali, and was called to lead soldiers from Naphtali and Zebulun against the formidable Canaanite* King Jabin of Hazor* (Judg 4:1–24). According to this same record (Judg 5:19) the clash of arms took place "at Taanach* by the waters of Megiddo.*" Taanach lies some 8 km. (5 mi.) to the SE of Megiddo, and, as at Ai* and Bethel,* the occupation of the sites was not generally simultaneous. Megiddo, for example, as careful analysis of the site has established, was unoccupied in Early Bronze Age III and IV, while Taanach flourished. Taanach was also strong and populous in the middle decades of the fifteenth century before Christ, while Megiddo housed only a small Egyptian garrison. The phrase from the record in Judges indicates some such situation. Taanach was the center, and Megiddo was a ruin. Excavation shows that after the destruction of Megiddo VII in the third quarter of the twelfth century, the site was deserted until the occupation by the people of Stratum VI, who struck out on entirely different lines in fortification and other building. They were followed in this, as in their pottery* types, by their successors of Stratum V. "It follows," Albright concludes, "that the song of Deborah* may be dated archaeologically about 1125 B.C., a date which agrees exceedingly well with the literary and political requirements of its contents."

BIBLIOGRAPHY: W. F. Albright, *The Archaeology of Palestine* (1951, rev. 1971), 117–18; M. Burrows, *What Mean These Stones?* (1941), 94, 123, 136–37.

EMB

BAR KOCHBA (bär kōk' bə). Simon Bar Kochba (or Simeon ben Kosiba) was the "desert Messiah" of Palestine's Second Revolt (A.D. 132). Jerusalem* was the camping place of the Tenth Legion and largely the ruin that Titus* had left in A.D. 70, but it was a ruin of passionately sentimental and religious significance to international Jewry. Great Jewish minorities in Cyrene, Alexandria,* and Cyprus* had risen in wild revolt seventeen years before, in the principate of Trajan, a prey to one of those waves of nationalism to which the race was prone, and had been put down with bloody reprisals. Hadrian,* an intellectual and farsighted ruler, displayed poor judgment in provoking the revolt of A.D. 132 by his proposal to rebuild Jerusalem* as a Roman foundation, Aelia Capitolina* (named after himself, Publius Aelius Hadrianus, and Capitoline Zeus*).

Bar Kochba boldly proclaimed an independent Jewish state. He issued coinage,* which survives, struck from defaced Roman currency. The Romans

Silver tetradrachm minted in A.D. 134/135 during Bar Kokhba revolt. Obverse: temple façade; legend: Shim'on. Reverse: *Lulav* with small etrog on left; legend: For the Freedom of Jerusalem. Courtesy Israel Museum, Jerusalem.

summoned Julius Severus from the governorship of Britain to crush the new rebellion, and it took three sanguinary years to stamp the resistance down. The rebel headquarters were in the tangled wadis* and cave-pitted cliffs where the Judean wilderness breaks in geological ruin into the Dead Sea.* Here, after photographic survey by helicopter, Yadin located a Roman commando camp on a cliff-top plateau, and the great inaccessible cave-complex where the rebels hid and were finally starved to death or driven to suicide by the waiting Romans.

The cave* was of large dimensions and was lined in one part by baskets of bones. There were metal objects made from looted Roman cult vessels, consisting of booty* from a Roman camp. There was another interesting discovery. In March 1961, in what came to be known as the Cave of Letters, a basket was found containing a bundle of papyrus* documents, women's sandals of the sort known among Israelis today as "Elath sandals," and farm and household implements. Among the documents was a file of twelve-years' content, ending significantly at the tragic year of A.D. 132, that gives a picture of life in a Jewish family a century after Christ. There are deeds, transfers, contracts, and agreements, showing the ordered life of a landowner on an estate between the two revolts. They even give some idea of the personalities of those in the family whose fortunes the documents follow. They showed that this group, natives of Zoar in the southern Judean highlands, had worked out a measure of cooperation with the local Roman garrison, for there is a note acknowledging a debt of sixty Tyrian silver dinars, borrowed at 12 percent interest from Valens, centurion of the First Thracian Cohort. It was dated May, A.D. 124, and the document runs: "I shall pay you monthly at the rate of one denarius in one hundred denarii. . . ." As security a piece of parental property was pledged. It is known that a cohort of Thracian auxiliaries was stationed at En Gedi,* and Valens's company was evidently a detachment sent down the S road for guard duty. Yehuda was the second husband of a woman named Babata, whose life is revealed in detail in the cache of documents. Yehuda came from En Gedi, where his father, Eleazar, had property.

There were other pathetic relics also. Along with the documents in the goatskin bag were beads, a mirror,* a comb—a whole toilet set, in fact—along with a powder and perfume container.

Among the letters cached in a remote rear corner of the cave were letters that appear to be from Bar Kochba himself. It is strange to read his terse orders. The documents are in varied hands, so we may not have the guerrilla leader's own handwriting. Adjutants were no doubt the scribes. "Whatever Elisha says, do," runs one command. Another orders the arrest of Tahnun Ben Ishmael and the confiscation of his wheat. Another calls for punishment of some who had repaired their homes, in defiance of a scorched earth policy. The cold, hard, and pitiable confiscation order is addressed to a couple named Jonathan and Masabala, who ruled a cultivated area at En Gedi—"From Shimon Bar Kochba to the men of En Gedi, to Masabala and Yehonaltan Bar Be'ayan: Greeting."

The warning of Jesus about false messiahs (Matt 24:24; Mark 13:22) were meaningless for the brave but unbelieving Jews of Hadrian's day. Christ's followers long since had left the storm centers of Jewish nationalism. It is to be supposed, therefore, that few Christians perished in either of these rebellions that reddened two separate decades with carnage.

BIBLIOGRAPHY: R. Harker, *Digging Up Bible Lands* (1972); Y. Yadin, *The Story of Masada* (1969); E. M. Blaiklock, *ZPEB*, 1 (1975), 474.

EMB

BARREL VAULT. A vault that has a roof in semicylindrical form.

BARROW. In archaeological terminology, a tumulus or grave mound.

BASHAN (bā'shən; Heb. בָּשָׁן, *bāšān*, "smooth," "fertile" or "fruitful"). In general that part N of the area E of the Jordan, a territory stretching from just below the Yarmuk River (S) to Mount Hermon* (N), from the Jebel Druze Mountains (E) to the hills E of the Lake of Galilee* (W). Bashan included the districts of Argob, Golan,* and Hauran, and a little of Gilead, and also the cities of Karnaim, Ashtaroth, Salcah, Kenath, and Edrei. Also included were the Greek cities of the Decapolis,* Hippos,* Dion,* and Abila.* In Greco-Roman times, the name of the area was Batanea.

At an altitude of c. 600 m. (2,000 ft.) above sea level, Bashan, with its high, rolling volcanic hills in the N, was suited for nomads, while with its volcanic craters and hollows of the S it was more adaptable to agriculture. The area was known for its "bulls" (Ps 22:12) and "cows" (Amos 4:1–3), as well as for its oak trees (Isa 2:13; Ezek 27:6).

Archaeological investigation of such structures as the megalithic* forts found in Bashan, as well as those at Rabbah Ammon, has revealed that this whole area was inhabited from the Early Bronze Age (c. 3000–2000 B.C.). A sixteenth-century Egyptian document of Thutmose III and the Amarna Letters* (early fourteenth century B.C.) both reveal a prosperous agricultural settlement in Bashan. It was this kind of settlement that the Israelites took over from the Am-

orite* King Og (Num 21:31–33; Deut 3:1–12).

In the centuries that followed the time of Christ, building developed there, as is illustrated in the Hauran area of Bashan, with its great reservoirs and aqueducts.* During the second and third centuries A.D. basilicas,* temples, and theaters* showed up in increasing numbers in the old cities.*

There is no written record of life in the Hauran earlier than the time of Trajan, except for a stray inscription such as to Herod, to Agrippa, and to Malichus II (A.D. 48–71) king of the Nabataeans.* However, from Trajan's time on, inscriptions abound. Names of emperors are to be found on almost all the ruins. In the Decapolis as well as in the Hauran, bits of basalt rock show on them evidence of some syllables of the title *Autocrator* (Greek for Imperator). Gods of the temples bear Semitic names or their Greek equivalents—such as Zeus,* Heracles, Athena, Tyche. The inscribed names of the benefactors who were responsible for building the temples show up as a Valens, a Caius, a Publius, and the like.

BIBLIOGRAPHY: G. A. Smith, *The Historical Geography of the Holy Land*, 23d ed. (1896), 549–52, 609ff.; I. Benzinger, "Batanaia," *PWRE*, III.1 (1897), 115–18; D. Mackenzie, "Dibon: The City of King Mesa," *PEQ* 13 (1882), 65–66; E. Epstein, "Hauran: Rise and Decline," *PEQ*, 40 (1909), 13–21; S. Cohen, "Bashan," *IDB*, A–D (1962), 363–64; J. Finegan, *The Archaeology of the NT* (1969), 61–62; F. B. Huey, Jr., *ZPEB*, 1 (1975), 485–86.

WHM

BASILICA (bə sil'i kə). The earliest Christian groups met in private houses (cf. Philem v.2). The early form of building dedicated to Christian worship was called a basilica (short for *basilica stoa*—"royal porch" or hall or perhaps *basilica oikia*—"royal house"). They tended to be oblong buildings with double colonades and a semicircular apse at the end and used for a court of justice or a place of assembly in pre-Christian times. The church adopted the form in a rudimentary fashion in the catacomb* chapels and later more completely above ground. W. M. Ramsay has a long and amply documented chapter on the origin of the term and an examination of surviving archaeological evidence in his *Thousand and One Churches* (1909), 297–324. A shorter but detailed description of architectural form is given in *ODCC* (1974), 139.

EMB

BASIN. A term describing a fairly sizable metal vessel* employed in religious rites of purification. The basin of the tabernacle (Exod 30:18; 31:9 et al.) was made of bronze* and was set on a base between the tabernacle door and the sacrificial altar.* Its function was to afford the priests facilities for ritual cleansing (Exod 30:20–21), and it may also have been used for purifying certain of the implements used in the sacrificial proceedings. The Solomonic Temple* boasted an ample supply of basins, the most prominent being the Sea, a large vessel of cast bronze which was made by Huram (or Hiram; not the king) of Tyre (1 Kings 7:13–14). The bowl was 4.5 m. (15 ft.) in diameter, nearly 2.4 m. (8 ft.) in height, and 7.5 cm. (3 inches) thick. It was set upon four groups of three bronze bulls facing the cardinal points of the compass. Its volume was 2000 baths (c. 44 kl. or 11,500 gals.; 1 Kings 7:26), and its exterior rim was decorated with the lily-work typical of contemporary Phoenician craftsmanship. The temple also contained ten smaller bronze bowls placed upon elaborate stands fixed to a wheeled base. The bowls held forty baths (c. 880 liters, or 230 gals.; 1 Kings 7:38), and the lower part of the bases was paneled and decorated with artistically executed figures of lions, palm trees, and cherubim,* in a manner typical of second millennium B.C. iconography. Finally these stands were sent to Assyria as scrap metal by Ahaz (2 Kings 16:17). Wheeled bases of this sort have been recovered by excavators in Cyprus,* while a tripod base was unearthed at Ras Shamra (Ugarit*).

See ABLUTIONS; BRONZE; CHERUBIM; CYPRUS; HIRAM; TYRE; UGARIT.

BIBLIOGRAPHY: W. F. Albright, *Archaeology and the Religion of Israel* (1946), 152–54.

RKH

BASKET. See VESSELS.

BAS-RELIEF (bä ri lēf'). A French term for carved figures raised less than half of their true proportion above the plane surface. It can be applied to the majority of Assyrian, Babylonian, and Egyptian reliefs. Also called low relief.

BATANEA. See BASHAN.

BATH, BATHING. See ABLUTIONS.

BEASTS, FIGHTING WITH. See THERIOMACHY.

BEATTY PAPYRI. See CHESTER BEATTY PAPYRI.

BED, BEDSTEAD. Furniture* for sleeping is rarely found in excavations. Exceptions include a wooden bed with bronze* fittings, dating from the Persian period (Iron III, 530–330 B.C.; see IRON AGE), found at Tell el-Far'ah (see TIRZAH), and a wooden couch in a good state of preservation from the Jericho* tombs. There was also a bronze bedstead found at Beth-pelet (Persian period), which the excavators identified as an import from Cyprus.*

Biblical literature abounds with references, one of the earliest being to the legendary iron bedstead of the giant King Og of Bashan* (Deut 3:11), which measured 9 by 4 cubits (over 4 by 1.8 m., or 13 by 6 ft.). From earliest times people, especially the poor, slept on the ground with their clothing* for covering. In view of this practice, the law forbade clothing being taken for a pledge (Exod 22:26–27). In the summer season the roof was a favorite place for sleeping. Near Eastern houses tend to have in the family room a raised platform (*mastaba* in Egypt) where the household activities such as cooking,* washing, weaving, etc., were carried out, and it was on this platform that the family slept at night. Very early houses often had earthen, clay*-covered couches extending along one side of the room. The raised bed originated the expressions "go up," and "come down"

from a bed (cf. Ps 132:3; 2 Kings 1:4, KJV). During the day carpets, pads, mats, and covers were folded and stored in alcoves in the room or in more elaborate storage places. The infant Joash was hidden in such a "bedroom" (2 Kings 11:2). Mattresses were often stuffed with wool, and pillowcases and coverlets were of fine fabrics, frequently decorated in great detail.

Wooden furniture was rare before the advent of bronze tools. At very early times, Egyptians made wooden bed frames, which held a woven mattress. Tombs at Saqqara (c. 2800 B.C.; see MEMPHIS) provide evidence for this type of Old Kingdom furniture. New Kingdom beds were of fine woods,* ornamented with gilding, glazes, inlays of ivory* and semiprecious stones. Cradles were in use in Palestine and were swung from tent poles or roof beams. In later times (during Iron II; see IRON AGE) the wealthy had elaborate, ornamented bedsteads, a luxury that incurred the wrath of the prophets (cf. Amos 6:4). "Beds inlaid with ivory" were also included in Hezekiah's tribute to Sennacherib* (*ANET*, 288). Beds were highly prized possessions in antiquity. Ten beds with silver* feet were sent by Ptolemy* to Eleazar the high priest in Maccabean times (Jos. *Antiq*. 12.2). They could also be used in payment of debt (Prov 22:27). The Persian beds of the ruling class were ornamented with gold and silver (Esth 1:6).

Canopied beds are referred to in the Song of Songs (3:10—a palanquin, as in RSV), while silken cushions and rich coverings are mentioned in several places (cf. Amos 3:12, ASV; Prov 7:16). A canopied bed in the tent of Holofernes is referred to in Jud 10:21. Perfumes were added by the adulteress (Prov 7:16–17). The canopy was prefigured by the raised platform beds devised in Mesopotamia,* the purpose being to provide cooler rest at night in the hot summers. They were made of four poles set upright that held a platform for sleeping.

NT beds, in addition to the simple raised platform in the houses, consisted of wooden frames. They could be carried easily, and on occasion used as a stretcher or bier (Matt 9:2; Luke 5:18; cf. 1 Sam 19:15; 2 Chron 16:14). Figurative speech made use of the bed, as in Isa 28:20, describing an insufferable situation; and the preparation of one's place, as in Sheol (Job 17:13). The uses of beds are set forth in many biblical passages. Some of these include, in addition to those mentioned above, sitting on, reclining at a table (for dining), the nap, conjugal relations, and private devotions.

See FURNITURE.

BIBLIOGRAPHY: H. Van-Lennep, *Bible Lands* (1875), 480; M. and J. Miller, *Encyclopedia of Bible Life* (1944), 248–49; C. Singer et al., *A History of Technology*, vol. 1 (1954); K. Kenyon, *Archaeology in the Holy Land* (1960), 191, Plate 38; H. G. Stigers, *ZPEB*, 1 (1975), 504.

MHH

BEERSHEBA. The present expanding city, 77 km. (48 mi.) SW of Jerusalem* and midway between the Mediterranean and the Dead Sea,* is two or three km. W of Tell es-Seba, which was evidently

Aerial view of excavation at Tel Beersheba (Tell es-Seba), showing (1) city gate, (2) storehouses, (3) site of horned altar, (4) water system, (5) deep trench through the fortifications, (6) rampart and glacis, (7) living quarters, (8) public houses. Courtesy Tel Aviv University, The Institute of Archaeology.

the ancient site. Several wells are identifiable in the area, one of them of considerable size, over 3.5 m. (12 ft.) in diameter and cut through 5 m. (16 ft.) of solid rock. One of the lining stones bears a date indicating that repairs were carried out in the twelfth century. When Conder discovered this inscription, the depth to the surface of the water was 11.5 m. (38 ft.).

Archaeological exploration of the area has no great significance. There are traces in the area of Bronze Age activity described by the Israeli Department of Antiquities in 1954. Copper ore was imported from Arabia* and refined there. The modern city is on the site of a Byzantine* town, but Iron Age* tombs have been located. From the Byzantine period come inscriptions and the foundation traces of houses and churches along with some graves, mostly the fruit of sporadic digging during the 1960s by Y. Yisraeli and R. Cohen. In 1969 a major project was set up at Tell es-Seba by the University of Tel Aviv and led by Y. Aharoni. The remains of a royal Israelite fortress were unearthed, and a number of Hebrew inscriptions were listed.

BIBLIOGRAPHY: A. Alt, *JPOS*, 15 (1935), 294–326; J. Perrot, *IEJ*, 5 (1955), 17–40, 73–84, 167–89; R. B. K. Amiran, *IEJ*, 5 (1955), 240–45; T. Josien, *IEJ*, 5 (1955), 246–56; M. Dothan, *IEJ*, 6 (1956), 112–14; Y. Aharoni, *IEJ*, 8 (1958), 26–38; S. Cohen, *IDB*, 1 (1962), 375–76; A. F. Rainey, *ZPEB*, 1 (1975), 507–9.   EMB

BEETLE. *See* SCARAB.

BEHISTUN INSCRIPTION (bə hi' stūn). Behistun (modern Bisitun) was a small village on the old caravan road from Ecbatana* to Babylon,* being located at the foot of a mountain range skirting the Plain of Karmanshah on the E. On one of the mountain peaks, in a most difficult position 90 to 120 m. (300 to 400 ft.) up the side of a 520 m. (1,700 ft.) peak, Darius* I (522–486 B.C.) commemorated the defeat of the rebellious Gaumata by means of a panel carved in relief and accompanied by many descriptive columns inscribed in Old Persian, Elamite (*see* ELAMITE WRITING), and Akkadian* characters. An Aramaic copy of this inscription has also been found at Elephantine* in Upper Egypt.* H. C. Rawlinson made the first copies in 1835 and deciphered part of the Old Persian. This in turn led to the decipherment of Elamite and Akkadian.

This trilingual inscription was the cuneiform* counterpart of the Egyptian Rosetta Stone,* which, with its Greek, demotic, and hieroglyphic texts gave the key to the decipherment of the last two languages of Egypt.*

See DARIUS.

BIBLIOGRAPHY: P. E. Cleater, *Lost Languages* (1959); E. Doblhofer, *Voices in Stone* (1961). (A good account of Rawlinson's feat in copying the three inscriptions in their inaccessible position, together with the problems of the decipherment of the text of Darius's account of his military operations, which is the theme of the inscription, is given in the June 1971 bulletin of the Australian Institute of Archaeology, *Buried History*, 7.2., 42–56.)   RKH

BEHNESA. See OXYRHYNCHUS.

BEIRUT (bā rūt'; Gr. βηρυτός, Bērytós). A city* on the coast of Lebanon at the foot of the promontory of Beirut (Ras Bairut). There is a well-populated plain to the E on the banks of the Nahr Bairut, the ancient Magoras River, and the coast is populated as well. The Nahr Bairut runs E c. 10 km. (6 mi.), forming St. George's Bay, and in the background to the E is the Lebanon range, with its steep terraces, green valleys, and a bare ridge on the summit.

Beirut (or Berytus, its older name) was one of the ancient cities on the Phoenician* coast and one of the main centers of the Gebalites (see GEBAL). The Amarna Letters* (fourteenth century B.C.) seem to indicate the place as the seat of the Egyptian vassal, Ammuniri (cf. ANET, 283–84).

At the time of the conquests of Alexander the Great, Beirut—along with the other Phoenician ports of Arvad, Byblos (Gebal*), and Sidon*—surrendered and gave its fleet to Alexander for his use. The Hellenistic town's streets were laid out on a grid plan, spaced at intervals, similar to the streets* of Berea, Damascus,* and Laodicea.*

The city became prominent when it was a Roman colony, its full name being Colonia Iulia Augusta Felix Berytus, according to CIL, 3, 161, 165–66, 6041 (cf. Plin. NH 5.20.78; Jos. War 7.3.1). On coins* at the time of Caracalla, it carried the name Antoniniana (J. H. von Eckhel, Doctrina numorum veterum, 3 [1792–1839], 357). During the times of the Herods (Herod the Great, Agrippa I and II; see HEROD, FAMILY OF) the city was embellished with some beautiful buildings including colonnades, temples, and market areas (see AGORA; FORUM) (Jos. War 1.21.11), and especially a theater* (Jos. Antiq. 19.7.5; 20.9.4). About that time there was completed a fine aqueduct* that brought water to the city from the Magoras River. According to an inscription (CIL, 10, 1634), there was in Puteoli* in the second century A.D. a colony of tradespeople from Berytus. The city was known for its law and its silkweaving until it was damaged by an earthquake in A.D. 29.

BIBLIOGRAPHY: E. Schürer, A History of the Jewish People, 2d rev. ed., div. 1, vol. 1 (1891), 436; I. Benzinger, "Berytus," PWRE, 3.3 (1897), 321–23; H. Guthe, "Phoenicia," New Schaff-Herzog, 9 (1950), 16; L. H. Grollenberg, Atlas of the Bible (1957), 102, 145; J. P. Rey-Coquais, "Berytus," PECS, R. Stillwell, ed. (1976), 152.

WHM

BEISAN. See BETH SHAN.

BEITIN. See AI.

BEIT LAHM. See BETHLEHEM.

BEIT MIRSIM, TELL. See DEBIR.

BELESYS. See NABOPOLASSAR.

BELSHAZZAR (bel shaz'ǝr; Akkad. Bēl šar uṣur, "Bēl has protected the king"). He was the ruler of Babylon* in 539 B.C., at the time of its fall to the Persians. He was son of, and coregent with, Nabonidus* (556–539 B.C.) and is unique in Assyrian annals in being the sole example of a crown prince who was officially recognized as coregent. He was probably a grandson of Nebuchadnezzar* II and was put in charge of the kingdom about 556 B.C., according to the Nabonidus Chronicle, while his father campaigned in Arabia.* An inscription from Haran* gave ten years as the period of Nabonidus's absence from Babylon. Two legal texts from the twelfth and thirteenth years of Nabonidus recorded oaths sworn by the life of Nabonidus the ruler, and Bēl-šar-uṣur the crown prince, which are without parallel in cuneiform* sources. Daniel appears to have dated events in his book in terms of the years of coregency (cf. Dan 7:1; 8:1), although contemporary annals were dated on the basis of the regnal years of Nabonidus. Other texts that give details of Belshazzar's religious and administrative activities in sixth century B.C. Babylon and Sippar* up to the fourteenth year of Nabonidus's reign show that he was exercising all the usual functions of a coregent. Possibly because of intrigue in Babylon, Nabonidus left Arabia c. 540 B.C. but arrived at his capital too late to prevent its fall and was subsequently captured. The king who died in Babylon in October, 539 B.C. was evidently Belshazzar (Dan 5:30), not Nabonidus, though nothing is actually known from Assyrian sources concerning his death. Kenophon (Cyropaedia, 7.5, 29–30) mentioned the incident but did not furnish names. Belshazzar is also rendered Balthaser (Baruch 1:11–12) and Ballasar (Jos. Antiq. 10.11.4).

See BABYLON; NABONIDUS; NEBUCHADNEZZAR.

BIBLIOGRAPHY: R. P. Dougherty, Nabonidus and Belshazzar (1929); C. J. Gadd, "The Harran Inscriptions of Nabonidus," An St, 8 (1958), 35–92; D. J. Wiseman, ZPEB, 1 (1975), 515–16.

RKH

BEMA (bē'mǝ; Gr. βημα, bēma, "raised place"). The term bema means literally a "step," a raised platform where, in a Greek assembly, the orator spoke. In the NT it occurs some ten times and is variously rendered, even within the same version (John 19:13—NIV "judge's seat," TCNT "Bench"; Acts 12:21—NIV, KJV "throne," WEY "tribunal," NEB "rostrum"; Acts 18:12—NIV "court," Beck "platform"; Acts 25:6, 10, 17—NIV "court," KJV "judgment seat," NASB "tribunal"; Rom 14:10; 2 Cor. 5:10—NIV "judgment seat," TCNT "bar").

One fine surviving example of a bema is highly relevant to the NT. The place of judgment, where Gallio* sat to hear the Jews'* case against Paul, only to dismiss it summarily, has been excavated with the Corinthian agora.* It was a structure near the middle of the agora, a high broad platform, raised on two steps, with a considerable superstructure. There is evidence of seating and ordered passages of approach. Constructed of white and blue marble, the bema must have been a remarkable feature of the agora, and, whether in its function as a speaker's platform or as the tribunal of justice, was visible to a large audience. The Corinthian (see CORINTH) agora probably dates from the forties of the first century, so was comparatively new when Paul was haled before it.

See AGORA; GALLIO.

BIBLIOGRAPHY: American School of Classical Studies at Athens, *Corinth, Results of Excavations* (1929–41); O. Broneer, *BA*, 14 (1951), 77–96; A. Rupprecht, *ZPEB*, 1 (1975), 960–64.

EMB

BENI HASAN (ben'ē hä'sän). An Egyptian nobleman Amen-em-het built a tomb at Beni Hasan some 240 km. (150 mi.) S of Cairo c. 1890 B.C. and covered the walls with murals portraying scenes depicting arts, trades (*see* TRADE GUILDS), and agricultural* pursuits of his day. One picture shows thirty-seven seminomadic tribesmen from Palestine, from the land of Shutu (central Trans-Jordan), led by Absha, their chief. The men were bearded, and the women used bands to hold their long hair in place. Their clothes* were multicolored, the men wearing short skirts and sandals and the women having calf-length dresses, which they fastened at the shoulder by means of a clasp. Instead of sandals, the women had shoes on their feet. One of the men carried a lyre, and on one of the donkeys were two bellows, indicating that at least some members of the group were traveling metalworkers.

BIBLIOGRAPHY: W. F. Albright, *The Archaeology of Palestine* (1960 ed.), 207, 209, fig. 61.

JAT

BERYTUS. *See* BEIRUT.

BETHANY (beth'ə nē; Gr. βηθανία, *Bēthania*; Semitic derivation uncertain). 1. A place on the E side of Jordan where John baptized (John 1:28). There are no remains.

2. A village on the Mount of Olives* 3 km. (almost 2 mi.) E of Jerusalem;* home of Lazarus (*see* LAZARUS, TOMB OF), Mary and Martha (John 11:1, 18; 12:1), and Simon the leper (Matt 26:6, Mark 14:3). With Bethphage* it was the last station on the road from Jericho* to Jerusalem (Mark 11:1; Luke 19:29). It was where Jesus stayed (Matt 21:17; Mark 11:11f.) and was the place of the ascension (Luke 24:50f.). Bethany is not named in the OT unless Ananiah (Neh 11:32) is the same place, as Albright suggests.

John 11:18 places this Bethany at 15 stadia (2.7 km., or less than 2 mi.) from Jerusalem. Eusebius (*Onomasticon*, 58) states it was at the second milestone from Aelia in a steep bank of the Mount of Olives, and the Bordeaux Pilgrim* (*CCSL* 125.18) says it was 1,500 paces E of the Mount of Olives, where the crypt of Lazarus is located. This distance is at the present village of el-Azariyeh (the Arabic name is derived from the Latin Lazarium).

Archaeological work in the area in 1914 revealed shaft tombs from the Canaanite* period, and new excavations in 1951–53 produced pits, caves,* cisterns,* tombs, and grave objects, showing almost continuous occupation from c. the sixth century B.C. to the fourteenth century A.D.

The traditional tomb of Lazarus consists of a vestibule chamber and then a small inner chamber with raised burial niches on three sides. In the fourth century a commemorative church was built here (cf. Jerome, in his revision of Eusebius's *Onomasticon*).

In 1949–53, the Franciscans excavated and found the tomb of Lazarus on the W and the church on the E with a connecting courtyard. The oldest Bethany church excavated (fourth century A.D.) shows an apse,* a nave, two side aisles, and remains of mosaic* pavements.

A second fifth-century church of the same plan was built 13 m. (about 45 ft.) E of the first one. In the twelfth century were built both a third church of the same basic plan and also, on the W end of the complex, a fourth church with a crypt connected to the Lazarus tomb. S of the churches was a large monastic abbey.

In 1953–54, a new church of Lazarus was constructed in the form of a Greek cross above the eastern part of the second and third churches, with the apses of the two earliest churches and parts of the mosaic pavement of first and second churches left visible.

See BETHPHAGE; LAZARUS, TOMB OF; MOUNT OF OLIVES.

BIBLIOGRAPHY: W. F. Albright, *AASOR*, 4 (1922–23), 158–60; E. G. Kraeling, *Bible Atlas* (1956), 393, 396–97, 410, 414; D. Baly, *The Geography of the Bible* (1957), 202; S. J. Saller, *Excavations at Bethany (1949–53)*, (1957); J. Finegan, *The Archaeology of the NT* (1969), 91–95; H. G. Andersen, *ZPEB*, 1 (1975), 528–29.

WHM

BETH-EGLAIM (beth eg'lä əm; Heb. בֵּית עֶגְלַיִם, *bêṯ 'eglāyîm*; Euseb. βηθαγλαιμ, *Bēthaglaim*, "house of the two calves"). Ancient name now applied commonly to Tell el-'Ajjul at the mouth of the Wadi Gaza, 4 miles SW of modern Gaza.*

Although there is no biblical reference to Betheglaim, the name is known from Eusebius in its Greek form, and a recollection of the Hebrew may be preserved in the Arabic name of the tell* with which Beth-eglaim is identified. This identification was first proposed by B. Maisler (now Mazar) in 1933 (*ZDPV*, 56 [1933]: 186–88) and confirmed by W. F. Albright, even though at the time the excavator, Sir Flinders Petrie, considered the tell to be ancient Gaza. More recently Tell el-'Ajjul has been claimed as the site of the great Hyksos* fortress of Sharuhen, a city prominent in Egyptian literary sources from the Fifteenth to the Eighteenth Dynasties (A. Kempinski, *IEJ*, 24 [1974], 145–52). The traditional identification with Beth-eglaim has, however, been upheld by O. Tufnell ("El-'Ajjul, Tell," *EEHL*, 1:52–61) and Y. Yisraeli ("Sharuḥen, Tell," *EEHL*, 4:1075–82).

Excavations by Petrie for the British School of Archaeology in Egypt* were conducted in four seasons from 1930 to 1934. The earliest evidence of occupation comes from a series of tombs ascribed by Petrie to the "Copper Age," but now designated MB I (or, with K. Kenyon, EB–MB, her "Amorite" phase), and dated between the twenty-first and nineteenth centuries B.C. Petrie dug two separate cemeteries, one

Late Canaanite gold jewelry from Beth-Eglaim (Tell el-Ajjul). Mother-goddess amulet-pendant, eight-pointed star pendant, crescent-shaped earring, two fly amulets, and a grape(?). Courtesy Israel Dept. of Antiquities and Museums. Photo: Israel Museum.

of which contained tombs marked by the single intact burial and the dagger offering. The other cemetery contained tombs with more pottery* and multiple burials of disarticulated skeletons. Other than the presence of the burials, there is no evidence of occupation during the MB I phase.

Clear evidence of occupation and fortification begins with the arrival, in the nineteenth century, of a people from the N called Hyksos. The use of bronze* is now common, and new types of pottery appear, clearly made on a fast wheel and showing affinities to types common in coastal Syria. That Tell el-'Ajjul had become an important link in the Hyksos fortification system is shown by the remnants of a massive sloping glacis* wall of packed earth rising to a height of a hundred feet. Around the glacis on three sides of the mound ran a moat 15 m. (50 ft.) wide, in the fashion now commonly known from remains of the same period at such sites as Hazor,* Gezer,* Lachish,* and the nearby Tell Farâ. Also during the Hyksos phase the great sandstone "palace" was constructed, upon whose foundation were built successive palaces long after the Hyksos themselves were driven from the area.

The end of Hyksos domination in Egypt marked the close of independent activity on the S coast of Palestine. From this time on Beth-eglaim became probably just another Eighteenth Dynasty station on the way to Gaza. Although various phases of the palaces were to continue through the Late Bronze Age* (Nineteenth Dynasty) and even into the Philistine* period, the city was never again what it had once

been. However, the tell is important for LB archaeological studies in the light of two finds: (1) apparent sacrificial burial of horses* with their warriors, and (2) a large cache of a special kind of bichrome pottery with affinities in style to Hurrian* materials. If the horse burials were not so late, they would be considered evidence of Hyksos influence; as it is, no firm explanation of the custom, so foreign to Semitic ways, is possible. The bichrome pottery has been extensively studied, and one writer, W. A. Heurtley, even suggested that it was the product of a single artisan who lived at Tell El-'Ajjul.

The last phase must be dated to the Philistine period, with both the palace and various dwellings uncovered, although the site was by this time overshadowed by neighboring towns.

See GEZER; HAZOR; HYKSOS; LACHISH.

BIBLIOGRAPHY: W. M. F. Petrie et al., *Ancient Gaza*, 1–4 (1931–34), 5 (1952); W. F. Albright, "The Chronology of a S Palestinian City, Tell el-'Ajjul," *AJSL*, 55 (1938), 337–59; K. M. Kenyon, "Tell Ajjul," *Archaeology of the Holy Land* (1970), 305, 322; E. K. Vogel, "Bibliography of Holy Land Sites," *HUCA*, 42 (1971), 83; and various articles on specialized topics.

CEA

BETHEL (beth'əl; Heb. בֵּית־אֵל, *bêṭēl*). A city located on the boundary separating Benjamin and Ephraim. In Josh 18:21–22 it was allotted to Benjamin but was lost to the Canaanites* in the Judges period. It was subsequently recaptured and resettled by the Ephraimites. Under the Canaanites the city was dedicated to El, one of the major deities in their pantheon. It was an important site in OT times, being second only to Jerusalem* in frequency of mention.

In the nineteenth century Edward Robinson identified Bethel with Tell Beitin, located on the watershed route 20 km. (12 mi.) N of Jerusalem. The site was excavated by Albright and others, the earliest levels going back to c. 2000 B.C. The city was well established in the Middle Bronze Age* (MB, c. 1950–1550 B.C.), and during this period Abram erected an altar* to God E of Bethel (Gen 12:8),

Part of cylinder seal from 13th century B.C., found in Bethel. The figure on the right is the goddess Astarte, whose name is written in Egyptian hieroglyphics in the center. On the left is the god Reshep. Courtesy Israel Dept. of Antiquities and Museums.

returning there after visiting Egypt* (Gen 13:3). Jacob experienced a theophany at Bethel, which he
then named "house of God" (Gen 31:13; 35:6–7).

Toward the end of MB a city wall* to the N, nearly
3.5 m. (11 ft.) thick and constructed of carefully fitted stones, was reinforced with a clay* revetment.
Bethel was an important Hyksos* fortress, and during Hyksos occupancy (c. 1600 B.C.) a defensive
complex was erected inside this wall, close to the
city gate.* While the archaeology of Bethel at this
period throws no light specifically on Abram and Jacob, the patriarchal narratives suit what is known of
MB admirably, and nothing in archaeology conflicts
with this dating sequence.

There are certain problems connected with Joshua's
attack on Ai* and Bethel. Ai, usually identified with
Et-Tell, has not revealed any thirteenth-century B.C.
occupation, and it has been suggested that the site
was an outpost for Bethel; that the names Ai-Bethel
are combined into a common episode, or that the
name Ai ("ruin") was intended to explain an impressive ruin as the work of Joshua. The burning of Bethel
(cf. Josh 12:7,16) was matched by a late-thirteenth-
century B.C. level of charred debris at the site that
was 1.5 m. (5 ft.) thick in places. The city subsequently rebuilt was crudely constructed by comparison with the Hyksos* city and marks the transition
to the Iron I Age.* Bethel was allotted to the Joseph
tribes, with the Ephraimites being prominent in its
capture (1 Chron 7:28). It was given its Hebrew name
of Luz (cf. Gen 35:6; Judg 1:23), and during the early
Judges period was the location of the ark (Judg 20:18–
28) prior to its removal to Shiloh.*

Bethel was burned twice, probably by the Philistines* before becoming the center of Jeroboam's cult-
worship in the early monarchy (cf. 1 Kings 12:26–33;
2 Chron 13:8–9). It was still a royal sanctuary in the
days of Amos (cf. Amos 4:4; 5:6 et al.), though the
cultic shrine still has to be located. Abijah incorporated Bethel into his kingdom (2 Chron 13:19), and
his son Asa may have demolished part of it (2 Chron
14:8). To date no traces of Assyrian destruction have
been recovered, but in the sixth century B.C. it was
certainly destroyed by fire. Returning exiles settled
there (Neh 11:31), and the city was fortified by Bacchides, c. 160 B.C. Vespasian* occupied it in A.D. 69,
and, after rebuilding, it survived until the Arab
conquest.

BIBLIOGRAPHY: W. F. Albright, BASOR, 55 (1935),
24–25; ibid., 56 (1935), 1–15; J. L. Kelso, BASOR,
137 (1954), 5–9; ibid., 151 (1958), 3–8; W. F. Albright and J. L. Kelso, The Excavation of Bethel,
AASOR, 39 (1968); H. M. Jamieson, ZPEB, 1 (1975),
532–34; J. L. Kelso, EEHL, 1 (1975), 190–93.

RKH

BETH HACCEREM (BETH HACCHEREM)

(beth hä kər'əm; Heb. בֵּית הַכֶּרֶם, bêṭ hakerem). In
the fifth century B.C. this place was the chief city of
a district governed by Malchiah, who repaired the
Dung Gate of Jerusalem* under Nehemiah's leadership (Neh 3:14). The city seems to have been on
an elevation, so that signal fires could be seen from
it (cf. Jer 6:1). Beth Haccerem was mentioned in the

Aerial view of Bethlehem: (1) The Church of the Nativity.
Courtesy Israel Government Press Office.

Pseudepigrapha* (2 Esd 13:14) and also in the Dead
Sea scrolls.* It has been identified with 'Ain Karem,
some six miles W of Jerusalem, but Aharoni favors
Ramet Rahel, a hill between Bethlehem* and
Jerusalem.

BIBLIOGRAPHY: Y. Aharoni, IEJ 6 (1950), 102–111;
137–157; ARC 18 (1965), 15–25.

RKH

BETHLEHEM (beth'lə hem; Heb. בֵּית־לֶחֶם, bêṭle-
ḥem). 1. A town in Zebulunite territory (Josh 19:15),
generally identified with Beit Lahm, c. 11 km. (7 mi.)
NW of Nazareth.*

2. A Judean town, home of David and birthplace
of Jesus, located about 10 km. (6 mi.) SW of Jerusalem* on a road linking that city with Hebron* and
the Negev.* It was first mentioned in the Amarna
Letters* (fifteenth to fourteenth centuries B.C.) in a
complaint about the town (Bit-Lahmi) going over to
the Habiru* (ANET, 489). The earlier name of Bethlehem was Ephrath (Gen 35:19), and it was known
as Bethlehem Judah or Bethlehem Ephrathah to distinguish it from the Zebulunite Bethlehem. In the
Middle Bronze Age* the area was visited by Jacob,
and there Rachel died (Gen 35:16ff.), being buried
between Bethel* and Bethlehem. The city was most
renowned because of its association with David and
the fact that it was also proclaimed as the birthplace
of the Messiah (Mic 5:2). No archaeological remains
of the first three Christian centuries have been recovered from the site, although a cave* where Jesus
was supposed to have been born (cf. Matt 2:1–16;
Luke 2:14f.; John 7:42) was mentioned by Justin
Martyr. In the fourth century Constantine constructed a basilica* over a group of caves, though
whether the one referred to by Justin Martyr was
included or not is unknown. Emperor Justinian (A.D.

527–65) rebuilt and extended Constantine's shrine, and in the medieval period further modifications were made. However, excavations at the Church of the Nativity have thrown no light upon the location of Christ's birthplace.

BIBLIOGRAPHY: R. W. Hamilton, *QDAP*, 3 (1933), 1–8; E. T. Richmond, id. 5 (1936), 75–81; L. H. Vincent, *RB* (1936), 545–74; F.-M. Abel, *Géographie de la Palestine*, 2 (1938), 276–77; J. W. Crowfoot, *Early Churches in Palestine* (1941), 22–30, 77–85; G. W. Van Beek, *IDB*, 1 (1962), 394–95; C. Kopp, *The Holy Places of the Gospels* (1963), 1–47; H. G. Andersen, *ZPEB*, 1 (1975), 538–40; M. Stekelis and M. Avi-Yonah, *EEHL*, 1 (1975), 198–206.

RKH

BETHPHAGE (beth′fə jē; Gr. βηθφαγή, *Bethphagé*). A village near Bethany* on the SE slope of the Mount of Olives;* referred to in Matt 21:1, Mark 11:1, and Luke 19:29; to be identified with Beth Page mentioned in the Talmud where it is suggested Bethphage was a suburb of Jerusalem* and lay outside the wall of the city.*

Bethphage has been located either beyond Bethany (Jerome, Letter 108,) or, rather, W of Bethany toward Jerusalem, about 1 km. (.5 mi.) E of the summit of the Mount of Olives. This last site was accepted by the Crusaders. Here in 1877 was found a stone with frescoes and inscriptions, one a picture showing the two disciples untying the donkey* and colt. The stone is preserved in the Franciscan Chapel at Bethphage. In the same vicinity were found caves,* coins,* cisterns,* pools,* a wine* press, and tombs of various types. All of this points to occupation from the second century B.C. to around the eighth century A.D.

Of special interest is the troughlike tomb twenty-one, with its rolling stone and its graffiti* inscriptions, one in Greek* and the other in archaic Semitic. It also showed signs depicting crosses, trees, palms, harps, and squares.

See BETHANY; MOUNT OF OLIVES.

BIBLIOGRAPHY: E. G. Kraeling, *Bible Atlas* (1956), 397–98; S. J. Saller and E. Testa, *The Archaeological Setting of the Shrine at Bethphage* (1961); *CCSL*, CLXXV (1965), 122; J. Finegan, *The Archaeology of the NT* (1969), 90–91.

WHM

BETHSAIDA (beth sā′ə də). The original home of Philip, Andrew, and his brother Peter, Bethsaida was located, it seems, E of the upper Jordan, not far from the debouchment of the river into the northern end of the lake. Remains in the locality suggest that there was a double site of considerable size some 90 m. (295 ft.) above lake level, one part standing c. 3.22 km. (2 mi.) from the shore, and the other, a fishing village, situated by the lake. The former may be the Julias which Philip the Tetrarch created out of Bethsaida and promoted to importance at the expense of the lakeside community. The site of the larger community is called Et Tell, that of the smaller el-'Araj. An aqueduct* and a road* of Roman type link the two places, and at Et Tell the remains of a

city wall* built of well-cut stone and an ancient mosaic* may be seen. The archaeological evidence therefore appears to support the geographical deductions to be made from the Gospels.

BIBLIOGRAPHY: C. Kopp, *Dominican Studies*, 3 (1950), 10–40; E. G. Kraeling, *Bible Atlas* (1956), 376–77, 386ff.; R. L. Alden, *ZPEB*, 1 (1975), 542–43.

EMB

BETH SHAN, BETH SHEAN (beth shan′, beth shē′ən; Heb. בֵּית שְׁאָן, *bêṯ šeʾān*). A town located at the junction of the Jordan and Jezreel valleys. Its ancient name, which appeared with variants in Egyptian, Akkadian,* and Hebrew texts from the fifteenth century B.C. onward, has been preserved in the modern village of Beisān, standing close to Tell el-Husn, the site of Beth Shan.

The earliest occupational levels went back to c. 3000 B.C., and in the Early Bronze Age* an important Canaanite* city was constructed there, though without any defensive wall. During the Amarna* Age it was occupied by Thutmose III after the battle of Megiddo* (c. 1468 B.C.) and fortified, presumably as a garrison town. This was the beginning of three centuries of dependence on Egypt,* reflected in the following century in one of the Amarna Letters,* which reported that "men of Gath-Carmel are garrisoned in Beth-Shan." Thirteen inscribed hieroglyphic* monuments or carved reliefs have been recovered from this period of Egyptian dominance. A statue* of Ramses III (Level VI) may have commemorated his second defeat of the Sea Peoples* in Galilee c. 1187 B.C.

Although Beth Shan had been allotted to Manasseh* (Josh 17:11), it was too difficult to overthrow (Josh 17:16; Judg 1:27) and became Israelite only under David. This would explain why no violent destruction has been found at the site between the Bronze and the Iron Age* levels. By 950 B.C. Beth Shan had been incorporated into Solomon's* fiscal organization, being included with Taanach* and Megiddo in the fifth administrative district (1 Kings 4:12). Under Rehoboam the city was sacked by Shishak* c. 926 B.C. (1 Kings 14:25) and was not founded again until Hellenistic times, when it was known also as Scythopolis.* It was one of the Ten Towns (the Decapolis*). It contained a mixed population of Jews* and Gentiles (2 Macc 12:29) who lived together peaceably. John Hyrcanus captured the city in 107 B.C., but it was later occupied by Pompey and remained a free city until the Arab conquest in A.D. 636. Many artifacts* from the Roman period have been recovered, including inscriptions and extensive mosaic* floors. There are some striking remains, notably the Greco-Roman theater.*

See SCYTHOPOLIS.

BIBLIOGRAPHY: A. Rowe, *The Topography and History of Beth-Shan* (1930); id., *The Four Canaanite Temples of Beth-Shan* (1940); G. M. Fitzgerald, in D. W. Thomas, ed., *Archaeology and OT Study* (1967), 185–96, with bibliography; J. M. Houston, *ZPEB*, 1 (1975), 543–45; F. James, A. Kempinski, and N. Tzori, *EEHL*, 1 (1975), 207–28.

RKH

Aerial view of Tell el-Husn and the Greco-Roman theater at Beth Shan. (*See also photo under* DECAPOLIS.) Courtesy Israel Government Press Office.

BETH SHEMESH (beth shē'mesh; Heb. בֵּית שֶׁמֶשׁ, *bêṭ šemeš*, "temple of the sun deity"). Several pre-Israelite settlements were known by this name. 1. A fortified Canaanite* city allocated to Naphtali (Josh 19:32–38), perhaps appearing in the nineteenth-century B.C. Egyptian Execration Texts* as *bwtšmš*. From the evidence of Judg 1:33 a site in upper Galilee* seems indicated, and Tell er-Ruweisi has been proposed accordingly.

2. In Josh 19:22 a Beth Shemesh near the Jordan is mentioned in connection with the border area between Issachar and Naphtali. The most probable site is Khirbet Shamsin in lower Galilee, although some authorities have suggested the modern el-'Abeidiyeh, S of the Sea of Galilee.

3. The most familiar town known as Beth Shemesh was located on the northern border of Judah* between Chesalon and Timnah* (Josh 15:10). It was also known as Ir Shemesh (Josh 19:41), and Mount Heres (Judg 1:35). The site was identified by E. Robinson with the modern Tell er-Rumeileh, to the W of 'Ain Shems and about 20 km. (12 mi.) W of Jerusalem.*

Excavations show the earliest settlements occurring c. 2000 B.C., and in the Middle and Late Bronze Ages* it was a heavily fortified Canaanite stronghold, though unmentioned in the Amarna Letters.* In Late Bronze Age levels a clay tablet written in the cuneiform* script of Ugarit* was discovered. Beth Shemesh was evidently captured in the period of the Judges (cf. Josh 21:16; 1 Chron 6:59) and was the place to which the plague-ridden Philistines* returned the captured ark* (1 Sam 6:10–7:2). David apparently strengthened the fortifications (Level IIa), but its occupation ended c. 918 B.C., when Shishak* invaded Judah (1 Kings 14:25–28). About 790 B.C. Joash of Israel defeated Amaziah of Judah near Beth Shemesh (2 Kings 14:11). It fell to the Philistines in the time of Ahaz (2 Chron 28:18) but was recaptured for Judah by Tiglath-Pileser* III. It was destroyed by Nebuchadnezzar* in the sixth century B.C.

4. An Egyptian city (Jer 43:13 KJV), also known as Heliopolis.*

BIBLIOGRAPHY: F.-M. Abel, *Géographie de la Palestine*, 2 (1938), 292; Y. Aharoni, *The Land of the Bible* (1966), 133, 150, 200–51, 286–87, 298–99; A. F. Rainey, *ZPEB*, 1 (1975), 545–48; G. E. Wright, in M. Avi-Yonah, ed., *EEHL*, 1 (1975), 248–53.

RKH

BETH ZUR (beth zûr; Heb. בֵּית צוּר, *bêṭ ṣûr*; LXX βηθσουρα, *bēthsura*, "house or place of rock"). A town in Judah* 6.5 km. (4 mi.) N of Hebron.* It was a Caananite* city assigned to the tribe of Judah (Josh 15:58). In 1 Chron 2:45 Beth Zur is a patronym of the Son of Maon, a descendant of Hebron. The occurrence of the names of several nearby towns in this ostensibly genealogical passage probably reflects the Hebrew settlement patterns in the centuries after the conquest. If so, the village was colonized by inhabitants of Maon, a town 16 km. (10 mi.) S of Hebron. Rehoboam fortified Beth Zur along with a number of other cities in the S of Judah (2 Chron 11:7). Apparently it was one of the places captured by Pharaoh Shishak* in Rehoboam's fifth year, when the Egyptians* invaded with "twelve hundred chariots* and sixty thousand horsemen and the innumerable troops of Libyans, Sukkites and Cushites" (2 Chron 12:3). A contingent from the "half-district of Beth Zur" contributed to Nehemiah's rebuilding of the wall of Jerusalem. The town later became a frontier fort between Judah and Edom.* As it commanded the southern highway from Jerusalem,* it figured largely in the struggles of the Maccabean* era, with Judas winning a major victory over the Seleucid general Lysias here in 165 B.C. and later being compelled to withdraw until Simon reoccupied it in 145 B.C. (1 Macc 4:28–35; 6:48–54; 11:65–67). Beth-sura was the strongest Hasmonean fortress in Judah, according to Josephus (Jos. Antiq. 13.5.6), but apparently it declined in the Byzantine period. The ruins of Beth Zur are located on a hill known in Arabic as Khirbet et-Tubeiqah, about .8 km. (.5 mi.) NW of the Crusader tower* called Burj es Sur. Archaeological excavations were undertaken here by the American Schools of Oriental Research under O. R. Sellers and W. F. Albright in 1931 and again in 1957. The archaeological evidence fits nicely into the biblical references. Middle Bronze Age* Hyksos* fortifications reflect the city's earlier history. It was apparently founded about 1750 B.C., but a destruction in the fifteenth century, presumably by Thutmose III, left the town vacant until the Israelite settlement in the early twelfth century.

The Maccabean remains were extensive, comprising houses,* shops, reservoirs, and fortifications which included a citadel fortress 35 by 40 m. (115 by 131 ft.) in size. Three successive fortresses were traced from the foundations as excavated. The first is probably from the Persian (see SUSA) period. The second, more oriental in plan, likely was built by Judas Maccabaeus between 165 and 163 B.C. The third is Hellenistic and was probably erected by Bacchides. There is a striking parallelism, according to Albright, between the dates indicated by the coins* and Rhodian jar handles and the history of the site as reported in The First Book of Maccabees.

See HEBRON; HYKSOS; JUDAH; MACCABEES; SHISHAK.

BIBLIOGRAPHY: O. R. Sellers and W. F. Albright, "The First Campaign of Excavations at Beth-Zur," BASOR, 43 (1931), 2–13; O. R. Sellers, "The 1957 Campaign at Beth-Zur," BA, 21 (1958), 71–76.

JEJ

BETROTHAL. See MARRIAGE.

BEZER. See BOZRAH.

BIAINI (BIAINILI). See URARTU.

BIREH. See AI.

BIRS NIMRUD. See BORSIPPA; CALAH.

BISHOP. See EPISKOPOS.

BISITUN. See BEHISTUN INSCRIPTION.

BIT GABBAR. See ZINJERLI.

BITHYNIA (bi thi′ ni ə; Gr. βιθυνια, Bithunia). A Roman province of Tracian origin, located in the NW part of Asia Minor,* bordered on the N by the Black Sea, on the W by the Propontis and the Thracian Bosporus, on the E by the city Heracleia, and on the S by the Mysian* Mount Olympus. Bithynia is mentioned in 1 Peter 1:1 and in Acts 16:7 where it is said the Holy Spirit did not allow Paul to carry the gospel to this place.

A number of Bithynia's cities show archaeological remains. Of two important western cities, Nicomedia shows evidences of Hellenistic and Roman citadel fortifications, while Nicaea has remains of a massive wall* from Roman times. Chalcedon had its copper mines and semiprecious stones, while Prusa at Mount Olympus, with its sulphur and thermal springs, appears to have been a medical center (see MEDICINE).

In the E mountainous area at Prusias on the Hypius River are remains of a strong fortification of ancient pre-Roman walls, as well as a Roman theater.*

The city of Bithynium farther to the E shows remains around the acropolis* of a wall of polygonal masonry, an evidence of early settlement. At Heracleia on the Black Sea, there can still be seen the remains of ancient moles,* or breakwaters, that enclosed its harbor.

BIBLIOGRAPHY: E. Schürer, A History of the Jewish People, 2.2 (1891), 222; D. Magie, Roman Rule in Asia Minor, I (1950), 302–20; C. F. Pfeiffer and H. F. Vos, The Wycliffe Historical Geography of Bible Land (1967), 387.

WHM

BIT-LAHMI. See BETHLEHEM.

BITUMEN. The "pitch," "slime," and "tar" of the OT (cf. Gen 6:14; 11:3; 14:10; Exod 2:3) is bitumen (Heb. kōpher, Akkad. kupru), a natural crude petroleum derivative. Pits of bitumen have been found at Kirkuk in Assyria and at Hit on the Euphrates, from where it was shipped down the river. Bitumen was used as mortar in the outer brickwork of the ziggurat* of Ur.* Abraham possibly was watching a petroleum-fed blaze when he saw judgment fall on Sodom* and Gomorrah.* Josephus calls the Dead Sea* the Asphalt Sea, and asphalt is a bituminous substance. The "oil from the flinty crag" (shale?—Deut 32:13) is almost an exact rendering of "petroleum" (petros—rock; oleum—oil).

See GOMORRAH; SODOM.

BIBLIOGRAPHY: W. Ault, ZPEB, 1 (1975), 623.

EMB

BLOOD GROUPING. In recent years blood grouping from very small quantities (as little as 10 mg.) of dried body tissue has been achieved successfully by Professor R. G. Harrison, Head of the Department of Anatomy, University of Liverpool. Polysaccharides extracted from tissue taken from the mummified bodies of Tutankhamen* and Smenkkhare were mixed with red cells of a group O person (i.e., with no factors A or B). The conventional agglutinative test on this gave the same blood group for each body—A2 and MN. This evidence that these two were brothers, sons of Amenhotep III, is supported by X-ray* examination of the bodies. Although no bodies of persons referred to in Scripture, except some pharaohs, have been recovered, this successful experiment opens the door to the establishment of possible relationships, where archaeological research uncovers skeletons with small quantities of tissue.

A striking example of the possible use of blood grouping has been found in Italy. It is an old controversy as to whether the Etruscans, whose empire held the center and N of the peninsula for centuries (*Roma* itself is an Etruscan word), came down the invasion routes from the N, or, as legend had it, from Asia. It has been found that the blood groupings of central Italy today still correspond to those in certain areas of Asia Minor,* and that in both cases the difference from surrounding peoples is clear. German migrants, in Hungary for some centuries, are similarly said to manifest the same general correspondence with the population of their place of origin. Such research is obviously difficult but could be useful in establishing racial identities and patterns of migration.

See PALAEOSEROLOGY.

GGG and EMB

BOATS. *See* SHIPS.

BODMER PAPYRUS. This manuscript of John's Gospel, complete for the first fourteen chapters, and containing a considerable portion of chapters 15 to 21, was written about the end of the second century. It appears to come from Upper Egypt.* Its discovery was announced by the Bodmer Library of Geneva in 1956, and hence the name.

See PAPYROLOGY; PAPYRUS.

BIBLIOGRAPHY: V. Martin, *Papyrus Bodmer II*, Bibliothèque Bodmer, Geneva (1956), chs. 1–14; id., *Papyrus Bodmer II Supplement* (1958, 1962); chs. 15–21; F. Filson, "The Bodmer Papyri," *BA*, 22.2 (1959), 48ff; J. W. B. Barns, *Muséon*, 75 (1962), 327–29; B. M. Metzger, *The Text of the NT* (1964), 26, 36–42, 80, plate 3.

EMB

BOGHAZKÖY (bō'gäz koi). A Turkish village that has given its name to the nearby ancient Hittite* capital of Hattusa, about 160 km. (100 mi.) E of Ankara. It is an elevated site bounded by valleys, and nearby are tangible evidences of ancient Hittite culture in the form of bas-reliefs* and the remains of large statues.* The site was first examined by a westerner in 1834, when the ruins of a great temple, some rock carvings, and the remains of a defensive wall* that had originally protected the upper part of the city, were described. Sixty years later a French archaeologist found tablets written in an unknown

cuneiform* language, and from 1900 the site was excavated by Hugo Winckler. Ten thousand tablets, most of them fragmentary, were unearthed, some of which were written in Akkadian* and gave evidence of comprising part of the royal archives of Hittite kings who had reigned during the fourteenth and thirteenth centuries B.C. The Hittite language, in which most of the tablets were written, was deciphered by Hrozný in 1915, and as a result the splendor and might of a once-prominent empire of the Bronze Age* came to light again. Since 1931 excavations have continued at the site, apart from an interval caused by World War II, and are being carried on.

From both older and more recent archives of tablets it is evident that Hittite territory was inhabited by several groups of people. The indigenous inhabitants were called Hatti, sometimes designated proto-Hittites, who apparently spoke a language unrelated to Hittite. This latter, Hatti language, which is Indo-European in form, was the mother tongue of another group which entered Anatolia somewhat before 2000 B.C., dispossessed the Hatti, and took over some of their traditions. In terms of the Great Fortress excavations, this period represents Level V, though it reveals virtually nothing about the time when the Hittites arrived, the extent of the indigenous population, or the rapidity with which the Hattic language became obsolete. Hittite itself comprised two major related dialects, Luwian, which was probably spoken in the S and most of Anatolia, and Palaic, which was apparently more common in the N. Hurrian,* in which some texts were written, was Mesopotamian* in origin.

Work at the Great Fortress has established the following levels: post-Hittite (Levels I–II), the Empire period (Level III, c. 1400–1200 B.C.), the Old Hittite period (Level IV), and pre-Hittite (Level V). An early Hittite king, Labarnas, extended his realm to the sea coasts, but the earliest texts come from the time of Hittusilis I, c. 1610 B.C., who conquered parts of northern Syria (*see* ARAM). His successor, Mursilis I, reduced Aleppo* and ended the First Dynasty of Babylon* by a victory c. 1595 B.C. From his archives come much contemporary knowledge of Hittite history and culture. Subsequent Hurrian pressure forced a retrenchment, but c. 1450 B.C. Tudhaliyas regained some Syrian territory, and in the following century the Hittites became a world power. Ramses II* tried unsuccessfully to reduce their influence in 1300 B.C., but a century later the Hittites were suddenly overwhelmed by the Sea Peoples* and became lost to history.

Hittite society was patriarchal, and many of the laws of Telepinus, codified c. 1525 B.C., had affinities with Pentateuchal legislation. However, the Hittites substituted compensation for the Semitic principle of lex talionis (an eye for an eye). The Hittites pioneered the smelting of iron* ore, for which they held a trade monopoly, and introduced the iron-fitted chariot* as a weapon (*see* ARMS AND WEAPONS) of war. Their feudal society stressed loyalty by oath, and from the Empire period there emerged the characteristic Hittite parity and suzerainty treaties. Hittite religion was highly syncretistic, exhibiting strong Hatti and Hurrian influences. Some Hittites may have migrated to Canaan* in the time of Abraham (cf. Gen 23), but otherwise the OT use of "*Hittite*" probably means "native Canaanite."

Palestine as such was always outside the territorial limits of the Hittite empire. When Hittite civilization ended c. 1200 B.C., Syria and Anatolia broke up into petty states, and it was to these Hittites that Solomon* sold Egyptian horses* (2 Chron 1:17). The center of Hittite influence by that time had moved from the ruined Boghazköy to Carchemish,* and the Hittite contemporaries of Ben-hadad were still formidable enough to command respect (cf. 2 Kings 7:6–7).

Individual Hittites are mentioned in OT narratives from Abraham to the early monarchy (cf. Gen 25:9; 26:34; 36:2; 1 Sam 26:6; 2 Sam 11:6 et al.), yet almost all of them bore typical Semitic names, which would reinforce the conclusion that *Hittite* was the rough equivalent of "native Canaanite" (cf. Gen 27:46) and was not a specifically ethnic designation. According to Ezek 16:3,45, Jerusalem* was founded on an admixture of Hittite and Amorite* stock. The Assyrians and Hebrews used the term Hittite to describe inhabitants of the empire and its dependencies, regardless of their ethnic affiliation. The presence of Hittites in Canaan poses certain historical problems, some of which can be explained if the people referred to are regarded as Horites (Hurrians) rather than as citizens of the Hittite Empire. Yet the OT regularly distinguished between the Hivites* (who were Hurrians) and the Hittites (cf. Exod 3:8, 17 et al.). Be that as it may, the ruined buildings at Boghazköy, the massive sculptures now on view, and the abundance of literary materials excavated, all testify eloquently to the stature of a once formidable Near Eastern power.

See HITTITES.

BIBLIOGRAPHY: O. R. Gurney, *The Hittites* (1952); I. J. Gelb, *IDB*, 2 (1962), 612–15; O. R. Gurney, *CAH*, 2, part 1 (1973), 228 passim.

RKH

BOOK OF THE DEAD. The common title for the collection of charms and magical spells written on papyrus* and buried with many mummies in Egypt* during most of its history. The book is known from a great many copies and fragments recovered from tombs. In the Old and Middle Kingdom the text was written in hieroglyphics* with the insertion of some small miniatures; in the New Kingdom it was written in hieratic.* There is a wide divergence in the number, form, and order of the incantations.* The text, which was difficult and obscure, was often corrupted and glossed by the scribes, the finest example being the Papyrus of Ani* in the British Museum which is over 26 m. (85 ft.) in length. The scrolls* were often written with blanks to be filled in after they were sold. They were available for any with the means to buy them, and the purchaser's name was inserted in the blanks left for the purpose. Acquittal in the court of the gods was supposedly assured by these documents—an abuse of religion and morality as gross as

the sale of indulgences in Luther's day. Chapter 125, which contains negative protestations of innocence and the declaration of the soul, are the most important for biblical scholarship. The custom of burying the Book of the Dead so degenerated that any old scrap was buried with the corpse in the Roman period.

BIBLIOGRAPHY: E. A. Wallis Budge, *The Book of the Dead* (1898); J. H. Breasted, *A History of Egypt* (1945), 175, 249–50, 571; J. Černý, *Ancient Egyptian Religion* (1952), 57, 87–91, 93–94.

WW

BOOTY AND TRIBUTE. Diligent cataloging by imperial states such as Egypt,* Assyria, and Babylon,* has left masses of information about exactions levied on defeated peoples and about property looted in the activities of imperial war. The lists are suggestive of suffering inflicted on smaller nations but also of the social patterns that produced the treasures carried off. For example, the records of Thutmose III tell of that pharaoh's campaign in Lower Galilee* (c. 1479 B.C.), listing the booty garnered and the people carried into slavery. Apart from Megiddo* the catalog included: "5 of their lords, 1,796 male and female slaves* with their children, 103 men; . . . flat dishes of costly stone and gold,* a large (two handled) vase of the work of Kharu [S Palestine], vases, flat dishes, bowls, drinking vessels, . . . (87) knives,* gold and silver* in rings." Further items were a statue* of beaten silver, with a head of gold and a staff with human faces; ivory,* ebony, and carob wood, wrought with gold; chairs and footstools;* tables of ivory and selected wood;* a staff wrought with gold and costly stones in the fashion of a scepter; and a statue* of the enemy-leader in ebony wrought with gold, the head of which was inlaid with lapis lazuli.*

It is instructive to note the standards of life and civilization in the conquered Canaanite* towns. In the next campaign "this same Pharaoh exacted from the chieftains of the country 103 horses,* 5 chariots* wrought with gold, 5 chariots wrought with electrum, 749 bulls, 5,703 small cattle, flat dishes of gold and of silver, a gold object, probably a horn, inlaid with lapis-lazuli, a bronze* corselet inlaid with gold, 823 jars of incense,* 1,718 jars of honeyed wine,* etc. . . . in addition to a 'chief's daughter with her ornaments of gold and lapis-lazuli,'* and 30 of her slaves, together with 65 other slaves, male and female. In the seventh campaign a tithe was levied on the harvest, which is recorded as comprising 'much grain, grain in the ear, barley, incense, green oil, wine and fruit. . . .' "

These lists were carved in hieroglyphs* in the temple of Amon at Karnak (*see* THEBES), quotations, apparently from written records in other form, for when the account of the storming and looting of Megiddo was described, the narrative used a formula similar to that which often appears in the OT. "Now all that his majesty did to this city, to that wretched foe and his wretched army, was recorded each day by its name . . . [and thereafter] . . . recorded upon a roll of leather* in the temple of Amon to this day" (cf. 1 Kings 14:19).

It was the same with Assyria. "Thus, in the annals

of the king inscribed on the large pavement slabs of the temple of Ninurta in Calah,* the royal residence built by the Assyrian king Ashurnasirpal II* (883–859 B.C.), we read: 'At that time I seized the entire extent of the Lebanon mountain and reached the Great Sea of the Amurru country. . . . The tribute of the sea coast—from the inhabitants of Tyre,* Sidon,* Byblos [see GEBAL], Mahallata, Maiza, Kaiza Amurru . . . gold, silver, tin, copper, copper containers, linen* garments with multi-colored trimmings, large and small monkeys, ebony, boxwood, ivory of walrous tusks . . . their tribute I received and they embraced my feet.' " Shalmaneser III (858–824 B.C.) records on the Black Obelisk (see SHALMANESER, BLACK OBELISK OF), "the tribute of Jehu, son of Omri;* I received from him silver, gold, a golden vase with pointed bottom, golden tumblers, golden buckets, tin,* a staff for the king. . . ."

Such lists, of course, are not necessarily indicative of the products of the defeated community. Thus the same Shalmaneser records that he received tribute from "the sea kings" and from "Arame, man of Gursi." He took in tribute, "silver, gold, large cattle, wine, a couch of whitest gold," but these luxuries were not necessarily part of the countries' normal range of goods.

The history of the conqueror sometimes finds reflection in the records. The Assyrian lists are at first meager. Subsequently, under a determined bureaucracy, they become so detailed as to suggest that tribute was an important and basic item in the empire's economy. Later, dating perhaps from the days of Sargon II,* the lists fall off. The vassal kingdoms, as distinct from the more ruthlessly exploited provinces, at times took a bold measure of the empire's weakness and refused tribute. A letter survives from a ruler of Ararat*: "As to the lapis-lazuli concerning which Your Majesty has written me as follows: 'They should requisition it'—does Your Majesty not know that lapis-lazuli is now high in price and that the country would rebel against me if I had actually requisitioned it? Rather—if it pleases Your Majesty—let a large body of troops come here and let them requisition the lapis-lazuli. And then the king must not consider it a crime [of mine] when I will not eat with

them [the Assyrian soldiers], nor drink water with them, nor accompany them, nor even rise before your messenger, nor inquire of him about Your Majesty's health, when they come here."

The inflow of wealth, as in the latter days of the Roman Republic, created vested interests and a vast bureaucracy, which, on the one hand, made for organized government, but was dangerous at times of royal succession. Great hatred among exploited and conquered peoples was built up, which often aided a new conqueror in overthrowing the present oppressor.

See SHALMANESER, BLACK OBELISK OF.

BIBLIOGRAPHY: J. Pedersen, *Israel: Its Life and Culture*, 3–4 (1940), 1–32; A. G. Barrois, *Manuel D'Archéologie Biblique*, 2 (1953), ch. 16.

EMB

BORDEAUX PILGRIM. An otherwise unidentified pilgrim to the Holy Land in A.D. 333, who recorded brief descriptions of sacred sites in a work entitled *Itinerarium Burdigalense*, translated into English under the title *Itinerary from Bordeaux to Jerusalem* (1887). It is the earliest recorded western pilgrimage to the Holy Land.

BORSIPPA. A Mesopotamian* city located 10 miles SW of Babylon,* famed for the staged temple-tower Ezida, shrine of the god Nabu (Nebo*), patron deity of writing and of scribes. In ancient times, the city* was situated adjacent to a lake, now dry. It is generally associated with Babylon in the texts as a suburb of the capital and is singular among S Mesopotamian cities in having never attained political power of its own apart from that city. It was the chief boast of the proud Babylonian kings that each was "Provider of *Esagila* [the temple of Marduk at Babylon] and of *Ezida*," and this formula was always the primary title in the inscriptions. In the important Akitu (New Year) festival, the king went to Borsippa by boat in order to fetch Nabu, who was to deliver his father Marduk as demanded by the ritual. The next day he returned with Nabu's statue* to Esagila amid general rejoicing.

The city is attested from the Ur* III period, where

One of four registers from black basalt Obelisk depicting tribute received by King Ashurnasirpal II (883-859 B.C.). This register shows men bearing tribute or booty of cloth, vessels, and furniture. Courtesy Carta, Jerusalem.

it is mentioned beside Babylon. It is also referred to in the prologue to the Code of Hammurabi* (iii.10) as a shrine honored by the king. The inscriptions of Shalmaneser (851 B.C.) (see SHALMANESER, BLACK OBELISK OF) and of Eriba-Marduk (782–763 B.C.) associated the city with Babylon. Borsippa joined in the Babylonian revolt of Shamashshumukin against Ashurbanipal* in 651 B.C., but was subdued three years later. The city was so celebrated for its learning that Ashurbanipal commanded its scholarly men specifically (of all the cities in his dominion) to make a collection of tablets from their personal libraries and the archives of the Borsippa temple.

Restless even under the rule of the Chaldean* dynasty, especially Nabonidus,* the city again endorsed revolts which flared under native kings in the Persian period, as attested by contracts dated in the year 482 B.C. Xerxes* crushed the uprising brutally, although the town continued to flourish and was to some extent prosperous, as reflected by the Murashu archive, but evidently the monuments were not repaired or rebuilt. Borsippa helped to preserve the Sumero*-Akkadian* culture through its temple astronomers* and scribes during the Seleucid period. The worship of Nabu continued until about the fourth century A.D., and the city was known even into the Arabic period.

Claudius Rich, as other travelers had done, imaginatively identified the ruin of Birs Nimrud with the Tower of Babel* of the Bible and the temple of Belus of the classical writers. Sir Henry Rawlinson excavated in 1854 to a depth of 5.2 m. (17 ft.) and marked off the size of the base by "laborious tunneling and careful measurement." He was rewarded by the dramatic discovery of a cylinder inscription which allowed him to announce that the ruin was the site of ancient Borsippa. Layard and Rassam added to the knowledge of the dimensions of the tower* in excavations conducted in 1880.

The ziggurat* stood in seven stages, with a base 83 m. (272 ft.) square and a preserved height of 47 m. (153 ft.). Levels 1-3 were each 7.9 m. (26 ft.) high, and stages 4-7 were each 4.6 m. (15 ft.) high, as was the shrine at the top. According to Rawlinson, each stage was supposedly colored according to Chaldean* astrological fancy: black, orange, red, gold, yellow, blue, and silver—representing the sun, moon, and the various planets. The name of the temple on the inscriptions is E-ur-imin-an-ki, "Temple of the seven spheres of heaven and earth."

The upper part of the brick mass is vitrified, this being probably responsible for the rise of Benjamin of Tudela's supposition that it was the Tower of Babel which had been struck by the lightning of divine wrath. Many legal and astronomical texts from the Neo-Babylonian* period and later are known to have come from the city, but scientific excavations have been largely lacking. The ziggurat and temple precinct were partially excavated by the Germans in 1902, but results were disappointing and the publication not extensive.

See ASHURBANIPAL; BABYLON; BABEL, TOWER OF; NABONIDUS; NEBO; ZIGGURAT.

BIBLIOGRAPHY: H. Rawlinson, *JRAS*, 17 (1860),

1–34; R. Koldewey, "Die Tempel von Babylon und Borsippa," *Wissenschaftliche Voroffentlichungen der deutschen Orient-Gesselschaft*, 15 (1911), 50–59; E. Unger, *Reallexikon der Assyriologie* 1 (1937), 402–29.

JEJ

BOTTLES. See VESSELS.

BOUNDARY STONES. Boundaries were marked between fields, districts, even national and tribal regions, by stones, often elaborately inscribed (cf. Gen 31:51–52). To remove a boundary stone was an offense under Babylonian law. When the Kassites* from the eastern hill country took over Babylonia (see CHALDEA) at the beginning of the sixteenth century B.C., the kudurru, or boundary stone, became a title deed, and the inscriptions that define their significance often contain valuable historical and geographical evidence, sometimes recording royal grants of land, reasons for the grant, and name of the donor. The usual conclusion consisted of a list of curses on anyone tempted to remove the landmark. For example, the kudurru of Ritti Marduk in the British Museum contains an account of a campaign of Nebuchadnezzar* I against the raiding Elamites. Amid fearful heat and sandstorm the chariot* commander Ritti Marduk did splendid service. In return he received a considerable gift of territory. The curse runs in part:

"Whensoever in after-time, a son of Khabban, or any other man who may be appointed governor of Namar or prefect of Namar, whether he be small or great, whoever he may be, in respect of the towns of Bît-Karziabku which the king has freed from the jurisdiction of Namar, shall not fear the king or his gods, . . . or shall incite a simple man, or a deaf man, or a blind man, or an evilly-disposed man, to break in pieces this memorial with a stone, or shall destroy it by fire, or cast it into the river, or bury it in a field where it cannot be seen; may all the great gods whose names are invoked in heaven and upon earth curse that man with a curse of wrath. . . ."

The Instruction of Amenemopet* similarly forbids interference, as do both Greek and Roman law. Deuteronomy twice warns against the offense (19:14; 27:17), which became a symbol of defection (Prov 22:28; 23:10). Defectors from the Qumran* community were called "removers of the landmark."

BIBLIOGRAPHY: C. Wilson, *Exploring Bible Backgrounds*, ill. facing 64; E. A. Wallis Budge, *Babylonian Life and History* (1925), 156–59; L. W. King, *Babylonian Boundary Stones in the British Museum* (1912); *ANET* (1955), 422.

EMB

BOW AND ARROW. See ARMS AND WEAPONS.

BOXING. Direct allusions to boxing in Ancient Near Eastern sources are sparse. Wrestling* was well known to both the Sumerians* and the Egyptians* and was depicted accordingly in artistic representations.

In one of his metaphors from the games,* Paul

writes: "Therefore I do not run like a man running aimlessly; I do not fight like a man beating the air" (1 Cor 9:26). Literary references to boxing are numerous and cover the whole range of Greek and Latin* literature. Archaeological evidence is meager, but a statue* of a boxer in the Louvre shows the cestus, or arrangement of leather* bands around knuckle and lower forearm, that protected the wearer. When reinforced with metal knobs and spikes, as in Roman boxing, it gravely damaged the opponent. Paul is referring to "shadow boxing," as it was called in Greek, a form of pugilistic training. He knew the fight was real. The methods of pugilism, along with the huge muscular development of the boxers, may be seen on the cone-shaped Boxer Vase and various seals* from Cnossos, the chief city of ancient Crete.

EMB

BOZRAH (boz' rə; Heb. בָּצְרָה, *bŏṣrāh*). (1) An Edomite city SE of the Dead Sea* and N of Petra,* identified with modern Buseirah. Biblical data mentions it as the home of an early king of Edom* (Gen 36:33). It was a principal city* of Edom, if not the only royal one, and would have been well situated to control the King's Highway.* Amos mentions the fortresses of Bozrah (Amos 1:12).

Excavations were conducted by Crystal M. Bennett from 1971–76 under the sponsorship of the British School of Archaeology in Jerusalem,* the British Academy, and the Palestine Exploration Fund. The city proved to be 7.8 ha. (19 a.) in size, with upper and lower cities situated on steep terraces above the Wadi Hamayideh.

The first two seasons opened exposures of over 700 sq. m. (7500 sq. ft.) and distinguished two main periods of occupation. Subsequent work defined two other periods, with subphases in some areas. The major building period was that of what the excavator called the "Plaster floor and wall people," found on the acropolis* in area A. Originally dated to the eighth century B.C., the finds were subsequently labeled eighth/seventh century and then dated mainly to the seventh century.

The buildings were undoubtedly administrative, palace, or temple structures guarded by a complex of buildings to the S (area C), which overlooks the only easy approach to the site. A massive fortification wall* was built on the terraces (which are likely those mentioned by Amos). In one period the wall was a casemate* structure. Six subphases of the stratification (*see* STRATIGRAPHY) were reported from the defenses. The "palaces" resemble Assyrian open court buildings, an indication of strong Assyrian influence in the period and a factor which comports well with the historical evidence.

The other periods of occupation include some reuse of the structures in the Persian period, with the latest evidence being Nabataean* and Roman. There is some evidence of an earlier level than the "palace" period, the so-called "mud-brick" phase. This could be ninth century B.C. at the earliest. The problem of the reasonably certain identification of the site with biblical Bozrah in spite of the absence of "Exodus period" evidence has been discussed by the excavator, but

without a solution. It should be pointed out that the passage in Num 20:17 does not specifically mention Bozrah, so there is no biblical requirement for the existence of the city at that time.

Domestic architecture was found in area D, and some of the most beautiful Iron Age II* pottery* ever found was located in area B. This strengthens the claim of the city to the title of royal citadel,* since the finds compare with those from Samaria.*

Important inscriptional evidence includes a Nabataean altar,* some graffiti,* a jar handle with two archaic letters (perhaps as early as the ninth century), and a three-line seal.* The seal was read by Lemaire as the name MLK B'L, "Baal* reigns," but corrected by Puech to "belonging to MLK LB' servant of the king."

(2) A city of Moab, the Bezer of the Mesha Stele,* perhaps Umm el-Amad near Madaba.

(3) A large town of the Hauran, modern Busra, or Busra Eski Sham, mentioned as Busruna in the Amarna letters.*

BIBLIOGRAPHY: M. Bennett, "Excavations at Buseira, Southern Jordan," *Levant*, 5 (1973); 6 (1974); 7 (1975); 9 (1977).

JEJ

BRAK. *See* HABOR.

BRASS. *See* BRONZE.

BRICK. *See* BUILDING MATERIALS.

BRICKKILN. *See* KILN.

BRIDLE. *See* HARNESS.

BRONZE. This metal is an alloy of approximately 90 percent copper and 10 percent tin;* it is harder and therefore more useful than pure copper. The secret of its manufacture was discovered during the fourth millennium B.C., and by c. 3000 B.C. it was rapidly replacing stone in the making of tools* and weapons (*see* ARMS AND WEAPONS). This was the start of the Bronze Age, which is generally divided into three periods: Early (c. 3000–2000 B.C.), Middle (c. 2000–1500 B.C.), and Late (c. 1500–1200 B.C.).

Archaeology has demonstrated that the use of bronze was introduced into Palestine c. 1900 B.C. There is no certain evidence that bronze was used in Palestine in the Early Bronze Age, and even in the Middle Bronze Age it was not common. It was brought into Palestine by Canaanite* infiltrators who settled in the area and whose culture overlaid that of the Amorites.* The Israelites entered Palestine during the Late Bronze Age. It was the Philistines* who brought the Iron Age* to Palestine. Their knowledge of iron* technology gave them an initial advantage over the Israelites, reflected in such OT passages as Judg 1:19 and 4:3. The fact that Goliath* had an iron spearhead is significant in this respect (1 Sam 17:7). The efforts of the Philistines to deny to the Israelites the knowledge of iron and so maintain their advantage over them are apparent in 1 Sam

13:19–21; and it was not until the Israelites, under Saul and David, conquered the Philistines that Israel passed from the Bronze to the Iron Age.

In the OT bronze is regarded as more valuable than iron but less valuable than gold* or silver* (Isa 60:17; cf. Dan 2:32–33); but there was a certain type of bronze that was as precious as gold (Ezra 8:27). Considerable use was made of it for decoration—*see* especially the account in 1 Kings 7:14ff. of bronze work in the temple,* for which Solomon* employed a skilled craftsman* from Tyre.* It was used also for armor (1 Sam 17:5–6), chains (Judg 16:21), cymbals (1 Chron 15:19), and bolts for doors (1 Kings 4:13). In its metaphorical use it denoted strength and durability (as in Job 6:12; 40:18; 41:27). God's invincible power is such that even bronze doors and iron bars cannot stop Him (Ps 107:16; Isa 45:2).

In Hebrew the same word denotes both bronze and pure copper; this is doubtless because of their similarity. The KJV uses the word "brass," which at that time denoted any alloy of copper. But "brass" now denotes an alloy of copper and zinc.

See GOLIATH; METALLURGY.

BIBLIOGRAPHY: J. R. Partington, *A Textbook of Inorganic Chemistry* (1950 ed.), 718, 722; D. R. Bowes, *ZPEB*, 1 (1975), 655–56.

WFR

BRONZE AGE. The historical/archaeological period of human history between the Stone Age (*see* PALAEOLITHIC; MESOLITHIC; NEOLITHIC) and the Iron Age,* lasting from c. 3000–1200 B.C. As the name implies, this period was characterized by the development and use of bronze* for making tools* and weapons (*see* ARMS AND WEAPONS).

See also the "Chronological Chart of Archaeological and Historical Periods."

BROOCH. The word *brooch* describes an ornamental clasp with a tongue and catch, which served functionally as a safety pin. The term may also refer to the bracelet (Exod 35:22) common in Palestine and usually made of bronze.* Later bracelets were occasionally made of glass,* and sometimes of iron* or silver.* Gold* bracelets were uncommon, although those referred to in Exod 35:22 were probably made from this metal. They appear to have been worn by both men and women. When the term *brooch* was being used, its most specific meaning was that of the fibula,* and this varied in shape from a design similar to that of a safety pin to a brooch of semicircular or triangular design. The brooch came into common usage in Palestine in the seventh century B.C. Earlier examples have been found, dating to the tenth century B.C., these perhaps being the immediate successors of the toggle pin. The brooch, worn by both sexes to fasten garments, appeared in a variety of ornamental designs, being made with both spring- and hinge-type pins.

Many brooches were found by Schliemann at Mycenae,* some dating to the thirteenth century B.C. Later ones proved to be of the common fibula type. The fibula Praenestina, dating from the seventh century B.C., is famous for its early Latin inscription

Elbow-type fibula from Iron Age II found at Tell Beit Mirsim. Courtesy Israel Dept. of Antiquities and Museums.

naming owner and maker. The brooch was found at Praeneste in Latium and was designed to hold a draped garment at the shoulder. It would seem to have been an emblem of rank. In Egypt* the term *brooch* sometimes referred to the pectoral which was worn as an ornament, often on the mummy of a king or high dignitary.

Judg 8:21,26 refers to ornaments and chains on the necks of camels* and the Hebrew is translated "crescents" in the RSV. These seem to have been moon-shaped brooches or pendants that the animals wore, either for superstitious purposes or to denote the rank of the owner. Isa 3:18 also mentions crescents (cf. 1 Macc 10:89; 11:58; 14:44). In general the buckles, pins, clasps, and brooches of the Ancient Near East have been classified by some writers in terms of the violin bow, the semicircular, the semicircular ornamental, the spring, and the hinge types. The antecedent of the fibula was the toggle, or shortened, pin.

This class of artifact* unfortunately has escaped typological analysis. Such items frequently receive little attention, and where they do are designated as pins, points, awls, and the like. Pins may be divided into two classes: (1) the pin with a self or curled head, and (2) the pin with a metal or wooden head attached. They are usually found in connection with human remains, which indicates their usage as fasteners for clothing.* Many pins were found in the Jericho* excavations. Kenyon suggested that pins were associated with female burials. However it seems most probable that they were used universally, as buttons are today. Both brooches and pins, their predecessors, evidently had uniform usage throughout Palestine.

BIBLIOGRAPHY: J. M. Myers, *IDB*, 1 (1962), 467, 733; M. H. Heicksen, *ZPEB*, 1 (1975), 657; H. G. Stigers, id., 881.

MHH

BROTHERS, STORY OF THE TWO. *See* TWO BROTHERS, STORY OF THE.

BUBASTIS (bū ba′ stis). A site in the eastern Delta region of Egypt,* about 56 km. (35 mi.) NE of modern Cairo, named in Ezek 30:17 (KJV "Pi-beseth," Heb. פִּיבֶסֶת), as ripe for judgment. It came to prominence in the Twenty-Second Dynasty of Egypt when a soldier of Libyan descent seized power about 945 B.C. and proclaimed himself pharaoh. This man, Sheshonk I, ruled from his palace at Bubastis and

(1) Canaanite arch (19th to 18th century B.C.) of the city of Laish (Dan) constructed of mud brick. The entrance of the arch was blocked in antiquity. (2) Stone steps leading to gate from E. (3) Revetment to strengthen tower (4). Courtesy Hebrew Union College, Jewish Institute of Religion.

became known to the Palestinians as Shishak.* In the fifth year of Rehoboam of Judah* he invaded Canaan* (1 Kings 14:25), bringing it within the sphere of Egyptian political influence once again, as it had been formerly in the Amarna* Age (fifteenth and fourteenth centuries B.C.). His campaign was commemorated in a relief, on a temple wall at Karnak (see THEBES). Among the Palestinian place-names included were Taanach,* Beth Shan,* Gibeon,* Bethhoron, Megiddo,* and Arad.* On this relief mention was also made of the "field of Abram." The site of Bubastis was described by Napoleon's band of savants in 1798 and was visited by Sir Gardiner Wilkinson in 1840 and by Naville for the Egyptian Exploration Fund in 1887–89.

BIBLIOGRAPHY: Herodotus 2.59 gives an account of the vast, obscene pilgrimage that was held every year, a sort of aquatic festival for Bastet, the cat-headed lioness deity; E. Naville, *Bubastis* (1891); B. Porter and R. L. B. Moss, *Topographical Bibliography of Ancient Egyptian Hieroglyphic Texts, Reliefs and Paintings*, 5 (1934), 27–35; A. Bowling, *ZPEB*, 4 (1975), 789.   RKH

BUCKET. *See* VESSELS.

BUILDING MATERIALS. *Stone.* Various forms of stone and rock building in Palestine range from Gal-

ilee* basalt to coastal sandstone (as at Caesarea*). Harder limestone was available in the hill country. A good deal of competently dressed stone for common building is to be seen in Israelite Samaria.* Hewn stone was very commonly used to reinforce rubble walls.* Herod's builders (see HEROD, BUILDING ACTIVITIES OF) were able to manage stone blocks up to 9 m. (30 ft.) in length. The great stones in the Wailing Wall,* and the other stonework associated with the foundation structure of Herod's temple* are surviving illustrations. Roman building set great store by the acquisition of the hardest stone, and one reason for the garrisoning of the Red Sea coast of Egypt* was to defend the quarries in the area. Trajan's column was built of this Red Sea stone. A word commonly used for square hewn stone in archaeological description is ashlar.*

Wood. Scientific analysis of wood* remains from drier parts of Palestine show that imported pine and cedar* were commonly used. Wood was quite common in Palestine until the days of Turkish deforestation, and the accounts of woodworking in the specifications for the Mosaic tabernacle and the Solomonic Temple show that craftsmen* were available who were completely familiar with this material. The successful extraction or tracing of wooden remains, especially in damp conditions, is a major technical problem of archaeology, described by Sir Mortimer

Wheeler in *Archaeology from the Earth* (1956), 99–103.

Bricks. Unburnt brick, dried in the sun, was a common building material. It was sometimes mixed with chopped straw that acted as a binding element even after decay, for the process of breakdown left chemical products that added flexibility to the material. In the tomb of Rekhmire, vizier* of Thutmose III, a mural was found depicting slaves* making bricks from Nile straw and sand. An accompanying inscription read: "The rod is in my hand; be not idle." Adobe (adorbi, *OCD*) is the name often given to sun-dried brick (see below). In Mesopotamian* areas, the bricks were frequently kiln*-baked, and Gen 11:3 is the first literary evidence for a product of some toughness—"they used brick instead of stone." R. Koldewey (*Excavations at Babylon* [1914], 75–82) has a description of Nebuchadnezzar's* brick making techniques. On Palestinian sites from the whole Bronze Age brick is common, in spite of the abundance of stone. Brick has the great advantage of prefabrication. The mudbrick of many sites, especially in Egypt, is a difficulty in archaeological investigation because of its similarity to the covering and surrounding soil. In such cases, as Sir Mortimer Wheeler puts it, "the trained workman is an asset . . . The texture of the earth, the feel of it, the sound of it as the pick or shovel strikes it, are all factors which . . . tell the experienced digger when he is, or is not, on a mudbrick wall" (*Archaeology From the Earth* [1954], 104). Bricks are frequently valuable in chronology.* They are sometimes stamped with the name of the reigning monarch; Nebuchadnezzar is most common. The Romans made a very good baked-clay brick and a chronology can be established for Rome* itself, though not, it appears, for elsewhere (Wheeler, op. cit., 54). The Roman brick was somewhat flat; hence *testa*, from *torreo* "to bake," meant both a brick and a tile. Combined generously with mortar, the Roman brick is recognizable in walls. Legionary engineers* stamped the number of their division on such bricks or tiles.

Mud brick with straw or stubble reinforcing may still be seen in the Middle East and even in Greece. Use of this binding was not invariable practice, however. An Egyptian papyrus* records the complaint of a contractor: "I am not provided with anything. There are no men for brick-making, and no straw in the district" (cf. Exod 5:7). At Pithom,* as at other Nineteenth and Twentieth Dynasty sites near Luxor* (*see also* THEBES), the builders used "bricks without straw," i.e., bricks having a finely-chopped stubble content rather than the more bulky straw from threshing operations.

See HEROD, BUILDING ACTIVITIES OF; NEBUCHADNEZZAR; PITHOM; VIZIER; WAILING WALL.

BIBLIOGRAPHY: N. Glueck, "Ezion-Geber—City of Bricks with Straw," *BA*, 3.4 (1940), 51–55; M. Wheeler, *Archaeology From the Earth* (1956), esp. ch. 6; S. G. Brade-Birks, *Teach Yourself Archaeology* (1953), ch. 16–17.

EMB

BUILDING METHODS, FORMS, AND FEATURES. *See* APSE; ARCH; ARCHITRAVE; ASHLAR MASONRY; ATRIUM; BARREL VAULT; BUILDING MATERIALS; CAPITAL; CAPSTONE; CASEMATE WALLS; CELLA; COLUMBARIUM; CORNICE; DOLMEN; ENGINEERING; ENTABLATURE; HYPOCAUST; HYPOSTYLE; LOCULUS; MASTABA; MENHIR; MORTAR; PEDIMENT; PLINTH; PROPYLAEUM. *See also* cross references under ART; BUILDINGS, STRUCTURES, AND EDIFICES.

BUILDINGS, STRUCTURES, AND EDIFICES. *See* ACROPOLIS; AMPHITHEATER; ANTONIA, TOWER OF; BABEL, TOWER OF; BABYLON, HANGING GARDENS OF; CASTLE; COLOSSEUM; ECCE HOMO, ARCH OF; HEROD, BUILDING ACTIVITIES; HERODIUM; HOUSE; PYRAMIDS; STOREHOUSES; SYNAGOGUE; TEMPLE, JERUSALEM; THEATER; TITUS, ARCH OF; TOWERS; WALLS; ZIGGURAT.

BULL. *See* OX.

BUQEIAH. *See* ACHOR, VALLEY OF.

BUSALOSSORUS. *See* NABOPOLASSAR.

BUSEIRAH. *See* BOZRAH.

BUSRA; BUSRA ESKI SHAM; BUSRUNA. *See* BOZRAH.

BUTLER. *See* CUPBEARER.

BYBLOS. *See* GEBAL.

BYZANTINE. When describing a period, it relates to a rather indeterminate era in Near Eastern history, beginning about the fourth century A.D. in Constantinople and associated areas of the Roman Empire. Architecturally it was characterized by the rich use of such ornamentation as domes, circles, round arches* and mosaic* work.

C

CAESAREA (ses ə rē'ə). The settlement lies on the open coast of Palestine. It is a rough and harborless littoral, comprising low sandhills swept by the sea winds and the Mediterranean surf. The coast is strewn with ancient harbor works, where engineers have striven to provide a haven for ships.* The sea has won in every case, and the endless assault of the waves has broken down and swallowed mole* and breakwater all the way up the old Philistine* coast to the jutting promontory of Carmel,* which provides Haifa* with a modicum of shelter from the SW winds.

At Caesarea the Mediterranean surge had its hardest task. Herod the Great (see HEROD, FAMILY OF) spent twelve years, from 25 to 13 B.C., building his great port there. His subtle diplomacy was aimed at serving Augustus,* whose eastern legions kept him in power, and simultaneously conciliating his restless and resentful Jewish subjects. Hence the apparent contradiction of a temple to Augustus, the perron of which can still be seen at Samaria,* and a temple* to Jehovah in Jerusalem.*

Caesarea gave the Romans an entry and a base. The sea wall was a notable triumph of engineering.* How the blocks of limestone, some of them 15 by 3 by 2.7 m. (50 by 10 by 9 ft.), were put in place to form the mole, itself some 61 m. (200 ft.) wide and standing in 180 ft. of water, is not known. It would tax all the resources of a highly mechanized society. The sea wall curved around to form a haven. Behind it, on the low sandy shore, a semicircle of wall protected the town—its houses, racecourse, theater,* and temples. The harbor, however, dwarfed the city, and a coin* of Nero bears the inscription: "Caesarea by the Harbor of Augustus."

Nothing of Herod's harbor is visible from the boulder-strewn shore today, although the dry dock for the galleys may still be traced. The theater with its high curve of seats is prominent. There Pilate for some reason set up an inscription, which was discovered by Professor Antonio Frova, the Italian archaeologist. This slab of stone bears Pilate's name, fragmented and half-obliterated but obviously his, and without accompanying titles or explanation. With the remnant of Pilate's name there are the letters ". . . IBERIEVM." Was the theater near a temple to Tiberius* (a "Tiberium") built by Pilate, so eager to be, as the Jews sneered, "friend of Caesar" (cf. John 19:12)? Further excavations may shed light on this matter.

The preparation of nearby building sites has uncovered the real water supply of the garrison town.

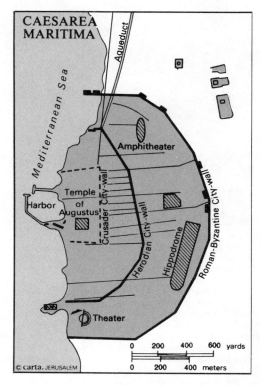

The exposed aqueduct,* so vulnerable to enemy action, was always difficult to reconcile with the prime need for security in Rome's* base and garrison towns. It appears from examination of this well-known structure that it was a task designed for two purposes. Primarily the building of it was to keep the cohorts hardened and occupied, but at the same time it screened the existence of another and less accessible supply of water.

BIBLIOGRAPHY: E. M. Blaiklock, Cities of the NT (1965), ch. 14.

EMB

CAESAREA PHILIPPI. Some archaeological material marks the site of this town, called Philip's Caesarea after the tetrarch who embellished it, to distinguish the town from the foundation on the coast, Herod's port of Caesarea,* which was the Roman bridgehead and garrison headquarters.

Grotto at Caesarea Philippi known as Banias (Arabic corruption of Paneas), dedicated to Greek god Pan. The niche above the grotto contained a statue of Pan as attested by the Greek inscription. Photo: Zev Radovan.

It was a center of worship of the god Pan long before the Roman occupation, and it was prized as being situated upon one of the chief sources of the Jordan. Sir George Adam Smith wrote in his *Historical Geography of the Holy Land* (1899, 474–75), "The place is a very sanctuary of waters, and from time immemorial men have drawn near it to worship. . . . This must have been one of the chief dwellings of the Baalim—perhaps Baal-gad* of the Book of Joshua. When the Greeks came in later times they also felt the presence of deity, and dedicated the grotto, as an inscription still testifies, to Pan and the Nymphs."

Coins contribute similar testimony. Smith's description continues: "The extraordinary mixture of religious and political interests which gathered upon this charming site during the first centuries of our era may be seen at a glance, in all its rich confusion, upon . . . the town's coins which De Saulcy has reproduced in his *Numismatique de la Terra Sainte*, 315, 316: Plate xviii, cf. No. 7 with No. 8. Here, on one coin,* we have the syrinx or pipe of Pan; on a second Pan leaning on a tree and playing a flute; on a third the mouth of the sacred cavern . . . and Pan within . . .; on others the laurelled head of Apollo, a pillared temple, and inside the figure of Poppaea, Nero's wife; . . . various emperors with their title Divus, and the town's own title, 'Caesarea—August,

Sacred and With Rights of Sanctuary—under Paneion.' "

The two religious systems were carried on together. Pan was worshiped in the grotto, while Caesar was worshiped in the white temple that probably stood on the cliff above, the site of the present Muslim shrine of Sheikh Khudr, or St. George. The exact location of Herod's temple is not known. Building stones are strewn all around the area.

See CAESAREA.

BIBLIOGRAPHY: F-M. Abel, *Géographie de la Palestine*, 2 (1938), 297–98; D. Baly, *The Geography of the Bible* (1957), 194–96.

EMB

CAESAR'S HOUSEHOLD. Paul refers to Christians of Caesar's household (Phil 4:22) and also to Christians in the household of Narcissus, the notorious freedman of Claudius.* The latter group probably joined Caesar's household on the fall of Claudius's secretary and the confiscation of his property. "Household," of course, refers to the slave* establishment. We have the testimony of Tertullian (*Apol.* 37.4) and that of Dionysius of Alexandria (quoted by Eusebius in *Hist. Eccl.* 7.10.3), for the presence of considerable groups of Christians in the imperial house, but it was not in the interests of Christians to announce their presence unnecessarily by name in the first three centuries, so archaeological evidence for their presence is of infrequent occurrence.

Professor G. Clarke of Melbourne University, writing recently in *HTR* (64.121–24), suggests that *CIL* 6.8987 is a Christian epitaph. It is of uncertain date, but possibly late second or early third century. It runs, "Alexander, Augg. ser., fecit se biuo Marco, filio dulcisimo, Caputa 5 fricesi, qui deputabatur inter bestito, res. qui uixit an.nis XVIII, mensibu VIIII, diebu. V. peto a bobis, 10 fra.tres boni, per unum deum, ne quis (h)un(c) tite.lo moles [tet] pos mort [em meam]. Rome. Via Salaria Vetus" ("Alexander, slave of the Augusti, erected in his own lifetime [this tomb] to Marcus his very dear son, a pupil of *Ad Caput Africae*, who was a keeper of the wardrobe and who lived 18 years, 9 months, and 5 days. I beg of you, kind brethren, by the one god, to prevent anyone molesting this tombstone after my death").

The invocation "by the one god" is unobtrusively worded, but obviously Christian, and "brethren" is a common form of Christian address. Here, then, are in all likelihood a Christian father and son. The school, *"ad Caput Africae,"* referred to in the epitaph was a prestigious school on the Caelian Hill, well staffed and equipped for the training of selected slaves for administrative posts. Professor Clarke comments of the college: "Its best pupils would be well read, well spoken; they would expect to marry non-servile wives (though not yet manumitted themselves), to own considerable property and other slaves, to receive entrée into (though not equal status with) the major social and governmental circles, and thus to wield themselves considerable *de facto* power."

"It is valuable to catch a glimpse from this inscription of Christians in Rome moving into such circles where good education might be obtained, wealth might be amassed, and political influence might be exerted. One can begin to understand why in 268 A.D. Christian *Caesariani* were thought important enough to be singled out in the second rescript of the persecution of Valerian."

It is possible that Alexander lived to see and perhaps suffer under Valerian's persecution.

See CLAUDIUS.

EMB

CALAH. This ancient city was established by Nimrod as part of an expansion of his kingdom in the land of Shinar* (Gen 10:10ff.). It became one of the capital cities of Assyria and appeared in cuneiform* texts as Kalhu. The modern site is known as Nimrud and is located 35.4 km. (22 mi.) S of Mosul, NE of the area where the Tigris and Upper Zab rivers flow together. Calah was one of the sites excavated by Sir Henry Layard between 1845 and 1851, during which time three palaces were discovered containing much sculpture and statuary, and from which the celebrated Black Obelisk of Shalmaneser* (859–824 B.C.) was recovered. Subsequent work by the British School of Archaeology in Iraq from 1947 to 1961 traced the occupation of the site from prehistoric times to the Hellenistic period. Pottery from the Tell Hassuna,* Tell Halaf (*see* GOZAN), and Tell al 'Ubaid* periods was recovered at the lowest levels of the site, indicating the antiquity of sedentary occupation there.

Some Sumerians* had settled at Ashur by about 3000 B.C., and for the next millennium they developed trade between the N and certain Sumerian cities including Ur.* When that center was destroyed by Amorite* invaders (c. 1990 B.C.), and the influence of the Mari* dynasty increased steadily thereafter, Calah and the Assyrian city-states went into political decline, especially when Hammurabi* finally incorporated Mari into his Babylonian Empire. Shalmaneser I (1274–1245 B.C.), one of the earliest kings of the Assyrians, rebuilt Calah as his capital and fortified it against attacks by the Urartians and Hurrians.* Under Ashurnasirpal II* (883–859 B.C.), Calah replaced Ashur as the capital of Assyria, and at this time its defenses were extended and strengthened. The city area itself was also enlarged and made more attractive by the addition of temples, a new citadel, and the beginnings of the great ziggurat.* When completed, the capital covered an area of approximately 4,144 ha. (16 sq. mi.). The powerful Assyrian army (cf. Nah 2:3f.; 3:2f.) marched from Calah under Shalmaneser III (859–824 B.C.) to attack a coalition comprising Israel, Damascus,* and the coastal city-states in 841 B.C. Jehu of Israel chose to become a tributary to the Assyrians, and the Black Obelisk of Shalmaneser possibly depicts a captive Jehu, or his emissary, kneeling and proffering tribute (*see* BOOTY). This incident is not recorded in the OT, although both Ahab* and Jehu were mentioned in contemporary Assyrian inscriptions.

Further attacks on the Palestinian kingdoms were launched from Calah in the time of Tiglath-Pileser* III (745–727 B.C.), who appeared on the NE frontier of Israel when Menahem (752–741 B.C.) was king (2 Kings 15:14), and the Assyrian king made him a

Black Obelisk of Shalmaneser III (bottom not shown) containing twenty panels in five rows running around four sides of obelisk like a continuous frieze and intended to be viewed from top to bottom. All the panels depict tribute being brought to Shalmaneser III. The second panel shows "Jehu, son of Omri" on his hands and knees paying tribute to the king. Reproduced by courtesy of the Trustees of the British Museum.

tributary. Pekah, who became ruler of Israel in 739 B.C., allied with neighboring states against Assyria in an effort to restore Israel's political fortunes. Inscriptions from the time of Sargon II* (722–705 B.C.) recorded that fresh attacks on Israel and Judah were mounted from Calah, and the Khorsabad annals (see KHORSABAD KING LIST) described the way in which Sargon had captured Samaria* and carried the northern tribes off as prisoners to Assyria. Some articles that are thought to have been part of the booty taken on that occasion have been recovered from the ruins of the citadel to the E of Nimrud. Babylonian and Medan attacks under Nabopolassar* from 616 B.C. brought about the end of the Assyrian Empire, resulting in the fall of Calah in 612 B.C. after a bitter battle at Nineveh.*

BIBLIOGRAPHY: M. E. L. Mallowan, *Twenty-five Years of Mesopotamian Discovery* (1956); id., *Nimrud and Its Remains* (1962).

RKH

CALENDAR. Originally the Hebrews had no means of accurate calendrical determination, marking the passing of time only by reference to lunar or solar months or to the seasons of the year. In patriarchal times the year may have been reckoned from the spring, but after the Amarna* Age it seems to have commenced in the autumn with the seventh month (Exod 23:16). Once Canaan had been conquered, the W Semitic lunar calendar was followed (1 Kings 4:7). This necessitated a periodic intercalation to make up the difference between a lunar and a solar year. The influence of Canaanite* names for months is evident from the Solomonic period, where Bul (1 Kings 6:37) and Ethanim (1 Kings 8:2) were mentioned in connection with the dedication of Solomon's* Temple. These two names appear in Phoenician* inscriptions, signifying "perpetual streams" and "produce" (or perhaps "cattle"), and show obvious agricultural* connections. The designations of the earlier months in the Hebrew calendar did not follow the names found in cuneiform* texts from Mari,* Alalakh,* and Ugarit,* though the Phoenician inscriptions contain names that may have been used periodically by the Hebrews.

In 1908 Macalister found a small limestone tablet at Gezer* that on translation proved to be a schoolboy's exercise or a farmer's almanac detailing agricultural activities for the year, beginning in the autumn. It dated from the tenth century B.C., and while translations differ, the contents depict an agricultural calendar in which specific periods were set aside for planting, hoeing, pruning, harvesting, and the like. In addition to lunar and agricultural calendars, events were dated either in terms of the regnal years of kings or by being coupled with some important natural event, such as the earthquake during Uzziah's reign (cf. Amos 1:1; Zech 14:5). Months were numbered from the Passover month (Exod 12:2), beginning in the autumn, though the Pentateuch does not describe a calendar as such.

BIBLIOGRAPHY: O. Neugebauer, *Exact Sciences in Antiquity* (1957 ed.); A. Jaubert, *VT*, 7 (1957), 35–61; J. Segal, id. (1957), 250–307; E. Kutsch, *VT*, 11

Gezer calendar, an inscription in ancient Hebrew script engraved on limestone tablet, 10th century B.C. The inscription records the annual cycle of agricultural activities. Replica—Courtesy Israel Dept. of Antiquities and Museums.

(1961), 39–47; J. Segal, *JSS*, 6 (1961), 74–95; J. Morgenstern, *JBL*, 83 (1964), 109–18; J. Baumgarten, *VT*, 16 (1966), 277–86; E. Bickerman, *Chronology of the Ancient World* (1968); J. Lilley, *ZPEB*, 1 (1975), 687–92.

RKH

CALF, GOLDEN. The golden (or gold*-plated) calf set up by Aaron in response to the pressure of the multitude, has two possible explanations. Aaron intended the idol to represent Jehovah (Exod 32:5, 8). Perhaps the Hebrew slaves* in Egypt* had been aware of the bull-god, Apis, an animal selected for worship at birth by virtue of certain markings considered divine. The bull was a symbol of fertility and strength and so became in more than one pagan cult a symbol of divine might. The bull-worship of Crete was a further example of this concept. The bull also appears in art and religious texts from Mesopotamia,* Asia Minor,* Phoenicia,* and Syria (see ARAM). The Syrian storm-god, Hadad, with a three-pronged trident representing lightning, is shown in an Aleppo* relief standing on the back of a young bull. K. A. Kitchen, who is of the opinion that the centers of Apis worship were too remote from Goshen* for the Hebrew expatriates to be strongly aware of the cult, mentions other forms of bull-worship in Egypt that may have played the same corrupting part. The horned statues of Apis that are connected with the worship of the bull-god come from the Saite period, at the end of Egypt's era of independent dynastic history.

The two golden calves of Jeroboam, inspired possibly by the Aleppo cult mentioned above, set up at Bethel* and Dan,* probably represented the throne of Jehovah, a corrupt version of the vacant mercy-seat on the ark of the covenant.*

A platform of stone has been unearthed at Dan (Tell el-Qadi), by A. Biram of the Israeli Department of Antiquities. It measures some 5.5 sq. m. (59 sq. ft.) and is built of dressed stone with a surrounding wall. In the opinion of the excavator, this is nothing other than the platform of Jeroboam's northern "golden calf." Adjacent gate structures date to the days of Jeroboam I, and they illustrate the importance of Dan as a cultic and administrative center. The northern part of the gate was extensively burned during the first half of the ninth century B.C., probably during one of the inroads of Ben-Hadad ("Son of the Storm-God") of Damascus* (1 Kings 20:22).

BIBLIOGRAPHY: Herodotus, History, 2.38; Pliny, NH, 8.184; E. Otto, Beiträge zur Geschichte der Stierkulte in Aegypten (1938), 6–8, 32–33; K. A. Kitchen, NBD (1962), 180; D. J. Wiseman, Illustrations from Biblical Archaeology (1959), 39, fig. 33; Buried History, QJAIA (March 1971), 7; R. A. Cole, Exodus, Tyndale OT Commentaries (1973), 214.

EMB

CALNEH (CALNO) (kal'ne). In Gen 10:10 Calneh was mentioned as one of Nimrod's principal cities and was associated with Babel, Erech,* and Akkad.* The site of Calneh has not been located up to the present, and some doubt has been cast on the very existence of the city by the suggestion that the Hebrew kullānāh can be repointed without consonantal change to read "all of them," as in Gen 42:36. Some scholars have identified Calneh with Nippur* because the place is mentioned along with Babylon* and Erech in the Babylonian Creation myth (CREATION EPIC, BABYLONIAN). Nippur was an important city,* which has yielded vast stores of literary and commercial tablets to archaeologists.

Other authorities claim that Calneh is Kullania (Calno, Kalno), mentioned in Assyrian tribute lists and overrun by Tiglath-Pileser* III in 738 B.C. Amos 6:2 and Isa 10:9 would seem to support this location, for the N Syrian cities of Carchemish,* Hamath,* and Arpad are associated in the same context. Kullania is most probably the modern Kullan Köy, about 9.6 km. (6 mi.) SE of Arpad.

See NIPPUR.

BIBLIOGRAPHY: I. J. Gelb, AJSL, 50 (1935), 189–91; W. F. Albright, JNES, 3 (1944), 254–55; J. Simons, The Geographical and Topographical Texts of the OT (1959).

EMB

CAMEL. This familiar desert quadruped occurs in two distinct varieties, the one-humped Camelus dromedarius, or Arabian* dromedary, and the two-humped Camelus bactrianus, or Bactrian camel, that appears to have originated in NE Iran. The Hebrew (gāmāl) and Greek (kamēlos) terms do not differentiate between the two species, and both kinds are represented on Ancient Near Eastern monuments.

Camels were first mentioned in Middle Bronze Age OT material in connection with Abraham and Jacob (Gen 12:16; 24:19; 24:35; 30:43; 32:7, 15), where they comprised part of the livestock. In Gen 24:10; 31:17, 34, they were mentioned as a means of transport for individuals. Otherwise in the Pentateuch, the only camel-riding groups were the Midianites* and Ishmaelites, who were desert traders (Gen 37:25) and found the "ship of the desert" indispensable for their livelihood. In the Late Bronze Age, camels were mentioned as beasts of burden in Egypt* (Exod 9:3) and were prohibited to the Hebrews for food in Lev 11:4; Deut 14:7.

Since camel nomadism only appears to have become prominent from about the twelfth century B.C. among Near Eastern nations with the exception of Egypt, many scholars assumed that the mention of camels in the Pentateuch was an anachronism. But Parrot discovered pieces of camel bones when excavating a house at Mari* belonging to the Pre-Sargonic period (c. 2400 B.C.) and also a jar on which the hindquarters of a camel were visible. This ceramic evidence was dated about 2000 B.C. Pierre Montet mentioned a stone container in the form of a camel from Egypt that went back to the same approximate period. D. J. Wiseman and A. Goetze recorded the mention of domesticated camels in a tablet from Alalakh* (JCS, 13 [1959], 29, 37), but their reading was disputed by W. G. Lambert (BASOR, 160 [1960], 42–43), who instead adduced a Ugaritic* source to provide evidence for the use of the camel in the Old Babylonian period, early in the Middle Bronze Age. From that same time came a jawbone of a camel from Tell el-Fara'h, while contemporary cylinder seals* from N Mesopotamia show riders on camels.

A relief at Byblos (Gebal*) in Phoenicia, dated in the eighteenth century B.C., depicts a camel in a kneeling position, and provided the occasion for a learned controversy between W. F. Albright and R. de Vaux. In Egypt, the Egyptian Faiyum furnished a camel skull belonging to the Middle Bronze Age, while from the Memphis* region came a thirteenth-century B.C. representation of a camel loaded with two water jars.

In India the camel was domesticated by the Early Bronze Age, as indicated by evidence from Mohenjo-Daro, though the animal was not as commonly found as in desert areas of the Near East. A tiny gold* camel in kneeling position, which had evidently been part of a necklace, was recovered from Ur* and dated in the Third Dynasty (c. 2070–1960 B.C.). Remains of camel bones unearthed on Bahrain, probably ancient Dilmun,* could well be as early as 3000 B.C.

In later times camels frequently appeared on reliefs, as in Assyria from the time of Tiglath-Pileser* III (744–727 B.C.) and Ashurbanipal* (669–627 B.C.). This brief selection from the mass of available evidence should, as R. K. Harrison has remarked, "be sufficient to refute the commonly held view that references to camels in Genesis are anachronistic touches introduced to make the stories more vivid to later hearers" (*Introduction to the OT* [1969], 311, and references).

BIBLIOGRAPHY: R. Walz, *ZDMG*, 101 (1951), 29–51; id., 104 (1954), 45–87; B. Brentjes, *Klio*, 38 (1960), 23–52; K. A. Kitchen, *NBD* (1962), 181–82; id., *Ancient Orient and OT* (1966), 79–80, with references; E. Yamauchi, *The Stones and the Scriptures* (1972), 36–37.   EMB

CANA (kā′nə; Gr. Κανά, *kaná*; probably from the Heb. קָנֶה, *qāneh*, "reed"). A village in Galilee,* where Jesus performed his first miracle (John 2:1, 11; 4:46), and the home of Nathaniel (John 21:2) and possibly also of Simon the Canaanite* (Matt 10:4).

Church tradition, from ancient and medieval times, has located Cana at Kefr Kennā, about 6.4 km. (4 mi.) NE of Nazareth,* on one of the routes to Tiberias,* a location convenient for pilgrims to visit on their way to the Sea of Galilee. But the doubling of the *n* in *Kanna* is hard to explain if *Kennā* is derived from *Kana*. Fragments of a mosaic* floor at Kefr Kennā containing a Hebrew-Aramaic inscription may have been part of a synagogue dating back to the second century A.D.

A better solution locates Cana about 14.5 km. (9 mi.) N of Nazareth at Khirbet Kānā, to the N of the El Battōf plain and near the Jewish fortress of Jatapata. Josephus (Jos. *Life*, 86) says that he stayed for a while at "a village of Galilee called Cana."

This Cana was on the summit of a hill and overlooked a marshy plain, where roads are still to be seen. The ruins at the top of the hill there have not been excavated, though potsherds and coins from the time of Christ have been recovered. Evidenced at the site are cisterns* and rock-cut tombs. There may be remains of the third century A.D. at the location, though this has not been confirmed.

BIBLIOGRAPHY: F.-M. Abel, *Géographie de la Palestine*, 2 (1938), 413; E. G. Kraeling, *Bible Atlas* (1956), 372–73; J. A. Thompson, *The Bible and Archaeology* (1962), 359; M. Pearlman and Y. Yannai, *Historical Sites in Israel* (1965), 76; J. Finegan, *The Archaeology of the NT* (1969), 66; M. H. Heicksen, *ZPEB*, 1 (1975), 700–1.   WHM

CANAAN, CANAANITES. In Gen 10:6, 15–18, Canaan was listed as the fourth son of Ham and ancestor of the Canaanites who were the inhabitants of Canaan, the older name of Palestine. The Canaanites are mentioned in a fifteenth-century B.C. inscription of Amenophis II as *kyn′n.w*, the equivalent of the Babylonian *kinnaḫḫu* that occurs in the Tell el-Amarna tablets (*see* AMARNA LETTERS). The origin of the name Canaan is obscure, and although it could possibly be traced to Hurrian* sources, earlier attempts to link it with the term *kinnaḫḫu*, "red purple," and to think of Canaan as the land of the murex mollusc from which the Phoenicians made their celebrated dye,* have now been shown to be incorrect linguistically. It is evident that the name came into prominence when Hurrian expansion westward was at its height, but anything beyond that is speculative.

In the Amarna Letters the Phoenician* coast is

described as the "land of Canaan," and as far as the Egyptians were concerned, it was a general designation for the whole of W Syria. In the OT the "land of Canaan" included all Palestine W of the Jordan (Num 34:3ff.). It comprised a rough pattern of four parallel strips produced by two mountain ranges. One of these ran from Lebanon along the W edge of the Jordan Valley, while the other stretched S from Mount Hermon* to the E of the Dead Sea* and continued to Mount Hor in Edom.* The parallel sections thus formed consisted of the maritime plain, the central mountainous region stretching S from Mount Hermon, the Jordan Valley, and the plateau of E Palestine. To the extreme S of Canaan lay the Negev,* an arid, inhospitable area of about 93,240 ha. (360 sq. mi.), of which Beersheba* was the chief settlement. The land of Canaan formed a bridge between the ancient Near Eastern centers of pagan civilization. From a geographic, historical, and cultural standpoint the term "Canaanite" is synonymous with "Phoenician." Consequently the former designation should only be used to describe the NW Semitic inhabitants of W Syria and Palestine, and their culture, prior to the twelfth century B.C.

Like the people themselves, the Canaanite language belonged to the NW Semitic group. Because

Potsherds with paintings representing Canaanite woman (top) and man, found in Beth Shan and dating from c. 1500 B.C. Courtesy Israel Dept. of Antiquities and Museums.

it was spoken over a wide area for a number of centuries, certain significant variations arose that have caused some doubts as to the homogeneity of the language. The nineteenth-century B.C. Egyptian Execration Texts* seem to indicate a strong Amorite* influence, but within a few centuries the impact of Hurrian appears equally evident. One of the languages of Canaan was Ugaritic,* deciphered in 1930 during excavations at Ras Shamra (Ugarit*) and surviving in an alphabetic cuneiform* script. It was found to be closely related to biblical Hebrew, which itself was probably a local Canaanite dialect similar to, but not identical with, the general speech of the sedentary Canaanites. Ugaritic, Canaanite, and OT Hebrew, along with the local tongue of Ebla (Tell Mardikh*) appear to be distinct though cognate linguistic forms of the NW Semitic group of languages. Ugaritic comprised an important link in the process by which the alphabet* seems to have developed from Egyptian syllabic or logographic writing to the Canaanite principles of alphabetism in cuneiform script, a process that may have been prompted originally by commercial needs.

The Middle Bronze Age in Palestine was notable for the level that Canaanite culture achieved. After 1700 B.C. stout-walled cities* were constructed along Hyksos* lines, and their excavation has revealed that the walls* had been constructed on the top of a steeply sloping earthen ramp made firm at the base by means of heavy retaining masonry. At this time some important Canaanite cities were enlarged, of which Hazor* (Tell el-Qedah) was one. The mound has proved to be among the largest in Palestine, and Canaanite expansions are represented by a large rectangular plateau just to the N of the tell,* flanked in places by a defensive wall, and on the W side by a large dry moat. There is no doubt that the construction techniques employed in building Canaanite walls were vastly superior to those of later structures erected by the Israelites.

So obvious were Hebrew deficiencies in this area that when King Solomon* launched his ambitious building program, he found it necessary to enlist the help of Phoenician craftsmen* when planning and constructing the temple in Jerusalem. Artisans sent by King Hiram* of Tyre* executed much of the work (1 Kings 7:13ff.), and from the appearance of contemporary buildings it seems that the Solomonic Temple* was a characteristically Phoenician structure. The ground plan described in 1 Kings 6:2ff. bears a close resemblance to that of the eighth-century B.C. chapel uncovered at Tell ta'Yinat* in Syria. Examples of the Proto-Aeolic pilaster capital* used in the Solomonic Temple have been unearthed from eleventh-century B.C. levels at Megiddo,* Samaria,* and Shechem.* The lilies and palmettes of the temple were typically Syro-Phoenician, while cherubim* were a common ingredient of W Asiatic iconography in the Middle Bronze Age and subsequent periods. The shape of the temple vestibule with its columns, the cedar* lining of the interior, the carved and inlaid decorative work, and other contemporary architectural features, testified eloquently to the advanced religious syncretism of the period.

The Canaanites also demonstrated superior ability in music* composition and in the playing of instruments. What has been described as the oldest sheet music in the world consists of two tablets from Ras Shamra inscribed with Canaanite musical notations and accompanied by a lyric of a rather romantic nature. The Beni Hasan Tableau* shows Palestinian nomads trudging behind their animals in Egypt* to the music of a lyre, and Egyptian monuments from 1550 B.C. onward refer to examples of Canaanite music. Ugaritic texts abounded with poetic sections, certain phrases of which were paralleled in the Hebrew Psalter. Ugaritic sources also referred to a division of temple personnel known as "sarim," who were analagous to the Hebrew singers of the monarchy and post-Exilic periods.

Politically, the Canaanites were organized into city-states, as were some other Near Eastern nations, and these social configurations were run along feudal lines. The Canaanite city-states relinquished their autonomy at the beginning of the Amarna* Age, when Palestine became an Egyptian dependency. The local princes then became subject to Egyptian jurisdiction but retained some infantry and chariots* for use in time of danger. After the Amarna Age ended, the corruption of Egyptian bureaucracy resulted in administrative and social decline in Canaan, and this doubtless contributed to the rapidity with which the Israelites occupied Canaanite territory under Joshua.

Tablets recovered from Ugarit afford a full description of the Canaanite pantheon, and they throw startling new light on the degrading, orgiastic nature of Canaanite fertility-worship. While the poetic texts present such a fluidity of function and personality that the exact relationships of the Canaanite deities are frequently very hard to determine, it is abundantly clear that the cult itself was a debased form of ritual polytheism. The chief deity was El, variously known as the "father of man" (abu adami) and the "father of years" (abu shanima), whose consort, Asherat, was familiar to the Israelites as Asherah.* Their offspring was the fertility-deity Baal,* the god of wind and storm, who was also known to his worshipers as Aliyn (Prevailer) and Zabul (Earthly Lord). The texts make it clear that Baal was a true "high god," and as such was the acknowledged head of the pantheon at Ugarit. The goddess Anat,* consort of Baal, was often depicted as violent and sadistic, and her functions as a divine courtesan gave formal sanction to ritual prostitution* in Canaanite religion. Along with Anat, Astarte and Asherah were also patronesses of sex and war. Other Canaanite deities included Mot, the god of death; Reshep, the god of pestilence; Shulman, the god of health; and Koshar, the god of crafts.*

Canaanite worship generally occurred outdoors at the "high places" that apparently were shrines located on the tops of hills. The rituals were conducted by priests and included prayer, the presentation of votive offerings, and indulgence in a sacrificial feast. One cult-object employed in worship was the asherah* (cf. 1 Kings 15:13 et al.), evidently a sacred tree or wooden symbol closely connected with the goddess Asherah. Another was the sacred pillar (massebah*), which may have been intended to represent a male deity. From Megiddo* came a small altar* of incense* of a kind found commonly in Canaanite sanctuaries after 1100 B.C. These altars were made of limestone and had projections or "horns" on each corner. One such structure recovered from Palmyra* in N Syria bore the inscription *ḥamman* or "altar of incense." From thirteenth-century B.C. levels at Lachish* were excavated the ruins of a shrine that had probably been destroyed while still in use. Originally it had plastered interior walls lined with benches for storing sacrificial offerings. At the front of the temple had been a raised area that had no doubt contained a small altar and possibly an idol of Baal or Asherah as well. The remains of sacrificial offerings indicate that at least four types of animals had been sacrificed, while the almost complete absence of charred bones show that the sacrificial meat had been boiled.

Ugaritic texts make it evident that Canaanite religion was of an intensely corrupt and immoral kind, which pervaded and even contaminated other Near Eastern religions and thoroughly merited the divine commands relating to the destruction of the devotees of Canaanite religion (Gen 15:16; Exod 23–24 et al.). Its gross and sordid nature was the very antithesis of the Sinai covenantal religion, and though pre-Exilic Israelites were strongly attracted at times by its seductiveness, it never gained complete hold upon Hebrew religious loyalties.

BIBLIOGRAPHY: D. J. Wiseman, *The Alalakh Tablets* (1953); W. F. Albright, *Archaeology and the Religion of Israel* (1953), 74ff.; id., *Yahweh and the Gods of Canaan* (1968); J. Gray, *The Legacy of Canaan* (1965); A. R. Millard, in D. J. Wiseman, ed., *Peoples of OT Times* (1973), 29ff.; J. A. Thompson, *ZPEB*, 1 (1975), 701–8.

RKH

CANDLESTICK. *See* MENORAH.

CANOPIC JARS. These small jars were made of stone or pottery* and used in ancient Egyptian burials to contain the viscera of the deceased. Soon after death an incision was made in the left side of the abdominal cavity and the soft viscera were withdrawn and embalmed. The actual jars were shaped to form an image of Osiris.* This was taken by the later Greeks to be the image of Canopus, the pilot of King Menelaus, who had been buried at Canopus on the Nile, hence the name of the containers.

The custom of using canopic jars began in the Old Kingdom period and died out in the New Kingdom period. Generally four canopic jars were buried in a separate decorated chest similar to the coffin. These jars were usually topped by lids with divine images carved on them, these being the four sons of Horus. In the tomb of Tutankhamen* four deities (Imset, Hapi, Dwamutep, and Kebehsenup) were summoned by means of incantations* to watch over the royal viscera. The tomb of Tutankhamen has very elaborate canopic jars in the form of small coffins, each topped by a bust of the king. These were placed in a four-part alabaster chest, which was in turn enclosed in a beautiful wooden chest. The whole was

Aerial photo of remains of early type of synagogue at Capernaum on shore of Sea of Galilee. The façade in the foreground faces south and is oriented toward Jerusalem. Courtesy Israel Government Press Office.

covered by many careful inscriptions, signets of goddesses, and the seals* of the cemetery (*see* NECROPOLIS). Not only are the jars and their inscriptions of some archaeological value, but more recently their contents have been subjected to palaeopathological* examination. Although the oils and alkalis, unguents and salves used in ancient Egyptian embalming* eroded or destroyed the soft tissues, some headway is being made in identifying pathological agents.

See OSIRIS; TUTANKHAMEN.

BIBLIOGRAPHY: J. Černý, *Ancient Egyptian Religion* (1952), 90, 105–6, 113.

WW

CAPERNAUM (kə pûr′ nā əm). The city on the NW shore of the Lake of Galilee that was the center of Jesus' Galilean ministry. Since the name disappeared and there was uncertainty over the site, it is only in modern times that this has been settled by archaeological work. One traditional site, Khirbet al Minyeh (linked with a reference in Jos. *Antiq.* 3.10.8) has been shown to be that of an Arab palace. The other, Tell Hum, which is 3.2 km. (2 mi.) to the NE, has been confirmed by the identification of its ruins. The meaning of the name is disputed. There is no tell* on the site, and it is suggested that the word may be a mutilated derivative from *telonion*, a customs post, which Kefar Nahum, "the village of Nahum," undoubtedly was. "Hum" is either a fragment of Nahum, or a word for "Brown."

Nothing remains from NT times. The foundations of a church have been identified, but of much greater interest are the considerable remains of a synagogue,* excavated by German archaeologists and the Franciscan fathers between 1905 and 1926. Some authorities have dated the structure to the late second or third century A.D., while others have placed it in the fourth century. Its size and design illustrate the vitality of Judaism at this period and also the extent of Greco-Roman influence. The basilica,* measuring 17.4 by 23 m. (57 by 75 ft.), was built of white limestone and contained two stories, with nave, two aisles, and transept on the ground floor and three galleries above. Columns with Corinthian capitals* below were matched by Doric-style columns in the galleries. The decorations of the entablature* show a remarkable latitude in comparison with Judaistic norms, with the featuring of mythological figures and animals.

It is possible that the synagogue in which Jesus taught stood on the same site and that the floor and foundations, both likely to have defied the efforts of ancient demolition teams, could belong to the first synagogue. The same applies to the decorations, many, as the present site demonstrates, salvageable.

BIBLIOGRAPHY: E. L. Sukenik, *Ancient Synagogues in Palestine and Greece* (1934), 7–21; J. S. Kennard, *JBL*, 65 (1946), 131–41; E. F. F. Bishop, *CBQ*, 15 (1973), 427–37; C. Kopp, *The Holy Places of the Gospels* (1963), 171–79; H. G. Andersen, *ZPEB*, 1 (1975), 746–48; N. Avigad, *EEHL*, 1 (1975), 286–90.

BFH and EMB

CAPITAL. The cap or highest part of a pillar or column, sometimes elaborately decorated.

CAPPADOCIAN TABLETS. These were commercial documents left by Assyrian traders in ancient Kanesh in Anatolia about 1900 B.C. They refer to patriarchal towns like Nahor (Gen 24:10) and Haran* (Gen 11:31; 12:4; 27:43 et al.) and make reference to deities under such titles as "the god of thy father," "the god of our fathers" (cf. Gen 28:13; 31:42, 53). They point to vigorous trade and travel at the time of the patriarchs. A few Indo-European names attest to the arrival of the Hittites.*

BIBLIOGRAPHY: W. F. Albright, *From the Stone Age to Christianity* (1957 ed.), 153–55.

JAT

CAPSTONE. An architectural term referring to a stone slab placed over a tomb to act as a cover or roof, or to the stone surmounting a pyramid.*

CARBON DATING. See DATING.

CARCHEMISH (kär'kə mesh). An important Syro-Hittite capital on the Upper Euphrates, identified with modern Jerablus 101 km. (63 mi.) NE of Aleppo.* Carchemish is well attested in cuneiform* records, being first mentioned in an eighteenth-century B.C. text as an independent trade center. Hittite* and Ugaritic* sources show that in the Amarna* Age it was an administrative city within the Hittite imperial system.

The sack of Carchemish by Sargon II* in 717 B.C.

was noted in Isa 10:9. Occupied by Neco of Egypt* in 609 B.C., it became a base for attack on the Babylonians but saw a massive Egyptian defeat in 605 B.C. by Nebuchadnezzar* II (cf. Jer 46:2). Archaeology has revealed traces of Neco's occupation of Carchemish and of the battle. A house has been uncovered, presumably occupied by an officer or official, that contained Egyptian bronze* figures, alabaster,* and blue frit vases (frit is the vitreous composition from which soft porcelain is made), clay-seal impressions (*see* SEAL) with the name of Neco, and a bronze ring with seal-bezel bearing the cartouche of Psammetichus. This house had been destroyed, and the ruins were littered with evidence of a desperate struggle. Everywhere, and especially in the doorways, were arrowheads in the hundreds and of many types. Javelin heads were numerous, a sword was found, and a remarkable bronze shield. In two rooms human bones were on the floor. The shield is of Ionian type belonging probably to a Greek warrior of Neco's army, an archaeological evidence of Greek mercenaries serving in Eastern Mediterranean armies. Pharaoh Neco fled through Syria and Palestine, pursued by Nebuchadnezzar. The find grimly illustrates the words of a section of the Babylonian Chronicles* translated by D. J. Wiseman in 1956. It was in 605 B.C. that, old and sick, Nabopolassar* handed over the army to Nebuchadnezzar, who did "fly like a vulture" (Hab 1:8) and marched up the Euphrates and fell on Carchemish. The text runs: "He crossed the river to go against the Egyptian army which lay in Carchemish. The armies fought with each other and the Egyptian army withdrew before him. He accomplished their defeat and beat them to nonexistence. As for the rest of the Egyptian army which had escaped from the defeat so quickly that no weapon had reached them, the Babylonians overtook and defeated them in the district of Hamath* so that not a single man escaped to his own country. At that time Nebuchadnezzar conquered the whole of Hatti-land."

BIBLIOGRAPHY: D. G. Hogarth and C. L. Woolley, *Carchemish*, 3 vols. (1914–52); D. J. Wiseman, *Chronicles of Chaldean Kings* (1956), 20–26; W. W. Hallo, in C. F. Pfeiffer, ed., *The Biblical World* (1966), 165–69, with bibliography; H. A. Hoffner, Jr., *ZPEB*, 1 (1975), 752–54.

RKH and EMB

CARIA (kâr'iə; Gr. καρία, *karía*). The name of the SW part of Asia Minor,* bounded on the N by the Maeander River area and Lydia,* on the E by Phrygia, on the SE by Lycia, and on the SW and W by the Mediterranean and Aegean seas.

There is no biblical reference to Caria itself, but two of its coastal cities play a part in the NT, Miletus* on the N (Acts 20:15–38) and Cnidus* (Acts 27:7) farther S. At Miletus, G. Kleiner, in 1961 and in subsequent years, investigated such parts as the theater* hill area with its remains from the Mycenaean* and archaic through the Byzantine* and medieval periods including some second-century A.D. villas with their mosaics.* Cnidus, located on the W end of a peninsula across from Halicarnassus, was built on terraces and had a double harbor, the moles* of which can still be seen. Concerning its religious celebrations, inscriptions bear testimony to the Doreia-Apollo Triopius festival held there in the first century A.D. (*Syll. Graec.*, 3d ed., 1065, 1066) as well as the festival of Artemis Hyacinthotrophos early in the second century A.D. (*Arch. Anz.*, no. 3 [1891?], 11; and *Fouilles de Delphes*, 3, Ecole francaise d'Athènes [1903?], 308).

Halicarnassus was famous for its fourth-century B.C. mausoleum, some sculptured parts of which are in the British Museum. Its foundation has also been excavated. The town of Cos on the island of that name, the birthplace of Hippocrates, has produced an altar from the fourth-century B.C. temple of Asclepius (P. Schazmann, *Asklepieion*, Arch. Inst. d. Deutsch Reiches [1932]). A Coan coin of the Roman Imperial period with the head of Hippocrates inscribed on it was also found (British Museum, B. V. Head, *Catalogue of the Greek Coins of Caria, Cos, Rhodes* [rep. 1897], 216, no. 216).

BIBLIOGRAPHY: A. H. M. Jones, *The Cities of the Eastern Roman Provinces* (1937), ch. 2; D. Magie, *Roman Rule in Asia Minor*, 1 (1950), 35–38, 50–52, 144–46, 155; C. F. Pfeiffer and H. F. Vos, *Wycliffe Historical Geography of Bible Lands* (1967), 370–74; M. J. Mellink, "Archaeology in Asia Minor," *AJA*, Miletus (1963), 185–87; ibid., (1967), 163, 169; ibid., Halicarnassus (1969), 219–20; ibid., Knidos (1969), 216–19; *OCD* (1970); H. Stillwell, ed., *PECS* (1976).

WHM

CARMEL, MOUNT. This notable Palestinian headland averages 457 m. (1500 ft.) in height and has given its name to the limestone mountainous range of which it is a part. It is located between the Palestinian coastal plain of Acco* to the N and the Plain of Sharon and Philistia* to the S. Although these two areas are joined by a narrow beach road, the people of antiquity preferred the inland passes when crossing the mountains, with the result that, aside from the Neolithic* settlers in the western caves, there was little occupation of Mount Carmel itself. In the Armarna* Age it was mentioned in lists from the time of Thutmose III and his successors, and at that period the delightful surroundings of Carmel were sacred to the cult of the Canaanite* god Baal.* One of its kings, Jokneam of Carmel, succumbed to Joshua, and the area was then assigned to the tribe of Asher (Josh 19:24–26), a move that gave the Asherites access to the Plain of Sharon. In the monarchy it was the scene of a notable defeat by Elijah of the Baal priests who were under the patronage of Jezebel,* wife of Ahab,* and whose activities were threatening to obliterate the traditional covenantal faith of the Hebrews (1 Kings 18:20ff.). Elisha mediated divine healing from Carmel (2 Kings 4:25ff.), and the area was most probably the place where Ahaziah's soldiers were destroyed when sent to arrest Elisha for his interference with Baal worship (2 Kings 1:9ff.). The attractiveness and productivity of the Carmel region are reflected in various OT writings (cf. Isa 35:2; Jer 50:19; Mic 7:14).

See AHAB; BAAL; JEZEBEL.

BIBLIOGRAPHY: D. Baly, *The Geography of the Bible* (1957), 136–37, 164, 180–82; C. F. Pfeiffer and H. F. Vos, *Wycliffe Historical Geography of Bible Lands* (1967), 99–100, 116.

RKH

CARRAWBURGH. *See* MITHRAS.

CARRHAE. *See* HARAN.

CARTOGRAPHY. The science of the construction and use of maps. Maps are of inestimable value in archaeological and historical study. The form most often used in archaeological exploration and recording is the topographic map, which represents certain selected man-made and natural features of a region or site, plotted to a definite scale. Scale is expressed on most maps as a ratio between distances on the ground and those on the map. The larger the scale, the greater the amount of information that can be conveyed. Features are shown by the use of conventional symbols, which are often explained in a legend. The devices used to show elevation on more technical maps are called contour lines. Relief on a map is shown by the spacing of these lines at regular intervals in relation to a known elevation. Contour lines never branch, fork, or cross one another. Closely spaced lines indicate a steep gradient; widely spaced ones mean the area is only slightly sloping.

Aerial photography* and stereoscopic viewing and drafting procedures are now widely used in technical mapping, which has also been greatly enhanced by the introduction of computer-aided laser mapping and recording devices.

JEJ

CARTOUCHE. A French term for the oval shape containing the hieroglyph* of a pharaoh's name.

CARYATID. In architecture, a female figure, normally clothed, which acts as a column in supporting a superstructure based on an entablature.* The term was derived from the name of a priestess of the Olympian goddess Artemis* (Roman Diana) at Karuai in Laconia.

CASEMATE WALLS. Casemate is a military term designating a chamber in a fort or an armored enclosure, as in a warship or fortification. The word, according to *ODEE* (1968), 149–50, derives from the Gr. *chásma* ("chasm" or "hollow"), mistakenly remodeled under the influence of the Italian *casa* ("house").

The wall construction comprises two parallel walls, built with an average space between of 1.5 to 2.1 m. (5 to 7 ft.). The outer wall was thickest (aver. 1.5 m., or 5 ft.), and the inner wall somewhat thinner (aver. 1.1 m., or 3½ ft.). The two walls were joined at intervals by cross walls, creating in effect a kind of rigid box girder and resulting in a series of chambers (or casemates) that were usually filled with rubble for added mass but were sometimes used for storage or other purposes. The casemate wall was widely used in Palestine in the eleventh and tenth centuries. Dr.

Aerial photo of part of upper city of Hazor: (1) Solomon's gate, (2) casemate wall, tenth century B.C., (3) storehouse. Courtesy Yigael Yadin, Jerusalem.

J. A. Thompson connects some of these tenth century fortifications, especially in SE areas of Palestine, with David's strategic defense against Philistine* intrusion. The type continued in sporadic use till late Iron II (see IRON AGE). Its design cleverly provided real (and even greater apparent) strength, with the least expenditure of labor and material.

Casemate fortifications were introduced in the Middle Bronze period and developed principally under the Hittite* Empire in the Late Bronze period (fourteenth–thirteenth centuries). The finest example of this LB fortification type may be seen at Hattusas (Boghazköy*), capital of the Hittites in Anatolia. This site had a citadel, upper and lower city complexes, all with walls,* and provides a classic demonstration of casemate design. The outer wall averaged 3.1 m. (10 ft.) thick, the inner wall 2.7 m. (9 ft.), and the space between 2.1 m. (7 ft.), giving an effective total thickness of 8 m. (about 26 ft.).

Rectangular bastions or towers were built at frequent intervals on the outer surface of the walls. In the period of the Neo-Hittite and Aramaic* kingdoms from the eleventh century B.C. on, the casemate system was widely adopted, being diffused into Syria, and thence to Palestine. Fortifications of this type were found at Zinjerli,* and the citadel of Saul at Gibeah* (end of eleventh century) is the earliest Palestinian example. It was rectangular in plan, c. 24 by 40 m. (79 by 131 ft.)—a minimum estimate; it was probably larger—and was built either of rough or dressed stones, with smaller chink stones. The double walls were connected by casemate partitions and had an elaborate corner construction to add strength.

Other examples appear at Tell en-Nasbeh (Mizpah*), Tell Beit Mirsim (Kiriath Sepher[?], see DEBIR), Beth Shemesh,* Gezer,* Hazor,* Megiddo,* Tell Qasile,* and in a number of isolated citadels in the Negev, including Arad.* Its most elaborate use was at Samaria* in the citadel of Ahab.*

There is little evidence of city fortifications during the period of the judges (twelfth–eleventh centuries). Most frequently the older Canaanite* walls were repaired and continued to function, as at Shechem* and Beth Shemesh. The distinctive casemate system used by the Hebrews was fundamentally different from the single massive Canaanite structures of rough stones. It was characteristic of the early Israelite period, and especially of Solomonic times, but gave way to heavier solid-wall construction made necessary by the introduction of the Assyrian battering ram in the early ninth century, which casemate walls were unable to withstand. The design, however, continued until about the end of the Iron II period, being used for inner city walls and minor fortresses where the chambers of the casemates were often used for dwelling or storage.

BIBLIOGRAPHY: R. Naumann, Architektur Kleinasiens (1955), 234–38, 288–89; W. F. Albright, The Archaeology of Palestine (1960), 120–22; L. Sinclair, "An Archaeological Study of Gibeah (Tell el-Ful)," AASOR, 34–35 (1960), 12–13, n.3,6; G. Wright, Biblical Archaeology (1962), 123, 187–89; L. Toombs and G. Wright, "The Fourth Campaign at Balatah (Shechem)," BASOR, 169 (1963), 49; Y. Yadin, The Art of Warfare in Biblical Lands, 1, 2 (1963), 91, 287–90; K. Kenyon, "Excavations in Jerusalem," BA, 27 (1964), 41; L. Sinclair, "An Archaeological Study of Gibeah (Tell el-Ful)," BA, 27 (1964), 54–55, 57–58.

MHH

CASTANET. See MUSIC.

CASTLE. A large building made of stone for purposes of defense and habitation is a feature not commonly found in the Semitic world. The term castle (or palace) is used to render a number of Greek and Hebrew words in the various versions (e.g., 1 Chron 11:7; Neh 1:1; 2:8; 7:2; Prov 18:19; Luke 11:21; Acts 21:34, 37; 22:24; 23:10, 16, 32). The Ancient Near East more often had fortified cities* with high walls,* narrow gates,* and ramparts for defense. However, a few pre-Christian forts have been found in Palestine. The castle of Saul at Gibeah,* modern Tell el-Ful, is the oldest. This castle had two rectangular walls over 30 m. (33 yds.) length interconnected at the corners. On each corner projecting outward were four strong siege towers.* Although small, the building was very durable. The remains of some Greek fortifications built by the Hellenistic princes have been located, but the great castles are of Roman de-

i

sign and construction. The Tower of Antonia, * built as a blockhouse on the NW corner of the Temple* Court in Jerusalem, * is indicative of the massive and enduring architecture of Roman castle building. Across Palestine today are many castles of the arched medieval type, with vaulting and great corbeled chambers, which were built during and after the Crusades. Such castles were developed as defense against the armored archer, cavalry, and chariotry.

BIBLIOGRAPHY: Y. Aharoni in D. W. Thomas, ed., *Archaeology and OT Study* (1967), 385–403; W. F. Albright in W. D. Davies, ed., *The Background of the NT and Its Eschatology* (1956), 158–59.

ww

CAT. The cat is not mentioned in canonical books of the Bible but does appear in the apocryphal (see PSEUDEPIGRAPHA) book of Baruch (6:22). It was domesticated in Egypt* before Joseph's time, and illustrations show cats destroying rats. In the days of immense grain storage promoted by Joseph, cats were no doubt commonly employed in this useful function. From the Old Kingdom period onward, the family cat was frequently taken on gaming and fowling expeditions in the marshes to act as a retriever of fallen game. With some consciousness of the plague-promoting activities of rodents, the priests may have placed the cat, the rodents' major foe, under the protection of the goddess Bastet, patron deity of the eastern half of the Nile Delta where the Israelites lived. The center of the cult was Bubastis* (cf. Ezek 30:17). Because of this veneration, cats, like crocodiles, * were mummified, and thousands of their remains exist. A good deal of art was expended on the theme. A painting on a cat-coffin in the Cairo Museum shows a holy cat sitting before an altar* loaded with sacrifices. In Thebes* a number of tomb reliefs show cats sitting under chairs, a ginger cat eating fish, and another grasping a goose.

BIBLIOGRAPHY: G. S. Cansdale, *All the Animals of the Bible Lands* (1970), 113–15; P. Dale-Green, *The Cult of the Cat* (1963), 1–7, ill. facing 15, 30–31, 46, 79.

EMB

CATACOMB (Gk. κατὰ κύμβας, *kata kumbas*, "at the ravine"). The word applies to subterranean burial places, consisting of galleries with recesses (*loculi*), and tombs. The word appears to have been applied first to the cemetery (see NECROPOLIS) under the Basilica* of Saint Sebastian on the Appian Way* under Rome, * in the fourth century. It was later extended to the whole vast complex of galleries in the tufa rock under Rome and much later to similar subterranean workings elsewhere. In Egypt* and Paris the galleries were old quarries* adapted for the reception of the dead. Roman law regarded places of burial as sacrosanct and so the catacombs of the city were available as a place of refuge, generally respected by the authorities. The Roman Catacombs, some forty in number and covering hundreds of kilometers, survive mainly NE and S of the city and are named after various saints—Callistus, Praetextatus, and Sebastian on the Via Appia; Domitilla on the Via Ardeatina;

Agnes on the Via Nomentana; Pancras on the Via Aurelia Vetus; and Commodilla on the Via Ostiensis. From the Christian point of view, the catacombs are important statistically for their preservation of Christian art and graffiti, * for the light thrown on Christian customs such as baptism. * Much archaeological work remains to be done.

BIBLIOGRAPHY: G. B. de Rossi, *Roma Sotterranea Cristiana* (1864–77); W. H. Withrow, *The Catacombs of Rome* (1890); M. Armellini, *Antichi Cimiteri di Roma e d'Italia* (1893); L. Hertling and E. Kirchbaum, *Le Catacombe Romane e i loro Martiri* (1949); E. M. Blaiklock, *Archaeology of the NT* (1970), 158–65.

EMB

CATAPULT. See MACHINES, WAR.

CATTLE. See Ox.

CAVE. Caves are common in the lime and sandstone of Palestine. A number of important cave sites used for human habitation, worship, or burial in ancient times have been discovered on the coast of the E Mediterranean. The earliest is the cluster of cave dwellings on Mount Carmel* used by Neanderthal communities (D. A. E. Garrod and D. M. A. Bate, *The Stone Age of Mount Carmel*, I [1937]). However, the practice of living as troglodytes was never widespread and only appeared during periods of climatic or political crisis (cf. Heb 11:38). Palestine shows nothing to parallel the Pueblo cliff-dwelling complexes of Indians of the southwestern U.S. A wide variety of Hebrew terms is used in the OT for the various types of Palestinian caves, although most of the famous ones, such as Machpelah, * were turned into shrines or churches during the Middle Ages, or overbuilt like the cave of the nativity of Bethlehem. * Cave archaeology is disappointing as there is little soil for excavation, and the commonplace habitation layers are not in evidence. Often the same cave site was used for hundreds of years as a temporary rest by hunting parties during the pre-Neolithic* period, and by traders in later periods. The most famous caves are those in the hills surrounding the Dead Sea, * where numerous groups found refuge during times of turmoil, from David's Adullam* to the refugees of Bar Kochba. * The Dead Sea Scrolls* were found in the caves above Qumran, * and in other caves of the region letters from the Bar Kochba period have been unearthed. There is no doubt that systematic examination of many more of the vast number of such crevices in the region will yield other finds. The unique atmospheric features of caves may preserve some materials not extant in other locations.

ww

CAVEA. A hollow or an excavated area. Used also of the spectators' benches section in Greek and Roman theaters. *

CEDAR. The wasteful exploitation of the Lebanon cedar forests by the Phoenicians is one of the first recorded examples of despoliation of the sort that has decimated the oak woods of England, the redwood forests of North America, and the New Zealand kauri. It is evident that Solomon,* in the process of his trading partnership with the Tyrians and his prestigious building projects in Jerusalem,* did much to promote the final ruin of the great stands of timber (see WOOD) on the Lebanon ranges. An Egyptian papyrus,* discovered in 1891, tells the story of a priest named Wenamon, who was sent to Phoenicia* in 1113 B.C. to secure timber for a funeral barge. It is a well-told and highly entertaining story, which throws light on the trade of the Palestine and Phoenician coast, and reveals details about the petty princedoms and port authorities of the eastern Mediterranean. The funeral barge of the pharaoh Khufu was discovered some years ago, and the first indication of its presence in the covered burial trench was the scent of cedar that marked the removal of the first flagstone.

BIBLIOGRAPHY: J. Baikie, *Egyptian Papyri and Papyrus Hunting* (1925), ch. 7; E. M. Blaiklock, *Word Pictures from the Bible* (1970), ch. 1.

EMB

CELLA. An ancient temple's inner sanctuary, which contained the cult image. In Bronze Age houses it was originally a shrine. The cella was walled on three sides, with an opening often facing the sunrise or moonrise. In front of the opening was a roofed porch supported by columns. In Greek and Roman temples the columns were often extended to form a colonnade.

CEMETERY. See NECROPOLIS.

CENCHREA (sen'kri ə; Gr. Κέγχρεαι, *kenchreai*). Modern Kechriais, on the Saronic Gulf, about 11 km. (7 mi.) from Corinth,* with which it was connected by a paved road,* was the eastern seaport of Corinth. Through it passed the city's trade with Asia. It is mentioned in Acts 18:18 as the place where Paul completed a Nazirite vow at the end of his eighteen-month stay in Corinth (A.D. 50–52) and in Rom 16:1 as the site of the church in which Phoebe was a deaconess. This was possibly a house-church associated with the city church of Corinth. Pausanias (second century A.D.) describes its harbor with temples of Asclepius and Isis at one side and of Aphrodite at the other, with a bronze* image of the sea-god Poseidon standing on a causeway running out into the sea. Ruins of ancient buildings and causeways are still to be seen.

FFB

CENOTAPH. An empty tomb or memorial for a deceased individual or group buried at another site.
See FUNERARY CUSTOMS, PALESTINIAN; NECROPOLIS.

CENSUS. See QUIRINIUS.

CERAMICS. See POTTER, POTTERY.

CHABOR. See HABOR RIVER.

CHAIR. See FURNITURE.

CHALCOLITHIC. A period in Palestinian archaeology dated roughly about 4500–3000 B.C. The term also describes levels and artifacts* from that period.

CHALDEA, CHALDEANS (kal dē'ə, -ənz; Heb. כַּשְׂדִּים, *kasdîm*; Aram. כַּשְׂדָּיֵא, *kasdāy'ē*; LXX χαλδαῖοι, *chaldaioi*). The inhabitants of the swampy, southern regions of Mesopotamia* who established the Neo-Babylonian Empire* (626 to 539 B.C.). In later periods magicians and diviners in possession of Babylonian astrological (see ASTROLOGY) lore were known as Chaldeans.

In many biblical passages the word "Chaldeans" is used as a synonym for "Babylonians" (Isa 13:19; 47:1, 5; 48:14, 20; Dan 9:1). In Daniel the term is also used to denote a group of wise men associated with magicians, astrologers, and soothsayers (Dan 2:10; 4:7; 5:7, 11).

1. *Origins and Ethnic Affiliation.* The origin of the Chaldeans is obscure. Some have suggested an infiltration from NE Arabia* based on the presence of an early Arabic script in southern Babylonia, which Albright called "Chaldean." Brinkman has analyzed the evidence as suggesting a W Semitic origin.

There may have been some original kinship with the Arameans,* who came to occupy adjacent territories in southern Babylonia to the N of the Chaldeans. Nonetheless the Chaldeans were consistently distinguished from the Arameans in the Assyrian documents (cf. 2 Kings 24:2 and Jer 35:11 where the Chaldeans are distinguished from the "Syrians" [Heb. Aram]).

2. *Language.* In the earliest periods, as far as we can discover, the Chaldeans used the Babylonian Akkadian (see AKKAD) language. It was only later that they adopted Aramaic.* That the Chaldeans in Dan 2:4 (cf. Dan 1:4) spoke to Nebuchadnezzar* in Aramaic (KJV "Syriack") simply reflects a period when Aramaic had become the common vernacular. It was therefore misleading for earlier scholars to call Aramaic the "Chaldee" language.

3. *Early History.* The Chaldeans first appear in the early first millennium B.C. in Assyrian inscriptions in the area of Kaldu, a region at the head of the Perisan Gulf which was also known as the Sea Lands. In the ninth-century inscriptions of Shalmaneser III (see SHALMANESER, BLACK OBELISK OF) we see the Chaldeans in settled areas with flourishing date plantations and in control of the Persian Gulf trade.

Their principal tribes from NW to SE were: the *Bit-Dakkuri*, occupying the area S of Babylon around Borsippa;*the *Bit-Amukani*, occupying the area between Isin and Uruk;*and the *Bit-Yakin*, occupying the area between Uruk and Ur.* The designation of Abraham's city as Ur of the "Chaldees" (Gen 11:28; cf. Acts 7:4) is a later gloss since to the Sumerians it was known as Urim.

4. *Under Tiglath-Pileser III.* Early in his reign in

Merodach-baladan II (left) presents an official with a grant of land. Inscribed on black marble. Height: 46 cm. Photo: Bildarchiv Foto Marburg.

745 Tiglath-Pileser* III came to the aid of Nabonassar, the king of Babylon, against the rebellious Chaldeans. Later in his reign the Assyrian king spent several years (731–729) seeking to suppress Mukinzeri, the chief of the Amukani. The Assyrians were able to subdue Mukin-zeri since the other Chaldeans failed to unite behind him. About a dozen of the letters found at Nimrud (see BORSIPPA; CALAH) shed light on the Assyrian attempts to suppress the Mukin-zeri revolt. Isa 23:1–14 has been considered an anachronistic reference to the Chaldeans, but it may instead be a reference to the devastation of Babylonia by the Assyrians at this time.

5. *Merodach-baladan II.* It was Merodach-baladan (Akkad. *Marduk-apla-iddina*, "Marduk has granted a son"), chief of the Bit-Yakin tribe, who was able to weld the Chaldean tribes into a unit. This Chaldean first appeared in the closing years of Tiglath-Pileser III and continued to be a troublemaker in the reigns of Sargon II* and Sennacherib.* After seizing Babylon in 721, Merodach-baladan fought the Assyrians at Der in 720 with the help of the Elamites, whose aid he had secured with costly gifts. We have three separate documents that claim the victory at Der for the Assyrians, for the Elamites, and for the Chaldeans. At any rate the Assyrians retired and left Merodach-baladan undisturbed for about a decade.

When Sargon again attacked in 710, Merodachbaladan abandoned Babylon without a struggle. After submitting to the Assyrians, he was permitted to remain as chief over the Bit-Yakin. With the accession of Sennacherib in 705, the Chaldean made another bid for power. It was about this time that Merodachbaladan sent his embassy to Hezekiah (2 Kings

20:12ff.; Isa 39:1–8), ostensibly a solicitous inquiry after the Judean king's health but apparently an effort to enlist his aid in an anti-Assyrian coalition. The revolts in the W that led to Sennacherib's famous invasion in 701 may have been coordinated with Chaldean agitation in the E. When Sennacherib turned against Bit-Yakin in 700, the last we hear of Merodach-baladan is that he had fled to Elam* bearing with him the images of his gods and the bones of his ancestors. By 694 his son had taken the place of leadership among the Chaldeans. On a black marble stele (VA 2663) in the Staatliche Museen in Berlin, is depicted a tall figure of Merodach-baladan wearing a pointed cap as he presents an official with a grant of land (cf. C. Pfeiffer, ed., *The Biblical World* [1966], 169).

6. *The Decline of the Assyrian Empire.* After the Elamites had captured Sennacherib's son, Ashurnadin-shum, who had been made king of Babylon, the Chaldean Mushezib-Marduk made himself king over Babylon. In 689 the Assyrians captured Babylon, devastated the city, and carried off the image of the patron god, Marduk. In 652 Nabubel-shumate, the grandson of Merodach-baladan, cast his lot with Shamashshumukin, the brother of Ashurbanipal* and ruler of Babylon, in his abortive revolt against the Assyrian king.

7. *The Chaldean Empire.* The Assyrians, however, had already begun to lose military supremacy. In the second half of the seventh century B.C. the Chaldeans, together with the Medes,* overthrew the Assyrians. Nabopolassar* in 626 began a brilliant if shortlived Chaldean Empire that included his illustrious son Nebuchadnezzar,* the ephemeral kings—Evil-Merodach,* Neriglissar, and Labashi-Marduk—and the enigmatic Nabonidus.*

8. *Chaldeans as Astrologers.* In the Persian, Hellenistic, and Roman periods the name Chaldean became a designation for astrologers. From the original association of the Babylonian priests with astrology, the term was then applied to Greeks who studied in the Babylonian schools. It also described charlatans who professed to read the future from the stars. The so-called "Chaldean Oracles" are theosophical works of Julian and his son, who lived in the second century A.D.

BIBLIOGRAPHY: R. P. Dougherty, *The Sealand of Ancient Arabia* (1932); C. Gadd, "Inscribed Barrel Cylinder of Marduk-apla-iddina II," *Iraq*, 15 (1953), 123–34; H. W. F. Saggs, "The Nimrud Letters, 1952-Part I," *Iraq*, 17 (1955), 21–50; H. Lewy, *Chaldaean Oracles and Theurgy* (1956); H. W. F. Saggs, "Ur of the Chaldees," *Iraq*, 22 (1960), 200–209; id., *The Greatness That Was Babylon* (1962); J. Brinkman, "Merodach-baladan II," in *Studies Presented to A. Leo Oppenheim* (1964), 6–53; A. Millard, "Another Babylonian Chronicle Text," *Iraq*, 26 (1964), 14–35; R. Biggs, "A Chaldaean Inscription from Nippur," *BASOR*, 179 (1965), 36–38; J. Brinkman, "Elamite Military Aid to Merodach-Baladan," *JNES*, 24 (1965), 161–66; id., *A Political History of Post-*

Kassite Babylonia 1158–722 (1968); M. Dietrich, *Die Aramäer Südbabyloniens in der Sargonidenzeit* (1970); A. Millard, "Baladan, the Father of Merodach-Baladan," *Tyndale Bulletin*, 22 (1971), 125–26; J. A. Brinkman, "Sennacherib's Babylonian Problem," *JCS*, 25 (1973), 89–95; J. Lindsay, "The Babylonian Kings and Edom, 605–550 B.C.," *PEQ*, 108 (1976), 23–39.

EY

CHANTING. See INCANTATION.

CHARCOAL. A form of carbon which enables identification to be made of the type of tree from which the original wood* came, by examining it in sections along its different planes. This test can also provide information regarding man's use of wood* in antiquity.

See DENDROCHRONOLOGY; DATING.

CHARIOT. The archaeological contribution to the history of Middle Eastern chariotry is considerable. The theme occupies a list of some fifty references in Yigael Yadin's monumental study—*The Art of Warfare in Biblical Lands in the Light of Archaeological Discovery*. His text and illustrations go back to the records of Lagash* and the armored warfare of Eonnatum. Chariots, in fact, judging from the evidence of vase paintings and other art, were known in Mesopotamia* in the first half of the third millennium B.C., a full thousand years before they were introduced to Egypt.* The well-known Standard of Ur,* an important artifact* from the third millennium, shows four-wheeled chariots, with crews of two, in a sequence meant to simulate a charge.

The hunting chariot, with spoked wheels, was light and swift and appears in Egyptian murals from the middle of the second millennium B.C. This is the prototype of the war chariot, a dangerous vehicle demanding the utmost driving skill. In an Egyptian painting from the tomb of the royal scribe Userhet, in the reign of Amenhotep II, and on a gold patera from Ugarit* of comparable date (first half of fifteenth century B.C.), the driver is shown with the reins round his waist and both hands free for the bow. There are similar murals from Egypt, and one shows a four-spoked chariot included in Canaanite* tribute.

Some of these vehicles have survived intact from 1400 B.C. onward, light and beautifully decorated, like that of Yuha, father-in-law of Amenhotep III. Recovered from the owner's tomb in the Valley of the Kings near Thebes,* it is in the Cairo Museum. A lighter vehicle of wood,* leather,* and metal, possibly a Canaanite type, is in the Florence Museum. Reliefs from the tomb of Thutmose IV show this light type of vehicle in military use. The pharaoh is standing in a chariot with eight-spoked wheels, the reins round his waist, and discharging arrows at retreating Asiatics. It is a vigorous piece of symbolic painting, showing strikingly the confusion of the battlefield.

The same mural shows an Asiatic charioteer pierced by a heavy arrow "between the joints of the armor" (1 Kings 22:34–35) and clinging wounded to the reins of his still galloping team. Such scale armor, good examples of which survive from Nuzi,* was vulnerable where the sleeve, or arm covering, joined the body armor. This was the point at which the English longbowmen aimed when their archery put an end to the reign on the battlefield of the medieval knight.

From the same period, a mural from the tomb of Menena shows the chariot, drawn by a spirited horse,* used as a farm transport vehicle. The lively chariot horse was almost a stylized tradition, for the team is shown in the same rearing pose, held by waist-bound reins, in both battle and hunting scenes. Tutankhamen's* tomb yielded a painted wooden chest, with a lively scene of the king, heavily supplied with arrows, bending a powerful composite bow, protecting the bow arm with an elaborate wrist-shield, and striking down lions,* after the fashion of some Assyrian lion-hunt reliefs. The difference is in the gaiety and decoration of the Egyptian scene.

With the evidence of reliefs only, it is difficult to determine whether the Assyrian war chariots were heavier than the Egyptian types; but on both sides, during the evil years of Assyrian aggression, the war chariot was a common feature of the battlefield. In the Sennacherib* reliefs depicting the assault on Lachish* and the removal of the booty, there is an illustration of a Judean battle-car, the only one of its kind found so far. It followed the model of the chariotry of Sargon* and Sennacherib and was drawn by four horses.

A variant feature in Assyrian chariotry is depicted on a relief of a chariot-charge showing Ashurbanipal.* His chariot has three horses, the third an "outrigger," while a third man in the royal vehicle carries a shield, no doubt a precaution against Ahab's fate (1 Kings 22:34). Characteristically, the Assyrians had solved the attendant difficulties of armored warfare. The murals from the second Ashurbanipal palace at

Shalmaneser III (858-824 B.C.), king of Assyria, followed by four attendants and a groom leading the horses of his chariot followed by a mounted horseman. Drawing of part of an engraving on the bronze reliefs from the gates of a palace of Shalmaneser III. These reliefs illustrate incidents from his military campaigns. Found in a mound near village of Tell Balawat. Now in British Museum. *(See also photos under* HARNESS; HORSE; QARQAR.) Courtesy Carta, Jerusalem.

Nimrud (see CALAH), according to Layard's drawings, show dismantled chariots carried across a river in a barge, with horses swimming and men on inflated skins.

The only NT reference to chariots would appear to be in Phil 3:13–14. Paul was in Rome* when, under Nero, the city was dedicated to chariot racing. A brilliantly depicted mosaic* from first-century Carthage depicts several four-horse chariots in full, violent action. The chariot-racing course, with semicircular ends and banked seating, was known as a circus.* An axial rib (spina), marked at each end of turning posts, divided the course into two runs. The laps were marked by balls at one end and dolphin-shaped objects suspended at the other. The Circus Maximus at Rome, in the Murcia Valley between the Aventine and Palatine hills, has been sufficiently exposed to see the shape of the course. The hippodromes of Alexandria* and Antioch* were famous. Paul had such a course in mind in Phil 3:12–16. Tiers of seats and the official stalls (the "cloud of witnesses" of Heb 12:1) are symbolically shown, and in the corner an official holds up a prize (or perhaps a flagman is signaling the lap).

BIBLIOGRAPHY: A. G. Barrois, *Manuel D'Archéologie Biblique*, 2 (1953), 98 seq.; Y. Yadin, *The Art of Warfare in Biblical Lands* (1963), passim; E. M. Blaiklock, *From Prison in Rome* (1963), 42–43; J. Gray, *The Legacy of Canaan* (1965), 7, 144, 232; J. Arthur Thompson, *ZPEB*, 1 (1975), 780–82.

EMB

CHARRAN. See HARAN.

CHEMICAL TECHNOLOGY. A great many of the ancient crafts* involved elements of technology that, while imperfectly understood, were nevertheless used consciously for the improvement of living conditions. What is perhaps the earliest evidence of chemical technology is seen in the glaze* (Heb. *spsyg*; cf. Prov 26:23 RSV) applied to Tell Halafian pottery* before it was baked at high temperatures in closed kilns. Specifically chemical processes were involved in such occupations as tanning, dyeing* and bleaching (see FULLER), and perfumery. The use of leather* for domestic furnishings as well as for sandals, skin containers, and military articles made tanning an important, if rather malodorous, industry. Surface hairs were usually burned off with lime,* and when the hides had dried, they were treated with a number of vegetable agents including pine and oak bark or leaves, while mineral salts such as alum were used for parchment* or thin decorative leather. Dyeing materials by means of vegetable stains was a craft almost as old as weaving itself. Scarlet dyes were made from crushed cochineal insects (cf. Exod 26:1, 31; Lev 14:4), while Tyrian purple (cf. Acts 16:14), made from the Mediterranean murex mollusk, was virtually a Phoenician* monopoly. The blue, purple, and crimson colors of the temple* veil (2 Chron 3:14) were merely variants of the basic dye used for the tabernacle fabric (Exod 28:5). Blue dye was also obtained from indigo plants in Syria and Egypt.* Excavations at Gezer,* Beth Zur,* and Beth Shemesh*

have uncovered the remains of ancient dye-vats, while at Tell Beit Mirsim (see DEBIR) more than twenty such dye-plants dating from the seventh century B.C. were found. Circular stone vats about .6 m. (2 ft.) in diameter and approximately the same in height were covered over and fitted out with channels for retrieving splashed dyes.

Along with dyeing frequently went the work of the fuller, who cleaned and whitened cloth* (cf. Mark 9:3) before any coloring matter was added to it. Customarily the cloth was "trodden out" on a large stone submerged in a stream and then spread out to dry in the sun (2 Kings 18:17; Isa 7:3). Nitre mixed with a light clay* was sometimes used as soap (Prov 25:20), but the burnt remains of the soda plant were also used by fullers.

In many Near Eastern countries the use of perfumes was often a substitute for bathing, and the compounding of perfumes and aromatic resins is a very ancient craft. In Exod 37:29 a perfumer (KJV, "apothecary") prepared the anointing oil and the incense,* most probably using Egyptian techniques in the process, and this function was still being carried on in the post-Exilic period (1 Chron 9:30; Neh 3:8). Near Eastern peoples made perfumes from myrrh, cassia, saffron, lotus blossoms, nard, cinnamon, stacte, and other aromatic substances. While the process of distilling essences was unknown in antiquity, many scented substances were compounded effectively with oil to produce a distinctive, lasting perfume. Such liquids were often kept in elaborate alabaster* flasks (cf. Matt 26:7) similar to those recovered from Tutankhamen's* tomb. Ugaritic society in the Amarna* Age boasted a special guild of craftsmen who manufactured a variety of perfumes from almugwood, oil of myrrh, and other aromatic and resinous substances.

Chemical technology in Mesopotamia,* Egypt, and at Ugarit* also involved the use of natural substances for purposes of healing (see MEDICINE). To the Egyptians went the distinction of establishing the synergistic relationship of ingredients in pharmaceutical prescriptions, a principle very much in the forefront of modern pharmacology. The Hebrews, however, did not possess pharmacopoeias of the Babylonian variety but on occasions resorted to popular therapeutic procedures (cf. Isa 38:21).

BIBLIOGRAPHY: R. J. Forbes, *Studies in Ancient Technology*, 1–6 (1955–58); R. K. Harrison, *Healing Herbs of the Bible* (1966).

RKH

CHEMOSH (kē'mosh). The name of the national god of the Moabites,* who are twice called "people of Chemosh" (cf. Num 21:29; Jer 48:46). Solomon* built a sanctuary to Chemosh "on a hill east of Jerusalem*" (1 Kings 11:7). This sanctuary, however, was later destroyed by Josiah (cf. 2 Kings 23:13–14). In one passage Chemosh is designated as the god of the Ammonites* rather than the Moabites (Judg 11:24). Some have suggested that this was an oversight on the part of the historian, but it is also possible that since Moab and Ammon were kindred nations descended from a common ancestor, Chemosh may well have been a deity common to both.

Drawing of Mesha Stele discovered at Dhiban in Transjordan and now in the Louvre. Courtesy Carta, Jerusalem.

is ascribed to some forms of Moabite worship only in biblical documents. There is no reference to such sacrifice in Moabite literature, nor have excavations produced physical proof of such a practice. The lack of evidence, however, does not negate the idea of human sacrifice but perhaps indicates that it was practiced on a limited scale.

BIBLIOGRAPHY: G. A. Cooke, *A Textbook of N Semitic Inscriptions* (1903), 1–14; W. F. Albright, *Archaeology and the Religion of Israel* (1953), 117–18; *ANET* (1950), 320–21; *DOTT* (1958), 195–99.

JJD

CHERUBIM. The discovery of the sarcophagus* of Ahiram* of Byblos (Gebal*) in 1923 gives some notion of the meaning of the phrase, "He who sits upon the cherubim" or "sits between the cherubim" (1 Sam 6:2 et al.). If the ivory panels from Samaria,* Megiddo,* Gebal,* and other places, with their representations of winged animals with a human face, rightly portray what the OT meant by cherubim, Ahiram's sarcophagus is significant. The stone casket shows the king with his feet on a three-stepped stool and the sides of his seat shaped like winged sphinxes. Some similar device is on a Megiddo ivory.* No idolatry is involved. Like the "living creatures" of Ezekiel and Revelation, the winged beings are purely symbolic, analogous to their function in the decorations of the Solomonic Temple.*

BIBLIOGRAPHY: P. Dhorme and L.-H. Vincent, *RB*, 35 (1926), 328–58; M. Haran, *Eretz Israel*, V (1958), 83–89; id., *IEJ* (1959), 30–38; W. F. Albright, *The Biblical Archaeologist Reader*, 1 (1961), 95–97; R. de Vaux, *Ancient Israel*, 2 (1965), 295–302, 304, 319–20; D. E. Acomb, *ZPEB*, 1 (1975), 788–90.

EMB

CHESTER BEATTY PAPYRI. The name of a group of biblical manuscripts acquired mainly in 1930 by A. Chester Beatty, an American collector. They had been discovered at Aphroditopolis, N of Memphis* in Egypt,* probably originating from the library of a Christian church.

The manuscripts are substantial portions of papyrus* codices (*see* CODEX): (1) seven from the OT, including large parts of Genesis, Numbers, Deuteronomy, Isaiah, Jeremiah, Daniel, Esther, and Ecclesiastes; (2) three from the NT, containing the Gospels with Acts, the Pauline Epistles, and Revelation; (3) one with part of the pseudepigraphical (*see* PSEUDEPIGRAPHA) Book of Enoch and a second century homily on the passion.

The number of surviving leaves in these codices varies greatly, the most remarkable being P[46] (Pauline Epistles and Hebrews) with 86 nearly complete leaves out of a total of 104. After Beatty acquired the original 10, the University of Michigan acquired another 30, and Beatty another 46, all from the same codex. This collection of papyri, dated to the second and third centuries A.D., provides important textual evidence for OT and especially NT prior to the great vellum (*see* PARCHMENT) codices of the fourth century and later.

BIBLIOGRAPHY: F. G. Kenyon, *The Chester Beatty*

Prior to 1868 the only significant information that scholars possessed on the identity and character of Chemosh came from the Bible itself. However, on August 19, 1868, the famous Moabite Stone* (*see* also MESHA STELE) was brought to a German missionary by Sheikh Zattam. The slab measured 1.2 m. (3 ft., 10 in.) high, .6 m. (2 ft.) wide, and 6.4 cm. (2½ in.) thick. It was rounded at the top and contained thirty-four lines of writing. The inscription referred to the triumph of Mesha, "son of Chemosh, king of Moab," whose father reigned over Moab for thirty years. He told how he threw off the yoke of Israel and honored his god Chemosh by building a high place* at Qarhoh. The date of the Mesha stone is roughly fixed by the reference to Mesha, king of Moab, in 2 Kings 3:4. On the basis of this information the date of the stone is placed variously between 840 and 820 B.C. In addition to the historical importance of the stone, we are able to learn a great deal about how the Moabite viewed his god Chemosh. In the Mesha inscription Chemosh is depicted as one who was angry, forsook his people, turned them over to their enemies, and then later delivered them. Mesha spoke of devoting people "to destruction" for the god "Ashtar-Chemosh."

At least one biblical reference seems to imply that, on occasion, human sacrifices were offered to this god (cf. 2 Kings 3:27). It seems that human sacrifice

Biblical Papyri, fasc. i–vii (1933–37); id., *The Text of the Greek Bible* (1937); B. M. Metzger, *The Text of the NT* (1964), 26–27, 36–42, plates II, XIVa.

BFH

CHIEF OFFICIAL. Used in KJV Acts 28:7 for the "prôtos" (πρῶτος) of Malta* (variously in other renderings; e.g., governor, TCNT; chieftain, RIEU; chief magistrate, NEB). The title was officially correct in Malta, as W. M. Ramsay first pointed out. It is epigraphically attested, e.g., IG, 24.601, where the title "first (man) of the Maltese" is applied to a Roman knight named Pudens. The Publius of Acts 28:7 was probably of the same rank. Also *CIL*, 10.7495, a fragmentary inscription, was restored with certainty to read: [munic]ipii Mel[itensium] primus omni[um]. The Greek and Latin inscriptions probably use a term adopted by the Roman administration from the existing nomenclature on the island—doubtless dating back to Carthaginian days. Rome's* policy was to use existing patterns of authority as far as possible. The praetor of Sicily held overriding authority (Cic.Verr. 4.18). Archaeology, in revealing an established Roman practice, underlines Luke's accuracy as a historian.

EMB

CHILD SACRIFICE. Numerous OT references to human sacrifice (cf. Lev 20:2; Deut 12:31f.; 2 Kings 16:3; Jer 7:31 et al.) make apparent the fact that the offering of human beings to a deity by means of ritual murder was not unknown in the Ancient Near East. That children were made the specific object of sacrifice in this way has been attested from N Mesopotamian* texts dated from the tenth to the seventh centuries B.C. From these sources it appears that certain rites celebrated in honor of the deity Hadad, the god of storms, involved the slaughter and cremation of young boys.

Several OT references appear to allude to this practice in connection with the Ammonite god Molech* (Lev 18:21; 2 Kings 23:10 et al.), probably the same deity as the Malik or Muluk worshiped during the Third Dynasty of Ur,* and also revered at Mari* c. 800 B.C. In 2 Kings 17:31 the men of Sepharvaim in E-central Syria burned their children as offerings to Adrammelech and Anammelech, the former being the Mesopotamian deity Adad-milki, a variant name for the Syrian Hadad. The cremation of male children in pursuance of this hideous practice is confirmed in N Mesopotamian texts of the tenth to seventh centuries B.C.

Precisely why these cults offered children in sacrifice is unknown, but it may have been to confirm a vow or solemn promise. According to Diodorus (20:14), children were placed before a statue of the Tyrian deity Melkart at Carthage and then deposited in a furnace. On the other hand, the OT references may merely allude to a practice current in Greece and elsewhere in the Aegean in which children were passed quickly through a flame in order to confer on them additional physical strength or ensure immortality. This custom was reflected in the classical stories of Thetis and Achilles (Apollodorus 3.13.6).

Archaeological evidence for child sacrifice is ambiguous, and though skeletons of children have been recovered in Palestine from Megiddo,* Gezer,* Taanach,* and other sites, they cannot be demonstrated unquestionably to be victims of sacrificial rites.

BIBLIOGRAPHY: W. F. Albright, *Archaeology and the Religion of Israel* (1953), 163.

RKH

CHINNEROTH. See GALILEE.

CHI-RHO (kī-rō). Chi and Rho, the first two letters (XP) of the Greek word for Christ, were, from the age of Constantine, frequently used as a Christian symbol, pre-Constantinian though the sign has been shown to be (e.g., M. Guarducci, *The Tomb of St. Peter* [1960], 111). They formed the "labarum" or battle standard of the emperor, replacing the legionary eagle* and the medallions bearing the emperor's portrait, which were carried on poles at the head of the cohorts (*see* ARMED FORCES IN THE NT). Examples from the catacombs* date back to the early years of Constantine and appear with all manner of accompaniment and stylization—on coins,* seals,* lamps,* vases, rings, gems. As far away as Britain we have the monogram on silver* spoons from the Mildenhall treasure, on stones in the Cotswold villa of Chedworth, in a villa mosaic* from Frampton in Dorset, and Roman pewter from Andover. Especially interesting is a fresco of the monogram from the Kentish villa of Lullingstone, which seems to show a knowledge of a representation on a fourth-century sarcophagus* now in the Lateran Museum. The dates of both pieces of funerary (*see* FUNERARY CUSTOMS, PALESTINIAN) art are around A.D. 350. On the Lateran coffin the monogram is supported by a cross with a surrounding wreath at which doves pick. This feature, which reappears in the villa fresco, suggests the blessed dead feeding on an immortal crown. On the sarcophagus two soldiers crouch below, signifying Christian warriors who have passed into rest.

BIBLIOGRAPHY: Of some interest is G. W. Meates, *Lullingstone Roman Villa* (1955), ch. 13. There is an important article on the sign by Matthew Black in a Festschrift presented to F. F. Bruce, *Apostolic History of the Gospel*, "The Chi-Rho Sign—Christogram and/or Staurogram" (1970), ch. 22 with bibliography.

EMB

CHISEL. See TOOLS.

CHOGA ZAMBIL. See ELAM.

CHORAZIN. See KORAZIN.

CHRONOLOGY. The study of temporal relationships is basic to historical and archaeological study because the search for formative influences, developmental trends, and relationships between events significantly controls the interpretation and synthesis of historiographic data. Two main types of chronology are usually mentioned in archaeological literature:

relative and absolute. Relative chronology is concerned with sequences and intervals. It is either unable to determine or is unconcerned with exact dates B.C. or A.D. Rather it seeks to establish, as a minimal requirement of the archaeologist's task, which features came earlier and which later. If possible, durations and intervals are assigned, for example, to the occupational levels of a house,* street,* or cave.* This "internal" chronology, assigned because of observable typological change or other durative phenomena such as radiocarbon decay, can then be compared to various "external" chronologies (i.e., those of other sites).

Absolute chronology, on the other hand, is concerned with establishing dates in accordance with a generally accepted dating* system or calendar. Regnal years were widely used in the ancient world for dating, as for example in the Bible. Eras were marked by the introduction of a dynasty (such as the Seleucid) or the founding of a city (Rome* and others) or a religion. The Sothic cycle in Egypt marked the introduction of an astronomical calendar.*

Establishing an absolute chronology and connecting relative with absolute dates is the most difficult aspect of historical study. Various modern methods have been used to bring greater precision to the task. Radiocarbon dating is useful for the more extended range of prehistoric activity. Dendrochronology* (tree ring dating) helps in areas where the record can be reconstructed by means of surviving timbers. Thermoluminescence is a technique which seeks to extract information from residual magnetism in earth and stone. The most commonly used dating technique among archaeologists, however, is typology.* Lithic or ceramic typology is extremely useful because of the abundance of the evidence, and has reached a level of refinement that guarantees considerable precision.

JEJ

CILICIA. A large area located in the SE coastal area of Asia Minor,* the W portion being known as Cilicia Tracheia and its E counterpart having the name of Cilicia Pedias. The latter was a fertile plain well watered by several rivers. Ancient trade routes between Asia Minor and Syria passed through the twin defiles known as the Cilician Gates and the Syrian Gates. Ancient tells* cover Cilicia Pedias, the earliest being Neolithic* in origin and related culturally to Mesopotamia.* In the second millennium B.C. Cilicia was known as Kizzuwatna, and in the fourteenth century B.C. it became part of the Hittite* Empire under Suppiluliumas.*

Cilicia was sacked when the Sea Peoples* overran the Hittites (c. 1200 B.C.), but by the eighth century B.C. it had recovered sufficiently to ally (c. 712 B.C.) with a Phrygian group against Sargon (see SARGON II) of Assyria, only to suffer another defeat. Cilicia became independent in the following century and fell under increasing Greek influence, particularly in the Persian period. Seleucus Nicator established Seleucid control in the Hellenistic period, but effective rule over the area only came with Pompey after 67 B.C. The two sections of Cilicia were divided at this time, but subsequently became reunified under Vespasian* about A.D. 72. The reference to Syria and Cilicia in Acts 15:23, 41 and Gal 1:21 are to Cilicia Pedias, which in the time of Luke and Paul was administratively a part of Syria.

BIBLIOGRAPHY: W. M. Ramsay, *The Cities of St. Paul* (1908); A. H. M. Jones, *The Cities of the Eastern Roman Provinces* (1937), 192–215; D. Magie, *Roman Rule in Asia Minor* (1950), 266–77; M. Gough, *AnSt*, 2 (1952), 85–150; ibid., 4 (1954), 49–64; ibid., (1956), 167–77; M. J. Mellink, *IDB*, 1 (1962), 626–28; E. M. Blaiklock, *ZPEB*, 1 (1975), 862–65.

RKH

CIRCUMCISION. See TEPE GAWRA.

CIRCUS. A chariot*-racing course, with semicircular ends and banked seating, sometimes called a hippodrome. An axial rib (*spina*), marked at each end by turning posts, divided the course into two runs. The laps were marked by balls at one end and dolphin-shaped objects suspended at the other. The Circus Maximus at Rome,* in the Murcia Valley (Lewis and Short, *Latin Dictionary* [1879], 1177, s.v. "Murcius") between the Aventine and Palatine hills, has been sufficiently exposed to see the shape of the course. The hippodromes of Alexandria* and Antioch* were famous. Paul has such a course in mind in Phil 3:12–16.

See GAMES.

BIBLIOGRAPHY: E. M. Blaiklock, *From Prison in Rome* (1964), 41–43.

EMB

CISTERN. The cistern of Palestine was commonly a pear-shaped reservoir into which water could run from a roof, tunnel, or courtyard. From about the thirteenth century B.C. it was plastered and its opening stopped by a suitably cut stone, large enough for protection, but sometimes quite heavy (cf. Gen 29:8–10). It must have been a frequent misfortune, in an earthquake-fractured land, to find the stored waters of a laboriously cut cistern seeping away through a new fissure in the rocks (cf. the imagery of an apostate people in Jer 2:13). In such abandoned reservoirs there is usually a mound of debris underneath the opening, consisting of dirt and rubbish, blown or knocked in, shattered remnants of water containers, and not infrequently skeletons. These may represent the result of accident, suicide, or some such incarceration as that which Jeremiah endured, although he did not experience the usual fatal end of exhaustion and drowning in water and mud. In one cistern at Gezer* archaeologists discovered a dozen or more male skeletons and the upper half of a female who had been sawn asunder at the waist (cf. Heb 11:37). These were prisoners who, unlike Joseph (Gen 37:20–29) and Jeremiah (Jer 38), were not rescued. Similar discoveries were made in cisterns at Ai* and Tell en-Nasbeh. Complex structures have been unearthed at Jerusalem,* Masada,* Samaria,* and other locations. Many cisterns constructed in antiquity are still in use.

BIBLIOGRAPHY: R. Macalister, *A Century of Ex-*

cavation in Palestine (1925), 220–21; W. F. Albright, The Archaeology of Palestine (1930), 113, 210; C. McCown, The Ladder of Progress in Palestine (1943); N. Glueck, Rivers in the Desert (1959), 94–97; R. de Vaux, Ancient Israel (1961), 238–40; R. Forbes, Studies in Ancient Technology, 1 (1964), 152; Y. Yadin, Masada (1966), 26–29.

EMB

CITADEL. A high fortified keep constructed to protect a city.* Sometimes the keep evolved into a "high place"* or a platform for a temple. Zion was originally the citadel of pre-Israelite Jerusalem,* and in the early monarchy it became a royal keep, the "city of David."

CITIES OF THE PLAIN. See PLAIN, CITIES OF THE.

CITY. Two types of collective dwellings are distinguished in the Bible, the city and the village. The city is understood to have been walled (see WALLS, CITY) (cf. Lev 25:29, 30) and to have had certain legal prerogatives. However, none of the cities of Palestine could be compared in size or structure to the great cities of Babylon,* Nineveh,* Persepolis,* Athens,* Corinth,* Carthage, or Rome.* There are three reasons: (1) The towns and cities of the most ancient East arose as cultic and market centers for farmers and herdsmen. These were the cities which represented the archaic-religious state, that total mixture of religion-ritual-government-business, such as Ur,* the composite aspects of whose life are evident from the extensive archaeological investigations on the site. The Hellenistic age ended this type of unified establishment everywhere but in Israel. (2) At no time did the Israelites ever build or control a large merchant fleet, sailing from a totally Israelite port and trading with Jewish colonies, as did the Greeks. The upland population was fairly homogeneous and had little intrusion other than of a military nature. Thus the cities were still serving their initial function long after the need had ceased and the great Greco-Roman thalassocracies had appeared. (3) The geography of Palestine, with the spine of the mountains from N to S and the deep valleys and deserts on either side did not support populations large enough for cities in the Greek sense, that is, large states with central participatory governments. Thus for many centuries after the fall of the archaic-religious state elsewhere we find its central form thriving in Israel, the dynamic of theocracy. While other cities of antiquity boasted dozens of shrines and temples (Babylon had 1,700 of them), all of Israel had only one, the great temple* in Jerusalem.*

The growth of the town, and later the walled city, is thought to have been a by-product of the development of food* producing over the previous practice of food gathering. Some believe this alteration is the theme behind the many Sumerian* dialogues and contests between hunter and farmer. This alteration in economic systems is the fundamental feature of the era called the Neolithic.* Although the primary archaeological evidence for the change is on

sites located in the upper foothills of the Zagros Mountains of Iraq, there is evidence for this same phenomenon around the shores of the fresh-water lakes left by the glaciers on a rough line across the N shore of the Mediterranean. One likely site is the shore of Galilee* where very ancient remains have been uncovered in the Valley of Ginossar. The Neolithic era certainly began in Palestine by 7000 B.C., possibly earlier. A number of ancient stone-walled towns have been excavated, usually situated near streams or springs. Jericho,* located on the flat lands NW of the Dead Sea,* is a prime example of this type of town. The ancient enclosed town lies within a few hundred feet of where the main spring issues out of the ground. The high stone walls and narrow streets go back at least ten thousand years.

Along with agriculture came the cultic center, and there is evidence that each little town had its temple to the tutelary deities of the district. The oldest known written records from Sumerian sites are all economic and yield data on the economic importance of the temples. It appears that in time the temples and the towns amassed wealth and power. Rulers of the towns became rulers of the land. In Genesis there are allusions to this state of affairs (Gen 6–11). Although Jericho is the oldest and most interesting example, other walled cities have been excavated in Palestine, namely Beth Shemesh,* Ramat-Rahel, Hebron,* Gibeon,* Hazor,* and many more.

With the increased manipulation of stored quantities, and the necessity for an impersonal technology to carry data and make it available to more than one location and time, the impetus for writing* developed. Thus the growth of the city and the practice of writing complimented each other from the earliest foundations of towns. Other technologies—ceramics (see POTTERY), weaving, brewing, and the like—increased greatly with the growth of cities. Over the centuries different types and methods of building cities and the city wall came into being. The earliest were simply rough-faced stones piled and fixed with mortar. In time casemate walls* consisting of cross walls to bolster two external walls were used. The Hyksos* custom of using beaten earth as fill for walls came to be used also. The building of cities by royal fiat brought the adoption of some form of planning, and some ancient city plans have been recovered. A central plaza-type market area was usually surrounded by the temple or castle* wall, and the houses* built up against it yielded a more or less concentric plan to the city. As the cities grew and altered, new streets* were dug through old walls and old houses and walls were quarried (see QUARRY) to provide material for new projects. The results are a bewildering puzzle of blocks and fragments which can only be sorted out with the greatest difficulty.

The size and extent of the ancient biblical cities were small, Jerusalem in David's time covering no more than ten acres. Most others were half as large. Streets were unpaved and rough, being completed and paved only in Greco-Roman times. Each small professional and trade group had its assigned sector of the city and all paid taxes to the court and temple.

BIBLIOGRAPHY: S. Piggott, ed., The Dawn of Civ-

ilization (1961); L. Mumford, *The City in History* (1961); Archaeological Institute of America, compiler, *Archaeological Discoveries in the Holy Land* (1967).

ww

CLAUDIUS. Tiberius Claudius Nero Germanicus (10 B.C.–A.D. 54; Acts 11:28; 17:7; 18:2) became *princeps* on the assassination of Caligula in A.D. 41. Two archaeological discoveries link Claudius with the NT: (1) The Nazareth Decree* is almost certainly a rescript of Claudius and contains a matter of evidential importance relating to the historicity of the Resurrection. (2) A papyrus* letter to the Alexandrians that is of great historical importance. The Jews of Alexandria* were a large, educated, and powerful community, having lived under their own ethnarch and racial council since the days of the Ptolemies (*see* PTOLEMY). Augustus,* in his pacification and organization of the provinces, had confirmed their privileges. In A.D. 41 there had been a good deal of tension and violence between the Alexandrians and the Jewish community, and Claudius sought to bring matters to order in a stern letter.* It was published by the proclamation of Lucius Aemilius Rectus, prefect of Egypt,* whose preamble illustrates the "name of blasphemy" that John saw on the heads of the Beast (Rev 13:1). It runs:

Proclamation by Lucius Aemilius Rectus. Seeing that all the populace, owing to its numbers was unable to be present at the reading of the most sacred and most beneficent letter to the city, I have deemed it necessary to display the letter publicly in order that reading it one by one you may admire the majesty of our god Caesar and feel gratitude for his goodwill towards the city. Year 2 of Tiberius Claudius Caesar Augustus Germanicus Imperator, the 14th of Neus Sebastus.

The concluding third of the letter deals with the ghetto troubles, and it seems to contain the first reference in literature to Christian missionaries, whose presence and preaching may indeed have caused some tension in the synagogue.* "Jewish visitors from Syria" are especially mentioned and described in severe terms as "fomenters of a general plague infecting the whole world."

The relevant section runs partly as follows:

As for the question which party was responsible for the riots and feud (or rather, if the truth must be told, the war) with the Jews . . . I tell you once for all that unless you put a stop to this ruinous and obstinate enmity against each other, I shall be driven to show what a benevolent prince can be when turned to righteous indignation. Wherefore once again I conjure you that on the one hand the Alexandrians show themselves forbearing and kindly towards the Jews . . . and on the other hand I explicitly order the Jews not to agitate for more privileges than they formerly possessed. . . . If desisting from these courses you consent to live with mutual forbearance and kindliness, I on my side will exercise a solicitude of very long standing for the city. . . . Farewell."

Perhaps the most learned of the emperors of the first century, Claudius earned unpopularity and ridicule because of his personal foibles, due probably to some form of cerebral palsy. He was nonetheless an able administrator, to whose reputation modern research has done some justice. A number of inscriptions, uncouth sometimes in language but wise in content, bear testimony both to Claudius's personality and to his shrewd administration. Statues of Claudius, always idealized, show the tension that arose from his physical disabilities and the faults of character that a painful and rejected childhood had inflicted on him.

BIBLIOGRAPHY: P. Lond., 1912, in F. G. Kenyon and H. I. Bell, *Greek Papyri in the British Museum* (1893–1917); Tac., *Ann.*, 11–12; Suetonius, *Dious Claudius*; A. Momigliano, *The Emperor Claudius and His Achievements* (1934); "The Augustan Empire," *CAH*, 10 (1952), 667–701.

EMB

CLAY. This substance was widely used for building, from the paleolithic cultures down to Roman times. In the irrigation* cultures of prehistoric Mesopotamia,* Egypt,* India, and the Danube Valley, clay, commonly bound with straw, was the most popular building material.* Clay cones with coloring added were used for decorative walls and façades at Uruk* and elsewhere in Sumer.* Clay figurines and pots were widely distributed even before the Neolithic Age.* The use of the potter's* wheel made possible new techniques in the forming of clay. The use of clay as a material for written or pictographic* communication dates from the fifth millennium B.C., and tablets from Rumania, as well as from several sites in Iraq, have messages impressed on them. Stamp seals* impressed on clay were in use by 3000 B.C. in Mesopotamia, Egypt, India, and many other areas. The addition of quartz sand and other grit to the natural clay added strength when fired. It is thought that the earliest copper smelting was possibly a by-product of the ceramic technology developed for clay. Since clays of various colors and characteristics were found around the Mediterranean, these, or artifacts made from them, were often traded. Clay mixed with lime or dung was also used as a plaster, while tempered pottery had many uses in agriculture. Broken sherds* from clay artifacts* were used as scrapers (Job 2:8), awls, and as writing materials called ostraca,* the latter proving of prime value to archaeologists.

See BUILDING MATERIALS; EGYPT; MESOPOTAMIA; OSTRACA; SUMER; URUK; WRITING, GENERAL.

BIBLIOGRAPHY: H. Wirsch, *Applied Mineralogy* (1968), 102–6, 119–26.

ww

CLOAK. Mentioned in Isa 3:22 and translating the word that in Ruth 3:15 is rendered "shawl" (ASV and RSV, "mantle"; KJV, "wimple"; Heb. *mitpahat*). In the Isaian context, it may mean a hooded cloak. Judean women shown in Assyrian reliefs wear a head covering which leaves the face free and falls down the back like a nun's veil.

CLOTH; CLOTHING. Vegetable fibers have been spun since Neolithic* times. Felt seems as old. From Sumer* have come tablets recording the amount of cloth woven by the weavers and the number of gallons of beer received as part of their pay. Red woolen cloth was particularly favored among the Sumerians. By Bible times evidence from the Near East shows that textiles were a major item of trade. A few types of cloth from biblical times have been discovered in Palestine, mostly from the dry desert regions of the Dead Sea* and the mountains around it. The two sources were animal and vegetable fibers. Animal fibers were common in Israel, but flax and cotton were imported from Egypt.* The wool fabric (largely men's and women's tunics) from the excavations of Masada* are the best examples ever found from the Roman Period. They had long warps with bands of color interspersed in the weft. The colors have faded over the centuries, but the dominant shades are brown, tan, reddish, and yellow, with stripes of black, blue, green, and other shades regularly used (cf. Ps 45:13–14).

Felt and leather* must have played an important role as trade goods in the patriarchal period, but no specimen has survived. Very wide kilts of woven flax and linen* are shown in various Egyptian paintings and carvings.

Although no clothing fragments from Palestinian excavations date from OT times, a number of artistic representations from other locations yield information on the styles of the peoples who lived in the Eastern Mediterranean. The best preserved of all are the representations from Egypt, particularly the Beni Hasan Tableau.* They show the N Semitic costume as a long shirt or tunic worn by both men and women. The areas of Palestine under Egyptian domination such as the NW coast show in their glyptic art the short kilt and bare chest of men's styles and the long short-sleeved or sleeveless gown. Men generally wore loin cloths, and women a baggy type of undergarment. However, artistic evidence shows a wide variation in hair and clothing styles over the centuries. It is known from the OT that men were bearded and women covered their heads. The cloth used in clothing and for head wrappings was brightly colored and frequently woven in patterns. Linen and even silk were known in Persian and Hellenistic times.

Except for ritual nudity (cf. 2 Sam 6:14–20) the Israelites were strictly dressed according to mood and social or religious position. Garments were decorated and adorned with jewelry and precious metals.

BIBLIOGRAPHY: L. Bellinger, "Cloth," *IDB*, 1 (1962), 650–55; R. J. Forbes, *Studies in Ancient Technology*, 4, rev ed. (1964); Y. Yadin, *Masada* (1966), 140, 154.   ww

CNIDUS (nī dus; Gr. χνίδος, *knídos*). A peninsula and also a city* on the Carian SW coast of Asia Minor* where Paul's ship on his voyage to Rome* touched, according to Acts 27:7, which is the only biblical reference to this place.

Cnidus, located across the Gulf of Cos from Halicarnassus at the end of the long peninsula (see also Pausanias 5.24,7), was beautifully situated, with terraces rising from the water to its acropolis.* The projecting cape of Triopium extending out along the coast and connected with it by a narrow isthmus supplied Cnidus with a double harbor, the moles* of which are still visible. At the top of the cape was the temple of Apollo, the patron god of the area whose festival was celebrated in common by the member cities. Cnidus itself seems to have been under the protection of Artemis* Hyacinthotrophus, in whose honor the city established a festival. The Dorian Federation met every four years at Cnidus to celebrate the Dorian Games (*see* GAMES).

At Cnidus are still visible, among other things, the remains of two temples (including the temple of Apollo Karneios and the temple of Aphrodite Euploia), town walls, other Greek structures, Roman period buildings, a stadium, a theater,* and Byzantine* churches. The important objects and other ruins are to be dated from the seventh century B.C. and before to the seventh century A.D., at which time Cnidus was abandoned. Inscriptions connected with Cnidus show reference to Apollo, Aphrodite, Artemis, Asklepios, Athena, Demeter and Persephone, Hermes,* Hestia, Isis, Kore, the Muses, Pluto, and Serapis.

BIBLIOGRAPHY: "Knidos," Pauly-Wissowa, *Real-Encyclopadie*, Band XI.1 (1921), 914–20; A. H. M. Jones, *The Cities of the Eastern Roman Provinces* (1937), 77; D. Magie, *Roman Rule in Asia Minor*, 1 (1950), 87; G. E. Bean and J. M. Cook, "The Cnidia," *Annual of The British School at Athens*, 47 (1952), 171–212; I. C. Love, "Preliminary Reports of the Excavations at Knidos, 1969–1971," *AJA*, 74 (1970), 149–55; *AJA*, 76 (1972), 61–76; ibid., 393–405; *OCD* (1970), 206; E. M. Blaiklock, *ZPEB*, 1:896; *The Princeton Encyclopedia of Classical Sites*, ed. R. Stillwell (1976), 459.   WHM

Beni Hasan Tableau depicting an Asiatic caravan coming to Egypt, from wall painting in tomb of

CODEX. The name for a collection of papyrus* sheets in book form. The Latin word "codex" (pl., codices) or "caudex" referred primarily to a wooden tablet coated with wax, a writing* material which remained common in Latin communities. But in the eastern and southern provinces of the Roman world the papyrus roll had been the norm. Its disadvantage lay in the difficulty of handling it; rolls were an average of about 25 cm. (10 in.) high, but as much as 10.5 m. (35 ft.) in length.

It was thus natural that the use of the codex evolved, substantially in the form of the modern book. Sheets of papyrus were laid on each other, folded in half and sewn together to form a quire (usually 10–12 sheets). Codices were made of varying numbers of quires, with numbered pages.

The only country in which papyrus codices survived was Egypt* (because of its extremely dry climate), and the numerous discoveries of sheets, rolls, and codices began late in the eighteenth century. One remarkable phenomenon was the rapid increase in the use of codices instead of rolls by the Christian communities in Egypt. These comprised about 74 percent of known Christian papyri by the fourth century, whereas non-Christian papyri show a much slower change. In the case of OT Greek manuscripts, this marked a break with the Jewish tradition of biblical scrolls. Although the earliest codex fragment (the John Rylands) dates to the early second century A.D., the major finds such as the Chester Beatty papyri* are from the late second and third centuries.

When from the fourth century vellum (*see* PARCHMENT) largely replaced papyrus as a permanent writing material, the codex form remained and has provided our most valuable biblical manuscripts—above all the Codex Vaticanus, C. Alexandrinus, C. Sinaiticus, C. Ephraemi, and C. Bezae. The discovery by Tischendorf of the Codex Sinaiticus in 1844 and its subsequent history is perhaps the best example of the archaeological role of the textual scholar.

See CHESTER BEATTY PAPYRI; PAPYRUS; PARCHMENT.

BIBLIOGRAPHY: J. Černý, *Paper and Books in Ancient Egypt* (1952); F. G. Kenyon, *Our Bible and the Ancient Manuscripts* (1958); P. R. Ackroyd and C. F. Evans, eds., *The Cambridge Ancient History of the Bible*, 1 (1970), ch. 1.

BFH

CODOMANNUS. *See* DARIUS.

COFFIN. *See* SARCOPHAGUS.

COFFIN TEXTS. These Egyptian* literary materials, which dealt against a magical background with man's future state, seem to have arisen from, or been profoundly influenced by, a collection of eschatological concepts, incantations,* and magical spells known as the Pyramid Texts, which were formulated for the Old Kingdom rulers and placed in their private tombs. From the First Intermediate period (Dynasties Seven–Eleven) these funerary inscriptions, which in brief reflected the deceased's desire to enjoy bliss beyond the grave and to be absorbed into the overall rhythm of cosmic activity, were extended to other members of the populace by being inscribed on the coffins of dead persons, hence the designation of these texts. After the Eleventh Dynasty they were written on papyrus* and placed in the coffin along with the deceased, and this development comprises the so-called Book of the Dead* stage of these inscriptions.

The ancient spells from the Pyramid Texts were augmented for the common people, but they still served the original purpose of safeguarding the existence and interests of the deceased by magical means when judgment was being meted out by Osiris* and his forty-two assessors. The reason why the texts were inscribed on the walls of coffins was to have the materials immediately at hand should the dead person need to consult them at any given moment. As time passed, the original idea of dependence upon magic for final felicity was modified by a more sophisticated concept, namely that happiness in eternity was conditioned by, and comprised the reward of, an earthly life lived according to morality and righteousness. Nevertheless, it was still thought prudent for the common man to be able to enlist the aid of magic in his deification, so that on entering the abode of the blessed dead he would be as his pharaoh. The Coffin Texts reflected the anticipated moral vindication of the deceased in such statements as, "My sin is dispelled, my error is wiped away," and "I go on the way which I have learned upon the Island of the Righteous." Although the Coffin Texts emerged from a period which saw the closest approximation of Egyptian life to the concept of democracy, they had very little to say about human rights or social justice apart from a short Middle Kingdom text from el-Bersheh, part of which was as follows: "I made the four winds that every man might breathe thereof in his time . . . I made the vast inundation that the

Khnum-hotep at Beni Hasan, c. 1890 B.C. *(See also photo under* LEATHER.*)*

poor man might have rights therein just like the rich . . . I made every man just like his fellow. . . ."

See BOOK OF THE DEAD; FUNERARY CUSTOMS; OSIRIS.

BIBLIOGRAPHY: J. Černý, *Ancient Egyptian Religion* (1952), 57, 87–94.

RKH

COINS. Barter was the normal method of exchange before the introduction of coinage, which probably occurred in the late eighth century B.C. in Asia Minor.* Although perishable foods* were sometimes used as currency, the most frequent medium of exchange was cattle, from which the Latin word for money, *pecunia* (from *pecus*, "cattle"), is derived. Wealth measured in the form of cattle is referred to in Gen 13:2, where Abraham is described as being "very rich in cattle, in silver, and in gold." Smaller animals, timber, wine, oil, and honey were sometimes used for barter and also for the payment of taxes* and tribute (*see* BOOTY) (cf. 1 Sam 8:15; 2 Kings 3:4; Ezek 45:13–16).

When the inconvenience of having a cumbersome object as a means of exchange became increasingly apparent, a commodity of more constant value and universal acceptability was found in metal. Copper was essential for the manufacture of weapons (*see* ARMS AND WEAPONS) and agricultural implements, while gold* and silver* were very highly prized metals from remote antiquity. Silver was also available in considerable quantities.

Estimating the true purity, weight, and value of metal by observation was not only difficult but unreliable. Ingots of uniform shape were molded, however, in addition to rings and bracelets of standard weight which could also be used for personal adornment. Gifts to Rebekah included "a gold nose ring weighing a beka and two gold bracelets weighing ten shekels" (Gen 24:22). The sons of Jacob purchased corn in Egypt with "bundles of money," presumably in the form of rings. Excavations at Gezer* yielded a molded ingot and a currency ring of gold, indicating the antiquity of this medium of exchange in Palestinian usage.

True values of these forms of currency could only be established by weighing the items, and cheating was prevalent as a result. It is recorded that when Abraham purchased the cave of Machpelah* he "weighed out for him . . . four hundred shekels of silver, according to the weight current among the merchants" (Gen 23:16). Weights that ensured a just balance were later stamped and declared sacred. "Honest scales and balances are from the Lord; all the weights in the bag are of his making" (Prov 16:11).

The transporting of a quantity of money such as a talent of silver or gold, or the heavy large flat discs of copper sometimes used as currency, continued to create difficulties in commercial transactions. The situation greatly improved when the stamping or authenticating of the value of a piece of metal began, and this in turn was the forerunner of the coin inscribed with symbols of local objects or the head of a king or god. Fraud continued to exist, however, and deep slashes in some silver coins testify mutely

to the doubt of a purchaser in ancient times and to his determination to find out for himself whether his coin contained pure silver or a less valuable metal which had been silver-coated. The milling of coin edges is a comparatively modern development, and because so many coins were clipped it was still necessary to weigh large quantities of silver to evaluate them precisely.

The earliest known coins seem to have been introduced in the seventh century B.C. almost simultaneously in Lydia* and Aegina. The first staters in electrum, an alloy of gold and silver, were attributed by Herodotus to Croesus of Lydia, although one dating to the reign of his father Alyattes (617–560 B.C.) has been excavated. Coins in the Bible only begin to be mentioned specifically in the post-Exilic period. Thus in Ezra 2:69 (RSV) the Jews on their return from exile donated "sixty-one thousand darics of gold (and) five thousand minas of silver" for the erection of the Temple. The Persian daric was a thick gold coin showing a detailed portrait of the king with a bow and arrow on the obverse and a simple die punch mark common to most early coins on the reverse. It was named after King Darius I* (521–486 B.C.), although the coin was in use at an even earlier period in the reign of Cyrus (550–530 B.C.). Writing at a later time, the author of the Book of Ezra was presumably using the local current term for the daric and applying it to the coins that Ezra carried with him. A similar explanation is probable for the form "daric" mentioned in 1 Chron 29:7 at the time of King David.

During the excavations at Shechem* in 1956, a coin of northern Greece dating from the sixth century B.C. was uncovered. In general the most familiar coins were the tetradrachmas exchanged by the Phoenician traders. Of these coins the Athenian tetradrachma had now developed into a coin which manifested both an obverse and reverse die, the result of which was a design of exceptional detail.

Yᵉhûdh, Jahud, the official name for the Persian province of Judea, was inscribed on a coin from the fourth century B.C., indicating that there was a local mint in the province. Persian satraps were authorized to mint silver coins, but not gold ones, which remained relatively rare.

With the expansion of Alexander's empire and the vast troop movements involved, a unified coinage was developed which consisted of gold staters and silver tetradrachmas. Many of these were minted at Tyre* and Sidon,* and they became the most acceptable silver coins of the period because of their high precious metal content. Excavations in Judah* to date have not recovered coinage from the period of Alexander the Great, although hoards of coins depicting his successors, the Ptolemies,* have been located.

From 198 B.C. Judah came under the rule of the Syrian Seleucids, and a period of political disturbance and persecution of the Jews* ensued. Some persons accommodated themselves to the Hellenistic ideology being forced on them by the Seleucids, but many withstood the attacks on the ancestral faith and found leadership in the Maccabee* family, which

Drawing of two coins from Persian Period, fourth century B.C. Left: coin showing owl-type head. Reverse: owl standing, facing small lily. Inscription: *YHD (Yahud)*. Silver, 7 mm. Right: Reverse: a god seated on winged chariot, holding falcon. Inscription: *YHD*. Silver, 15 mm. *(See also photos under* PTOLEMY; TIBERIAS; VESPASIAN.*)* Courtesy Carta, Jerusalem.

organized systematic revolt. So successful were the Maccabees in this that the Syrian governor even granted Simon Maccabee the right to mint coins, stating, "I give thee leave to coin money for thy country with thine own stamp" (1 Macc 15:6).

The copper coins minted soon afterward were simple and unpretentious but were remarkable in that they did not show portraits. Adhering strictly to the second commandment, the Jewish people would not allow any portrait to appear on coins, which instead frequently bore agricultural designs such as the cornucopia and the poppy head, signifying abundance. Paleo-Hebrew script (*see* EPIGRAPHY, HEBREW), familiar on the coins of Tyre and Sidon, was in use on these first Jewish copper coins. Once thought to have been minted about 111/110 B.C., they are now believed to date from the reign of Alexander Yannai (Jannaeus), 104–78 B.C. The lack of a portrait design may have been one of the reasons for the slow development of coinage in Judea.

During the Roman period coins from earlier Greek times as well as those from Rome were regarded as acceptable currency. The silver coin, the denarius, was similar in size, weight, and value to the earlier drachma, and the denarius became the acknowledged price of a day's labor. In the KJV the word is translated as "penny," which, until recently, in English coinage was written with the symbol "d," the abbreviation of "denarius."

With so many different types of coinage in circulation, the need for moneychangers was obvious, particularly in cosmopolitan cities and at locations such as the temple. At the great feasts, when there were so many strangers in Jerusalem who needed to pay the tax into the temple treasury, the moneychangers set up their stalls in the court of the Gentiles, where in Matt 21:12; Mark 11:15; Luke 19:45–46, and John 2:15 it is recorded that Jesus overthrew the tables because of the dishonest practices of the moneychangers.

Herod I (36–4 B.C.; *see* HEROD, FAMILY OF), Archelaus* (4 B.C.–A.D. 6), and Herod Antipas (4 B.C.–A.D. 39) minted coins which bore a date and a Greek inscription, but in deference to Jewish ideology they were similar in pictorial design to earlier Judean coins.

Philip (4 B.C.–A.D. 34), the tetrarch of an essen-tially non-Jewish area, minted the first local coins with the head of the Roman emperor on the obverse. Herod Agrippa I (37–44) was the first to put his own portrait on a Jewish coin. Coins struck by Pontius Pilate showed an augur's wand and other emblems familiar to Roman priests. Augury was popular with Tiberius,* and Pilate had apparently been a member of the college of augurs. However, it has now been established that the design was current before the reign of Tiberius, and thus it could not have been minted originally only in deference to that particular emperor.

With regard to the actual value of coins, the terms "shekel" and "talent" as they occur in 1 Kings 10 referred to weight rather than an actual coin—a shekel being 11.5 grams of silver or approximately .4 ounce, while a talent was 3,450 grams. The value of coins can be established best in terms of their purchasing power. In the time of Solomon,* 600 shekels of silver purchased a chariot* and 150 shekels a horse* (1 Kings 10:29; cf. Lev 5:15). A field was purchased by Jeremiah for 17 shekels of silver (Jer 32:9), while Abraham bought a cave* and associated land for 400 shekels (Gen 23:15–16). In larger international dealings gold was also used as a medium of exchange. Thus Hezekiah paid tribute of 300 talents of silver and 30 talents of gold to Sennacherib (q.v., 2 Kings 18:14), while the Assyrians received 1,000 talents of silver from Menahem (2 Kings 15:19).

Greek coins were valued at 100 silver drachmas to a mina and 6,000 to a talent. In 300 B.C. one drachma bought a sheep, and five an ox.* The tetradrachma or four-drachma coin is mentioned in Matt 17:27 as the value of the temple tax for two people. The Roman silver denarius, translated as "penny" in the KJV, was 16 times the value of the *as*, sometimes translated as "farthing." One quarter of the *as* was the quadrans, the smallest Roman coin, which was the equivalent of the widow's mite (Mark 12:42). Two denarii were paid to the innkeeper by the Good Samaritan to cover the cost of food, care, and shelter for the person he had befriended (Luke 10:35).

BIBLIOGRAPHY: R. A. S. Macalister, *The Excavation of Gezer*, 2 (1912), 259; G. F. Hill, "Palestine," in *A Catalogue of Greek Coins in the British Museum* (1914); J. G. Milne, *Greek and Roman Coins in the Study of History* (1939); P. Romanoff, *Jewish Symbols on Ancient Jewish Coins* (1944); G. R. Halliday, *Money Talks about the Bible* (1948); A. Reifenberg, *Israel's History in Coins from the Maccabees to the Roman Conquest* (1953); F. A. Banks, *Coins of Bible Days* (1955); *The Numismatic Chronicle*, 18 (1958), 187–93; M. Grant, *Roman History from Coins* (1958), 50, 64, 65; W. C. Prime, *Money of the Bible* (n.d.); J. Y. Ankermon, *Numismatic Illustrations of the Narrative Portions of the OT* (1966); Y. Meshorer, *Jewish Coins of the Second Temple Period* (1967); J. P. Lewis, *Historical Backgrounds of Bible History* (1971), 155–65.

HWP

COLLAGEN CONTENT. See DATING.

COLLEGIA. See TRADE GUILDS.

Colosseum in Rome. Photo: Fratelli Alinari.

COLOSSE (kə los′ə; Gr. Κολοσσαί, *Kolossai*, "purple wool"[?]). The location of this town very near Laodicea* and farther up the Lycus Valley was fixed by W. J. Hamilton in 1835. He recorded fragments of stonework, the acropolis,* traces of the theater,* and cemetery (*see* NECROPOLIS) area. The depletion of the remains since the virtual abandonment of the site in the eighth century accounts for this obliteration. Like Hadrian's Wall,* Colosse became a quarry for cut stone. Herodotus's reference (7.30) to Colosse as "a great city of Phrygia," a remark confirmed by Xenophon (*Anabasis*, 1.2.6) a century later, cannot be dismissed. Hierapolis* and Laodicea probably drained life and commerce away, and Strabo, at the beginning of the Christian era, spoke of Colosse as a small town (12.8.13). Inscriptions and coins* of small importance confirm another two or three centuries of continuing habitation. As at Laodicea, archaeology would probably prove rewarding but would hardly alter the suggestion of Lightfoot (*Commentary*, 16), that Colosse was the least important of the churches to which Paul wrote. The letter, of course, was also to be read in the considerable church community of Laodicea. Hierapolis, Laodicea, and Colosse were almost a conurbation.

BIBLIOGRAPHY: D. Magie, *Roman Rule in Asia Minor* (1950), 126–27, 985–86; M. J. Mellink, *IDB*, 1, 658; E. M. Blaiklock, *ZPEB*, 1 (1975), 913–14.

EMB

COLOSSEUM. The medieval name given to the Flavian Amphitheater, the great memorial built to honor his family and dynasty on the site which Nero had designed for an artificial lake in his "Golden House." The axes of the structure measure 186 by 156 m. (610 by 512 ft.) and it stands some 48.50 m. (159 ft.) high. Just before his death in A.D. 79, Ves-

pasian* dedicated two stories faced in travertine (a white limestone quarried* in Italy) and treated respectively in Doric and Ionic arcades. Titus* added a third level in Corinthian style, and a fourth tier of arcades pierced by windows. This carried the structure that supported the enormous awning. There were three tiers of seating with standing room above with magisterial and official box seating. The arena was floored with timber, covering cells for wild beasts, gladiators' accommodation, and a mass of lifting and elevator machinery. The numbers over the street level entrance portals may still be seen. This was part of an efficient scheme to regulate the entrance and exit of some 45,000 spectators. Nerva and Trajan did some restoration work, but it is only in recent years that the structure has been in any real danger. This arises from the vibration of traffic. Earlier, of course, the ruthless despoiling in the Middle Ages and Renaissance days did immense damage to the structure.

Considering that Jerusalem fell in A.D. 70, it may be supposed that thousands of Jewish slaves* formed the mass of the laboring force in the decade of building devoted to the great propagandist pile. Vespasian had to show that he was no Nero but a leader of a new age with a care for the Roman multitude. Inscriptional evidence related to the Colosseum is listed in *OCD*, 214.

EMB

COLUMBARIUM (Lat., "dovecote"). A chamber fitted with niches for containers of ashes of the cremated dead. Dating from Etruscan times, the earliest Italian types occurred near Veii, a city destroyed by Rome* in 396 B.C. Niches at Hareshah and Masada* proved too small to contain an urn but were possibly used without a container, being closed off by means of a tile.

COOKING. Cooking is mentioned frequently in the OT, and the Israelites were given specific instructions both negative and positive to separate their practice from the idolatry and sacrifice of the Canaanites* and other pagan peoples. Hearths, cook pits, clay* ovens,* and numerous utensils have been recovered from all over Palestine. The common methods were roasting over an open fire and boiling, as for a stew or soup. Querns* and mortars* for grinding grain and flat stones for baking bread have turned up in the older levels of Jericho,* Hazor,* Ramat Raḥel, Beth Shemesh,* and many of the early occupation levels. Exod 23:19 and similar passages apparently refer to the Canaanite custom of performing some sort of Baal* sacrificial rite, which is alluded to in the Ugaritic* texts.

In the main, the lower classes had only a gruel or porridge made from grain and flavored with onions, salt,* and the like. The grains in common usage were wheat, barley, rye, spelt, millet, and fitches. Wheat was the preferred cereal, of which both wild and cultivated were found in Palestine. All of the grains used were cooked in some manner before being eaten. Meat, aside from fish, was expensive and almost unattainable. Hence the royal gift of 2 Sam 6:19, which was the remainder of the offering made to the Lord.

Many types of vessels of pottery,* iron,* and precious metals have been excavated. The palace kitchens of Ramses III are depicted on an Egyptian wall. Although the modeling and the embellishments altered the general shape and use of Israelite utensils, their functions changed little over the centuries. Most cooking vessels were shallow and wide, allowing for easy access to the contents. A spherical pot with a small aperture and two handles was probably used for heating water. Eighth- and seventh-century B.C. Palestinian cooking pots generally bore the trademark of the potter,* as in modern times. Metal pans and vessels* were in limited usage because of cost.

An important element in Palestinian cooking was the oven (tannûr), many examples of which have been recovered by archaeologists. It had the appearance of an inverted basin and was commonly

Reconstructed kitchen in Israelite house c. tenth century B.C. Tel Aviv, Ha'aretz Museum of Mediterranean Art. Photo: Israel Government Press Office.

built over a hole in the ground about a yard wide and a foot deep. The oven was insulated by means of a clay lining, and a fire was lit so as to heat the inside thoroughly. Subsequently the bread was placed on flat stones or on the inside walls of the oven to cook. If the oven had a smooth plaster exterior, the flat loaves of bread were sometimes put there to bake also. In larger cities* there were public ovens to which women could take their bread for baking. The housewife usually supervised the cooking of meals, although work was often delegated to servants (cf. Gen 18:6–7). Royal households had their own cooks and bakers because of the quantities of food involved (cf. Gen 40:1). At certain periods officials were appointed to taste the food before the king himself consumed it, to guard against attempts at poisoning.

BIBLIOGRAPHY: J. L. Kelso, *The Ceramic Vocabulary of the OT* (1948); id., *IDB*, 1, 679–80; M. H. Heicksen, *ZPEB*, 1 (1975), 956–57.

ww

COPPER. *See* BRONZE.

COPPER AGE. *See* CHALCOLITHIC.

COPTIC. *See* WRITING.

CORD. *See* ROPE.

CORINTH. Most of the visible remains of Corinth, largely the result of extensive work by the American School of Classical Studies in Athens,* are from the ruins of the Roman foundation of Julius Caesar in 46 B.C. The famous commercial and naval city-state of Corinth, which played an important part in half a millennium of Greek history, had, at the time of Caesar's rebuilding, lain in ruins for exactly a century. The Romans obliterated it when they finally crushed the Achaean League in 146 B.C. The remaining columns (seven of an original thirty-eight) of the temple of Apollo on the ridge which dominates the site, are the principal relics of the older city.* For pious reasons the god's temple was spared, to inspire, perhaps, a vivid metaphor in Paul's second letter to the Corinthian church (2 Cor 6:16). The Apollo temple dates from 540 B.C.

The archaeological investigation of the city reveals that it was linked to the great acropolis* of the Acrocorinthus and to the western haven on the Corinthian Gulf (Lechaeum) by long fortifications. A wide paved street, 6–7.5 m. (20–25 ft.) wide, connected Lechaeum with the marketplace or agora.* The agora, the central feature of the existing remains, was entered through a propylaeum,* where a Roman arch* seems to stand on the site of an earlier Greek one. The remains of the buildings which housed and controlled the copious fountain of Peirene lie on the E of the Lechaeum street. These ruins are from the buildings of the great patron and benefactor of Athens and Greece, Herodes Atticus (A.D. 101–77). The agora was bounded on three sides (W, NW, and S) by porticoes, the longest being the southern stoa* which is 160 m. (525 ft.) long. Behind this portico stood a senate house and a second basilica.* The first may be traced to the W, in front of the terrace where the temple of Apollo stands—a rectangular structure divided by two lines of columns. Behind the southern basilica began the road to the eastern port of Cenchreae,* on the Saronic Gulf. There were shops to the NW and SW of the agora, and directly opposite the propylaea,* dividing a lower from a higher level of the agora, was the bema,* the raised platform on which Gallio sat at the trial of Paul (Acts 18:12–17). As the apostle turned away after the abrupt termination of the trial, the high columns of Apollo's temple against the sky must have dominated his view. A large theater,* dating from the earlier Corinth, lies to the N of the Apollo temple. Two other items of interest to NT archaeology are a fragmented plinth* from the Jewish synagogue* and a first-century pavement (S of the theater) which was laid by one Erastus. The inscription runs, "Erastus, at his own expense, in commemoration of his aedileship." Writing to the Roman church from Corinth (Rom 16:23), Paul mentions a city official named Erastus.* There is no proof that this is the same Erastus as the administrator who dedicated the pavement for his fellow citizens, but the probability remains.

BIBLIOGRAPHY: J. G. O'Neill, *Ancient Corinth* (1930); H. J. Cadbury, "Erastus of Corinth," *JBL*, 50 (1931), 42–58; O. Broneer, "Corinth, Center of St. Paul's Missionary Work in Greece," *BA*, 14 (1951), 77–96; American School of Classical Studies, *Ancient Corinth, A Guide to the Excavations*, 6th ed. (1954); A. Rupprecht, *ZPEB*, 1 (1975), 960–64.

EMB

CORNICE. The horizontal band of masonry supporting the pediment* of a classical building.

COSMETICS. In antiquity cosmetics were widely used and traded. There were perfumers in Jerusalem in Nehemiah's day (Neh 3:8 NEB). Jars, beakers, mortars,* and palettes used to make and store cosmetics have been recovered from many sites, frequently from womens' tombs. Characteristic palettes were recovered from Iron Age* Megiddo.* They comprised small limestone bowls about 10 cm. (4 in.) in diameter and had a decorated flat rim.

The chief ingredients of cosmetics were natural organic dyes* derived from flowers, roots, berries, and invertebrates. Texts from Mesopotamia* have yielded recipes for unguents and perfumes, some of them involving sublimation and fractional distillation. Vessels for carrying out these procedures have been excavated from Mari* and other Mesopotamian sites.

Some ointments were stored in ivory* boxes and less frequently in expensive alabaster* jars (cf. Luke 7:37). Instead of using water for bathing, Near Eastern women often employed perfumes and ointments,* much as some Arab women still do today. The Egyptians used skin ointments to offset the ravages of their climate, and as a medicinal procedure they put astringent substances such as kohl and malachite on the eyelids to prevent ophthalmic disease. Subsequently this usage became cosmetic as well as preventive. Remains of toilet sets containing these

and other materials have been recovered from numerous Egyptian graves.

Excessive use of cosmetics was thought to be the indicator of moral decline, and such is stated in the OT and elsewhere, particularly where the use of eye paint was being considered (cf. 2 Kings 9:30; Jer 4:30; Ezek 23:40).

In Hellenistic times hair dyeing, tattooing, and ritual scarification became more popular with the general trend toward orientalization. Grecian and Roman cosmetics and cosmetic instruments have been recovered from Pompeii* and Palestine, as well as Roman Africa.

See CHEMICAL TECHNOLOGY; MEDICINE.

BIBLIOGRAPHY: G. Wright, *BA*, 28 (1958), 50–79; J. A. Thompson, *IDB*, 1, 701–2; R. K. Harrison, *Healing Herbs of the Bible* (1966), 49–54; M. H. Heicksen, *ZPEB*, 1 (1975), 981.

WW

COTTON. See CLOTH.

COUNCIL, JEWISH. See SANHEDRIN.

COURT. See BEMA.

COVENANT, COVENANTS. One Hebrew word (בְּרִית, *berîth*) serves several purposes in the OT. It denoted agreements between individuals like Abraham and Abimelech (Gen 21:27); between kings of Israel and neighboring kings, as Solomon* and Hiram* the king of Tyre* (1 Kings 5:12); or such as between the king of Judah and Nebuchadnezzar* (Ezek 17:15). But it also denoted the solemn commitment between Yahweh the God of Israel and His people Israel (Exod 19:5). It had both secular and religious meanings.

Modern excavations have produced treaty documents and agreements of many kinds written on stone or baked clay* tablets from sites reaching from Babylonia (see CHALDEA) to Asia Minor,* Palestine, and Egypt,* and extending in time from the third millennium B.C. to the middle of the eighth century B.C.

The number of personal agreements is legion. In general the document contains the names of the parties in a preamble, the substance of the agreement, a list of witnesses with their seals,* and very often a curse clause promising dire results for those who might break the agreement.

Treaties between states were of two kinds, (1) the parity treaty between states of more or less equal status, and (2) the suzerainty treaty, as imposed by a ruler on a defeated or submissive smaller state.

The best extant example of a parity treaty is that between Ramses II* of Egypt* and Hattusilis the Hittite* ruler. It is preserved in Egypt on the walls of the temple of Amon at Karnak (see THEBES) and of the Ramesseum, as well as on a baked clay document found in Anatolia. These are almost exact duplicates.

Numerous examples of suzerainty treaties, complete or fragmentary, are also available. Many treaties between the Hittites and their vassals come from

Anatolia and others from Ugarit.* Two similar treaties come from Alalakh* and a number from Assyrian excavations, the best known being those of Esarhaddon* and eight of his vassals from Media, uncovered in Nimrud (see BORSIPPA; CALAH) in 1955.

The structure of these Ancient Near Eastern treaties remained fairly constant over the centuries. The text normally comprises (1) the preamble, which identifies the author of the treaty and gives his titles and attributes; (2) the historical prologue in which the benevolent deeds of the great king on behalf of the vassal are recounted and made the ground of the suzerain's appeal to the vassal to render future obedience in gratitude for past benefits; (3) the treaty stipulations—general clauses that lay down principles on which future relations were to be based, as well as specific stipulations; (4) the divine witnesses and guarantors of the treaty; (5) sanctions, maledictions, and curses on those who would break the treaty and blessings on those who would keep it. In addition to these standard elements there was provision for depositing the treaty documents in the sanctuaries of the two parties, for periodic reading of the treaty document, for an oath of acceptance, and for a religious ceremony, often including blood sacrifices by which the treaty was ratified.

It was at first thought that only second-millennium treaty documents carried the historical prologue, because first millennium documents seemed to lack this item. But a first-millennium B.C. document with a historical prologue is now known.

The people of Israel seem to have adapted this secular political model to describe their relationship with Yahweh, whom they saw as their Great Suzerain, with themselves as His vassals. The treaty (covenant) literary pattern as outlined above can be discerned behind such passages as Exod 19:3–8; 20:1–17; 24:3–8; Josh 8:30–35; 24; the book of Deuteronomy as a whole, and many of its parts. The covenant idea in Israel could well be as old as Moses. Much of the vocabulary in covenant passages in the OT shows links both etymologically and semantically with that of the Near Eastern treaty language. Some aspects of the teaching of the prophets takes on a new aspect when viewed against this background, and the treaty pattern is important in the literary criticism of numerous passages of the OT. An important theology of the OT has been written with the covenant idea as its unifying theme.

BIBLIOGRAPHY: V. Korosec, Hethitische Staatsvertrage (1931); G. E. Mendenhall, "Law and Covenant in Israel and the Ancient Near East," BA, 17 (1954), 24–46, 49–76; D. J. McCarthy, Treaty and Covenant (1963); J. A. Thompson, The Ancient Near Eastern Treaties and the OT (1964); K. A. Kitchen, Ancient Orient and OT (1966), 91–96; id., The Bible in Its World (1977), 79–85.

JAT

COW. See Ox.

CRAFTS, CRAFTSMEN. These may be defined broadly as encompassing any manual processes which involve particular skills or dexterity. One of the very earliest was the making of pottery,* and Neolithic* levels in Mesopotamia,* Syria (see ARAM), Palestine, and elsewhere attest to the coarse, plain nature of the products from that period. But by the Chalcolithic* Age at Tell Halaf, a superior painted pottery was in vogue, fired at a great heat in closed kilns* to produce a delicate, porcelainlike finish. This period also saw the development of weaving, which might in fact go as far back as the late Neolithic Age. The lowest levels at Susa* (c. 4000 B.C.) revealed traces of linen* cloth,* showing that the craft was already being practiced there at that time. Carpet weaving commenced about the same period also, giving great antiquity to the Ghiordes and Sehna knots of subsequent Persian and Chinese carpets. In the OT the "craftsmen" were normally woodworkers (2 Sam 5:11; 2 Kings 12:11; Isa 44:13 et al.) and they may only have begun to develop their skills from the Solomonic period under Phoenician* influence (cf. 2 Sam 5:11; 2 Kings 22:6). An ancient tradition associated the beginnings of metallurgy* with Tubal-Cain (Gen 4:22), the "Cain" probably being connected with the Kenites who mined copper and iron* deposits in the Wadi Arabah, and with whom the later Kenizzites were associated (1 Chron 4:14f.). Evidence of metallurgical products fashioned as early as the third millennium B.C. at Metsamor in the center of the Ararat* plains was discovered by Russian archaeologists in 1965–66, lending credence to the tradition about Tubal-Cain. From references such as Num 10:29 and 21:9, it would appear that Israelites learned the craft of metalworking from the Kenites.

Near Eastern craftsmen seldom used slaves,* for reasons which are not clear. Canaanite craftsmen were organized into guilds (see TRADE GUILDS), a practice adopted in post-Exilic Judea (Neh 3:8). Such groups often occupied a particular area of the town (cf. Isa 7:3; Jer 37:21; Neh 11:35) and frequently worked in the open air. Countless examples of exquisite craftsmanship in metals, fabrics, wood,* and semiprecious stones have been recovered from sites in the Near East, testifying to the advanced manual skills of the artisans of antiquity.

BIBLIOGRAPHY: A. Lucas, Ancient Egyptian Materials and Industries (1948); R. J. Forbes, Metallurgy in Antiquity (1950); Guidebook, Museum of History of the Metsamor Mining and Metallurgical Works (1970).

RKH

CREATION EPIC. The usual title of the Babylonian cosmological myth is Enuma Elish, which gives poetic expression to ancient Mesopotamian dualistic pantheism. The text was recovered from the library of Ashurbanipal* (668–626 B.C.) and a number of other older fragments have been excavated. The epic divides the making of the world into the creation of the world-stuff and the creation of the world order. Mankind is formed from the mixture of the blood of a slain god and the clay of Mesopotamia.* The text was written sometime after the First Dynasty of Babylon on seven tablets and was read as part of the ritual of the annual New Year's Day, the akitu festival in which the king would impersonate the high god Marduk/Ashur and slay the sea hag, Tiamat, in a sympathetic magical rite. Enuma Elish is typical of the primitive myths of cosmogony of the ancient world, but yields valuable comparative material. Its significance for biblical scholarship lies in the contrasting restrained dignity and firm monotheism of the Genesis account. The basic difference is that which lies between truth and its corruption.

See ASHURBANIPAL; ATRA-HASIS EPIC; BABYLON; MESOPOTAMIA.

BIBLIOGRAPHY: A. Heidel, *The Babylonian Genesis* (1963 ed.); W. G. Lambert, "A New Look at the Babylonian Background of Genesis," *JTS*, n.s. 16 (1965), 287–300.

WW

CROCODILE. The Hebrew word לִוְיָתָן (*liwyāṯān*; whence "leviathan") is found six times in the OT and is rendered "leviathan,*" in all cases save Job 3:8 ("raise up their mourning") in KJV. The RSV renders it "who are skilled to rouse up Leviathan." The word seems to refer to any monster of the deep, but in most contexts (e.g., Job 41:1 in most modern translations) it refers to the crocodile—the *crocodilus niloticus*, native to the Nile Valley from earliest times. In Ps 104:25–26 it may be the whale or the porpoise that "plays" or "frolics."

The crocodile in Egypt was venerated as a symbol of sunrise and became a hieroglyph* for this word. Mummified crocodiles attest the worship of the creature and have been found in many places (e.g., at Ombi and Tebtunis, where Grenfell and Hunt found the remains of the saurians stuffed with papyri*). The Greek traveler and historian Herodotus mentions the matter (2.148), describing the training and care of the animals while alive and their mummification when dead.

A Faiyum papyrus refers to a pending visit of a Roman senator and gives directions for his proper entertainment, including the wherewithal to feed the sacred crocodiles.

In the Pyramid Texts (*see* COFFIN TEXTS) the crocodile appears as an enemy of the dead, likely to rob him of the sacred charms that help him through the ordeal of his journey beyond the grave.

Reflecting the language of Job is a simile in the hymn of praise written for Thutmose III by the priests of Amon. The god says in stanza 4:

I have come, giving thee to smite those who are in their marshes,
The lands of the Mitanni tremble for fear of thee;
I have made them see thy majesty as a crocodile,
Lord of fear in the water, inapproachable.
—H. Breasted, *History of Egypt*, 319

In Palestine, the Carmel* caves* contained crocodile remains from the Pleistocene period. They were probably to be found in a river that debouched near Caesarea.* The Crusaders mentioned crocodiles also and the Bedouins allege their existence in Palestine into this century. The crocodile must have vanished from the Euphrates and Tigris before the eighth

century B.C.; otherwise it is unlikely that Tiglath-Pilser I* would have received one as a present from Egypt.

BIBLIOGRAPHY: G. S. Cansdale, *All the Animals of the Bible* (1970), 195–97.

EMB

CROCODILOPOLIS (krok ō di lop' ə lis). This name, meaning *"city of the crocodile,"* was given by the Greeks to several towns in Egypt* where the crocodile-god Sobek was worshiped, but especially to the ancient city of Shedet in the Faiyum, c. 160 km. (100 mi.) SSW of modern Cairo. Under the Ptolemies (*see* PTOLEMY), as Arsinoe, this town was the center of a province greatly extended by land reclamation and irrigation; its successor is modern Medinet el-Faiyum. The town is only one of many (inside and outside the Faiyum province) whose Greco-Roman ruin-mounds have yielded masses of Greek papyri,* including early Christian manuscripts, both biblical and otherwise.

BIBLIOGRAPHY: B. P. Grenfell et al., *Faiyum Towns and Their Papyri* (1900); Alan H. Gardiner, *Ancient Egyp. Onomastica*, 2 (1947), 116–17; id., *The Wilbour Papyrus II Commentary* (1948), 43ff.

KAK

CROMLECH. *See* MEGALITHIC MONUMENTS.

CROSS-DATING. *See* DATING.

CROWN. The crown, universal symbol of royalty, may be illustrated widely from archaeological sources, as for example the famous "double crown" of Egypt, and the truncated conical cap of the Assyrian kings. (See D. J. Wiseman, *Illustrations From Biblical Archaeology* [1958], 41, 65.)

CRUCIFIXION. For all the relic lore of the Middle Ages, no remnants of the cross as an instrument of punishment survive. Roman nails,* on the other hand, some of them in new condition, were discovered recently at Inchtuthill, in Scotland, a supply abandoned by Agricola when he withdrew from his reconnaissance into Scotland, in A.D. 78 (I. A. Richmond, *JRS*, 1944). The nine-inch and six-inch spikes, sharp, heavy-headed, quadrilateral, in tough iron* were like the nails of the cross.

Philological and literary evidence seems to point to a T-shaped cross. The upright stake (*stipes*) was a fixture at the place of execution. The cross-piece was a beam carried by the condemned victim, bound to his arms and across the nape of the neck. This evidence has been competently assembled by a French surgeon, Pierre Barbet (*The Passion of Our Lord Jesus Christ*, ch. 2, [1954]). Dr. Barbet's object is to prove, by examination of the pathology of the death of Christ, the authenticity of the Turin Shroud. But the relic cannot be traced back beyond the fourteenth century.

Archaeology might have been expected to have some decisive word to say, but this is not the case. A satirical third-century graffito* from the Palatine shows a line drawing of a crucified ass, worshiped by

Drawing based on anatomical study of remains discovered in a Jerusalem cave, of man crucified with knees flexed. Courtesy Carta, Jerusalem.

a standing figure and labeled: "Anaximenos worships his god." The cross appears to be T-shaped, but an upward protusion behind the head of the animal could suggest the traditional form.

The primitive Christian church shrank from all representation of the Passion, and scarcely a score of crosses can be collected from the graffiti of the catacombs.* An early crucifix, an ivory object in the British Museum, seems to have been made in the late fifth century and is of traditional shape. The same is the case with the oldest representation of the crucifixion, a rough miniature in a Syrian evangelarium, dated A.D. 586, now in the Laurentian Library in Florence.

In one or two rare catacomb inscriptions, the cross, in the form of a T, seems to be inserted in the midst of a martyr's name: ΔΙΟΝΤΥCΙΟΥ (Dionysion), for example, in the catacomb of Saint Peter and Marcellinus. M with a bar above it (representing the horizontal beam of the cross?) seems to be a similar indication of martyrdom inserted into an epitaph, e.g., VERICMVNDVS (Vericundus). The T-device dates from the second and third centuries, and may support the contention that this was the common shape of the cross.

Important light on the crucifixion was shed by a discovery in 1968. In a Jerusalem cave,* Israeli archaeologists unearthed the first material evidence of a crucifixion. It could indicate that Jesus Christ might have been crucified in a position different from that shown on the traditional cross. A detailed anatomical study of the remains of a man crucified at about the same time as Christ (a young man named Yehohanan) showed that the victim was nailed to the cross in a sitting position, both his legs slung together sideways, with the nail penetrating the sides of both feet just below the heel. The remains were discovered during excavations in an ancient cemetery at Givat

Hamivtar in NE Jerusalem (q.v.).

The anatomical study carried out by Dr. Nico Haas, of the Hebrew University anatomy department, indicated that the man was crucified "in a compulsive position, a difficult and unnatural posture," evidently to increase the agony. The feet were joined almost parallel, both transfixed by the same nail at the heels, with the legs adjacent. The remains of the nail were embedded in the ankle bones. It was easier for those who took the body down to break the nail from the wood than to remove it from the feet.

The knees were doubled in a semiflexed position, the right one overlapping the left. The trunk was contorted, and the arms were stretched out, each apparently stabbed by a nail in the forearm, and not in the palms. This supports a contention by the French surgeon already quoted that the nails used in the crucifixion of Christ penetrated the solid structure of the wrist bones.

Traditional crucifixions show Christ with both palms nailed to the cross, His legs stretching straight downward with a nail transfixing the feet frontally near the instep.

Some scholars in Jerusalem believe that the posture revealed in the anatomical report indicates the usual position for crucifixion used in the city at that time.

The evolution of the symbolism of the cross may be illustrated from archaeology. One of the reasons for its comparative rarity in early Christian art is the abhorrence in which the Romans held the symbol (W. H. Withrow deals with this theme in his eighty-year-old, but still valuable, publication, *The Catacombs of Rome*, 260–80). Hence the Palatine wall-scratching from the days of Septimus Severus, to which reference has already been made. The symbolism of the cross first appears in mystical statements by Jerome and Justin, and the appearance of the Chi-Rho* symbol in the Catacombs from A.D. 331 onward. The alleged discovery of the true cross by the Empress Helena heralded the adoration of the cross as an image. A curious archaeological comment on this practice has come from an apocryphal fragment discovered in the Nile Valley during the busy digging which sought to anticipate the filling of the Aswan* High Dam. University of Chicago archaeologists discovered, in the ruins of a tenth century Coptic monastery, an ancient prayer book containing an alleged conversation of Christ. Its legendary character is apparent, but it illustrates the advances made by this century in the adoration of the cross.

BIBLIOGRAPHY: J. Finegan, *FLAP* (1946), 252, 292, 431; M. Gough, *The Early Christians* (1961), 83, 97, 180–82; Pierson Parker, *IDB*, 1, 746–47; H. D. Drumwright, Jr., *ZPEB*, 1 (1975), 1040–42.

EMB

CRYPTOGRAM, CRYPTOGRAPH. A communication written in a special system of characters to preserve the secrecy of the material. A cipher, code, or system of writing in cipher or code.

CUBIT. *See* WEIGHTS AND MEASURES.

Cuneiform tablet in Assyro-Babylonian language. Letter written by Abimilki of Tyre to Akh-en-Aton king of Egypt in early 14th century B.C. Found at Tell el-Amarna. *(See also photo under* TAANACH.) Courtesy of The Metropolitan Museum of Art, Rogers Fund, 1924.

CUNEIFORM (kū nē′ə fôrm). This wedge-shaped, impressed script was introduced in Mesopotamia* and used throughout the W Asian world until Hellenistic times. The origin was pictographic,* and probably somewhat hieroglyphic,* in that it was used by a class of priests to record the temple accounts. Four major types of signs to be pressed on clay* as cuneiform can be identified as the script developed.

1. *Archaic-pictographic.* This is the oldest type, in which the signs are stylistic outlines of common objects. There is some evidence that this was in use in other areas as well as in Mesopotamia. It is just possible that some early pre-Sumerian culture developed this writing system. The extant texts all seem to be ownership stamps or simple ledgers. One illustration shows such a tablet from Djemdet-Nasr, originating around 3500–3000 B.C.

2. *The script.* This is the second phase, still further abstracted and stylized, and employed by the Sumerians* and the Akkadians* of the Sargonic *(see* SARGON OF AKKAD) period. It is a complex syllabary in which each sign stands for a whole syllable such as a vowel, a consonant plus vowel, a vowel plus consonant, or a consonant plus a vowel plus another consonant. Since the Sumerian language consisted basically of all open syllables (consonant followed by vowel or vowel followed by consonant) without any consonantal clusters, the syllabary system worked

very well, as it does for modern Japanese. However, when a complex Semitic language such as Akkadian was written in this manner, synthetic syllables had to be concocted. Thus, England would have had to be written out as en-eg-la-an-ed. Over the centuries the original complex of some 1,500 signs was reduced, as it was found unneccessary to use some, and others absorbed similar, less common syllables. The result was a lowering of the number of signs to about 400. The signs were still drawn in highly linear and very precise fashion, illustrated by a Sargonic inscription of King Naram-Sîn from about 2270 B.C.

3. *Later developments.* The Assyrian and Babylonian traditions divided, as did the geographic spheres of the northern and southern areas of Mesopotamia. The later signs became even more reduced, and as more vocabulary was added and a wide variety of subjects were treated in the clay compositions, the script became more stylized, and separate scribal traditions grew up. The precise etched lines of the older styles were compacted to the tiny pyramidical indentations seen in the hundreds of thousands of tablets that have been unearthed in Iraq. During the period from 2000 B.C. to 450 B.C. cuneiform script and the dialects of Akkadian, Assyrian, and Babylonian became the lingua franca of the entire Near East, and texts in these languages, written by native scribes, have been excavated from Hittite,* Egyptian, Iranian, and West Canaanite sites. The linguistic dominance of the script and the language encouraged other cultures to adapt the wedge-shaped signs to their own languages.

4. *Peripheral cuneiform.* This is the last stage, when the script was transformed as a vehicle of many other languages, Indo-European Hittite,* W Semite Ugaritic, Eblite or Eblaic, Northern Vannic, and Persian. A finely inscribed Persian bowl has very well-designed cuneiform signs carved into the lip. Cuneiform signs had now been so greatly reduced in number and organization as to border on being alphabetic,* which unfortunately the system never became.

Until the conquest of Persian areas by Roman armies there were still scribes who read and wrote the ancient script. Some may have lingered on into the early decades of the Christian era. However, certainly by one hundred years after Christ, the knowledge of the script and most of the languages had disappeared. The recovery, decipherment, and translation of the cuneiform script, and the dozen or more languages written in it, are among the great intellectual triumphs of Western European scholars. The first attempt was made soon after Sir Henry Rawlinson brought back his copies of the trilingual inscription on the cliff face at Behistun *(see* BEHISTUN INSCRIPTION) in 1835. Since Greek classical writings included the names of some of the Persian kings and the forms of their titles, groups of signs could be isolated. While individual insights had been made into the nature and values of the signs by eighteenth-century scholars, it was the German teacher, G. F. Grotefend (1775–1853) who first read Old Persian with some success. Delving independently and cooperating at certain points, a small group of scholars, following Rawlinson, were able to begin translating Babylonian by 1850. Within forty years F. H. Weissbach had proven that Sumerian was a separate language and by the second decade of the twentieth century, it too could be translated. Other decipherments followed, with the Czech F. Hrozný reading Hittite by World War I. The progress on the very earliest cuneiform has gone somewhat slower, but grammars, lexica, and translations are now becoming available. Cuneiform written on nearly imperishable stone or baked clay comprises the best sources of historical data for our understanding of the ancient world. Although it is an old science by modern measure, there is as much, if not more, unread and unknown cuneiform material in the museums of the world as at any time in the nearly two centuries since the study was introduced.

See AKKAD; BEHISTUN INSCRIPTION; MESOPOTAMIA; PICTOGRAPHY; WRITING.

BIBLIOGRAPHY: R. Labat, *Manuel D'Epigraphie Akkadienne* (1959); K. Jaritz, *Schriftarchäologie der altmesopotamischen Kultur* (1967); W. White, "Writing," *ZPEB*, 5 (1975), 995–1015, with references.

ww

CUP. See UTENSILS.

CUPBEARER. Cupbearers or butlers (cf. Gen 40:1–23; 1 Kings 10:5; Neh 1:11) acquired immense power in Egypt.* Of eleven known from Egyptian monuments of Ramses III, five were foreign slaves* in places of influence. The position was like that of the Egyptian sultans in the Middle Ages. Queen Tiy, an ambitious member of Ramses III's harem, seeking to secure the succession for her son, Pentewere, plotted against her ailing husband along with the "chief of the chamber," Pebekkamen, and the royal cupbearer or butler, Mesedsure. Points of contact with the Joseph story are immediately apparent. How the plot was uncovered, its investigation committed to a commission of fourteen officials, seven of them royal "butlers," and the scandals which followed, may be read in H. Breasted's *History of Egypt* (1945), 497–500. Whether Solomon's* cupbearers held similar influence is not known. They were a legacy from both Sumerian and Canaanite royalty. An ivory* from Megiddo,* dated around the twelfth century, shows a king sitting on his throne, flanked by winged, human-headed lions.* He drinks from a bowl with a cupbearer behind him. Thirteen centuries earlier still, a relief from Sumer* shows the king of Lagash* sitting bare-chested and elaborately kilted, and drinking from a bowl, while a cupbearer, two vessels in hand, stands behind him. Similar illustrations, reminiscent of Nehemiah and his office, come from Assyria.

The most famous of all illustrations comes from Knossos in Crete and dates from the middle second millennium B.C. Sir Arthur Evans uncovered the great palace in March 1899. On April 5 he chanced on a fresco, described in part as follows: "Early in the morning the gradual surface uncovering . . . re-

vealed two large pieces of Mycenaean fresco. . . . One represented the head and forehead, the other the waist and part of the skirt of a female figure [later realized to be male] holding in her hand a long Mycenaean 'rhyton' or high funnel-shaped cup. . . . The figure was life-size. . . . In front of the ear is a kind of ornament and a necklace and bracelet are visible."

H. E. L. Mellersh comments (*The Destruction of Knossos* [1970], 45): "Evans, it may be noted, was being modest, calling his find Mycenaean, from their similarity to some of Schliemann's; soon, however, he would take courage and name them with his own invention, Minoan.* In fact he had uncovered the famous 'cup-bearer' wall-painting, the slightly epicene figure of a handsome youth walking in procession."

BIBLIOGRAPHY: E. W. Heaton, *Everyday Life in OT Times* (1956), 164, fig. 80, both illustrate Megiddo ivory; H. Frankfort, *Art and Architecture in the Ancient East* (1954), plate 89; H. E. L. Mellersh, op. sup. cit., facing 89; W. F. Albright, *The Archaeology of Palestine* (1960), 123, fig. 31.

EMB

CUSH. See ETHIOPIA; NUBIA.

CYCLOPEAN MASONRY. An ancient style of building which used massive, irregular stones, thought to have been placed in position by the fabled giant Thracian race known as the Cyclops. Such myths were applied to Stonehenge, the approach to the Lion Gate at Mycenae,* and even to the gigantic masonry at the Wailing Wall* in Jerusalem.*

CYLINDER SEALS. See SEALS.

CYMBAL. See MUSIC.

CYPRUS. An island shaped like an animal skin, 225 by 96 km. (140 by 60 mi.) with its neck toward Syria c. 96 km. (60 mi.) away and lying 66 km. (41 mi.) S of Asia Minor.* Christianity had already been brought to Cyprus (Acts 11:19) when Paul visited there (Acts 13:4). It was known as Kittim in the OT (actually the name of the city, Kition), and its oldest attested name was Alashia, as evidenced from cuneiform* texts from Mari* (eighteenth century B.C.), Ugarit,* and Tell el-Amarna (see AMARNA) (fourteenth–thirteenth century B.C.). Homer calls it Cyprus (*Il.* 11, 21; *Od.* 4, 83), and in the Assyrian inscriptions of the late eighth and seventh century B.C., it is named Iadanana or Iadnana (*ANET*, 290,1).

1. *General Archaeological Picture.* Recent archaeological excavations on Cyprus have revealed a high quality of Neolithic* culture lasting from c. 4000 to 3000 B.C., followed by a native Bronze Age showing increased prosperity. The fifteenth century B.C. demonstrates direct contact with Mycenaean Greece and also with Asia Minor and Syria. Most major areas of Mycenaean* urban life and culture are seen, among these being a mode of writing,* a variant of Minoan script, brought by Mycenaean colonists.

This Cypriot script of the Bronze Age continued

into the classical period and was used to transmit Greek (*see* EPIGRAPHY, GREEK) down to c. 400 B.C. The continuance of this script seems to show that the island survived any catastrophic change at the time of the Iron Age,* when the Dorian invasion occurred. Inscriptions also demonstrate the survival in the classical period of a non-Greek language.

2. *Excavations of Particular Sites.* The sites excavated on the island include, from E to W, Salamis, Enkomi, Kourion (on the S coast), Lapithos (on the N coast), and Palaipaphos (Old Paphos) and Nea Paphos (New Paphos, on the SW coast).

In the late nineteenth century, excavations were conducted at such places as Kouklia (Palaipaphos), where Roman and earlier buildings were found, and at Salamis,* one of the very important cities of Cyprus, located c. 6.5 km. (4 mi.) N of Famagusta, with extensive ruins of gymnasium, baths, theater,* agora,* Temple of Zeus Olympios, two early Christian basilica* churches, royal tombs, etc. In the eleventh century B.C. it must have succeeded the Mycenaean city of Enkomi c. 2 km. (1¼ mi.) inland. In the 1930s to the 1950s there were further excavations at such locations as Sotira (a hilltop Neolithic settlement), Lapithos (an early Bronze Age cemetery), the Kouklia area of Palaipaphos (Late Bronze sites), and of Nea Paphos, Kourion (Late Bronze Age finds with Mycenaean affinities), and Enkomi (a few miles SW of Salamis) where there was found evidence of Late Bronze Mycenaean culture. Kition (Larnaca) on the S coast was occupied in the Early Bronze Age and founded as a city in the Late Bronze Age. Twenty-two km. (13½ mi.) to the NW is Idalion (one of the ancient kingdoms of Cyprus), located by the River Yialias, with remains extending to the S of the modern town of Dhali. The ruins, coming from the Late Bronze Age, Archaic, Classical, Hellenistic, and Roman periods, include a fortified cult center that later became the sanctuary of Athena, which the Phoenicians* associated with Anat.

Excavations have also provided additional evidence of the Archaic to the Hellenistic periods, such as those at the locality Litharkés near Meniko, and on the slopes of the Kaphizin hill near Nicosia, with finds of inscribed fragments of Hellenistic pottery.*

Evidences of the Greco-Roman and later periods have come from excavations at Kourion (cf. the bath building with the mosaic* pavements), at Phterikoúdhi and Polemídhia (tombs of the Roman period containing glass,* lamps, and coins*), and at Salamis.

Of interest are the milestones found in the region of Paphos,* a city (probably founded in the last half of the fourth century B.C. by Nikokles, the last of the Paphian kings) that was for much of the Ptolemaic and for the whole of the Roman imperial period the capital of the island. These milestones were connected with that section of the Roman road* from Kourion to Old Paphos (with its famous ancient temple of Aphrodite). The milestones demonstrate that the route along the S coast of Cyprus was originally a part of the official imperial road system. It is to be remembered that Paul traveled from Salamis (E coast) to Paphos (Acts 13:4–6) and may well have used this road. The first-century Greek inscription found at Kytheria with part of the word "Sergius" in it may possibly refer to the Sergius Paulus of Acts 13:7.

See MARI; PAPHOS; SALAMIS; UGARIT.

BIBLIOGRAPHY: E. Oberhummer,   "Kupros," *PWRE*, 12.1 (1924), 59–117; *Swedish Cyprus Exploration* 1–4 (1934–38); F. H. Stubbings, *Mycenaean Pottery from the Levant* (1951); C. F. A. Schaeffer, *Enkomi-Alesia* (1952); A. H. S. Megaw, "Archaeology in Cyprus, 1952," *JHS*, 73 (1953), 133–37; id., "Archaeology in Cyprus, 1954," *JHS*, 75 (1955), supplement, 29–34; T. B. Mitford, "Three Milestones of Western Cyprus," *AJA*, 70 (1966), 89–99; J. Deshayes, *La Necropole de Ktima* (1963); Vassos Karageorgis, *The Ancient Civilization of Cyprus* (1969); B. Van Elderen, "Some Archaeological Observations," *Apostolic History and the Gospel*, ed. W. W. Gasque and R. P. Martin (1970); *American Expedition to Idalion, Cyprus*, ed. L. E. Stager, A. Walker, and G. E. Wright (Cambridge, Mass: The American Schools of Oriental Research, 1974); *PECS*, ed. R. Stillwell (1976), 256–57.

WHM

CYRENIUS. *See* QUIRINIUS.

CYRUS. (sī'rəs; Heb. כּוֹרֶשׁ, כֹּרֶשׁ, *kôresh, kōresh*; LXX κῦρος, *Kyros*; Old Pers. *Kūrush*; Akkad. *Kurashu*). Cyrus II, or Cyrus the Great, was the greatest Achaemenid king and the founder of the Persian Empire (*see* PASARGADAE). He reigned over the Persians from 559 until 530 B.C.

I. *Biblical References.* Isa 44:28 and 45:1 speak of Cyrus as the Lord's shepherd and His anointed. Daniel (1:21; 6:28; 10:1) was in Babylon* when Cyrus captured it in 539. 2 Chron 36:22–23 and Ezra 1 speak of the Persian king's generosity to the Jews* in captivity after his capture of Babylon. Numerous references in Ezra relate how Cyrus aided the Jews in their return to Judah* and how he granted them permission to rebuild their temple.*

II. *Extra-Biblical Sources.* A. *Old Persian.* A few brief trilingual (Old Pers., Akkad., Elamite) inscriptions in which Cyrus speaks in the first person have been found at Pasargadae.* Borger and Hinz, who believe that paragraph 70 of the Behistun Inscription* indicates that Darius (q.v.) was the first to use Old Persian, attribute the inscriptions at Pasargadae to him. On the other hand, Ghirshman and Hallock believe that these Old Persian inscriptions should be credited to Cyrus. B. *Akkadian.* In addition to a number of minor inscriptions in the way of seals from Ur (q.v.) and Uruk (*see* ERECH) economic texts, and so on, there are two noteworthy quasi-historical, propaganda documents: (1) The famous Cyrus Cylinder,* found by Rassam in Babylon in 1879, depicts the joyous welcome accorded to the king by the people of Babylon. (*See ANET*, 315–16.) (2) the Verse Account describes the erratic behavior of Nabonidus,* the king of Babylon, in contrast to the reverential attitude of Cyrus. (*See ANET*, 312–15.) Of great

Drawing of tomb of Cyrus II at Pasargadae.

value is the Chaldean* Chronicle of Nabonidus, first published by Smith and retranslated by Wiseman. (*See ANET*, 305–7.) C. *Greek.* Herodotus I. 95–216 gives us an extensive and relatively trustworthy account of Cyrus. Quite tendentious is Xenophon's *Cyropaedia* or "Education of Cyrus," which presents an idealized portrait of the king reflective of Xenophon's admiration of Cyrus (c. 400 B.C.), the pretender to the throne of Artaxerxes II. At the other extreme is the account of Ctesias, Greek physician of Artaxerxes II, who depicts Cyrus as the son of a bandit.

III. *Ancestry and Family.* A previous Cyrus is known as a contemporary of Ashurbanipal* c. 640 B.C. Cyrus II was born to Cambyses I, a Persian, and to Mandane, daughter of the Median king, Astyages, c. 598. When Cyrus was about twenty he married Cassandane, who became the mother of Cambyses II, his successor. Another wife was Amytis.

IV. *Accession and Rise to Power.* Cyrus began ruling over the Persians in 559. In the "Dream Text" from Sippar (cf. *DOTT*, 89–90), Nabonidus is assured that Cyrus, the young servant of Marduk, would liberate Harran from the Ummān-manda (Medes*) by Nabonidus's third year (554/553). It therefore appears that Cyrus began to rebel against his Median grandfather Astyages by this time.

V. *Conquests.*
A. *Conquest of Media (550 B.C.).* The Nabonidus Chronicle confirms the Greek accounts (Herodotus 1. 127f.) that Cyrus was aided in his victory in Nabonidus's sixth year (550/549) by the defection of Astyages's (Ishtumegu) army. After the capture of Ecbatana,* Cyrus transferred the valuables to Anshan, his homeland, which was the area near Pasargadae. The Medes continued to play an honored and important role under the Persian Achaemenid kings.
B. *Conquest of Anatolia (547–46 B.C.).* In the following years Cyrus seems to have conquered Bactria* and other regions to the E (Herodotus 1. 153). As the Persian armies advanced N then E, Armenia, Cappadocia, and Cilicia in eastern Anatolia, followed by Cyprus,* submitted to Persian arms.

Croesus, the king of Lydia* in western Anatolia, had been misled by an oracle from Delphi which had advised him that "if he should send an army against the Persians he would destroy a great army" (Herodotus 1. 53). He consequently advanced across the Halys River. After an indecisive battle with the Persians near Pteria, Croesus withdrew, inasmuch as winter was approaching. Cyrus surprised him by continuing his pursuit. In 547 he captured Sardis,* the Lydian capital. A pyramid* tomb at Sardis, similar to Cyrus's own tomb, may have belonged to a Persian soldier who died in the campaign.

Herodotus (1.86) maintains that Cyrus spared Croesus from a fiery death on a pyre. The Chaldean Chronicle in a broken passage may be reconstructed and interpreted to mean that Cyrus killed the king of Ly[dia]. Mallowan, however, argues that the word *iduk* does not always mean "kill" and defends the classical tradition.

The conquest of Lydia and of the Greek settlements in Ionia in W Anatolia would shortly bring the Persians and Greeks into open conflict under Darius* and Xerxes.*
C. *Conquest of Babylon (539 B.C.).* Herodotus and Berossus state that Cyrus had subjected the rest of "Asia" by the time he turned against Babylon, his erstwhile ally. Morale in Babylon had been lowered by the studied neglect of the god Marduk on the part of Nabonidus, who had removed himself to Teima in Arabia,* leaving Babylon in the hands of his son Belshazzar,* who is depicted as de facto king in the book of Daniel. Nabonidus's return to Babylon just before Cyrus's attack was too late to muster an adequate defense.

Among others, Ugbaru, the governor of Gutium, defected to the Persians. Many of the inhabitants of Akkad* also defected when the Persians attacked Opis. Sidney Smith suggests that the Tigris was diverted before this attack. Herodotus (1.191) indicates that the Euphrates River, which bisects Babylon, was diverted at a time when the confident Babylonians were celebrating a festival (cf. Dan 5). The great city fell in October 539, and Cyrus was welcomed as a liberator.

Cyrus found that the inhabitants resembled skeletons. He ordered his troops not to terrorize the people and instituted slum clearance: "I brought relief to their dilapidated housing." A fragment in the Yale Babylonian Collection, identified in 1970 by P.-R. Berger as part of the Cyrus Cylinder, informs us that as Cyrus restored the city's inner wall* and moats, he took note of the inscription of his "predecessor," Ashurbanipal.

Cyrus further pleased the Babylonians by having his son Cambyses observe the neglected New Year's rite of Marduk. He restored to their cities gods from Sumer and Akkad which had been removed by Nabonidus.
D. *Restoration of the Jews.* Cyrus's decree in 538 (2 Chron 36:22–23; Ezra 1:1ff.) permitting the Jews* in Babylonia to return to Judea and to rebuild their temple is therefore quite consonant with his general policy of toleration. Later in the reign of Darius, a memorandum in Aramaic* of his decree was found at Ecbatana (KJV "Achmetha," Ezra 6:2).

VI. *Cyrus's Religion.* Most scholars, including A.

Jackson, E. Herzfeld, H. Nyberg, and A. Christensen, believe that Cyrus was an Iranian polytheist. A number of scholars, however, noting the continuity of religious thought between Cyrus and Darius, have sought to attribute the magnanimity of Cyrus to the teachings of Zoroaster. Among those who suggest that Cyrus may have been a Zoroastrian are A. Jirku, S. Smith, M. Mallowan, and D. Stronach.

VII. *Later Campaigns and Death.* Though nearly 70, Cyrus campaigned in the distant NE part of his realm against the nomadic Massagetae (Herodotus 1.201–4). He had established an outpost on the Jaxartes River called Cyropolis (Cyreschata, modern Kurkath) against them. He was killed in battle in 530, and his body was transported about a thousand miles to Pasargadae.

VIII. *Building Activities.* Evidence of Cyrus's building was discovered by Woolley at Ur. He had the inscriptions of Nabonidus defaced and set up his own inscription in the gate of the temenos* of Nanna, a text which recalls his proclamation in Daniel. The moon god Sin was restored to his shrine by Cyrus.

Also at Uruk, Cyrus rebuilt the temple of Ishtar. From texts from Uruk now in Florence, we learn that the making of woolen garments (*see* CLOTH, CLOTHING) for the cult statues suffered no interruption during the Persian takeover in 539–538. Cyrus maintained a force of bowmen at Uruk to guard the shepherds there.

In 1971 a new palace of Cyrus was discovered about 20 miles from the Persian Gulf near the highway connecting Bushire and Borazjan. Excavations by Safaraz have uncovered two lines of beautifully carved column bases.

For the palaces and tomb of Cyrus at his capital and the recent excavations there by D. Stronach, *see* PASARGADAE.

BIBLIOGRAPHY: C. Simcox, "The Role of Cyrus in Deutero-Isaiah," *JAOS*, 57 (1937), 158–71; S. Smith, *Isaiah Chapters XL–LV* (1944); E. J. Bickerman, "The Edict of Cyrus in Ezra 1," *JBL*, 65 (1946), 249–75; A. T. Olmstead, *History of the Persian Empire* (1948); A. Champdor, *Cyrus* (1952); R. Kent, *Old Persian* (1953); R. Ghirshman, *Iran* (1954); D. Wiseman, *Chronicles of Chaldaean Kings* (1956); R. Borger and W. Hinz, "Eine Dareios-Inschrift aus Pasargadae," *Zeitschrift der Deutschen morgenländischen Gesellschaft*, 109 (1959), 117–27; A. Burn, *Persia and the Greeks* (1962); L. Woolley and M. Mallowan, *Ur*

Excavations, 9 (1962); M. Smith, "II Isaiah and the Persians," *JAOS*, 83 (1963), 415–20; W. Culican, *The Medes and Persians* (1965); R. Ghirshman, "A propos de l'écriture cunéiforme vieux-perse," *JNES*, 24 (1965), 244–50; H. Tadmor, "The Inscriptions of Nabunaid . . . ," *Studies in Honor of Benno Landsberger*, ed. H. Güterbock and T. Jacobsen (1965), 351–63; R. Hallock, "On the Old Persian Signs," *JNES*, 29 (1970), 52–55; G. Hanfmann and J. Waldbaum, "New Excavations at Sardis . . . ," *Near Eastern Archaeology in the Twentieth Century*, ed. J. Sanders (1970), 307–26; W. Shea, "An Unrecognized Vassal King of Babylon in the Early Achaemenid Period," *Andrews University Seminary Studies*, 9 (1971), 51–67, 99–128; R. de Vaux, "The Decrees of Cyrus and Darius on the Rebuilding of the Temple," *The Bible and the Ancient Near East* (1971), pp. 63–96; J. Harmatta, "The Rise of the Old Persian Empire: Cyrus the Great," *Acta Antiqua* (Budapest), 19 (1971), 3–15; id., "The Literary Patterns of the Babylonian Edict of Cyrus," *Acta Antiqua* (Budapest), 19 (1971), 217–31; W. Eilers, ed., *Festgabe deutscher Iranistan zur 2500 Jahrfeier* (1971); D. Stronach, "A Circular Symbol on the Tomb of Cyrus," *Iran*, 9 (1971), 155–58; M. Mallowan, "Cyrus the Great," *Iran*, 10 (1972), 1–17; C. Walker, "A Recently Identified Fragment of the Cyrus Cylinder," *Iran*, 10 (1972), 158–59; J. Whitcomb, "Cyrus in the Prophecies of Isaiah," *The Law and the Prophets*, ed. J. Skilton (1973), pp. 388–401; *Commémoration Cyrus* (1974); P.-R. Berger, "Der Kyros-Zylinder mit dem Zusatzfragment BIN II Nr. 32 . . . ," *Zeitschrift für Assyriologie*, 64 (1975), 192–234.

EY

CYRUS CYLINDER. When Cyrus* the Persian (557–529 B.C.) conquered Babylon* in 539 B.C. he issued a decree inscribed on a clay* cylinder discovered by Hormuzd Rassam in the nineteenth century. After outlining the misdeeds of Nabonidus* and Belshazzar* and their neglect of the worship of Marduk, he told how that god chose him as legitimate ruler, having "scanned and looked through all the countries, searching for a righteous ruler willing to lead him [Marduk] in the annual procession." He decreed the restoration of proper worship in Babylon, the return of captive gods to their own temples and captive peoples to their own lands. This decree provides the background to Ezra 1:1–3; 6:3–5.

BIBLIOGRAPHY: J. P. Pritchard, *ANET* (1955), 3–5–16.

JAT

D

DABERATH (dab'ə rəth). This levitical city of Issachar (Josh 21:28; 1 Chron 6:72) is usually identified with ruins near the village of Daburiyeh, at the foot of Mount Tabor.

DABURIYEH. *See* DABERATH.

DAGON (dā'gon; Heb. דָּגוֹן, *dagon*). A major Philistine* deity worshiped in Gaza* (Judg 16:23), Ashdod* (1 Sam 5:2–7). In the latter city the shrine survived to Maccabean times (1 Macc 10:83–84), at Gaza (Judg 16:30) and also at Asher* (Josh 19:27). The origin of the name and the nature of the god are rather uncertain. "Dagon" was an element of theophoric names in Amorite* culture (e.g., Dagantakala), but there is no evidence that it was derived from the Hebrew *dag* ("fish") thus making Dagon a fish-deity. Some relationship to the Hebrew *dagan* ("grain," "corn") seems more probable. From 2500 B.C. temples dedicated to Dagon existed in Mesopotamia,* Syria, and northern Phoenicia. The cult was firmly established at Ugarit,* and his temple rivaled that of Baal.* In some Ugaritic texts the dying-and-resurgent Baal was described as the "son of Dagon," which may indicate some stage in the development of Baal as a vegetation-deity. At Beth Shan* the excavated temple may perhaps be the one mentioned in 1 Chron 10:10. Other Palestinian shrines were probably located at two sites, each called Beth Dagon (Josh 15:41; 19:27).

RKH

DALMANUTHA. *See* MAGADAN.

DALMATIA. *See* ILLYRICUM.

DAMASCUS (də mas'kus; Heb. דַּמֶּשֶׂק, *Dammeseq*; Gr. Δαμασκός, *Damaskós*). A city of ancient OT Syria (Aram*) and capital of NT Coelesyria and of modern Syria, located in the plain E of the Anti-Lebanon range and NE of Mount Hermon.* Since it bordered the desert to the E and was supplied with water through the Abana (the Nahr Barada) and Pharpar (Nahr el-'Awaj) rivers, Damascus played an important role in commerce, military activity, and religion. Damascus is mentioned several times in the OT (cf. Gen 14:15; 2 Sam 8:5–6; 1 Kings 11:24; 2 Kings 8:7, 9; Isa 7:8 et al.). It is also referred to in the NT (Acts 9:2ff.; 22:5f., 10ff.; 26:12, 20; 2 Cor 11:32; and Gal 1:17).

It is not certain that today's Damascus was the main part of the early second millennium B.C. city, since in the Damascus area there are several tells* with remains of ancient settlements. Such are Tell es-Salijeh c. 9 miles E of Damascus on the Nahr Barada (Abana) River and Tell Deir Habiyeh c. 9 miles SW of Damascus. Both sites were centers of civilization in the Old Babylonian period, c. eighteenth to seventeenth century B.C.

In the Amarna* Age Egyptian* domination is evident, as indicated by Damascus being listed among the places conquered by Thutmose III (1490–1436 B.C.) (*ANET*, 242). This period also seems to show connection between the city and Mycenaean civilization* since pieces of Mycenaean pottery* were discovered at Tell es-Salijeh. Many of these are now in the Museum of Damascus.

By the end of the second millennium, Damascus was the head of the Aramaean kingdom that for several centuries vied for power with the Assyrians. Besides the OT (cf. 2 Kings 16:9; Isa 7:8ff.), inscriptions give evidence of this. Compare the fight of Shalmaneser III (858–824 B.C.) against the Aramaean coalition that included Damascus (*ANET*, 278–81); also the inscription of the conquest of Tiglath-Pileser III* (744–727) over the city (*ANET*, 283). Another inscription reports the revolt of Damascus and others against Sargon II* (721–705) (*ANET*, 285). Later the city was conquered by the Babylonians, Persians, and Alexander the Great (the latter in 332 B.C.).

In 65 B.C. Rome conquered the area and a Nabataean* governor ruled Damascus.

Archaeology has illuminated particularly the Roman period and several centuries of the Christian era. Straight Street (lined with colonnades in the Roman period) has been identified (*PEQ*, 11:42), and there have been discovered remains of a massive Roman arch* (*PEQ*, 12:40) and a Roman gateway (*PEQ*, 24:72–73). Also identified has been remains of a heathen temple of Jupiter Damascenus; about a dozen Greek inscriptions (probably third century A.D.) from the temple have to do with the activities of various commissions of temple stewards (ἱεροῖαμίαι, *hieroiamiai*) who in succession presided over the temple (*PEQ*, 12:150–53).

Later the Church of St. John the Baptist and Arcadius was built on the same site; the area is now occupied by the Mosque of the Omayyads, and near it in 1909 there was found the fragment of a column with a Greek inscription relating to the rights of protection afforded by the earlier Church of St. John (*PEQ*, 11:42–51; 12:206–9).

Although the small chapel of the so-called house of Ananias (below ground level) is not ancient, re-

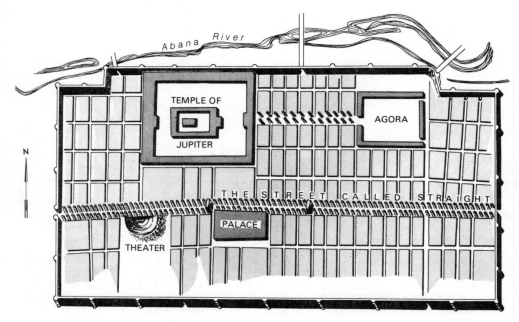

Damascus: plan of city. Courtesy Carta, Jerusalem.

mains of an ancient church at the back of it, with part of a wall from the Byzantine* period, give some authenticity to the site.

BIBLIOGRAPHY: E. Schürer, *A History of the Jewish People in the Time of Jesus Christ*, 1.2 (1891), 352–57; *PEQ*, assorted articles from 1897 to 1955; J. Sauvaget, *Les Monuments historiques de Damascus* (1932); J. B. Pritchard, ed., *ANET* (1955); A. Haldar, "Damascus," *IDB* (1962), 757–58; *PECS* (1976), 256–57.

WHM

DAMASCUS DOCUMENT. *See* ZADOKITE FRAGMENTS.

DAN. An important biblical city* at the northern limits of Israelite territory in O.T. times. Not originally a part of the inheritance of the tribe of Dan, it was captured by a contingent of 600 Danite warriors when their patrimony proved to be difficult to hold against the Canaanites.* In a famous incident they pressed into their own service a young Levite attached to the household of Micah, an Ephraimite (Judg 18). The idols* introduced by this priest became a snare for the subsequent inhabitants, and Dan never lost its reputation for heterodoxy. The prominent place of Dan in the religious reforms of Jereboam I marked it out, along with Bethel,* for condemnation.

Geographically Dan is frequently linked with Beersheba* in a bipolar phrase signifying the extent of Israelite territory. "From Dan to Beersheba" became restricted during the divided monarchy to "from Dan to Bethel."

The mound (tell*) of ancient Dan, called Tell el-

Qadi (Mound of the Judge), is at the foot of Mount Hermon* and covers 20 ha. (50 a.). It rises 20 m. (65 ft.) above the level of the plain. A tremendously powerful spring emerging beside the tell is fed by underground sources derived from the melting snows of Hermon. The resultant spring forms one of the main sources of the Jordan River and the shape of the tell was apparently governed by the stream. The earliest major fortifications were those of the Middle Bronze II* period.

Historical records from Egypt* and Mesopotamia* recognize the importance of the city in pre-Israelite times. Originally called Laish (or Leshem) according to the Bible, the city is found among those men-

Bilingual inscription in Greek and Aramaic on a plaque from Tel Dan found in area of high place, dated c. second century B.C. The text reads: "To the god who is in Dan Zoilos made a vow." This formula is indicative of a tradition from the days of Jeroboam I to the Hellenistic period. See 1 Kings 12:28-30 and Amos 8:14. Courtesy Hebrew Union College, Jewish Institute of Religion.

tioned in the Egyptian execration texts* of the nine-teenth–eighteenth centuries B.C. The Mari* tablets (eighteenth century B.C.) also preserve a valuable reference to the city. Its name was changed to Dan by the invading Danites, who took advantage of its distance from the nominal Sidonian sphere of influence.

Archaeological work began under Avram Biran in 1966 and has continued annually by the same excavator with sponsorship by the Israel Department of Antiquities.

Stratification. The early picture of the sequence and chronological (*see* CHRONOLOGY) extent of each stratum has had to be modified several times, but the overall scheme is fairly clear. Substantial Early Bronze Age deposits have been attested, but served as fill for the later constructions, and thus have been insufficiently investigated in undisturbed contexts. The huge MB II wall* and rampart were partially dug into the EB strata. The city seems to have flourished in the eighteenth and seventeenth centuries, until a destruction occurred c. 1625–1575 B.C. Following this, there was some slight occupation in LB I, with significant finds from LB II A-B (Stratum VII).

At the end of the Late Bronze Age there was a partial destruction level of ash and charred material which the excavator connects with the original Danite onslaught. Level VI is characteristically Early Iron I,* with some Late Bronze material. Levels V-I are Iron Age II, and span the tenth-eighth centuries, with some late occupation reaching down to the end of the seventh and the beginning of the sixth centuries. Level III, containing some important remains, is dated to c. 925–875 B.C. Among the tombs, number 387 yielded a rich hoard of objects from LB II (fourteenth century B.C.). Included in the finds were 15 bronze* arrowheads and a bronze sword, as well as an abundance of Cypriot (*see* CYPRUS) and Mycenean* pottery.* A large rare Mycenean chari-oteer vase was dated to the middle of the fourteenth century.

Defenses. The original MB fortifications consisted of a thick stone core 10 m. (33 ft.) high and 6.5 m. (21 ft.) wide, flanked by a sloping glacis* of approximately 40–45 degrees. The earth ramparts were of typical Hyksos* type and were covered by a layer of hard yellow plaster.*

The Iron Age wall covered an enlarged area. It averaged 3.6 m. (12 ft.) thick and was probably built during the tenth century B.C. by Jereboam I. The city gate* of this period is the largest and best preserved in all of Palestine, measuring 19 by 26 m. (62 by 85 ft.) and consisting of four roomlike areas. It was paved with large basalt slabs and contained an interesting pedestal or rostrum for a throne or cult statue.* The excavator conjectured that the decorated stone bases supported a canopy under which the king probably sat on state occasions. A bench 4.5 m. (15 ft.) long was also found in the gate area. A paved street* ran through the gate. Its 10 m. (33 ft.) width was traced 70 m. (230 ft.) into the city. The gate was burned in the early ninth century B.C., pre-

sumably by the Syrians under Ben Hadad of Damascus* in 885 B.C.

One of the most startling and impressive discoveries of recent Palestinian archaeology was the unearthing of a large MB II mudbrick gateway complete with intact arch,* which had apparently been used for only a decade or so when it was covered over entirely in order to raise the level of the walls. It remains the finest surviving example of a defense system of the period.

Sanctuary. In area T on the NW corner of the mound, a structure termed the *bama*, or "high place,*" was discovered. It proved to be a large stone platform, built over several centuries, but with part of the masonry made in the style found at Israelite Samaria.* The structure measures 18.2 by 18.7 m. (59½ by 61 ft.), with walls of header-stretcher construction c. 1.5–2.3 m. (5–7½ ft.) wide. It was elevated on a stone core and formed a broad esplanade paved with flat basalt stones. A flight of monumental stairs 8 m. (26 ft.) wide faced the town on the S side. A small horned incense* altar* of Israelite type from the ninth or tenth century was found near the stairs in 1974. The platform was first built in the MB II period and was gradually enlarged. It is probable that Jereboam I was responsible for the early Israelite additions, but the pottery supports a date of the mid-ninth century for the stairs, which were presumably added by Ahab.* The *bama* was subsequently enlarged and reused in the Hellenistic and Roman periods. A second-century B.C. Greek* and Aramaic* bilingual text with a vow "to the god of Dan" was discovered in 1975.

The size of the city of Dan, its geographical position, and its historical and biblical importance guarantee that continuing excavations will provide many more important facts for scholarly research. The reconstructionist school of biblical criticism has yet to deal seriously with the implications of the sanctuary for the religious and literary history of Israel.* Likewise, the impact of the "Danite" destruction level on the question of the date of the Israelite conquest has not yet been fully appreciated.

BIBLIOGRAPHY: Avraham Biran, "Tel Dan," *IEJ*, 16 (1966); 17 (1967), 121–23, 144–45; 19 (1968), 121–23, 239–41; 20 (1970), 92–94, 118–19; 22 (1972), 164–66; 23 (1973), 110–12; id., "Tell Dan," *BA*, 37 (1974), 26–51; *BA* 43.3 (1980), 168–82; *BAR* 7.5 (1981), 20–37.

JEJ

DANUNA. *See* SEA PEOPLES.

DAPHNAI. *See* TAHPANHES.

DARIUS (də rī′əs; Heb. דָּֽרְיָ֫וֶשׁ, *dāryāwesh*; LXX Δαρεῖος, *Dareios*; Old Pers. *Dārayavaush*, from *Dāraya-Vahumanah*, "He Who Sustains Good Thought"; Akkad. *da-ri-ia-muš*; Elamite *da-ri-ia-ma-u-iš*). The name of three Persian kings: (1) Darius I, or Darius the Great (522–486 B.C.), whom we shall refer to simply as Darius; (2) Darius II (423–404 B.C.), who is known as Nothus; (3) Darius III (336–330 B.C.), who is known as Codomannus.

I. *Biblical References*. Darius is mentioned prominently in Ezra 4–6 (cf. Hag 1:1, 15; 2:10; Zech 1:1, 7; 7:1) as the Persian monarch under whom the temple* at Jerusalem was finally reconstructed after the Jewish return from exile in Babylonia.

"Darius the Persian" in Neh 12:22 is probably Darius I, but Nothus and even Codomannus have been suggested. "Darius the Mede" in Dan 5:31; 6:1 et al. was a ruler set over Babylonia under Cyrus* (Medes II).

II. *Sources for Darius*. A. *Cuneiform Texts*. The royal inscriptions of Darius were often written in trilingual cuneiform* versions: (1) Old Persian; (2) Elamite, the language of Susa*; and (3) Akkadian, the Semitic language of Babylon.

Borger and Hinz have interpreted section 70 of the Behistun Inscription* (DB) to assert that Darius invented the Old Persian script (*Cyrus* II.A, and *Pasargadae* IV.C.2). Lewy and Ghirshman, however, conclude that this passage simply means that Darius permitted copies of his inscriptions on tablets and on parchment to circulate.

In any case, OP was used exclusively by kings. We have fifty-six different OP inscriptions of Darius including those on weights and seals,* or nearly one hundred if we include duplicates. This is more than all other Achaemenid kings combined. The inscriptions after Darius are often but imitations of his texts.

These include: (1) from Persepolis* trilingual and OP texts on two gold* and two silver* plates (discovered in 1936), and on numerous architectural pieces; (2) from Naqsh-i-Rustam a long trilingual carved on the cliff; (3) from Susa trilingual and OP on clay* tablets and column fragments; (4) from Mount Elvend, SW of Hamadan, a trilingual; (5) from Hamadan a trilingual on gold and silver plates, discovered in 1926; (6) from near Suez in Egypt* trilinguals on granite stelae;* (7) from Pasargadae,* a fragmentary inscription formerly attributed to Cyrus; and (8) longest and most important is the trilingual text carved at Behistun. 1. *The Behistun Inscription*. The site known in modern Pers. as Bīsitūn (Arabic *Behistūn* from Old Pers. *bagastāna*, "Place of the God") is located 20 miles E of Kermanshah on the road to Hamadan. Between 520 to 518 B.C. on a sheer cliff 107 m. (350 ft.) above the plain, Darius had carved a monumental record of his rise to power. The texts cover a space over 6 m. (20 ft.) high and about 18 m. (60 ft.) wide.

In relief are sculptured from left to right two attendants, Darius treading upon the pretender Gaumata, then eight bound rebel leaders—including a Scythian* with a peaked hat who was added later. Above the captives hovers the winged symbol of Ahura-Mazda.

Persian Muslims thought the relief depicted a teacher beating his pupils; Persian Christians thought that it represented Christ and His twelve disciples. The first European to discover the monument was a Frenchman named Otter, in 1734. It was the Eng-lishman H. Rawlinson who in 1835–37 and 1847 succeeded in copying the inscription, at times as he was perched precariously on top of a ladder resting on a narrow ledge! His copies provided the key to the decipherment of cuneiform script.

Fragmentary copies of the text have been found in Akkadian on a diorite block from Babylon* and in Aramaic* on a papyrus* from Elephantine,* Egypt. 2. *The Elamite Persepolis Texts*. In 1933–34 several thousand fragments and tablets inscribed in Elamite were found in the fortification wall of Persepolis,* along with a single Greek text. Some two thousand of these Fortification Tablets were published in 1969 by R. Hallock. They date from the thirteenth to the twenty-eighth year of Darius (509–494 B.C.). These texts deal with the transfer and payment of food* products.

In 1936–38 additional Elamite texts were discovered in the Treasury of Persepolis. A little over a hundred of these texts have been published by G. Cameron in 1948, 1958, and 1965. They date from the thirtieth year of Darius to the seventh year of Artaxerxes (492–458 B.C.). In addition to payment in kind they include supplementary payment in silver coins,* an innovation introduced c. 493 B.C. (Darius is also noted for his gold coins known as darics.)

Though we now have only the Elamite copies made by accountants transferred from Susa, the original orders were probably dictated in OP and also written in Aramaic on perishable materials.

B. *Classical Texts*. In addition to the classical sources of Herodotus, Ctesias, Strabo, Polyaenos, etc., we have the interesting Gadates Inscription in a Greek copy from about the time of Tiberius.* This is a communication from Darius to his official Gadates, commending him for the transplanting of fruits from Syria to Asia Minor* but condemning him for his treatment of the gardener of the temple of Apollo near Magnesia on the Maeander.

III. *Ancestry and Accession*. Darius, who was born in 550, came from a collateral Achaemenid line. His grandfather and his father, Hystaspes—the satrap of Parthia and Hyrcania—were still alive when he seized the throne. He was serving as a spear bearer among the "Immortals" with Cambyses II, when the latter died in July 522 on his way back from an invasion of Egypt. According to the official account on the DB and in Herodotus III. 61–79, Cambyses had murdered his brother Smerdis (Bardiya), and a Magian, Gaumata, posing as Smerdis, had seized the throne in March 522. Olmstead, however, believes that the man Darius deposed was not a Pseudo-Smerdis but the brother of Cambyses.

Together with six other Persian nobles, Darius killed the (Pseudo-)Smerdis in September. To reinforce his claim to the throne Darius married two daughters of Cyrus,* including Atossa, who bore Xerxes.* His right to rule was strongly contested and, as he informs us in the DB, he had to defeat nine rebels in nineteen battles in his first three years.

Among the rebels he suppressed were a Nidin-tu-Bel, who claimed to be Nebuchadnezzar III, and an Armenian, Arakha, who claimed to be Nebuchad-

Limestone relief of King Darius seated on throne with Crown Prince Xerxes, attendants, and guards behind him; from Persepolis. Courtesy The Oriental Institute, University of Chicago.

nezzar IV. The former occupied Darius from September to December 522, and the latter from September to November 521.

IV. *Conflicts and Achievements.* A. *Scythia.* On the basis of the *Tabula Capitolina*, a chronological summary in Greek (dated A.D. 15), most historians have assumed that Darius fought against the eastern Scyths and later, c. 513, against the European Scyths. Balcer has suggested that the king's object was to obtain gold from the Scyths. B. *Egypt.* A revolt in Egypt was easily suppressed by Darius in 518. An Egyptian named Udjahorresne, who had served under Cambyses, was commissioned by Darius to reopen a medical school at Sais in the Delta. The Demotic Chronicle informs us that Darius ordered the codification of Egyptian laws. The temple of Amon at Hibis in the Khargah Oasis, built under Darius (510–490 B.C.), was excavated in 1941 by H. Winlock.

Darius ordered the completion of a canal to connect the Pelusiac arm of the Nile with the Red Sea* (Herodotus 2. 158). This account has been confirmed by the discovery of a series of granite stelae* inscribed in Egyp., OP, Akkad., and Elamite which read: "Saith Darius the King: I am a Persian; from Persia I seized Egypt; I gave order to dig this canal from a river by name Nile . . . to the sea which goes from Persia."

In 1972 excavators found at Susa a larger than life-size statue* of Darius, minus its head. It is the first such freestanding Achaemenid statue to be discovered. It is made of local limestone and is inscribed in four languages: OP, Elamite, Akkad., and Egyp. It was made probably between 500–490 B.C., probably as a copy of an original statue set up in Egypt. The inscription reads in part, "Behold the statue of stone which Darius the King ordered made in Egypt in order that in the future whoever sees it will know that the Persian rules Egypt." C. *India.* Western India (now W Pakistan) had been subdued

by Darius before 513. He sent an expedition under a Carian* seaman, Scylax, to explore the route from the headwaters of the Indus River to its mouth and then across the Indian Ocean around Arabia* to Suez (Herodotus 4. 44). D. *Palestine.* After the revolt in Babylon had been suppressed, Ushtannu was installed as governor over Babylonia and areas to the W known as *Athura* (Assyria) or *Ebir-nāri* ("Trans-Euphrates" or "Beyond the River"; cf. Ezra 5:3 RSV). Palestine was governed by Tatnai (Tattenai), who was correctly identified by Olmstead in 1944 with *Ta-at-tan-ni* in cuneiform texts. This governor temporarily stopped the building of the Jewish temple* (Ezra 5–6) until the record of Cyrus's permission could be confirmed. Through the encouragement of Haggai and Zechariah, the temple was completed in 515. E. *Ionia and Greece.* The Ionian Greeks rebelled against the Persians in 499–494. They were given token aid by Eretria and Athens.* After a punitive expedition was shipwrecked at Mount Athos in 492, a second force captured Eretria but was defeated by the Athenians at Marathon in 490 (Herodotus 6. 103–17).

The *Soros*, a mound about 30 feet high, marks the spot where the 192 Athenian dead were buried at Marathon. In 1970 S. Marinatos discovered another mound, 3.3 m. (11 ft.) high, 2 km. (1¼ mi.) SW of the Soros, which covered the burial of Athens's Plataean allies. Excavations brought to light the remains of several young men about 20–25 years old and a cremation of a 10-year-old lad. At Olympia were dedicated the helmet* of Miltiades, the Athenian leader, and a helmet taken from the "Medes," discovered by the Germans in 1961.

V. *Constructions.* A. *Persepolis.* The construction of the new capital at Persepolis,* though begun by Darius in 518, was not completed until 460. Excavations have been conducted at the site by E. Herzfeld in 1931–34 and by E. Schmidt in 1935–

39. Since the 1940s the site has been excavated and reconstructed by the Iranian archaeological service. In 1972 the Iranians celebrated the nation's 2500th birthday with festivities at Persepolis.

On the artificial terrace, 275 by 457 m. (900 by 1500 ft.) and 12 m. (40 ft.) high, Darius built: (1) his palace; (2) the Tripylon; (3) the Treasury; and (4) the Apadana or audience hall, 59.5 m. (195 ft.) square, which could accommodate 8,000 guests. The last two structures were completed by Xerxes.* B. *Babylon.* Darius used Babylon as an occasional winter residence. He built there an arsenal, a palace for the crown prince, and an apadana for his own palace on the Southern Citadel. A fragment of his DB inscription on a diorite stele* was found in the ruins of Nebuchadnezzar's* old palace museum. C. *Susa.* Susa* was also used as a winter residence. Not only have the ruins of Darius's apadana been recovered but also an inscription that details the various materials used: (1) cedar* from Lebanon, (2) gold from Sardis* and Bactria,* (3) lapis lazuli* from Sogdiana, (4) silver and ebony from Egypt, (5) ivory* from Ethiopia* and Sind, etc.

The Royal Road which ran 2735 km. (1700 mi.) from Susa to Sardis was traversed by caravans in ninety days, but by royal couriers, changing horses, in a week. Herodotus's (8.98) description of these couriers serves as a motto of the New York post office: "These are stayed neither by snow nor rain nor heat nor gloom. . . ." D. *Naqsh-i-Rustam.* Four miles N of Persepolis is the site of Naqsh-i-Rustam, where there are two altars* and a quadrangular tower, the *Ka'aba-i-Zardusht* ("The Cube of Zoroaster") which are similar to structures at Pasargadae* (*Pasargadae* IV.A and IV.C.1).

Carved on the cliff are four tombs. The second from the E is identified by a trilingual inscription as that of Darius. The facade of his tomb is in the form of a cross 22 m. (73 ft.) high and 11 m. (36 ft.) wide. The cross beam contains a panel with a relief of Darius on a throne supported by representatives from thirty nations. The interior contains three vaults and nine cists for Darius and members of his family. Darius died in 486 at the age of sixty-four.

VI. *His Religion.* A number of scholars including E. Meyer, Clemen, Moulton, and Wilber, hold that Darius was a Zoroastrian. Herzfeld, Olmstead, and others identify Hyastaspes, the father of Darius, with the Gushtasp converted by Zoroaster. Some scholars even believe that Cyrus was a Zoroastrian (*Cyrus* VI.). Though Zoroaster is not named in Darius's inscriptions, and none of the Achaemenids are mentioned in the Avesta, these scholars believe that they can detect Zoroastrian elements in the texts of Darius. Ahura-Mazda alone is mentioned by name, and "Truth" is exalted against the "Lie."

Other scholars who do not believe that Darius was a Zoroastrian include Prášek, Jackson, Nyberg, Christensen, and Cameron. Ghirshman notes that Darius and the other Achaemenids were buried in tombs instead of being exposed, as required in the Avesta and as practiced by the Magi. On the Naqsh-i-Rustam panel Darius worships the sacred fire but without the *patidana*, the cloth mask required by later Zoroastrian ritual. In view of Zoroaster's denunciation of the haoma cult, it is interesting to note the presence of mortars* and pestles for the cult from Persepolis (dated to Xerxes' reign).

BIBLIOGRAPHY: A. Jackson, "The Religion of the Achaemenian Kings," *JAOS*, XXI (1900), 160–84; L. King and R. Thompson, *The Sculptures and Inscriptions of Darius the Great on the Rock of Behistun in Persia* (1907); F. W. König, *Relief und Inschrift des Königs Dareios I am Felsen von Bagistan* (1938); R. Parker, "Darius and His Egyptian Campaign," *AJSL*, LVIII (1941), 373–77; G. Cameron, "Darius, Egypt and the 'Lands Beyond the Sea,'" *JNES*, II (1943), 307–13; P. Junge, *Dareios I, König der Perser* (1944); G. Cameron, *Persepolis Treasury Tablets* (1948); A. Olmstead, *History of the Persian Empire* (1948); G. Cameron, "Darius Carved History on Ageless Rock," *National Geographic*, XCVIII.6 (1950), 825–44; R. Kent, *Old Persian* (1953); E. Schmidt, *Persepolis I* (1953); J. Lewy, "The Problems Inherent in Section 70 of the Bisutun Inscription," *HUCA*, XXV (1954), 169–208; J. Harmatta, "A Recently Discovered Old Persian Inscription," *Acta Antiqua* (Budapest), II (1952–54), 1–16; G. Lanczkowski, "Zur Entstehung des antiken Synkretismus Darius als Sohn der Neith von Sais," *Saeculum*, VI (1955), 227–43; W. Benedict and L. von Voigtlander, "Darius' Bisutun Inscription . . . ," *JCS*, X (1956), 1–10; K. M. T. Atkinson, "The Legitimacy of Cambyses and Darius as Kings of Egypt," *JAOS*, LXXVI (1956), 167–77; E. Schmidt, *Persepolis II* (1957); G. Cameron, "Persepolis Treasury Tablets Old and New," *JNES*, XVII (1958), 161–76; V. Strouve, "The Religion of the Achaemenids and Zoroastrianism," *Cahiers d'histoire mondiale*, V (1959–60), 529–45; G. Cameron, "The Monument of King Darius at Bisitun," *ARC*, XIII (Sept., 1960), 162–71; R. T. Hallock, "The 'One Year' of Darius I," *JNES*, XIX (1960), 36–39; A. Burn, *Persia and the Greeks* (1962); R. Ghirshman, *The Art of Ancient Iran* (1964); G. Cameron, "New Tablets from the Persepolis Treasury," *JNES*, XXIV (1965), 167–92; W. Culican, *The Medes and Persians* (1965); C. Nylander, "Old Persian and Greek Stonecutting and the Chronology of Achaemenian Monuments," *AJA*, LXIX (1965), 49–55; G. Cameron, "An Inscription of Darius from Pasargadae," *Iran*, V (1967), 7–10; L. Trümpelmann, "Zur Entstehungsgeschichte des Monumentes Dareios' I. von Bisutun . . . ," *Archäologischer Anzeiger* (1967), 281–98; H. Bengtson et al., *The Greeks and the Persians* (1968); R. Hallock, *Persepolis Fortification Tablets* (1969); A. Rainey, "The Satrapy 'Beyond the River,'" *AustBibArch*, I (1969), 51–78; D. Wilber, *Persepolis* (1969); S. Marinatos, "Further News from Marathon," *Athens Annals of Archaeology*, III (1970), 153–66; E. Schmidt, *Persepolis III* (1970); F. Vallat, "Table élamite de Darius Ier," *Revue d'assyriologie*, LXIV (1970), 149–60; R. Hallock, "The Evidence of the Persepolis Tablets," *The Cambridge History of Iran*, II (1971), ch. 1; W. Hinz, "Zu den Elamischen Burghaus Inschriften Darius I aus Susa," *Acta Antiqua* (Budapest), XIX (1971), 17–24. J. Balcer, "The Date of *Herodotus* IV.1, Darius' Scythian Expedition," *Harvard Studies in Classical Philology*, LXXVI (1972), 99–132; M. Kervran, "Une statue de Darius découverte à Suse," *Journal asiatique*, CCLX (1972), 235–39; D. Stronach, "Description and Comment," ibid., 241–46; F. Vallat, "L'inscription cuneiforme trilingue (DSab)," ibid., 247–52; J. Yoyotte, "Les inscriptions hiéroglyphiques Darius et l'Égypte," ibid., 253–66; F. Vallat, "La triple inscription cunéiforme de la statue de Darius Ier," *Revue d'assyriologie*, LXVIII (1974), 157–66; M. A. Dandamaev, *Persien unter den ersten Achämeniden* (tr. from Russian by H.-D. Pohl, 1976); E. Yamauchi, "The Achaemenid Capitals," *NEASB*, VIII (1976), 5–81; W. Hinz, *Darius und die Perser* (1976); E. von Voigtlander, *The Bisitun Inscription of Darius the Great* (1978).

EY

DATING. The ability to assign reasonable dates to strata and individual artifacts* alike is obviously of great importance in any archaeological endeavor. The dating procedures were of a rather haphazard character until Sir Flinders Petrie established a system of ceramic dating with reference to the various phases of Minoan* culture. So reliable has this proved to be that it is an essential technique for all situations in which pottery* is present. Earlier methods of dating have now been reinforced by procedures based on modern science, and some of these will be surveyed briefly.

1. *Potassium-Argon Dating.* Potassium 40, one kind of potassium atom, is radioactive and decays slowly into argon. The age of a mineral containing potassium can thus be calculated by measuring the amount of the original potassium that has decayed. The procedure is far from simple, and allowance must be made for loss, with the result that only broad geological time scales can gain advantage from it.

2. *Carbon-14 Dating.* In the upper atmosphere there exists a radioactive isotope of carbon with an atomic weight of 14 instead of 12. It is created when nitrogen-14 atoms are bombarded by cosmic rays. The proportion of C14 and C12 remains constant in the atmosphere, and both are absorbed, as carbon dioxide, into the substance of plants. Of such vegetable matter wood* is particularly durable, lasting sometimes for thousands of years. In the wood the C14 disintegrates and is not replaced, so that, with the process of time, the proportion of C14 to C12 decreases continually and evenly. The half-life of the carbon-14 atom has been estimated at 5,500 years, though some scientists believe this figure is too low. On this basis a sensitive radiation counter can measure the residue of carbon-14 in the specimen, with a current margin of error of plus or minus 100 years. This has been tested on material of an age known from historical data and found to constitute a fairly reliable dating method, provided that there is no extraneous radio-active contamination.

3. *Fluorine Dating.* This is a scientific technique for determining the relative age of fossil bones. It depends upon the fact that bones and teeth absorb the element fluorine, which hardens them. When bones or teeth lie in permeable earth containing fluorides they absorb fluorine progressively and at a constant rate, so that two bones which have lain in the same place for the same length of time will be found to have absorbed roughly the same amount. This amount can then be determined by chemical analysis. The rate at which fluorine is absorbed varies from place to place, so that the method cannot be used to provide absolute dating. Its sole function is to provide a relative dating by establishing which of two (or more) bones found on the same site has been there the longer.

4. *Thermoluminescence Dating.* This technique is based on the fact that all minerals emit visible light if heated to red hot. Some minerals when so heated exhibit an additional light output called thermoluminescence (TL), which arises from release of energy stored in the substance. This storage process occurs as the mineral absorbs minute levels of nuclear radiation from its surroundings.

As geological material, pottery constituents will have been exposed to radiation over an extremely long period and will have stored a very high level of TL energy. But this geological TL will have been driven off during the process of kiln-firing, so that immediately after its manufacture, the pottery's stored level of TL energy is nil.

A time-zero has been set by the kiln-firing and consequently relates directly to the age of pottery. For from that time, reaccumulation of energy occurs in response to the radiation environment in which the pottery finds itself and is subject to scientific measurement.

The importance of the time-zero setting mechanism is peculiar to pottery. Many other materials, such as marble, sandstone, and jade used for carving, and precious stones used for decoration, are geological in origin. TL analysis of these would therefore yield a geological age, not a date related to when the material was worked in antiquity. Thus the distinction between an authentic ancient art ceramic and one of modern origin (either an imitation or a forgery) becomes apparent. The modern article will yield only a fraction of the TL observed from the ancient.

5. *Collagen Content.* Collagen is a protein occurring in animal bone. The fats are dissipated after death, whereas the collagen remains, although in decreasing quantities. An analysis of the existing nitrogen content will indicate the amount of bone protein which has survived. There is sufficient uniformity in the processes of decay to enable uncomplicated deposits of bones of various dates to be separated by means of this method, which is normally used in conjunction with other dating methods.

6. *Chronology.* A process of prime importance in archaeology. Much dating is relative, giving information about the order of events rather than furnishing specific dates. In the absence of historical records which could be expected to provide a rea-

sonably detailed chronology, relative archaeological dating employs such methods as stratigraphy,* typology,* cross-dating, sequence-dating, collagen content, fluorine testing, and radiometric assay. Closer to absolute dating are radiocarbon dating, dendrochronology,* varve dating, thermoluminescence, potassium-argon dating, and pollen analysis (see PALYNOLOGY).

7. *Archaeomagnetism.* A method of dating ferromagnetic artifacts in terms of the nature of their magnetic field at the period when they finally cooled after baking, as with clay* objects, which normally contain magnetic oxides of iron.* The success of the method depends upon its correlation with other archaeological dating techniques and is accurate to plus or minus fifty years for a two-thousand-year period.

8. *Geochronology.* A comprehensive term covering the various techniques employed for dating artifacts against the background of geophysical changes. Such methods include radiocarbon and potassium-argon dating, thermoluminescence, dendrochronology, fluorine testing, and varve dating.

9. *Cross-Dating.* A means of dating by comparing artifacts from different cultures—as for example, where a type of pottery from City A recovered from City B is contemporary with or later than A. Cross-dating is generally employed when other types of geophysical tests are lacking.

BIBLIOGRAPHY: M. Wheeler, *Archaeology from the Earth* (1954), 49; S. Rapport and H. Wright, *Archaeology* (1964), 46–59.

EMB, JEJ, and HWP

DEAD SEA. From the second century A.D. this was a popular name for the unique salt-laden lake located at the mouth of the Jordan River. In the OT it was called the Salt Sea (Gen 14:3; Num 34:12 et al.), the Sea of the Plain (Deut 3:17; 4:49 et al.), and the eastern sea (Ezek 47:18; Joel 2:20). Some early writers such as Josephus (Jos. *War* 4.7.2) also referred to it as the Asphalt Sea.

It comprises the deepest part of a large rift-valley lying at the southern extremity of the Jordan, and it has no natural exit. On average it is 17 km. (10 mi.) wide and 69 km. (43 mi.) in length. The surface is 394 m. (1292 ft.) below the level of the Mediterranean Sea, but the lowest levels of the Dead Sea are at least as deep again, and soundings in the NE section have gone down more than 1300 ft. On the E and W the Dead Sea is shut in by rocky cliffs, while two-thirds of the way down the E side a large promontory juts westward into the sea for about 13 km. (8 mi.). As contrasted with the NE corner under the hills of Moab,* the S end of the Dead Sea is only between 2.5 and 4.5 m. (8 and 14 ft.) deep. The depth and extent of the sea at the latter extremity varies with the severity of the rainy season.

The Dead Sea is thus a large, enclosed inland lake and is fed by the Jordan and about five smaller streams that pour an estimated six million tons of water into

it each day. These waters have a high saline content derived from the heavy salt* deposits near the shores of the sea. Petroleum and sulphur also form an important part of the local geological picture, and these, along with other minerals such as calcium, sodium, and potassium, have been the object of commercial extraction in some areas. The heat and dryness in the rift valley combine to produce a high level of evaporation in the Dead Sea waters, and this balances the liquid inflow while building up a high concentration of mineral particles. As a result, the Dead Sea is comprised of about 25 percent solid material, and this contributes to the buoyancy and extreme bitterness of the water. It is impossible for marine life to exist in the Dead Sea, though it can be found in pools near the mouths of the springs and wadis* that flow into the sea.

The cities of the valley (Gen 10:19; 13:10ff. et al.) were apparently located S of the promontory known as el-Lisan, and they were most probably submerged by the waters of the south-eastern part of the Dead Sea when the cities were destroyed (Gen 19:24ff.). This situation obviously precludes their excavation by conventional methods. Some seismic disturbance appears to have precipitated the catastrophe, which also involved combustible bituminous* substances (Gen 19:28). An early city of Judah in the wilderness district (Josh 15:62) was known as the City of Salt, identified by most scholars with Khirbet Qumran,* where remains of Iron Age* buildings go back to about 900 B.C. A road leading down the Wadi Qumran to the S and W may have been constructed in the Iron Age II period to link the City of Salt with the outposts in the Valley of Achor.* In the Maccabean period Khirbet Qumran accommodated a monastic group that bequeathed to modern scholarship the celebrated Dead Sea Scrolls.* The only challenge to the universally-accepted barrenness of the Dead Sea was that offered by Ezekiel's vision (Ezek 47:1ff.), which contemplated its re-creation by a lifegiving stream flowing from beneath the temple.*

BIBLIOGRAPHY: D. Baly, *The Geography of the Bible* (1957), 202ff.   RKH

DEAD SEA SCROLLS. In 1947 a Bedouin goatherd by the Dead Sea* threw a stone into a cliff-side cave,* heard the splintering of earthenware, and gave the world the first of the documents now known as the Dead Sea Scrolls, the religious library of a desert sect who lived for two full centuries at Qumran* near the NW corner of the inland sea which provides the name. Since then investigation has probed more of the caves on the barren cliffs by the Dead Sea, and added largely to the collection.

Fragmented or amazingly intact, the ancient documents may be seen in Jordan's Archaeological Museum or in Israel's Shrine of the Scrolls. They are carefully preserved under regulated conditions of temperature and humidity. Few documents have been so intensively studied and few so recklessly interpreted.

The texts from the caves are of varied interest and importance. There are manuscripts of every OT book

Section of the Thanksgiving Scroll, one of few sectarian scrolls found in Qumran cave. The complete scroll contains about forty hymns stylistically similar to psalms. Courtesy The Shrine of the Book, D. Samuel and Jeane H. Gottesman Museum of Biblical Manuscripts, Israel Museum, Jerusalem.

except Esther, a thousand years older than anything scholarship possessed before this. There are commentaries on the prophets but they are of no great value as commentaries. There is a Manual of Discipline, from which it is possible to gain some notion of the life lived in the desert community. The Temple* scroll, the last major one to be translated, was acquired after the Six-Day War in 1967. The document, 8.5 m. (28 ft.) long, contained regulations to be enforced when the Qumran sect ultimately returned to Jerusalem. * Laws of purity for the sect prohibited coition and defecation within the Holy City on the Sabbath. The ruler of the future theocracy could have only one wife, though he was permitted to remarry after her decease. Polygamy was thus strictly forbidden to the sectaries, and regulations regarding divorce were the same as those taught by Christ (Mark 10:2–12).

There is a mystic story of a war between "the children of light" and the forces of darkness, with some allusion to a "teacher of righteousness" done to death by the hierarchy.

This mysterious figure at first gave rise to some controversy. As far as substance can be given to the shadowy personality, the teacher was probably the founder of the sect in the second century B.C., a good man who rose to protest the corruption of contemporary Jewish religion and met martyrdom. Attempts to identify him with Christ, who died in the full blaze of recorded history, have encountered in-

superable chronological difficulties. Nor did the people of Qumran think of their teacher of righteousness as a messiah. In their eschatology, while they regarded themselves in some sense as the corporate fulfillment of Isaiah's "Servant" and Daniel's "Son of Man," they looked for the appearance at the end of the age of three figures—a priestly messiah, a military messiah, and Moses' "prophet," with which the coming of Christ hardly accords.

While it is true that some of the sectaries' expressions may be found in the utterances of Christ, a teacher of the common people of the land, whom they "heard gladly," would be expected to seek a vocabulary close to that of contemporary religious usage. The fact that the imagery of light and darkness, so common in John's writings—phrases like "eternal life" and the double "amen," or "verily, verily I say . . ." appear in the Scrolls—only demonstrates that Christ spoke the common language of His day. It was Christ's way to emphasize old truth and set it in a more compelling light.

It is also a fact that, in direct contrast with the rigid discipline of the sectaries, Christ was no ascetic. His foes held that against Him. He also contradicted their ethical teaching, notably in His firm command to love one's enemies. Qumran counseled hate for "the foes of light." "Love the Children of Light," runs the Qumran text, "and hate the Children of Darkness." It is a behest from the allegorical document found among the Scrolls, "the War of the Children of Light and the Children of Darkness," a curious compilation built out of the detailed study of the OT wars and what appears to have been a Roman military manual. Nothing could be more alien to Christ's teaching. Indeed, He was surely quoting when He said, "You have heard it said: Thou shalt love thy neighbour and hate thine enemy, but I say to you. . . ."

In short, it is historically impossible to identify the well-documented life of Christ with the exotic allegorizing of this desert sect.

It became apparent, as scholars went to work on Qumran and its library, that the true interest and meaning of the discovery lay in the people as much as in the scrolls. But the study of the community of Qumran added little to that which was plain to see in the NT. It merely sharpened understanding.

The Pharisees and Sadducees dominate the gospel story in the NT. The first-named were the defenders and exponents of the Law, the second a cynical priestly hierarchy, collaborators and simonists. Both hated Christ, the former because He exposed the hypocrisy of their legalistic pretentions, the latter because He menaced their profits and their comfort. But it is obvious that there was a "third force" in Palestine, a core of faithful folk who kept true religion alive in an age of disillusionment and materialism. These people were the NT representatives of what the OT calls "the remnant," and "seven thousand who had not bowed the knee to Baal," "God's poor," the faithful in all ages.

Mary and Joseph and the parents of John the Baptist belonged to this group; so did the Bethany family; so did the fisher-folk of Galilee and the erstwhile disciples of John; so did the widow in the treasury, who dropped a tiny contribution into the box. . . . They were all there, in the story, quite clear to the reader. The scrolls seem to give them added life.

It should occasion no surprise that, around the time of Christ, a protest movement should have sought the wilderness, retreat to which was deep in the Jewish consciousness. Isaiah's writings are prominent among the scrolls, and a verse from Isaiah could have been the marching order and directive of the Qumran community. "In the wilderness," it runs, "prepare the way of the LORD. In the desert make straight a pathway for your God."

Nor can it be an accident that these very words find echo and repetition in the recorded sayings of John the Baptist. He was "a voice," he said, "crying in the wilderness: Make straight a pathway for your God." The desert preacher, whose whirlwind ministry forms a prelude to the Christian story, was obviously under the influence of the desert religious communities, or perhaps a member of one of them. His activities were centered a dozen miles from Qumran. His disciples, who became Christ's "fishers of men," were converts who went back to their daily ways of living and carried into industrial and urban life the breath of the wilderness devotion.

The fact that there was a protest movement in Jewish religion during this period has always been known. The Essenes were described in the first century. Indeed, Pliny, the Roman writer whose scientific curiosity led him to his death in the eruption of Mount Vesuvius in August A. D. 79, actually described a community by the Dead Sea which could easily be the people of the scrolls. He had doubtless talked with many soldiers who had fought through the Jewish War of A. D. 66 to 70, during which the community at Qumran was broken up, leaving its library in the sheltering caves.

With the library from the caves to point the way, archaeologists turned to a ruin at Qumran and found it to be just such a place as Pliny described, a sort of monastery without celibacy, as skeletal remains of both men and women reveal, the home of a dedicated fellowship given to discipline, the preservation of the Scriptures, and to holy living. The community was established about 135 B.C. It continued for almost exactly two hundred years. In A.D. 66 came the mad revolt of the Jews against the Romans, over three years of awful warfare, the destruction of Jerusalem, and the systematic ransacking of Palestine for all remnants of Jewish opposition. To the Romans, in the days of the Great Revolt, such folk were partisans, and Vespasian's* troops destroyed the Qumran buildings. The inhabitants, no doubt, escaped, for they had time to hide their books in the caves. "This treasure we have in earthen vessels," said Paul, and he was alluding to a custom observed at Qumran and elsewhere. The books were concealed in great jars of earthenware.

The meaning of the Dead Sea Scrolls for Christians today may be summed up in three exhortations. Let them seek simplicity in their faith and avoid the perils of social compromise. Let them find unity in a common devotion to their God. Let them be pre-

pared to see the benison of heaven rest rather on the devoted than the proud, on the humble rather than the great.

But such has ever been the theme and purport of the NT, and if Qumran is, in Edmund Wilson's phrase, to rank with Bethlehem and Nazareth as "a cradle of Christianity," it is only in this sense that the tendentious words could be true. John translated passive protest and retreat into action, "withdrawal and return," if Toynbee's formula may be applied. And since John's converts provided the first Christian disciples and prepared the land for the impact of Christ, Qumran, if John was influenced by the group, may claim a preparatory part.

Textually, the scrolls have provided some enlightenment. They have clarified a handful of inconsiderable textual corruptions and thrown light on some minor difficulties of interpretation. Until 1947, for example, the oldest text of Isaiah was dated A. D. 895. A major item among the scrolls is an Isaiah manuscript a full thousand years older. It has cleared up some problems. There is, for example, no break between chapters 39 and 40. How, in the light of this, is the theory, first propounded in 1892 by Bernhard Duhm, that there were three Isaiahs, conflated and fused in the first century, to stand? Here is a book, dated at the latest about the end of the second century before Christ, which obviously knows nothing about such editing. Some individual texts have also been elucidated. Consider Isa 21:8, which, in the KJV, is quite without meaning. The verse runs: "And he cried, a lion: My Lord, I stand continually upon the watchtower in the daytime. . . ." Hebrew was originally written in consonants only, with the vowel marks inserted later. The consonants of the word for "see" ($r'h$) were transposed at some stage in textual transmission to read $'ryh$, or "lion." The better reading would therefore be: "And he who saw cried: 'My Lord. . . .'" Sense is thus restored to a confused text.

There is another mistranslation, due to incorrect vocalization, in Isa 49:12. The older versions speak of "the land of Sinim" which could only refer to China. To the disappointment of those who cherish so farflung a text, the scrolls show that the reading should be "Syene," that is Yeb in Upper Egypt.* In Isa 20:1, the proper name Tartan, which occasioned some difficulty, reads in the scroll "turtan," and is correctly rendered in RSV as "commander-in-chief." There is also a brief phrase in Isa 53:11 where the scroll follows the Septuagint, to read: "After the travail of his soul he will see light, he will be satisfied. . . ." rather than the Masoretic text, on which our Bibles are based. The conclusion is that the Isaiah Scroll demonstrates the astonishing accuracy of the text which has been transmitted.

It also demonstrates the general accuracy of the Septuagint, clearing up in the process a NT text. In Acts 7:14, Stephen remarks that Jacob's tribe came to Egypt, "three score and fifteen souls." Genesis, on the other hand, said "three score and ten." A Qumran text of Genesis reads Stephen's figure. Hebrew numerals are delicate to write, and Stephen's correct quotation had become corrupted in the later manuscripts behind our version.

Again, what did Christ mean when he blessed "the poor in spirit"? A Qumran text shows that the phrase was used in religious parlance as the opposite of "the hard-hearted." Pity, it may be said, came into the world with Christ. Another text shows that "poor" meant "faithful" in noneconomic contexts.

Apart from such pieces of notable usefulness, the scrolls have given little. There are commentaries (one, for example, on Habakkuk), but the exposition is symbolic and mystical, and remote from the plain meaning of the text. There are some biblical romances, embroiderings of the OT story of no great value. Here, for example, is the purport of an excerpt from a scroll in the Hebrew University of Jerusalem. Badly preserved and brittle, the two-thousand-year-old, Aramaic* scroll is the last of seven found in the Qumran caves. It enlarges on the story of Abraham's journey to Egypt with Sarah, as related in Gen 12. Just before entering Egypt, Abraham persuaded her to pose as his sister, according to the biblical account: "Abraham said: I know that you are a woman beautiful to behold; and when the Egyptians see you, they will say, 'This is his wife'; then they will kill me, and keep you. Say you are my sister."

The newly deciphered scroll adds a vivid description of Sarah: "And how beautiful the look of her face. And how fine is the hair of her head; how fair indeed are her eyes and how pleasing her nose and all the radiance of her face. Her arms were goodly to look upon and her hands how perfect. How fair her palms and how long and fine all the fingers of her hands. And all maidens and all brides that go beneath the wedding canopy are not more fair than she. Above all women she is lovely and higher in her beauty than that of them all, and with all her beauty there is much wisdom in her. And the tip of her hands is comely."

The scroll then gives Abraham's account of how his fears about Sarah's beauty were justified when the pharaoh heard she was "very beautiful." Abraham tells in the scroll how he prayed that God would show His "mighty hand" and descend upon the Egyptian king, and "that night the Most High God sent a pestilential wind to afflict him and all his household, a wind that was evil, And it smote him and all his house and he could not come near her."

Abraham's account ends with a description of how, after two years, the ruler of Egypt sent for him and restored his wife, asking him to pray that the plagues might cease. As the Bible relates, he tells how he was permitted to leave Egypt "exceedingly rich in cattle and also in silver and gold." Observe that there is no shadow of discrepancy with the Genesis account, only imaginative amplification.

BIBLIOGRAPHY: F. F. Bruce, *Second Thoughts on the Dead Sea Scrolls* (1956); Millar Burrows, *The Dead Sea Scrolls* (1955); id., *More Light on the Dead Sea Scrolls* (1958); William Sanford LaSor, *Amazing Dead Sea Scrolls and the Christian Faith; A Bibliography of the Dead Sea Scrolls, 1948–1957* (1958); J. C. Trever, *The Untold Story of Qumran* (1965), W. S. LaSor, *ISBE*, I, 883–97.

EMB

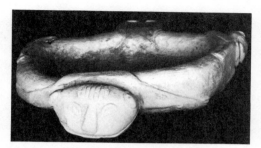

Stone libation tray decorated by head of female lion and heads of two lion cubs, found at Debir (Tell Beit Mirsim), Late Bronze Age II. Courtesy Israel Dept. of Antiquities and Museums.

DEBIR (deb'ir; Heb. דְּבִיר, *deḇîr*). A city* in the Judean hills inhabited originally by the Anakim until the Canaanite* structure was sacked by Joshua (Josh 11:21). The Heb. "Kiriath Sepher" ("scribe city") may not preserve accurately the earlier Canaanite meaning (cf. Josh 15:15, 49). When Judah was reorganized administratively, Debir became a Levitical city (Josh 21:15) and the district capital of the S uplands. Locations such as Zahariyeh, Khirbet Zanuta, and Khirbet Tarrameh, all about 19 km. (12 mi.) S of Hebron,* have been suggested as the site of Debir by various authors, but Albright identified it with Tell Beit Mirsim, the same distance SW of Hebron. Excavations there between 1926 and 1932 showed that the site had been settled originally in the Early Bronze IV period c. 2300 B.C. The Middle Bronze I settlement may have been visited by Abraham, but in the early Hyksos* period it was destroyed and then reconstructed, being protected by a beaten earth wall.* Well-built houses,* metal work, and ivory* inlays testify to the prosperity of the city at that period. When the Late Bronze Age occupation was destroyed it was replaced by a poorer culture, but whether this was Kenizzite in nature as Albright postulated is unknown. How far this information is sufficient to support Albright's identification is uncertain, particularly since K. Galling (*ZDPV*, 70 [1954], 135–41) criticized it on topographical and archaeological grounds. His own proposal of Khirbet Rabud seems to accord better with the topography of Judg 1:15, since several fresh water springs occur in the area. The site was excavated in 1968 and 1969, when Late Bronze Age artifacts* were recovered in quantity.

Debir is first mentioned in Josh 10:38 as a Canaanite royal city inhabited by the Anakim (Josh 11:21). When the land was apportioned to the Israelite tribes, Debir along with other Shephelah* settlements was assigned to Judah.* Debir came under Philistine* influence in the twelfth century B.C., being destroyed by them about 1050 B.C. at the battle of Ebenezer (1 Sam 4). In his ascendancy David fortified Debir with a casemate wall* and gateway* of the kind found at Beth Shemesh.* Shishak* destroyed the city in 918 B.C., but Asa (911–869 B.C.) rebuilt it. Debir was an important center for textile dyeing,* reaching its peak in the eighth century B.C. In the final quarter of the following century Debir began to decline, was destroyed in 587 B.C. by Nebuchadnezzar* at the time when Jerusalem* fell, and was never rebuilt.

BIBLIOGRAPHY: W. F. Albright, *AASOR*, XII (1930–31); ibid., XIII (1931–32); ibid., XVII (1936–37); ibid., XXI–XXII (1941–43); Y. Aharoni, *The Land and the Bible* (1967), 18 passim; *EEHL*, I, 171–78; M. Kochavi, *Tel Aviv* 1 (1974), 2–33; K. A. Kitchen, *The Bible in Its World* (1977), 12, 90.

RKH

DEBORAH AND MIRIAM, SONGS OF (deb'ər ə, mir'ē əm; Heb. דְּבוֹרָה, *deḇôrāh*; מִרְיָם, *mirᵉyom*). Canaanite* literary texts dealing with the mythological exploits of Baal* and Anath,* and the epic adventures of heroes, have confirmed the antiquity of Deborah's and Miriam's songs of victory (Exod 15; Judg 5). The editor of the corpus of Canaanite religious poetry (C. Virolleaud), mainly discovered by C. F. A. Schaeffer between 1929 and 1933 at Ugarit,* has pointed out that style, vocabulary, and poetic structure were identical with that of Hebrew poetry of the thirteenth and twelfth centuries B.C. W. F. Albright, drawing examples from the Ugaritic Baal-song and Ps 92:9, and a poem addressed to the hero Aqhat and the song of Deborah (Judg 5:30), convincingly demonstrated the identity of the form, one which had fallen out of use by the tenth century except in a few contexts of designed archaism or quotation. A species of "repetitive and climactic parallelism," characteristic of this early date in Canaanite, Egyptian,* and Assyrian contexts, confirms the early date of both the song of Deborah and the earlier song of Miriam. This, as Albright concludes, "cannot be accidental, particularly as the literary genre of the triumphal poem, celebrating military victory, was then at the climax of its popularity." In the case of the song of Miriam, the phrase "the mountain of thine inheritance" (Exod 15:17) was taken by liberal critics as a reference to Zion and to either the temple* of Solomon* or the temple of Zerubbabel. This led to a late dating of the song. One of the Canaanite epics, which cannot be dated later than 1400 B.C., places Baal's dwelling likewise "on the mountain of thine inheritance." The conclusion is obvious—there is no valid reason, either on grounds of poetic form or of language, to date Miriam's triumphal song later than the thirteenth century (Albright's interesting discussion of the relevance of the Ugaritic texts is found in his *Archaeology of Palestine* [1960], 230–35).

BIBLIOGRAPHY: W. F. Albright, *The Bible and the Ancient Near East* (1961), 339; Y. Aharoni, *Near Eastern Archaeology in the Twentieth Century* (1970), 255–64 (where questions about the destruction of Taanach are raised); A. C. Myers, *ISBE*, I, 904–5.

EMB

DECAPOLIS (də kap'ə lis; Gr. Δεκάπολις, *Dekapolis*). The ten towns, for this is what the name means, occupied an area principally E of Jordan and Galilee,* on the inner curve of the Fertile Crescent. The cities formed a political and a military, as well as a geographical, complex and emerged, with their predominantly Greek migrant populations, after Alexander's penetration of the Middle East and the Greek diaspora that followed. Two (Pella* and Dion*) of the ten towns, which were doubtfully located, bore Macedonian names and were evidently colonies of Alexander's veterans, almost after the Roman fashion of planting demobilized veterans at imperial strongpoints.

Another was Philadelphia,* the OT Rabbath-Ammon, which is now Amman, the modern capital of Jordan. A fine stone theater,* that consistent sign of Greek occupation, still stands in Amman's business center. Gadara,* the modern Umm Qeis, on the eastern edge of the Jordan cleft, has not been excavated, but it is known that it was a city* 2 miles in circumference, predominantly Greek, with two theaters, a colonnaded street,* and baths. Coins* suggest shipping activities and indicate that Gadara's territory extended to the lake, as the story of the maniac implies. Legionary tombs are in the vicinity. Gerasa,* the modern Jerash, 42 km. (26 mi.) N of Amman, is one of the most extensive ruin complexes in the area, a place of intense interest, with temples, shopping colonnades, a high-set theater, and a unique oval forum.* The whole place suggests the vigor of the commercial, social, and cultural activity of these centers of Greco-Roman life which guarded Rome's most vulnerable frontier.

The lists vary, as between, for example, Pliny, Ptolemy,* and Josephus. Whether Damascus,* far to the N, is to be included in the ten is a moot point, and the precise location of other of the towns still awaits the investigation of geographical survey and archaeology. Patterns of privilege, areas of administration, government, and political functions vary with the changing structures of Greek, Roman, and Herodian control. Coinage, as collections are extended and interpreted, associated inscriptions, as they come to light, will no doubt build up a more complete picture of this immensely sensitive and important cosmopolitan area. Clarification could thus probably emerge of the varied use of "Gadarenes," "Gerasenes," and "Gergasenes" in texts of Matt 8:28; Mark 5:1; and Luke 8:26. Each of the Decapolis cities controlled surrounding territory, and probably separated enclaves of land. There is no reason why Gerasa should not, by privilege or purchase, have controlled territory by the lake which was geographically Gadarene. Gadara's long aqueduct* alone shows it must have been important to that community to control land necessary to its life, commerce, and convenience. All such questions are likely to find solution in archaeological evidence, numismatics (*see* COINS), and epigraphy.*

Scythopolis,* the ancient Beth Shan,* and known from Egyptian,* and Akkadian,* as well as Hebrew texts, is the only city of the Decapolis lying today inside Israeli territory. It is at the intersection of the valleys of Jezreel and Jordan, strategically commanding the entrance to the Plain of Esdraelon, and one of the most important nodal points of communication in the region. Two inscribed stelae of Seti I (c. 1313–1292 B.C.), a stele* of Ramses II* (c. 1292–1225 B.C.), and a statue* of Ramses III (c. 1198–1167 B.C.) sug-

Statue of Ramses III found at Beth Shan. Courtesy Israel Dept. of Antiquities and Museums.

gest an Egyptian presence and strategic interest over a vital century and a half of Palestinian history. Culturally, the Scythopolis of the Decapolis (its new name being probably a relic of Scythian intrusion) was possibly a point at which the Gentile life of the Decapolis made contact with that of Galilee. Perhaps the story of the prodigal son illustrates this confrontation. On the other hand, the Lord's own visits to the eastern shore of Galilee reveal that travel to it was not restricted to land.

The road* systems of the Decapolis itself mingled the two worlds of which the NT, from the Gospels to Paul's Epistles, is a document and are a further theme for detailed archaeological study, clear though the general pattern of the network is. An important Roman road, the Trajan Way (Via Traiana) built toward the beginning of the second century, goes straight to the Decapolis from the deep S of the land. The highway, one element of that great system which was a Roman tool of empire, was largely the work of the Ninth Legion. It drove N, with some typical Ro-

man engineering,* especially in the Wadi-el-Mujib 80.5 km. (50 mi.) S of Amman, and through Amman (Philadelphia) to Gerasa, where surviving milestones still mark its triumphal course. The Trajan Way entered Gerasa by a triumphal arch,* and ran into the oval forum to form the colonnaded main street of the city, which can be walked today, with the original white limestone paving still in place. An inscription marks the exit: "Built by Claudius Severus, legate of Trajan." It sweeps on to Damascus, Rome's strong interpretation in military stone of the ancient caravan route of the Fertile Crescent, which linked the vanished empires of the river civilizations.

BIBLIOGRAPHY: "Jerash in the First Century," R. Fink, *JRS* (1909); G. A. Smith, *HGHL*, 623–38; E. M. Blaiklock, *ZPEB*, 2 (1975), 81–84; V. P. Hamilton, *ISBE*, 1, 906–8.

EMB

DEMOGRAPHY. The study of population through the use of vital statistics.

DEMOTIC. *See* WRITING.

DENARIUS (de når′ē əs; Gr. δηνάριον, *dēnarion*). This was a silver* coin* dating back to Roman Republican times. It was first issued about 180 B.C. and continued as a common medium of exchange into NT times. It was commonly a day's wage for a laborer in the early first century, the only clue to any attempt to value its purchasing power. The KJV translation, "penny," influenced, no doubt, by the surviving symbol *d* (for denarius) for that coin, was one of the more lamentable errors of the translators. The Republican denarius bore on its obverse the head of Roma as a guardian goddess wearing a winged helmet.* This was changed to Britannia on the old British penny. Often *X* also appeared, signifying that the coin had ten times the value of the *as*. Devices varied on the reverse—Castor and Pollux or Jupiter in a quadriga or four-horsed chariot.* Commemorative themes often intruded. For example, one denarius, struck in 58 B.C. to honor Pompey's general Marcus Aemilius Scaurus, marked the annexation of Judea* by showing the Nabataean* ruler Aretas* kneeling by his camel* and offering the laurel of victory to Rome.* It was about this time that coinage began to commemorate individual heroes—Pompey, first conquerer of Jerusalem for Rome, being an example. The denarius of Augustus* was a coin of great beauty and that of Tiberius* followed the model of his stepfather. This was the coin of the famous saying of Christ (Matt 22:21). A denarius of Titus* bears on its reverse the same device as that used in a victory coin (a sestertius) of his father Vespasian.* There is an exultant emperor and the words JVDAEA CAPTA (Judaea subdued)—a weeping woman pictured eight centuries before by Isaiah (3:26) "desolate upon the ground." There are some twenty Flavian coins by which the emperors Vespasian and Titus kept Rome aware of their triumph over Judea. The fact emphasizes the formidable character of Jewish opposition to the Empire in the days of its strength. The silver denarius has, of course, a long history interwoven with five hundred years of Rome's story, Republican and Imperial, but this note covers its biblical significance.

BIBLIOGRAPHY: F. A. Banks, *Coins of Bible Days* (1955), passim; John Yonge Akermon, *Numismatic Illustrations of the OT* (1966).

EMB

DENDERA (den'də ra). A site in upper Egypt* on the W Bank of the Nile about 50 km. (31 mi.) N of Luxor. Marked as the place of a cult as early as the Old Kingdom, Dendera (Gr. *Tentyra*) was successively enlarged, leaving the standing remains primarily from the Ptolemaic and Roman periods. The celebrated temple of Hathor is typical of late Egyptian architecture and is beautifully preserved. The façade has six columns with Hathor-faced capitals* linked by a lower screen wall. The cornice* has a winged disk in the center. Altogether there are twenty-four Hathor columns in the hypostyle* hall, which formed a forecourt for the inner chambers of the temple. The reliefs are richly worked on the inner and outer walls of the sanctuary, and commemorate such diverse personages as Cleopatra, Augustus,* Tiberius,* Caligula, Claudius,* and Nero. All worship the goddess Hathor, her consort, Horus, and her son, Ihy. The famed zodiac of Dendera, now in the Louvre, came from the roof of this temple. Among the other ruins at Dendera are an Isis temple, a sacred lake, Roman baths, two *mamisi* (of Nectanebo I and of the Roman period), each celebrating the birth of Ihy, and a Coptic church, as well as a great wall surrounding the precinct. The wall, built in the reign of Domitian,* measures nearly 305 m. (1000 ft.) on each side.

JEJ

DENDROCHRONOLOGY. The word derives from the Greek *dendron* "a tree" and *chronos* "time" and has been devised as a name for the use of the growth rings in the wood* of forest trees as a means of dating* associated events and processes. Growth rings in the cut trunks of huge kauri trees in New Zealand show the pattern of the seasons, dry or wet, back through the major portion of the Christian era. The moist and comparatively even climate of the New Zealand rain forest and the lack of associated timber from Polynesian building in the small area in which the kauri is indigenous deprives the dendrochronological record of the great trees of any archaeological usefulness.

Not so in the western United States where the ancient redwoods, the strong undulations in rainfall, and the abundance of cut and even charred timber in Pueblo sites have proved of immense archaeological value. It has been possible by matching wood from such sources, cut timber, fossil timber, and even fragments from ancient fires to make a complete sequence back to very early days of human occupation and the development of the maize-using societies of the area. Periods of migration, resettlement, and the occupation and abandonment of inhabited places can be dated with something near absolute precision by the simple evidence of the annual rings in the trees.

So far dendrochronology has played no part in the archaeological investigation of biblical history, though the great cedars* of Lebanon might have provided a calendar* as exact as that of the redwoods. The lack is of a continuous record, for unless an ancient log or wood fragment can demonstrate a continuity with trees cut at a known recent date, the sequence fails. A funeral barge of Lebanese timber, retaining its characteristic aromatic smell, was discovered in a pharaonic burial area. If it were possible to overlap its growth rings with progressively more recent timber through such cedar-using periods as that of Solomon's* golden age and secure a contact with a log of modern lumbering, a most desirable and exact dating calendar would be in the hands of the archaeologist. The denudation of the Lebanese cedar forests, with the fearful sequence of burning and destruction which swept Palestine between Solomon and Hadrian,* has rendered such aid to archaeology most unlikely.

BIBLIOGRAPHY: F. E. Zeuner, *Dating the Past* (1950); S. Rapport and H. Wright, *Archaeology* (1964), 49–50.

EMB

DERBE (dûr'bē; Gr. Δέρβη, *Derbē*). The site of Derbe was fixed, along with that of Lystra,* by J. R. Sterrett in 1885. The town played a small part in history, as far as the meager records of this remote Lycaonian* region go, and the site was long disputed. It is now reasonably certain that it is a fair-sized mound at a locality known as Kerti Hüyük, for here a dedicatory inscription honoring Antoninus Pius and set up by the people of Derbe in A.D. 157 was discovered. Milestones mark an Imperial road to Antioch.*

BIBLIOGRAPHY: W. M. Ramsay, *The Historical Geography of Asia Minor* (1890), 336–37; M. Ballance, "The Site of Lystra, a New Inscription," *AnSt*, 7 (1957), 147–51; M. J. Mellink, *IDB*, 1, 825–26.

EMB

DEREA. See DION.

DIANA. See ARTEMIS.

DIBON (di'bon; Heb. דִּיבוֹן, *diḇôn*). A city* of Moab* 21 km. (13 mi.) E of the Dead Sea* and 4.8 km. (3 mi.) N of the Arnon River. In 1868 the famous Moabite Stone* was found there. Excavations were conducted in 1950–56 by the American Schools of Oriental Research, and show that the city was occupied in the Early Bronze Age. Evidence is lacking for the Middle and Late Bronze Ages (an unexplained gap from 1800 to 1300 B.C.), but the site was actively occupied in the Iron Age* from which the Moabite remains come. Later occupations in the Nabataean,* Hellenistic, Roman, and Byzantine* periods have been demonstrated. The town was strongly fortified in all periods and the heaviest wall (2.3 to 3.3 m., or 7½ to 10¾ ft. thick) dates to the days of Mesha (2 Kings 3:4). Carbonized grain from Iron Age levels is dated by the Carbon 14 (*see* DATING) test to 858 plus or minus 165 years. The recovery of pottery* and architectural features has increased our knowledge of ancient Moab considerably. A small fragment of basalt carrying some Moabite letters gives hope that yet other inscriptions may be found.

BIBLIOGRAPHY: "The Excavations at DIBON (DHIBAN) in MOAB, Part I: The First Campaign, 1950–1951, F. V. Winnett; Part II, The Second Campaign, 1952, W. L. Reed," AASOR, 36–37 (1957-58), pub. 1964; A. D. Tushingham, "Excavations at Dibon in Moab, 1952-1953," BASOR, 133 (1954); W. H. Morton, Report of the Director of the School in Jerusalem, BASOR, 140 (Dec. 1955), 5–7; W. H. Mare, ZPEB, 122–24; EEHL, 1, 330–33.

JAT

DIBSEH. See TIPHSAH.

DICAEARCHIA. See PUTEOLI.

DICE. See GAMES.

DILEAN. See TELL NAGILA.

DIOSPOLIS. See THEBES.

DILMUN (dil'mun). An ancient island mentioned in cuneiform* sources as early as Ur-Nanshe of Lagash* (c. 2520 B.C.) and frequently thereafter, especially in the important Sumerian* myth, Enki and Ninhursaĝ, in which Dilmun is eulogized as a sort of primeval paradise. H. Rawlinson first recognized the name in 1861 and identified it with Bahrain in the Persian Gulf. G. Bibby and the Danish Arabian Expedition have been excavating the sites in S Arabia* and Bahrain since 1953. They have discovered a series of occupations from Neolithic* to Medieval Arab times. Whether they have located Dilmun is still debatable.

BIBLIOGRAPHY: S. N. Kramer, The Sumerians: Their History, Culture, and Character (1963), 53 passim; G. Bibby, Looking for Dilmun (1969).

WW

DION (di'on). A city* (Latinized, Dium) of the Decapolis,* a little SE of Pella* according to Ptolemy.* Most modern geographers place it some 14 5 km. (9 mi.) N of Edrei (identified with Deraa halfway between Damascus* and Amman). Coins* from the time of Caracalla depict a Syrian god. Literary evidence is collected in a long footnote by G. A. Smith (Historical Geography of the Holy Land, 598).

EMB

DISEASE. See MEDICINE.

DISHES. See UTENSILS.

DISPLAY INSCRIPTION. This is the name given to an inscription of Sargon* at Khorsabad* in which the monarch boasts of his suppression of a rebellion by Merodach-baladan, the Chaldean* ruler of Babylon* from 721–710 B.C. (cf. 2 Kings 20:12; Isa 39:1).

It runs in part: ". . . Merodach-baladan, son of Iakin, king of Chaldea, seed of a murderer, prop of a wicked devil, who did not fear the name of the lord of lords, put his trust in the Bitter Sea with its tossing waves, violated the oath of the great gods, and withheld tribute. . . . Twelve years he ruled and governed Babylon, the city of the lord of the gods, against the will of the gods . . . I made ready my battle chariot,* set my camp in order, and gave the word to advance against the Chaldean, the treacherous enemy. And when Merodach-baladan heard of the approach of my expedition, he was seized with anxiety for his safety, and fled from Babylon to the city of Ikbi-bel, like a bat by night." Sargon died five years later (705 B.C.). The so-called Limmu List reports that "A soldier entered the camp of the king of Assyria [Sargon], and killed him in the month Abib. And Sennacherib* sat on the throne."

BIBLIOGRAPHY: ARAB, II, 66.

EMB

DIUM. See DION.

DIVORCE. See MARRIAGE.

DJANET. See TANIS.

DOG. Dogs were known to Neolithic* man, some of the earliest skeletons coming from Denmark. Remains are also found, associated with human habitation, from the earliest levels of Jericho.* Three breeds can be distinguished from predynastic Egypt* (i.e., before 3000 B.C.). From times quite as early, pottery* dogs of a greyhound type, emerge from sites round the whole curve of the Fertile Crescent. The large hunting mastiff was known in Mesopotamia* before Abraham's time. There is abundant archaeological evidence for the worship of Anubis in Egypt. This jackal-headed god was generally regarded as a dog-totem ("latrator Anubis,") says Vergil in his account of Actium (Aen. 8.698). The negative Hebrew attitude toward the dog, evident in the OT could date from the days of Egyptian servitude.

BIBLIOGRAPHY: G. S. Cansdale, All the Animals of the Bible Lands (1970), 121–24.

EMB

DOG RIVER. See NAHR AL KALB.

DOLMEN (dōl'men). The term dolmen, meaning, perhaps, "tablestone," or related to the Cornish tolmen, "a hole of stone," is of Celtic origin and describes a structure consisting of large unhewn stones erected on their bases or edges so as to form a rectangular enclosure. They were then covered over with a megalith,* or with several smaller stones, the finished structure being generally used as a tomb. The cromlech of Cornwall, Wales (there is also one in Ireland), is a very closely related structure. It is a group of erect stones covered by a flat megalith. When there is no capstone,* however, the structure is more properly known as a menhir.* While the more primitive dolmens have a single chamber, whether circular or rectangular, others from later periods sometimes had ancillary chambers to the main en-

View of mound and remains of harbor at Dor. Courtesy Israel Dept. of Antiquities and Museums.

closure joined together by means of a corridor. At some Indian and W European sites a tumulus was formed by covering the dolmen over with a mound of earth. Exposed European dolmens may have been concealed in this way originally but denuded either by natural erosion or the cultivation of the terrain.

Dolmens are common in Jordan, especially to the W of the river, and in the area of the Dead Sea.* They are rare E of the Jordan. These structures, both single and double chambered, are very ancient and Neolithic,* but they point to the existence, perhaps five thousand years before Christ, of an organized civilization, agricultural* in nature and with abundant surplus labor—perhaps the "mighty men" of Gen 6:4. They belonged to the time of the first foundation of Jericho.*

BIBLIOGRAPHY: G. Daniel, *Scientific American*, 243, 1 (1980), 78–90.

RKH

DOMITIAN (do mish'ən). Titus Flavius Domitianus (A.D. 81–96) was the son of Vespasian,* and the brother and successor of Titus.* It was probably during his tyrannical principate that John was relegated to Patmos.* Rev 6:6 may support this conjecture, for an edict of A.D. 92, designed to restrict viticulture and promote the production of wheat, roused wide resentment in western Asia Minor.* A curious event of seeming Christian significance took place just before Domitian's assassination in A.D. 95. The prince's niece, Flavia Domitilla, was accused, along with her husband, Flavius Clemens, first cousin of the emperor and consul, of "atheism" and was exiled to Pandateria. This charge was commonly leveled against Christians.

The coins from Domitian's time depict him as having a small head with thick neck muscles. The fact that his features resemble those of Nero probably indicate a stylized representation.

BIBLIOGRAPHY: J. Moffatt, *Exp.* (1908), 359–69; S. Reinach, *Revue Archéologique* (1902), 350–51; E. M. Blaiklock, *The Century of the NT* (1962), 116–26.

EMB

DONKEY. According to G. S. Cansdale (*Animals of Bible Lands*, 1970, 71) the donkey (*equus asinus*) is a domesticated Nubian* variety. The Atlas Mountains variety, known from rock paintings and Roman mosaics, disappeared by the third century A.D. The domesticated donkey appears as early as 2650 B.C. in the realistic art of the tomb of Ti at Saqqara (*see* MEMPHIS). One scene shows a stubborn animal tugged by leg and ear and belabored from behind (Hermann Rauke, *The Art of Ancient Egypt* [1936], plate 213). The word *ass* seems to derive from the Sumerian* *ansu*, through Greek and Latin. The animals shown drawing the chariot* on the Standard of Ur* (2500 B.C.) are thought to be onagers because of their bushy tails—tamed "wild asses" (Cansdale, 95). The riding donkey of the queen of Punt is shown in a fresco of 1500 B.C. from the temple of Deir el-Bahari. A text from Mari* as early as the seventeenth century B.C. shows that the donkey was considered the proper animal for royalty (cf. Zech 9:9; Matt 21:1–7).

EMB

DOR (DORA) (dôr, dôr ə; Heb. דֹּאר, דֹּור, *dō'r, dôr*; Gr. Δώρ, Δώρα, *Dōr, Dōra*, "habitation" or "circle"). Toponymic studies indicate that many places were named after particular buildings characterizing a settlement in its earlier stages or after the general form of its dwellings, as is the case with Dor.

A coastal city* SW of Mount Carmel,* and about

one-half the distance from present Haifa* to Caesarea.* It was one of the small harbors developed during the Bronze Age by the Phoenicians, although an alternate opinion holds it to be founded as a naval base by the Egyptians of the New Empire. It seems most probable that it was a Sidonian colony, exploiting the abundant murex shellfish, necessary for the Tyrian dyeing* industry. The terms Naphoth Dor (Josh 11:2; 12:23; 1 Kings 4:11), meaning "coast [and/or] heights of Dor," were descriptive of the region pertaining to the city. It retained continuous importance into Roman times. The present small harbor town of et-Tanturah lies next to the ruins of Dor, with remains of a tower called el-Burj, which may have been a citadel guarding the harbor in Canaanite* and subsequent times.

The harbor consists of two small bays enclosed by rocks. It occupies a formation called the Lower Kurkar, which is a hard layer of solidified ancient dune sand beneath the surface, extending inland a short distance. Further inland is the Upper Kurkar, the narrow line of low hills bordering the coast from Joppa* northward, and well developed in the region of Dor, which doubtless played an important part in the defense of the town. The harbor marks a division point between the coastal sands—siliceous to the S, derived from external sources (Egypt), and calcareous to the N, resulting from coastal erosion in that area. The Plain of Dor had as its boundaries the Carmel promontory at the N, and the Crocodile River (Nahr es-Zerka) about 32 km. (20 mi.) to the S. It consisted of a two-mile area between the sea and the mountains, marshy in part.

Dor is shown by archaeological investigations as one of the few towns along the coast whose occupation began in the Late Bronze period. The others include Tell Abu Huwam, at the mouth of the Kishon River, and Ashdod.* Excavations by the British School of Archaeology were carried out in 1923–24 and provided stratigraphic* evidence for its period of importance. It was the western anchor of a chain of fortress cities across N Palestine, including Jokneam, Megiddo,* Taanach,* Ibleam, and Beth Shan,* and must have shared in the wealth accruing from greatly expanded sea trade during the fourteenth century B.C. The thirteenth century, however, with its upheavals and invasion by the Sea Peoples* during the half-century after 1225 B.C., hindered its development, and it passed into the hands of the Thekel (who may be akin to the Sikel in Homer's *Odyssey*, who gave their name to Sicily), becoming their headquarters. They probably became amalgamated with the Philistines* to the S.

The Egyptian traveler Wen-Amon describes Dor as a place he visited, with some cause to remember, during his journey to Phoenicia. He called the inhabitants the Tjeker (*ANET*, 26). The Israelites were not able to gain possession of Dor during the conquest, though it figures in the record. Its king became allied with Jabin of Hazor* and was conquered along with him (Josh 11:1–14; 12:23), but Dor was not then occupied (cf. 17:11; Judg 1:27; 1 Chron 7:29), and probably did not come under control of Israel until the unification of the kingdom. It was duly as-

signed to Manasseh, though geographically on the borders of Asher (cf. Jos. *Antiq.* 5.1.22). In the middle of the eleventh century, Dor joined Ashkelon* in a rebellion and besieged Sidon,* whose inhabitants were forced to flee to Tyre.* Manasseh failed to drive out the Canaanite settlers, but by the time of Solomon* it had become one of his twelve administrative districts, likely the fourth. Solomon's official there, Ben-Abinadab, was married to one of his daughters (1 Kings 4:11). After the division of the kingdom it remained within the territory of Israel. After 722 B.C. it passed into control of the Assyrians. Tiglath-pileser* III captured and set a governor over the city, and later established it as one of the three Assyrian provinces in the Palestinian region: (1) "the way of the sea" (Dor); (2) "the land beyond the Jordan" (Gilead); (3) "Galilee of the Gentiles" (Megiddo). Only a small area around Samaria* remained to Hoshea, the last king of Israel (cf. Isa 9:1).

During the period of Persian occupation the various harbors of Palestine were turned over to Tyre and Sidon as bases for coastal shipping. From an inscription on the coffin of Eshmun 'azar, king of Sidon, we learn that he received Dor and Joppa as grants from the Persian king (*ANET*, 662). In 219 B.C. Dor was beseiged by Antiochus III, who forced Trypho (Tryphon) the governor to flee to Apamia (1 Macc 15:10–14; Jos. *Antiq.* 13.7.2). Josephus notes two additional matters concerning Dor—first, an act of impiety in the Jewish synagogue,* involving high Roman officials in its settlement (Jos. *Antiq.* 19.6.3), and secondly, that Apollo was worshiped at Dor by the Gentiles who inhabited the city (Jos. *Apion*, 2.10).

Dor was granted autonomy by Pompey in 64 B.C., but this was the end of its importance, for the new harbor at Caesarea* built by Herod took the sea traffic it had depended upon. Sea trade explains the special importance of Dor within the framework of the Israelite monarchy, as a harbor town with a marine tradition. When this ceased, the city inevitably declined as it had no hinterland to fall back on. The Via Maris ("way of the sea") also by-passed Dor in the main, hence there was little possibility of land trade.

BIBLIOGRAPHY: Jos. *Antiq.* 5.1.22; 13.8.2; 14.4.4; 19.6.3; G. Dahl, "Materials for the History of Dor," *Transactions of the Connecticut Academy of Arts and Sciences*, 20 (1915), 1–131; *IEJ*, I (1950–51), 249; D. Baly, *Geography of the Bible* (1957), 131–33; Y. Aharoni, *The Land of the Bible* (1967), 16–18, 41, 46, 237–38, 361–62, passim; Y. Aharoni and M. Avi-Yonah, *The Macmillan Bible Atlas* (1968), 59, 62, 63, 66, 67, 113, 147; G. Foerster, "Dor," *EEHL* (1970), 130–32, Hebrew; *DDB*, 4th ed. (1972), 188.

MHH

DOTHAN (dō'thən; Heb. דֹתַיִן, *dōṯayin*, דֹּתָן, *dōthon*; Gr. Δωθαΐμ, *Dōthaim*, Δωταια, *Dotaia*, Δωτεα, *Dotea*). The modern Tell Dotha, a site located 21 km. (13 mi.) N of the city of Samaria.* Excavated from 1953 under Joseph P. Free of Wheaton College, the 6-ha. (15-a.) location proved to have been first occupied at the end of the Chalcolithic* period (c. 3000 B.C.). In the Early Bronze Age (c. 3000–2000 B.C.) the settlement at Dothan was pro-

Sewage drain beneath city gate from Tell el-Fa'rah. *(See also second photo under* TAANACH.*)* Courtesy Israel Dept. of Antiquities and Museums.

tected by a sturdy wall,* perhaps originally 7.6 m. (25 ft.) high, about 2.7 m. (9 ft.) thick at the top and some 3.4 m. (11 ft.) thick at the base. From the evidence of shards* there were seven occupational levels in the Early Bronze period.

Dothan is first mentioned in Scripture in connection with the Middle Bronze Age (c. 2000–1500 B.C.) activities of the sons of Jacob (Gen 37:13–17). At that time Dothan was fortified by a solidly built citadel* and a thick defensive wall, outside which was a wide stairway leading from the city to the plain below. The Middle Bronze Age at Dothan was also represented by two occupational levels, the second of which seems to have continued into the Late Bronze Age (c. 1500–1200 B.C.). This phase was also marked by two occupational levels which yielded many potsherds. A tomb dated about 1300 B.C. on the W slope of the site was found to contain hundreds of clay* lamps* and small jugs, with about 150 separate skeletons as well as considerable crushed osseous material.

Iron Age I (c. 1200–1000 B.C.) occupation of the site was again marked by two levels, one of which possessed another burial chamber adjacent to the Late Bronze Age tomb. The Iron Age II (c. 1000–600 B.C.) phase exhibited four occupational levels, the earliest of which contained the remains of an administrative building from the early monarchy period. Free uncovered the ruins of the city that must have fallen c. 725 B.C. to the Assyrians (2 Kings 17:5–6), and it was in this city that Elisha must have lived over a century earlier. At that time the Syrian king

endeavored to arrest Elisha for revealing secret plans to the Israelite king (2 Kings 6:8–14). The site was occupied thereafter to the Byzantine* period, though the density of the population in the exilic and post-exilic periods is unknown. Scattered remains from the Persian era (c. 500–300 B.C.) suggest a light occupational history. Dothan was mentioned in the apocryphal book of Judith (3:9; 4:6; 7:3) as the site of military activity in the intertestamental period, a time that is well attested by Hellenistic levels (c. 300–50 B.C.). Dothan is a most attractive site, presenting as it does a remarkably good pattern of Palestinian culture over a period of about three and a half millennia.

BIBLIOGRAPHY: J. P. Free, *ZPEB*, 2, 157–60.

RKH

DRAGON. *See* LEVIATHAN.

DRAIN. A means of drainage, as a channel, trench, pipe, sewer, sink, or ditch. Earliest drainage seems to have been related to agricultural* practices in Mesopotamia* where it appears as a corollary of irrigation.* Drains must have been used in early towns to carry off surplus rainfall, and in dry areas to provide water storage when natural basins or impervious stone for cisterns* occurred. With the innovation of hydraulic lime plaster* in the Late Bronze Age, the cistern and drains to fill it became ubiquitous, every flat roof top and empty space providing storage.

Late Bronze houses* of the wealthy consisted of open courts surrounded by single- or double-storied rooms. Several of these were found at Ur,* Mari,* Megiddo,* Taanach,* Bethel,* and other places. At Bethel a remarkably well-built system of stone-lined drains ran under the plastered floors and carried drainage outside the city wall to an undetermined storage or disposal. Excavations in the Solomonic levels at Dothan uncovered numerous stone-lined drains in excellent condition. They were rectangular in section, c. 25 cm. (10 in.) wide and 20 cm. (8 in.) deep, covered with flat stones. These drains received water from the housetops, as connections between the gutters or downspouts were visible, and conveyed it to storage facilities or to waste. From the ninth century B.C. on, nearly every Palestinian house had its own cistern for the storage of winter rain. It received relatively clean water from housetops instead of from streets* and courts. Subterranean drains were increasingly used to keep the interior of towns as dry as possible.

Sophisticated water storage and supply systems were engineered by both Greeks and Romans. An example is the double tunnel system to regulate the water level and drainage of Lake Copais in Boetia, built during the time of Alexander the Great. A complex canal system was used by the Romans to drain the marshes S of Rome,* which had a primary effect of controlling malaria-carrying mosquitoes. While lead* pipes for domestic water supply were frequently used, clay* or terra-cotta pipes proved adequate for drainage.

Sewage and garbage problems arose with the first urban settlements. Drainage for these appear in early times in the Indus Valley (e.g., Mohenjo-Daro), Mesopotamia, and Crete. Roman facilities were excellent, and indeed ancient sanitation was often far superior to that developed in later times, including medieval Europe.

Dikes and drainage had to be built by the early farmers of Mesopotamia, but evidence of their work in the fields has been much obscured by development in later times. Also our knowledge of drainage in the great river valleys in ancient times depends on textual evidence that is largely incomplete. Basin-irrigation, using flood-water from the Nile, was common in ancient Egypt, and artificial drainage was not much needed. Agricultural drainage techniques were little developed in Palestine because of the well-drained hills and valleys of limestone formation. Drains, therefore, had to do primarily with housing and cities.

In the irrigation techniques of the classical world, draining was very important. Much potentially fertile land in the Greek domain was covered with marshes, swamps, and shallow lakes, and emphasis was placed on drainage, though little information concerning methodology has been passed on to us.

The Romans were far more active in the use of drainage. Channels with stepped-back stone embankments were common, and water tunnels similar to the Near Eastern *qanats* were used. A twofold advantage was obtained by building navigable canals. Dikes were also built to protect the flatlands.

BIBLIOGRAPHY: C. Singer et al., *A History of Technology*, 1 (1954), 520–55; 2 (1956), 678–80; W. F. Albright, *The Archaeology of Palestine* (1960), 101, 210; R. Forbes, *Studies in Ancient Technology*, 2 (1965), 75–79; H. Hodges, *Technology in the Ancient World* (1970), 211, 222.

MHH

DRILL. See TOOLS.

DUBU. See TOB.

DUMAH (dū'mä; Heb. דּוּמָה, *dûmāh*). A son of Ishmael (Gen 25:14; 1 Chron 1:30). His name became tribal and then geographical, hence its application to the local head town of Gawf, modern Arabic Dumat-al-Gandal, or el-Jof, Assyrian Adummatu, attested by Assyrian and Babylonian royal inscriptions of the seventh and sixth centuries B.C. The place is an oasis midway between the head of the Gulf of Aqaba and the head of the Persian Gulf. It had the distinction of being overrun by Sennacherib,* Esarhaddon,* and Nabonidus.* Its strategic significance, lying far E of the Fertile Crescent* communication lines, must therefore have been real.

Dumah was also the name of a town in the Judean uplands (Josh 15:52). A suggested identification is with the present ed-Domeh 10 km. (6 mi.) SW of Hebron.*

BIBLIOGRAPHY: S. Cohen, *IDB*, 1, 874–75; H. Jamieson, *ZPEB*, 2 (1975), 171.

EMB

DUMAT-AL-GANDAL. See DUMAH.

Plan of church at Dura Europos. Courtesy Carta, Jerusalem.

DURA EUROPOS (dū'rä yoŏ rō'pəs). A ruin on the right bank of the Euphrates, about halfway between Aleppo* and Baghdad. It has been called "the Pompeii* of the Syrian desert." It was discovered accidentally by a British army officer in 1921 and has attracted the attention of some notable archaeologists. A preliminary survey by the Egyptologist J. H. Breasted was conducted immediately after the discovery of the site. Systematic excavation was undertaken by F. Cumont over the next two years (1922–23), and from 1928 to 1937 the Yale University and the French Academy of Inscriptions worked on the site. The city was a Seleucid fortress on an indeterminate frontier and later a Parthian caravan town. The Romans held it from A.D. 165 for about a century. The Empire's eastern frontier was one which the Romans never stabilized, and the abandonment of Dura in the middle of the third century was illustrative of a wavering policy some three centuries old. Dura has yielded some extraordinary finds: (1) a third century fragment of Tatian's Diatessaron, the harmony of the four Gospels which went far to demolish much radical criticism of John's Gospel; (2) the earliest known Jewish synagogue,* dated approximately A.D. 245; (3) of slightly earlier date, the first known example of a Christian church. It was part of a house, like the chapel at the Lullingstone villa in Kent, in SE England, possibly contemporary, and had been made by joining two rooms and providing a platform. A third room was used as a baptistry.

BIBLIOGRAPHY: J. H. Breasted, *Oriental Forerunners of Byzantine Painting, First-Century Wall Paintings from the Fortress of Dura on the Middle Euphrates* (1924); M. I. Rostovtzeff, ed., *The Excavations at Dura-Europos* (1929–); id., *Dura-Europos and Its Art* (1938), 10–30.

EMB

DUR-KURIGALZU. See AQAR QUF.

DUR-SHARRUKIN. *See* KHORSABAD.

DUWEIR, TELL ED-. *See* TELL ED-DUWEIR.

DYE; DYEING. The coloring of cloth* and other materials was an ancient art highly prized from a very early period of human activity. The most common dyes were those derived from plants and shellfish. These were fixed by dipping the dyed fabric in lime* or similar solutions. There is some evidence that the name given to the purple fluid obtained from the sea snails such as *Murex*, as mentioned in many ancient sources, was Hurrian *kinaḫḫu*, meaning "purple," which later became the familiar name Canaan.* These small reddish to white mollusks are still common on all the shores of Asia Minor,* and vats and other facilities for extracting and applying the dye have been excavated at a number of Iron Age* sites in Israel. A fine dye works has been found just W of the Herodian temple* wall in old Jerusalem.* The works was built very early in the Christian era. Samples of dyed cloth are rare, but a few specimens from the desert areas of S-central Israel are extant. Another dye works has been discovered at Tell Beit Mirsim (cf. W. F. Albright, *AASOR*, 21–22 [1941–43], 55–62, and pls. 116, 51c–d, 52–53). Here the evidence suggests that the industry was home-based. Many rooms in houses,* 3–6 m. (10–20 ft.) long, were equipped with two round stone vats, with the accompanying drains,* basins,* and benches. Although it was always a cottage industry in Israel, foreign craftsmen* were brought in to refine the techniques (2 Chron 2:7). Since ancient peoples held to a strict dressing by rank, dyed cloth was always an object of value and trade.

BIBLIOGRAPHY: C. Singer et al., eds., *A History of Technology* (1954), 245–50; R. J. Forbes, *Studies in Ancient Technology*, 4 (1964).   ww

E

EAGLE. Ancient zoologists did not differentiate carefully between the various species of the genus *Aquila* (but cf. Pliny, *NH*, 10.3,4,7), so that vultures, eagles, and ospreys were commonly subsumed under the designation of eagle. Such birds were notable for their flight (Prov 23:5; Obad 4), their inaccessible nests (Job 39:27; Jer 49:16), and the care with which they tended their young (Deut 32:11). As the largest of the Palestinian flying birds, the eagle was a most impressive sight, and it is not surprising that it appeared in the literature of Near Eastern peoples. Thus the swiftness of the eagle's flight (Deut 28:49) was matched by similar allusions in Ugaritic* literature (cf. the Legend of Aqht, 3,11,20,28,32).

Mesopotamian* art demonstrated a close connection between the eagle and several deities of the pantheon (cf. E. Ebeling and B. Meissner, *Reallexikon der Assyriologie*, I [1932], 37). In Greek mythology the majestic eagle was the bird chosen by Zeus to convey a fawn to the Achaeans (*Iliad* 8.247–52). In both Republican and Imperial times, the eagle was the device of choice on the standards of the Roman legions. Hence the purport of the Lord's apocalyptic remark in Matt 24:28. Among the fresco decorations at Capernaum* (Tell Hum) is a representation of two eagles, back to back but with reflexed necks, holding between them a wreath. It is said to be the crest of the famous Tenth Legion which saw long service in Palestine and was perhaps the unit to which the centurion of Capernaum belonged (Luke 7:1–10).

BIBLIOGRAPHY: C. H. Gordon, *Ugaritic Literature* (1949), 92–93.; *Fauna and Flora of the Bible*, (United Bible Societies *Helps for Translators*, XI) (1972), 82–84. EMB

EANNATUM, VICTORY STELE OF. *See* VULTURES, STELE OF.

EAST SEA. *See* DEAD SEA.

EBLA. *See* TELL MARDIKH.

EBODA. *See* AVDAT.

ECBATANA (ek bat' ə nə; Aram. אַחְמְתָא, *Aḥmetā'*; from Old Pers. *Hagmatāna*, "place of assembly"; Akkad. *Agamatanu*; LXX A Ezra 6:2 'Αμαθά, *Amathá*; Greek writers 'Αγβάτανα, *Agbatana*, or Εκβάτανα, *Ekbátana*). The ancient capital of the Medes* located at modern Hamadan, which has preserved the name.

1. *Site*. Situated in the Zagros Mountains in NW Iran,

halfway between Tehran and Baghdad, Ecbatana, as its name implies, was an ancient crossroads. It commanded the major route from Mesopotamia* traversing the Zagros Mountains to points E.

Ecbatana was located in a high synclinal basin, 16 km. (10 mi.) wide and 24 km. (15 mi.) long, at an elevation of about 1830 m. (6,000 ft.) above sea level. It is enclosed by mountains, most notably by the 3,049-m. (11,700-ft.) high Mount Alvand to the W. Winters are severe with temperatures dropping to 20 degrees below zero F. and with snow 6 m. (20 ft.) deep in the passes. On the other hand, since the area is delightful in the summer, Ecbatana was used as a summer residence by the Persian kings.

2. *Biblical and Apocryphal References*. The sole OT reference is Ezra 6:2 where the KJV has transliterated the Aramaic* as *Achmetha*. This passage refers to the discovery at Ecbatana of a record of the decree of Cyrus* concerning the Jewish temple.*

Sarah, a demon-tormented woman who became the bride of Tobias, dwelt in Ecbatana (Tobit 7:1). Judith 1:1–4 describes the construction of Ecbatana by a fictional king, Arphaxad. 2 Macc 9:3 refers to the retreat of Antiochus Epiphanes from Persepolis* to Ecbatana.

3. *Classical Descriptions*. Herodotus 1.98 gives us a fanciful description of Ecbatana as it was constructed by Deioces, a Median* chief who lived in the eighth century B.C.: the city* was surrounded by seven concentric walls,* each of a different color with the two innermost walls coated with silver* and gold.* Ctesias, the Greek physician of Artaxerxes II (404–360), asserts that the legendary Semiramis built a palace at Ecbatana.

Polybius 10.27 describes the city at the time of its capture in 209 B.C. by Antiochus III. It was a city without walls but with a strong citadel.* The palace had been stripped of its cedar* woodwork and its gold and silver ornaments had been plundered by Alexander and his successors. Antiochus was able to carry off from the temple of Aena (Anaitis) gold bricks and silver tiles totaling about four thousand talents.

4. *History*. Scholars who question Herodotus's ascription of Ecbatana's foundation to Deioces suggest that the Median capital may have been established under Cyaxares II (625–585 B.C.). Cyrus captured Ecbatana in 550 when he rebelled against his Median grandfather, Astyages. The city was captured in 521 by Darius* after a brief Median revolt.

Alexander came to Ecbatana in his pursuit of Darius III and later revisited the city after his campaigns in the E. Antiochus III plundered the city, and Antiochus IV renamed it Epiphaneia.

The Parthians continued to use Ecbatana as a summer palace (Strabo 11.13.1). The town declined somewhat under the Sassanians. It was captured by the Muslims in A.D. 645, and served as the Seljuk capital from 1150–1200. Hamadan now boasts the tomb of the famed Avicenna (d. A.D. 1037). An alleged tomb of Esther and Mordecai is lacking in any authenticity.

5. *Discoveries*. Inasmuch as the occupation of the ancient site by the modern city of Hamadan has prevented systematic excavations, evidence has been limited to a few accidental finds.

A brief dig by Virolleaud and Fossey in 1913 uncovered a damaged bronze* jug which can be identified as Median from its resemblance to a Persepolis relief. A flood in the 1930s revealed the "Hamadan Treasure," only a part of which was recovered. This hoard included two gold swords, one now is in the Metropolitan Museum and the other in Tehran. In these two museums are two gold rhytons, which probably originated from Hamadan.

A number of important OP inscriptions have been recovered from Hamadan: (1) a gold tablet of Ariaramnes, the great-grandfather of Darius, published by Herzfeld in 1930; (2) a similar gold tablet of Ariaramnes' son, Arsames, published by Kent in 1950. If these are authentic, as maintained by Herzfeld and Ghirshman, they would be our oldest OP inscriptions. Most scholars, however, believe that they are propaganda documents inscribed perhaps by Artaxerxes II c. 400 B.C.

In 1923 a trilingual inscription of Darius on a gold tablet was found in Hamadan, while a duplicate in silver was also recovered. Three inscriptions of Artaxerxes II have been found, two on column bases and one on a gold tablet. They inform us that he had built an apadana with stone columns in Ecbatana.

At the SE outskirts of Hamadan is a gigantic stone lion,* which may have been erected by Alexander the Great in honor of his companion Hephaistion.

6. *Hamadan and Ecbatana*. On the SE border of Hamadan is a large bare hill, the al-Musalla, which Jackson believed was the site of ancient Ecbatana. Aerial photographs taken in 1937 by E. Schmidt revealed the true site of the ancient mound under houses in the NE sector of Hamadan. In 1956 Dyson examined a section of the mound which had been cut through by Ecbatana Street. The overthrow of the Shah in 1979 ended plans to excavate the Median capital.

BIBLIOGRAPHY: E. Weissbach, "Ekbatana," A. Pauly and G. Wissowa, eds., *Real-Encyclopädie der classischen Altertumswissenschaft*, 5 (1905), cols. 2155–58; A. V. W. Jackson, *Persia Past and Present* (1906), 144–74; E. Herzfeld, *Archaeological History of Iran* (1935), 22–27; R. de Vaux, "Les decrets de Cyrus . . . sur la reconstruction du temple," *RB*, 46

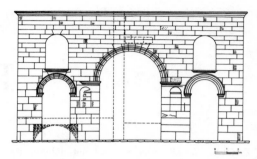

Ecce Homo Arch. A diagrammatic reconstruction from *Carta's Historical Atlas of Jerusalem* by Dan Bahat.

(1937), 29–57; E. Schmidt, *Flights over Ancient Cities of Iran* (1940), 74f.; R. Kent, "The Oldest Old Persian Inscriptions," *JAOS*, 66 (1946), 206–12; id., *Old Persian* (1953); E. Schmidt, *Persepolis I* (1953), 36–38; C. Wilkinson, "Assyrian and Persian Art," *Bulletin of the Metropolitan Museum of Art*, 13 (1955), 220–22; R. North, *Guide to Biblical Iran* (1956), 27–33; R. Dyson, "Iran 1956," *University Museum Bulletin*, 21 (1957), 31–33; L. van den Berghe, *Archéologie de l'Iran ancien* (1959), 108–10; A. L. Oppenheim, *Ancient Mesopotamia* (1964), 139, 394; C. H. Gordon, *The Ancient Near East* (1965), 255, 281–82; H. Luschey, "Der Löwe von Ekbatana," *Archäologische Mitteilungen aus Iran*, NF 1 (1968), 115–22, pl. 45–50; R. de Vaux, "The Decrees of Cyrus . . . ," *The Bible and the Ancient Near East* (1971), 63–96; P. Calmeyer, "Zu einiger Vernaghläsigten Aspecten Medischer Kunst," *Proc. of the 2nd Annual Symposium on Arch. Research in Iran* (1974), 112–27; E. Yamauchi, "The Achaemenid Capitals," *Near East Archaeological Society Bulletin*, 8 (1976), 14–19, 56–58, 77; O. Muscarella, "Excavated and Unexcavated Archaemenid Art," *Ancient Persia*, ed. D. Schmandt-Besserat (1980), 31–35.

EY

ECCE HOMO ARCH (ek'e hō' mō). This arch,* part of which is visible on the Via Dolorosa, is identified by tradition as the place where Pilate showed Jesus to the people and said "Here is the man!" (John 19:5). The present arch is later than the time of Christ and is a part of the new city* called Aelia Capitolina,* built by Hadrian* in A.D. 117–38. It was actually the monumental NE entrance gate* to the city. The arrangement is depicted on the Medeba Mosaic Map.*

However, its location is definitely associated with the place called Gabbatha,* or "The Stone Pavement" (John 19:13), later known as the *Lithostrōtos*. Extensive excavations by Père L. H. Vincent of the Dominican Bible School in Jerusalem, who also established the location and plan of the Tower of Antonia* at the NW corner of the temple* area, revealed a well-built pavement, several meters below the level of the present street. This is nearly below the Arch of Ecce Homo and under the modern quarters of the Sisters of Zion. The paving stones consist of large blocks of hard limestone, 1 m. by 1 m. by 30 cm. (3 by 3 by 1 ft.) in size, and cover an area of about

15 sq. m. (165 sq. ft.). Those paving the sloping portion have well-defined transverse grooves cut into the surface, to prevent slipping by pedestrians and horses.* It is certainly very probable that this is the pavement described in John 19:13. Scratched on the stones is a game board, evidently used by the Roman soldiers of the Tenth Legion, as it includes their insignia, a scorpion.

There is divided opinion as to whether Pilate would have been staying at the Tower of Antonia or at Herod's Palace, near the Joppa* Gate, but a consensus seems to indicate the former. If this is established, the currently known Via Dolorosa is the course of Jesus' last journey and the Ecce Homo Arch is erected on or above the traditionally known place.

BIBLIOGRAPHY: M. Avi-Yonah, *The Madaba Mosaic Map* (1954), 52; W. F. Albright, *The Archaeology of Palestine* (1960), 155, 245–46; J. Finegan, *Light from the Ancient Past* (1961), 320–21; E. Hoade, *Guide to the Holy Land* (1962), 158–60, 162–63; G. E. Wright, *Biblical Archaeology* (1962), 226.

MHH

ECIRKOY. *See* HIERAPOLIS.

ECOLOGY AND ARCHAEOLOGY. Man's modification of his environment is a constant preoccupation of archaeology, in Bible lands as elsewhere. The literary evidence is voluminous, and Homer, Plato, and Vergil are not the only writers who provide abundant information about the deforestation of Mediterranean lands which left the harbor works of Ephesus* so far from the modern coastline. "At the present day," wrote Ramsay at the turn of the century, "Ephesus has all the appearance of an inland city. The traveller who wanders among its ruins, may be at first unconscious of the neighbourhood of the sea . . . at the foot of the hill lies the ancient harbour, now a marsh dense with reeds. . . ." That landscape has since been modified by modern efforts to heal the ancient damage to the land, but the failure of Ephesus to remain the port for which the evidence— literary, numismatic,* and archaeological is plentiful—is indicative of what happened to the whole peninsula of Asia Minor.* Man's age-old folly of deforestation, consequent erosion, destruction of the natural water system, climatic and thence social and political change, may be read in all the ruins of the valley plains.

Lebanon likewise saw its ranges denuded of the valuable cedar,* without replacement of the forest cover, and in the act promoted the growth of desert and wilderness in its own and neighboring lands. The problems of renascent Lebanon today go back to Phoenician* mishandling of the land's resources, for which the archaeological and literary evidence is abundant.

Palestine also was once a less arid land. Forests are mentioned in the OT which no longer exist, and the evidence of olive* growing and rock mulching to protect the trees extends as far as desert areas of the Negev. Israeli dry-farming technicians have learned much from Nabataean* water systems recovered by archaeological research in the arid S of Israel. "By

careful terracing the control of catchment areas to regulate flood water into concentrated areas of cultivation, and the protection of vines from evaporation by raising them on mounds, the Nabataeans were indeed able to make the desert blossom as the rose," writes J. M. Houston (*ZPBA*, 21). Ceylon and the Euphrates Valley are similarly areas where man's ancient battle to keep the water flowing have been revealed by archaeological research.

Water, man's waste and conservation of it, are prominent in the archaeology of Bible lands. "Wherever in the Near East I have found water," writes Nelson Glueck, "there I have found traces of ancient civilisations, and sometimes a continuous record of settlement from the earliest historical times. Thus it is that, not only on the top of the plateau of Gilead, which overlooks the Yarmuk from the S and where the fairest lands of all Transjordan may be found, but even in the depths of the Yarmuk Gorge, I have found remains of ancient settlements, large and small, early and late, eloquent of man's creative activity, and of his frenzied attachment to the soil" (*The River Jordan*, 119). He might also have listed sites from Caesarea Philippi* to Jericho,* which owed its ancient origin to a flowing spring.

In the same survey (127–29), Glueck describes a Roman artesian system between Jabbok and Nimrin, an arid region some 16 miles E of Jordan. There is evidence of some sane Roman conservation in the area, with forest retention, and a wide system of cisterns* and aqueducts.* There are indications that the trenching of a course of water on the E side of the hills had led the ancient water engineer* deeper and deeper into an underground water table, which was finally traced by vertical shafts connected by a tunnel. It was an artesian system discovered again in modern times—literally water in the desert produced by striking its rock (cf. Exod 17:6).

Aerial view of experimental farm near Avdat. It uses methods of farming and irrigation originating in *Middle Bronze Age*, I, developed during Israelite period, and perfected by the Nabataeans. Courtesy Michael Evenari.

Edomite pottery from seventh century B.C. found at Tel Malhata (Tell el-Milh). Courtesy Tel Aviv University, Institute of Archaeology.

Archaeology in the Euphrates Valley plain has been able to establish the continual recession of civilization up the river, from Ur* to Babylon,* as progressive salinization,* aided and unaided by human pollution of irrigation* canals and trenches, destroyed the capacity of occupied agricultural land to grow first wheat, then barley, and then dates. Archaeology provides a somber record of the decline of river valley cultures by the modification of the environment under human occupation. Monuments to the same process may be found in the river valleys of Asia Minor, as illustrated by the contiguous remnants of Colossae,* Hierapolis,* and Laodicea.*

Occupation debris is, of course, the archaeologist's stock in trade, and not infrequently reflects a major modification of the environment. Layard's description of Babylon* in the early days of modern archaeology is a case in point. "To the vast mound of Babel* succeed long undulating heaps of earth, bricks and pottery.* Other shapeless heaps of rubbish cover for many an acre the face of the land. On all sides fragments of glass,* marble and inscribed brick are mingled with that peculiar nitrous and blanched soil which, bred from the ruins of ancient habitations, checks and destroys vegetation and renders the site of Babylon a naked and hideous waste" (A. Layard, *Nineveh and Babylon* [1853], 484).

The remains of mud bricks no doubt produced the infertility which the pioneer archaeologist mentioned. Frequently the ancient site became a source of matured and fertile compost for the local peasantry. It was while grubbing for such soil at the Amarna* mound, the ruined site of the Pharaoh Ikhnaton's unique capital, that a peasant woman discovered in 1887 the cache of correspondence which became famous as the Amarna letters.* Early Indo-European immigrants into Italy are known as the terramaricoli ("the black earth people") because their occupation sites are marked by the fertile black earth of the settlement's own making. The tells* of the Bible lands are hills created by man-made ruin, his

discarded possessions, houses,* and the other debris of continued human presence.

In a word, it is the consistent lesson of archaeology that, since Neolithic* times, man has polluted and damaged his environment.   EMB

ED-DOMEH. *See* DUMAH.

ED-DUWEIR, TELL. *See* TELL ED-DUWEIR.

EDESSA. *See* URFA.

EDFU (ed'fū). A prominent Upper Egyptian city during the period when the kings of the Macedonian Greek dynasty governed Egypt* (c. 323–330 B.C.). It contains all that remains of one of the world's best preserved edifices, the temple of the falcon-deity Horus. This huge building was commissioned in 237 B.C. by Ptolemy* III (c. 280–221 B.C.) to replace an earlier temple at the site. Granite from this latter structure was used to fashion a niche which then formed part of the inner sanctuary. In the following century the temple was enlarged by Ptolemy VI, who decorated it with beautifully carved columns, thereby adding to its imposing appearance. The only other significant addition occurred under Ptolemy VIII and Ptolemy IX, when a huge forecourt was constructed. Smaller shrines built by Ptolemy VI (180–146 B.C.) and Ptolemy VIII have also survived in a reasonable state of preservation. The influence of Greek elements in the architecture of the buildings is discreet but noticeable.

See PTOLEMY.

BIBLIOGRAPHY: J. Černý, *Ancient Egyptian Religion* (1952), 23, 46–47, 143.   RKH

EDOM; EDOMITES (ē'dəm, ē'dəm īts; Heb. אֱדוֹם, *'edôm*). A land and people, the latter being descended from Edom, the Esau of Gen 36:1–17. The territory extended for about 160 km. (100 mi.) from the Wadi Zered to the Gulf of Aqaba and encompassed the Wilderness of Edom. A rugged area with mountain peaks rising to 1616 m. (5,300 ft.) it nevertheless possessed good areas for cultivating crops (cf. Num 20:17,19). In the Middle Bronze Age the King's Highway* passed along the eastern plateau (Num 20:14–18). Excavations have shown that there was a pre-Edomite culture of a Hurrian* variety (Gen 14:6) in the land between the twenty-third and twentieth centuries B.C., which was apparently terminated by the raids of Chedorlaomer (Gen 14:1). From about 1850 B.C. to about 1350 B.C. the territory seems to have been unoccupied except for the activities of roving Bedouin tribes. By the thirteenth century B.C. the biblical Edomites were well established there under the leadership of tribal chiefs (Gen 36:15–19) and kings (Gen 36:31–39). The pharaohs Merneptah (c. 1124–1114 B.C.) and Ramses III (c. 1198–1167 B.C.) claimed to have subjugated Edom, though how completely is unknown.

The Israelites were refused permission to traverse Edomite territory at the time of the Exodus (Num 20:14–21), and when Joshua divided Canaan* up among the Israelite tribes, the borders of Edom remained unviolated (Josh 15:1,21). King Saul came into conflict with the Edomites (1 Sam 14:47), and his successor David effectively conquered them (2 Sam 8:13). Though meeting with some Edomite opposition (1 Kings 11:14–22), Solomon* built a port at Ezion Geber* and developed the smelting of copper in the region, as excavations at the site have illustrated. In the time of Jehoshaphat (870–848 B.C.), Edom was ruled by a deputy (1 Kings 22:47), who joined with Israel and Judah in a campaign against Moab* (2 Kings 3:4–27). Under Jehoram (848–841 B.C.), Edom remained independent for half a century, but Amaziah of Judah* partially recaptured Edomite territory (2 Kings 14:7). For a brief time the Edomites gained revenge on Judah (2 Chron 28:17) when Ahaz (732–716 B.C.) was ruling, but about 736 B.C. Tiglath-Pileser* III made Edom a vassal. When Judah fell in 587 B.C. some Edomites settled S of Hebron,* but in the next century they came increasingly under Arab* control. The Nabataeans* overran Edom in the third century B.C. and assimilated some of the natives into their own culture. Edomite wealth came principally from trading in natural resources, such as copper and iron,* and from the imposition of tolls on the caravan trade.

BIBLIOGRAPHY: N. Glueck, *The Other Side of the Jordan* (1940), 114–34; D. Baly, *The Geography of the Bible* (1958), 8 passim; S. Cohen, *IDB*, II, 24–26; R. K. Harrison, *ZPEB*, 2 (1975), 201–5.

RKH

EDREMID. See ADRAMYTTIUM.

EGLON. See TELL EL-HESY; TELL NAGILA.

EGNATIAN WAY (VIA EGNATIA). Built in the late second century before Christ, this W-E highway traversed Greece from Dyrrachinm to Thessalonica,* thence following the Thracian coast to Byzantium. Its length was 869 km. (540 mi.). It was traveled by Paul in his journeys in N Greece. Milestones, still occasionally recovered, marked the course of this great strategic highway. Its biblical significance lies only in the fact that Philippi,* Amphipolis,* and Thessalonica* were cities on its route.

EMB

EGYPT (ē' jipt; Heb מִצְרַיִם, *misrayim*; Gr. Ἀιγυπτος, *Aigyptos*. Meaning of Heb. is uncertain; LXX [Gr.] derives from Egyp. Hat-ku-Ptah, a name of Memphis). A nation in the NE corner of Africa, along the course of the lower Nile and its delta on the Mediterranean, the seat of an ancient civilization.

1. *The Land of Egypt.* The real Egypt is not the countless acres of desert flanking the Nile Valley, but strictly the long narrow strip of cultivation along either bank of that river in the valley, and the lands of the flat delta at its mouth. There alone, where the waters support plant life, is any settlement possible. Geographically, there is also a great contrast between the broad expanses of the delta and the long, narrow, cliff-hemmed valley S of it—hence the duality of the old Egyptian state and monarchy: "the two lands" and pharaoh as "King of Upper & Lower Egypt" in the inscriptions. The Heb. dual form *misrayim* may also conceivably reflect this fact. In this rainless land, all life depended on the annual Nile flood, product of the rains and melting snows of Ethiopia.* The division of Egypt was known to the OT writers. Their Pathros is Egyp. *pa-ta-resi*, "Southland," the Upper Egyptian valley, while Naphtuhim (Gen 10:13) may represent the delta of Lower Egypt (*na-p[a-i]dhu*).

2. *Historical Background.* The long line of pharaohs was divided by Manetho* into thirty dynasties or royal families—a scheme of reference still used today. These dynasties, however, are now grouped into larger significant periods of history, following the rise and fall of the Egyptian state and civilization. After prehistory, before c. 3100 B.C., these are:

B.C.	Period	Dynasties
c. 3100–2700	Archaic Period—emergence of united monarchy	I–II
c. 2700–2200	OLD KINGDOM—Pyramid Age, first era of greatness	III–VI
c. 2200–2040	First Intermediate Period—decline and dissention	VII–X
c. 2134–1786	MIDDLE KINGDOM—reunion and recovery	XI–XII (1991-1786)
c. 1786–1552	Second Intermediate Period—decline and division	XIII–XIV; XV–XVI (Hyksos*); XVII
c. 1552–1070	NEW KINGDOM—reunion and empire in Syria and Nubia*	XVIII–XX
c. 1070–332	Late Period—decline with occasional brief recovery	XXI–XXX; XXXI

Subsequently, Egypt was ruled by Alexander, the Ptolemies, the Romans, and the Arabs.*

From the biblical viewpoint, Egypt was a contemporary of OT events from the Middle Kingdom onward. The elaborate state organization, massive architecture (e.g., pyramids*), superb art, and earliest literature of the Old Kingdom illustrate clearly, as does contemporary Sumer,* the high level of cultural achievement in the centuries before Abraham. Circulating between Ur* and Egypt (Gen 11:31; 12:10), Abraham was no savage born in the night of prehistoric time but a traveler among advanced cultures.

The visits of Abraham and Jacob's sons to Egypt in time of famine (Gen 12:42–44) can be illustrated from a Middle Kingdom tomb scene at Beni Hasan* of thirty-seven Asiatics visiting Egypt (nineteenth century B.C.). With Abraham's escort out of Egypt (Gen 12:20), one may compare that for Sinuhe returning there (ANET, 21 and n. 39). Both the Middle Kingdom/Second Intermediate period and the New Kingdom yield colorful background for the narrative of Joseph.*

The New Kingdom was the period of Hebrew sojourn in, and exodus from, Egypt, and the era of Egypt's greatest political power. The conquests of Thutmose III (c. 1490–1436 B.C.) were largely lost under Akhenaton* (c. 1374–1358 B.C.), and partly recovered under Sethos I (c. 1315–1290 B.C.) and Ramses II* (c. 1290–1224 B.C.).

During the New Kingdom, texts and pictures document the presence of many Semites, Horites, and other foreigners in Egypt at all levels—from slaves,* laboring on buildings like the Hebrews, to cupbearers* like Ben-Ozen or Pen-Hazuri ("He of Hazor") attendant upon the pharaoh. Semitic dialects were known to the scribes as well as Egyptian (e.g., ANET 477 and n. 41), and the geography of Canaan* well-understood (ANET, 476–78). Young foreigners were brought up and educated in royal harems (cf. Exod 2), so that the childhood of Moses fits the cultural context well.

With the Israelites' escape route from Egypt, one may compare that of runaway slaves under Sethos II (c. 1210–1204 B.C.), from Rameses* via Succoth (Tjeku) to a Migdol and the desert (ANET, 259). Finally, the Libyan war stele* of Merneptah (c. 1224–1214 B.C.) mentions Israel as in W Palestine in his fifth year (c. 1220) alongside Gezer* and Ascalon; his Amada stele and its parallels reinforce Merneptah's claim to have raided Palestine. Earlier (while the Israelites were in Sinai ?), Ramses II* had invaded Moab,* including Dibon* and other cities.

After c. 1200 B.C., Ramses III (c. 1170) had to fight off the Sea Peoples,* and under Ramses IV–XI, the empire crumbled away in a welter of inefficiency and corruption. Even the tombs of the pharaohs were robbed in the Valley of Kings.

The Late Period began with the weak Dynasty XXI, whose kings in Tanis* (c. 1070–945 B.C.) ruled all Egypt only by giving recognition to the rule of the S by a high-priestly line in Thebes.* Not until Siamun did Egypt actively intervene in Palestine, when he raided Philistia,* giving Gezer to Solomon* with a daughter's hand in marriage. The next Dynasty (XXII) was founded by Shoshenq I, the Shishak* who raided the Hebrew realms after Solomon was safely dead (1 Kings 14:25; 2 Chron 12). But under his less shrewd successors, civil war and local princely ambitions split Egypt asunder, so that by c. 725 B.C., So (Osorkon IV) was utterly powerless

to aid Hoshea against Assyria (2 Kings 17:4), and as Shilkanni actually bought off Sargon II* in 716 B.C. Thereafter, the Nubian Twenty-fifth Dynasty encouraged Palestinians such as Hezekiah against Assyria, as in 701 B.C. by Tirhakah as prince, later king.

Assyria sacked Thebes in 663 B.C., and in fact from 664 a new line of princes from Sais, the Twenty-sixth Dynasty (NW Delta), began to rebuild the unity and prosperity of Egypt around itself. The interventions of Neco II* (610–595 B.C.) and Hophra (589–570 B.C.) against Babylon* were unsuccessful, but otherwise the Saite dynasty ruled a flourishing realm until conquest by Cambyses of Persia in 525 B.C. Jews* in Egypt at this epoch are known at Elephantine.* During c. 400–341 B.C., Dynasties XXVIII-XXX secured independence, until a Persian reconquest (Dynasty XXXI) in 341–332 B.C., which ended in Hellenistic rule from Alexander the Great onward.

3. *Cultural Background.* a. *Religion.* In religion, the Egyptians were polytheists who revered many deities, personifying natural forces (Nile, sun, air, earth, etc.) which were sometimes expressed in animal life (bull, falcon, jackal, etc.), in abstract principles (Maat, "truth," "right order"), and in human states (e.g., Osiris, just ruler, god of the dead). The link between deity and man depended basically upon correct performance of prescribed ritual by priests in specified temples, rather than on personal heart devotion. However, consciousness of sin and human limitation was present, certainly in the New Kingdom period (cf. ANET, 380–81). As background for the OT, Egyp. religion is instructive (1) by contrast and (2) in illustrating incidentals, such as the early use of music,* annual feasts, set rituals and offerings, tabernacle structures, etc., long before any Babylonian exile, or even Moses' time. b. *Literature.* Religious literature (hymns, prayers, spells, etc.) begins with the Pyramid Texts in the third millennium B.C., and through the Coffin Texts,* Book of the Dead,* and other materials, runs on till the Roman period. Lyric poems from the New Kingdom contribute to the intellectual background of Song of Songs, and the long series of "Wisdom books" are valuable in showing how early the type of structure and style in Proverbs had arisen. The abundance of narratives, especially Middle and New kingdoms, likewise exhibit literary techniques often misused by OT scholars to produce imaginary "constituent documents" of OT writings.

BIBLIOGRAPHY: *Land and General Reference.* B. Porter and R. L. B. Moss, *Topographical Bibliography of Anc. Egyp. Texts*, 1-7 (1929–51), 2nd ed., 1-2 (1960–71); J. M. A. Janssen et al., *Annual Egyptological Bibliography, 1947ff.* (1948ff.); H. Kees, *Ancient Egypt, A Cultural Topography* (1961); G. Posener et al., *A Dictionary of Egyptian Civilization* (1962); W. Helck and E. Otto, *Lexikon der Ägyptologie* (1972ff.).

History. CAH, 1, part 2 (1971ff.), 145–207, 404–531; E. Hornung, *Untersuchungen, Chronologie und Geschichte, Neuen Reiches* (1964); K. A. Kitchen, *Third Intermediate Period.*

Religion and Literature. A. Erman and A. M. Blackman, ed. W. K. Simpson, *The Ancient Egyptians, A Sourcebook* (1966); E. Hornung, *Der Eine und die Vielen* (1971); K. A. Kitchen, *Ancient Orient and OT* (1966), ch.6 (literary criticism).

KAK

EGYPT, DESCENT TO. A monument of Haremhab (1350–1314 B.C.) provides a parallel to the invitation of pharaoh to Jacob's tribe to settle in Egypt.* It records how a community of shepherds from the N petitioned Egypt to grant them pasturage, "as was the custom of the father of their fathers from the beginning." On the tomb of Tehuti-hetep at el-Bersheh there is a picture of a drove of Syrian cattle entering Egypt and the words, "Once you trod the Syrian sands. Now here in Egypt you shall feed in green pastures."

BIBLIOGRAPHY: *FLAP* (1951), 102, fig. 48.

EMB

EIN FESHKA. See DEAD SEA SCROLLS; QUMRAN.

EKRON (ek'ron; Heb. עֶקְרוֹן, *'eqrôn*; LXX Ἀκκαρών *Akkarōn*; the meaning of the original Hebrew may have been "deep-rooted"; cf. the play on words in Zeph 2:4). The northernmost of the five major Philistine* cities (Josh 13:3; 1 Sam 6:17), Ekron together with Gath* was located in the interior rather than near the coast.

1. *History*. Ekron was first assigned to the tribe of Dan* (Josh 19:43). The Israelites were evidently not able to capture it effectively (according to the LXX of Judg 1:18; the MT, on the other hand, affirms the capture of Ekron, Gaza,* and Ashkelon* by Judah*). The border of Judah passed along the ridge N of Ekron (Josh 15:11).

In the ninth century B.C. Ahaziah was rebuked for consulting the god of Ekron, Baal-Zebub (2 Kings 1:2–16). The name Baal-Zebub "Lord of Flies" (cf. Matt 12:24–29) is a derisive alteration of Baal-Zebul "Lord of the High Place." Amos (1:8) pronounced judgment upon Ekron and the other Philistine cities.

Ekron is quite prominent in Assyrian inscriptions which describe the conquest of Philistia. A letter from Calah* (Nimrud) refers to Ekronites bearing tribute to Sargon II.* Sargon's forces besieged Ekron in his campaign of 712. The siege is depicted in a relief of Hall V at Dur-Sharrukin (Khorsabad*); Ekron is spelled *Amqarruna* in Akkadian. When Sargon died in 705, the local nobility of Ekron rebelled against the Assyrian yoke. Hezekiah intervened and imprisoned the pro-Assyrian ruler of Ekron, Padi.

In his invasion of Palestine in 701, Sennacherib* assaulted Ekron and killed the rebellious patricians. Common citizens guilty of minor crimes were made prisoners; Padi, liberated from Hezekiah, was reinstated as the ruler. Territory taken from Judah was given to Ekron (*ANET*, 287–88; *DOTT*, 66–67).

Ikausu, king of Ekron, was called up to Nineveh* by Esarhaddon* (*ANET*, 291; *DOTT*, 74). Unlike the names of most Philistine rulers known to us which are Semitic, this seems to be an originally Philistine

name. Ikausu also paid tribute to Ashurbanipal* as the latter marched toward Egypt in 663 B.C. (*ANET*, 294).

The history of Ekron during the Neo-Babylonian* and Persian periods is not known except for prophecies pronounced against the city (Jer 25:20; Zeph 2:4; Zech 9:5, 7). In 147 B.C. Alexander Balas gave Ekron and its territory to Jonathan Maccabeus (1 Macc 10:89). According to Eusebius, Ekron still had a large Jewish population c. A.D. 300.

2. *Identification*. As in the case of Gath, the identification of Ekron remains disputed. In the nineteenth century Edward Robinson identified Ekron with 'Âqir, an Arab village c. 8 km. (5 mi.) SW of Ramle. No ancient remains, however, have been discovered here.

Qatra, a site 4.8 km. (3 mi.) SW of 'Âqir, was proposed as Ekron in 1923 by Albright on the basis of a remark by Eusebius, which seemed to indicate that in passing from Ashdod* to Jabneel one could see Ekron to the E.

Khirbet el-Muqanna', surveyed by J. Naveh in 1957, now seems to be the most likely candidate for Ekron. Located 13 miles due E of Ashdod, it is in a position to command the Valley of Sorek. Although it is a low-lying tell, its area of 16 ha. (40 a.) is larger than that of any other Iron Age* site known. Fortification walls* including a gate* were traced. From the surface shards it appears that Philistines founded the Early Iron Age II city on an abandoned Early Bronze site. After enjoying considerable prosperity during the tenth–sixth centuries, the city seems to have declined after the Neo-Babylonian* invasions of Nebuchadnezzar.*

The features of Khirbet el-Muqanna' have convinced most scholars that it should be identified with Ekron, with the notable exception of Albright, who wished to reconsider the site of 'Âqir (1966).

BIBLIOGRAPHY: E. Robinson, *Biblical Researches in Palestine*, 2, 3rd ed (1867), 226–29; W. F. Albright, "Contributions to the Historical Geography of Palestine," *AASOR*, 1-2 (1923), 1–17; H. W. F. Saggs, "The Nimrud Letters, 1952—Part II," *Iraq*, 17 (1955), 126–34; H. Tadmor, "The Campaigns of Sargon II of Assur," *Journal of Cuneiform Studies*, 12 (1958), 83; J. Naveh, "Khirbet al-Muqanna'—Ekron," *IEJ*, 8 (1958), 87–100, 165–70; B. Mazar, "The Cities of the Territory of Dan," *IEJ*, 10 (1960), 65–77; G. E. Wright, "Fresh Evidence for the Philistine Story," *BA*, 29 (1966), 70–86; H. Tadmor, "Philistia under Assyrian Rule," ibid., 86–102; W. F. Albright, *The Amarna Letters from Palestine; Syria, the Philistines and Phoenicia* (1966), 26, n. 3; E. Hindson, *The Philistines and the Old Testament* (1971); K. A. Kitchen, "The Philistines," *Peoples of Old Testament Times*, ed. D. J. Wiseman (1973), 53–78; A. F. Rainey, "The Identification of Philistine Gath," *Eretz Israel*, 12 (1975), 63–76; Y. Aharoni, *The Land of the Bible* (rev. ed., 1979), 270ff.

EY

ELAM (ē'ləm; Heb. עֵילָם, *'ēlām*). The region east of the Tigris river incorporating the plain of Khuzi-

Relief from Nineveh depicting two Elamite soldiers. Courtesy S.P.Q.R. Musei Capitolini, Rome.

stan, the natural extension of the Mesopotamian* plains, and the Bakhtiari (or Zagros) mountains is ancient Elam. Genesis 10:22 lists Elam as one of Shem's sons. Archaeological research has established that man has been in this area since the Late Stone Age, with the painted pottery* of Susa* and other sites, the finest in prehistoric Iran, going back to the fourth millennium B.C. Both Awan, where the first recorded dynasty was established about 2600 B.C., and Susa are referred to in ancient records as the main centers of Elamite civilization. The Old Elamite period commenced about 1900 B.C., the Middle dating from about 1500 to 1000, while the Neo-Elamite era ended with Assyrian invasions about 640. In the following century Elam was incorporated into the Achaemenian empire.

Excavations conducted at various sites, supplemented by written records from Mesopotamia, enable an outline of Elamite history to be reconstructed (see R. Ghirshman, Iran). Four key sites have been investigated.

Susa (Shushan). A sizeable village in the latter fourth millennium B.C. and the center of a powerful Elamite dynasty in the mid third millennium, Susa reached its golden age with Elamite civilization as a whole in the twelfth century B.C. It continued as a significant center after Cyrus* the Great's rise to power in 550, becoming the capital of the Susiana satrapy, or province (Dan 8:2). Excavations were conducted in 1854 by W. H. Loftus, and by French archaeologists in 1884 and then continuously from 1897 to the present. The importance of trade contacts with Mesopotamia and the Indus Valley are well illustrated here and at Tepe Yahya.

Anshan. Tell i Malyan, located 46 km. (28½ mi.) north of Shiraz, has now been identified as Anshan by means of bricks inscribed in Elamite (see ELAMITE WRITING). Prior to this the city* was known only from third and second millennia B.C. documents as

the capital of Awan. Excavations by the University of Pennsylvania in 1971–72 have provided evidence of occupation from the third millennium down to about 1000 B.C. and have unearthed forty Elamite and seven proto-Elamite clay* tablets.

Choga Zambil. Located 60 km. (37 mi.) SE of Susa, this site has one of the best preserved ziggurats* of the ancient Near East, 150 m. (492 ft.) square at the base and originally 52 m. (170 ft.) high, involving five stories. It was built about 1280 B.C., during the Mosaic age, in honor of In-Shushinak, the Elamite chief god. The city was destroyed in the 640 B.C. Assyrian invasion.

Haft Tepe. The name means "seven mounds" (although over 12 are here), and the site is 30 km. (18½ mi.) SE of Susa. Excavations since 1965 reveal occupation from the sixth millennium to the Elamite city of the late second millennium B.C. and have filled in a gap in Elamite history between 1500 and 1300. Over 500 tablets have been recovered.

There was constant interaction of Elam with Mesopotamia: Sargon of Akkad,* Gudea* of Lagash,* Shulgi and kings of Ur* (Dynasty III) dominated Elam. Early in the second millennium, a new national dynasty was established under rulers referred to as the "divine messenger, father and king." This was also an era of expansion, until checked by Hammurabi* of Babylon* (c. 1724–1682 B.C.). Twenty-one tablets from Nippur* record a 435-line poem of lamentation over Ur following its destruction by the Elamites about 1936 B.C.—"O Nannar (Moon God), Ur has been destroyed, its people have been dispersed" (ANET, 460). Southern Babylonian cities, such as Isin, Uruk, and even Babylon, came under Elamite domination. This is the farthest expansion documented in the era to which Genesis 14 belongs. Chedorlaomer, although a compound of two Elamite names, is unknown in the king lists.

Elam was one of the first states to revive after the Kassite* domination in the Near East leading to the Golden Age of the thirteenth century B.C. One king of this dynasty, Shutruk-Nahhunte, successfully raided Babylon about 1200, taking the famous Hammurabi Stele (see HAMMURABI, CODE OF) back to Susa as a trophy, where it was discovered in 1902–3 and sent to the Louvre.

During the first half of the first millennium, the Elamites opposed the might of Assyria, sometimes acting in concert with the Chaldeans* in Babylonia. Excavated documents from Mesopotamia describe the ebb and flow of fortunes, although generally the Assyrians had the ascendancy (ANET, 300ff.). Merodach Baladan (Marduk-apal-iddina), the Chaldean who, with his sons, regularly rebelled against Assyria, was supported both by the Elamites and by Hezekiah (2 Kings 20:12; Isa 39). Babylon revolted again in 694, at Elam's instigation, and, although the allies at first defeated Sennacherib,* the Assyrian king destroyed Babylon in 689. Elam's warlike actions are alluded to in the prophetic writings (Isa 22:6; Jer 49:34–39; Ezek 32:24).

The continuous struggle between Assyria and Elam ended about 640, when Ashurbanipal* wreaked vengeance on Elam, his own claim being that he destroyed twelve Elamite districts (see, possibly, Ezra 4:9). Evidence of his victory is obvious at Susa and Choga-Zambil. This effectively ended Elamite power, as may be seen in a possible reference to their avoiding battle with Nebuchadnezzar* in 596. The Achaemenian rulers of Persia became the dominant leaders in the Near East with the rise of Cyrus (550), and Elamites could have been involved in the fall of Babylon to him in 539 (Isa 21:2–10).

Under Cyrus and his successors Elam became one of the Persian satrapies (provinces), Susiana, with the ancient center of Susa remaining the capital. In this role it appears in a number of biblical passages (Dan 8:2; Neh 1, Esth).

Excavations at Susa have revealed something of the glory of the city in the Persian era prior to its surrender to Alexander the Great in 331 B.C. and its devastation by fire (whether accidentally or deliberately is undetermined) four months later. Foundation tablets, 34 by 34 by 9 cm. (13 by 13 by 3½ in.), discovered in the inner doorway of the palace of Darius* I, one written in Babylonian and one in Elamite, describe the king's ancestry, his building the palace, and the source of the workmen and materials—bricks from Babylon, cedar* wood from Lebanon, gold* from Sardis* and Bactria* (Afghanistan), silver* and ebony from Egypt,* ivory* from India and Ethiopia,* materials for paint* from Ionia, lapis lazuli* and other stones from what is now Russia, and stone columns from Elam. The inventory provides an interesting comparison with Ezek 27, where Tyre's* imports are listed.

Both Nehemiah (1:1) and Esther (1:2 et al) are associated with Shushan, the palace or the citadel.* In the palace area (250 by 150 m., or 820 by 492 ft.) Darius* built his residence based on three courtyards, running E to W, the rooms around the smaller, more enclosed, central court most likely being the royal apartments. To the N was the apadana, or audience hall, with its thirty-six magnificent columns with their double-headed bull capitals.* Glazed* brick panels at the entrances to the palace depicted the king's bodyguards, the famous "Immortals."

Elamites were present in Jerusalem with Parthians and Medes,* peoples from the same region, on the day of Pentecost (Acts 2:9).

Our knowledge of Elamite religion is limited by the terse nature of the known records. It appears, however, that from a diversity of city-state gods a national pantheon came into being in the pre-Sargonic era (mid third millennium B.C.). Other changes occurred with time. The earlier supreme deity, the goddess Pinikir, was replaced as head by a male god, and gradually became less significant. Likewise, the chief god of Susa, In-Shushinak, slowly eclipsed the main deities of earlier times. The character of the gods was ill defined partly because their ineffable nature placed them beyond the scope of human language.

Mesopotamian religion often influenced Elamite ideas, and Babylonian gods in particular were associated with the pantheon. Nahhunte, the sun god, was the god of justice, just as was Shamash in Babylonia. As in Mesopotamia, semidivine beings, half human and half animal or plant, were common, often acting as temple guardians. Both cultures believed in good and bad demons. In Elamite religious art a most important motif was the serpent.* Originally part man and part snake, he gradually became less animal. While the serpent god was periodically significant in Mesopotamia, it was continuously more important in Elam.

BIBLIOGRAPHY: Details of Elamite history, political structure and religion will be found in CAH, 3rd ed., 1.2; 2.1,2.

GGG

EL-AMARNA, TELL. See AMARNA.

ELAMITE WRITING.
Current excavations are enlarging and modifying our understanding of the development and use of Elamite (see ELAM) writing. There seems little doubt that the concept came from Mesopotamia,* the Sumerian* sign for milk being found at Choga Mish in an early context. The Elamites, however, at first developed their own semi-pictographic script, known as Proto-Elamite. First, numerals occur on clay* bullae at Susa, followed soon after by script on clay tablets, mainly lists. These have been regarded as the earliest evidence of Proto-Elamite, but the discovery of seven written tablets and thirty blanks at Tepe Yahya, dated to about 3200 B.C. show a wider spread of its early origins. The several hundred signs first employed were later reduced to considerably fewer.

In the mid third millennium B.C. the cuneiform* script of Mesopotamia was adopted for writing Elamite, and Akkadian* was also introduced, probably due to the conquests of Sargon* and Naram Sin. However, Proto-Elamite tablets found at Anshan in recent years, dating to about 2000 B.C., demonstrate that this script also was still used. The revived Elamite nationalism early in the second millennium saw the introduction of many indigenous words in the Akkadian business documents.

Elamite proper, in cuneiform script, was employed from the second millennium, forty tablets from Anshan dating to the last quarter of this era. In Achaemenian times Elamite was used as one of the three standard scripts, with Babylonian and Old Persian, on monuments and building records, such as the famous Behistun Inscription* of Darius* I and a gold* foundation record of the same king. This language was deciphered between 1843 and 1852 by Westergaard and Norris, but Proto-Elamite still remains essentially a puzzle.

GGG

EL-AREINI. See TELL SHEIKH AHMED EL-AREINI.

ELATH
(ē' lath; Heb. אֵילַת, 'ēlaṯ). A town located on the northern tip of the Red Sea,* at the junction of the eastern gulf (the Gulf of Aqaba) with the Arabah, the broad valley extending 177 km. (110 mi.) northward to the southern end of the Dead Sea.* Elath probably received its name from the Edomite chieftan Elah (Gen 36:41), particularly since the name immediately following is apparently the Punon lo-

cated in the Wadi Arabah. It is generally associated with Ezion Geber* in the earlier biblical texts, and some confusion exists over the use of three names for the same locality: El-Paran, Ezion Geber (KJV Gaber), and Elath* (Eloth).

The name El-Paran in the famous story of the "battle of the four kings against the five" (Gen 14:6) is generally assumed to refer to Elath. Aharoni (*The Land of the Bible*, 182) reads it El(ath) Paran, identifying it with biblical Elath. The second element is derived from its proximity to the extensive Paran wilderness.

Elath is mentioned along with Ezion Geber in Deut 2:8 as a way station of the Exodus route. Many scholars have assumed that the two are identical by virtue of their close association and that one is merely an amplification of the other; i.e., "Elath, even Ezion-geber." The clearest evidence, however, comes in 1 Kings 9:26, which has "Ezion Geber, which is near Elath," perhaps indicative of two very close but separate localities. In the divided monarchy the name Ezion Geber drops out of use in the biblical text after the time of Jehoshaphat, and Elath is used instead. Uzziah (Azariah) "rebuilt Elath and restored it to Judah*" (2 Kings 14:22), and it was later recovered by Rezin of Syria in the reign of Ahaz, at which time the Jewish population was forcibly replaced by Arameans* (2 Kings 16:6). These OT references seem to demand two places in close proximity to each other.

The problem, however, is that only one ancient site prior to the Nabataean* period has been found so far on the mainland in the vicinity of the N end of the Gulf of Aqaba. This site, Tell el-Kheleifeh, about 2.4 km. (1½ mi.) W of the modern town of Aqaba, was first proposed by Fritz Frank in 1934 as the location of ancient Ezion Geber. Excavations were undertaken between 1938 and 1940 by Nelson Glueck and the American Schools of Oriental Research.

Glueck's work was singularly important in revealing a Judean fortress, warehouse, and trading station at the junction of the land and sea routes. It also provided new evidence for the little-known Edomite material culture and ceramic sequence. The claim that the major installation was a copper refinery* was eventually retracted by the excavator, the celebrated "flues" being nothing more than apertures for crossbeams bonding the mud-brick walls together according to an architectural pattern noted elsewhere. Originally constructed in the time of Solomon* or a little later, the fortress went through several phases of rebuilding. Phase I saw the erection of a 12-by-12 m. (40-by-40 ft.) structure in the tenth century surrounded by a mud-brick glacis* and a 41-m. (135-ft.) square casemate wall.* Phase II, presumably built by Jehoshaphat, greatly enlarged the area and added a triple gateway. Phase III contained a seal of Jotham, son of Uzziah. This level correlates well with the rebuilding by Uzziah specifically mentioned in Scripture (2 Kings 14:21), presenting a strong probability that Tell el-Kheleifeh is indeed the Elath of the Bible. Period IV is clearly Edomite, which again squares with the biblical evidence (2 Kings 16:6). Inscribed Edomite jar stamps and an Aramaic* ostracon* were found in this level. The last

phase (V) ended in the fifth–fourth centuries B.C., with glazed Attic blackware in evidence. Thereafter the tell* was abandoned and Elath was moved 2.4 km. (1½ mi.) to the E, to the site of the modern Jordanian city* of Aqaba. It was known in the Roman-Byzantine period, and even into the early Arabic* period, as Aila, a place frequently attested in historical literature from the Roman occupation onward.

It is clear that the excavations have solved some problems and raised some new questions. The El-Paran/Elath/Ezion Geber equation, although generally valid since all were in the same region, remains problematical in specific topographical terms. The absence of Bronze Age ruins on the tell points to the likelihood that El-Paran was simply an oasis on the border of the Paran desert delimiting the extent of the Horite territory, and perhaps not a fortified settlement at all. In this respect it is analogous to the situation at Beersheba* in the patriarchal period. It is difficult to determine if it should be located at Tell el-Kheleifeh or in the vicinity of Aqaba, where the water supply and other environmental factors are better. The evidence is not yet conclusive. Elath is very probably the same place as El-Paran. The names have a similarity of meaning and may be etymologically related (the "tall tree[s] of Paran" and "grove of tall trees," i.e., an oasis). Probably palms rather than terebinths are intended. Somewhere in the Aqaba vicinity is indicated as the likely location for Elath, since Aila, as Aqaba was formerly called, has been the major oasis in the region at least since Roman times and continuously thereafter. Elath and Aila are also linguistically related. The fact that no occupational evidence earlier than the Nabataean period is known from Aqaba, together with the fact that Tell el-Kheleifeh is the only place along the coast where Iron Age* remains have been found, combines to make the precise identification with the tell almost certain. The excavations perfectly fit the textual evidence for the history of the site in the biblical period. Evidently Tell el-Kheleifeh is biblical Elath. There may, however, be more of the town than has been found to date. What has thus far been excavated represents the fortified royal Judean warehousing and transshipment establishment. Glueck fully expected that someday a fort on the hill and a town at the oasis would probably be found to round out our picture of Elath. The most problematical reference is to Ezion Geber. Without the use of this etymologically unrelated place-name, near Elath but separate from it, there would be no difficulty in identifying Elath with Tell el-Kheleifeh, and the matter would be simply resolved. Scholars have approached the problem in a number of ingenious ways. Glueck thought that the town had its name changed from Ezion Geber to Elath by Uzziah just as he changed Sela to Joktheel (2 Kings 14:7; 2 Chron 26:1,2). Glueck used the two names as referring to one and the same place, and his reports speak rather confusingly of Ezion Geber III (Elath I), in his terminology for level III. Consequently, in his view, the use of Elath as a toponym could have resulted only from the late composition or late scribal updating of Deuteronomy. Aharoni, on the other hand, located Ezion Geber at

Tell el-Kheleifeh and assumed that Elath was located at Aqaba. A new archaeological survey after the Israeli occupation of the Sinai Peninsula in 1967 prompted the suggestion that the Island of Jaziret Phara'on some 10 miles S of modern Eilat might be Ezion Geber. This possibility corresponds well to the Phoenician* preference for utilizing offshore islands as maritime bases, as at Arwad and Tyre* on the Phoenician coast. If Solomon built a seaport and base for his fleet on the island with the help of Hiram,* king of Tyre, and also constructed a fort and transfer facility on the mainland, this would account for all the requirements of the biblical record. It would also account for the change of names after Jehoshaphat, whose fleet was disastrously wrecked at Ezion Geber (1 Kings 22:48). Apparently the port was then abandoned, because the name dropped out of history at that point.

BIBLIOGRAPHY: F. Frank, "Aus der 'Arabah, I: Tell el-chlefi," *ZDPV*, 57 (1934), 243–45; N. Glueck, "Ezion-geber: Solomon's Naval Base on the Red Sea," *BA*, 1 (1938), 13–16; "The First Campaign at Tell el Kheleifeh," *BASOR*, 71 (1938), 3–17; "The Topography and History of Ezion-geber and Elath," *BASOR*, 72 (1938), 2–13; "The Second Campaign at Tell el-Kheleifeh (Ezion-geber: Elath)," *BASOR*, 75 (1939), 8–22; "The Third Season at Tell el-Kheleifeh," *BASOR*, 79 (1940), 2–18; N. Glueck, *The Other Side of the Jordan* (1940), 89–113; id., *Rivers in the Desert* (1949), 157–63; B. Rothenberg, "Ancient Copper Industries in the Western Arabah," *PEQ* (1962), 5–65; N. Glueck, "Ezion-geber," *BA*, 28 (1965), 70–87. JEJ

EL-AZARIYEH. See LAZARUS, TOMB OF.

EL-BUSAIREH. See BOZRAH.

ELEPHANTINE (el ə fan tē′ nə). A small island in the Nile just below and N of the first cataract, opposite Aswan.* In antiquity it was the seat of the governor of the first and southernmost province of Upper Egypt.* In the Pyramid* Age (third millennium B.C.), such governors conducted trade expeditions into Nubia,* obtaining gold* and tropical products for the pharaohs. Remains of several temples are known, especially of the creator-god Khnum.

Under the Persian Empire, a mercenary garrison including Aramaic*-writing Jews* was posted on the island, these having a temple of Yaho ("Jehovah") associated in cult with other divine names. The remains of that settlement have yielded a series of Aramaic papyri* and ostraca* of great value for background study of the Persian period of Jewish history.

See ELEPHANTINE PAPYRI.

BIBLIOGRAPHY: B. Porter and R. L. B. Moss, *Topographical Bibliography of Ancient Egyptian Texts . . .*, 5 (1937), 222, 224ff.; E. G. Kraeling, *The Brooklyn Museum Aramaic Papyri* (1953), 21ff.; Boulos Ayad Ayad, *The Topography of Elephantine according to the Aramaic Papyri* (1967). KAK

ELEPHANTINE PAPYRI. The name given to a series of papyrus* documents written in Aramaic* script

and language (closely akin to Hebrew; *see* EPIGRAPHY, HEBREW), belonging to members of an Aramean* and Jewish garrison at Elephantine* in S Egypt* during the Persian Empire. They range in date from 495 to 399, thus spanning most of the fifth century B.C. They fall into various categories.

1. *Literary Works.* Among more prosaic documents an Aramaic version of the famous Behistun Inscription,* which vaunts the greatness of Darius I,* was recovered. This illustrates the statement of Darius that he sent documents into all lands for the peoples (compare this practice in Dan 6:25; Ezra 1:1; Esth 1:20–22; 3:12–14; 8:9). Still more valuable was a fragmentary MS of the Words of Ahikar, a wisdom text (cf. Proverbs) much elaborated in other versions in later times (*ANET*, 427ff.).

2. *Religious Documents.* No specifically religious writings have so far been found. But references to the Sabbath occur in letters, while one papyrus of 419 B.C. (fifth year of Darius II) is almost certainly a command to keep the Passover (*see* PASSOVER PAPYRUS), a feast mentioned also in two ostraca.* Another contemporary document is a list of subscribers at two shekels a head to (the temple of) Yaho (Cowley No. 22), while the temple and its sacrifices and destruction are featured in various letters, including petitions for rebuilding the temple (Cowley No. 30, etc.).

3. *Social Documents.* Under this head come a long series of legal scripts—marriage* contracts, an adoption,* a manumission (release from slavery), and a series of "conveyances" of property (sale, gift, etc.). Contacts with OT legal usage and language are slight. Both bodies of data are parts of a larger and variegated whole—the multifold legal traditions of the Ancient Near East that lasted millennia.

4. *Others.* Quite a variety of letters exists, along with lists of names, grain accounts, and a command to repair a boat. These provide useful incidental background on special topics and are especially valuable for the study of biblical Aramaic.

BIBLIOGRAPHY: A. E. Cowley, *Aramaic Papyri of the Fifth Century* B.C. (1923); E. G. Kraeling, *The Brooklyn Museum Aramaic Papyri* (1953); H. L. Ginsberg in *ANET* (1950, 1955, 1968); R. Yaron, *Law of the Aramaic Papyri* (1961); K. A. Kitchen in D. J. Wiseman et al., *Notes on Some Problems in the Book of Daniel* (1965); B. Porter, *Archives from Elephantine* (1968). KAK

EL-FARA. See TIRZAH.

EL-FUL, TELL. See TELL EL-FUL.

EL-HUSN, TELL. See BETH SHAN.

ELIEZER (ē li ā′ zər; Heb. אֱלִיעֶזֶר, *'elî'zer*). The fifteenth-century B.C. Nuzi* tablets elucidate Semite adoption* customs. A childless couple would adopt a son to ease their old age and provide proper burial. He would be the heir, failing the birth of a natural son subsequent to his adoption.

Alalakh* Tablet 16, which is contemporary with the Nuzi documents, mentions the same custom. Ilimilimma makes Tulpuri his "father," who, in return for his property when he dies, requires Ilimilimma's support while he lives. Although it is possible that Tulpuri was using this method to gain royal patronage, it reflects the custom as described in the Nuzi tablets. The custom is relevant to Abraham's prayer in Gen 15:2–3 concerning Eliezer, his chief servant.

Alalakh Tablet 16 also makes it clear that the father had the right to choose his heir though he might pass over, in the process, older children. Early Assyria, Ras Shamra (see UGARIT), and Nuzi had the same custom. For example, Alalakh Tablet 92 states in a marriage contract between Irihalpa and Naidu: "If Naidu does not give birth to a son (then) the daughter of his brother Iwassura shall be given (to Irihalpa as wife) . . . if (another wife) of Irihalpa gives birth to a son first and after that Naidu gives birth to a son, the son of Naidu alone shall be first-born."

The choice of Isaac and the promotion of Joseph over Reuben are thus illustrated (Gen 48:21–22). The practice also explains the promotion in status of Ephraim and Manasseh.*

BIBLIOGRAPHY: C. H. Gordon, *BA*, 3 (1940), 1–12.

EMB

EL-JEZER, TELL. See GEZER.

EL-JOF. See DUMAH.

EL-KHALIL. See HEBRON.

EL KHAMSA. See EMMAUS.

EL-MASKHUTA, TELL. See PITHOM.

EL-MISHRIFEH. See QATNA.

EL-MUTESELLIM (MITESSELIM), TELL. See MEGIDDO.

EL-OHEIMIR, TELL. See KISH.

ELOQUENT PEASANT. He is the chief character in an Egyptian work of fiction dating from the Ninth and Tenth Dynasties, the troubled times of the Intermediate period between the Old and Middle kingdoms. It tells of the peasant's protest to the pharaoh Akhtoy Nebkaure', whose name is known from only one other place. Some official of Egypt's* overwhelming bureaucracy had wronged the man, and his protests were so eloquent that he was at last brought to pharaoh so that his language could be enjoyed. In point of fact, it is so loaded with poetic verbiage and metaphor that it is almost impossible to translate adequately. It does, however, give a touch of common life such as the NT and the nonliterary papyri* provide. The text was popular in later ages,

and copies and fragments are abundant.

BIBLIOGRAPHY: A. H. Gardiner, "The Story of the Eloquent Peasant," *JEA*, 9 (1923), 5ff.; *Berlin Papyrus* 3023 and 3025.

WW

ELOTH. See ELATH.

EL-PARAN. See ELATH.

EL QARIE. See ABU GHOSH.

EL QUBEIBEH. See EMMAUS.

EL QUDEIRAT, AIN. See AIN EL-QUDEIRAT.

ELTEKEH (el te′kə; Heb. אֶלְתְּקֵא, *elt^eqē′*). A city* of Dan's* inheritance, later Levitical (Josh 19:44; 21:23). Sennacherib,* in his annals of 701–702 B.C., mentions the place (as Altaku) along with Timnah,* among his conquests (Chicago Cylinder 3.6; Taylor Cylinder 2.82, 83). In 701 B.C. there was a significant confrontation there between Sennacherib and the allied forces of Ethiopia* and Egypt.* It has been identified with Khirbet el Muqannah, 40 km. (25 mi.) W of Jerusalem, but if this place proves to be Ekron,* Eltekeh remains in geographical obscurity.

BIBLIOGRAPHY: W. F. Albright, *BASOR*, 15 (1924), 8; D. D. Luckenbill, *The Annals of Sennacherib* (1924), 24.

EMB

EL YEHUDIYEH (YAHUDIYA). See LEONTOPOLIS.

EL-ZAKARIYEH. See AZEKAH.

EMBALMING. Although practiced in other cultures, it is the Egyptian custom of mummification (the term derived from the Persian-Arabic words for bitumen*), the earliest known, that is referred to in the OT. The art of preserving the body after death was not employed in Palestine, as the many tombs and graves excavated there clearly demonstrate. Gen 50:2 and 26 state that both Jacob and Joseph* were embalmed in Egypt,* while v. 3 gives the period of embalming as forty days and of mourning as seventy days.

At that time, about 1700 B.C., the Egyptians had not established a uniform method of mummification and, in fact, never were completely successful in their aim of preserving the body. The practice almost certainly owes its origin to the natural preservation of corpses buried in the hot, dry sand, which acted as a drying agent, in the predynastic period (pre-3000 B.C.). When burial in tombs, intended to help conserve the body, led to putrefaction, many attempts were made to counter this, including the tight wrapping of the body and even of the individual members. The first steps toward success, however, were the removal of the internal organs and the use of natron to conserve them and the body.

The basic dehydration process was established by the New Kingdom era (1570–1085 B.C.), reaching a peak in the twenty-second Dynasty (935–730 B.C.) and declining thereafter. First, following an early

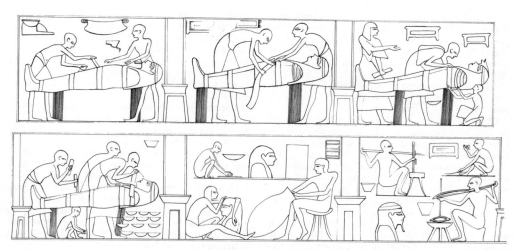

Drawings from painting on tomb of Amen-em-Opet (1350-1200 B.C.) at Thebes showing process of mummification. Courtesy The British Library.

ritual involving a flint knife* and the flight of the priest using it, an incision was made in the left side for the removal of the viscera, excluding the heart, while the brains were removed through the nostrils by a hooked instrument. The body was then packed in dry natron for about forty days, contrary to earlier claims that it was immersed in a natron solution. Natron, a drying agent, is a combination of salts— sodium carbonate, sodium bicarbonate, sodium sulphate, and common salt* in varying proportions— readily available in Egypt and having a purificatory significance which ordinary salt alone lacks. The process was similar to the salting of fish, the Greek term Ταριχεύω (taricheuō) being used by Herodotus both for the pickling of fish and for mummification, for which he describes three methods, all of which used natron (Herodotus 2.88f.,77).

Following the desiccation of the body, it was anointed with ointments,* spices, and resin before being wrapped in bandages and sheets, in an attempt to restore the body to its normal proportions. The body cavity had already been packed with resin-impregnated linen* or other materials.

Preparation of the corpse took place in a temporary structure known as the "House of Purification" or the "House of Stench." A special table of wood* or stone, or as in Tutankhamen's* case apparently a series of polished limestone blocks, was provided for the manipulation of the body during the embalming.

The whole process, as two papyri* of the Greco-Roman period and two inscriptions of the fourteenth century B.C. record, took seventy days, thirty of which were for the wrapping process and accompanying rituals. Gen 50, therefore, notes correctly the times involved. Finally, the mummy was placed in one or more coffins for the burial rites.

Special care was accorded the heart because of its supposed role in the judgment before Osiris,* the god of the dead. "Heart scarabs*" were placed over the breast, many of which bore engraved instructions

for the heart not to witness against the deceased. The viscera were usually stored in four canopic jars* in a natron solution, in later times with the lids representing the four sons of Horus, the protective deities. As the natron and other items used in preparation of the body were regarded as unclean, they were not placed in the tomb, but caches have been found nearby containing these because of their close association with the body.

With certain exceptions, such as the bulls of Memphis,* mummification of animals was rare before the Greco-Roman period.

References in Scripture to the use of spices (2 Chron 16:14, King Asa; John 19:34–40, Jesus) and the wrapping of the body in linen cloth* are not indications of a form of embalmment but are merely ceremonial preparations for burial.

BIBLIOGRAPHY: P. Montet, *Everyday Life in Egypt* (1958), 300–30; L. Cottrell, *Life Under the Pharaohs* (1960), 221–36; B. Mertz, *Temples, Tombs and Hieroglyphs* (1964), 64–113; M. R. Wilson, *ZPEB*, 2 (1975), 297–98.   GGG

EMMAUS (e má əs; Gr. Ἐμμαοῦς, *Emmaus*). A Judean village mentioned once in the NT (Luke 24:13), where it is stated that the place was 60 stadia (c. 11 km., or 7 mi.) from Jerusalem* (according to such MS evidence as P75 [early third century], B, etc.; some other MSS, as Sinaiticus, read 160 stadia [c. 29 km., or 18 mi.]). But since the direction from Jerusalem is not given, there is difficulty in determining its exact location.

Two unlikely locations toward the S from Jerusalem which have been conjectured as Emmaus are el Khamsa (over 60 stadia SW of Jerusalem) and Artas, S of Bethlehem* where Roman baths were found.

Another unlikely site, Abu Ghosh,* also known as Kiryat el 'Enab, located about 14.5 km. (9 mi.) W of Jerusalem, has been thought by some to have been NT Emmaus. A Crusader church was built here over a Roman fort that contains an inscription indicating that part of the Roman Legion X was stationed at the place. Also conjectured is modern Kaloniyeh, 6.4 km. (4 mi.) W of Jerusalem, which is identified with an Emmaus at which Vespasian* is said to have settled eight hundred soldiers (cf. Josep. *War* 7.6.6).

According to the MSS evidence, the two main sites best considered for NT Emmaus are el Qubeibeh and 'Amwas.

El Qubeibeh, 11 km. (7 mi.) NW of Jerusalem and beyond Nebi Samwil,* goes back to the times of the Crusaders, who found there a Roman fort, Castellum Emmaus. In the late nineteenth century the Franciscans who built a church there found remains of a Crusader basilica,* with evidence within of what might have been a Byzantine* church (or a Roman house*). Further excavation in 1943 revealed a first-century A.D. village nearby.

The modern town of 'Amwas (or, Imwas), which preserves in its Arabic form the name Emmaus, is c. 32 km. (20 mi.) WNW of Jerusalem. After the Roman destruction of Jerusalem, this Emmaus had its name changed to Nicopolis. Although Eusebius (*Onom.*, 90) identifies this village with that of Luke 24:13, some have thought it to be too far away. Excavations begun here by the Dominicans in 1875 were finished in 1924–30. There were found a small twelfth-century Crusader church, a small basilica dating from the fifth or sixth century A.D., a large basilica (with nave, two aisles, and three apses*) dated from the third to the sixth centuries, and a house of either the second–third or fifth century A.D.. There were also found a baptistry* and mosaics* featuring birds and plants.

BIBLIOGRAPHY: F.-M. Abel, "La distance de Jerusalem a Emmaus," *RB*, 34 (1925), 347–67; L.-H. Vincent and F.-M. Abel, *Emmaüs sa basilique et son historie* (1932); Antonine De Guglielmo, "Emmaus," *CBQ*, 3 (1941), 293–301; J. Finegan, *The Archaeology of the NT* (1969), 177–80; M. Avi-Yonah, *The Holy Land* (1966), 84, 95, 115, 159; The *PECS*, R. Stillwell (1976), 302; *EAEHL*, ed. M. Avi-Yonah, 2 (1976), 362–64.   WHM

EN GEDI (en ged'ē; Heb. עֵין־גֶּדִי, 'ên-geḏi). "The name, meaning spring of the goat," (Arab. 'Ain Jidi) designated an important source of fresh water on the W of the Dead Sea,* about 56 km. (35 mi.) SE of Jerusalem,* which has maintained its ancient name up to modern times. It is near the modern settlement of 'Ain Jidi. The location of the oasis made it possible to produce semitropical vegetation such as palm trees, vineyards, and balsam (cf. Song of Songs 1:14; Ecclus. 24:14). One of the discoveries of the large Israeli program of excavation in 1961, in which the Hebrew University cooperated with the Israel Exploration Society was evidence of a perfume industry based on the balsam tree. The balsam, as both Pliny and Josephus say, was common in the area. En Gedi was occupied in the Early Bronze Age by Amorites,* who were conquered in the time of Abram by a Mesopotamian* coalition headed by Chedorlaomer (Gen 14:7–9). At that time En Gedi was known as Hazazon-tamar. In the conquest period the area was included in the barren regions of Judah.* David hid there from Saul's pursuit (1 Sam 23:29; 24:1–22), and in the time of Jehoshaphat it was a rallying point for the Moabite,* Ammonite,* and Meunite armies prior to the conflict at the Ascent of Ziz (2 Chron 20:2). In his vision Ezekiel saw fishermen* plying their trade in the Dead Sea* from En Gedi to En Eglaim (Ezek 47:10).

Excavation has been fairly continuous from 1949, but it was the campaigns of the early sixties which sorted out occupation levels from Josiah to Nebuchadnezzar.* The place was revived as an active settlement on the return from Exile, and it enjoyed some measure of prosperity in Persian days. Jar handles marked "Yehud," the Persian province of Yehudah (Judah), date from this time. Remains, in fact, date from the fourth millennium B.C. up to early Byzantine* times. Considerable fortifications, dating from Hellenistic and Hasmonean times, must have been a prominent feature of the ancient oasis and religious center in NT days.

BIBLIOGRAPHY: V. R. Gold, *IDB*, 2, 101–2.
                                              RKH and EMB

EN GEV (en gev'; Heb. עֵין־גֵּב, 'ên-geḇ). A large Israeli kibbutz* under the Golan* Heights almost opposite Tiberias.* It is near the site of interesting prehistoric remains which throw some light on the Neolithic* inhabitants of Palestine, the fauna of the land (gazelles, roedeer, wild oxen*), on the first fishermen* of Galilee,* and the climate of early Palestine. *See* TIBERIAS.

                                              EMB

ENGINEERING. The precision of ancient engineering may be illustrated from many archaeological sites, and the technical processes involved are not always easy to describe. The Parthenon in Athens,* with its inward-tilted columns and optical adjustments to the whole complex of its lines (a sophisticated feature, incidentally, to be found first in the ziggurat* of Ur*); the acoustic perfection of the Greek theater* (esp. Delphi and Epidaurus); the alignments and construction of the pyramids*—these are only a few examples of advanced technology. The achievement of prefabricated stonework in Solomon's* Temple* cannot be dismissed as an idle boast. 1 Kings 6:7 asserts that the stone was cut at some distance from the site and fitted into place after being transported to the building site, so that no irreverent noise of axe or hammer should be heard. There must have been exact plans and specifications for the varied shapes and sizes of stone.

Tunneling was another example of engineering precision. 2 Kings 20:20 mentions the Siloam Tunnel (*see* SILOAM INSCRIPTION) and a point about its inscription (W. F. Albright, *ANET*, 321), which describes how the two crews of tunnelers met in the middle, is sometimes overlooked. It is not a royal boast, but a rough piece of work, perhaps suggested by the engineer in charge. The impression is that the feat was not unique, but it does presuppose some accurate measuring devices and techniques. Megiddo* has an earlier example of such tunneled water conduits. It consists of a large vertical shaft from the ground level inside the city wall* to the level of the spring outside the fortifications. A horizontal shaft was then begun from both ends and met in the solid rock with an error of only a couple of feet (C. C. McCown, *The Ladder of Progress in Palestine* [1943], 183–85). The date of this tunnel is not precisely known, but it is Solomon's work (Kathleen Kenyon, *Royal Cities of the O.T.* [1971], 67–68, 102–3). "At a time when no compasses, theodolites or other scientific instruments to measure direction and levels were available, it is a most remarkable achievement," says Dr. Kenyon. "It also indicates a very considerable control of manpower, for to hew a way through solid rock for this depth and distance, and to carry out and dispose of the residual debris, was a colossal undertaking."

Other tunnels are known, showing that this method of quarrying* was common, but the evidence for accurate measurement is not so clear. For example, in Gezer,* excavated in the early 1900s by R. A. Macalister, there was found a tunnel cut 29 m. (95 ft.) through the solid rock down to a cave* in which is a spring. It is slanting and about 7 m. (23 ft.) high by 4 m. (13 ft.) wide, with eighty steps allowing descent to the waters. It allows direct access to the spring rather than simply conducting the water elsewhere. It is impressive engineering for the Bronze Age.

BIBLIOGRAPHY: R. A. Macalister, *The Excavation of Gezer, 1902–5 and 1907–9*, 1-4 (1912).   EMB

ENGINES. *See* MACHINES.

ENMISHPAT. *See* KADESH BARNEA.

EN-NASBETH, TELL. *See* MIZPAH.

ENROLLMENT. *See* QUIRINIUS.

ENTABLATURE. In architecture, a wall or beam spanning the capitals* of the columns and supporting structures above it.

ENUMA ELISH. *See* CREATION EPIC, BABYLONIAN.

EPHESUS (ef'ə sus; Gr. Ἔφεσος, *Ephesos*). Immense contributions to the history of Ephesus have come from a full century of archaeology. The city,* located at the mouth of the Cayster, between the Sea and the Koressos Mountains of Asia Minor,* was in a state of decline in NT times. It had been bypassed by the major movements of trade, and it was outside the main streams of history and was living on the reputation which great cities like Athens* acquired. It was still, as coinage shows, "the Landing Place," the port at which the proconsul of Asia landed, and where he had his seat, but the harborworks, far from the sea, show the process of silting and destruction (*see* ECOLOGY) which has demoted Ephesus from her primacy in trade, before the city's name appears in the history of the church. The city had its tourist and pilgrim trade. The great temple of Artemis* stood

there, and the dependence of the city on this trade, and such myths as "the Thing which Fell from Heaven," explains the story of the riot told so vividly in Acts 19. Charles Seltman, it may be noted, advances with some plausibility the thesis that a curious stone object, at present in the Liverpool City Museum, is actually this cult object—perhaps a piece of meteoric stone (*Riot in Ephesus* [1958], 86–87). The image of Artemis herself, known from figurines and coins,* is a strangely ornamented female figure, with a shrine and a basket on her head, a veil decorated with beasts, long necklaces, embroidered sleeves, legs sheathed with empaneled animals and with multiple breasts, or, as some say, an apron covered with clusters of grapes or dates, a symbol of Artemis's role as the nourishing spirit of nature. The temple was a shrine of great splendor which endured until the Goths sacked the city in A.D. 263. The ruins are located in a marsh one and a half miles NE of the city. The temple is widely represented on coins, but from such sources it is impossible to verify the ancient report that it was four times the size of Athens's Parthenon. A fine boulevard ran through the city from the harbor to Mount Pion, where the great theater* was cut into the natural hillside. The curve of the slope at that point provided the Greek engineers* with their basic structure. It is a magnificent memorial of the great days of Ephesus and a vivid framework for Acts 19, for it is still virtually in use, seating 24,000 spectators. The agora* is SW of the theater, though the present ruins are largely from the third century when the marketplace was reconstructed. The remains of a Neronian hall are, however, distinguishable on the E side, apparently destroyed by an earthquake. The S gate,* according to a fragmentary inscription, was built about 4 B.C. in honor of Augustus* and is the best preserved. The marketplace has proved epigraphically* rich. A colossal statue of the notorious enemy of the Christians, Domitian,* last of the Flavians, has been found in fragments. It was evidently the main piece of a temple of the Caesar-cult. The basilica* of John, whose later life and death was associated with Ephesus, can be traced back through various buildings and restorations to subterranean grave chambers under a mausoleum, which could give substance to the tradition that John was buried there. On the NE slope of Panajir Dagh, into which the theater is cut, was the so-called Catacomb of the Seven Sleepers. The Christian interest attaching to this well-known legend is an inscription of the fifth century, the date when the seven youths gave their final testimony. A rectangular stone, once the base of a statue* of Artemis, and on which a cross had been set, bore an inscription: "Demeas has removed the deceitful image of the 'demon' Artemis and put in its place this sign which drives idols away, to the praise of God and the cross, the victorious, imperishable symbol of Christ."

BIBLIOGRAPHY: W. M. Ramsay, *The Letters to the Seven Churches* (1904); A. H. M. Jones, *Cities in the Eastern Provinces* (1937); E. M. Blaiklock, *The Christian in Pagan Society* (1951); id., *The Cities of the NT* (1965); id., *ZPEB*, 2 (1975), 324–32.   EMB

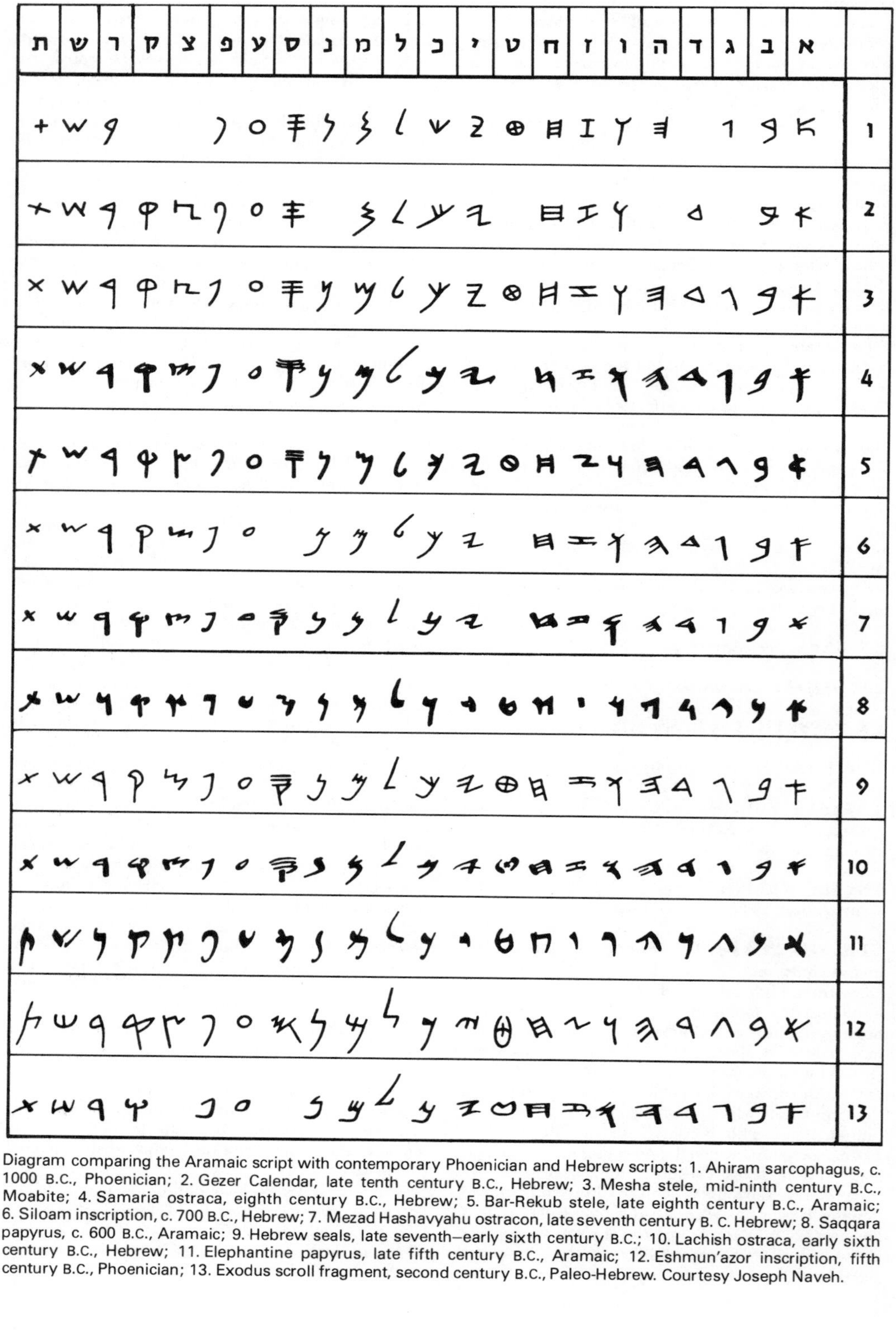
א ב ג ד ה ו ז ח ט י כ ל מ נ ס ע פ צ ק ר ש ת
1
2
3
4
5
6
7
8
9
10
11
12
13

Diagram comparing the Aramaic script with contemporary Phoenician and Hebrew scripts: 1. Ahiram sarcophagus, c. 1000 B.C., Phoenician; 2. Gezer Calendar, late tenth century B.C., Hebrew; 3. Mesha stele, mid-ninth century B.C., Moabite; 4. Samaria ostraca, eighth century B.C., Hebrew; 5. Bar-Rekub stele, late eighth century B.C., Aramaic; 6. Siloam inscription, c. 700 B.C., Hebrew; 7. Mezad Hashavyahu ostracon, late seventh century B. C. Hebrew; 8. Saqqara papyrus, c. 600 B.C., Aramaic; 9. Hebrew seals, late seventh–early sixth century B.C.; 10. Lachish ostraca, early sixth century B.C., Hebrew; 11. Elephantine papyrus, late fifth century B.C., Aramaic; 12. Eshmun'azor inscription, fifth century B.C., Phoenician; 13. Exodus scroll fragment, second century B.C., Paleo-Hebrew. Courtesy Joseph Naveh.

EPHRATH. See BETHLEHEM.

EPIGRAPHY, GENERAL. The study of epigraphy (lit. "upon-writing") is the study of inscriptions in durable materials such as stone or bronze;* in this it contrasts with paleography.* It is usually divided into Greek, Hebrew, Latin* epigraphy, etc., each of these divisions being a specialized study on its own. It has in general two branches, the paleographical and the historical.

Paleography studies such matters as the form and shape of letters, the use of abbreviations, and the direction of writing.* Inscriptions that read from right to left are said to be retrograde. Some of the earliest Greek inscriptions are of this type. The term *boustrophedon* (lit. "ox-turning") refers to a later style in which the lines of writing go alternately from left to right and from right to left throughout the inscription. In Greek this style was abandoned during the sixth century B.C. in favor of a standardized left-to-right pattern. The term *stoichedon* (lit. "row by row") refers to the actual arrangement of letters on the stone: in the stoichedon style the letters form not only horizontal but also vertical lines, which means that every line contains an equal number of letters, each of which is written vertically beneath the corresponding one of the line above. The fact that the number of letters in the line is constant can be of great assistance to the epigraphist in restoring lost or damaged words in a stoichedon inscription.

In inscriptions, as on papyrus* or parchment,* styles of lettering change in the course of time, albeit slowly; and, as in the case of paleography, this fact can be used to help date an otherwise undated inscription. In the case of early Greek inscriptions, where the alphabetic script was still in its childhood, there is variation in the number of letters in the alphabet,* and this may give a useful clue not only to date but also to place of origin. Abbreviations are a natural space-saving device, and their study is also included in the paleographical branch of epigraphy.

The historical branch is concerned with the content of inscriptions. Such materials are classified by content, the broadest common distinction being between public and private inscriptions. Public inscriptions include all texts dealing with matters of state, such as treaties, decrees, public dedications, or public memorials. A feature of public inscriptions is their tendency to make considerable use of conventional formulae, and this known propensity sometimes enables epigraphists to restore large portions of public inscriptions which have been damaged or defaced. The reconstructed portions of the Gallio* inscription at Delphi are of this type. Private inscriptions include tombstones (the commonest type within this category) and a variety of legal documents such as property contracts or wills. These reveal a great deal about home life and social institutions in their own age. Indeed, it has been said of Greek inscriptions that "there is no aspect of Hellenic thought or speech, writing or action on which they do not throw valuable light" (*OCD*, "Epigraphy, Greek"). The content of an undated inscription will often help to date it if, for example, it refers to persons, events, or things

of which the date is already known from other sources.

It is the function of epigraphy in its widest sense to bring out all the historical, antiquarian, and linguistic significance of the inscriptions available for study. As new inscriptions are constantly being found, the study is never-ending; and the size and importance of the contribution which it makes to every aspect of our knowledge of the ancient world are great.

BIBLIOGRAPHY: A. G. Woodhead, *The Study of Greek Inscriptions*, 2nd ed. (1981).

WFR

EPIGRAPHY, HEBREW. As currently understood by Near Eastern scholars, epigraphy (*see* EPIGRAPHY, GENERAL) is concerned with the inscribed records of antiquity, the materials used in the process and the methods employed, the languages of the inscriptions, the type of writing* used and the relation between the two in such matters as spelling, along with the historical or social conditions which prompted the incidence of the particular material under study. Inscriptions occurred in both Mesopotamia* and Egypt* from an early period, but among the Hebrews they tended to be rather sparse, perhaps in an attempt to avoid the making of graven images which sometimes formed a part of Near Eastern inscriptional activity. Possibly the earliest epigraphic source connected with the growth of an alphabetic* linear script in Palestine is the "pseudo-hieroglyphic*" writing on a badly weathered stele* from Balu'ah in ancient Moab,* which may go back to about 2000 B.C.

Inscriptions recovered from the ancient Sinaitic turquoise mines in 1904 appear to be dated half a millennium later, at about 1500 B.C. According to Albright, who deciphered them, they contained an alphabetic script used by Semitic slaves* who were working the mines* in the time of Thutmose III. Potsherds (*see* SHARDS) found at Gezer,* Lachish,* Hazor,* and Beth Shemesh* were also inscribed in a similar type of script. A plaque recovered from Shechem* bore a form of writing that may be at least a century older.

Early Canaanite* alphabetic inscriptions from the thirteenth and twelfth centuries B.C. have been recovered from Byblos (*see* GEBAL), Beth Shemesh, and Lachish. In biblical tradition Joshua was credited with writing a copy of the law of Moses on the altar* stones on Mount Ebal (cf. Deut 27:2; Josh 8:32), and this material, following Egyptian practice, would be inscribed on a plaster* surface placed on the bare rock. This inscription, along with other similar contemporary literary efforts, has not survived. Iron Age* epigraphy is represented by an inscription on the tomb of Ahiram* of Byblos, about 1000 B.C., where the script was written horizontally from right to left, as it had been for at least a millennium.

The tenth-century B.C. limestone tablet from Gezer, dealing with a succession of agricultural* activities, is one of the earliest Hebrew inscriptions, while about 850 B.C. the activities of Omri* of Israel were reflected in the celebrated Moabite Stone,* erected by King Mesha of Moab.* The thirty-four lines of well-cut inscription illustrate the use of Hebrew script on a monument outside Canaan proper and at the same time provide the only significant inscription in the Moabite dialect. From the time of Hezekiah came the Siloam Inscription,* about 701 B.C., describing the construction of a water conduit (cf. 2 Kings 20:20; 2 Chron 32:2–4, 30), while from roughly the same period and location emerged the tomb inscription of the Royal Steward. The Samaritan Ostraca,* written between about 778 and 770 B.C., show the development of the cursive style of writing, whereas the Uzziah plaque and the Hezir tomb inscription at Jerusalem,* both occurring at the beginning of the Christian era, illustrate clearly the transition to monumental square Hebrew character.

BIBLIOGRAPHY: I. J. Gelb, *A Study of Writing* (1952); G. R. Driver, *Semitic Writing from Pictograph to Alphabet* (1954 ed.); A. Murtonen, *Early Semitic* (1967).

RKH

EPIPHANEIA. See ECBATANA.

EPISCOPOS (e pis' ko poi; Gr., Ἐπίσκοπος, *episkopos*). A Greek term meaning "overseer" or "guardian" and used in the NT as a synonym for *presbyteroi* (cf. Acts 20:17, 28; Titus 1:5–7), who were the leaders of the NT church (cf. Acts 14:23; Phil 1:1).

In nonbiblical Greek contexts prior to, during, and after NT times, *episkopos* was used of gods and of persons having a definite function or fixed office within a group. This shows up both in literature (cf. Hom. 2. 22. 254f.) and archaeologically in inscriptions, papyri,* and coins.* In a second-century A.D. inscription the Furies, as *episkopoi*, are used to threaten those who molest graves;* (*IG* 12. 9, 1179); a διαμόνιον (*daimonion*, "divinity") also has the role of *episkopos*, according to a second-century B.C. papyrus (*P. Par.* 63, Col. IX, 47ff.). In education, an *episkopos* was a tutor (Plato *Leg.* 795d).

In ancient times *episkopos* was used to describe both state officials, and local officers of religious and nonreligious societies. In fifth- and fourth-century B.C. Athens* *episkopoi* (state officials) were supervisors chosen by lot from Athenian candidates and sent out to the cities of subject members of the Attic League. They had to deal with public order and exercised some judicial powers. The inscriptions from Erythrae (*IG* 1.10,11) show the Athenian *episkopoi* as civil officials involved in the arrangements for the new constitution set up at Erythrae and also involved in appointing the first assembly under the constitution. State officials in Egypt* (*P. Petr.* III, No. 36a, 17; third century B.C.) are seen as discharging judicial functions, and a coin from Claudius's* time calls the officer in charge of the Ephesian mint an *episkopos* and uses the term four times.

The term *episkopos* is more commonly used for local officers of societies. At Rhodes* such *episkopoi* are listed as civic officials along with prytanes and praetors (*IG* 12,1,49,42ff.). Uses of the term in cultic contexts are illustrated by a Rhodian inscription (*IG* 12.1,731) where an *episkopos* holds responsibility with others for the maintenance of the Apollo

sanctuary at Rhodes. A cultic society on the island of Thera instructs two *episkopoi* to invest money donated for the deity Anthister (*IG* 12.3, 329; second century B.C.).

The verb *episkopeō* may be used, as it is in a Syrian inscription (A.D. 253) in Canata (Waddington 2412f.) to indicate supervision of the construction of a public building. Such supervision possibly entailed also the control of the construction money in the case of three *episkopoi* mentioned in a Der'at inscription (Ditt.*Or*, 2.614). In another inscription from Syria, *episkopoi* are said to control the temple funds (Waddington 1911, 1989, 1990) while in still another the city magistrate has *episkopē* supervision over the building of an aqueduct and a temple of Athena (Waddington 2298, 2308). Christian bishops mentioned on building inscriptions after the fourth century A.D. are not to be understood as functioning in the same capacity as these overseers just mentioned.

The question of whether the title "overseer" is of Jewish origin arises from a study of the word *mebaqqer* in the Damascus Document (published 1910) where the term means the overseer or inspector of membership, discipline, and finances in the camp. *Mebaqqer* also recurs in the Dead Sea Scrolls* from Qumran* (Manual of Discipline 6.12–20; cf. *CDC* 9.18–22; 13.7–19; 14.11–13; 15.8,14) and seems to be comparable to the steward (Ἐπιμελητής, *epimelētēs*) of the Essenes (Jos. *War* 2.8,3).

BIBLIOGRAPHY: W. H. Waddington, *Inscriptions Grecques et Latines de la Syrie* (1870); Ditt. *Or*; Ditt. *SIG*; *Syria*, Publications of the Princeton Univ. Archaeological Expeditions to Syria (1904, 1905, 1909); M. H. Shepherd, Jr., "Bishop," *IDB*, A–D (1962) 441–43; H. W. Beyer, "Ἐπίσκοπος" *TDNT* (1964), 599–622; L. Morris, *Ministers of God* (1964); D. G. Stewart, *ZPEB*, 1 (1975), 617–20.

WHM

EPONYM. A term applied to a person giving his name to a place or people; also the name itself.

ERASTUS (e ras'tus; Gr. Ἔραστος, *Erastos*). It seems unlikely that the considerable person (the *aerarius civitatis*) mentioned in Rom 16:23 as the "director of public works" (*oikonomos*) of Corinth* was the Erastus of Acts 19:22 and 2 Tim 4:20. Some light is thrown, perhaps, on the historicity of this member of the Corinthian church by an inscription dated in the second half of the first century and naming one Erastus as an official who paved a street. He was an aedile. The words run: "Erastus pro aedilit[at]e s[ua] p[ecunia] stravit": Erastus, by virtue of his aedileship, had this paved at his own expense. The inscription was discovered by the American School of Classical Studies (*ASCSA, Ancient Corinth. A Guide to the Excavations* [1954], 74). Erastus was not an uncommon name, and there is no guarantee that the friend of Rom 16:23 and the paver of the Corinthian mall were identical.

BIBLIOGRAPHY: *BS* 88 (1931), 342–46; Emilio Gabba, *Inscrizioni Greche e Latine per lo Studio della Bibbia* (1958), 109–10.

EMB

ERECH. Erech in the Bible (Gen 10:10; Ezek 4:9), otherwise known as Uruk, was one of the most important of the ancient Sumerian* city-states. It is identified with a group of mounds called Warka located about 281 km. (175 mi.) SE of Baghdad. It has been excavated from 1912 on by the German Orient Society and has been taken as a type site for the Uruk period (fourth millennium B.C.).

The pottery* at Uruk was a distinctive red ware as well as some black and grey; both types were made on a genuine potter's wheel and were polished but unpainted.

The earliest example of a ziggurat* (a holy tower or mound) was discovered at Uruk; at its top was the White Temple with its original whitewash still visible. The White Temple had replaced six earlier temples.

Cylinder seals* first developed at Uruk. These were rolled over moist clay* objects as a seal* of ownership and were in use for about three thousand years after this time all over the ancient world. Two square plaster* tablets found in the White Temple had impressions of cylinder seals.

The people at Uruk invented a pictographic* script writing illustrated by two thin clay tablets from the Red Temple. This marks the beginning of the Proto-literate period, and the writing* gradually develops into cuneiform* as the pictures are reduced to more abstract symbols.

The first stone construction also comes from Uruk in the form of a small section of limestone pavement. The city was not quite as prominent after the rise of the Third Dynasty of Ur,* but Uruk continued to be occupied down to the Parthian period, having a life span of over four thousand years.

BIBLIOGRAPHY: A. Falkenstein, *Archaische Texte aus Uruk* (1936); *CAH*, 1, Part 1, 328 passim; *CAH*, 1, Part 2, 41 passim; L. L. Walker, *ZPEB*, 5 (1975), 339–40.

BCC

ERIDU (er' i dū). A Sumerian* city-state located c. 161 km. (100 mi.) NW of Basra and some 8 km. (5 mi.) due S of ancient Ur.* It was mentioned in the Sumerian King List, a chronological compilation of early rulers which was apparently made during the celebrated Third Dynasty of Ur (c. 2070–1960 B.C.). The List commenced with a statement about kingship being "lowered from heaven" and placed in Eridu* under Alulim and Alalgar, who reigned for 28,800 and 36,000 years respectively, according to the List. These and six other kings from Badtibira, Larak, Sippar,* and Shuruppak* ruled for exaggerated lengths of time before a devastating flood terminated activities in southern Sumer for a time. The numbers in the King List are reminiscent of those which recorded the ten patriarchs from Adam to Noah (Gen 5), although the principles of computation are unknown in both instances. Subsequently an unnamed deity founded five cities which included a rebuilt Eridu. An early temple excavated there indicated that Enki, a water-god, was the tutelary deity in postdiluvian times. Since Enki was known as the "Lord of Wisdom," Eridu was evidently the ancient seat of Sumerian culture.

BIBLIOGRAPHY: S. N. Kramer, *The Sumerians: Their History, Culture and Character* (1963), 31 passim; *CAH*, 1, Part 1, 60 passim; id., Part 2, 72 passim.

RKH

ER-RAHMAN. *See* HEBRON.

ER-RETABA, TELL. *See* PITHOM.

ESARHADDON (e sər had' ən; Heb. אֵסַר־חַדֹּן, *ēsarḥadon*). Ruler of Assyria and Babylonia, 681–669 B.C., succeeding his father Sennacherib,* of whom he was a younger son when Sennacherib was murdered (2 Kings 19:37; Isa 37:38). He had been designated crown prince some months earlier and speedily avenged his father's death by pursuing the murderers, apparently his brothers, into southern Armenia. He quelled rebellious movements in Nineveh* and Asshur and moved his forces to protect his northern frontier against such marauders as the Cimmerians. Civil strife in southern Babylonia led him to campaign against the Elamites,* and some Babylonians were later deported to Samaria* (cf. Ezra 4:2). When Egypt* tried to foment rebellion in Palestine and Syria, Esarhaddon marched against Sidon* and Kundi in 677 B.C. and the following year made vassals of the Edomite, Moabite,* and Ammonite* rulers. His first attack on Egypt in 675 B.C. was of limited success, but eventually he defeated Pharaoh Taharqa and compelled him to flee to Upper Egypt. Esarhaddon tried to rule Egypt from Memphis* using native officials, a policy which produced indifferent results. From Palestine he secured help in rebuilding cities in Babylonia and Assyria, and cuneiform* letters mentioning tribute received from Palestinian states can be assigned to this period. The visit of Manasseh* to Babylon (2 Chron 33:11) is probably connected with this phase of Esarhaddon's activities. In 672 B.C. his younger son Ashurbanipal* was made crown prince, and Esarhaddon's brother Shamash-shumukin became ruler of Babylon. A group of treaties with the Medes,* recovered from Calah* (Nimrud), recorded their assent to this arrangement. The Egyptians rebelled in 670 B.C., and Esarhaddon was on his way to crush the uprising when he fell ill at Haran* and died in 669 B.C., being succeeded by Ashurbanipal.

The story of his dynamic reign is almost completely reconstructed from archaeological sources. His vassal treaties were discovered at Nimrud in 1955 and deal with the appointment of the king's sons as crown princes of Assyria and Babylonia in May 672 B.C., together with the oath of allegiance sworn to them. The usual comminations, or denunciations, are included in the text: "May Sarpanitu who gives name and seed, destroy your name and seed . . . ; May Adad, controller of the waters of heaven and earth dry up your ponds. . . ."

BIBLIOGRAPHY: R. Borger, *Die Inschriften Asarhaddons, Königs von Assyrien* (1950); D. J. Wiseman, *Iraq*, 20 (1958), 1–99; id., *ZPEB*, 2 (1975), 340–42; *ARAB*, 2, 199–289.

RKH

ESCHATOLOGY. This word, signifying "doctrines of last things," reflects an expectation common to many cultures and religions. The basic ingredient appears to be the enlarging of locally-experienced catastrophes into cosmic proportions and their interpretation in terms of human activity, whether negatively as punishment for wickedness or positively for the renewal of society, particularly in an "endtime." Pagan eschatological traditions began in Sumeria,* where early kingship as listed on the Weld-Blundell prism was interrupted abruptly by a flood that inundated Shuruppak* and its environs. It is not clear how these traditions relate to the biblical account of the Deluge, but Sumerian texts accounted for the occurrence by stating that the deities had regretted creating mankind and had decided that drowning would be a suitable fate for turbulent humanity. This general tradition was a feature of Near Eastern literature, surviving for many centuries in differing versions. Eschatological elements prominent in the Babylonian Gilgamesh Epic* include the crossing of the waters of death, an experience of the underworld, and the revelation to Gilgamesh of a plot by the gods to drown mankind. The Genesis flood narrative shows clearly that the catastrophe was prompted by moral considerations that culminated in judgment upon the contemporaries of Noah. In ancient Egypt* all life was interpreted eschatologically, and from his earliest years an individual was in a state of continual preparation for what would happen immediately after death. The Coffin Texts* and many Egyptian gnomic writings indicate that persons would be judged at their decease according to the morality of the life lived here, while temple murals frequently depicted in harrowing detail the supposed ceremonies of judgment after death.

Archaeology has little to say on biblical eschatology before the days of the first Christians and their archaeological relics. The ancient Hebrews, though possessing no detailed doctrine of life after death, still looked forward to a time when God would redeem the righteous in judgment and cleanse the earth of evil (cf. Amos 5:18; Joel 1:15; 3:14–18; Isa 2:2ff.; Zech 14:9). NT writers saw the historic Christ as an eschatological figure appearing in the "last days" (cf. Heb 1:2), though the divine kingdom still remained to be consummated (cf. Mark 10:25,30; Eph 1:21 et al.). While hanging on the cross, Jesus gave some support to a concept of paradise current in His day (cf. Luke 23:43; Rev 2:7). Archaeological inscriptions in Latin,* relevant to the eschatological theme of the Apocalypse, using the numerical values of letters reflect the enigmatic enumeration of the beast in Rev 13:18, while the wicked woman of that same book may perhaps be illustrated by a coin* from the time of Vespasian,* representing Rome* as a woman seated on the seven hills of the city.

RKH

ESHKALON. See ASHKELON.

ESHNUNNA (esh nōō′nə). This site, the modern Tell Asmar, is located about 42 km. (26 mi.) NE of Baghdad. Excavations indicate that the ancient city* was founded in the Jemdet Nasr* period of predynastic Babylonia. At Early Dynastic levels a small square temple was unearthed which contained stone statues* of the fertility god Abu and his consort, the mother-goddess. These very early examples of Sumerian* statuary are finely executed, and may well represent the beginnings of what later became a stereotyped artistic form. The statue of Abu was about 76 cm. (30 in.) high and depicted the deity wearing a full beard. The mother-goddess was attired in a calf-length cloak that passed under the right arm and fastened on the left shoulder. Abu wore a skirt that reached just below the knees and had a pleated decorative border all around. From the same site came a gypsum statue of a participant in worship, again depicted wearing a flowing beard. The eyeballs were made of a yellow substance set in bitumen* and gave the statue a recognizably devout appearance.

Until the time when the Elamites* and Amorites* began to invade the cities of Sumer, Eshnunna enjoyed political independence. But about 1960 B.C., when Ur* fell to the Elamites, a man named Kirikiri took over control of Eshnunna. This state of affairs did not last for long, however, for when Hammurabi* defeated Rim-Sin, the last king of Larsa,* he absorbed Sumer into his burgeoning Semitic empire, along with Elam, Mari,* and Eshnunna.

BIBLIOGRAPHY: S. N. Kramer, *The Sumerians: Their History, Culture, and Character* (1963), 72; *CAH*, 1, part 1, 198, 209–10, 372.

RKH

ES-SEBA, TELL. See BEERSHEBA.

ESSENES (es sēnz′). Our knowledge of this sect of Judaism, belonging to the first centuries B.C. and A.D., is still largely dependent upon literary evidence. Philo of Alexandria* concerned himself principally with their religious life and their social customs (*Quod Omnis Probus Liber Sit*, 11; *Hypoth.*, 11), and Pliny the Elder, writing a few years after the fall of Jerusalem* in A.D. 70, gives more on the latter (*HN*, 5.15). Josephus, however, has provided the most factual and detailed information, particularly on the Essene initiation rites and the spread of the Essene movement throughout Judea* in both monastic communities and the urban centers (Jos. *War* 2.8,2 seq.; Jos. *Antiq*. 18.1.5).

The discovery of the Dead Sea Scrolls* and the excavations at Khirbet Qumran* in 1951–55 have been adduced by many scholars as evidence for the nature of Essene life. The community known to Pliny the Elder lived on the W side of the Dead Sea* above En Gedi, which corresponds to the Qumran site. More important still, the ground plan of the Qumran settlement is in harmony with the descriptions given in the literary accounts of the Essene way of life.

Early investigators, following Dupont-Sommer, treated Khirbet Qumran as an Essene settlement and interpreted the scrolls as illuminating Essene life more fully and accurately than any of the ancient writers had done. However, a careful comparison of the Qumran material with what Philo, Pliny, and Josephus had to say about the Essenes reveals significant differences between the two groups. Whereas the Essenes were pacifists, the Qumran sectaries were decidedly militaristic, as their War Scroll quite clearly shows. The Qumran group also included women, which was contrary to predominant Essene practice. Whereas the latter gave great prominence to sabbath observance, the Qumran literature gave no specific instructions on this matter. Thus if the monastic group at Qumran can be called "Essene" at all, it can only be in the most general of senses.

BIBLIOGRAPHY: F. F. Bruce, *Second Thoughts on the Dead Sea Scrolls* (1956), 110–24; H. Sérouya, *Les Esséniens* (1959); H. Kosmala, *Hebräer-Essener-Christen* (1959); R. K. Harrison, *The Dead Sea Scrolls* (1961), 94–99; W. S. LaSor, *The Dead Sea Scrolls and the New Testament* (1972), 131–41.

BFH

ES-SULTAN. *See* TELL ES-SULTAN.

ETAM (ē'tam; Heb. עֵיטָם, 'ēṭām). 1. A place in the Judean* uplands between Tekoa and Bethlehem.* Rehoboam fortified it as an outpost when Israel became an independent kingdom (2 Chron 11:6; cf. LXX of Josh 15:59; 1 Chron 4:3). It is usually identified with Khirbet el-Hoh, about 10.5 km. (6½ mi.) SSW of Jerusalem.* The site is probably the Etam referred to by Josephus (Jos. *Antiq*. 8.7.3) as having fine gardens* and an ample water supply. Perhaps the latter was tapped in Hellenistic times by the reservoirs and the aqueduct* which supplied Jerusalem with water (cf. Jos. *Antiq*. 18.3.2; Jos. *War* 2.9.4).

2. A Simeonite village (1 Chron 4:32) of uncertain location that may be identified with 1. above, or with 'Aitum, a place about 18 km. (11 mi.) WSW of Hebron.*

3. A rocky cleft in which Samson* hid from the Philistines* (Judg 15:8,11). A W Judean location is indicated, but it is impossible to identify it with certainty.

BIBLIOGRAPHY: L. H. Grollenberg, *Atlas of the Bible*, trans. J. M. H. Reid and H. H. Rowley (1956), 149; H. J. Kraus, *ZDPV*, 72 (1956), 152–62; R. C. Ridall, *ZPEB*, 2 (1975), 380.

RKH

ETANA (e tan'ə). A legendary king of Kish.* According to the Sumerian King List, which describes him as one who "consolidated all lands" and who lived for 1,560 years, he was the thirteenth postdiluvian king. Other sources describe him as the first king after the Flood.*

Etana is the subject of a myth that is preserved in the Old Babylonian, Middle Assyrian, and Neo-Assyrian fragments. The myth first describes the conflict between an eagle* and a serpent,* who had been partners. The serpent has placed the eagle in a pit to punish him for his treachery.

Etana, who is childless, aids the eagle. In gratitude, the eagle offers to bear Etana on his back so that he may secure the plant of birth. The myth describes in vivid passages the ascent skyward as the

earth and sea below continue to decrease to the size of a furrow and a bread basket. Panic-stricken, Etana loses his grip and plummets downward. Just at this critical juncture, our extant fragments fail us.

Etana did have a son called Balikh, so his mission must have been successful. A fragment published in 1969 describes how the plant of birth was used to ease the labor pangs of Etana's wife.

The Gilgamesh Epic* (7.4.49) and the Pushkin Elegy refer to Etana's presence in the nether world. His ascent to heaven was a favorite subject of cylinder seals from as early as the Old Akkadian period (twenty-third century B.C.).

BIBLIOGRAPHY: O. R. Gurney, "A Bilingual Text Concerning Etana," *JRAS* (1935), 459–66; T. Jacobsen, *The Sumerian King List* (1939), 80–81; *ANET* (1955), 114–18, 265; S. N. Kramer, "Death and Nether World according to the Sumerian Literary Texts," *Iraq*, 22 (1960), 59–68; A. L. Oppenheim, *Ancient Mesopotamia* (1964), 266–67; J. V. K. Wilson, "Some Contributions to the Legend of Etana," *Iraq*, 30 (1969), 8–17; *ANE*, 517; W. W. Hallo and W. K. Simpson, *The Ancient Near East* (1971), 40–41.

EY

ETHIOPIA (ē thĭ ō' pĭ ə; כּוּשׁ, Heb. kūš; LXX, Αἰθιοπία, Aithiopia; Heb. from Egyp. *Kš*).

1. *Definitions*. The name Ethiopia is now borne by the E African empire known also as Abyssinia. But in biblical times, the Gr. term "Ethiopia" was equivalent to the land of Cush (Egyp. and Heb.), now termed Nubia*—an area along the middle Nile from its first to fourth cataracts in S Egypt* and N Sudan (N part, now flooded by Lake Nasser behind the new High Dam near Aswan*).

2. *History and OT Relevance*. In the Pyramid Age (third millennium B.C.), the pharaohs sent expeditions S to trade for central African products and set up a base at Buhen near the second cataract. In the Middle Kingdom, Egypt occupied Nubia beyond that point, losing control in the Hyksos* period. In the New Kingdom (c. 1550–1070 B.C.), Nubia as far as the fourth cataract was incorporated entirely within the Egyptian Empire, partly colonized, and its gold* mines, quarries,* and trade routes fully exploited. The pharaoh ruled it through a "viceroy of Nubia." After the Empire, Nubia was again lost to Egypt. There arose an independent Nubian kingdom ruled by princes imitating pharaonic culture and constituting a "shadow Egypt." Thus, Egypt lapsing into political chaos in the eighth century B.C., Nubian kings intervened in Egypt in the persons of Piankhy (c. 730 B.C.) and Shabako, who founded the Twenty-fifth Dynasty there from c. 715 B.C. Most famed king of this line was Tirhakah, who was involved with Hezekiah against Assyria in 701 B.C. But the Nubian kings were better temple-builders than soldiers. After the sack of Thebes* by Assyria (664 B.C.) and the rise of the northern Twenty-sixth Dynasty, the rule of Nubian kings was confined to Nubia, developing eventually into the kingdom of Meroe. From this realm came the eunuch of Queen Candace (Acts 8:27),

who was met by Philip after leaving Jerusalem.* Candace is the title borne by the influential queen-consorts of that kingdom; the identity of the particular Candace whose minister features in Acts remains uncertain. Thirteen centuries earlier, Moses' Cushite wife, perhaps a Nubian he had married in Egypt, was the object of family contention (Num 12:1).

BIBLIOGRAPHY: W. Y. Adams, "Post-Pharaonic Nubia in the Light of Archaeology, I–III," *JEA*, 50 (1964), 102–20; 51 (1965), 160–78; 52 (1966), 147–62; W. B. Emery, *Egypt in Nubia* (1965); P. L. Shinnie, *Meroe* (1967).

KAK

ETHNARCH. See ROMAN GOVERNMENT, ADMINISTRATION OF PROVINCES.

ET-TAWIL. See AI.

ET TELL. See AI; BETHSAIDA.

EVIL-MERODACH (ē' vəl mâr' ə dak; Heb. אֱוִיל מְרֹדַךְ *'ewil merōdak*; LXX Εὐιαλμαρωδέκ *euialma-rōdek*; Akkad. *Amēl-Marduk*, "The Man of Marduk"). The son of Nebuchadnezzar,* who reigned briefly after his father's death in October 562 B.C., until his own death in August 560.

According to Berossus as cited in Josephus (Jos. Apion 1.146) Evil-Merodach after an arbitrary and licentious reign was assassinated by his brother-in-law, Neriglissar.

According to the Bible (2 Kings 25:27–30; Jer 52:31–34), Evil-Merodach in his first regnal year (561) released the Judean* king Jehoiachin* from imprisonment after thirty-six years of captivity and treated him kindly.

BIBLIOGRAPHY: E. Weidner, "Jojachin, König von Juda, in babylonischen Keilschrifttexten," in *Mélanges Syriens offerts à M. René Dussaud*, 2 (1939), 923–35; W. F. Albright, "King Jehoiachin in Exile," *BA*, 5 (1942), 49–55; *DOTT*, 84–86; R. H. Sack, *Amēl-Marduk 562–560 B.C.* (1970); W. H. Brownlee, "Aftermath of the Fall of Judah according to Ezekiel," *JBL*, 89 (1970), 393–404; H. Orlinsky, *Understanding the Bible through History and Archaeology* (1972), 210–12.

EY

EXECRATION TEXTS. Egyptian* rulers in the Middle Kingdom period (c. 1990–1790 B.C.) sought to control their enemies by writing curses against them on pottery* bowls or clay* figurines and breaking these in a temple to release the curses. Two groups of such texts indicate that the Amorites* were present in Palestine and Syria early in the second millennium B.C. The Berlin texts, 1925–1875 B.C., purchased in Thebes* and written on pottery bowls, list some thirty Palestinian and Syrian chieftains but few towns. The Brussels texts, from fifty to a hundred years later, inscribed on figurines were obtained from Saqqara and list more towns and fewer chieftains, thus suggesting that nomadic Amorites were settling

down. These were the forerunners of the Amorites in later Palestine (Num 21:21f.; Josh 10:5).

BIBLIOGRAPHY: *ANET* (1955), 328–29.

JAT

EXEDRA. An open room or vestibule, either in a gymnasium or private house, where conversation could be held.

EXILE, JUDEAN. Archaeological excavations in Palestine and Babylonia have furnished a good deal of evidence for the historicity of OT narratives dealing with the Judean exile. Apart from circumstantial accounts in Kings, Ezekiel, and Ezra, the considerable depopulation of the land can be verified archaeologically. It was obviously a case of a much larger transfer of population than the removal of a few leaders of the community. W. F. Albright points out that a considerable number of occupied sites and fortress towns have been excavated with some thoroughness in Judah,* and others examined sufficiently to determine the date of their final occupation. "The results," he writes, "are uniform and conclusive: many towns were destroyed at the beginning of the sixth century B.C. and never again occupied; others were destroyed at that time and partly reoccupied at some later date; still others were destroyed and reoccupied after a long period of abandonment, marked by a sharp change of stratum and by intervening indications of use for non-urban purposes" (*Archaeology of Palestine* [1960 ed.], 141–42). In fact, there is not one identifiable case of a town of Judah which was in continuous occupation over the period of the exile. Bethel* forms a sort of "control" for this conclusion. It was sited just outside the northern boundary of Judah and so did not suffer with its neighbors. It was occupied continuously over the entire period.

War casualties in shocking numbers must have also depopulated the land. Assyrian records commonly boasted of human massacre, and there is no reason to suppose that Babylonian warfare was more sparing of human life. The tensions of society in the southern kingdom which were increased by the realization that the Babylonian assault on Jerusalem in 597 B.C. could not be resisted successfully were reflected clearly in the Lachish* ostraca (*see* LACHISH LETTERS). For example, Letter VI contained a complaint by an official in Jerusalem about the effects of utterances by the ruling coterie, claiming that they were undermining morale in Judah (W. F. Albright, *ANET*, 321–22). The fierceness of the assault on Lachish has been revealed by the debris of excavation, from which was recovered a seal which was inscribed: "Gedaliah, who is over the house." This was evidently the man appointed governor by Nebuchadnezzar* II to administer the southern kingdom after 597 B.C., and who was subsequently murdered (2 Kings 25:22; Jer 41:1–3).

No evidence of the extent of death and deportation suffered by the population survives from this period, but Babylon* was eager to leave no Egyptian sphere of influence or intrigue along the road from their land to the Nile.

There is evidence enough from the Babylonian

records for the presence in the capital city of the deported Jews.* The ration lists of Evil-Merodach* for the family of King Jehoiachin* (or Yaukin, as he is called in the texts) have survived (cf. *BA*, 5 [1942], 49–55), and there are references, among others, to deportees from Ashkelon.* The records cover the tenth to the fifteenth year of Nebuchadnezzar's reign, i.e., 595 to 570 B.C., the period of his depopulation policy.

Cyrus* II initiated the contrary policy of a strong buffer area, and as his records show, "gathered together all the exiles and returned them to their homelands," encouraging the reestablishment of cohesive religions ("Cyrus Cylinder,*" *ANET*, 315). This is an important archaeological contribution to the historicity of Ezra.

BIBLIOGRAPHY: H. G. May, *AJSL*, 56 (1939), 146ff.; O. Tufnell et al., *Lachish III (Tell ed-Duweir) The Iron Age (Text)*, (1953), 21–23, 331–39; *DOTT*, 212–17.

EMB

EXODUS, THE. See ISRAEL STELE.

EXORCISM. This was an important part of medical* therapy in the Ancient Near East because of the demonic theory of disease. The priest-physicians of Mesopotamia* employed a wide variety of therapeutic substances, the efficacy of which was supplemented by the use of invocations to Ea and Marduk, and by a variety of incantations.* Part of an Assyrian incantation intended for use by the sufferer himself runs: "Be off. Be off. Go away. Your wickedness like smoke rises heavenward. By the life of Shamash the Mighty [i.e., the Sun god], in truth, be exorcised. By the life of Asaraludu [i.e., Marduk], the gods' priest of incantations, be exorcised . . . From my body, in truth, be parted."

The name of Jesus was used in rituals of exorcism by certain renegade Jews* in Ephesus* (Acts 19:13–17). A third-century papyrus* quotes the Lord's name in just such an invocation. Olive* branches were to be placed before the possessed. The exorcist was to stand behind him and say, "Hail, spirit of Abraham; hail, spirit of Isaac; hail, spirit of Jacob; Jesus the Christ, the holy one, the spirit—drive forth the devil from this man. O Demon, whoever you are by the God Sabarbathioth [repeated four times], come out demon . . . I chain you with adamantine chains not to be loosed. I give you over to black chaos in utter destruction."

BIBLIOGRAPHY: R. C. Thompson, *The Devils and Evil Spirits of Babylonia* (1903–4); id., *Semitic Magic* (1908); J. A. Montgomery, *Aramaic Incantation Texts from Nippur* (1913), 9, 26, 36; E. Reiner, *Šurpu. A Collection of Sumerian and Akkadian Incantations* (1958); I. Mendelsohn, *IDB*, 2, 691.

EMB

EZION GEBER (ēz′yon gē′ bər; Heb. עֶצְיוֹן גֶּבֶר, ʿeṣyôn geḇer). This settlement is first mentioned as a stopping place during Israel's wilderness journeyings (Num 33:35–36; Deut 2:8). It apparently was near the Gulf of Aqaba, the E arm of the Red

Sea* (cf. Num 21:4). During the time of David, this site was evidently under Edomite* control, and it was from this people that David took the territory (cf. 2 Sam 8:13–14; 1 Chron 18:12–13). The site was later developed during the reign of Solomon* (1 Kings 9:26–28). With Phoenician* help, Solomon was able to develop a seagoing fleet of some significance. This extended his trade program beyond the borders of Israel as far as Ophir.* There is no further information on this fleet after the death of Solomon. It may be that its service was concluded during the turbulent years of the division of the kingdom and the rise of Edom* against Israel (cf. 1 Kings 11:14–22, 25; 2 Kings 8:20–22; 2 Chron 21:8–10). It is also possible that the fleet was either destroyed or came under the control of Pharaoh Shishak* when he swept through Judah* and Israel about 918 B.C. Another possibility is that the fleet was destroyed by a storm much like that during the days of Jehoshaphat. In the early ninth century B.C. King Jehoshaphat attempted to reinitiate seagoing trade with the use of such large vessels at this port (2 Chron 20:35–37). This venture, however, was unsuccessful because of a violent storm bringing about the destruction of the fleet. About fifty years later Amaziah recaptured Edom (1 Kings 14:7) and enabled his son Azariah to rebuild the city,* which was then called Elath.* Archaeological evidence, along with a comparison of Deut 2:8 with 1 Kings 9:26, indicates that Elath was indeed the later name of Ezion Geber.

The initial identification of Tell el-Kheleifeh with the biblical site of Ezion Geber was first suggested by Fritz Frank in 1934. This small low mound is located approximately in the center of the N shoreline of the Gulf of Aqaba. It is about 457 m. (500 yd.) from the actual shoreline today and, according to Nelson Glueck, may have been some 274 m. (300 yd.) or more distant several millennia ago. However, it does not appear that there has been any significant change in the shoreline since the site was first occupied in the tenth century B.C. That Tell el-Kheleifeh is the site of Ezion Geber is also supported from the biblical description which locates Ezion Geber "near Elath" (1 Kings 9:26).

The excavations conducted at Tell el-Kheleifeh by Glueck indicated that the site contained five major occupational periods with numerous phases extending from the tenth century B.C. to the fourth century B.C. Unfortunately, excavations to virgin soil did not produce any materials which could be associated with the fifteenth-century B.C. exodus and the presence of Edomites in the area. Period I at the site is approximately the Solomonic period beginning about 1000 B.C. and continuing for some years after Solomon's reign. One of the more interesting discoveries of Period I was a large building which measured 12 m. by 12 m. (40 ft. by 40 ft.) and was divided into three small rooms to the N and three large rectangular rooms to the S. All of the walls of this building had two rows of tile set into them, one row above the other. The lower row of tile* was about .9 to 1.2 m. (3 to 4 ft.) above the floor level and went completely through the walls, while the upper row of tiles led into a channel within the wall. Glueck had initially

Seal signet ring, c. eighth century B.C., with inscription "Belonging to Jotham." Underneath the inscription is a horned ram and in front of it a bellows or metal bar. Found at Tell el-Kheleifeh. Courtesy Smithsonian Institution Photo No. 489A.

concluded that the building was a copper refinery* or smelter and that the apertures served as flue-holes during Period I of this building. He concluded that strong winds from the NW would enter into the furnace* rooms of the structure, thus providing a natural draft to fan the flames. This viewpoint, however, was abandoned by Glueck in favor of an alternate suggestion on the part of Beno Rothenberg. It was pointed out by Rothenberg that there was a noticeable absence of great amounts of slag which seems strange if this building was indeed a large smelting place. Also it was observed that there were numerous analogies to this kind of construction, both inside and outside Palestine. The apertures, it turned out, resulted from the decay and/or burning of wood* beams laid across the width of the walls for bonding or anchoring purposes. Examples of this kind of construction of mud-brick walls have been found at Sendschirli, Boghazköy,* Tell Ta 'Yinat,* Tell Halaf, and also at Troy* and Knossos (see BA, 28.3 [1965], 73). The general conclusion is that the building was used as a storehouse* or granary.* This conclusion, however, does not mean that the site was not used at all for metallurgical* activities during the time of Solomon and later. The small amount of slag at the site is explained as being the indication of a difference in metallurgical operation as compared to other sites in Wadi Arabah in which great quantities of slag have been found. It was Glueck's speculation that Tell el-Kheleifeh was utilized mainly to remelt the globules of copper ore obtained through several metallurgical processes in the Wadi Arabah smelting sites.

The ingots would be shaped in such a way as to prepare them for manufacturing or shipping purposes. This process, therefore, would have produced little or no slag.

Period II is characterized by a completely new series of massive fortification walls made of mud brick. The system became a double-walled system with regularly spaced insets and offsets, often parallel to the earlier outer wall of the enclosure, strengthened by a glacis* built of brick laid in a crisscross fashion for additional strength, as opposed to the header-stretcher method used elsewhere in walls of buildings at this time. The new outer mud-brick fortification consisted of a large inner wall and a smaller outer wall with a dry moat between the walls. The inner wall stood to a height of about 7.6 m. (25 ft.) and was 4.6 m. (15 ft.) thick at the base, including the glacis. The wall itself was about 2.3 to 2.7 m. (7½ to 9 ft.) thick. The outer wall stood to a height of 3 m. (10 ft.) and was about 1 m. (3 ft.) thick plus a glacis similarly constructed as the inner one. The total fortified complex covered an area of about .6 ha. (1½ a.) and was entered by one of three gates.* Significant discoveries from Period II included the bones of a man, his camel,* and bowls with bones of a fish, a bird, and a small animal. These may have been remnants of a funerary* meal for the deceased or perhaps an offering to his god. This burial was discovered in a large mastaba*-like grave* located between the two walls of the main enclosure. Period II at Ezion Geber probably represents a reconstruction of the site by Jehoshaphat of Judah. Period II occupation at the site was ended by a great fire, as was the case in Period I. It is interesting that after the time of Jehoshaphat the site is no longer mentioned in biblical literature.

Period III at Ezion Geber has been tentatively connected with the time of Amaziah (Uzziah) and his son Jotham. Since Amaziah changed the name of the Edomite capital, Sela, to Joktheel (2 Kings 14:7; 2 Chron 26:1–2), it is possible that he also changed the name of Ezion Geber to Elath. Period III fortifications of the site were basically the same as those previously used. The ninth-century gateway was modified by walling up the entrances to the two sets of facing guardrooms, producing a casemate* effect. The third gate was narrowed by placing a mud-brick pillar against both piers. The courtyard, which was previously open, was now filled with dwellings. A ring with a copper-enclosed seal* bearing the inscription lytm ("belonging to Jotham") with a ram depicted on it was discovered in the debris of this period. It is speculated that the ring may have belonged to the governor of Elath during the administration of Jotham.

Period IV at Ezion Geber is considered to have been basically under Edomite control. The fortification walls were reused from the previous two periods. Ezion Geber IV had at least three phases. The first of these extended down into the seventh century B.C., coming to an end perhaps during the expedition of Ashurbanipal* against Egypt in 663 B.C. A number of stamped jar handles were found in these levels. Four large stone jars were found in a storeroom of a later phase of city IV, one of which contained a sweet smelling resin. A clay* plaque bearing a crude representation of the pregnant mother goddess was found in another house. A number of foundation offerings were found beneath the walls of the houses consisting of pots with fruit, fish, and fowl. Jar handles with a stamp coming from the early phases of Period IV had an Edomite inscription reading, "Belonging to Qausanal, the servant of the king." The first part of the name is associated with a well-known Edomite deity, Qaus or Qos which subsequently became a Nabataean* deity. The Babylonian conquest under Nebuchadnezzar* brought an end to Edomite rule over Elath of Period IV. It was destroyed before the end of the sixth century B.C.

Period V represented a new industrial city built over Period IV. It probably existed under Persian administration. That trade was conducted on extensive scale with Arabia* is evidenced by Aramaic* ostraca* including wine* receipts. Shards* of fifth- to fourth-century B.C. black-glazed Greek pottery* indicate widespread trade with the western and northern Mediterranean world. With the end of Period V comes the end of specific archaeological information concerning the history of the site. It is not impossible, of course, that earlier and later settlements were there of a more transitory nature. The use of numerous perishable materials by seminomadic peoples makes archaeological determination of population density most difficult. Ezion Geber, however, is a fine example of an ancient seaport with its multi-faceted interests.

See ELATH.

BIBLIOGRAPHY: N. Glueck, *BASOR*, 71 (1938), 3–18; 72 (1938), 243; 75 (1939), 8–22; 79 (1940), 2–18; 80 (1940), 3–10; 82 (1941), 3–11; 85 (1942), 8–9; 159 (1960), 11–14; 163 (1961), 18–22; id., *The Other Side of the Jordon* (1940), 50–113; id., *Smithsonian Report for 1941*, 453–78; id., *Rivers in the Desert* (1959), 153–68; B. Mazar, *VTs*, 4 (1957), 57–66; Nelson Glueck, "The Negev," *BA*, 22 (1959), 89–94; N. Avigad, *BASOR*, 163 (1961), 18–22; B. Rothenberg, *PEQ*, 94 (1962), 44–56; N. Glueck, *BA*, 28 (1965), 70–87; W. B. Coker, *ZPEB*, 2 (1975), 468–70.

JJD

EZ-ZIB. *See* ACCO.

F

FAIENCE. A glazed* paste manufactured mostly from quartz sand and applied to earthenware, which is so named.

FAKHARIYA, TELL. See GOZAN.

FAMINE. Times of dearth and the drought that occasions them (Gen 12:10; 26:1; Acts 11:28) are part of the meteorological history of the earth. Undulations in the radioactivity of the sun are sometimes the cause, and archaeology can relate the movements of Pueblo and Navajo Indian cultures in the western United States to the periodic onset of drought, a record accurately recorded in the rings of the redwood trees (see DENDROCHRONOLOGY). It is traceable through living trees, timber in the cliff dwellings of the tribes, and even charcoal.* According to a theory of Professor Rhys Carpenter, the shift of rain belts by variations in the Sahara and cyclical desiccation of large areas in temperate and tropical zones, account for the unexplained collapse of the Mycenaean* civilization in the twelfth century B.C. and the difficulties of Byzantium from A.D. 400 to 750. In the former case archaeology can establish the shifting of habitation to rainy slopes and the abandonment of important centers of habitation. Whether the drought in Jacob's and Elijah's day is to be explained thus is not clear, but periods of major change, according to Carpenter's theory, break up in a series of shorter periods of desiccation and famine.

Periodic droughts of the first century A.D. may have been man-made, and archaeology provides abundant evidence of the effects of deforestation (see ECOLOGY) in Asia Minor,* for example, the silted harbor of Ephesus.* A bas-relief* from the pyramid* causeway of Pharaoh Unis at Saqqara, dating about 2400 B.C., shows typical famine figures, a woman and two men, with ribs showing and emaciated limbs. They are probably Semites. A wall painting* of six centuries earlier shows a similarly emaciated herdsman leading three oxen* as a gift to Ukh-hotep. The Nile often cushioned Egypt* against the impact of drought.

BIBLIOGRAPHY: Rhys Carpenter, *Discontinuity in Greek Civilization* (1968); F. C. Hibben, *Treasure in the Dust* (1953), ch. 9.   EMB

FARA. See SHURUPPAK.

FARAH, TELL EL-. See TIRZAH.

FARMING. See AGRICULTURE.

FEINAN. See PUNON.

FELIX, ANTONIUS (fē'liks an tō'ni əs). Antonius Felix, a freedman of the Roman House of Claudius (Acts 23:23–24:27). It is a matter of some curiosity that no epigraphical (see EPIGRAPHY, GENERAL) information or archaeological comment has emerged on Felix's eight years in Samaria* and Judea* (A.D. 52 to 60). The recent and fragmentary Pilate inscription from Caesarea Maritima is practically the total of such information for the procurators of Palestine.

The main literary sources are Acts, Josephus, Tacitus, and Suetonius. The Emperor Claudius* made Felix, a brother of the influential freedman Pallas, procurator of Palestine in A.D. 52, an appointment which testifies to the pernicious influence such freedmen had in Claudius's court. Felix was probably a freedman of Antonia, the emperor's mother, his name thus being Antonius Felix. Felix married three royal women, one of whom was the granddaughter of Mark Antony and Cleopatra (Suetonius, *Claudius* 28). This marriage brought Felix into relationship with the court of Claudius. Another wife, the Jewish princess Drusilla, daughter of Agrippa I and sister of Agrippa II, had been married to Azizus, king of Emesa.

Tacitus (*Ann.* 12.54) in a bitterly hostile passage, relates that Felix and Cumanus governed for a while concurrently in Palestine, Felix over Judea and Samaria,* and Cumanus over Galilee.* But Josephus's account (Jos. *Antiq.* 20, 6.3 to 7.1; Jos. *War* 2.21.8) is preferable in stating that Felix succeeded Cumanus as procurator of Palestine. This chronological difficulty is one which archaeological and epigraphical studies eventually could resolve.

BIBLIOGRAPHY: E. Schürer, *A History of the Jewish People in the Time of Jesus Christ*, 1.2 (1891), 174–84; P. von Rohden, "Antonius," *PWRE*, 1.2 (1894), 2616–17; *OCD* (1968), 360; Jack Finegan, *The Archaeology of the New Testament* (1969), 80; E. M. Blaiklock, *ZPEB*, 2 (1975), 526–28.

WHM

FERMENTATION. This process involves the transformation of organic substances by a process of chemical change, accompanied generally by a degree of effervescence. The purpose is to break down complex material into simpler forms. Ordinary or alcoholic fermentation involves the conversion of certain kinds of sugar into alcohol and carbon dioxide and occurs whenever yeast is added to sugar solutions under appropriate conditions. While the starchy components of bread dough do not undergo alcoholic fermentation as such, they can be broken down into simpler substances which will ferment.

The principle of liquid fermentation was well known to the people of the Ancient Near East. The Sumerians* and Babylonians made a potent alcoholic drink from the sap of the palm tree, while, according to tablets found at Ur,* a form of beer was made by fermenting barley. Viticulture, employing the common grapevine *Vitis vinifera L.*, was first mentioned in the OT in connection with Ararat* (Gen 9:20), perhaps the original habitat of the plant. The vine also grew in Egypt,* and paintings* on the walls of tombs depicted the various stages of wine* making. The Egyptians, like the Philistines, also brewed beer from barley. In Palestine, the valleys of Eshcol and Sorek were notable, with En-gedi, for their high quality grapes and wines.

To produce fermentation in starch, a small amount of decomposing dough reserved from a previous batch of bread was added to "leaven" the lump. No fermenting agent other than sour dough was mentioned in the Bible, though by NT times a number of other substances were in vogue (cf. Pliny, *NH*, 18.16).

BIBLIOGRAPHY: R. J. Forbes, *Studies in Ancient Technology*, 3 (1965).

RKH

FERTILE CRESCENT. This name was given in 1916 by J. H. Breasted to a great alluvial tract in western Asia which forms a rough semicircle with its open side pointing toward the S. The western extremity is the SE corner of the Mediterranean Sea; the central area lies directly N of Arabia,* while the eastern end leads into the Persian Gulf. It constitutes the cultivable area between mountain and desert, likened by Breasted to the shores of some desert bay behind which the mountain ranges rise. The dry sands made this alluvial crescent all the more hospitable, and it is not without reason that the earliest cultures, with their abundant archaeological remains, were established along the waterways and communication lines of the region. This same phenomenon occurred outside the Fertile Crescent in connection with the early village cultures of the Indus Valley and the Neolithic* settlements along the Nile River. Toynbee's theories of the river origins of some major human cultures can be widely documented archaeologically. Even in the third millennium B.C. seminomadic peoples were moving back and forth along the length of the crescent, and at the beginning of the second millennium B.C. there were migrations of various kinds, some of which resulted in the formation of distinctive national groups such as the Hittites.* Ancient cities including Ur,* Mari,* Nuzi,* and Alalakh,* from which many Bronze Age texts and other artifacts* have been recovered, were prominent cultural centers in the Fertile Crescent through which a great many persons passed in their travels. Sumerians,* Akkadians,* Assyrians, Horites, Hittites, Mitanni,* and other peoples and groups made their home in or near the crescent, and their vast legacy of artifacts tells of the rise and fall of ancient empires in this alluvial cradle of humanity.

RKH

FESHKA, AIN. See AIN FESHKA.

FIBULA. An anatomical term describing the slender, outermost bone of the leg. In antiquity such animal bones served as pins, which were later copied in metal and shaped in the form of a safety pin. Generally made of bronze,* the fibula was used with draped garments. Some fibulae were made in one piece, others in two, and because of the many varieties in different areas, types of fibulae are often associated with specific districts and particular times. As a result, they are extremely useful in typological* dating.*

HWP

FILIBEDJIK. See PHILIPPI.

FISH, SIGN OF. See ACROSTICS.

FISHING; FISHERMEN. All Near Eastern nations were familiar with fishing as a means of food,* pleasure, or trade. From Neolithic* settlements at Deir Tasa in Upper Egypt,* as well as in other locations, there have been recovered primitive fishhooks made from shell or horn. Fishhooks made from bone have also been recovered from Natufian* deposits in Palestine. Bone fishhooks, of course, are common discoveries in archaeological sites from Europe to Polynesia, and iron* hooks of Solomon's* time, come from Ezion-Geber, and a very shapely bronze* hook was found at Gaza,* dating from the Middle Bronze Age (cf. Job 41:1; Isa 19:8; Amos 4:2; Hab 1:15; Matt 17:27).

As a sport, fishing was popular among the Egyptian royalty and upper classes, while the mere commercial aspects were illustrated as early as the Fourth Dynasty, where a tomb relief of Rahotep (c. 2500 B.C.) showed three fishermen engaged in lifting to the surface a net containing fish. A painting* from the tomb of Simut (fifteenth century B.C.) shows a well-dressed sportsman spearing fish in a papyrus* swamp with a two-pronged spear, plied from a raft of papyrus stems.

In the Amarna* Age the Phoenicians* developed fishing as a commercial enterprise and were also prominent in this activity during the post-Exilic period (Neh 13:16). The Tigris and Euphrates also contained fish, and these were valued highly as food supplements by the Babylonians and Assyrians. An eighth-century Assyrian relief shows line fishing. The fisherman, judging from the protruding tails of the fish in the basket on his back, had done well. A monument recovered from Nineveh* and dated in the sixth century B.C. showed an Assyrian fishing in a river and depositing his catch on the bank beside him.

Fishing occurred in the Nile (Isa 19:8), the Sea of Galilee* (Matt 4:18), and the Mediterranean (Neh 13:16), as well as in the smaller rivers, lakes, and marshes. The ancient Hebrews apparently did not fish for sport, and while the harpoon (Job 41:7) and the line and hook were used (Isa 19:8) when they needed food on a small scale, hand nets thrown into the water from land (Eccl 9:12) or dragnets slung

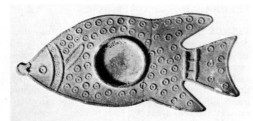

Flat clay fish plaque with circular "mirror" inlay found in fifth-century grave near Bet Govrin along with other Christian objects. The plaque is probably a Christian artifact. Note what appears to be a ladder in the tail of the fish. It has been suggested that the ladder was one of the instruments of the Passion. Courtesy Israel Dept. of Antiquities and Museums. Exhibited and photographed at Israel Museum, Jerusalem.

from boats (Matt 13:47; Luke 5:4–7) were favored commercially.

The symbol of a fish and the acrostic* ἰχθύς (ichthús) both of which have been recovered archaeologically, were popular in the early Christian church to remind believers of the need to be "fishers of men" under the lordship of Christ, Son of God, and Savior.

In the Church of Santa Maria Antiqua, which appropriated the Library of Augustus* in the Forum during the fifth century, Professor Boni discovered in 1901 a Christian sarcophagus* with two fishermen, stripped almost naked, drawing ashore a net full of fish.

BIBLIOGRAPHY: G. Dalman, *Arbeit und Sitte*, 6 (1939), 343–70.   RKH and EMB

FLAVIAN AMPHITHEATER. *See* COLOSSEUM.

FLAX. *See* CLOTH; LINEN.

FLOODING. Any devastating inundation of water, whether of short or more lengthy duration. Such flooding as resulted from the periodic rise of the Nile was in sharp contrast to the sudden, violent floods of Mesopotamia,* which often wrought enormous devastation. Once the surface of the land there had been inundated, the comparatively high water table could sustain a flood for a considerable period of time.

Flood traditions were part of the lore of numerous ancient peoples and were by no means confined to the inhabitants of Mesopotamia. Catastrophic deluges seem to have been a regular part of ancient Sumerian* life, however, and the tradition of a great flood, or a series of such inundations, became firmly established in the early dynastic period of Sumerian history. The Weld-Blundell prism, an ancient Sumerian King List which may have been compiled during the Third Dynasty of Ur* (c. 2070–1960 B.C.), recorded the names of the kings who reigned in Sumer before a great deluge disrupted society. This source indicates that Shuruppak* was inundated, along with Kish,* Eridu,* and other neighboring areas. The presence of a flood stratum at a tell* is usually thought of in terms of a clean clay* or alluvial

deposit, above and beneath which can be found the debris of other occupational levels.

Excavations at the Late Jemdet Nasr* levels at Shuruppak uncovered the presence of a large alluvial deposit, while at Kish a somewhat later flood left a 45.5-cm. (18-in.) layer of sediment a little above the Jemdet Nasr levels. At Ur, Woolley found an 8-foot thick water-laid clay deposit dating from the Middle Obeid period, which had undoubtedly been occasioned by a devastating flood. From Nippur,* a fragmentary tablet dated in the third millennium B.C. preserved an account of an inundation of major proportions, occasioned by angry Sumerian gods who wished to destroy mankind. Enka, the powerful water-deity, forewarned Ziusudra, a pious king-priest, of the impending disaster, enabling him to escape in a large boat from the worst effects of the flood. Precisely what relation this early deluge-tradition has to other similar sagas of antiquity, and to the Noachian flood in particular, is very hard to determine. Attempts to correlate the archaeological data from the various sites excavated to date has also proved difficult. The alluvial deposits at Ur and Kish have been shown to come from different periods, while the flood levels found at Shuruppak, Uruk, and Lagash* are not contemporary with the stratum at Ur. When Watelin excavated Kish he uncovered a number of alluvial layers, indicating the prevalence of floods in that part of Sumer. But at Tell-el-Obeid, about 6.4 km. (4 mi.) from Ur, no indications of water-laid strata were found during Woolley's activities at the site.

As remarked above, the precise relationship between these inundations and the one described in Genesis is extremely difficult to establish. However, the various sedimentary levels discovered to date show clearly that periodic inundations were an unfortunate feature of Mesopotamian life, and it may well be that more than one such local flood was being commemorated in the epics. Since the excavations have shown that not all Sumerian cities were equally flooded, some scholars believe the Noachian deluge may itself have been a comparatively localized inundation, drowning the world that was familiar to Noah and his family.

At Kish, Watelin discovered cylinder impressions of Gilgamesh (*see* GILGAMESH EPIC), the legendary hero of Babylonian epic narrative, at levels below the ones which Langdon had identified with the Genesis flood. Obviously the Babylonian flood story was already familiar to the inhabitants of Kish, making it an extremely ancient religious tradition in Mesopotamia. In the light of current evidence it is impossible to state with certainty the origin or interrelationship of either the Mesopotamian or Hebrew accounts of the deluge which was commemorated in their writings, or to relate the Genesis narrative to any specific archaeological level in Mesopotamia.

See ATRA-HASIS EPIC.

BIBLIOGRAPHY: *FLAP* (1946), 23–30; A. Heidel, *The Gilgamesh Epic and OT Parallels* (1946); R. K. Harrison, *OT Times* (1970), 45–47, 61–63.

RKH

Winery at Gibeon dating from eighth and seventh centuries B.C. The rock-cut cellars contained 9¾-gallon wine jars maintaining a constant temperature of 18°C. Reproduced by permission of The University Museum, University of Pennsylvania.

FLUORINE DATING. See DATING.

FOOD; FOOD PROCESSING. In the earliest phases of human existence (cf. Gen 1:29; 2:16) dietary items were predominantly of a vegetable and cereal nature. With the Fall came the necessity for manual labor, accompanied by a presumed diversity of dietary elements. Near Eastern archaeological discoveries at second-millennium B.C. levels have confirmed that cereals, bread, dairy products, and wine* were popular, along with lentil soup (cf. Gen 25:29–34), veal (Gen 18:6–8), fish, lamb, and game caught in the desert areas (Gen 27:3–4). Eighteenth-century B.C. texts from Mari* show that honey was a favorite food of the royalty and upper-class citizens, while pistachio nuts were deemed suitable gifts for kings (cf. Gen 43:11). Egyptian foods enjoyed by the Hebrews in captivity included abundant fish, onions, garlic, leeks, and cucumbers (Num 11:5).

Vegetables did not grow very readily in most parts of Palestine, hence the staple items of diet were grain, wine, and olive* oil (Deut 7:13 et al.). The latter was prepared either by means of a pestle and mortar* (Exod 27:20) or by using a large stone roller to produce a pulp that was then trodden out (Deut 33:24) or pressed still further. Stone presses hewn out of the solid rock have been discovered at Megiddo,* Taanach,* and Jerusalem.* The vine provided fresh grapes (Deut 23:24 et al.), raisins (1 Sam 25:18 et al.), unfermented grape juice (Joel 1:5 et al.), and wine itself. Acidulous wine ("vinegar") was diluted with water and used as a refreshing drink (Ruth 2:14; cf. Ps 69:21; Matt 27:34). In Mesopotamia,* Egypt,* and Philistia,* beer was a popular beverage, but the Hebrews preferred to drink wine. Figs were commonly used in the form of cakes, and the sycamore fig, which needed to be punctured in order to mature (Amos 7:14), was especially valued by the poor, for whom it was a staple item of diet.

The majority of people only ate meat occasionally, whether it was the fatted ox* (Prov 15:17) or the calf, kid, or lamb prepared for guests (cf. Judg 6:19; 2 Sam 12:4 et al.). The dietary laws of the Torah (Lev 11:1–23; Deut 14:3–21) specified clean and unclean foods and had hygienic as well as other considerations in view. In the Ancient Near East, food served to implement a bond of fellowship, as in covenant meals (cf. Gen 31:54; Josh 9:3–15 et al.). This concept reached new heights of symbolism in the Last Supper, where the bread and wine were employed by Christ to typify His broken body and shed blood (Matt 26:26–28 et al.).

See AGRICULTURE.

BIBLIOGRAPHY: H. N. and A. L. Moldenke, *Plants of the Bible* (1952); M. S. and J. L. Miller, *Encyclopedia of Bible Life* (1955), 199 seg.; J. P. Lewis, ZPEB, 2 (1975), 581–87.

RKH

FOOTSTOOL. Ancient footstools generally consisted of a low square or rectangular support for the feet of a person who was sitting upon an elevated seat such as a throne. In the early Hebrew monarchy Solomon's* throne had six steps and its own gold* footstool (2 Chron 9:18), and this is the only literal use of the term *kebhesh* in the OT. Footstools were popular among Egyptian* royalty.

The famous tomb of Tutankhamen* provided a tastefully carved footstool on which the enemies of Pharaoh were represented in stylized form, amid their double bows, prostrate beneath the monarch's feet. Semites with pointed beards and Africans were commonly presented in this way, symbolizing their subjection and the ruler's calm superiority.

A Theban tomb painting showed Pharaoh's enemies actually forming the royal footstool (cf. Ps 110:1).

Three Blacks, dressed identically, wore ostrich feathers in their hair, necklaces, bracelets, earrings, and short skirts. Two types of Syrians were shown: to the left was a bearded figure with a bald or shaved head and wearing a shawl over a long white garment. To the right the bearded figure wore a white band around black hair and was clothed in a long-sleeved garment which reached down to the ankles. The five figures were depicted kneeling with upstretched hands in a gesture of worshipful submission. They decorate the seat of the enthroned Amenhotep III (c. 1413–1377 B.C.).

See FURNITURE.

BIBLIOGRAPHY: Nina de Garis Davies and Norman de Garis Davies, *The Tombs of Menkheperrasonb*, etc. (1933), plates 41, 43; N. M. Davies and A. H. Gardiner, *Ancient Egyptian Paintings*, 2 (1936), plate 58; J. B. Pritchard, *BASOR*, 122 (1951), 36–41.

EMB

FOOTWASHING. The washing of feet was both necessary and desirable in the Ancient Near East and was one of the acts of hospitality preferred by a host to his guests. In the earlier phases of the custom it was the practice for water to be poured over the guests' feet, but at a later period built-in footwashing basins* began to be used.

W. F. Albright described a rectangular court by the western gate* of Tell Beit Mirsim (Debir*). This lime*-paved court gave access to six rooms similarly paved, each with a stout door. "Wall cupboards," he wrote, "a built-in basin for washing, and other conveniences suggested at once that this was the official guest-house of the pre-exilic town" (*Archaeology of Palestine*, [1960], 139–40). Portable footbaths also came into use, as illustrated by a specimen from Samaria, and these had a raised support for the foot in the middle (cf. Luke 7:44; John 13:2–11).

See ABLUTIONS.

BIBLIOGRAPHY: *AIs* (1965), 460.

EMB

FORTIFICATIONS. *See* CASEMATE WALLS; GLACIS; TOWERS; VALLUM; WALLS, CITY.

FORTRESS. *See* CASTLE.

FORUM. The marketplace of a Roman city* where the public assembled for business and sometimes heard judicial decisions handed down. It is equivalent to the Greek agora.*

FOSSE. *See* VALLUM.

FOUNDATION SACRIFICE. This term refers to one of the variant forms of human sacrifice familiar in the Ancient Near East. It was alluded to in Josh 6:26, where Joshua laid a curse on the man who attempted to rebuild Jericho* (Tell es-Sultan). If the poetic couplet reflected contemporary practices accurately, the first-born son alone was deemed a suitable foundation offering to the deity involved, who would then supply protection for the city in the future.

Near Eastern superstitions also required the sacrifice of a male child as a deposit under the foundation stones of city gates* if they were to be truly efficacious in warding off evil powers of hostile persons. To date, archaeological evidence has failed to support such practices at Jericho as those alluded to by Joshua, and the only child burial uncovered there by Garstang, in what he understood as a Neolithic* shrine, was of a nonsacrificial character. Similarly, Kathleen Kenyon failed to find foundation sacrifices at Jericho, although she recovered something quite similar from beneath a ruined temple that had apparently been built in the Early Bronze Age.

In 1 Kings 16:34 an attempt to rebuild Jericho in defiance of Joshua's curse was undertaken by Hiel of Bethuel, at a cost of his first-born and his youngest son, in fulfillment of Joshua's prediction. Precisely how these individuals died, however, is uncertain. Foundation sacrifices sometimes involved the walling-up of a living victim near the foundation stone instead of a religious ritual involving human sacrifice. While traditions of this kind were widespread in antiquity, they have proved far from easy to substantiate archaeologically.

BIBLIOGRAPHY: J. and J. B. E. Garstang, *The Story of Jericho* (1948), 62; K. M. Kenyon, *Digging up Jericho* (1957), 193f.

RKH

FRIEZE. In classical architecture a frieze is part of an entablature,* between the architrave* and the cornice,* often sculptured in bas-relief.*

FRUIT. *See* FOOD.

FUKHKHAR, TELL EL. *See* ACCO.

FUL, TELL EL-. *See* TELL EL-FUL.

FULLER; FULLERY. The fuller was one whose occupation it was to "full" (i.e., tread) cloth* in order to clean or thicken it. The agent for this purpose was "fuller's earth," a hydrous silicate of alumina.

At Pompeii* there was a guild of fullers (*fullones*) according to inscriptions from that city, and murals from the same town give realistic impressions of life and work in a fullery. All the fulleries so far discovered there were in private houses,* or houses adapted for the purpose. One belonged to Marcus Vesonius Primus, a councillor in office in A. D. 34. The vats for the fuller's earth (*creta fullonia*) and the vats for rinsing and scouring are visible. Similar equipment is in the considerable establishment of Lucius Veranius Hypsaeus in the Via di Mercurio of Pompeii. One of the tufa pillars used for drying contains a pictorial record of the washing, scouring, treading, carding, and brushing of the cloth and the final bleaching over basketwork spreaders where it was exposed to sulphur fumes.

BIBLIOGRAPHY: R. J. Forbes, *Studies in Ancient Technology*, 4 (1956), 81–89; Amedio Maiuri, *Pompeii* (1960), 120–27.

EMB

FUNERARY CUSTOMS, PALESTINIAN. For the Hebrews, death was invariably a traumatic emotional

"Shell" sarcophagus from the Jewish necropolis in Beth She'arim, second to fourth centuries A.D. *(See also second photo under* ALPHABET *and photos under* CYRUS; HESHBON; KIDRON; SARCOPHAGUS. *Courtesy Israel Government Press Office.*

experience, and grief was expressed in a variety of mourning customs which included weeping, the tearing of one's garments, and wearing sackcloth (Gen 37:34), as well as fasting, loosening the hair, and beating the breast. Pagan Canaanite* customs prohibited to Israel included lacerations* of the skin, the trimming of the beard and temple area of the head, and the offering of tithes to the deceased (cf. Deut 26:14). Mourning ceremonies could last for between seven (cf. Gen 50:10) and thirty (cf. Num 20:29f., Deut 34:8ff.) days, and during the monarchy in the case of certain notable persons the customs included the reciting of a poetic lament especially composed for the occasion (cf. 2 Sam 1:17ff.; 2 Chron 35:25). Professional mourners began to be employed by bereaved families in the pre-Exilic period (cf. Jer 9:17–20; Amos 5:16), and this practice was still in vogue in NT times (cf. Matt 9:23–24), when the normal period of mourning was seven days.

From the Middle Bronze Age onward, members of a family were interred in the same tomb (*see* GRAVE) whenever possible, as with Sarah, Abraham, Isaac, Rebekah, Leah, and Jacob (Gen 23:19; 25:9; 49:31; 50:13), all of whom were interred in the Cave of Machpelah in the Hebron* district. Where this was not possible, as in the case of Rachel (Gen 35:19f.), the deceased person was buried in a separate tomb. Because of climatic conditions and the belief that contact with the dead caused ceremonial defilement, it was the custom to dispose promptly of corpses. The embalming* of Jacob and Joseph* reflected Egyptian* practices, which involved removing the brain and viscera, soaking the corpse in natron, and wrapping it in linen* strips, a process which could take as long as seventy days.

Burial places could consist of caves,* tombs excavated from the rock of hillsides or some area under the house floor or courtyard. Ceremonies attending the burial usually included the bearing of the corpse on a bier rather than in a coffin (cf. 2 Sam 3:31), though precisely what other rituals took place in the

OT period cannot be determined. At all events, improper burial of any kind was to be deplored (cf. 1 Kings 13:22; Jer 16:6). In the Iron Age,* wealthy persons or families often had their own underground tombs dug into the slopes of hills. A courtyard entrance led to an inner chamber, the sides of which were lined with shelves cut out of the rock. Poor people would often be interred together in a small area of land in the vicinity of a city,* as with Jerusalem* (cf. 2 Kings 23:6; Jer 26:23), though cemeteries (*see* NECROPOLIS) as such were comparatively uncommon. Cremation was not favored by the Hebrews, although it was undertaken occasionally as a preliminary to burial in a family tomb (cf. 1 Sam 31:12f.). Some kind of fire in honor of the deceased would form part of royal burials from time to time (cf. 2 Chron 16:14; 21:19f.; Jer 34:5), though the origin and significance of this custom are obscure. During and after the monarchy the bereaved would sometimes prostrate themselves on the ground (2 Sam 13:31), wear mourning apparel (2 Sam 14:2), and cut off their hair (Jer 7:29; Ezek 7:18; Amos 8:10) in addition to engaging in more regular funerary customs.

NT sources mention that the deceased were first washed (Acts 9:37) and then anointed (Mark 16:1) before being wrapped up in linen in which fragrant spices (*see* OINTMENT) had been placed (John 19:40). A cloth napkin (John 11:44) was placed over the face of the corpse as one of the last acts of preparation for burial. By NT times burial space had become so limited in certain areas of Palestine that the bones of long-dead ancestors were removed from their tombs and stored in chests known as ossuaries* to make room for more recently deceased persons. During the Roman period decrees were promulgated which prohibited the removal of stone coverings of tombs and the theft or mutilation of their contents. A few wealthy Palestinian families began at this time to decorate tombs in emulation of the more elaborate Hellenistic practices, but the poorer classes were content to whitewash the exteriors (cf. Matt 23:27). Aside from decorative purposes, the white color may have served to warn passers-by of the contents of the structure and thus prevented defilement.

BIBLIOGRAPHY: W. L. Reed, *IDB*, 1, 474–76; K. A. Kitchen, *NBD*, 170–72.

RKH

FURNACE. Ovens for the purpose of smelting (*see* REFINING) ore or baking pottery,* bricks, or lime were made of brick or stone, and varied in design according to the use to be made of the structure. As early as the Chalcolithic* Halafian period, closed kilns* were employed to fire pottery at high temperatures. Discoveries by Russian archaeologists at Metsamor in 1965–66 included two types of smelting furnaces dating back to the second millennium B.C. and perhaps even earlier. In the subsequent Bronze and Iron Ages* furnaces were widely used for smelting metallic ores, heating metal ingots prior to forging, making bricks, and firing pottery and other ceramics. Copper-refining furnaces in Palestine have been excavated at Beth Shemesh,* Tell Quasileh, and elsewhere (*see* METALLURGY), and representa-

Early Iron Age copper-smelting furnace from site 2 at Timnah. Courtesy Institute of Mining and Metals, Tel Aviv.

tive iron*-smelting furnaces from such sites as Gaza,* Ali,* Ain Shems, and Tell Jemmeh. The latter contained crucibles (Heb. *kûr*) placed over a firebox to which draughts were fed by means of a flue. At Megiddo* three wishbone-shaped furnaces were excavated, measuring about 3 by 2.5 m. (10 by 8 ft.). Air entered under the furnace door, blew through both channels of the furnace, and came out through a rear flue. The smelting furnace seems indicated in Deut 4:20; Prov 17:3; Jer 11:4 et al., while the kiln was most probably referred to in Gen 19:28; Exod 9:8; 19:18. The furnace (*'attûn*, cf. Akkad. *utūnu*, "oven") of Dan 3:6–26 may have been used for smelting metals. In figurative language the furnace appears in Deut 4:20; 1 Kings 8:51; Isa 48:10; Matt 13:42; 1 Peter 1:7 and elsewhere to describe divine punishment or God's tempering of man.

See MEGIDDO; METALLURGY; OVEN; POTTER, POTTERY.

BIBLIOGRAPHY: C. Singer, *A History of Technology* (1954), 391–97; R. J. Forbes, *Studies in Ancient Technology*, 6 (1958), 66 seq.; *Guidebook of the Museum of History of the Metsamor Mining and Metallurgical Works* (1970), 14.

RKH

FURNITURE. Despite considerable literary evidence of furniture in the ancient world, comparatively few actual pieces have survived. One of the reasons for this disparity is that often the furniture of antiquity was not furniture as we understand it today. For example, the word *shulḥan* ("table") means properly a hide spread out, like the *sugrah* of the Bedouin, around which the company squatted, as did Joseph's* brothers when the foreign caravan drew near (Gen 37:25), or like Isaiah's table with the Persian rugs spread round (21:5), or in Ruth that of Boaz on the Bethlehem threshing floor. Cicero paid a large sum for a table of citron wood,* but few wooden objects withstand the centuries. Apart from stone

tables or work benches visible at such places as Qumran* and Pompeii,* art remains the one archaeological source. A banquet scene from Khorsabad* shows four nobles on benches or stools round a small table. In Egypt* the low table was the common choice for dining as pictures of Akhenaton* show. Chairs have been recovered from Tutankhamen's* tomb, and the high-backed ceremonial chair or throne may be seen in the palace of Knossos. A cupboard or small table stands beneath the cross in the Christian house at Herculaneum.* A bed* with its strappings is also to be seen at Herculaneum. The Egyptians, like the Babylonians, commonly slept on a spread mat, and the former supported the neck with a stand which, to our mind, would be very uncomfortable.

About 2600 B.C. in Egypt there was fashioned a prefabricated portable bed-canopy for Queen Hetepheres I, mother of Cheops, the builder of the Great Pyramid. This wooden framework was overlaid with gold* and was constructed with tenon and socket joints. Fragments of canopy poles from a First Dynasty tomb at Saqqara show that this kind of royal furniture was extremely ancient. A mural from the tomb of Ti at Saqqara depicted a carpenter using a chisel and mallet (*see* TOOLS) as he made furniture, while two others were using copper saws to make boards. Excavations in a Middle Bronze Age tomb at Jericho* have provided examples of the low tables popular in Mesopotamia,* as well as couches, beds, chairs, boxes, carved bowls, and spoons. The elaborate and exquisite furnishings of the Egyptian Amarna* Age were brought to modern notice with the discovery of Tutankhamen's tomb, depicting vividly the splendor of that period of cultural revival in Egypt.

Woodcarving was evidently a specialized occupation undertaken by a few furniture makers (cf. Exod 31:5; 35:33), and in the Iron Age* these people probably did much of the ivory* inlay work which was popular among wealthy Palestinians (cf. Amos 3:15) and others. In general, furnishings in the homes of people prior to the monarchy were austere, but after

Three tables made of plastered mud brick (reconstructed and on display at Rockefeller Museum, Jerusalem), found in the Scriptorium at Qumran. First century A.D. Courtesy Israel Dept. of Antiquities and Museums.

that period became more elaborate and plentiful. This reflected the influence of Phoenician* craftsmen,* who in the time of Solomon* decorated the royal palace, as they did the temple,* with a variety of fine-quality grained woods. Excavations at Samaria* have revealed beautiful ivory inlays from Omri's palace, and this building also was constructed by Phoenician workmen. In the NT period the height of luxury was reached in Herod's palace in Jerusalem* and in his winter residence at Jericho.

The royal throne, a distinctive and unique piece of furniture, was modeled on the high-backed chair found in the middle- and upper-class homes, and in the case of Solomon (1 Kings 10:18–20) it had wide armrests of the kind depicted on the sarcophagus* of Ahiram,* king of Byblos (see GEBAL) in Phoenicia, c. 1000 B.C. An even earlier (c. thirteenth century B.C.) ivory plaque from Megiddo* showed bearers of tribute approaching a throne which had a lion* carved in relief on the side and wings stretched backward. A backless throne was depicted on a stele from Zinjirli,* and on each corner of the structure there was a bull's head. In general the styles of Hebrew domestic furniture were copied with little variation from those of contemporary nations. Excavations at Ur* by Woolley showed that, about 2500 B.C., the furniture in a middle-class Sumerian* home comprised low tables, high-backed chairs, and beds with wooden frames.

BIBLIOGRAPHY: M. S. and J. L. Miller, *Encyclopedia of Bible Life* (1944), 246–52; A. C. Bouquet, *Everyday Life in NT Times* (1955), 30–32, 38–46; E. W. Heaton, *Everyday Life in OT Times* (1956), 74, 208–10, plates 22, 24, 27, 110.   RKH and EMB

G

GABBATHA (gab'ə thə; Gr. Γαββαθᾶ, *Gabbathá*). The Gr. transliteration of an Aramaic* word, the etymological derivation and meaning of which is still uncertain. The term is only used in Scripture in John 19:13, referring to a locality in Jerusalem which also had the Gr. name λιθόστρωτον (*lithostrōton*), the *Pavement*. The Praetorium is also identified with the area (Matt 27:27; Mark 15:16; John 19:9).

Since Paul was kept by the Roman procurator Felix in the Praetorium of Herod* (Acts 23:35), it seems probable that this building was appropriated by Roman procurators for their official business. There were two such chief residences of Herod in Jerusalem* and both have been claimed as having the Gabbatha-Lithostrōton pavement where Christ was judged.

The one building that Josephus calls a palace (Jos. *War* 5. 4, 4) and fortress of the upper city (Jos. *War* 5. 5, 8) was adjacent to the three towers* of Hippicus, Phasael, and Marianne, located on the W side of the present walled city.* This building could have satisfied the needs of a procurator, but no paved court has been uncovered in the area.

Gabbatha-Lithostroton pavement under the Convent of Our Lady of Sion in Jerusalem. Courtesy Notre Dame de Sion, Jerusalem.

The other building was located at the NW corner of the temple.* Josephus calls it a fortress (Jos. *Antiq.* 15. 8, 5) with the appearance of a tower, and he also describes it as resembling a palace (Jos. *War* 5. 5, 8). Such a building, called the Antonia* in ancient times, would also have satisfied the needs of a procurator. In this area a large stone pavement has been found and excavated, extensive portions of it being under the Convent of the Flagellation, the Convent of Our Lady of Sion, and the Greek Orthodox Convent. The preserved pavement extends over an area of c. 32 m. (105 ft.) from W to E and 48 m. (157 ft.) N to S, a total of over 1,500 sq. m. (16,140 sq. ft.). Architectural remains in the area reveal an impressive courtyard with surrounding galleries. The large limestone paving stones are square or rectangular and each side is as long as two to three meters on a side. Channels for water drainage are cut in some paving stones, while on others evidence of a game board points to Roman soldiers having been garrisoned here. It is likely that this is the location for the Gabbatha-Lithostrōton.

BIBLIOGRAPHY: G. Dalman, *Sacred Sites and Ways* (1935), 335; M. Burrows, "The Fortress Antonia and the Praetorium," *BA*, 1 (1938), 17–19; L.-H. Vincent, "Le Lithostrosos Evangélique," *RB*, 59 (1952), 513–30; L.-H. Vincent, *Jerusalem*, 1 (1954), 216–21; K. W. Clark, "Gabbatha," *IDB*, 2 (1962), 332; J. Finegan, *The Archaeology of the NT* (1969), 156, 160–61; J. B. Payne, *ZPEB*, 2 (1975), 618.

WHM

GADARA (gəd'ə rə; Gr. Γαδαρά, *Gadara*). A city of the Decapolis* mentioned in the Bible only in the Gospel accounts regarding the demoniac: in Matt 8:28, the best texts read "Gadarenes" (Aland-Metzger *Gr. Testament*); and some of the MSS read the same in Mark 5:1 and Luke 8:26, 37. In each of these passages, there are variant readings of "Gerasenes" and "Gergesenes." Gadara (modern Umm Queis or Mukes) is located c. 8 km. (5 mi.) SE of the Lake of Galilee,* S of the Yarmuk River and built on a projection of land on the E edge of the Jordan Valley so that it overlooks the lake. According to the Peutinger Table Gadara was 16 miles from both Tiberias and Capitolias. During Seleucid times it was also called Antiochia and Seleucia, and in the late Roman times an inscription gives its name as Colonia Valentiniana Gadara. The city's territory included the hot springs of el Hamme, and since coins* found there indicate interest in shipping, the territory no doubt extended to the lake itself. Excavations at Gerasa* (Jerash) have yielded clear evidence of the Roman culture in these cities of the Decapolis and as Gadara is being excavated, undoubtedly further evidence will be produced. This Greek city had a circumference of 3.2 km. (2 mi.) and shows in its visible remains two theaters,* a basilica,* a colonnaded street,* and baths. Currently the Germans and the Danes are excavating at the site.

BIBLIOGRAPHY: F.-M. Abel, *Géographie de la Palestine*, 2 (1938), 145, 176, 323; E. G. Kraeling, *Bible Atlas* (1956), 382–83; D. C. Pellett, "Gadara," *IDB* (1962), 335; M. F. Unger, *Archaeology and the NT*

(1962), 139–41; M. Avi Yonah, *The Holy Land* (1966), 40, 51, 69, 75 et al.; J. C. DeYoung, *ZPEB*, 2 (1975), 622–23; *PECS* (1976), 341.

WHM

GAIUS JULIUS CAESAR OCTAVIANUS. *See* AUGUSTUS.

GALATIA. The land of the *Galatae* (Gauls or Celts), whether in Western Europe (Latin* *Gallia*) or, more especially, in N-central Asia Minor,* where three Galatian tribes settled in the mid-third century B.C. The Galatian territory in Asia Minor, formerly Phrygian,* stretched over 320 km. (200 mi.) from SW to NE, between 31° and 35° E and between 39° and 40° 30' N. The Romans conquered the Galatians in battle (189 B.C.) but allowed them to retain much independence. Galatia thenceforth preserved its friendship with Rome and augmented its territory in various directions. In 64 B.C. it received from Rome the status of a client kingdom, which it retained until Amyntas, its last king, fell in battle against the marauding Homanadensians from the Taurus highlands (25 B.C.); it was then reorganized by Augustus* as a Roman province. Its royal capital, Ancyra* (modern Ankara), became the seat of the Roman governor (*legatus pro praetore*). By this time Galatia included much territory that was not ethnically or linguistically Galatian. In apostolic times the province of Galatia stretched between Pontus on the N (bordering on the Black Sea) and Pamphylia on the S (bordering on the Mediterranean). In later Roman times its limits were reduced by reason of new provincial groupings.

Twice in Acts Paul traverses part of Galatia while journeying westward through Asia Minor (16:6; 18:23); several churches planted by him and Barnabas during their tour described in Acts 13:13–14:23 were in the southern part of the province—Antioch of Pisidia,* Iconium,* Lystra,* and possibly Derbe.* An unresolved problem of NT criticism is whether these were the "churches of Galatia" addressed in Gal 1:2 (cf. 3:1) or whether the churches addressed lay farther N, in "ethnic Galatia," in Ancyra and other cities. We have no clear evidence of Paul's evangelizing "ethnic Galatia"; Christianity is not attested in Ancyra until well after Paul's time. Paul's missionary program is most consonant with his following the main routes through S Galatia. The references in Acts 16:6; 18:23 should probably be understood in this sense.

The cities,* roads,* and frontiers of Roman Galatia have been increasingly identified by archaeological data—inscriptions and milestones as well as buildings and walls. Apart from Iconium (modern Konya), the other S Galatian cities evangelized by Paul have had to be located by archaeological testimony. Pisidian Antioch—3.2 km. (2 mi.) E of modern Yalvaç, SW of Akşehir, a Greek city which (with Iconium) was added to the Galatian kingdom by Antony in 36 B.C.—received the status of a Roman colony from Augustus thirty years later. Excavations have exposed much of the ancient site—walls,* gates,* squares, theater,* and aqueduct.* The ancient cult of Mēn Askainos in its vicinity persisted for a long period. Mēn appears on coins* of Pisidian Antioch (of which an exceptionally large number is extant) well into the third century A.D. As for "Lystra and Derbe, cities of Lycaonia" (Acts 14:6), the former was located at Zostera, near Hatunsaray, on epigraphic grounds, by J. R. S. Sterrett in 1885; the latter was not identified until 1957 and the following years, when two inscriptions showed that it stood at or near Kerti Hüyük, about 24 km. (15 mi.) NNE of Laranda (modern Karaman). It is not certain whether it lay within the provincial frontier of Galatia or in the part of Lycaonia* belonging to the kingdom of Commagene.

BIBLIOGRAPHY: *FLAP*, 260–64; *FLAP* rev, 340–45; F. F. Bruce, "Galatian Problems, 2," *BJRL*, 52 (1969–70), 243–66.   FFB

GALILEE (gal'ə lē; Gr. Γαλιλαία, *Galilaía*; from Heb. גָּלִיל, *gālîl*, "circle, district," or strictly גְּלִיל הַגּוֹיִם, *gelîl haggôyim*,"district of the Gentiles";Aram. גְּלִילָא, *gelîlā*). An area of N Palestine.

1. The Boundaries. Before the Exile* the boundaries of Galilee were vague and variable, but afterward and specifically in the NT period, Galilee was described more definitively. According to Josephus (Jos. *War* 3.3.1–2) this area was bounded on the W and N (Northern or Upper Galilee) by Phoenicia* and Syria, on the S (Southern or Lower Galilee) by the territory of Samaria,* and Scythopolis,* and on the E by the territory of Hippos* and Gadara,* and by Gaulanitis. After the time of Herod* the Great, Galilee was administered by Herod Antipas (cf. Luke 23:6, 7) until A.D. 39.

The large lake in E Galilee was known in the OT as the Sea of Chinnereth or Chinnoreth (Num 34:11; Josh 12:3; 13:27), in 1 Macc 11:67 and Josephus as the Sea of Gennesar, and in the NT as the Sea of Gennesaret (Mark 6:53), the Sea of Tiberias (John 21:1) or, the Sea of Galilee (John 6:1 et al.).

2. The Old Galilee District. Settlements in Old Galilee included Hazor,* which Albright calls the Canaanite* capital of Galilee, as indicated by Josh 11:10 and verified by the early fourteenth-century B.C. Amarna letters.* Considerable excavations have been conducted at Hazor.

The summit of the Horns of Hattin (Qrûn Ḥaṭṭîn), located NW of Tiberias,* have revealed ancient ruins including fortifications coming from the Early Bronze but mostly the Late Bronze Age. Albright argues that this is the site of the Canaanite royal city of Madon conquered by Joshua and occupied by Israel (Josh 11:1; 12:19). The ruins of Khirbet Madin, a half mile NW, preserve the ancient name.

On the isolated hill, Tell el-'Oreimeh, located above Tabgha,* on the NW side of the Sea of Galilee, there is evidence of a Bronze Age settlement covering the top of the hill; the acropolis* there seems to have been settled for a brief period in the Early Bronze Age. This may be the site of the ancient Canaanite and Israelite town of Chinnereth (Deut 3:17; Josh 19:35) (so Albright and Dalman).

Other Old Galilee sites which show evidence of

Bronze Age settlement include: et-Tell, just N of the Sea of Galilee and less than 1.6 km. (1 mi.) E of the Jordan River, where Early, Middle, and Late Bronze Age shards* have been found; Beth Shan,* with its evidence of the religious services of the Canaanites; and the large tell el-Kerak, ancient Beth-yerah, the city of the moon, located at the SW corner of the Sea of Galilee, which was evidently important in the Early Bronze period. Other important cities of the Old Galilee district include Kedesh-Naphtali, a few kilometers NW of Lake Huleh, and Hazor S and E, where extensive excavations have been conducted, revealing Early Middle and Late Bronze and Iron Age remains.

3. New Testament Galilee. A number of important Galilean towns and villages of this period, which are mainly located near the Sea of Galilee, have been subject to archaeological investigation.

Tiberias, a town named after the emperor by Herod Antipas and built about A.D. 18 by Herod in the place of his former capital at Sepphoris, is located on the SW shore of the Sea of Galilee. The remains of a Roman acropolis bear testimony to Herod's time. About 2.4 km. (1½ mi.) S of Tiberias were the warm springs of Hammath* (cf. Josh 19:35), and a village that Josephus (Jos. *Antiq.* 18.2, 3) calls Ammathus. In mounds adjacent to the springs and excavated by Slousch (1921) and Moshe Dothan (1961) were found remains of the southern gate* of the city and of baths of the Israelite period, and also a building used in part as a synagogue* probably as early as the first century A.D. In the early fourth century the synagogue had a mosaic* floor with an inscription including the words, "Amen, Amen." In the fifth century the small rectangular building was enlarged into a basilica* with an apse.*

About 3.2 to 4.8 km. (2 to 3 mi.) N of Tiberias is the present settlement of Migdal (or Mejdel) which no doubt preserves the ancient location of Magdala, or Magadan* (cf. Matt 15:39; 27:56) or Tarichaea as Josephus calls it (Jos. *War* 3.9, 7–30, 5). Whether the Dalmanutha of Mark 8:10 and Magdala are names for the same place is uncertain.

Farther N is the site of Tell el-Oreimah, which lay uninhabited in Jesus' time. Beyond this, about .8 km. (½ mi.) is the area of et-Tabgha, a corrupt name in Arabic* for the Gr. *Heptapegon*, "the place of Seven Springs," but at the springs there was no NT town. However, nearby at the bottom of a hill known as the Mount of Beatitudes is the Heptapegon Basilica (with some fourth-century A.D. mosaics* preserved), a church commemorating the multiplying of the loaves and fishes. Also there was the Chapel of the Beatitudes and the rock on which the risen Lord was supposed to have laid the fish (John 21:9).

Capernaum* (Tell Hum), located at the lake about 2.4 km. (1½ mi.) NE of et-Tabgha, is important for its fourth-to-fifth-century A.D. synagogue and the ruins of a fifth-century octagon Byzantine* church under which are remains of a first-century A.D. fisherman's* quarters (cf. Mark 1:29–31) used a little later for Christian worship.

At Chorazin (Korazin*) or Kerazeh (cf. Matt 11:21–

23; Luke 10:13–15) about 3.2 km. (2 mi.) up in the hills to the NW were discovered remains of a synagogue of about A. D. 200 and a large stone seat (cf. Matt 23:2).

At Kefar Bir ʿam in the hills W of the Huleh Valley have been found well-preserved third–fourth-century synagogue ruins with an inscription of the second–third century. Among other places in Upper Galilee that have been excavated are Meiron,* Khirbet Shĕma', Gush Halav (the Giscola mentioned by Josephus [Jos. Life, 43–45]), and en-Nabratein, all of which produced remains of synagogues. In 1981 excavators uncovered at en-Nabratein an architectural fragment of a Torah shrine belonging to the late Roman synagogue there, projected as the successor to the ancient ark of the covenant in late Jewish tradition.

To the NE of Capernaum and on the E of the Jordan River as it flows into the Sea of Galilee is the area of Bethsaida Julias (named by Philip the tetrarch in honor of Julia, daughter of Augustus*). Two sites are possible for this "Bethsaida of Galilee" (John 12:21): Khirbet el-ʿAraj, right on the lake shore, or et-Tell, a mound about a mile N of the lake. Some have surmised Julias at et-Tell and Bethsaida,* a fishing village, at el-ʿAraj.

SW of the lake was Nazareth,* which does not preserve in what has been found there much that is authentic from NT times, except the Spring of Mary.

Beth Sheʿarim, a village in southern Galilee, is mentioned by Josephus (Jos. Life, 119) as Besara, where in the first century A.D. produce was stored for Queen Berenice. In the second century, several Jewish scholars lived in Beth Sheʿarim, and from this time on it was famous for its Jewish cemetery (see NECROPOLIS). The town was destroyed about A.D. 351. Considerable excavations have been conducted there, particularly in the cemetery. The city had its synagogue and also an extensive basilica,* probably a public building.

BIBLIOGRAPHY: G. A. Smith, The Historical Geography of the Holy Land (1896), 411–63; W. F. Albright, "Among the Canaanite Mounds of Eastern Galilee," BASOR, 29 (1928), 1–8; G. Dalman, Sacred Sites and Ways (1935), 5–9, etc.; E. G. Kraeling, Bible Atlas (1956), 29, 373–87; K. W. Clark, "Galilee," IDB, 1 (1962), 757, 2 (1962), 344–47; N. Glueck, The River Jordan (1968), 39–75; J. Finegan, The Archaeology of the NT (1969), 43–60; Carol L. Meyer et al., "Excavations at Meiron in Upper Galilee, 1971–72," BASOR, 214 (1974), 2–25; EEHL, 2 (1976), 406–8, 474–94, 3 (1977), 856–62; Carol L. Meyer, ed., "The Meiron Excavation Project," BASOR, 230 (1978), 1–24; "Preliminary Report on the 1977 and 1978 Seasons at Gush Halav (el-Jish), BASOR, 233 (1979), 33–58; E. M. Meyer, "Shema' Khirbet," EEHL, 4 (1978), 1094–97; S. Loffreda, "Dating the Synagogue at Capharnaum," The Holy Land (1981), 55-61; Eric M. Meyers, James F. Strange, and Carol L. Meyers, "The Ark of Nabratein—A First Glance," BA, vol. 44, no. 4 (Fall,1981), 237-43; Eric M. Meyers et al., Excavations at Ancient Meiron, Upper Galilee, Israel 1971-72, 1974-75, 1977 (1981).   WHM

GALLIO. The brother of the Roman Stoic Seneca and governor of Greece when St. Paul was brought to trial in Corinth* (Acts 18:12ff.). His full name was L. Junius Gallio Annaeanus and he is known from the fragmentary inscription S.I.G. 801 D (= Smallwood, 376) from Delphi. The emperor's titulature on the inscription dates it to A.D. 52. If the inscription refers to Gallio's successor, and Gallio's governorship is dated from May 51 to May 52, Paul's sojourn of eighteen months in Corinth (Acts 18:11) may be placed in the period from the winter of 49/50 to the summer of 51. But if, as seems more likely, the inscription is to be assigned to Gallio's own governorship (more traditionally dated from July 51 to July 52), Paul's sojourn in Corinth can be placed a year later, i.e. from 50/51 to 52.

BIBLIOGRAPHY: F. J. Foakes Jackson and K. Lake, The Beginnings of Christianity, 5 (1933, rep. 1966), 4604ff.; A. Plassart, L'inscription de Delphes mentionnant le proconsul Gallion, Revue des Études Greques, 80 (1967), 372ff.; R. Jewett, Dating Paul's Life (1979), 38ff.

DBS

GAMES. 1. Old Testament. Such games as those which cruelly surrounded Samson's* end, or those in which he took part (Judg 14:12), or the children's games of Zechariah's idyll (8:5), have left no material of archaeological relevance—unless some of the clay* figurines passed off as cult images, and found on many sites, are, in fact, dolls. A relief from the Sixth Dynasty (2350–2200 B.C.) tomb of Mereruka at Saqqara, shows boys engaged in a tug of war. Gaming boards have been found at Ur* (2500 B.C.), in Tutankhamen's* tomb (1361–1352 B.C.), and on Palestinian sites (e.g., Kirjath-Sepher (Debir*), Tell el-ʿAjjul, Beth Shemesh,* Gezer*). The surviving gaming boards are elaborate and ornate, inlaid with ivory,* shell, and gold* and are of varied shapes. Some have a series of holes for pegs. At Umm el-Biyara, a fort guarding Nabataean* Petra,* as at Mizpah,* squares for gaming were cut into the rock, as at the Pavement (Gabatha*) in Jerusalem, but in no case is there a clue to the nature or rules of the game.

An ancient Egyptian game played by putting pebbles in a series of holes, similar to the modern game of Kala, is thought to have been the ancestor of backgammon. There is a sixth-century Greek vase showing Athena, Achilles, and Ajax playing dice. The scene is on active service. Shields lean against nearby trees. Helmets,* corselets, and greaves are worn. Swords and spears are in hand.

2. New Testament. Paul frequently draws vivid metaphors from the Greek athletic festivals, chiefly from the foot-racing events, and from the Isthmian Games especially (1 Cor 9:24–27; Heb 12:1, 2; Gal 2:2, 5:7; Phil 2:16; 2 Tim 2:5). The Greeks had four athletic festivals—the Olympic Games, in honor of Olympian Zeus,* held at Olympia in the Alpheus River valley, in the NW Peloponnese; the Pythian Games, in honor of Apollo, at Delphi; the Nemean Games at Argos, and the Isthmian Games at Corinth.*

The Isthmian Games were athletic contests held every second year in Corinth, in honor of Poseidon.

Tau limestone game board found at Beth Shemesh; an ivory teetotum and ten blue faience playing pieces found at Tell Beit Mirsim; Middle Bronze Age IIB. Courtesy Israel Dept. of Antiquities and Museums.

They were established in 581 B.C., and a contest, then, would have been held while Paul was in Corinth, for the Gallio* Inscription at Delphi dates this as A.D. 50 and 51. The Athenians, rejecting the Corinthian legend, claimed that the games were founded by their own founding hero, Theseus. This gave a reason for the manner in which the Athenians patronized the games of their ancient rival on the isthmus. More practical reasons were the easy journey from Athens* to Corinth and the fact that Corinth was the pleasure city of the Central Mediterranean. The games, based in an urban environment, afforded more facilities for entertainment than those of the remote religious centers of Delphi and Olympia.

The Games offices were located in the southern stoa* of Corinth, and the contests took place some 9.7 km. (6 mi.) away to the eastern coast of the isthmus where stood a large stadium and a temple to the god Poseidon. The prize was a "corruptible crown" indeed—one of wild celery. Boxing* was included as well as running. Hence Paul's metaphor (1 Cor 9:24–27).

The Olympic Games were held every four years at Olympia where extensive remains are to be seen, including the palestra* or wrestling ground, and the recently excavated stadium. The work was begun early in the century by French archaeologists and still continues. A well-preserved stadium is to be seen at Delphi above the oracle's temple and the theater.* On both sites, elaborate remains of temples illustrate the fact that, like the associated theater at Delphi, the games were a religious occasion.

Little is known of the Nemean Games save that the site, the great altar to Zeus, the gymnasium, and the palestra have been excavated on the northern borders of the Argolid at Cleonae.

Phil 3:14 may refer to the Roman chariot* race. The site of the Circus* Maximus in Rome,* where such contests were held, is known, but none of the appurtenances beyond the shape and formation of the course survives. The best preserved site is the Circus of Maxentius on the Via Appia (Appian Way*), but this racecourse was not dedicated until A.D. 309 and so cannot have been associated with the racing fever at Rome in Nero's day, which may have prompted Paul's metaphor.

BIBLIOGRAPHY: W. F. Albright, *Mizraim*, 1 (1933), 130–34; *ANEP* (1954), figs. 212–19; E. W. Heaton, *Everyday Life in OT Times* (1956), 91–92; W. H. Morton, *BA* 19 (1956), 33–34; R. F. Schnell, *IDB*, 2, 352–53; C. E. De Vries, *ZPEB*, 2, 649–52; E. N. Gardiner, *Greek Athletic Sports and Festivals* (1910), esp. 218; id., *Olympia* (1925); E. M. Blaiklock, *Two Letters from Prison* (1964), 42–43.

EMB

GARDENS. The Bible makes some ninety references to gardens, but archaeological material on the theme is meager. Gardens, in fact, are not of a nature to leave archaeological evidence, save such paving as that which betrays a submerged villa-garden of Tiberius's* day, off Corfu. The Anct tablets of Egypt* show rows of sycamore fig trees and date palms. Ornamental pools often formed part of large Egyptian gardens, but they were decorative in nature, not meant for use by swimmers. A picture in a Theban tomb of early date shows beds of poppies and papyrus* growing in ordered ranks by a canal. This must have been known in towns on the sister-river, the Euphrates, since Balaam, who came from there, spoke thus of Israel (Num 24:6). The tribes, whose ordered tent lines showed far below his vantage point, were, he said, "like long rows of palms, like gardens by a river, like aloes planted by the Lord, like cedars beside the water. . . ." An Assyrian relief, typically sanguinary, shows a royal garden party—such as the one in Esther's story (1:5; 7:7–8)—in which the head of a rebel prince swings from the branch of a tree.

Babylon* certainly knew such places of pleasure, and according to Herodotus, nine-tenths of Babylon in the days of Nebuchadnezzar* II consisted of public parks and gardens. The "hanging gardens," one of the so-called wonders of the world, were terraced gardens of some size, held high on great stone arches.* This corresponds with descriptions in Diodorus and Strabo. The place has been identified by archaeologists as a complex of heavily built walls in the palace area. These walls would be the foundations of a garden on terraces hydraulically watered from the Euphrates. The beautiful little park stood on an asphalt-proofed platform. Koldewey, in his excavations early in the century found fourteen large arched vaults, and in the basement a structure that he thought was a hydraulic device similar to the dolab (water bucket), used today in the neighborhood to provide a continuous flow of water.

Of the gardens of the Persians, the huge parks or *paradeisoi*, and the formal gardens of the palace precincts, no traces remain, but the latter must have been like the gardens in the wall paintings of Pompeii. In the British-Roman villa at Fishbourne archaeological research is reconstructing the formal garden, and it may be possible, by the study of the pollen grains, to reconstruct its hedgerows and flowerbeds.

BIBLIOGRAPHY: R. Koldewey, *The Excavations at Babylon* (1914), 91.

EMB

GATE; GATEWAY. The gate was the entrance to a walled* city* or town, often mentioned along with its component parts (cf. Neh 3:3, 14). The number of gates varied from city to city. Jericho* had only one, but the ideal Jerusalem* of Ezekiel had twelve gates (Ezek 48:30–35). Excavations in Palestinian cities have shown that the city gate served as a center for mustering defensive troops to ward off an attacking enemy. At most sites it was located at the only open area within the walls, the rest of the land being occupied by buildings or narrow streets. The gate naturally attracted merchants because of the available space and hence was the center of commercial and trading activity in each city. The judges also assembled in that area to hear cases and render their decisions (cf. Gen 19:11; Amos 5:10 et al.). In Middle Bronze Age Palestine, fortress gates were constructed along lines long employed in Mesopotamia,* familiar from the palace complex of Zimri-Lim at Mari* (eighteenth century B.C.).

Excavations at Megiddo* and Shechem* have demonstrated that this type of gateway actually comprised two or three gates, each of which was flanked by a pair of massive stone piers in symmetrical alignment, and usually augmented by means of defensive towers.* A modification of this structure appeared in the Iron Age* gateway at Megiddo. Dating from the time of Solomon, it comprised three pairs of long narrow piers separated by two pairs of deep recesses and resembled the tenth-century B.C. gateways at Carchemish.*

A later gate at Megiddo is more like a new design which appeared commonly in the eighth century. It was described fully by W. F. Albright in connection with Tell Beit Mirsim in seventh- and early sixth-century levels. It involved an indirect approach. The city walls were made to overlap, thus precluding a direct intrusion, and compelling an assault party to run a gauntlet between the two overlapping ends along a corridor exposed to downward fire. The E gate of Mizpah* (Tell en-Nasbeh) is a fine example. The approaching enemy was compelled to expose his right unshielded flank to defenders on the protected inner wall as he turned along the approach corridor. In connection with this Tell en-Nasbeh gateway excavated at ninth-century B.C. levels, archaeologists uncovered long stone benches in the partly enclosed area just outside the gate, where the elders and judges sat (cf. 2 Sam 15:2–6; Job 29:7–10, 21, 22 et al.).

The Damascus* Gate in old Jerusalem gives the best surviving idea of an ancient city gate.

BIBLIOGRAPHY: W. F. Albright, *The Archaeology of Palestine* (1960), 89–90, 126–27, 138–39; *Views of the Biblical World*, 2 (1960), 94, 107, 221, 262; ibid.,

3 (1960), 137, 151; *AIs* (1961), 152–53, 155, 166–67, 233–34; S. Barabas, *ZPEB*, 2, 655–56.

RKH and EMB

GATH. (gath; Heb. נַת, *gat*). 1. A prominent Philistine* city,* one of the famous pentapolis which included Gaza,* Ashdod,* Ashkelon,* and Ekron.*

In biblical history, Gath is first mentioned as the home of the Anakim (Josh 11:22) and later as a Philistine stronghold where the ark of the covenant* was taken (Josh 13:3; 1 Sam 5:7–10). It was also the home of Goliath* and, ironically, the city where David resorted for refuge from Saul and eventually became the vassal of Achish, king of Gath (1 Sam 21:10; 27:2–4). Gath figured in the frequent wars between the Philistines and Israelites. Both Samuel and David fought against the city (1 Sam 7:14; 1 Chron 18:1), while Rehoboam fortified it, and Uzziah later destroyed its walls (2 Chron 11:8; 26:6). By the time of Amos (c. 760 B.C.) the place was evidently in ruins (Amos 6:2). Sargon II* campaigned in the vicinity when he destroyed Ashdod in 715 B.C. Whereas the location of the first three has always been known, and that of Ekron is fairly well established, much debate has surrounded the precise site representing Philistine Gath.

The British survey of Palestine placed Gath at Tell es Safi. W. F. Albright tried to argue for a location further S, which he did so successfully that both the tell* he claimed as the site and a sizeable modern Israeli town nearby were both named "Gat." His candidate, Tell esh-Sheikh Ahmad el- 'Areini* (Tel 'Erani or Tel "Gat"), near the ruined Arab village of Iraq el-Menshiyeh, was disproved by the excavations of S. Yeivin from 1956–61. The archaeological finds did not fit the historical description of the city of Gath. An Early Bronze Age city with a small Iron Age* fortification on the summit without a Philistine level could not be the famous Gath of the Philistines.

Benjamin Mazar followed Albright but was forced by textual evidence to theorize another Gath (Gittaim) even further S, so he proposed Tell Nagila.* R. A. Mitchell and Ruth Amiran dug at Nagila in 1962–63, but again no Philistine level was found in the Canaanite*-Hyksos* city.

G. E. Wright was driven to search even further S by the same logic that had caused Albright and Mazar to look for a southern Gath: Tell es Safi was too close to Ekron (Tel Muqanna). Therefore Wright proposed Tell esh-Shari'ah in 1966. Y. Aharoni and the Israeli school, however, have maintained that the proper reading of 1 Sam 17:52–53 indicates that Gath was in or near the Valley of Elah. Samuel, too, apparently campaigned only in the N of Philistia, and, if so, the reference in 1 Sam 7:14 would support a northern Gath. Tell es Safi is now once again the foremost candidate for the site of Gath. The earlier excavations by F. J. Bliss and R. A. S. Macalister for the Palestine Exploration Fund in 1899 had uncovered abundant Philistine materials, a fact which makes the identification probable, if not certain.

Since the word Gath means "winepress," it is found to occur frequently in Palestinian place-names, sometimes in compound with other elements to dis-

Gate area on north side of Tell Megiddo: (1) earliest gate, nineteenth century B.C., (2) Late Bronze Age gate, (3) street and basalt steps leading from Late Bronze Age gate, (4) eastern part of Solomonic gateway (tenth century B.C.), (5) part of Ahab's gate (ninth century B.C.). Photo: PICTORIAL ARCHIVE (Near Eastern History) Est.

tinguish the various towns. Gath Hepher* (Josh 19:13) and Gath Rimmon (Josh 19:45) were small villages compared with the primary Gath "of the Philistines." The small town of Moresheth, birthplace of Micah (Jer 26:18; Mic 1:1), was an outlying village in the vicinity of the larger Philistine Gath, and so was termed Moresheth-Gath.

Both the Ras Shamra (see UGARIT) tablets and the Amarna* tablets (see AMARNA LETTERS), as well as Egyptian conquest lists of Thutmose III and Sheshonk I, mention numerous Gaths. It is inevitable that some literary confusion, not to mention geographical confusion, exists as a result of the frequent use of this common name.

2. Gath Hepher, the birthplace of Jonah (2 Kings 14:25), is probably to be identified with Khirbet ez-Zurra' near the village of Meshshed in Galilee,* which boasts one of the many traditional tombs of Jonah to be found in the Near East. Potsherds (see SHARDS) recovered from the site since 1929 indicate probable occupation from the Late Bronze to the end of the Iron II Age* (c. 1000–600 B.C.).

3. Gath Rimmon appears in two tribal lists, that of Dan (Josh 19:45 and Josh 21:24), where it is to become a Levitical city, and that of Manasseh* (Josh 21:25). The latter reference has been thought to be a textual error resulting from a scribal miscopying of the previous verse, because 1 Chron 6:70 leaves it out of the Manasseh list. In any case, the Danite Gath Rimmon is now thought to be properly fixed at the site of Tell el-Jerishe on the Yarkon River near Ramat Gan. Excavations by E. L. Sukenik intermittently from 1927–40 showed that the town was occupied from the Early Bronze Age to about the tenth century B.C., with a large Hyksos glacis* (eighteenth–seventeenth centuries) and important Late Bronze deposits. The northern Gath Rimmon may be Rummana near Taanach,* an identification supported by El Amarna 250.46.

BIBLIOGRAPHY: F. J. Bliss, "The Excavations at Tell es-Safi," PEFQSt (1899), 183–99, 317–33; ibid., (1900), 16–29; F. J. Bliss and R. A. S. Macalister, Excavations in Palestine During the Years 1898–1900 (1902), 1–43; W. F. Albright, AASOR, 2–3 (1923), 7–12; E. L. Sukenik, "Tell el-Jerishe," QDAP, 4 (1935), 208–9; ibid., 6 (1937), 225; ibid., 10 (1944), 198–99; S. Yeivin, First Preliminary Report on the Excavations at Tel "Gat," 1956–1958 (1961); cf. Department of Antiquities, "tell Gath," IEJ, 6 (1956), 258–59; ibid., 7 (1957), 264–65; ibid., 8 (1958), 274–76; ibid., 9 (1959), 269–71; S. Yeivin, "Early Contacts Between Canaan and Egypt," IEJ, 10 (1960), 122–23, 193–203; ibid., "tel Gath," IEJ, 10 (1961), 191; B. Mazar, "The Cities of the Territory of Dan," IEJ, 10 (1960), 65–77; S. Bulow, R. A. Mitchell, "An Iron Age II Fortress on Tel Nagila," IEJ, 11 (1961), 101–10; R. Amiran and A. Eitan, "A Canaanite-Hyksos City at Tell Nagila," ARC 18 (1965), 113–23; G. E. Wright, "Fresh Evidence for the Philistine Story," BA, 29 (1966), 78–86; A. F. Rainey, "Gath of the Philistines," CNI, 17:2–3 (1966), 30–38; ibid., 17:4 (1966), 23–34; C. F. Pfeiffer, The Biblical World (1966), 249–50; S. Barabas, ZPEB, 2 (1975), 658–59.

JEJ

GATH HEPHER (gath hē' fər). A border town in Lebanon (Josh 19:13), also mentioned as the home of Jonah the prophet (2 Kings 14:25).

Since 1929, when surface explorations were conducted, Gath Hepher has been identified with Khirbet ez-Zurra', a large site 4.8 km. (3 mi.) NE of Nazareth* and close to the spot where one tradition places the tomb of Jonah. Shards gathered on the site indicate probable occupation from Late Bronze through Iron II (c. 1600–600 B.C.).

BIBLIOGRAPHY: E. G. Kraeling, Bible Atlas (1956), 292, plates VI, VII, VIII, IX, X.

CEA

GAWF. See DUMAH.

GAWRA, TEPE. See TEPE GAWRA.

GAZA. The southernmost town of the Philistine Pentapolis (Five Towns) called by the Hebrews Azza, the Azzati of the Amarna letters.* The town had no harbor although the Roman city* extended to the coast. Modern Gaza, 4.8 km. (3 mi.) inland, the site mentioned by Arrian in connection with Alexander's siege, appears to be the location of the ancient "caravan city," the gateway between Palestine and Egypt.* Biblical and other literary references are numerous; twenty references occur in the Bible alone. The rest of the evidence is from archaeological sources. The Annals of Thutmose III imply Egyptian possession of the town in 1468 B.C. for the pharaoh

Detail from mosaic floor in ancient synagogue at Gaza. King David, dressed as a Byzantine king, is depicted as Orpheus playing the lyre. Courtesy Asher Ovadia, Israel Dept. of Antiquities and Museums.

used the city as his first staging post on the campaign of that year (also Taanach,* Letter 6. *BASOR*, 94 [1944], 24–27). The Amarna letters mention the danger to the town, shared by most of Palestine, at the time of the Habiru* invasion (about 1360 B.C. in the latter years of the Eighteenth Dynasty). Fluctuations in the strength of the Egyptian hold over her buffer areas in the N are thus implied, a process which may be deduced from the records of Joshua and Judges. Philistine control became established and even resisted the S extension of Solomon's* power.

Amos (1:6–7) condemned Gaza for its slave trade with Edom,* a commerce to be expected from Gaza's position on the Fertile Crescent* trade routes, and confirmed by a S Arabian* inscription concerning a female temple slave.* This would have occurred in the middle of the eighth century B.C.

Over the next century, the city appears in the Assyrian royal records (Tiglath-pileser* III; Sargon II;* Sennacherib;* Esarhaddon;* and Assyria's last strong king, Ashurbanipal*) and the undulations in the fortunes of a strongpoint lying near the limits of Assyrian military contacts may be seen in the documents. The denunciation of Gaza by Zephaniah (2:4–7, 13–14) may reflect a period during which a Philistine puppet of Assyria held Judean borderlands.

As predicted by Jeremiah (25:20; 47:5), the successor empire, Nebuchadnezzar's* Babylon, overran Gaza, and the kings of Gaza and other petty realms are shown as captives in the conqueror's inscriptions.

A plausible interpretation of Acts 8:26 implies that ancient Gaza was a deserted site, with the new Roman foundation, in accordance with its role, nearer the coast. There is therefore much likelihood that significant remains are covered by modern occupation. W. J. Pythian-Adams had little success in his trial diggings of 1923.

In 1966 synagogue* ruins were discovered somewhat S of the site, picturing the familiar Jewish decorations of the menorah* (branched candlestick), the shofar (ram's horn), and the palm branch. There is a mosaic* floor, showing David as Orpheus, named in Hebrew characters, but depicting animals charmed by his lyre, as in Greek legend. It is sixth-century work like the mosaics of Shekel and Maon.

BIBLIOGRAPHY: J. B. Pritchard, *ANET*, 529; E. G. Kraeling, *Bible Atlas* (1956), 417–18; W. H. Mare, *ZPEB*, 2 (1975), 662–65.

EMB

GEBAL (gē′ bəl; Heb. גְּבָל, *geḇal*; Gr. βύβλος, *Byblos*; Ugar. *Gbl*; Amarna *Gubla*; meaning "hill"). A city* of the N Phoenician* coast between Beirut* (Berytus) and Tripoli. 1. *Excavation*. Gebal was identified in 1860 by E. Renan and work was begun as early as 1921, first with Pierre Montet, and then under the direction of Maurice Dunand, whose career is synonymous with excavation of the famed city. Early work on the tell,* which lies on a small bluff immediately to the S of the modern town of Jebeil (Arab. for Gebal), revealed almost continuous occupation from Neolithic* times through the Crusader period. Among the many highlights were the discovery of a Neolithic necropolis* with over seven hundred

tombs, an abundance of pottery,* inscriptions from various periods, and houses* and fortifications typifying almost every important period of Syrian archaeology.

2. *History of the city*. The Neolithic people who lived in Gebal as early as 5000 B.C. were a coastal variation of a culture found in such Palestinian inland sites as Shaar Hagolan and Yarmuk. Decorated pebbles and stylized figurines, incised ceramic patterns of varying degrees of artistry, impressed cord pottery, various flint tools* and burial patterns are common to many sites from the N Syrian coast to northern Palestine. Chalcolithic* Gebal has many similarities to this culture, though differences indicate strong new elements. Multiple burials (up to twenty-six adults in one vault) enter at this period; curvilinear or rectilinear houses are grouped on cobbled streets;* silver* and a little copper is refined; and various pots, tripod bowls, and other combed ware is found.

It is not clear what happened to Chalcolithic Gebal, but by about 3100 B.C., when Egypt* was becoming united under the early dynasties, a new urban civilization arose, both in Byblos and in the rest of Syria-Palestine. Gebal quickly became a leading port for Egyptian goods, with oil, wine,* perfumes, grains, and honey among items of trade. Cedar* wood was an obvious choice for the return journey, as the Palermo Stone* (twenty-seventh century, *ANET*, 227) tells us. Other important innovations include the first city walls* in Gebal, the use of a potter's wheel, and the introduction of bronze.* Also during the early third millennium was built the first temple to Baalat Gebal ("The Lady of Gebal"), soon to be followed by new and larger temples, which continued to about 2200 B.C.

In the period 2100–1900 the so-called Amorite* Invasion took place across Palestine-Syria, and Gebal was burned at the very start of that phase. Names of kings from the city that followed indicate probable Amorite control, and by the nineteenth and eighteenth centuries the Execration Texts* (*ANET*, 328ff.) show a definite breakdown in relations between Egypt and Gebal, though other indications point to a strong trade between the two countries at times during the Twelfth Dynasty.

In the Hyksos* and Amarna* periods, Gebal apparently reflected the general culture of its day. Royal names are preserved in the Mari* texts, and scarabs* of one ruler, Yantin'ammu, have been found in several places. Of the city in Hyksos times we have no specific knowledge, but following the demise of these "foreign rulers" Gebal became a vassalage of the New Kingdom pharaohs for over three hundred years. During this period about sixty letters from a ruler of Gebal, Rib-addi by name, pleaded with Pharaoh for help against ever-increasing pressures from such outside forces as the king of Amurru and the internal machinations of disloyal princes (*ANET*, 483ff.). By c. 1100 B.C., the Egyptian traveler and merchant, Wenamon, was finding considerable independence on the part of the natives (*ANET*, 25ff.), and it is shortly after this that the great period of Phoenician expansion begins.

During this important phase perhaps the most significant archaeological remains are the various inscriptions and tablets that illumine our knowledge of alphabetic* writing.* Although cuneiform* alphabetic inscriptions are known earlier from Ugarit,* the idea of a linear alphabet seems first to be used extensively in Gebal. Details of the development are still in dispute, but by c. 1000 B.C., on the sarcophagus* of King Ahiram* (discovered 1923) we have a clear and readable Canaanite-Phoenician script, using characters that were to remain standard for a thousand years. This alphabet was, apparently, taken over by the Greeks in the centuries that followed, and both the names of the letters (e.g., alpha, beta, etc.) and their order continued Phoenician traditions. So famous did Gebal become for its writing that the Greeks called the city after the name of scrolls* seen there, and Byblos, or "book," eventually became the name by which the city was known in the West.

The trading world of Byblos survived invasions of Assyrians, Babylonians, and Persians. Some decline was evident at the onset of the Hellenistic period, though the city followed many others in accepting Greek culture. From the Roman period there is evidence of considerable building, and the remains of a bath, a basilica,* and a theater* are to be seen. The last important archaeological period is represented by the Crusader castle,* which dominates the site to this day.

BIBLIOGRAPHY: P. Montet, *Byblos et l'Egypte* (1928); M. Dunand, "Rapport préliminaire sur les fouilles de Byblos en . . . ," Bulletin du Musee de Beyrouth, beginning with vol. 1 (1937) and continuing regularly through vol. 22 (1969); id., *Fouilles de Byblos*, 1 (1939); id., *Biblia Grammata* (1945); V. G. Childe, *New Light on the Most Ancient East*, 4th ed. (1952), 220–24; S. H. Horn, "Byblos in Ancient Records," Andrews University Seminary Studies, 1 (1963), 52–61; M. Dunand, *Byblos, son histoire, ses ruines, ses légendes* (1964); W. F. Albright, "Gebal," *EBi*, 2 (1964), 404–11; id., "Further Light on the History of MB Byblos," *BASOR*, 179 (1965), 38–43; O. Tufnell and W. A. Ward, "Relations between Byblos, Egypt and Mesopotamia at the End of the Third Millennium B.C.," *Syria*, 43 (1966), 165–241; K. Branigan, "Further Light on Prehistoric Relations between Crete and Byblos," *AJA*, 71 (1967), 117–21; K. A. Kitchen, "Byblos, Egypt, and Mari in the Early Second Millennium B.C.," *Orientalia*, 36 (1967), 39–54; F. B. Huey, Jr., *ZPEB*, 2 (1975), 666–68; C. Mesnil Du Buisson, "Le cylindresceau archaïque de Byblos réexaminé," *Berytus*, 24 (1975–76), 89–119; P. K. McCarter and R. B. Coote, "Spatula Inscription From Byblos," *BASOR*, 212 (Dec 1973), 16–22; F. M. Cross, "A Recently Published Phoenician Inscription of the Persian Period From Byblos," *IEJ*, 29 (1979), 40–44.

CEA

GEDALIAH (ged ə lī' ə; Heb. גְּדַלְיָהוּ, g^edalyāhû; "Yahweh is great"). Governor of Judah* during the Exile (2 Kings 25:22–26; Jer 40–41).

Several Gedaliahs are mentioned in Scripture (1 Chron 25:3, 9; Zeph 1:1; Jer 38:1–6; Ezra 10:18), but only the one mentioned above is connected with

any archaeological find. A clay* seal* impression with marks of papyrus* on the back was found at Lachish* inscribed with two lines: "(belonging) to Gedaliah, (w)ho is over the hou(se)." The style and writing accord with a date c. 600 B.C., making it probable that this official is identified with the Gedaliah of biblical records.

BIBLIOGRAPHY: J. C. L. Gibson, *Textbook of Syrian Semitic Inscriptions* (1971), 62, 64.

CEA

GEHENNA. See HINNOM.

GENEALOGIES. Genealogies comprised one of the earliest forms of Ancient Near Eastern historiography. Among early Sumerian* texts are a number of tablets bearing genealogies, set out in the same "staccato style," to use D. J. Wiseman's phrase, as that found in the genealogies of Genesis. Such texts were also found in considerable numbers when Chiera excavated Nuzi* (Yorgan Tepe) from 1925. Often they were inscribed on the backs of tablets which had been used to record other matters. Such materials proved to be Hurrian "family trees," and their usage follows closely that of similar material in Genesis, particularly if that book can be regarded as comprising in part some eleven tablets written in the fashion of ancient Mesopotamian* historiography (cf. R. K. Harrison, *Introduction to the OT* [1969], 543–53). Genealogies were the property of the families who owned the tablets on which they were written, and comprised the only history that most people ever encountered. Many modern Arabs* can recite their genealogies backward from their own generation. The remark in Heb 7:1–3 about Melchisedek* being without genealogy is meant to imply that he founded his own dynasty.

EMB

GENESIS APOCRYPHON. The Genesis Apocryphon was one of the first of the now famous Dead Sea Scrolls* to be found. A Bedouin goat tender accidentally discovered what was later called Cave 1 of the eleven manuscript caves* in the vicinity of Khirbet Qumran* and carried off several of these scrolls.* This scroll, now called the Genesis Apocryphon (1QApGen), was not opened immediately in 1948 because of its advanced deterioration. It was at first identified by some of the fragments broken off in handling, as was the Scroll of Lamech. When it was finally opened and published in 1956, it proved to be written in literary Aramaic* of the first century B.C. It contains a paraphrase of the Genesis accounts of Lamech, Enoch, Noah, and Abraham, with some added fantastic and legendary material. The name Apocryphon was given because its embellishments and poetic legends seemed to put it in a class with *Enoch*, *Jubilees*, and other apocryphal (*see* PSEUDEPIGRAPHA) books. Some scholars argue convincingly that the scroll should rather be classed as a targum, since even where the embellishments occur it follows the pattern of the Hebrew text of Genesis verse by verse. At any rate, the Genesis Apocryphon is linguistically significant as an example of literary

Palestinian Aramaic in the century before Jesus Christ.

BIBLIOGRAPHY: N. Avigad and Y. Yadin, *A Genesis Apocryphon* (1956).

BCC

GENIZAH. This term (meaning "hiding-place") was used of the storeroom or depository in a synagogue* in which worn-out Hebrew and other manuscripts were placed. According to Rabbinic tradition, works of a heretical nature were also put in the genizah to prevent them from influencing the public (cf. *Shab.* 13b, 30b; *Pes.* 62). The most notable genizah of modern times is the one in the old synagogue near Cairo, which had once been a Christian church. In the storeroom Solomon Schechter discovered a fragment of the original Hebrew of Ecclesiasticus in 1896, and after that time other material was recovered from the same source and published. Many ancient synagogues had genizahs, and it was not unusual for their contents to be taken out periodically and buried in a cemetery. On occasions such material has been disinterred, as at Alexandria* in 1898, but with little significant result. The Qumran* caves, though a depository for precious manuscripts, did not comprise a genizah, since the writings seem merely to have been stored pending future usage.

BIBLIOGRAPHY: E. N. Adler, *JE*, 5, 612–13.

RKH

GENNESAR; GENNESARET. See GALILEE.

GENTILES, COURT OF THE. Gentiles were forbidden the inner temple* areas, and even Roman citizenship did not protect a Gentile who intruded into prohibited areas. Josephus (Jos. *War* 5, v, 2; cf. Jos. *War* 6, ii, 4; Jos. *Antiq.* 15. xi, 5; Philo *Leg.* 212) says: "Proceeding across this [the open court] towards the second court of the temple, one found it surrounded by a stone balustrade, three cubits high and of exquisite workmanship; in this at regular intervals stood slabs giving warning, some in Greek, others in Latin characters, of the law of purification, to wit that no foreigner was permitted to enter the holy place, for so the second enclosure of the temple was called." One of these warning notices was discovered in 1871 by Clermont-Ganneau. It runs: "No

Greek plaque, attached to the Soreg, forbidding Gentiles to pass beyond that point. Courtesy Israel Dept. of Antiquities and Museums.

man of another nation to enter within the fence and enclosure round the temple. And whoever is caught will have himself to blame that his death ensues" (cf. Acts 21:26–30).

BIBLIOGRAPHY: F. Clermont-Ganneau, *RA*, 23 (1872), 214–34, 290–96 and plate x; A. Edersheim, *The Temple, Its Ministry and Services* (1874), 23–24; E. Schürer, *A History of the Jewish People in the Time of Jesus Christ*, 1 (1890), 2, 74; id., 2 (1890), 1, 266; H. G. Stigers, *ZPEB*, 5 (1975), 645–56.

EMB

GEOCHRONOLOGY. See DATING.

GERAR (jē'rär; Heb. גְּרָר, *geʿrar*). Tell Jemmeh was the original suggestion for this site, a few kilometers S of Gaza* and excavated by W. J. Pythian-Adams (1922) and W. F. Flinders Petrie five years later. The latter's excavations penetrated to the sixteenth century B.C. The identification was challenged by D. Alon who named Tell Abu Hureirah a short distance further from Gaza to the SE in Wadi Es-Sariah. The survey showed that the eminence was indeed a tell,* occupied since Bronze Age times, and not a natural hill, as was originally thought. The community was prosperous in the Middle Bronze Age, the time of the patriarchs (cf. Gen 10:19; 20:1, 2; 26:6, 20). This would both confirm the story of the relations of Abraham and Isaac with Abimelech (probably a dynastic name) and also support the contention of Kelso that the patriarchs were desert sheiks of wealth, influence, and authority, with whom the communities of Palestine did well to come to terms.

BIBLIOGRAPHY: Y. Aharoni, "The Land of Gerar," *IEJ* 6 (1956), 26–32. For the earlier view, W. F. Petrie, *Gerar* (1928); W. H. Mare, *ZPEB*, 2 (1975), 698.

EMB

GERASA. This town is identified with modern Jarash (Jerash) in Jordan, where excavations by four important archaeological schools have revealed the commercial and political importance of this town of the Decapolis.* The ruins visible today date from the second to the seventh centuries and reveal a considerable city* with fine temples, public buildings, and shopping malls, appropriate enough for one of the "caravan cities" of the Fertile Crescent.* The ruins have been heavily plundered, the modern village, Jarash, itself having been built on the nearby hill of stones removed from the ancient city. A notable and unique feature was an oval forum* ringed by columns, large sections of which still stand in place, Ionic columns here, though Corinthian capitals are the commonest order in the city. A theater* occupies a typical site on a hillside overlooking the city. Of Christian interest is a fifth-century inscription noting the official recognition of Christian worship and the discontinuance of pagan. The display of this edict was no doubt necessary in a center devoted to the worship of Artemis.*

BIBLIOGRAPHY: W. A. Thomson, *The Land and the Book* (1882), 333, 338, 353, 359; C. H. Kraeling, *Gerasa, City of the Decapolis* (1938); K. Sim, *Desert*

Roman forum at Gerasa in Jordan. Courtesy Israel Dept. of Antiquities and Museums.

Traveller: The Life of Jean Louis Burckhardt (1969), 118–19.

EMB

GERASENES; GERGESENES. *See* GADARA.

GERIZIM, MOUNT (ger′ə zim; Heb. הַר־גְּרִזִים, *har gᵉrizzîm*). A mountain (Tell er-Ras, Tananir) on the S side of the pass in which modern Nablus and ancient Shechem* are located. The pass runs EW and Gerizim lies opposite Mount Ebal on the N.

Gerizim has, from earliest antiquity, been an important site. Although infrequently mentioned in the biblical record (Deut 11:29; 27:12; Josh 8:33; Judg 9:7; cf. also reference to "this mountain," John 4:20–21), the mountain commands a prominent overview of two well-traveled highways and has a long history, continuing to the present, of religious associations. That it was important to the premonarchal nation of Israel is clear from the references above, as well as from its undoubted association with the nearby covenant center of Shechem (Tell Balaṭa, below in the valley). Both Josephus and the NT indicate that the mountain was the site of an important Samaritan* temple, built, according to Josephus, c. 335–330 B.C. and destroyed by the Maccabean ruler John Hyrcanus in 128 B.C. In the Christian era, several writers of the fourth and fifth centuries refer to a great temple to Zeus* Hypsistos on Mount Gerizim built by the Emperor Hadrian,* a testimony which is confirmed by pictorial representations, on coins* struck between 138 and 253 A.D., of a colonnaded structure with steps leading up to it.

The mountain is made up of three peaks, the highest of which (on the SE) contains the Samaritan high place currently in use, a Muslim weli, the remains of the Theotokos Church built by the Emperor Zeno c. 484 A.D., and other fortifications added by Justinian. Two ridges extend from the peak, one to the W and one to the N, the latter covered by a small

mound known as Tell er-Ras. In addition to the structures on top of the tell,* interest has recently been shown in a site known as Tananir on the lower N slope, about 300 yards from Tell Balaṭa. Excavations in 1968 by the American Schools of Oriental Research uncovered what is considered to be a Middle Bronze temple and other structures of the same period (*see* Bibliography). A further site, possibly to be identified (after excavation) with the lost Samaritan city of Loza, is on the S and SW slopes, where extensive remains indicate Hellenistic occupation.

Preliminary excavations on Tell er-Ras were undertaken by C. W. Wilson for the Palestine Exploration Society in 1866 with little result. In 1930 A. M. Schneider and a German expedition cleared the beautiful Theotokos Church and the accompanying fortifications on the SE peak but did nothing on the tell itself. Attention was again attracted to Tell er-Ras in 1962 when a Joint Expedition was working at Shechem and a number of unidentified Aswan* granite column fragments were found near the tell. In 1964 and 1966 full-scale excavations were conducted, led by R. J. Bull of Drew University, and extensive remains both of the great Roman Zeus temple and the stairway leading up to it were uncovered. It was found to have been erected on a massive filled platform with walls 2.7 m. (9 ft.) thick and 6 m. (20 ft.) high, while the temple itself measured 14 by 20 m. (46 by 66 ft.) and was dated to the period of Hadrian, c. 130 A.D. A series of six square cisterns* on the N side of the platform were excavated and dated, from coins and inscriptions, to a destruction in the fourth century A.D. Of special interest was evidence of additional construction in the sixth century when the temple was apparently reused by Byzantine* monks.

The 1966 excavations had indicated that the Roman temple was built on top of an earlier structure, the construction of which was of unhewn stone and mud mortar. In 1968 this building was shown to have been of Hellenistic origin (Samaritan period), surrounded by a high temenos* wall also from the Samaritan period, measuring about 18 m. (60 ft.) square with a height of 9 m. (30 ft.), and resting on bedrock. While archaeologists in the field are convinced this is the temple of the Samaritans noted by Josephus, it is conceded that further work needs to be undertaken in various parts of this important site.

If this site was in fact that of the Samaritan temple, the ruins (from the destruction of 128 B.C.) of both the temple and the altar would have been visible to Jesus and the woman during their dialogue at Jacob's well* (John 4:20).

BIBLIOGRAPHY: A. M. Schneider, "Romische und Byzantinische Bauten auf dem Garizim," ZDPV, 68 (1951), 211–34; R. J. Bull, "The Excavation of Tell er-Ras on Mount Gerizim," BA, 31 (1968), 58–72; R. G. Boling, "Bronze Age Buildings at the Shechem High Place: ASOR Excavations at Tananir," BA, 32 (1969), 81–103; E. F. Campbell, Jr., "Tell Balatah and Tell er-Ras," Newsletter No. 10 of the American Schools of Oriental Research (1968–69); E. K. Vogel, "Bibliography of Holy Land Sites," HUCA, 42 (1971), 62–63; R. J. Bull, "Er-Ras, Tell," EEHL, 4 (1978), 1015–22; R. J. Bull, "Archaeological Footnote to 'Our Fathers Worshiped on This Mountain,' John 4:20," NTS, 23 (1977), 460–62; R. J. Bull, "Archaeological Context for Understanding John 4:20," BA, 38 (1975), 54–59; G. G. Garner, "The Temples of Mt. Gerizim. Tell er Ras—Probable Site of the Samaritan Temple," Buried History, 11 (1975), 33–42.

CEA

GETHSEMANE. This place (the name is Aramaic* for "oil-vat") was a garden* (John 18:1) of olives.* The location "across the Kidron* torrent," as John puts it, must lie within a narrow compass on the slopes of the Mount of Olives.* The Armenian, Greek, Latin* (the Franciscan order), and Russian churches possess properties round about, and the Franciscan Basilica of the Agony, a modern structure, is built over fourth-century ruins. Within is the traditional rock of the agony described by the seventh-century pilgrim Arculf. This is as far as archaeology can go in identifying the site. The present olive trees in the precinct go back to the seventh century, but since olive roots are practically indestructible, the trees may grow from the remaining roots of those destroyed by Titus* in the siege of A.D. 70.

BIBLIOGRAPHY: W. E. Thompson, The Land and the Book, 634 (This ninety-year-old classic is still readable.); G. Dalman, Sacred Sites and Ways (1935), 321ff.; C. Hollis and R. Brownrigg, Holy Places (1969), 45–50, 59, 82–83.

EMB

GEZER (gē'zər; Heb. גֶּזֶר, gezer). The site of this city* of the Shephelah* was identified in the course of investigations between 1870 and 1873 by C. Clermont-Ganneau at Tell el-Jezer, near the village of Abu Shusheh. A bilingual inscription in Greek and Hebrew, discovered by him in 1874, clinched the matter. It reads: "the confines of Gezer-Alkos." R. A. S. Macalister worked on the site from 1902 to

1905, and again from 1907 to 1909. Subsequent excavations were conducted by G. E. Wright and W. G. Dever. All periods from Bronze Age work to Hellenistic and Roman are now distinguished. Y. Yadin has discovered a Solomonic level, missed by Macalister. The Hebrew Union College expedition has relocated the "high place,*" described by Macalister and made numerous corrections to the work of earlier investigations.

BIBLIOGRAPHY: For an exhaustive bibliography to 1970 see A. F. Rainey, ZPEB, 2 (1975), 709.

EMB

GHASSULIAN CULTURE. This culture, which occurred in the early Chalcolithic* period (c. 5600–3000 B.C.), is the Palestinian counterpart of the cultures of Tell Halaf in Mesopotamia* and Badari in Upper Egypt.* While copper was being employed increasingly from the beginning of the Chalcolithic period, flint implements were still being used extensively in the Near East, and this situation is reflected in all contemporary levels excavated. Ghassulian culture derived its name from Teleilat Ghassul,* a place close to Jericho* and N of the Dead Sea,* where Palestinian Chalcolithic deposits roughly contemporary with those of Tell Halaf and Badari were found. Although Ghassulian pottery* was by no means as fine or elegant as its Halafian counterpart, it nevertheless exhibited some variation and improvement over that of earlier periods. Houses* excavated at Teleilat Ghassul were made of mud brick with a plastered interior on which fresco designs had been painted.* One elaborate geometrical pattern was based upon an eight-pointed star and was surrounded by the remains of other geometrical figures. Another fresco depicted a bird, which had been executed by the ancient artist with great precision and attention to detail. Ghassulians buried their dead in stone-lined graves,* along with ornaments and pottery vessels, the latter undoubtedly having contained food.* This would perhaps indicate some rudimentary belief in an existence after death, though there may well have been other reasons why the vessels were interred with the deceased person. At Khedheirah, the bones of dead Ghassulians were deposited in house-urns, fashioned in the shape of normal Ghassulian adobe houses on stone foundations, suggesting that the dead may have been thought to be living in the afterlife much as they had done previously.

BIBLIOGRAPHY: A. Mallon et al., Teleilat Ghassul I (1934); CAH, 1.1, 521–25.

RKH

GHOSH, ABU. See ABU GHOSH.

GIBEAH (gib'ē ə; Heb. גִּבְעָה, gib'āh, "a hill"). Tell el-Ful,* 4.8 km. (3 mi.) N of Jerusalem.* "Gibeah of Saul," as the hill is called in Isaiah's dramatic passage on the war bulletins of the swift Assyrian attack rolling down on Jerusalem (Isa 10:28–32). According to Josephus, Titus* camped there on the night before he reached Jerusalem. There is a fine view from the hilltop—hence King Hussein's choice of the royal location for a palace in 1965. The site was identified as early as 1843 and first explored for the Palestine Exploration Fund in 1868, a project which the excavator, Lieutenant Charles Warren, seems to have left undescribed. The major archaeological investigation was undertaken by W. F. Albright in 1922, 1923, and 1933. Albright described five periods of occupation, but fixed the Early Iron Age, * perhaps in the last generation of the thirteenth century as the first substantial exploitation of the two-acre hilltop site. The Hebrew settlement covered roughly two centuries and ended in some catastrophe reflecting possibly the horrible events of Judg 19 and 20. A deep layer of ash marks a great conflagration. Albright's major discovery was a fortress which took final shape in the time of Saul, about 1000 B.C. It was originally of Philistine* construction, destroyed by Saul after his victory over the Philistines (if "Gibeah" is read for "Geba" in 1 Sam 13:3, 16). Albright discovered the substantial remains of the SW corner of a subsequent fortress-palace superimposed by Saul on the earlier ruins as his royal stronghold. Bronze* arrowheads and an iron* plowpoint vividly illustrated the point of transition from the Bronze to the Iron Ages. *

The building that Albright uncovered was probably the palace in which David endured the paranoiac jealousy of Saul (1 Sam 18:10–11). The site was abandoned after the death of Saul, and, in spite of its commanding position was not occupied again for some three centuries.

More recently, in 1964, in order to forestall the obliteration of the site by the Jordanian palace, Paul Lapp undertook further investigation which largely confirmed Albright's findings. He was able to add some details. N of the SW wall tower from which Albright projected the size and shape of Saul's stronghold, a portion of the W wall, to the length of 3 m. (10 ft.), was uncovered. This point of reference tended to confirm Albright's projections and answer the objections expressed by de Vaux, but cast doubt on Albright's belief that the fortress had casemate walls. * A single wall, some 1.2 m. (4 ft.) thick, seems to be indicated. Lapp also challenged the view that a Philistine fort lay beneath Saul's restoration. He found no evidence of distinctive Philistine occupation, and indeed no typically Philistine pottery* was recovered by Albright, who explained the deficiency by assuming that the Philistines had been so assimilated culturally that no distinctive types need be expected.

Generally, Saul's palace-fort was an austere structure, reflecting the poverty of a period just emerging from a "dark age," and yet to confirm its unity and find the strength and purpose which unity brings. It was, as H. T. Frank remarks, "like Saul himself, a symbol of transition. Hardly impressive in the light of the royal Hebrew magnificence which, in less than a century, would dominate Solomon's capital only 4.8 km. (3 mi.) away, it was nonetheless, like Saul himself, monumental in the promise it embodied" (*Bible Archaeology and Faith* [1971], 120–24).

BIBLIOGRAPHY: W. F. Albright, "Excavations and Results at Tell el-Ful," *BASOR*, 4 (1924); L. A. Sin-

"Pool of Gibeon" with its spiral staircase of seventy-nine steps. Reproduced by permission of The University Museum, University of Pennsylvania.

clair, "An Archaeological Study of Gibeah (Tell el-Ful)," *AASOR*, 34 (1960); W. F. Albright, *The Archaeology of Palestine* (1960 ed.), 120–21; G. G. Swaim, *ZPEB*, 2 (1975), 711–12.

EMB

GIBEON; GIBEONITES. Mentioned forty-five times in the Bible, the Gibeonites are famous for their deception of Joshua during the conquest. For having tricked him into a peace treaty, they were in turn cursed to become "hewers of wood and drawers of water." There are hints that Gibeon was well known for its water supply. The contest of Abner and Joab was located at the "pool of Gibeon" (2 Sam 2:13), and the usurper, Ishmael, was found by the "great waters in Gibeon" (Jer 41:12).

Al Jib, 12.8 km. (8 mi.) N of Jerusalem, * has now been conclusively proven as the site of Gibeon. It was excavated between 1956 and 1962 by James Pritchard for the Museum of the University of Pennsylvania and the Church Divinity School of the Pacific. Pritchard found abundant ceramic evidence for habitation during the entire Bronze Age (3100–1200 B.C.), Iron Age* (1200–550 B.C.), Persian period (539–330 B.C.), and Roman period (63 B.C.–A.D. 325). There was definite evidence of occupation during Joshua's campaigns: imported wares from Cyprus, * local pilgrim flasks, boxes, lamps, * and jugs, as well as scarabs* of Thutmose III (1490–1436 B.C.). The most remarkable finds were from the Iron Age. Identification of the site was made by over twenty-five inscriptions with the name "Gibeon," and one with the name, "Hananiah," which occurs in Jer 28:1. The water systems were the most extensive ever excavated in Palestine. A system of tunnels had been cut through 118.6 m. (389 ft.) of solid rock; steps cut from the rock totaled more than 179, including the spiral stairs around the pool,* and the great pool itself which was 11 m. (36 ft.) in diameter and 9 m. (30 ft.) deep and was carved from the rock. Another large chamber or cistern* was discovered at the end of a tunnel from the pool 15 m. (49 ft.) lower than the pool, and cool, sweet water was found in it although it had been sealed for twenty-five centuries.

Other finds of the Iron Age included: a pillar-supported house* with kitchen and storage room, the city wall,* eighty jar handles stamped with the royal seal,* and an industrial complex with vats and storage jars indicating that Gibeon was the center of a large wine* industry.

BIBLIOGRAPHY: J. B. Pritchard, "The Water System at Gibeon," *BA*, 19 (1956), 66–75; id., "Industry and Trade at Biblical Gibeon," *VTSup*, 7 (1959), 1–12; id., *Gibeon, Where the Sun Stood Still* (1962); R. L. Alden, *ZPEB*, 2 (1975), 714–17.

BCC

GIHON, SPRING OF. This source of water is possibly the modern 'Ain Sitti Margam, the spring E of Jerusalem* from which Hezekiah cut his conduit, the famous Siloam tunnel (*see* HEZEKIAH'S TUNNEL) to supply water to the Pool of Siloam.* According to 2 Chron 33:14 it was still outside Manasseh's* wall. During the Greek period the spring proved unequal

Rock-cut entrance to Spring of Gihon. *(See also photo under* HEZEKIAH'S TUNNEL.) Courtesy Israel Government Press Office.

to the demands made on it by the citizens of Jerusalem, and water was ultimately brought from a distance by means of aqueducts,* one of which was either constructed or reconstructed by Pontius Pilate.

BIBLIOGRAPHY: K. M. Kenyon, *Jerusalem: Excavating 3000 Years of History* (1967), 15–16, 31, 69–77.

EMB

GILGAMESH EPIC. An epic poem concerning the legendary Gilgamesh, fifth king of the first dynasty of Uruk* following the flood. It includes a Babylonian account of a great flood* (Tablet XI).

The first copies of the epic to be found and published were part of the great library of Ashurbanipal* found at Nineveh* by A. H. Layard and his successors. George Smith startled the European world in 1872 with a paper entitled "The Chaldean Account of the Deluge," in which the now-famous flood epic of Tablet XI first came to public notice. In the years since then, additional copies of the text and various fragments have been uncovered throughout the entire Near East, and publications on the subject have become voluminous. Versions of some part of the epic are now available in Sumerian (from which the epic probably originated), various dialects of Akkadian,* Hittite,* and even Hurrian.* Published editions are legion, and the modern English reader can choose from any one of several translations.

The flood story, though justly the most famous part of Gilgamesh's epic, is but one of twelve tablets. The others recount various exploits of the hero and his friend Enkidu and seem to be teaching a moral. The lesson is that death comes to all, and there is nothing better than to enjoy life now. The flood story is of secondary importance and helps illustrate this theme. Similarities between the Gilgamesh Epic and the biblical account of Noah are immediately noticeable, but the essential difference in theme and outlook makes any direct dependence of the one on the other extremely doubtful. The more available and important recent studies of the subject are listed in the bibliography.

See ATRA-HASIS EPIC.

BIBLIOGRAPHY: A. Heidel, *The Gilgamesh Epic and OT Parallels* (1949); E. A. Speiser, *ANET*, 2d ed. (1955), 72–98, 104–6; S. N. Kramer, *ANET* (1955), 42–44; J. V. Kinnier Wilson, *DOTT* (1958), 17–26; P. Garelli, ed., *Gilgameš et sa Légende* (1960); A. R. Millard, "A New Babylonian Genesis Story," Tyndale Bulletin XVIII (1967), 3–18; A. K. Grayson, *The Ancient Near East; Supplementary Texts and Pictures*, J. B. Pritchard, ed. (1969), 503–7, 512–14; W. G. Lambert and A. R. Millard, *Atra-hasis: The Babylonian Story of the Flood* (1969); J. Hansman, "Gilgamesh, Humbaba and the Land of the Erin-Trees," *Iraq*, 38 (1976), 23; R. E. Simmons-Vermeer, "Mesopotamian Floodstories; A Comparison and Interpretation," *Numen*, 21 (1974), 17–34; D. J. Wiseman, "A Gilgamesh Epic Fragment From Nimrud," *Iraq*, 37 (1975), 157.

CEA

GIZA (gē'zə). Giza (Gizeh) was the necropolis* of the city of Memphis* (capital of the Egyptian* Old

Kingdom) and site of the world famous pyramids.* Located on the desert plateau directly W of the modern city* of Cairo, the site is actually some 8 km. (5 mi.) from the town of Giza. The name "Giza" attached itself to the pyramids because it was the closest town prior to the twentieth century.

The great pyramid of Khufu is deserving of the title "one of the seven wonders of the world," but the entire complex of monuments on the Giza plateau is massive beyond comparison. The three major royal tombs (the pyramids of Khufu, Khafre', and Menkaure) are surrounded by six smaller pyramids, the name of only one of which is known, that of Khamerenebty II, queen of Menkaure. Tombs of family members and nobles comprise an estimated 5000 additional structures, many of which are inscribed or have subterranean chambers which are decorated with painted reliefs. This vast tomb field is but one component of the Memphite cemetery, stretching for many miles from Abu Roash to Meidum. Each major pyramid had its own mortuary temple and stone causeway reaching down to the edge of the cultivation where another (valley) temple was located. Pits containing solar boats (one 46 m., or 150 ft., long) surrounded the base of the pyramid. In one shaft in the bedrock nearly 31 m. (100 ft.) deep, grave* goods from the burial of Queen Hetepheres were found. She was the mother of Khufu, builder of the great pyramid.

The great pyramid originally rose to a height of 147 m. (481 ft.), but is today only 137 m. (449 ft.). It covered approximately 5.3 ha. (13 a.) and consisted of nearly two and one-half million blocks, weighing between two and three tons each. The largest stones (roofing the king's chamber) weigh close to 40 tons each. The orientation of the base and the leveling of the first course are marvels of precision. All of this structure was prepared as the sepulchre for the reigning pharaoh. The prevailing solar cult was the key to the tomb's significance, and the benben (capstone*) was of the greatest religious significance. Nummulitic limestone from the site made up most of the core or packing stones, and the entire edifice was faced with a smooth casing of white Tura limestone, almost all of which is missing today. The interior arrangement of chambers is simple, with two major rooms (called the king's and queen's chambers) and an ascending shaft, the grand gallery.

The Chephren (Khafre') pyramid originally stood 143 m. (470 ft.) high, and that of Mycerinus (Menkaure) was much smaller (65 m., or 218 ft.). At the side of the Chephren valley temple stood the famous Sphinx, a native rock outcropping carved into the likeness of the king as Re-Harakhty, god of the sunrise. Nearby was a huge wall,* fronting a city constructed for those who would erect and care for the monuments and the funeral rites.

Besides the pyramids, there is much at Giza of archaeological importance. From the reign of Cheops (Khufu) in Dynasty IV (c. 2600 B.C.) down to the end of Dynasty VI (c. 2250 B.C.), the cemeteries have provided a great part of our knowledge of society, art, titles, and burial customs of the Old Kingdom. Nobles and officials from the courts of the kings were buried in mastaba* tombs, which were arranged in an orderly fashion between "avenues" running N and S, and "streets," which intersect at right angles. The order of the cemetery and the placement of tombs deteriorated as the Old Kingdom progressed beyond Dynasty IV. Later tombs were built utilizing already existing structures for a portion of their support and still other tombs were constructed without regard for the previous regularity of the cemetery, taking any space that was available. The subterranean chambers of this vast tomb-field, particularly those which are inscribed and painted, reveal a plethora of delightful scenes from Egyptian daily life as well as religious and funerary practice (cf. FUNERARY CUSTOMS).

Numerous life-like painted* limestone statues,* as well as a few unpainted "reserve heads," have come from the tombs. The tomb chamber of Hetep-heres, mentioned above, contained remnants of a canopy, a sedan chair, and other items of furniture* inlaid with silver* and gold.* The body of the queen was missing, however, leaving a mystery which has never been completely solved. The recently restored solar boat of Cheops is one of the most impressive remains of ancient Egyptian civilization.

BIBLIOGRAPHY: Ahmed Fakhry, The Pyramids (1961); I. E. S. Edwards, The Pyramids of Egypt (1961); B. Porter and R. Moss, Topographical Bibliography of Ancient Hieroglyphic Texts, Reliefs and Paintings, 3; G. A. Reisner, Giza Necropolis I–II.

JEJ

GLACIS (glā'sis). A military architectural term (Fr., originally "a slope made slippery by frozen rain," OED), denoting the slope from the top of the counterscarp of a fortification toward the open country. It is applied archaeologically to a sloping feature built at the base of city* walls* to hinder enemy attack. Glacis were known earlier, but were most highly developed in the ninth century B.C., in direct response to the threat of the Assyrian battering ram, which was a heavy, cumbersome machine that must be brought close to the wall to operate, under covering mantlets such as those described in Roman military literature (e.g., Julius Caesar's Commentaries).

The glacis was designed to expose the attackers to the defenders' missile fire from above, and, if it had a packed clay* covering, could be rendered quite slippery at a focal point of attack by pouring water or oil on it from above. Countermeasures to the glacis were the building of long gradual ramps to the wall or the digging out of a section of the glacis itself. An example of such a ramp may be seen at Masada,* which had a natural glacis. It was built by the erosion debris around Masada, and this talus slope is common near any similar outcrop of stone.

Excavations at Jericho* by K. Kenyon revealed a Middle Bronze Age defensive system, including a glacis at the base of the city wall, presumed by the excavator to be for defense against Hyksos* chariots.* The steep slope was covered with plaster,* or alternatively by a stone revetment with a mud-brick parapet at the foot of the slope. Several glacis were found frequently at the Late Bronze city of Hazor,*

Iron Age sloped stone glacis from Tell Malhata. Courtesy Tel Aviv University, Institute of Archaeology.

Sloping assault ramp on the western side of Masada. Courtesy Israel Government Press Office.

built of *terre-pisée* (or *pisé*; "beaten earth") as a part of the walls. Some of them, however, were built with a battered stone construction.

Both types of glacis seem to have been used first in Anatolia and Syria, in response to military tactics developed in those areas. The *terre-pisée* type is the earlier (cf. excavations at Jericho, Lachish,* and Tell Beit Mirsim). Albright dates this type at the beginning of the seventh century or at the end of the eighteenth century and the stone glacis in the late seventeenth or early sixteenth centuries B.C. *Terre-pisée* glacis appear in nearly all excavated Middle Bronze sites and are best represented in Alalakh* (Tell 'Atshana) in Syria; and in Palestine at Jericho (Tell es-Sultan), Lachish (Tell ed-Duweir), Tell Beit Mirsim, Tell el-'Ajjul, Tell Far'ah, and other sites. Sometimes the defenses were increased by a fosse or moat at the foot of the glacis. The best example of stone slopes are seen at Shechem* (Balâtah), Tell Beit Mirsim, Jericho, and at several Anatolian sites. There is a fine glacis at Tell en-Nasbeh (Mizpah*).

BIBLIOGRAPHY: W. F. Albright, *The Archaeology of Palestine* (1960 ed.), 75, 88–89; FLAP rev, 157–58, 164; AIs, 233.

MHH

GLASS. This common compound consists mostly of some kind of silicate, an alkali such as soda or potash, and a base which generally comprises lime or lead* oxide. It can be made easily and cheaply by modern methods, but in the Ancient Near East it was not

common, and until the Roman period was regarded by the Hebrews as semiprecious in nature. Consequently there are few references to it in Scripture (Job 28:17; Rev 4:6; 15:2; 21:18, 21). Discoveries by Soviet archaeologists at the foot of Mount Ararat* have revealed the presence of smelting furnaces* which were able to reduce metallic ores and also to make glass. Since these smelters appear to be dated about 2500 B.C., they are considerably older than any other known means of glass manufacture in the Near East. Perhaps it was from this kind of technology that the Sumerians* derived their knowledge of glass.

In Palestine the art of making glass was first practiced by the Phoenicians,* although the substance was also familiar to the Egyptians* after the Amarna* period. Glass beads, trinkets, and ornaments are found regularly in Egyptian graves,* but to what extent they were of native origin is not always certain. The Egyptians appear to have copied the Phoenician technique of bonding glass rods around a core of clay* to make a hollow vessel when the core was removed. But only from the Roman period onward was technology sufficiently advanced for large containers or sheets to be fabricated. Many buried glass beakers, vials, and bowls recovered from that period have become oxidized through contact with chemicals in the soil, and in consequence they have acquired a beautiful iridescent appearance.

BIBLIOGRAPHY: D. R. Bowes, *ZPEB*, 2 (1975), 729–30.

RKH

GLAZE. A shiny, transparent coating generally used on pottery,* glaze was made by applying a paste of powdered glass* to the surface of the pottery and baking it until the small glass particles fused. The glaze formed an intact surface on the pottery, preserving whatever painted* designs were underneath it, making the artifact suitable as a container for liquids where necessary, and affording it a degree of attractiveness and durability which it would not otherwise have possessed.

HWP

GNOSTICISM; GNOSTICS. See NAG HAMMADI PAPYRI.

GOAT. The earliest evidence for the domestication of the goat comes from prepottery levels in Jericho.* Two types, with corkscrew and scimitar horns, are distinguishable from very early times in northern Mesopotamia.* Varieties in color, illustrating Jacob's genetical scheming of Gen 30, are known from very early illustrations in Egypt.* Rams' skins dyed red were used in the tabernacle, and this implies a developed tanning process, but it is not known when roughly dried hides were replaced by the dressed leather* mentioned twice in the Bible (2 Kings 1:8; Matt 3:4). As early as the thirteenth century B.C., goat skins (and sheep skins) were made into parchment,* and a manuscript of Isaiah dated 150 B.C. is on this material.

BIBLIOGRAPHY: G. S. Cansdale, *All the Animals of the Bible Lands* (1970), 44–48.

EMB

GOLAN. This area, to the NE of the Sea of Galilee,* has long been known as the locale of ancient sites reaching back to the Ghassulian* period of the fourth millennium B.C. The importance of surveying them and excavating selected areas was made more acute by the wars of 1967 and 1973 as they affected the Golan Heights. Since 1967, the maneuvers by the Israeli forces combined with attempts at land development have posed serious threats to the existence of the ancient sites. An archaeological survey was begun in 1967 in the area, one result of which was to demonstrate the presence of Chalcolithic* settlements in the Golan. Excavations commenced in 1974 to trace the remains of walls observable from the surface. A number of rectangular houses* built in parallel chains were uncovered at Rasm Ḥarbush in 1978 and 1979, leading to the conclusion that the settlement was large by Chalcolithic standards. Pottery,* flint, and basalt artifacts* were recovered, along with several house-god statues.* The latter may have been standing originally on a shelf or on the top of an unroofed wall, judging by the position in which they were found on the floor. Pieces of charcoal* were identified as having come from olive* trees, and many carbonized olive pits were also recovered. Nothing resembling an oil press was found, however, suggesting that oil was only extracted on a small scale for ordinary domestic purposes.

Some distinctive styles of pottery vessels were recovered from Golan sites, the ornamentation comprising impressed rope-pattern bands and horizontal incised decorations. Hafted hoes, flint sickle blades, adzes, and pointed tools* indicate the pastoral pursuits (*see* AGRICULTURE) of the Chalcolithic communities in the Golan. Occupation of the area appears to have been intermittent during the biblical period and beyond.

BIBLIOGRAPHY: Clare Epstein, *BA*, 40 (1977), 57–62; *IEJ*, 29 (1979), 225–27.

RKH

GOLD. By virtue of the fact that it is found pure in the earth and in streams, gold may easily have been the first metal known to man. It is mentioned throughout the Bible, and because of its durability and resistance to chemical decomposition, gold has survived in large quantities from most early civilizations, from the Mayas and Incas to the Sumerians.* Craftsmanship* in gold is found to be astonishingly mature even among peoples not notable for other forms of plastic art—the early Celts of Ireland, for example, and the prehistoric tribes of the Crimea. Egyptian* reliefs from Mereru-ka's tomb at Saqqarah (*see* MEMPHIS), dating from twenty-three centuries before Christ, show the weighing, recording, melting, and casting of gold. Various OT terms for gold must indicate various degrees of quality and color. Precision is impossible, but the rough renderings "pure gold," "fine gold," "choice gold," etc., indicate a maturity of craftsmanship in the use of the metal which surviving gold objects abundantly illustrate—for example, the Mycenae gold death masks, the Vaphio cups (both in the Athens Archaeological Museum), the Dublin Museum's collection of early Celtic gold ornaments, and hundreds of ornaments from Palestine, Egypt, and other parts of the Middle East. In antiquity gold was commonly obtained from W Arabia,* the Persian and Armenian mountain ranges, the Aegean Islands, and W Asia Minor.*

BIBLIOGRAPHY: J. R. Partington, *A Text-Book of Inorganic Chemistry* (1950 ed.), 745–47; E. M. Blaiklock, ed., *ZPBA* (1969), 438–43; D. R. Bowes, *ZPEB*, 2 (1975), 771–72.

EMB

GOLGOTHA (gol′gə thə; Gr. Γολγοθᾶ, *Golgothá*). A term meaning "skull" (cf. Matt 27:33; Mark 15:22; Luke 23:33; John 19:17; Latin* *colva*, "calvary"), the name of an execution site near Jerusalem,* so called either because skulls were left there or because the hill looked like the face of a skull. The NT does not specifically locate Golgotha but indicates it was somewhere outside the Jerusalem wall* (John 19:20; Heb 13:12–13) and seemingly on a hill, for it could be seen from a distance (Mark 15:40). Eusebius (Euseb. *Onom.*, 74) puts Golgotha in Aelia N of Mount Zion. This area fits the two sites now called Golgotha: a place in the Church of the Holy Sepulcher* and Gordon's Calvary.

When the Christians fled Jerusalem the 80.5 km. (50 mi.) to Pella* on the eve of the Jewish War (Euseb. *Hist.* 3.5.3), they were still close enough to keep the knowledge of Golgotha fresh in their minds; a knowledge which probably was carried on through

Christians in Jerusalem in Hadrian's* time and later (Euseb. *Hist.* 4.6).

Jerome (Letter 58 to Paulinus, *NPNFSS*, 6, 120) in A.D. 395 says that Hadrian's marble statue* of Venus put up on Golgotha and the statue of Jupiter that stood on the resurrection site continued to Constantine's day. Eusebius states (*Life of Constantine* 4.64) that Constantine, in removing the statue of Venus, also uncovered a tomb which was understood to be Christ's. In A.D. 326 the Emperor Constantine ordered a church, a basilica,* to be built there (*Life of Constantine* 3.31). The Bordeaux Pilgrim* also locates Constantine's basilica in this same area (*CCSL*, 175, 17), where the Church of the Holy Sepulcher now stands.

The Kenyon excavations S of the church in 1962–63 have shown the area occupied by the church to have been outside Josephus's Gennath or second wall (i.e., the wall of Jesus' time). Quarrying remains and pottery* finds show that the area was a quarry* outside the town from the seventh century B.C. to the second century A.D. Further verification that the area was outside the city came from study showing that Josephus's second wall on the W side of the city ran N, to the E of the church.

Since tombs would have been proscribed within the walls, remains of ancient rock-cut tombs at the site also point to the area as being outside the city.*

The Madaba Mosaic Map* (A.D. 560) shows the Church of the Holy Sepulcher as prominent, with doors, with Martyrion, Calvary, and the Anastasis. The church was destroyed and rebuilt several times, the church built there by the Crusaders enclosing the rock of Golgotha.

Gordon's Calvary (first suggested by Thenius in 1842) is the hill above the Grotto of Jeremiah, a quarry area N of Solomon's Quarry and the present Jerusalem N wall. It has physical features resembling a human skull. There are Byzantine*-type tomb remains nearby, including the Garden Tomb. The latter probably only goes back to the third century A.D. at the earliest.

In 1976, Dr. Christos Katsimbinis, excavating at the Church of the Holy Sepulcher, uncovered a 10.7 m. (35 ft.) high mound of grey rock which in the time of Jesus would have stood outside the city's N wall. The excavation of the mound uncovered two small caves* which gave the rock a skull-shaped appearance. This discovery seems to confirm the authenticity of the traditional site of Christ's crucifixion and shows that Christ was not crucified on some remote hill but close to a busy street leading out of Jerusalem.

BIBLIOGRAPHY: Gustaf Dalman, *Sacred Sites and Ways* (1935), 346–81; Kathleen Kenyon, "Excavations in Jerusalem, 1963," *PEQ*, 96 (1964), 14ff.; K. Kenyon, "Excavations in Jerusalem, 1965," *PEQ*, 98 (1966), 85–87; P. B. Bagatti, *L'Eglise de la gentilite en Palestine* (1968), 140–53; J. Finegan, *The Archaeology of the NT* (1969), 109, 135–37, 163–71.

WHM

GOLIATH, ARMOR OF. The Philistines* were Europeans and Goliath wore Aegean armor (1 Sam

17:4–7), well-enough known from Greek vase paintings. The scale armor, of which Yadin provides numerous illustrations, required great technical skill in manufacture if the three essential prerequisites were to be met—lightness, complete protection, and freedom of movement.

Goliath's javelin was "like a weaver's beam" because the block of wood* which separated the threads of the warp to allow free passage to the threads of the weft had loops of cord attached to it. The Hebrew historian was seeking to describe a type of throwing javelin not familiar in Palestine. A fifth-century Greek kylix in the British Museum shows such a weapon. Caught between the warrior's fingers is a loop like that on a weaver's beam. As the javelin was released the cord unwound to give the weapon spin, and therefore greater accuracy and penetration.

Goliath's mistake was in not throwing first. Instead, he threw back his head to laugh, and his opponent was first with his shot. The stone caught Goliath on the forehead because he lacked the protection of a visor. It was important, with this type of armor, to keep the head down. A relief from the palace of Kapara at Tell Halaf in the British Museum shows how the slinger pulled the thongs taut, converting the leather pad into a bag for the stone. He held the bag in his left hand and the ends of the two thongs in his right above his head. The sling was whirled with the right hand and at the proper point of momentum one thong was released to open the bag and free the stone. Michelangelo's statue* of David is accurate in this regard and shows the young man concealing his preparation to throw.

BIBLIOGRAPHY: Y. Yadin, *The Art of Warfare in Biblical Lands*, 354–55, 364.

EMB

GOMORRAH. One of the "cities of the plain"* (Gen 13:12) destroyed by God. It was mentioned in Gen 4:2, 8 with Sodom,* Admah, Zeboiim, and Bela (Zoar), though it was generally linked with Sodom in biblical references. The place was first mentioned in connection with a description of Canaanite* territory (Gen 10:19), and it was the object of an attack by a Mesopotamian* coalition led by Chedorlaomer (Gen 14:2, 8). The cities of the plain had apparently been tributaries to Babylonia for some twelve years but had finally revolted. The campaign by Chedorlaomer in the Valley of Siddim was evidently intended to crush the rebellion and bring the area under Babylonian control once more.

At one time the cities were thought to have been located N of the Dead Sea* where the Jordan Valley opens into the "circle" or "plain." Subsequent researches indicate that they most probably lie submerged under the shallow waters of the southern part of the Dead Sea. To the S of the peninsula known as el-Lisan ("the Tongue") the Valley of Siddim evidently lay in antiquity. It had been a fertile pasture land originally, amply watered by five streams which still flow from the E and SE into this area of the Dead Sea. About 2000 B.C. a catastrophe occurred here which ended settled occupation of the area for six hundred years. It was probably an earthquake with concomitant explosions of gaseous deposits, a telling illustration of divine judgment on human depravity and is held up in Scripture frequently as a warning against perversion and other forms of sin (cf. Deut 29:23; Isa 1:9; Jer 49:18; Amos 4:11; Luke 17:29; 2 Peter 2:6 et al.). The names became symbolic of moral rebellion.

Of the cities themselves, it is possible that underwater archaeology,* or other forms of submarine investigation in the shallow Dead Sea, may provide further information.

See POMPEII.

BIBLIOGRAPHY: W. F. Albright, *BASOR*, 14 (1924), 5–7; id., *AASOR*, 6 (1924–25), 58–62; F. G. Clapp, *AJA* (1936), 323–44; J. P. Harland, *BA*, 5 (1941), 17–32; id., 6 (1943), 41–54; id., *IDB*, 4, 395–97; R. L. Alden, *ZPEB*, 2 (1975), 775.

RKH

GOSHEN (gō′shən; Heb. גֹּשֶׁן, *gōšen*). A territory in the E Delta of Egypt,* where Joseph* settled his family. By Moses' time, it was deemed to be in the "land of Rameses*" (Gen 47:11; cf. Exod 12:37, Num 33:3, 5). This latter equivalence connects Goshen with the territory dependent eventually on the great Delta residence later built and used by Ramses II and his successors, in the environs of modern Qantir. This fact puts Goshen in the general triangle of land between the E arm of the Nile and Wadi Tumilat, in a fertile and productive region, a characteristic observed separately by both the biblical author (Gen 47:6, 11 "best of the land") and Egyptian scribes praising the rich countryside of Rameses (*ANET*, 470–71). An Egyptian word is sometimes read *gsm* and identified with Goshen; but its true reading may be *šsm*, and thus entirely unrelated. The Goshen of Josh 10:41, 11:16, and 15:51 is a town in S Judah,* unconnected with Goshen in Egypt.

BIBLIOGRAPHY: A. H. Gardiner, *JEA*, 5 (1918), 218–23; E. Naville and A. H. Gardiner, *JEA*, 10 (1924), 25–32, 94–95; J. van Seters, *The Hyksos* (1966), 146, 148; K. A. Kitchen, *ZPEB*, 2 (1975), 777–79.

KAK

GOZAN (gō′zən; Heb. גּוֹזָן, *gôzān*; Akkad. *guzanu*). An ancient city* on the Upper Habor River* (N of the middle Euphrates), now the mound of Tell Halaf.

The first settlement at Tell Halaf goes far back into Mesopotamian* prehistory (sixth–fifth millennia B.C.), a certain type of painted* pottery* being named after this site.

More famous is the first-millennium township of Guzana which during the tenth and ninth centuries B.C. was capital of a small Aramaean* state. Its best-known king was Kapara son of Khadianu (the latter name perhaps related to that of Hezion of 1 Kings 15:18), of the ninth century B.C. He built a palace with a striking façade of statue-columns. By 808 B.C., Guzana had been incorporated into the system of provinces of Assyria under a governor. A rebellion in 759 B.C. was crushed in 758, a fact reflected in Sennacherib's* later message to Hezekiah of Judah (1 Kings 19:12). To the river Habor, in the district

of Gozan, some Israelites were deported after the fall of Samaria* in 722 B.C. (2 Kings 17:6), as were some by Tiglath-pileser* III a little earlier (1 Chron 5:26). Two main groups of cuneiform* texts were found: one series from c. 800 B.C., and another of c. 648 B.C. and later. An altar* (ninth century B.C.) and some clay* tablets (c. 648 B.C.) were inscribed in early Aramaic.*

BIBLIOGRAPHY: M. von Oppenheim, *Tell Halaf* (1931); J. Friedrich et al., *Die Inschriften vom Tell Halaf* (1940); M. von Oppenheim, R. Naumann, A. Moortgat, B. Hrouda, *Tell Halaf*, 1–4 (1943–62); A. Moortgat, *Archäologie und Altes Testament, Festschrift für K. Galling* (1970), 211–17.

KAK

GOZLU KULE. *See* TARSUS.

GRAFFITI. A consistently popular form of literary expression, used from antiquity to the present day. Sometimes of a subcultural variety, graffiti employ words, inscriptions, and drawings which are inscribed on surfaces ranging from walls and rock faces to small pieces of pottery.*

HWP

GRAIN. *See* AGRICULTURE; GRANARY.

GRANARY. Grain storage in pits, and in large pots or jars, goes back at least to the Chalcolithic.* Nearly all sites of this period in Palestine (e.g., Teleilat el-Ghassul, Haderah, Tell Abu Matar, and Jiftlik) contain remains of these features. Excavations at Tell Jemmeh in 1953 revealed many large grain pits, up to 8 m. (26 ft.) in diameter, and at Beth Shan* a brick silo, c. 3 m. (10 ft.) wide and nearly as deep, was uncovered. Kenyon cleared a single room in Middle Bronze Jericho* containing more than a dozen large storage jars. Caves* were also used, as well as dry cisterns.* During the Late Bronze and Iron I periods large central granaries became common in Palestine. Community granaries were discovered by

Model of set of twelve granaries found in tomb at el-Kab, Egypt; IV Dynasty. Courtesy Dagon Collection, Archaeological Museum of Grain Handling in Israel.

Albright at Tell Beit Mirsim. Excavators at Dothan found a storage complex with large stone-lined grain pits and adjacent buildings filled with pottery* measuring jars, probably indicating that the site was a tax-collection center. At Gezer* Macalister found many granaries, some of which were evidently public while others were attached to private houses.* Sizes varied, and sometimes several compartments served to separate different kinds of grain. In many of the storage places remnants of grains, sometimes charred, remained, indicating the varieties of grain, which included wheat, barley, oats, millet, and lentils. When tested for germination, all the grains were found to be completely carbonized.

Store-cities, with warehouses for government storage of various supplies, especially grain, were common from high antiquity. Temples in Mesopotamia* and elsewhere were often centers for this purpose. They were well known in Egypt,* as at Tanis* (Rameses*) and Tell Retabah (Pithom,* Exod 1:11), the latter surrounded by massive walls enclosing a space of 167 sq. m. (200 sq. yd.), with many large brick chambers. A clay* model from early Egypt shows features of a granary, including closed walls with roof openings through which grain was poured, a terrace with a place for the recording scribes to sit, and an open court in front. In Palestine, David had stores in various locations (cf. 1 Chron 27:25); Solomon* built storehouses* in different parts of the country to accumulate supplies for his palace commissariat (1 Kings 4:7ff.; 9:19) and also had warehouses in border regions, as at Tadmor* (2 Chron 8:4–6; cf. 1 Kings 9:18, 19). This city (Palmyra*) was a commerce-control center, a kind of bureaucracy for handling food and other supplies. Jehoshaphat (2 Chron 17:12–13; 32:27–29) and Hezekiah also followed this plan. Such granaries and food* depots became logical objectives of invaders, as in the case of Ben-hadad of Syria, who smote the store-cities of Naphtali (2 Chron 16:4).

Masada* had a very extensive storage complex, with many parallel magazines for storage of grains and other commodities. These were first described by Josephus and were excavated by Yadin in the 1960s.

One of the greatest storage complexes from antiquity is to be seen at the excavations of the port city of Ostia, near Rome. Many of the warehouses (*horrea*) date from the first century of the Christian era. Huge pottery jars, reminiscent of an earlier storage center at Troy,* were found dug down into the floors of the granaries. Ostia had its streets* named for the granaries and the mills, and other features related to the ships* and crews that engaged in the very extensive grain trade between Alexandria* and Rome.*

BIBLIOGRAPHY: G. Barton, *Archaeology and the Bible* (1937), 175; K. Kenyon, *Archaeology of the Holy Land* (1960), 271–72, 279; Y. Yadin, *Masada* (1966), 87–106.

MHH

GRAVE. A grave is any area excavated specifically for the interment of the dead, including tombs, the latter being natural or artificial caves* which were used for the same purpose. From most biblical pas-

Seven storage jars and cremation krater from Iron Age (c. ninth to eighth centuries B.C.) grave at Aczib. Courtesy Israel Dept. of Antiquities and Museums.

sages it is difficult to determine whether the place of interment was a grave or a tomb, since the writers did not distinguish carefully between them. A great many examples of both have been excavated in Near Eastern countries, with tombs being more prominent because of their greater physical durability.

Grave burials as such are best represented from very early times in Egypt,* where the dry sands desiccated the corpse and preserved it in a reasonably recognizable form. Such interments from the pre-dynastic period (c. 5000–2900 B.C.) can be seen in most large museums, usually in the form of a box burial. In such cases the corpse is invariably in the contracted or fetal position, adopted by the Egyptians as a means of economizing on labor when excavating the grave and placed originally facing the W, the supposed abode of the blessed.

Cemeteries (*see* NECROPOLIS) from later periods of Egyptian history have been excavated at Abydos* and elsewhere. In Palestine, graves have also been uncovered at various sites, one of the more promising being that at Khirbet Qumran.* There the graves were found to be austere in nature, which was consonant with the nature of the religious sect from which the deceased had come. As a result the graves exhibited neither funerary offerings nor ornamentation of the corpses. The graves themselves were shafts sunk about 1.5 m. (5 ft.) deep into the marl and had a mortuary chamber hollowed out under one of the long axes of the shaft. In this the body was laid without being placed in a coffin, and the head was positioned so that it pointed to the S. As a result of this type of burial the skeletal remains were in poor condition when discovered but were nevertheless distinguishable as comprising both male and female bones.

Contemporary Palestinian archaeologists are paying increased attention to grave-excavation in an attempt to learn, if possible, about the nature of pathological conditions which precipitated death in biblical times.

See EMBALMING; FUNERARY CUSTOMS, PALESTINIAN.

BIBLIOGRAPHY: *AIs* (1961), 56–61; S. Barabas, *ZPEB*, 2 (1975), 807–9.

RKH

GREEK LANGUAGE, NT. The basic material for the study of most languages may be classified as archaeological. The vital importance of the Rosetta Stone* and the Behistun Inscription* is well known. Whole literatures, and the linguistic knowledge they contain, lie in cuneiform* texts and surviving papyri.* The history of the Latin* language begins with the *Praenestine fibula* with its fragment of very early Latin, and the *Senatus Consultum de Bacchanalibus*, whose Latin text antedates most literary remains (*CIL* 1.196). The Greek dialects find their most distinctive monuments in epigraphical* remains. In like manner the Koinê or Common Greek, the language of the NT, finds its principal documentation in the nonliterary papyri of Egypt.*

The great linguistic fact which made the spread of Christianity in the first-century Mediterranean world possible, was the bilingualism of the whole area, following the conquest of the E by Alexander, and the equally significant conquest of the W, Italy and Rome* itself, by Greek culture. For this there is abundant evidence, from inscriptions in a multitude of places, to the graffiti* of Pompeii.* The Greek colonies, dotted round the whole littoral of the Mediterranean Sea and its connected waters, laid the foundations for this linguistic infiltration. Writing in 13 B.C., Horace, the Roman poet, remarked: "Captive Greece took captive her fierce conqueror," and at the end of the first century of the Christian era, the mordant satirist Juvenal, who, as an indigent and struggling poet, could not abide the universal presence in Rome itself of busy and successful Greek immigrants, wrote: "Romans, I cannot endure a Greek city" (*Sat.* 3.60,61). It would obviously have been possible to live in Rome without knowing Latin, provided one knew Greek. It was not Italy, but Africa, which first demanded a Latin Bible.

As J. H. Moulton remarks: "The historian marks the fact that the Gospel began its career of conquest at the one period of the world's annals when civilization was concentrated under a single ruler. The grammarian adds that this was the only period when a single language was understood throughout the countries which counted for the history of that Empire" (*Grammar of NT Greek*, 1.6).

The Common Dialect, the medium of this vast movement of communication, was the global heir of the Greek of Athens,* the language of most of the major works of surviving Greek literature, a subtle and efficient mode of speech varying with the writer in competence, polish, and power. Nonetheless, whether it be the Greek of the Apocalypse, the epistles, or the narrative parts of the NT, it is still demonstrably the Greek of everyday use, and it is here that archaeology has its decisive and illuminating word to say. Both contemporary inscriptions and masses of papyri show that the writers of the NT used the Greek of the common people, of the home, the street, and the marketplace, and that fact has enormous significance. The major monuments of this dialect have become available only with the realization, largely during this century, of the importance of the nonliterary papyri of Egypt. They cover a wide range of language. J. H. Moulton writes (op. cit., 27–28): "The

papyri, to be sure, are not to be treated as a unity. Those which alone concern us come from the tombs and waste paper heaps of Ptolemaic and Roman Egypt; and their style has the same degree of unity as we should see in the contents of the sacks of waste paper sent to an English paper-mill from a solicitor's office, a farm, a school, a shop, a manse, and a house in Downing Street. Each contribution has to be considered separately. Wills, law reports, contracts, census-returns, marriage-settlements, receipts and official orders largely ran along stereotyped lines . . . private letters are our most valuable sources; and they are all the better for the immense differences that betray themselves in the education of their writers. The well-worn epistolary formulae show variety mostly in their spelling; and their value for the student lies primarily in their remarkable resemblances to the conventional phraseology which even the NT letter-writers were content to use."

Archaeology, or papyrology* to be more precise, has taken us into the realm of daily speech and writing—a phenomenon not to be paralleled in the study of any other ancient language.

Inscriptions are a second source of nonliterary Greek, but, being written to last, and not casual utterances of ordinary folk careless of literary style or elegance of composition, their value lies rather in corroborating the linguistic evidence of the papyri. They reveal, for example, that within the range of the Common Dialect, there was little difference between the speech of Italy and that of Syria. The Greek of the NT was therefore a mode of universal communication.

See ALPHABET; BEHISTUN INSCRIPTION; CUNEIFORM; LETTERS; PAPYROLOGY; PAPYRUS; ROSETTA STONE; WRITING.

BIBLIOGRAPHY: Volume 1 (*Prolegomena*) of J. H. Moulton's *Grammar of NT Greek* remains the best and most readable introduction to the subject of the Common Dialect. *See* also F. P. Dinneen, *An Introduction to General Linguistics* (1967), 70–113; W. White, Jr., *ZPEB*, 2 (1975), 826–34, with bibliography.

EMB

GRID LAYOUT. A method of approaching the archaeological exploration of a site by dividing the area into squares to facilitate the recording of the site's features and the artifacts found there. Frequently a square trench is dug within the grid square and is separated from other similar trenches by a strip of earth left standing so as to be useful in identifying the strata.

HWP

GROVES. *See* ASHERAH.

GUDEA. A Sumerian* governor at Lagash* who helped to prepare the way for the last great resurgence of Sumerian culture in the Neo-Sumerian period (c. 2070–1960 B.C.). He was a provident and kindly ruler whose piety was comparable to that of Solomon* in a considerably later age (cf. 1 Kings 8). Purportedly in a vision, he was instructed to restore the temple Eninnu at Lagash, which had apparently been constructed originally at the end of the Jemdet Nasr* period. Following detailed instructions, Gudea laid the first brick himself and supervised the entire process connected with the extensive reconstruction of the temple complex. In his inscription which dealt with this project, Gudea stated that the timber required for the work had been imported from a mountainous region in N Syria. This area was part of the same geological structure as the Lebanon range, from which, in a later period, Solomon was to take trees to build his temple* at Jerusalem* (1 Kings 5:6). A number of statues* of Gudea have survived and show that he had abandoned the earlier Sumerian custom of wearing a full beard.

BIBLIOGRAPHY: S. N. Kramer, *The Sumerians, Their History, Culture, and Character* (1963), 22, 66–67, 99, 137–40, 260, 276.   RKH

GUILDS. *See* TRADE GUILDS.

GUZANI. *See* GOZAN.

H

HABBAKUK COMMENTARY. *See* DEAD SEA
SCROLLS.

HABIRU (hä be´rū). A group with diverse characteristics attested in about two hundred texts, mainly
of the second millennium B.C., throughout the Near
East.

Spelling and Etymology. It is apparent from Hittite* treaties, tax lists from Ugarit,* etc., that the
Sumerian* logogram SA.GAZ and its variants are to
be read as "Habiru." In the Amarna letters* the logogram is used rather than the syllabic spelling, except for the letters from Abdi-Ḫeba of Jerusalem.
Lexical texts also gloss SA.GAZ as ḫabbātum,
"robber."

The Akkadian* syllabic spelling ḫa-BI-ru may stand
for either "Habiru" or "Hapiru." The Egyptian form
'pr.w is not decisive. The discovery in 1939 of a
Ugaritic tablet with the spelling '-p-r indicates that
the first consonant of the original W Semitic word
was an *ayin* and that the second consonant was probably a *p*. (For convention's sake we shall use
"Habiru.")

Goetze and Greenberg have suggested an etymology from the Akkadian *epēru* "to supply with necessities," so that a Habiru would be one who was
dependent on others. Dhorme, Borger, and Albright
suggest a derivation from Akkadian *eperu* "dust," so
that a Habiru would be a "dusty one."

Attestation. The earliest appearances of the SA.GAZ
are now known to be in Sumerian texts dating c.
2500 B.C., whereas the earliest appearance of the
word *hapiru* is in a nineteenth-century B.C. text from
Alishar in central Turkey. The Habiru/SA.GAZ appear in diverse roles in Mesopotamia* in the Agade,
Ur* III, and Old Babylonian period as agricultural
workers, mercenary soldiers, marauders, etc. At
Nuzi* in the fifteenth century they appear as aliens
from Assyria and Akkad who sell themselves into voluntary slavery. An important fifteenth-century inscription describes how Idrimi spent seven years in
exile from Alalakh* among the Habiru. At Alalakh
one tablet lists some 1400 Habiru, of whom 80 owned
or drove chariots.*

Ugaritic texts seem to indicate that slaves sought
to run away to Habiru territory under the Hittites.
The Habiru appear both in Old Kingdom (1740–1460
B.C.) and Empire (1460–1200 B.C.) Hittite texts as
troops and as a lower social class.

The Habiru appear as 'pr.w in a number of Egyptian texts: (1) the story of the taking of Joppa* by a
general of Thutmose III; (2) Amenophis II claims the
capture of 3600 Habiru; (3) the Beth Shan* stele* of
Seti I describes an attack of the Habiru of Yarmuta;
(4) under Ramses* II–IV they appear as slaves* of
the temple of Re at Heliopolis* and as workers with
stone.

The most important references to the Habiru are
in about sixty of the famous Akkadian Amarna letters
(fourteenth century B.C.) found in Egypt,* representing futile pleas from loyal vassals in Syria and
Palestine against the marauding Habiru. The Habiru
were seizing control everywhere because of the in-
action of Amenophis IV. The loyal chiefs called their
enemies "Habiru" with the sense of "traitor" or
"rebel." Two tablets recently discovered at Kamed
el-Loz in Lebanon describe the deportation of some
of the Habiru to Nubia.*

The last references to the Habiru are in thirteenth–eleventh-century texts from Mesopotamia
which call them *'Abirâya*.

The Habiru as an Ethnic Group. A number of the
references can be interpreted in a way which would
represent the Habiru as an ethnic group. The Mari*
and Alalakh texts assign territories to the Habiru,
and the Hittites swear treaties by their gods. Though
this view has been recently championed by M. Kline,
R. de Vaux, and others, the widespread dispersion
of the Habiru and the variety of names which they
bear bespeak otherwise.

The Habiru as a Social Class. The majority of
scholars, following a suggestion made by B. Landsberger in 1930, view the Habiru as a social
class of diverse origins. Although this does not explain all references, what the majority of Habiru seem
to have in common is a status of being uprooted,
propertyless, aliens, or refugees, who sought to make
a living either by servitude, as at Nuzi, or by brig-
andage. In some cases, as at Ugarit and Alalakh, on
the other hand, the Habiru had acquired property
and some influential positions.

The Habiru and the Hebrews. Since the first revelation of the Habiru in the Amarna texts late in the
nineteenth century scholars have been tempted to
associate the Habiru with the biblical *'ibrîm* or "Hebrews,"—a word that occurs thirty-four times in
the OT, usually either by foreigners or in the presence of foreigners. This view, which received support from the date of a 1400 B.C. destruction of

Jericho* proposed by Garstang, was popularized by C. Marston.

Most scholars reject any direct identification of the Hebrews with the Habiru in view of the following objections: (1) philological difficulties in the equation; (2) the probability that Habiru is an appellative term describing a class, whereas *'ibrî* is an ethnic term; (3) the considerable differences in the distribution, activity, and character of the two groups.

Many scholars would still maintain some indirect connection, however, suggesting that the Hebrews were but a small part of the larger Habiru movement.

Albright, who has interpreted the Habiru as "dusty ones" in the sense of donkey caravaneers, believes that Abraham and his descendants were indeed Habiru in this sense. This view has not been well received.

Cazelles would identify the Habiru with the Hebrews (but not with the Israelites) as a class linked with the Hurrians.*

BIBLIOGRAPHY: J. A. Wilson, "The *'Eperu* of the Egyptian Inscriptions," *AJSL*, 49 (1932–33), 275–80; J. Bottéro, *Le problème des Habiru* (1954); M. Greenberg, *The Hab/piru* (1955); M. Kline, "The Ha-BI-ru*—Kin or Foe of Israel?" *WTJ*, 19 (1956), 1–24, 170–84; id., 20 (1957), 46–70; R. Borger, "Das Problem der 'apīru ('Habiru')," *Zeitschrift des Deutschen Palästina-Vereins*, 74 (1958), 121–32; E. Campbell, "The Amarna Letters and the Amarna Period," *BA*, 23 (1960), 2–22; J. Gibson, "Some Important Ethnic Terms in the Pentateuch," *JNES*, 20 (1961), 217–38; W. F. Albright, "Abram the Hebrew," *BASOR*, 163 (1961), 36–54; G. Mendenhall, "The Hebrew Conquest of Palestine," *BA*, 25 (1962), 66–86; W. Helck, *Die Beziehungen Ägyptens zu Vorderasien . . .* (1962), 526–35; M. B. Rowton, "The Topological Factor in the Hapiru Problem," *Studies in Honor of Benno Landsberger*, ed. H. Güterbock and T. Jacobsen (1965), 375–87; W. F. Albright, *The Amarna Letters from Palestine . . .* (1966); 14–20; F. F. Bruce, "Tell el-Amarna," *Archaeology and OT Study*, ed. D. Thomas (1967), 3–20; R. de Vaux, "Le Problème des Hapiru après quinze années," *JNES*, 27 (1968), 221–28; W. F. Albright, *Yahweh and the Gods of Canaan* (1968), 73–91; R. Saidah, "Archaeology in the Lebanon 1968–1969," *Berytus*, 18 (1969), 126–29; M. Weippert, *The Settlement of the Israelite Tribes in Palestine* (1971), 55–102; H. Cazelles, "The Hebrews," *Peoples of OT Times*, ed. D. J. Wiseman (1973), 1-28.   EY

HABOR RIVER. A tributary of the Euphrates flowing into it from the NE, and known in Assyrian records as Khabur, or Chabor. It meandered through a heavily settled valley whose ancient remains are marked by such sites as Tell Halaf, Tell Chagar Bazar, Tell Brak, and Tell Hamudi. The first truly great culture of antiquity, the Chalcolithic,* was centered in northern Mesopotamia* and was represented in the area watered by the Habor. The river is now the only permanently flowing tributary of the Euphrates in Mesopotamia. In the ninth year of Hoshea, some of the Israelites were exiled to the banks of the Habor

(2 Kings 17:6; 18:11; 1 Chron 5:26), settling in an unidentified location.

BIBLIOGRAPHY: *CAH*, 1, part 2, 308, 316, 318, 323, 328–29, 331, 437, 557, 597, 625.

RKH

HADAD RIMMON (hā'dad rim'ən; Heb. הֲדַדְרִמּוֹן, *hᵃdadrimmôn*). A composite name, both parts of which may refer to Baal* as a thunder deity; it may also refer to a place somewhere in the Plain of Megiddo.*

No place-name exactly fits, although Rimmon (modern Rummaneh) N of Nazareth* (cf. Josh 19:13) may reflect the second part of the name. However, both Hadad and Rimmon (Assyrian Ramanu) are known as titles for the Canaanite* god Baal.

BIBLIOGRAPHY: D. W. Thomas, ed., *Documents from OT Times* (1958), 133.

CEA

HADATU (hä dä'tū; possibly Akkad., "pleasant"[?], or else Aram., from חדת, *ḥdṭ*, "new" [-town?]). An ancient city, now the mounds of Arslan Tash, some 35.4 km. (22 mi.) due E of Carchemish* and the Euphrates River. The early history of this city remains unknown. During the Assyrian Empire it became a provincial center, provided with a palace for visits by the Assyrian kings. It was rebuilt several times, certainly by Tiglath-pileser III* (c. 745–727 B.C.) and probably by Sargon II* (c. 722–705 B.C.). The town was enclosed within a roughly circular wall* of brick, with three principal gates.* These and other structures were adorned by large stone lions,* bulls, etc., in the Assyrian manner. A temple of Ishtar* was also found at the site. Biblically, the most interesting discovery was the ivory* carvings that had formerly belonged to Hazael, Aramaean* king of Damascus* and oppressor of Israel,* one piece even bearing his name. He perhaps had sent them in his tribute to Adad-nirari III of Assyria.

BIBLIOGRAPHY: F. Thureau-Dangin et al., *Arslan Tash* (1931); cf. A. Parrot, *Archéologie mésopotamienne*, I (1946), 464–71, 519 n. 8.

KAK

HADRAMAUT. *See* ADRAMYTTIUM.

Stone relief of three soldiers from Arslan Tash; Tiglath-pileser III (745-727 B.C.). Courtesy Museum of Ancient Orient, Istanbul.

HAFT TEPE. See ELAM.

HAGAR. The handmaid of Sarah who was given as a concubine to Abraham and became the mother of Ishmael. Abraham probably acquired her when visiting Egypt* (Gen 12:10). Her name is Semitic rather than Egyptian and may mean "departure." The custom by which Sarah gave Hagar to Abraham to produce children was paralleled by the activities of Rachel and Leah somewhat later on (Gen 30:3, 9) and illustrated also by tablets from Nuzi* and Ur.* These latter showed that a marriage* contract generally included a clause requiring an infertile married woman to give her maid to her husband as a concubine in order to raise a family. This may be documented from surviving codes from Abraham's day.

The pregnant Hagar despised her mistress and, in consequence, had to flee from her anger. A theophany persuaded her to return, and Ishmael was later born into the household. Ultimately, Sarah herself conceived and gave birth to Isaac, but during the latter's weaning-feast the boy Ishmael apparently mocked him, resulting in the expulsion of Hagar and her son. God's destiny for Ishmael (cf. Gen 21:9-14) took him to north-eastern Sinai,* where he became a hunter. He married an Egyptian woman and had children, one of his daughters marrying Esau (Gen 28:9; 36:3, 10). How far there is a relation between the Hagrites (cf. Ps 83:6; 1 Chron 5:10, 19f.) and Hagar is uncertain, but it seems at least probable, if only because two of Ishmael's sons were Hagrites (1 Chron 5:19).

BIBLIOGRAPHY: J. A. Thompson, *Archaeology and the OT* (1959), 24-31; D. W. Thomas, ed., *Documents from OT Times* (1962), 27-37; S. Barabas, *ZPEB*, 3 (1975), 9-10.   RKH

HAIFA. The vigorous Israeli seaport at the foot of Mount Carmel,* which handles the bulk of Israeli trade, is modern, but overlays ports more ancient. The protruding end of the Carmel highland provides a small measure of shelter from S gales, and on a harborless coast it was inevitable that the site would be occupied. As with many modern cities, of which London and Rome* are prime examples, extensive building not merely covers possible archaeological material but provides only piecemeal glimpses of what lies beneath. Work at Haifa has revealed Roman remains, and it appears that the Roman Castra Samaritanorum, a fortified post settled by Samaritans, was in the area. Whether Haifa is Eusebius's Hefa, and whether Sycaminum or Shikoma were on the site, cannot be stated with certainty. Acre (*see* ACCO) overshadowed the place until modern times.

BIBLIOGRAPHY: E. G. Kraeling, *Bible Atlas* (1956), 453.

                                                    EMB

HALAF, TELL. See GOZAN.

HALICARNASSUS. See CARIA.

HAM. 1. One of Noah's three sons, apparently the second (Gen 5:32; 6:10 et al.) bore this name. With others of the family of Noah, he survived the Flood and shared in the divine covenant* (Gen 9:1-18). He became the ancestor of many descendants, listed in the table of nations (Gen 10:2-11:9; cf. 1 Chron 1:5-23), of whom the principal members were Cush (Ethiopia*), Mizraim (Egypt*), and Canaan.* The name was used in Pss 78:51; 105:23, 27; 106:22 of Ham as the eponymous* father of the Egyptians in this same sense. Anthropologists do not recognize a Hamitic race as such, though the term is applied to a group of languages of which Egyptian is one. In OT times descent from a specific ancestor is all that is meant, not necessarily a common language, race, or habitat.

2. An early site in Trans-Jordan whose inhabitants were overcome by Chedorlaomer (Gen 14:5). The location of the area is unknown.

BIBLIOGRAPHY: T. C. Mitchell, *NBD* (1962), 500; S. Barabas, *ZPEB*, 3 (1975), 20-21.

                                                    RKH

HAMA. See HAMATH.

HAMADAN. See ECBATANA.

HAMATH (hā'məth; Heb. חֲמָת, ḥamāṯ; LXX Ἐμάθ, *Hemath*; meaning very uncertain; "walls"?). Hamath is the name of several towns of ancient Syria-Palestine. The most famous one mentioned in the OT is now Hama on the middle Orontes River. From about 1000 B.C., Hamath was the capital of an independent state reaching from the borders of Aram*-Damascus* N and NE to the Euphrates River. Its kings bore partly Neo-Hittite* and partly W Semitic names. David's victory over Hadadezer of Aram-zobah freed Toi, king of Hamath, from the latter's yoke (2 Sam 8:9-11), so that Toi sent his son with a gift. He probably became a subject-ally of David, so that by conquest and alliance, David's realm indeed reached as far as the Euphrates. After Solomon's* loss of the intervening territory of Damascus (1 Kings 11:23-25), Hamath regained full independence. The Hittite Hieroglyphic* inscriptions of Urhilina, king of Hamath (c. 850 B.C.), indicate that he drew upon men of Laqe (beyond Euphrates) and Naharma (probably Naharaim) among others for his works and suggest the extent of the Hamathite realm. The Assyrian kings turned the kingdom into a province by 720 B.C. (cf. 2 Kings 17:24; 18:33-34). Prior to that date, Hamath had experienced decline for a century. A usurper, King Zakir (*see* ZAKIR STELE) from the Lu'ash province of the realm (capital, Hadrach), had had to fight off a hostile coalition, c. 780 B.C. (*ANET²,³*,501-2), as recorded on his stele.* Later, within c. 770-750 B.C., both Damascus and Hamath seemingly came under the ascendancy (and possibly rule) of Jeroboam II of Israel* (2 Kings 14:28) and perhaps Uzziah of Judah.* Excavations at Hamath have produced remains of a monumental gateway* to, and other buildings within, the citadel;* also, some small Aramaic* and other inscriptions.

BIBLIOGRAPHY: H. Ingholt, *Rapport préliminaire, première campagne, fouilles de Hama* (1934); id., *Rapport préliminaire, sept campagnes de fouilles* à *Hama en Syrie* (1940); E. Fugmann, *Hama . . . l'architecture des périodes préhellénistiques* (1958); K. A. Kitchen, *Hittite Hieroglyphs, Aramaeans & Hebrew Traditions* (forthcoming), Table V.

KAK

HAMMER. See TOOLS.

HAMMON (HAMMOTH) (ham'ən; Heb. חַמּוֹן, ḥammôn, "hot spring"?). 1. A border town in Asher (Josh 19:28), identified with Umm el-'Awamid, on the coast 8 km. (5 mi.) NE of Rosh ha-Nigra—at the present-day border between Israel* and Lebanon.

2. A Levitical town in Naphtali (1 Chron 6:76), identified generally with the Hammoth-dor of the Levitical lists in Josh 21:32. It is considered to be the well-known Hammath of Naphtali (Josh 19:35), located at Hammam Tabariyeh, the site of an important hot spring just S of Tiberias* on the Sea of Galilee.* Most of the remains at the latter site are from the second century A.D. and include a lovely synagogue* floor from the second or third century.

BIBLIOGRAPHY: *Macmillan Bible Atlas*, 71, 113; L. H. Vincent, "Les Fouilles Juives in d'el-Hamman, a Tibériade," *RB*, 31 (1922), 115–22; Y. Aharoni, *Land of the Bible* (1967), 105, 271.

CEA

HAMMURABI (hä mə rä'bi). The sixth and most famous king of the First Dynasty of Babylon,* the son of Sinmuballit and the father of Samsuiluna. There is some difficulty about the dating of his reign, but it is generally thought that the period 1792–1750 B.C. is correct. Some, arguing from the date of the conquest of Mari,* would push the period on for something near half a century. It was once thought that Hammurabi had been one of the world's first great empire builders, but it is now becoming clear that he was only one of a large group of rulers spread across the W Asian plateau and that he held his power by treaty and vassalage as much as by conquest. His reign of forty-three years was not equaled by any other king of his age.

Two classes of cuneiform* tablets have survived from this period, consisting of inscriptions by Hammurabi or about him, as well as tablets from the E Semite kingdom of Mari on the middle Euphrates River. The documents reveal an able diplomat securing his position in a cosmopolitan age, when no single Near Eastern power had complete power, and temporary confederations often shifted the balance. He was contemporary with Rim-Sin of Larsa,* Shamshi-Adad of Assyria, Iasmah-Adad of Mari, Ibalpiel II of Eshnunna,* and the last pharaohs of the Twelfth Dynasty of Egypt.* During Hammurabi's reign, all of these rulers died or lost their thrones, including the last rulers of Isin. Hammurabi played a part in all of the successions except in Egypt.

The social system of Babylon under Hammurabi was a complex mixture of agrarian feudalism and royal trading. This diverse organization is brought out in the texts, which show a confusing hierarchy of social castes, vassals, tenants, princes, merchants, and slaves.* Taxes* and tariffs on traded goods in kind

were the chief revenue of the state. It is clear from the code that Hammurabi was attempting to bring some semblance of order out of the dealings of private traders, landed aristocrats, and foreign mercenaries, a situation which he had inherited. Although paying lip service to all of the ancient gods, Hammurabi appears to have relied cannily on careful planning, for which he demonstrated considerable ability. He was, after all, an Amorite* and although there is a very strong Sumerian* cultural undercurrent in all of his inscriptions, he seems to have effectively reduced Sumerian influence in his court, and in fact, Sumerian cultural influence declined steadily after his time. For students of the Bible, his code of laws (*see* HAMMURABI, CODE OF) has been of interest for over half a century. Unfortunately, the water table of the site of ancient Babylon has not allowed any major buildings of Hammurabi's time to be identified, but his inscriptions show that his building activities must have been considerable among a people for whom architecture had become a notable art.

There is much evidence that such great national epics as *Gilgamesh** were composed during his long reign. In the centuries after Hammurabi, his exploits became legendary and his reign was seen as a golden age. In his days the vast and highly developed literature of the Sumerians was copied and studied, not as a living force in society but as a remnant of the past, and without this impetus during Hammurabi's long years of peace, nothing of Sumerian literature would have survived.

The records of Hammurabi demonstrate that between the time of Abraham and Moses there was an extensive development of petty states in the Middle East, supported by a literate class of traders and agriculturalists who had a sophisticated love of the arts and a developed culture. Although the name Hammurabi, "(the god) Ham is great," has been frequently related, if not equated, to the Amraphel of Gen 14:1, 9, there is little evidence to support the contention.

BIBLIOGRAPHY: F. M. T. Böhl, *Hammurabi* (1946); H. Schmökel, "Hammurabi von Babylon . . . ," *Berichte zur Weltgeschichte* 11 (1958); C. J. Gadd, "Hammurabi," *CAH*, 1 part 2, 88, 90, 636, 639, 643, 662.

WW

HAMMURABI, CODE OF. The name ascribed by most scholars to the inscription of nearly 282 laws in Old Babylonian cuneiform* on a diorite stele,* along with a historical prologue and a literary and religious epilogue. The stele was inscribed sometime around 1765 B.C. in Babylon,* and was carried off by the Elamites under Šutruḥ-Naḥunte (c. 1200 B.C.) to their capital at Susa,* the biblical Shushan. It was unearthed by a French expedition in 1901–2 on the site of the old acropolis* of Susa and moved to the Louvre. The top of the stele, itself a pillar of black diorite, 2.4 m. (8 ft.) high, is decorated with a bas-relief* of Hammurabi* receiving the command to inscribe the laws, but not the laws themselves, from the E Semite deity, Shamash. It is now known that

1. Clay anthropoid sarcophagi, Deir el-Balah, thirteenth century B.C. Courtesy Israel Museum, Jerusalem.

2. Clay Astarte figurine from Tel Zeror in supine position with legs positioned on a double base and hands holding her breasts, Late Bronze Age. Collection of Israel Dept. of Antiquities and Museums. Exhibited and photographed at Israel Museum, Jerusalem.

3. Cult stand from Taanak, end of tenth century B.C. Bottom register: nude Astarte grasping ears of lions. Second register: two winged sphinxes. Third register: goats eating from "tree of life" flanked by two lions. Top register: calf, winged sun disk flanked by columns with voluted decoration. On each side is an ibex. Collection of Israel Dept. of Antiquities and Museums. Exhibited and photographed at Israel Museum, Jerusalem.

4. Inscribed and decorated seals of the second quarter of the first millennium B.C. in Hebrew, Ammonite, Moabite, Phoenician, and Aramaic. From the collections of the Israel Dept. of Antiquities and Museums and the Israel Museum. Exhibited and photographed at the Israel Museum, Jerusalem. Description of the two large seals in the center of the collection: Left: seal of WYKL, quartz, Aramaic, seventh century B.C., provenance unknown; scaraboid seal—in upper register four-winged female shown frontally holding staff (lotus plant?); in lower register the name of the owner. Right: seal of Jezebel, grey opal, Phoenician, ninth to eighth centuries B.C., provenance unknown; scaraboid seal— in upper register a crouching sphinx holding *ankh* in forelegs; in lower register hawk flanked by uraei, before it a stylized floral design, above it a winged solar disk. Letters of owner's name dispersed in lower register.

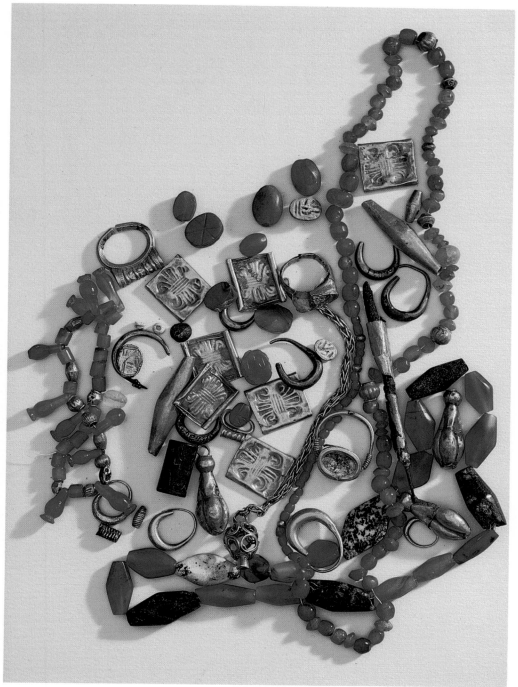

5. Jewelry hoard of early Israelite Period from Beth Shemesh. The hoard consists of more than two hundred items including carnelian, jasper, and gold beads; gold and silver earrings; and various uninscribed scarabs. From the collection of the Israel Dept. of Antiquities and Museums. Photo: Israel Museum, Jerusalem.

6

7

8

9

6. Philistine krater with two tilted horizontal handles from Ashkelon, Iron Age II. Collection of Israel Dept. of Antiquities and Museums. Exhibited and photographed at Israel Museum, Jerusalem. 7. Phoenician-type jug from Achziv, Iron Age II C. Collection of Israel Dept. of Antiquities and Museums. Exhibited and photographed at Israel Museum, Jerusalem. 8. Bichromeware krater with two shoulder handles from Tell Nagila, Late Bronze Age I. Collection of Israel Dept. of Antiquities and Museums. Exhibited and photographed at Israel Museum, Jerusalem. 9. Imported Mycenaean kylix excavated in Fosse Temple I at Lachish, Late Bronze Age I. Collection of Israel Dept. of Antiquities and Museums. Photo: Israel Museum, Jerusalem.

Finds from the Cave of the Letters in Nahal Hever, c. A.D. 135. Photographs (10-13) courtesy of The Shrine of the Book, Israel Museum, Jerusalem.

10. Goat-hide waterskin that contained various possessions of a woman (see figure 13) and fifteen letters from Simeon Bar Kosiba (Kokhba) to the leaders of the revolt in the En Gedi region. 11. Section of a large woolen rug that covered the burial in the niche.

12. Household vessels and utensils found in the Cave of the Letters.

13. Well-preserved woven willow basket. Contents of waterskin (figure 10), besides the fifteen letters: jewelry; cosmetic utensils of glass, wood, and bone; several balls of dyed spun wool and a bundle of purple-dyed unspun wool; a baby's tunic (not shown in photo); and a metal disk mirror set in a wooden frame and found alongside the waterskin.

14. Aerial view of Khirbet Qumran looking NE. In the foreground is the marl terrace containing caves dug out of the marl soil to form dwellings. In the background are the excavated remains of Khirbet Qumran, situated on a spur of the marl terrace. Photo: Werner Braun, Jerusalem.

15

15. Aerial view of the synagogue at Capernaum in the foreground. The octagonal building south of the synagogue is now defined as a church built above the remains of St. Peter's house in the first half of the fifth century A.D. In the background is the Sea of Galilee. View to SW. Photo: Werner Braun, Jerusalem.

16. Aerial view of Tel Hazor looking E. In the background is the kibbutz Ayelet Hashahar. Photo: Werner Braun, Jerusalem.

17. Aerial view of the Temple Mount in Jerusalem, looking NE. In the foreground along the southern wall of the
Temple Mount one can see the excavations. To the left are the remains of the Umayyad structures and to the right
are the steps leading to the Hulda Gates. Photo: Werner Braun, Jerusalem.

18. Photograph of the entrance to the Cave of the Letters when it was excavated in 1960 under the direction of Y. Yadin. The cave is located in the northern bank of Nahal Hever near the Dead Sea about four km. SW of En Gedi. The cave contained skeletons and skulls, metal vessels, metal and wood utensils, leather objects, woven baskets, clothing and wool, keys, glass plates, Bar Kokhba letters, biblical scrolls, and the Babata Archive. Photo: Hirshbain-Kneller, Jerusalem.

19. Photograph of the entrance to the Cave of the Treasure when it was excavated in 1960 under the direction of P. Bar-Adon (descending the ladder). The cave is located in Nahal Mishmar near the Dead Sea, about seven km. SW of En Gedi. The cave contained a huge Chalcolithic cache of metal vessels, pottery, stone vessels and ornaments, textiles, straw and wicker objects, leather objects, food, cereals, vegetables and fruit, and a weaving loom. Photo: Hirshbain-Kneller, Jerusalem.

20. One of the largest quarried stones in the world—cut but left unused in ancient times at Baalbek. Photo: Ben Chapman.

21. Temple of Bacchus at Baalbek. Photo: Ben Chapman.

22. Mesopotamian prayer tower. The tradition of ziggurats, high places, and holy mountains came from ancient Sumer. Photo: Ben Chapman.

23. Glazed relief from the walls of ancient Babylon. Photo: Ben Chapman.

24. A dolmen from a site in Jordan near the Dead Sea. Photo: Garo Nalbandian, Jerusalem.

25. Petra: The Palace Tomb (extreme left) and the Corinthian Tomb next to it. Photo: Garo Nalbandian, Jerusalem.

26. The Medeba mosaic map fragment in situ. Photo: Garo Nalbandian, Jerusalem.

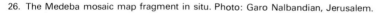

27. Gerasa: The south tetrapylon where the southern Decumanus crosses the Cardo, which is lined with Corinthian columns. In the foreground one can see three of the four pedestals situated in the circular piazza. Photo: Garo Nalbandian, Jerusalem.

28. Theater at Ephesus overlooking the Arcadian Way, which led to the harbor. Photo: Ben Chapman.

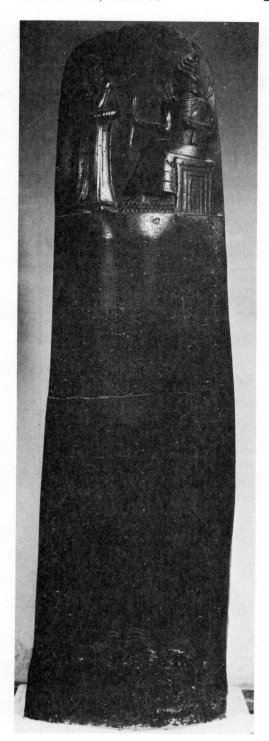

Hammurabi stele. Courtesy Musées Nationaux, Paris.

this was a custom among the kings of certain Sumerian and Akkadian-Babylonian dynasties. The laws are similar to those of other older codes and indicate a harsh caste system based on the economic values of a farming and trading people, prescribing arbitrary justice to three recognized levels of society. Although often compared with the OT laws, there is a very wide divergence in form as well as content, the chief difference being in the superstition and polytheism which underlies the code. The prologue and epilogue are written in the mathematically precise Hymnal-Epic dialect of the language and are a beautiful example of archaic Babylonian cuneiform. The laws, as distinct from the prologue and epilogue, are written in prose in a slightly different dialect.

The code is the longest Babylonian inscription which has survived, comprising 2614 lines out of an original total of 4000. Thirty-two offenses carried the death penalty. Some of the specified offenses—for example, sorcery, false witness, theft of sacred or state property, receiving stolen goods, kidnapping, faulty construction, incest, adultery, striking a parent, and murder—are also offenses dealt with in the Mosaic Code.

Bodily mutilation, following a system of *lex talionis*, was a common penalty, namely, eye for eye, bone for bone, and so on. Fines and restitution were specified, as was also a scheme of fixed fees and wages, with medical charges adjusted to the rank of the patient. Boatmen, reapers, threshers, and herdsmen were paid annually, while brickmakers, carpenters, masons, and other artisans worked on a daily basis. This was also the case for the hire fees for various forms of road and water transport. The social reasons for many of these policies are far from clear.

The code's prologue acknowledges the gods and their goodness in elevating the lawgiver from shepherd to king. The epilogue lauds the king's achievements in battle and administration and enjoins obedience on all who carry out the laws, with fearful curses on transgressors.

The outstanding difference between the Hammurabi and Mosaic codes lies in the latter's recognition of God as the only source of law and righteousness.

BIBLIOGRAPHY: F. M. Böhl, *King Hammurabi of Babylon in the Setting of His Time* (1946); W. J. Martin, "The Law Code of Hammurabi," *DOTT* (1958); D. J. Wiseman, *ZPEB*, 3 (1975), 24–27.

ww

HAMUDI, TELL. *See* HABOR RIVER.

HANA; HANAENS. *See* TERQA.

HANGING GARDENS OF BABYLON. *See* BABYLON, HANGING GARDENS OF.

HANNATHON (ha'nə thon; Heb. חֲנָתֹון, *ḥᵃnnoṯôn*). A border town in Zebulun, Hannathon was, during both the Late Bronze* and Iron ages,* an important town, as references in two Amarna letters* (EA, nos. 8, 245) and the annals of Tiglath-pileser III* show. It appears in the border list of the tribe of Zebulun

(Josh 19:14) between Neah (unidentified) and the Valley of Iphtahel (probably the Wadi el-Malek, NW of Nazareth*). Various locations have been proposed for Hannathon, with a majority of scholars favoring Tell el-Bedeiwiyeh (Hebrew, Tell Hannaton), a site 9.8 km. (6 mi.) N of Nazareth which guards the W outlet of the Sahl el-Battof Valley. If the identification is correct, Hannathon stood astride an important road across Lower Galilee* from the Jordan Valley to the Plain of Acco.* In biblical times the same highway, because of its higher altitudes, also served as an alternate to the Via Maris. Surface explorations by Albright in 1923 point to occupation of the tell in MB, LB, Iron I, and the Islamic periods. Some scholars have identified Hannathon, or Tell el-Bedeiwiyeh, with Asochis of NT times.

BIBLIOGRAPHY: W. F. Albright, "Some Archaeological and Topographical Results of a Trip through Palestine," *BASOR*, 11 (1923), 11; id., "Contributions to the Historical Geography of Palestine," *AASOR*, 2–3 (1923), 23–24; F.-M. Abel, *Géographie de la Palestine*, 2 (1938), 63, 343; B. Mazar "Hannathon," *EBi*, 3 (1958), 220f.; Y. Aharoni, *The Land of the Bible*, (1967), 25, 56, 331.

CEA

HAPIRU. See HABIRU.

HARAM EL-KHALIL. See MACHPELAH.

HARAN (hā'ran). This city,* whose Assyrian name means "main highway," was located about 32 km. (20 mi.) SE of Edessa, on the main trading route from Nineveh* to the Euphrates and Aleppo.* As a commercial center it was also linked with such Mediterranean ports as Tyre* (Ezek 27:3). Excavations at Haran (spelled "Harran" in the cuneiform* texts) indicate that the site was occupied in the third millennium B.C. The fact that Haran was a center of the moon cult of Babylonia suggests that it had been founded during the third dynasty of Ur,* perhaps about 2000 B.C. Certain tablets from Mari* refer to the moon cult indirectly.

Because of its strategic location it came under Assyrian influence at a comparatively early period. About 1310 B.C. it was fortified by Adadnirari I, serving thereafter for some centuries as the capital of an Assyrian province. 2 Kings 19:12 indicates that the ancestors of Sennacherib* had sacked Haran in 763 B.C., along with other cities, but under Sargon II* and his successors it was restored and the temple rebuilt. When Nineveh fell in 612 B.C. Haran housed the remains of the Assyrian army until it was overthrown in 609 B.C. by the Babylonians. Haran was restored during the Chaldean* period, and the elderly mother of Nabonidus was installed as high priestess. The present ruins at the site are those either of Roman, Sabean,* or Islamic times. For several centuries after Christ, Haran remained a center of lunar paganism.

In the second millennium B.C. Terah settled at Haran after leaving Ur (Gen 11:31), and Abram left it to go to Canaan (Gen 12:1). Albright suggested that the patriarchal trade activities on the Fertile Crescent* caravan routes found a useful center in Haran (*BASOR*, 163). Jacob sought refuge at Haran from Esau (Gen 27:43), and there he met his future wife (Gen 29:4).

The unbroken occupation of the site has had limited archaeological investigation. T. E. Lawrence surveyed the position, but actual digging, and that of limited scope, did not begin until the joint Anglo-Turkish expedition of 1951–52. Apart from a few Babylonian inscriptions, little of biblical interest was found, despite the connection of Haran with Abram's and Terah's story. The excavations ended for some time with the death of D. S. Rice in 1956.

The history of Haran, and its involvement with the successive movements of imperialism in the area may be traced on through the writings and inscriptions of some 1500 years, but no great biblical significance emerges from the record.

Haran, of course, occurs in late Roman Republican history as Carrhae, the scene of the Parthian victory over Crassus's three legions, which might have changed the history of the world had the Parthian king recognized the full significance of the hour.

BIBLIOGRAPHY: W. F. Albright, *JBL*, 43 (1924), 385–93; S. Lloyd and W. Brice, *AnSt*, 1 (1951), 77–111; W. F. Albright, *From the Stone Age to Christianity* (1957), 155, 236–37, 263, 315; J. A. Thompson, *The Bible and Archaeology* (1962), 20–22, 135, 148, 166, 170; S. Barabas, *ZPEB*, 3 (1975), 32–33.

RKH and EMB

HARARI, TELL. See MARI.

HARMAL. See TELL HARMAL.

HARNESS. The Hebrew term 'aṣar was used in Jer 46:4 of harnessing horses but in 1 Sam 6:7 of the yoking of cows. Specific items of harnessing do not always appear to have had names. The word commonly rendered "bridle" in Greek and Hebrew includes the whole controlling harness of the horse's head. The Hebrew *metheg* commonly means "bridle" but includes the bit (Isa 30:28; 37:29), while

Mede bringing two horses as tribute to King Sargon II (722-705 B.C.), Fragment of wall relief from Sargon's palace at Dur-Sharrukin, modern Khorsabad. The horses have most of the elements of a contemporary riding bridle. *(See also photo under* HORSE.) Courtesy The Metropolitan Museum of Art, gift of John D. Rockefeller, Jr., 1933.

resen means "halter" (Gesenius, *Hebrew Lexicon*, 607). The word *metheg* is used figuratively only at 2 Sam 8:1, if the word of which it forms a part in a difficult text can be rendered "the bridle of the mother-city" (*NBD*, 818, *sub.voc. Metheg-ammah*).

The NT uses *chalinos* twice. In James 3:3 the meaning is undoubtedly "bit," that is, properly the *stomion* or mouthpiece, as distinct from the *hēniai* or reins. This synecdoche may be paralleled from Aeschylus, Sophocles, and Euripides (Liddell and Scott, *Greek Lexicon*, *sub.voc.*). In Rev 14:20 the opposite is the case. *Chalinos* is there the reins. The same semantic phenomenon is to be seen in the overlapping of *frenum* and *habena* in Latin (Lewis and Short, *Latin Dictionary*, *sub.voc.*). The Roman *frenum lupatum*, or sawtoothed bit, could be a very cruel and damaging piece of harness.

Archaeology can illustrate only the bit, since bridles were perishable. In the Rockefeller Museum in Jerusalem is a bit of Syrian origin from the second millennium B.C. with spiked rings, with the spikes turned inward at each end. It was designed to prick the outside of the animal's mouth. There is a jointed bit, of modern form, from the same era.

BIBLIOGRAPHY: C. V. Wolf, *IDB*, 1, (1962), 443; E. M. Blaiklock, *ZPEB*, 1 (1975), 620.

EMB

HAROSHETH (ha'rō sheth). Properly Harosheth-Hagoiim ("Harosheth of the Gentiles") and a town of Sisera, it is a doubtful locality variously identified with Tell 'Amr or Tell el-Harbaj (*BBSAJ*, 2.12; 4.46). If it is to be identified, as some have suggested, with the Muhrashti of the Amarna letters, * the locality should be sought in the Plain of Sharon.

BIBLIOGRAPHY: E. G. Kraeling, *Bible Atlas* (1956), 151.   EMB

HARP. See MUSIC.

HARRAN. See HARAN.

HARSHA. See TEL HARSHA.

HASSUNA. See TELL HASSUNA.

HATRA. A desert city* located in the Jazira area of modern Iraq between the Tigris and Euphrates rivers. Hatra flourished from the mid-first to the mid-third centuries of the Christian era, having much in common with other caravan cities of the period such as Petra* and Palmyra.* The city owed its existence to the trade route, which ran east to Persia and west to the Mediterranean.

Unlike the more fertile lands of Akkad* and Sumer* to the S and of Assyria to the NE, the barren territory of Hatra was an extension of the Syrian desert. Caravans were still plying these routes with long trains of heavily-laden camels* even up to recent times. The pre-Islamic Arab merchants who built Hatra grew rich on the exchange of goods, which included textiles (*see* CLOTH), spices, and luxury items such as jewelry.

A vast walled city with splendid monuments in its

heyday, Hatra is still one of the most impressive ruins in Mesopotamia.* Early researches were undertaken by Tor Andrae, who was able to produce a map of the site. The Directorate of the Antiquities Department of Iraq conducted excavations from 1951–55, and has made the city the principal site in the antiquities restoration program since 1960. Work has continued at the great iwan, with the two smaller iwans, or halls, now formed into a site museum. Much of the great temenos,* including the E façade and two propylaea,* has also been restored.

Many dedicatory monuments and statues* of royalty, priests, and nobles have been found, some with Aramaic* inscriptions. Hatra is celebrated among art historians for its unique blending of oriental and occidental motifs. Both Indo-Persian and Hellenistic elements can be traced in the architecture and sculpture found at the site.

The religious history is equally interesting and multifaceted. A small temple in pure Hellenistic style has been found, unlike anything else at Hatra, in which fragments of statues of at least nine of the Olympian gods have been identified. A structure called the "fire temple" was shown to have contained a series of royal statues, with inscriptions identifying only Senatruq I and Senatruq II. Another, Andre's temple C, was dedicated to the Semitic deity Shulman.

BIBLIOGRAPHY: J. Teixidor, "Aramaic Inscriptions of Hatra," *Sumer*, 20 (1964), 77–82; id., "The Altars found at Hatra," 21 (1965), 85–92; id., "The Kingdom of Adiabene and Hatra," *Ber.*, 17 (1967), 1–12; J. Orchard, "Recent Restoration Work in Iraq," *Iraq*, 24 (1962), 73–77; id., "Recent Archaeological Activity in Iraq," *Iraq*, 25 (1963), 104–9.

JEJ

HATTASAS; HATTUSAS. See BOGHAZKÖY.

HATTI. See HITTITES.

HATTINA. See TELL TA YINAT.

HAUSH, TELL. See BAAL GAD.

HAZARMAVETH (hā zər mā'veth). A Semitic tribe descended from Shem through Joktan and mentioned in Gen 10:26 and 1 Chron 1:20. They settled in the Wadi Hadramaut in S Arabia,* a flourishing valley controlling the incense routes with Shabwa as its capital. Two archaeological surveys of the area have produced no results of biblical relevance. A fascinating account of the area is given in Freya Stark's *Southern Gates of Arabia* (1936).

BIBLIOGRAPHY: G. Caton-Thompson, *The Tombs and Moon Temple of Hureidha* (1944); W. L. Brown and A. F. L. Beeston, *JRAS* (1954), 43–62; S. Barabas, *ZPEB*, 3 (1975), 49–50.

EMB

HAZAZON-TAMAR. See EN GEDI.

HAZOR (hā'zōr). The name seems to mean "enclosure" or "settlement" and was therefore used of several OT localities (cf. Josh 15:23, 25; Neh 11:33; Jer 49:28–33). The most important of these, however, was a fortified site in Naphtali (Josh 19:36), identified with Tell el-Qedah and located 8 km. (5 mi.) SW of Lake Huleh and 16 km. (10 mi.) N of the Sea of Galilee.* The tell* dominates the Plain of Huleh, with the city* tell comprising 10 ha. (25 a.) along with an additional 50 ha. (150 a.) to the N. The site was identified by Garstang in 1926, but major excavations only commenced under Yadin in 1955. The city tell was apparently founded in the third millennium B.C., while the remainder, presumably of Hyksos* origin, was established in the second millennium B.C. Hazor was mentioned in the nineteenth-century B.C. Execration Texts* from Egypt,* in the eighteenth-century B.C. Mari* tablets, in lists of conquered cities from the time of Thutmose III, Amenhotep II, and Seti I (fifteenth to fourteenth centuries B.C.), as well as in the fourteenth-century B.C. Amarna letters* and OT passages. Its importance in antiquity was undoubtedly due to the fact that it was located on a major caravan-trade route from Egypt to the N and E. In the time of Joshua, Hazor was a Canaanite* city-state whose ruler, Jabin (probably a dynastic name), organized a coalition against the advancing Israelite forces (Josh 11:1). His plans were unsuccessful, however and ended in the death of Jabin and the sacking of Hazor (Josh 11:1–15; 12:19). The burning of the city was probably an indirect testimony to its importance, since no other city in the northern campaign suffered this fate. About a century later Deborah and Barak* led an attack upon another ruler of Hazor described as "Jabin king of Canaan" (Judg 4:2, 24). His military commander, Sisera, had nine hundred iron-fitted chariots* at his disposal, but despite this formidable opposition the Israelites were able to gain a victory at the battle of Taanach* c. 1125 B.C. (Judg 4–5). About two hundred years later Solomon* rebuilt and fortified Hazor in order to protect the Plain of Huleh (cf. 1 Kings 9:15), and a casemate wall* typical of the period was recovered from Level X. City gates,* characteristic of their Solomonic counterparts from Gezer* and Megiddo,* were also found in the same stratum. Under Ahab Hazor was reconstructed, and from this period came a large building and a heavily fortified citadel* on the western edge of the tell. From the succeeding city were recovered Hebrew inscriptions belonging to the time of Jeroboam II (892–753 B.C.), while on top of this was the heavy layer of ashes, a yard thick in places, which marked the destruction in 732 B.C. under Tiglath-pileser III* of Assyria (2 Kings 15:29). At a later period Hazor was rebuilt but was subsequently abandoned early in the seventh century B.C. The citadel was used by the Persians in the fifth and fourth centuries B.C. and saw its final service as a military outpost in the Hellenistic period. In a stratum belonging to the Late Bronze Age* was found the remains of a Canaanite* temple whose plan comprises the earliest "prototype" of the Solomonic Temple* yet discovered.

In 1962 an American tourist visiting Hazor picked up a cuneiform* tablet from the surface of the tell. It was published in 1975 and proved to be a description in Akkadian* of a lawsuit brought before the king of Hazor. Dated between 1800 and 1600 B.C., the material illustrates the extent to which Babylonian culture was influencing Canaanite life in the Middle Bronze Age.

BIBLIOGRAPHY: Y. Yadin et al., *Hazor I, Hazor II, Hazor III-IV* (1958–61); W. W. Hallo and H. Tadmor, *IEJ*, 27 (1977), 1–11.

RKH

HEADDRESS. As an article of official or sacred livery, the headdress was widely adopted in antiquity. Paleolithic* cave* art shows some types of headdress on figures who may have been shamans of the cult. Early in Egyptian history the *ḥ ḏ t* "white crown" of Upper Egypt* and the *d š r t* "red crown" of Lower Egypt were combined in the hieroglyphic* usage into the *s ḥ m t y* "double crown" of the pharaohs. Exquisite headdresses have been excavated from Egyptian tombs and from the burial pits of Ur.* The Mesopotamian* headdresses were made of gold,* silver,* and electrum (an amber-colored alloy of gold and silver) and decorated with carnelian (a reddish variety of quartz) and lapis lazuli.* The texts reveal that headdresses of feathers, wool, linen,* and even flowers were worn on festival occasions and for royal functions. Battle helmets* of all types have been discovered from Sumer,* Elam,* Babylon,* Egypt, Persia,* Greece, and Rome.* In the OT the Egyptian loan word for "cap" is used in Hebrew and remnants of such leather* headpieces have been found in Palestine.

WW

HEALING. See CHEMICAL TECHNOLOGY; INCANTATION; MEDICINE.

HEBREW LANGUAGE. See EPIGRAPHY, HEBREW.

HEBREW PEOPLE. See HABIRU; JEW.

HEBREW RELIGION. Up to the nineteenth century, studies in this field regarded the various elements of Hebrew faith as parts of one large body of truth originating with Moses at Sinai.* From the Judges period this corpus encountered occasional lapses from the monotheistic ideal up to the Exile* and subsequently emerged in the form of a theocracy based on the rites and ceremonies of the ancient Law, a pattern which survived to the Christian era.

The nineteenth-century positivist approach to history, however, minimized metaphysical influences and stressed the more factual elements of history and culture instead. Wellhausen adopted these premises and used the evolutionary concepts of Hegelian philosophy to reconstruct Israelite religion. His conclusions were that OT religion gradually evolved from purely naturalistic origins through the phases of popular, prophetic, and priestly belief and practice, respectively. For him, the earliest phases of this process were marked by such primitive religious forms as animism, tabu, totemism, and ancestor worship, all of which he purported to recognize in the pre-Mosaic period. However, in reaching these conclusions,

Wellhausen ignored an increasing corpus of archaeological knowledge which even then was making it clear that the religion of the Hebrew patriarchs was far more sophisticated in origin and nature than he could ever have imagined. It is now abundantly clear from a comparative study of literary texts from Babylonia, Ugarit, * and elsewhere, that such practices as animism had left the Near Eastern scene long before the time of the Hebrew patriarchs. Temples dedicated to "high gods" existed in Mesopotamia* from the fourth millennium B.C., and the evidence relating to the environment of early Israel suggests, not merely a significant degree of cultural attainment, but also equally sophisticated concepts of a personal god. This new knowledge of the nature of Ancient Near Eastern religion demands renewed consideration of the arguments for a primitive monotheism.

The OT narratives dealing with patriarchal religion give the impression of a general monotheistic tradition modified somewhat by Mesopotamian polytheism (cf. Josh 24:2). The patriarchs participated in a personal faith-relationship with the Deity and utilized circumcision as the token of membership in the divine covenant.* Ugaritic archaeology has shown convincingly that the patriarchal names for God compounded with "El" were genuinely pre-Israelite in character. The Hebrew patriarchs seem to have worshipped the same deity under a variety of names, but the clear beginnings of Hebrew monotheism *per se* must be sought in the Mosaic era, when the religious system of the Israelites was established. Basic to this monotheism was the revealed name of God as YHWH and the establishing of a divine covenant with Israel,* the structure of which parallels exactly

that of the second millennium B.C. Hittite* suzerainty treaties recovered from Boghazköy.* As a focus for worship in the wilderness period, Moses was ordered to construct a tabernacle whose nature and design has been illustrated archaeologically by similar structures from Egyptian and Arab* sources, a fact which firmly plants the record in the right period of history. An outstanding feature of contemporary religious legislation was the aniconic emphasis which prohibited idol worship in any form (Exod 20:4; 34:17). This ancient legislation has been supported by Palestinian archaeology, since no figurine representing the Hebrew deity has ever been recovered from any site, in contrast with the series of pagan male figurines prominent in Canaanite* archaeological levels. An elaborate sacrificial ritual was also enacted in the Mosaic era, in which animals or cereals were offered by prescription to secure forgiveness for confessed sins of omission or inadvertence.

Excavations at Ras Shamra (Ugarit), from 1929, have thrown new light on Hebrew religion by revealing the nature of the syncretism occurring after the Conquest period. The sordid sexuality of Canaanite religion, and its infiltration into Hebrew worship from the time of Jeroboam I (931–909 B.C.) onward, has become abundantly clear, setting the strictures of the prophets concerning true morality in infinitely sharper focus. Thus the conflict between Elijah and the Baal priests (1 Kings 18) involved the fundamental ethical quality of the Hebrew deity rather than purely nationalistic or ritualistic considerations. Canaanite archaeology has also shown the extent to which Solomon's temple* followed contemporary Phoenician* patterns of design and decor, while still

Detail of fourth-century A.D. mosaic pavement in synagogue at Hamman Tabariyeh (Hammath). The middle and largest section of the mosaic is a circle with Helios holding the sun in his hand surrounded by the twelve signs of the zodiac. The representation of images was permitted by the sages of Tiberias, as is attested by the written sources (see TJ., Av. Zar, 3:3 42d). Courtesy Israel Government Press Office.

retaining its own individuality. The use of music* in the Davidic Age of worship has also been verified by archaeological discoveries in Palestine.

The bull-worship of the northern kingdom typified the syncretism of the depraved religion of Canaan and the worship of the Hebrew God. Pre-Exilic prophets such as Amos and Hosea repeatedly denounced this corruption and foretold disaster unless the nation repented sincerely of its idolatry. Spiritual obduracy led to successive captivities for Israel and Judah, and during the Exile Hebrew religion was purged of all its idolatrous associations. A nonsacrificial form of worship was followed in which prayer, confession, and the reading of the Law were prominent. From this period emerged the beginnings of the synagogue,* which thereafter became a permanent feature of Jewish religious life. The second temple was constructed after the Exile* from about 535 B.C., and many of the offices and traditions of the early monarchy were reestablished. In 444 B.C. Ezra, a Jewish scribe from Babylonia, guided the struggling Jewish theocracy toward a rededication of itself to the Mosaic Law and thereby established the pattern of normative Judaism. Jerusalem* became the focal point of national worship, and the temple was the scene of the great religious festivals prescribed in the Law. Side by side with this, however, was the weekly worship held in the synagogues, which were established in villages and towns throughout the land. Here the Law was read and expounded much as it had been in the days of Ezekiel. When the Jerusalem temple was demolished by the Romans in A.D. 70, the religion of dispersed Judaism was preserved by means of synagogue worship. A number of ruined synagogues have been unearthed in Palestine and elsewhere, some of which have yielded elegant mosaic* pavements incorporating pagan astrological signs.

BIBLIOGRAPHY: G. E. Wright, *An Introduction to Biblical Archaeology* (1960); R. K. Harrison, *Introduction to the OT* (1969), 362–414; id., *ZPEB*, 3 (1975), 94–107.   RKH

HEBRON (heb'rən; Heb. חֶבְרוֹן, *ḥeḇrôn*, "league" or "confederacy"). This is one of the most important cities in S Palestine. It is located about 30.6 km. (19 mi.) S of Jerusalem* in the hill country at an altitude of 790 m. (2600 ft.) above sea level. The area around Hebron is characterized by the presence of beautiful vineyards, orchards, and large olive* groves. With an annual rainfall of 20.3 to 25.4 cm. (8 to 10 in.) the widespread use of cisterns,* wells,* and pools* was an obvious necessity. The site of ancient Hebron (el-khalil, er-Rahman) has made it one of the most revered cities of Islam. At the center is a mosque said to be built over the tomb of the patriarchs.

Abraham lived in the vicinity of Hebron for considerable periods of time. In his days the resident population of the area was the "sons of Heth" (Hittites*) and the Amorites* (Gen 23:7–8; 14:13). Originally, Hebron was called Kiriath Arba ("four-fold city," "tetropolis," Gen 23:2; 35:27; Josh 15:54; 20:7; 21:11; Neh 11:25). According to Num 13:22 Hebron "was built seven years before Zoan in Egypt.*" This

Royal ("Lamelekh") seal impression on pottery jar handle. From Lachish, late seventh century B.C. Top register: "Lamelekh" [Belonging] to the king). Middle register: two-winged scarab. Bottom register: "Hebron." *(See also photo under MACHPELAH)* Courtesy Israel Dept. of Antiquities and Museums.

reference probably relates its foundation to the "Era of Tanis*" (c. 720 B.C.). Abraham purchased a cave* to serve as a family sepulcher from local Hittite landowners (Gen 23:17). It was in this cave of Machpelah* that all of the patriarchs and their wives were buried except Rachel (Gen 49:30ff.; 50:13).

Under Moses the spies visited Hebron and its environs during the wilderness journey (Num 13:22ff.). During the Occupation period under Joshua the city was successfully conquered (Josh 10:1–27), and its inhabitants, along with those of neighboring cities,* were put to death (Josh 10:36–37; 11:21–22). Not long after this, however, it was reoccupied by the Anakim clans. It was finally recaptured and subjugated by Caleb and his soldiers after the death of Joshua (Josh 14:12–15; 15:13–14; Judg 1:19–20). Hebron was designated as a Levitical city and a city of refuge (Josh 20:7; 21:10–13). It also became an important district capital of that area (Josh 15:54). When David was a fugitive he received help from the people of this city (1 Sam 30:31). It was here that Abner was treacherously slain by Joab at the gate (2 Sam 3:27). After Saul's death David was anointed king there (2 Sam 5:3) and reigned there for seven and one-half years until Jerusalem was made the new capital (2 Sam 5:5). Six sons were born to him while resident in this city (2 Sam 3:2). It was at Hebron that Abner consulted with David on the proposed union of Israel* with Judah* (2 Sam 3:12–32). The site was an important fortress for Rehoboam (2 Chron 11:10). During the Exile,* the Edomites* probably occupied the city, although it appears from Neh 11:25 that Jewish exiles did colonize the site to some extent. Later, Judas Maccabeus drove the Edomites from Hebron and the surrounding regions (1 Macc 5:65; Jos. *Antiq.* 12.8.6). It is believed that Herod* was responsible for extensive building operations around the sacred precincts presumed to be the patriarchal burial cave, and some of the masonry of the great Haram at Hebron would seem to support this tradition (see W. F. Albright, *The Archaeology of Palestine* [1961], 156).

In A.D. 1165 it became the see of the Latin bishop, but twenty years later it fell to the armies of Saladin. During the Crusades, this city was known as "Castle of Saint Abraham" and was a link in a chain of fortresses protecting the Latin kingdom of Jerusalem. Since the fall of the city to Saladin, however, Hebron has been an important Muslim shrine.

Because of this continuous occupation of the site, archaeological work has encountered great difficulties. During the summer of 1963, Philip C. Hammond of Princeton Theological Seminary conducted extensive surveys of the area. A year later, between July and September, an American expedition to Hebron was led by Hammond, who worked with five other cooperating institutions. A trench was opened in the Wadi Tuffah on the western outskirts of Hebron. This produced only late Islamic fill above the bedrock. Two probes were conducted on Jebel Batraq, to the N of Hebron. Shards* from Islamic, Byzantine,* and the Roman periods were found. Excavations were carried on to bedrock in those areas as well. The most important areas investigated, however, were located on the slopes of Jebel er-Rumeide located just W of modern Hebron. Stratigraphic* indications pointed to occupation during the Islamic, Byzantine, Late Roman, Iron I and II (*see* IRON AGE), and Late Bronze I and Middle Bronze I (*see* BRONZE AGE) periods. Various periods were represented by a series of complex house walls and plastered floors. Two Middle Bronze, sub-floor burials were also uncovered in these areas. Near the end of the excavation, materials from the Early Bronze I period were just beginning to come to light. Traces of the ancient city wall* were also located in this vicinity. A number of caves and burial sites were located with the aid of the proton-magnetometer. One such cave contained materials from the Early Bronze I and Chalcolithic* periods. The excavators concluded that there was generally continuous occupation at the site from the Early Bronze period onward, although further excavation is needed to determine particular phasing and occupational gaps.

That Hebron was a royal city of some importance is further confirmed by discoveries at the site of biblical Gibeon* (el-Jib). Some eighty royal stamp impressions on jar handles were found in the first two seasons of excavations at this site. The seals* usually bore the impressions of either a winged beetle or a winged sun disk. Above the design were four Hebrew letters (*lmlk* "for the king") and below, there generally appeared one of the four ancient place names, Hebron, Socoh, Ziph, or Memshath. The handles which bear these impressions once belonged to large, four-handled storage jars which held approximately 38 liters (10 gal.) of liquid. The wide distribution of such handles indicates that there existed a lively trade throughout the area of Hebron in the OT kingdom period.

BIBLIOGRAPHY: James B. Pritchard, *Gibeon, Where the Sun Stood Still* (1962), 117; Gerald A. Larue, "American Expedition to Hebron, 1964," *JBR*, 33 (1965), 337–39; P. C. Hammond, "Hebron," *RB*, 72 (1965), 267–70; ibid. (1966), 566–69; ibid., 75 (1968), 253–58; id., "David's First City; The Excavation of Biblical Hebron, 1964," *Princeton Seminary Bulletin* (1965), 19–28; id., "Archaeological News from Jordon: Hebron," *BA*, 28 (1965), 30–32.

JJD

HELIOPOLIS (hē lē o′ pǝ lis; Gr. Ἐλίουπόλις [LXX], for Egypt. ʼIwnw, meaning uncertain). The site of ancient Heliopolis is today marked by the ruin-mounds of Matariyeh, Tell Ḥisn and its environs, about 16 km. (10 mi.) N of central Cairo. It was an early center of sun-worship in Egypt,* and fragments of temple decoration by Djoser, builder of the Step Pyramid (c. 2650 B.C.), were found there. Achieving great prominence during the Pyramid* Age (c. 2700–2300 B.C.), the theological influence of its priests was then and thereafter rivaled in Egypt only by the cult of Osiris.* One such was doubtless Joseph's father-in-law, the "priest of On," Potiphera, whose very name includes (appropriately) that of the sun-god Re (Gen 41:45, 50).

Heliopolis was perhaps most splendid in the Middle and New Kingdoms (c. 1991–1786, c. 1551–1070 B.C.) when many pharaohs adorned its temples, especially with obelisks.* These were tall shafts, capped with miniature pyramids that caught the first and last rays of the sun. Reference to Heliopolis in Isa 19:18 is uncertain, but Jeremiah (43:13) prophesied God's breaking of the "pillars" or obelisks of Heliopolis. Today, only one still stands there; the rest have long since been removed or reduced to fragments, and not only by Nebuchadnezzar.* In Ezek 30:17, On for Heliopolis is vocalized Awen, perhaps as a pun on Heb. ʼawen "trouble, wickedness."

BIBLIOGRAPHY: B. Porter and R. L. B. Moss, *Topographical Bibliography of Anc. Egypt. Texts . . .* , 4 (1934), 59–65 (principal remains; recent excavations remain unpublished); Sir A. H. Gardiner, *Ancient Egyptian Onomastica*, 2 (1947), 144–46:400; H. Kees, *Der Götterglaube im alten Ägypten* (1956), 214–86; P. Montet, *Geographie de l'Egypte Ancienne*, 1 (1957), 155–71, fig. 17–19; H. Kees, *Ancient Egypt, A Cultural Topography* (1901), 147–82; K. A. Kitchen, *ZPEB*, 3 (1975), 113–14.

KAK

HELKATH (hel′kath; Heb. חֶלְקָת, *ḥelqāt*). A Levitical city (Josh 21:31) just inside the border of Asher (Josh 19:25), called Hukok in 1 Chron 6:75. It may have been mentioned about 1460 B.C. in topographical lists of the pharaoh Thutmose III and may possibly be located at Tell el-Harbaj near Haifa,* or at Tell el-Kussis, farther S. RKH

HELLADIC. Relating in some manner to Hellas, ancient Greece.

HELMET. There is richly abundant archaeological illustration of the helmets of the ancient world. Illustration ranges from the Standard of Ur* (third millennium) which shows the tight-fitting, metal Sumerian* helmet, designed to cover the back of the neck and cheek, to the decorated feather-topped, or disk and horn-topped helmets of the Lydians and Sea Peoples* routed by Ramses III* and depicted in the amazingly detailed colored reliefs of Medinet Habu near Thebes,* to tenth-century B.C. conical helmets of Aramean* cavalrymen from Tell Halaf and the crested helmets of the Assyrian bowmen of Tiglath-pileser III* and Sargon II.* Greek helmets, heavily crested and visored, are well known from Greek vase paintings. The name Goliath* is possibly Lydian (Alyattes is a name found in Western Asia Minor), and Goliath's helmet was probably of the Homeric type, designed to be worn by sword and spear fighters, with the head down over the shield rim and the visor protecting the brow. Goliath lost the protection of his highly sophisticated headgear when he threw back his head to laugh.

Roman helmets, not unlike the Greek, but typically neater and more compact, may be seen on Trajan's column and the arches of Severus and Constantine.

BIBLIOGRAPHY: S. E. Ellacott, *Armour and Blade* (1962); Y. Yadin, *The Art of Warfare in Biblical Times* (1963), illustrations passim; E. Yamauchi, *The Stones and the Scriptures* (1973), 95 and f.n. refs.

EMB

HERCULANEUM (hûr kyə lā′ nē əm). This Roman city,* neighbor of Pompeii,* perished in the eruption of Vesuvius in August A.D. 79. It was a more elegant and residential town than its neighbor and more heavily sealed by the solidification of its volcanic covering. It appears to have been overwhelmed by an immense flood of super-heated mud.

The section opened up lies in a mighty hole, 167 sq. m. (200 sq. yd.), and this must be only a small portion of the town. The undistinguished modern town of Erculaneo still forbids wider digging, and it will be extremely expensive to carry on beyond the present works. Whereas Pompeii was a busy market town, with a cross section of population, Herculaneum seems to have been more genteel, being the residential town of richer Romans, whose houses stood up to two and three stories high. The streets are wide by the standards of the time.

The excavations, begun seriously in 1927, produced much of classical interest, but, like Pompeii, Herculaneum does add a fragment or two to the archaeology of the Bible. A house,* for example, in what appears to be the sort of private chapel to be seen in the Lullingstone Villa, shows the marks on the wall where a wooden cross had been burned during the eruption—further evidence of the early date at which the cross had become a symbol. Below the cross, and almost a ruin, stand the remains of what might have been a sort of altar, or at least a small table to carry the food and drink of the Christian love feast. One hesitates to think that the Christian Communion or Eucharist took so formal a shape so early in the history of the church, but how else can we explain the furnishing of this strange little room?

Christianity reached Italy in the reign of Claudius,* perhaps in the late forties of the century. A group of Christians, sufficiently well organized and in contact with others to know of the apostle Paul's arrival under military escort, met him at Pozzuoli, the ancient Puteoli,* which is not far away. That was somewhere near A.D. 60 or a little later.

BIBLIOGRAPHY: J. J. Deiss, *A City Returns to the Sun* (1966); "Rome and Herculaneum," *Buried History*, 10.1 (1974), 10–15.

EMB

HERES, MOUNT. *See* BETH SHEMESH.

HERMES. Hermes' house* (Rom 16:14) has been located under the church of San Sebastiano, originally called the Basilica Apostolorum from the tradition that the bodies of Peter and Paul lay there after their martyrdom. Excavation has revealed a first-century A.D. Roman house with associated burial places with inscriptions and wall decorations. One inscription records that Hermes, at the age of seventy-five, emancipated his household of slaves,* probably in consequence of his conversion or in the adjustments preceding the end of his life. The house dated from A.D. 40 and a change in the interior decorating, from pagan to Christian, may also point to the conversion of the owner.

BIBLIOGRAPHY: S. L. Caiger, *Archaeology of the NT* (1939), 130–31; K. Kirschbaum, *The Tombs of Saint Peter and Saint Paul* (1959), 196–97; A. G. Mackinnon, *The Rome of the Early Church* (1930), 129.

EMB

HERMON. The Mount of the Transfiguration, N of Caesarea Philippi,* is strictly a range 29 km. (18 mi.) long. It is called Sirion (Deut 3:9) in the Execration Texts* of the eighteenth and nineteenth centuries of Egypt,* and in documents from Ugarit.* In a fourteenth-century treaty between a Hittite* and a Syrian ruler, the deities of Lebanon and Sirion are called upon as guarantors of the contract. A document of Tiglath-pileser III* refers to Hermon as Saniru.

BIBLIOGRAPHY: S. Barabas, *ZPEB*, 3 (1975), 125–26.

EMB

HEROD, BUILDING ACTIVITIES OF. A common mark of the empire builder and autocrat (and examples are as varied as Augustus* and Nero, Solomon* and Nebuchadnezzar*) is a zeal for building. In this respect the first Herod runs true to form. He financed buildings as far away as Rhodes,* Nicopolis, the Syrian Antioch,* Tyre,* Sidon,* and Damascus.* He rebuilt Omri's* old fortress of Samaria,* calling it Sebaste ("*sebastos*" is the Greek for the Latin adjective "*augustus*," from which Augustus took his imperial name). At Sebaste (the name is still reflected in the village of Sebastiyeh) Herod built a temple to Olympian Zeus* in honor of Augustus. Its forecourt alone was some 76 m. (250 ft.) square. A forum* and a stadium* are adjacent. Typical of Herod's clever dual policy was the temple* (forty-six years in building—John 2:20) which he adorned so lavishly in Jerusalem* in honor of Jehovah. He built Caesarea* as a fortress and bridgehead for the Romans, and as the ruins emerge they give a greater and greater impression of the magnificence of the port. In addition to the temple, Jerusalem had Herod's palace and fortifications which included the citadel* of Antonia.* Ashkelon* experienced Herod's building enthusiasm, and his palace at Masada* was a triumph of architectural engineering.* At Herodian Jericho* (in the neighborhood of Tulul Abu el-'Alayiq) Herod had a palace, and a gymnasium, apparently of his building, has been excavated.

EMB

HEROD, FAMILY OF. Herod the Great was not a true Jew but an Idumaean who was appointed king of Judea* and its surrounding districts by the Romans in spite of Jewish hostility to him. He died in 4 B.C. Luke 1:5 and Matt 2 (cf. Acts 23:35) narrate his part in the Slaughter of the Innocents at Bethlehem* at the birth of Jesus Christ. Several of his coins* (and of coins issued by his descendants) survive and a few inscriptions to him have been recorded. One is in Athens,* honoring him for a benefaction to the city: *ho dēmos basilea Herōdēn Philorōmaion euergesias heneken kai eunoias tēs eis heauton (OGIS 414)*— "the people have honored king Herod, the friend of the Romans, on account of his good services and good will towards the city."

His son Archelaus (briefly mentioned in Matt 2:22) succeeded him in Judea and Samaria,* not as king, but as ethnarch. His rule lasted from 4 B.C. to A.D. 6 and proved as unpopular with the Jews as that of his father. His name appears on a fragmentary Palestinian inscription (*CIG* 4537 and *add.*). Another of the sons of Herod the Great who features in the NT was Herod Antipas, tetrarch of Galilee* and Peraea from 4 B.C. to A.D. 39. He is famous for ordering the execution of John the Baptist (Matt 14; Mark 6; 8:15; Luke 3; 8:3; 9:7; 13:31). In Luke 23:7ff. (cf. Acts 4:27) he is assigned a part in the trial of Jesus. He is honored on two Greek inscriptions (*OGIS* 416–17). A third son of Herod to be named in the Gospels (Luke 3:1; cf. Matt 16:13; Mark 8:27) was Philip, tetrarch of Trachonitis and other districts N of Judea from 4 B.C. to A.D. 34. His relation to the Philip of Matt 14:3 and Mark 6:17 is unclear.

The next generation is represented by Herod Agrippa, so-called, and Herodias his sister, the children of another of Herod's sons (Aristobulus). Herod Agrippa's actual name was Julius Agrippa, and he is generally referred to dynastically as Agrippa I. In A.D. 37 he was made king of the tetrarchies previously administered by his uncle, Philip, and by Lysanias. (Lysanias,* mentioned in Luke 3:1, was tetrarch of Abilene, a district of Ituraea, under Tiberius* and is named on the inscription *OGIS* 606.) He acquired Galilee and Peraea from another of his uncles, Herod Antipas, in 39. In 41 he became king of Judea itself, which he ruled until his death in 44. In Acts 12, where he is simply called Herod, he is responsible for the beheading of James and the arrest of Peter. On one of his coins he appears as AGRIPPAS PHILOKAISAR BASILEUS MEGAS—"the great king Agrippa, the friend of the emperor" (Smallwood, 209a). The inscription *OGIS* 418 also refers to him. His sister Herodias is said to have been married to a Philip (cf. above) in the Gospels: in other sources her first husband is called a Herod. No doubt attaches to her second husband, her uncle Herod Antipas, whom she incited to the death of John the Baptist. (It may be noted that Herod Antipas himself had been previously married to the daughter of Aretas,* the king of Nabataean* Arabia* mentioned in 2 Cor 11:32).

The third generation is represented by Herodias's daughter Salome and the children of Agrippa I. Salome, who danced for the head of John the Baptist, is not mentioned by name in the Gospels (Matt 14:6ff.; Mark 6:22ff.). She married her great-uncle Philip the tetrarch (cf. above). Acts names three of the children of Agrippa I. M. Julius Agrippa, dynastically Agrippa II, was considered too young to succeed his father as king of Judea on the latter's death in 44. However, he showed a deep interest in the affairs of Judea after it had reverted to provincial status in 44 and often intervened in Jewish matters. In 49 he became tetrarch of Chalcis, a district in Ituraea, but in 53 was transferred to a tetrarchy over Trachonitis and other NE districts, including Abilene,* Galilee, and Peraea. While on a visit to Caesarea* he became involved in the trial of Paul (Acts 25f.). Monuments recording his name are relatively frequent. On one he is styled, "the great king Agrippa, friend of the emperor, god-fearing and friend of the Romans" (*OGIS* 419). His sister Bernice, who accompanied him on his visit to Caesarea (Acts 25:13, 23), bore

STEMMA OF THE HERODS

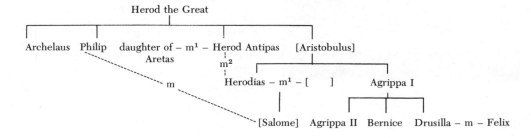

the full name of Julia Berenice. She is grandiloquently called "great queen, daughter of king Julius Agrippa, and the descendant of great kings who were benefactors of the city" (*OGIS* 428) on an Athenian inscription, while in Beirut* a stone records her having restored a building originally built by Herod the Great (Smallwood, 212b). The sister of Agrippa II and Bernice, who is known from Acts, is Drusilla, and was married to the Roman procurator Felix and present with him when he gave Paul the opportunity to expound his faith soon after his formal accusation by the Jews (Acts 24:24).

BIBLIOGRAPHY: For the coins of the Herods, cf. *BMC;* for a comprehensive treatment of the family, A. H. M. Jones, *The Herods of Judaea,* (1938, rev. 1967); R. D. Sullivan, The Dynasty of Judea in the First Century, in *Aufstieg und Niedergang der römischen Welt* (Festschrift F. Vogt) 2, 8 (1978), 296–354.

DBS

HERODIUM. A fortress and mausoleum situated 6.4 km. (4 mi.) SE of Bethlehem,* on the "Hill of Paradise." It was built by Herod the Great (*see* HEROD, FAMILY OF) after his victory over the Jews* in 40 B.C., and he was buried there (cf. Matt 2:19). The cone-shaped hill was an artificial device, enclosing a citadel* with four round towers* and high retaining walls. Inside it Herod laid out an imposing palace, and beyond it at the foot of the hill he constructed further royal apartments which combined Greek and oriental styles. Josephus (Jos. *War* 1.21.10) describes the Herodium before its destruction in A.D. 72 as one of the last three citadels of Jewish resistance, mentioning particularly the two hundred mar-

Aerial view from north to south, of Herodium showing remains of fortress at summit with its round eastern tower and three semicircular towers. Courtesy Israel Government Press Office.

ble steps leading up to it and the aqueduct,* of which traces remain.

A Hebrew document has recently been found, dated to A.D. 133, which shows that the disused fort was made into a supply depot in the rising of Bar Kochba.*

BIBLIOGRAPHY: M. Avi-Yonah, *A History of the Holy Land* (1969), 136ff.; M. Pearlman and Y. Yannai, *Historical Sites in Israel* (1969 ed.), 245ff.

BFH

HESHBON. This city is mentioned thirty-eight times in the Bible as a large city* with many dependent villages (Num 21:25; Josh 13:17). In the time of the Exodus and conquest, Israel,* after being refused permission to travel the highway through the land, successfully defeated Sihon, king of the Amorites,* who lived in Heshbon; Israel then settled there (Num 21:21–26). It had attractive pasture lands (Deut 21:39), and "pools in Heshbon" was a figure of beauty (Song of Songs 7:4). It was still a prosperous city in the time of Isaiah and Jeremiah (Isa 16:8; Jer 48:45) and was important enough in the Christian era to have a representative bishop (*see* EPISKOPOS) at the Council of Nicaea in A.D. 325.

Heshbon is located in the Trans-Jordan region about 75 km. (47 mi.) straight E of Jerusalem.* The site is occupied today by a very small village called Hisban.

Andrews University has sponsored several campaigns at Heshbon beginning in 1968.

Excavators have found evidence of habitation at Heshbon in the Arabic period (A.D. 638–1517) illustrated by public and private structures (notably an Islamic bath complex), several water channels, cisterns,* one with a capacity of over 265,000 liters (70,000 gallons), a hoard of Mameluke coins* in a small lamp, an infant burial, and numerous other artifacts.*

A large basilica* church on the summit of the hill was the major witness to the Byzantine* period (A.D. 323–638). It had been reconstructed several times, and some of the stones and pillars may have come from an earlier Roman temple or public building. Other evidence of the Roman period included a partitioned* cave workshop, tombs (especially a tomb with a rolling stone door like the tomb in which Jesus was buried), a monumental stairway to the acropolis,* a wall that may have been part of a defense system, traces of the Roman road to Jericho* and Jerusalem, a rare Elagabalus coin minted in Heshbon, and numerous glass* and ceramic vessels (*see* POTTERY).

Although there was abundant ceramic evidence for the Iron II* period (900–539 B.C.), other archaeological evidence of pre-Roman Heshbon was scarce. Several ostraca* (broken pottery with writing on it) were found, one in Aramaic* script from the sixth century B.C.; part of what was interpreted as a large water reservoir was dated in the Iron II period. Some Iron I pottery and a possible wall are the only indications of life in Heshbon prior to the time of Isaiah and Jeremiah so far discovered at the site.

BIBLIOGRAPHY: *AUSS,* 9 (1971), 147–60; ibid., 11 (1973), 1–114, plates 1–16; ibid., 12 (1974), 35–46,

Early Roman Period (before A.D. 70) rolling-stone tomb, first of its kind found east of the Jordan from Tell Ḥesban. Courtesy Professor L. T. Geraty, Andrews University.

plates I–II; ibid., 13 (1975), 101–247, plates I–XVI.

BCC

HESY (HESI), TELL EL-. See EGLON.

HEZEKIAH'S TUNNEL. Referred to in 2 Kings 20:20; Isaiah 22:9ff.; 2 Chronicles 32:30-31, it was built by Hezekiah (c. 715–686) to bring water from the Spring of Gihon* within the walls* of Jerusalem.* The tunnel, discovered in 1880, was cut through solid rock for 518 m. (1700 ft.) from both ends, probably just before Sennacherib's* attack in 701 B.C.

See SILOAM INSCRIPTION.

BIBLIOGRAPHY: W. F. Albright, *The Archaeology of Palestine* (1960), 135, 221; N. Shaheen, "The Sinuous Shape of Hezekiah's Tunnel," *PEQ* (July-Dec. 1979), 103-8.

JAT

HIBA, AL-. See AL-HIBA.

HIBBEH, AL. See AL-HIBA.

HIERAPOLIS (hī ər a' pō lis; Gr. Ἱεράπολις). Modern Eçirköy, Hierapolis is sometimes known from its silica-draped terraces of lukewarm water (Rev 3:15, 16) as Pamukkale or "cotton castle." It is a town of the Lycus Valley, mentioned in Col 4:13, along with the neighboring cities of Laodicea* 9.6 km. (6 mi.) S and Colosse,* as the home of a Christian group over which Epaphras exercised pastoral care. Later in the first century Philip and his daughters moved there from Palestinian Caesarea,* and early in the second century Hierapolis had Papias as its bishop (*see* EPISKOPOS). Its name, meaning "holy city," marks it out as a cult center of the Anatolian mother goddess, identified locally with Leto, mother of Artemis.* Its hot springs were valued for their healing properties. The villagers of Eçirköy still stand the water in stone jars to cool it before they drink it. The limestone deposited by the water as it falls over precipices S of the city has formed terraces edged with white cascades, visible for miles around. Hierapolis must have been a popular "spa" resort to judge by its opulent and extensive remains. The Romans were partial to such resorts, and there is evidence of a considerable Roman element in the population—another source of wealth for the affluent neighboring marketplace of Laodicea.*

Although it has not been systematically excavated, the city* plan is recognizable. It was based on the grid principle: the main street with its colonnades runs NW and SE, and other streets cross it at right angles. Among public buildings still discernible are Roman baths associated with a gymnasium, a Roman cemetery and marketplace, notable for the fine locked stone of its arches,* and a theater* overlooking the city and the Lycus Valley. The Roman tone of the spa town could have been a motive for the establishment of a Christian cell there—especially if the foundation dated from Paul's period in Ephesus* (Acts 19:1, 10).

BIBLIOGRAPHY: E. M. Blaiklock, *ZPEB*, 3 (1975), 152–55.

FFB and EMB

HIERATIC. One of the developed phases of Egyptian* hieroglyphic* writing. Because the pictorial symbols of the "sacred carving" were normally used on stone, and only occasionally written on papyrus* with a pen, a simplified "cursive" form of hieroglyphic was developed early in the Old Kingdom period (c. 2900–2200 B.C.). This script, known as "hieratic" or "priestly writing," was characterized by a modification of the earlier hieroglyphic signs and was used along with its precursor as late as the third century A.D. Whereas hieroglyphic was normally written from right to left, though occasionally in the reverse manner also, hieratic was written from right to left in vertical columns until about 1900 B.C., as was originally the case with hieroglyphics, but after that time it occurred principally in horizontal lines. Hieratic was admirably suited to papyrus documents, and many such artifacts* have survived from various periods in Egyptian history, furnishing invaluable information about a wide range of human activities.

BIBLIOGRAPHY: A. H. Gardiner, *Egyptian Grammar* (1950), 10.

RKH

HIEROGLYPHS; HIEROGLYPHIC. These terms, meaning "sacred writing," were applied to the earliest types of pictographic* symbols employed in written communications by the ancient Egyptians. Hieroglyphic writing* appeared in a fully developed form at the end of the fourth millennium B.C. and was most probably influenced originally by elements of the Sumerian* system of writing, including ideograms,* determinative symbols, and other linguistic features. Hieroglyphic developed independently, however, and the form of specific signs changed very little during the prolonged written history of the Egyptian language. Hieroglyphic long outlasted cuneiform,* occurring in a degenerate form as late as the fifth century A.D. Such writing was as much an ancient form of art as a means of communication, as the many elegantly executed inscriptions from ancient Egypt* testify. Whereas cuneiform was syllabic, hieroglyphic was consonantal, and since vowels were not included in the script, it is virtually im-

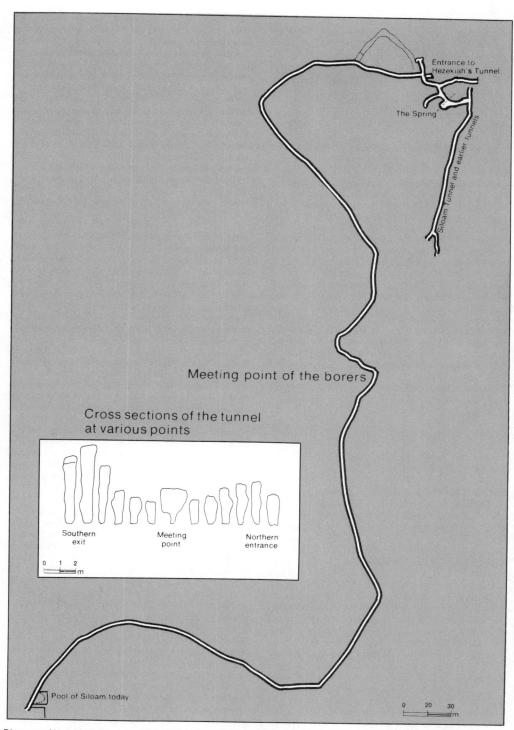

Entrance to
Hezekiah's Tunnel

The Spring

Siloam tunnel and earlier tunnels

Meeting point of the borers

Cross sections of the tunnel
at various points

Southern
exit

Meeting
point

Northern
entrance

0   1   2
▭▭▭ m

Pool of Siloam today

0   20   30
▭▭▭▭ m

Diagram of Hezekiah's Tunnel, which carried water from the Gihon Spring in the Kidron Valley to the Pool of Siloam in the Tyropoeon Valley. *(See also photo under* SILOAM.*)* Courtesy Carta, Jerusalem.

possible to determine just how the words were pronounced in antiquity. While there were many ideograms in the language, there were also sufficient symbols comprising a single consonant to have made an alphabetic* system entirely possible. In the event, however, this latter was achieved by the Semitic population of Palestine. Hieroglyphic was originally written in vertical columns from right to left, as in Hebrew, but on occasions occurred in the reverse order. At a later period the Egyptian scribes began to write hieroglyphic in horizontal lines. Two subsequent variations of hieroglyphic were the hieratic* and demotic scripts, both of which survived well into the Christian era.

BIBLIOGRAPHY: A. H. Gardiner, *Egyptian Grammar* (1950), 4 passim.   RKH

HIGH PLACE.

This was the elevated center of ritual in Canaanite* and other Near Eastern religions, and in the OT it was usually associated with a shrine located on a mountain or hill. Some *bāmāhs*, however, were situated in valleys (cf. Jer 7:31; 19:5 et al.). The kind of high place known as *rāmāh* or "mound" was mentioned by Ezekiel (16:24–25, 31, 39). Elevations seem to have been preferred in order to bring the worshiper closer to the heavens and thus to his god, who was thought to dwell there.

The Canaanites employed sacrificial high places long before the Israelites occupied the land. Thus at Megiddo,* excavators discovered a shrine of this type dated about 3000 B.C., with a large altar* for sacrificial rituals. More elaborate high places from the Bronze Age* had platforms, altars, benches, and rooms in which priests and worshipers could partake of sacrificial offerings. The high places were so frequently associated with pagan cults that they became symbols of false worship (2 Kings 23:4–20). Jeroboam's golden calves were set up in "high places" (1 Kings 12:28–33). After the captivity of Judah the high place disappeared from the cultic scene.

BIBLIOGRAPHY: C. C. McCown, *JBL*, 69 (1950), 205–19; W. F. Albright, *Archaeology and the Religion of Israel* (1953 ed.), 103–7; id., *VTSup*, 4 (1957); C. E. DeVries, *ZPEB*, 3 (1975), 155–58.
                                                            EMB

Large round altar (diameter: 8 m.; height: 1.4 m.) c. 2500-1850 B.C., built of small rubble stones and found at Megiddo. In the foreground is one of three additional temples erected in the vicinity of the round altar. Note the square altar with steps leading up from the east. Courtesy Israel Dept. of Antiquities and Museums.

HINNOM.

The name occurs thirteen times in the OT as the name of a man after whose son a valley was named. Since all the references are to the valley, Hinnom may be taken as the name of the valley. Hinnom is located just W and S of the city* of Jerusalem;* this valley joins the Kidron Valley* just S of the Gihon Spring.*

The Hinnom Valley is notorious as the site of Topheth, where many of the Israelites worshiped false gods and sacrificed their children by burning them (2 Kings 23:10). The sin was so displeasing to God that Jeremiah changed the name of the valley to "Valley of Slaughter," and he predicted that it would become a terrible, open graveyard for Jerusalem, defiling the city (Jer 7:30–34). By the time of Jesus, the place had become a place where rubbish was burned, so that He used the phrase "the fiery Hinnom Valley" as a symbol for hell. The Greek transcription of the Hebrew words "Valley of Hinnom" is *Gehenna*; it is usually translated "Hell" in all twelve of its NT occurrences.

There are some Jewish and Christian tombs on the S hillside of the Hinnom Valley which have been dated to the Byzantine* and Roman periods. Some traditions make this the site of the "Potter's Field," which had been bought with the blood money Judas had been given to betray Jesus.

BIBLIOGRAPHY: E. G. Kraeling, *Bible Atlas* (1956), 308–9, 336.
                                                            BCC

HIPPODROME.

See CIRCUS.

HIPPOS.

The name of this city of the Decapolis* derives from the Greek for horse (*hippos*). Similarly, the Hebrew *sus* ("horse") lies under the city's Hebrew name, Susita. Excavations reveal a well-fortified city* on a naturally strategic height near Engev* on the E shore of Galilee* opposite Tiberias.* Coins* bear the city's symbol, a horse* or the head of a horse. The city, excavated in the early 1950s by the Israeli Department of Antiquities, was well fortified and walled, laid out round a central axis, equipped with a large internal reservoir and a bath. The Byzantine* period saw some architectural splendor, churches and a cathedral. There were also docking facilities, since barge traffic was able to shorten considerably the distance from middle Galilee to Damascus* by cutting across the lake from Tiberias to Hippos.   EMB

HIRAM.

A king of Tyre* who reigned from approximately 969 to 936 B.C., he was the son of Abi-Ba'al. The name appears in several forms in the OT. The usual form is *ḥîrām* (cf. 2 Sam 5:11). In 1 Kings 5:10, 18; 7:40 the form is *ḥîrôm*, while it is uniformly *ḥûrām* in the book of 1 Chron. A treaty involving commercial agreements was established between David and this king. In this treaty King David was able to obtain cedar* wood, masons, and carpenters for the construction of his palace in Jerusalem* (2 Sam 5:11; 1 Chron 14:1). Later Hiram concluded a treaty with Solomon,* in which he provided cedar wood and skilled workmen (1 Kings 5:1–18) in exchange for wheat and olive oil. Solomon also depended on Hiram for the provision of ships* and experienced seamen in order to complement his wide trade program. Solomon's merchant fleet operated principally from Ezion Geber* (cf. 1 Kings 9:26–28; 10:11, 22; 2 Chron 8:17, 18; 9:10, 21). Later he offered Hiram 20 cities in Asher for 120 talents of gold* (1 Kings 9:10–14). The proposal, however, met with something less than enthusiasm on the part of Hiram, and it is therefore not clear that the arrangement was ever settled.

In Phoenician* records Hiram appears as a conqueror and ruler. He was victorious over various colonial revolts. According to Josephus (Jos. *Apion* 1:17–18) he began to rule at the age of nineteen. He pulled down the old temples of Heracles and Astarte and rebuilt them. According to some scholars this occurred in his eleventh and twelfth year (see H. J. Katzenstein, *JNES*, 24 [1965], 116–17). He may have been responsible for the great expansion of Phoenician interests in the western Mediterranean world. His predecessors must have exerted considerable influence on the northern tribes of Israel*—Asher, Naphtali, and Dan.* Deborah, the prophetess, lamented the fact that some of these tribes became more interested in commercial enterprise rather than the defense of their own countrymen (cf. Judg 5:16–18).

BIBLIOGRAPHY: H. J. Katzenstein, "Is There Any Synchronism between the Reigns of Hiram and Solomon?" *JNES*, 24.1–2 (1965), 116–17; Jos. *Antiq.* 8:5:3; Jos. *Apion* 1:17–18; W. F. Albright, *Archaeology and the Religion of Israel* (1956), 132; John Bright, *A History of Israel* (1959), 182–84; S. Barabas, *ZPEB*, 3 (1975), 161–62.

JJD

HISBAN. See HESHBON.

HISSARLIK. See TROY.

HITTITE LAW. A collection of laws found in fragmentary form in the ruins of Hattušaš (modern Boghazköy*), the imperial capital of the Hittites* in central Asia Minor. These laws, which represent several stages of development, date probably from the earlier, or Old Kingdom period, through the close of the Hittite Empire (c. 1450–1200 B.C.).

Hittite law is of interest to biblical scholars both for its similarities to and its differences from biblical law. Of the over two hundred extant Hittite regulations (*ANET*, 188–97), almost all civil and criminal categories are included, with the notable exception of adoption,* inheritance, and contract laws. The basis for the codes (although they were apparently never promulgated as codes in the usual sense) seems to be the Indo-European principle of compensation rather than the more generally Semitic principle of lex talionis (eye for an eye). However, since biblical law employs both a compensatory principle and the lex talionis principle, we would do well to avoid too rigid a distinction in form.

The element of progression provides the most unusual feature of these laws. The phrase often employed by the editor of the extant version incorporates both a former and a later penalty. "Formerly (karu) . . . , but now (kinuna) . . ." is used commonly, and in general the former penalty is heavier than its later equivalent. Additional modernizing tendencies are seen in the elimination or reduction of corporeal punishments and the replacement of capital punishments (possibly represented in such things as "exposure to the bee sting," law 92) with a monetary compensation.

The laws discovered included almost complete versions of two tablets, each with one hundred clauses, and there is some evidence that originally a third tablet existed. Scholars feel that the laws were part of a consecutive series, and all contemporary publications reflect this in their numbering of the works.

BIBLIOGRAPHY: F. Hrozný, *Code hittite provenant de L'Asie Mineure* (1922); A. Goetze, "The Hittite Laws," *ANET* (1950); E. Neufeld, *The Hittite Laws* (1951); O. R. Gurney, *The Hittites* (1952), 88–103; J. Friedrich, *Die Hethitischen Gesetze* (1959, rep. with additions 1971); H. A. Hoffner, *The Laws of the Hittites* (unpublished Ph.D. dissertation, 1963); supplementary technical bibliography: J. H. Hospers, *A Basic Bibliography for the Study of Semitic Languages* (1973), 96f.; A. Kempinski, "Hittites in the Bible: What Does Archaeology Say?" *Biblical Archaeology Review* 5 (4-5, 1979), 20–45.

CEA

HITTITES (hi'tīts; Heb. חִתִּים, *ḥittîm*; LXX χέττοι, *Chettoi*. From Anatolian *Hatti*, meaning unknown). The name refers to the ancient peoples of Anatolia and N Syria.

Definitions. The term Hittites has several different applications both in the Near East and in the OT. The original term Hatti applied to the population of Central Anatolia in the third millennium B.C., who were speakers of the peculiar Hattian language. Those who spoke an Indo-European language called Nesian in the cuneiform* texts, took over control of Anatolia, absorbing much Hattian religion and culture in the process, and named their own kingdom "Hatti." It is these Nesians who are today the historical Hittites *par excellence*, so known because of their kingdom being named Hatti. This term then passed into Egyptian, Assyrian, and Hebrew alike, to produce the term Hittite. These Hittites proper may be reflected in Genesis, although this is disputed. The Hittite realms in N Syria to the thirteenth–twelfth centuries B.C. are certainly intended in Josh 1:4 and Judg 1:26. Finally, after c. 1200 B.C., when the Hittite Empire was swept away, a series of lesser states sprang up, to be subdued gradually by Assyria down to 700 B.C. Their rulers are the "kings of the Hittites" of Solomon's* day and later (1 Kings 10:29; 2 Kings 7:6). These rulers had hieroglyphic* inscriptions in Luwian, a language closely related to Nesian (cuneiform Hittite), the so-called Hittite hieroglyphs.

History. The fusion of Hattians and Nesites or Hittites proper was already well under way by the nineteenth century B.C., as shown by the Cappadocian Tablets* from Kanesh (Kultepe*). Sometime thereafter, the Hittites established a central mon-

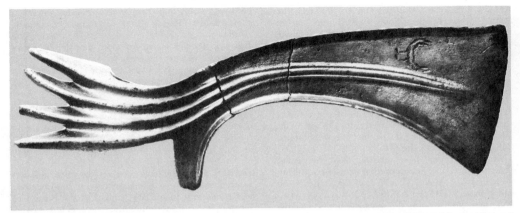

Syro-Hittite hand-shaped bronze axehead; c. 1417-1362 B.C., from Beth Shan. Courtesy Israel Dept. of Antiquities and Museums.

archy based on Hattušaš (now Boghazköy). Greatest kings of the Hittite Old Kingdom were Hattusil I and Mursil I, the latter even raiding Babylon* c. 1595 B.C. Then internal dissension at court, plus Hurrian pressure in the E, reduced the realm drastically. Telepinus stabilized the monarchy with his rule of succession, but not until the accession of Suppiluliuma I,* founder of the New Kingdom, c. 1380 B.C., was the tottering kingdom transformed into a stable empire reaching S into Syria to Lebanon and the borders of Damascus.* His successors Mursil II, Muwatallis, Mursil III, and Hattusil III all in turn clashed with Egypt,* but the last-named made peace with Ramses II* of Egypt by c. 1270 B.C., bringing over fifty years of relative peace to the Levant. Tudkhalia IV was a great builder (especially at Hattušaš) and a religious renovator. But population movements in the Near East broke into the Anatolian homeland, despite the valor of the last emperors (ending with Suppiluliuma II), and swept the Hittite state into oblivion. Part of the Luwian-speaking population of Cilicia* seems to have moved eastward into N Syria as a consequence, where they initially maintained Hittite culture and traditions.

Thus, after c. 1200 B.C., there arose a "shadow empire" based in Carchemish,* whose rulers boasted—like their imperial predecessors—of the title "Great King," claiming more than local status. The overlordship of Carchemish probably reached as far N as Marash and Malatya in the Taurus Mountains and as far S as Hamath,* until roughly 1000 B.C. By then, several vassals had claimed full independence or been overcome by others (e.g., Hamath by Aram-Zobah), and Carchemish became merely one Neo-Hittite city-state among others, and its kings just kings. Thus when, in the tenth century B.C., David vanquished Hadadezer of Aram-Zobah and had the grateful Toi of Hamath as subject-ally, the power of Carchemish was already over, except as a prosperous trading state on an important route crossing of the Euphrates. The realm of Hamath reached the Euphrates further SE, and therewith also David's dominance. The "kings of the Hittites" contemporary with

the Hebrew monarchies included the rulers of Hamath, Hattina, Gurgum (Marash), Milid (Malatya), Que (Cilicia), Carchemish, and Bit-Adini (Beth-Eden, cf. Til-Barsip*). The latter, plus Sam'al, Arpad and eventually Hamath, became Aramean* in this general period. Outlines of the dynasties and history of these Neo-Hittite and Aramean kingdoms can be glimpsed from a scatter of Hittite hieroglyphic* and Old-Aramaic* inscriptions and the Assyrian annals, down to their political extinction by the end of the eighth century B.C.

Cultural Background and OT. The cuneiform archives of Hattušaš yield much detail on life, culture, and structure of the Hittite Empire; besides Hittite proper, and texts in related Luwian and Palaic dialects, they include documents in Hurrian (Horite), Babylonian, and other tongues. The treaties between Hittite emperors and their vassals show a literary form (fourteenth–thirteenth centuries B.C.) analogous to that of the Mosaic and Joshua covenants of the OT. Their function, of course, was different in each case. The religious rituals of the Hittites likewise illustrate as early as Moses' time the formulation of proper religious rites, with "author" title-lines (cf. headings, "the Lord spoke to Moses . . . ," etc., in Lev), and such concepts as offering pure and whole (not blemished) sacrifices in temples, and that of the scapegoat. Thus there is no need whatever to relegate such concepts in Lev to a period subsequent to the Babylonian Exile (*see* EXILE, JUDEAN). Similarly, Hittite law can be utilized to give background to OT law and usage, and narratives as background to a book like Job. Neo-Hittite and Aramean texts likewise give some background to the narratives of Kings and Chron. With the fate proclaimed for Jezebel,* namely to be eaten by the dogs (1 Kings 21:23; cf. 2 Kings 9:36), one may compare the curse on a Carchemish slab, "may the dogs of Nikarawas eat off his head!" This was addressed to anyone destroying the inscription.

BIBLIOGRAPHY: O. R. Gurney, *The Hittites* (1952); A. Goetze, *Kleinasien*, 2 (1957); A. Goetze, O. R. Gurney, *CAH*, 1, part 2, 311–12, 428–38, 683, 694,

830–37, 856–57; E. Akurgal, *The Art of the Hittites* (1962); H. A. Hoffner, "Some Contributions of Hittitology to OT Study," *Tyndale Bulletin*, 20 (1969), 27–55; K. A. Kitchen, *Hittite Hieroglyphs, Aramaeans & Hebrew Traditions* (forthcoming).

KAK

HIVITES (hī'vīts; Heb. חוּים, *ḥiwwîm*; LXX Εὐαιος, *Heuaios*). The name of a people in Syria and Canaan,* among a series of peoples to be overcome by the Hebrews. They are attested from the age of the patriarchs (Gen 34:2 et al.) to the time of Solomon* (1 Kings 9:20–21) in the OT.

At present there is no extra-biblical mention of these people. But the alternation of Hivite and Horite as origin of Zibeon (Gen 36:2, cf. 20) and of Hivite and Horite as between NT and LXX (so, e.g., in Gen 34:2) has given rise to the suggestion that the two are related, whether as groups of people, or simply as variant forms of the same name (Hurwi becoming both Hurri, or "Horite," and Hiwwi, or "Hivite"). This is theoretically possible, but far from certain. Provisionally, it may be wiser to retain the identities as those of two groups of people.

See HURRIANS; JEBUSITES.

BIBLIOGRAPHY: E. A. Speiser, *AASOR*, 13 (1932), 29–31; H. A. Hoffner, Jr., *Tyndale Bulletin*, 20 (1969), 27–37; id., *ZPEB*, 3 (1975), 172.

KAK

HOR-DEDEF, INSTRUCTION OF PRINCE. This fragmentary composition has survived in two copies from Thebes,* both dated at the end of the Nineteenth Dynasty (c. 1220 B.C.), though the language used might point to a time of composition within the Amarna* Age. The author was traditionally one of the wise men of Egypt,* who followed the pattern adopted by Pharaoh Amen-em-het and others in giving instruction to his son. Hor-dedef, a son of the Old Kingdom Pharaoh Khufu, became legendary for his wisdom, and the *Instruction* purported to enshrine his teachings. The few lines which have survived encouraged humility and proper preparation for the afterlife, but they are much inferior to similar gnomic material from Egypt and to the Hebrew proverbs from the period of the monarchy.

BIBLIOGRAPHY: *ANET*, 419–20, 432, 467, 476.

RKH

HORITES. See HIVITES; HURRIANS.

HORIZONTAL STRATIGRAPHY. See STRATIGRAPHY.

HOR, MOUNT. See AARON'S TOMB.

HORNET. An insect of the order *Hymenoptera*, capable of inflicting a very serious sting. Hornets are widely distributed throughout the Mediterranean area and were well known in antiquity. They are mentioned in the Bible in Deut 7:20; Josh 24:12; and in other ancient texts. Fragments of hornet nests have been excavated and the figure of the hornet, particularly *Vespa orientalis*, was used in the art of many

cultures. Kings and conquerors took the hornet as their totem. Hence John Garstang's suggestion (*Joshua-Judges* [1931], 112ff., 258ff.), based on Egyptian scarabs* from Jericho,* that the hornet of the above references represented the Egyptian power in Canaan,* and its softening of the land for Hebrew conquest. It has also been suggested (Koehler in Koehler-Baumgartner *Lexicon sub.voc.*) that "hornet" is a mistranslation, the correct rendering being rather "discouragement" and the reference being to a wave of shattered morale paralyzing the doomed tribes.

WW

HORSE. Among biblical peoples the horse was not used in agriculture* or for transporting burdens, but was prominent in warfare* and in the pleasures of the wealthy. Second millennium B.C. records of Hebrew life do not mention horses particularly, the camel* or donkey* being the favored means of transport (Gen 24:64; Num 22:23 et al.). The common Hebrew term *sûs* and its Egyptian *ssm.t* and Akkadian (*see* AKKAD) *sîsû* counterparts seem to be Aryan in origin and might indicate that the domestication of the horse occurred in the central Asian region. The nineteenth-century B.C. Cappadocian Tablets* mentioned horses occasionally, but it was about a century later that they came into prominence when the Aryan Mitanni, who at one phase of their history held the balance of military power between the Hittites* and Egyptians, introduced the two-wheeled war chariot,* complete with horses. The Kassites,* who were attacking Babylonia at that period, adopted the new weapon and quickly conquered the country, bringing with them the so-called Babylonian "Dark Ages." From the eighteenth to the sixteenth centuries B.C. the Hyksos* developed the horse-drawn chariot as a weapon, and with it they conquered Egypt.* In the later Amarna* Age the chariot companies were the monopoly of the Egyptian aristocracy. From the cuneiform* correspondence found at Tell el-Amarna, the horse seems to have been used in Palestine by the fourteenth century B.C. Horses are mentioned as tribute on the walls of Hatshepsut's unfinished temple. From the later days of Egypt, as

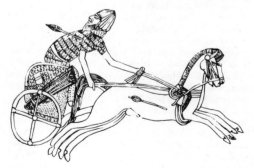

Wounded Asiatic charioteer, detail from drawing on chariot of Thutmose IV (1425-1417 B.C.) showing king riding in his chariot over battlefield of wounded Asiatics. *(See also photo under HARNESS.)* Courtesy Carta, Jerusalem.

the great empire broke up, we meet one Piankhi who held the kingdom of the Upper Nile from 741 B.C. from which he extended his power northward for some score of years. In the archaeology of the horse he merits mention for a statement on the so-called Piankhi Stela. Namlot was captured, and after an inspection of the palace and treasury, the king went to "the stables* and the quarters of the foals. He saw that they suffered hunger and said: 'I swear as Re loves me it is more grievous to my heart that my horses suffer hunger than any evil deed thou hast done. . . .' "

Cavalry units as such were apparently introduced by the Medes* and employed with considerable success in Mesopotamia* from the twelfth century B.C. onward. The simple nomadic ideals of the Hebrews regarded the horse as a pagan luxury (cf. Deut 17:16; 1 Sam 8:11), or token of the triumph of brute force instead of faith in the Lord (cf. Isa 31:1; Ezek 17:15). Solomon* ignored these concepts, however (1 Kings 4:26), as did Ahab* (1 Kings 18:5). The Annals of Shalmaneser III (859–824 B.C.) recorded that the latter ruler provided two thousand war chariots in the concerted attack against Assyria. One band on the magnificent gates* of this king, a masterpiece of Assyrian art, shows them attacking Parga in Syria and also crossing a river by a pontoon bridge. Cavalry in a battle charge associated with chariotry are depicted in wall reliefs in the palace of Ashurnasirpal II,* discovered by Layard. Later Assyrian kings were served by highly skilled cavalrymen, mounted bowmen, forerunners of the Parthian cavalry of later centuries, riding without saddle or stirrups. Reliefs from the palace of Sargon* show, in stylized form, the cavalry of the king at work in hilly country. Another, from Sennacherib's* palace, shows cavalry moving in column through wooded terrain. With typical realism, an officer is shown with his hand to his mouth shouting orders.

Only the wealthy normally rode on horses (cf. 2 Kings 5:9; 14:20; Esth 6:8–11; Jer 22:4 et al.), and there are abundant reliefs from Egypt, Assyria, and Persia which depict such circumstances.

BIBLIOGRAPHY: Y. Yadin, *The Art of Warfare in Biblical Lands*, 382ff., 402–3, 456ff.

RKH and EMB

HOUSE. A comprehensive term referring equally well to a peasant's dwelling and to a royal home. Excavations in northern Mesopotamia* have shown that Neolithic* villages comprised groups of small huts made of reeds and mud. These houses became more sophisticated in appearance when sun-dried mud bricks came into use in Mesopotamia as building materials. The inside walls of such structures were often plastered with mud and decorated with mosaics* of small baked clay* cones which were sometimes painted red or black. Early Bronze Age houses as found at Ur* seem to have been built on three sides of a quadrangle, and in the case of poorer persons a house consisted of one story only. Upper class houses were normally two stories in height, the bottom one being perhaps built of rough fieldstones and the upper portion of sun-dried mud bricks. The

two floors of such a structure were connected by means of a brick stairway.

In general in the Ancient Near East the availability of local materials dictated the type of construction, so that while mud or sun-dried mud bricks were commonly used in Egypt* and Mesopotamia, stone was more popular in Palestine. An important technological improvement in the manufacture of mud bricks occurred with the addition of finely chopped straw and similar vegetable material (cf. Exod 5:7), which had the effect of increasing the plasticity of the clay threefold during decomposition. Even from early times Near Eastern houses were often impressive structures with thick walls, as excavations of Early Bronze Age* levels at Ai* have shown. At Debir,* the foundations of houses of Middle Bronze Age construction were designed to hold firm, solid walls. The houses of Sodom* (Gen 19:1ff.) were most probably of this sturdy character also. In OT times, only royal residences and the homes of the rich were made of hewn stone (cf. 1 Kings 7:9; Isa 9:10) or of even more costly white marble (1 Chron 29:2). Where mortar was used in the Ancient Near East, the builders could choose from bitumen* (Gen 11:3), clay, lime,* or gypsum (Isa 33:13; cf. Deut 27:4). Local timbers were used for beams, doorposts and the like, with sycamore (Isa 9:10), olive,* sandalwood, cypress, and cedar* being prominent in more elaborate carpentry or carved work (1 Kings 7:2; Jer 22:14 et al.). With the exception of palaces, Palestinian houses in biblical times seem to have been one-story structures, and this may have been a consequence of the inferior Israelite building technology current at the time of the entrance into the Promised Land. Houses in Palestinian cities were arranged in a purely haphazard manner, and excavations have shown that they manifested increasingly inferior constructional characteristics when Israelite cities first began to experience overcrowding from the eighth century B.C.

The typical Palestinian dwelling was in appearance a rather plain and unattractive building, being whitewashed both outside and inside with gypsum or lime. Only palaces seem to have varied from this decor, being sometimes painted* in brighter colors (cf. Jer 22:14). The roof was flat, and in poorer houses simply comprised a layer of clay stamped into the rafters which formed the ceiling of the room below (cf. Mark 2:4; Luke 5:19).

The better class houses had roofs made of tile* or thin slabs of stone. On all houses some sort of low protective railing was erected on the outer edge of the roof to prevent people from falling off (cf. Deut 22:8), either as they slept (1 Sam 9:26), talked with one another (1 Sam 9:25), or engaged in a variety of other activities (Josh 2:6; 2 Kings 23:12; Jer 48:38; Matt 10:27 et al.). Pillars were very important constructional elements for supporting flat roofs. Some Middle Bronze Age houses had two or more tiers of balconies held up by central pillars, so that if the latter were dislodged great damage could result (Judg 16:26).

Commonly found in Egyptian homes, the porch was comparatively rare in Palestinian dwellings, being mentioned only in connection with the temple* and

Reconstruction of Israelite house, c. tenth century B.C. *(See also photo under* COOKING.) Courtesy Ha'aretz Museum, Ceramics Museum, Tel Aviv.

Solomon's* palace (1 Kings 7:6f.; Ezek 40:7), or, in NT times, the high priest's palace (Matt 26:71), this latter "porch" probably being the street entrance to the house. In royal palaces the porch was a place where judgments were rendered (1 Kings 7:7f.). House doors were often made of wood (cf. S of Songs 8:9), though excavations in Syria have uncovered doors made of single slabs of stone several inches thick and as much as 3 m. (10 ft.) in height. These heavy structures turned either on stone pivots or on bronze* hinges, examples of which have been recovered from several Near Eastern sites.

Palestinian houses were usually built to enclose a space known as the court. The homes of some wealthy persons had as many as seven of these open areas in which wells* (2 Sam 17:18), baths (2 Sam 11:2), and shade trees could be found. In colder weather a fire was often kindled in the court (cf. Luke 22:55). Kitchens formed part of inner courts, comprising a raised brick platform which had hollowed-out containers for charcoal (cf. Ezek 46:23). Home furnishings included such basic items as a bed,* lamp,* chair, and table (cf. 2 Kings 4:10), along with cooking and dining utensils (*see* also FURNITURE). Beyond these necessities the tastes and wealth of families would dictate the presence or absence of ivory*-inlaid bedsteads (Amos 6:4) and tables (Prov 9:2), soft pillows for reclining (Ezek 13:18), and oriental carpets for floors or wall hangings.

BIBLIOGRAPHY: G. Conteneau, *Everyday Life in Babylon and Assyria* (1954); A. Badawy, *Architec-* *ture in Ancient Egypt and the Near East* (1966); H. G. Stigers, *ZPEB*, 3 (1975), 217–21.

RKH

HUKOK. *See* HELKATH.

HUNTING. An activity frequently mentioned in the OT, literally and metaphorically. Two early biblical hunters were Nimrud and Esau (Gen 10:9; 25:27). There is ample archaeological illustration of hunters and hunting both from Assyria and Egypt.* Hunting with dogs* in pre-Israelite Palestine is mentioned in the Egyptian tale of Sinuhe,* the exiled noble who fled to Syria on the death of Amenhotep I (2000–1970 B.C.) and returned to Egypt with a record of adventures in old age (J. H. Breasted, *History of Egypt* [1945], 203). From the tomb of Amenhotep at Beni Hasan, comes a vivid picture of hunting in the desert with bows and nets. The tomb of Ti at Saqqara, of much earlier date (2650 B.C.), shows a hunt for hippopotamus in papyrus* swamps, a favorite place for fowling. Decoration on an ivory* box from Tell el-Far'ah shows another such scene. Hunting was a royal sport. The Lion Hunt Relief of Ashurbanipal* at Nineveh (883–859 B.C.) shows great mastiffs straining at the leash, and two footmen with shields and daggers are depicted perilously cooperating with the king's chariot* whence, with bow and arrow, he shoots at aggressive lions* and lionesses. In another part of the relief he is shown in single combat with a lion which rises on its hind legs to attack him (cf.

1 Sam 17:34–36). A similar maned lion attacks a riderless horse* below (G. S. Cansdale, *Animals of Bible Lands*, [1970], illustrations facing 97 and 160). Hunting for wild donkeys* appears in another of Ashurbanipal's reliefs. The king was obviously in Nimrud's tradition. It was certainly ancient enough, for a hunters' camp has been found at Hassuna in Iraq, dating from the fifth millennium B.C. It contained weapons, tools,* and storage jars.

BIBLIOGRAPHY: *ANEP* (1954), 56–60.

EMB

HURRIANS. A people widely scattered throughout the Ancient Near East, they are alluded to in the OT as Horites, Hivites,* and Jebusites.* Originating perhaps in Armenia, the Hurrians had settled in historic times in Anatolia, Syria, central Palestine, and as far E as modern Kirkuk. The Hurrians were most prominent from the middle of the third millennium to the close of the second millennium B.C. They drew heavily upon Mesopotamian* culture of the early third millennium B.C. and consequently were able to enrich the Hittites* of Anatolia in the areas of religion, literature, law (*see* HITTITE LAW), and art. They also left their mark on Hittite vocabulary, which possesses a great many Hurrian loan words. However, their greatest political and social achievement was the establishing of the Mitanni* Empire, whose center lay in the region of the biblical Haran* in the middle Euphrates Valley. The Hurrians were an important religious and political force at Mari* during the time when Hammurabi* (c. 1792–1750 B.C.) was consolidating his Babylonian Empire. Excavations at the Horite city of Nuzi* (Yorgan Tepe) have uncovered thousands of clay* tablets written in the native Babylonian language, which on translation were found to have preserved a remarkable record of Hurrian culture. While many of the texts came from the fifteenth century B.C., which is a little later than the biblical patriarchs, they furnish remarkable insights into the life and times of Abraham and his offspring and set them firmly against a background of second millennium B.C. Assyrian society.

As the dominant ethnic group in the Near East during the second millennium B.C., the Hurrians established themselves firmly in the region between Media and the Mediterranean during the patriarchal period. From the middle of the sixteenth century B.C. they held undisputed sway in such centers at Boghazköy,* Alalakh,* and Nuzi, and for a century and a half the Horite expansion of the original Mitanni kingdom of northern Mesopotamia maintained a balance of power between the Hittites, Assyrians, and the Egyptians.* But under the Hittite ruler Suppiluliumas I* (c. 1395–1350 B.C.) the Mitanni Empire was reduced to something approaching a buffer state between Anatolia and Assyria. The political influence of the Hurrians finally came to an end with their defeat by the resurgent Assyrians about 1150 B.C.

In the OT the ancient inhabitants of Edom,* who were defeated by Chedorlaomer and his Mesopotamian alliance (Gen 14:5–6), were spoken of as descendants of Seir the Horite (Gen 36:20). The sons of Esau finally dispossessed them (Deut 2:12, 22), though Esau himself may have been married to a Hurrian woman (Gen 36:25). Under the designation of Hivite, Hamor was associated with Shechem (Gen 34:2), while other Hivite settlements were located at Gibeon* (Josh 9:7; 11:19), Mount Lebanon (Judg 3:3), and Hermon* (Josh 11:3). This equation of the terms Hurrian and Hivite is reflected in the Hebrew of Gen 36:2, 20, while in Gen 34:2 and Josh 9:6–7, the LXX read "Horite" for the KJV, RV "Hivite." It thus seems clear that terms such as "Jebusites" and "Hivites" were local designations for the Hurrians. There is also independent archaeological evidence for the existence of the Hurrians in central Palestine during the Amarna* Age (fifteenth and fourteenth centuries B.C.). Cuneiform* tablets recovered from Tell Ta'annek (Taanach*) have preserved lists which contain a significant proportion of Horite personal names. Another contemporary tablet found at Shechem* also appears to contain names which are most probably Hurrian in origin. One of the fourteenth-century B.C. Tell el-Amarna tablets (AMARNA LETTERS) consisted of a Mitanni letter written in classical Hurrian by Tuslaratta to Amenhotep IV of Egypt, while in others the ruler of Jerusalem,* which was a Jebusite center at that time, bore a Hurrian name, Arad-khepa. Both from their connection with Haran and their place in the pre-Israelite population of Palestine it is clear that the Hurrians exercised considerable influence over the forbears of the Hebrew people. However, the two groups were far from pursuing a consistently harmonious relationship, as the incident narrated in Judg 9 demonstrates. Shechemite opposition to Abimelech rested in part on their claim to true Hurrian descent (Judg 9:28), i.e., from Hamor, whereas Abimelech was only Hurrian in the sense of being the son of Gideon by a Shechemite concubine. Hurrian influence over biblical Hebrew can be seen in the spirantization of certain consonants, a pattern otherwise foreign to Semitic speech but characteristic of Hurrian.

BIBLIOGRAPHY: I. J. Gelb, *Hurrians and Subarians* (1944); E. A. Speiser, *Introduction to Hurrian* (1941); H. G. Güterbock, *Journal of World History*, 2 (1954), 383–94; H. A. Hoffner, Jr., *ZPEB*, 3 (1975), 228–29.

RKH

HUSN, TELL EL-. See BETH SHAN.

HÜYÜK. The Turkish equivalent of tell.*

HYKSOS (hik'sos; Gr., from Egypt., becoming *hiqšos*, "rulers of foreign lands," later misinterpreted as "shepherd kings"). The name given to the kings of the Fifteenth–Sixteenth dynasties in Egypt,* c. 1700–1542 B.C. During the Thirteenth Dynasty (c. 1786–1632 B.C.), large numbers of W Semites came gradually into Egypt, e.g. as servants and slaves* (as was Joseph*). Some appear to have become local rulers of districts in the E Delta ("Sixteenth Dynasty," c. 1700–1650 B.C. ?); one such prince took over the rule of Egypt, perhaps by a coup d'état, at the capital, Memphis,* so founding the Fifteenth Dynasty

(c. 1650–1542 B.C.), and reducing the Thirteenth-Dynasty princes to a line of vassal rulers at Thebes* in the S. Memphis was retained as the central capital. In the E Delta, replacing an old Twelfth-Dynasty residency, a new Delta residency and camp, Avaris, was founded, on or near the site of the future city of Rameses.*

While during the Thirteenth Dynasty W Semites had already held high office in Egypt (cf. also JOSEPH), this trend continued under the Hyksos. The chancellor Hur probably belongs in this period. The most powerful Hyksos* pharaohs were Khyan and Apopi or Apophis (who used three throne-names). The Hyksos in Egypt were essentially W Semites like the Hebrews, Amorites,* and others; Hurrian and Indo-Aryan theories of their origin remain discredited on the clear evidence of Semitic proper names mixed with Egyptian. During 1600–1550 B.C., the Theban kings (Seventeenth Dynasty) led Egyptian opposition to Hyksos rule, and Ahmose I finally expelled Apopi's successor in his own eleventh year,

c. 1542 B.C. Excavations at Tell el-Dab'a in the E Delta (near possible site of Avaris) have yielded Middle-Bronze Age* pottery,* emphasizing the links with Palestine. The Egypto-Semitic milieu of the Thirteenth and Hyksos Dynasties formed an appropriate setting for such as Joseph.

BIBLIOGRAPHY: J. van Seters, *The Hyksos* (1966); end-date of Hyksos, cf. K. A. Kitchen, *Chronique d'Égypte*, 43.86 (1968), 314.

KAK

HYPOCAUST. A hollow space or duct beneath a floor or between masonry through which heat was conveyed for warming rooms or baths.

HYPOSTYLE (Gk. "resting on pillars set underneath"). An architectural term used to describe a building with a flat stone roof, such as the Amun Temple at Karnak, which is supported by pillars beneath. The halls and chambers of the structures are described as hypostyles.

I

ICONIUM. A city of S-central Asia Minor* mentioned six times in the Bible. The apostle Paul preached there on his first missionary journey (Acts 14:1–7). The modern Turkish city* is Konya. The successes as well as the persecutions of Paul and Barnabas at Iconium are indicated not only by the biblical references but by inscriptions there that reveal the presence of a thriving Christian community from the third century onward. Iconium was the setting for the *Acts of Paul and Thecla*.

In Acts 14:6, Paul and Barnabas escaped from Iconium and went on to the "cities of Lycaonia,* Lystra* and Derbe.*" Here Luke could be understood as suggesting that Iconium was not in Lycaonia at this time. Other writers show that not only was Iconium in Lycaonia, but was once (39 B.C.) its capital. William M. Ramsay was convinced by archaeological evidence that Luke was quite correct in Acts 14:6, for at the time Iconium was a Phrygian* city, and the borders of Lycaonia had fluctuated. Even after this time when they were politically part of Lycaonia the people of Iconium preferred to call themselves Phrygians.

BIBLIOGRAPHY: W. M. Ramsay, *Cities of St. Paul* (1907), 317–82; *FLAP* (1946), 260–64; T. S. Kepler, *IDB*, 2 (1962), 672–73; E. M. Blaiklock, *ZPEB*, 3 (1975), 240–41. BCC

IDEOGRAM. An original picture or character expressing a concept without actually naming or sounding it.

IDOL. The word is a transliteration of the Greek *eidōlon*, an image, and in the language of the Bible refers to any form of representation in wood,* stone, or metal of a deity. It can be, and at all times has been, extended to cover any symbol of the supernatural (e.g., the image on coins,* or Roman standards), a representation of a living being, and even an abstract obsessional entity of worship.

In the Bible the term includes images, probably anthropomorphic, of cult objects (Gen 31:19, 34–35), equally with the "idols" of Athens, themselves extending from the phallic herms (Hermes*) at the doors of houses* to the splendid statues* of Athene on the Acropolis,* to which Paul made scarcely concealed reference in his speech to the Areopagus* court (Acts 17:29).

The archaeological evidence is coextensive. From the Late Bronze Age* and Early Iron Age* to classical times, idols exist which go far to explain the Hebrew loathing for such objects of cult ritual and

Seated clay Neolithic (c. 5500 B.C.) mother goddess idol, probably fertility symbol, of *dea nutrix* type, in nursing attitude; found at Horvat Minha in the Jordan Valley about 15 km. (9 miles) south of Sea of Galilee. Courtesy Israel Dept. of Antiquities and Museums. Exhibited and photographed at Israel Museum, Jerusalem.

worship. Clay* molded figurines of naked women with vastly emphasized pudenda and breasts are the earliest examples of those fertility cults which extend to NT times, modified into merely superstitious amulets in the herms of Athens.* The magnificent surviving statues of the Greeks which have excited the admiration of another world, are, within the circle of biblical thought, simply examples of idols, as were the boxed clay figures found under the floors of Mesopotamian houses to represent, like the Roman lares and penates, the guardian spirits of the home.

It is unnecessary here to list the art objects from all the cultures surrounding Israel* which would have been idols to Hebrew observers. The Hebrew revolt, signified strikingly in the empty mercy seat and the absence of any figure in the Holy of Holies of the tabernacle or the temple,* was not the only example of such a spiritual conception of God. The temple at Hazor,* at one stage at least, appears to have had a "holy place," an adytum,* without an image of any sort.

See TERAPHIM.

BIBLIOGRAPHY: R. Dussaud, *Les Découvertes de Ras Shamra (Ugarit) et l'AT* (1971); A. G. Barrois, *Manuel D'Archéologie Biblique* (1953), 389–98; J. Gray, *IDB*, 3 (1962), 673–75.

EMB

IDRIMI. See ALALAKH.

IDUMEA. See EDOM.

ILLYRICUM (i lir′ ə kum; Gr. Ἰλλυρικόν, *Illyrikon*). A district across the Adriatic Sea from Italy, officially known in ancient times as Dalmatia (*Illyricum Superius*) and Pannonia (*Illyricum Inferius*), in the area of modern Albania. It is cited in the Bible only in Romans 15:19. The Greeks came into contact with the Illyrians in the eighth century B.C. (Strabo 6.269; 7.315), and in later centuries Greek colonies were established notably at Salona and Spalato. The Illyrians became famous as pirates and more than once were defeated by Roman forces. Excavations were conducted in 1963–64 by B. Dautaj at the fortress of Krotine, located on a peak of the Shpragrit Mountains, E of Apollonia in what was Southern Illyricum. There were revealed two summits inside the city* with its wall* of 2,400 m. (7,872 ft.) in circumference. The excavation of the acropolis,* the higher summit, showed stamped tiles of the Hellenistic period, some carrying the name *Dimallitan*. The name of the city at that time was Dimallon, a Greek name meaning "of double fleece." Significantly the place overlooks the rich pasture lands of Myzeqija (Apollonia). The earliest coins* in the acropolis were those of Epidamnus, dating from 320–270 B.C. The city may have been founded by Pyrrhus or his successors c. 290 B.C.

BIBLIOGRAPHY: Vulić, "Illyricum," *PWRE*, 9.1 (1914), 1085–88; J. Knox, "Exegesis of Roman," *IB* 9 (1954), 645–46; Burhan Dautaj, "La découverte de la cite illyrienne de Dimale," *Studia Albanica*, 1 (1965), 65–71; N. G. L. Hammond, "Illyris, Rome and Macedon in 229–205 BC," *JRS*, 58 (1968), 1–21; "Illyricum," *OCD*, 2d ed. (1970), 541.

WHM

IMHOTEP (im hō′tep; Egypt., "he who comes in peace"). The famed chief minister of King Djoser, builder of the Step Pyramid (Third Dynasty, c. 2650 B.C.) at Saqqara near ancient Memphis,* and modern Cairo. A statue* base of the king found there bears the name and titles of Imhotep, probably the famous Imhotep. He is reputed to have composed a wisdom book, first of a long series of such works by Egyptian sages, analogous in form and content with Proverbs. However, of Imhotep's work, nothing has yet been recovered. In later ages, he was deified—as sage, architect, and as a patron of medicine,* identified by the Greeks with Asklepios. He personifies the type of the learned sages of the great past so dear to later Egyptians (cf. *ANET*, 432 and n. 4; 467), and is accurately reflected by Isaiah (19:11–13) in his scathing dismissal of pharaoh's worldly counselors.

BIBLIOGRAPHY: K. Sethe, *Imhotep, der Asklepios der Aegypter* (1902); J. B. Hurry, *Imhotep* (1926); B. Gunn, *Annales du Service des Antiquités de l'Égypte*, 26 (1926), 190–96.

KAK

IMMORTALITY. The reality of a life beyond death was the theme of a deepening faith in pre-Christian times, and to trace the emergence and shaping of that conviction does not concern this article. The OT spoke of alien cults with unqualified condemnation, and, if the beliefs of pagan neighbors or conquerors played a part in the implantation among the Hebrews of faith in survival, it could hardly have been in other fashion than by promoting, in more thoughtful and devoted thinkers, the conviction that, if such beliefs held truth, then God must have something more pure and more satisfying for His people.

It is the present object to mention the archaeological evidence for beliefs in immortality, and it is sometimes a difficult task to define the limits of the archaeological evidence. For example, is the Gilgamesh Epic* to be considered as literary or archaeological evidence for an early Babylonian belief in "another world"? Where does the Egyptian Book of the Dead* stand when its text is recovered from inscriptions and fragmentary papyri?

Archaeological investigation does demonstrate the universality of a belief in human survival after death. Without boundary of race or place it appears as a common conviction, as burial customs vividly illustrate. In some Central Asian burial grounds skeletons have been discovered sitting in a circle around the ashes of a great campfire. So they slept in life. Weapons by their side, they rested with head on knee. Springing to wakefulness at a night alarm, the combined vision of the circle of warriors covered every point of the compass. Not dead, it might appear, but sleeping, as they had so often slept on the windswept plain, ready to spring to life and action at the trump of another world. The dead beneath the cellar floors in Ur* sleep on their sides with legs drawn up in the position of the human embryo. Death, the symbolism suggests, is but rebirth into another life.

In Egypt, scene of Israel's* servitude, life was interwoven with death. Box burials recovered from predynastic times showed that the corpse had been buried in the so-called "fetal position" with its face looking westward to the abode of the departed. The pyramids,* munificent modes of burial, fantastically protected graves,* and the whole elaborate science of mummification, (*see* EMBALMING) were all practices fundamentally devised to keep a body intact, in some ill-defined conviction that a disembodied personality was thereby comforted or aided.

Orphism and other cults tell the same story, but their remains and documents are to be classified rather as literary than archaeological. The Athenian cult of the Eleusinian mysteries, however, has left considerable remains in a great temple complex near Athens.* These "mysteries" were of unknown antiquity. We know that they were practiced seven centuries before Christ, and that they extended four centuries into our era, when Alaric the Goth destroyed the sanctuary in the modern Athenian suburb. In this cult, life after death was taken for granted. To be initiated into the rites, which, based on the worship of the Earth Goddess, Demeter, suggest an origin in nature worship, meant rebirth of the soul and happiness beyond the grave. Part of the mystic ritual seems to have been the exhibition of an ear of corn which stands for death and resurrection. Other mystery cults symbolized the same thought in a rite of baptism* by immersion.

The Christian belief in immortality, was, as Paul insisted, intimately interwoven with the historical fact of the resurrection. The evidence for a faith in another life and in a resurrection is found in many catacomb* inscriptions. Here are examples: "MACVS PVER INNOCENS ESSE IAM INTER INNOCENTES COEPISTI QVAM STAVILIS TIBI HAEC VITA EST QVAM TE LAETVM EXCIPET MATER ECCLESIA MVNDO REVERTENTEM COMPREMATVR PECTORVM GEMITUS STRVATVR FLETVS OCVLORVM"—"Macus, innocent boy, thou hast begun to be among the innocent. Unto thee how sure is thy present life. Thee how gladly thy mother, the church, received returning from this world. Hushed be the bosom's groaning, dried be the weeping of eyes." Of similar sort are also the following: "SALONICE SPIRITVS TVVS IN BONIS"—"Salonicus, thy spirit is among the good"; "REFRIGERAS SPIRITVS TVVS IN BONIS"—"Thou refreshest thy spirit among the good"; "CORPVS HABET TELLVS ANIMAM CAELESTIA REGNA"—"The earth has the body, celestial realms the soul"; "AGAPE VIBIS IN ETERNVM"—"Agape, thou livest forever"; "DORMIT ET VIVIT IN PACE XO"—"He sleeps and lives in the peace of Christ"; "MENS NESCIA MORTIS VILIT ET ASPECTV FRVITVR BENE CONSCIA CHRISTI"—"The soul lives not knowing death, and right consciously rejoices in the vision of Christ"; "PRIMA VIVIS IN GLORIA DEI ET IN PACE DOMINI NOSTRI XR"—"Prima, thou livest in the glory of God, and in the peace of Christ, our Lord."

The Christian doctrine of resurrection appears more clearly in these: "HIC REQVIESCIT CARO MEA NOVISSIMO VERO DIE PER XPO CREDO RESVSCITABITVR A MORTVIS"—"Here rests my flesh; but at the last day, through Christ, I believe it will be raised from the dead"; "RELICTIS TVIS IACES IN PACE SOPORE MERITA RESVRGES TEMPORALIS TIBI DATA REQVIETIO"—"You, well-deserving one, having left all you have, lie asleep in peace—you will arise as you deserve—a temporary rest is granted you"; "RECEPTA CAELO MERVIT OCCVRRERE XPO AD RESVRRECTIONEM PRAEMIVM AETERNVM SVSCIPERE DIGNA"—"Received into heaven, she deserved to meet Christ at the resurrection, worthy to receive an everlasting reward"; "CREDO QVIA REDEMPTOR MEVS BIBIT (sic) ET NOBISSIMO DIE DE TERRA SVSCI-

TABIT ME IN CARNE MEA VIDEBO DOM"—"I believe, because that my Redeemer lives, and in the last day shall raise me from the earth, that in my flesh I shall see the Lord"; "IVSTVS CVM SCIS XPO MEDIANTE RESVRGET"—"Justus, who will arise with the saints through Christ"; "HIC IN PACE REQVIESCIT LAVRENTIA QVAE CREDIDIT RESVRRECTIONEM"—"Here reposes in peace Laurentia who believed in the resurrection."

There are inscriptions more brief. Two loculi, for example, in one place adjoin each other. A few fragments of bone lie in one recess, marked as those of Ulpia, who, says the inscription, had been "decorated"—clothed in the glory of another life. Nearby a marble slab records the fact that Eutychia, "happiest of women," lies there in the rock recess. On Eutychia's breast is a glass* locket depicting Christ bearing the fruit of the tree of life. She was a martyr. A glass patera embedded in cement below her loculus shows the raising of Lazarus (see LAZARUS, TOMB OF) as a Roman scene.

The Christian archaeologist finds the contrast with the tombs on the Appian Way* above a striking demonstration of what Christianity was bringing to a disillusioned and already disintegrating Roman society. The inscriptions show the world-weariness and loss of faith which may be read in first-century literature and the declining years of the Republic. "MISCE, BIBE, DA MIHI," runs one—"A cocktail, please, for you and me." High philosophy had brought no comfort to so many at this day. A forced and sullen submission to the inevitable is all that many of the inscriptions have to say. "DOMUS AETERNA, SOMNO AETERNALI," "In eternal sleep"; and frequently there is the accompaniment of the inverted torch, the emblem of despair. So they run: "INFANTI DVLCISSIMO QVEM DII IRATI AETERNO SOMNO DEDERVNT," "To a very sweet child whom the angry gods gave to eternal sleep"; "QVOD EDI ET BIBI MECVM HABEO QVOD RELIQVI PERDIDI," "What I ate and drank I have with me; what I left I have lost"; "BALNEA VINVM VENVS CORRVMPVNT CORPORA NOSTRA SED VITAM FACIVNT V V," "Baths, wine and lust ruin our constitutions, but they make life, farewell."

H. P. V. Nunn sums up the question of relevant literature well in his useful little book *Christian Inscriptions* (1952). He writes: "The most interesting inscriptions are those which give us information about the beliefs of those who erected them, especially with regard to their opinions about the sacraments and the after life. Most inscriptions of this kind are rather late. They have naturally been used in controversy on both sides. The literature dealing with Christian archaeology in Rome* is enormous. Little of it is accessible to the English reader, however, as it is written in Latin,* Italian, and French in books that are now almost unobtainable. Some of them are strictly scientific, like Diehl's *Inscriptiones Latinae Christianae Veteres*, De Rossi's *Roma Sotterranea*, *Inscriptiones Christianae* and his articles in the *Bullettino di Archaeologia Cristiana*."

EMB

INANA, DESCENT OF. *See* Ishtar, Descent of.

INCANTATION. Ritual proceedings, including the chanting of spells, were commonly used in the Ancient Near East by priests, magicians, and physicians for dispossessing demons, the supposed etiological factor in illness, and for restoring the sick to health, as well as for a wide range of purely prophylactic purposes not directly connected with physical health (*see* Medicine). The verbal formula was particularly prominent in Babylonia when incantations were being used in cases of sickness. It became the major element in the various chants, assumed a stereotyped form, and thus was able to be collected into an "Incantation Series," which proved to be a very accessible compendium for the incantation priests.

Though material adjuncts such as water and herbal composites were also used in the healing rituals, the incantation apparently relied heavily upon psychological suggestion. This involved an identification with a prominent deity, the naming of the evil spirit and its exorcism, the result of which would be the healing of the sufferer. In Babylonia, Ea, the water-deity, was usually brought into contact with the sufferer by means of a ceremonial "baptism," after which the particular ailment was related diagnostically to one of a number of underworld demons. The stereotyped formula "by heaven be exorcised, by earth be exorcised" concluded the incantation. Egyptian* priests in the Old Kingdom period used similar exorcist* rituals, and these also were compiled in the form of a manual. In such incantations the all-powerful sun deity Re was the focus of all healing aspirations. Yet side by side with this magical approach to healing, the ancient Egyptians practiced an empirico-rational form of therapeutics, as is evident in an extant surgical papyrus.*

No Palestinian texts dealing with incantations have survived from any cultures, but the fact that there may well have been such material in circulation may be gleaned from allusions to "whispering" or "muttering" (cf. Ps 58:5). Jewish exorcist practices of the first century A.D. are reflected in Acts 19:13, where the name of Jesus was an important element of the prescribed formula. The incantation manuals from which such spells were pronounced were subsequently burned (Acts 19:19).

BIBLIOGRAPHY: R. C. Thompson, *The Devils and Evil Spirits of Babylonia*, 2 vols. (1903–4); id., *Semitic Magic* (1908); id., *ERE*, 4, 742–44; G. Foucart, *ERE*, 4, 750; S. H. Hooke, *Babylonian and Assyrian Religion* (1953), 77 passim; F. Jonckheere, *Les Médecins de l'Egypte Pharaonique* (1958); R. K. Harrison, *IDB*, 3 (1962), 331–34.

RKH

INCENSE. In the OT it was the prerogative of the high priest to offer incense which was made according to a special formula (Exod 30:34–38). The incense was burned on the altar* of incense (Exod 30:1ff.; 40:5; Lev 4:7) which stood before the veil of the Holy of Holies. Lists of items used in the worship of tabernacle and temple* include incense vessels (Num 7:14, 20, 84–86; 1 Kings 7:50). The Hebrew term

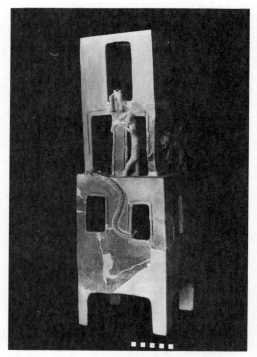

Reconstructed pottery incense burner from Beth Shan, c. 1200–1000 B.C. *(See also photo under* AI.*)* Courtesy Israel Dept. of Antiquities and Museums.

kap means literally "palm of the hand." The use of incense in temple worship was not unique to Israel.* Canaanites* and others of Israel's neighbors used it. Excavations have produced a wide variety of items such as horned incense altars, pottery* incense stands, small shallow stone bowls, some with a hand carved in relief on the bottom so that the interior of the bowl looks literally like the palm of a hand, metal spoons, etc. which testify to the wide use of incense in the worship of W Asiatic peoples in biblical times.

BIBLIOGRAPHY: M. Haran, "The Use of Incense," VetTest, 10 (1960), 113–29; G. E. Wright, "Solomon's Temple Reconstructed," *BA*, 4 (1941); H. G. May, *Material Remains of the Megiddo Cult* (1935); R. K. Harrison, *Healing Herbs of the Bible* (1966), 43.

JAT

INCRIPTIONS. *See* Epigraphy, Hebrew.

INK AND PEN. Archaeological evidence shows that the ink referred to in 3 John 13 consisted of soot and gum diluted with water, making a compound of remarkable durability. On the other hand, such ink did not penetrate the fibers of papyrus* documents and so was washed off easily (cf. Col 2:14; Rev 3:5). A metallic type of ink was made from soot, gum acacia, water, and iron oxide. Both varieties of ink were found in dried-up form in the scriptorium at Qumran.*

The common scribal practice of writing on the side on which the shorter fibers of the papyrus lay horizontally was dictated by a desire to use the surface best suited to the pen. Not merely did that side furnish a smoother surface and facilitate rolling, but it also provided the equivalent of ruled lines. The need for economy and a long script sometimes led to writing on the opposite side (*in verso*). An example is a long papyrus on magic in the British Museum (121 in the catalog of *Greek Papyri*). Although what appear to be pens have been illustrated pictorially from the Egyptian Old Kingdom period in scenes depicting scribes at work, it is impossible to say for certain if any of the pointed instruments excavated to date were specifically used for purposes of writing. The Hebrew *ḥereṭ* (Isa 8:1) was probably a stylus with a hard point for use on a metal surface, while the term *'eṭ* described either an iron stylus (Job 19:24; Jer 17:1) or a reed pen (Jer 8:8; Ps 45:1), the latter being used for writing in ink on potsherds or papyrus. It comprised a reed which had been split or frayed at one end to form a brush, which in ancient Egypt* was flattened so that strokes of varying thicknesses could be made easily. During the Old Kingdom period reeds were pointed and split to form something like a quill pen, the *kalamos* of 3 John 13. This type of pen was used principally on parchment.* A triangular stylus was employed for the writing* of cuneiform.* Such fragile implements were hardly likely to survive. We are reduced to inference from the writing they executed.

See SCRIBAL TRAINING, EGYPTIAN.

BIBLIOGRAPHY: G. R. Driver, *Semitic Writing* (1948), 17ff.

EMB

INN. No archaeological researches have been able to identify with certainty the "inns" of either OT or NT times. Such establishments as that which Rahab may have kept by the walls* of Jericho* (Josh 2:1), or of Chimham, descendent of David's host, in the vicinity of Bethlehem* (Jer 41:17), cannot be located definitely in any ancient ruin. The phrase "Geruth Chimham" in Jer 41:17 can be rendered "Chimham's Habitation" or "Chimham's Inn." How far this inn survived the calamitous end of Judah* between 597 and 587 B.C. is unknown. Luke uses two words, one meaning an "unloading place" (κατάλυμα—*kataluma*, 2:7) and the other meaning "a common hostel"

Three pottery inkwells from Qumran, first century A.D. Courtesy Israel Dept. of Antiquities and Museums.

(*pandocheion*, 10:34). The rough khan thus mentioned, on the Jericho road, may indeed be the very place which the Lord had in mind in his story of the Samaritan. This place, the "Good Samaritan's Inn," or Khan Hatrur, is typical of such staging posts, a building with an arched doorway leading into a central courtyard with a well.* In the ruins of ancient towns such rough resorts could be imagined in more than one complex of walls and foundations.

A Greek inscription of the first century says that one Theodotus, son of Vettemus, possibly, on the evidence of his Latin* name, an emancipated Jewish slave,* provided a synagogue* and a guesthouse* for strangers. The fragment was found in a cistern* on the S-eastern hill of Jerusalem.*

Inns generally had an unsavory reputation, and the Christian insistence on hospitality found additional motive in this fact. A fragment of an unknown gospel speaks of a leper who tells the Lord that he contracted his disease by eating with lepers in an inn. He uses the word that Luke uses in 10:34. The papyrus came probably from Oxyrhynchus* and is dated about the middle of the second century. The passage (lines 32 to 37) runs: "And a leper approached Him saying, Rabbi Jesus, I myself became a leper by traveling with lepers and eating with them in the inn. If you will, I am made clean. And the Lord said to him, It is my will, be clean. . . ." It is possibly the incident referred to in Matt 8:2–3 and parallels Mark 1:40–42, Luke 5:12–13.

BIBLIOGRAPHY: H. I. Bell and T. C. Skeat, *Fragments of an Unknown Gospel* (1935); G. Dalman, *Sacred Sites and Ways* (1935), 41–43, 244–45; E. F. F. Bishop, *Jesus of Palestine* (1955), 41–45; J. A. Thompson, *IDB*, 2 (1962), 703–4.

EMB

IPU-WER. A sage who appeared in the presence of pharaoh in the "Time of Troubles" which followed the Pyramid* Age, to deliver a message of doom. His message has survived in one papyrus* (Berlin Papyrus 3024) in which, in the manner of Isa 24, he pictures the overturning of established order. According to Ipu-Wer, "noble ladies are now gleaners, and nobles are paupers. He who never slept even on a plank, now has a bed.* He who knew not the lyre, now has a harp. The bald man who had no oil, has now become the owner of sweet myrrh. She who had no box, now has a trunk. She who looked at her face in the water is now the owner of a mirror." The writer then appears to look for a righteous king, who will restore just rule and "bring cooling water to the flame." He shall be called "the shepherd of the people. Verily he shall smite evil. . . ." J. H. Breasted is fanciful when he suggests a link between this nostalgic remembrance of the better days of the Old Kingdom and Hebrew messianic prophecy, but Ipu-Wer does represent man's ancient and universal longing for peace and justice. He lacks Isaiah's diagnosis (24:5) and clear vision of the coming Servant of God (25:6–12; 26; 27).

BIBLIOGRAPHY: *ANET*, 442; J. H. Breasted, *History of Egypt* (1945), 204–5.

EMB

Iron tools from Tell Jemmeh; tenth century B.C. Courtesy Israel Dept. of Antiquities and Museums.

IRAQ EL-MENSHIYEH, TELL. See TELL SHEIKH AHMED EL-AREINI.

IRON. This metal does not exist in its pure state in the earth's crust, and the Iron Age* merely dates man's discovery of the smelting (see METALLURGY; REFINING) and working of the extracted metal. The Iron Age began at various times for various peoples. It was not until 500 B.C. that it came to Britain. In the story of the Hebrew occupation of Palestine is caught the record of a moment of transition. There was iron in Canaan,* for it was part of the spoil of Midian* and Jericho* (Num 31:22; Josh 6:24; 22:8), and the invaders, not equipped with iron weapons or chariotry, were unable to cope with native peoples thus armed in territory favorable to chariot* tactics (Josh 17:16; Judg 1:19; 4:3). The metal was still in short supply at the time of the Philistine* expansion, and the Philistines went to some trouble to withhold the knowledge of ironworking from their largely bronze*-armed foes. It was David who seems to have remedied this defect in Hebrew weaponry (2 Sam 8:8; 1 Chron 22:3).

Archaeology confirms the implications of this story. Iron is found in Mediterranean and Middle Eastern sites as early as 3000 B.C., but it is mostly space debris. Beads of meteoric iron are very ancient, and it was probably meteoric iron that is found in Mycenaean* jewelry.

The earliest Near Eastern iron smelters are most probably those discovered by Russian archaeologists in the area of Ararat* about 1972. These smelters, which employed a surprisingly sophisticated technique, are thought to date back to about 2500 B.C. In the Timnah* Valley in southern Israel, Beno Rothenberg discovered an iron mine in 1971 that may have been worked by the Egyptians* as early as 1250 B.C.

The Hittites* began their smelting activities about 1600 B.C., and it seems that in both Akkadian* and Hebrew the term for iron was a Hittite loan word. Early iron was of uncertain quality, and bronze was generally preferred in the initial period of iron metallurgy.* The failure of bronze supplies was the first factor that led to the use of iron, which appeared as metal for weapons somewhat before the time when the Philistines* introduced iron to Palestine. The propensity of iron to rust away has destroyed much of the evidence, but a surviving letter of Hattusilis III (1275–1250 B.C.) suggests a Hittite export trade in the metal: "As for the good iron about which you wrote to me, it is not available in my storehouse at Kizzuwatna. . . . They will produce good iron, but as yet they have not finished. I am sending you herewith an iron daggerblade." Ancient furnaces probably did not produce very good cast iron, and as a result weapons may have been of mild steel. Quenching was known as early as Homer, while the Romans, who understood carburization and annealing, could produce sword blades that were not brittle.

Plow points were made of iron at least as early as one millennium B.C. Other iron implements have also been found (see AGRICULTURE).

BIBLIOGRAPHY: H. H. Read, *Rutley's Elements of Mineralogy* (1970 ed.), 513–23; D. R. Bowes, *ZPEB*, 3 (1975), 307–9.   EMB

IRON AGE. Iron* was utilized for tools* and weapons as early as 2700 B.C. in Mesopotamia* and Egypt,* but it did not come into general use until much later. In Palestine iron was in general use by about 1200 B.C. and continued until tempering became common in Roman times. Archaeologists are not in complete agreement about the ending of the Iron Age; perhaps the most popular use of the designation is for the period 1200–300 B.C. It is divided as follows: Iron Ia (1200–1150), Ib (1150–1025), Ic (1025–950), Id (950–900); Iron IIa (900–800), IIb (800–700), IIc (700–600); Iron III (600–300). Some archaeologists prefer to use only two divisions that both cover the same period; others designate Iron III as the Persian period and make the division at 539 B.C. The whole Iron Age is sometimes called the Israelite period as opposed to the Bronze Age,* which is called the Canaanite* period in Palestine. The reigns of all the kings of Israel* and Judah* occurred during the Iron Age.

Biblical references indicate the prominence of iron in Palestine in this period. Weapons are mentioned in 1 Sam 17:7; chains in Ps 105:18. 2 Sam 8:14 and 1 Chron 22:3 seem to be corroborated and illustrated by the explorations of Nelson Glueck in Trans-Jordan and the Arabah. David, after conquering the Edomites, exploited the mines,* and this became the source of Israel's iron. Before this time ironworking was mainly carried on by the Philistines* (who probably learned it from the Hittites*), and the Israelites depended on them for making and servicing implements (1 Sam 13:19–23).

Iron Age sites are not usually identified by the abundance of iron since it oxidizes so quickly. Distinctive local pottery* types as well as some imports from Cyprus* and Rhodes* together with known architectural techniques are more important. Saul's citadel* at Gibeah* shows how the Israelites adopted a northern system of casemate walls* for their defenses. An Iron Age plow point unearthed from the tell and dated about 1010 B.C. is one of the earliest datable iron implements recovered so far from the Palestinian uplands. The age of Solomon* shows improved building techniques; the city* gates* at Hazor,* Gezer,* and Megiddo* all follow the same plan. Official buildings from the time of Omri* at Samaria* have parallels at Beth Shan,* Hazor, and Megiddo. A series of forts around Amman, formerly dated in the Iron Age by Nelson Glueck, have now proved to be Roman. Heshbon,* also in Trans-Jordan, yielded an abundance of Iron Age pottery and possibly even the "pools of Heshbon" mentioned in S of Songs 7:4.

BIBLIOGRAPHY: G. A. Wainwright, *Antiquity*, 10 (1936), 5–24; R. J. Forbes, *Ex Oriente Lux*, 9 (1944), 6–14.   BCC

IRRIGATION. Water is the most frequently mentioned natural resource in the Bible, but there are few references to irrigation. The most likely is in Gen 2:6, where "mist" (KJV, RV, RSV) should probably be translated "river" or "irrigation canal." Perhaps Pishon and Gihon, two of the four subdivisions of the river which flowed from Eden (Gen 2:10), were also large irrigation canals. Eccl 2:5–6 alludes to watering trees from pools* (reservoirs, cisterns*); Isa 58:11 mentions watered gardens,* and Deut 6:11 speaks of the Promised Land as having already cisterns which the Israelites would not have to dig.

Archaeology seems to illustrate the fact that irrigation was less systematized or mechanized in Palestine than in other eastern lands; this was partially because of the terrain and climate. The Gezer Calendar names the various agricultural activities as determined by the seasons. The early rain softens the ground, and this is the time for cultivation. Heavy rain falls in December and January; January and February are the time for planting, etc. Summer fruits had to be watered by hand from cisterns and pools (see the figure in Num 24:7). The land along the Jordan is too low for irrigation and does not need it anyway; mountain ridges border the valley. About the only way to get water in the dry season in Palestine aside from springs and streams, which are scarce, is to draw it from a cistern or public reservoir. Almost every excavation in Palestine discovers numerous cisterns. Some of these were gigantic like those at Qumran* and Masada,* holding thousands of gallons of water. Water channels are often found leading from open collecting areas to the cisterns with filtering basins near them. Cisterns were for general water consumption, which could include irrigation.

Nelson Glueck found interesting systems of irrigation in Trans-Jordan. At et-Telah he found a spring with a large reservoir and below this in the plain a large area of walled square fields; the site had not been used for 2000 years. Another Nabataean* site called Khirbet Ayun Ghuzlan had a small aqueduct* of finely cut stones with channels in them leading from a spring to terraced fields.

Egypt* and Mesopotamia* were better suited for developing systems of irrigation, and there it was absolutely necessary to any type of agriculture.* The wealth of Babylon* was to some extent related to fertile flood* deposits and a system of small and large irrigation canals. Reference is made to these water rights in the Code of Hammurabi* (1728–1626 B.C.). Sennacherib's* aqueduct at Jerwan has been excavated by the Oriental Institute; it is the oldest and dates to 700 B.C. The Pools of Solomon* (before 200 B.C.) provided water by means of an aqueduct to Jerusalem* 11.3 km. (7 mi.) away; the aqueduct was repaired by Pilate in the first century. A very famous aqueduct at Caesarea* provided water for that Roman city. It may be that some of the water from these aqueducts was used for irrigation.

BIBLIOGRAPHY: M. S. Drower in C. Singer, *A History of Technology*, 1 (1954), 530–57; R. O. Whyte and L. D. Stamp, *A History of Land Use in Arid Regions* (1961), 57–118; G. R. Lewthwaite, ZPEB, 3 (1975), 309–10.

BCC

IR SHEMESH. See BETH SHEMESH.

ISDUD. See ASHDOD.

ISHTAR, DESCENT OF. A poetic myth from Mesopotamia,* discovered in two recensions, an older Assyrian version from Ashur* (second millennium B.C.), and a later Neo-Assyrian version from the library of Ashurbanipal* (668–626 B.C.). Although the theme of the tale was derived from the Sumerian story of the "descent of Inanna" in search of Dumuzi (recovered from tablets found at Nippur*), the Semitic version was a singular creative effort. Ishtar, the Babylonian-Assyrian fertility goddess (known in other cultures as Astarte, Ashtartu, Ashtoreth; see Judg 2:13), goes down into the nether world, the "land of no return," where she is ceremonially stripped of her awesome livery until she is totally at the mercy of the goddess of the dead, Ereshkigal. She is slain and impaled. However, a clever trick by Ea, acting through a eunuch, Asushunamir, revives Ishtar and brings her back to the land of the living, where sexuality and fecundity again appear on the earth. The reason for her descent is most likely to search for her lost lover, Tammuz, but this has been contested, for Tammuz does not return after the manner of the typical "vegetation god" but appears as a deity of the nether world. The myth is written in high literary style, with many words and phrases of Sumerian* origin. The myth is also filled with psychological and sexual symbolism and has been studied widely for insight into ancient personality. It is unfortunate that no more than 150 lines of what must have been a major poem cycle have survived. The text reveals the hedonistic quandaries of paganism, against which the religion of Israel* had to contest. If Jer 7:18 is correctly rendered for "the queen of heaven," as in most versions, the reference is to Ishtar and her worship, infiltrating into Israelite popular superstition. A similar intrusion of the Babylonian cult was the "wailing for Tammuz" of which Ezekiel complains (8:14).

BIBLIOGRAPHY: *Larousse Encyclopedia of Mythology* (1959), 57–58; J. Nougayrol and J.-M. Aynard, *La Mésopotamie* (1965), 41–44.

WW

ISRAEL. A name given to Jacob, later used as a designation for the twelve tribes, and after the division of the monarchy a term usually meaning the northern kingdom (as distinct from Judah*).

In most of the Hebrew Bible the sons of Jacob and their descendants are referred to by some term including the name Israel. They are originally (and subsequently) thought of as the "Sons of Israel," or the "Tribes of Israel," or the "People Israel." Israel as a land is a secondary concept, as the notion of a geopolitically based national state developed only later.

The earliest archaeological reference to Israel comes in the stele of the Egyptian* Pharaoh Meneptah (c. 1230 B.C.), where Israel is given the determinative for people rather than land, indicating that possibly they were still not fully settled into a territory. In the annals of the Assyrian king Shalmaneser III (858–824), the name Israelite is used, with the country determinative (matSir-'i-la-a-a), in describing Ahab.* The same king pictures Israelite porters bearing tribute (*see* BOOTY) and refers to their King Jehu as a son of Omri* (Hu-um-ri) and then mentions Israel by the name "land of Omri" (matHu-um-ri). Also from the late ninth century B.C. comes the Mesha Stele,* king of Moab,* in which there are two clear references to "Israel" as the land over which Omri and his son ruled. By the time of Tiglath-pileser III* (744–727 B.C.) and Sargon II* (721–705), Israel is referred to as the "House (or Land) of Omri" (Bit Hu-um-ri-a), while Menahem,* the king, is identified with the capital city Samaria.*

Although the Southern Kingdom existed alone after 722/1 B.C., it was still called Judah rather than Israel, and Assyrian records refer to Hezekiah as the Jew (amelIa-u-da-ai). However, after the return from Exile* it is apparent that the little community in Jerusalem* considered itself the commonwealth of Israel, and the name is utilized extensively in the books of Ezra and Nehemiah as well as in 1 and 2 Chronicles.

BIBLIOGRAPHY: *ANET*, 3d ed. (1969), 279–84, 320, 378; *ANEP*, 2d ed. (1969), 120–22.

CEA

ISRAEL STELE. The so-called Israel Stele is a large granite stele* which was found in Meneptah's mortuary temple W of Thebes* by Petrie. It originally belonged to Amenhotep III and was usurped by Meneptah and placed in his own funerary temple. Meneptah was the son and successor of Ramses II* and ruled from c. 1224 to c. 1214 B.C. The stele is actually a commemorative series of hymns relating to Meneptah's victory over the Lydians in the spring of his fifth year. At the top is a representation of Meneptah and the god Amun, with Mut, the wife of Amun, and Khonsu, their son, in the background. The text itself is comprised of twenty-eight lines in which the pharaoh boasts of his triumph over the

Merneptah stele. Courtesy Encyclopaedia Judaica.

Lydians and other foreigners. This monument attracted wide attention because Israel* is mentioned in the last section, this being one of the rare references to Israel in ancient nonbiblical documents. Meneptah's victory over the enemies to the N are described in normative poetic expression for such commemorative hymns. His reference to Israel is as follows: "Israel is laid waste, his seed is not; Hurru is become a widow for Egypt." The reference to Hurru is related to the Hurrians,* or the biblical Horites (*see* HIVITES).

For Bible students the inscription is extremely important. First, it is an official recognition of a people called Israel in extra-biblical documents and is the earliest mention of Israel known to us in such literature. The words "his seed is not" are a conventional phrase applicable to any defeated or plundered people. It should not, therefore, be applied to the slaying of male children of the Israelites by the Egyptians,* as some writers have suggested. Similar expressions are found at least five times referring to other people.

In contrast with other enemies, preceded by the

determinative for "nation," the word *Israel* is designated as a "people." The fact that such a determinative was used preceding the name Israel might indicate that from an Egyptian viewpoint they were considered a people not yet permanently resident in the political (national) sense of the term. It is also possible, however, that the hymn suffers from the carelessness of late Egyptian scribes, who, in copying documents were notorious for their inattention to some of these smaller matters (*see* SCRIBAL TRAINING, EGYPTIAN). What is significant, however, is that Israel was located in Palestine at the time of Meneptah. It could be that the tribes of Judah, Dan, Simeon, and Benjamin offered some resistance to the northern campaigns of Meneptah but were defeated in the process. The stele, therefore, is a significant complement to the history of the latter days of the judges and indeed may have a bearing on the date of the conquest.

BIBLIOGRAPHY: *ANET*, 376–78; Pierre Montet, *Egypt and the Bible* (1968), 24–30; James Henry Breasted, *Ancient Records of Egypt*, 3 (1906), 256–64; Sir Alan Gardiner, *Egypt of the Pharaohs* (1961), 270–75.

JJD

ITALIAN BAND (COHORT; REGIMENT). *See* ARMED FORCES IN THE NT.

IVORY. Ivory became known as an object of wealth and luxury in Palestine after the initiation by Solomon* of eastern trade with the merchant states of Tyre* and Sidon.* Rhodes* (Dedan) is mentioned in Ezek 27:15 as one of the clearing houses and perhaps processing places for tusks. There were elephants in Northern Syria in the second millennium B.C., and elephant hunts are mentioned in connection with Amenenheb, an officer of Thutmose III who captured 120 of the animals (*ANET*, 241); Tiglath-pileser,* two centuries later, slew elephants in Haran* (*ARAB* 1.247), and Ashurbanipal,* two centuries later still, killed many elephants and stocked a zoo with captured specimens (*ARAB* 1.519,20). The Black Obelisk of Shalmaneser III* speaks of elephant tusks used as tribute. Lists of booty* mention ivory objects Thutmose III took from Megiddo* in 1468 B.C.— "six sedan chairs of ivory and carob wood worked with gold" (*ANET*, 237). Adadnirari (810–783 B.C.) took, in the form of tribute from Damascus,* beds* and couches inlaid with ivory. Sennacherib* reports similar articles of furniture* collected as offerings from Hezekiah in 701 B.C. (*ANET*, 288). Archaeological digging has produced ivory ornaments and fragments of laminated ivory, from Cyprus* to Ur.* Megiddo and Samaria* produced major stores of such material, particularly from the period 1350–1150 B.C. Intricately carved objects and decorations, gaming boards, panel sheathing, boxes, and many other treasures from Megiddo especially, suggest a collector's activities.

BIBLIOGRAPHY: J. W. and G. M. Crowfoot, *Early Ivories from Samaria* (1938); G. Loud, *The Megiddo Ivories* (1939); *ANEP* (1954), figs. 125–32; R. D. Barnett, *A Catalogue of Nimrud Ivories and Other Examples of Ancient Near Eastern Ivories* (1957); N. B. Baker, *ZPEB*, 3 (1975), 346.

EMB

IZMIR. *See* SMYRNA.

J

JACOB'S WELL. The place near Sychar* where Jesus encountered the woman of Samaria.*

Although various OT traditions from the area around Shechem* relate both to Joseph* and his father Jacob, there is no explicit reference either to a field (but cf. Gen 48:21–22) or to a well* in the vicinity dug by Jacob. The Gospel of John (4:5ff) first mentions a well, in "a city of Samaria called Sychar, near to the parcel of ground that Jacob gave to his son Joseph." Christian tradition from the fourth century (and possibly much earlier) connects this incident with a well about 23 m. (75 ft.) deep not far from Tell Balaṭa, most certainly the site of ancient Shechem. The well, known as Bir Ya'kûb (Jacob's Well), fits perfectly the requirements for the biblical story. This well is now topped by a large stone with a hole in it but the well widens as it goes down into the soft limestone base.

As early as the time of Jerome (404 A.D.) there is record of a cruciform church with the well in the center of its crypt. After successive destructions and rebuilding, the church was rebuilt by the Crusaders, only to be completely destroyed in 1187. In 1860, work began on another church, but nothing has been done since 1914. The opening of the well is now about fifteen steps below the surface of the ground.

BIBLIOGRAPHY: G. Dalman, *Orte und Wege Jesu* (1919), 207–11; id., *Sacred Sites and Ways* (1935), 212–15; R. J. Bull, "Archaeological Context for Understanding John 4:20," *BA* 38 (1975), 54–59; R. J. Bull, "Archaeological Footnote to 'Our Fathers Worshipped on This Mountain,' John 4:20," *NTS* 23 (1977), 460–62. CEA

JAFFA. *See* JOPPA.

JARASH. *See* GERASA.

JAZIRAH. *See* MITANNI.

JAZIRET EL-ARAB. *See* ARABIA.

JEBEL HAROUN. *See* AARON'S TOMB.

JEBEL MUSA. *See* SINAI.

JEBUSITES (jeb' yə sīts; Heb. יְבוּסִי, *yᵉḇûsî*). The name of the clan which occupied the city* of Jerusalem* (Josh 15:8; 18:16, 28), known from the name of its inhabitants as Jebus (Judg 19:10; 1 Chron 11:4–5) before its capture by David.

According to Gen 10:16 the Jebusites were derived from Canaan* (Jos. *Antiq.* 7.3.1, describes the Jebusites as members of the Canaanite race). In the lists of the inhabitants of Canaan before the conquest the Jebusites are placed along with the Amorites* in the hill country (Num 13:29; Josh 11:3).

At the time of the conquest, Adonizedek the king of Jerusalem, was the leader of the Amorite kings who opposed Joshua at Gibeon* (Josh 10:5). Though the Israelites were able to capture Jerusalem and set fire to it (Judg 1:8), the Jebusites evidently regained the city and continued as an enclave in the midst of the Israelites (Josh 15:63; Judg 1:21). This situation is illustrated by the story of the Levite who did not wish to lodge in Jerusalem because it was the city of strangers (Judg 19:10–12).

Despite the confidence of the Jebusites in their well-fortified city, Jerusalem was captured by David's general Joab by means of the ṣinnôr (KJV "gutter") shortly after 1000 B.C. (2 Sam 5:6–8; 1 Chron 11:4–6). Many expositors have thought that this term described an underground water shaft of the kind found at Megiddo.* (See K. Kenyon, *Jerusalem*, pp. 22, 30 and the articles by Y. Shiloh.)

After David's conquest Jerusalem is no longer called Jebus. David purchased the threshing floor of Araunah the Jebusite (2 Sam 24:16–25) called Ornan (1 Chron 21:15–28) as the site of the Lord's altar.* In Zech 9:7 we are told that Ekron* shall be as a Jebusite, that is, the Philistines* will be absorbed by the Israelites as was Araunah the Jebusite.

E. A. Speiser has argued that the peoples known in the conquest lists as Jebusites, Hivites,* and Hittites* should be considered as branches of the Hurrians* or Horites. R. de Vaux has offered some cogent criticisms of such a pan-Hurrian theory. Nonetheless the identification of the Jebusites of Jerusalem as a Hurrian group is supported by both biblical and nonbiblical evidence. The name *Araunah* (2 Sam 24:16, Kethib *Awarnah*) can be analyzed as the Hurrian *ewri*, "ruler," plus the Hurrian determinative singular *ne*. The Amarna letters of the fourteenth century B.C. indicate that the chief of *Urisalimmu* (Jerusalem) was *Abdi-Khepa*, a man with a Hurrian name.

In excavations in 1923–24 R. A. S. Macalister identified a wall on the ridge of Ophel, the southeastern hill of Jerusalem, as a Jebusite structure. Kathleen Kenyon in excavations conducted from 1961 to 1967 demonstrated that the so-called "tower of David" is from the Maccabean* period (second century B.C.). In 1978-80 Y. Shiloh cleared the adjacent sloping structure and redated it to the tenth century

Eastern slope of the Ophel: (1) thick Jebusite wall at foot of ridge and (2) Israelite wall above it, probably of David's city. Photo: D. Eisenberg.

B.C. Some 27 m. (89 ft.) down the slope of Ophel Miss Kenyon discovered a corner of a true "Jebusite" wall. The massive wall was built by the Amorites c. 1800 B.C. and was used by the Jebusites and later by the Israelites until the eighth century B.C. A secret water shaft, which rises 15 m. (50 ft.) vertically from the Gihon Spring* to a point within this Jebusite wall, was part of the underground water system. This shaft was discovered by Captain Warren in his investigations of Hezekiah's Siloam Tunnel* in 1867.

Miss Kenyon's exploratory shafts indicated that the Jebusite city covered only the ridge of Ophel, just S of the southeastern corner of the present walled city of Jerusalem. The city of David was less than 76 m. (250 ft.) wide and c. 396 m (1300 ft.) long, or a little less than 4.5 ha. (11 a.). This area would also include the terraced eastern slopes of Ophel, which seem to be the *millo* or "filling" which required constant repair by David (2 Sam 5:9) and by Solomon* (1 Kings 9:15). The southwestern hill of Jerusalem, which is today called Mount Zion, seems not to have been occupied until the time of Herod* Agrippa I (A.D. 40–44).

BIBLIOGRAPHY: C. Wilson and C. Warren, *The Recovery of Jerusalem* (1871), 238–58; E. A. Speiser, "The Hurrian Participation in the Civilisations of Mesopotamia, Syria and Palestine," *Journal of World History*, 1 (1954), 311–27; K. Kenyon, "Biblical Jerusalem," *Expedition*, Vol. 1 (1962), 32–35; Y. Yadin, *The Art of Warfare in Biblical Lands* (1963), 267–

70; K. Kenyon, "Excavations in Jerusalem," *BA*, 27 (1964), 34–52; E. A. Speiser, "Hurrians and Hittites," B. Netanyahu, ed., *The World History of the Jewish People* 1 (1964), 158–61; R. de Vaux, "Les Hurrians de l'histoire et les Horites de la Bible," *RB*, 74 (1967), 481–503; K. Kenyon, *Jerusalem* (1967), 18–41, 49–53; id., *Royal Cities of the OT* (1971), 24–35; A. D. Tushingham, "Jerusalem," D. Baly, ed., *Atlas of the Biblical World* (1971), 155–62; R. North, "The Hivites," *Biblica*, 54 (1973), 43–62; H. A. Hoffner, "The Hittites and Hurrians," in *Peoples of Old Testament Times*, ed. D. J. Wiseman (1973), 225–28; *Jerusalem Revealed*, ed. Y. Yadin (1975); B. Mazar and K. Kenyon, "Jerusalem," *EEHL*, ed. M. Avi-Yonah, 2 (1976), 580–97; T. Ishida, "The Structure and Historical Implications of the Lists of Pre-Israelite Nations," *Biblica*, 60 (1979), 461–90; Y. Shiloh and M. Kaplan, "Digging in the City of David," *BAR*, 5.4 (1979), 36–49; Y. Shiloh, "The Rediscovery of Warren's Shaft," *BAR*, 7.4 (1981), 24-39; H. Shanks, "New York Times Misrepresents Major Jerusalem Discovery," *BAR*, 7.4 (1981), 40-43.

EY

JEHOIACHIN. The second last ruler of Judah* carried captive to Babylon* by Nebuchadnezzar* in 598 B.C. This capture of Jerusalem* is described in the chronicles of the Chaldean* kings, and Jehoiachin's presence in Babylon is attested on three clay* tablets that are receipts for oil, barley, and other substances issued to Jehoiachin (Yaukin) and his five sons. The tablets are dated from the tenth to the thirty-fifth year of Nebuchadnezzar* II (i.e., 595–570 B.C.). A date of 592 B.C. has been assigned to one of the tablets in which the name Jehoiachin occurred. A seal* belonging to Eliakim, the steward of Jehoiachin, was unearthed at Beth Shemesh.*

BIBLIOGRAPHY: W. F. Albright, *JBL*, 51 (1932), 77–106; H. G. May, *AJSL*, 56 (1939), 146–48; E. F. Weidner, *Mélanges syriens . . .*, 2 (1939), 923–35; W. F. Albright, *BA*, 5 (1942), 49–55; *ANET*, (1955 ed.), 308; D. J. Wiseman, *Chronicles of Chaldean Kings* (1956), 32–35, 72–73; H. G. May, *IDB*, 3 (1962), 811–13; J. Lilley, *ZPEB*, 3 (1975), 416–18.

JAT

JEMDET NASR. A site in central Mesopotamia* about 32 km. (20 mi.) NE of the place where the later Babylon* was erected. Its culture marks a phase in early Mesopotamian history at the end of the fourth millennium B.C., which saw the first use of bronze* in Mesopotamia. The pottery* excavated at the site was painted* ware, showing black and yellow patterns imposed on a red background. Some tablets were found written in a semipictographic* script which was more complex than that of the Uruk* (Warka) phase. Sculpture in stone was another innovation of the period and is also represented at contemporary levels from Ur* and Uruk. The Jemdet Nasr Age also saw the beginnings of international commerce, and archaeological discoveries have furnished evidence of contemporary Mesopotamian influence upon ancient Egypt* in such matters as cylinder seals and the construction of buildings based upon the architectural principle of the recessed niche, which was Mesopotamian in origin.

BIBLIOGRAPHY: *CAH*, 1, Part 1, 151 passim; id., Part 2, 72 passim.   RKH

JEMMA IN. See TIRZAH.

JERABLUS; JERABIS. See CARCHEMISH.

JERASH. See GERASA.

JERICHO. The famous biblical site of Jericho, often called "the city of palm trees," is mentioned in several separate settings in the OT. The first is in the context of Joshua's capture of the city* (Josh 5–6). After the fall of Jericho, Joshua placed a curse on it (6:26). The site itself was not inhabited again till much later. Meantime the oasis and the spring that supported it were occupied. Eglon, king of Moab,* occupied the area for a time (Judg 3:13). David's envoys rested here after their insulting treatment by Hanun of Ammon* (2 Sam 10:5; 1 Chron 19:5). In the days of Ahab* (c. 874/3–853 B.C.) Hiel the Bethelite refounded Jericho proper but lost his eldest and youngest sons because of the curse (1 Kings 16:34). The nearby village was frequented by Elijah and Elisha (2 Kings 2:4–5, 18–22). Later the Babylonians captured Zedekiah on the plains of Jericho (2 Kings 25:5; 2 Chron 28:15; Jer 52:8). After the Exile* there seem to have been a village in the area (Ezra 2:34; Neh 7:36). In NT times the town of Jericho was situated to the S of the old mound (Matt 20:29; Mark 10:46; Luke 10:30–37; 18:35; 19:1). An important road led from Jerusalem* to Jericho (Luke 10:30–37).

In archaeological terms we are concerned with three Jerichos: the ancient mound which claimed little history after Joshua captured it, the oasis village, and the NT site. Important archaeological work has been carried out on the ancient mound and in the NT site. The major part of this discussion is concerned with ancient Jericho, which has proved to be a remarkable source of historical and archaeological data over many years. However, serious denudation of the mound both by rain and by removal of surface materials by local farmers has disrupted nearly all the deposits belonging to the second half of the second millennium B.C. This means that direct evidence about the period of the Israelite occupation is very scanty. There is, nevertheless, an enormous amount of information about the centuries and millennia preceding the Israelites. In particular, recent archaeological work has provided us with a fine insight into certain aspects of the culture of the Canaanites* among whom the Israelites settled.

The site of ancient Jericho can be identified with certainty as Tell es-Sultan, an impressive mound on the western outskirts of modern Jericho. There are other tells* in the area, but this is the most impressive and lies at the source of the perennial spring of Ain es-Sultan. Despite erosion the tell stands 21 m. (70 ft.) at its highest point above the surrounding plain and covers an area of about 4 ha. (10 a.), some 366 m. (1200 ft.) from N to S and 182 m. (600 ft.) across at its broader northern end.

Jericho lay in a very strategic position, opposite the main ford over the lower Jordan and at the entrance to important passes which led from the Jordan Valley to the highlands. Moreover it controlled a vital water supply. Hence it was a key point for all invaders. Throughout its history there is strong evidence that nomadic invaders descended on Jericho on a number of occasions, among whom were the Israelites.

Excavation began here over a century ago when Sir Charles Warren sunk some trial shafts to a depth of about 9 m. (30 ft.) into the tell in 1867. He reported that nothing much of significance was to be found at the site. We know today that one of his shafts cut the Early Bronze Age* town wall,* and the other cut into the prepottery Neolithic* levels neither of which could be recognized at the time. Perhaps he was looking for gigantic stone statues such as were then known from Nineveh.*

During the years 1907–9 an Austro-German expedition led by E. Sellin and C. Watzinger traced the line of the wall surrounding the summit, investigated a considerable area of the upper levels at the northern end, and cut a deep trench from E to W. They lacked the techniques of modern archaeology and the knowledge of Palestinian pottery* so that much of their work was unreliable.

Between 1930 and 1936 John Garstang of the University of Liverpool undertook a major excavation at Jericho. He devoted much of his attention to the mud-brick walls discovered by the previous excavators and cut trenches across these at various points. He assigned these to four stages, two to the Early Bronze Age, one to the Middle Bronze Age, and one to the Late Bronze Age. It was he who popularized the view that the destruction of the latter wall by fire and earthquake marked the period of the Israelite attack under Joshua. We now know that this wall was in fact an Early Bronze Age wall. He made other erroneous conclusions. Certain structures and tombs were taken by him as providing evidence that the site was occupied down to about 1400 B.C. on the basis of pottery finds. Since his day the study of Palestinian pottery has made considerable progress and dating evidence for a Late Bronze Age occupation is too meager to allow conclusions to be drawn. If it once existed it has largely disappeared. In any case current scholarship would date the Exodus to the early thirteenth century with an entry into Palestine of about 1250 B.C. However, evidence from the thirteenth century is virtually lacking.

The definitive work of Dr. Kathleen Kenyon was carried out between 1952 and 1958. Soundings at a number of places in all parts of the mound have now provided evidence of the story of Jericho from its first occupation to its final abandonment.

The archaeological history of Jericho is virtually a summary of the whole archaeological history of Palestine. From Mesolithic* beginnings c. 8000 B.C. the site developed through a proto-Neolithic into a full Neolithic* town by about 7000 B.C. During the seventh and for most of the sixth millennium the city achieved a remarkable state of culture with a massive city wall and an impressive defense tower.* In fact,

Mound of Tell es-Sultan, site of ancient Jericho: (1) Early Bronze Age city wall, (2) retaining wall of Middle Bronze Age, II glacis, (3) glacis, (4) Kenyon's trench I, (5) trench II, (6) trench III, (7) modern road, (8) reservoir near spring. Photo: PICTORIAL ARCHIVE (Near Eastern History) Est.

the succeeding pottery-Neolithic was a pale shadow of the earlier town. The occupants could make a coarse pottery but lived in partly sunken huts for a long time. Eventually they began to build freestanding houses* on stone foundations with a superstructure of mud bricks.

It was only in the Early Bronze Age, which began about 3100 B.C., that Jericho and the rest of Palestine began to assume the appearance of the land to which the Israelites came. Numerous small towns in strategic positions arose all over the land.

Jericho became a walled city with walls around the crest of the mound that already contained several layers of occupation. These walls had a very checkered history from about 3000 B.C. to about 2300 B.C. They were rebuilt in places, patched, and refaced many times. Some of the repairs were localized. Some were needed because of earthquake damage, some because of fire perhaps caused by an enemy attack, others because of erosion at the foot of the wall. Dr. Kenyon found one area on the W side where seventeen stages were identified, fourteen on the same line and the last three representing a rebuilding 7 m. (23 ft.) down the slope of the mound giving the appearance of a double wall. None of this can be ascribed to Joshua as earlier excavators proposed. There was no double wall of the Late Bronze Age. The period of the Early Bronze Age is represented by numerous excellent tombs well furnished with a wide variety of pottery types. As the Early Bronze Age developed, Jericho became a flourishing town closely settled by solid substantial houses although without any clear town planning.

The Early Bronze Age at Jericho, as at other sites in Palestine, came to a calamitous end when nomadic invaders destroyed the urban life of the land. The evidence is particularly clear at Jericho. The Early Bronze Age town wall was destroyed by fire. The story of the tombs shows that the communal graves* of the Early Bronze Age which sometimes contained up to three hundred burials gave place to single burials. Completely new pottery and weapons are found in the tombs of the nomads. But they did not build the same substantial houses. The nomads camped all over the mound as well as down the slopes and in the surrounding areas. The first houses were slight and entirely different from those of the Early Bronze Age town with small rooms and of irregular shape. This period, known archaeologically as the Early Bronze-Middle Bronze Intermediate Period, lasted till about 2000 B.C. when a new wave of immigrants submerged these people and gave rise to the beginnings of the Middle Bronze Age, which lasted from about 2000 to 1500 B.C. The culture of this age was that which the Israelites met when they entered the land in strength during the Late Bronze Age.

At Jericho the Middle Bronze Age was preserved in a continuous succession of town levels. Dr. Kenyon was able to elucidate the story by careful excavation in a small area and by a close study of the tombs. There is evidence of a basic continuity of culture. During this period the Hyksos* conquerors fortified Jericho by building their typical sloping earth bank around the city instead of the older freestanding wall.

Inside the walls, however, life went on as elsewhere in Palestine. At one stage a violent destruction hit Jericho and left houses buried beneath collapsed debris. This destruction of the final period of Middle Bronze Age Jericho took place early in the sixteenth century B.C. and is probably to be connected with the expulsion of the Hyksos from Egypt.* The debris covered the town of the age and excavation has revealed the layout of the city. Cobbled streets ascend the slope of the mound by means of shallow steps. Shops and storerooms opened onto the streets with living quarters above. A wealth of domestic objects was found in the ruins. The tombs of the age have been well preserved and contain not only the usual pottery but a considerable amount of furniture* and personal possessions. If the tomb equipment represents the normal needs of these people during their lives, we are now able to reconstruct the contents of the typical home. They sat and slept on rush mats on the floor. They normally had a long low wooden table with two legs at one end and one at the other. Some had stools and a few had wooden beds.* The household vessels were all of pottery. Enough seeds, stores, and other pieces of food* remain to give us a good idea of their normal diet. On the whole life was simple with only very few items of value. There is interesting evidence of contact with Egypt from the presence of scarabs,* alabaster* and faience* vessels, and the style of the wooden furniture. After the destruction of the mid-sixteenth century B.C. Jericho was abandoned. It was only a faulty identification of pottery at Beth Shan* which was then used to date Jericho pottery which led to the claim by Professor Garstang that Jericho was occupied down to about 1400–1380 B.C. It was during the period of abandonment after about 1550 B.C. that the mound suffered erosion by wind and rain.

There is evidence that there was an occupation of Jericho in the second part of the Late Bronze Age. A few tombs and some traces of a house remain. No evidence of the defenses remains. Dr. Kenyon suggests that the site was reoccupied about the beginning of the fourteenth century but abandoned about the middle of the century. This would be the town of Joshua's day, although practically no evidence remains.

As to the occupation of the Iron Age* (1 Kings 16:34) there is no evidence, although one tomb provides some evidence of an occupation of the site.

There are indications of a town here in the seventh century, but this came to an end with the Babylonian invasions. Thereafter the old site was abandoned.

NT Jericho was to the S of the ancient site. Herod* the Great (40/37–4 B.C.) built a winter palace and ornamental gardens* here. Excavations in recent years have laid bare a fine structure, part of which goes back to Herodian times. A large cistern* and traces of an aqueduct* which brought water down from the Wadi Qilt to the N have been brought to light. There is a considerable area of ruins in the vicinity awaiting excavation.

BIBLIOGRAPHY: J. L. Kelso, *AASOR*, 29–30 (1955); K. M. Kenyon, *Digging Up Jericho* (1957); id., "The Tombs Excavated 1952–4," *Excavations at Jericho*,

1. The three Herodian towers: (1) Hippicus, (2) Phasael, (3) Mariamne. From scale model of Jerusalem in A.D. 66 located at Holyland Hotel in Jerusalem. Courtesy Israel Government Press Office. 2. C. N. Johns' excavation at Jaffa Gate Citadel: (1), (2) two Hasmonean fortifications, (3) remains of Herod's Phasael tower. Courtesy Israel Dept. of Antiquities and Museums. 3. Herodian masonry on southwestern corner of Temple Mount at South wall excavation by B. Mazar. Courtesy Israel Government Press Office. 4. Blocked-up Triple Gate (top right) in southern wall of Temple Mount. The buildings below are Byzantine structures uncovered by Mazar in the South Wall excavation. The domed building at the top left is the Al-Aqsa Mosque. Courtesy Israel Government Press Office.

1 (1960); id., "The Tombs Excavated 1955–8," *Excavations at Jericho*, 2 (1965); id., *Archaeology in the Holy Land* (1965; see Index under "Jericho"); id., "Jericho," D. W. Thomas, ed., *Archaeology and OT Study* (1967), 264–75; K. A. Kitchen, "Jericho," *NBD* (1962), 611–13; J. B. Pritchard, "The Excavations at Herodian Jericho," *AASOR*, 32–33 (1958); id., "The 1951 Campaign at Herodian Jericho," *BASOR*, 123 (1951), 8–17; H. M. Jamieson, *ZPEB*, 3 (1975), 451–55; E. Netzer, "The Winter Palaces of the Judean Kings at Jericho at the End of the Second Temple Period," *BASOR*, 228 (1977), 1-14.

JAT

JERUSALEM, NEW TESTAMENT. First century A.D. Jerusalem was situated on two hills separated N and S by the shallow Tyropoeon Valley, at an elevation of about 762 m. (2500 ft.). The city* was defended on the S and W by the Hinnom* Valley and on the E by the Kidron* Valley, with only its N flank left without natural defense.

First-Century Structures. On the E side of the city N of the Spring of Gihon* (1 Kings 1:33) was located the temple* area, the place in which Herod* built his magnificent temple. The Herodian temple, called the *ho naos* (Matt 27:40), was surrounded by the temple area, the *to hieron* (Matt 26:55), which consisted of an outer court of the Gentiles with its walls lined with cloisters of double rows of marble columns roofed with carved cedar,* the ones on the E called "Solomon's Porch" (John 10:23) and those on the S, the "Royal Porticoes" with their four rows of columns and three aisles (Jos. *Antiq.* 15.393.411). Inside this was the inner court which Josephus calls the "second court of the temple" into which no Gentile could enter (Jos. *War* 5.193; Jos. *Antiq.* 15.417). Two stone inscriptions have been found warning Gentiles against entering on pain of death. This inner area was composed first of the Women's Court, and then farther on, the Court of Israel (or the Men's Court), and finally the Court of the Priests, where, in front of the temple itself, the priests offered altar* sacrifices (cf. Jos. *Antiq.* 15.419).

This structure was destroyed in A.D. 70 (cf. Matt 24:2), but Titus* left some of the retaining wall foundation around the temple, a good part of which Herod the Great had built with characteristic massive blocks of stone incised around the edges. Large portions of this foundation are to be seen at the SE corner of the temple area as well as on the W side at the Wailing Wall* and also S of the latter where recent excavations have been conducted by B. Mazar. Further evidence of Herod's construction is to be seen in the remains of two gates* in the S wall—the present walled up Double and Triple Gates, those known in

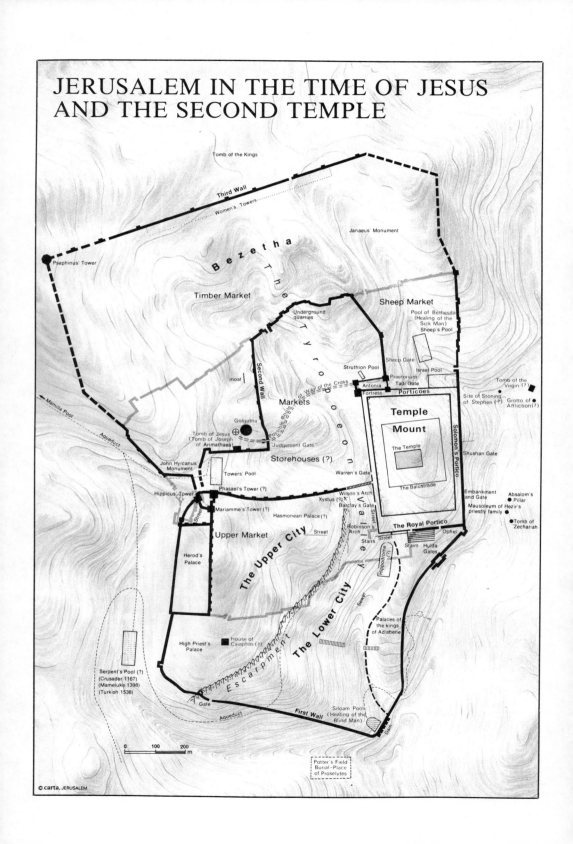

JERUSALEM IN THE TIME OF JESUS AND THE SECOND TEMPLE

Tomb of the Kings

Third Wall

Women's Towers

Janaeus' Monument

B e z e t h a

Psephinus' Tower

Timber Market

Sheep Market

Underground quarries

Pool of Bethesda (Healing of the Sick Man)

Sheep's Pool

Second Wall

Sheep Gate

Israel Pool

Tomb of the Virgin (?)

moat

Struthion Pool

Praetorium
Tadi Gate

Site of Stoning of Stephen (?)

Grotto of Affliction (?)

Mamilla Pool

Aqueduct

Way of the Cross

Antonia Fortress

Porticoes

Markets

Temple Mount

Golgotha

The Temple

Tomb of Jesus
(Tomb of Joseph of Arimathaea)

Judgement Gate

Shushan Gate

Solomon's Portico

John Hyrcanus Monument

Storehouses (?)

Warren's Gate

The Balustrade

Towers' Pool

Wilson's Arch

Embankment and Gate

Absalom's Pillar

Hippicus' Tower

Phasael's Tower (?)

Xystus (?)

Barclay's Gate

Mausoleum of Hezir's priestly family

Mariamme's Tower (?)

Hasmonean Palace (?)

Robinson's Arch

The Royal Portico

Tomb of Zechariah

Upper Market

Street

Stairs

Stairs Hulda Gates

Ophel

The Upper City

Herod's Palace

Hippodrome (?)

Palaces of the kings of Adiabene

The Lower City

High Priest's Palace

House of Caiaphas (?)

Serpent's Pool (?)
(Crusader 1167)
(Mameluke 1398)
(Turkish 1538)

E s c a r p m e n t

Gate

Aqueduct

First Wall

Siloam Pool
(Healing of the Blind Man)

Dam

0   100   200
m

Potter's Field
Burial-Place of Proselytes

© carta, JERUSALEM

the Jewish *Middoth* (I, 1 and 3) as the two Huldah Gates,—no doubt those referred to by Josephus (Jos. *Antiq*. 15.411) when he says, "the fourth front of this court, facing south, also had gates in the middle."

At the W wall of the temple complex are remains of ancient arches* of two bridges jutting out to cross the Tyropoeon Valley W, the one to the N called Wilson's Arch and the other at the SW corner called Robinson's Arch. This corresponds to Josephus's description that at A.D. 70 there was a "passage to the upper city where the bridge joined the temple" (Jos. *War* 6.325). Not far south of Wilson's Arch was Barclay's Gate, also known as the Coponius Gate (named for the Roman Procurator Coponius, A.D. 6–9).

To the N of the present temple area are archaeological remains of the ancient Castle of Antonia* with its massive striated courtyard pavement stones (*see* GABBATHA) found under the present Convent of our Lady of Sion and the Franciscan Convent of the Flagellation. According to Josephus, the Antonia had been rebuilt by Herod the Great and renamed for Mark Antony (Jos. *Antiq*. 15.293; 15.409).

On the NW corner of the SW hill of old Jerusalem Herod the Great constructed a palace. On the N he built three towers* of white marble from 18–37 m. (60–120 ft.) high, named Hippicus, Phasael, and Mariamne, probably in that order from W to E. They contained chambers and living quarters (Jos. *War* 5.161–175). To the S and adjoining these towers Herod built his palace with its own enclosed wall and banquet halls, guest chambers, cloisters, and gardens* (Jos. *War* 5.176–183). In his destruction Titus razed the Antonia but left standing the three towers and part of the western city wall (Jos. *War* 6.93; 7.1–2). Excavations were conducted here in this area called the citadel* by C. N. Johns from 1938–48 and by Ruth Amiran and A. Eitan in 1968–69 (cf. Magen Broshi's related work in 1971 in the *Armenian Garden*). Much of the present castle* is of Arab mameluke work of the fourteenth century, following the pattern of the twelfth-century Crusader castle there. Present in the NE angle is the prominent structure known as the Tower of David, whose substructure, following Josephus's measurements (Jos. *War* 5.166) must be that of Herod's Phasael Tower.

N and E of the Antonia in the vicinity of the Church of St. Anne are excavated ruins of the pool(s) of Bethesda (cf. John 5:1–16) where two cisterns* have been found with fragments of columns and capitals* which show that beautiful balustrades and galleries surrounded the pools.* That there was a place called Bethesda with a pool(s) in Jerusalem at Jesus' time is confirmed in the Hebrew text of the early first-century A.D. Qumran* copper scroll (3Q15, *DJD*, 3.297). Further first-century evidence are the remains of Roman columns and capital fragments and a Hebrew graffito* found there. That Bethesda's geographical location N of the temple area is correct is supported by the remains of a fifth-century church built over the pool but later destroyed by the Persians (A.D. 614). The Crusaders built a new basilica* of St. Anne to the E of the pools which, after subsequent Moslem use, was restored in modern times by the Catholic church. The Crusaders ran a stairway

down into the ancient Roman cistern which is the way to the cistern today.

The Pool of Siloam* (cf. 2 Kings 20:20; John 9:1–7), located at the SE of the city just below Ophel Hill was the reservoir into which the water flowed through Hezekiah's tunnel* (2 Chron 32:30) from the Spring of Gihon.* Just above the present Pool of Siloam in a 1913–14 excavation R. Weill discovered the remains of a bastion tower, 10 m. (33 ft.) wide and about 13 m. (43 ft.) long, evidently the tower spoken of in Christ's day (Luke 13:4). Later a Byzantine* domed basilica was built above Siloam (cf. Anonymous of Piacenza, A.D. 570, *CCSL*, 175.166, and the Madaba Mosaic* Map). This basilica had a nave and side aisles, according to the 1897 excavations of F. J. Bliss and A. C. Dickie, confirmed also by K. Kenyon in her excavations in the 1960s at Jerusalem. She indicates that there was preserved there a fine inscribed mosaic.

The Walls of Jerusalem: The question of the walls of Jerusalem existent at the time of Christ and the first century A.D. is related to the location of the crucifixion* and burial place of Jesus.

The First Wall. The First Wall, called by Josephus the "most ancient" wall (Jos. *War* 5.142) seems, in the light of his description, to have been in existence up to and including Josephus's own day. This Jewish historian seems to think that this wall goes back in part to at least the time of David and Solomon* and their successors, although Kenyon thinks that its northern extremity was of Maccabean origin.

There is general acceptance, though without conclusive evidence, that the first "old" wall crossed the Tyropoeon Valley from the Herodian Citadel on the W to the temple platform on the E in a line approximately that of the present E-W David Street.

This corresponds to Josephus's statements (Jos. *War* 5.143–45) that the First Wall began on the N at the Hippicus Tower and extended E to terminate with the temple's western porch. On the S Josephus says the First Wall went down and then E above the Pool of Siloam to the E porch of the temple.

Thus, it is to be observed according to the requirements of Heb 13:12 ("without the gate"), that since both the Church of the Holy Sepulcher* or Gordon's Calvary and Garden Tomb (*see* GETHSEMANE) are outside the First Wall, either place could have been the site of the crucifixion and burial of Christ.

The Third Wall. The southern extremity of the Third Wall of Jerusalem has been shown by excavations in 1961 to have encircled the southern end of the western ridge of the Jerusalem complex but not before the first century A.D., according to Kathleen Kenyon. Her map of this time not only shows a trace of a post-Exilic wall running S beyond Siloam, but also a part of a wall and gate of Agrippa's time located below Siloam at a point near the joining of the Hinnom and Kidron valleys. However, N. Avigad in excavations in the Jerusalem Jewish Quarter in 1970 and 1971 has found evidence of a new wall on the eastern edge of the western ridge which goes back to the eighth century B.C. and may well argue for a wall connecting the eastern and western ridges on the S in OT times. If such a southern wall was rebuilt by Herod Agrippa I (A.D. 37–44), it was no doubt destroyed by the Romans at A.D. 70, as is indicated by the stratigraphical* evidence pointed out by Kenyon.

As to its northern extremity, the Third Wall has been argued to have been in line approximately with the present N wall of the Old City, but it has also been argued that it ran farther N and is to be connected with wall remains in the vicinity of the Albright Institute of Archaeological Research. M. Avi-Yonah thinks that this "outer" wall, remains of which were excavated by Sukenik and Mayer in 1925–27, is the Third Wall planned by Herod Agrippa I. Kenyon disagrees because the visible portions of that "outer" wall seem to face S, which would fit Titus's siege wall (Jos. War 5.491–511) which he used as he faced Agrippa's Third Wall to the S. Sara ben-Aryeh in 1972 excavated again along this outer wall and uncovered substructures of the wall with shards* of the Herodian period and remains of a tower that bulged northward some 9 m. (30 ft.) for a length of 45 m. (148 ft.) between the Nablus Road and the Road of the Engineering Corps. The wall was about 4 m. (14 ft.) wide. She and B. Mazar of the Temple Mount Excavations also think that this was Josephus's Third Wall.

Kenyon holds a commonly held view, namely, that the Third Wall of Herod Agrippa I is that wall approximately in line with the N wall of the present Old City. She maintains this view because of portions of Herodian masonry found near the Damascus Gate. J. B. Hennessy, in excavating at the Damascus Gate in 1964–66, found also a coin* there of A.D. 42–43. He argues that the wall there is part of Herod Agrippa's Third Wall never finished by him and that the gate complex there certainly seems to have been reconstructed and incorporated into Hadrian's version of Jerusalem, Aelia Capitolina.*

Josephus (Jos. War 5.147–51) describes the northern course of this Third Wall as going N from the Tower Hippicus (the area of the present-day Citadel) and then E below the Helena monuments (the so-called "Tombs of the Kings") through the royal caverns (of Solomon's Quarry) and over to the Kidron Valley. This also corresponds closely with the course of the present N wall.

The Second Wall. Josephus states that the Second Wall started from the Gennath (Garden) Gate in the First Wall and, enclosing only the northern district of the town, went up as far as Antonia (Jos. War 5.146). At one other place (Jos. War 5.158) Josephus remarks that the Second Wall, which he now calls "the middle wall," had fourteen towers (presumably, from what he says, they were at 200-cubit [300-foot] intervals). The conclusion is that Josephus's Second Wall ran a relatively short distance.

Apart from the mention of Josephus, the Gennath Gate is unknown. It does not seem to have been located at Herod's towers, for Josephus does not mention the towers with the Second Wall as he does in describing the First and Third Walls. So the Gennath Gate must have been located farther E in the First Wall which ran along the line of the present David Street. Josephus says the Second Wall started N from this gate.

In her excavations at Site C, located directly S of the Church of the Holy Sepulcher and N of the old First Wall, Kenyon has shown that this area was outside the city wall until the second century A.D. This is seen by evidence of a quarrying in the rock bed there over which was put a fill of dirt. This dirt fill contained enough seventh-century B.C. and first-century A.D. pottery* and enough second-century A.D. pottery to suggest that the fill was put there after the time of Christ by Hadrian* in A.D. 135. Kenyon states, "It can therefore be said confidently that the area was a quarry,* outside the town walls in the seventh cent. B.C. and remained outside them until the second cent. A.D."

Kenyon then observes that though the exact location of the Gennath Gate and the northern run of the Second Wall are not known, the evidence of the quarry and pottery of Site C argues that the Gennath Gate was in the center of the First Wall and that the Second Wall thus extended N from the Gennath Gate just E of the quarry and the present site of the Church of the Holy Sepulcher. The area of the Church of the Holy Sepulcher was, therefore, "without the gate" in Jesus' day.

Kenyon's projected location of Josephus's Second Wall may fit in with the findings of N. Avigad in his excavations on a new wall in the nearby vicinity of the Jewish Quarter, a new wall which goes back to the eighth century B.C., but may have continued to A.D. 70. So argues Ruth Amiran, but M. Avi-Yonah doubts it.

Location of Calvary and the Tomb of Jesus. Two alternate views present themselves as to the location of Calvary and the tomb of Jesus.

Gordon's Calvary and the Garden Tomb, which have been suggested as the site, are located a short distance N of the present Damascus Gate and just E of Nablus Road.

As to location, Gordon's Calvary fits the biblical requirements of being outside the gate. Although the side of the hill looks like the face of a skull (see GOLGATHA) this may be due to man-made cuttings in the hill. The biblical reference to Calvary as the place of a skull (Matt 27:33 et al.) may mean that it was shaped like a skull, or simply that skulls of crucified criminals could be found there.

The nearby rock-hewn Garden Tomb, though aesthetically satisfying, is not of the first century A.D. It contains a Byzantine* (fourth to sixth centuries A.D.) trough-type burial place, and two Byzantine crosses were found painted on one wall.

A second main view posits the Church of the Holy Sepulcher as the site for Calvary and the tomb, a view that is almost certainly correct. It has already been seen that quarry Site C and the nearby area on which the Church of the Holy Sepulcher was to be built were, in the days of Jesus, located to the W and outside of Josephus's Second Wall, though later

The two domes of Church of the Holy Sepulcher. Courtesy Keren Hayesod United Israel Appeal, Photo Archives.

enclosed by Agrippa's Third Wall.

In addition to this evidence, the presence of the church of ancient Jewish tombs called the Tomb of Joseph of Arimathea situated on the west edge of the Rotunda argues for the area at that time being outside the city walls. Certainly a cemetery would not be located within the city walls. Further, the presence of tombs agrees with the biblical statement of John 19:41, which indicates the close proximity of the tomb to Calvary, a requirement which is fulfilled by the large hill of rock which the church also encloses. Early Christian tradition in the witness of Jerome, Eusebius, and others, also bears testimony to this church being the site of the cross and tomb.

It was evidently this strong tradition that persuaded Queen Helena, along with Constantine, to locate the Church of the Holy Sepulcher in the early fourth century A.D. on this very site. In contrast to Heb 13:12, the site was then within the walls of the city—something they would not have known was not true in the time of Christ. In 1976 excavations conducted by Dr. Christos Katsimbinis in the Church of the Holy Sepulcher uncovered a 10.5 m (35 ft.) high mound of grey rock containing two small caves which gave it a skull-shaped appearance. This hill, which is claimed as the genuine Calvary, would have been located just outside the N wall of Jerusalem in Christ's time, standing in a corner where the wall formed an angle.

The archaeological and literary evidence thus points to the Church of the Holy Sepulcher as the authentic site of Calvary and the tomb of Jesus.

The Pavement. The location of the Praetorium (Matt 27:27 et al.) and the pavement (see GABBATHA) (John 19:13) where Pilate judged Jesus has been argued as being either at the tower of Herod's Palace at the W wall of the city, or at the Antonia,* on the NW corner of the temple area.

Magen Broshi, excavator in 1971 at the area of Herod's palace, believes the square that was in front of the palace was the place of the Praetorium.

Finegan argues quite effectively for the fortress palace of Antonia on the basis of its large paved courtyard of striated stones (cf. the pavement of John 19:13) and on Josephus's testimony (Jos. *War* 5.244;

2. 224–27; Jos. *Antiq.* 20.106–12) that a Roman cohort was permanently stationed there and military precautions were taken in that area at festival times. Such a place for the Roman governor's military force would be logical in case of upheaval at the temple area (cf. Acts 21:30–37).

At any rate, whether the pavement and Praetorium are to be located at the Antonia or Herod's towers, the distance for Christ to have gone to Calvary at the Church of the Holy Sepulcher would not have been too great.

The Via Dolorosa. Although the traditional and modern Via Dolorosa with its fourteen stations of the cross, project quite definitely the route Jesus took to Calvary, Scripture does not tell us the way He went. It only says He was led off to be crucified and that they came to Golgotha, the place of the skull (cf. Matt 27:31–33 et al.).

BIBLIOGRAPHY: F. J. Bliss and A. C. Dickie, *Excavations at Jerusalem, 1894–1897* (1898), 178–210; G. Dalman, *Sacred Sites and Ways* (1935), 250–310; A. Parrot, *Golgotha and the Church of the Holy Sepulcher* (1957); FLAP (1963), 315–30; ibid., *The Archaeology of the NT* (1969), 109–76; K. Kenyon, *Jerusalem* (1967); B. Mazar, *The Excavations in the Old City of Jerusalem* (1969); N. Avigad, "Excavations in the Jewish Quarter, 1970, 1972," *IEJ*, 20, nos. 3–4 (1970), 134–35; ibid., 22, no. 4 (1972), 193–95; J. B. Hennessy, "Preliminary Report on Excavations at the Damascus Gate, Jerusalem, 1964–66," *Levant*, 2 (1970), 22–24; R. Amiran, "The First and Second Walls of Jerusalem Reconsidered in the Light of the New Wall," *IEJ*, 21, nos. 2–3 (1971), 166, 167; M. Avi-Yonah, "The Newly Found Wall of Jerusalem and Its Topographical Significance," *IEJ*, 21, nos. 2–3 (1971), 168, 169; E. Hoade, *Guide to the Holy Land* (1973), 109–454; K. Kenyon, *Digging up Jerusalem* (1974), 273, 274; B. Mazar, *The Mountain of the Lord* (1975), 82–84; J. Wilkinson, "The Church of the Holy Sepulchre," *Archaeology*, vol. 31, no. 4 (1978), 6-13.

WHM

JERUSALEM, OLD TESTAMENT. The place known today as Jerusalem is situated on the central Palestinian plateau. It is a little over 32 km. (20 mi.) W of the N end of the Dead Sea,* and more than 48 km. (30 mi.) E of the Mediterranean Sea. The altitude of the present city* is about 762 m. (2500 ft.) above sea level, but the plateau is very uneven, and the earliest settlement was actually on the lowest of the hills in the immediate vicinity.

In antiquity the plateau was carved up even more deeply than at present by valleys and ravines, some of which have been filled in by debris over the centuries. To the E lay the Kidron Valley,* while to the W and S ran the Valley of Hinnom* (Wadi al-Rababi). A third valley traversed the site from a northerly to a southerly direction, making for two unequal parts.

From excavations in the Valley of Rephaim, located to the W and SW of Jerusalem, it would appear that the earliest movements of peoples in the area can be traced back to prehistoric times. Flints, arrowheads, and scrapers from the Paleolithic* and Neolithic* periods have been recovered and shown to have been of indigenous origin. Occupation of the area later to be known as Jerusalem commenced toward the end of the fourth millennium B.C. with a settlement on the narrow upland section located SE of the area subsequently named Ophel. The choice of this site was obviously dictated by the need for water, for below the hill on the W edge of the Kidron Valley was the Spring of Gihon* (1 Kings 1:33). Nearly 910 m. (1000 yds.) further S was another spring, known in the OT as En Rogel (2 Sam 17:17), which combined with Gihon would ensure an adequate water supply for the primitive settlers. Another important consideration, the defense of the site, would have been accomplished quite readily by the simple expedient of erecting a stone wall across the narrow N end of the promontory. These earliest inhabitants of the site were evidently Semites, and some of their rough metal implements and crude pottery* have been unearthed by excavators.

In the third millennium B.C. some settlers lived in a cave* in the area later known as Mount Zion. The pottery they left behind has been assigned to Early Bronze Age I,* and traces of defensive walls of the same general age have also been discovered in the locality. At the southern extremity of the hill, archaeologists discovered a stairway hewn out of the rock. The fact that it has proved difficult to associate any other local structures with the period of its construction may well indicate that the stairway represents the very first attempts by the primitive settlers to establish some means of defense. Toward the end of the third millennium B.C. the occupants of the area as a whole seem to have begun a process of expansion northward, and in the second millennium B.C., in the Middle Bronze Age, walls were continued along the E border of the Ophel area.

From 1961 onward, Kathleen Kenyon excavated the Middle Bronze Age II city wall, which had been built about 49 m. (160 ft.) below the top of the ridge, apparently to protect the water supply of the Spring of Gihon. By this period (c. 1800 B.C.), if not earlier, the pre-Israelite inhabitants of the site had excavated a horizontal tunnel which tapped the spring and allowed the water to flow back into the settlement. There a shaft had been sunk for the convenience of the settlers, and it was this structure that Warren discovered in 1867.

What are perhaps even earlier attempts to divert the spring water consisted of two surface canals discovered on the E slope. An even more primitive canal, dating almost certainly from the third millennium B.C., consisted of a short trench about 1.5 m. (5 ft.) deep which drew the spring water into a hollow in the rock. All these structures indicate the concern which the early settlers had for maintaining adequate supplies of water for personal and irrigation* purposes. Precisely how the W edge of the pre-Israelite city was fortified has yet to be determined, but the remains of a large gate* found on the NW area of the hill may have marked an access point to the

settlement through a defensive wall. The gate seems to have been Late Bronze Age in origin, and thus of Jebusite* construction.

The Middle Bronze Age was almost certainly the period in which Abraham encountered the Mesopotamian* coalition which invaded Palestine under Chedorlaomer (Gen 14). Consequently, it has been thought that the "Salem" of Gen 14:18 is to be identified with Jerusalem. However, there are a number of considerations which merit caution on this whole matter. Until the discovery in 1976 of the Eblaite texts from Syria, in which the reference to Jerusalem (U-ru-sa-li-ma) antedated other allusions to this ancient site by at least five hundred years, the first mention of the site by name was in the nineteenth-to-eighteenth-century B.C. Egyptian Execration Texts* from Luxor* in the approximate form Urushalimma. This name most probably meant "the foundation of Shalem," i.e., the center of worship of the pagan deity Shalem ("completion"), who, with his twin Shahar ("day star") is known from texts recovered from Ras Shamra (Ugarit*). Shalem, the evening manifestation of the Venus star, was evidently the deity worshiped by the pre-Israelite population of the area. In the fourteenth-century B.C. Tell el-Amarna tablets (see AMARNA LETTERS) the settlement was called Urusalim but was also known under the form Beth-Shalem, which again drew attention to the local deity and his cultic center.

If the place mentioned in Gen 14:18 is to be identified with the Shalem mentioned above, it is not particularly easy to see, firstly, how the name could have been Hebrew in origin, and secondly, how the Middle Bronze Age king of the pre-Israelite city of Shalem could have been such an outstanding priest of the most high God as to have had his spirituality perpetuated into NT times (Heb 5:6; 7:1 et al.)—especially if the Jebusites came from Amorite* stock (cf. Gen 10:16). If, however, the "Salem" of Gen 14:18 is not to be identified with Shalem, but instead with the well-watered region of Salim, which witnessed in a much later age the activities of John the Baptist (John 3:23), it could well have been located E of Jordan in the area known in NT times as Perea.* This is supported by the statement that it was the king of Sodom* who went out to meet Abraham at the Valley of Shaveh, which suggests a location in the Jordan Valley rather than in the central plateau region. The story of a subsequent visit of Abraham to the area (Gen 22:1–19) described his journey to one of the mountains "in the land of Moriah,*" but whether "Moriah" is a genuine place-name, or a corruption of "Amorite," as the Syriac version implies, is open to some doubt.

The prosperous Middle Bronze Age II phase of Palestinian life yielded some ground to the Hurrians* (Horites), who entered Palestine about the Late Bronze Age I period. This occurred at the beginning of the Amarna* Age, when Egypt* dominated the Near East, and at a time when Jerusalem was little more than a fortified outpost in the central Palestinian plateau. The entire region was under Egyptian political and military control, and a fourteenth-century B.C. vassal-ruler of Jerusalem named Abdi-

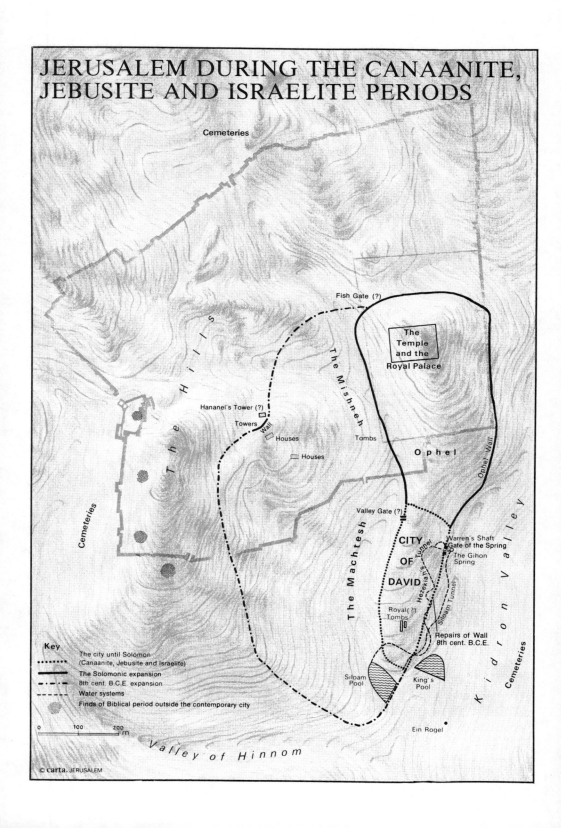

JERUSALEM DURING THE CANAANITE, JEBUSITE AND ISRAELITE PERIODS

Cemeteries

Fish Gate (?)

The Temple and the Royal Palace

The Hills

The Mishneh

Hananel's Tower (?)

Towers

Wall

Houses

Tombs

Houses

Ophel

Ophel Wall

Cemeteries

Valley Gate (?)

CITY

OF

DAVID

The Machtesh

Warren's Shaft
Gate of the Spring

The Gihon Spring

Hezekiah's Tunnel

Siloam Tunnel

Royal (?) Tombs

Repairs of Wall
8th cent. B.C.E.

Kidron Valley

Cemeteries

Siloam Pool

King's Pool

Ein Rogel

Key

⋯⋯ The city until Solomon
(Canaanite, Jebusite and Israelite)

—— The Solomonic expansion

—·— 8th cent. B.C.E. expansion

--- Water systems

Finds of Biblical period outside the contemporary city

0   100   200
m

Valley of Hinnom

© **carta**. JERUSALEM

City of Jerusalem: (1) Dome of the Rock, (2) Al-Aqsa mosque, (3) remains of Umayyad structures from Mazar's excavation at southwestern wall of Temple Mount, (4) excavations by Mazar of southern wall of Temple Mount, (5) "Ophel Wall" excavation by Charles W. Warren, 1867-70, (6) The segment of wall named the "Jebusite Bastion" by its discoverer, Macalister (1925), and later restudied by K. M. Kenyon—probably a part of Jerusalem's fortifications from the fifth century B.C. to A.D. 70. (7) Gihon spring. (8) Siloam pool. The City of David and the Ophel were located on the southeastern ridge below the Temple Mount. Photo: Werner Braun, Jerusalem.

Hiba, who was doubtless of Hurrian ancestry, wrote certain of the celebrated Amarna letters to Egypt, requesting military aid against the marauding Habiru.* Excavations have shown that the Hurrians constructed a strong defensive rampart on the E slope of Ophel, and another similar structure to the S. As with earlier inhabitants, they too were concerned to safeguard their water supplies, and early in the Late Bronze Age they cut several tunnels and conduits into the rock to divert the waters of Gihon.

With the decline in Egyptian power at the end of the Amarna Age came increasing independence for Jerusalem and other Palestinian vassal-states. By this time the control of Jerusalem had passed into indigenous Jebusite hands, and in the days of Joshua its ruler allied with four other kings in an attack on Gibeon* (Josh 10:1–5). Even though the king of Jerusalem, Adoni-zedek, was killed, his city was not captured (Josh 10:6–43), although it was allotted to Benjamin when Palestine was divided among the tribes (Josh 18:28). Jerusalem's independence survived throughout the Judges' period (cf. Judg 19:10–12) but terminated when David captured the apparently impregnable Jebusite stronghold of Zion (2 Sam 5:6–7; 1 Chron 11:4–6).

In the OT the name "Jebus" was used to designate the pre-Israelite phase of occupation, as indicated in the MT of Josh 18:28, "the Jebusi, which is in Jerusalem." The means by which David gained access to this heavily protected mountain fortress have occasioned some debate among scholars. The mention of a ṣinnôr or "water shaft" (2 Sam 5:8 RSV; "watercourse" RV; "gutter" KJV) led to the belief that David's men had entered the city via the shaft discovered by Warren, but Albright showed that the term ṣinnôr was a Canaanite* word meaning a grappling iron (so NEB) or hook, thus implying that the conquering Israelites actually scaled the walls to conquer Jebus. Discussion has also centered on the question as to whether or not the "stronghold of Zion" was actually the same as Jerusalem. Current archaeological opinion mostly regards Zion as referring originally to the Jebusite-fortified SE ridge area and takes Jerusalem as a description of the environs as a whole.

Davidic occupational remains have not been easy to identify, partly because of the reuse in later periods of suitable building materials. However, it seems probable that in repairing the city (2 Sam 5:9) David rebuilt the terraces constructed in the fourteenth century B.C. on the E slopes of the hill as a means of enlarging the original site. The Millo ("Filling") which David undertook was apparently part of his repair work also, and alludes to an area of land, or of a breached wall, which was filled in. The Kenyon excavations of 1964 uncovered a strong retaining wall on Ophel in the neighborhood of the Amarna-Age terraces, and if it is Davidic in origin, as seems probable, it would constitute a portion, if not all, of the Millo.

David's residence was established within the perimeter of the city after its capture, and its location (2 Sam 5:11; 1 Chron 14:1; cf. Neh 12:37) seems to have been at the S end of Ophel on the E side. The Davidic mausoleum was also in the same area and

according to 1 Kings 2:10ff. housed the king's remains and those of a dozen of his successors. This portion of the City of David was excavated by Raymond Weill, but although several tombs were uncovered, the locality had already suffered heavily at the hands of Roman stonecutters, making attempts at identification of individual tombs impossible.

Iron Age II* occupational levels N of the Jebusite defensive N wall indicate that Solomon* enlarged David's city by extending the NE wall further N above the Kidron Valley,* and it was probably here that the royal "upper house" (Neh 3:25) was constructed, along with other buildings, as part of the temple* complex (cf. 1 Kings 3:1; 7:1). Excavations along the E crest of the ridge overlooking the Spring of Gihon uncovered a massive wall which ran S from the N limit of David's city. Dated in the early monarchy, this structure may have formed an inner wall protecting some of the royal buildings.

The temple, Solomon's outstanding constructional achievement, was built on the site of Araunah's threshing floor, and in design was a typically Phoenician* edifice. The ground plan (1 Kings 6:2ff.) is very similar to that of an eighth-century B.C. chapel excavated at Tell Tainat* in Syria, which comprised a rectangular structure with three rooms leading from a portico fronted by two columns. The inner shrine (cella*) had a raised platform, and the entire structure was most probably lined with cedar* planks. Examples of the proto-aeolic pilaster capital* used in the temple have been recovered from eleventh-century B.C. levels at Shechem,* Megiddo,* and Samaria,* to supplement the one found below the ridge overlooking the Spring of Gihon.

Any constructional traces of the Solomonic Temple have long since been obliterated by the enormous structures raised on the site by Herod the Great (see HEROD, BUILDING ACTIVITIES OF), and the most that archaeologists can do nowadays is to uncover the Herodian masonry to the S and W of the temple mount. Equally disappointing is any attempt to locate the irrigation pools credited to Solomon (Eccl 2:6), though certain sites above the mount of the Tyropoeon Valley and the lower end of the SE hill above Gihon have been suggested. Nor do there appear to be any traces of the numerous pagan altars* which Solomon built for his foreign wives, unless a structure uncovered at ninth-century B.C. levels in an area N of Gihon represents one such altar.

Excavations at Iron Age II levels still have to locate accurately certain constructions mentioned in the OT. The conduit of the Upper Pool (Isa 7:3; 36:2) was obviously close to an adequate water supply, but whether that was Gihon or En Rogel has not been determined. The Upper Pool may have been a large underground reservoir which was replaced by the Pool of Siloam* in the days of Hezekiah (see HEZEKIAH'S TUNNEL). This celebrated structure, first discovered in 1880, was an attempt to strengthen Jerusalem against a siege by Sennacherib* about 701 B.C. by bringing the waters of Gihon into the SE corner of the city (2 Kings 20:20; 2 Chron 32:30).

The conduit was excavated through solid rock for nearly 546 m. (600 yds.), the workmen laboring hurriedly from opposite ends and meeting in the middle. An inscription (*see* SILOAM INSCRIPTION) on the right-hand wall some 6 m. (20 ft.) in from the Siloam entrance was written in eighth-century B.C. Hebrew script (c. 701 B.C.) to commemorate the achievement. Needless to say, this rare specimen of pre-Exilic Hebrew writing* is of great value to the palaeographer.*

What may have been the remains of an Iron Age II irrigation system linked to the modern Birket el-Hamra near the opening of the central valley has been discovered, though the dam which blocked the valley's mouth has still to be located and excavated. The "two walls" which contained a reservoir (Isa 22:11) and a gate (Jer 52:7f.) were probably part of this general structure, though this is uncertain, as is also the topography of the city walls built by Hezekiah and Manasseh* (2 Chron 32:5; 33:14).

Under Nehemiah the city was expanded to the W, and the wall which he built most probably coincided with the boundaries of Jerusalem as they existed in the subsequent Hellenistic age. The descriptions of his wall are topographical, and archaeologists have experienced difficulty in delineating the structure accurately. Where the wall departed from recognizable Iron Age foundations it was built on ground which contained no previous sedentary traces. Although many elements of Nehemiah's wall are extremely difficult to identify, it is thought that the lowest levels of the celebrated Wailing Wall* come from his period. Another part of Nehemiah's structure ran along the crest of the ridge above the slopes of the Kidron Valley, and here, at the S peak of the ridge, was most probably the staircase of the city of David (Neh 12:37). It led from the top of the ridge to the valley, where there was a gate. The lower reaches of the stairway were traversed by one of the Iron Age conduits, indicating that the stairway may well have been constructed in the early monarchy.

In the Maccabean* and Hasmonean periods the city plundered by Antiochus IV (1 Macc 1:29ff.) and his successors (1 Macc 9:54) was rebuilt and extended (1 Macc 10:11; 12:36f.; 13:10), paving the way for further work under the Herods.

BIBLIOGRAPHY: R. Weill, *La Cité de David*, 1 (1920); J. Simons, *Jerusalem in the OT* (1952); L.-H. Vincent, *Jérusalem de l'Ancien Testament* (1954); R. Amiran, *The Ancient Pottery of Eretz Yisral* (1963); K. Kenyon, *BA*, 27 (1964), 34–52; id., *Jerusalem: Excavating 3000 Years of History* (1967); *CAH*, 1, Part 1, 531, 534–35; ibid., Part 2, 211, 231, 509, 555.

RKH

JESUS, LIKENESS OF. The human appearance of Jesus has always been a matter of speculation, and a long, but not necessarily reliable, tradition may be traced from the art of the catacombs* to the spurious letter of Publius Lentulus. This document, written in passable Latin,* first appeared around the fourteenth century. It purported to be a report of one Publius Lentulus, a Roman officer in Judah* in the time of Christ. It is without authority and derives rather from the representations of the Lord in later

Roman-Christian art after the severer philosophic type became prevalent.

In the rough art of the catacombs, Jesus is represented variously as the Good Shepherd, opening the eyes of the blind, healing the woman with the issue of blood, and blessing a child. He is invariably shown youthful and beardless and, as far as one can be dogmatic about art so simple, of gentle and benign expression.

Some of the great men of the past built a tradition of ignoble appearance, uncomeliness, and ugliness. Justin Martyr, Tertullian, Clement, Origen, and Basil agree in this tradition—again, with no shadow of authority save Isa 52. Jerome, on the other hand, with another patristic group, following the Song of Songs and some prophetic psalms, argued for a quite contrary tradition of comeliness. Chrysostom, Gregory of Nyssa, Ambrose, and Augustine were at one in this view.

No authentic portrait of Christ was cited by them, though Eusebius said that he had seen portraits of Jesus, Peter, and Paul. How reliable such portraits in the third century might be can be judged from the fact that the same Eusebius does not dismiss entirely a tradition that a statue* said to stand at Caesarea Philippi* bore "the likeness of Jesus." It is more likely to have been Vespasian* or Hadrian,* if such a statue existed, with the supplicant province, in the form of a woman, bowed before him. Imagination read into it the story from Luke.

The oldest surviving likeness is one in imitation of mosaic* and removed to the Vatican Museum from the Catacomb of St. Callixtus. It is probably from the fourth century—as far removed from genuine memory as we are from Shakespeare. The mosaic portrays a smooth-browed adult with long brown hair, large thoughtful eyes, long narrow nose, and serene countenance. The spurious Lentulus's epistle may have derived much from it.

In the Catacomb of Sts. Nereus and Achilles, the head and bust of Christ form a medallion in the vaulted ceiling, reflecting the early Christian practice of covering the faces of the dead with a handkerchief bearing the likeness of Christ. Thomas Heaphy, who spent a lifetime searching for such portraiture, believed that this representation was early second century, but it is not clear upon what arguments he based this claim, except that the position suggests that the catacombs were still used for burial. Domitilla's husband, the consul Flavius Clemens, was put to death just before Domitian* died, in A.D. 95, and Nereus and Achilles were her chamberlains, but it is impossible to claim that the likeness approaches living memory.

The early Christians probably had a deep inhibition against all such portraiture, and the fact that the Emperor Alexander Severus had images of Christ along with those of Abraham and Orpheus in his household lararium is indication enough that the fear was justified.

Representation in portrait and mosaic became common enough with the coming of the church buildings and basilicas,* but they have no historical value. There is a mosaic picture of Christ dating back to the fourth or fifth century and dug up on a villa site at Hinton St. Mary, in Dorset. At least, a male portrait is associated in the design with the Chi-Rho* sign. The portrait adds nothing to knowledge.

We must only conclude that we know nothing from art, archaeology, or description of the appearance of Christ. The fact that Suetonius describes in his *Lives of the Caesars*, the appearance of emperors a century before his time, opens the remote possibility that the Catacomb of Sts. Nereus and Achilles could just possibly have retained a thread of memory.

BIBLIOGRAPHY: C. C. Dobson, *The Face of Christ* (1933).

EMB

JEW. Originally, a member of the southern kingdom, or the tribe of Judah;* later, of the nation of Israel* as distinct from Gentiles.

In pre-Exilic (*see* EXILE, JUDEAN) times the normal term applied to Judeans, as distinct from Ephraimites or Israelites, is "men of Judah." The term "Jew" or "Jews" is not used biblically until 2 Kings 16:6 (where RSV still reads "men of Judah"), but the term becomes commonplace in post-Exilic literature. In extra-biblical records, Hezekiah (c. 700 B.C.) is called by Sennacherib* a Jew (ᵃᵐᵉˡIa-u-da-ai) in his Assyrian Annals. Later the term was to become common, both in Jewish records (cf. *ANET*, 491f.) and in the literature of their neighbors. Whether it referred primarily to a religious community or to the descendants of the exiles is a question only a modern man could ask. From NT times it has been the standard designation for all Israelites.

BIBLIOGRAPHY: J. Jocz, *ZPEB*, 3 (1975), 585–86.

CEA

JEWELS. *See* MINING.

JEZEBEL. The wife of Ahab* and daughter of Ethbaal, priest-king of Tyre* and Sidon.* Her marriage was a political contract whereby Israel* hoped to calm the hostility of Damascus.* As a personal favor, Jezebel was permitted to retain her own religion, the worship of Baal,* together with her attendant prophets numbering many hundreds. A battle for religious supremacy between the god of the Hebrews and the worshippers of Baal ensued, culminating in the incident on Mount Carmel* (1 Kings 18:17–40). Throughout her life Jezebel remained in constant conflict with Elijah.

Her unscrupulous use of Ahab's seal which resulted in the death of Naboth showed that she stopped at nothing to achieve her ends. A woman of strong character, Jezebel was a divisive, undermining influence in the kingdom of Israel, and when her power was finally overthrown ten years after Ahab's death, she dressed herself regally, painted her face, and looked out of a window. This final act, unseemly in biblical times, could have been expected only from a prostitute. Jezebel was thrown from her palace to the feet of Jehu, who trampled her to death beneath his horse's hoofs. Subsequently there were few remains left for burial, fulfilling Elijah's prophecy that the dogs* would eat her flesh. By NT times her name was already a byword (Rev 2:20). Ostraca* from the

ninth and seventh centuries B.C. found at Samaria* contain many names of which "Baal" is an element. This indicates the pervasive influence of the Baal worship which was introduced by Jezebel to the land of Israel. Of the many thousands of ivory* fragments recovered from Samaria, some are unquestionably from the "ivory house" (1 Kings 22:39) which Ahab built for his willful, fastidious queen.

BIBLIOGRAPHY: J. W. Crowfoot and K. Kenyon et al., *Samaria II, Early Ivories at Samaria* (1938); W. F. Albright, *Archaeology and the Religion of Israel* (1942), 160; G. F. Owen, *Archaeology of the Bible* (1961), 290–93.

HWP

JOPPA (jop'ə; Heb יָפוֹ, *yāpô'*; LXX Ἰόππη *Ioppē*, meaning "beautiful" or "beauty"). It was called *Yapu* in Egyptian and in Akkadian; in Arabic it is called *Yâfâ*, from which comes its modern name Jaffa. In the KJV the Hebrew is at one point (Josh 19:46) transliterated "Japho."

Joppa is a seaport located 56 km. (35 mi.) WNW of Jerusalem.* In view of the straight Palestinian coastline formed by the deposition of Nile silt even such an inadequate harbor as Joppa's, formed by a breakwater of rocks 90–120 m. (300–400 ft.) offshore, was important. Joppa's strategic importance was enhanced by its proximity to the Via Maris, the coastal highway between Egypt* and points N, and by the fact that it was the closest port to Jerusalem. The ancient citadel* of Joppa was situated on a small hill a little over 30 m. (100 ft.) high at the foot of which were some perennial springs.

Joppa was known to classical writers as the site where Andromeda was chained before her rescue by Perseus. Marcus Scaurus, Pompey's aide, was said to have brought back to Rome the 12-meter (40-ft.) bones of the monster which threatened Andromeda, and Pliny the Elder (Pliny *NH*, 5.14.69) reported that the people of Joppa could point out the rock where she had been chained!

1. *Biblical References*: Joppa was assigned to the tribe of Dan* (Josh 19:46), which was forced by the Philistines* to migrate N. It fell to the Israelites in the time of David. Both in the days of Solomon* (2 Chron 2:16) and in the days of Ezra (Ezra 3:7) cedar* logs were floated from Lebanon to the vicinity of Joppa, perhaps to the river port of Tell Qasile.* It was at Joppa that Jonah embarked on a Tarshish* vessel (Jonah 1:3) to flee from the Lord.

Joppa is quite prominent in the NT as the town of Tabitha, or Dorcas (Acts 9:36–42) and of Simon the tanner (Acts 9:43). It was on the roof of Simon's house,* which was by the sea (Acts 10:6–18), that Peter had his famous vision which heralded the entrance of Cornelius and other Gentiles into the church. The Church of St. Peter on the citadel of Joppa dates back to A.D. 1654. The little mosque near the lighthouse pointed out as the site of Simon's house dates from A.D. 1730.

2. *The History of Joppa in Extra-Biblical References*. Joppa was captured by Thutmose III (1490–1435 B.C.). The clever capture of the city by phar-

aoh's general, Thoth, who used an Ali Baba type of ruse, is celebrated in the Papyrus Harris 500 (*ANET*, 22–23). Joppa, whose prince was one of the hostages taken to the Egyptian court, appears twice in the fourteenth-century Amarna letters.* In the thirteenth-century satirical Papyrus Anastasi I (*ANET*, 478) Hori claims that a fair maid of Joppa made a fool of his rival.

When Sennacherib* invaded Palestine in 701, one of the cities which he captured was Joppa (*ANET*, 287). From the inscription of King Eshmunazar of Sidon,* discovered in 1855, we learn that c. 450 B.C. Joppa along with Dor* to the N came under the control of Sidon.

After Artaxerxes III destroyed Sidon in 351 B.C., Joppa enjoyed a very brief period of independence before falling prey to Alexander the Great. Under the Diadochi Joppa changed hands frequently. It was subject to the Ptolemies from 301 until 197 B.C., when it was seized by Antiochus III. In 146 B.C. Jonathan captured Joppa, and four years later his brother Simon forced the Greek inhabitants to leave the city. This victory provided the new Jewish state with a seaport (1 Macc 13:11, 14:5; Jos. *Antiq*. 13.6.4).

In 66 B.C. Pompey established Roman hegemony over Palestine. In 47 B.C. Caesar returned Joppa to the Jews.* Herod* the Great captured Joppa in 37 B.C. (Jos. *Antiq*. 14.15.1) to begin his campaign to establish his rule over Palestine. Herod's construction of a deeper port at Caesarea* severely undercut Joppa's importance.

The Jewish sources (Mishnah, Talmud, Tosefta) refer to a miracle which occurred at Joppa to preserve a bronze* gate* donated for the temple* at Jerusalem by Nicanor. In the course of a voyage from Alexandria, sailors threw overboard one of the gates to lighten the ship* during a storm. When the ship arrived at Joppa, the gate was found under the ship's keel.

Joppa played a key role during the First Jewish-Roman War. In A.D. 66 Cestius Gallus attacked the rebellious city and killed the population of 8,400 (Jos. *War* 2.18.10ff.). The Jews, however, reoccupied the city and used it as a base to harass the grain shipments from Egypt to Rome.* In A.D. 67 the Romans entered the city by surprise, forcing the inhabitants to take refuge in their ships. The N winds of a storm sank their ships; the bodies of 4,200 washed ashore (Jos. *War* 3.9.2–4). On the ruins of the city Vespasian* erected a fort called Flavia Joppa. The Flavian emperors celebrated the defeat of the small Jewish navy by issuing coins* with the inscriptions "Judaea Navalis" and "Victoria Navalis."

In the post-Roman period Joppa became the seat of a Christian bishop (*see* EPISKOPOS) in the fifth century A.D.

During the Crusades Joppa was once again the bone of contention between rival forces. Saladin took the city in 1187; Richard the Lion-Hearted captured it four years later. Napoleon conquered the city in 1799, and Allenby seized it from the Turks in 1917.

In the nineteenth century Jews began to settle in Jaffa, which remained largely Arab until the war of 1948 established Israel's independence. In 1909 Jews had begun to settle in the sand dunes N of Jaffa in an area which was eventually to become the flourishing city of Tel Aviv, to which Jaffa was affixed in 1950. By 1968 Jaffa was a town of 60,000 Jews and 6,500 Muslims and Christians.

3. *Excavations*. The incomplete written record of Joppa's long history has been supplemented recently by excavations. Prior to 1948 Arab houses covered the citadel area. The first excavations were conducted in 1948–50 by P. L. O. Guy for the Department of Antiquities. The same area was investigated by J. Bowman and B. Isserlin in 1952 for the University of Leeds. Since 1955 J. Kaplan has conducted over ten seasons of excavations for the Tel Aviv–Jaffa Museum in Area A in the eastern part of the citadel, in Area B in the vicinity of the Turkish Bath, and in Area C near the Church of St. Peter.

The Leeds expedition demonstrated that the ancient city did not cover the entire hill. Kaplan's work unveiled Hyksos* ramparts enclosing a great square. A topographical survey indicates that more than half of this square has been destroyed by shore erosion caused by the gradual sinking of the coastline.

Among Kaplan's most interesting discoveries is a thirteenth-century gate with an inscription of Ramses II uncovered in Level V of Area A. It is possible that the destruction of this level was the work of invading Sea Peoples.* In the succeeding Level IV the excavator uncovered the heavy bronze door hinge of the city gate. This level was burned c. 1230, perhaps by Meneptah.

There is some evidence of Philistine* shards* in an ash pit in Area A. Joppa was evidently under the control of Ashkelon* during the early Iron Age.*

Pre-Philistine temple, c. end of 13th century beginning of 12th century B.C., excavated at Joppa. The skull of a lion was found on the floor of the temple, suggesting the practice of a lion cult in the temple. Courtesy Israel Government Press Office.

From a temple of this stratum, excavated in 1971, comes a unique lion's* skull, perhaps once embalmed* for use in a cult.

Remains of the settlement of Joppa under Sidonian control from c. 450 B.C. include imports of Attic pottery.* A Phoenician inscription discovered at the end of the nineteenth century indicates that there was a Sidonian temple to the god Eshmun at Joppa. In 1970–71 a large building, perhaps a temple, of this period was uncovered.

From the Hellenistic period has emerged an agora* with a double row of shops. An inscription bearing the names of Ptolemy Philopator (221–204 B.C.) and his wife Berenice has been discovered. From the Maccabean (see MACCABEES) period has come a hoard of 851 coins of Alexander Jannaeus, dated c. 90–85 B.C.

Evidence of the destruction wrought in the First Jewish-Roman War has been uncovered. Three identical Greek inscriptions record that a certain Judah held the office of *agoranomos*, an inspector of weights and measures, under the Romans just before the Jewish revolt under Trajan in A.D. 115–17.

BIBLIOGRAPHY: F.-M. Abel, "Le littoral palestinien et ses ports," *RB*, 11 (1914), 556–90; S. Tolkowsky, *The Gateway of Palestine: A History of Jaffa* (1924); id., "The Destruction of the Jewish Navy at Jaffa in the Year 68 A.D.," *PEFQSt*, 60 (1928), 153–63; A. Kindler, "The Jaffa Hoard of Alexander Jannaeus," *IEJ*, 4 (1954), 170–85; J. Bowman et al., "Archaeological Expedition to Jaffa 1952," *Proceedings of the Leeds Philosophical Society*, VII (1955), 231–50; Y. Karmon, "Geographical Aspects in the History of the Coastal Plain of Israel," *IEJ*, 6 (1956), 33–50; J. Kaplan, *The Archaeology and History of Tel Aviv–Jaffa* (Heb., 1959); id., "The Fifth Season of the Excavation at Jaffa," *JQR, N.S.* 54 (1963), 110–14; id., "Jaffa's History Revealed by the Spade," *ARC*, 17 (1964), 270–76, reprinted in *Archaeological Discoveries in the Holy Land*, J. B. Pritchard, ed. (1967), 113–18; J. Kaplan, "The Archaeology and History of Tel Aviv–Jaffa," *BA*, 35 (1972), 66–95; J. L. Kelso, *ZPEB*, 3 (1975), 683–84.

EY

JOSEPH. The eleventh and favorite son of Jacob, his first by Rachel.

I. *General Period.* The beautiful and brilliantly told narrative of Joseph is intimately linked with the fortunes of the patriarchs who, on various grounds, can be referred to the earlier part of the second millennium B.C.. On the basis of a thirteenth-century B.C. date for the Exodus, the datum in Exod 12:40–41, 51, that Israel* left Egypt* 430 years after arriving there, it is reasonable to suggest c. 1700 B.C. as a round figure for Joseph's own arrival in Egypt. On Egyptian chronology as at present understood, the Eighteenth Dynasty began c. 1552 B.C., Ahmose I expelling the Hyksos* about his eleventh year, c. 1542 B.C. The 108 years of the Hyksos Fifteenth Dynasty thus began c. 1650 B.C., when it relegated the Thirteenth Dynasty to vassal status in Thebes.* On this basis, Joseph would have been sold into the Egypt of the late Thirteenth Dynasty and possibly have grown up to serve an early Hyksos pharaoh—but of course, there is no absolute certainty of this. However, culturally, it must be emphasized that late-Thirteenth-Dynasty Egypt had already a strong W Semitic element, including some pharaohs with Semitic names or reference (Khandjir; Ameny the Asiatic), and W Semites working in Egypt (cf. on Papyrus Brooklyn, below). And similarly, the Hyksos employed Egyptian officials, not only Semites. Thus, the Egypto-Semitic blend of the Joseph-narrative fits well into the late Thirteenth and early Fifteenth Dynasties alike; there is no great contrast here.

II. *Egyptian Background.* In general terms, ancient Egypt supplies a useful backcloth for Joseph. A. *Gen 37,39.* Apart from being well attested by Middle Bronze Age* remains, Shechem* is also mentioned in Egyptian documents of the Twelfth Dynasty (*ANET*, 230) and early Thirteenth Dynasty (*ANET*, 329, n.8). The twenty shekels of silver* (one-third mina) paid for Joseph is the correct average price for a slave* about the eighteenth century B.C. (cf. Code of Hammurabi,* 116,214,252; *ANET*, 170,175–76, etc.). When sold into Egypt, in the Late Middle Kingdom, Joseph was but one of many W Semites there then—witness the many "Asiatics" in Twelfth-Dynasty records (Posener), and especially the more than forty "Asiatic" servants in a large Egyptian household in distant Thebes c. 1750 B.C. in Papyrus Brooklyn 35.1446. Many of them bear good Semitic names comparable with, e.g., Menahem, Shipra(h), (J)acob, (Is)sachar, and so on. Then, like Joseph who was "in the house" of his master, several of these people were *hery-per*, i.e., domestic servants. As Joseph rose to be overseer of his master's house or estate, so one may compare the Egyptian *imy-r per*, or steward with this role. Potiphar in Hebrew is termed *sarîs*. Later this meant "eunuch," but in earlier days, as here, simply "dignitary," "official." And Potiphar's wife was not the only Egyptian adulteress in literature (Papyri Westcar, D'Orbiney). B. *Gen 40–44.* Butlers, or better, cupbearers,* are attested in most periods in Egypt. Papyrus Brooklyn, already cited, began as part of the register of criminals in the Great Prison at Thebes and illustrates Egyptian prison usage. Prisonkeepers are well attested. Dreams were always significant in the biblical Near East, which produced manuals of dream interpretation. An Egyptian manual is known from the thirteenth century B.C. (Papyrus Chester Beatty* III) but originating before Joseph's time. Egypt in antiquity was famed for her grainfields and (to Egyptians) notorious for famine when the Nile flood was inadequate; inscriptions attest both aspects. With the fine linen,* gold* collar, and royal signet ring given Joseph on investiture, one may compare the signet ring and fringed scarf(?) and gold collar received by, e.g., the Viceroy of Nubia,* Huy, at his investiture under Tutankhamen.* In the Late Middle Kingdom, evidence for horses* in the Nile Valley (Buhen) may be indirect evidence for the chariot* as a novelty in Egypt by Joseph's time. Like many Asiatics in Papyrus Brooklyn (and others in the New Kingdom, later), Joseph was given an Egyptian name; his wife's and father-in-law's names are also good Egyptian. C. *Gen 45–50.* That Joseph's family should be settled in the E Delta (Goshen*) and to keep the royal cattle fits well with known Egyptian internal colonization in the Delta, and with the preferred role of the Delta for keeping cattle (so also, King Kamose, sixteenth century B.C.—*ANET,* 232 and n.5). That the priests should have separate estates is consonant with usage. The embalming* of Jacob, and later Joseph, reflects Egypt's millennial-long custom of mummification.

BIBLIOGRAPHY: N. de G. Davies, *The Tomb of Huy* (1926), 11, pls.V–VI; W. C. Hayes, *A Papyrus of the Late Middle Kingdom in the Brooklyn Museum* (1955), cf. *ANET*[3], 553–54; W. F. Albright, *JAOS,* 74 (1954–55), 222–33; G. Posener, *Syria,* 34 (1957), 145–63; J. Vergote, *Joseph en Égypte . . .* (1959), cf. K. A. Kitchen, *The Joseph Narrative and Its Egyptian Study of the Biblical Story of Joseph* (1970); K. A. Kitchen, *The Joseph Narrative and Its Egyptian Background* (forthcoming).

JUDAH (JUDEA). The name by popular etymology meant "praised" (Gen 29:35). Judah was a son of Jacob and the eponymous* ancestor of the tribe of Judah.

Archaeological investigation of the earliest period in Judah is part of the larger quest for information as to the conquest and settlement of the Israelite tribes in Palestine. Attempts to correlate the data in Josh with Judg 1:1–21 and fix the whole in the context of archaeological findings from the area in question have remained speculative for want of a firm scheme for the overall picture. Excavation in Jerusalem has provided perhaps the clearest indication of a definite penetration of Judah that can be pegged chronologically.

Whether, as has been argued by A. Alt and others, Judah was originally and historically a separate entity must be largely determined on the ground of biblical rather than archaeological evidence.

After the division of the kingdom of Israel* following the death of Solomon,* Judah is both the dominant tribe in the S and the name by which the southern kingdom is known. Its relative isolation from the struggles of the great powers apparently accounts for the lack of mention of Judah in secular writings until the time of Ahaz (c. 740 B.C.), who was tribu-

tary to Tiglath-pileser III,* and his son Hezekiah, whose kingdom was attacked by Sennacherib,* c. 701 B.C. (*ANET,* 282,287f.). Archaeological evidence for the destruction of the kingdom in 586 B.C. comes from Jerusalem,* Lachish,* Tell Beit Mirsim,* and other sites.

The resettlement of Judah, beginning with the edict of Cyrus* the Persian in 538 B.C. concerning the restoration of the Jerusalem temple,* was a slow process. Results of excavation have yielded relatively little firm data on the period, and it is not until the third century that any density of population is recovered. Although during all of this period Judah is to be considered a province of the Persian Empire, both coins* and jar handles have been found with the inscription "Yehud" stamped on them. In 332 B.C. Judah, together with the rest of Palestine, passed under the control of Alexander the Great, and until the victories of the Maccabees* in the second century B.C. it was part of the Ptolemaic and Seleucid empires. Though relatively lacking in monumental evidence, Palestine has produced sufficient evidence to confirm the historical picture of extensive Hellenistic influence in Judah.

The Hasmonean period (165–37 B.C.), during which a succession of Maccabbean priest-kings restored the kingdom of Judah, is well-illustrated archaeologically, particularly from remains at Beth-zur, Gezer, and Marisa. The limits of Judean power were constantly altered as both Idumeans to the S and the ever-present Seleucids* strove with the renascent state for control of the land. In the spring of 63 B.C. the Roman power was invited into Judea to settle what had become a shameful civil strife, and the end of the kingdom of Judah was effectively reached, though the name and a form of Judean government persisted through the dynasty of Herod the Idumean (*see* HEROD, FAMILY OF) and a succession of Roman procurators until the final destruction of Jerusalem by the Romans in A.D. 70.

BIBLIOGRAPHY: H. H. Rowley, *From Joseph to Joshua* (1948); *ANET* (1955), 282, 287ff.; W. F. Albright, *The Archaeology of Palestine* (1960); Albrecht Alt, *Essays on OT History and Religion* (tr.1966), 133–260; K. M. Kenyon, *Jerusalem* (1967).

CEA

JUDAS MACCABAEUS. *See* MACCABEES.

JUDGMENT SEAT. *See* BEMA.

JUPITER. *See* ZEUS.

K

KADESH BARNEA (kā'desh bär nē'ə; Heb. קָדֵשׁ
בַּרְנֵעַ, *qaḏēš barnēa*). A site in the Negev* about
80 km. (50 mi.) SW of Beersheba,* and marked by
four springs ('Ain Qedeis, 'Ain el-Qudeirat, el-Qo-
seimeh, and el-Muweilah). 'Ain el-Qudeirat has been
suggested as the original Kadesh in preference to
'Ain Qedeis (which preserves the name Kadesh or
"holy") because it has a considerably larger water
supply.

The site was mentioned in Gen 14:7 as En Mishpat
("spring of judgment") in connection with the invasion of the Mesopotamian* alliance and its search for
minerals. Abraham stopped at Kadesh Barnea for
supplies in journeying to and from Egypt* (Gen 20:1),
and the theophany to Hagar occurred also in this
general vicinity (Gen 16:7–14). Kadesh Barnea was
an eleven-day journey from Mount Horeb, and in
the time of Moses it bordered Edomite* territory
(Num. 20:16). The site was notable for being the
departure point of the spies sent to Canaan* (Deut
1:20) and the subsequent rebellion against Moses.
For that act the Israelites were condemned to stay
in the wilderness for a generation, and much of that
time seems to have been spent near Kadesh Barnea.
Miriam died there (Num 20:1), and Aaron (*see*
AARON'S TOMB) also ended his life on nearby Mount
Hor (Num 20:23–29). In Numbers 34:4, Kadesh Barnea was located at the S end of Israel's* territory,
and was officially incorporated into the Promised Land
by Joshua (Josh 10:41), after which time it remained
unmentioned in Hebrew historical narratives.

No buildings from the Mosaic period have been
uncovered at Kadesh Barnea, although the area was
occupied from the Chalcolithic* and Early Bronze
ages.* The remains of a Judean fortress, first noticed
by Woolley and Lawrence, were excavated by Dothan and found to go back to about the ninth century B.C. The fortress walls were of casemate*
construction, and had eight defensive towers.* The
building was destroyed by Edomites, probably in the
fifth century B.C. Subsequently the area was occupied by Nabataeans.*

BIBLIOGRAPHY: C. L. Woolley and T. E. Lawrence, *The Wilderness of Zin* (1936 ed.); M. Dothan,
IEJ, 15 (1965), 135–51; J. L. Kelso, *ZPEB*, 3 (1975),
775–77.

RKH

KADESH (ON THE ORONTES) KAH. Also called
Kinza and Qizza (Amarna *qidsi*), it was a city* in
Syria in the Plain of Homs, identified with present-
day Tell Nebi Mend, 72.5 km. (45 mi.) S of Hamath.*

Kadesh, usually further specified by its location on
the Orontes River (Nahr el-Asi) to distinguish it from
other cities by that name, was an important city in
Late Bronze-Age* Canaan.* Although there is no
clear reference to Kadesh in the Bible (with a possible exception in the Lucianic Greek reading *chittim
qadesh* [Kadesh of the Hittites] in 2 Sam 24:6), the
city was an important fortress in the Canaanite world
which the incoming Israelites penetrated.

Egyptian* sources, from which the most written
information comes, first mention Kadesh in the various campaign reports of Thutmose III (c. 1490–
1436 B.C.). Kadesh is seen as the leader of a coalition,
reported in Egyptian sources as consisting of no less
than 330 princes, that met Thutmose and his forces
in the Galilean city of Megiddo* (*ANET*, 235). The
sixth campaign of that same pharaoh was directed
against Kadesh itself (*ANET*, 239), and the city was
destroyed. Subsequent rulers, including Amenophis II (c. 1436–1413 B.C.), considered the city a
vassal, although the records of correspondence from
Tell el-Amarna (*see* AMARNA LETTERS) indicate that
for a time at least the vassalage was somewhat
nominal.

In the Nineteenth Dynasty a scene from Karnak
left by Seti I (c. 1309–1291 B.C.) shows that king attacking a mountainous settlement called in the description "the town of Kadesh" (*ANET*, 254). In the
fifth year of the following king, Ramses II* (c. 1290–
1224), a great battle was fought in Kadesh between
the Egyptian monarch and the Hittite* ruler Mu-
watalliš, with the result something of a stalemate. A
covenant between Ramses and the later Hittite ruler
Hattušiliš confirmed the division of influence somewhere in the neighborhood of Kadesh.

Tell Nebi Mend, a large mound stretching along
the banks of the river, was excavated by the French
Académie des Inscriptions et Belles Lettres under
the direction of M. Pézard in the years 1921–22.
Four occupation levels were discovered, from the
lowest city which was fortified with a Hyksos* glacis*
wall (Middle Bronze) through Hellenistic and Roman
periods. In between there was evidence of Late
Bronze occupation (the period illuminated by Egyptian records), and indeed a partial stele* of Seti I was
among the finds. A third level showed that the city
continued to flourish during the Phoenician* period
of the Iron Age* before its final glory under the Seleucid* and Roman rulers.

BIBLIOGRAPHY: M. Pézard, *Qadesh: Mission archéologique à Tell Nebi Mend, 1921–1922* (1931).

CEA

KALHU. *See* CALAH.

KALNO. *See* CALNEH.

KALONIYEH. *See* EMMAUS.

KANESH. *See* KULTEPE.

KAPARA. *See* GOZAN.

KARATASH. *See* ADRAMYTTIUM.

KARATEPE (ke rə te' pe; Turkish, "black mountain"). An ancient site in SE Turkey, in the valley of the Ceyhan River, roughly 50 km. (31 mi.) NE of Adana.* In antiquity it was a walled citadel* built by one Asitiwata, king of Que (Cilicia*) and named after himself Asitiwatayya, "(city of) Asitiwata," cf. "city of David," or "Pi-Ramesses." The date of the king and his citadel is disputed but is certainly within the ninth–eighth centuries B.C. The gateways* and their inner approaches were adorned with Neo-Hittite sculptures of poor style and with sets of corresponding inscriptions in Old Phoenician* language and alphabet* and in Hittite* hieroglyphs.* This remarkable discovery thus paved the way for a full decipherment of the so-called Hittite hieroglyphs, a task previously well begun but with limited results. The Phoenician text is itself valuable for its linguistic information and the twin texts for their picture of Near Eastern kingship in the time of the Hebrew monarchy.

BIBLIOGRAPHY: F. Rosenthal in *ANET*[2,3], 499–500, with references; H. T. Bossert et al., *Karatepe, First, Second Preliminary Reports* (1946–47) and . . . *Ausgrabungen, Erster Vorbericht* (1950). Popularly treated by C. W. Ceram, *Narrow Pass, Black Mountain* (1956).

KAK

KARIM SHAHR (kä'rim shär). A prehistoric site near Jarmo on the Chemchemal Plain in Mesopotamia.* The site was excavated by Robert J. Braidwood of the Oriental Institute of Chicago, together with the American Schools of Oriental Research in Baghdad, in 1951. He concluded that the site contained but a single stratum, and occupation was c. 6000 B.C., making it earlier than Jarmo and thus the oldest Neolithic* settlement of Mesopotamia. Industries included flint, stone grinding, some domestication of animals, and possibly food* production. Subsequent to 1951, similar finds from the period have been unearthed at Gird Chāi, M'lefaat, and Asiab and at least one scholar, Abdul J. Jawad (a student of Braidwood) has redated the Karim Shahr materials from 9000–7000 B.C.

BIBLIOGRAPHY: R. J. Braidwood, "Cave to Village," *BASOR*, 124 (1951), 12–18; H. E. Wright, Jr., "Geological Setting of Four Prehistoric Sites," *BASOR*, 128 (1952), 11–24; R. J. Braidwood and B. Howe, *Prehistoric Excavations in Iraqi Kurdistan* (1960); A. J. Jawad, *The Advent of the Era of Townships in Northern Mesopotamia* (1965); *CAH*, 1, Part 1, 253, 256, 260.

CEA

KARKAR. *See* QARQAR.

KARNAK. *See* THEBES.

KASSITES. The Kassites were originally from the Zagros Mountains and were in control of Babylonia for at least four centuries in the latter half of the second millennium B.C., which was longer than any other Babylonian dynasty. With the exception of a few conflicts with the Sealand to the S and Assyria to the N, the Kassite era was characterized by peace—some would say, by stagnation. The Kassites quickly and completely adopted Babylonian ways and succeeded in conserving the older Sumerian* and Akkadian culture.

Original Homeland and Name. The homeland of the Kassites lay somewhere in the Zagros Mountains of western Iran. Specific suggestions have ranged from the area W of Hamadan to the Luristan or Pushti-Kuh areas of the Zagros.

The Babylonians called the Kassites *Kaššu* (in the Nuzi* texts *Kuššu*). The Greeks called them *Kossaioi* (in Hecataeus *Kissioi*), derived from the Aramaic* *Qussaye*. Hence some of the older English works called them Kossaeans.

E. A. Speiser suggests that the land of Cush (Gen 2:13; cf. 10:8) through which the Gihon River of the Garden of Eden winds is not the traditional Cush, S of Egypt* but is the homeland of the Kassites.

Linguistic and Ethnic Affinities. We have no long connected texts in the Kassite language but only a few dozen words and a few hundred names, some of which appear in bilingual lists with Akkadian renderings. Kassite appears to be an agglutinative language which is related to Elamite.* A few stems such as *burias* (cf. the Greek deity *Boreas*), *šurias* (cf. Indo-Aryan *suryah*, Latin *sol*, "sun"), and possibly *murattas* (cf. Indo-Aryan *Marut*, a pest god), have been analyzed as Indo-European. These can be explained as loan words, however, and are not sufficient evidence to establish the Kassites as Indo-Europeans. It is true that like many Indo-European groups the Kassites were especially devoted to horses.*

Sources of Information. Our sources are relatively scanty for such a long period of time for which thirty-six Kassite kings are listed. This is particularly true of the first two centuries of the Kassite period—a veritable dark age—for which we have virtually no material evidence and no contemporary inscriptions. The bulk of the material remains belongs to the so-called Middle Kassite period of kings, nos. 16 to 26 (mid-fifteenth to mid-thirteenth century B.C.).

We have about two hundred royal Kassite inscriptions written in Akkadian, which are brief and not very informative. In addition there are a few letters and some legal and administrative documents, chiefly from Nippur.* The most interesting of these latter texts describes the conduct of a temple hospital for female patients.

The most instructive sources are extra-Kassite texts such as the Assyrian Synchronous History, which is quite anti-Babylonian, and the Akkadian Amarna letters* found in Egypt, which include the correspondence of the Kassite kings with Amenhotep III and Amenhotep IV (Akhenaton*).

History. The Babylonian King List claims that the 36 Kassite kings reigned for 576 years. (In the following discussion the number in brackets indicates the place of the kings in this list. For a complete list see Jaritz [1958], 201–2). The end of the Kassite era is quite firmly fixed at c. 1160 B.C. What is in question is how seriously the total length of the Kassite era can be taken and when the beginnings of the era should be placed.

The Old Babylonian Empire of Hammurabi* and his successors was suddenly toppled by the blitzkrieg of the Hittite* king Muršilis I in 1595. Before this event the Kassites had been infiltrating into Mesopotamia,* perhaps as horse trainers. Samsu-iluna (1749–11), Hammurabi's immediate successor, claimed a victory over a "Kassite Army" in his ninth year.

The chronological problems are rendered even more complex by the disagreement among scholars as to the chronology of the preceding Old Babylonian Dynasty, whose end is variously placed at: (1) 1650 B.C. (high chronology of A. Goetze), (2) 1595 B.C. (middle chronology of S. Smith and H. Lewy, adopted by the revised *CAH*), and (3) 1531 B.C. (low chronology of W. F. Albright). There seems to be a growing consensus in favor of the middle chronology, which we have assumed as our framework.

After the destruction of Mari* by Hammurabi, the most important settlement in the middle Euphrates area became Terqa,* which served as the capital of the kingdom of Hana. Among the kings of Terqa appears a Kaštiliaš, a Kassite name, c. 1736, which may confirm the claim of the Babylonian King List (576 plus 1160 equals 1736) that the Kassites were established this early. It has therefore been suggested by S. Smith, B. Landsberger, and W. Hallo that it may have been from Terqa that the Kassites took over Babylon* after the Hittites had attacked and withdrawn.

After a very brief interlude in which a king from the Sealand momentarily seized Babylon, the first Kassite king to rule over Babylon was Agum II [no. 9], whose great achievement was the recovery of the idols of Marduk and his consort, Sarpanitum, which had been carried off by the Hittites some twenty-four years before to the land of Hana. In the mid-fifteenth century Ulamburiaš [no. 13] crushed the independent Sealand at the head of the Persian Gulf, reuniting for the first time in two centuries the whole of Babylonia under one rule.

The sixteenth king Karaindaš (late fifteenth century B.C.) is the first Kassite king with contemporary inscriptional evidence. Kurigalzu I [no. 18] built a new capital Dur Kurigalzu c. 1400. He and his two successors were in close diplomatic contact with the Egyptians, sending the pharaohs their daughters in marriage.

The Amarna letters reveal that the Kassite kings were constantly begging the Egyptians for gold.*

Burnaburiaš III [no. 20] (1375–47 B.C.) complained to Amenhotep III that his messengers had been robbed in Canaan,* and later he wrote to Amenhotep IV, taking umbrage because the pharaoh had sent no condolences when he had been sick. The Babylonian king asked the Egyptians not to correspond with the Assyrians. Later, however, the growing strength of Assyria after the collapse of Mitanni* to the Hittite Suppiluliuma* made it expedient for Burnaburiaš to contract a marriage alliance with Ašur-Uballit of Assyria. A surprising evidence of Burnaburiaš's enterprise comes from a discovery in 1963 of a cache of inscribed cylinder seals* found at Thebes* in central Greece.

When the Kassites revolted against the son of the Babylonian-Assyrian marriage and installed a usurper, Ašur-Uballit intervened and set up his own candidate, Kurigalzu II [no. 22]. The twenty-eighth king Kaštiliaš IV (1242–35) tried to assert Babylon's independence but was defeated by the great Assyrian conqueror, Tukulti-Ninurta, who placed his feet upon the neck of the hapless Kassite king. Thereafter Babylonia was ruled by a succession of weak and ephemeral Kassite kings. About 1160 the Elamites under Šutruk-Nahhunte and his son Kutir-Nahhunte swept over Babylonia, ending the long Kassite dynasty and carrying off to Susa* such treasures as the Hammurabi Law Code* and even the statue* of Marduk.

In the first millennium B.C. the Assyrians continued to encounter in the Zagros Mountains people called Kaššu, who opposed them at times and provided them with fighting men at other times. The mountaineers who threatened the passage of the Achaemenids, Alexander the Great, Seleucus, etc. through the Zagros may well have been descendants of the Kassites.

Culture. The Kassites not only continued the worship of the Babylonian deities but even revived the cult of a number of ancient gods whose worship had been discontinued. A text from Nippur describes the refurbishing of the Ekur, the temple of the Sumerian god Enlil, who was identified with the Kassite god Harbe.

The most important site of the Kassites is the new capital of Dur Kurigalzu established by Kurigalzu I c. 1400 B.C. This capital flourished until the end of the Kassite period. Dur Kurigalzu is at Aqar Quf* some 48 km. (30 mi.) W of Baghdad. It was excavated by the Iraqis under Taha Baqir from 1943 to 1945. Aqar Quf has the distinction of having the highest standing ziggurat,* a landmark some 52 m. (170 ft.) high. The excavators cleared the base of the ziggurat, part of a palace, and three temples to Enlil, Ninlil, and Ninurta—Sumerian deities. Fragments of a colossal statue of Kurigalzu with a long Sumerian inscription were recovered, as were unique frescoes.

One distinctive architectural innovation of the Kassites was the use of molded brick to form designs, a device which was later used by the Assyrians, Neo-Babylonians,* and Persians.

A prominent feature of the later Kassite period was the increased use of *kudurru* stones. These stelae,* covered with symbols of deities, marked the

Kassite *kudurru,* black limestone; height: 0.68 m.; 12th century B.C., found at Susa. The text on back of this stone deals with a grant made to Marduk-apal-iddin, son of the king, and lists the gods who will curse anyone who does not respect the grant. The face of the stone shown here has twenty-four symbols representing various deities. Courtesy Musées Nationaux, France.

grants of land to the king's retainers. The word *ku-durru* means "boundary," but most kudurrus have been found in cities where they had been set up in temples, rather than in open fields. Kassite art also includes some excellent animal sculptures in terra cotta and cylinder seals* inscribed with vivid animal designs and landscapes.

André Godard has argued that the most highly decorated Luristan bronzes were the work of the Kassites after they had been forced from Babylonia back to their homeland in the Zagros Mountains. The

prime difficulty with this theory is that no Luristan bronzes have ever been found in Mesopotamia proper from the Kassite era.

BIBLIOGRAPHY: J. A. Knudtzon et al., *Die El-Amarna-Tafeln* (1908, 1915); S. A. B. Mercer, *The Tell el-Amarna Tablets* (1939); T. Baqir, "Iraq Government Excavations at 'Aqar Qūf," *Iraq Supplements* (1944, 1945); id., *Iraq*, 8 (1946), 73–92; S. N. Kramer et al., "Fragments of a Diorite Statue of Kurigalzu . . .," *Sumer*, 4 (1948), 1–29 [cf. *ANET*, 57–59]; K. Balkan, *Kassitenstudien I: Die Sprache der Kassiten* (1954); E. D. van Buren, "The Esoteric Significance of Kassite Glyptic Art," *Orientalia*, 23 (1954), 1–39; F. el-Wailly, "Synopsis of Royal Sources of the Kassite Period," *Sumer*, 10 (1954), 43–54; K. Jaritz, "Die kassitischen Sprachreste," *Anthropos*, 52 (1957), 850–98; id., "Quellen zur Geschichte der Kaššû-Dynastie," *Mitteilungen des Instituts für Orientforschung*, 6 (1958), 187–265; id., "Die Kulturreste der Kassiten," *Anthropos*, 55 (1960), 17–84; A. Parrot, *Sumer: The Dawn of Art* (1961), 313–37; T. H. Carter, "Studies in Kassite History and Archaeology" (unpublished dissertation, Bryn Mawr, 1962); A. Goetze, "The Kassites and Near Eastern Chronology," *JCS*, 18 (1964), 97–101; N. Platon and E. Stassinopoulou-Touloupa, "Oriental Seals from the Palace of Cadmus," *Illustrated London News* (28 Nov. 1964), 859–61; G. Roux, *Ancient Iraq* (1964), 216–39; E. Speiser, "The Historical Framework," B. Netanyahu, ed., *The Word History of the Jewish People*, 1 (1964), 212–19; R. Biggs, "A Letter from Kassite Nippur," *JCS*, 19 (1965), 95–102; J. Brinkman, *A Political History of Post-Kassite Babylonia, 1158–722* (1968); M. S. Drower, "Syria c. 1550–1400 B.C.," *CAH*, 2, Part 1, 3rd ed. (1973), 417–525; J. Brinkman, "Notes of Mesopotamian History in the Thirteenth Century," *Bibliotheca Orientalis*, 27. 5–6 (1970), 301–14; W. W. Hallo and W. K. Simpson, *The Ancient Near East* (1971), 97–109; P. R. S. Moorey, "Towards a Chronology for the 'Lūristān Bronzes," *Iran*, 10 (1971), 113–29; C. J. Gadd, "Assyria and Babylon c. 1370–1300 B.C.," *CAH*, 2, Part 2, 3rd ed., (1975), 21–48; A. Godard, *The Art of Iran* (1965), 45–86; D. J. Wiseman, "Assyria and Babylonia c. 1200–1000 B.C.," *CAH*, 2, Part 2, 3rd ed. (1975), 443–81; J. M. Munn-Rankin, "Assyrian Military Power 1300–1200 B.C.," *CAH*, 2, Part 2, 3rd ed. (1975), 274–306; J. E. Reade, "Kassites and Assyrians in Iran," *Iraq*, 16 (1978), 137–43.   EY

KAVALLA. *See* NEAPOLIS.

KECHRIAIS. *See* CENCHREA.

KEEP. *See* CITADEL.

KEFR KENNA. *See* CANA.

KEILAH (kē'i lä). A frontier strongpoint (Josh 15:44; 1 Sam 23:1–13; Neh 3:17,18) which David defended against a Philistine* assault, only to receive less than the gratitude he merited from the local population. The strategic importance of the place is underlined by the fact that it is mentioned, as a source of contention between the princelings of Hebron* and Jerusalem,* in the Amarna letters* (1369–1353 B.C.). It is identified with Khirbet Qila, about 13 km. (8 mi.) NW of Hebron.

BIBLIOGRAPHY: *ANET*, 487–89.

EMB

KERTI HÜYÜK. *See* DERBE.

KEY. Keys were usually made of bronze,* in the Ancient Near East, and were used for locking or unlocking gates* or doors. A key such as that mentioned in Judg 3:25 was probably designed to move a slotted bolt or bar. More sophisticated bronze keys had a right-angled projection at the bottom instead of the tapering or more stubby point of the simpler variety. One key recovered from a Palestinian site may have been used in connection with an early tumbler lock, for in addition to the right-angled projection at the bottom it terminated in three upright prongs which were much like a trident in appearance. Biblical usage of the term is predominantly symbolic, including the power to admit to or exclude from the kingdom (Rev 3:7), the authority to bind and loose (Matt 16:18–19), and the preeminence of the position which the risen Christ holds over death and hell (Rev 1:18).

BIBLIOGRAPHY: P. S. Minear, *IDB*, 3 (1962), 8.

RKH

KHABUR. *See* HABOR RIVER.

KHELEIFEH, TELL. *See* EZION GEBER.

KHIRBEH. An Arabic term meaning "a ruin."

KHIRBET AL MINYEH. *See* CAPERNAUM.

KHIRBET AR ARAH. *See* AROER.

KHIRBET EL-HOH. *See* ETAM.

KHIRBET EL MUQANNAH. *See* EKRON; ELTEKEH.

KHIRBET ET-TUBEIQAH. *See* BETH ZUR.

KHIRBET EZ-ZURRA. *See* GATH HEPHER.

KHIRBET KANA. *See* CANA.

KHIRBET KERAZEH. *See* KORAZIN.

KHIRBET QILA. *See* KEILAH.

KHIRBET RABUD. *See* DEBIR.

KHIRBET SHAMSIN. *See* BETH SHEMESH.

KHORSABAD. This site, otherwise known as Dur-Sharrukin, was the scene of early Near Eastern archaeological activity, when in 1843 Paul Émile Botta, the French consular agent at Mosul, began excavations which ultimately uncovered the palace of Sar-

gon II* (722–705 B.C.). This structure with its associated buildings occupied an elevated area of about 10 ha. (25 a.), this being one-thirtieth of the entire city.* The palace contained reception halls decorated with inscriptions, sculptures, and bas-reliefs,* winged animals cast in bronze,* and other artifacts* that demonstrated the high level of Assyrian art at this period. Many of the wall-carvings portrayed scenes from the daily life, religious practices, and military activities of the Assyrians at a time when they were enslaving nations such as the northern kingdom (cf. 2 Kings 17:5–6) and demonstrated in a memorable way the virility of the Sargonid regime. Nearly a century after Botta's explorations, the Oriental Institute of the University of Chicago conducted an extensive reinvestigation of the site and recovered additional texts and inscriptions from the royal palace. These included the so-called Khorsabad Annals,* which describe events in the reign of Sargon II. The most important occurrence in the first year of his reign was the fall of Samaria,* and the Annals recorded how he had taken the people captive, rebuilt the city, and placed a governor in charge of it. This event was noted again in the Khorsabad "Display Inscription," a summary of happenings in the first decade and a half of his reign. Heavily-armed warriors depicted on alabaster* reliefs in the palace indicate dramatically the kind of ferocious enemy which attacked Samaria.

BIBLIOGRAPHY: G. Loud, *Khorsabad I* (1936); G. Loud and C. B. Altman, *Khorsabad II* (1938); *FLAP* (1951), 168, 174–76.

RKH

KHORSABAD KING LIST. A list of Assyrian rulers from the remains of the palace of Sargon* in Khorsabad,* discovered in 1932–33 during excavations by the Oriental Institute, University of Chicago. For similar, earlier lists, cf. *ANET*, 269.

BIBLIOGRAPHY: A. Poebel, *JNES*, 1 (1942), 247–306, 460–92; ibid., 2 (1943), 56–90; E. F. Weidner, *Archiv für Orientforschung XIV* (1944), 362ff.; A. K. Grayson, "Assyrian and Babylonian King Lists," W. Roellig, ed., *Lišān mitḫurti, Festschrift W. F. von Soden* (1969), 105–18.

CEA

KIDRON. There are twelve biblical references to Kidron as the stream bed, valley, or wadi* which runs S between Jerusalem* and the Mount of Olives* down to the Hinnom* Valley, and then winds through the wilderness down to the Dead Sea.* There is no stream in that part of the Kidron Valley that lies directly E of the city of Jerusalem today. The present level of the valley, though it is very deep, is from 3 to 12 m. (10 to 40 ft.) higher than it was in ancient times, which means that there is less drainage into it. The main source of water before the time of Hezekiah was the Gihon Spring,* and this is now diverted through Hezekiah's Tunnel* to the Pool of Siloam.* The Kidron was also called the Valley of Jehoshaphat in Joel 3:2,12.

The Kidron Valley has always been a natural border for the city,* and several of the biblical refer-

Section of Kidron Valley with Mount of Olives in background and three tombs in foreground; left to right: Pillar of Absalom, tomb of Benei Hezir, tomb of Zachariah. Courtesy Israel Government Press Office.

ences mention it in this way. Some interesting archaeological items associated with the valley are the Garden of Gethsemane* where remains of two earlier churches lie beneath the present church, the tomb of Mary where some elements go back to Byzantine* times, the Pillar of Absalom (which probably dates rather to the period of the Greek domination of Palestine), the Cave of Jehoshaphat (also Hellenistic), the Gihon Spring with its tunnels, and En Rogel Spring. In Hezekiah's Tunnel, which was explored by Charles Warren in 1867, was discovered the famous Siloam Inscription* dating from the eighth century B.C. Excavations in 1961 and 1962 above the Gihon Spring revealed a section of the Jebusite* wall which had remained in use down to the seventh century B.C.

BIBLIOGRAPHY: *FLAP* (1946), 149, 159, 236; G. E. Wright, *Biblical Archaeology* (1957), 126, 221; F. B. Huey, Jr., *ZPEB*, 3 (1975), 790–93.

BCC

KILN. It is difficult to distinguish smelting furnaces (*see* REFINING) from kilns for the firing of bricks or pottery, but at Megiddo* three wishbone-shaped structures were discovered, two of them still containing pottery.* These were probably of the same form as brickkilns. The air was sucked in down the two arms and escaped by a rear flue. The Megiddo kilns measured 3.05 by 2.44 m. (10 by 8 ft.). Other kilns, serving perhaps both for brick and ceramic work, were found at Tell Qasile* and Tell en-Nasbeh. The Babylonian brickkiln (cf. Dan 3:6), a tool of Nebuchadnezzar's* punishment, may have looked like the pottery kiln excavated in Nippur* (see also B. Beissner, *Babylonien und Assyrien* [1920], 234 and figs. 55–56; R. Koldewey, quoted under BUILDING MATERIALS). Incidentally, a Babylonian letter of about 1800 B.C. and an Assyrian regulation of some seven centuries later, mention the sadistic punishment of Dan 3 (G. R. Driver, *Archif für Orientforschung* 18 [1957], 129; E. F. Weidner, ibid., 17 [1956], 285–86).

EMB

KING'S HIGHWAY. This was a trade route S from Damascus* (through Bashan,* Gilead, Moab,* and Edom*) to the Gulf of Aqaba and was in use well before 2000 B.C. The road was mentioned by name in Num 20:17; 21:22; and Deut 2:27. The raiders of Genesis 14 followed this route, and their invasion is marked by the destruction of the northernmost of the line of fortresses which defined and guarded the route. The fact that there was no restoration of these interconnected fortifications for six centuries shows that the raid was no small invasion in spite of the spectacular success of Abraham's counterattack. The obvious apprehension of Abraham, recorded indirectly in Genesis 15:1, was justified. The fortress line was ultimately restored, became a Nabataean* trade route, and a Roman road* under Trajan after the subjection of the Nabataeans. A modern road in Jordan, bearing the same name (Arabic Tariq es-Sultani), follows the same route.

BIBLIOGRAPHY: N. Glueck, *The Other Side of the Jordan* (1940), 10–16; J. A. Thompson, *Archaeology and the OT* (1957), 57–58; S. Cohen, *IDB*, 3 (1962), 35–36; D. E. Hiebert, *ZPEB*, 3 (1975), 824.

EMB

KINSA. *See* KADESH KAH.

KIRIATH ARBA. *See* HEBRON.

KIRIATH-BAAL. *See* KIRIATH JEARIM.

KIRIATH JEARIM (KIRJATH-JEARIM). The "city of forests" was one of the four leading cities of the Gibeonites* (Josh 9:17) and a boundary point on the Benjamin-Judah border (Josh 18:14,15). It was also known as Kiriath-baal and Baalah (a contraction of the same, Josh 15:9,10), an earlier name identifying it as a former Canaanite* high place* (cf. 1 Chron 13:6). In connection with their exodus to the N, the people of Dan camped there briefly (Judg 18:12), an excellent stopping place in view of its large springs.

Kiriath Jearim is perhaps best known as the place where the Ark of the Covenant remained for more than twenty years after the conquest of Shiloh* c. 1050 B.C. (1 Sam 7:1–2; 2 Sam 6:2). David's first attempt to bring it up to Jerusalem* resulted in the tragic death of Uzzah and it was left again, this time in the house of Obed-edom where it remained for three months. Another effort by David was successful (1 Chron 13:5,6; 2 Chron 1:4).

As a border town it evidently belonged first to Benjamin, and in an administrative reorganization was transferred to Judah* (cf. Josh 15:60; 18:28). Other references include a note that it was the hometown of Uriah, a prophet who came to a sad end (Jer 26:20–23); and mention of the return of some of its people from the Babylonian Exile* (Neh 7:29; Ezra 2:25).

Although other identifications have been made and proposed, that with Abu Ghosh,* about 15 km. (9 mi.) to the W of Jerusalem (this corresponds with Eusebius's description), on the main road to Lod and Tel Aviv,* is well founded. This town got its name from a bandit leader, who during the early part of the nineteenth century, set up a self-imposed toll collection station on this important and well-traveled road. Actually the town of the biblical period was located just to the NW of Abu Ghosh, on a hill now called Deir el Azhar, because of the religious buildings and ruins located there. It seems to have migrated to its present location during Roman times. The Romans built a fort on this hill, which was garrisoned with troops from the Tenth Legion (*Fretensis X*). They added to the large spring a reservoir, whose walls were later incorporated into the construction of a large medieval church. Earlier, the site was distinguished by a Byzantine* basilica.*

Abu Ghosh is today a popular resort for Jerusalemites, due to its fine facilities for bathing and swimming. Recent excavations in its environs by a French group have been directed primarily to the recovery of prehistoric materials.

BIBLIOGRAPHY: F.-M. Abel, *RB*, 30 (1921), 97–102; F. D. Cooke, *AASOR*, 5 (1923–24), 105–20; W. F. Albright, *BASOR*, 24 (1926), 15; F.-M. Abel, *RB*, 43 (1934), 349–52; *QDAP*, 11 (1945), 113; *IEJ*, 1 (1951), 248; Y. Aharoni, *The Land of the Bible* (1967), 224–27, 287, 301; A. F. Rainey, *ZPEB*, 3 (1975), 825–27.

MHH

KIRIATH SEPHER; KIRJATH-SEPHER. *See* DEBIR.

KISH. An important Sumerian city* of the third millennium B.C., Kish is located SE of Babylon,* which replaced the city in prominence, beginning perhaps as early as the Akkadian* period, but certainly from the Old Babylonian period on. Its significance can be seen from the fact that it was mentioned in the Sumerian King List as the first to rule all of Sumer* after the Flood. It also formed a part of the titulary of the Mesopotamian* kings for centuries, continuing long after the decline of the city.

The site, called Tell el-Ukheimir today, was excavated in 1914 and the years following (up to World War I) by the French under de Genouillac. From 1923–33 a joint Anglo-American project under Stephen Langdon was sponsored by the Ashmolean Museum and the Field Museum. Among the discoveries which have generated the most interest for biblical scholars are tablets written in cuneiform* with parts of the Babylonian creation story *Enuma Elish* (*see* CREATION EPIC, BABYLONIAN). The layer of silt believed by Langdon to be flood evidence from the time of Noah is now thought to be only one of several floods* of different periods found in a number of Mesopotamian* cities, including Ur.*

Kish has been the subject of more recent researches by MacGuire Gibson of the Oriental Institute, University of Chicago.

JEJ

KITTIM. *See* CYPRUS.

KIZZUWATNA. *See* CILICIA.

KNIFE. Of various shapes and lengths, having either a single or a double edge, and made variously of flint, bronze,* copper, or iron,* the knife was a domestic implement, as opposed to the dagger, which was used in warfare.* Flint knives have been found at many Neolithic* sites and were in use in Palestine from about 3500 B.C., in the Chalcolithic* period. Knives made of copper are known from the time of Abraham to the period of the early monarchy, some of them having blades as long as 25 cm. (10 in.). Fastening wooden handles to the metal was far from easy, but in places where this was done the handles were secured by a tang or by rivets. When iron was introduced in the early monarchy it rendered other materials increasingly obsolete. Flint knives continued to be used for such religious functions as circumcision, however (cf. Josh 5:2–3), pointing to the antiquity of the kind of rite for which an early type of knife was alone deemed suitable. The practice of "breaking bread" no doubt also arose from an inhibition against using a new material in an ancient context. Flint knives were also preferred for such tasks as shaving, because they held a much better edge than their bronze or copper counterparts. Limestone molds were frequently used to cast the blades of metal knives, and from Tell Beit Mirsim one such mold was recovered which had originally been employed to cast a 40.6 cm. (16 in.) long blade. Knives of this length may well have been used for other than purely domestic purposes, however (cf. Judg 19:29). The "penknife" of Jer 36:23 is elsewhere rendered "razor" in the RSV, pointing to similarity of form and function. The only metaphorical use of "knife" to denote a rapacious generation is in Prov 30:14.

BIBLIOGRAPHY: A. G. Barrois, *Manuel d'Archéologie Biblique*, 1 (1939); C. Corswant, *A Dictionary of Life in Bible Times* (1956), 164.

RKH

KONYA. *See* ICONIUM.

KORAZIN (CHORAZIN) (kō rā' zin; Gr. Χοραζίν, *Chorazín*). A town in Galilee* that Jesus con-

Basalt chair found in third-century A.D. synagogue at Korazin; believed to be "seat [*cathedra*] of Moses" (see Matthew 23:2). The inscription in Judeo-Aramaic commemorates the benefactor, Judah son of Ishmael. Courtesy Israel Dept. of Antiquities and Museums; exhibited and photographed at Israel Museum, Jerusalem.

demned, with nearby Capernaum* (Tell Hum), for its unbelief (Matt 11:21; Luke 10:13).

Korazin is evidently to be located about 3 km. (2 mi.) N of Tell Hum at the ruins of Khirbet Kerazeh; this location is in agreement with Jerome's view that it was about this distance from Capernaum (De situ et nominibus locorum hebraicorum 194).

Extant are remains of a third-century A.D. synagogue* (excavated early in the twentieth century) made of basalt rock, with evidence of decorations of flora, fauna, mythological figures, astrological symbols, and geometrical designs. The structure was a basilica* type, rectangular with rows of columns and accompanying aisles, with the ornamental façade and sacred enclosure for the Torah characteristically on the side nearest to Jerusalem.* With the ruins was found a "seat of Moses" (cf. Matt 23:2) made of basalt and carrying the inscription in Aramaic,* "Remembered for good be Judan, son of Ishmael, who made this stoa and its staircase."

The Israel Department of Antiquities excavated in the area surrounding the synagogue in 1962 and found on the E remains of a large public building. On the N were structures connected to the synagogue including what seemed to be a ritual bath (see ABLUTIONS). On the W were basalt-built houses,* while on the S the presence of at least two olive* presses points to an industrial section. All this constituted a town covering 6 ha. (15 a.). The building activity occurred basically in the early A.D. centuries.

BIBLIOGRAPHY: J. Ory, "An Inscription Newly Found in the Synagogue of Kerazeh," PEFQS (1927), 51–52; F.-M. Abel, Géographie de la Palestine, 2 (1938), 299–300; C. Kopp, "Christian Sites around the Sea of Galilee, 3, Chorazin," in Dominican Studies, 3 (1950), 275–84; Z. Yewin, in IEJ, 12 (1962), 152–53; J. Finegan, The Archaeology of the NT (1969), 52, 57–58.

WHM

KUE (kū' e). Cilicia* is probably Kue. The KJV is incorrect in translating it "linen yarn" in 1 Kings 10:28; 2 Chron 1:16. Egypt* is mentioned in the same verse as another place whence Solomon* imported horses,* but the true reading is probably Musri, another region of Asia Minor,* naturally associated with Cilicia,

and not Mizraim (Egypt).

Kue is authenticated archaeologically. It appears in the annals of Shalmaneser III (858–824 B.C.). The local ruler opposed the Syrians. Inscriptions from Calah* list tribute received from Kue by Tiglathpileser* (745–727 B.C.) a century later. The region was mentioned in a text from the time of Nebuchadnezzar II* and dated between 595 and 570 B.C., as well as occurring in the Istanbul stele* of Nabonidus.*

BIBLIOGRAPHY: M. H. Heicksen, ZPEB, 3 (1975), 842–83.

EMB

KULLANIA. See CALNEH.

KULLAN KÖY. See CALNEH.

KULTEPE (kul te' pe). The modern Turkish name for the mound of the ancient city* of Kanesh; the site lies about 20 km. (12.4 mi.) NE of Kayseri, in the basin of the Kizil Irmak (Halys) River. In the early second millennium B.C., Kanesh was the seat of a local Anatolian city-state ruler, one dynasty among several in Anatolia that flourished prior to the establishment of a central and far-reaching Hittite* kingdom. Outside the town proper was a trading settlement of Assyrian merchants, the "karum." Here have been found large numbers of cuneiform* tablets in Old Assyrian, the so-called Cappadocian Tablets* which were the archives of those merchants. These tablets give a vivid picture of the trade, wide travel and customs, and concepts of that epoch ("early patriarchal" in OT terms, perhaps; the concept of "the God of the fathers" is seen in these texts, and is thus very old). The destruction of this merchant colony (an institution found at other Anatolian cities) was later followed by a brief renewal in the decades before Hammurabi* of Babylon.*

BIBLIOGRAPHY: Outline and full references, A. Goetze, Kleinasien, 2nd ed. (1957), 67–81; Cf. also P. Garelli, Les Assyriens en Cappadoce (1963); N. Ozgüc, ARC, 22 (1969), 250–55; CAH, 1, Part 2, 385–86, 399, 682–99, 708–16, 723.

KAK

KUYUNJIK. See NINEVEH.

L

LACERATION. The wild passion of the priests of Baal* on the occasion of the Carmel* contest with Elijah (1 Kings 18:28) partook of features common to the lamentation for the dead nature god or spirit of vegetation from which, curiously enough, and by devious paths, Greek drama emerged. The practice was denounced by the prophets (Isa 65:4; Ezek 8:14). From Ras Shamra (*see* UGARIT) a *threnos* or lamentation for Baal has survived which actually records the self-mutilation of Elijah's opponents: "Dead is Baal the Mighty, Perished is the Prince, Lord of the Earth. Then the kindly El, the Merciful, Comes down from his throne . . . He lets down his turban in grief . . . He tears asunder the knot of his girdle; He makes the mountain re-echo with His lamentation . . . Cheeks and chin He rends, His upper arm He scores, His chest as a garden-plot, Even as a valley-bottom his back He lacerates."

BIBLIOGRAPHY: *DOTT*, 128–33.   EMB

LACHISH. One of the largest cities of southern Judah,* Lachish was a fortress tcwn from the tenth to the sixth centuries B.C. lying halfway between Jerusalem* and Gaza.* Today it is marked by the impressive mound Tell ed-Duweir.* The town was known to the Egyptians in the days of Thutmose III (c. 1490–1437 B.C.), and is mentioned five times in the Amarna letters* as *Lakisu* or *Lakišu* c. 1400–1360 B.C.

The area around Lachish was occupied in palaeolithic* times (c. 8000 B.C.), and natural cave* dwellings were in use in the Chalcolithic* (c. 3000 B.C.) and Early Bronze Ages* (c. 3000–2000 B.C.). About 2800 B.C. settlement was concentrated on the present hill, where it remained more or less continuously until c. 150 B.C., when it was finally deserted. The tell* and some of the surrounding areas were excavated between 1932 and 1938.

In the patriarchal period there was a town here, and in the days of the Hyksos* rulers, c. 1700 B.C., the city* was protected by a fosse (ditch) and a plaster-covered glacis* (sloping ramp) probably crowned by a brick wall.* During the period 1600–1200 B.C. a small Canaanite* temple was built in the fosse which underwent several changes before it was destroyed possibly by the Israelites c. 1200 B.C. It is one of the best examples of a Canaanite temple found in Palestine. Rubbish pits around the shrine have yielded bones of sheep, goats,* oxen,* and gazelles—all young. Many right forelegs and shoulders were found among the bones (cf. Lev 7:32).

In the corresponding city on the mound important inscriptions were found which, although very fragmentary, give evidence of the use of alphabetic* writing* in Palestine in the period c. 1500–1200 B.C., before the arrival of the Israelites. In the late Bronze Age the city also had a temple on the mound as well as in the fosse, as excavations of 1975–77 have shown.

The mound was deserted during the twelfth and eleventh centuries in the days of the judges, but the city was revived in the days of David and Solomon* and became part of the fortification system of Judah. A palace for a provincial governor was erected on a large platform about 32 m. (105 ft.) square, built over earlier ruins. The summit of the mound was surrounded by a wall of sun-dried bricks about 5.8 m. (19 ft.) thick. Farther down the mound was an outer wall of stone and brick about 4 m. (13 ft.) wide. This double wall arrangement continued for three centuries. It is depicted on an Assyrian monument from the days of Sennacherib* (705–681 B.C.). On the W of the mound was a gate* protected by a large tower,* which was later incorporated into the outer wall. A sloping road led into the city at this point and turned right up the slope of the tell.

During the late eighth century a shaft was dug into the rock at the SE corner of the inner wall, presumably to store water. The city was taken by Sennacherib, and the work was not completed. A layer of ashes on the roadway, many arrowheads, an Assyrian bronze* helmet* crest and a spearhead, give evidence of Sennacherib's attack. The scene is depicted on a relief discovered in the palace of Nineveh.*

After the Assyrian withdrawal Lachish was refortified. A new stone wall replaced the upper wall, and the protective tower near the gateway was joined into the outer wall. Nebuchadnezzar* attacked this city in 586 B.C. Lachish was one of the last cities to fall (Jer 34:7). Something of the frenzy of these last days can be discovered in the Lachish Letters* written on broken pottery* pieces and discovered in a room of the gate tower.

Between 586 B.C. and c. 450 B.C. Lachish lay in ruins, but it revived under Persian and Greek rulers. A fine provincial palace was erected on the site of the old citadel* with a cultic building nearby in which was found a small limestone altar* and a crude relief of a human figure in a posture of adoration, dating to the second century B.C.

Excavations have produced vast quantities of pottery, as well as inscriptions, seals,* stamped jar handles, ornaments, tools,* and weapons (*see* ARMS AND WEAPONS). Problems still remain about the exact stratification of Lachish.

BIBLIOGRAPHY: H. Torczyner, L. Harding, A. Lewis, and J. L. Starkey, *Lachish I: The Lachish Letters* (1938); O. Tufnell, *Lachish II: The Fosse Temple* (1940); id., *Lachish III: The Iron Age* (1953); id., *Lachish IV: The Bronze Age* (1958); id., "Hazor, Samaria and Lachish: A Synthesis," *PEQ*, 95 (1959), 90–95; G. E. Wright, "Judean Lachish," *BA*, 18 (1955), 9–17; *ANET* (1955), 321f.; R. D. Barnett, "The Siege of Lachish," *IEJ*, 8 (1958), 161–64; J. A. Thompson, *ZPEB*, 3 (1975), 850–58; D. Ussishkin, "Excavations at Tel Lachish: 1973–1977, a Preliminary Report," *Tel Aviv*, 5 (1978), 1–97.

JAT

LACHISH LETTERS. These documents were written on pieces of broken pottery* and were discovered in the ruins of the last Israelite city* of Lachish.* In 1935 eighteen were found and three more in 1938, making twenty-one in all. They represent correspondence between the military commander of Lachish, a certain Yoash, and outpost commanders, in the days when Nebuchadnezzar* was closing in on Jerusalem.* Most of these letters are poorly preserved, but six of them give useful information about the time. They depict a state of urgency with messengers moving to and fro; one outpost watching for the fire signals of Lachish because those at Azekah* have gone out (cf. Jer 34:7); requests for detailed information from outposts; the visit of Coniah, the commander of the army, to Egypt;* warnings; exhortations; rumors; oaths. They are written in classical Hebrew prose and have unusual philological value quite apart from the light they shed on the days of Jeremiah.

Reverse side of Lachish Letter No. III. The sender, Hoshaiah, writes to Yoash, apparently the military commander at Lachish, regarding the suspicion by the king that Hoshaiah has read one of the confidential royal letters sent by the king to Yoash. *(See also photo under* AZEKAH.) Courtesy Israel Dept. of Antiquities and Museums.

BIBLIOGRAPHY: H. Torczyner et al., *Lachish I, The Lachish Letters*, (1935); W. F. Albright, "A Supplement to Jeremiah. The Lachish Ostraca," *BASOR*, 70 (1938) 11–17; id., "A Re-examination of the Lachish Letters," *BASOR*, 73 (1939), 16–21; id., "The Lachish Letters After Five Years," *BASOR*, 82 (1941), 18–21; *ANET* (1955), 321–22; D. Winton Thomas, *DOTT* (1958), 212–17.

JAT

LADDER. Ladders were frequently used in the ancient world. On the Ur-Nammu* stele* ladders are shown as part of the equipment needed for the construction of a ziggurat.* Fifth and Sixth Dynasty (2750–2470 B.C.) Egyptian friezes show scaling ladders used in siege operations. The same device is visible in Assyrian war reliefs. The Assyrian relief from Tell Halaf shows a date picker ascending a date palm by means of a conventional ladder.

Jacob's vision, however, was based on a different kind of imagery. Rock strata around Bethel,* where the fugitive slept, resemble flights of stairs, and this may have reminded Jacob of stories told by his grandfather of the stairs up the ziggurat of Ur,* with their crowds of ascending and descending people. Abraham's own last sight of Ur, through the clear air, could have been the high temple mound with the prominent stairways and their still visible traffic.

BIBLIOGRAPHY: Y. Yadin, *The Art of Warfare in Biblical Lands* (1963), 146–47, 228–29, 346, 392, 398, 406, 424–25, 448–49, 462.

EMB

LAGASH (lä' gäsh). A Sumerian* city in southern Mesopotamia,* formerly identified with the mound at Tello(h) and now considered to have included Tello but to have had its center at the nearby site of Al-Hiba.* Both mounds lie slightly E of the Shaṭṭ-el Hayy, a river which connects the present Tigris and Euphrates prior to their junction in the Shaṭṭ-el Arab. Lagash was the chief city* of at least two Sumerian dynasties in the late third millennium B.C.

Much of the material from Tello and Al-Hiba belongs to the end of the Early Dynastic III period (c. 2550–2370 B.C.), though the second great period of the city's history (the time of Sumerian revival associated with the Lagashite ruler Gudea,* c. 2230–2100 B.C.) produced the finest sculpture and a wealth of inscriptions. The site of Tello was originally excavated surreptitiously by the French vice-consul at Basra, Ernest de Sarzec, from 1877 to 1901, in a series of eleven campaigns. Although it was de Sarzec who uncovered most of the great tablets and striking monuments connected with the site, it remained for his successors, Captain G. Gross, Abbe de Genouillae, and especially André Parrot, to provide a working chronology* of the city. Parrot, who dug from 1931 onward, published the materials through 1933, and all subsequent work on Sumerian culture has made rich use of the finds. Since 1966 a French expedition has done work at Tello and Al-Hiba, the results of which are now becoming available.

Lagash, though not a biblical site, is one of the richest sources of information on the Sumerian civilization, a people whose language, culture, and religion greatly influenced both the following Assyrian and Babylonian peoples, and also through them, the family of Abraham. In both periods of Lagash's greatness, her closest cultural affinities seem to be with Ur, the great Sumerian city from which Abraham began his pilgrimage. Thus, the life and work of Sumer,* perhaps best illustrated in Lagash of all the Sumerian cities, become part of the heritage of Israel* and through Israel, the Christian world.

The archaeological history of Lagash begins in the predynastic period, though most of the remains consist of rubbish and graveyards. It is with the rise of Enkhegal and his successor Ur-nanshe, in the latter part of the Early Dynastic period that the city comes into its own. Ur-nanshe's dynasty, founded about 2550, for a time ruled the entire land of Sumer, and from the days of the kings Eannatum, Entemena, and Urukagina, we have the richest finds of the period. Ur-nanshe himself is the first ruler to claim trade in timber with the legendary Dilmun, and from his relics we have a classic relief in Sumerian style of the king bearing on his head a basket of earth, with which to inaugurate the building of a temple (ANEP, 149). Features include the half-skirt, the pointed nose, and the rather stiff appearance of subsequent Sumerian art.

Eannatum, whose disputes with neighboring Umma* were typical of the entire dynasty, is best known for his Stele of Vultures,* so called because in bold relief are pictured a flock of vultures carrying away parts of the corpses of the Umma enemies (ANEP, 94ff.). The stele* also features a phalanx of soldiers in close order with lances and shields. From the time of Urukagina,* whose entry into Lagash seems to have been rather abrupt, comes the notable list of "reforms" designed to redress the grievances then being felt by the poor against local officials and tax-gatherers (see TAXES). Although the kingship was shortly to fall before Lugalzaggisi of Umma, whose rule then gave way to the great Sargon* of Akkad,* the reforms of Urukagina provided a model for all subsequent uprisings against entrenched and uncontrolled officialdom, and even have their echo in the book of Amos.

Lagash experienced a revival of her power in the years c. 2230–2100 B.C. under one Ur-Baba and his successor, the mysterious Gudea. Under the former ruler temples and irrigation* works were rebuilt, and a beginning was made in the stone sculpturing techniques that, under Gudea, became the "most finished masterpieces of Babylonian statuary" (CAH, 458). The statues* communicate an element of solidarity and humility, almost as if the figure portrayed were aware that his place in history was settled but slightly undeserved (ANEP, 450f.). Gudea's great achievement was the rebuilding of the temple E-ninnu, for which he imported stone and cedar* from the Amanus Mountains (probably Syria or Lebanon). Also preserved is a plan for a temple or fort (ANEP, 234), together with many inscriptions. The latter represent the greatest flowering of the classical Sumerian language, a development that was to be envied and copied by Assyrian successors for well over a thousand years.

BIBLIOGRAPHY: F. Thureau-Dangin, Les cylindres de Goudea: transcription, traduction, commentaire, grammaire, lexique (1905); H. de Genouillac et al., Fouilles de Telloh, I, Epoques Présargoniques (1934); A. Parrot, Tello: vingt campagnes de fouilles, 1877–1933 (1948); id., Glyptique mésopotamienne: fouilles de Lagash (Tello) . . . 1931–1933 (1954); E. Solberger, Corpus des inscriptions "royales" pre-sargoniques de Lagaš (1956); T. Jacobsen, "La géographie et les voies de communication du pays de Sumer," RA, 52 (1958), 127ff.; id., "The Waters of Ur," Iraq, 22 (1960), 175ff.; J. E. Wooten, Mesopotamian Sculpture from the Proto-literate Period to the Agade Dynasty (1965); A. Falkenstein, Die Inschriften Gudeas von Lagaš, Vol. 1, Einleitung (1966); T. Jacobsen, "Some Sumerian City Names," JCS, 21 (1967), 100–103; C. Virolleaud, Tablettes économiques de Lagash (1968); CAH, 1, Part 2 (1971), 114–20, 138–44, 288, passim.   CEA

LAISH. See DAN.

LAKISU. See LACHISH.

LAMENTATION OVER THE DESTRUCTION OF UR. See UR, LAMENTATION OVER THE DESTRUCTION OF.

LAMP. The earliest lamps, simple stone containers for oil to feed a wick of twisted flax and so provide a light of some continuity, were a Neolithic* invention. Examples of immense antiquity showing signs of the burning wick date from Stone Age Pyrenaean caves.* In Britain, chalk lamps from 2000 B.C. come from the Neolithic flint mines near Cissbury in Sussex.

In Middle Eastern countries the sea shell seems to have provided the first oil container, and the British Museum has samples of conch shells used as lamps dating from the fourth millennium. Ur* of the Chaldees* has provided examples of alabaster* lamps im-

Seven-wicked pottery lamp found at Tell el-Kheleifeh (seventh to sixth centuries B.C.). Courtesy Smithsonian Institution, Photo No. 42379-K.

itating the conch shell, just as early Phoenician* lamps preserved the shape of the scallop shell. Sophistication of design came at an early period. A very ancient Neolithic stone lamp in the museum of St. Germain-en-Laye shows a head of an ibex and has a clearly defined spout. A bronze* lamp from Ur is in the shape of a crocodile,* antedating by many centuries a Roman predilection for animal shapes.

Pottery* early gained currency in lamp making. The Wellcome expedition (1937–38) on the site of Tell ed-Duweir* found square pottery lamps of high quality, containers pinched into shape with four spouts. They dated from the third millennium. Amorite* immigrants to the area introduced the lamp which the Hebrew newcomers took over. Developments may be traced, but household utensils of such simplicity varied according to the whim of the individual craftsmen.* In the Iron Age,* containers grew deeper to lengthen the life of the light, spouts grew longer, bases flatter for safe handling, wicks multiplied, and stands were invented.

The Greek lamp, which became common in the fourth and third centuries before Christ, was a better article. It dated back to the fine open lamps of Minoan* and Mycenaean* times, but the Greeks were more inventive in their craftsmanship. They cast their lamps on the potter's wheel, introduced the mold for mass production, curved the lips to minimize spilling, and covered the nozzle or the whole lamp. The influence of the Greek lamp may be discerned from the fifth century but is dominant in the covered lamps of Hellenistic times. Older types dating from Maccabean* times may reflect the archaism of that period.

BIBLIOGRAPHY: F. W. Robins, *The Story of the Lamp* (1939); R. H. Smith, "The Household Lamps of Palestine in OT Times," *BA*, 27 (1964), 1–31; id., ". . . in Intertestamental Times," *BA*, 27 (1964), 101–24; id., ". . . in NT Times," *BA*, 29 (1966), 1–27; J. Rea, *ZPEB*, 3 (1975), 865–66.

EMB

LAMPSTAND. *See* MENORAH.

LANGUAGE. *See* ALPHABET; ARAMAIC; EPIGRAPHY, GENERAL; EPIGRAPHY, HEBREW; GREEK LANGUAGE; HIERATIC; HIEROGLYPHS; IDEOGRAM; LATIN; PALAEOGRAPHY, GENERAL; PALAEOGRAPHY, HEBREW; WRITING, GENERAL; WRITING, PICTORIAL.

LAODICEA. The ruins of ancient Laodicea, at the junction of the Lycus and Maeander valleys, cover many acres, but no thorough investigation of the site has yet been undertaken. The end of the aqueduct* which brought in Laodicea's vulnerable water supply has been traced and described, but little else has been adequately mapped or recorded. It is possible to trace the line of the city* wall,* and an inscription dedicates a threefold eastern gate* to Vespasian,* to whom also a stadium, in a poor state of preservation, is dedicated. Two theaters* are visible and a large building, dating from Hadrian,* which may have been a bathhouse. As with too many ancient sites, from Hadrian's Wall* to the Roman cities of N Africa, the dressed stone of the cities has been quarried* ruth-

lessly by local inhabitants for their own buildings. Only three of the cities of "the seven churches" (Rev 1:4) have been excavated with any vigor—Ephesus,* Pergamum,* and Smyrna.*

BIBLIOGRAPHY: M. J. Mellink, *IDB*, 3 (1962), 70–71; E. M. Blaiklock, *Cities of the NT* (1965), 124–28; W. White, Jr., *ZPEB*, 3 (1975), 877–79.

EMB

LAPIS LAZULI. A complex silicate containing sulphur and sometimes spangled with iron pyrites to form a rich blue gemstone common in ancient seals* and inlays from Sumer.*

LAQA. *See* TERQA.

LARSA. An ancient Sumerian* and later Amorite* city,* located at the modern site of Senkereh, in southern Mesopotamia* between Ur* and Erech (Uruk*).

The period of Larsa's greatest glory was during the so-called "Isin-Larsa Age" (c. 2030–1763 B.C.) in the interregnum between the Third Dynasty of Ur and the rise of Hammurabi's* First Dynasty of Babylon.* A series of fourteen kings with originally old Amorite, later W Semitic and finally Elamite* names came to the throne. Larsa coexisted with her rival Isin, a scant 88.5 km. (55 mi.) to the NW, an indication that neither power was particularly strong. Gungunum, the fourth successor of the original ruler Naplanum, took control of Ur (possibly by military conquest) thereby establishing Larsa's greatest territorial control. In the waning years of the period when Isin declined and Babylon was on the rise, Larsa was taken over by one Kudurmabuk, a sheik with an Elamite name, whose second son Rim-Sin was to become one of the greatest, as well as the last of Larsa's independent rulers. Rim-Sin, who finally reduced the rival Isin, apparently coexisted with Hammurabi for almost thirty years before the rivalry between them came to a head. With the incorporation of Larsa into an administrative district of Hammurabi's empire, the great days of the city were at an end. A recently discovered stele* of Nabonidus,* the Babylonian monarch in the sixth century, lists Larsa as one of the cities that revolted in the incident that sent Nabonidus to Haran,* but other than that Larsa does not figure prominently in history.

Excavations conducted from 1854 onward by W. K. Loftus and the Assyrian Exploration Fund produced artifacts,* particularly tablets, but no clear stratigraphy* for the tell* was determined. It remained for André Parrot, who began excavations in 1932, to fully correlate the finds which included tablets from Ur III down to the Neo-Babylonian* period. The French excavations were reopened in 1967 and continue to produce worthwhile material.

In addition to inscriptional material covering such important items as the reigns of Larsa kings and the sexagesimal nature of Larsa mathematics, the work has uncovered a ziggurat,* temples, and palaces. Work has also focused on the water system, a feature of early Babylonia which was often the key to the prosperity of a particular city.

BIBLIOGRAPHY: F. Thureau-Dangin, "La chronologie de la Dynastie de Larsa," *RA*, 15 (1918), 288ff.; A. Parrot, "Tello et Senkerah-Larsa Campagne," *RA*, 30 (1933), 169–82; L. Matous, "Zur Chronologie der Geschicte von Larsa bis zum Einfall der Elamiter," *ArOr*, 20 (1952), 288ff.; A. Parrot, *Glyptique mésopotamienne Fouilles de Lagash et de Larsa* (1954); J. van Dijk, "Une insurrection générale au pays de Larsa avant L'avènement de Nuradad," *JCS*, 19 (1965), 1ff.; M. B. Rowton, "Watercourses and Water Rights in the Official Correspondence from Larsa and Isin," *JCS*, 21 (1967), 267–74; M. Birot, "Découvertes epigraphiques a Larsa (campagne 1967)," *Syria*, 45 (1968), 241–47; A. Parrot, "Fouilles de Larsa," *Sumer*, 24 (1968), 39–44; id., "Fouilles de Larsa, 1967," *Syria*, 45 (1968), 205–39; id., "Scènes de guerre à Larsa," *Iraq*, 31 (1969), 64–67 and plates; S. Walters, *Water for Larsa* (1970); *CAH*, 1, Part 1, 149, 208–9, 351, 358; *CAH*, 1, Part 2, 599, 628, 633, 636, 641–43.   CEA

LATIN. As the language of Rome, it became one of the official languages of Palestine during Roman occupation but has left few archaeological traces in the area. It was one of the three languages forming the inscription on the cross of Christ. Paul's Gentile name was Latin, a reflection, no doubt, of his prized Roman citizenship. The Nazareth Decree,* most probably a rescript of Claudius,* seems to reflect in its Greek a Latin original. There are some twenty-five Latin words in the NT but written in Greek form and script. Some legionary tombs and a few tiles bear brief Latin inscriptions. So do some of the coins* then current in Palestine. The earliest remains of Latin, for example, the Praenestine fibula,* and the famous S Italian decree against the worship of the Bacchanals, are archaeological material but lie outside the scope of biblical archaeology.   EMB

LAUNDERER. *See* FULLER.

LAVER. *See* BASIN.

LAW, HITTITE. *See* HITTITE LAW.

LAW, MESOPOTAMIAN. *See* MESOPOTAMIAN LAW.

LAZARUS, TOMB OF. The tradition of Lazarus's tomb at el-Azariyeh, the village named after him on the eastern slopes of the Mount of Olives, goes back to the Pilgrim of Bordeaux* in A.D. 333. The steps down into the tomb are comparatively modern (seventeenth century). Excavating in 1949 to 1953, S. J. Saller was able to demonstrate that a church stood near the traditional site at the end of the fourth century.

BIBLIOGRAPHY: *FLAP* (1951), 236.

EMB

LEAD. The use of lead for various weights is well illustrated archaeologically, the chief use probably being for plummets or leads on fishing nets (Exod 15:10). Figurines of lead have been unearthed in Egyptian* and Phoenician* excavations. Some parts of the Darius* inscription at Behistun* illustrate Job's figure (19:24)—". . . an inscription, cut with an iron tool and filled with lead . . . in hard rock" (NEB).

The Greeks used lead cramps to hold stonework in place, the method being to pour the molten lead into a precut hole. The holes, from which the metal has been dug by thieves and vandals, are frequently the only archaeological record of the practice. One expensive technique the Romans used in making roads was to set the stone blocks in molten lead. Medieval theft ensured that few traces of this engineering* remain. A lead "pig," weighing 83.5 kg. (184 lbs.), has been discovered in Britain, near Mansfield, Nottinghamshire.

Lead sulphide is found in Asia Minor* and was an item of Tyrian* trade (Ezek 27:12). Egyptian* and Lesbos women used the white paste formed from lead sulphide as a cosmetic, and no doubt suffered forms of lead poisoning as a result. The Romans were also exposed to such toxicity by their lead piping for

Jewish lead sarcophagus from Beth Shearim, fourth century A.D. Courtesy Israel Dept. of Antiquities and Museums. Exhibited and photographed at Israel Museum, Jerusalem.

water, of which many examples exist. Vitruvius, Augustus's* architect and military engineer, wrote an accurate description of such poisoning and was even aware of the source (Vitr. *De Arch.*, 8.6.10, 11).

BIBLIOGRAPHY: J. R. Partington, *A Textbook of Inorganic Chemistry* (1950 ed.), 833–34; D. R. Bowes, *ZPEB*, 3 (1975), 899.   EMB

LEATHER. Flint scrapers from prehistoric sites attest the early treatment of hides to form leather garments (Gen 3:21). A tannery discovered in Egypt* shows that various vegetable tanning agents were used, and tomb paintings* show the soaking and drying of hides and their working on a wooden tripod. They were softened with oil and beaten with a wooden mallet. Peter was housed by a tanner in Joppa (Acts 9:43). Hebrew tanning technique is described in rabbinical literature but has no archaeological attestation. Leather bags, belts, and sandals come from the Judean caves,* and their quality indicates an efficient technology. The Isaiah scroll from the Qumran* cave (c. 150 B.C.) is made up from seventeen sheets of coarse skins sewn together, with the writing on the outer surface.

BIBLIOGRAPHY: H. Jamieson, *ZPEB*, 3 (1975), 901.   EMB

LEONTOPOLIS (lē ən to' pō lis). A Greek name, meaning "city of lion," applied to at least two ancient Egyptian settlements. One in the E-central Delta is now the ruins of Tell Muqdam; it was a seat of the Twenty-third Dynasty (c. 820–720 B.C.) but otherwise undistinguished. The other, about 16 km. (10 mi.) N of Heliopolis, strictly "Heliopolitan Leontopolis," was an estate of Ramses III* (c. 1170 B.C.), Nayu-tehut-Ramesses, abbreviated to Nathō, and dependent on Heliopolis. There he had a palace and temple. The ruins of Tell el Yehudiyeh mark the site. By the Hellenistic period, a colony of Jews* was living there (cf. modern name just given; and Greco-Jewish gravestones found). This was the Leontopolis where the priest Onias IV fled and established a smaller temple based on that at Jerusalem (c. 162 B.C.). The prophecies of Isa 19:18–22 are sometimes referred in part to this place and its temple, though certainty in this regard is not possible. Petrie claimed to find evidence of Jewish cult-practice, a claim doubted by Peet.

BIBLIOGRAPHY: Jos. *Antiq.*, 12.9; 13.3; Jos. *War*, 1.9; 8.10; W. M. F. Petrie, *Hyksos and Israelite Cities* (1906), 2,19–27; T. E. Peet, *Egypt and the OT* (1922), 207–27; Sir A. H. Gardiner, *Anc. Egyp. Onomastica*, 2 (1947), 146ff.

KAK

LESHEM. See DAN.

LETTER WRITING, NEW TESTAMENT ERA.

Address. The address on papyrus letters was brief, for they were not sent by public post, but merely carried by a responsible bearer, several of whom are named in the NT (e.g., 2 Cor 2:13; 7:6,13; Eph 6:21). There is a parallel to this last reference in a letter of 103 B.C. in which the writer enjoins the messenger

Plaits and leather sandal of a young woman *in situ*, found at Masada. Courtesy Y. Yadin and Israel Exploration Society, Jerusalem.

"to pass on his greetings" with the letter. There is a "letter of commendation" (see below) in the Cairo Museum collection simply inscribed: "To Philoxenos," and another from Oxyrhynchus* addressed "to Tyrannus the Procurator" (*OP*, G&H 2.292). Likewise the well-known letter from Hilarion to Alis, directing the exposure of an unwanted child is addressed: "Hilarion to Alis, deliver." The original titles to the epistles would run likewise: "To the Romans," "to the Hebrews," and so on.

Greetings. In Paul's letters, the papyri,* the opportunity is often taken to send a kindly word to friends and acquaintances. "Give my regards to . . ." is Paul's frequent word (Rom 16:3,5ff.; 1 Cor 16:20f.; and in a score of similar contexts).

Farewell. The word of farewell at the end of a letter was often in the hand of the author, not of the amanuensis (e.g., 1 Cor 16:21; Gal 6:11). A. Deissmann quotes a papyrus* (Deiss*LAE*, 170ff.), in which, without comment or preamble, "goodbye" is added in what is quite clearly another hand.

Dictation of. Letters in the ancient world were commonly dictated. Writing on papyrus was an irksome process and demanded expertise as well as penmanship (Ps 45:1). Illiteracy, complete or partial, was the common reason for dictation. Many surviving documents are marked by the writer on behalf of such and such a person, "because he does not know letters" (e.g., *OP*, G&H 2.262ff.; 275.43—dated A.D. 66). In the same collection, 3.212ff.; 497.24, dated early second century, is a marriage contract marked: "I write on his behalf seeing that he writes slowly." A Tebtunis papyrus of a Nile fisherman, named Ammonius, dated A.D. 99, was written by a friend for the same reason (*Tebtunis Papyri*, Grenfell, Hunt, and Goodspeed, 2.118f.; 316). Peter and John, the Galilean fishermen, may also have employed amanuenses. 1 Peter 5:12 states that it was written "by Silvanus." A medieval tradition names one Prochorus as the scribe of John. For Paul's practice see 2 Thess 3:17–18; Col 4:18; and especially Rom 16:22. A parallel to Tertius's postscript in Romans is a third-century letter from one Helene's father, Alexander: "And I, Alexander, your father send hearty greetings." There is no change of hand.

It is easy to see how the varied skill, responsibility, or understanding of the writer might modify sentence structure, grammar, or vocabulary of the letter in a manner in no way diminishing authenticity and authority, for the finished message would be read back to the author and sanctioned. Nonsense is thus made of computerized methods of determining authorship.

There was also tachygraphy or shorthand, authenticated from Cicero (*Cato Minor* 23), the papyri, and Pliny (*Ep.* 3.5.14, 9.36.2). A papyrus of A.D. 155 contains a contract of a citizen of Oxyrhynchus* apprenticing his slave* to a tachygraphist for no less than two years (*OP*, G&H 4.204f., 724). "I have placed," so he begins after customary greeting, "with you my slave Chaerammon to be taught the signs which your son Dionysius knows." And then, after a reference to the salary already agreed upon between them, he proceeds: "You will receive the second instalment consisting of forty drachmae when the boy has learnt the whole system, and the third you will receive at the end of the period when the boy writes fluently in every respect and reads faultlessly."

Copying of. Paul's directions regarding an interchange of letters between Colosse* and Laodicea* no doubt involved copying, for letters were considered, in general, as confidential to the addressee, or, at least, within his discretion and disposal (see Col 4:16). If others were in the writer's mind to be included in reading the correspondence, directions were specific, as in the case of an Oxyrhynchus papyrus (*OP* 10.1349) published in 1914. It runs: "To my lady mother, Germania, greetings. Since I came away from you yesterday without telling you about the pot, take and copy my letter and give it to my lady mother Apraxis for my sister Hagia. Well, do not forget. I pray that you are well."

The Colossian footnote must have been one of the first movements of multiplication which gave Paul's communications the status they won as NT documents.

Bearers of. Taking a hint from Col 4:7–9 ("All my affairs shall Tychicus make known to you . . . I have sent him for this reason . . . with Onesimus . . . They will give you a full account of what is happening here"), A. S. Way justifies a good deal of expansion in his rendering of Paul's letters (*Letters of St. Paul and Hebrews* [1935], x–xiii).

A papyrus in the Loeb collection, edited by A. S. Hunt and C. C. Edgar (1932–34—Loeb Classical Library), and dated 168 B.C., contains a bitter com-

plaint addressed to a delinquent husband. It answers an unsatisfactory letter from him, and the letter was evidently expanded by means of verbal communication from the bearer. The concluding paragraph runs: "As, moreover, Horus who delivered the letter, has brought news of your having been released from detention, I am thoroughly ill-pleased. Notwithstanding, as your mother also is annoyed, for her sake as well as mine please return to the city, if nothing more pressing holds you back. You will do me a favour by taking care of your bodily health. Goodbye."

Letters of Commendation. The practice of writing a letter to introduce its bearer or secure his or her acceptance was a common and established practice to which the NT frequently refers (Acts 9:2; 22:5; 1 Cor 16:3; Rom 16:1; 2 Cor 3:1; 3 John 12—and, of course, Philemon, with which a similar letter of Pliny may be compared). Cicero's surviving correspondence contains many examples (e.g., *Fam.* 7.5, introducing Trebatius to Caesar). There is even an example, exquisitely tactful, among Horace's poetic epistles, that last flowering of the Roman *satura* (Epist 1).

Papyrology* has contributed numerous examples. A papyrus from Oxyrhynchus (*OP*, 12.1587) uses the very phrase of 2 Cor 3:1. Another Oxyrhynchus papyrus (*OP*, 2.292), discovered by Grenfell and Hunt, and in the Cambridge University Library, demonstrates the popular form. It runs: "Theon to his esteemed Tyrannus, many greetings. Heraclides, the bearer of this letter, is my brother. I therefore entreat you most with all my power to treat him as your protégé. . . . You will confer upon me a very great favour if Heraclides gains your notice. Before all else you have my good wishes for unbroken health and prosperity. Good-bye."

Letters of the Papyri. Consideration of the light thrown on the epistolary literature of the NT by archaeological discovery brings us inevitably to the Egyptian papyri.* The fact that people in the ancient world wrote letters was, of course, well enough known from Latin* literature, even before the Egyptian documents came to light. The letters of Cicero provide invaluable information on that stormy generation which saw the end of senatorial rule and the establishment of the dictatorship which we call the Roman Empire. The letters of Pliny the Younger show Roman society at its best at the turn of the first century of the Christian era. Its surviving books contain Pliny's official communications with the Emperor Trajan when the writer was governor of Bithynia,* and much information about the first clash between the state and the church.

The letters of both Romans survive in their own right as literature. The surprise of the papyri has been the vast extent of ancient literacy and the volume of the everyday correspondence between private persons on all manner of subjects of daily interest. The letters of the NT, although at times they touch the heights of literary power, have as their prime object information and exhortation in the plain and simple speech. And the discovery of Egypt's* mass of proletarian correspondence, besides providing much linguistic information, has shown the class of writing* to which the letters of Paul, Peter, John, Jude, and James belong.

There is no perceptible difference between the style of the private letters of the first and the fourth century. They are innumerable and repay careful examination by the NT scholar. It is revealed, for example, that Paul observed with some care the forms of polite address common in his day. There is an opening word of salutation, followed by thanksgiving and prayer for the person or group addressed. Then comes the special subject of communication, greetings to friends, and perhaps a closing word of prayer.

In the sphere of language the papyri have provided much information for the student of the NT epistles, and for the Bible as a whole. The nonliterary papyri have revealed that Paul and his fellow writers used the vernacular of the day and the speech of common communication. What else could be expected? The aim of the NT writers was to be taken seriously, and its authors in consequence deliberately use the speech of ordinary folk in their daily round. Luke begins his Gospel with a piece of elaborate Greek worthy of Thucydides. Then as though in demonstrable and deliberate renunciation of all literary artifice, he rounds off his sentence and adopts the vernacular.

The same vernacular, recovered from the papyri, is the speech of the NT letters, and indeed of the Gospels. It is not without grace and power; it is not incapable of poetry, as more than one chapter of Paul's writings demonstrates. At the same time, it is in the full stream of contemporary Greek. It is the vocabulary of that contemporary language which has thrown light on passages in the Epistles obscure to the scholars who, before the coming of papyrology,* approached the text only from the angle of classical and literary Greek.   EMB

LETTERS, ANCIENT NEAR EASTERN. Al-
though the desire for epistolary communication was apparently not the original reason for the invention of writing, possibly about 3500 B.C., it gradually expressed itself as the parameters of this important cultural innovation widened. The latter half of the third millennium B.C. in southern Mesopotamia* saw the origin of a diversified group of Sumerian literary compositions that included myths concerning creation, the gods, and ancient heroes and a variety of hymns, wisdom compositions, and essays. Excavations at sites such as Nippur* and Lagash* have uncovered thousands of unilingual Sumerian administrative, economic, legal, and grammatical writings. Letters in the form of military dispatches have survived from the Third Dynasty of Ur* and have furnished important information about the nature and functioning of the Sumerian kingdoms and their relations one with another. Thus Shulgi, son of Ur-Nammu* who established the dynasty about 2070 B.C., received an unpromising intelligence letter from one of his officials stationed in turbulent Subir, and this document, along with Shulgi's displeased response, has survived in the same archive. Ibbi-Sin, a weak successor of Shulgi, corresponded from Ur

with his own provincial governors in an attempt to shore up his crumbling domain, and the text of some of his royal correspondence has also survived. Political instability, intrigue, disloyalty, and double-dealing on the part of officials are all reflected in these letters (S. N. Kramer, *The Sumerians* [1963], 331–35).

In the second millennium B.C. the rulers of the Old Babylonian period (c. 1830–1550 B.C.) communicated with allies and officials by means of letters and military dispatches. At Mari,* Parrot excavated over twenty thousand tablets, of which about five thousand were letters written in Babylonian liberally interspersed with west-Semitic terms and grammatical forms. These documents included correspondence between Hammurabi* (c. 1792–1750 B.C.) and the ambassadors of Zimri-Lim, the last king of Mari, showing how friendly the two kings were prior to Zimri-Lim's defeat at Hammurabi's hands (cf. G. E. Mendenhall, *BA* XI, No. 1 [1948], 13). Hammurabi was also very cordially disposed toward Rim-Sin of Larsa* before conquering him about 1780 B.C., referring to him in gracious terms while winning his confidence.

The days of Hammurabi saw the rise of a well-organized courier system for the delivery of dispatches and letters. Documents increasingly began to be enclosed in clay envelopes, on the outside of which was a statement of the contents, and in the case of business and contracts a separate attestation by the parties making an agreement. Material transmitted in this manner proved to be completely safe from any tampering.

Perhaps the most celebrated official correspondence was the literature discovered at El-Amarna* in 1887. It consisted mainly of diplomatic letters and dispatches sent to the pharaohs Amenhotep III and Amenhotep IV between about 1400 and 1350 B.C. from the governors and rulers of Egyptian-controlled territory in western Asia. The letters followed the general Akkadian format and normally began with the addressee, who was named by title. The sender then identified himself by name and position, and frequently indulged in polite and solicitous salutations, which might also include an invocation of divine blessing on the recipient. The preliminaries having been dispensed with in this manner, the main part of the message then followed, in which the writer reported on his status and made whatever requests were necessitated by the situation. Akkadian letters often concluded with a request for tidings about the recipient's well-being, though this element did not always appear in the Amarna correspondence.

From these letters it is evident that the incursions of the Habiru* were weakening Egyptian domination of western Asia, and this, combined with the political ambitions and intrigues of the governors themselves, presented serious difficulties for the Egyptian administration. In one letter (Knudtzon 288), Abdiheba, a governor of Jerusalem, complained that "the land is lost" and that he had encountered enemies of the Egyptians "as far as the territories of Seir and as far as Gath-Carmel." Apparently the Habiru had taken all the pharaoh's cities in his area, and if archers were not sent soon, everything would be lost to Egypt. The desperate need for reinforcements, especially archers, was a recurrent theme in such letters, as with a diplomatic message from Akizzi of Qatna* to Akhenaton* urgently requesting help against his enemies in Syria and Hatti-land.

Letters recovered from Ugarit* (Ras Shamra) reflected the general purpose and style of other Amarna-age correspondence. One communication made an urgent appeal for reinforcements in the face of impending defeat (H. L. Ginsberg and B. Maisler, *JPOS* 14 [1934], 243–97; 15 [1935], 181–84). A more personal letter from a slave to "the Queen, my lady" consisted of a polite enquiry as to the recipient's welfare (H. L. Ginsberg, *BASOR*, 42 [1938], 19), and this was evidently a favored style of personal correspondence at Ugarit.

A record of Sargon II's* invasion of Urartu* in 414 B.C. occurred in the form of a letter addressed to Ashur, god of Assyria. It furnished a detailed description of the expedition that had been mounted against Rusa I (c. 735–714 B.C.) and which resulted in his defeat. Other Assyrian monarchs whose letters have survived include Esarhaddon* (680–669 B.C.).

Many of the ostraca* discovered by J. L. Starkey at Lachish* in 1935 proved to be letters, while others were military dispatches and lists of names. The sixth-century B.C. script had deteriorated badly in many instances, making the deciphering of the messages very difficult. It is clear, however, that the situation reflected in the letters was one of great anxiety, standing as Lachish was on the brink of disaster. Ostracon III mentioned a certain "prophet" who has otherwise remained unidentified, while Ostracon IV complained about communications sent out by one of the royal officials that on receipt were having a demoralizing effect on the populace. This charge of "weakening the hands" was ironically enough the very one that the royal officials had laid against Jeremiah in the reign of Zedekiah (Jer 38:4).

The papyri discovered at Elephantine* in Upper Egypt in 1903 and dated between 500 and 400 B.C. included a number of Aramaic* letters written by Jews who were members of a military colony stationed on the island. For the Bible student the most important letter was one addressed to Bagoas, the governor of Judah. It complained, in 410 B.C., that the colony's temple had been destroyed, apparently as the result of an anti-Semitic movement among the Egyptians of the locality, and requested help in the rebuilding of the structure. The sons of Sanballat,* the governor of Samaria,* were also named in the document, as was Johanan, the high priest of Jerusalem* (cf. Neh 12:12; 13:28). According to another letter, the colony was still in existence in 397 B.C.

Letters are mentioned occasionally in the OT, and sometimes quoted in part or whole (cf. 2 Sam 11:15; 1 Kings 21:8-10; Ezra 7:11-26; Jer 29:1-28).

BIBLIOGRAPHY: A. H. Sayce and A. E. Cowley, *Aramaic Papyri Discovered at Assuan* (1906); A. Ungnad, *Aramäische Papyrus aus Elephantine* (1911); J. A. Knudtzon and O. Weber, *Die El-Amarna-Tafeln* (1915); C. A. Keiser, *Letters and Contracts from Erech* (1917); A. E. Cowley, *Aramaic Papyri of the Fifth Century B.C.* (1923); A. Parrot, *Mari, une ville perdue* (1935); E. Chiera, *They Wrote on Clay* (1938); G. Dossin, *Syria*, XIX (1938), 105–26; H. Torczyner, *The Lachish Letters* (*Lachish I*), (1938); id., *Te'udot Lakhish* (1940); *ANET*, 480–92; *DOTT*, 212–17, 256–69.   RKH

LEVIATHAN. The identity of this monster is variously interpreted. According to D. G. Stradling (*NBD*, 729–30), the reference in Isa 27:1 is to the swift flowing Tigris and the "winding" (RV) Euphrates. W. F. Albright (*The Archaeology of Palestine*, 235) finds a clue in the Baal* Epic of Ugarit* where "Leviathan" (or Lotan) is called a viper and attracts the same adjectives as those found in the Isa context. The metaphor remains intact. The "dragon of the sea" (*tannîn*) appears in the same documents from Ugarit. The impression of a cylinder seal* recovered from Tell Asmar and dated in the Akkadian* period (c. 2360–2180 B.C.) depicts deities killing a seven-headed serpent-dragon. The idea may reflect Early Mesopotamian* cosmogonic myths.

BIBLIOGRAPHY: T. H. Gaster, *IDB*, 3 (1962), 116; H. L. Ellison, *ZPEB*, 3 (1975), 912.   EMB

LIME. This chemical is a caustic, highly infusible white solid when pure, described chemically as CaO, which is obtained by calcining limestone, shells, bone, or the forms of calcium carbonate (also called quicklime, burnt lime, or caustic lime). Quicklime develops great heat when slaked with water, forming a crumbly mass of slaked lime, or hydrated lime, which is calcium hydroxide.

Its use and processing date from very ancient times in the Near East. There were very many lime kilns* in early Palestine that made use of the abundant source material of limestone. This stone was formed during the numerous marine invasions in the geologic history of the country, and most of the visible outcroppings in both Palestine and Trans-Jordan are from the Cretaceous Period and of the Cenomanian and Senonian Series.

Lime was used fairly early in the preparation of leather,* and its antiseptic properties were similarly not unknown. The development of waterproof, or hydraulic, lime plaster became an important factor in the thirteenth-century settlement of the Israelites in the hill country of Palestine. This ability to build adequate cisterns* enabled them to settle in any place where there was rain, in contrast to the earlier Canaanites,* whose occupation was restricted to sites near perennial streams or springs. Some earlier use of raw lime plaster, limy marl, or stone more naturally impervious is known, but proved inadequate for the cisterns needed for sizable settlements.

Lime did not become an important component of mortar for building purposes until Hellenistic times. The ancient Egyptians* used gypsum (hydrated calcium sulphate) and its derivatives, including plaster of Paris, in their mortar. That bones provided a source for lime production is evident from Amos 2:1, though this passage shows this use of human bones was an act of vengeance.

BIBLIOGRAPHY: J. R. Partington, *A Textbook of*

Inorganic Chemistry (1950 ed.), 754–55; D. R. Bowes, *ZPEB*, 3 (1975), 936–37.

MHH

LIMES (lī' mēs). A Latin word for a fortified boundary or frontier and often used in archaeology for the line thus traced along the limits of an occupied territory, marked by an integrated pattern of traces, e.g., along the Rhine and the Danube, and less regularly on the east of Rome's ancient Middle Eastern provinces.

LINEAR A. A simplified form of pictographic* script written on tablets and used c. 1750–1450 B.C. in Minoan* Crete. It is little understood, and may only have survived for about two centuries. It was evidently not a form of Greek, and suggestions that it was a script employed in the writing of Akkadian* are purely speculative.

LINEAR B. A later form of writing than Linear A,* originating perhaps c. 1400 B.C. As well as occurring in "Mycenaean"* Crete, it was used also on the mainland. It may have been an adaptation of Linear A, and possibly formed a very early type of Greek.

LINEN. It is the product of the flax plant, the fibers of which are made into yarn. When woven, a rough-textured, discolored material results, necessitating bleaching in order to produce a white cloth.* It is remarkable that material so fragile should become the stuff of archaeological investigation at all, but enough traces and fragments have survived to show that the linen of antiquity was of the highest quality and equal to any vegetable fabric of today. The date for cutting the flax was noted in the Gezer* Calendar, and linen weaving took place in the area of Beth Shan* and Arbela. Surviving fragments of Egyptian* linen from royal tombs are so finely woven that only magnification can distinguish the material from silk. From the tomb of Tutankhamen* colored linen has come, and blue linen threads are found in some of the textile materials from Qumran.*

BIBLIOGRAPHY: L. M. Wilson, *Ancient Textiles from Egypt* (1933); L. Bellinger, *BASOR*, 118 (1950), 9–11; G. M. Crowfood, *PEQ* (1951), 5–31.

EMB

LIONS. Lions are mentioned over one hundred times in the Bible in both literal and figurative senses. They were well known all over the biblical world in ancient times, although today they are extant only in Africa and India. Archaeology has uncovered many examples of the use of lions in art to symbolize royalty, divinity, and strength. The earliest temples at Warka (before 3000 B.C.) displayed carvings of lions as symbols of deity. At Hazor,* a lion guarded the entrance to a Canaanite* temple; 1958 excavators also found the stone head of a lioness. Lions were also part of the decorative motif in the Solomonic Temple* (1 Kings 7:29, 36). There are many lions in the reliefs from the palace of Ashurbanipal* at Nimrud.* The Processional Street at Babylon* was decorated with blue glazed reliefs of lions, and a huge

Lion head found in Philistine strata at Ashdod, c. 12th century B.C. Courtesy Israel Dept. of Antiquities and Museums.

basalt lion was found in one of the palaces nearby. In 1967 four lion heads were found in the excavation of a sixth-century B.C. temple of Athena at Smyrna;* the lion was also represented on their coins.* A stamp seal* from the Museum in Amman, Jordan, was recently published displaying a roaring lion; the lion is a frequently occurring animal in glyptic art and is found on stamp seals from the tenth century B.C. to the Persian Period. The lion was the symbol of both Israel* and Judah,* as illustrated on the famous seal found at Megiddo* bearing the inscription of Shema the servant of King Jeroboam. Lions are also frequently found in the decorations of Jewish synagogues,* and many recently discovered Byzantine* churches have lions with other animals depicted in mosaic* floors. Jesus Christ is represented symbolically as "The Lion of the tribe of Judah" (Rev 5:5).

BIBLIOGRAPHY: F. S. Bodenheimer, *Animal and Man in Bible Lands* (1960), 17, 42–43, 100, 104; *Fauna and Flora of the Bible*, United Bible Societies Helps for Translators, 11 (1972), 9, 50–51, 192; G. S. Cansdale, *ZPEB*, 3 (1975), 939–41.

BCC

LIPIT-ISHTAR. This man was king of Isin c. 1932–1906 B.C. and instituted a program of social reforms which was associated with one of the earliest collections of Sumerian* laws. Extant copies have come mostly from Nippur,* and like the later Code of Hammurabi* depicted Lipit-Ishtar as divinely appointed to establish justice in the land. The legal material has not been preserved in its entirety, but about two-thirds can be reconstructed. There were about sixty laws inscribed on a stele,* beginning with a prologue and ending with an epilogue. They were grouped according to subject matter, and dealt with slavery,* marriage,* and inheritance, the renting of boats, recompense for damages sustained, and other matters. With the code of Ur-Nammu* (c. 2113–2096 B.C.) they comprise the earliest extant Sumerian laws.

BIBLIOGRAPHY: *CAH*, 1, Part 2, 634–37.

RKH

LIVER. Ezekiel 21:21 ironically pictures the king of Babylon at his task of divination. The liver of a sacrificed animal was consulted for its markings. Perhaps the abnormal structure of the hepatic lobes or pattern of the blood vessels had some significance in terms of the signs of the zodiac. At any rate, among the Babylonians, and among the Etruscans, who handed on haruspicy (the inspection of the liver) to the Romans, the practice was a superstitious art. Models of livers in baked clay* come from Picenza (Etruscan), Boghazköy* (Hittite), Mari,* and Babylonia. These devices were probably used in the temple schools to instruct the neophytes in the divinatory art. Significantly, the Levitical law prescribed that the caul above the liver be burnt on the altar, and Josephus maintains that this included the organ itself (Jos. *Antiq.* 3.9.2.).

BIBLIOGRAPHY: "Haruspices," *OCD*, 2d ed., 489.
EMB

LOCULUS. A diminutive form of locus (Lat., "little place"). The term is used of a coffin and of the niches cut for the dead in the walls of the catacombs.*

LOCUST. The locust (Lev 11:21–22; Matt 3:4; Pliny, *NH*, 6.35; 7.2) dried or cooked is in fact a rich food* with a 75 percent protein content along with vitaminous elements, carbohydrates, and minerals. A relief from the palace of Nineveh* shows attendants carrying to Sennacherib's* table strings threaded with pomegranates and locusts (about 700 B.C.). Along with the wild honey, John the Baptist therefore had a fairly well-balanced diet, not despised by kings.

BIBLIOGRAPHY: F. S. Bodenheimer, *Insects as Human Food* (1951); G. S. Cansdale, *ZPEB*, 3 (1975), 948–50.
EMB

LOESS (lō′ es). A sand or loam deposit of Pleistocene origin, which sometimes exhibits stratification.* Its flora attracted herbivores and carnivores as well as Neolithic* man, and the resultant artifacts* include bones and worked flint implements.

LOGIA. See AGRAPHA.

LOTAN. See LEVIATHAN.

LOTS. In the OT, lots were often cast in an attempt to discover God's will for a given situation. The objects known as Urim and Thummim (Exod 28:30) which were part of the priest's ephod, may have been used in this connection, although there is no direct evidence available. Decisions which involved the casting of lots included the choice of a scapegoat (Lev 16:7–10, 21–22); the division of the land of Canaan* (Josh 14:2; 18:6); the service of the Solomonic Temple* (1 Chron 25:7–8); and establishing the guilt or innocence of persons suspected of criminal activities (1 Sam 14:42).

Numerous ostraca* were found at Masada,* all marked by letters or names, and Yigael Yadin suggested that they had been used for the drawing of rations. One group of eleven had a single name on each, and all were different, though apparently written by the same hand. Yadin thought that these referred to Eleazar Ben Ya'ir, commander of the ill-fated garrison, who survived with his ten commanders for the final act of defiance against the Romans.

BIBLIOGRAPHY: F. E. Hamilton, *ZPEB*, 3 (1975), 988.
EMB

LUCIAS SERGIUS PAULLUS. See SERGIUS PAULUS.

LUKA. See SEA PEOPLES.

LUXOR. The modern town built on the southern part of the site of ancient Thebes,* the capital of Upper Egypt* in the Eleventh Dynasty, and the most splendid city* of the Two Lands between the Eighteenth and Twenty-first Dynasties. At its height, Thebes was a center of art, learning, religion, and politics, and was noted for its towering obelisks,* stately buildings, and magnificent temples.

Located about 675 km. (420 mi.) south of the present city of Cairo, Luxor grew up around the splendid temple built by Amenhotep III and dedicated to Amon-Re, his wife Mut, and his son Khons. The structure was marked by a colonnade of stately pillars, and an outer court which was added by Ramses II.* The building was heavily damaged by an earthquake in 27 B.C., and at that time the site was abandoned.
RKH

LUZ. See BETHEL.

LYCAONIA (lĭ cə ō′nē ə). This was a high, treeless plateau in S-central Asia Minor.* There are two references to the region in the Bible. In Acts 14:6, Paul and Barnabas escaped from Iconium* and went on to the "cities of Lycaonia, Lystra,* and Derbe.*" The implication of Luke is that Iconium was not in Lycaonia at the time. Other writers show that Iconium was not only in Lycaonia but was its capital in 39 B.C. William Ramsay demonstrated from archaeological evidence that Luke was quite correct in his statement in Acts 14:6, for at the time Iconium was a Phrygian* city and the borders of Lycaonia had fluctuated. In Lystra, a city* of Lycaonia, Ramsay found an inscription that dedicated a statue to Zeus* and Hermes;* special local interest in these deities provides an interesting background to Acts 14:11–12. Derbe,* another important city of Lycaonia, was tentatively identified by Ramsay on the basis of surface survey and limited excavation with a mound called Gudelisin. New epigraphical* evidence (three inscriptions) has now made possible a new location for Derbe, 48 km. (30 mi.) E of Ramsay's site, at Kerti Hüyük. In the general area there are ruins of more than fifty Byzantine* churches.

BIBLIOGRAPHY: A. H. M. Jones, *The Cities of the Eastern Roman Provinces* (1971 ed.), 75–109; H. W. Hoehner, *ZPEB*, 3 (1975), 1009–10.
BCC

LYDIA. The name of a merchant woman mentioned in Acts 16:14, 40, who came from Thyatira,* a city* in the province of Lydia. The country was a territory in W Asia Minor,* bounded on the N by Mysia,* on the E by Phrygia,* and on the S by Caria.* In it were such well-known cities as Sardis.* The coastal cities of Cyme, Smyrna,* Ephesus,* etc., were sometimes reckoned as belonging to Lydia and sometimes to Aeolis and Ionia. Lying mostly in river valleys, Lydia included on the N the Hermus Valley (modern Gediz), in the center the Cayster (modern Küçük Menderes) and on the S border the Meander Valley (modern Büyük Menderes). The capital Sardis was inland in the Hermus Valley.

Based on what little excavations have been done on the preclassical periods, the inland region was more conservative, while the coastal area was more active in commerce and warfare.*

That Lydia was exposed to Hittite* cultural penetration (second millennium B.C.) is seen in two rock-cut monuments with inscriptions in Hittite hieroglyphs:* in one case inscribed on the "Niobe," an image of a seated goddess found near Magnesia ad Sipylum; and in the other, reliefs of a warrior (god?) near Karabel, which Herodotus mentions (2.106).

Extensive excavations have been conducted at Sardis,* under George Haufmann and Harvard University; and other excavations have also been undertaken at Ephesus.

The Lydians became powerful, especially under their kings, Gyges (c. 685–652 B.C.) and Croesus (560–542 B.C.), the latter being famous for his wealth and for his interest in Greek culture, which is demonstrated by his subsidy to the building of the archaic temple of Artemis* at Ephesus on which his inscribed name has been preserved.

Knowledge of the Lydian language is obscure, although a number of inscriptions have been found at Sardis. The language seems to belong to the Anatolian group of Indo-European. From the royal names of Myrsilos, Sadyattes, and Alyattes, it may be gathered that the Lydian kingdom had connections with the second millennium when names in -attes (as Maduwattash) appeared in W Asia Minor and when Murshilis was a Hittite royal name.

BIBLIOGRAPHY: L. Burchner, J. Keil, and G. Deeters, "Lydia," PWRE, 13.2 (1927), 2122–202; D. Magie, Roman Rule in Asia Minor (1950), 45–50; M. J. Mellink, "Lydia," IDB, 3 (1962), 190–92; OCD, 629; A. H. M. Jones, The Cities in the Eastern Roman Provinces (1971 ed.), passim; H. W. Hoehner, ZPEB, 3 (1975), 1011–13.

WHM

LYRE. See MUSIC.

LYSANIAS. He was tetrarch of Abilene,* who, according to Luke 3:1, ruled at the time of the Emperor Tiberius,* the Procurator Pontius Pilate, and the tetrarchs, Herod Antipas (see HEROD, FAMILY OF), and Philip.

An earlier Lysanias, a successor to his father Ptolemaeus, ruled from 40 to 36 B.C. over a large area from the region of Caesarea Philippi* to Laodicea,*

with Chalcis as the capital. He was executed by Mark Antony.

The man mentioned in Luke is undoubtedly a second and later Lysanias of the time of A.D. 25 to 30, to whom the statements of Josephus also most naturally refer. The expressions "Abila of Lysanias" (Jos. Antiq. 19.5.1), "the kingdom of Lysanias," distinguished from "the kingdom of Chalcis" (Jos. War 2.11.5), and "Abila the Tetrarch of Lysanias" (Jos. Antiq. 20.7.1) do not fit the earlier Lysanias whose kingdom was much larger than Abila and had Chalcis as the capital.

Two inscriptions agree with Luke 3:1 and Josephus regarding the existence of a second Lysanias who ruled in the period of the NT tetrarchies. Inscription CIG 4523 speaks of a Lysanias and of a "Zenodotus of Lysanias the tetrarch," thus indicating the existence of two men in this general period with the same name.

Inscription CIG 4521 found at Abila mentions Lysanias the tetrarch as governing at the time when the Roman Empire is said to be ruled by more than one Augustus* (the plural Sebastoi is used), which occurred for the first time in the reign of Tiberius* (A.D. 14–37; cf. Tac. Ann. 1.8).

BIBLIOGRAPHY: E. Schürer, A History of the Jewish People, 1.2 (1891), 335–39; R. Savignac "Texte complet de l'inscription d'Abila relative a Lysanias," RB, 9 (1912), 533–40; H. Leclercq, "Lysanias d' Abilene," Dict. d' Arch, 10 (1931), 405–11; J. M. Creed, The Gospel According to St. Luke (1957), 307–9; E. Gabba, Iscrizioni greche e latine per lo Studio della Bibbia (1958); D. E. Hiebert, ZPEB, 3 (1975), 1013.

WHM

LYSTRA. The site of this Lycaonian* town was confirmed by an inscription discovered in 1885 by J. B. Sterrett, which confirmed the early suggestion by Leake in 1820, that Lystra was a ruin-mound a little N of Hatsunaray. The mound revealed habitation levels as far back as the third millennium B.C. The first century A.D. city was not confined to the tell,* and little systematic investigation of the scattered remnants around the site has taken place. The name itself is probably old Lycaonian, a language unknown to Paul (Acts 14:6–21). The place was, no doubt, a market town, and shared the changing fortunes of the administrative areas of Lycaonia itself and neighboring Galatia* in Hellenistic and Roman days. Augustus's* establishment of a "colonia" there about 6 B.C. under the name of Julia Felix Gemina Lustra, and the appearance of consequential inscriptions and Augustan coinage, led to the geographical identification (CIL 3.6786). The ruins of the temple of Zeus* (Acts 14:13) remain for excavation at the foot of the mound.

BIBLIOGRAPHY: W. M. Ramsay, The Cities of St. Paul (1908), 407–18; E. M. Blaiklock, Cities of the NT (1965), 31–34; A. H. M. Jones, The Cities of the Eastern Roman Provinces (1971 ed.), 134–35; H. W. Hoehner, ZPEB, 3 (1975), 1015.

EMB

M

MACCABEES. A name traditionally given to the brothers and associates of Judas Maccabaeus, the Jewish liberator (d. 160 B.C.), whose surname represents either Hebrew *maqqabah* "hammer" or the acrostic* formed by the initial letters of the slogan *Mi Kamokha Ba'elohim Yahweh*, "Who is like thee among the gods, O Lord?" (cf. Exod 15:11), perhaps emblazoned on his banner. The name "Maccabees" is also attached to four documents of the first century B.C., two of which (1 and 2 Macc) are among our primary documents for the liberation struggle led against the Seleucid forces by Judas and his brothers.

When Judas fell in battle, he was succeeded as leader of the Jewish insurgents by his brother Jonathan, who accepted the high priesthood from the Seleucid pretender Alexander Balas in 152 B.C. When Jonathan was captured and killed in 143, he was succeeded by Simon, last survivor of the brothers, under whom Judea* gained political independence. He became the founder of the Hasmonean dynasty of priest-kings, which ruled until the Roman conquest in 63 B.C.

Under this dynasty the boundaries of Jerusalem* were extended to cover part of the western hill, which was joined to the temple* area by the First N Wall. In the upper city,* facing the temple from the western side of the Tyropoeon Valley, there was built a Hasmonean residence; fortifications of Maccabean date have been uncovered there. The city wall on the eastern side (S of the temple area) was also added to and strengthened in Maccabean times.

Beth-zur,* on the Judeo-Idumaean frontier (between Jerusalem and Hebron*), when excavated by O. R. Sellers in 1941, yielded extensive Maccabean remains, including a fortress built by Judas (cf. 1 Macc 4:61). At Marisa (Mareshah*), modern Tell Sandahannah in the Shephelah,* a whole town of the period has been unearthed. The ruins of Simon's fortress at Gezer* (1 Macc 13:43, 48) were brought to light by R. A. S. Macalister. The mausoleum which Simon built for his parents and brothers at Modin, with seven pyramids,* remained a notable monument for several centuries.

BIBLIOGRAPHY: W. R. Farmer, *Maccabees, Zealots and Josephus* (1956), 47–158; Y. Aharoni and M. Avi-Yonah, *The Macmillan Bible Atlas* (1968), 110–28; H. W. Hoehner, *ZPEB*, 4 (1975), 2–8.   FFB

MACE. *See* ARMS AND WEAPONS.

MACEDONIA. In NT times, a mountainous region N of Achaia and SW of Thracia, extending from the Aegean Sea to the Adriatic. Although it contained several fertile plains, its principal cities* were on the coast of the Aegean Sea. In the third millennium B.C. migrations of people from Europe and the E were followed by tribes of Thracians, Macedonians, and some maritime peoples.

The Macedonian kingdom was established early in the seventh century B.C., but it was only three centuries later that the warring Macedonian tribes were finally unified under Philip II of Macedon (359–336) and proceeded to exercise hegemony over mainland Greece. When Philip was assassinated, his son Alexander the Great succeeded him, ruling from 336 until his premature death in 323. During his short reign he managed to found the largest Near Eastern empire in antiquity, imposing Greek culture on peoples from the Levant to the Indus Valley.

After his death a period of instability followed in Macedonia, until the territory was absorbed into the Imperial system subsequent to the victory of Aemilius Paullus in 168. Macedonia became a full Roman province in 148 B.C., with which Achaia was combined between A.D. 15 and 44. Roman rule resulted in the construction of the famous Via Egnatia (*see* EGNATIAN WAY) which traversed the mountains from W to E from twin starting points on the Adriatic, and went beyond Thessalonica,* Philippi,* and Nicopolis to terminate in Thrace.

Paul doubtless traveled along this road on his missionary journeys in Asia Minor,* establishing flourishing Christian churches in the process (Acts 16:8–17:15). Some of Paul's traveling companions were Macedonians (Acts 19:29; 20:4), while the believers in that province were notable both for their contributions to alleviate poverty in Jerusalem (Rom 15:26) and also for their support of the apostle himself (2 Cor 8:1–5; Phil 4:15).

Excavations at the main sites in Macedonia have furnished clear indications of Hellenistic structures, although there is frequently a considerable amount of Byzantine* overlay. Thus only the foundations of the city wall* at Thessalonica can be regarded as original, and the same is true of other structures there and elsewhere. An inscription from the Vardar Gate, where the Via Egnatia entered Thessalonica, mentioned certain officials known as politarchs.*

BIBLIOGRAPHY: W. A. Heurtley, *Prehistoric Macedonia* (1939); J. Finegan, *IDB*, 3 (1962), 216–17; A. Rupprecht, *ZPEB*, 4 (1975), 22–25.   RKH

MACHINES, WAR. In 2 Chron 26:15 it is recorded that Uzziah, in strengthening the defenses of Jeru-

Balls of stone used during the Bar Kokhba revolt (A.D. 132-135) and found in Herodium. *(See also photos under* ARMS AND WEAPONS.*)* Courtesy Israel Government Press Office.

salem, * equipped the walls * with stone-throwing devices. There seems to be no archaeological illustration from Middle Eastern war for such machines, but literary evidence from both Greek and Roman centuries is abundant (*OCD* under "Siegecraft," 837–38). Two types of artillery were used by the Romans, the *catapulta* (invented in Syracuse about 400 B.C.) and the *ballista*. The former shot heavy arrows, and a skeleton of a defender of Maidun Castle in Dorset, besieged by Vespasian, * holds such a metal shaft between the shattered vertebrae. Originally a shaped wooden shaft had probably been attached, but this has rotted away. The machines that propelled such missiles, based on swinging beams and twisted ropes, have likewise disappeared. Evidence is meager and confined to art, where no indication is given of structure or working. Around Masada * are numerous balls of stone that had been propelled by the vanished machines of both besieger and besieged (Y. Yadin has illustrations in his *Masada*, 162–63). A catapult is also shown on the tombstone of Caius Vedennius Moderatus of the Legio XVI (Dessau, *Inscriptiones Latinae Selectae*, 1892–1916, no. 2034), and Trajan's Column seems to show some war machines. This is the limit of archaeological evidence. The rest can only be conjectured from literary evidence (*see Companion to Roman Studies* [1935], 480–81).

In Ezek 26:9 reference is made to "engines of assault" (KJV; "battering rams" NIV, NASB). Assyrian illustrations of siegecraft, startlingly realistic and detailed, show various forms of battering rams and the covering mantlets by which they were moved into positions of assault against a wall or gate. * Y. Yadin, in *The Art of Warfare in Biblical Lands* (1963), has numerous striking illustrations, principally from Assyrian frescoes.

See also ARMS AND WEAPONS; WARFARE.

EMB

MACHPELAH (mak pē ′lə; lit., "the double cave" — Gen 23:19; 25:9; 49:31; 50:13). The place of Abra-

ham's family tomb is fairly certainly located at the site of the Moslem shrine, Haram el-Khalil, at Hebron. * An Arab and Latin * account of some medieval "archaeology" in June A. D. 1119 alleges the discovery there of the bones of the patriarchs. Since the site had been alternately occupied by Moslem and Christian buildings, no certainty can be attributed to the account, although Jew, * Moslem, and Christian are one in honoring the patriarchal family.

The modern archaeological interest attaches rather to the vivid account of an Eastern sale and purchase detailed in Gen 23. V. R. Gold (*IDB*, 3 [1962], 219) describes it as "a typical example of land purchase under Hittite law, * the point being that Ephron the Hittite was anxious, by including the surrounding property, to transfer to the purchaser his feudal obligations under Hittite law." Hittite * documents also add a note of trees growing on the property under transfer.

The Alalakh * tablets add some further authenticating details. Tablets 18 to 23 show that silver was the common currency (*see* COINS) in the eighteenth century B.C., a situation, no doubt, centuries old. Copper superseded silver * only three centuries later. Tablets 33 and 48 refer to the shekel "according to the weight of Aleppo." Tablets 52–53, 56, and 58 use the phrase "at its full price." The last-named tablet uses the formula: "The full price is paid and the vendor is satisfied" (cf. Gen 23:16).

BIBLIOGRAPHY: M. Lehman, on the theme of Abraham's purchase, *BASOR*, 129 (1953), 15–18; R. de Vaux, *Dictionnaire de la Bible*, *Suppl.* 5 (1953), cols. 618–27; H. G. Stigers, *ZPEB*, 4 (1975), 26–28.

EMB

MADABA. *See* MEDEBA.

MADAI. *See* MEDES.

MADDER ROOT. The red dye * of the madder root, or cloth * dyed with the product, was probably the merchandise which Lydia * was selling at Philippi * (Acts 16:14). Madder is a herbaceous climbing plant (*rubia tinctorum*), with rough hairy stems and small

Aerial view of mosque, Haram el-Khalil, built over Cave of Machpelah in modern Hebron. Courtesy Israel Government Press Office.

yellow flowers, cultivated for its crimson dye. It was also considered to have medicinal* qualities. Archaeologically, the plant and its products have assumed unexpected relevance at Qumran.* Red-stained skeletal remains were studied by Dr. Nicu Haas, a senior lecturer in Anatomy at the Hebrew University-Hadassah Medical School, in Jerusalem,* in 1968. These were the remains of six men, four women, and a child of two, proving, incidentally, that the sect was not an all-male community. This, together with archaeological findings, indicated an early collective settlement at Qumran. "The presence of females was only the first discovery," says Dr. Haas. "Another was a purplish-red stain found in the bones." Chemical analysis led to the conclusion that the stain was from alizarin, the pigment of the madder root, common in the region, and which was used as a natural dye for clothes.

It is not thought that the dye came from burial clothes, which were not commonly used, but was ingested from drink made from the root, a medicinal practice mentioned by Josephus and apparently under some rabbinical ban. This may account for the absence of stain in the child's remains and in that of a septuagenarian, a non-Jew, as certain oriental characteristics show, who must have joined the community after his bone growth was completed.

The use of the madder root drink has persisted along the Mediterranean, in the Balkans, and southern France, and by the Arabs, as a morning drink; but its function has changed from disease prevention to the warding off of the "evil eye."

New findings, S of the Qumran site, dating back to the same period, have shown the same collective pattern of life as well as analogous practices, substantiated by similarly red-stained skeletons.

EMB

MAGADAN (MAGDALA) (mag'ə dan; Gr., Μαγαδάν, *Magadan;* Μαγδαλά, *Magdala*). A place probably to be located just N of Tiberias* on the Lake of Galilee.* The parallel passage, Mark 8:10, has Dalmanutha.

Magdalēnē ("woman from Magdala") was the surname of a Mary (Matt 27:56 et al.), who was probably from the town of Magdala. The place name remains in the Arabic* Mejdel, a village on the road c. 4.4 km. (2¾ mi.) N of Tiberias.

The site is at the junction where the ancient road from Nazareth* came down the Wadi el-Hamam (Valley of Pigeons), past the cliffs of Arbela; the Jews fought the Syrians at Arbela (1 Macc 9:2), and Josephus fortified the village of the Cave of Arbela in the war with Rome (Jos. *Life* 37; 188). This is in harmony with the location being named Magdala which derived from Heb. *migdal* "tower," i.e. guard tower.* This is no doubt the same place as the Talmud's Migdal Nunaija ("fish tower") located near Tiberias (Pesahim 46a, *SBT* 2.4.219) and Josephus's Tarichea (probably from *Tárichos* "salted fish"; Jos. *War* 3.9, 7; 445), also located near Tiberias.

Christian pilgrims found the place carrying the name Magdala. Theodotus (A.D. 530) says in going N from Tiberias 3.2 km. (2 mi.), he came to Magdala

"where the Lady Mary was born" (*CCSL*, 175.115).

There must have been a Byzantine* church located at Magdala, for Eutychius (d. 940) says, "The Church of Magdala near Tiberias shows that here Christ expelled the 7 demons which were in Mary Magdalene" (*The Book of Demonstration*, ed. Watt, *CSCO*, 193.136). The church is not now identifiable.

The other names, such as Magadan, etc. (with the possible exception of Dalmanutha), witnessed to in the Greek MSS of Matt 15:39 and Mark 8:10 may well be just variants of Magdala, Migdal "tower."

BIBLIOGRAPHY: W. F. Albright, "Contributions to the Historical Geography of Palestine," *AASOR*, 2–3 (1923), 29–46; G. Dalman, *Sacred Sites and Ways* (1935), 125–26; C. Kopp, *The Holy Places of the Gospels* (1963), 190–96; Finegan, *The Archaeology of the NT* (1969), 44–48.   WHM

MAGDALA. See MAGADAN.

MAGIC. See EXORCISM; INCANTATION.

MAJUSCULE SCRIPT. See PALAEOGRAPHY, GENERAL.

MALTA (môl'tə; Gr., Μελίτη, *Melitē*). A small island mentioned in Acts 28:1 (Melita KJV), lying to the S of Sicily, 30 km. (18 mi.) long and 13 km. (8 mi.) wide. The largest harbor is on the NE side at the modern city* of Valetta. The traditional St. Paul's Bay is c. 13 km. (8 mi.) farther NW. There are two other islands in the group, Gaulus (or Gozo) and Kerkina.

Archaeological investigation has revealed numerous prehistoric sites on Malta and Gozo, with some materials dating from 2300 B.C. to 1400 B.C. including pottery,* flints, shells, and megalithic* structures in double oval form, probably for cult practices. Other prehistoric material dates from 1400 B.C. to 800 B.C.

Following the Phoenician* and Carthaginian influence, the Romans took control of the islands which at first were under the province of Sicily, as shown by a Maltese coin* of c. 35–27 B.C. Under the Roman Empire, the islands were placed under a procurator, as evidenced by a Latin inscription (*CIL*, 10.7494). In the time of Tiberius,* a Greek inscription speaks of a L Castricius Prudens as "chief" (*prōtos*), i.e., the leading official, of Malta, the same title given Publius in Acts 28:7. The traditional site for the villa of Publius, where Paul was received when shipwrecked, is San Pawl Milqi, located on the slopes above Bur Marrod, near Salina Bay.

At the center of Malta, where the ancient city of Melita was located, a few Roman tombs have been found. Also near Birzelbugia, in the S of Malta, work has been done on a Roman villa whose mosaics* and sculptures testify to the high degree of Maltese culture. On Malta are a number of Jewish and Christian catacombs.*

BIBLIOGRAPHY: T. Ashby, "Roman Malta," *JRS*, 5 (1915), 23–80; T. Zammit, *Malta, the Islands and Their History* (1926); H. Leclercq, "Malte," *Dictionnaire d' archéologie chretienne et de liturgie*, 10.1 (1931), 1332–39; J. D. Evans, *Malta* (1959); R. C.

Stone, *ZPEB*, 4 (1975), 46–48; *PECS* (1976), 568–69.
WHM

MAMRE (mäm′rə; Heb. מַמְרֵא, *mamrê*; LXX
Μαμρη, *Mamrē*). A site or location c. 3.2 km. (2 mi.)
N of Hebron,* associated with Abraham's stay in the
area. Locally called Ramet el-Khâlil, it was, according to Gen 14:13, 24 named after Mamre, an Amorite* whose brothers Eshcol and Aner were also
attached to Abraham in his battle with Chedorlaomer's army.

Abraham built an altar* "by the great trees of
Mamre" (Gen 13:18), and it was here that he enter-
tained three heavenly visitors and interceded with
them for Sodom* and Gomorrah* (Gen 18:20–33).
Nearby to the SE was the cave* of Machpelah,* which
he purchased for a family burial place.

The extensive ruins at the great oak and spring in
Mamre include the church which was built in response to a letter to Constantine from his mother-in-
law, Eutropia, who visited the site and observed a
pagan cult located there. This was not built over the
tree and spring but toward the eastern end of an
enclosure 49 m. (160 ft.) wide by 65 m. (214 ft.) long.
In the SW corner of this enclosure was the spring or
well* and formerly a tree thought to be the oak of
Abraham. The tradition of patriarchal association is
evidently very ancient, as the excavators found a
pavement dating to the ninth–eighth centuries B.C.
A hiatus in this pavement just NE of the well may
signify the location of an oak tree. The basilica* was
small, 20 m. (66 ft.) wide and 16.5 m. (54 ft.) deep.
Excavation of the site during the 1920s was directed
by A. E. Mader whose work satisfactorily established
its identification with both the site of Mamre and the
Constantinian church. Continuing Christian tradition located Mamre here. This tradition is referred
to by Jerome (fourth cent), Eucherius (sixth cent),
Areulpus (A.D. 700), and by Benjamin of Tudela (A.D.
1163). Fourth-century travelers describe an oak at
this site, though Josephus indicates it as being
nearer—six furlongs (1.2 km.)—to the city* of Hebron (Jos. *War* 4.9.7; Jos. *Antiq.* 1.10.4). To this day
some visitors are shown an aged oak tree a short
distance to the NW of Hebron, which may reflect
this earlier identification. However, the tree is a
Holm oak, not indigenous to Palestine, but presumably introduced by the Crusaders.

The courtyard, or *haram*, unmistakably reveals
Herodian masonry similar to the enclosures around
the Jerusalem* temple* area and the cave of Machpelah in Hebron. It was destroyed in A.D. 70, but
was rebuilt by Hadrian.* In his day it was the location of a terebinth market ("Fair of Terebinthos") and
a Roman temple. A huge altar near the center of the
enclosure marked the scene of continuing pagan activities. In A.D. 135 Jewish prisoners from the Second Revolt, led by Bar Kochba,* were sold here as
slaves,* an insult to one of Judaism's most sacred
shrines. Despite the building of the Constantinian
church, and destruction of the altar in the fourth
century, pagan cults continued active until the Arab
conquest. The basilica had been torn down by the
Persians in A.D. 614 and partially rebuilt. The com-

pressed plan is very interesting, containing an "inscribed apse" (built within the rectangle of the church)
with a narthex running all the way across its façade
and the courtyard, as well as sacristies displaced to
the outside of the side aisles. Two similar designs are
known in N Syria and at Binbirkilisse in Anatolia.

BIBLIOGRAPHY: A. Mader, *Mambrie, Die Ergeb-
nisse der Ausgrabungen im heiigen Bezirk Râmet el-
Ḥalîl in Südpalästina*, 2 vols. (1957); *FLAP*, 537–38;
G. Armstrong, "Imperial Church Building in the Holy
Land in the Fourth Century," *BA* (1967), 95–96;
R. L. Alden, *ZPEB*, 4 (1975), 48.

MHH

MANASSEH. The discrepancy imagined between
2 Kings 21 and 2 Chron 33 in the matter of Manasseh's repentance receives some light from archaeology. "Manasseh King of the Jews" appears in a list
of twenty-two Assyrian tributaries of imperial Assyria
on both the Prism of Esarhaddon* and the Prism of
Ashurbanipal* (*ANET*, 291, 294). It is reasonable to
assume that Manasseh was put in a very difficult position by the four-year rebellion of Shamashshumukin, Ashurbanipal's brother, and governor of Babylon*
(652–648 B.C.). Whatever side Manasseh chose, there
was a chance of hostile confrontation. Perhaps late
in life, being a listed vassal, he suffered either a period of imprisonment in Assyria, or Babylon (which
became Ashurbanipal's capital), or was summoned
there for a painful scrutiny of loyalty. The experience
could have disillusioned the aging Manasseh with his
imported pagan worship. The problem spawned a
crop of Jewish rehabilitation legends, and the little
apocryphal classic of devotion, the Prayer of
Manasseh.

BIBLIOGRAPHY: H. B. MacLean, *IDB*, 3 (1962),
254–55; A. C. Schultz, *ZPEB*, 4 (1975), 61–65.

EMB

MANETHO (man′ə thō). The Greek version of an
Egyptian name not identifiable with certainty. Manetho was an Egyptian priest from Sebennytos in the
central Delta, who is principally famed for having
written a history of Egypt* (the *Aigyptiaka*) besides
other works of uncertain number and attribution. He
produced his history under Ptolemy II Philadelphos
(282–246 B.C.).

The history has been entirely lost except for occasional citations (as by Josephus, Jos. *Apion*) and
the late versions of an *Epitome*, or outline-lists of the
Egyptian dynasties, naming many kings with their
lengths of reign, and the place of origin and length
of years of each dynasty. These versions come to us
in the works of Julius Africanus and Eusebius. As a
priest at Heliopolis,* Manetho would have had access to very valuable chronological material; however, by his time, errors had already lodged in
Egyptian tradition, and his copyists and excerptors
served him ill. As a result, his basic division of the
line of pharaohs into thirty or thirty-one "dynasties"
is sound and still used. However, the lists of kings
and reigns are often corrupt, although valid data can
be gotten from them, especially in comparisons with
inscriptional evidence.

BIBLIOGRAPHY: W. G. Waddell, *Manetho*, Loeb ed. (1940).

KAK

MANGER. A box or trough containing fodder for domesticated animals. The crib or stall is referred to in Job 39:9; Prov 14:4; Isa 1:3, a roofed stall in 2 Chron 32:28, and a pen in Hab 3:17. In the Megiddo* stables,* oblong feed boxes cut from long blocks of limestone are found, measuring about 1 by .6 by .5 m. (3 by 2 by 1½ ft.). Masonry mangers were found in a stable at Lachish* dating to about 1200 B.C. Crusader mangers of similar pattern are found at Acre (Acco*). The Lachish manger was in a cave* used as a stable. The heavy wooden mangers of medieval Christian art were foreign to Ancient Near Eastern usage, which commonly employed natural stone mangers.

BIBLIOGRAPHY: W. White, Jr., *ZPEB*, 4 (1975), 66–67.

EMB

MANTLE. *See* CLOAK.

MANUAL OF DISCIPLINE. *See* DEAD SEA SCROLLS.

MAPS. *See* CARTOGRAPHY.

MARDIKH. *See* TELL MARDIKH.

MARESHAH (mə rē'shə; Heb. מָרֵשָׁה, *mārēshāh*). A Canaanite* city* in the Judean lowlands, identified with Tell Sandahannah, which under Joshua became the principal city of that part of the Judean Shephelah* (Josh 15:44). Mareshah was fortified (2 Chron 11:8) by Rehoboam (c. 922–915 B.C.) and reinforced by Asa (c. 913–873). Near the city an attacking force from Gerar* was defeated by Asa and forced to flee home (2 Chron 14:9–14). Mareshah's destruction was prophesied by Micah (1:15), and in the exilic period it became an Edomite* capital under the name Marisa. In the middle of the third century B.C. it was a notable center for Idumean slave* trading, and contemporary painted tombs, when excavated, furnished a number of Phoenician,* Greek, and Idumean names, including that of the national deity Qos. Excavations at Hellenistic levels uncovered remains of a city patterned on Greek constructional lines, with blocks of houses,* and some streets* intersecting at right angles.

BIBLIOGRAPHY: W. F. Albright, *The Archaeology of Palestine* (1960), 152–53; V. R. Gold, *IDB*, 3 (1962), 263–64; R. F. Gribble, *ZPEB*, 4 (1975), 73.

RKH

MARI (mä'rē). This once-flourishing cultural center is now identified with Tell Hariri near the Euphrates River, about 11 km. (7 mi.) N of Abu Kemal in SE Syria. Its importance arose from its being located at the intersection of two caravan routes, one of which crossed the Syrian desert while the other comprised one of the main highways from Assyria to Babylonia. Excavations were carried out at the site from 1933 to 1960, uncovering such important ruins as a temple

Statue of Puzur-Ishtar, governor of Mari, Ur III period (c. 2060-1955 B.C.). Courtesy Staatliche Museen zu Berlin.

complex dedicated to Ishtar,* the latest building coming from the First Dynasty of Babylon; a royal palace from the same general period; and a large ziggurat,* or staged temple tower. The royal palace belonging to the eighteenth-century B.C. rulers Iasmaḫ-Adad and Zimri-Lim contained three hundred rooms extending over 6 ha. (15 a.), and from its archives were recovered over twenty thousand tablets written mostly in Akkadian. These have furnished a wealth of historical, geographical, religious, and cultural information about contemporary northwestern Mesopotamia.*

Mari was first mentioned in the middle of the third millennium B.C. in an inscription recording its fall to the king of Lagash.* Mari was subsequently conquered by Sargon I* of Agade, but by the time of the Third Dynasty of Ur* (c. 2070–1960 B.C.), Mari was under Sumerian* control. A prince of Mari, Ishbi-Irra, helped overthrow Ur, but the independence thus gained was soon lost to Shamshi-Adad I of Assyria (c. 1818–1786 B.C.). Zimri-Lim gained control of Mari about 1780 B.C. but was defeated in battle by Hammurabi* c. 1760. However, he continued as vassal ruler for nearly twenty years, until the Kassites* sacked Mari about 1745. Mari was an Amorite* cultural center, which exercised a rather inadequate degree of control over neighboring nomadic and seminomadic peoples. One such group, the aggressive "Bene Yamina," are thought to have some affinities with the OT Benjaminites. Another, the Habiru,* were of equally obscure origin but appeared as mercenaries, musicians, captives, servants, and government employees. To what extent they are related to the OT Hebrews is uncertain. The same group appeared in texts from Alalakh,* Ras Shamra (see UGARIT), and Tell el-Amarna (see AMARNA).

The Mari Amorites probably controlled the Haran* district to which Abram and his father Terah migrated (Gen 11:31). Certainly the family connection with the area seems preserved in sites S of Haran such as Serug, Peleg, and Terah, though a positive connection has yet to be demonstrated. The Mari Amorites frequently ratified a treaty by killing a donkey,* a custom favored by the descendants of Shechem (cf. Josh 24:32).

The terminology of the royal census at Mari involving enrollment, purification, disciplinary measures, and the like, has striking parallels to OT terminology (e.g., Exod 30:13–14).

BIBLIOGRAPHY: A. Parrot, *Mari, une ville perdue* (1935); *CAH*, 1.2, 97 passim.   RKH

MARISA. See MARESHAH.

MARRIAGE. I. *Mesopotamian Marriage.* A. *Preparations for Marriage.* Marriages were arranged by parents. The Eshnunna* Code invalidated a marriage which lacked parental permission.

The betrothal created an inchoate marriage. The violation of a betrothed maiden was considered a capital offense since she was legally regarded as a wife according to the Code of Hammurabi.*

The betrothal was sealed by the transfer of the *terhatu* ("bride price") from the groom to the father of the bride. The *sheriqtu* ("dowry") was given by the father of the bride to his daughter. From the Old Babylonian period the dowry was commonly larger than the bride price.

B. *The Celebration of Marriage.* Some Ur* III court documents indicate that marriages could be arranged by oral agreements. *CH* 128 ruled that a woman is not a wife without a *riksātu* ("contract").

Contracts could include special provisions. Nuzi* contracts obliged the barren wife to provide her husband with a handmaid to bear children (cf. *CH* 146; Gen 16).

Marriage was a civil affair which required no religious sanctions. During the wedding the bride's face was covered. The Middle Assyrian Laws (*MAL* 40) prescribed severe penalties for wives who went out on the streets unveiled.

C. *The Dissolution of Marriage.* A man could divorce his wife for a variety of reasons. A wife who had neglected her house could be sent out empty-handed or reduced to the status of a slave* (*CH* 141, cf. 143). The Assyrians could divorce their wives at will and send them away without anything (*MAL* 37).

Divorce by the woman was more difficult and at times not permitted. A blameless woman who had been disparaged by her husband could sue for divorce before the city council of Babylon* (*CH* 142).

II. *Ugaritic Marriage.* A. *Preparations for Marriage.* In the mythological text of the wedding of Nikkal and the Moon, Yarih (the Moon) offers to give a *mhr* ("bride price") of a thousand pieces of silver* and ten thousand of gold* for Nikkal.

Nikkal's dowry (*tlh*) and wedding gifts (*mlg*) are mentioned. One text speaks of a widow's *trht* (cf. Akkad. *terhatu*) of eighty shekels which she brought with her as a dowry.

B. *The Dissolution of Marriage.* A series of Akkadian* and Ugaritic* texts deal with a case of royal divorce. King Ammistamru II (1250–40 B.C.) divorced Piddu and sent her back to Amuru with her children and with her property. Fisher has argued that Piddu is to be identified with "the Great Lady who committed a great sin," i.e. adultery, who is mentioned in other texts. He suggests that it was her daughter who was put to death, perhaps because she was the issue of the adultery (cf. 2 Sam 12:14).

III. *Egyptian Marriage.* A. *Preparations for Marriage.* Girls were married between twelve and fourteen, and young men between fourteen and twenty years old. The woman's father was usually the one who drew up the contract with the groom. A deed from 536 B.C. is the first evidence of a contract between the groom and the bride herself.

Certain deeds, dating from 517 B.C. to the Ptolemaic period, are based on "the money to become a wife," in which the bride gave a sum to the husband, who then promised to maintain her.

The dowry included toiletry articles, vessels,* garments, etc., which remained the wife's property.

B. *The Celebration of Marriage.* Marriages could be concluded without any written documents. Most of the marriage documents are proprietary in character, dealing with the disposition of property.

There is no evidence that any religious ceremonies were involved in marriage. The father of the bride conducted her, accompanied with rich gifts, to the groom's house where a great feast was held.

C. *The Dissolution of Marriage.* From 364 B.C. some deeds stipulated that a rather high fine had to be paid by the husband who divorced his wife. From 542 B.C. women were given deeds that guaranteed their freedom to marry again after a divorce.

IV. *Jewish Marriage.* A. *Preparations for Marriage.* Sepulchral inscriptions of Jewish families buried in the catacombs* at Rome* in the early Christian era give the ages of brides in six cases: two married at twelve, two at fifteen, one between fifteen and sixteen, and one between sixteen and seventeen. Males were advised to marry between fourteen and eighteen.

Aramaic marriage document from Elephantine, dated 449 B.C., of Tamut, handmaiden of Meshullam b. Zaccur, to Ananiah b. Azariah. Tamut remained a handmaiden even after her marriage. Courtesy The Brooklyn Museum. Bequest of Miss Theodora Wilbour.

In the Elephantine papyri* the bride herself was not an active participant in the contract, but in the Bar Menasseh marriage deed (first century B.C.) the bride's consent was recorded.

Ordinarily a year intervened between the Jewish betrothal, or *qiddûshîn* ("consecration"), and the nuptials, or *niśśu'în* ("taking up"). Once made, the betrothal was legally binding and could not be broken save by death or by divorce.

The Elephantine papyri list the *muhra* ("bride price") in one case (Cowley, Aramaic Papyri No. 15) as five shekels and in another (Kraeling, Papyrus 7) as ten shekels. In these fifth-century B.C. texts the bride price was given to the woman as part of her dowry. In the period of the rabbis the bride price became purely nominal.

B. *The Celebration of Marriage*. The *ketubah* was the marriage contract which the husband provided to his wife. Its provision was made an obligatory condition by Rabbi Meir in the second century A.D.

Three relatively complete and four fragmentary Aramaic* contracts, which are called *s^epar 'intu* ("document of wifehood"), have been recovered from Elephantine. From Murabba'at have been recovered two Aramaic marriage documents (one dated to A.D. 117), and two Greek contracts, including one of a remarriage (A.D. 124). From Nahal Hever we have a well-preserved *ketubah* (between A.D. 128–30) of the second marriage of Babata.

C. *The Dissolution of Marriage*. To validate a divorce the husband had to give a *gēṭ* ("bill of divorce") to his wife and have the divorce registered in a Jewish court.

The Elephantine texts, influenced by Egyptian custom, permitted either the man or the woman to initiate divorce without any objective grounds being necessary. Whoever initiated the divorce had to pay a penalty of *ksp śn'h* ("divorce money").

V. *Greek Marriage*. A. *Preparations for Marriage*. Girls were married as early as twelve, but more usually between fourteen and twenty. On the other hand, men usually wed when they were closer to thirty.

A woman was always subject to a male *kurios* ("guardian"). She was therefore the object of marriage negotiations and her consent was not required.

In the early period a necessary preliminary to marriage was the betrothal, or *egguēsis* (from the verb "to put into the hand"). This was a formal transaction, usually before witnesses, in which the father of the bride promised his daughter to the groom.

B. *The Celebration of Marriage*. Greek marriage contracts dating at the earliest from the late fourth century B.C. have been preserved on papyri* from Egypt.* The husband promised that he would not maltreat his wife, nor introduce any other woman into the house. His wife was not to leave the house either by day or night without his consent.

The act of *ekdosis* ("giving up") marked the formal conveyance of the bride to the groom and sealed the marriage. In Hellenistic times with the weakening of the Greek family the *ekdosis* was replaced by a *de facto* joining of the pair.

C. *The Dissolution of Marriage*. A couple could agree to separate simply to recontract a more suitable union. The husband had the right to divorce his wife without any valid reason.

The wife, with the aid of her male guardian, could sue for divorce before the eponymous* archon if her husband had been flagrantly unfaithful.

VI. *Roman Marriage*. A. *Preparations for Marriage*. By the time of Augustus* the legal minimum age for marriage for girls was set at twelve, and for boys at fourteen, a standard which was later adopted by church canon law.

A study by Hopkins of 145 Latin inscriptions revealed that over half of the girls were married by fifteen. Grooms were generally men in their twenties, with an average age of twenty-five.

Marriages were usually preceded by a betrothal, or *sponsalia*. The *dos* ("dowry") was a very important factor in most marriages. Its size would be fixed after hard bargaining between the families.

B. *The Celebration of Marriage*. No ceremonies of a legal character were required to form a valid marriage. In the early Empire contracts (called the *tabulae nuptiales*) listing the dowry were inscribed as a record of the marriage.

The ceremonies were completed by the *deductio in domum mariti*, the formal transfer of the bride to her new home. The groom would then carry the bride over the threshold to prevent her from stumbling, which would have been an unlucky omen.

C. *The Dissolution of Marriage*. In the early history of Rome divorce was rare. The Twelve Tables of law inscribed in 451 B.C. record the formula for divorce: *Res tuas tibi habeto*, "Take your things with you."

By the late Republic and early Empire, divorces had become quite common among the upper classes, often for political reasons. In this period a wife could initiate divorce proceedings.

BIBLIOGRAPHY: *Mesopotamian Marriage*. C. Gordon, "Biblical Customs and the Nuzu Tablets," *BA*, 3 (1940), 1–12; A. van Praag, *Droit matrimonial assyro-babylonien* (1945); S. Greengus, "Old Babylonian Marriage Ceremonies and Rites," *JCS*, 20 (1966), 55–72; id., "The Old Babylonian Marriage Contract," *JAOS*, 89 (1969), 505–32.

Ugaritic Marriage. A. van Selms, *Marriage and Family Life in Ugaritic Literature* (1954); A. Rainey, "Family Relationship in Ugarit," *Orientalia*, 34 (1965), 10–22; L. Fisher, *The Claremont Ras Shamra Tablets* (1971).

Egyptian Marriage. W. Edgerton, *Notes on Egyptian Marriage* . . . (1931); P. Pestman, *Marriage and Matrimonial Property in Ancient Egypt* (1961).

Jewish Marriage. A. Cowley, *Aramaic Papyri of the Fifth Century* B.C. (1923); M. Burrows, *The Basis of Israelite Marriage* (1938); E. Neufeld, *Ancient Hebrew Marriage Laws* (1944); L. Epstein, *Sex Laws and Customs in Judaism* (1948); E. Kraeling, *The Brooklyn Museum Aramaic Papyri* (1953); D. Mace, *Hebrew Marriage* (1953); P. Benoit et al., *Les Grottes de Murabba'at* (1961), 104–17, 243–56; Y. Yadin, *Bar-Kokhba* (1971), 222–53.

Greek Marriage. W. Erdmann, *Die Ehe im alten Griechenland* (1934); H. Wolff, *Written and Unwritten Marriages in Hellenistic* . . . *Law* (1939); id., "Marriage Law and Family Organization in Ancient Athens," *Traditio*, 2 (1944), 43–95; W. Lacey, *The Family in Classical Greece* (1968).

Roman Marriage. P. Corbett, *The Roman Law of Marriage* (1930); G. Williams, "Some Aspects of Roman Marriage Ceremonies and Ideals," 48 (1958), 16–29; M. Hopkins, "The Age of Roman Girls at Marriage," *Population Studies*, 18 (1964–65), 309–27. EY

MARS HILL. See AREOPAGUS.

MASADA (mä sä′də). When Titus* had destroyed Jerusalem* in A.D. 70 he went home to his triumph but left behind for methodical subjugation a great stronghold situated by the Dead Sea.* This was the fortress of Masada so meticulously described and magnificently illustrated in the volume, *Masada*, by Israel's soldier archaeologist, Yigael Yadin. Professor Yadin spent three years on the scientific investigation and reconstruction of Masada. The results confirm the awful story told at great length by Josephus.

The stronghold of Masada was one of three mighty forts, built in the rugged eastern hills of Judea* by the first Herod (*see* HEROD, FAMILY OF), who ruled the Jews* as a puppet king of Rome from 40 to 4 B.C. The strongholds were Herodion, Machaerus, and Masada, and the last named was fortified in 36 B.C., over a century before Rome ended the great siege. In that almost impregnable place, it is possible to imagine Herod's fear-haunted soul and the shadow of the deepening paranoia, which darkened Bethlehem* (cf. Matt 2:16).

It is possible, also, to see a facet of Roman policy. When the land was subdued, Vespasian,* survivor of the four contenders for the principate of A.D. 69, was compelled to demonstrate his authority, and also to confirm the fact that he was not irresponsible in marching a substantial legionary force to Italy in the midst of the Jewish War.

Aerial view of Masada, looking southeast. In the foreground is the three-terraced northern palace and behind the upper terrace is a complex of buildings that include storerooms and a large bathhouse. *(See also second photo under* GLACIS *and photo under* LEATHER.) Courtesy Israel Government Press Office.

The fort of Masada was solidly built of casemate walls* and battlements (*see* GLACIS). Reservoirs, voluminous enough to hold 396,200 cu. m. (14 million cu. ft.) of water, cleverly channeled out to take advantage of the flash floods which are a feature of the violent climate, were chipped out of the solid core of the rock. One of the royal palaces stood on the projecting southern promontory of the summit plateau, skillfully built on three different levels, with a sheer drop beneath. Hence the phrase "the hanging palace," which recurs in Professor Yadin's account. It was a magnificent piece of architecture and engineering*—a Roman palace, complete with bathhouse and hypocaust,* the very symbol of that pro-Roman policy, allied with subtle conciliation of the Jews,* which the able Herod family pursued successfully for a whole century. Wine* jars, stamped with the name of C. Sentius Saturninus, consul for 19 B.C., tell the same tale of skillful collaboration. The jars were marked: "To King Herod of Judaea," the earliest inscription ever discovered containing Herod's name. The wine was evidently Augustus's present to the useful Jewish king. The view across the sinister waters of the Dead Sea was superb and appropriate. A secret staircase, "the serpent path" mentioned by Josephus, helped in the identification of the vast ruins.

"This path," says the historian, "is broken off at prominent precipices of the rock, and returns frequently into itself, and lengthening again by little and little has much ado to proceed forward . . . for on each side is a vast, deep chasm and precipice, sufficient to quell the courage of everybody by the terror it infuses into the mind."

Josephus describes, with details of area and length, the fortifications and architecture of Herod's fortress and its two royal abodes, after the fashion which makes him so uninteresting at times to read, but most rewarding for archaeologists. He describes, too, the storehouses of dates and corn laid up for a siege, all of which, he alleges, in the clear dry air of the locality, remained edible and fresh for years in the rock reservoirs. Remnants have been found in the long storerooms. It was a well-stocked and well-armed stronghold which fell into the possession of the last desperate Jewish fighters of the great rebellion. Trees grew by the art of the Masada cultivators, and animals were fed on the rock platform. It was like a modern kibbutz, well-stocked and self-sufficient, as Yadin's investigations make plain.

The walls of circumvallation and the assault ramp may still be seen, and confirm Josephus's story of Silva's attack. The ascent on the landward side is still gained by this path if visitors are prepared for the arduous climb. A cable car on the seaward side offers a less arduous and less historical approach.

Inside the fortress are the undoubted memorials of the mass suicide which the historian describes. Ten men were chosen by lot to slay the rest. These lay down by the bodies of their families, and the ten executioners went to work systematically. One man was then chosen by lot out of the ten, and he killed his nine companions. The very lots, fragments of pottery* bearing the names of the ten, have been found, the letters still legible on the baked clay.* The lots were thrown, no doubt, into a helmet, and one was drawn. Left alone in the charnel house, the lone survivor went around the ranks of the dead and made sure with a thrust here and a slash there that none remained with vestige of life, and then, says Josephus, he drove his sword through his own body. For some reason, two women and five children escaped the slaughter.

Qumran,* the locale of the Dead Sea Scrolls,* is 48 km. (30 mi.) away, and in the ruins of Masada were found considerable pieces of writing exactly like that in some of the Dead Sea Scrolls. This might suggest that some surviving members of the Qumran community had joined the desperate resistance fighters at Masada, although direct evidence is lacking.

BIBLIOGRAPHY: Y. Yadin, *Masada. Herod's Fortress and the Zealots' Last Stand* (1967).   EMB

MASKHUTA, TELL EL-. *See* PITHOM.

MASONRY. *See* ASHLAR MASONRY; BUILDING MATERIALS; CYCLOPEAN MASONRY.

MASSEBAH (ma sē′bə; pl., masseboth). A term for the many sacred pillars, which, along with the asherim, were cult symbols of "the abominations of the Canaanites*" (cf. Lev 26:1; Deut 16:21–22; 27:15; Isa 44:19 et al.). It is not certain whether they were, all or in part, phallic emblems, or whether, in their strength and durability, they stood to remind the worshiper of the presence of the god. An extraordinary sample was found in the temple at Hazor* by Yigael Yadin. The thirteenth-century B.C. shrine was almost intact. Some small basalt stelae* were ranged round a central massebah, which itself bore a relief of two hands lifted in adoration of the sun. The head, as though in desecration, had been thrown down. A storeroom contained replacements for the stones, some in process of manufacture. Yadin is of the opinion that this is the only shrine in Palestine depicting the masseboth of the OT. They represented a concept quite different from that marked by the Hebrew memorials of stone (e.g., Jacob's at Bethel,* Gen 28:11–18, and Moses' twelve stones, Exod 24:4).

EMB

MASTABA (mäs tä′bə). An oblong, flat-topped stone or marble tomb, normally containing a mortuary chapel and other rooms. The outside of a mastaba was frequently concealed with sand so that only the top was visible.

"Shrine of the stelae" from Hazor, series of basalt stelae discovered in ritual niche above temple floor. One relief stele shows two hands raised in prayer toward a moon crescent. On the left is a statuette of a seated man and on the right is a lion orthostat. Late Canaanite Period. Courtesy Israel Dept. of Antiquities and Museums. Exhibited and photographed at Israel Museum, Jerusalem.

MATAR, ABU. *See* ABU MATAR.

MATARIYEH. *See* HELIOPOLIS.

MEASURES. *See* WEIGHTS AND MEASURES.

MEAT. *See* FOOD.

MEAT MARKET. The word (*makellon*) used by Paul (1 Cor 10:25) is found as early as 400 B.C. in an inscription from Epidaurus and the Latin* equivalent (*macellum*) is in the earliest Latin literature (Plautus and Terence). The Latin word is also found in a Corinthian inscription, which, however, does not identify the exact locality. It dates from the early years of Tiberius* and was found on the road to Lechaeum, Corinth's northern port. In the agora* of Corinth,* on the southern side where the judgment seat, or bema,* stands, another fragmentary inscription seems to refer to a piscarium or fish market, and in the same locality there are thirty-three shops with wells* connected with the Peirene Fountain. An inscription refers to "Lucian the butcher," indicating that the *macellum* was probably here.

BIBLIOGRAPHY: BAG, 488, lists the references exhaustively.

EMB

MEDEBA (MADABA) (med'ɔ ba; Heb. מֵידְבָא, *mêḏᵉḇāʾ*). A city in Trans-Jordan, taken by Israel* from the Amorites* (Num 21:30) and given to Reuben (Josh 13:16). The city* had evidently belonged earlier to Moab* and formed part of the border area that alternated between the kingdoms of Moab, Israel, and Ammon.* At the beginning of the united monarchy, Ammonites seem to have been in control (1 Chron 19:7), but subsequently Mesha, king of Moab, told in his inscription (the Moabite Stone*) how Omri,* king of Israel, had captured the city and kept it for at least two generations. Mesha himself returned the city to Moab, though it may have again gone over to Israel in the conquests of Jeroboam II (2 Kings 14:25). In Hellenistic times it formed the northern limit of the Nabataean* kingdom, though at times the city was in Maccabean* hands. From the Roman period come additional Nabataean inscriptions, as well as Roman ruins in the grand style of Jerash. Toward the end of the Byzantine* period the city was the seat of a bishopric and is mentioned in the articles of the Council of Chalcedon in A.D. 451. A period of abandonment followed, until c. 1880 the town was resettled, a state continuing to this day.

The antiquities of Medeba were best seen in the nineteenth century; little remains today. With the exception of an Iron-Age* tomb excavated in 1950 by G. L. Harding, all that remains is one cistern* and a few mosaics* from Byzantine days. One of the mosaics, however, discovered in 1890 in the construction of a new church, was a sixth-century map (*see* MEDEBA MOSAIC MAP) of Palestine that constitutes one of the few important graphic sources of topographical information for the period. Unfortunately most of the map was destroyed, but the parts preserved include a fine picture of Jerusalem,* parts

Detail of Medeba mosaic map showing Jerusalem as an oval, walled city. Courtesy Israel Dept. of Antiquities and Museums.

of the Jordan Valley, and a section of the Negev.*

BIBLIOGRAPHY: G. L. Harding, "An Early Iron Age Tomb at Madeba," *PEFA*, 6 (1953), 24–33; M. Avi-Yonah, *The Madaba Mosaic Map* (1954); E. K. Vogel, "Madeba," *HUCA*, 42 (1971), 57; E. B. Smick, *Archaeology of the Jordan Valley* (1973), 141–53 (an analysis of the Medeba Map with illustrations); P. A. Verhoef, *ZPEB*, 4 (1975), 147–48; *EEHL*, 3 (1977), 819–23.

CEA

MEDEBA MOSAIC MAP. Medeba* was situated in the fertile uplands E of the Jordan and, after the Hebrew conquest of Canaan,* was allotted to the Reubenites (Josh 13:9). Being choice land, the area was attractive to others than the Israelites, and the Moabite Stone* (*ANET*, 320) indicates the interest which the Trans-Jordanian peoples had in the area (cf. 1 Chron 19:7; Isa 15:2).

During the Maccabean* period one of the sons of Mattathias was killed by a certain Jambri of Medeba, for which swift vengeance was exacted by Jonathan and Simon (1 Macc 9:36–42).

After the death of Antiochus Epiphanes the city* was occupied by John Hyrcanus (Jos. *Antiq.* 13.9. 1), and in the early Christian period it became a center of Christianity, ultimately having a bishop (*see* EPISKOPOS) of its own.

In 1884 an ancient map of Palestine, dating back to about the sixth century A.D., and executed in mosaic,* was discovered in the Greek Orthodox church at Medeba. Although there are areas of the map which have suffered considerable damage when reconstruction at the site was being undertaken, it is nevertheless of significance in showing the way in which the land of Palestine appeared to the geographers of the Byzantine* period. The map has now been incorporated into the pavement of the church.

BIBLIOGRAPHY: D. Baly, *The Geography of the Bible* (1957), 30, 172, 236; M. Avi-Yonah, *The Madaba Mosaic Map* (1954).

RKH

MEDES (MEDIA) (Heb. מָדַי, *Māḏay*; LXX Μῆδοι, *Mēdoi*, except at Gen 10:2, which has *Madoi* and 1 Chron 1:5, which has *Madaim*, which English versions have transliterated as "Madai"). An Indo-European people who dominated the highland area of northwestern Iran in the first half of the first millennium B.C. until the ascendancy of the Persians under Cyrus.* They were closely related to the Persians and were not always distinguished from them by the Assyrians, Egyptians, or Greeks, who called both groups "Medes."

1. *Geography.* The heartland of the Medes was located in the northern Zagros Mountains, in modern Kurdistan and Luristan. Media is a highland region from 915 to 1,525 m. (3000 to 5000 ft.) above sea level, divided by mountains into parallel valleys trending NW to SE. The capital of Media was Ecbatana,* modern Hamadan, on the major route from Mesopotamia* to the E. The Assyrians noted that the Medes were found as far E as Mount Bikni (Demavend), NE of Tehran. Levine has argued that Mount Bikni is Elvend near Hamadan.

The climate in Media is temperate during much of the year, and Persian kings used Ecbatana as their summer capital. Winters, however, are severe. Though rain is sometimes scanty in the valleys, there is considerable precipitation in the form of snow.

2. *Biblical References.* There are numerous references to the Medes for the period before the Exile* (e.g., 2 Kings 17:6; Isa 13:17; Jer 25:25; 51:11, 28), and especially for the Exilic period itself (Ezra 6:2; Esth 1:19; and Dan 5:28; 6:8, 12, 15). References (Dan 5:31; 9:1; 11:1) to Darius the Mede,* who, by this name, is not found in nonbiblical sources, led H. H. Rowley to maintain that Daniel erroneously conceived of a Median empire, i.e. the second kingdom in his apocalypses (Dan 7). Conservative scholars hold that the second kingdom was the Medo-Persian Empire, and that Darius the Mede may be either Gubaru (according to Whitcomb), or a title for Cyrus (according to Wiseman).

The sole NT reference to Medians is in the list of places represented by those who heard the message on the day of Pentecost (Acts 2:9).

3. *Extrabiblical Sources.* As we have no connected texts in the Median language, we are dependent primarily upon Assyrian, Neo-Babylonian, and Greek documents. The *Māda*, or Medes, are first mentioned in 836 B.C. in the reign of Shalmaneser III. They occur in the texts of every Assyrian king thereafter until Ashurbanipal.* The Medes occupy a prominent place in Neo-Babylonian documents as they were partners with the Chaldeans* in bringing an end to the Assyrian Empire. In these texts the Medes are sometimes called *Ummān-Manda*, a generic word for "hordes."

Herodotus provides us with valuable information on the Medes and the Persians; some of his data can be integrated with the cuneiform* texts.

4. *Median History.* Assyrian kings, beginning with Shalmaneser III in the ninth century B.C. encountered Iranian tribes, including "the mighty Medes" and "the distant Medes" in the area around Ecbatana

and as far E as the region S of the Caspian Sea.

According to Herodotus (1.96–99) a certain Deioces established a capital at Ecbatana and united the Medes. A chief named *Daiaukku* was captured by Sargon II* in 715 and deported to Hamath* in Syria. A year later Sargon also defeated a Median prince, Metatti, who ruled over Zakirtu, a region SE of Lake Urmia.

In 672 when Esarhaddon* installed his son Ashurbanipal as crown prince, he imposed vassal treaties on Median princes. The texts of these treaties, which include some of the largest cuneiform tablets ever discovered—one measures 45.7 by 30.5 cm. (18 by 12 in.)—were discovered in 1955 at Nimrud (Calah*) and published by Wiseman in 1958. The treaties had been deliberately smashed by the Medes when they captured Nimrud in 612 B.C.

During Esarhaddon's reign, omen texts refer to Kashtariti (the Assyrian form of the Median *Khshathrita*, the word for "kingship"). He was a chief of the Kar-Kašši in the central Zagros who sought to unite Medians, Mannaeans, and Cimmerians in an anti-Assyrian coalition. He has been identified with Herodotus's Phraortes (675–653), a son or grandson of Deioces. According to Herodotus (1.102), Phraortes also subdued the Persians.

Herodotus (1.103 and 3) describes a twenty-eight-year interregnum by nomadic Scythians,* who were finally expelled by Phraortes' son, Cyaxares II (625–585). Cyaxares is the Greek form of *Huvakshatra*; in Akkadian texts he is called *Ummakishta*. Herodotus credits Cyaxares with the creation of a disciplined Median army. Allied with the Neo-Babylonian Nabopolassar,* the Medes were primarily responsible for the fall of Ashur* in 614 and of Nimrud and Nineveh* in 612, and of Harran (Haran*) in 610. During the last five years of his reign Cyaxares fought with Alyattes of Lydia* (Herodotus 1.73–74), a conflict which was ended by the prediction of an eclipse by Thales and the mediation of Labynetus, i.e. Nabonidus.* A Lydian princess was married to Astyages, son of Cyaxares.

Astyages (585–550) is the Greek for *Arshtivaiga; Ishtumegu* in Akkadian.* His daughter, Mandane, married a Persian, Cambyses I and gave birth to the famous Cyrus.* The half-Median and half-Persian Cyrus rebelled against his grandfather in 553 and led the Persians to a complete victory in 550.

Thereafter the Medes played a subordinate though important role under the Persians in the Achaemenid period.

5. *The Arrival of the Medes.* The date of the arrival of the Medes is a matter of dispute. R. Ghirshman placed their arrival at 1000 B.C. from the evidence at Tepe Siyalk.* From the gabled tombs at Siyalk, Ghirshman postulated a northern origin from the direction of the Caucasus.

More recently T. Cuyler Young, Jr., has argued for an earlier migration c. 1300 B.C. from the Gurgan Plain SE of the Caspian Sea. Young asserts that there is no major archaeological break in the Iron II* (1000–750 B.C.) period comparable to the beginning of the Iron I Age. The earlier period is characterized by the

Head of Mede from Persepolis stairway relief; Darius I (521-486 B.C.) to Xerxes (485-465 B.C.) Period. Courtesy the Oriental Institute, University of Chicago.

widespread distribution in the W, e.g., at Hasanlu, Giyan, and Siyalk of a uniform gray pottery,* with possible roots in the culture of Tepe Damghan and Tepe Hissar in the Gurgan area in the E. A possible objection to Young's thesis is the long gap between the Hissar IIIC (2000–1850) ware and the Iron I ware. Deshayes believes that the settlers of Tureng Tepe in the Gurgan Plain were the Indo-European ancestors of the Iranians.

Possibly linked to an early Iranian migration is the rich Iron I (fourteenth–thirteenth centuries B.C.) cemetery uncovered by E. Negahban at Marlik a short distance from the SW shore of the Caspian Sea.

6. *Median Art and Archaeology*. The Medes are depicted on the Persepolis* reliefs wearing domed felt caps, short curled beards, knee-length leather* tunics, and high-laced shoes. They are armed with rectangular shields and short swords carried in decorated scabbards.

The only certain example of Median art is a decorated gold* scabbard from the Oxus Treasure. Barnett has suggested that the figure depicted on the scabbard is Astyages. The decorations include Assyrian, Scythian, and Urartian* elements.

Certain tombs carved in cliffs have been regarded as Median by Herzfeld and Ghirshman. The tomb at Qyzqapan has a relief of two men in Median dress.

Until 1965 we had no examples of Median architecture. Recent excavations at three sites S of Hamadan have provided us with the first Median

structures. C. Meade suggests that the people who settled Baba Jan Tepe, in Luristan were Medes. Excavations by Young at Godin Tepe have brought to light a Median manor house. Excavations at Nush-i Jan, 58 km. (36 mi.) S of Hamadan, by Stronach in 1967 uncovered Median buildings (c. 750–550 B.C.), including a structure with blind windows which anticipates the famous Ka'ba-i Zardusht at Naqsh-i Rustam and the Zendan-i Sulaiman building at Pasargadae.*

BIBLIOGRAPHY: A. T. Olmstead, *History of Assyria* (1923); H. H. Rowley, *Darius the Mede and Four World Empires in the Book of Daniel* (1935); C. C. Torrey, "Medes and Persians," *JAOS*, 46 (1946), 7–15; A. T. Olmstead, *History of the Persian Empire* (1948); R. Ghirshman, *Iran* (1954); D. J. Wiseman, *Chronicles of Chaldaean Kings* (1956); id., *Vassal Treaties of Esarhaddon* (1958); J. Whitcomb, *Darius the Mede* (1959); R. Labat, "Kaštariti, Phraorte et les débuts de l'histoire mède," *JA*, 249 (1961), 1–12; R. D. Barnett, "Median Art," *Iranica Antiqua*, 2 (1962), 77–95; R. Ghirshman, *The Art of Ancient Iran* (1964), 84–91; id., "Le trésor de l'Oxus, . . . et l'art mède," K. Bittel, ed., *Vorderasiatische Archäologie*, (1964), 88–94; E. Negahban, *Marlik* (1964); W. Culican, *The Medes and Persians* (1965); R. Dyson, "Problems of Protohistoric Iran as Seen from Hasanlu," *JNES*, 24 (1965), 193–217; E. Porada, *The Art of Iran* (1965), 137–41; G. Thompson, "Iranian Dress in the Achaemenian Period," *Iran*, 3 (1965), 121–26; D. J. Wiseman et al., *Notes on Some Problems in the Book of Daniel* (1965); T. C. Young, Jr., "A Comparative Ceramic Chronology for Western Iran, 1500–500 B.C.," *Iran*, 3 (1965), 53–85; H. von Gall, "Zu den 'medischen' Felsgräbern in Nordwestiran und Iraqi Kurdistan," *Archäologischer Anzeiger* (1966), 19-43; T. C. Young, Jr., "The Iranian Migration into the Zagros," *Iran*, 5 (1967), 11–34; R. Dyson, "The Archaeological Evidence of the Second Millennium B.C. on the Persian Plateau," *CAH*, 2 (1968); C. Meade, "Luristan in the First Half of the First Millennium B.C.," *Iran*, 6 (1968), 105–34; J. Deshayes, "New Evidence for the Indo-Europeans from Tureng Tepe, Iran," *ARC*, 22 (1969), 10–17; C. Goff, "Excavations at Baba Jan," *Iran*, 7 (1969), 115-30; W. Hinz, *Altiranische Funde und Forschungen* (1969), 63–94; D. Stronach, "Excavations at Tepe Nushi-i Jan, 1967," *Iran*, 7 (1969), 1–20; T. C. Young, Jr., *Excavations at Godin Tepe* (1969); L. Levine, "The Iron Age Revealed," *Expedition*, 13.3–4 (1971), 39–43; id., "Geographical Studies in the Neo-Assyrian Zagros," *Iran*, 10 (1973), 1–78, 99–124; M. Roaf and D. Stronach, "Tepe Nūsh-i Jān, 1970," *Iran*, 13 (1973), 129-40; F. Bagherzadeh, ed., *Proc. of the IInd Annual Symposium on Archaeological Research in Iran* (1974); R. Ghirshman, *L'Iran et la migration des Indo-Aryens et des Iraniens*, (1977); G. Komoróczy, "Ummān-Manda," *Acta Antiqua*, 25 (1977), 43-67; C. Goff, *An Archaeologist in the Making* (1980).   EY

MEDICINE. From very early times the people of Mesopotamia* and Egypt* in particular initiated and developed a system of medical practice which came under the supervision of a branch of the priesthood. The superstitious Mesopotamians regarded disease as the result of bodily invasion through the apertures of the head by malignant demons from the underworld. Hence exorcism* was an extremely important priestly technique in medical practice. A series of Babylonian tablets described the depredations of the "headache demon," and it is probable that the ailments alluded to included meningitis, cerebro-spinal fever, intracranial pressure from tumors, malaria, and other diseases. Not all pathogenesis had superstitious attributions, however, for one cuneiform* text described with great clinical accuracy the condition of a man suffering from the effects of overindulgence in alcohol.

The Sumerians* were the first to discover the curative properties of herbs, and a tablet from the last quarter of the third millennium B.C. contains the world's oldest pharmacopoeia. The Code of Hammurabi* recognized the professional status of the physician a:.d established guidelines for the pursuit of his vocation. The earliest written Egyptian medical traditions almost certainly go back to the end of the third millennium B.C. and show that, as in Mesopotamia, magic and superstition were dominant in therapeutics. While galenicals (herbal extractions) were used, they generally were thought to stand in need of an incantation to increase their effectiveness. Nevertheless, one Egyptian papyrus,* a surgical casebook, proved to be quite free from magical influences. Along with the establishing of the four basic elements in a compound prescription, the Egyptians were the first to discover how to reduce a dislocated jaw. A mine of information and archaeological illustration on his country's ancient medicine and therapeutic practice is to be found in the study published in 1963 by Professor Paul Ghalioungui of the Cairo Ain Shams Medical Faculty, entitled: *Magic and Medical Science in Ancient Egypt*.

Because God was the sole healer (Exod 15:26), the Hebrews placed little reliance upon physicians until the kingdom period (cf. 2 Chron 16:12). Their religious traditions disavowed magic completely and placed the incidence of disease either on a demonstrably empirico-rational or on a spiritual basis. The "physicians" of Gen 50:2 were embalmers, and those mentioned in narratives from the monarchy can have been little more than herbalists, as their counterparts in Amarna Age Ugarit* had been. Popular sayings of a rather derisive nature had arisen about physicians by the time of Jesus (Matt 9:12; Luke 4:23), but by contrast Luke was referred to in Col 4:14 as the "beloved physician." The Bible has little to say about medical treatment, though noting that boils, wounds, and putrifying sores had various medicinal remedies applied to them (cf. 2 Kings 20:1–7; Isa 1:6; Luke 10:34; 1 Tim 5:23). In general the biblical emphasis seems to have been on prevention rather than cure, this being especially prominent in the Mosaic hygienic code of the Torah. Surgical instruments of some sophistication have survived from the first century, notably from Pompeii,* overwhelmed when Vesuvius erupted in August A.D. 79.

BIBLIOGRAPHY: R. Labat, *Traité akkadien de*

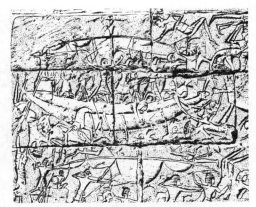

Drawing of wall carving from Medinet Habu. The detail is from a large scene of the naval battle of Ramses III (1198-1166 B.C.) with the Sea Peoples. Courtesy Carta, Jerusalem.

diagnostics et prognostics medicaux (1951); F. Jonckheere, *Les medicins de l'Egypte pharaonique* (1958); P. Ghalioungui, sup. cit.

RKH

MEDINET EL-FAIYUM. CROCODILOPOLIS.

MEDINET HABU (me dē'net hä'bū). A modern Arabic name applied to a group of ruined temples and later settlement near the S end of W Thebes.*

On the W bank of the Nile in Thebes, Ramses III erected his great funerary temple, southernmost of a long series, c. 1180 B.C. It followed the normal New Kingdom pattern of a stone structure, pylons, open colonnaded courts, hypostyle* halls, dark inner sanctuaries and stores, the whole surrounded by brick houses for priests and storage of dues in kind, within a massive enclosure wall. Here, the wall also included an older small temple of Amun. The great temple is the best preserved of its type, and is famous for its carved scenes of wars of Ramses III, including against the Sea Peoples,* picturing the Philistines.* Other invaluable records include the vast calendar of religious festivals and reliefs showing festivals of Min and Sokar. The entire temple and precinct was admirably dug, recorded, and published by the Oriental Institute, University of Chicago.

BIBLIOGRAPHY: *OIC*, 5, 7, 10, 15, 18 (1929–34); *Medinet Habu*, 1–8 (1930–70); *Excavations at Medinet Habu*, 1–4 (1934–54); W. F. Edgerton and J. A. Wilson, *Historical Records of Ramses III* (1936); B. Porter, R. L. B. Moss, and E. W. Burney, *Topographical Bibliography of Anc. Egyptian . . . Texts*, 2, 2d ed. (1971), on W Bank temples.

KAK

MEGALITHIC MONUMENTS. A structure of this kind is one that has been made out of large upright stones that were probably covered with slabs of the same material. Such monuments are to be found in various parts of Europe and the Near East, and have been regarded as a product of the closing phases of the Neolithic* era. The megaliths of the Near East

Model of reconstructed city of Megiddo: (1) gate area, (2) water pit, (3) south stable complex, (4) south palace. *(See also photos under* ALTAR; SHISHAK; STABLES) Courtesy Israel Government Press Office.

seem to have been mostly burial monuments, whereas those at Stonehenge apparently comprised a second-millennium B.C. temple.

Known variously as cromlechs, menhirs,* and dolmens,* these monuments were towering structures that were normally unadorned in any way, and their distribution in the uplands of Palestine, Syria, Asia Minor,* and Armenia would suggest that they were the products of pastoral groups. The Palestinian megalithic burials have been dated to the sixth and fifth millenniums B.C., but to date have defied all attempts at identifying the religious attitudes of those who constructed them, other than the obvious importance to them of life after death.   RKH

MEGIDDO (mə gi′dō). The modern Tell el-Mutesellim was strategically situated on a hill overlooking the outlet of the mountain pass connecting the Plain of Esdraelon to the coastal plain. Excavations have been conducted here by G. Schumacher in 1903–5, C. S. Fisher (1925–27), P. L. O. Guy (1927–29), and G. Loud (1935–39). Later excavators determined to excavate the entire mound, but after five strata had been removed they concentrated on large trenches in various areas of the mound. In 1960 Y. Yadin undertook limited soundings to clear up some stratigraphical problems of Solomon's* period.

Excavations revealed twenty strata of occupation. Levels XX to XVI were all prepatriarchal age and cover the close of the Chalcolithic,* Proto-Urban, and Early Bronze ages.* An early shrine was found in level XIX and a remarkable oval altar* of burnt offerings* approached by steps in level XVI. The debris around the altar contained many animal bones (Exod 20:26).

The Middle Bronze Age,* the most probable period of the patriarchs, is covered by levels XV to X. After a break of two centuries Megiddo was reoccupied in the twenty-first century B.C. The great altar continued in use, but in level XV three small shrines were associated with it. The influence of the Hyksos* begins in level XIII and continues till level X. It is marked by scarabs,* and later by a sloping glacis* outside the city wall.* Fine houses,* jewelry, tools,* bone inlay, and tombs well stocked with pottery* attest an age of wealth.

The Late Bronze Age is covered by levels IX to VII. The Hyksos rulers were expelled from Egypt,* and Egyptian control extended to Palestine once again. Level IX was probably destroyed by Thutmose III (c. 1550–1468), after he had defeated a coalition of local rulers. Level VIII (fourteenth century B.C.) had a fine city gate,* and a new temple was built over the ruins of earlier shrines. There was an attractive palace here beneath the floor of which was discovered a hoard of gold* and ivory* objects. This was probably the city of Prince Biridiya, who wrote several of the Amarna Letters.* A fragment of the Flood epic found by a shepherd in 1955 seems to belong to this city. Level VII, covering the thirteenth and most of the twelfth centuries, contained a fine palace. The famous water system which consisted of a vertical shaft dug through the debris of earlier cities and then through the rock beneath to a point where it was possible to drive a horizontal shaft out to a cave* where there was a fine spring was once thought to belong to this city. Modern opinion places it in level IVA in the days of King Ahab. During the twelfth century the Israelites occupied the land, although Megiddo was not captured till later (Judg 1:27). After level VII the city lay in ruins for a time. Some historians argue that the battle of Judg 5 took place at this time, because the narrative refers to Taanach* by the waters of Megiddo (v. 19), as though only Taanach was occupied.

With level VI, which covered the first half of the eleventh century, the Iron Age* began. The large Canaanite* temple ceased to exist at this time. The city was destroyed by a great fire but was soon rebuilt toward the end of the century as city VB, possibly by the Israelites during the days of Saul. Little remains of city VB. The later phase VA, and city IVB, belong to the time of Solomon,* when Megiddo was transformed into one of the royal chariot* cities. Originally the remarkable stable* complexes, now thought to be storehouses, were attributed to Solomon, but Y. Yadin later showed that the northern storehouses belonged to phase IVA from the time of Ahab.* A fine residence stood in level IVB, and the city was surrounded by a casemate wall.* The road into the city entered a gateway protected by towers,* turned at right angles, and crossed an open space to pass through another entrance protected by towers. Pharaoh Shishak* damaged this city c. 918 B.C. A part of a stele* of Shishak was found in the ruins. The city recovered, and new stable complexes were built on the NE, probably by Ahab. The city survived till the end of the ninth century when it was destroyed, possibly by Hazael of Syria c. 815 B.C. (2 Kings 13:3–7).

Level III belonged to the eighth century. It was well planned and prosperous. Here stood an enormous grain storage bin (see GRANARY) which held some 460 cu. m. (12,800 bu.). It was 6.4 m. (21 ft.) deep, 10.7 m. (35 ft.) in diameter at the top, and 6.4 m. (21 ft.) in diameter at the base. A seal* from this city carries the words: "belonging to Shema the servant of Jeroboam"—perhaps an officer of Jeroboam II (c. 786–746 B.C.). This city was destroyed, probably by the Assyrian Tiglath-pileser,* during his campaign in the Galilee* area in the days of Pekah (2 Kings 15:29).

Level II was an Assyrian city, the capital of the Assyrian governor of the province of Megiddo. It was destroyed about the end of the seventh century, probably by Pharaoh Necho* in 609 B.C. (2 Kings 23:29–30).

The last city, level I, was unwalled and was largely residential. It ceased to exist early in the fourth century B.C.

BIBLIOGRAPHY: R. S. Lamon and G. S. Skipton, *Megiddo I: Seasons of 1925–1934* (1939); G. Loud, *Megiddo II: Seasons of 1935–1939* (1948); H. G. May, *Material Remains of the Megiddo Cult* (1935); R. S. Lamon, *The Megiddo Water System* (1935); G. Loud, *The Megiddo Ivories* (1935); G. E. Wright, "The Discoveries at Megiddo, 1935–39," *BA*, 13 (1950), 28–46; Y. Yadin, "New Light on Solomon's Megiddo," *BA*, 23 (1960), 62–68; I. Dunayevski and A. Kempinski, *IEJ*, 16 (1966), 142; J. N. Schofield, in D. W. Thomas, ed., *Archaeology and OT Study* (1967), 309–28; Y. Yadin, *Hazor* (1972), 147–64; A. F. Rainey, *ZPEB*, 4 (1975), 164–76.

JAT

MEIRON (mī'ron). The town is not mentioned in the Bible, although it is important as the home of some famous Jewish rabbis during the first century B.C. That the town was significant in ancient times may be deduced from the fact that it occurs in the lists of cities conquered by Thutmose III, Ramses II, * and Tiglath-pileser III.* Meiron is a rather common name that has various spellings, and there may be a connection with the biblical "waters of Merom," where Joshua defeated the king of Hazor* and his allies (Josh 11:5, 7). The town is located 8.9 km. (5½ mi.) NW of Safed in Galilee.*

Near the village are the ruins of a synagogue, * dating from the second century A.D. The main entrance is flanked by two side doors, and the W wall was carved from the rock against which the synagogue was built; the basilica* was 27 m. (86 ft.) long, and 13.5 m. (44 ft.) wide. Hillel's Cave is shown as the burial place of the famous scholar of the Torah of the first century B.C. Nearby is the tomb of Rabbi Shammai, his opponent. The Throne of the Messiah is the name of a high rock here where the Messiah is supposed to sit in the last days when he appears to deliver Israel.* Meiron is still the site of an annual festival called Lag ba-Omer.

BCC

MEJDEL. See MAGADAN.

MELAH. See TELL-MELAH.

MELCART STELE. This monument was discovered in a village about 8 km. (5 mi.) N of Aleppo* in northern Syria in 1940, and the text of the inscription which it contained was published in 1941 by Marice Dunand, who had excavated Byblos (see GEBAL). Precisely how the stele* arrived at the site is unknown. Although there were Roman ruins in the area, there was no evidence of earlier occupational levels. Even if it arrived in Roman times, as seems probable, there appears no good reason why it should have been taken there at that point. The stele is dated by epigraphy* to the middle of the ninth century B.C., more accurately c. 870, and if it came originally from nearby Aleppo it would furnish evidence of the extent to which the Syrian Empire of the ninth century B.C. had expanded. However, the monument may well have been brought to Aleppo from Damascus, * the Syrian capital, though certainty on this matter is lacking.

The bas-relief* figure of Milqart (Melcart), wearing a Syrian loincloth, strikes a militant attitude. Beneath his feet is the following Aramaic* inscription, "The monument which Bah-hadad, son of Tabrimmon, king of Aram,* erected for his lord Milqart, which he vowed to him, and he listened to his voice." This stele is the earliest inscribed monument recovered to date which bears the name of an Aramean ruler, namely Benhadad I. The wording on the stele describing him is identical with that in 1 Kings 15:18. What is particularly valuable about this monument is that, with the Zakir Stele, * it supplies the only extrabiblical historical material recovered to date from Syria which describes the century and a half of warfare* between the Damascus regime and the northern kingdom of Israel. *

The text of the inscription is weathered, and consequently poorly preserved in places, particularly where the names of Tabrimmon and Hadyan (Hezion) occur in the writing. The opening line appears to follow a stereotyped form, as indicated by its parallel in the Zakir Stele. * While the Melcart inscription has provided general confirmation of the list of Damascene rulers in 1 Kings 15:18, it says nothing about the identity of Rezon, who captured Damascus in the time of Solomon, * and from whom the subsequent dynasty was descended. Since Rezon also established the traditionally hostile character of the Syrian regime toward Israel, it seems improbable that there is confusion in 1 Kings 15:18 between Rezon and Hezion. The inscription raises fresh questions about the number of Benhadads who ruled in Syria. Before the stele was recovered, three were normally distinguished, but Albright, who translated the Melcart inscription in 1942, held that the Benhadads of 1 Kings 15:18 and 20 were one and the same person. This person, in such case, reigned about forty years (c. 880–842 B.C.). 1 Kings 20:34 implies that a Benhadad who was contemporary with Ahab* had defeated Omri, * but Albright rendered "father" by "predecessor," thus removing difficulties in the way of a single identification. The inscription, however, does nothing to support this identification, and though the stele is usually attributed to Benhadad I, the loss of the patronymic throws some doubt on even this assumption.

BIBLIOGRAPHY: W. F. Albright, BASOR, 87 (1942), 23–29.

RKH

MELCHIZEDEK (mel ki′zə dek). On the majestic person of Melchizedek, king of Salem in Canaan, archaeology has few words to say. Hebrews 7:1–3 describes him as "without father or mother," which simply means that he founded his dynasty. Another "king of Salem" states in the Amarna letters* of 1380 B.C.: "Behold, this land, neither my father nor my mother gave it to me. The hand of the mighty King gave it to me."

Something of a parallel to the patriarchal monarch of Salem has been recovered from the documents of the Euphrates Valley. Into a troubled page of the history of Larsam, a principality in Elam, * came a strange character known as Kudur-Mabug, of the royal family of Elam. In his inscriptions he avoids the title "king" and uses "adda" or "patriarch." He worshiped the deity Nannar, but with a humble piety which suggests that his religion contained some flavor of an original revelation. In an inscription found at Ur, * he tells us: "When Nannar had responded to my prayer and had delivered into my hand the enemies who had razed the summit of E-barra, verily I brought back the cities of Mashganshabra and Karra-Utu to Larsam. Nannar, thou art my king. Thou hast done it! I, what am I? Because of this thing [he repaired the temple E-nunmah for Nannar] for my life and for the life of my son Warad-Sin, king of Larsam . . . Because of my work, may Nannar, my king,

rejoice over me. A destiny of life, a good reign, a throne of firm foundation, may he give me for a gift. The dear shepherd of Nannar may I be, and may my days be long!"

BIBLIOGRAPHY: P. Carleton, Buried Empires (1939); H. Vincent, Jerusalem de l'AT, 2 (1956), 612–13.

EMB

MELITA. See MALTA.

MEMPHIS. The name of the pyramid town of Pepi I, which later extended to whole city, * Memphis is traditionally said to have been founded by Menes, first pharaoh of all Egypt. * Certainly throughout most of Egyptian history it was the effective administrative capital, being uniquely situated near the junction of the Upper Egyptian valley and Lower Egyptian Delta, constituting the link and control point for both lands. Modern Cairo is in this respect its direct successor.

Memphis was the real capital for the entire Pyramid Age, and a southern extension (Ithet-tawy) likewise in the Middle Kingdom. It shared the role of capital with Thebes* (for the S) and Rameses* (Delta residence) in the New Kingdom. But both then and throughout the Later Period—when it was effective as a co-capital with Delta dynastic cities like Tanis* or Sais—Memphis remained the real center of Egypt. Most of the ancient city has disappeared. The vast cemeteries (see NECROPOLIS) of Saqqara, Giza, * Dahshur, etc., marked out by Old and Middle Kingdom pyramids* and tomb-chapels of the nobles, still hint at its former extent and splendor. The chief god was Ptah, a craftsman* like Vulcan; his consort was the lioness-goddess Sekhmet. The local god of the dead, later linked also with Osiris, * was Sokar. The Apis bull was the sacred bull of Ptah; the Serapeum was the burial vaults of the sacred bulls. The prominence of Memphis is reflected in Hos (9:6) and Isa (19:13), likewise by Jer (2:16; 46:14). Jews, * like many other foreigners, dwelt there (Jer 44:1), and it featured in Ezekiel's prophecies of judgment (30:13).

BIBLIOGRAPHY: W. M. F. Petrie, Memphis, 1–6 (1909–15); B. Porter and R. L. B. Moss, Topographical Bibliography of Anc. Egyp . . . Texts . . . , 3 (1931); M. T. Dimick, Memphis (1956); A. M. Badawi, Memphis als zweite Landeshauptstadt im neuen Reich (1948); R. Anthes et al., Mit Rahineh 1955 (1959); id., Mit Rahineh 1956 (1965); H. Kees, Ancient Egypt, A Cultural Topography (1961), 147ff.; C. E. DeVries, ZPEB, 4 (1975), 179–83.

KAK

MENAHEM (men′ə hem). Archaeology sheds a ray of ironic light on the amount of the tribute paid by this cruel king (2 Kings 15:14–22) to the Assyrians. A sum of fifty shekels was collected from leading citizens of Israel. * Tablets from Nimrud (see CALAH) suggest that, at about this time, fifty shekels was the price of a competent slave. * It was the sort of crude joke which Pul (Tiglath-pileser III*) might have enjoyed. The king records receiving tribute (see BOOTY) from Menahem of Samaria* along with other rulers overrun in his westward sweep. A fragmentary text records that Menahem, "overwhelmed like a bird in a snowstorm," fled and bowed at the royal feet. He was pardoned on the acceptance of a tribute—the one thousand talents mentioned by the Hebrew historian. The Assyrian boasts that he took Israel and all it had to Assyria.

BIBLIOGRAPHY: *ARAB*, 1, 816; J. Lilley, *ZPEB*, 4 (1975), 183–84.

EMB

MENES. *See* NARMER, PALETTE OF.

MENHIR (men' hîr). A term of Celtic origin meaning a "long stone." As used by archaeologists it describes a prehistoric monument comprising a single erect stone, left generally in its rough state though on occasions surviving in a partly shaped form. While the menhir properly stood alone, a group of such monoliths was sometimes aligned in parallel lines or in circular form. Menhirs have been described in Brittany, India, Algeria, and elsewhere and seem to have been erected originally either as a memorial to some deceased person of note, or as a commemorative marker of a battlefield. The menhir should be distinguished from the obelisk* which is a square monumental shaft tapering gently upward from the base and crowned by a pyramidal top. Several examples survive from ancient Egypt*—the Cleopatra's Needle in Central Park, New York City, and the one on the Thames embankment in London, which was actually from the time of Thutmose III. The menhir is also different in character from the stele,* the latter often being an elaborately sculptured or inscribed slab of stone generally intended for public enlightenment or use, as with the stele containing the law code of Hammurabi,* the commemorative slab of Shishak* unearthed at Megiddo,* the Benhadad stele found in 1940 near Aleppo,* and many others. Sculptured menhirs, carved to represent a human or divine personage, have been found in France, Italy, and Spain.

See also DOLMEN; MEGALITHIC MONUMENTS.

BIBLIOGRAPHY: G. Daniel, *Scientific American*, 243.1 (1980), 78–90.

RKH

MENORAH (mə nōr'ə). The Hebrew word might refer to any lampstand, but in the OT it signified especially the seven-branched lampstand (KJV "candlestick") of the tabernacle and the temple,* which, through the medium of prophecy (Zech 4:2, 11) became a Jewish symbol (e.g., from Jewish graves* in many parts of the ancient world to Israeli Jerusalem* today). The actual object was taken to Rome* in the spoil of Jerusalem, and, as the Arch of Titus* shows, was carried, along with other sacred objects, in the triumphal procession of Vespasian* in A.D. 70. The menorah stood in the Temple of Peace for almost four centuries. In A.D. 456 Genseric and his Vandal army sacked Rome and the lampstand was carried to Carthage, Genseric's headquarters, where it was lost from history.

BIBLIOGRAPHY: A. R. Mitchell, *NBD* (1962), 708; L. E. Toombs, *IDB*, 4 (1963), 64–66.

EMB

MENSHIYEH, TELL IRAQ EL-. *See* TELL SHEIKH AHMED EL-AREINI.

MERCHANT. The ancient Babylonians, Canaanites,* and Greeks were the outstanding merchants of the Ancient Near East, the word "Canaanite" becoming a synonym for "trader" in OT times (Prov 31:24; Hos 12:7). Business activities were conducted from the ziggurats* by the industrious Sumerians,* and various types of merchandise were exported as far afield as India and Egypt.* Sumerian pottery* has been recovered from Mohenjo-Daro in the Indus Valley, suggesting a ship* trade with that region by way of the Persian Gulf. Many business documents have been recovered from sites such as Mari* and Nuzi,* and these illustrate the activities of the ancient Babylonian merchants. The Code of Hammurabi* set a standard in commerce by regulating weights and measures, as did the Mosaic law (Deut 25:14–15). From very early times merchants traveled great distances to pick up their goods, following overland trading routes and calling at established seaports. (cf. Gen 41:49; Exod 1:11; 1 Kings 10:28), and at an early period the sons of Jacob began trading with Egypt (Gen 43:11), although the pre-Exilic Hebrews were not particularly notable as merchants. The Beni Hasan tableau* furnishes an idea of the appearance of trading Asiatics during the late Middle Kingdom period

Fragments of earliest known representation of the Temple menorah (c. 37 B.C.-A.D. 4), found in 1969 excavations of the Old City of Jerusalem. A representation of an altar may be on the right. Courtesy Israel Government Press Office.

of Egypt. Texts recovered from Kultepe* and Bogh-azköy* in Asia Minor* tell of Assyrian merchants about 2000 B.C. trading in textiles, copper, and tin,* the two latter metals (see METALLURGY) furnishing the Hittites* with the components for manufacturing bronze.* The Assyrian merchants enjoyed free movement between countries and had a high social status based upon a firm code of business ethics.

During the Exile* many Jews* became wealthy merchants under the Babylonians and the later Persians, and archaeological excavations at Nippur* and Babylon* have uncovered documents belonging originally to large commercial firms, in which many Jewish names occur. Traveling merchants brought their goods to bazaars (cf. Neh 3:31; 13:19–20) and engaged in noisy trading. Like his Semitic counterpart, the Greek emporos was also a traveler (Matt 13:45) and operated from marketplaces (see AGORA) in which his business activities were regulated by the local authorities, as at Alexandria.*

BIBLIOGRAPHY: J. L. Kelso, Archaeology and Our OT Contemporaries (1966); id., ZPEB, 5 (1975), 784–91.

RKH

MERI-KA-RE, INSTRUCTION FOR. A work composed by an Egyptian pharaoh for the edification of his son, Meri-ka-re. Biblical relevance is slight, save that the document reveals the ideas on conduct, social and personal, and the notions of leadership current in the world of Abraham's day. The part which named the attributive author has survived in damaged condition, but there can be little doubt that he was Khety II, who lived in the First Intermediate Period (2200–2000 B.C.) of ancient dynastic rule. This was a time of weak government and social unrest in Egypt* in which the noble families of Thebes,* Memphis,* and Herakleopolis were contesting for supremacy. Khety belonged to a group from Herakleopolis and probably reigned between 2150 and 2080 B.C.

Three papyrus* copies of the Instruction are extant, all written about seven hundred years after the original was composed. There is no reason to question the genuineness of the Instruction or its royal author, if only because it reflected so faithfully the instability and uncertainty of the times. Although it dealt in part with such pressing issues as the maintaining of strong frontier outposts and the quelling of revolts, its main theme was that of the importance of individual moral conduct and proper social relationships. The king was to set an example of uprightness and justice to his subjects, ruling them wisely for the greatest good of all. The exhortations concerning the promotion of justice and the protection of the oppressed can be paralleled in Isa 1:17; Jer 22:3; and Ps 82:3–4, where an analogous social situation is reflected. The thought of the Instruction on life after death contrasts sharply with OT concepts, however. The Egyptians sought to perpetuate physical existence after death as part of their doctrine of immortality.* The Instruction derided those who scoffed at eternal life and commended those who pursued lives of uprightness.

BIBLIOGRAPHY: J. A. Wilson, ANET, 414–18; T. W.

Thacker, DOTT, 155–61.

RKH

MERNEPTAH STELE. See ISRAEL STELE.

MEROM. See MEIRON.

MESCHECH AND TUBAL (mē'shek, tū'bəl). According to cuneiform* inscriptions, Meschech and Tubal (Gen 10:2; 1 Chron 1:5; Ezek 27:13; 32:26; 38:2, 3; 39:1) were tribes in Asia Minor.* They are also mentioned by Herodotus as the Moschoi and Tiberenoi. The Mushki, as the Assyrians called Meschech, appear first in texts of Tiglath-Pileser,* who defeated them in a battle near the Euphrates. The sequence of events is unknown, but it was probably part of the turmoil associated with tribal assaults on the Hittite* Empire around 1100 B.C. Four centuries later, Sargon* seems to have found Mita, king of the Mushki, a doughty opponent; for over a full generation they were a major frontier problem for the Assyrians. They had progressed solidly in power since the days when they were mentioned in a thirteenth-century Hittite* text as a disloyal vassal of the Armenian hill country. The Midas of Phrygia,* known in Greek tradition, was no doubt Mita. His capital, Gordian, in the W of his domains, and out of Assyrian reach, has yielded archaeological evidence of a highly developed metallurgical* craft* (Ezek 27:13).

BIBLIOGRAPHY: IDB, 4 (1962), 357–58; ibid., 5, 717–18.

EMB

MESHA STELE. A lengthy inscription in Moabite discovered at Dibon* in 1868, recounting the exploits of Mesha, king of Moab* (2 Kings 3:4).

See also MOABITE STONE.

MESOLITHIC. The Middle Stone Age, c. 9000–7000 B.C.

MESOPOTAMIA. In its narrower sense (northwest portion), Mesopotamia is mentioned five times in the Bible (Gen 24:10; Deut 23:4; Judg 3:8, 10; 1 Chron 19:6) and is a translation of Aram Naharaim which means "Aram* of the two rivers." Twice in the NT (Acts 2:9; 7:2) it seems to be used in the larger sense of Greek usage to mean the whole of the land between the Tigris and Euphrates rivers from the ancient Persian Gulf to the Masius Mountains in Syria.

Mesopotamia was the matrix of the OT Hebrew culture since Abraham was divinely led out of the highly developed culture of Ur* in lower Mesopotamia. It is of inestimable importance because of its influence on Palestine. There developed the roots of pagan Semitic religions and myths, codified laws, writing,* agriculture,* architecture, medicine,* business, and history. It is the beginning of the Fertile Crescent* and the cradle of civilization. Almost every aspect of eastern archaeology is concerned with Mesopotamia. It was the home of the Sumerians,* Amorites,* Assyrians (see ASSYRIOLOGY), Chaldeans,* Babylonians,* Hittites,* and (during the Exile*) the Hebrews.

Among the major cities excavated in Mesopotamia

are: Jarmo, Hassuna, Kirkuk, Nineveh,* Samarra, Halaf, Eridu,* Ubaid, Uruk, Jemdet Nasr,* Shuruppak,* Asmar, Ur,* Lagash,* Isin, Larsa,* Mari,* Khorsabad,* and Nuzi.* The archaeological contributions of these and other Mesopotamian sites with their palaces, temples, and tablets make it easier to understand the highly developed civilization from which Abraham, the father of the Jews,* came. He was not originally a nomad. The whole history of the OT is thus illustrated against the background of the Mesopotamian peoples with whom Israel* interacted.

BIBLIOGRAPHY: C. H. Gordon, *IDB*, 3 (1962), 359; R. L. Alden, *ZPEB*, 4 (1975), 196.

BCC

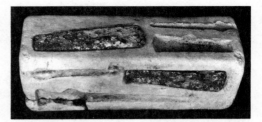

Pottery mold for casting implements with two axes or chisels in place, from Tell Balatah (Shechem) Middle Bronze Age (2200-1500 B.C.). Courtesy Israel Dept. of Antiquities and Museums.

MESOPOTAMIAN LAW. Law was highly developed very early in Mesopotamian history. Archaeological evidence shows that there were regulations concerning labor and management, navigation, agriculture,* family life, business transactions, marriages,* wills, adoptions,* and almost every conceivable situation where truth and justice might be upheld. These laws provide a broad cultural background for understanding the laws God gave to Israel* in the OT.

Four important codes of laws have been discovered which illustrate ancient Mesopotamian law. The Lipit-Ishtar Code* of the king of Isin is an example of pre-Babylonian law. It appeared in fragments found at Nippur* at the beginning of this century and was only recently dated to a period about 175 years before the Hammurabi* code.* The fragments contain about thirty-five laws concerning slaves,* boats (*see* SHIPS), gardens,* families, and the treatment of oxen.* They are written in Sumerian (*see* SUMER). The most famous and complete law code of ancient Mesopotamia* is the Code of Hammurabi (1792–1750 B.C.), which was found at Susa* in 1902 on a black stele* about 2 m. (7 ft.) tall that had been carried off by the Elamite* captors of Babylon.* A relief at the top of the stele shows Hammurabi receiving the law from the sun-god. Besides a prologue and an epilogue, there are about three hundred laws inscribed on the stone in cuneiform.* These are thought to have been selected from a larger corpus for emphasis. Another important code is the Law of Eshnunna* discovered at Tell Abu Harmal, near Baghdad. It is dated about 150 years before Hammurabi, and, among other laws similar to those in the codes mentioned above, it includes royal decrees on price fixations of oil and grain. The Code of Ur-Nammu* has also been deciphered from fragments on a tablet from Nippur and it dates from the reign of this king (c. 2070–2052 B.C.).

RKH

METALLURGY. The working of metal derived from ore was practiced widely in the Ancient Near East, with gold* and copper most probably being the first metals thus used. The techniques for deriving the metals from their ore bodies were doubtless discovered independently in several areas. Thus, copper working in Egypt* exhibits different stages of complexity, suggesting that the processes were indigenous in origin. Ancient copper mines and slag heaps have been discovered in Sinai,* the Wadi Arabah, Anatolia, Iran, and elsewhere. About 1972 Russian archaeologists discovered in the vicinity of Mount Ararat* a great many furnaces* used about 2500 B.C. for smelting iron,* copper, zinc, and other substances. Soviet authorities have claimed the area to be the oldest large-scale metal processing center in the world. This discovery may well have an important bearing upon the location and metallurgical activities of Tubal-Cain (Gen 4:22), described as a forger of every sort of bronze* and iron tool. Whereas earlier views of his activities saw him as cold-forging meteoric iron and native copper, it now appears that he was in contact with a culture which had already discovered how to smelt iron ore and to produce other metallic alloys as well. An important Edomite* mining center was located at Punon* (modern Feinan), where copper was first smelted about 2000 B.C. for probable shipment to Egypt. Excavations at Mene'iyyeh and Khirbet en-Nahas show that in the Iron Age I–II* period, considerable smelting was carried out in the area. At Khirbet el-Jariyeh archaeologists discovered that the smelting furnace was roughly circular in shape and approximately 2.7 m. (9 ft.) in diameter. At Timnah* in 1941, Nelson Glueck discovered a large slag heap which pointed to the operation of a copper smelter. In 1971 Beno Rothenberg uncovered a complex network of copper mines in the area dating from about 1400 B.C. An iron mine was also found at Timnah, and Rothenberg thought that the Egyptians, who had worked the area originally, had used the iron oxide as a flux before discovering the value of iron in its own right as a metal. The Early Iron furnace at Tell Jemmeh had its flues aligned so as to catch the prevailing westerly winds, but others were worked by means of bellows (cf. Jer 6:29) similar to those depicted in the nineteenth-century B.C. wall paintings in the tomb of Khnumhotep III at Beni Hasan.* Bronze, an alloy of copper and tin,* may have been manufactured first at Ur* about 2500 B.C., and subsequently in Anatolia, Egypt, and Syria between 2000 and 1800 B.C. This would be somewhat later than comparable activity carried on in the region of Mount Ararat. The earliest bronze objects from Palestine were found at Jericho* and dated about 2100 B.C. In the monarchy, bronze objects were cast near Succoth* (cf. 1 Kings 7:46; 2 Chron 4:17).

See also LEAD; MINING; REFINING.

BIBLIOGRAPHY: J. L. Kelso, *BASOR*, 122 (1951), 26–28; G. M. A. Haufmann and J. C. Waldbaum in J. A. Sanders, ed., *Near Eastern Archaeology in the Twentieth Century* (1970), 310–15; R. J. Forbes, *Studies in Ancient Technology*, 9 (1972).

RKH

METALS. See BRONZE; GOLD; IRON; LEAD; METALLURGY; REFINING; SILVER; TIN.

MIDDEN. A refuse dump of antiquity, the contents of which often furnish invaluable information to archaeologists.

MIDIAN; MIDIANITES. A country or district, probably in the NW part of Arabia,* inhabited by a seminomadic people.

The "Land of Midian" to which Moses fled from Egypt* (Exod 2:15–16) seems to have been located in the Sinai* Peninsula, though additional references in biblical texts clearly locate Midian farther to the E, a fact that may reflect the transient nature of these tribes. Genealogically, Midian as an eponymous* ancestor of the tribe is traced to Abraham through his wife Keturah (Gen 25:2). He, together with the other sons of the concubines, was sent away to the E, to the "land of Qedem" (Gen 25:6). In the Joseph* story, Midianites, with Ishmaelites, are involved in trade between northern Israel* or Syria and Egypt. At the same time of the conquest, they appear in confederation both with Moab* (Num 22–25, 31) and the Amorite* king Sihon (Josh 13:21), although the previously friendly relations between Moses and the Midianites (Num 10:29) have led to the conclusion that there were various tribes of loosely connected peoples. In the time of Gideon, tribes of Midianites regularly penetrated into the Esdraelon Valley as camel-riding nomads, again apparently from the E. From this time on Midian does not appear in historical records, but the name may be preserved in the Greek *Modiana* of Ptolemy's *Geography* (6.7, 27) or the *Madiam* of Eusebius's *Onomastica* (136.31, ed. Lagarde). The name, which apparently refers to a city* on the E coast of the Gulf of Aqaba, reappears in Arab sources.

Of the archaeological history of the Midianites nothing can be said. The question of Midianite cities is part of the larger problem of identification and classification of the scanty remains in the desert areas of Trans-Jordan from the second millennium B.C. The problem of Midianite camels* and the exact date of their first use in the area, together with the question of Midian's exact relation to her neighbors Moab and Edom,* has attracted most of the attention of biblical scholars.

BIBLIOGRAPHY: O. Eissfeldt, "Protektorat der Midianiter Uber Ihre Nachbarn im Letzten Viertel des 2. Jahrtausends v.Chr.," *JBL*, 87 (1968), 383–93; W. F. Albright, "Midianite Donkey Caravans" H. T. Brank and W. L. Reed, eds. *Translating and Understanding the Bible* (1970), 197–205; R. L. Alden, *ZPEB*, 4 (1975), 220–22.

CEA

MILCOM. See MOLECH.

MILETUS (mī lē'təs). An Ionian city* on the W coast of Asia Minor,* at the mouth of the Maeander River. It was visited by Paul on his third missionary journey, and there he said farewell to the Ephesian elders (Acts 20:15–21:1; cf. 2 Tim 4:20). German excavations were first conducted from 1899–1914, then in 1938 and 1955. Although there is evidence of a fortified site from the Minoan* and Mycenaean* periods, Miletus did not become famous until the seventh and sixth centuries B.C. as the Ionian capital and the greatest colonizer of the Greek world. It was connected by a Sacred Way with the temple of Apollo at Didyma 16 km. (10 mi.) S, of which imposing ruins survive.

In the fifth century, after Miletus had been destroyed by the Persians in the Ionian Revolt, the city was replanned by Hippodamus, but the greatest period of building was the Hellenistic, with two marketplaces (see AGORA), a theater,* and council chamber. The theater, rebuilt about A.D. 100, is the best survival of the Roman period and an inscription in the fifth row of seats attests the importance of Jews* and proselytes: "the place of the Jews, also called the God-Fearing." Other remains are of the shrine of Delphian Apollo, the Nymphaeum, and the Baths of Faustina, wife of Emperor Marcus Aurelius.

The commercial importance of Miletus had lessened in NT times, largely owing to the silting up of the mouth of the Maeander; today the ruins are 8 km. (5 mi.) from the sea.

BIBLIOGRAPHY: T. Wiegand, ed., *Milet, ergebnisse der ausgrabungen und untersuchungen . . .* (1906–15); G. E. Bean, *Aegean Turkey: An Archaeological Guide* (1966), 219–30, Plates 55–59; R. C. Stone, *ZPEB*, 4 (1975), 225–27.

BFH

MILL; MILLSTONE. Fragments of mills or millstones are found in surface surveys and excavations throughout the biblical world. The grinding of grain for the daily baking of bread was done in the morning by the women or maidservants, and sometimes by male prisoners (Exod 11:5; Judg 16:21; Isa 47:2). When the sound of grinding was no longer heard in the settlement, it was a sign of desolation (Eccl 12:4; Jer 25:10; Rev 18:22). Broken millstones sometimes became anchors for fishermen's boats, and even missiles used in siege defense (cf. Judg 9:53).

Several kinds of millstones were used in ancient times, most of which were made from the black basalt stone that is plentiful in Bashan,* the Galilee* region, parts of Anatolia, and in other volcanic regions. This is a hard vesicular stone, providing a long-wearing surface, and the many cavities make an ideal series of cutting edges.

The mortar and pestle.* This method of grinding by pounding the cereal or other foodstuff in a hollow with the end of a long stone is probably the earliest method used and survives until the present time among many primitive peoples. The OT mentions this means of grinding (Num 11:8; Prov 27:22).

The quern and muller.* These Old World terms

Limestone servant figure using quern and muller for grinding grain; Giza, Fifth Dynasty (c. 2494-2345 B.C.). Courtesy Museum of Fine Arts, Boston.

have the New World equivalent of mano and metate, meaning two stones rubbed together to produce flour from grain introduced between them. The bottom stone was larger, of varied size, perhaps averaging some 33 cm. (13 in.) wide by 65–75 cm. (25–30 in.) in length. It is frequently called a "saddle quern" by archaeologists because through long usage the top surface was worn concave. The smaller hand stone (muller) had a shape similar to a small loaf of bread and was used in the classic washboard fashion. Grain was introduced at the top of the sloping quern and issued as flour at the end farthest from the operator. This explains the statement, "the maidservant is behind the mill" (Exod 11:5). The upper stone was called the "rider" (cf. Deut 24:6). Making flour in Egypt* was part of the housewife's task, who ground the cereals with quern and muller from the earliest historic times. The rubbing stone was called in the Egyptian texts the "son of the millstone." Only after 1500 B.C. do we learn of the existence of professional millers in Egypt, the hieroglyph* for "miller" being a kneeling man. By the Pyramid Age (c. 2700 B.C.) the saddle quern was placed on an inclined base, with a trough arrangement at the lower end to collect the flour. No trace of a rotary mill is found before Hellenistic times (300 B.C.), and then they seem to have been imported from Mesopotamia.*

Provenience of saddle querns and their rubbing stones includes the entire Eastern Mediterranean, from Neolithic* times onward. They began to decline in usage toward the end of the Bronze Ages.*

In Mesopotamia several forms of the quern and muller were used, each adapted to the grain to be ground, e.g., cereals, sesame, or dates. At a very early time they evidently had also several types of rotary hand mills.

The rotary hand mill. This is archaeologically known best from Assyrian times on (especially after 1000 B.C.). The earliest example of a rotary mill with handle peg inserted in the side of the upper stone is from Tell Halaf, in Syria, dating to the ninth century B.C. Biblical references are quite early with mention of the upper and lower stones (cf. Judg 9:53; 2 Sam 11:21; Job 41:24), though the first of these may apply to the quern. The use of the rotary mill

became widespread in Palestine during early Hellenistic times. It might have averaged from 38 to 46 cm. (15 to 18 in.) in diameter, the lower stone being somewhat thicker than the upper so as to provide stability. A convex surface was fashioned in the top of the lower stone, and the upper was made concave to fit into it. Refinements consisted of a hole bored near the edge of the top stone for the insertion of a wooden handle, and a funnel-shaped hole in its center to receive the grain. As the stone was turned, requiring the combined effort of two people using the long handle (Matt 24:41), flour came out around the perimeter of the mill. A very early form of circular mill was found at Gezer,* having no handle, the upper part which could only have been moved back and forth in all directions by the hands of the operators. The classical portable rotary hand mill with its two flat stones was intimately connected with the armies of Greece and Rome, as every army had to make its own flour in the field. Each group of ten men was provided with one hand mill and enough grain to supply each man with flour for thirty days.

The powered rotary mill. These mills, characteristic of Roman times, were much larger and were turned by slaves* or draft animals. They are well exemplified by those seen in the excavations at Pompeii.* This first mechanization of the mill was large, standing higher than a man. The lower stone had a conical top (with slopes of 30–40 degrees from the

Rotary hand-mill: basalt upper millstone from Roman Period found at Kfar Nahum on Sea of Galilee. *(See also photo under QUERN.)* Courtesy Dagon Collection— Archaeological Museum of Grain Handling in Israel.

horizontal). The upper stone had a sort of hourglass shape with the interior consisting of two converging funnels, the lower one fitting the cone of the base, and the upper serving as a hopper, receiving the grain to be ground. Its waist carried two large ears or sockets, into which poles were inserted to provide leverage for turning it. Power was applied to these by harnessed animals, and sometimes slaves. By metonymy the upper stone was called a "donkey" in Greek and gave rise to the common name of "donkey mill." The base of the whole included a wide ledge to receive the milled flour from above.

The crushing mill. This was customarily used for crushing olives, * preparatory to their being pressed to extract oil. It was, however, on occasion used for grinding many other food materials. It consisted of a large circular base, perhaps 1.2 to 1.8 m. (4 to 6 ft.) in diameter, lying horizontally, with a height of some 76 cm. (30 in.). The flat surface had a rim around its edge, and a boss in the center from which a vertical shaft projected. This provided a means of hinging a beam for rolling a thick, heavy stone wheel with flat rim around in the lower depression. Draft animals were hitched to the outer end of the beam. When turning, the grinding action was a combination of a rolling and wiping movement, due to the geometry of its construction, effectively crushing the material placed below it. This mill, still in use in some areas, was extremely widespread, and evidently highly efficient.

The roller mill. This was used primarily for the production of olive oil and was mechanically more efficient even than the crushing mill. It was called mulè, or mole olearia, and consisted of two cylindrical wheels or millstones rotating on a horizontal axis. The base and vertical shaft were identical to that of the crushing mill. A further refinement of this type was called a trapetum, in which the rotating wheels moved a fixed distance from the trough, to prevent breaking the olive stones. An illustration of this Roman mill may be seen in the Pompeiian wall paintings. There is no mention of crushing or roller mills in the OT, since they were not used in Palestine until the Hellenistic period.

BIBLIOGRAPHY: H. Van-Lennep, *Bible Lands: Their Modern Customs and Manners* (1875), illus., 87; C. Singer et al., *A History of Technology*, 1 (1954), 273–74; ibid., 2 (1954); R. J. Forbes, *Studies in Ancient Technology*, 3 (1965); H. Hodges, *Technology in the Ancient World* (1970); L. J. Wood, *ZPEB*, 4 (1975), 227.

MHH

MINING. Little reference occurs to this type of activity in Scripture, the allusion in Job 28:1 being to a source of silver* ore. The term "boring," mentioned in the Siloam Inscription* (c. 701 B.C.), elsewhere described the excavating of a cistern* (cf. Deut 6:11; Jer 2:13). The mining of metals, principally copper and to a lesser extent iron, * occurred in Palestine in the Timnah* Valley and elsewhere, where there

were rich veins in the sandstone. At Punon,* copper was first mined about 2000 B.C., and in the Iron Age* I and II periods, extensive mining was carried on in the Arabah at Khirbet en-Nahas, Khirbet el-Jariyeh, Mene'iyyeh, and at other locations.

In 1971 Beno Rothenberg discovered a group of copper mines in the Timnah Valley in S Israel,* not far from where Nelson Glueck had encountered a large slag heap in 1941. The mines found by Rothenberg were located in the white sandstone cliffs, and the tunnels extended for hundreds of yards in all directions. So sophisticated was the arrangement of tunnels, air shafts, and stairways that mining engineers* were needed to help in the work of excavating. The mines were worked at different levels, and these were joined by vertical shafts up to 15 m. (50 ft.) in depth. The ore was hauled up the shafts by means of ropes, * which wore grooves into the upper rims of the shafts. With these mines went a large copper smeltery, a circular structure with a diameter of about 36.5 m. (40 yd.). Rothenberg has estimated that mining activity was first carried out at the site about 4000 B.C. An iron mine was also discovered at Timnah, and its use may have helped to usher in the Iron Age in Palestine and Egypt* about 1100 B.C. These mines are at least a millennium older than others of the same general size in the Near East, and certainly far more sophisticated in their construction.

In Trans-Jordan, an ancient mine may have been located at Magharat Warda, and perhaps accounts for the tradition relating to Og of Bashan* (Deut 3:11), who had an iron (NEB "basalt") sarcophagus. * The latter (KJV, "bed"; RSV, "bedstead") may in fact have been an iron throne similar to that occupied by an earlier Hittite* monarch.

Although there are no gem deposits in Palestine and Syria, small quantities of semiprecious stones and decorative minerals were in existence in the Late Bronze Age, * as shown by the fifteenth-century B.C. collection recovered from Megiddo, * as well as the agate, carnelian, and glass* beads from Ezion Geber. * The art of the gem cutter was assumed in Exod 28:9–11, though stones such as those used by the Hebrews were generally mined from deposits in either Mesopotamia* or Egypt. * There are no certain indications that mining was ever an occupation with which the Hebrews were thoroughly familiar, although local labor was most probably used at Palestinian mines.

BIBLIOGRAPHY: O. R. Gurney, *The Hittites* (1954), 20, 83; F. V. Winnett, *IDB*, 3 (1962), 384–85; D. R. Bowes, *ZPEB*, 4 (1975), 230–32.

RKH

MINOA; MINOAN CIVILIZATION. This Bronze Age* of Crete is an area in which biblical and Aegean archaeology touch. If Caphtor (Amos 9:7) was Crete, the Philistines* may have had some connection with the long Aegean island, and it may have been the catastrophes which fell on Minoan Crete in the later centuries of the second millennium B.C. which set the Sea Peoples* wandering and impinging on the coasts of Egypt* and the Middle East. The pressure of the Dorian inroad, and natural disasters such as the volcanic eruption that befell Santorini, may have played a part. Minos was a king of Knossos, whose name (like Caesar) became a dynastic title. There were other centers of culture in Crete, but there is abundant archaeological evidence for the supremacy of Knossos. The sea power of the Cretans, evident from their unwalled towns, is the factor which, by its promotion of maritime migration, trade, and colonization may have played a part in OT history.

BIBLIOGRAPHY: H. J. Kantor, *The Agean and the Orient in the Second Millennium B.C.* (1947).

EMB

MINUSCULE SCRIPT. *See* PALAEOGRAPHY, GENERAL.

MIRIAM. *See* DEBORAH AND MIRIAM, SONG OF.

MIRROR. In the ancient world a mirror was made of a flat, circular piece of metal that was polished so as to obtain a reflection. Mirrors go back at least to the Early Bronze Age,* and many of them had at-

Late Bronze Age bronze mirror of Egyptian origin from tomb in plain of Acre. Courtesy Israel Dept. of Antiquities and Museums. Exhibited and photographed at Israel Museum, Jerusalem.

tractively sculptured handles. One from Abydos* in Egypt* had a fine bone handle and suggests the sort of bronze* mirror used by the Israelite women (cf. Exod 38:8; Job 37:18).

The Amarna letters* refer to a gift of mirrors from Pharaoh Amenophis IV to Burnaburiash the Hittite* king, indicating that mirrors were considered to be a valuable and desirable gift. Specimens have also been discovered in Palestine. One from Tell el-'Ajjul near Gaza* had a handle designed like a lotus flower and was probably of Egyptian manufacture. The reflected image was far from perfect, as Paul's reference, no doubt to the fine bronze mirrors made in Corinth,* indicates (1 Cor 13:12). A mirror with some trinkets in a goatskin bag is a pathetic relic from the Bar Kochba* revolt, found in a Dead Sea* cave. The art of silvering glass* was not known until the thirteenth century, and glass mirrors of any sort were not in existence until Roman times. The KJV translation "looking-glass" or "glass" (Job 37:18 and 1 Cor 13:12) are therefore anachronisms.

BIBLIOGRAPHY: G. Bénédite, *Catalogue general des antiquités égyptiennes du musée du Caire, Miroirs* (1907); N. Hugedé, *La metaphore due miroir dans les épitres de St. Paul aux Corinthiens* (1957); J. A. Thompson, *ZPEB*, 4 (1975), 251.

EMB

MISHRIFEH. *See* QATNA.

MITANNI (mi tan 'ē). The name is found in certain cuneiform* texts of the second-millennium B.C. Hurrian* (Horite) kingdom of Jazirah. The twentieth-century B.C. Hurrians who lived in the Upper Tigris and Euphrates area had infiltrated into Syria by about 1800 B.C., and two centuries later the Hurrians were dominant in N Iraq and N Syria. The Mitannians proper seem to have constituted one Indo-European segment of Hurrian society, and during the Amarna* Age (fifteenth and fourteenth centuries B.C.) they were in control of a kingdom which occupied the district watered by the Balikh and Khabur rivers. The Kassite* period of dominance in Babylonia (c. 1600–1145 B.C.) contrasted sharply with the imperialistic tendencies of the then defunct Hammurabi* regime and was matched among the Hittites* by a similar lack of interest in an expansion of territorial holdings. Into this political vacuum the Mitannians moved in strength under the vigorous direction of their military commanders and soon built up an influential political and commercial empire in N Syria and the steppe land between the Euphrates and Tigris.

At the beginning of the Amarna period the Mitannians held the balance of power between the Hittites and the Egyptians. Accordingly, the latter regarded the Mitanni kingdom as the real threat to their dominance of Syria, and about 1480 B.C. Thutmose III commenced what was to be a lengthy campaign to conquer Syria and end Mitanni influence. His aims were only partly successful, for in Syria the Mitanni leaders were able to retain control of Carchemish* and Alalakh* for use as bases from which uprisings could be fostered in those areas which they had had to surrender. Amenophis II (c. 1435–1421 B.C.) launched several Egyptian campaigns against N Syria, but with only moderate success. Under Thutmose IV (c. 1420–1411 B.C.) military aggression against the Mitanni kingdom was replaced by diplomacy. An alliance was established between Egypt* and the Mitanni capital of Washukkanni, and this was cemented by the marriage* of Amenhophis III to the Mitannian princess Kilu-Hepa. Mitannian military fortunes were eclipsed by the rise of the energetic Hittite ruler Suppiluliumas,* about 1375 B.C., who, in a sudden E movement of troops, gained control of many important Mitannian spheres of influence, including Qatna,* Ugarit,* Alalakh,* and Qadesh. Rival claimants for the throne in Mitanni brought about intrigue and civil strife, which was complicated by attempts to secure support from both the Hittites and the resurgent Assyrian Empire. When Tushratta was murdered about 1360 B.C., his successor, Mattiwaza, was unable to retain control of the Mitannian throne, and fled to Boghazköy* in an attempt to muster Hittite support for his cause. The Assyrians, under Ashuruballit (c. 1365–1330 B.C.), occupied the area still left under Mitannian control and brought the kingdom to an effective end. Subsequent Hittite attempts to restore Mattiwaza as the Mitannian king proved futile, and by the time Suppiluliumas died the Assyrians had replaced the Mitannians as the second major power in the Near East. The Mitannians were typical products of Horite culture at one of its most vigorous phases (see NUZI). Letters from Mitanni rulers were discovered among the Tell el-Amarna tablets (see AMARNA LETTERS). Mitannian monuments generally reflect Hittite influence in both size and other physical characteristics. If Level IV at Alalakh is dated correctly within the period c. 1550–1473 B.C., it would harmonize with the domination of N Syria by the Mitanni rulers Parratarna and Saustatar.

BIBLIOGRAPHY: G. Roux, *Ancient Iraq* (1964); *CAH* 2, Part 1, 152–53, 229–30; H. A. Hoffner, *ZPEB*, 4 (1975), 253–54.   RKH

MITHRAS (mith′rəs). The Iranian god of war and light, apparently venerated by the Hittites* and Greeks. Mithraism constituted a strong rival to the Christian faith in the first centuries of its expansion, and on this theme archaeology has a fascinating chapter to add.

In the autumn of 1954, from the bombed ruins E of St. Paul's Cathedral in London, emerged a little shrine of Mithras, the Persian god of the sun. The existence of this shrine had been long suspected, since a piece of Mithraic sculpture was found not far away in Bond Court by the Wallbrook. The fragment came from a statuette of the god and bore the inscription: "Ulpius Silvanus, discharged soldier of the Second Legion, pays his vow."

Ulpius no doubt came up from Monmouth, where the Second Legion was quartered, and visited the shrine of the soldier's god as a modern visitor to London might attend divine service in Westminster Abbey or St. Paul's Cathedral. Mithras was peculiarly the god of the legionnaires, brought from the

Middle East by the Syrian legions. It was probably the swelling notes of the hymn to Mithras, sung by thousands of lusty voices as the sun came up, which once chilled the hearts of a Roman army waiting to defend northern Italy (Tac. *Hist.* 3.24). It was a sign that the soldiers from the E had marched down through the NE passes and were gathered beneath their standards in the camp opposite. That was in A.D. 69, when the Roman occupation of Britain was recent news. When Ulpius Silvanus paid his vow, the religion which had first found acceptance with the garrisons of the Middle East was widely disseminated through the whole Roman Army.

The London Mithras shrine is one of a series. There is another on the Welsh border, while another lies somewhere under the walls and buildings of York, still awaiting discovery. On Hadrian's Wall, the ruins of which still run from Newcastle to Carlisle, are two shrines. One is in a cave* at Borcovicium. This Roman camp sits on the crags 32 km. (20 mi.) from Hexham, near the little village of Wall-on-Tyne. This area marks the best preserved portion of Hadrian's great engineering work, and it is here, on a southward-sloping hillside, that Borcovicium still shows its streets and walls, the foundations of its granaries,* and the worn cobblestones which speak eloquently of the Romans' four centuries of sojourn in the British Isles.

A team of archaeologists was able to demonstrate the periodic destruction and restoration of one Roman shrine according as Mithraism or Christianity won the ascendancy among the commanding officers of the local garrison. The building was finally destroyed in the time of Constantine, when the Empire became officially Christian.

In the early Persian religion, where his figure first appears, Mithras, like the Roman Jupiter (see ZEUS), was associated with light. He is one of the powers of good, who struggled against the forces of darkness and evil. It was a natural step to associate him with the sun, especially at its rising.

BIBLIOGRAPHY: F. Cumont, *Textes et monuments figurés relatifs aux mystères de Mithra* (1896, 1899).

EMB

MITYLENE (mi tə lē′nē; Gr. Μιτυλήνη, *Mitylene*). The chief city* of the island of Lesbos off the NW coast of Asia Minor.* Paul's ship stopped there briefly (Acts 20:14). Mitylene, located on the eastern side of the island, was on a long promontory which had an islet at its end, supplying two good commercial harbors.

Of the ancient buildings, only the theater* is still visible, with its semicircle clearly indicated on the slopes of the hill on the W side of the city. Newer excavations have revealed parts of the edge of the orchestra and the graduated rows of theater seats. Evidence of a platform between the semicircle of seats and the orchestra makes it likely that at a later time (i.e., in the Roman period) the theater was used for such as gladiator combat, as indicated by inscription (*IG*, 12.2.447ff., Papajeorjiu, no. 11). Some of the significant remains found in the area of the city gates* relate to Roman times, including a number of pieces of mosaic* floor (*Arch. Anz.* [1931], 285).

A number of inscriptions related to Mitylene have been discovered which show among other things interest in the cult of many gods. In Roman times a festival, like that of Zeus,* was established in the city in honor of Augustus* whose statue was erected with the inscription stating that he was the common benefactor and the savior and founder of the city (cf. *IG*, 12.2.58, 152–57). The citizens showed their appreciation for the benefits bestowed on them by Augustus's administrator, Marcus Agrippa, in several inscriptions in which the latter is called, "god, savior and founder of the city" (cf. *IG*, 12.2.166, 168, 171–72, 203).

BIBLIOGRAPHY: G. F. Hill, *JHS*, 17 (1897), 86; R. Herbst, "Mytilene," *PWRE*, 16.2 (1935), 1411–27; D. Magie, *Roman Rule in Asia Minor*, 1 (1950), 83–84, 468; ibid., 2 (1950), 1330; *OCD* (1970), 595.
WHM

MIZPAH (miz′pə). Mizpah, or Mizpeh, is mentioned nearly fifty times in the Bible, but it is not always the same town. One town with this name (Gen 31:49) was in N Gilead, but its exact location is unknown. A region known as the Land of Mizpah (Josh 11:3) was probably in the northern part of Palestine. There was also a small town called Mizpeh of Judah* (Josh 15:38) somewhere in the Shephelah.* Another Mizpah (1 Sam 22:3) was in Moab.* The Mizpah that figures most importantly is Mizpah of Benjamin. It was in Judah, near the border between Judah and Israel.* On several important occasions the whole nation gathered before the Lord at Mizpah: the murder of the Levite's concubine (Judg 20, 21), the return of the ark* from the Philistines* (1 Sam 7:5–6), the inauguration of Saul as king (1 Sam 10:17). Mizpah was fortified by Asa (1 Kings 15:22).

There are two possibilities for the site. Nebi Samwil* is 6.4 km. (4 mi.) N of Jerusalem* and is the traditional site, although it has not been excavated. Tell en-Nasbeh has been excavated (1926–35) and has yielded some evidence in favor of its being Mizpah of Benjamin. An early phase of habitation of the site was indicated by the presence of some Early-Bronze* (3200–2100 B.C.) pottery.* The main period of occupation was in the Israelite period (after 1200 B.C.), and two sets of city walls* were excavated. The earlier walls were made of rubble about 1 m. (1 yd.) thick and were replaced by a much stronger system of fortification constructed of limestone blocks laid in clay* mortar.* The later walls were about 4 m. (13 ft.) thick and 10 m. (32 ft.) high. There were several towers* in the wall, and the gate* was made between the walls where they overlapped on the NE side of the city. The gate was the first of its kind to be excavated and provided an example of the typical oriental gate where business was conducted. The houses* were mostly simple stone enclosures with roofs, but there were some pillar houses. Some ostraca* from the Persian period give possible, but not conclusive, evidence for the name Mizpah. Even more important was the seal* of Jaazaniah (2 Kings 25:23), which tends to confirm the identification. Also significant were the eighty-six jar handles stamped "to the king."

BIBLIOGRAPHY: N. Glueck, *BASOR*, 92 (1943), 10ff.; J. Muilenburg, in C. C. McCown, ed., *Tell en-Nasbeh*, 1 (1947); J. L. Kelso, *ZPEB*, 4 (1975), 254–57.
BCC

MIZRAIM. See EGYPT.

MOABITE STONE. A basalt slab carrying over thirty lines of writing in ancient Moabite found at Dibon* in 1868. The date of the stone is fixed approximately by its reference to Mesha (2 Kings 3:4) and is generally placed between 840 and 820 B.C., perhaps about 830 B.C. The monument records how Omri,* king of Israel,* subdued Moab* because of the anger of the god Chemosh,* and how his son Ahab* also ruled the land. Israel occupied the land for forty years (figuratively). Then Chemosh enabled Mesha to reoccupy the lands lost to Israel. A military campaign is described. In the campaign Mesha took Nebo,* put the people to the sword, and devoted them to destruction for Chemosh (cf. Josh 6:17–18, 21). The name Yahweh is mentioned in line eighteen. The monument is significant for history, for religion, and for the language and syntax of Moabite. It is the longest inscription yet found in Palestine.

BIBLIOGRAPHY: *ANET*, 320–21; *DOTT*, 195–98; F. I. Andersen, "Moabite Syntax," *Orientalia*, 35 (1966), 81–120.
JAT

MOAB; MOABITES. A country and a people in southern Trans-Jordan, between the rivers Arnon and Zered, extending at times N of the Arnon. In pre-Exodus times the area had settled villages till c. 1900 B.C. Then for several centuries it was largely occupied by nomads, until the emergence of the Moabite kingdom, with settled towns, just before 1300 B.C. The Moabites had frequent contact with Judah* and Israel* until the fall of Jerusalem* in 587 B.C. Thereafter Moab fell on evil times and reverted to semi-nomadic occupation until the last centuries B.C.

At the time of the Exodus the Israelites sought to traverse Moab along the Kings' Highway,* but were forbidden (Judg 11:17). Balak, king of Moab, invited Balaam the diviner to curse Israel (Num 22–24). In the days of the judges, Eglon of Moab subdued part of Israel (Judg 3:12–30). Later Elimelech, a Bethlehemite, migrated to Moab. His daughter-in-law Ruth married Boaz and became an ancestress of David (Ruth 1:1–2; 4:18–22). David subdued Moab (2 Sam 8:2, 12), but after Solomon's* death Moab broke free until subdued again by Omri* of Israel. The story is told on the Mesha* or Moabite Stone.* Moab broke free under Ahab,* whose son Jehoram was unable to reconquer the land (2 Kings 1:1; 3:4–27). The Moabites were in a confederacy that invaded Judah (2 Chron 20:1–30), and Moabite bands raided Israel on Elisha's death (2 Kings 13:20). Moab was eventually subdued by Assyria in the eighth century and is mentioned frequently on Assyrian inscriptions. After the fall of Assyria in 609 B.C., Moab broke free but was subdued by Nebuchadnezzar* and lost her independence, thereafter falling successively under the control of Persians, Nabataeans,* and Romans.

There has been significant but limited archaeological work in Moab. Important excavations have been carried out at Dibon* and Aroer,* some work has been done at Medeba* and Heshbon,* and a considerable amount of surface survey work has been undertaken.

Inscriptions found in Moab include the Moabite Stone, the almost illegible Balu'ah Stele, from the thirteenth or twelfth century B.C., and the fragmentary inscription from Dibon.

At Aroer on the brink of the Arnon River excavations commenced in 1964. The site goes back to the end of the third millennium. In the days of Mesha there was a fortress here. Excavations at Heshbon have just begun. Ruins found at Medeba so far are from the Christian era. Surface surveys have produced a wide range of potsherds (see SHARDS). Tombs have yielded a range of intact pottery,* seals,* and many figurines of fertility goddesses, though no figure of the god Chemosh* has yet been found.

BIBLIOGRAPHY: N. Glueck, *AASOR*, 14 (1933), 1–114; ibid., 15 (1935); ibid., 18–19 (1939); ibid., 25–28 (1951); id., *The Other Side of the Jordan* (1945); E. Olavarri, "Fouilles à Aro 'er sur l'Arnon. Les niveaux du Bronze Intermédiaire," *RB* (1969), 230–59; G. L. Harding, *The Antiquities of Jordan* (1959, rev. 1967); A. H. Van Zyl, *The Moabites* (1960); D. J. Wiseman, *ZPEB*, 4 (1975), 257–67.

JAT

MOLE (mōl). A large structure, usually of stone, erected for use as a pier or breakwater; also sometimes designates the harbor itself that is so protected.

MOLECH (MOLOCH) (mō'lek). A deity to whom human sacrifice was offered (2 Kings 23:10; Jer 32:35), and worshiped in Ammon* (1 Kings 11:7; Heb. *milcom*). The name is an element in many Ammonite names such as Adad-milki. The god was known in other lands and occurs on the Mari* documents, c. 1700 B.C.

The custom of sacrificing children to Molech (Lev 18:21; Jer 7:31) has found illustration from Carthage, the powerful N African colony of Tyre* and major rival of the Roman Republic in the second and third centuries B.C. Modern Tunis, expanding over the site, has accelerated archaeological work, and discoveries in Carthaginian cemeteries provide evidence for the burning of babies by fire.

BIBLIOGRAPHY: W. F. Albright, *Archaeology and the Religion of Israel* (1953), 162–64; id., *Yahweh and the Gods of Canaan* (1968), 235; B. K. Waltke, *ZPEB*, 4 (1975), 269–70.

JAT

MONEY. See COINS.

MONUMENTS; MEMORIALS. See AARON'S TOMB; BEHISTUN INSCRIPTION; BENI HASAN TABLEAU; CENOTAPH; CYRUS CYLINDER; DISPLAY INSCRIPTION; DOLMEN; ECCE HOMO, ARCH OF; HERODIUM; ISRAEL STELE; LAZARUS, TOMB OF; MASSEBAH; MASTABA; MEGALITHIC MONUMENTS; MELCART STELE; MESHA STELE; MOABITE STONE;

NATIVITY, CHURCH OF THE HOLY; NESTORIAN MONUMENT; OBELISK; PYRAMIDS; RACHEL, TOMB OF; ROSETTA STONE; SARCOPHAGUS; SEPULCHER, CHURCH OF THE HOLY; SHALMANESER, BLACK OBELISK OF; STATUES; STELE; UNKNOWN GOD, ALTAR TO THE; VULTURES, STELE OF; ZAKIR STELE; ZIGGURAT.

MONUMENTUM ANCYRANUM. See ANCYRA.

MONUMENTUM ANTIOCHENUM. See ANTIOCH, PISIDIAN.

MORDECAI (môr'də kī). Mordecai's name seems to relate to Marduk, the Babylonian god, and Esther's to Ishtar,* a goddess of the same pantheon. The names are those accepted or imposed after the fashion mentioned in the story of Daniel. Perhaps they mark the compromise and pagan integration of the Jews* who settled down in Exile.* To interpret the story as a myth describing the cosmic conflict of related gods and the alternation of the seasons, is exegesis worthy rather of the last century than of this. Archaeology has only a small contribution to make—a cuneiform* text not precisely dated names one Marduka as a treasury officer under Xerxes I.* This mad monarch, who launched the mighty and ill-starred assault on Greece in 480 B.C., is fairly well characterized in the story of Esther, and the tablet, as A. Ungnad has argued, may be a small contribution to the historicity of the book.

BIBLIOGRAPHY: A. Ungnad, *ZAW*, 58 (1940/41), 240–44; ibid., 59 (1942–43), 219; J. B. Scott, *ZPEB*, 4 (1975), 273–74.

EMB

MORIAH (mō rī'ə). This name occurs twice in the Bible. In Gen 22:2 Abraham was commanded to go to the land of Moriah and offer his son as a burnt offering. The only note of location in the text is that the place was three days distant from Beersheba.* The other biblical reference is 2 Chron 3:1, which names the site of the building of Solomon's* temple as Mount Moriah. Christian tradition has related both references to the site of the Dome of the Rock mosque, where there is a huge rock 17.7 by 15.5 m. (58 by 51 ft.), called the Sacred Rock. The rock appears as though it may have been used for sacrifices in ancient times. There are channels cut into it, and there is a large room cut out of the rock beneath. There is no archaeological evidence to date the use of the rock for sacrifices, but there is little doubt that this was the site of the temple* and the threshing floor of Araunah, which David purchased to make his offering to God.

BIBLIOGRAPHY: B. K. Waltke, *ZPEB*, 4 (1975), 276.

BCC

MORTAR. 1. The Hebrew terms *mᵉdhōkāh* and *makhtēsh* (cf. Prov 27:22) described a basalt or limestone container in which various substances were pulverized by means of a pestle. Grains were chiefly prepared in such a way, although herbs, pigments, resins, and liquids often found their way into mortars. Excavations have uncovered various kinds of these containers, ranging from the very simple slab with a central depression to elaborately decorated ones standing on carved feet. From Megiddo* several circular and rectangular mortars were recovered which were characteristic of the varieties occurring in Palestine.

2. As a building material, the Hebrew *ḥōmer*, "clay, *" described the binding compound which was used to hold layers of bricks together. Soft clay often mixed with straw, the latter having the effect of increasing the strength and plasticity of the material threefold, was applied to the bricks while damp, and when hardened it resulted in a rigid, unified structure. In the Tower of Babel* narrative, bitumen* (*ḥēmār*) was used as a mortaring agent (Gen 11:3), there being ample supplies of the substance. Again, the use of bitumen in this manner guaranteed a durable structure, especially if the brick had been baked in a kiln. *

BIBLIOGRAPHY: R. W. Funk and D. R. Sellers, *IDB* (1962), 439–40; E. Russell, *ZPEB*, 4 (1975), 276–77.

RKH

MOSAIC MAP, MEDEBA. See MEDEBA MOSAIC MAP.

MOSAICS. The ability to make designs or pictures by fitting together and cementing selected pieces of flat rock or stone of different colors is one of the most characteristic expressions of oriental decorative art. Mosaic art had multiple origins. It was practiced in Sumeria, * Egypt, * India, the Aegean, and especially by the Romans and Byzantines. * The Byzantine church, in particular, specialized in it. One early example is seen in the so-called "Standard of Ur,*" a wooden panel about .6 m. (2 ft.) long and 23 cm. (9 in.) wide, recovered from a royal tomb at Ur* and dated about 2500 B.C. It was inlaid with mosaic work on both sides, and although the wood* had decomposed completely when the artifact* was unearthed, the mosaic inlay had remained in position, enabling accurate restoration of the panel to be made. Many sites in Egypt and Palestine have furnished evidence of mosaic pavement work at widely differing archaeological levels. The one from the Persian period at Susa's* royal palace was alluded to in Esth 1:6 and is in contrast to the "pavement" (Gabbatha*) of John 19:13, which in all probability was merely an open area paved with large flat stones. A beautiful mosaic panel in almost undamaged condition was recovered from the second-century B.C. synagogue* of Beth Alpha in Palestine, and curiously enough it included the signs of the zodiac as well as baskets of bread and bunches of grapes. Early Christian or Byzantine* mosaics, which have been recovered, included one of loaves and fishes at et-Tabgha, an oriental mosaic in a church at Gerasa, * a circular panel from Seleucia Pieria, and the Medeba Map. * The et-Tabgha (Galilee*) mosaic is in the Church of the Multiplication. A basket of loaves is flanked by two Galilee mullets ("Peter's fish") beneath the altar. * The floor is a fine picture guide to the flora and fauna of the lake.

To move a little outside the theme of biblical archaeology, a mosaic depicting a swastika, the first ever discovered as appearing prominently in an ancient synagogue decoration, has recently been uncovered at En Gedi* by archaeologists of the Jerusalem University and the Government Antiquities and Museums Department.

It was found in a mosaic pavement dating to the early third century A. D. which was excavated after the fifth century mosaic pavement of the En Gedi synagogue had been lifted and transferred to the Israel Museum in Jerusalem for treatment and conservation.

A symbol of disputed origin, dating back thousands of years, the swastika was used in areas as far separated as China, Egypt, Scandinavia, and the Americas. It has been found in the Catacombs* of Rome, * on textiles of the Inca period, and on relics unearthed at the site of ancient Troy*—now in a third-century synagogue in Israel as well. Perhaps representing the sun, infinity, and continual re-creation, it serves to this day as one of the sacred signs of Buddhism. Its more recent use as the emblem of Nazism originated in the mistaken belief that it had been created in India as a symbol of the Aryan race.

The En Gedi synagogue had two or three entrances on its N side—the side facing Jerusalem. The mosaic pavement is one of the oldest known in Israel and is the earliest mosaic pavement of a synagogue.

BIBLIOGRAPHY: C. Hollis and R. Brownrigg, *Holy Places* (1969), 115–16, 129, 146, 152, 167, 184, 187; A. Gurnett, *Mosaics* (1967); N. Avigad, *EEHL*, 4 (1975), 187–90.

RKH and EMB

MOSERAH. See AARON'S TOMB.

MUGHARAH, WADI EL (mug'ha rə). This wadi* ("valley of caves") runs S of Mount Carmel,* and from some of its caves* have come artifacts* from the Stone Age which are important for the origins of Palestinian culture. Four sites were excavated between 1929 and 1934 by D. A. E. Garrod and T. D. McCown, who led an expedition sponsored by the British School of Archaeology. Three caves yielded parts of human skeletons and artifacts made from stones and marine shells, all of which were dated in the Old Stone and Middle Stone ages. The Natufian* culture, so named by Miss Garrod, who discovered it in a neighboring area, the Wadi en-Natuf, was also represented in the Mugharah caves. The Natufians are generally dated in the Middle Paleolithic* period. The Natufians lived in the pre-pottery phase of human culture and are credited with instituting agricultural* activity in the Near East. Their artifacts at Mugharah included pestles, rough knives* and scrapers, while flint sickles, stone mortars* and pestles have been found at other Natufian sites. The artistic abilities of the Natufians were represented in the Mugharah caves and elsewhere by small portraits of the human head and the carving of tiny figures. There are no allusions to the Wadi el-Mugharah in biblical history.

BIBLIOGRAPHY: D. A. E. Garrod and D. M. A.

Skeleton from the Cave of the Valley belonging to the Natufian Period (Mesolithic—10,000-7500 B.C.). Note that the body is laid in a tightly flexed position and wearing a necklace of dentalia and bone ornaments—characteristic of Early Natufian. The head rests on a layer of stones. Courtesy Israel Dept. of Antiquities and Museums.

Bate, *The Stone Age of Mount Carmel*, 1 (1937); T. D. McCown and A. Keith, *The Stone Age of Mount Carmel*, 2 (1939); W. F. Albright, *The Archaeology of Palestine* (1960 ed.), 37, 59–61; E. Anati, *Palestine Before the Hebrews* (1963), Parts 2, 3; R. L. Alden, *ZPEB*, 4 (1975), 309.   RKH

MUKES. *See* GADARA.

MUMMIFICATION. *See* EMBALMING.

MUQDAM, TELL. *See* LEONTOPOLIS.

MURABB'AT, WADI. *See* DEAD SEA SCROLLS.

MURATORIAN FRAGMENT. It is difficult to decide whether this famous list of NT canonical books is to be regarded primarily as an archaeological contribution or as a literary one. The list was discovered by Ludovico Antonio Muratori (1672–1750), librarian and archivist to the Duke of Modena, in the Ambrosian Library of Milan, Italy. The library was founded early in the seventeenth century by Frederico Borromeo and was the first great European collection of books to be open to the public. Muratori came across the list of NT books in an eighth century MS, and the writing* would appear to date from the late second century since Pius I, Hermes, and Montanus are listed as the writer's contemporaries. There are eighty-five lines beginning with a mutilated notice on Mark

and continuing with Luke and John, who are recorded as the third and fourth of the Gospel writings. It lists all NT books save Hebrews, James's and Peter's letters and rejects a group of noncanonical writings. The Latin* is so bad that some regard it as a transliteration of a Greek text. The *ODCC*, under "Muratori" and "Muratorian Canon," gives an exhaustive bibliography.

      EMB

MUSIC; MUSICAL INSTRUMENTS. In the Ancient Near East music was a normal and regular part of everyday living, reflected alike in song and dance, festal celebrations, laments, certain aspects of military life, liturgical worship, and private devotion. In Sumer* and Akkad,* instrumental and vocal music were prominent in both the temples and the royal palaces, with some musicians being court functionaries. Magnificent harps and lyres were recovered from the "royal" tombs at Ur,* and dated between 2700 and 2500 B.C. in the First Dynasty. Most of the poetry recovered to date celebrated the praises of the deities, which is hardly surprising since music was under the control of professional priest-musicians. Aside from the use of trumpets, the extent to which music occurred in Egyptian temple rituals prior to the Amarna* Age is uncertain, but the magnificent "Hymn to the Sun," a product of the religious reformation of Amenhotep IV (c. 1396–1346 B.C.; *see* ATON, HYMN TO THE; AKHENATON), at least demonstrated the poetical expertise of the Aton priests. The musicians of Canaan* had long been famous for their vocal and instrumental skills, and the Beni Hasan tableau* (c. 1900 B.C.) indicated that such Semites took their instruments with them on their journeys.

A tablet from Ras Shamra (Ugarit*) dated about 1850 B.C. has been decoded and found to contain not only the words of a love ballad but also certain markings which represented the music and which directed how it was to be played and sung. These markings had prevented earlier translations of the

Reconstructed lyre with sound box from Great Death Pit at Ur, 2700-2500 B.C. *(See also photo under* DEAD SEA SCROLLS.) Courtesy University Museum, University of Pennsylvania.

material being made because the flag-like cuneiform* symbols had proved impossible to understand. In 1972 after fifteen years of research, Anne D. Kilmer deciphered the symbols and established the nature of the composition. The tablet has been described as "the oldest sheet music in the world," antedating the Greek form of written western music by about 1500 years. It suggests also that Israelite as well as Canaanite singers could have had written music from which they sang and played (cf. Ps 137:2). The music from Ugarit was basically western rather than eastern, because it employed a seven-tone scale rather than the five-tone scale typical of Oriental music.

Egyptian monuments from 1550 B.C. refer explicitly to examples of Canaanite music, while at Ugarit excavations reveal the existence of a class of temple personnel known as "sarim," analagous to the Hebrew singers from the time of David onward. At Megiddo,* an ivory* inlaid plaque was discovered which showed a royal person drinking from a bowl while a musician played on a lyre.

The Hebrew tradition which associated the invention of music with the harp and flute (Gen 4:21) testifies to the antiquity of these instrumental types and finds support from archaeological discoveries in the Near East. The instruments show the connection between music and pastoral life. The Hebrew ʿûghāḇ (cf. Job 30:31) was actually a generic term covering all wind instruments, just as kinnôr designated stringed instruments. The harps recovered from the First Dynasty of Ur found their counterparts in the chordophones from the Egyptian Amarna Age and the New Kingdom period. The Hebrews considered the kinnôr (harp or lyre) to be the noblest of all instruments, since it was that used by David and the Levitical priests. The only stringed instrument mentioned in the Pentateuch (Gen 4:21; 31:27), it was small in size (cf. 1 Sam 10:5) and thus able to be carried around without difficulty. However, it is uncertain if it was played by hand or with a plectrum (1 Sam 16:23). The number of strings on Near Eastern lyres varied from three to twelve. The nēbhel (KJV "psaltery") was also a stringed instrument, perhaps a twelve-stringed harp, used on religious occasions, though sometimes (Isa 5:12; 14:11; Amos 5:23) for secular entertainment also. The "lyre" in Dan 3:5, 7, 10, 15 was probably the Akkadian sabitu, or seven-stringed lyre, one of which was recovered from Ur. A development of the simple reed pipe or whistle (cf. Judg 5:16; Dan 3:5, 7, 10, 15) can be seen in the elegant silver* flute, also found at Ur. The Babylonian "twin pipes" (ḥalḥallatu) comprised an early form of the flute (cf. Isa 30:29; Matt 9:23), and in antiquity were in considerable demand at weddings, funerals, and banquets. Trumpets of the kind illustrated on Assyrian and Egyptian monuments were an early development among the Hebrews, with silver trumpets being mentioned in Num 10:1–2. The shôphār, made of animal horn, was also used frequently on military and religious occasions.

Percussion instruments included cymbals (cf. 1 Chron 16:5), which accompanied trumpets (cf. Ezra 3:10) or lyres (cf. Neh 12:27), and which may have been referred to in 1 Cor 13:1. Assyrian reliefs from the time of Ashurbanipal* (669–627 B.C.) depicted army musicians playing lyres to the accompaniment of drums and horizontal cymbals. Another relief showed a musician playing vertical cymbals.

The term sûmphônyâ ("pipe") of Dan 3:5, 10, 15 is not now recognized as referring to any specific musical instrument, and instead seems to refer to the ensemble playing of all the preceding orchestral instruments. A collective term for "stringed instruments" occurs in Pss 45:8; 150:4.

Music was employed to cheer a departing guest (cf. Gen 31:27), after victory in battle (Exod 15:1ff.; Judg 5:1ff.), and at feasts (Isa 5:12), especially wine festivals (Isa 16:10). The whole range of the population from the king (cf. 2 Sam 19:35) to the shepherd boy (1 Sam 16:18) and the prostitute (Isa 23:16) enjoyed musical entertainment. As in life, so in death (cf. 2 Sam 1:18–27; Matt 9:23), music formed an important part of the occasion commemorated. Although 1 Chron 15:16–24 describes the Davidic choir and orchestra in detail, it is otherwise difficult to assess the precise character of temple* music.

BIBLIOGRAPHY: C. H. Cornill, Music in the OT (1909); J. Stainer, The Music of the Bible (1914); C. Sachs, Musik der Antike (1924); S. B. Finesinger, HUCA, 3 (1926), 21–77; F. W. Galpin, The Music of the Sumerians (1937); R. Lachmann, The Rise of Music in the Ancient World (1943); P. Gradenwitz, The Music of Israel (1949); E. Werner, IDB, 3 (1962), 457–76; A. D. Kilmer, RA, LXVIII (1974), 69-82; H. M. Best and D. Huttar, ZPEB, 4 (1975), 311–24; IDB Supp. Vol. (1976), 610-12.

RKH

MUTESELLIM, TELL EL-. See MEGIDDO.

MYCENAE; MYCENAEAN CIVILIZATION (mī cē′nē). Mycenae was an ancient fortified site in the NE of the Peloponnese, and gave its name to the Late Bronze Age* (c. 1450–1100 B.C.) culture of mainland Greece and the Aegean islands except Crete, which was Minoan* in culture. Schliemann was the first to excavate Mycenae in the nineteenth century, and subsequent studies have shown that Mycenaean culture was built on the foundations established by the Minoan civilization.

Mainland Greece had been settled sporadically in the third millennium B.C., but at the end of the Early Bronze Age invaders destroyed most of the dwellings in the S mainland and built less sophisticated houses for themselves. This fact, along with the presence of burial sites within the settlement areas, might suggest that the invaders were from Anatolia, where such customs were followed. Certainly the group that occupied some of the Cycladic islands were from W Anatolia, as indicated by their pottery.* The culture of the mainland migrants remained comparatively undeveloped during the Middle Bronze Age, although elaborate jewelry dating to the sixteenth century B.C. was recovered from some Mycenaean graves.* Cretan pottery was imported into the Peloponnese, and certain refinements in pottery making appear to have been adopted from the Cyclades migrants.

From about 1600 B.C., Cretan influence affected both the Aegean islands and the mainland, and this is reflected in artifacts* recovered from the royal shaft graves at Mycenae. Six of these were excavated by Schliemann in 1876, but 75 years passed before another related group was discovered outside the Late Bronze Age walls* of the city.* The graves were elaborately constructed and decorated, and with the dead were interred some magnificent specimens of gold* and silver* vessels,* dress ornaments, tiaras, and a wide variety of bronze* weapons (see ARMS), some of which were decorated with gold, silver, and electrum inlays.

Pottery from the second group of graves in particular was of local manufacture, perhaps originating in Messenia. Under Cretan influence such ware became more sophisticated in the Late Bronze Age, which resulted in its being regarded as characteristic of Mycenaean civilization. Another feature of that culture was the use of family tombs cut into the rock, with a passage leading to the burial chamber. Another kind of tomb, the *tholos*, was built in the style of a primitive beehive, and was also approached through a long passageway.

An outstanding element of Mycenaean civilization was the language, known as Mycenaean Greek. It was used for court annals and inventories, and was written in a syllabic script to which the scholars have given the name of Linear B.* It was recovered principally from Mycenae, Tiryns, Thebes,* and Messenia, though some tablets were excavated at Knossos in Crete.

After the conquest of Crete and the Cyclades by maritime invaders about 1450 B.C., the cultural influence of Crete declined steadily, and by the thirteenth century Mycenae seems to have been the capital of an empire that included Crete and other Aegean islands. Some apparent threat of invasion caused strong defensive walls to be built around Mycenae, Tiryns, and even Athens,* where the acropolis* was fortified. Though justified, these precautions ultimately proved to be of no avail, since by the end of the thirteenth century B.C. most of the mainland Mycenaean centers were destroyed. The invaders, of uncertain identity, kept some Mycenaean traditions alive, but these were modified further when the Dorians invaded the Peloponnese.

BIBLIOGRAPHY: M. Ventris and J. Chadwick, *Documents in Mycenaean Greek* (1956); J. Chadwick, *The Decipherment of Linear B* (1958); E. T. Vermeule, *Greece in the Bronze Age* (1964); G. E. Mylonas, *Mycenae and the Mycenaean Age* (1966).

RKH

MYRA (mī'rə; Gr. Μύρα, *Myra*). An old city* inhabited by Lycian speaking people, located on the SW coast of Asia Minor* where Paul's ship landed (Acts 27:5) on his way to Rome.*

Myra lay a few miles back from the coast and its territory included the port of Andriace about 6.4 km. (4 mi.) SW, where Paul's ship landed. The importance of the city in the Persian period is shown by the many Lycian inscriptions of that time which have been found there. Later in the Roman times Myra bestowed on Augustus* and then on Tiberius* the title of "Imperator of land and sea, Benefactor and Savior of the whole Universe" (*IG Rom.*, 3.719, 721). Tiberius was also called *theos* ("god") by the people of Myra (*IG Rom.*, 3.715, 720–21) as well as by those of Eresus, Mitylene,* and Cos.

In addition, the public assembly of Myra honored Germanicus Caesar (Tiberius's brother's son) and his wife Agrippina by erecting statues* for them and calling this military commander "Savior and Benefactor" (cf. *IG Rom.*, 3.715–17, 719, 721).

In the second century A.D., through special gifts granted to it, Myra built a public portico and theater.* In its necropolis* are a number of Syrian type rock tombs. Not far away is found a well-preserved granary* of Hadrian, containing the busts of Hadrian and Faustina in the front wall.

BIBLIOGRAPHY: W. M. Ramsay, *St. Paul the Traveler and Roman Citizen* (1896), 297–300; W. Ruge, "Myra," *PWRE*, 16.1 (1933), 1083–89; A. H. M. Jones, *The Cities of the Eastern Roman Provinces*, 2nd ed. (1971), 9, 100, 102, 106–7; D. Magie, *Roman Rule in Asia Minor*, 1 (1950), 497–98, 502, 520, 529; ibid., 2 (1970), 1360–61, 1386; Ekrem Akurgal, *Ancient Civilizations and Ruins of Turkey* (Istanbul, 1973), 263–64; *PECS* (1976), 603–4.   WHM

MYSIA (mish'ē ə; Gr. Μυσία, *Mysia*). A province in the NW region of Asia Minor* with borders as follows: W, the Aegean Sea; N, the Hellespont and Propontis; E, Bithynia,* and Phrygia;* and S, Lydia.* Paul went through Mysia to Troas* (Acts 16:7–10). Later the apostle visited Troas and also went on to Mysian Assos* on the coast (Acts 20:5–14). Other Mysian cities of the NT were Adramyttium* and Pergamum.*

In Roman times the proconsul worked, for judicial purposes, through a grouping of communities into circuits (*dioeceseis* or *conventus*). One such conventus, that of Adramyttium, included an inland valley town of Pericharaxis, mentioned in an inscription which indicated that in the third century A.D., the town had a city organization with an annual *prytanis* and magistracies. In the next valley, the Mysian tribe of the Abbaeitae lived in villages and carried their tribal organization and name (as did some other Mysian tribes) into the first century B.C. and beyond as indicated by their coins.* Cities* in the area also issued their coins as evidenced by those issued in the reigns of Nero and Hadrian.

Among its metals was silver,* mined in the NW part of Mysia at Argyria (which gave its name to the metal) and at Pericharaxis.

BIBLIOGRAPHY: A. H. M. Jones, *The Cities of the Eastern Roman Provinces* (1937), 33, 37, 88–91; D. Magie, *Roman Rule in Asia Minor*, I, (1950), 43–44; E. M. Blaiklock, *ZPEB*, 4 (1975), 326–27.

WHM

MYTILENE. *See* MITYLENE.

N

NABATAEANS. An Arab people who played an important part in the history of Palestine in the last centuries B.C. and the first centuries A.D. They are of uncertain origin. Possibly being the desert raiders of Mal 1:1–5, they became known in historical documents in 312 B.C. when they refused to submit to Alexander's successor, Antigonus. They gradually occupied all of ancient Moab,* Edom,* and part of the Negev.* We can trace their line of kings from Aretas I* (c. 150 B.C.) to Rabbel II (A.D. 70–106), when they fell to the Romans. Considerable archaeological evidence is available. As skilled agriculturists,* they left many dams and cisterns* to support population in areas previously sparsely settled. They were fine artists and left an abundance of the beautiful Nabataean ware. They hewed remarkable buildings—temples, houses,* shops, etc.—out of the mountain face. Their finest architecture is preserved at Petra.* Egyptian and Greek influence is evident in the tombs and mausoleums and elsewhere, with their gables, mouldings, and cornices.* They left numerous "high places"* or open air sanctuaries from the early period (fourth to first century B.C.). Numerous inscriptions written in a distinctive Aramaic* alphabet* have been found. A number of Nabataean papyri* have been discovered in the Qumran* area. Surface surveys attest the spread of their considerable achievements throughout Trans-Jordan and in the southern parts of western Palestine.

BIBLIOGRAPHY: N. Glueck, *The Other Side of Jordan* (1940), 158–200; J. Starcky, "The Nabataeans, A Historical Sketch," *BA*, 18 (1955), 89–106; G. L. Harding, *The Antiquities of Jordan* (1959); S. Cohen, *IDB*, 3 (1962), 491–93; B. Van Elderen, *ZPEB*, 4 (1975), 347–51.

JAT

Painted Nabataean dishes used at funerary meals, found in topsoil near tombs of Nabataean necropolis at Kurnub; first half of first and first half of second centuries A.D. Courtesy Professor Abraham Negev.

NABONIDUS (nab ō ni′dəs). This Akkadian* name, meaning "Nabû is awe-inspiring," belonged to the last king of Babylon,* who ruled from 555–539 B.C. Though authors such as Herodotus and Xenophon deal with the events of his reign, surprisingly little detailed historical narrative material has survived to supplement the scanty information relating to his rule and the final collapse of Babylon. A basalt stele* dealing with his rise to power seems to defend rather than explain the circumstances which led him to seize the throne from Labashi-Marduk, son of Neriglissar, in 555 B.C. Another Nabonidus text from Haran* narrated the story of his mother's life, while a further source referred to the "king of the Medes" in the tenth year of Nabonidus. From available evidence he apparently rose from the position of a military commander to be king of Babylon, perhaps through a palace rebellion. Shortly after his accession he marched westward to Cilicia,* where, according to Herodotus, he settled differences between the Lydians* and the Medes.* He also rebuilt the temple of Sin in Haran, of which he was a native, and after a period of illness he marched against the northwestern oasis of Tema,* killed the inhabitants, and established his capital there for the next ten years. His absence from the New Year festival in Babylon during that time was a matter of acute embarrassment to the religious authorities. Explanations adduced for this strange behavior have ranged from considerations of international policies to resistance by the Babylonians to his proposed substitution at Haran of Sin, the moon-god, for the local Bel-Marduk as chief deity. One of the Haran monuments seems to support the latter suggestion, indicating that opposition to the plans of Nabonidus for Haran caused him to indulge in self-exile at Tema in a fit of pique. However, his son Belshazzar* acted as coregent in Babylon during his absence, a situation which made Daniel the third member of the ruling triad (Dan 5:29). Cyrus,* a vassal of Astyages, king of Media, presented a threat to Babylon by revolting against his suzerain about 550 B.C., and thereafter the Medes menaced Babylonian security. With the defeat of Croesus of Lydia and the fall of Sardis* in 546 B.C., the Median danger to Babylon became acute. Babylonian sources say virtually nothing about the next six years, but during this period Nabonidus returned to a weakened and divided Babylon. He may have attempted to come to terms with the religious authorities by bringing all the images from Babylonian temples into the capital. When Cyrus entered Babylon on October 16, 539 B.C., Nabonidus fled but did not long escape the fate which overtook Belshazzar (Dan 5:30). With his death the Neo-Babylonian or Chaldean* period ended and that of the Achaemenids began.

BIBLIOGRAPHY: R. P. Dougherty, *Nabonidus and Belshazzar* (1929); J. Lewy, *HUCA*, 19 (1946), 405–59; A. L. Oppenheim, *ANET*, 308–14; id., *IDB*, 3 (1962), 493–95; C. J. Gadd, A-S, 8 (1958), 35–92; D. J. Wiseman, *ZPEB*, 4 (1975), 351–52.

RKH

NABONIDUS, PRAYER OF. From the fourth Qumran* cave a MS fragment dated about the second half of the first century B.C. preserves a prayer attributed to Nabonidus,* the last king of the Neo-Babylonian Empire,* who ruled from 555 to 539 B.C. According to this MS, Nabonidus confessed his sin when he was "smitten with a serious inflammation by the command of the Most High God" while he was residing at the oasis of Tema* in Arabia.* After this a priest was sent from among the Babylonian exiles, and he interpreted something of the significance of the ailment for the benefit of Nabonidus. Some scholars have adduced this MS scrap as indicating that an affliction attributed in Dan 4 to Nebuchadnezzar* should instead have been credited to Nabonidus. However, Nebuchadnezzar's illness is a well-attested clinical form of psychosis, whereas the symptoms described in the "Prayer of Nabonidus" merely indicate some inflammation of the tissues. Certain other symptoms mentioned seem to have nothing in common with recognizable pathological conditions, which makes at best a rather bizarre description of disease, in sharp contrast with the account in Dan 4. The "Prayer" seems to be haggadic in character and to comprise a previously unknown apocryphal accretion to the canonical Daniel.

BIBLIOGRAPHY: J. T. Milik, *RB*, 63 (1956), 407–12; R. K. Harrison, *Introduction to the OT* (1969), 1117–20.

EMB

NABOPOLASSAR (na bo po laz′ ər; Akkad. *Nabū-apal-uṣur*, "Nabu protect the son"). The king (626–605 B.C.) of the Chaldeans,* who was the father of Nebuchadnezzar* and the founder of the Neo-Babylonian Empire.* In Greek sources he is also known as Busalossorus in Abydenus, as quoted by Eusebius, and as Belesys in Diodorus Siculus (2, 24.2ff.).

The most important documents for his reign are portions of the Chaldean Chronicles published by C. Gadd in 1923, covering the years 616–609 B.C., and other sections published by D. J. Wiseman in 1956, covering all but the king's fourth through his ninth years.

Although it has been suggested that Nabopolassar was the son of Bel-Ibni, the Chaldean viceroy over the Sealands under the Assyrians, Nabopolassar described himself as "the son of a nobody" whom Marduk chose because of his piety.

The background of Nabopolassar's rise to power is not clear as the dates of the last Assyrian rulers over Babylonia are uncertain and disputed. It seems that Ashurbanipal* was served in Babylon* by a king Kandalanu, whose name some scholars have interpreted as but another title for Ashurbanipal. After 627 came two sons of Ashurbanipal, Ashur-etillu-ili and Sin-shar-ishkun.

After gaining Sippar,* Nabopolassar claimed kingship over Babylon in November 626. A three-cornered struggle seems to have taken place between Nabopolassar; Ashur-etillu-ili, the Assyrian king; and the latter's brother Sin-shar-ishkun, who gained the Assyrian throne about 623.

One of Nabopolassar's first acts was the return from Uruk* of the gods which had been taken from Susa,* a move designed to win Elamite* support. In 624 the Assyrian garrison was subjected to a severe siege at Nippur,* which fell into Nabopolassar's control by 622. By 620 the Chaldeans had gained control of Uruk from Sin-shar-ishkun. What is more important, by this time Nabopolassar had joined hands with Cyaxares, the king of the Medes.*

There is an unfortunate hiatus in the chronicles until 616. By this time Nabopolassar was in complete control of Babylonia. In 615 the Chaldeans attempted an unsuccessful attack upon Ashur.*

In 614 the Medes succeeded in breaching the walls* of Ashur and then proceeded to massacre the inhabitants. Nabopolassar arrived only after the city* fell. According to classical sources, a marriage* alliance was sealed between the two allies with Nabopolassar's son, Nebuchadnezzar, marrying Amytis, the daughter of Cyaxares.

In 612 Nabopolassar joined the king of the Umman-manda (lit., "hordes," who are probably the Medes, though some have suggested that they were Scythians*) for the final assault on Nineveh* (cf. Nah 3). According to classical traditions, Nineveh was taken with the aid of an abnormally high Tigris River; the Assyrian king Sardanapallus (i.e., Sin-shar-ishkun) is reported to have cast himself into the flames as the city burned.

A remnant of the Assyrians, led by Ashur-uballit, fled W to Haran,* where they received support from their new allies, the Egyptians.* In 610 Nabopolassar marched with the Medes against the garrison at Haran, forcing the Assyrians to withdraw even farther westward beyond the bend of the Euphrates. In

609 after the last spasms of resistance Ashur-uballit seems to have fled northward.

What is of interest for biblical studies is the knowledge that it was in a futile attempt to block Egyptian aid to the embattled Assyrians that Josiah, king of Judah, * met his death at Megiddo* in 609 (2 Kings 23:29; cf. 2 Chron 35:20–23). 2 Kings 23:29 should be translated accordingly: "Pharaoh Necho king of Egypt went up to (rather than 'against' as in the KJV) the king of Assyria."

After 607 Nabopolassar, because of old age and perhaps ill health, left the command of the army to his son, Nebuchadnezzar. Nabopolassar died on August 15–16, 605, in his twenty-first year as king.

BIBLIOGRAPHY: C. Gadd, *The Fall of Nineveh* (1923); A. T. Olmstead, *History of Assyria* (1923), 633–44; S. Smith, *Babylonian Historical Texts* (1924); I. Price, "The Nabopolassar Chronicle," *JAOS*, 44 (1924), 122–29; A. Oppenheim, "Siege Documents from Nippur," *Iraq*, 17 (1955), 69–89; D. Wiseman, *Chronicles of Chaldaean Kings* (1956); A. Parrot, *Babylon and the OT* (1958), 79–87; H. W. F. Saggs, *The Greatness That Was Babylon* (1962), 135–39; R. Borger, "Der Aufstieg des neubabylonischen Reiches," *JCS*, 19 (1965), 59–77; J. Macqueen, *Babylon* (1965), 133–40; J. Reade, "The Accession of Sinsharishkun," *JCS*, 23 (1970), 1–9; D. Baltzer, "Harran nach 610 'medisch,' " *Welt Orients*, 7 (1973), 86–95; L. L. Walker, *ZPEB*, 4 (1975), 352–53.

EY

NAG HAMMADI PAPYRI. Nag Hammadi is in Upper Egypt, * some 48 km. (30 mi.) N of Luxor, * the place where, in 1946, a group of peasants unearthed the library of a deviant Christian sect which consisted of some thousand pages of Coptic MSS translated from earlier Greek originals. The documents date from the early fourth century and are of importance for the light they throw on mystical gnostic doctrines which had infiltrated certain areas of Christian thinking. Overshadowed by the discovery of the Dead Sea Scrolls* in the following year, and concealed and withheld alike by the discoverers and the Egyptian authorities, the Nag Hammadi papyri took a decade to reach publication in the West. Apart from the so-called Gospel of Thomas, * the collection is of interest only to students of early heresy and mystical religion. It is obvious that gnosticism in its varied forms was a major problem in the church, and the value of the Nag Hammadi documents is that they make gnostic sources directly available for the first time. Previously, from John's writings onward, these varied forms of mystical heresy were known or inferred only from the writings of those who took in hand to refute or to rebut their teaching. Nag Hammadi has supplied originals.

BIBLIOGRAPHY: A. Guillaumont et al., *L'Evangile selon Thomas* (1959); W. C. Van Unnik, *Newly Discovered Gnostic Writings* (1960); B. Gärtner, *The Theology of the Gospel According to Thomas* (1961); J. E. Ménard, *L'Evangile selon Philippe* (1964); R. M. Wilson, *Gnosis and the NT* (1968).

EMB

NAGILA. See TELL NAGILA.

NAHARIYAH (nä hä rē′yə). This little town on the coast near the Israeli—Lebanese border was the scene, in 1954 and 1955, of Israeli excavations. An interesting temple was discovered, founded in the middle of the eighteenth century B. C., and enlarged a century later. Outside was a circular stone structure with related objects marked as a high place, * or place of sacrifice, though such places did not require a topographical elevation. This place of sacrifice was in a court which was the center of the associated worship. Near the altar* was a stone box, apparently to receive such votive offerings as the metal figurines of animals and doves found on the site. The high place was still greasy from libations of oil and the acts of sacrifice. Vessels* containing seven cups were no doubt associated with the libations and were discovered in the court. Beads, jewelry, and silver* and bronze* images of female deities suggested a fertility cult. The naked bodies, with overemphasis on sexual characteristics, indicate the cult of Asherah, * known from the Bible and the Ugaritic text as a fertility goddess, worshiped at Tyre* and Sidon, * not far up the coast. Here, at any rate, is a typical Canaanite* high place of the sort denounced by Amos (7:9 and 2 Kings 23:8). Similar institutions have been found at Megiddo* and Byblos (Gebal*).

EMB

NAHR AL KALB. On a cliff face beside this river ("Dog River") which debouches between Beirut and Byblos (Gebal*) passing conquerors have recorded their achievements. There are boastful words of the great Ramses II* who marched N in 1298 B. C. against the Hittites. * The inscription is old and almost obliterated, but the record of the pharaoh's passing strikingly illustrates the well-known passage in George Adam Smith's *Historical Geography of the Holy Land* (112) in which the great geographer spoke of the influence on the OT of the tides of history which swept N and S over the lands of the Bible. In 671 B. C. Esarhaddon* of Assyria recorded a victory over Egypt. * Nebuchadnezzar* added his destruction of Jerusalem* in 586 and his thirteen-year siege of Tyre. * The roll ends with tablets from World War I in English and French and one set up in 1946 proclaiming Lebanon's independence.

EMB

NAIL. *Fingernails.* Captive women were required to pare their fingernails in order to prevent them from marring their beauty by scratching their faces in grief and defiance, thus reducing their value as slaves. *

A peg, or pin. These were driven into a wall (Isa 22:23–25) or used as tent pegs (Judg 4:21–22; 5:26).

Nails for construction. Nails and pegs for construction might be made of wood, * bone, stone, copper, bronze, * iron, * gold, * or silver. *

Metal nails came into use during the Early Bronze Age* and have been found in Palestinian excavations throughout the biblical period. The earliest nails were of bronze; later long iron nails appear, and bronze continued to be used in the smaller sizes. Those of precious metal were, of course, primarily ornamental. In general, sizes of nails were similar to those now used, except for our smallest.

Frequently wood is found adhering to excavated nails (see CRUCIFIXION for the story of the 1968 discovery of the bones of Shimon Hagagol). At Samaria* a variety of nails was found—long iron spikes 17.8 to 22.9 cm. (7 to 9 in.), as well as differing lengths of shorter nails, many in the 2.54 to 3.8 cm. (1 to 1½ in.) range. These had small squared heads, and some were made with broad flat-domed heads. Most have squared shanks similar to American colonial cut nails and were made with broad flat-domed heads covered with gold foil. Similar gold- and silver-coated nails occur in the Nuzi* finds, and doubtless this type was used for ornamental purposes. Short bronze nails from Tell Abu Hawam, near Acco,* from the thirteenth century B.C., show traces of gold foil. These samples of ornamental nails may give some idea of what the "gold nails" for the temple (2 Chron 3:9) were like. Nails were sometimes used in making idols (cf. Jer 10:4).

A reason for the relatively few nails found in Palestinian excavations is probably related to their somewhat limited use in antiquity. They were in fact an expensive item, and other, cheaper methods of fastening were readily available. No doubt the practice, still prevalent in the Mediterranean countries, of binding structural members together with cord, was ordinarily used.

The ancient Greeks used iron nails more freely, frequently to fasten terra-cotta facings to timber or stone structures, as well as for more usual purposes. An early use of bronze (later brass) nails was for fastening leather* coverings over wooden articles. Subsequently nails were extensively used for applying fittings such as hinges, locks, bolts, etc. The crude handmade nails required the use of an awl or bit to make a hole before they could be driven.

The vast hoard of nails discovered at Inchtuthill in Scotland gives an idea of what the nails of the cross (John 20:25) were like. It is difficult to explain how the nails came to be in Scotland, for the Roman reconnaissance there seems not to have involved a policy of extensive fortification. Perhaps the nails were from sabotage of a supply train sent up from Corfinium (Corbridge).

BIBLIOGRAPHY: R. Forbes, Studies in Ancient Technology, 8 (1964), 130; C. Singer et al., A History of Technology, 2 (1965), see index.

MHH and EMB

NAIN (nān; possibly from Heb. נעים, "pleasant, delightful"). A town of S Galilee* only mentioned in the Bible in Luke 7:11, its name surviving in the Arabic* Nein which is located on the NW side of Nebi Dahi (or, Jebel edh Dhahi), a hill between Gilboa and Tabor,* known in the OT as the hill of Moreh (Judg 7:1). Nain looks out over the Plain of Esdraelon. The location is c. 8 km. (5 mi.) SE of Nazareth* and c. 40 km. (25 mi.) from Capernaum.*

According to Luke 7:12, NT Nain was walled, and the visible ruins indicate that the town then was of some importance, compared to the modern small village of Nein. Above the village to the SE there are tombs and caves* in the rock of the hill.

Today there can be seen a small Franciscan church built on the ruins of a medieval church (probably the one Peter the Deacon saw c. A.D. 1137; CCSL 175, 98), and nearby there are ruins of another shrine containing deteriorated sarcophagi.*

BIBLIOGRAPHY: G. Dalman, Sacred Sites and Ways (1935), 190–92; F.-M. Abel, Géographie De la Palestine, 2 (1938), 394–95; E. G. Kraeling, Bible Atlas (1956), 380–81; Atlas of Israel (1970), map 10.

WHM

NAIRI. See URARTU.

NARMER, PALETTE OF. It is possible that Narmer was a religious title given to Menes, the uniter of Egypt* (3400 B.C.?). The famous palette, one of those dedicated in the temple of Horus at Hierakonpolis, is both a sample of early Egyptian art and a document of the barbarous imperialism of the period. The king is shown followed by his sandal-bearer and preceded by four standard-bearers inspecting the decapitated bodies of his foes. Lower on the same side, the king is shown as a bull, breaching a city* wall* and trampling his foes. On the reverse stands the tall figure of the king who lifts a heavy mace with pear-shaped head of white stone to crush the skull of his enemy whom he grasps by the hair. Fallen foes again adorn the bottom.

BIBLIOGRAPHY: J. E. Quibell, Hierakonpolis, 1 (1900), 10; Manetho, Manetho, W. G. Waddell, trans. (Loeb, 1940), 27–29; J. H. Breasted, History of Egypt (1945), 35–45; FLAP, 73–74; pl. 28.

EMB

NASBEH, TELL EN-. See MIZPAH.

NASH PAPYRUS. A page containing the Decalogue (Exod 20:2–17) and the Shema (Deut 6:4–5), of some palaeographical* interest. The page, which came allegedly from a Fayum papyrus* deposit, was acquired by W. L. Nash at the turn of the century (he was secretary of the Society of Biblical Archaeology) and was published first in 1903 by S. A. Cooke. The angular form of the writing* suggests a date c. 150 B.C.

BIBLIOGRAPHY: S. A. Cooke, "A Pre-Massoretic Biblical Papyrus," PSBA, 25 (1903), 35–56; W. F. Albright, "The Nash Papyrus," JBL, 36 (1937), 145–76; id., BASOR, 115 (1949), 10–19.

EMB

NATHO. See LEONTOPOLIS.

NATIVITY, CHURCH OF THE. The tradition that the "stable" of the nativity story was a cave* goes back to Justin Martyr, who was born near Samaria* about the end of the first century at Neapolis* (modern Nablus). Jerome worked in a cave at Bethlehem* near the traditional site at the end of the fourth century. Jerome mentions that Hadrian, at the time of the Second Jewish Rebellion, desecrated the traditional cave by consecrating it to Adonis, and that Helena, Constantine's mother, built a church above it in the fourth century. All that archaeology can add

Nave of Justinian's Church of the Nativity, looking east, showing fragments of floor mosaics below present church floor. Courtesy Israel Dept. of Antiquities and Museums.

is that examination in 1934 and again in 1948 to 1951 has shown that there are floor mosaics* 0.8 m. (2½ ft.) below the present church floor. These almost certainly belong to the Constantinian basilica.*

BIBLIOGRAPHY: FLAP (1951), 431, 438–42; pls. 191–92.   EMB

NATRON. See EMBALMING.

NATUFIANS (nə tū'fi unz). These were Mesolithic* people scattered through parts of Palestine and elsewhere, but called after the type site, in the Wadi en-Natuf in W Palestine, dug by Dorothy A. E. Garrod and Theodore D. McCown from 1929–34.

The Mesolithic culture of W Palestine forms a bridge civilization between the food-gathering and food-producing people. Just what influences caused the changes are still unknown, and the dates when Mesolithic culture arose are not uniform in all parts of the world. In the Natufian culture from the caves* of Mount Carmel* and the surrounding area basket weaving, the use of bows, traps for animals, and various kinds of fishnets (see FISHING), and probably the domestication of animals become common. Small flint tools* are characteristic (microliths), and the Natufians, unlike other Mesolithic peoples, who specialized in highly schematic designs, developed a unique naturalistic art. Animal and human figures seem to predominate, some of which may be purely decorative and some of which are definitely erotic and probably connected with fertility rites.

Burials were conducted within these earliest known settlements, leaving us a rich hoard of material for study. There were two subtypes of burial, each with a body lying on its side in a basically flexed position, one of which is tightly flexed and the other loosely. The difference, according to Garrod, seems to have been one related to space available. In other situations skulls were buried, without the rest of the body, and, unlike the Paleolithic* burials, group graves* are normal. Decorations of shell, bone, and various kinds of jewelry accompanied the body to burial, and apparently the body was coated with some kind of red ocher. One very strange burial of twelve mutilated bodies, including those of children, was found in the cave of El-Wad, for which no explanation has ever been fully given.

The generally accepted dates for this culture are c. 12,000–10,000 B.C. for its beginning and c. 7500 B.C. for its termination with the development of the Neolithic* Age. Main sites include Jericho, Einan, Nahal Oren, and the various caves of Mount Carmel.

BIBLIOGRAPHY: D. A. E. Garrod and D. M. A. Bate, *The Stone Age of Mount Carmel*, 1 (1937); T. D. McCown and A. Keith, *The Stone Age of Mt. Carmel*, 2 (1939); E. Anati, *Palestine Before the Hebrews* (1962), 139–78; E. K. Vogel, "Bibliography of Holy Land Sites," *HUCA*, 42 (1971), 61 (Mount Carmel Caves), 66 (Nahal Oren); *CAH*, 1, Part 1, 86, 95, 120–21, 251, 499–500, 503; D. O. Henry, "Natufian Site of Rosh Zin; A Preliminary Report," *PEQ*, 105 (1973), 129–40; P. A. Larson, Jr., "Ornamental Beads From the Late Natufian of Southern Israel," *Journal of Field Archaeology*, 5 (1978), 120–21.
                                              CEA

NAZARETH (naz'ə rəth; Gr. Ναζαρέθ, *Nazareth*). A town in the hills of Galilee,* just to the N of the Plain of Esdraelon, the hometown of Jesus (Matt 2:23 et al.).

Recent archaeological evidence shows that Nazareth was inhabited long before as well as during the early Roman period. This is evidenced by the ancient skull found near the town as well as by Middle Bronze-

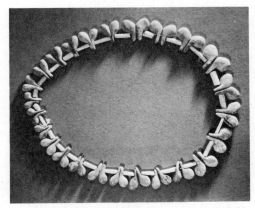

Natufian period necklace of dentalia and bone found in grave in Cave of the Valley. (*See also photos under* AGRICULTURE; MUGHARA, WADI EL.) Courtesy Israel Dept. of Antiquities and Museums. Photo Israel Museum, Jerusalem.

Mary's Well under altar of Greek Orthodox Church of the Annunciation in Nazareth. Courtesy Israel Government Press Office.

Age* pottery* from burial caves* in the upper part of the city.* Also, near the Church of the Annunciation there have been found grain silos of the type that were as early as the Chalcolithic Age* but in which the earliest pottery was of Iron II* (900–600 B.C.). Other pottery there consisted of a little from the Hellenistic period, more from the Roman and most from the Byzantine* period. Of the twenty-three tombs found c. 450 m. (500 yd.) from the church most were of the kokim type (i.e., horizontal shafts or niches off a central chamber) known in Palestine from c. 200 B.C. and which became the standard Jewish type. Two tombs had in them artifacts* (lamps,* etc.) to be dated from the first to fourth centuries A.D. Four tombs sealed with rolling stones typical of the late Jewish period testify to a considerable Jewish community there in the Roman period.

Testimony to a town at Nazareth in the first century A.D. comes from fragments of an inscription containing the name Nazareth in Hebrew, found in the Hebrew University excavation in Caesarea* in 1962. As Talmudic material showed, the complete text gave a list of the twenty-four priestly courses (cf. 1 Chron 24:7–19; Luke 1:5) and added were the names of the Galilean towns where the courses were located. This transfer of courses to Galilee* must have occurred after A.D. 70.

The most authentic Christian site in Nazareth is the spring on the N side of the present city, known from the twelfth century as Mary's Well; the water comes from above the Church of St. Gabriel and is piped down to the main road that goes from Nazareth to Tiberias.*

Among other shrines, the earliest remains of the Church of the Annunciation come from about the beginning of the fifth century. The Crusaders built a much larger church on the site, and then in 1730 another church was built which was never finished but was demolished when the recent church was built. Both the Byzantine and Crusader churches were of a basilica* type. In subterranean grottoes there is a fifth-century mosaic* inscription which reads, "from Conon, deacon of Jerusalem."

During the construction of the Church of the Annunciation opportunity was afforded to investigate the ground below. A pool was found belonging to the nave of the Byzantine church, which had graffiti* on stones with letters such as IH (the abbreviation for Jesus' name), fragments of invocations to God, etc. Under the floor of a small monastery were eight stones of an older building, column bases, moldings, ends of arches,* and jambs of doors. Many of the stones still contained white plaster and graffiti in charcoal,* with several crosses formed, a reference to the passage on the annunciation in Luke, a boat (a symbol connected with Jesus), fragments of another invocation to God, and a male figure holding a cross-headed staff in his right hand. All this was part of an early church before Constantine's time, a church built on a synagogue plan.

The site of the ancient synagogue of Luke 4:16–29 is in doubt although several locations have been suggested. In 1969 Bagatti distinguished two synagogues* in Nazareth, one of the Jews* (located NW of the Franciscan monastery) and one of Jewish Christians.

BIBLIOGRAPHY: G. Dalman, *Sacred Sites and Ways* (1935), 57–78; F.-M. Abel, *Géographie De la Palestine*, 2 (1938), 203, 395; E. G. Kraeling, *Bible Atlas* (1956), 358–59; J. Finegan, *The Archaeology of the NT* (1969), 27–33; S. J. Saller, *Second Revised Catalogue of the Ancient Synagogues of the Holy Land* (1972), 70–71; E. M. Blaiklock, *ZPEB*, 4 (1975), 388–92; *EEHL*, 3 (1977), 919–22. WHM

NAZARETH DECREE. An interesting archaeological discovery which appeared first in the Froehner collection of antiquities was labeled: "Slab of marble sent from Nazareth, 1878."

As translated by Michel Rostovtzeff in 1930 it reads: "Ordinance of Caesar. It is my pleasure that graves and tombs remain undisturbed in perpetuity for those who have made them for the cult of their ancestors, or children, or members of their house. If, however, any man lay information that another has either demolished them, or has in any other way extracted the buried, or has maliciously transferred them to other places in order to wrong them, or has displaced the sealing or other stones, against such a one I order that a trial be instituted, as in respect of the gods, so in regard to the cult of mortals. For it shall be much more obligatory to honor the buried. Let it be absolutely forbidden for anyone to disturb them. In the case of contravention I desire that the offender be sentenced to capital punishment on charge of violation of sepulture."

The Greek is an indifferent version of the Latin,* and the inscription has been attributed to Claudius* (10 B.C.–A.D. 54). This emperor experienced periodic difficulties with his Jewish subjects in different parts of the empire. One of his letters, written in A.D. 41, endeavored to regulate the behavior of the Jews* in Alexandria.* According to Acts 18:2, he also expelled all the Jews who were living at that time in Rome.* The Roman historian Suetonius credited the expulsion from Rome in A.D. 49 to rioting over "one Chrestos," which would give added force to the Nazareth rescript.

BIBLIOGRAPHY: A. Momigliano, *The Emperor Claudius and His Achievements* (1962); E. M. Blaiklock, *ZPEB*, 4 (1975), 391–92.

EMB

NEAPOLIS (nē a' pə lis). A port of Macedonia* (modern Kavalla) about 16 km. (10 mi.) SE of Philippi,* where Paul first set foot in Europe (Acts 16:11). From the classical Greek period there survives a shrine of Parthenos (the maiden goddess), from the Roman period various inscriptions which bear names known also at Philippi.

BIBLIOGRAPHY: G. Balalakis, "Neapolis," *JAA* (1936), 1–48; P. Collart, *Philippes, ville de Macédoine* (1937), 102–32; R. C. Stone, *ZPEB*, 4 (1975), 393–94.

BFH

NEBI MEDN, TELL. *See* KADESH KAH.

NEBI SAMWIL (ne'bi sam'wil). A prominent hill just N of Jerusalem* overlooking Gibeon* and the upper reaches of the Ajjalon Valley. It is the present site of the mosque of the Prophet Samuel (hence its name), housing a cenotaph* and boasting a tall minaret from which one may view both the Dead Sea* and the Mediterranean on a clear day. The Crusaders dubbed it "Mountjoy" because they caught their first glimpse of the Holy City from its heights.

Such a striking eminence could scarcely have escaped becoming a high place* in the Canaanite* period, and it is likely that its delineation as a sacred precinct antedates the Hebrew and Muslim eras. It cannot be the actual burial place of Samuel, since 1 Sam 25:1 explicitly states that the prophet was buried, according to the custom of the time, in his house at Ramah. In fact, another mosque commemorating Samuel stands a few kilometers N at er-Ram (generally identified with Ramah of Benjamin).

The proper biblical identification of the site has been puzzling. The earlier suggestion that Nebi Samwil should be identified with Mizpah* by virtue of the strong association with Samuel's name has been generally discarded in favor of the Tell en-Nasbeh/Mizpah equation. One attractive possibility is that Nebi Samwil was the great high place of Gibeon mentioned in 1 Kings 3:4 and 2 Chron 1:3–13. The proximity of the site to Gibeon is sufficient to account for the appellation, while the pronounced elevation

visible from Jerusalem serves to explain why it should be favored with the tabernacle of the congregation, the brazen altar* of Bezaleel, and, most important, the inaugural sacrifice of a thousand burnt offerings by Solomon.*

The site was a strategic defensive position for Jordan's Arab Legion between the years 1948–67, and extensive trenches mark the hilltop facing the former Israeli frontier.

Excavations have not yet been undertaken at Nebi Samwil. A few shards* of the late Israelite monarchy period have been found on the hill, but the full illumination of the site's archaeological history remains for the future.

JEJ

NEBI YONUS. *See* NINEVEH.

NEBO. 1. The mountain in Trans-Jordan from which Moses viewed the Promised Land, identified with Ras es-Siyagha between Medeba* and Heshbon.*

The Bible speaks of the range as the Abarim Mountains, with Pisgah being the central ridge or massif facing the Dead Sea.* Mount Nebo itself is the topmost pinnacle, providing a commanding vista of Cis-Jordan, especially in the early morning in springtime when the air is clear. The Israelites camped near Mount Nebo (Num 33:47), and Moses died here after pronouncing a blessing on the tribes (Deut 32:49–50; 34:5–6—although chap. 33 may have been conveniently inserted here). The location of Moses' burial place, somewhere in the valley opposite Beth-Peor, was forgotten in antiquity.

Excavations at Ras es-Siyagha by the Franciscan Biblical School under Father Bagatti and Father Saller in 1933, 1935, and 1937 revealed a propheteum, a Byzantine* church erected to the memory of Moses. Churches honoring prophets were rare, but another at Tekoa commemorating Amos is known. The excavations at Mount Nebo revealed a triple-aisle church with trefoil apse,* beautiful mosaics,* and two sub-

Fourth-century A.D. basilica (apse oriented to the east) situated on hill of Siyagha (traditionally associated with the death of Moses). It is located near the hill of Khirbet el-Mukhaiyet, which is generally identified as the town of Nebo. Courtesy Studium Biblicum Franciscanum, Jerusalem.

sidiary chapels, one containing a quatrefoil baptistry. The church and surrounding monastery covered a rectangular area 60 by 80 m. (65 by 87 yd.). Elaborate pictures of trees, fruits, birds, and animals, as well as geometric motifs and dedicatory inscriptions covered the floors.

2. A town in Moab* belonging originally to the tribe of Reuben (Num 32:3, 38; Isa 15:2; Jer 48:1, 22). Mesha, King of Moab, captured it from Israel* c. 830 B.C.

Khirbet Ayn Musa has been suggested as the location of the site, but it is probably Khirbet el-Mekhayyat, also excavated by the Franciscans in 1933, 1935, 1937, 1939, and 1948. The area surrounding the town yielded materials from the Stone Age to the Middle Bronze Age,* while the khirbeh* itself contained pottery* of Iron Age I and later.

3. A town in Judah* (Ezra 2:29; Neh 7:33) of which little is known. It may be reflected in the Arabic place-name Beit Nube, or Nuba.

4. A Babylonian deity, properly Nabu, mentioned in Isa 46:1. Nebo, or Nabu, was the son of the chief god Marduk (the "Bel" of Isa who figured prominently in the Akitu new year festival and procession). His most notable temple and ziggurat* were at Borsippa* (Birs Nimrud).

BIBLIOGRAPHY: S. J. Saller, *The Memorial of Moses on Mount Nebo* (Ras Siyagha), 1–2 (1941); S. J. Saller and B. Bagatti, *The Town of Nebo (Khirbet el-Mekhayyat)* (1949); H. Schneider, *The Pottery*, 3 (1950); S. J. Saller, "Iron Age Tombs at Nebo, Jordan," *SBFLA*, 16 (1966), 165–298, figs. 1–37; V. Corbo, "Nuovi Scavi Archaeologici nella del Battistero della Basilica del Nebo (Siyagha)," *SBFLA*, 17 (1967), 241–58, figs. 1–7; F. B. Huey, Jr., *ZPEB*, 4 (1975), 394–95.

JEJ

NEBUCHADNEZZAR (NEBUCHADREZZAR) (neb ə kəd nez′ər; Akkad. *Nabū-kudurri-uṣur,* "Nabu protect my boundary stone," or "Nabu has protected the succession-rights"; the Heb. נבוכדראצר, *n^ebûkadre′ṣṣar,* used in Jer and Ezek is closer to the Akkad.; the variant נבוכדנ[א]צר, *n^ebûkadne[′]ṣṣar,* may be derived from an Aramaic* form; LXX Ναβουχοδονοσόρ, *Nabouchodonosor*).

The son of Nabopolassar,* Nebuchadnezzar was the greatest of the Neo-Babylonian* or Chaldean* kings, reigning from 605 to 562 B.C. He is mentioned almost a hundred times in the OT.

I. *Sources.* Until 1956 apart from references in the Bible and Josephus we had little more than building inscriptions as contemporary evidence for this great king. Then D. J. Wiseman published portions of the Babylonian Chronicles* which give us detailed political and military information of the first magnitude for the first ten years of Nebuchadnezzar's reign. It appears that these Akkadian tablets from the British Museum were being prepared for publication by L. W. King before his death in 1919, after which they lay neglected for nearly four decades.

II. *Military Activities.* A. *Carchemish (605).* While his aged father, Nabopolassar,* remained in Babylon,* Nebuchadnezzar led the Babylonians in a decisive victory over the Egyptians at Carchemish* on the western bend of the Euphrates in May or June 605 (cf. 2 Chron 35:20; Jer 46:2). Excavations at Carchemish in 1912–14 by C. L. Woolley and T. E. Lawrence (of Arabia*) uncovered evidences of the battle: Egyptian sealings of Neco II,* vast quantities of arrowheads, layers of ash, and a shield of a Greek mercenary fighting for the Egyptians.

Nebuchadnezzar pursued the fleeing Egyptians to Hamath* in Syria and then "conquered the whole land of Hatti," i.e., Syria and Palestine. According to Josephus (Jos. *Antiq.* 10.86–87) he by-passed Judah* and reached the border of Egypt* (cf. 2 Kings 24:7).

B. *The Accession of Nebuchadnezzar (605).* When Nebuchadnezzar heard of his father's death on August 15, he raced over 805 km. (500 mi.) in about two weeks to arrive in Babylon on September 7. After receiving the crown, he returned to Syria and continued to receive tribute (*see* BOOTY) until early in 604. He then returned to celebrate the Babylonian New Year in Nisan (March/April), the date from which his first regnal year was counted according to the postdating system employed by the Babylonians.

C. *The Subjugation of Judah (605–604).* The apparent contradiction between Dan 1:1, which relates that Nebuchadnezzar besieged Jerusalem in Jehoiakim's third year, and Jer 46:2, which dates the battle of Carchemish in Jehoiakim's fourth year, may be resolved if we assume that Daniel used the postdating system and that Jeremiah used the antedating system which counted the accession year. Though no actual siege of Jerusalem is mentioned in the Babylonian Chronicles, it was during the campaigns of 605–604 that Jehoiakim made submission and that Daniel was deported to Babylon.

D. *The Capture of Ashkelon (604).* In his fifth year Jehoiakim proclaimed a fast (Jer 36:9), in the ninth month, or Kislev (Nov./Dec.). This was no doubt occasioned by Nebuchadnezzar's advance against Ashkelon* in Kislev, 604. Ashkelon's resistance was sustained by a hope for Egyptian aid, as an Aramaic letter from its king Adon to the pharaoh informs us. This letter, which is one of the oldest Aramaic documents from Palestine, was found in Egypt in 1942.

An interesting feature of the battle of Ashkelon is the presence of Antimenidas, the brother of the famous poet Alcaeus, fighting on the side of the Babylonians. The presence of Greek words in Daniel becomes less problematical with further evidence of Greek mercenaries in the Near East in Nebuchadnezzar's day. A fortress of Greek mercenaries at a site between Ashdod* and Jaffa (Joppa*), dated just before 609, was discovered in 1960, and inscribed ostraca* concerned with supplies for *Kittim* or Greek mercenaries, dated to c. 600, were discovered at Arad.*

E. *A Battle With the Egyptians (601).* The Babylonian Chronicles reveal a hitherto unknown battle in which the Babylonians and Egyptians mauled each other. Nebuchadnezzar had to spend the next year reequipping his army. This turn of events may have encouraged Jehoiakim to rebel against the Babylonians in spite of the warnings of Jeremiah (27:9–11).

F. *Raids Against the Arabs (599).* In 599 from a base in Syria the Babylonians conducted raids against the Arab tribes just as Jeremiah (49:28–29) had prophesied.

G. *The Capture of Jerusalem (597).* Late in 598 Nebuchadnezzar personally led the Babylonian army W against Judah. Just before the invaders' arrival Jehoiakim died, and his eighteen-year-old son Jehoiachin* came to the throne. He was to rule a little over three months (2 Chron 36:9) before Jerusalem fell on March 16, 597. The Chronicles laconically report: "He then captured its king and appointed a king of his own choice"—namely, Zedekiah, Jehoiachin's uncle (2 Kings 24:17). Nebuchadnezzar sent back to Babylon great treasures (2 Kings 24:13) and ten thousand captives (2 Kings 24:14), including Jehoiachin and members of his family. Their presence in Babylon is attested by ration tablets discovered there (*see* EVIL-MERODACH).

H. *Events of 596–594.* In 596 Nebuchadnezzar evidently campaigned against Elam* to the E (cf. Jer 49:34–39). As a rule his alliance with the Medes* kept his eastern frontier secure.

Late in 595 Nebuchadnezzar was faced with an insurrection at home which he efficiently suppressed. A tablet dated to the following year records a sentence of death passed upon a landowner of high rank, perhaps implicated in the revolt.

In 594 Nebuchadnezzar marched again to Syria. Zedekiah seems to have been obliged to appear personally in Babylon (Jer 51:59) at this time.

I. *The Destruction of Jerusalem (587–586).* Psammetichus II, who had become pharaoh in 594, won a signal victory over the Sudan in 591. Perhaps this turn of events encouraged the Judean exiles to come to Ezekiel to make an inquiry before the Lord (Ezek 20:1). One of the Lachish Letters* reports that a Judean commander had gone down to Egypt, perhaps for military aid. In any case Zedekiah had chosen to rebel against the Babylonians by 589.

Unfortunately, the extant Babylonian Chronicles do not cover Nebuchadnezzar's final attack upon Jerusalem. Letters written on ostraca found at Lachish* offer vivid contemporary evidence for the approaching invasion. One of the letters bears the dramatic message: "we are watching for the signals of Lachish. . . . for we cannot see Azekah." This may mean that the fortress of Azekah,* which was halfway between Lachish and Jerusalem, had already fallen to the Babylonians (Jer 34:7).

Scholars are divided as to the year of Jerusalem's capture and destruction. 2 Chron 36:11 informs us that Zedekiah reigned eleven years. Scholars such as Albright, Freedman, Tadmor, and Wiseman, who believe that the Jews* used a calendar beginning in Nisan (April), would date the fall of Jerusalem to the summer of 587. Others such as Thiele, Malamat, Horn, Redford, and Saggs, who believe that the Jews used a calendar beginning in Tishri (Sept.), would date the fall of Jerusalem to the summer of 586. The latter date would seem to better accord with Ezek 33:21 which informs us that the Judean exiles in Bab-

ylonia learned the news of the disaster from a fugitive in December 586.

The devastation wrought by the Babylonians may be seen from the archaeological evidence. Virtually all of the fortified towns in Judah were destroyed. Of all the excavated cities only Samaria* and Gezer* have revealed fairly continuous occupation throughout the Exilic and post-Exilic periods. Of a population of c. 250–300,000 in eighth-century Judah, only about half may have survived the onslaught.

In spite of this crushing defeat, the Jews seem to have mustered their forces for a final show of resistance in 582 (Jer 52:30).

J. *The Siege of Tyre.* Josephus (Jos. *Apion* 1.156; Jos. *Antiq.* 10.228) cites Phoenician* authorities for the tradition of a thirteen-year siege of Tyre* by Nebuchadnezzar. Most scholars would date this siege to the period immediately after the final siege of Jerusalem. Though Josephus does not tell us this, the siege must have been successful, inasmuch as a number of later documents list Tyre under Babylonian control.

In the Wadi Brissa N of Beirut are two inscriptions in which Nebuchadnezzar boasts of his success in opening up roads to secure the cedars* of Lebanon (*ANET*, 307).

K. *Invasion of Egypt (568).* A text, which is unfortunately very fragmentary, seems to describe an attack against Amasis of Egypt (cf. Jer 43:8–13) in Nebuchadnezzar's thirty-seventh year.

III. *Domestic Achievements.* A. *Buildings.* Nebuchadnezzar's boastfulness (Dan 4:30) was based on the fact that he had made Babylon the greatest city* in the ancient world, covering 1,011 ha. (2,500 a.), only a part of which was excavated by Koldewey from 1899–1917. Herodotus, who visited the site in the fifth century B.C., left us an accurate description of the city.

Among the most noteworthy structures are the beautifully decorated Ishtar Gate, the king's palace, the ziggurat,* and Marduk's temple. A structure near the Ishtar Gate with fourteen vaulted chambers has been identified by Koldewey as the substructure of the famed Babylon Hanging Gardens,* which Nebuchadnezzar is reputed to have built for his Median

General view of Ishtar Gate at Babylon, from north. From "The Excavations at Babylon," R. Koldewey, London, 1914. By permission of Macmillan, London and Basingstoke.

wife, Amytis, who missed the vegetation of her homeland.

A large court in the citadel,* 17 by 52 m. (56 by 170 ft.), has been identified as the king's throne room. It is decorated with Ionic columns which seem to be the handiwork of Greek artisans. Koldewey visualizes this as the site of Belshazzar's feast (Dan 5).

Nebuchadnezzar's hand is also seen at Ur,* where he practically rebuilt the city. His transformation of the temple E-Nun-Mah from a building for secret ritual into a spacious structure is associated by Woolley with the public ceremonies related in Dan 3:1–16.

B. *Justice.* A cuneiform* text published in 1965, though it does not name the king by name, is probably to be ascribed to Nebuchadnezzar. It describes a king who is so devoted to justice that "he did not rest night or day." A criminal guilty of a second offense is decapitated and a stone image of his head is displayed as a warning.

IV. *Dementia and Demise.* Some scholars have proposed the thesis that the story of Nebuchadnezzar's madness in the book of Daniel is a distorted reflection of Nabonidus's exile in Arabia.* It is now clear from the new Haran* inscriptions that Nabonidus was in exile for ten years and not for seven as had been thought previously (Dan 4:32 speaks of "seven times"). Among other objections to this theory is the fact that this interpretation was based on Sidney Smith's rendering of a line in the Persian Verse Account, which is no longer tenable (cf. *ANET*, 313). Nabonidus's behavior may seem erratic but he was not mad.

Unfortunately we have few details about the last thirty years of Nebuchadnezzar's life. He died soon after October 562 and was succeeded by his son Evil-Merodach.

BIBLIOGRAPHY: R. Koldewey, *The Excavations at Babylon* (1914); A. Olmstead, "The Chaldaean Dynasty," *HUCA*, 2 (1925), 29–55; O. Ravn, *Herodotus' Description of Babylon* (1942); M. Vogelstein, "Nebuchadnezzar's Reconquest of Phoenicia and Palestine and the Oracles of Ezekiel," *HUCA*, 23 (1950–51), 197–220; D. Wiseman, *Chronicles of Chaldaean Kings* (1956); A. Malamat, "A New Record of Nebuchadrezzar's Palestinian Campaigns," *IEJ*, 6 (1956), 246–56; H. Tadmor, "Chronology of the Last Kings of Judah," *JNES*, 15 (1956), 226–30; A. Parrot, *Babylon and the OT* (1958); D. W. Thomas, ed., *DOTT* (1958), passim; A. Parrot, *The Arts of Assyria* (1961); J. Quinn, "Alcaeus 48 (B16) and the Fall of Ascalon (604 B.C.)," *BASOR*, 164 (1961), 19–20; J. Naveh, "The Excavations at Meṣad Ḥashavyahu . . . ," *IEJ*, 12 (1962), 89–113; H. W. F. Saggs, *The Greatness That Was Babylon* (1962); C. L. Woolley and M. E. L. Mallowan, *Ur Excavations IX: The Neo-Babylonian and Persian Periods* (1962); J. Bright, *Jeremiah* (1962); J. Fitzmyer, "The Aramaic Letter of King Adon to the Egyptian Pharaoh," *Biblica*, 46 (1965), 41–55; W. Lambert, "Nebuchadnezzar King of Justice," *Iraq*, 27 (1965), 1–11; J. Macqueen, *Babylon* (1965); D. Wiseman et al., *Notes on Some Problems in the Book of Daniel* (1965); Y. Aharoni, "Hebrew Ostraca from Tel Arad," *IEJ*, 16 (1966), 1–7; S. Horn, "The Babylonian Chronicle and the Ancient Calendar of the Kingdom of Judah," *AUSS*, 5 (1967), 12–27; E. Yamauchi, *Greece and Babylon* (1967); G. Larue, *Babylon and the Bible* (1969); S. Weinberg, "Post-Exilic Palestine: An Archaeological Report," *Proceedings of the Israel Academy of Sciences and Humanities*, 5.5 (1969); K. Freedy and D. Redford, "The Dates in Ezekiel in Relation to Biblical, Babylonian and Egyptian Sources," *JAOS*, 90 (1970), 462–85; E. Yamauchi, "The Greek Words in Daniel in the Light of Greek Influence in the Near East," J. Payne, ed., *New Perspectives on the OT* (1970), 170–200; T. W. Overholt, "King Nebuchadnezzar in the Jeremiah Tradition," *CBQ*, 30 (1968), 39–48; A. van Selms, "The Name Nebuchadnezzar," in *Travels in the World of the Old Testament*, ed., M. S. van Voss et al. (1974), 223–29; S. Singer, "Found in Jerusalem: Remains of the Babylonian Siege," *Biblical Archaeology Review*, 2 (1976), 7–10; W. H. Shea, "Nebuchadnezzar's Chronicle and the Date of the Destruction of Lachish III," *PEQ*, 111 (1979), 113–16; D. Weisberg, *Texts From the Time of Nebuchadnezzar* (1980). EY

NECO (NECHO) (nē'kō; Heb. נְכֹו, *neḵō*; LXX Νεχάω, *nechaō*). Neco I was king of Sais and the W Delta and father of Psammetichus I, founder of the Twenty-sixth Dynasty of Egypt.* Neco II, son of Psammetichus I, who reigned 610–595 B.C. is the biblical Neco.

This Neco marched into Palestine in c. 609 B.C. to support the last Assyrian king, Assur-uballit II, against the rising power of Babylon* and the Medes. However, Josiah of Judah* was determined to assist Assyria's fall and, in battle with Neco, was slain (cf. 2 Kings 23:29ff.; 2 Chron 35:20ff.).

Neco's object was probably to ensure Egypt's succession to the Assyrian imperial heritage. The project failed, but the fact that Egypt occupied a coastal strip of Assyrian territory for a short time is indication of Neco's ambitions. This archaeologically-based knowledge enables translators to clear up the confusion in KJV 2 Kings 23:29. The NIV, e.g., reads: "Pharaoh Neco king of Egypt went up to help the king of Assyria by way of the Euphrates."

Assyria fell, and Babylon succeeded her. Meanwhile, Neco replaced Jehoahaz with Jehoiakim as vassal (2 Kings 23:31–35; 2 Chron 36:1–4). In the battle of Carchemish* (605 B.C.), the Babylonians defeated and chased the pharaoh out of Syria-Palestine (2 Kings 24:1, 7; cf. Jer 46:2ff.). But when Nebuchadnezzar* marched against Egypt in 601 B.C., the pharaoh successfully warded him off. Within Egypt, Neco II fostered trade, encouraging Greek merchants; sent Phoenicians* to sea who circumnavigated Africa; and began a canal from the Nile to the Red Sea.*

BIBLIOGRAPHY: D. J. Wiseman, *Chronicles of Chaldaean Kings 626–586 B.C.* (1956); A. H. Gardiner, *Egypt of the Pharaohs* (1961), 357–59; J. A. Thompson, *Buried History* (1974), 47; id., *ZPEB*, 4 (1975), 400–1. KAK

NECROPOLIS (nə krop'ə lis). A cemetery; lit., "city of the dead."

NEEDLE. Needles discovered on excavated sites are remarkably modern in size and structure. They cover all periods, from bone needles of the earliest periods to the more common bronze* instruments of the OT times. Making the hole in the end to hold the thread was a task of some delicacy, which seems to have been effected with great skill by craftsmen* both in bone and in bronze.

In regard to Jesus' statement regarding the eye of a needle, there is no archaeological or papyrological confirmation for reading *kamilos* ("cable" or "rope") for *kamelos* ("camel") (Matt 19:24; Mark 10:25; Luke 18:25), as some scholars have proposed.

Bone needles blunt at both ends were discovered at Megiddo.* They are of very early date and would seem to be part of a weaving shuttle.

EMB

NEGEV (NEGEB) (ne'gev; Heb. נֶגֶב, *negeb*, "the dry land," with derived meaning, "the southland"). The Negev is the southern region of Palestine, formed roughly by a triangle stretching from the Gulf of Aqaba on the S, northward to Gaza* on the W and the Dead Sea* on the E.

The area receives little rainfall, from a high of just over 20 cm. (8 in.) annually in the N around Beersheba* to a low of less than 5 cm. (2 in.) at the head of the Gulf of Aqaba. For this reason, cultivation has never been consistent in the region, a factor in the intermittent nature of sedentary occupation throughout recorded history. Water sources in antiquity included the occasional spring or well,* together with the natural reservoirs or cisterns* for which the area is noted. In dry years the latter were undependable, sometimes forcing whole cities* to abandon their settlements. Truly arable soils are limited to the valleys, with the best soil made up of the alluvial, dusty loess* common to the broad plain around Beersheba.

The general climate in the Negev has, apparently, been consistent since the close of the last ice age. Settlement, which throughout history appears to have fluctuated sharply, is therefore a reflection of human factors rather than of any drastic shift in the natural environment. Periods of high population are usually related either to a need for additional arable lands for an agricultural society to the N, or to an increased requirement for security and stability in the region relating to use of caravan and trade routes throughout the Negev. Occasional settlements have also resulted from mining* and smelting (*see* REFINING) activities. The usual cycle of settlement was a growth from a small beginning to a highly developed and secure life, followed by an attack from the ever-present tribes in the desert such as the Amalekites. The land would then return to relative emptiness, to await the transformation of the latest wave of Bedouins from nomadic life to tillers of the soil.

Earliest evidence for settlement in the Negev goes back to Paleolithic* times, and continues through the Neolithic,* Chalcolithic,* and Early Bronze ages.* A flourishing Chalcolithic civilization, 5000 years re-

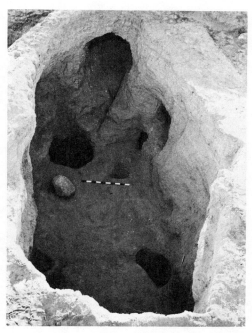

Early subterranean dwelling from Beer Safad near Beersheba dated to the second half of the fourth millennium. Courtesy Centre de Recherches Prehistoriques Français de Jérusalem.

moved from us, was unearthed by the extensive excavations of Jean Perrot at Bir Abu Matar (*see* ABU MATAR) (a suburb of Beersheba), by Yohanan Aharoni at Arad,* and by various surface explorations, particularly those of Nelson Glueck. Following the decline of this impressive civilization in the northern loess valleys, there is evidence of continued inhabitation during Early Bronze (Tell Ira near Beersheba), followed by a fallow period of several hundred years. Between the twenty-first and nineteenth centuries B.C. (Middle Bronze I or Early Bronze–Middle Bronze), another flourishing agricultural and commercial society arose in the area surrounding Beersheba, chronicled by Nelson Glueck as the scene of a "Pax Abrahamitica" and more recently the object of an extensive reexamination by the Central Negev Highlands Project (1978). Many a small village or seminomadic center has been uncovered for this period, the characteristic mark being the ubiquitous "cup-hole," a hollowed-out section of the underlying rock about 13 cm. (5 in.) in diameter. In the nineteenth century B.C. this society was completely destroyed, possibly in connection with an invasion such as that described in Gen 14, leaving the land again unsettled for hundreds of years.

When the Israelite exodus traversed the region it was inhabited by seminomadic Amalekites (Num 13:29), though Canaanites* are recorded in the region around Arad (Num 21:1). With the exception of Arad and the little-known "city of Amalek," later overcome by Saul (1 Sam 15:5), little was known of sedentary occupation during the period before the 1972–1975 excavations at Tell Masos, possibly to be identified with biblical Hormah. The reference to the "city of Amalek," ingeniously but unconvincingly identified with Avaris and placed in the Wadi el Arish by I. Velikovsky (*Ages in Chaos*, 1952), remains an enigma. Later the tribes of Judah* and Simeon were to occupy parts of the northern Negev, together with other tribes of uncertain origin (1 Sam 27:10; 30:14).

The first real expansion, following the Middle Bronze I period, came during the united Israelite monarchy. Numerous inhabited sites have been uncovered with evidence from a town like Arad* pointing to at least five destruction and rebuilding phases within the period of Iron II alone. Of special interest archaeologically are the remains in Arad, of what is alleged to be an Israelite sanctuary (tenth to seventh centuries B.C.) and various ostraca.* More recently evidence has come from the Beersheba Valley in the N, as well as from the central Negev highlands, of extensive tenth-century settlements, connected with expansion of forts and trading under King Solomon.* Although the Beersheba area (Tell Ira) continued active throughout the Iron Age, settlement in the Central Highlands after Solomon is restricted to the important oasis of 'Ain el Qudeirat (Kadesh Barnea*) on the western extremity of the highlands. Another important site occupied through the later Israelite period and rich in artifacts* is Aroer,* a site which, like Arad, has yielded a number of ostraca with Hebrew lettering (*see* EPIGRAPHY, HEBREW).

After the destruction of Jerusalem* in 587/86 B.C., the tides of empire bypassed the Negev. With the exception of an Idumean caravanserai at Mampsis (Kurnub), major settlement had to await the coming of the Nabataeans,* who not only reoccupied old sites but built an impressive semiurban civilization in many hitherto uninhabited places. Particularly impressive from this period are the ruins of Avdat* (Oboda), Subeita, Elusa, Mampsis, Aroer, Ruheiba, and Nessana. Population figures show that the Nabataean Negev then supported more people than at any time previously and was to be surpassed only in the high period of Byzantine* occupation in a civilization that was built on the ruins of the Nabataean.

In the year A.D. 106, the Nabataean kingdom passed under the control of Rome,* and the whole area was incorporated into the Province of Arabia.* The Romans were by no means unaware of the importance of the Negev, although their primary interests lay elsewhere. Several important Nabataean settlements continued under Roman overlordship, but it remained for the Byzantine civilization, with its renewed interest in the eastern part of the empire, to bring the zenith of Negev development. The hiatus following the decline of the Nabataeans in the second century was not long nor were its effects on the land severe. Old watercourses, cities, cultivation, and even descendants of the earlier population continued with no major break. Pagan motifs were incorporated into Byzantine art, the remains of which provide rich treasures for archaeologist and tourist alike. The sixth century was the high point for the Byzantine Negev. Within a hundred years after the Moslem conquests,

the diversion of trade routes, the decline of commerce and agriculture, and the general demoralization of the Christian population caused a shift from the desert centers to elsewhere. From that time until the recent Israeli penetration into the area, neither settler nor archaeologist has given the region major attention.

In addition to the excavations noted above, major Nabataean and Byzantine centers have recently been extensively explored, with an impressive yield in fresh knowledge of these civilizations' art, architecture, and writing.* The magnificent churches of Nessana, Avdat (Oboda), Mampsis, and Subeita, with their lovely mosaic* tile floors are but one sample of the riches awaiting the visitor to these long-forgotten cities.

BIBLIOGRAPHY: W. F. Albright, "Egypt and the Early History of the Negeb," *JPOS*, 4 (1924), 131–61; C. L. Woolley and T. E. Lawrence, *The Wilderness of Zin* (1936); G. E. Kirk, "Archaeological Exploration of the Southern Desert," *PEQ* (1938), 211–35; id., "The Negev or Southern Desert of Palestine," *PEQ* (1941), 57–71; Y. Aharoni, "The Negeb of Judah," *IEJ*, 8 (1958), 26–38; M. Evenari and Y. Aharoni, "The Ancient Desert Agriculture of the Negev," *IEJ*, 8 (1958), 230–68, and 9 (1960), 97–111; B. Rothenberg, *God's Wilderness* (1961); N. Glueck, "Further Explorations in the Negev," *BASOR*, 179 (1965), 6ff.; Y. Aharoni, "The Negeb," *Archaeology and Old Testament Study*, ed. D. W. Thomas (1967), 385–404; N. Glueck, *Rivers in the Desert*, 2nd ed. (1968); A. Negev, "The Nabatean Necropolis of Mampsis (Kurnub)," *IEJ*, 21.2–3 (1971), 110–29; id., "Nabatean Sigillate," *RB*, 79.3 (1972), 381–98; A. E. Marks, "Prehistoric Sites in the Central Negev," *IEJ*, 23.2 (1973), 105–6; id., "Negev Central," *RB*, 80 (1973), 396–99; A. Negev, "Nabatean Capitals in the Towns of the Negev," *IEJ*, 24.3–4 (1974), 153–59; id., "Churches of the Central Negev: An Archaeological Survey," *RB*, 81 (1974), 400–422; Z. Meshel and Y. Tsafrir, "Nabataean Road from 'Avdat to Sha'ar-Ramon," *PEQ*, 106 (1974), 103–18; L. E. Stager, "Farming in the Judean Desert During the Iron Age," *BASOR*, 221 (1976), 145–58; A. Biran and R. Cohen, "Aroer 1976," *IEJ*, 26 (1976), 139–40; A. Negev, "Early Beginnings of the Nabataean Realm," *PEQ*, 108 (1976), 125–33; Z. Meshel, "Horvat Ritma—An Iron Age Fortress in the Negev Highlands," *Tel Aviv*, 4 (1977), 110–15; A. Biran and R. Cohen, "Aroer 1977," *IEJ*, 27.4 (1977), 250–51; A. Negev, "Subeita," *EEHL* (1978), 1116–24; A. Biran and R. Cohen, "Aroer in the Negev," *Qadmoniot*, 11 (1978), 20–24; R. Cohen and W. G. Dever, "Preliminary Report of the Pilot Season of the 'Central Negev Highlands Project,'" *BASOR*, 232 (1978), 29–45; R. Cohen, "The Israelite Fortresses in the Negev Highlands," *Qadmoniot*, 12 (1979), 38–50; M. Kochavi, "Rescue in the Biblical Negev," *Biblical Archaeological Review*, 6.1 (1980), 24–27.   CEA

NEIN. See NAIN.

NEMRUD DAGH (nem'rəd däg). An area of Syria about 130 km. (80 mi.) NNW of Haran.* It is traditionally associated with the activities of Nimrod (Gen 10:8–12), as are many other Mesopotamian* sites in which the form *Nimrud (Nemrud)* occurs. The location was included in the westward expansion of the Hurrians* in the nineteenth and eighteenth centuries B.C. and was part of the subsequent Mitanni* kingdom. By the middle of the fourteenth century B.C., it had been absorbed by the resurgent Assyrian Empire. Some artifacts* from the earlier period of Babylonian history have been recovered from the area, as well as Mitannian remains, but these are of little significance for the biblical story.

RKH

NEO-BABYLONIAN EMPIRE.

The names Babylon, Babylonia, and Babylonians occur almost three hundred times in the Bible, with about half of the references coming from Jeremiah. None of the biblical references alludes to the first Babylonian kingdom, founded by Hammurabi* (1728–1626 B.C.), and, except for a few possibly symbolical allusions in the NT, the Neo-Babylonian Empire is always in view. Babylon* is mentioned so often because its king, Nebuchadnezzar,* devastated Judah* and took the people captive (*see* EXILE).

Babylon, the capital of the Neo-Babylonian Empire, is located 80 km. (50 mi.) S of modern Baghdad. After its prominence under Hammurabi, it was often overrun by the Hittites,* Kassites,* Elamites,* and Assyrians. The eleventh and last dynasty of Babylon was that of the Chaldean,* or Neo-Babylonian, kings: Nabopolassar,* Nebuchadnezzar II, and Evil-Merodach.* Four weaker kings, Neriglissar, Labashi-Marduk, Nabonidus,* and Belshazzar,* were involved in the decline. The span of the Neo-Babylonian Empire was 626–539 B.C.

The city of Babylon of Nebuchadnezzar's time was excavated by Koldewey in 1899–1917. The city* plan was determined, the remains of the ziggurat* with a temple to the patron god Marduk was identified, and other fortifications, palaces, and the substructure of the famous Babylon Hanging Gardens* were excavated. The best preserved monuments of the empire were the Procession Street and the Ishtar Gate with its decorations of bulls, dragons, and lions* in colored relief on blue-glazed tiles. Inscriptions and extensive chronicles published by D. J. Wiseman illustrate the accuracy of the biblical details of Nebuchadnezzar's Palestine campaign. A large, well-equipped army was in the field constantly to keep the tribute coming in. Much of this money was used in building projects in Babylon.

BCC

NEOCAESAREA. See PHILADELPHIA.

NEOCHORI. See AMPHIPOLIS.

NEOLITHIC.

The "new," or late, Stone Age (c. 8000–4000 B.C.), during which animals were first domesticated and agriculture,* pottery,* and textiles (*see* CLOTH) were developed.

NESIANS; NESITES. See HITTITES.

NESTORIAN MONUMENT.

Here is a footnote to the story of the resurrection, and a facet of its archaeology comes, oddly enough, from ancient China.

In Sianfu, in 1625, an inscribed stone was found which had lain buried for nine centuries. Workmen digging foundation trenches came upon a large monument, some 2.1 m. (7 ft.) high and 1 m. (3 ft.) wide. Set up in A.D. 781, it contained a statement of Christian belief, and a description of the arrival, in A.D. 635, at Sianfu, then a capital of the Tang Dynasty, of a missionary from Tutsin, or Syria, named Olopan. There was also an account of the fortunes of the church which he founded.

It was a document of early Christianity in China, and undoubtedly genuine. The Christianity was of the Nestorian variety, and the persecution which the followers of the fifth-century Syrian bishop Nestorius endured in the homeland was repeated in China. European scholars denounced the Sianfu inscription as a forgery, a charge which persisted until the time of Renan. Nestorian Christianity in China apparently failed because, while it sought to communicate the gospel to the people, it eroded biblical teaching by omitting the atonement and resurrection of Christ.

The Japanese scholar P. V. Saeki, who has studied the Nestorian inscription intensively, believes that the Nestorian Church still exists in two forms. The twenty million Moslems of China contain a host of its descendants, but were left with only a vague monotheism.

EMB

NIMROD; NIMRUD. See CALAH.

NIMRUD, BIRS. See BORSIPPA.

NINEVEH.

It may be fairly conjectured that Xenophon, the Athenian soldier of fortune, was the first to notice the tell* of Nineveh. His retreating force of Greeks, bravely setting out to cut their way home from the heartlands of Persia, saw a complex of ruins, which appears to be in the right locality (Xen. *An.* 3.4.10). Jonah's city* of "three days' journey" (Jonah 3:3) must, of course, have been through the whole complex of associated villages and centers of habitation, bound together by one irrigation* pattern from the Tigris. The center which has engaged the attention of archaeologists for almost a century and a half, would be the palace and administrative area, where durable remains would have been likely to congregate. The wider region could be profitably surveyed from the air.

There are two associated mounts, Kuyunjiq and Nebi Yunus, on the E side of the Tigris directly opposite the modern Mosul. A circumference of some 12.8 km. (8 mi.) can be traced. The second-named ruin-pile is inaccessible because of modern habitation. The former, and considerably the larger, has received British archaeological attention, for a period extending from Layard's major excavations in 1845, to the five intensive years of scientific digging by Campbell Thompson, Hutchinson, Hamilton, and Mallowan from 1927 to 1932.

The credit for the first investigation of the site

must go to P. E. Botta, French consul at Mosul in 1842. Layard entered into Botta's labors, somewhat roughly, displacing Botta's successor on the site and in the consulate, Victor Place. Layard thus secured the looting, for early archaeology was little more, of the palaces of Ashurbanipal* and Sennacherib, * with their wealth of art and cuneiform* tablets. George Smith, the pioneer epigraphist, and Sir E. Wallis Budge worked on the tell without distinction, and it was not until this century, that Assyriologists were able to reduce some order into the rich but confused mass of material torn unsystematically from one of the most rewarding of all ancient archaeological sites. It was with the coming of the scientific archaeologists, and the five years' work already mentioned between World Wars I and II, that the area was more thoroughly explored, stratigraphic* investigations made, and excavation carried to the virgin soil, no less than 25 m. (82 ft.) down. It was here that Nineveh's protohistory began, 5000 years before our era.

Nebi Yunus ("the tomb of Jonah") remains the traditional burial place of Jonah, a mosque and a village complete with cemetery (see NECROPOLIS). Any prospect of discovering the treasures which must lie beneath appears slim. If it were possible to remove the 14,500,000 tons of rubble in the first mound, and the 6,500,000 tons in the other, there is no calculating how the knowledge stores of Assyriology* might be increased.

Stratigraphic excavation has at least revealed the antiquity of human occupation on the site, as it has done at Jericho. * It far antedated literary reference. Nineveh is first mentioned in a cuneiform tablet in the twenty-first century B.C. where an ideogram, * a fish in a city enclosure, represents its name. Later, Hammurabi* (1792–1750 B.C.) spoke of himself as "the king who in Nineveh glorified the name of the goddess Ishtar." An inscription of Shamshi-Adad, one of Ashur's early rulers (1823–1791 B.C.), similarly links the name of Ishtar with Nineveh. Ishtar was, it appears, venerated there, typically as the warrior goddess. She was, incongruously, the deity of love and war, and the elevation of the latter role is typical of the most war-minded of ancient peoples. Her temple has been identified. A second temple has been identified as that of Nabu, god of writing, another appropriate object of worship among a people whose recovered records amount to thousands of clay* tablets, and whose surviving vocabulary gives a word count higher than that of the ancient Greeks, in Liddell and Scott's famous lexicon.

Impressive remnants of the palaces of Shalmaneser I (1273–1244 B.C.), Tiglath-pileser I* (1114–1076 B.C.), Adadnirari II (911–891 B.C.), Tukulti-Ninurta II (890–884 B.C.), Ashurnasirpal* (883–859 B.C.), Sennacherib* (705–681 B.C.), and Ashurbanipal (669–628 B.C.) have been located. Tyrants and imperialists have commonly shown a tendency to build grandiosely—as evidenced by Augustus's* Rome ("I found Rome built of brick and left it built of marble"), Nero's Golden House (Suet. Aug., Ner.), and Nebuchadnezzar's Babylon ("Is not this the great Babylon I have built . . . for the glory of my majesty?" [Dan 4:30]). Sometimes such architectural activity is a sign of a whole people's confidence and pride. Karnak and the Acropolis* of Athens* provide illustration. In Assyria such remains speak of the arrogance and self-assertion of a strong, ruthless imperial people— the character which their doings in the OT so richly suggest.

Nineveh was not the only seat of Assyrian power. Other royal cities of the upper Tigris were Ashur (Qalaat Shergat), Kalakh (Nimrud, or Calah*), and, some 20 km. (13 mi.) away, Dur Sharrukin (Khorsabad*), to whose building Sargon II* devoted his power. It was on Sargon's early death that his son Sennacherib made Nineveh supreme, aided by the immense resources of an empire stretching from the Mediterranean to the Persian Gulf. Esarhaddon* and Ashurbanipal, Sennacherib's successors, continued the vast program of pretentious building, artistic embellishment, and mighty fortification. It is curious to find that these bandit kings, ruthless and sanguinary conquerors, were great patrons of literature, and set out to preserve in well-stocked libraries the sacred and secular works of all past centuries. Archaeology is deeply in their debt.

It was Tiglath-Pileser I* (1114–1076 B.C.) who first reached the Mediterranean in the days of the Judges of Israel, * and the long and evil story of Assyria's conquests runs on, through the records of the conquerors, who listed campaigns, the totals of loot and tribute (see BOOTY), the record of sadistic punishments, reprisals and acts of genocide, slaves,* hostages, and victims of all sort through reign after reign. It was with Shalmaneser III (858–824 B.C.) that the records first mention a biblical character. Ahab* (A-ha-ab-bu) of Israel was one of a group of eleven who sought to stop the Assyrian drive to the S. Ahab, according to the listing (given on the monolith inscription of Kurkh), provided the considerable contribution of two thousand chariots* and ten thousand infantry. Since chariots were probably an import from Egypt, * and horses from Cilicia, * this indicates the immense prosperity of Israel under Ahab, with the Phoenician* trade at its height. The Assyrian account of the battle of Qarqar, * in which Shalmaneser claimed to have routed the allies, is typical of the bloodthirsty ways of the conqueror. It runs: "With the supreme power with which the Lord Ashur endowed me . . . I fought against them. From the city of Qarqar as far as Gilzau I attacked them. I overthrew 14,000 warriors of their armies. . . . I filled up the Orontes [river] with their bodies. I captured in the battle their chariots, their horsemen, their horses and their armour."

The subjugation of Jehu (Ia-w-a), descendant of Omri* (Hu-um-ri-i), is also given in a record of Shalmaneser III. The Israelite king, or his representative, is pictured on the Black Obelisk, * discovered at Calah and now in the British Museum.

The huge tribute exacted by Pul (Tiglath-Pileser III), as described in 2 Kings 15:19–20, is mentioned in the Assyrian documents, stone slabs at Calah. So, too, is the vassalage of Ahaz (2 Kings 16:10–18).

Ahaz's appeal for help against Damascus, * shortsighted though it was, found answer in Tiglath-pileser's punishment of Israel and Syria, an action

Stele depicting King Esarhaddon holding two royal captives. Courtesy Staatliche Museen zu Berlin.

carried out with Assyria's usual ruthlessness (2 Kings 15:30), and with Hoshea placed on Samaria's throne. "The house of Hu-um-ri-a (Omri, i.e. Israel) . . . all his people, and their goods, I sent away to Assyria. They overthrew their king Pa-qa-ha (Pekah) and I made A-u-si (Hoshea) king over them. I received from them ten talents of gold . . . and I carried them away to Assyria" (ANET, 284).

The end of Samaria* after three year's investment, begun by Shalmaneser in 724 B.C. and concluded by Sargon II, is commemorated in an inscription from the latter monarch's palace at Dur-Sharrukin near Nineveh. It runs: "Sargon, conqueror of Samaria and of all Israel." The so-called Display Inscription* gives details of spoil.

Sennacherib, son of Sargon (705–681 B.C.), placed Hezekiah under tribute during the fourteenth year of the latter's reign (2 Kings 18:13–18). Hezekiah's subjection was also alluded to on a bull from Nineveh and in a text from Nebi Yunus (ANET, 288).

The only archæological record from the Hebrew side is the tomb of Shebna,* one of the plenipotentiaries of the story (Isa 36:3ff.) and something of a controversial figure (IEJ, 3 [1953], 137–52).

The capture of Lachish* in the same sequence of events is depicted in a relief from Nineveh, whose accompanying inscription runs: "Sennacherib, king of the world, king of Assyria, seated on his throne, inspects the plunder from La-ki-su."

The art is vivid and uninhibited, plainly showing the fierce attack with every manner of weaponry, the refugees, impaled captives, and the desperate defense.

Esarhaddon (687–642 B.C.), who succeeded the assassinated Sennacherib, was also a man of ferocious energy. The sadistic treatment of captive notables prophesied by Amos (4:2) is depicted on the stele* of Esarhaddon, found at Tell Ahmar. He holds two captive princes on strings tied to hooks through their lips. The same vicious conqueror boasts: "I hung the heads of Sanduarri and of Abdimilkutte round the neck of their nobles . . . to demonstrate to the population the power of Ashur, my lord, and paraded [thus] through the wide main street of Nineveh with singers [playing on] . . . harps."

Manasseh,* king of Judah,* is mentioned in the list of the defeated monarchs from the same coastal campaign (2 Chron 33:11). Esarhaddon penetrated Egypt and justified Isaiah's lack of confidence in them (Isa 20:3–6). Egyptian sculpture found at Nebi Yunus in 1954 may be part of the spoil.

Ashurbanipal, one of Esarhaddon's successors, was one of the last of the grim line of Nineveh's kings and, in his attack on defecting Egypt, touched biblical history in that he exacted a military contribution from Manasseh. Ashurbanipal's reign was long (669–628 B.C.) and typical, but Nineveh's story, from this point on, ceases to have relevance within the sphere of biblical archaeology.

BIBLIOGRAPHY: A. H. Layard, Nineveh and Its Remains, 2 vols. (1849); id., The Monuments of Nineveh From Drawings Made on the Spot, 2 vols. (1849–53); id., Discoveries in the Ruins of Nineveh and Babylon (1853); G. Smith, Assyrian Discoveries (1875); D. D. Luckenbill, Ancient Records of Assyria and Babylonia (1925–27); R. C. Thompson and R. W. Hutchinson, A Century of Exploration at Nineveh (1929); ANET (1950), 265–301; ANEP (1954); FLAP (1951), 174–77, 181–83; A. Parrot, Nineveh and the OT (1955); D. J. Wiseman, ZPEB, 4 (1975), 440–44.

EMB

NIPPUR (ni poor'). This city* was the chief religious center of Sumer* and the most important Sumerian site to be excavated.

The Site. Nuffar, as the site is called in Arabic, is located about 160 km. (100 mi.) S of Baghdad; in antiquity it was located about 88 km. (55 mi.) SE of

Clay map of Nippur with legends showing locations of temple, walls, gates, and canals. Courtesy The University Museum, University of Pennsylvania.

Babylon* and 160 km. (100 mi.) NW of Ur.* It was on a canal of the Euphrates but is now surrounded by sand dunes. The canal survives as a wadi,* the Shatt-en-Nil, which bisects the ruins from NW to SE.

The Tell. The tell* consists of a series of mounds covering 73 ha. (180 a.) and rising to an average height of 14 m. (45 ft.) above the canal bed. We have an accurate map of Nippur from c. 3000 B.C., indicating the locations of buildings, gates,* etc.

Excavations. It was at Nippur that Americans first entered Mesopotamian* archaeology with expeditions sponsored by the Babylonian Exploration Fund and the University of Pennsylvania. These excavations which were conducted between 1889 and 1900 under the successive direction of J. P. Peters, J. H. Haynes, and H. V. Hilprecht were plagued by disease and troubled by fighting Arab tribes. After the first season, which was a dismal failure, the following seasons proved to be spectacularly productive. To the W of the wadi the excavators found about eight thousand cuneiform* tablets, including the Murashu Archive from Persian times, and incantation bowls from the pre-Islamic period.

The excavations to the E of the wadi were even more rewarding. Part of the "Temple Hill" around the ziggurat* was cleared. To the S of this religious quarter, the excavators unearthed about twenty thousand cuneiform texts at the so-called "Tablet Hill." This was believed to be a school, but later excavations have shown that this was the residential quarter of scribes, so that the site is now known as the "Scribal Quarter."

Modern excavations were resumed in 1948 and have been conducted in alternate years, so that twelve seasons were completed as of 1973. The expeditions have been sponsored by the Oriental Institute and the University of Pennsylvania (up to the fourth season), and by the American Schools of Oriental Research (after the fourth season). The excavations have been directed successively by D. E. McCown, R. C. Haines, J. Knudstad, and McGuire Gibson.

In the Scribal Quarter the excavators have found the longest stratified sequence for middle Mesopotamia, extending from the Akkadian through the Achaemenid period. The recent achievements include further clearing of the ziggurat and the temple of Enlil, the discovery of an immense temple of Inanna (in 1952), and the recovery of a few thousand texts.

Texts. Of the over thirty thousand texts found at Nippur most are in Sumerian and date from 2500–1500 B.C. Among the most interesting of these are some two thousand Sumerian literary texts—comprising 80 percent of the corpus of such works—many of which have been published by S. N. Kramer. The texts from Nippur include the only fragment of the Sumerian Flood Story recovered (*see* ZIUSUDRA), the Ur-Nammu* Law Code, the earliest law code, as well as the next oldest, the Lipit-Ishtar* Code.

Pre-History. Nippur seems to have been founded c. 4500 B.C. Its Inanna temple can be traced back almost to Uruk* times (c. 3400 B.C.). From an analysis of myths and legends, Jacobsen has set forth the thesis that Nippur was the center of a prehistoric primitive democracy.

Third Millennium B.C. Nippur enjoyed its greatest glory in Sumerian times as it was the city of Enlil, the head of the Sumerian pantheon, and the site of his famed temple precinct, the E-Kur ("Mountain House"). According to myth Enlil separated heaven from earth at Nippur.

Sumerian theologians taught that it was on account of the desecration of the E-Kur by the Akkadian king Naram-Sin that the gods brought down the barbarous Gutians to destroy Agade, paving the way for the Sumerian renaissance of the Ur III period (twenty-first century B.C.). Ur-Nammu, the founder of the Ur III dynasty, built the ziggurat at Nippur. Its base measures 39 by 58 m. (128 by 190 ft.). The temple of Enlil was located NE of the ziggurat. To the SW of the ziggurat lay the enormous temple of Inanna, measuring 90 by 100 m. (295 by 328 ft.). Its history can be traced over three thousand years to the Parthian period.

Shulgi, the second king of the Ur III dynasty, established a storage city at Drehem a few kilometers SE of Nippur. From the thousands of Ur III economic texts it appears that all the Sumerian cities—except Nippur, which functioned as the center of an amphictyony—were required to send provisions to Drehem for the Enlil cult at Nippur.

Second Millennium B.C. Ishbi-Erra, the founder

of the Isin dynasty, seized Nippur to strengthen his claim as the successor to the Ur III dynasts. After being partially destroyed by invaders, Nippur was restored by Ishme-Dagan (1953–1935 B.C.), as recorded in "The Lamentation for Nippur." With the exaltation of Marduk, god of Babylon, by Hammurabi, Enlil and his city Nippur lost their supremacy. In the Old Babylonian period Nippur still flourished as a center of scribal education. Perhaps because of a shift in the Euphrates, Nippur suffered a drastic decline from 1700 until the reign of the Kassite king, Kadashman Harbe I, c. 1400 B.C. In the Kassite* period the temple of Enlil was rebuilt, and a palace erected on a western mound.

First Millennium B.C. Nippur, as one of the favored cities under the Assyrians, was exempt from taxes. Fragments of cylinders of Esarhaddon (680–669 B.C.) record the king's restoration of the E-Kur. Nippur was one of the last cities in the S to remain loyal to the Assyrians during the revolt of the Chaldeans.* Documents have been recovered which record how the citizens of Nippur were forced to sell their children during the siege of Nabopolassar.*

Some of the most important texts of the Persian period have come from Nippur. These include 730 tablets, dating from 455 to 403 B.C., from the archives of the banking family of Murashu. Murashu and his family were not Jews,* as is sometimes stated, but did number Jews among their clients. The economic texts show a rise in interest charged from 10 percent in Neo-Babylonian* times up to 50 percent charged by Murashu and Sons.

First Millennium A.D. Substantial Parthian remains of the first and second centuries A.D. were found at Nippur, including an immense fortress which covered the ziggurat area. In the subsequent Sassanian period (A. D. 226–637) there was a large Jewish community at Nippur. From this phase have come numerous incantation bowls inscribed in Aramaic,* Syriac, and Mandaic. Arabic historians record that Nippur was the site of a Christian bishopric as late as the twelfth century A.D.

BIBLIOGRAPHY: J. P. Peters, *Nippur* (1897); J. A. Montgomery, *Aramaic Incantation Texts from Nippur* (1913); ANET (1950), passim; G. Cardascia, *Les archives des Murashû* (1951); V. E. Crawford, "Nippur, the Holy City," *ARC*, 12.2 (1959), 74–83; W. W. Hallo, "A Sumerian Amphictyony," *JCS*, 14.3 (1960), 88–114; D. Hansen and G. Dales, "The Temple of Inanna, *Queen of Heaven*, at Nippur," *ARC*, 15.2 (1962), 75–84; A. Goetze, "Esarhaddon's Inscription from the Inanna Temple in Nippur," *JCS*, 17 (1963), 119–31; D. Hansen, "New Votive Plaques from Nippur," *JNES*, 22 (1963), 145–66; E. M. Yamauchi, *Mandaic Incantation Texts* (1967); D. E. McCown and R. C. Haines, *Nippur I: Temple of Enlil, Scribal Quarter, and Soundings* (1967; this is the final report of the 1948–52 excavations); G. Buccellati and R. D. Biggs, *Cuneiform Texts from Nippur* (1969). For interim reports on excavations after 1952 see: *Sumer*, 11 (1955), 107–9; *ILN* (Sept. 6, 1958), 386–89; *ILN*

(Sept. 9, 1961), 408–11; *Sumer*, 17 (1961), 67–70; *Sumer*, 22 (1966), 111–14; *Sumer*, 23 (1968), 95–106; S. N. Kramer, "Lamentation over the Destruction of Nippur," *Eretz Israel*, 9 (1969), 89–93; ANE (1970), 573–76; 582–84, 645–51; A. Goetze, "Early Dynastic Dedication Inscriptions from Nippur," *JCS*, 23 (1970), 39–47; O. R. Gurney, "The Tale of the Poor Man of Nippur and Its Folktale Parallels," *AnSt*, 22 (1972), 149–58; M. Gibson, "Nippur, 1972–73," *Expedition*, 16.1 (1973), 9–14; M. D. Coogan, "Life in the Diaspora: Jews at Nippur in the Fifth Century B.C.," *BA*, 37 (1974), 6–12; M. Gibson, "The Twelfth Season at Nippur: Fall, 1973," *Expedition* 16.4 (1974), 23–32; id., *Excavations at Nippur: Eleventh Season* (1975); M. D. Coogan, *West Semitic Personal Names in the Murašû Documents* (1975); id., "More Yahwistic Names in the Murashu Documents," *Journal for the Study of Judaism*, 7 (1976), 199–200; M. W. Stolper, "The Genealogy of the Murašû Family," *JCS*, 28 (1976), 189–200; id., "A Note on Yahwistic Personal Names in the Murašû Texts," *BASOR*, 222 (1976), 25–28; A. Guinan et al., "Nippur Rebaked," *Expedition*, 18.3 (1976), 42–47; M. Gibson, "Nippur: New Perspectives," *ARC*, 30 (1977), 26–37.

EY

NO. *See* THEBES.

NOPH. *See* MEMPHIS.

NOTHUS. *See* DARIUS.

NUBIA; NUBIANS. Nubia is the area S of ancient Egypt* which extends up the Nile from Aswan* into the Sudan, but its limits are not strictly defined. Nubia is the biblical Cush, which is often Ethiopia* in the English Bible, following the Greek translation. Ethiopia or Ethiopians occur thirty-eight times. When Egyptian rulers were weak, from about 750–650 B.C., Cushite rulers controlled Egypt. One of these, Tirhakah, is mentioned in Isa 37:9 as leading his forces against Sennacherib* when the latter was threatening Jerusalem.* In later times there were several queens with the name Candace, one of which is mentioned in Acts 8:27 in connection with the Ethiopian eunuch who was converted.

Excavations in Nubia in the 1960s revealed some massive mud-brick fortresses for defense against the Egyptians and a trading post at Buhen. Some mass burials of servants with royalty seemed to indicate that the servants allowed themselves to be buried alive with their masters in order to accompany them to the next world. Statues* and other objects may have come from Egyptian merchants in the period 1720–1567 B.C. A large temple was found at Sulb on the W bank of the Nile; it had granite lions* and rams at the entrance. The ram, especially, was a symbol of divinity among the Cushites. In 1958 some interesting evidence of the spread of Christianity in the region of Nubia was found at 'Ain Fara. A large square mosque gave evidence of having been formerly a Christian church. Nearby was another church and monastery complex. An ostracon* at the site carried the Christian symbol of a fish and a cross; another piece of pottery* had a dove's head and a cross.

BIBLIOGRAPHY: H. C. Leupold, *ZPEB*, 4 (1975), 1047–48.

BCC

NUFFAR. *See* NIPPUR.

NUZI (NUZU) (nū´zē). This city, the modern Yorghan Tepe was not a biblical site but is biblically significant because of documents discovered in the palace and in private homes, which illuminate the customs of Northern Mesopotamia* in the fifteenth century B.C.

The excavations between 1925 and 1931 revealed an important provincial town which was under Hurrian* domination during the fifteenth and fourteenth centuries B.C. The twenty thousand clay* tablets written in a Babylonian dialect, in cuneiform* script, cover some four or five generations and include the complete archives of several people. Important parallels in customs, law, and social conditions with the society of the patriarchal narratives are evident. Many of these customs are now known to be much older than the fifteenth century B.C., so that they reflect the practice of Northern Mesopotamia and Syria in the preceding centuries when the patriarchs were living. On the other hand, some of the customs were current quite late in the second millennium B.C. and some continued even into the first millennium. They are therefore difficult to use for dating the patriarchal age. Even so, there are useful insights into Mesopotamian life.

One group of documents deals with inheritance. Normally a man's estate passed to his eldest son who received a "double portion." Where a man had no son he would "adopt" a relative or a freeborn man outside the family, or even a slave.* Such a "son" would care for the man in his old age, give him a proper burial, continue to observe the religious rites of the family, and carry on the family name. Such practices are reminiscent of Abraham's adoption of Eliezer (Gen 15:2–4). Another practice was common, in which a childless wife gave to her husband a secondary wife who might bear a son, who would become the heir, and was regarded as the son of the true wife. The parallel with Gen 16:2 is clear. In such a case, should the first wife subsequently bear a son, this later son became the heir, but the temporary heir was to be given a share in the family inheritance and not to be cast out. When Sarah drove out Hagar and Ishmael (Gen 21:10–11) the thing was therefore grievous in Abraham's eyes.

It was possible in the Nuzi society for a man to dispose of his birthright. One text tells of a brother who gave "three sheep in exchange for his inheritance share." We are reminded of Jacob and Esau (Gen 25:30–34). This practice is known in older Assyrian and Babylonian texts.

In some documents the possession of the household gods was the prerogative of the head of the family. These passed to the heir on the death of the former head. There is possibly a reflection of this custom in Rachel's action in carrying away the "gods" of Laban in an attempt to secure the inheritance for Jacob (Gen 31:30).

Oral blessings and deathbed statements uttered in the presence of witnesses carried legal significance at Nuzi. One young man was able to marry the girl of his choice, despite the opposition of his brothers, when he produced witnesses who had heard the dying father declare that this was his wish. There may be a parallel here to the blessings of Jacob (Gen 27) and Isaac (Gen 49).

Numerous such parallels provide valuable background information to the patriarchal narratives and provide evidence for the reliability of the social and legal background of these narratives.

It should be recognized that some of the above proposals represent rather free interpretations of the evidence and have been modified by some writers. Certainly the Nuzi material should not be treated in isolation from material from other documents.

BIBLIOGRAPHY: C. H. Gordon, "Biblical Customs in the Nuzi Tablets," *BA*, 3 (1940); E. A. Speiser, "New Kirkuk Documents Relating to Family Laws," *AASOR*, 10 (1930), 1–73; id., "One Hundred New Selected Nuzi Texts," *AASOR*, 16 (1936), 7–168; I. J. Gelb et al., *Nuzi Personal Names* (1943); F. R. Steele, *Nuzi Real Estate Transactions* (1943); M. Greenberg, *The Hab/piru* (1955), 65–70; A. A. MacRae, *ZPEB*, 4 (1975), 470–73; M. J. Selman, "The Social Environment of the Patriarchs," *Tyndale Bulletin*, 27 (1976), 137–47; J. Van Seters, *Abraham in History and Tradition* (1975); T. L. Thompson, *The Historicity of the Patriarchal Narratives* (1974); N. Weeks, "Man, Nuzi and the Patriarchs," *Abr Nahrain*, 16 (1975–76), 73–82.

JAT

NYSA. *See* SCYTHOPOLIS.

O

OATHS. According to Cicero's discussion (Cic. *Off.* 3.27–32) an oath "is an assurance backed by religious sanction."

I. *Definition and Descriptions of Oaths.* An oath, which is a solemn declaration made under divine sanction, may be assertive, promissory, or exculpatory. An assertive oath calls God to witness the truth of a statement (cf. 1 Kings 18:10). An oath may be promissory with regard to future undertakings, as is often the case in business transactions. An exculpatory oath seeks to clear a person from an accusation (cf. the Code of Hammurabi,* laws 20, 23, 103, 107, etc.; *ANET*, 163ff.).

A. *The Implied Curse.* In biblical oaths the implied curse attendant upon a nonfulfillment of an oath is often expressed in the vague statement, "May the Lord do so to me and more also, if . . ." (Ruth 1:17; 2 Sam 3:35; 1 Kings 2:23 et al.). On rare occasions, the full implications of the curse are spelled out (Ps 7:4–5; Ps 137:5–6; Num 5:19ff.). In order to demonstrate his sincerity, Job quite boldly called upon himself diverse curses (Job 31), uttering dreadful things which were normally left unspecified. Peter, in his betrayal of the Lord, progressively denied Christ (Matt 26:70), denied with an oath (v. 72), and finally cursed, i.e., called down curses upon himself (v. 74).

Other cultures were quite imaginative in stating clearly the consequences of breaking an oath or of swearing a false oath. In Mesopotamia,* if one perjured himself his head was to be covered with hot asphalt or worse. In Egypt,* one swore: "If I speak not the truth, let my nose and ears be cut off"; "may I be thrown to the crocodile," etc.

B. *The Importance of Oaths.* The oath was quite significant in the OT. Two of the Ten Commandments pertain in part to oaths: the third commandment (Exod 20:7) forbids vain oaths, and the ninth commandment (Exod 20:16) forbids false oaths. Even if one swore to his own disadvantage, he was obliged to keep his oath (Ps 15:4).

C. *Words Rendered "Oath."* The Hebrew word for oath is *šebûʿâ*, which is related to the word for "seven"; cf. Beersheba,* which means either "the well of seven" (Gen 21:28–30), or "the well of the oath" (Gen 21:31). Another Hebrew word which is sometimes translated "oath" is *ʾālâ* (e.g., Gen 24:41; 26:28; Deut 29:12 et al.) and more properly connotes the implicit curse (cf. Zech 5:3).

The Akkadian word for oath is *māmîtu*, from the root "to pronounce," and the word *nîš* from the root

"to live," as in the phrase "by the life of. . . ." The Egyptian word for oath, *ᶜnh*, (pronounced ankh), is also derived from the verb "to live." The Greek word for oath is *horkos*. The Latin* is derived from the verb *iurāre*; our related English word "juror" is one who has sworn under oath. The Arabic word for oath, *yamîn*, originally meant the right (hand), by which the oath was sworn.

II. *Praxis.* A. *Formulae.* In making promises to men Jehovah swears by Himself (Gen 22:16), lifting up His hand, as it were (Exod 6:8; cf. Isa 62:8; Ezek 20:5) and making asseverations on His life (Ezek 17:16; Zeph 2:9). God can offer no stronger confirmation of His promise than His oath (Heb 6:13–18).

Men swore by the formula, "as the Lord lives," (Judg 8:19; 1 Sam 14:39). Aramaic* ostraca* from Egypt record oaths sworn "by the life of YHH." Despite the prohibition against the invocation of other gods (Exod 23:13), there is considerable evidence that the Israelites swore oaths in the names of the pagan deities (Jer 5:7; 12:16; Amos 8:14; Zeph 1:5). The fifth-century B.C. Aramaic documents from Elephantine* indicate that the Jews* there swore by pagan gods.

In Egypt and in Mesopotamia oaths were commonly sworn by the life of the king. By NT times, the Jewish populace, in seeking to avoid a direct reference to Jehovah, were swearing by everything from "the fig-picker" to "heaven" (Matt 23:16–22). *Corban* (Mark 7:11; cf. Matt 15:5), though usually a vow, could also indicate an oath (Jos. *Apion* 1.166–67).

B. *Actions.* Various actions reinforced the solemnity of the swearing of oaths. The raising of one's hand (Gen 14:22; Rev 10:5–6) or hands (Dan 12:7) was a frequent gesture, as it still is today. Abraham's servant placed his hand under his master's "thigh" (Gen 24:2) in swearing his oath. The later Jewish practice of grasping a phylactery* may be the prototype for our practice of swearing upon the Bible.

Dramatic acts depicting the conditional curses accompanied covenants or treaties which are elaborations of oaths. The word for treaty in Akkadian, Hittite, and Aramaic is taken from the word for "oath." Treaties were inviolable because of the oaths that were sworn (Josh 9:15–20). The phrase for making a covenant in Hebrew and in Greek is literally "to cut" a covenant or oath, referring to the ritual of cutting animals (Gen 15:9, 10, 17) in twain and passing between the pieces as an object lesson of what would happen to transgressors (Jer 34:18–20).

The Shurpu magical texts refer to "an oath sworn by slaughtering a sheep and touching the wound." Abba-El gave the city* of Alalakh* to Yarimlim and took an oath by cutting the neck of a lamb and saying, "(May I be cursed) if I take back what I gave you." In the eighth-century treaty signed between Ashurnirari V and Mati'ilu of Arpad in Syria, we read: "If Mati'ilu sins against this treaty, so may, just as the head of this spring lamb is torn off . . . the head of Mati'ilu be torn off . . ." (*ANE*, 532). Similar curses are found in the Aramaic treaties of Mati'ilu found at Sefire (*ANET*, 503–4), and the vassal treaties of Esarhaddon* (*ANE*, 534–41). In the ceremonies of the Hittite* soldier's oath (*ANET*, 353–54) wax was burned, salt* was scattered, malt loaves were ground, and a blind woman and a deaf man were led before the soldiers. In a text from Mari* deities swearing to protect the city swallow the dissolved brickwork of Mari (cf. Num 5:21–22).

III. *Uses of Oaths*. A. *Legal*. Oaths were used for a variety of purposes. In Egypt a husband swore at a wedding, "As Amon lives, as Pharaoh lives, . . . if I wish to divorce her and I love another woman . . . I am the one who must give her the things recorded above." In Mesopotamia business transactions involved oaths which were sworn before judges or priests and before witnesses, and which were duly recorded in writing.*

B. *Juridical*. In the face of the lack of witnesses or of conflicting evidence, oaths were used as a kind of ordeal to determine the truth (1 Kings 8:31; Exod 22:7–11). It was assumed that the guilty party would fear to take the oath (Eccl 9:2). Detailed evidence is available from Nuzi.* There oaths were used more frequently than the river ordeal. Defendants who refused the oaths lost their cases, but records reveal that even two of those who did take the oath were deemed insincere by the judges. The Elephantine papyri* also disclose the use of the oath to determine court cases. In Athens* jurors swore to judge fairly and recited: "May there be many blessings on me if I keep my oath, but if I break it may there be destruction on me and my family."

C. *Political*. The oath was the core of most treaties. Usually the vassals swore oaths of allegiance to their sovereign (*ANE*, 534ff.), but a letter from Shamshi-Adad of Assyria indicates that this king also swore an oath to his vassal (*ANE*, 628; cf. Deut 26:17–19). The same letter indicates that some vassals were quite cavalier about their oaths: "He becomes the ally of a king and swears an oath, [then] he becomes the ally of a[nother] king and swears an oath, while becoming an enemy of the first king with whom he was allied."

IV. *The Abuse of Oaths*. By the NT period the populace was accustomed to swear oaths on every occasion. According to Philo (*De spec. leg*. 2.8): ". . . they do not blush to use name after name, one piled upon another, thinking that the continual repetition of a string of oaths will secure them their object." The rabbis tried to distinguish between valid and invalid oaths (Mishnah, *Nedarim*, and *Sheb-*

uoth). In general the rabbis held that only the word *sheᵇbuᶜa* or its substitutes, or the mention of God's name or His attributes, constituted valid oaths. Jesus condemned the fine distinctions which were drawn by rabbinic casuistry (Matt 23:16–22).

Indeed, Jesus taught that it was preferable not to swear at all (Matt 5:33–37; James 5:12). Some rabbis also taught that one sinned in swearing a true oath if there was no urgent need for it. Philo (*Decalogue* 17.84–19.95) held that it was best not to swear at all. According to Josephus (Jos. *War* 2.135) the Essenes* "refrain from swearing, considering it worse than perjury; for, they say, the man who cannot be believed unless he calls on God as witness condemns himself" (cf. Clem. Al., *Strom*. 7.8.50).

BIBLIOGRAPHY: S. Mercer, *The Oath in Babylonian and Assyrian Literature* (1912); J. Pedersen, *Der Eid bei den Semiten* (1914); J. Cronin, *The Athenian Juror and His Oath* (1936); J. Wilson, "The Oath in Ancient Egypt," *JNES*, 7 (1948), 129–56; S. Blank, "The Curse, Blasphemy, the Spell, and the Oath," *HUCA*, 23 (1950–51), 73–95; D. Wiseman, *The Vassal-Treaties of Esarhaddon* (1958); M. Tsevat, "The Neo-Assyrian and Neo-Babylonian Vassal Oaths and the Prophet Ezekiel," *JBL*, 78 (1959), 199–204; R. Hayden, "Court Procedure at Nuzu" (unpublished Brandeis University dissertation, 1962), 34–39; M. Pope, *IDB*, 3 (1962), 575–77; A. Crown, "Aposiopesis in the OT and the Hebrew Conditional Oath," *Abr-Nahrain*, 4 (1963–64), 96–111; D. McCarthy, "Three Covenants in Genesis," *CBQ*, 27 (1964), 179–89; J. Priest, "*ᵒorkia* in the *Iliad* and Consideration of a Recent Theory," *JNES*, 23 (1964), 48–56; G. Buchanan, "Some Vow and Oath Formulas in the NT," *HTR*, 58 (1965), 319–26; S. Lieberman, *Greek in Jewish Palestine*, 2d ed. (1965), 115–43; J. Fitzmyer, *The Aramaic Inscriptions of Sefire* (1967); N. Lohfink, *Die Landverheissung als Eid* (1967); B. Porten, *Archives from Elephantine* (1968), 151–58; M. Weinfeld, "The Covenant of Grant in the OT and in the Ancient Near East," *JAOS*, 90 (1970), 184–203; J. Plescia, *The Oath and Perjury in Ancient Greece* (1970); M. Weinfeld, "The Covenant of Grace in the Old Testament and in the Ancient Near East," *JAOS*, 90 (1970), 184–203; H. C. White, "The Divine Oath in Genesis," *JBL*, 92 (1973), 165–79; T. M. Gregory, *ZPEB*, 4 (1975), 476–79; M. Weinfeld, "The Loyalty Oath in the Ancient Near East," *Ugarit Forschungen*, 8 (1976), 379–414; S. Parker, "The Vow in Ugaritic and Israelite Narrative Literature," *Ugarit Forschungen*, 11 (1979), 693–700. EY

OBELISK. A tapering stone monument originating in Egypt* at Heliopolis and probably representing the descending rays of the sun. The KJV "Beth Shemesh*" of Jer 43:13 is Heliopolis ("temple of the sun" NIV), and the "image" of that verse is sometimes translated "obelisk" (RSV), or as "sacred pillar" (NIV).

OBODA. See AVDAT.

OCTAVIAN. See AUGUSTUS.

OFFERINGS. The Hebrew sacrificial calendar provided both for intermittent and continual offerings to God. The latter comprised an immolated animal, accompanied by a cereal offering and a libation (Exod 29:38–42; Lev 6:12–13 et al.), the procedures for which varied somewhat at different times. The schedule of offerings detailed in Num 28–29 has its counterpart in practices contained in the Uruk* material, the latter, however, being considerably more elaborate. The OT "bread of the Presence" (Exod 25:30 et al.) was paralleled by the Mesopotamian "food of the presence" (akâl pâni), which, as with the Hittite* sacrificial rituals, often consisted of twelve loaves and was unleavened. A guilt offering ('aṭm) corresponding to the Hebrew 'āshām was mentioned in Hurrian* (Horite) documents. Prescriptions for Ancient Near Eastern offerings were related to the social standing of the worshiper, as also in the OT (Lev 4:23–32; 12:8; cf. Luke 2:24). Thus the Hittite Yuzgat tablet allowed a poorer man to offer a smaller sacrifice, this practice being paralleled in Babylonian and Phoenician* texts also. The nature of acceptable offerings specified in Ugaritic texts included cattle, sheep, oxen,* doves, and cereals, as in the OT, while the third-century B.C. Phoenician tariff from Marseilles included the ox, goat,* ram, wild fowl, and certain game birds. Babylonian sacrificial texts mention honey, cream, garlic, and wine* as well as animal flesh, and a similar situation existed at Ugarit.* The Babylonians, Hittites, and Egyptians insisted, with the Hebrews, that sacrificial offerings should be of the highest quality.

RKH

OHEIMIR, TELL EL-. See KISH.

OIL. See FOOD; MILL; OLIVE.

OINTMENT. Natural scents combined with pastes or other vehicles were very popular trade items throughout Near Eastern history. Bas-reliefs* from Egypt* and Mesopotamia* and texts from all parts of the ancient world present the importance of such resins and oils that could be used for perfuming or scenting the body and clothing.* A fine text containing instructions for making perfumes has been excavated from Assyria. While the W Semite literature frequently refers to unguents, the OT employs both the term sēmēn, "oil" and merqāḥ, "salve." Ugaritic uses both in the phrase, šmnrqḥ, "perfumer's oil." Tiny vessels for unguents, some still containing traces of the substances, have been excavated from most large sites of the Near East.

BIBLIOGRAPHY: R. K. Harrison, *Healing Herbs of the Bible* (1966), 49–54; F. B. Huey, Jr., ZPEB, 4 (1975), 515–18.

WW

OLIVE. The *Olea europaea* L., one of the most valuable trees of the eastern Mediterranean region, was probably a native of western Asia despite its botanical name. Its first OT mention was in connection with the Flood* (Gen 8:11), and since then it has become the symbol for peace (cf. Ps 52:8). In early Meso-

potamian art the olive was occasionally represented as the Tree of Life. Thus it is probably the branched tree depicted on many Babylonian cylinder seals,* which often show goats* standing on either side on their hind legs, rather like the "supporters" of more modern heraldry. The gold* and silver* representation of a male goat caught in a thicket which Sir Leonard Woolley recovered from the Early Dynastic period of Ur* is most probably in the same general tradition. Excavations in Palestine have shown that olives, when harvested, were processed by being placed in a shallow hole in a rock and crushed by means of a large upright millstone.* At a later period the stone was fastened to the middle of a hinged beam, thus enabling greater pressure to be applied when the oil was being extracted. This latter appeared as a therapeutic substance in extant pharmaceutical texts from Babylonia, Assyria, and Egypt,* being most probably the vegetable oil mentioned in the oldest pharmacopoeia known to man, a Sumerian tablet from the third millennium B.C. Olive wood was highly esteemed through the Near East for decorative carpentry (cf. 1 Kings 6:23) because of its rich amber grain when seasoned and polished. Excavations at sites in the Negev* have revealed traces of stone-mulched dust which is probably all that remains of ancient olive stumps, suggesting the dry-farming techniques of antiquity, and a period when the area was more productive than at present.

The slow maturing of the olive also made it a symbol of peace. There was small incentive for its culture unless a people could see a generation of peace free from the trampling and "scorched earth" of ruthless invaders. Olive trees were frequently, in ancient times, the first casualty of war, as digging at Lachish* has strikingly illustrated. When he stormed the stronghold, Nebuchadnezzar* cut all the olive trees round about and piled them for a mighty holocaust against the limestone walls.* As the calcined stones flaked he drove his battering rams through the fire. In the breach, through which his storming parties gained entry, the powdered limestone may still be seen full of olive stones.

BIBLIOGRAPHY: H. N. and A. L. Moldenke, *Plants of the Bible* (1952), 157–60; R. K. Harrison, NDB (1962, rev. 1970), 907; W. E. Shewell-Cooper, ZPEB, 4 (1975), 528.

RKH

OLIVES, MOUNT OF. This ridge is a part of the N–S mountain range, located just E of Jerusalem,* across the Kidron* Valley. It is about 4 km. (2½ mi.) long, with three summits. The northernmost and highest, called Ras el-Mesharif, 820 m. (2,690 ft.) above sea level, is the Mount Scopus area. The middle summit at 811 m. (2,660 ft.) is the Mount of Olives proper, directly E of Jerusalem (Zech 14:4); the Arabic name is et-Tur and the village there Kefar et-Tur. The S summit is above the present town, Silwan, and probably is the Mount of Corruption or Mount of Offense (2 Kings 23:13).

The name occurs twice in the OT, in 2 Sam 15:30 and Zech 14:4. In the NT this mount is important especially in the events of the Passion Week and of the Ascension (Luke 24:50; Acts 1:12).

The Mount of Olives is rich in ancient finds, some from the OT period, but most from the time of Christ and much later.

At the southeastern end of the subsidiary ridge, Ras esh-Shiyah, which runs SE from the middle summit, is the present village el-Azariyeh, no doubt ancient Bethany.* Here have been found grave remains from the Canaanite* period and from the sixth century B.C. to the fourteenth century A.D., as well as the traditional tomb of Lazarus* and remains of several successive church structures from the fourth century A.D. on.

About 0.8 km. (½ mi.) NW of Bethany at the NW end of the Ras esh-Shiyah ridge is the site thought to be Bethphage,* a site showing occupation from the second century B.C. to c. the eighth century A.D. There is now a Franciscan chapel at the location.

About 20 m. (65 ft.) S and a little W of the middle summit, et-Tur, are the ruins of the Eleona Church with its cave crypt where probably, according to tradition (cf. Eusebius *Life of Constantine* 3.43), Helena, mother of Constantine, built a church (Etheria, A.D. 385, calls it Eleona) over this cave* in which Jesus was thought to have revealed to his disciples his secrets about the end of the age (Matt 24). In excavating the ruins, beginning in 1910, the Dominicans found a basilica*-type church; mosaic* pavement was also found. The church was destroyed by the Persians in 614, but in the Middle Ages a chapel was erected there to commemorate Christ's giving the Lord's Prayer; the present Church of the Creed and the Church of the Pater Noster (with the prayer inscribed in forty-six languages in wall panels) was built subsequent to 1868.

An octagonal church was built about 385 on the middle summit of the Mount of Olives, the place of the Ascension, according to Etheria's testimony. The church was destroyed in 614, rebuilt by the Crusaders, and then taken over by the Moslems and made into a mosque which remains to the present. All of the original that is preserved are the foundations of the octagon and the central shrine.

The Dominus Flevit ("the Lord wept") Franciscan Chapel, the site where, by tradition from the fourteenth century on, Jesus was thought to have wept over Jerusalem (Luke 19:41), is located in a northwesterly direction about halfway down the W slope of the mount. The Franciscans in their excavations from 1953 have uncovered a large ancient cemetery used from 135 B.C. to A.D. 70 and in the third and fourth centuries. Ruins of a Byzantine* church with some mosaic pavement were found under and adjacent to the present chapel.

Gethsemane* is to be located somewhat opposite the so-called Golden Gate on the lower W slope of the mount. Excavations have revealed two ancient churches: the first, a fourth-century basilica was destroyed in 614; and the second, a Crusader church superimposed on the first but at an angle. The Franciscans in 1924 completed a modern basilica on the site next to the garden* in which there are many old olive trees.

Lower on the slope and to the N of Gethsemane a Byzantine church was built (perhaps fifth century) over what was then regarded as the tomb of Mary, the mother of Jesus. The Crusaders reconstructed it from ruins and added beside it a large monastery, the Abbey of St. Mary of the Valley of Jehoshaphat. Excavations have revealed remains of sixth-century mosaic floors and Crusader pavement and masonry. The modern church is known as the Church of the Tomb of Mary.

NW of the middle summit is an olive grove where, according to folklore, the disciples, at the Ascension were called "Men of Galilee" (Acts 1:11).

More recently built structures on the mount are: the Russian Church of St. Mary Magdalene (just above Gethsemane); the Russian Monastery on et-Tur; and the Augusta Victoria Hospital on the S end of Mount Scopus.

BIBLIOGRAPHY: H. Vincent and F.-M. Abel, *Jerusalem Nouvelle*, 1–2 (1914), 301–419; ibid., 4 (1926), 808–10, 821–31, 1007–13; M. Avi-Yonah, *QDAP*, 2 (1932), 164–66; G. Dalman, *Sacred Sites and Ways* (1936), 261–68; F.-M. Abel, *Géographie de la Palestine*, 1 (1938), 372–75; G. A. Barrois, "Mount of Olives," *IDB*, 3 (1962), 596–99; P. B. Bagatti, *L'Eglise de la gentilité en Palestine* (1968); J. Finegan, *The Archaeology of the NT* (1969), 88–108.

WHM

OMRI (om'rī; Heb. עָמְרִי, *'omrî*). Omri was a king of Israel* (c. 884–873 B.C.), who usurped the throne and moved the capital from Tirzah* to Samaria* (1 Kings 16:23–27). Excavations at Samaria have revealed that he built in a grand style with magnificent masonry on bedrock. Excavations at Tirzah reveal a decline in this city* after the middle of the ninth century B.C. Omri was known to the Assyrians and gave his name to Israel on Assyrian monuments—Bit Humri (house of Omri). The Moabite Stone* tells of his conquest of Moab.* He was a man of military strength and of greater international significance than one would realize from the Bible.

BIBLIOGRAPHY: K. M. Kenyon, *Archaeology of the Holy Land* (1960), 260–69, 318–19; Y. Aharoni, *Land of the Bible* (1960), 294–95; J. Lilley, *ZPEB*, 4 (1975), 533–35.

JAT

ONOMASTICON. A vocabulary or list of proper names, usually in alphabetical order.

OPHIR (ō'fər). The location of Ophir is obscure. Attempts to identify it on linguistic grounds and from the evidence of the cargoes brought thence to Solomon's* port of Ezion Geber* (1 Kings 10:11; 1 Chron 29:4) have variously placed Ophir from Zimbabwe (Rhodesia) to Supara just N of Bombay (Supara—Sopher [Jos. *Antiq.* 8.6.4]—Ophir). The only archaeological reference is found on a Tell Qasile* ostracon* of the sixth century B.C.: "Gold of Ophir to Beth Horon . . . thirty shekels." The two likeliest places are the southern tip of Arabia,* the modern Yemen, and ancient Sabaea (*see* SABEANS), or Somaliland. Archaeology is not easy in the first named locality owing to the condition of the land and the obstructive attitude of authority. The ancient Sabean territory of the Yemen is a rich and largely unexplored archaeological field (see Wendell Phillips, *Qataban and Sheba* [1955]), but when research can examine this difficult region without impediment, much light could be thrown on the period of Solomon, and the location of Ophir in that area could possibly be established, but a case can be made for Somaliland, the other possible claimant, which contains the Egyptian Punt area. A detailed record of Princess Hatshepsut's trading expedition to that area, along with the cargoes, is in existence. The three-year journey (1 Kings 10:22) by Hebrew reckoning, need only have been parts of three years, perhaps no more than fourteen months. Egyptian records for trade with the Punt area extend from the Fifth Dynasty in the middle of the third millennium through fully fifteen centuries of Egyptian history.

BIBLIOGRAPHY: G. Ryckman, *Supplément au Dictionnaire de la Bible* (1959), cols. 744–51; G. W. Van Beek, *IDB*, 3 (1962), 605–6; W. White, Jr., *ZPEB*, 4 (1975), 540–41.

EMB

OPHRAH. See AFFULEH.

OSIRIS (ō sī'ris; Gr. from Egyp. *Wsir*, meaning uncertain). An ancient Egyptian god, Osiris first emerged clearly in the Old Kingdom, or Pyramid Age (third millennium B.C.), as a royal god of the dead. A king not only might join the sun-god in heaven, but he could also be identified with Osiris as ruler of the realm of the dead. In later periods (especially from c. 2000 B.C.), ever-wider circles of Egyptians came to look to Osiris as their hope in the afterlife. Hence numberless funerary inscriptions request his benefits. Osiris, moreover, became judge of the dead; the spells of the Book of the Dead* were intended to guide a deceased person past that judgment into the blissful realm of Osiris with its abundant harvests. A rich mythology grew up around Osiris as the good king, a founder of civilization, murdered by his evil brother Seth and succeeded by his young son and avenger Horus, son of the wily goddess Isis. The most famous cult-center of Osiris was at Abydos* in Upper Egypt. His cult illustrates a developed belief in an afterlife contemporary with (but very distinct from) OT religion and culture.

BIBLIOGRAPHY: H. W. Helck, "Osiris," *PWSup*, 9 (1962), 469–513; J. G. Griffiths, *The Origins of Osiris*, 2nd ed. (1980).

KAK

OSNAPPAR; OSNAPPER. See ASHURBANIPAL.

OSSUARY. A stone chest (Lat. *ossuarium*) used as a container for bones. Bone fragments were placed in an ossuary when burial sites were cleared for renewed use. Found near Jerusalem* and in funerary caves,* they contain inscriptions in Hebrew, Aramaic,* and Greek.* The most common come from the Roman era.

See also FUNERARY CUSTOMS, PALESTINIAN.

OSTRACA (os'trə kə). The Greek name for potsherds (*see* SHARDS), the cheapest and most common of ancient writing* materials. Since they did not lend themselves to incised writings, they have rarely been found in Mesopotamia,* but in Egypt* go back to the Old Kingdom. Most, however, are from the Valley of the Tombs of the Kings and the New Kingdom, and among these the nonliterary ostraca have thrown the most light on biblical history, with a wide range of information about the daily life of Egypt from the period of the Israelite sojourn.

Ostraca have been of more direct historical use in Palestine, particularly at Lachish.* During the Wellcome-Marston expedition there (1935–38) twenty-one ostraca were found in the burnt guard-room, dated to 588–87 B.C. and called the "Lachish Letters.*" The script is important for our knowledge of Hebrew at this period, and the letters illustrate vividly the relations between the military governor of Lachish and his subordinate nearby, shortly before Nebuchadnezzar's* capture of Jerusalem* (2 Kings 25:1f.; Jer 29:1f.).

In Egypt many thousands of shards have been discovered relating to the NT period, written in Greek* and Latin,* also Aramaic* and Coptic. The great majority provide detail for the social rather than the political history of Greco-Roman Egypt, but some have assisted with the understanding of NT Greek terms.

BIBLIOGRAPHY: V. Wilchen, *Griechische Ostraka aus Agypten und Nubien* (1899); J. Černý, *Chronique d'Égypte*, 6.12 (1931), 212–24; *DOTT* (1958), 204–8, 212–17; O. Tufnell, "Lachish," in D. W. Thomas, ed., *Archaeology and OT Study* (1967), 305–7.

BFH

Pottery ossuaries shaped like houses or ovoid jars, from Chalcolithic Period, found at Hederah, Azor, and Bene-Berak. The openings are large enough to receive a skull. The ossuaries are usually decorated with some anthropomorphic feature (a simple nose or beak). Courtesy Israel Dept. of Antiquities and Museums.

OVEN. Reliefs from Assyria and Egypt* have given a clear idea of the structure of ancient ovens. The basic shape was cylindrical, the inside of which was lined with a layer of burnt clay.* The floor was covered with pebbles, on which a fire was built. When the oven was adequately heated, the pebbles were cleared of ashes and the dough was placed on them or else against the walls of the oven. A typical Iron Age* oven excavated at Megiddo* was found to have

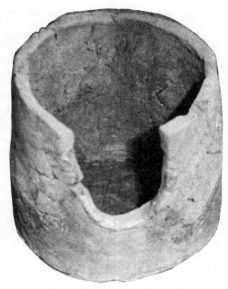

Clay oven found at Arad from Iron Age II. Courtesy Dagon Collection—Archaeological Museum of Grain Handling in Israel.

been covered with a plastered layer of potsherds (*see* SHARDS) as a means of insulating the outside of the clay-lined oven. A fine baker's oven, with bread still inside, may be seen in Pompeii.* In antiquity, as also among many modern Palestinian peasants, the fuels used consisted of dry grass (cf. Matt 6:30; Luke 12:28), bushes from the desert, and cakes of animal dung mixed with straw and dried in the sun. Commercial bakers generally followed the pattern of other professions in occupying specific areas of cities (cf. Neh 3:11; 12:38).

BIBLIOGRAPHY: G. A. Barrois, *Manuel d'Archéologie Biblique*, 1 (1939), 320–22; id., *IDB*, 3 (1962), 612–13; W. White, Jr., *ZPEB*, 4 (1975), 553–54.

RKH

OVERSEER. *See* EPISKOPOS.

OX. Palestinian oxen were evidently of the same genus (*bos*) as those of other Ancient Near Eastern countries. The ox was domesticated at an early period and constituted a significant indication of personal wealth (cf. Gen 13:2). Reliefs from various periods of Near Eastern life depict the ox as a draft animal which pulled plows (cf. Deut 22:10; Prov 14:4) and wagons (Num 7:3; 2 Sam 6:6) and helped to thresh grain (Deut 25:4; cf. 1 Cor 9:9). Mosaic legislation in the Torah displayed great concern for the care of such animals, requiring them to rest on the Sabbath day (Exod 23:12) and be subject to the law of firstlings (Lev 27:26).

The ox was a clean animal (Deut 14:4) but nevertheless was used for food only on important occasions (cf. 1 Kings 1:19; Matt 22:4). Ancient Near Eastern peoples offered oxen up as a sacrifice, as evidenced in Babylonian and Ugaritic* sources, and also in a comparatively late (third to second century B.C.) Phoenician* sacrificial tariff from Marseilles, attesting to the antiquity of the practice in Exod 20:24. Oxen pastured on grass (cf. Num 22:4; Job 6:5), but also fed on straw (Isa 11:7) when grass was scarce. The dung was frequently used as a fuel.

The ox was prominent throughout western Asia as a symbol of deity and fertility, the worship of the Apis bull in Egypt* being typical. The "golden calves" of Jeroboam I were Israelite adaptations of this cultus. In the Solomonic Temple* the huge laver* rested on the backs of a dozen bronze* oxen (1 Kings 7:25), reflecting Phoenician iconography. One of the cherubs in Ezekiel's vision (Ezek 1:5–10) bore the face of an ox.

BIBLIOGRAPHY: W. S. McCullough, *IDB*, 3 (1962), 614; G. S. Cansdale, *ZPEB*, 1 (1975), 764–67.

RKH

OX, WILD. The unicorn of the KJV (Num 23:22; 24:8; Deut 33:17; Job 39:10; Ps 22:21; 29:6; Isa 34:7) is the wild ox, once called the aurochs, the ancestor of domesticated cattle. The last recorded aurochs (*bos primigenius*) died in A.D. 1627 in a Polish park. The bull was a huge animal, some 2 m. (6 ft.) at the shoulders, black or dark brown, with forward pointing horns. The famous prehistoric cave* drawings of Lascaux show some obvious examples. Thutmose III (about 1500 B.C.) hunted the aurochs. One hunt in which this pharaoh claimed 176 kills, is commemorated on a scarab.* The latest Egyptian evidence, where a hunt from chariots* is shown, is to be dated in the reign of Ramses III, about 1190 B.C. The Assyrian kings, never to be outdone in hunting, rode the aurochs down on horseback, as did the plains Indians with the American buffalo.

BIBLIOGRAPHY: G. S. Cansdale, *All the Animals of the Bible Lands* (1970), 82–84.

EMB

OXYRHYNCHUS (ok si rin´kəs). This Egyptian town, modern Behnesa, was on the Bahr Yusuf, the leading canal of the thickly populated Fayyum, 16 km. (10 mi.) from the Nile, and 418 km. (260 mi.) from Alexandria.* Of the town itself few remains are visible, but Oxyrhynchus has proved the richest of all sources of papyri.* The first thorough exploration of the area was by Grenfell and Hunt toward the end of the last century, and their published documents and those of their successors run into a score of volumes. Most of the texts are from the Roman and Byzantine* centuries. They provide a vivid picture of daily life in the town and have richly added to the non-biblical records of Christianity. Two pages of "*logia*," that is, sayings of Jesus, have been found, fragments of apocryphal gospels, and many documents illustrative of the common life in which the early followers of Christ lived.

BIBLIOGRAPHY: B. P. Grenfell and A. S. Hunt, *Oxyrhynchus Papyri* (1898–); C. M. Cobern, *The New Archaeological Discoveries* (1922), passim; M. S. Enslin, *IDB*, 3 (1962), 614–16; W. White, Jr., *ZPEB*, 4 (1975), 556–57.

EMB

P

PADDLE. Ancient Near Eastern paddles appear to have had a blade at one end of the shaft only. The paddle was operated by hand and worked independently of a fixed rowlock. Clay* models of boats from Egypt* dated about 3500 B.C. have shown that a paddle-like device was inserted into the forked stern of river boats to act as a rudder.* Lightweight vessels on the inland waterways of Mesopotamia* and Egypt were generally propelled by means of paddles, and models of boats from these countries have illustrated the stance of the operator. Large seagoing Phoenician* vessels (cf. 1 Kings 9:26–27) were propelled by rows of oars, and this constituted a development of paddle operation. The most ancient paddles in existence were found in a Neolithic* site in a swamp in Yorkshire, England.

BIBLIOGRAPHY: *ANE* (1970), pls. 105, 676.

RKH

PAHEL. *See* PELLA.

PAINT; PAINTING. The use of colored pigments and similar substances for decorating a wide variety of articles occurred from the Neolithic* period. Painted pottery* was found at Tepe Gawra,* Jericho,* Tell el-Judeideh, and other locations, setting a pattern for the much more elaborate work of the Chalcolithic* period as represented at Tell Halaf, Tell el-Obeid, and elsewhere. The practice of painting patterns on the clay* cone mosaics* used on the inner walls of houses* arose in the al 'Ubaid period, the colors favored being red and black. The Neolithic houses of Jericho frequently had painted walls, and in succeeding periods it became fashionable for houses to be decorated by means of painted designs, as at Teleilat el-Ghassul. Late Bronze Age* levels at Megiddo* (Stratum VIIA) revealed that the plastered walls of a palace had been painted in several colors, following traditions established in Assyria and Egypt,* where animal figures carved in bas-relief* were often painted (cf. Ezek 23:14 KJV). From the beginning of the Old Kingdom period the Egyptians indulged in elaborately painted coffins (*see* SARCOPHAGUS) whose colors are often vivid millennia later.

Painting is seldom mentioned in the Bible, and at that mostly in a negative fashion, as with the eye paint of Jezebel* (2 Kings 9:30), the decor of Jehoiakim's palace (Jer 22:14), or the shields of the Medes* and Babylonians when they attacked Nineveh* (Nah 2:3).

Green malachite paint was used from about 4000 B.C. onward as a cosmetic,* as indicated from exca-

. Silver boat model with leaf-blade paddles found in tomb of "King's Grave" at Ur; 25th century B.C.. Courtesy University Museum, University of Pennsylvania.

vations at the lowest levels of Susa* and elsewhere. This substance was a mild astringent and was originally employed to treat or prevent ophthalmia but quickly became popular as an aid to beauty. Cosmetic palettes have been recovered from Iron Age II* (c. 800–600 B.C.) levels in Palestine, consisting of several round bowls about 10 cm. (4 in.) in diameter and standing on a flattened base. Babylonian and Egyptian women used rouge, while paint sticks were discovered in a toilet set found at Ur* and dated about 2500 B.C. In the Annals of Sennacherib,* Hezekiah of Judah* contributed stibnite, a form of antimony used in eye paint, as part of his levy for the Assyrians. From the New Kingdom period onward the Egyptians also used lead sulphide for cosmetic purposes.

BIBLIOGRAPHY: R. J. Forbes, *Studies in Ancient Technology*, 3 (1956).

RKH

PALACE. *See* CASTLE.

PALAEOBOTANY. The scientific examination of prehistoric and other forms of vegetable material. Prehistoric remains of especial value have been recovered from moist areas such as marshes or bogs, where the water has assisted in preserving the artifacts.* In Mesopotamia* and elsewhere, the character of woven articles such as mats can be determined from the imprint left behind in the moist clay,* long after the original material has disintegrated. Valuable information on early crop cultivation has also been obtained by these studies.

HWP

PALAEOGRAPHY, GENERAL. The study of palaeography (lit., "ancient writing") is the study of lettering on such materials as papyrus* and parchment.*

In this it contrasts with epigraphy.* It is normally divided into Greek* palaeography, Latin* palaeography, etc., each of which is a specialized study.

In the study of palaeography two distinctions are fundamental. The first is between book hands and documentary hands. Book hands are the careful and conservative styles of writing* used in the copying of books; documentary hands are the freer and more rapid styles used in documents and letters. Documentary hands, in which speed of execution was of prime importance, develop and alter more quickly than book hands, and so diverge rapidly from them. Speed of execution is achieved in particular by simplifying the shapes of the letters and joining the letters to each other; the result is the type of writing called cursive (literally "running"), a feature of documentary hands.

The other fundamental distinction is between majuscule and minuscule scripts. Majuscule scripts are those in which all the letters lie between two parallel lines (as, e.g., A B K Y); minuscule scripts are those in which the letters lie between four parallel lines (as, e.g., a b k y). Majuscule scripts are historically the earlier; minuscule scripts are generally developed from cursives.

There are various types of majuscule scripts; for Greek the most important is that known as uncial. The uncial script in Greek is characterized principally by the rounded shape of the letters ε, C, and ω (which developed in the first half of the third century B.C.); it continued thereafter with minor modifications as the sole book hand for over one thousand years, being eventually replaced during the ninth century A.D., by which time it had become too heavy and elaborate for common use. The Codices Sinaiticus, Alexandrinus, and Vaticanus are all in uncials (see CODEX).

The Greek documentary hand, like the uncial script, developed from the type of majuscules known as epigraphic capitals (which are characterized in particular by the angular shape of the letters E and Σ); but it diverged early and became cursive during the third century B.C. This cursive script supplied the pattern for the Greek minuscule book hand which was developed by scribes in Constantinople in the ninth century A.D. and superseded the uncials. It continued in use with minor modifications until the invention of printing.

Because both the book and the documentary hands change and develop with the passage of time, it is possible to date a manuscript or document from its script. Dating by this means is not always necessary, as many manuscripts and documents carry their own date upon them; but where the date is not so given the evidence from writing can provide a useful approximation. Some of the major signposts for dating Greek writing have already been indicated; two others may be mentioned: (a) the replacement in the fourth century A.D. of papyrus by parchment as the main material for book production; the use of parchment encouraged a more careful and heavier style of uncials with the vertical strokes thicker than the horizontal ones; (b) the practice of suspending minuscule letters from the line rather than standing them upon

it, which began near the end of the tenth century A.D.

The variant forms of individual letters enable one to date both book and documentary hands more closely within these broad outlines.

BIBLIOGRAPHY: *OCD*; L. Whibley, *A Companion to Greek Studies* (1905).

WFR

PALAEOGRAPHY, HEBREW. This field of study (*see* PALAEOGRAPHY, GENERAL) does not afford the investigator as much material as can be found in cuneiform,* although even before the beginning of the Late Bronze Age,* about 1500 B.C., there were inscriptions being written in a primitive script, variously described as early Canaanite,* proto-Phoenician, or proto-Sinaitic. Such alphabetic* scripts must have been used by Moses (cf. Exod 24:12; 34:27), Joshua (cf. Josh 8:32), Samuel (cf. 1 Sam 10:25), and contemporary literate officials (cf. 1 Chron 4:41 et al.). This form of writing* evidently comprised a development of the Canaanite* "pseudo-hieroglyphic" script of about 2000 B.C. No "book hands" are extant from this period, and the script has only survived on more durable substances such as stone and potsherds (shards*). A later phase of the proto-Sinaitic script occurred in inscriptions from Byblos (Gebal*), Lachish,* and Beth Shemesh,* and these were followed chronologically by the tenth century B.C. script found on the Iron Age* sarcophagus* of Ahiram* (c. 1000 B.C.).

The writing on the Gezer* calendar* is by an unskilled person, and contrasts forcibly with the carefully inscribed Moabite Stone* (c. 850 B.C.), whose letters already showed a cursive tendency. Appar-

Drawing of Mesad Hashaviahu (near Yavne Yam) ostracon, late seventh century B.C., an example of cursive Hebrew script from First Temple Period. The text is a letter from a reaper to the governor complaining that an officer had unjustly confiscated his garment. Courtesy Carta, Jerusalem.

ently the Arameans* adopted the Phoenician* script about 1000 B.C. and subsequently introduced certain consonants to indicate final long vowels, a feature present in both Moabite and Hebrew texts from the ninth century B.C. onward. Hebrew script, both lapidary and cursive, was a descendant of the Phoenician. The earliest group of cursive texts is the Samarian ostraca,* dated in the reign of Jeroboam II, which were written in a clear, professional script related to that occurring in the Siloam tunnel inscription* (c. 701 B.C.). A more developed cursive form was found in the Lachish Letters* (c. 590 B.C.), which were written in good classical Hebrew and employed dots as word dividers.

Aramaic* script became increasingly cursive from c. 600 B.C. onward, as on the Bar Rekub stele* and also on a papyrus* document sent from Palestine to Egypt* about 604 B.C. Persian Aramaic produced a semiformal script about 225 B.C., resembling those of the Palmyrene and Nabataean* inscriptions. Early in the following century the Palestinian Jews* adopted modified Aramaic square characters, an early phase of which appeared in the Nash Papyrus* (c. 150 B.C.). The angular Phoenician script was perpetuated by the Samaritans,* and also survived in a modified form on second-century B.C. coins* and in some Dead Sea* materials. These latter exhibit a mixture of archaic and contemporary lettering, and these are of great importance for the study of the formal and cursive hands used between the third century B.C. and the second century A.D. Scripts emerging from the Herodian (30 B.C.–A.D. 70) and post-Herodian periods can be recognized readily and dated accurately. Throughout the OT period and well into the medieval Christian era, all Hebrew writing was in consonantal form, and aside from the use of certain vowel-letters no attempt was made to indicate how the words were to be vocalized.

BIBLIOGRAPHY: I. J. Gelb, A Study of Writing (1952); S. Birnbaum, The Hebrew Scripts II (1954–57).

RKH

PALAEOLITHIC. The Old Stone Age, before 10,000 B.C.

PALAEOPATHOLOGY. A study of ancient human bones and other tissues as a means of gathering information on disease, fractures, malnutrition, and dental decay in early ages of man's history. The conditions under which a person lived or died can often be revealed by an examination of human bones, which sometimes also show evidence of wounds and deformities. Modern methods of reconstituting and staining the tissues of Egyptian mummies occasionally reveal the presence and nature of ancient bacterial bodies. Palaeopathology has also been applied to the bones of prehistoric animals.

HWP

PALAEOSEROLOGY. A method of testing the circulatory system of human bodies in which amounts of blood have been preserved, either by being dried or cooled at a rapid rate. Such tests have occasionally yielded some information about ancient blood groupings.* The method is still highly experimental and at present depends too heavily upon variables in the nature and content of the available samples to be at all reliable.

HWP

PALERMO STONE. A celebrated Egyptian artifact* recording the union of Upper and Lower Egypt* under one king. By the Fifth Dynasty it had become customary in Egypt to inscribe historical material on pieces of stone, and the Palermo fragment contains one of these annals. It is a small black diorite rectangle, about 41 cm. (16 in.) high, 25 cm. (10 in.) wide, and nearly 7.6 cm. (3 in.) thick. It is divided neatly into rows of oblong spaces containing hieroglyphic* signs furnishing names of rulers in Lower Egypt and annals from the First Dynasty. The Cairo fragment of the Palermo Stone included predynastic rulers and recorded the invasion of Asia by King Djer (Athothis II). Lines 2 and 3 furnish records from the period of the First Dynasty, though the beginning of that dynasty is missing from the inscription. Lines 4 and 5 deal with the Second Dynasty, and the Third Dynasty commences in some detail with Line 6. Most of the Fourth Dynasty is missing, and the record of the stone ends during the Fifth Dynasty.

See EGYPT.

BIBLIOGRAPHY: FLAP, 70, 74, and pl. 27.

RKH

PALESTRA (PALAESTRA) (pə les′trə). A school or a structure devoted primarily to training in wrestling,* though often used for training and exercise in other sports (see GAMES) as well.

PALIMPSEST. A parchment* or papyrus* sheet in which new material has been written upon a used, and mostly erased, original. This latter writing is frequently quite valuable and can be recovered to some extent by infrared photography.

PALMYRA (pal mī′rə). Probably to be identified with OT Tadmor,* a city about 193 km. (120 mi.) NE of Damascus* which was built by Solomon* as part of his policy of opening and consolidating trade routes linking Israel* with Syria and Mesopotamia* (2 Chron 8:4). The Roman name Palmyra ("date palm") arose from a confusion between the names Tadmor and Tamar (Semitic word for date palm), the latter being in Judea.*

The excavations have been carried out by archaeologists of many nations, most recently Swiss (1954–56) and Polish (1957–). Artifacts* show that the oasis was occupied from the second millennium, but the earliest ruins on the very extensive site of Roman Palmyra are those of the sanctuary of Bel. They consist of a large courtyard 205 by 210 m. (672 by 688 ft.), with the temple itself at the center, entered by a propylaeum* 35 m. (115 ft.) wide. Here were worshiped not only Bel (assimilated by then into the Greek Zeus*) but also Jahribol the sun-god and Aglibol the moon-god. An inscription dates the foundation to A.D. 32, but beneath the temple inscriptions belonging to its predecessor date from 44 B.C. In the Valley of Tombs the "tower-hypogeum" type also dates to the early Imperial period. The Christian basilicas* belong to the late Empire.

BIBLIOGRAPHY: T. Wiegand, *Palmyra* (1932); J. Starcky, *Palmyre* (1952); D. Schlumberger, *La Palmyrène du Nord-Ouest* (1951); K. Michalowski, *Palmyra* (1970).

BFH

PALYNOLOGY. A study, also called pollen analysis, of the character and distribution of grains of pollen with reference to the changing nature of vegetational zones. In northern Europe, these latter have been dated (*see* DATING) precisely by radiocarbon techniques, and a chronology* has been established. Pollen samples can thus provide invaluable information about the environment at the time when the sites were settled originally. As with some other forms of analysis, palynology is not without its difficulties and limitations.

HWP

PAMUKKALE. *See* HIERAPOLIS.

PANNONIA. *See* ILLYRICUM.

PAPHOS (pā'fos). A town on the SW coast of Cyprus,* capital of one of its four districts and called New Paphos (modern Baffo) to distinguish it from Old Paphos nearby, famous for the shrine of the Phoenician* goddess Astarte, whose cult the Greeks adapted to the worship of Aphrodite. Tacitus in describing the visit of Titus* in A.D. 69 calls the temple "renowned among both natives and foreigners" (Tac. *Hist.* 2:2), and its (Phoenician) foundations were discovered in 1888, including a Greek inscription of the period of Tiberius (*OGIS* 2.585).

At New Paphos Paul met the Roman proconsul Sergius Paulus* (Acts 13:6–12), perhaps the L. Sergius Paullus of an inscription of the same Claudian (*see* CLAUDIUS) period (*CIL* 6.31545). Considerable Roman remains have been found—harbor moles,* city wall,* amphitheater,* and temple.

BIBLIOGRAPHY: E. Oberhummer, "Paphos," *RE* (1896–1913); G. Hill, *A History of Cyprus*, 1 (1949); J. M. Houston, *ZPEB*, 4 (1975), 588–89.

BFH

PAPYROLOGY. This branch of archaeological, literary, and historical studies derives its material from surviving papyrus* documents and has to do with their discovery, identification, and decipherment. Speaking to an Oxford audience in 1937, Sir Frederic Kenyon mentioned the surprising fact that the word "papyrology" was first used only in 1898, and somewhat apologetically, in a review of the second British Museum catalog. The word *papyrus* is old, going back to Theophrastus in the fourth century before Christ, and its lineal descendant *paper* is a common word today.

With few exceptions—notably three, certain Greek papyri from the excavated ruins of the Campanian town of Herculaneum,* overwhelmed by Vesuvius

in August A.D. 79, a few samples from Dura-Europos* on the Euphrates, and some medieval documents from Ravenna—surviving papyri come from Egypt* S of the Delta. There are papyri in Egyptian, Hebrew, Greek,* and Latin.* There are literary papyri which have proved important contributions to the corpus of Aristotle and to Greek elegy comedy. The nonliterary papyri date from 311 B.C. to the seventh century. They come from the wrappings of mummies, the stuffed bodies of sacred crocodiles,* and from mere wastepaper heaps—all manner of documents which have the same degree of unity one might find in the sacks of wastepaper sent to a modern paper mill for pulping.

They have proved, wrote J. H. Moulton half a century ago (*Grammar of NT Greek*, I, Prolegomena, 3), "a treasure which has been perpetually fruitful in surprises. The attention of the classical world has been busy with the lost treatise of Aristotle and the new poets Bacchylides and Herodas, while theologians everywhere have eagerly discussed new sayings of Jesus. But even these last must yield in importance to the spoil which has been gathered from the wills, official reports, private letters, petitions, accounts, and other trivial survivals from the rubbish heaps of antiquity."

References to papyri go back to the middle of the eighteenth century and are scattered through the sparse records of early nineteenth-century archaeology, but it was not until the last decade of the century that the unique value of the papyrus documents was recognized and systematic search and preservation begun.

In the season of 1889–90 Sir Flinders Petrie, excavating in the Fayyum, found a number of mummies encased in a cartonnage (linen and papyrus glued together in many thicknesses) of papyrus. This casing was found to be composed of Greek documentary and literary texts dating from the third century B.C. They are now known as the Petrie Papyri and include parts of the *Laches* and *Phaedo* of Plato written down within a hundred years of his death, some more Homer, and about a hundred lines of the lost *Antiope* of Euripides.

The oldest surviving literary papyrus, the *Persae* of Timotheus, seems to be the only document certainly antedating Alexander's conquest of Egypt* in 332 B.C. The earliest dated document is a marriage* contract from Aswan,* of 311 B.C. The latest extend beyond the Arab conquest of A.D. 642. The papyrus documents from Egypt, then, cover a thousand years of Hellenistic, Roman, and Byzantine* history. Their immense variety has provided a picture of life over all these vital centuries, amazing in detail. At least 20,000 texts have already been published, including some 1500 literary texts. The mass of as yet unpublished material cannot be assessed.

In a bundle of papyri acquired by Sir Wallis Budge were writings by Isocrates, Demosthenes, and Hyperides, as well as a lost treatise by Aristotle. In 1956 the collection of the sayings of Christ known popularly as the *Gospel of Thomas** was brought out of Egypt. In 1959 a lost play of Menander from a recently discovered papyrus was produced in Geneva, and the famous Greek writer of comedies, without whom the Romans would not have had Plautus and Terence, achieved a modern triumph by appearing in the Third Programme of the BBC. His newly discovered play, *Dyscolos*, or *Grumpy Man*, was acted on that occasion.

Light thrown on the NT by the papyrus documents is wide and varied. There are private letters without number which show the nature of letter writing* in the ancient world. Their contents are of invaluable social significance, casting intimate light on life as it was lived on common levels. There are legal documents which illustrate many pages of the NT. The Common Greek of the NT is often paralleled and explained by the language of the nonliterary papyri. So, too, is the historical background—the census returns and associated documents, for example.

BIBLIOGRAPHY: Nonliterary papyri: A. S. Hunt and C. C. Edgar, eds., *Select Papyri*, 2 vols. (Loeb, 1932–34). Recent material: New books, newly edited texts, and all associated papyrological material appear in the annual bibliography of Greco-Roman Egypt in the *JEA*. A brief treatment of papyrology relating to NT studies: E. M. Blaiklock, *The Archaeology of the NT* (1970), passim.

EMB

PAPYRUS (pə pī´rəs). The *cyperus papyrus* is a sedge which still grows plentifully in the Sudan, where it reaches the height of nearly 8 m. (25 ft.). In ancient days, as abundant evidence proves, the papyrus grew also in the northern Nile Valley, especially in the rich swamplands of the Delta. Very early in Egyptian history it was adopted as an emblem in Lower Egypt,* to match the lotus emblem of the upper division of the land. The papyrus is a graceful plant and may be seen in pictures of Egyptian goddesses, held in the hand as a symbol of divinity; its clustered buds gave the architect a theme for decoration.

The papyrus stem had manifold uses. Bound in bundles, for example, it provided handy rafts or canoes, for use in those bird-hunting expeditions in the fenlands loved by Egyptian sportsmen. But above all, the tough pellicles of the stem gave mankind its first cheap and practicable writing* material.

Pliny the Elder, the Roman admiral and scientist, has left a long description of the manufacture of writing material from the papyrus stem. This was called hieratic* paper because it was devoted in earlier times only to the writing of books of religion. Placed crisscross on the board, the slices of reed were beaten together and pressed until the natural glue of the plant bound the sheets into a strong thin lattice of fiber.

According to Pliny, the Emperor Claudius,* most scholarly of the Roman rulers of the first century, took some interest in the quality of papyrus. Pliny writes: "The reason was that the thin paper of the period of Augustus* was not strong enough to stand the friction of the pen, and, moreover, as it let the writing show through, there was a fear of a smudge being caused by what was written on the back, and the great transparency of the paper had an unattractive look in other respects. Consequently, the foun-

Cyperus papyrus plant growing around Lake Huleh in Galilee (before the lake was drained). Courtesy Israel Government Press Office.

dation was made of leaves of second quality and the woof or cross layer of leaves of the first quality. Claudius also increased the width of the sheet, making it a foot across. There were also eighteen-inch sheets called *macrocola*, but examination detected a defect in them, as tearing off a single strip damaged several pages. On this account Claudius' paper has come to be preferred to all other kinds."

The surface was smoothed with pumice, and the result was a durable writing paper. If kept dry, it survives well to this century and probably will survive well into the future. South of Cairo it never rains, and in fortunate consequence the writings of dwellers in Egypt under five empires—Egyptian, Persian, Greek, Roman, and Islamic—have survived to charm, amuse, or instruct the modern world.

Papyrus farming was big business in Egypt, for the commercially-minded rulers of Alexandria* speedily recognized its value, and the system of control devised by the Ptolemaic bureaucracy covers comprehensively the harvesting and sale of the plant. There are numerous contracts in existence, themselves on surviving papyrus, which indicate the legal thoroughness with which a meticulous officialdom governed the industry.

BIBLIOGRAPHY: A. S. Hunt and C. C. Edgar, eds., *Select Papyri*, 2 vols. (Loeb; 1932–34).

EMB

PAPYRUS ANASTASI. Egyptian material dating about the thirteenth century B.C., comprising a miscellany of texts compiled for educational purposes.

PARADISE, HILL OF. *See* HERODIUM.

PARCHMENT. Eumenes II of Pergamum* (197–158 B.C.) is said to have promoted the manufacture of this rival to the Egyptian papyrus.* Hence "pergamena carta," whence "parchment." It was made from sheep or goat* skin, or sometimes, for the superior variety known as vellum, from calf or kid skin. It was naturally much more expensive than papyrus. The parchments of 2 Tim 4:13 were probably OT Scriptures but could have been documents of citizenship.

Much parchment has demonstrated its durability by surviving for modern examination and scrutiny. Samples have been found as far from Pergamum as Dura on the Euphrates and dated within the early years of Eumenes's reign (king of Pergamum, 197–158 B.C.; 1 Macc 8:8). Papyrus was replaced by its more expensive rival material in the early Christian centuries. Jerome records that worn papyri in the library of Caesarea* were replaced by vellum, and Constantine's edict supplying fifty copies of the Bible to the churches of his capital specified vellum. The Vatican and Sinaitic codices (*see* CODEX) of the Bible are vellum.

EMB

PASARGADAE (pə sär′gə dē). The capital of Persia chosen by Cyrus.* The name may be a variant of *Parsagard*, "Camp of the Persians," *Parsagert*, "The Fortress of Fars," or *Parsagadeh*, "The Throne of Fars."

I. *The Site.* Pasargadae is located in Fars (the province of ancient Persia [*see* SUSA] in SW Iran), 44 air km. (27 air mi.) NE of Persepolis* or about 80 km. (50 mi.) by road. It lies in the Mashhad-i-Murghab or plain of the Pulvar River over 1,830 m. (6,000 ft.) above sea level. It is almost entirely surrounded by mountains. To the SW is the gorge of the Tang-i-Bulaqi, where an ancient road can be traced. The area is bitterly cold in winter and hot in summer.

The buildings of Pasargadae are scattered over a wide area as befits the first capital of the half-nomadic Persians. There are no outer walls* to define its limits.

II. *History.* Though there seem to be some pre-Achaemenid deposits, Pasargadae became a major settlement after Cyrus chose it as his capital to commemorate his victory over the Medes* in 550 B.C. Most of the buildings date from 546 to 530. Darius* contributed some work on the citadel* and on Palace P. Even after Darius established his new capital at Persepolis, Pasargadae served as the religious center where Persian kings were inaugurated. According to Plutarch, the new king, dressed in the robe of Cyrus, was crowned in the sanctuary of a goddess (Anahita).

Alexander the Great seized Pasargadae without fighting and removed from its treasury some six thousand talents of bullion. He paid his respects at the tomb of Cyrus and upon his return from India was outraged to discover that the tomb had been looted.

III. *Excavations.* Near Cyrus's tomb Muslims established a cemetery and built a mosque in the thirteenth century A.D. It was R. Ker Porter in the nineteenth century who was the first to identify the tomb as that of Cyrus from classical descriptions.

The first excavations were conducted in 1928 by E. Herzfeld. Ali Sami of the Iranian Archaeological Department conducted excavations at the site for five years beginning in 1949. D. Stronach of the British Institute of Persian Studies excavated at Pasargadae from 1961 to 1963, primarily in the citadel area.

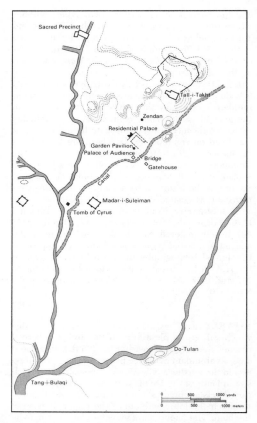

Sketch plan of Pasargadae from D. Stronach, "Excavations at Pasargadae, Third Preliminary Report," *Iran*, III (1965).

IV. *Monuments.* The monuments are concentrated in four major areas: (1) the Sacred Precinct to the NW; (2) the Citadel about a km. (nearly 1 mi.) to the SE of the Sacred Precinct; (3) the Palace area 500 to 1,000 m. (580 to 1,150 yd.) SW of the Citadel; (4) the tomb of Cyrus 1,500 m. (1,600 yd.) SW of the Palace area.

A. *The Sacred Precinct.* There are two altars of white and black limestones, cubical in shape, and about two m. (6 ft.) high. Olmstead suggests that these were twin altars* to Ahura-Mazda and to Anahita, Godard that they were altars to the sacred elements of fire and of water.

A nearby terrace, about 70 by 40 m. (75 by 43 yd.), is built upon a natural rock outcrop. The terrace seems to be of a later construction than the altars, which date from Cyrus's settlement. There is no evidence that the terrace served as a foundation for a temple; the sanctuary of Anahita must therefore have been located elsewhere.

B. *The Citadel.* The citadel of the *Tall-i-Takht*, "Hill of the Throne," or *Takht-i-Madar-i-Suleiman*, "The Throne of the Mother of Solomon," as it is called, is an impressive terrace, built upon a hill rising 50 m. (54 yd.) above the plain. The terrace proper rises 12 m. (39 ft.) high and is built of well-drafted limestone blocks fitted together with metal butterfly-shaped clamps over an inner core of rubble. The platform covers an area 200 by 130 m. (216 by 140 yd.).

Stronach's investigations have revealed three major occupational periods: (1) Period I, the original establishment of Cyrus; (2) Period II, from 522 to 280 B.C.; (3) Period III, 280 to 230 B.C. There was also a brief occupation during the late Sassanian or early Islamic period.

The unfinished platform of Cyrus was transformed by Darius into a mud-brick citadel. An aerial photograph (see AERIAL PHOTOGRAPHY) by E. Schmidt also revealed a polygonal circuit of mud-brick walls about the citadel. Neo-Babylonian* booty found in the wall indicates that it was begun by Cyrus. A limestone cover over a drain in the citadel turned out to be a copy of Xerxes'* Daiva inscription. Period II was ended by violence in 280 B.C., perhaps by a national revolution at the time of the death of Seleucus I, whose coins* are included in two hoards which were discovered.

C. *The Palace Area*. 1. *The Zendan-i-Suleiman* or "Prison of Solomon" was a quadrangular tower 600 m. (656 yd.) SW of the Tall-i-Takht. All that stands today is one wall about 13 m. (16 yd.) high with three rows of false windows. A better preserved and nearly identical structure is the Ka'aba-i-Zardusht at Naqsh-i-Rustam near Persepolis. It has been suggested that Darius may have built the Ka'aba to take the place of a ruined zendan.

The function of these two towers is much in dispute. There are three theories: (1) It has been suggested that they were tombs (Dieulafoy, Herzfeld, Sami) or temporary repositories for the dead (Godard, Goldman); (2) Others (Hinz, Ghirshman, Zaehner, Duchesne-Guillemin) have suggested that they were fire temples; (3) Henning and Mallowan believe that they were repositories for archives or royal objects.

2. *The Residential Palace*, or Palace P, is located 300 m. (328 yd.) SW of the zendan. It is a structure 77.5 by 44 m. (83 by 48 yd.) that had six rows of five columns. Nylander concludes from the presence of toothed chisel marks that this was one of the latest of Cyrus's structures. Borger and Hinz have identified an inscription from this palace as that of Darius. Not all would agree with their conclusion that all the Old Pers. inscriptions at Pasargadae were inscribed by Darius.

3. *The Palace of Audience*, or Palace S, is located 300 m. (328 yd.) S of the Residential Palace. It was a hypostyle* hall, 45 by 56 m. (49 by 60 yd.), with black stone bases and white columns.

4. *The Gatehouse*, or Palace R, is a monumental entrance to the palace area 200 m. (220 yd.) SE of the Palace of Audience. It measured but 22 by 26.5 m. (24 by 28 yd.). In Herzfeld's day the main doorways were flanked by colossal winged bulls, not a trace of which remains today. One white limestone jamb bears a figure who wears a triple Atef Egyptian crown, four wings, and an Elamite* garment. Mallowan suggests that it may represent Cyrus himself. More plausible

is Barnett's identification with the Phoenician* god Baal.* A broken jamb from Palace S depicts a man clad in a fish garment of an Assyrian type. Barnett suggests that these may represent iconographically Cyrus's religious toleration.

5. *The Garden and the Bridge*. Excavations by Stronach in 1963 uncovered two new structures. Between the Palace of Audience and the Gatehouse Stronach uncovered the remains of a bridge which had five rows of three stone columns about 2 m. (6 ft.) high. The superstructure may have been wooden.

Between the Palace of Audience and the Residential Palace a garden* pavilion was discovered. In this area the excavators found a jar with thirty-seven different kinds of precious objects, including gold* bracelets, earrings, bells, silver* spoons, coral, and pearl beads. The objects, which date between 450 to 350 B.C., may have been hidden as Alexander approached.

D. *The Tomb of Cyrus*, called the *Qabr-i-Madar-i-Suleiman*, or "The Tomb of the Mother of Solomon," was described by many classical writers. They inform us that the tomb was surrounded by a wooded park and that Magi offered daily sacrifices of sheep and monthly sacrifices of horses.* Arrian (Arr. *Anab.* 6.29.8) reports that there was an inscription which read: "Mortal! I am Cyrus son of Cambyses, who founded the Persian empire, and was Lord of Asia. Grudge me not, then, my monument."

The imposing tomb of white limestone, 5.5 m. (6 yd.) high, rests upon a six-level base also 5.5 m. (6 yd.) high. The structure may be patterned after a ziggurat,* but many of the features are Ionian and Lydian* in origin. There is a small entrance to the inner chamber which once held the golden sarcophagus* of Cyrus.

The gabled roof is formed of five enormous stones which are arranged around a relieving hollow space, discovered by Sami in 1951. In 1969 Stronach discovered the faint design of a rosette on the NW pediment, perhaps a symbol of Ahura Mazda (supreme creative deity), which inclines him to believe that Cyrus may have been a Zoroastrian.

In 1950 a cruder parallel to Cyrus's tomb was discovered in a valley SW of Kazerun in the Sar Mashhad region. The monument of white limestone is called the *Gur-i-Dokhtar* or "The Tomb of the Daughter."

BIBLIOGRAPHY: A. Jackson, *Persia Past and Present* (1906), 278–93; E. Herzfeld, "Pasargadae," *Klio*, 8 (1908), 1–68; id., "Bericht über die Ausgrabungen von Pasargadae 1928," *AMI*, 1 (1929–30), 4–16; E. Schmidt, *Flights over Ancient Cities of Iran* (1940), 18–19; A. Olmstead, *History of the Persian Empire* (1948), 59–67; E. Schmidt, *Persepolis* I (1953), 20–25; R. Ghirshman, *Iran* (1954); R. Barnett, "Pasargadae and the Source of Achaemenid Art and Architecture," *Iraq*, 19 (1957), 74–77; R. Borger and W. Hinz, "Eine Dareios-Inschrift aus Pasargadae," *ZDMG*, 109 (1959), 117–27; H. Treidler, "Pasargadae," *PWRE*, Supplement 9 (1962), cols. 777–99; D. Stronach, "Excavations at Pasargadae, First Preliminary Report," *Iran*, 1 (1963), 19–42; R. Ghirshman, *The Art of Ancient Iran* (1964), 12–34; D. Stronach, "Excavations at Pasargadae, Second Preliminary Report," *Iran*, 2 (1964), 21–39; B. Goldman, "Persian Fire Temples or Tombs?" *JNES*, 24 (1965), 305–8; G. Jenkins, "Coin Hoards from Pasargadae," *Iran*, 3 (1965), 41–52; D. Stronach, "Excavations at Pasargadae, Third Preliminary Report," *Iran*, 3 (1965), 9–40; G. Cameron, "An Inscription of Darius from Pasargadae," *Iran*, 5 (1967), 7–10; D. Stronach, "Urartian and Achaemenian Tower Temples," *JNES*, 26 (1967), 278–88; C. Nylander, "Who Wrote the Inscriptions at Pasargadae?" *Or-Suec*, 16 (1967–68), 135–78; R. Barnett, "Anath, Ba'al, and Pasargadae," *MUSJ*, 45 (1969), 407–22; C. Nylander, *Ionians in Pasargadae* (1970); D. Stronach, "A Circular Symbol on the Tomb of Cyrus," *Iran*, 9 (1971), 155–58; T. Kawami, "A Possible Source for the Sculptures of the Audience Hall, Pasargadae," *Iran*, 10 (1972), 146–48; E. Yamauchi, "The Achaemenid Capitals," *NEASB*, 8 (1976), 20–25; D. Stronach, *Pasargadae: A Report on the Excavations Conducted by the British Institute from 1961 to 1963* (1978). EY

PASSOVER PAPYRUS. This letter, one of the Assuan (Aswan*), or Elephantine, papyri* was sent to the Jewish garrison at Elephantine* in the fifth year of Darius II, 419 B.C. It is a heavily damaged text but appears to concern a festival in Nisan from the fourteenth to the twenty-first day on which leavened bread is prohibited. The Passover preceded the Festival of Unleavened Bread. This appears to be archaeological evidence for the observance of the Passover, although the word is not used. Furthermore, it is evidence for the observance in a place other than Jerusalem* (a geographical limitation which would seem to follow from Deut 16:5–8). The colony, of course, already had a temple, infringing Deut 12:5.

The fact that the letter bears the royal authority is illustration of documents in Ezra bearing the authority of the king although dealing with Jewish religious matters. It further illustrates the Persian policy of fostering Jewish religion, in recognition of its purity and political usefulness. The text, as given in *DOTT*, 259, is as follows: "[To] my [brethren Yedo]niah and his colleagues the [J]ewish gar[rison], your brother Hanan[iah]. The welfare of my brethren may the gods [seek..]. Now this year, the fifth year of King Darius, an order was sent from the king to Arsa[mes, saying '... Jew]ish [garrison].' Now therefore do you count four[teen days of the month Nisan and ke]ep ..., and from the fifteenth day after the twenty-first day of [Nisan .....]. Be ritually clean and take heed. [Do] n[o] work [... ..no]r drink ..., and anything whatever [in] which the[re is] leaven [do not eat ... from] sunset until the twenty-first day of Nis[an..... do not br]ing [it] into your houses, but seal [it] up between [these] day[s]. [......ki]ng. [To] my brethren Yedoniah and his colleagues the Jewish garrison, your brother Hanan[iah]." EMB

PATARA (pat'ə rə; Gr. Πάταρα, *Patara*, a name that is linked with Patarus, son of Apollo). An im-

portant seaport of Lycia, a rugged area in southwestern Anatolia. Located about 11 km. (7 mi.) E of the mouth of the Xanthus River, Patara served as the harbor for the city of Xanthus but was important in its own right as one of the six largest cities* of the Lycian league. Its ruins are located near the modern village of Gelemish.

Biblical Reference. On his last journey to Jerusalem* Paul sailed into Patara from Rhodes.* There he transferred to a ship* that was sailing directly to Phoenicia* (Acts 21:1–2). Codex* D suggests that it was at the port of Myra,* a Lycian* city to the E, that Paul made the transfer.

The Oracle. Patara was noted for an oracle of Apollo, where the god spent his winter months while absent from his more famous home at Delos.

History. Herodotus (fifth century B.C.) refers to Patara's oracle (1.182). The city surrendered to Alexander the Great in the winter of 334–33. In 275 B.C. Ptolemy* II seized the port and renamed it after his wife Arsinoe. A century of Egyptian domination prospered the city's trade. Antiochus III captured Patara in 197. In the peace of Apameia, Lycia was allotted to Rhodes until 167 B.C., when the Lycians were permitted to organize an independent federal league under the protection of the Romans.

Patara fell to Brutus in 42 B.C. But for the most part the Lycians enjoyed their independence for two centuries until Claudius* annexed it in A.D. 43 and joined Lycia to Pamphylia to form one Roman province. Some late sources say that the legendary St. Nicholas (fourth century) was born at Patara, though he is usually associated with Myra.

Monuments. Patara was rediscovered by Francis Beaufort in the British Admiralty survey of southern Turkey in 1811–12. The entrance to the port, which was 250 m. (270 yd.) wide and 1 km. (c. ½ mi.) long, is now covered with sand, with marshes further inland. Numerous travelers in the nineteenth century and a few in the twentieth century have reported on the visible ruins. Still to be seen are parts of the city wall,* a triple-arched gate,* open sarcophagi,* and a granary* erected by Hadrian. Outstanding is a fine theater* dating from the time of Tiberius and refurbished in A.D. 147.

Numerous inscriptions have been recorded. One of them reports the building of a bath at Patara by Vespasian* but mainly through local funds. Quite noteworthy are the number of Patarans in the second century A.D. who rose to prominent positions in the Roman government and who were able to make generous benefactions to the city.

In 1952 a brief salvage operation was conducted at Patara by F. J. Tritsch and A. Dönmez. In 1974 a survey of the visible monuments was conducted by G. K. Sams and A. Bilgütay.

BIBLIOGRAPHY: W. J. Conybeare and J. S. Howson, *The Life and Epistles of St. Paul*, 2 (1857), 225–27; O. Treuber, *Geschichte der Lykier* (1887);

E. Kalinka, ed., *Tituli Asiae Minoris*, 2.1 (1920), 141–81; G. Radke, "Patara," *PWRE*, 18 (1949), col. 2555–61; D. Magie, *Roman Rule in Asia Minor*, I (1950), 516–39; F. J. Tritsch and A. Donmez, ". . . a Colossal Head of Apollo, and Other Discoveries in the Ancient Cities of Lycia," *ILN*, 202 (March 21, 1953), 450–51; F. Stark, *The Lycian Shore* (1956); S. Jameson, "Two Lycian Families," *AnSt*, 16 (1966), 130–37; D. Ferrerro, *Teatri Classici in Asia Minore*, 2 (1969), 123–33; E. Akurgal, *Ancient Civilizations and Ruins of Turkey* (1970), 261–62; G. K. Sams, "Investigations at Patara in Lycia, 74," *ARC*, 28 (1975), 202–4; G. E. Bean, *Lycian Turkey* (1978).

EY

PATINA. A term for the greenish carbonate of copper film (aerugo) formed on copper and bronze* after prolonged exposure to dampness or contact with acid. The underlying metal is thereby protected from further contact with oxidizing substances.

PATMOS. A small volcanic island in the SE Aegean, in the group called the Sporades. It lies about 56 km. (35 mi.) W of Miletus,* and is 40 km. (25 mi.) in circumference. On the isthmus at its center the ruins of a Greek settlement have been excavated, but better known is the traditional site of the vision of John (Rev 1:9-11), a cave* on a hill in the southern part of the island below the monastery of St. John the Divine.

BIBLIOGRAPHY: *PWRE*, 18, 4th ed. (1949), 2174–91.

BFH

PAVEMENT. *See* GABBATHA.

PEDIMENT. In classical architecture, the triangular area forming the gable of a roof, and frequently decorated by elaborate carvings.

PEDOLOGY. A study, also called soil analysis, of the buried soil of a site in order to determine the environmental conditions at the time of the burial. Confirmation of results can frequently be obtained by means of pollen analysis (*see* PALYNOLOGY) and phosphate analysis.*

HWP

PELLA. Originally a Canaanite* city* called Pahel, on the E side of the Jordan Valley (the site of modern Tabaqat Fahil). The name occurs in Egyptian records of the second millennium, but the city perished in local wars before the Israelite conquest. Some pottery* of the Bronze* and Iron ages* survives.

The site was resettled by Macedonian Greeks after 332 B.C. and given the similar name Pella (from the Macedonian capital). Josephus states that it was restored by Pompey (Jos. *Antiq.* 13.15.4), and the remains of a theater* and tombs survive from the Greco-Roman period. In A.D. 66 the Christians left Jerusalem* for Pella, in view of the predictions of the city's destruction (Mark 13:14), but the history of the church in Pella lies beyond biblical times. The site has not been excavated but was surveyed in 1933 and 1958.

BIBLIOGRAPHY: N. Glueck, *The Other Side of the Jordan* (1940), 158–200; id., *AASOR*, 25–28 (1951), 254–57; R. Smith, *AASOR Newsletter*, 9 (1967–68); R. L. Alden, *ZPEB*, 4 (1975), 672.

BFH

PEN. *See* INK AND PEN.

PENNY. *See* DENARIUS.

PEREA (pə rē′ə). Perea was the Greek term for the Trans-Jordan, and in particular signified that area of Herod the Great's kingdom bounded on the E by Heshbon,* Philadelphia,* and Gerasa,* while its N limit was situated at Pella.* The capital was Gador, modern Tell Gadur. In the original allocation of Canaanite* territory to the Israelites, the area was to be taken from the Ammonites,* Moabites,* and Gileadites, and given to Reuben, Gad, and the half-tribe of Manasseh. Because of its position as a buffer for the territory W of the Jordan, it was always open to attacks from the E. In the Maccabean* period, Judas Maccabeus transported an oppressed Jewish minority from Perea to Judah* for safety (1 Macc 5:9–54). John Hyrcanus (135–104 B.C.) and Alexander Janneus (103–76 B.C.) each conquered and Judaized Perea, and in 57 B.C. the city of Amathus, apparently the N capital of Perea beyond the Jabbok, became a district of Palestine. On Herod the Great's death, his son, Herod Antipas (4 B.C.–A.D. 39) inherited the territory.

Perea is only mentioned once in the NT, in a variant reading of Luke 6:17, but its citizens were included in the crowds that followed Jesus and experienced His healing (cf. Matt 4:25; Mark 3:8). The place where John was baptizing (John 1:28) was the city of Bethany,* located in Perea. When Christ and His disciples left the Galilee* area to come to Jerusalem* (Matt 19:1), they stayed for a time in Perea before journeying along the Jordan valley to Judea.

The area has been occupied intermittently since Chalcolithic* times. Rabbah,* modern Amman, which was named Philadelphia in the intertestamental period, is the oldest continually occupied city in the world.

BIBLIOGRAPHY: G. Dalman, *Sacred Sites and Ways* (1935), 233–39; N. Glueck, *Explorations in Ancient Palestine III*, *AASOR*, 18–19 (1939), 140, 143; E. W. Saunders, *IDB*, 3 (1962), 728–29; R. L. Alden, *ZPEB*, 4 (1975), 695–96.

RKH

PERFUME. *See* CHEMICAL TECHNOLOGY; OINTMENT.

PERGA. One of the principal cities of Pamphylia, a Roman province of Asia Minor.* It was built on a rocky elevation in the plain of Pamphylia, about 13 km. (8 mi.) from the coast and close to an E-W road. The site may have been occupied as early as the Middle Bronze Age,* and by the late Mycenaean* period it was a Greek colony, dedicated to the cult of Artemis.*

Little is known about the history of the city* prior to Alexander the Great, who passed through it twice. After his death it came under Seleucid control, and subsequently rose to prominence under the Romans. The ruins at the site, located near modern Murtana, comprise an acropolis* on a rocky outcrop, a lower city which was perhaps Hellenistic in origin, and some other monuments. The lower city has attractive remains including a stadium,* traces of colonnaded streets* and shops, a theater,* and public baths. No trace of the cult temple of Artemis has been found to the present.

Perga was visited twice by Paul and Barnabas on their first missionary journey (Acts 13:13), once on their way to Antioch* in Pisidia, and the second time on their return (Acts 14:25). The earliest Christian churches at the site only date to the fourth century A.D.

BIBLIOGRAPHY: A. M. Mansel and A. Akarca, *Excavations and Researches at Perga* (1949); A. M. Mansel, *Arch. Anz.* (1956), 99–120.

RKH

PERGAMUM (PERGAMOS) (pûr′gə mum). Of all the seven churches of Asia mentioned in Rev 2–3, Pergamum contains perhaps the most archaeological material. It has been well excavated but suffered much wanton damage during World War II. It is situated in a commanding position, with a view of far ranges, the sea, and the purple peaks of Lesbos, and had been, when John wrote, a city-seat of government for fully four hundred years. It was a capital city* in pre-Roman days, and when the last of her kings bequeathed his kingdom to the Romans in 133 B.C., Pergamum became the chief town of the new province of Asia. It was natural, then, that the first temple of the imperial cult, the worship of the emperor on which the Christians looked with such deep abhorrence, should be located there. A temple to Rome* and Augustus* was erected in Pergamum in 29 B.C. But other cults beside that of Rome were endemic at Pergamum. There was the worship of Asklepios, the god of healing, whose symbol was a serpent. The Asklepion, or temple of healing dedicated to this deity, was largely excavated in the 1930s, complete with its dormitory accommodations. A coin* of Pergamum, commemorating an imperial visitor, shows the Emperor Caracalla standing, spear in hand, before a great serpent coiled around a bending sapling. The emperor raises his right arm in the exact gesture of the Nazi salute.

The letter to Pergamum is addressed to those who live "where Satan has his throne" (Rev 2:13), and Christians must have found something peculiarly satanic in the town's preoccupation with the serpent image. Pausanias of Lydia,* the Greek traveler who wrote many descriptions of ancient cities, spoke of Asklepios as "sitting on a throne with a staff in his hand, and his other hand upon the head of a serpent." The serpent was, in fact, a totem of the god, and harmless varieties of snakes had free run of such shrines. The church in Pergamum obviously found the surrounding symbolism of paganism quite diabolical.

Pausanias also mentions the magnificent throne-like altar* to Zeus* that stood on the acropolis* crag dominating the city. The altar commemorated the defeat of a Gallic invasion of Asia. Recovered by German archaeologists, the great block of decorated stone was taken to Berlin where it forms a major exhibit in the East Berlin Museum, rebuilt after the fashion of twenty centuries ago in a huge silent hall, uniquely lighted. Its base is some 36 m. (118 ft.) long and nearly the same width. It rises to a height of perhaps 15 m. (50 ft.). In form it might be the entrance to some gigantic temple. Above three sides of the base a graceful colonnade runs, set with dozens of slender pillars. A flight of twenty-six wide marble steps rises up to its center, which contains a small sanctuary. Immediately below the colonnade are set the friezes* that are the altar's chief glory.

They tell the story of the legendary struggle between the gods and goddesses of Olympus and the giants. Athene, her face long since obliterated, clutches the hair of a rising giant. Hekate thrusts a torch into the face of another, and there stands Artemis,* her shattered arm still poised to hold a bow. The giants, in accordance with Pergamum's prevailing obsession, are represented as a brood of Titans, with snakelike tails. Curiously enough, examination by experts from the British Museum of a battered marble figure of a giant, which has been lying for some years in the junkyard of the Workshop Town Council in a London suburb, has led to the startling conclusion that the statue* may be one of the missing figures from the frieze surrounding the altar of Zeus.

BIBLIOGRAPHY: E. M. Blaiklock, *The Cities of the NT* (1965), 103–6; id., *ZPEB*, 4 (1975), 701–4.

EMB

PER-RAMESSES. See RAMESES, CITY OF.

PERSEPOLIS (pûr sep′ə lis). Capital city* of Darius I,* son of Hystaspes, who was king of the Persians 521–486 B.C., then of his son Xerxes,* 485–465 B.C. (for the former, see Ezra 4:5, Hag 1:1, Zech 1:1; for the latter, Ezra 4:6, Esth 1:1 [KJV, Ahasuerus]). Although second in importance to Susa,* Persepolis was renowned for its buildings before their destruction by Alexander. The ruins are situated N of modern Shiraz in SW Iran and have been excavated chiefly by E. Herzfeld, E. F. Schmidt, and the Iranian government.

The central feature is a huge terrace with retaining walls, into the W side of which were built two flights of monumental stairs. On the terrace were Darius's audience hall (Apadana) and palace, also Xerxes' "hall of a hundred columns," palace, and harem. Bas-reliefs* of the Apadana and stairs vividly portray Persian soldiers and subject nations.

BIBLIOGRAPHY: E. F. Schmidt, *Persepolis*, 2 vols. (1953–57); R. Ghirshman, *Iran* (1961); W. White, Jr., *ZPEB*, 4 (1975), 707–9.

BFH

PERSIA. See SUSA.

PETER, HOUSE OF. The Franciscan G. Orfali excavated a street* paved with basalt at Capernaum*

Remains of apadana, or audience hall, at Persepolis, begun by Darius (521-486 B.C.) and completed by Xerxes (485-465 B.C.).

(Tell Hum) and uncovered hand mills* and olive* presses. This was over half a century ago. In 1968 V. Corbo, in a probe beneath a fifth-century octagonal church, discovered the traces of a fisherman's* quarter. Pilgrims' graffiti* convinced him that he had discovered Peter's house, but no certainty can attach to these claims.

BIBLIOGRAPHY: V. Corbo, "St. Peter's House Rediscovered," *Christian News from Israel*, 20.1–2 (1969), 39–50; V. Corbo and S. Luffreda, *Ricordi di S.Pietro sul Lago di Tiberiade* (n.d.).   EMB

PETER, TOMB OF. That Peter as well as Paul was martyred at Rome* under Nero is a natural inference from statements made by successive Christian writers from Clement of Rome (c. A.D. 96) onward; it was so well known that most of them assume it rather than state it. Dionysius, bishop of Corinth* (c. A.D. 170), states it explicitly (Eus. *Hist.* 2.25.8); a decade or two later the Roman presbyter Gaius goes farther when he says that he can point out the "trophies" or monuments of the two apostles on the Vatican and the Ostian Way respectively (Eus. *Hist.*, 2.25.7). It was in the belief that Peter was actually buried at the site indicated by Gaius that Constantine (306–337) excavated the side of the Vatican hill to accommodate the foundations of his basilica* of Peter. The present basilica was erected on the same site in the sixteenth and seventeenth centuries, after its predecessor had been demolished to make way for it. Reports of excavations and discoveries in the foundations were made at that time, but by present-day archaeological standards their formulation is unsatisfactory and their significance ambiguous.

Fresh excavations undertaken in 1939 and the following years led to the discovery of an extensive pagan necropolis* of the second and third centuries beneath the basilica. Of special importance for our present subject was the discovery of a small columnar monument in relation to which Constantine's whole basilica appears to have been oriented. If this monument is of comparable date with a water channel near it, which was constructed in the time of Marcus Aurelius (and probably before his accession as emperor in A.D. 161), it was a generation old when Gaius mentioned the "trophy" of Peter on the Vatican, and is almost certainly to be identified with that trophy. But it need not have marked the tomb of Peter; it may have been erected at or near the place of the apostle's martyrdom. That Nero's circus,* where many of his Christian victims met their death, stood on the Vatican hill we know from the elder Pliny (Pliny *NH* 36.11.74) and Tacitus (Tac. *Ann.* 14.14.4). But, whatever the original intention of Peter's monument was, it came to be accepted that his actual tomb lay beneath what is now the high altar* of St. Peter's.

The matter might rest there, were it not for the *Memoria Apostolorum ad Catacumbas*, under the basilica of St. Sebastian at the third milestone on the Appian Way.* From the mid-third to the mid-fourth century it was popularly believed that the remains of both Peter and Paul lay here, and it was a well-frequented place of pilgrimage. The abundance of graffiti* on this site (excavated in 1915) invoking Peter and Paul contrasts with the absence of such inscriptions in the neighborhood of the Vatican monument. The coexistence in Rome of two sites claiming to be Peter's last resting place was inconvenient, and Pope Damasus (366–383) set up an inscription at the site on the Appian Way which said in effect: "Peter and Paul used to live here, but you will find them here no more." The two claims have been reconciled by the theory that Peter's remains were moved to the Appian Way under Valerian (A.D. 258) and brought back to the Vatican hill by Constantine; but of this there is no evidence. Quite probably his body was not recovered after his execution, and the best that could be provided for him was a cenotaph.*

BIBLIOGRAPHY: O. Cullmann, *Peter: Disciple-Apostle-Martyr* (1953); B. Van Elderen, ZPEB, 4 (1975), 733–39; J. M. C. Toynbee and J. B. Ward-Perkins, *The Shrine of St. Peter and the Vatican Excavations* (London, 1956).

FFB

PETHOR (peth'ər). A city* of Mesopotamia* and the home of the venial prophet Balaam, Pethor (Num 22:5; Deut 23:4) in 'Amaw is the Pitru of Hittite* texts and described as Ashur-utir-aṣbat in Assyrian records. It was located near the confluence of the Sagur (modern Sajur) and the Euphrates rivers. A fifteenth-century B.C. Egyptian text mentions chariot* timber from 'Amaw, "the god's land" (i.e., the East) "in the hill-country of Naharen" (i.e., hills overlooking the two rivers).

BIBLIOGRAPHY: *ANET*, 278; *BASOR*, 118 (1950), 15–16, n. 13.

EMB

PETRA (pē'trə). The ruins of this Nabataean* city,* situated in the Trans-Jordan on the E side of Wadi Arabah, were discovered by Burckhardt in 1812. Petra has sometimes been identified with OT Sela (Judg 1:36; 2 Kings 14:7; Isa 16:1), both words meaning "rock" or "cliff," but the oldest tomb remains of Petra do not go back further than the sixth century B.C., following the occupation of Edom* by the Nabataean Arabs. Sela may be the name of several sites in the vicinity of Petra, but it is principally identified with the Edomite stronghold which was taken when Amaziah slaughtered ten thousand Edomites in the Valley of Salt, and which was renamed Joktheel (2 Kings 14:7). This has been identified by N. Glueck with the settlement on a plateau 305 m. (1,000 ft.) above Petra, Umm el-Biyyara, with artifacts* belonging to the Early Iron Age.*

The chief remains of the later, or "classical," Nabataean period are the monumental tombs and the open-air sanctuaries. Of the former the most notable are el-Khayneh and Qasr Far'on; of the latter the "Conway" High Place* within Petra itself, and the Great High Place excavated by G. L. Robinson. This is marked by a rectangular court and two altars,* all hewn from solid rock. These sanctuaries have thrown light on the OT "high places" of the Iron Age.

For Aretas IV,* last of the Nabataean kings, see 2 Cor 11:32. The famous rock-cuts or mausoleums of Petra belong to the second century A.D., when the city was capital of Roman Arabia* and at the height of its fame for the caravan trade. It dominated the major routes in Syria and Palestine.

It was early in the last century that Jean Louis Burckhardt, first of modern travelers, visited Petra. His journals, with ample commentary, have recently been published by Katherine Sim (*Desert Traveller* [1969]), and it is easy to catch the note of wonder and awe that the ruins have inspired in visitors from Hadrian in A.D. 131 to H. V. Morton between World Wars I and II. The place captured the imagination of the last century, inspiring Dean Burgon's sonnet with its well-known concluding line: "A rose-red city half as old as time."

The Treasury is Petra's gem. It is a temple to Isis built by Hadrian, placed artistically opposite the very mouth of the cleft in the rock, which is the rock city's only western gate. Other Roman remains include paved streets,* a theater,* and some ruined buildings.

BIBLIOGRAPHY: G. L. Robinson, *The Sarcophagus of a Vanished Civilization* (1930), 1–171; W. G. Albright, *The Archaeology of Palestine*, 160ff.; id., "The High Place in Ancient Palestine," *Volume du Congrès* (1957), 242–58.

BFH and EMB

PHILADELPHIA. This ancient city* in the valley of the Cogamus, named by Attalus II Philadelphus of Pergamum* in honor of the "brotherly love" (Gr. *philadelphia*) he held toward his brother Eumenes, retains nothing of archaeological interest. The modern Turkish country town of Alasehir no doubt covers much of significance. Numismatics (*see* COINS) contains some evidence of a change of name in gratitude for the relief given by imperial bounty after the great earthquake of A.D. 17 (Tac. *Ann.* 2.47). The name given was Neocaesarea and appears on a few coins but did not survive. The "new name" of Rev 3:12 no doubt refers to this.

BIBLIOGRAPHY: W. M. Ramsay, *The Letters to the Seven Churches of Asia* (1904), 391–412; E. M. Blaiklock, *The Cities of the NT* (1965), 120–23; id., ZPEB, 4 (1975), 753–54.

EMB

PHILIP, GOSPEL OF. A NT apocryphal gospel forged in the name of Philip, a disciple of Christ. One such document is cited by Epiphanius (*Panarion* 26.13.2–3) who quotes it as saying, "The Lord revealed to me what the soul must say in its ascent to heaven, and how it must answer each of the powers above."

A Coptic Gospel of Philip (written in Sahidic) was found in 1945 with other gnostic documents in thirteen codices in upper Egypt,* near Nag Hammadi* and near ancient Chenoboskion. It is not absolutely clear whether this "gospel" is the same as the one cited by Epiphanius.

This pseudonymous (*see* PSEUDEPIGRAPHA) Coptic document of thirty-six pages of text consists of a continuous discourse of exposition of 127 sayings. Philip's name was possibly attached to the work because the biblical Philip baptized Simon of Samaria* (Acts 8:12f.), who was thought by some to be the founder of Gnosticism. This Coptic document seems to have been associated with the Valentinian type of Gnosticism, although there are parallels to teachings in

Khaznet Far'un at Petra; Roman temple-like tomb, c. A.D. 25, according to Abraham Negev. The façade consists of two Corinthian orders placed one above the other. The portico has three entrances leading to lateral halls. In the upper order, at the center is a Tholus and on its sides, two pavilions each bearing a broken pediment. In the space between the columns are remains of reliefs probably representing female figures. Photo courtesy of Inguar Karmhed.

other schools of Gnosticism.

The original *Philip* was probably written in Greek, and since the writer considers himself a Christian (cf. Sayings 6, 102) and to be within the apostolic tradition (Saying 47), this original version was probably written not later than c. A.D. 200. The Coptic version found in Egypt probably comes from the fourth or fifth centuries A.D.

BIBLIOGRAPHY: J. Doress, *The Secret Books of the Egyptian Gnostics* (1960), 144, 221–25; E. Hennecke, *NT Apocrypha*, W. Schneemelcher and R. McL. Wilson, ed. (1963), 271–78; R. McL. Wilson, *The Gospel of Philip* (1962); A. K. Helmbold, *The Nag Hammadi Gnostic Texts and the Bible*

(1967), 64–71; R. McL. Wilson, *ZPEB*, 4 (1975), 759.

WHM

PHILIPPI. A Roman colony and the leading city of that district of Macedonia (Acts 16:12) where, following Paul's visit, a notable Christian church was founded. The site (modern Filibedjik) was excavated by the French from 1914–38. Called earlier "The Springs," it was established as a city-state by Philip II of Macedon, taking his name. From this period a wall,* citadel,* and theater* have been identified. Under Rome Philippi lay at the E end of the Via Egnatia (*see* EGNATIAN WAY), which ran between the citadel and the forum;* it gave its name to the famous battle of 42 B.C. fought by the Ganga River W of the city.*

As Luke has recorded, Philippi had been settled as a colony of Roman citizens in the early Empire; it was one of six such foundations and the full title appears on coins,* "colonia Julia Augusta Philippensis" (compare the references to citizenship in Phil 1:27; 3:20). The account in Acts is notable for some technical terms which are verified by inscriptions: *archons* ("authorities") and *strategoi* ("magistrate"; 16:19–20), *hrabdouchoi* ("officers"; Lat. *lictors*; 16:35). As might have been expected with a mixed Thracian, Greek, and Roman population, religious practices were diverse; temple sites and inscriptions show the dominant Greco-Roman deities, together with Cybele, Bendis, Isis, and Sarapis.

Lydia, "a dealer in purple cloth" (Acts 16:12–14), was the first Christian convert (the word [PU]RPURARI on an inscription is further evidence of the trade in purple dye), and there is some speculation as to the location of the place of prayer "outside the gate" by the riverside (16:13). Rather than the gate* in the wall* of the city, it is more likely to have been the Roman arch,* of which ruins survive, to the W, by the Ganga River.

BIBLIOGRAPHY: P. Collart, *Philippes, ville de Macédoine*, 2 vols. (1937); id., *Philippes et la Macédoine orientale a l'époque chretienne et byzantine* (1945); P. Lemerle, *Philippes et la Macédoine orientale*, 2 vols. (1945); A. Rupprecht, *ZPEB*, 4 (1975), 759–62.

BFH

PHILISTINES. Known in antiquity as Pulusati, the Philistines comprised one of a number of maritime groups, collectively described as the Sea Peoples,* who exerted a political and cultural influence in the Near East during the second millennium B.C., and finally overran much of the eastern Mediterranean at the end of the Bronze Age.* They are usually thought to have been Aegeans, but they were not basically mariners, preferring instead to establish their cities* somewhat away from the sea coast.

In the Patriarchal period, which is usually equated with the Middle Bronze Age,* Philistine beginnings were traced back to Casluhim, son of Mizraim, son of Ham (Gen 10:14). The mention of Egypt* (Mizraim) may well reflect what appear to be the Egyptian origins of Minoan* culture, and perhaps allude also to the possibility of contacts with the Aegean world in the Middle Bronze Age I period. Abimelech, the Philistine king of Gerar,* bore a Semitic name, but that of his general Phichol is of unknown origin and is certainly non-Semitic in character, a situation which might also suggest a mixed origin for the Philistines. There are no known archaeological deposits associated with these peoples at this time, and Philistine artifacts* as such only begin to be attested toward the end of the second millennium B.C. However, it is probable that the Babylonian *Kaptara* and the Egyptian *kftyw* in Middle Bronze-Age documents are related to the OT Caphtor and refer to some Aegean location, probably Crete. There is now clear evidence of an expansion of Aegean trade during the Middle Minoan period (c. 1900–1700 B.C.), which

corresponds to the early part of the Middle Bronze Age. Aegean artifacts coming from this period have been unearthed at Hazor,* Ugarit,* Abydos,* and elsewhere.

Fourteenth-century B.C. Ugaritic sources referred to Ashkelon* and Ashdod* as trading centers, while the Amarna letters* mention Gath,* Gaza,* Joppa,* and Ashkelon, as well as noting the incidence of raids by the piratical Lukku (Lycians). Fourteenth-century B.C. pottery* from Aegean sources has also been found at Ashkelon, Gaza, and Tell Jemmeh. The foregoing evidence suggests that it is a mistake to regard the mention of the Philistines in the patriarchal narratives as an anachronism. Instead, it seems highly probable that the Philistines of the Middle Bronze Age had definite Aegean origins and were in fact early representatives of the same maritime group which subsequently gave the land of Palestine its familiar name. Late-Helladic* IIIB (thirteenth-century B.C.) material has been excavated at Ashkelon, Tell el-Hesy* and Tell Jemmeh, while a number of Cretan seals* discovered near Gaza have been taken as indicating the existence of an indigenous industry in Philistia.

The conquest of Canaan* included the capture by Judah of Gaza, Ashkelon, and Ekron* (Judg 1:18), and excavations at Isdud (Ashdod) appear to support this tradition. Archaeologists have found clear evidence of violent destruction there during the middle of the thirteenth century B.C., the best explanation of which relates it to the Israelite conquest of Canaan* under Joshua. What is most probably the precursor of Philistine pottery appeared in Cyprus* and elsewhere in the Aegean at the end of the thirteenth century B.C. In the following century this variety of pottery (Late Helladic IIIC) occurred in Palestine for the first time at Tell el-Farah, and for the next one hundred years it was represented in all the major areas of Philistine occupation as well as in the adjacent sites of the Negev* and the Shephelah.* The pottery of the Philistine plain was quite distinctive, being a composite imitation in local clay* of the later Mycenaean* wares. Typical of Philistine pottery are large two-handled bowls of cream-ware, decorated with stylized birds. Beer jugs of the same ware generally had one handle and a strainer spout and bore geometric designs in red and black. The size and frequency of these jugs indicate that the Philistines consumed large quantities of beer. Cylindrical jars were also typical of Palestinian pottery in the Settlement period. During the time of Ramses* III, the Canaanites adopted the Egyptian practice of burying their dead in clay coffins which resembled large storage jars. The body was lowered into the container through an opening in the upper part, which was then closed by means of a matching piece of clay. On this latter surface were molded human features of a stylized nature, along with other occasional engravings (*see* COFFIN TEXTS). One such thirteenth-century B.C. coffin bearing a hieroglyphic* inscription was unearthed at Lachish.* The Philistines seem to have taken over this practice from the Canaanite population, for in twelfth- and eleventh-century B.C. tombs at Tell el-Farah in the Negev and from Iron

Left: Philistine stirrup jar from Gezer. Right: krater from Ashkelon. Both c. 1200-587 B.C. The decorations on the Philistine ware are usually in the upper band, which is divided into metopes by straight or curvy lines. The drawings include spirals enclosing a cross and stylized birds with heads turned backward. Courtesy Carta, Jerusalem.

Age levels at Beth Shan,* these anthropoid containers were found in association with Philistine pottery. Similar coffins have been unearthed outside Philistine territory in some parts of the Nile Delta, which would suggest that the Egyptians were adopting these containers in preference to their own wooden ones.

From the mortuary temple of Ramses III* at Medinet Habu* come battle scenes which depicted three contemporary groups of Sea Peoples, namely the Peleset, Tjekker, and Sherden. Their military uniform included headdresses, kilts, round shields, daggers, and swords. One iron* sword recovered from twelfth-century B.C. levels near Jaffa (Joppa*) was of the same variety as those portrayed in the mortuary temple carvings. During the Judges period (twelfth and eleventh centuries B.C.) the Philistines were apparently the dominant group in a wave of Sea Peoples which occupied the coastlands of southern Canaan. They may, however, have included some of the Sherden, who had served as Egyptian mercenaries and who may perhaps have been settled by the Egyptians at strategic places in the Philistine plain as garrison troops. When the Hittite* Empire collapsed about 1200 B.C., the Philistines took over the smelting of ore (see REFINING) and the manufacturing of iron implements, this being previously a Hittite monopoly. During the next century they built up a flourishing trade in implements and weapons, and this, along with their distinctive pottery,* made the Philistines an important cultural force in Canaan at the end of the Judges period. The excavation of Philistine houses* has supported the tradition relating to the death of Samson* (Judg 16:25–30). This redoubtable opponent of the Philistines died in a building where he was able, by pulling on the central pillars, to bring about the collapse of the entire structure and the death of many Philistines. How this feat was possible has been made clear at several Philistine sites, where ruins have shown that some of their larger houses were built around a central hall. This in turn was bisected by a row of columns which bore the weight of the upper story and the roof.

Just prior to the Hebrew monarchy the Philistines overran Canaan, and at one stage defeated the Israelites at Shiloh.* Excavations there have shown

that in addition they burned the town to the ground. Its ruins were still in existence in the time of Jeremiah and were used by the prophet to teach a somber lesson to the Judeans (Jer 7:12–14). By the time of Samuel the Philistines were exercising full control over the manufacture and distribution of iron tools and weapons (see ARMS; cf. 1 Sam 13:19–20). Excavations at sites such as Tell Qasile,* near Tel Aviv,* and Gerar* throw some light on the nature of contemporary technology in Philistia. Both copper and iron had been processed at these sites, and the available evidence would indicate that iron implements were being used in the Philistine plain before being in general circulation in the uplands where the Israelites lived. The Philistine copper refinery at Tell Qasile was dated about 1000 B.C., at the end of Iron Age I and roughly contemporary with Saul and David. It was circular in shape, standing about 1.2 m. (4 ft.) in height with an open chimney at the top. The outside was insulated by means of a stone facing, while inside at the bottom was a tiled base on which the clay crucibles containing the ore were placed. An air channel dug into the ground and lined with mud bricks fed the prevailing winds to the coals beneath the crucibles. An Early Iron Age furnace* at Tell Jemmeh had flues on both sides. Others may perhaps have employed bellows (cf. Jer 6:29) either for use when there was insufficient wind or to function as the air supply when the ducts became choked with sand. During the excavation of Tell el-Ful* (Gibeah*), Albright found an iron plowpoint in the tell,* and dated it about 1010 B.C. As such it is one of the earliest iron implements recovered to date from the Palestinian highlands and recalls the barrier to Israelite material prosperity which the Philistines presented. Remains of wagons from the same general period indicate that they were made of wood,* while the relief of Ramses III shows that they were restricted to light loads and were usually drawn by a pair of oxen.* Egyptian records also make it clear that the Philistines engaged in a vigorous mercantile trade based on the sea lanes between Egypt* and Phoenicia.* The eleventh-century B.C. story of Wen-Amon, who had been sent to Phoenicia by the Pharaoh to purchase cedar* for the sacred barque of Amun at Thebes,* furnishes interesting sidelights on this aspect of Philistine culture, in which the Israelites may even have been partially involved. As a result of the conquests of David the Philistines went into decline, and their culture seems to have been absorbed by the Phoenicians.

BIBLIOGRAPHY: R. A. S. Macalister, The Philistines, Their History and Civilization (1914); W. F. Albright, AASOR, 12 (1932), 53–58; C. H. Gordon, Antiquity, 30 (1956), 22–26; T. C. Mitchell in D. W. Thomas, ed., Archaeology and OT Study (1967), 405–27; K. Kenyon, Archaeology in the Holy Land (1970), 221–39; E. E. Hindson, The Philistines and the OT (1971); J. C. Moyer, ZPEB, 4 (1975), 767–73.

RKH

PHOENICIA. A name used by the Greeks to designate ancient Canaan* and apparently not current earlier than about 800 B.C. The term originated from *phoinix* or ("purple dye") and was to the Greeks what the Hurrian* *kinaḫḫi* ("purple dye") apparently was to the Mesopotamian* traders and merchants. Whatever the intent of the Hurrian term, the Greek *phoinix* occurred in the Linear B* tablets from the Mycenaean* culture, indicating a trading relationship between Greece and Phoenicia as early as about 1200 B.C.

The land was approximately 193 km. (120 mi.) in length, with its S border at Mount Carmel* and its N extremity at the Eleutherus River (the modern Nahr el-Kebir). To the E Lebanon formed a natural defensive barrier as well as producing the supplies of almug, cedar,* and pine, for which the region was famous in antiquity. In the narrow coastal plain that was only about 8 km. (5 mi.) wide at its widest point, crops such as wheat, barley, garlic, and onions grew, along with grapes, date palms, olives,* and fig trees (*see* FOOD).

From excavations at Gebal* (Byblos) it appears that the area was inhabited about 4000 B.C. by a group that had cultural contacts with Sumer* and Egypt.* A millennium later invaders from the E settled along the coast, and these roving bands included some Semitic elements. They were contained in the Syria-Lebanon area by Sargon* I and others, and by the eighteenth century B.C. they were engaged in vigorous trade with Egypt, probably competing with the Syrian city-state of Ebla (Tell Mardikh*) in the process.

Phoenician cities suffered destruction at the hands of the Hyksos,* but were rebuilt and from about 1500 were spheres of Egyptian political influence. Toward the end of the Amarna* Age the Egyptians invaded Phoenicia, probably to thwart Hittite* interests, and again destroyed a number of Phoenician cities without, however, reducing Sumur, Beirut, and Sidon.* The Hittites were reasserting their interest in Phoenicia about 1385 B.C., probably with a view to imperial expansion, but in the event both nations were engulfed in destruction by maritime invaders about 1200 B.C.

A renewed Phoenicia was invaded a century later by Tiglath-pileser I* of Assyria, but under Hiram* of Tyre* (c. 981–947 B.C.) Phoenicia enjoyed its "Golden Age," forming successive alliances with David and Solomon* (2 Sam 5:11; 1 Kings 5:1). Phoenician sea trading was widespread in the Mediterranean, and one result of this was the establishing of colonies in such places as N. Africa, Sardinia, and Asia Minor.* Quite probably Phoenician vessels traded with producers in such areas of Britain as Cornwall and the Mersey district.

As discoveries at the Phoenician city of Ugarit* have shown, the religion of Phoenicia (a name that at the end of the Bronze Age* was synonymous with Canaan) was of a highly orgiastic and immoral nature. Its influence affected the Israelites under Ahab* of Israel* (c. 874–853 B.C.) and was one of the causes underlying the collapse and exile of the N kingdom in 722 B.C. A few years earlier, Tyre and Byblos had paid tribute to the vigorous Assyrian leader Tiglath-pileser III (745–727 B.C.), and this was reinforced when in 701 B.C. Sennacherib* of Assyria (704–681

B.C.) marched into Phoenicia, deported many inhabitants, and installed a puppet ruler over the remainder.

When Assyrian power collapsed in 612 B.C., the Babylonian ruler Nebuchadnezzar* II (604–562 B.C.) besieged Phoenicia and carried out further deportations. Phoenicia then experienced a serious decline in influence and trading ability, and ironically some of its own colonies took over the nation's trade in the W Mediterranean. A coalition of Phoenician cities supported the Persian rulers Cambyses (530–522 B.C.) and Xerxes I* (485–465 B.C.) against the Greeks, but suffered severely when Persian power in the Near East disintegrated under the attacks of Alexander the Great.

Phoenicia became Hellenized subsequently, and produced a famous philosopher named Zeno (*see* ZENO PAPYRI) the founder of Stoicism. The land fell under Seleucid rule after Alexander's death, and was incorporated into the Roman empire in 64 B.C. From 31 B.C. the "pax Romana" brought new prosperity to Phoenicia, and in NT times it was a prominent trading area once more, supplying dyed goods, timber, glassware,* fruits, grains, and fish (*see* FISHING) to the Levant and elsewhere. Some Phoenicians accepted the gospel (Mark 3:7; 7:24) and were also objects of early Christian evangelization (Acts 11:19; 15:3; 21:2).

The greatest contribution of Phoenicia to human culture was in the part played in the development of an alphabet* (*see also* WRITING). The Phoenicians improved upon Egyptian hieroglyphic* attempts at alphabetizing by integrating the alphabetic concept with cuneiform* writing. Alphabetizing was then transmitted through the Phoenicians and Hebrews to the Greeks, and subsequently to the Romans. Far more sinister was the influence of their sensuous fertility Baal* religion, which by some estimates was the most pervasive and depraved that the world has known.

BIBLIOGRAPHY: P. K. Hitti, *History of Syria, Including Lebanon and Palestine* (1951); W. F. Albright in G. E. Wright (ed.), *The Bible and the Ancient Near East* (1961), 328–362; A. S. Kapelrud, *IDB*, 3 (1965), 800–805; D. Harden, *The Phoenicians* (1962); J. Gray, *The Canaanites* (1964); H. A. Hoffner, *ZPEB*, 4 (1975), 778–82.   RKH

PHOSPHATE ANALYSIS. A study of the residue of phosphates left by decayed animal organic matter. Percolating water slowly removes the phosphate from the deposit, enabling a chemical assay to be made. The technique has been employed extensively in the examination of caves* to determine the nature of the occupation, on settlement sites to distinguish residential from industrial areas, and on burial grounds to establish the locale of a decomposed body.

    HWP

PHRYGIA. An ill-defined tract of territory in W Asia Minor* that had N and S extensions. The Phrygians have been traced back to Macedonia* and Thrace, and apparently made their first major occupation of W Asia Minor toward the end of the second millennium B.C. They were related to the Trojans, and during the epic period of Homer they were energetic and enterprising settlers (cf. Hom. *Il.* 3.184) who engaged in trading and viticulture. It is possible that the rock cities and sculptures of the "Phrygian Monument" territory S of Dorylaeum reflect this period of culture and commercial prominence, which declined immediately when Gyges of Lydia* (685–652 B.C.) extended his empire into W Asia Minor.

Phrygia became subject in turn to the Persians and Greeks, with its final subjugation occurring under the Romans between 133 and 25 B.C., when the territory became the imperial provinces of Asia and Galatia.* The Phrygian region of Galatia is mentioned in Acts 16:6, but it is improbable that Paul ever preached in the towns of the Lycus valley such as Hierapolis,* Laodicea* and Colosse.*

BIBLIOGRAPHY: A. H. M. Jones, *Cities of the Eastern Roman Provinces* (1937); D. Magie, *Roman Rule in Asia Minor* (1950); F. V. Filson, *IDB*, 3 (1965), 805–8; E. M. Blaiklock, *ZPEB*, 4 (1975), 784–86.

RKH

PHYLACTERIES. Known in Hebrew as *tefillin*, these were receptacles containing verses of Scripture bound on the forehead and arm during prayer or as a permanent demonstration of piety, in literal following of such passages as Exod 13:9–16 and Deut 6:8; 11:18. A complete head tefillin has been discovered at Qumran.* "Now," Professor Yadin says, "we can for the first time understand and visualize the shape and composition of the Tefillin in this early period."

Open capsule of head phylactery (*tefillin*) containing four separate compartments each with folded parchment, found at Qumran and dated c. first half of first century A.D. Courtesy Y. Yadin and Israel Exploration Society, Jerusalem.

He notes that the pious wore the Tefillin, especially that of the head, all day. "Now we see that the size and shape of the box were perfectly suited for this purpose." Furthermore, now for the first time, we can study such technical problems as the nature of the leather* used in making the box, the parchment* strips containing the biblical passages inserted into the box, and the threads of tendon and hair used to hold it all together.

BIBLIOGRAPHY: *SBK*, 4 (1928), 250–76; D. Barthélemy and J. T. Milik, *Qumran Cave I* (1953), 72–76; G. H. Davies, *IDB*, 3 (1962), 808–9; J. A. Thompson, *ZPEB*, 4 (1975), 786–88. EMB

PHYSICIAN. *See* MEDICINE.

PI-BESETH. *See* BUBASTIS.

PICTOGRAPHY. Literally "picture-writing," this is the earliest stage in the evolution of true writing.* A simple narrative or sequence of ideas is expressed by means of a series of pictures which carry the actions or ideas through to their conclusion; each picture is called a pictogram.

The most important point about pictography is that it is not confined to the representation of single, unconnected images but can follow through a narrative. It is this ability to present a sequence that justifies its being regarded as the earliest stage of true writing rather than merely as a forerunner. But pictograms are distinguished from alphabetic* scripts in that they have no phonetic connection with the language concerned. The pictures stand, not for sounds, but for things, and a narrative in pictographic writing could be read and understood by speakers of different languages. In this respect it might be regarded as superior to alphabetic writing (in which the signs denote sounds, not things); but from other points of view the alphabetic system is far more useful and convenient, as it can function with relatively few signs where a pictographic system requires a great many.

From pictograms developed ideograms,* in which each picture may denote not only the thing represented, but also analogous ideas, so that, e.g., a picture of the sun denotes not only the sun but also light, warmth, etc. Ideograms are one of the components of the Egyptian hieroglyphic* script.

See also WRITING, PICTORIAL.

BIBLIOGRAPHY: D. Diringer, *Writing* (1962); Y. Bar-Hillel, *Language and Information* (1964).

WFR

PICTORIAL WRITING. *See* WRITING, PICTORIAL.

PILATE, PONTIUS. *See* CAESAREA.

PIPE. *See* MUSIC.

PITCH. *See* BITUMEN.

PITCHERS. *See* VESSELS.

PITHOM (pi'thom; Heb. פִּתֹם, *pitom*; LXX, Πειθω, *Peithō*; from Egyp. *P[r]-[ʾ]tm*, "Mansion" or "Estate of Atum"). Pithom is mentioned only once in the OT, as a store-city built by the Israelites, along with Rameses,* on the eve of the Exodus (Exod 1:11). The name corresponds clearly to Egyptian Per-Atum, but this name is applicable to any center of worship of Atum. Succoth* (at Tell el-Maskhuta) had such a temple and so is by some thought to be biblical Pithom. However, as Succoth, not Pithom, fits and appears in the itinerary of the Exodus, it is possibly preferable to locate biblical Pithom about 14.5 km. (9 mi.) W of Tell el-Maskhuta, at Tell er-Rataba, where also Ramesside remains of a temple of Atum have been found. The question remains open for the present. A recent attempt by Uphill to identify Pithom with Heliopolis* goes against the known proper terminology for Heliopolis (Per-Re, rather than Per-Atum). The Hebrew for Heliopolis is *On*, and Heliopolis is too distant from Rameses to be linked with it as the scene of the Hebrews' labors.

BIBLIOGRAPHY: A. H. Gardiner, *JEA*, 5 (1918), 261–69; ibid., 10 (1924), 95–96; B. Porter and R. L. B. Moss, eds., *Topographical Bibliography of Anc. Egypt. Texts* . . . , 4 (1934), 53–55; ibid., 55; E. P. Uphill, *JNES*, 27 (1968), 292–99.

KAK

PITRU. See PETHOR.

PLAIN, CITIES OF THE. These five settlements, also called the cities of the valley, at the S end of the Dead Sea* included Sodom,* Gomorrah,* Admah, Zeboiim, and Zoar. The Valley of Siddim (i.e., of the Dead Sea) is part of the deep geological rift that is a prominent feature of Palestinian topography, and the Dead Sea lies in its deepest part. While earlier opinions concerning the location of these cities varied, some placing them at the N end of the Dead Sea, there is now a general consensus among scholars that they occupied the area now covered by the body of water S of the Lisan Peninsula. Baly speaks of this area as "a large and shallow bay," and suggests that the land may have subsided by reason of an earthquake, thus causing its flooding from the main body of water to the N. These cities were destroyed by the Lord (Gen 19:23–29) because of their wickedness and are referred to throughout Scripture as the prime example of divine retribution for sin. While geologists and archaeologists are in agreement concerning this location, no professional excavations have yet been undertaken.

The destruction of these cities is of great interest because of the frequent biblical references and the writings of early chroniclers, including Diodorus, Josephus, Strabo, and Tacitus. Brimstone (sulphur) and fire are referred to, and the catastrophic nature of the event is emphasized. Volcanic activity may have been involved, though Clapp denies its possibility. Certainly there was an earthquake, and burning asphalt along with natural gas may have been ignited by lightning or otherwise. Bitumen* and petroleum seepages still occur, especially under water, and large chunks may "calve" (break off) and rise to the surface. Geological investigation confirms the existence of bitumen deposits, with evidence of natural gas, especially in the vicinity of Jebel Usdum (Arabic, "Mount of Sodom"). This unique mountain of salt* and related petrographic materials extends some 10 km. (6 mi.) in length and is from 198 to 220 m. (650 to 720 ft.) in height. Winter storms have eroded its sides into fantastic pinnacles and shapes, some of which may have been identified with Lot's wife (cf. Gen 19:26). Pits of bitumen are referred to in Gen 14:10 as a deterrent to the battle in which Lot and his household were captured. The Lord warned Abraham in advance of His intention to destroy these wicked cities, giving the righteous an opportunity to escape.

There may be an inference in Gen 14:3 to the filling of this area with water. Historically, the end of contacts with these cities is indicated in the corpus of pottery* found at the site of Bab edh-Dra'* in the Lisan Peninsula. A time of between 2300 and 1900 B.C. is evident, and some feel that Abraham could have been involved at this early date.

1. *Sodom.* This city* is frequently mentioned in the Bible (thirty-six times) and often associated with Gomorrah as the epitome of a wicked city. Lot chose this area to reside in (cf. Gen 13:10–12; also note Gen 10:19). Its king was Bera, who was attacked by Chedorlaomer and his Mesopotamian* allies. Sodom may have been located near the W side of the embayment, near Jebel Usdum, on a stream called Seil en-Numeirah, or more centrally in the Wadi Arabah.

2. *Gomorrah.* As in the case of several of the other cities, this is also referred to in outlining the territory of the Canaanites* (Gen 10:19). Its King Birsha was also attacked by the Mesopotamian coalition. The location of Gomorrah is unknown but seems to have been adjacent to Sodom, in the fertile Valley of Siddim, before the rising waters of the Dead Sea covered it. In that case it could be located on the banks of the stream known as Seil 'Esâl. Together with Sodom it is frequently referred to as an example or warning because of its licentiousness (cf. Deut 29:23; 32:32; Isa 1:9–10; 13:19; Jer 23:14; 49:18; 50:40; Amos 4:11; Zeph 2:9; Matt 10:15; Rom 9:29; 2 Peter 2:6; Jude 7).

3. *Admah.* This settlement was included in the fate of the others. Its king was Shinab (Gen 14:2). Of uncertain location, it may be projected somewhere between Seil 'Esâl and Seil en-Numeirah. Along with Zeboiim, it is selected for special reference by the prophet Hosea (11:8).

4. *Zeboiim.* This city was also mentioned in connection with the boundaries of the Canaanites (Gen 10:19) and as one of the five cities attacked by Chedorlaomer and his confederates. Its king was Shemeber, who was defeated by the invaders (Gen 14:2, 8, 10). Its fall was referred to by Moses (Deut 29:23) and Hosea (11:8). Its location may have been on one of the streams flowing into the Dead Sea from its SE corner.

5. *Zoar.* Another of the "cities of the valley," its

king was called Bela ("little one"). It was to this settlement that Lot and his family finally escaped, and
it seems that it was not (at first) destroyed along with
the others, since the Lord allowed Lot to escape from
Sodom to Zoar. Perhaps it was located on somewhat
higher ground, on the banks of Seil el-Qurahi.

BIBLIOGRAPHY: M. Kyle, *Explorations in Sodom*
(n.d., prob. 1928), gen. ref.; B. Wyllie, "The Geol-
ogy of Jebel Usdum, Dead Sea," *The Geological
Magazine*, 68 (1931), 366–72; F. Clapp, "The Site of
Sodom and Gomorrah," *AJA* (1936), 323–44;
N. Glueck, "Explorations in Eastern Palestine II,"
AASOR, 15 (1934–35), 7–9; id., *BASOR*, 67 (1937),
19–26; G. Wright, *The Pottery of Palestine* (1937),
78–81; id., "The Chronology of Palestinian Pottery
in Middle Bronze I," *BASOR*, 71 (1938), 27–34;
J. Harland, "The Location and Destruction of the
Cities of the Plain," *BA*, 5 (1942), 17–32; ibid., 6
(1943), 41–54; D. Baly, *The Geography of the Bible*
(1957), 205–6; J. P. Harland, *IDB*, 4 (1962), 395–97;
G. H. Livingston, *ZPEB*, 1 (1975), 781–83.

MHH

PLASTER. Two substances for covering the inner,
and occasionally the outer, walls of buildings were
used by the peoples of the Ancient Near East. The
simplest of these was a layer of wet clay* (cf. Lev
14:42–43), which when hard formed a smooth, impervious surface. A more durable material was made
by heating powdered gypsum or limestone. When
applied carefully, this type of plaster provided an
even surface which could be engraved (cf. Deut 27:2,
4) or painted.* The plastering of floors and walls of
houses* was practiced from Neolithic* times, as shown
by excavations at Tell el-Obeid, Tepe Gawra,* Jericho,* and many other sites. At the beginning of the
Iron Age* the Israelites developed a thick, waterproof plaster which they applied to the inside of domestic cisterns,* basins, and underground silos. Most
probably they had learned the art of compounding
plaster from the Egyptians, who themselves used
plastered surfaces extensively in homes, temples, and
tombs. The plaster of Dan 5:5 (Aram. *gîrâ*) was actually the glazing* on the brickwork of the palace
wall (cf. Isa 27:9).

RKH

PLINTH. The square stone base of a column, pier,
or architrave.*

POLITARCH. One of the tests of Luke's accuracy
as a historian is found in the exactitude of the terminology used in the *Acts of the Apostles* for Roman
officials and the imperial government. Archaeology
provides a striking example in the case of the word
"politarch." In Acts 17:6, 8, Luke twice uses the term
politarches to denote rulers of Thessalonica. Since
the term had not been discovered elsewhere, critics
of the historian had dismissed the word as a mistake.
Today it can be read high and clear in an arch* spanning a street of Salonika (modern Thessalonika); and
sixteen other examples occur. It is accurately documented in extrabiblical sources as early as the 1882

edition of Liddell and Scott's *Greek-English Lexicon*.
It appears from epigraphical (*see* EPIGRAPHY,
GENERAL) evidence that there were five or six politarchs, but the number may not have been fixed,
and it is not possible to detail their functions. A relevant inscription runs as follows: "In the year 76 of
Augustus . . . To the Emperor Tiberius Claudius
Caesar Augustus Germanicus, pontifex in the fourth
period of his tribunician power, consul designate
for the fourth time, eight times acclaimed 'imperator,' father of his country, the city dedicates [i.e.,
probably 'this statue'] while Nicaratos, son of
Theodas, and Heracleides, son of Demetrius were
politarchs. . . ."

BIBLIOGRAPHY: D. G. Hogarth, "Inscriptions from
Salonica," *JHS*, 8 (1887), 360–61; E. D. Burton, "The
Politarchs," *AJT*, 2 (1898), 598–632; W. D. Fergu-
son, "The Legal Terms Common to the Macedonian
Inscriptions and the NT," *Historical and Linguistic
Studies in Literature Related to the NT*, Second Se-
ries, Vol. 2, Part 3 (1913), 65–66; E. Gabba, *Iscri-
zioni greche e latine per lo studio della Bibbia*; E. M.
Blaiklock, *The Archaeology of the NT* (1970), 95–
111.

EMB

POLLEN ANALYSIS. *See* PALYNOLOGY.

POMPEII. This Campanian town of SW Italy was
covered by the ash of Vesuvius in the great eruption
of August A.D. 79 and is remarkably preserved. Excavation, some of it disastrously destructive, has proceeded for the last two centuries, and something like
half of the town, which covers 65 ha. (160 a.) has
been laid bare. It has presented a detailed picture
of Roman provincial city* life in the first century,
but has little biblical relevance, save in its demonstration of the sort of city life, vices, and religious
activities, the first Christians confronted. According
to Josephus (Jos. *Antiq.* 20.7.2), Agrippa, son of Drusilla (Acts 24:24), perished in the eruption, but the
only archaeologically verified evidence of Jewish or
Christian presence in the town is a graffito* reading,
"SODOMA GOMORA," no doubt intended to be a
comment on the corruption of the place.

BIBLIOGRAPHY: Pliny, *Ep.* 6.16, 20; H. H. Tan-
zer, *The Common People of Pompeii: A Study of the
Graffiti* (1939).

EMB

POOL. A term describing different types of artificial
reservoirs. Seen at Gezer,* Megiddo,* Gibeon,* Jerusalem,* and in Bethlehem's* Valley of Urtas, the
pools, with fragments of connecting aqueducts,*
formed part of the water systems of antiquity.

POPULATION ESTIMATION. An intensely interesting study based on educated guesses. Estimators
can employ the number and size of houses* and their
population density, or for larger areas can utilize the
number of settlements occupied at any given time.
A cemetery (*see* NECROPOLIS) often provides information, which must be tempered by questions about
whether persons of all ages and all levels of society
were buried there, as well as about how many per-

sons from that settlement died elsewhere, possibly during trading expeditions, while traveling, in battle, or at sea.

HWP

PORCH. *See* HOUSE.

POTASSIUM-ARGON DATING. *See* DATING, ARCHAEOLOGICAL.

POTSHERD. *See* DATING, ARCHAEOLOGICAL; SHARD.

POTTER; POTTERY. Every Near Eastern tell* exhibits abundant quantities of pottery at different levels (cf. Job 2:8), if only because of the simple technology involved in the making of most ordinary pottery vessels.* The earliest levels of some sites such as Jericho* furnish prepottery phases of culture, but later periods of the Neolithic* show the widespread usage of pottery. At the lowest levels of Nineveh* and Tepe Gawra* the Neolithic ceramic ware was coarse and plain, but at Tell Halaf, the pottery of the succeeding Chalcolithic* period was elegantly crafted (*see* CRAFTS) and attractively painted.* It was handmade, glazed* (Heb. *spsyg*, Hittite *zapzagaya*; cf. Prov 26:23), and fired at an intense heat in closed kilns* to produce the finest ware of its kind in antiquity. In Palestine, Neolithic pottery was coarse, and the clay* was often mixed with finely chopped straw which, unknown to the potters, had the chemical effect of increasing the plasticity and strength of the mixture by some 300 percent, as is now known from studies in colloidal chemistry. Palestinian Chalcolithic pottery shows obvious points of contact with Mesopotamia* and Syria, while in the succeeding Early Bronze* period pottery bowls and pitchers were exported from Palestine to Egypt.* The spread of Hyksos* influence was accompanied by attractive pottery forms, and this was matched in the Middle and Late Bronze Ages by the importing of handsome Mycenaean* pottery along with jugs and bowls from Cyprus. Early Iron Age* Philistine* pottery imitated Mycenaean styles, as illustrated by the large beer jugs and the two-handled deep bowls which were attractively decorated with red and black designs, and sometimes with birds. During the monarchy the pottery of the Israelites included the so-called Samaria ware, consisting of thin, elegant bowls and other containers of varying depths which bore colored patterns beneath the rims. Greek influence became evident in Palestinian pottery from the Persian period onward, the most characteristic imitation being that of the amphora,* which constituted an advance over certain kinds of Middle Bronze and Iron Age storage jars.

Originally all pottery was handmade, but late in the fourth millennium B.C. the potter's wheel was invented. Fragments of one early wheel from Ur* were recovered by Woolley and dated in the fourth millennium B.C. Such wheels usually consisted of two stones (cf. Jer 18:3), one pivoted above the other in such a way that the potter could turn the upper stone as he molded the clay. Such a workshop was

Potter's wheel, basalt, Late Canaanite Period (1550-1200 B.C.) from Hazor. *(See also photos under* AI; EDOM, EDOMITES; HEBRON; LAMP; NABATAEANS; OSSUARY; PHILISTINES; SAMSON; VESSELS.) Courtesy Israel Dept. of Antiquities and Museums. Exhibited at and photographed by Israel Museum.

unearthed at 1800 B.C. levels at Lachish,* as well as at Qumran.* From Iron-Age strata at Megiddo,* Gezer,* and Hazor* have been recovered smaller potters' wheels, the upper one being socketed into the lower and having an attachment which enabled it to be turned by the potters' feet. With this type of wheel the lower stone was usually set in a shallow pit, as at Qumran. Coarse clay was the preferred material for utilitarian ware, though for more expensive vessels* the potter first refined his clay by treading it out in water (Isa 41:25). Israelite clay frequently turned reddish-brown when fired, as opposed to the cream, buff, grey, or brown ware of some other nations. Large pottery jars were often used in the Near East for storage purposes, holding such diverse things as food,* liquids, cuneiform* tablets, title deeds (Jer 32:14), and scrolls,* the latter as at Qumran. Broken pieces of pottery (shards*) were frequently used as material on which to write brief notations or messages.

BIBLIOGRAPHY: J. L. Kelso, *Ceramic Vocabulary of the OT* (1948), 1–48; R. B. K. Amiran, *Antiquity and Survival*, 2.2.3 (1957), 187–207; H. Jamieson, *ZPBE*, 4 (1975), 824–29.   RKH

POTTER'S VESSEL. See EXECRATION TEXTS, EGYPTIAN.

POUCH. See PURSE.

POZZUOLI. See PUTEOLI.

PRAETORIUM. See JERUSALEM, NT.

PROCONSUL. See ROMAN GOVERNMENT, ADMINISTRATION OF PROVINCES.

PROCURATOR. See ROMAN GOVERNMENT, ADMINISTRATION OF PROVINCES.

PROPRAETOR. See ROMAN GOVERNMENT, ADMINISTRATION OF PROVINCES.

PROPYLAEUM (prop ə lē'əm; pl. propylaea, often construed as sing.; lit., "in front of the gate"). The term was used to describe such things as the pillared entrance to the precinct of the Parthenon or the arched* entrance of the Corinthian agora.*

PROSTITUTION, CULTIC. This practice was especially widespread in the Ancient Near East, involving the female and at times male devotees of goddesses of fertility, who dedicated their earnings to their deity. One of the motives of the practice, particularly in Mesopotamia,* where the king engaged in an act of *hieros gamos* ("sacred marriage") with a temple prostitute, was to insure the fertility of the land and people through sympathetic magic. Other practices of temporary temple prostitution seem to have involved the ritual defloration of virgins by strangers before their marriage to their husbands.

The English word *hierodule*, which is a transliteration of a Greek word which literally means "sacred slave," is commonly used to designate a female sacred prostitute.

1. Mesopotamia. Cultic prostitution was listed by the Sumerians* along with kingship, justice, and truth, etc., as one of the divinely ordained institutions. The Mesopotamian goddess of fertility was the Sumerian Inanna, who was identified with the Akkadian* Ishtar.* An unpublished Old Babylonian hymn describes Ishtar as a hierodule whom 120 men could not exhaust.

In the Sumerian city* of Uruk* the sacred marriage* rite was probably repeated annually between a hierodule who represented Inanna and the king who represented Dumuzi (Tammuz). We have a number of sensuous love songs celebrating the love between Inanna and Dumuzi from the Ur III period (twenty-first century B.C.). From a text of Iddin-Dagan of the Isin Dynasty we learn that the rite was performed on New Year's Eve. There are possible illustrations of the rite on some cylinder seals.*

A number of categories of priestesses seem to have functioned as hierodules, though explicit references are lacking. The Sumerian NU.GIG, and the corresponding Akkadian *qadištum* (and its variants *qadiltum*, *qaššatum*), mean "tabooed" or "dedicated," and are usually translated "hierodule." From legal texts we learn that the *qadištum* could marry and bear children, or if unmarried could adopt children. It is assumed that marriage ended the *qadištum*'s role as a sacred prostitute. A Babylonian proverb, however, warns: "Do not marry a prostitute, whose husbands are legion, a temple harlot, who is dedicated to a god, a courtesan, whose favours are many."

Men "whose manhood Ishtar has changed into womanhood" appear to be male hierodules.

In the Gilgamesh Epic* VI.165f. Enkidu is tamed by a *ḫarimtu*, a cult prostitute of Ishtar. Lambert has interpreted the Gilgamesh Epic IV. 34–36 as a reference to the practice of *ius primae noctis*, the ritual defloration of virgins. He interprets the famous passage in Herodotus 1.199 as related to this practice rather than to cultic prostitution proper. Herodotus wrote that every Babylonian woman was required once in her life to have relations with some stranger in the temple of Aphrodite (i.e., Ishtar; cf. Strabo 16.1.20, and the apocryphal Epistle of Jeremiah 43).

2. Palestine. In the OT the feminine *qᵉdēshâh* and the masculine *qādēsh*, translated by the KJV as "harlot" or "whore," and "sodomite," are now generally interpreted as female and male cult prostitutes. In Gen 38:21–22 Tamar is described as a *qᵉdēshâh*, though there are no references to a cult; in Gen 38:15 the common word for harlot, *zônâh*, is used. In Hos 4:14 *qᵉdēshôth* and *zōnôth* are used in parallel lines in a cultic context.

Some scholars such as H. G. May have therefore jumped to the conclusion that the word *zônâh* and its many derivatives refer not just to prostitution but to cultic prostitution. In the 1930s it became quite common for scholars to find allusions to cultic prostitution everywhere in the OT.

Clear references to cultic prostitution are to be found in the following passages. In Deut 23:17–18 the contemptuous phrase "dog" refers to a male cultic prostitute. In Rehoboam's time according to 1 Kings 14:23–24 the presence of male prostitutes was one of the abominable practices which became prevalent. 1 Kings 15:12 relates how Asa put away the male prostitutes from the land. Still later Asa's son, Jehoshaphat, had to repeat this cleansing (1 Kings 22:46). According to 2 Kings 23:6–7 Josiah pulled down the houses of the *qᵉdēshîm* (a plural which may refer just to male prostitutes or to both male and female prostitutes), where women wove vestments in honor of Asherah.*

The following passages may contain possible allusions to sacred prostitution: Num 25:1–2; 1 Sam 2:22; Jer 13:27; Ezek 16; and Amos 2:7–8.

2 Macc 6:4 asserts that among the abominations introduced into the Jerusalem temple* area by Antiochus IV was debauchery with prostitutes; the Megillat Ta'anit likewise comments: "The Gentiles built there a sacred place and brought prostitutes there. . . ."

3. Syria and Phoenicia. In Ugaritic* texts of temple personnel we find listed next to the *khnm* "priests," the *qdšm*, probably male cultic prostitutes.

Lucian (*Syr.D.* 6) in the second century A.D. informs us that in ceremonies in memory of Adonis at the temple of Venus of Byblos (Gebal*) all women who would not shave themselves had to prostitute themselves.

The practice of the prostitution of women in the service of Venus at Heliopolis* (Baalbek*) is attested as late as the fourth century A.D. by the historians Socrates, Eusebius, and Sozomen. Constantine destroyed the temple and erected a church upon its ruins.

Augustine (August. *De Civ. D.* 4.10) knew that the Phoenicians* prostituted their daughters to Venus before giving them in marriage.

4. Cyprus and Cythera. There is good reason to believe that Phoenician influence is responsible for the importation of cultic prostitution as part of the Greek worship of Aphrodite by way of Cyprus* and Cythera, an island just off the SE Peloponnesus.

The worship of Aphrodite had its center at Old Paphos* in SW Cyprus. Cinyras, the father of Adonis, was said to have instituted the custom of religious prostitution there. According to numerous writers, women had to prostitute themselves to strangers at this temple. Tacitus (Tac. *Hist.* 2.1.2) records how Titus* visited the shrine of the Paphian Venus. Excavations at the end of the nineteenth century unearthed the remains of the famous building. Recent excavations at the village of Kouklia, which covers the site of Palaipaphos, have now uncovered evidence that the sanctuary dates back to the Late Bronze Age,* lending some confirmation to the legend of its foundation in the Mycenaean* era. Coins* give us some idea of the temple's appearance in antiquity.

Herodotus 1.105 notes that the temple of Aphrodite on Cythera was founded by Phoenicians (cf. Pausanias 1.14.6). Pausanias 3.23.1 calls the sanctuary of Aphrodite at Cythera the most ancient of all the temples of the goddess in Greece.

The association of Aphrodite with Cyprus and Cythera was already recognized by Homer in the eighth century B.C.

5. Greece. Farnell points out that Aphrodite was nowhere regarded as a divine ancestress except at Thebes,* which had very strong Phoenician associations. There were also very strong Phoenician elements at Corinth,* the main center of her worship in Greece.

Strabo 8.6.20 asserted that the temple of Aphrodite on the Acrocorinth had more than a thousand *hierodoulous* ("temple slaves") or *hetairas* ("courtesans"), whom both men and women had dedicated to the goddess. He claimed that the prosperity of Corinth was in no small measure dependent upon these hierodules. Sacred prostitution had been established at Corinth before the fifth century B.C., as we have a record of the prayers of the hierodules during the Persian invasion. Xenophon of Corinth, a participant in the Olympic games* of 464 B.C. vowed that if he won he would dedicate a hundred girls to the temple of Aphrodite. The charms and the wiles of the Corinthian hierodules are described by Pindar, Aristophanes, and Athenaeus. When Paul warned his congregation in Corinth against immorality (1 Cor 6:13–20), he was warning them not against ordinary prostitutes but against hierodules.

A thorough investigation of the Acrocorinth by C. W. Blegen in 1926 revealed some finely worked porous blocks, probably of Aphrodite's temple which had been displaced by an early Christian church. Classical sources speak of the temple as a small building so the hierodules must have lived elsewhere. Coins offer contradictory evidence for the appearance of the temple, but agree in depicting the statue* of the goddess as naked to the waist.

6. Carthage and Sicily. It is of more than passing interest that Dido of Phoenicia, the legendary founder of Carthage, stopped off at Cyprus on her way to N Africa. There the high priest of the goddess Astarte and eighty maidens destined for sacred prostitution joined her. Evidence from Carthage, however, is scanty. Representations of "temple boys" on

"Astarte" or Dea Nutrix pottery figurines, Judaean types, seventh century B.C. Left: pillar-shaped with human head. Right: bird-headed. Courtesy Israel Dept. of Antiquities and Museums. Photo Israel Museum, Jerusalem.

stelae* at Carthage have been interpreted as male temple prostitutes.

Some miles inland from Carthage at Sicca Veneria in Numidia women took part in prostitution at the temple of Venus.

Sicca was founded by colonists from Eryx in western Sicily, which had been founded by Phoenicians. The numerous hierodules at the temple of Astarte-Aphrodite-Venus at Eryx were, no doubt, engaged in temple prostitution. In Strabo's (6.2.5) time their numbers had declined. It is interesting that the importation of the worship of Venus Erycina into the Roman capital in 215 B.C. did not bring with it the practice of sacred prostitution.

7. Armenia and Anatolia. We are told by Strabo 2.14.6 that the Armenians at Acilisene honored the Persian goddess Anaitis by dedicating their daughters to her for sacred prostitution before their marriages.

Herodotus 1.93 describes how young girls in Lydia* in western Anatolia practiced prostitution to earn their dowries. Ramsay cites an inscription of the second century A.D. as evidence of the continuation of cultic prostitution at Tralleis.

Large numbers of sacred prostitutes plied their vocation in honor of the goddess Ma at two sites named Comana and at other sites in Cappadocia in eastern Anatolia (Strabo 12.3.36).

8. Egypt. Clear references to sacred prostitution in Egypt* occur only in late authors such as Strabo (17.1.46), who associates the practice with the cult of Amon-Zeus at Thebes. There young girls prostituted themselves before marriage. There are also some possible allusions in Herodotus (1.182; 2.60, 126). An inscription of Ramses* III has been interpreted by Breasted to be a reference to sacred hierodules. On the other hand, Hempel and Albright do not believe that sacred prostitution was native to Egyptian religion.

9. *Female Figurines.* Numerous nude female figurines found in excavations may be related, indirectly at any rate, with the glorification of sexuality in cultic prostitution. Pritchard, in analyzing 294 examples from Palestine, has detected six basic types: (1) an archaic type with earflaps, derived from Mesopotamia; (2) a figure holding her breasts, imported from Mesopotamia and appearing in Palestine from the Middle Bronze to the Late Bronze periods; (3) a figure with arms hanging to the side, associated with Hyksos* scarabs;* (4) the "Qadesh" type in which the figure holds lilies or serpents (one example in the Winchester College Collection dated to Ramses III is explicitly labeled "Qudshu-Astarte-Anath"); (5) a figure holding a disc, found at Megiddo,* Taanach,* etc., from the eleventh–seventh centuries B.C.; (6) a pregnant figure also from the eleventh to the seventh centuries B.C.

Artistic confirmations of the eastern affinities of the Greek Aphrodite may be seen in ivory* inlays of an alluring goddess peering out of a window, which in Mesopotamia were ascribed to Ishtar and in Greece to Aphrodite. Astarte plaques imported from the E into Corinth served as the models for figurines of Aphrodite.

BIBLIOGRAPHY: D. G. Hogarth et al., "Excavations in Cyprus, 1887–88, Paphos," *JHS*, 9 (1887), 147ff., 193ff.; L. R. Farnell, *The Cults of the Greek States* (1896); G. A. Barton, "Hierodouloi," *HERE*, 6 (1917), 671–76; D. Luckenbill, "The Temple Women of the Code of Hammurabi," *AJSL*, 34 (1917), 1–12; R. Herbig, "Aphrodite Parakyptusa," *OLZ*, 30 (1927), 917–22; B. H. Hill, "Excavations at Corinth 1926," *AJA*, 31 (1927), 70–79; H. Zimmern, "Die babylonische Göttin im Fenster," *OLZ*, 31 (1928), 1–3; J. O'Neill, *Ancient Corinth I* (1930), 50–52; H. G. May, "The Fertility Cult in Hosea," *AJSL*, 48 (1932), 73–98; A. Westholm, "The Paphian Temple of Aphrodite and Its Relation to Oriental Architecture," *Acta Archaeologica* (1933), 201ff.; B. Brooks, "Fertility Cult Functionaries in the OT," *JBL*, 60 (1941), 227–53; J. B. Pritchard, *Palestinian Figurines in Relation to Certain Goddesses . . .* (1943); P. J. Riis, "The Syrian Astarte Plaques and Their Western Connections," *Ber.*, 9 (1948–49), 69; K. Mlaker, *Die Hierodulenlisten von Ma'in* (1943); R. Schilling, *La religion romaine de Vénus* (1954); I. E. S. Edwards, "A Relief of Qudshu-Astarte-Anath in the Winchester College Collection," *JNES*, 14 (1955), 49–51; J. P. Asmussen, "Bemerkungen zur sakralen Prostitution im Alten Testament," *ST*, 11 (1957), 167–92; A. Parrot, *Le Musée du Louvre et la Bible* (1957), 60–69; W. G. Lambert, "Morals in Ancient Mesopotamia," *Ex Oriente Lux*, 15 (1957–58), 184–96; id., "Divine Love Lyrics from Babylon," *JSS*, 4 (1959), 1–15; *Éléments orientaux dans la religion grecque ancienne* (1960); H. Herter, "Die Soziologie der antiken Prostitution im Lichte des heidnischen und christlichen Schrifttums," *Jahrbuch für Antike und Christentum*, 3 (1960), 70–111; F. Henriques, *Stews and Strumpets; A Survey of Prostitution I* (1961); V. Bullough, *The History of Prostitution* (1964); R. Patai, "The Goddess Asherah," *JNES*, 24 (1965),

37–52; M. C. Astour, "Tamar the Hierodule," *JBL*, 85 (1966), 185–96; J. Renger, "Untersuchungen zum Priestertum in der altbabylonischen Zeit," *ZA*, 58 (1967), 178–88; R. Stadelmann, *Syrisch-palästinensische Gottheiten in Ägypten* (1967); E. Yamauchi, *Greece and Babylon* (1967), 47–53; S. Moscati, "Sulla diffusione del culto di Astarte Ericina," *Oriens Antiquus*, 7 (1968), 91–94; S. N. Kramer, *The Sacred Marriage Rite* (1969); W. Herrman, "Aštart," *Mitteilungen des Instituts für Orientforschung*, 15 (1969), 6–51; D. R. Hillers, "The Goddess with the Tambourine," *ConTM*, 41.9 (1970), 94–107; T. Jacobsen, *Toward the Image of Tammuz* (1970); F. G. Maier, "Alt-Paphos auf Zypern," *Antike Welt*, 1 (1970), 3–15; 2 (1971), 3–14; S. N. Kramer, "Le rite de mariage sacré Dumuzi-Inanna," *Revue de l'histoire des religions*, 181 (1972), 121–46; E. Yamauchi, "Cultic Prostitution: A Case Study in Cultural Diffusion," *Orient and Occident*, ed. H. Hoffner (1973), 213–22; M. Delcor, *Religion d'Israël* (1976), 55–71, 86–94; L. Durdin-Robertson, *The Goddesses of Chaldaea, Syria and Egypt* (1974); V. Karageorghis, "A Representation of a Temple on an 8th Century B.C. Cypriot Vase," *Rivista di Studi Fenici*, 1 (1974), 9–13; D. Boedeker, *Aphrodite's Entry into Greek Epic* (1974); S. B. Pomeroy, *Goddesses, Whores, Wives and Slaves* (1975); H. W. Attridge & R. Oden, *De Dea Syria* (1976); E. Fisher, "Cultic Prostitution in the Ancient Near East?" *Biblical Theology Bulletin*, 6 (1976), 225–36; G. Grigson, *The Goddess of Love* (1976); R. Oden, "The Persistence of Canaanite Religion," *BA*, 39 (1976), 31–36; B. L. Trell, "Architecture on Ancient Coins," *ARC*, 29 (1976), 6–13; M. Price & B. L. Trell, *Coins and Their Cities* (1977), 79, 147, 236; K. Nicolaou, "Archaeological News from Cyprus, 1976: Palaipaphos," *AJA*, 82 (1978), 528–29; P. Friedrich, *The Meaning of Aphrodite* (1978); I. Michaeolidou-Nicolaou, "The Temple of Aphrodite as Depicted on Clay Sealings from Paphos," *AJA*, 84 (1980), 223; P. Dion, "Did Cultic Prostitution Fall into Oblivion during the Postexilic Era?" *CBQ*, 43 (1981), 41–48.   EY

PROVINCE, ROMAN. See ROMAN GOVERNMENT, ADMINISTRATION OF PROVINCES.

PSEUDEPIGRAPHA (sū də pig'rə fə). This term strictly indicates those written works penned under a false or fictitious (pseudo) name. The corpus of literature included a large group of Jewish writings outside the OT canon and composed originally in Hebrew, Aramaic,* and Greek* between c. 200 B.C. and A.D. 100–200. Because some of these Jewish works carried such names as Adam, Moses, and Enoch, these writings became known among Protestants as Pseudepigrapha, but in the Roman Catholic Church, by ancient Christian usage, they were termed Apocrypha.

The corpus in the main includes apocalypses (such as the Apocalypse of Baruch and the Assumption of Moses), histories (as the First and Second Books of Maccabees), collections of psalms (as the Psalms of Solomon), and wisdom literature (such as the Wisdom of Solomon).

Of special interest are the Dead Sea Scrolls* material found at Qumran* from 1947 on. The Qumran site itself was excavated early in the 1950s. Some of the works found in caves* in the vicinity were MS copies of biblical material. Among the finds were discovered a number of apocryphal extrabiblical books that help to shed light on the life and beliefs of the Jews* of the period in general and of the Qumran community in particular. Among these extrabiblical books from Qumran, some were already known from other sources, these being the books of Jubilee, Enoch, the Damascus Document, and the Testament of Levi. Other extrabiblical books, not known from other sources, are: the Genesis Apocryphon;* a pseudo-Jeremianic work; apocalyptic works (i.e., the War Scroll [1QM], the Description of New Jerusalem, the Three Tongues of Fire, the Book of Mysteries, and collections of Messianic passages from the OT); hymnic works (Hodayoth [1QH], and Psalms of Joshua); and peshers, or commentaries. Fragments of such commentaries were found on Isaiah, Hosea, Micah, Nahum, Psalms, and Habakkuk.

Besides the Pseudepigrapha of the intertestamental period, there are books that could be called NT Pseudepigrapha, works written mainly from the second to the fifth centuries A.D. These works, which are usually called NT Apocrypha, and some of which carry false titles, include some of the gnostic works (such as items in the corpus found in the late 1940s at Nag Hammadi,* Egypt*) and give so-called sayings (logia) of Jesus or describe, with embellishments, events in his life, as well as expand on events in the life of the early church. Such works include the Gospel of Thomas,* the Gospel of Philip,* the Gospel of Judas, the Gospel of Bartholomew, the Apocryphon of James, the Protevangelium of James, the Infancy Story of Thomas, and the Gospel of Nicodemus. The apostolic and early church writings, pseudepigraphical works, strictly so-called, include the Kerygma of Peter, the Epistle to the Laodiceans, the Pseudo-Titus Epistle, the Acts of John, the Acts of Peter, the Acts of Paul, the Acts of Andrew, the Acts of Thomas, the Apocalypse of Peter, the Apocalypse of Paul, and the Apocalypse of Thomas.

This corpus of material with its embellishments and differences is useful for comparison with the NT text and can be helpful in the study of Gnosticism and other teachings that developed in and around the early church.

BIBLIOGRAPHY: R. H. Charles, ed., The Apocrypha and Pseudepigrapha of the OT in English, 2 vols. (1913); B. M. Metzger, An Introduction to the Apocrypha (1957); Y. Yadin, The Message of the Scrolls (1957), 73–155; M. Burrows, More Light on the Dead Sea Scrolls (1958), 387–409; J. T. Milik, Ten Years of Discovery in the Wilderness of Judaea (1959), 61–80; C. T. Fritsch, "Pseudepigrapha," IDB, 3 (1962), 960–64; T. H. Gaster, ed., The Dead Sea Scriptures (1964); E. Hennecke, New Testament Apocrypha, W. Schneemelcher and R. McL. Wilson eds., 2 vols. (1963, 1965); J. M. Robinson, The Nag Hammadi Codices (1974).

WHM

PTAH-HOTEP, INSTRUCTION OF (ptä-hō'tep). Ptah-Hotep was a vizier* of the Egyptian Fifth Dynasty who died, it is said, at the age of 110, some twenty-five centuries before Christ. What he had learned about good speech and wisdom, he wrote down for his son, after the manner of the Hebrew proverbs. "There is no one born wise," declares Ptah-Hotep, but by observation wisdom may be acquired. Here are some samples of such proverbial wisdom: "Wrongdoing has never brought its undertaking into port. . . . It may be that a fraud gains riches but the strength of justice is that it lasts. . . . Let not your heart be puffed up because of knowledge, and be not confident because you are a wise man. Take counsel with the ignorant as well as with the wise. . . . Good speech is more hidden than the emerald but it may be found with maidservants at the grindstones. . . . Be thoroughly reliable on a mission. Carry out your errand as if he who sends you has spoken. Grasp hold of the truth and do not exceed it. Strive against making words worse, thus making one great man hostile to another through vulgar speech. . . . If you wish to make friendship last in a home to which you have access as a master, a brother or a friend, beware of approaching the women. . . . Love your wife as is fitting. Fill her stomach. Clothe her back. Make her heart glad. She is a profitable field to her Lord."

BIBLIOGRAPHY: ANET (1950), 412–13; J. H. Breasted, History of Egypt (1945), 73, 107, 204; J. B. Pritchard, Archaeology of the OT (1958), 228–32.

EMB

PTOLEMAIS. See ACCO.

PTOLEMY (tol'a mi; Gr. Πτολεμαῖος, Ptolemaios). Primarily the title of king, particularly the dynasty of Hellenistic kings ruling in Egypt* from 323 to 30 B.C. and on.

Ptolemy I (Soter, Savior), one of the generals of Alexander the Great and the one from whom the name and dynasty began, was satrap of Egypt from 323–305 B.C. and king of the country from 305–283. Coins* of Ptolemy I include one from the street* E of Villa at Libyan Ptolemais, and a silver* tetradrachma struck at Paphos* on Cyprus* (305–285 B.C.; Ptolemy's diademed head on the obverse and his name flanking an eagle* on the reverse); some coins bear the head of Alexander on one side and the name Ptolemaiou Basileus ("King Ptolemais") on the other, the use of basileus here fixing the date as within 305–285 B.C., when Ptolemais called himself king.

Ptolemy II, Philadelphus (283–247 B.C.) advanced Hellenistic and literary culture (witness the LXX) and material prosperity, as the Zeno papyri* bear witness. On coins are to be seen such as the heads of the king and his daughter Berenice who married the Seleucid king Antiochus II (cf. Dan 11:6); a gold* tetradrachma shows the two heads of Ptolemy II and Arsinoe II, his sister-wife, on the obverse, and on the reverse their parents Ptolemy I and Berenice I are pictured as gods.

From the time of Ptolemy III (246–221 B.C.), who struggled with the Seleucid kingdom, Greek inscriptions give evidence of Jewish synagogues,* called

Drawing of coin of Ptolemy I. Left: obverse; right: reverse. Courtesy Carta, Jerusalem.

proseuchai (i.e., places of prayer) at Schedia and at Leontopolis,* Egypt. Some gold coins show the bust of Ptolemy III as radiate (like rays of the sun) with aegis, trident, and scepter on the obverse and the inscription Basileus—Ptolemaiou and a radiate, filleted cornucopia on the reverse (Head, *Historia Numorum*, 853). Libyan Ptolemais was founded probably near the beginning of Ptolemy III's reign by this ruler from whom it received its name.

Ptolemy IV, Philopater (221–203 B.C.) a ruler vengeful toward the Jews* witnessed the declining power of his kingdom. Coins show the bust of Ptolemy IV and the inscription *Ptolemaiou Philopatoros* and the queen Arsinoe III and the inscription *Arsinoēs Philopatoros* (Head, 854).

Ptolemy V, Epiphanes (203–181 B.C.) struggled with the Seleucid king, Antiochus III, and during his reign, all foreign Egyptian possessions were lost except Cyprus and the Cyrenaica. Rare gold tetradrachms (Head, 855) show the bust of Ptolemy V, radiate or diademed, and with either of the following inscriptions: *Ptolemaiou Epiphanous* or *Basileus Ptolemaiou*.

Ptolemy VI, Philometer (180–146 B.C.) made it possible for Jews under Onias to build a Jewish sanctuary in Leontopolis, province of Heliopolis,* after the Jerusalem model. Some coins show the regency of his mother with him through the words *Kleopatras* on the obverse and *Basileus Ptolemaiou* on the reverse (Head, 856).

Ptolemy VII, Eupator, murdered shortly after his accession (146 B.C.), was followed by Ptolemy VIII, Euergetes II (or Physcon; 146–117 B.C.), whom coins designate as ruler by *Basileus Ptolemaiou Euergeto* ("the beneficence of King Ptolemy"; Head, 847). Ptolemy IX, Lathyrus, was coregent with his mother, Cleopatra (116–107 B.C.). This period, along with the reign of Ptolemy X (Alexander I) down to c. 80 B.C., is a confused picture.

Ptolemy XII's nineteen-day reign (80 B.C.) was followed by that of Ptolemy XIII, Neos Dionysos, or Auletes, who was deposed in 56 B.C. Coins of his time show a πα, and on a rare drachma appears the bust of Auletes. His daughter, Cleopatra VII, of Mark Antony association, dominated the Egyptian scene in the next years (51–30 B.C.). Coins show the head of Cleopatra on the obverse and the words *Basilissēs Kleopatras* ("Queen Cleopatra") on the reverse (Head, 859).

BIBLIOGRAPHY: G. F. Hill, *Historical Greek Coins* (1906); B. V. Head, *Historia Numorum* (1911);

S. Zeitlin, *History of the Second Jewish Commonwealth* (1933); R. H. Pfeiffer, *History of NT Times* (1949); F. A. Banks, *Coins of Bible Days* (1955); V. A. Tcherikover and A. Fuks, *Corpus Papyrorum Judaicarum* (1957); V. A. Tcherikover, *Hellenistic Civilization and the Jews* (1959); C. H. Kraeling, *Ptolemais, City of the Libyan Pentapolis* (1960); S. B. Hoenig, "Ptolemy," *IDB*, 3 (1962), 962–67; G. F. Hill, *Ancient Greek and Roman Coins* (1964); id., *Historical Roman Coins* (1966); K. A. Kitchen, *ZPEB*, 4 (1975), 951–54.

WHM

PUL. See TIGLATH-PILESER.

PULUSATI. See PHILISTINES; SEA PEOPLES.

PUNON. A well-watered locality (modern Feinan) E of the Arabah, with evidence of occupation from 2000 B.C. Copper appears to have been smelted (*see* REFINING) there at this time, and the Arabah trade route no doubt took ore to Egypt.* When Israel* camped here (Num 33:43) in the years after the Exodus, the place was in decline. The Nabataeans* resumed the copper mining which continued up to Roman times. Eusebius reports that Christian prisoners were used in the mines. A Christian presence from Byzantine* times is attested by the ruins of a basilica* and a monastery. In the latter an inscription refers to a bishop Theodore of the sixth century.

BIBLIOGRAPHY: N. Glueck, *AASOR*, 15 (1934–35), 32–35.

EMB

PURPLE. See DYE, DYEING.

PURSE. A leather* pouch ("scrip" KJV, "wallet" RV; Gr. *pēra*), differentiated from the *ballantion*, the "bag" in some of the relevant contexts (Matt 10:10; Luke 9:3; 10:4; 22:35). In Judith 13:10 the words *tōn brōmatōn* ("food-bag" NEB) are added, suggesting, in fact, what the contexts imply, that the word meant simply a leather bag for carrying provisions. It was commonly used by Ancient Near Eastern shepherds and may have been a more substantial version of the *kophinos*. Leather has small survival capacity, but a leather bag of goat* skin has been found in the Bar Kochba* cave* complex.

EMB

PUTEOLI (pu te'ə li). A city* (now Pozzuoli) on the N side of the Gulf of Naples, founded in the sixth century B.C. as Dicaearchia and later named Puteoli under the Romans, who made it an important port city for its eastern imports and exports (Strabo 5.245; Loeb).

Puteoli successfully opposed Hannibal in his campaign in 215 B.C. In 199 it received a customs post and in 194 became a maritime colony. The city received colonial status under Sulla or Augustus* and was certainly so honored by Nero and Vespasian.* Its population is estimated to have been nearly 65,000.

Its special road, the Via Domitiana, connected with the famous Via Appia (Appian Way*). In the days of its prosperity Puteoli was a villa resort for such as Sulla, Cicero, and Hadrian. Here Paul landed on his way to Rome* (Acts 28:13).

Among the ancient remains of Puteoli are the market hall (macellum), often called the Serapeum (a statue* of Serapis was discovered there), and a temple of Augustus (cf. *CIL*, 10.1613–14), subsequently replaced by the cathedral of San Proculo. Of the two amphitheaters,* the older one was probably the place where Nero gave a gladiatorial performance in A.D. 66 (Cass. Dio 62.3.1), which Paul could have seen. A later amphitheater (*CIL*, 10.1789), from the time when Puteoli was a Flavian colony, and thus not earlier than Vespasian, has left well-preserved ruins. It could accommodate 40,000 to 60,000 spectators, thus being the third largest such structure in Italy—smaller only than those at Rome and Capua. Also in the upper town were the baths of Trajan (or Janus), a circus,* an aqueduct,* and other structures.

A number of Christian inscriptions have been found there.

BIBLIOGRAPHY: C. Dubois, *Pouzzoles Antique Histoire et topographie* (1907); H. Leclercq, "Pouzzoles et Cumes," *Dictionnaire d'Archéologie Chretienne et de liturgie*, 14.2 (1948), 1673–87; J. Finegan, "Puteoli," *IDB* 3 (1962), 971–72; R. F. Paget, "The Ancient Ports of Cumae," *JRS*, 58 (1968), 163–66; *OCD* (1970), 901; *PECS*, 743–44.

WHM

PYRAMIDS. Pyramids were both tomb and monument for ancient Egyptian kings, or pharaohs. The first one was an edifice of six "steps," each one smaller than that below it—the Step Pyramid of King Djoser, reputedly built by his minister Imhotep.* Later kings of the Third Dynasty imitated this design, which betokened a stairway to heaven for the deceased king, as well as a fitting tomb for his mummified body. In the Fourth Dynasty (c. 2700 B.C.), Snofru turned to building true pyramids (pentahedrons with four smooth, triangular sides built on a square base). At Giza* his successors, Cheops (Khufu) and Khefren, built the Great Pyramid (146 m., or 480 ft. high) and the Second Pyramid (144 m., or 471 ft. high), respectively. These reflect remarkable accuracy of construction and architectural and engineering ingenuity of the highest order. Some blocks of the Great Pyramid are estimated to weigh over 54,400 kg. (60 tons).

Later pyramids in the Old and Middle Kingdoms were usually considerably smaller and less solid. In the New Kingdom, a very small pyramid sometimes capped private tombs. Royalty never used pyramids again except for the Twenty-fifth Dynasty and its successors in Nubia.*

Pyramids exemplify the early perfection of state organization in the Near East long before Solomon.* Quaint ideas about their being granaries* of Joseph, observatories, or repositories of esoteric eschatology* are unfounded.

BIBLIOGRAPHY: I. E. S. Edwards, *The Pyramids of Egypt* (1947; 2d ed. 1961); L. Cottrell, *The Mountains of Pharaoh* (1956, rep. 1963).

KAK

PYRAMID TEXTS. *See* COFFIN TEXTS.

Q

QALAAT SHERQAT (kä′ lə ät shûr′kət). Qala‘at Sherqat is a site on the Tigris River about 40 km. (25 mi.) due S of Tell Hassuna* in Mesopotamia* and is the modern name for Ashur.* This latter was the designation of the national god of Assyria and was used in addition both for the city* of Ashur and the Assyrian Empire. The site was occupied in the prehistoric period, and artifacts* have been recovered from that era which reflect closely the culture of nearby Tell Hassuna for the corresponding period.

The earliest references to the city of Ashur occurred in cuneiform* texts found at Nuzi* and dated in the Old Akkadian* period (c. 2360–2180 B.C.). Ashur was the place where a Sumerian* *ensi*, or governor, ruled during the Third Dynasty of Ur.* When that brilliant period of Sumerian culture came to an end, about 1960 B.C., Ashur was ruled by a series of overseers and became an important commercial center. Texts from Boghazköy* and Kultepe* have detailed Assyrian trade in such items as copper, tin,* and textiles. This trade ceased after more than a century, and only under Shamshi-Adad I (c. 1748–1716 B.C.) did Assyria regain its independence. Ashur then became the administrative and political center of his regime and was adorned with a splendid temple of the national deity, Ashur. When Shamshi-Adad I died his burgeoning empire disintegrated quickly under pressure from Hammurabi,* the Hurrians,* and the Amorites,* and it was only when the Mitanni Empire* suffered defeat in the time of the Hittite* ruler Suppiluliumas* that Ashur began to assume prominence once more as capital of a resurgent Assyrian Empire.

The aggressive, militant spirit of the nation led to the conquest of Babylon* under Tukulti-Ninerta I (c. 1224–1208 B.C.), but thereafter Babylonian cultural concepts infiltrated Assyria and came to dominate most of the important areas of Assyrian life. Their international treaties, for example, were modeled on lines familiar to other Near Eastern nations, as with the treaty between Ashurnirari VI (754–746 B.C.) and a ruler of Upper Syria, or one between Esarhaddon* (681–669 B.C.) and a king of Tyre.* From the Assyrian imperial period (c. 1100–633 B.C.) came the "charter" of Ashur, granted by Sargon II* (722–705 B.C.) to the city in return for support prior to his accession, and the oath of loyalty sworn by Assyrian officials, a legal document which unfortunately has only survived in fragmentary form.

The earliest excavations at Ashur were undertaken by Layard, Rassam, and Place. The site was excavated much more extensively from 1903 to 1914 by a German expedition under Koldewey and Andrae. Layard's activities uncovered a black basalt statue* on which was an inscription of Shalmaneser III, as well as fragments of boundary markers, inscribed bricks, and some pillaged tombs from a comparatively late period. In 1853 Rassam discovered two foundation tablets (*see* RASSAM CYLINDER) at the base of the ziggurat* of the deity Ashur, which recorded that the temple had been erected in 1820 B.C. and subsequently reconstructed by Tiglath-pileser I* (c. 1110–1103 B.C.). Andrae's expedition made it clear that Ashur had been occupied continuously from the early third millennium B.C. down to Parthian times. There were several occupational levels at the site, and from the artifacts recovered it appears that the city had been at its highest levels of prosperity in the nineteenth, thirteenth, twelfth, and ninth centuries B.C. Many inscriptions were recovered, along with quantities of pottery* and tablet material. Between the inner and outer S wall* of the city were discovered a row of steles* of Assyrian rulers from Adad-nirari I to Ashurbanipal.* Tombs and sarcophagi* of other kings were also discovered, but most of them had been plundered. Under Sargon II Ashur was replaced as the capital city, first by Calah* and Nineveh,* and then by Dur-Sharrukin (Khorsabad*).

BIBLIOGRAPHY: W. Andrae, *Das wiedererstandene Assur* (1938); S. Smith, *Early History of Assyria to 1000* B.C. (1928); *FLAP*, 51, 168ff.; D. J. Wiseman, *ZPEB*, 1 (1975), 369–70.

RKH

QANTIR-KHATAANA-TELL DABA. *See* RAMESES.

QAREIT EL ENAB. *See* ABU GHOSH.

QARQAR (kär′kär). A site on the central Orontes River in Syria which was the scene of a famous battle fought between Shalmaneser III and an anti-Assyrian coalition in 853 B.C. The site has been identified with Tell Qerqūr in the village of Qarqar. Though the battle is not mentioned in the OT, it is important because it sheds light on the foreign policy of Ahab* of Israel* and provides our earliest known synchronism with Assyrian documents.

I. *Sources for Shalmaneser III (859–824 B.C.)*. We are fortunate in possessing several editions of the annals of Shalmaneser III which describe the battle fought in his sixth year. The most accurate text is found on the monolith inscription found at Kurkh on the Tigris in 1861. It was inscribed shortly after the

Engraved and hammered bronze band XIII from Balawat Gates. The upper register depicts the Assyrian assault on a town in Hamath. The lower register depicts charioteers driving away, leading a line of female captives. Reproduced by courtesy of the Trustees of the British Museum.

battle. Later editions of the annals include a text from his seventeenth year inscribed on a tablet, published by Cameron in 1950. This is almost identical with the inscriptions on two bull colossi from Nimrud (Calah*). An edition from his twentieth year inscribed on a marble slab was published by Safar in 1951. The famous Black Obelisk (*see under* SHALMANESER) comes from the end of the king's reign and is a poor source, inasmuch as later revisions tended to be compressed and distorted. For example, the monolith lists the enemies' casualties as 14,000; this figure is progressively inflated in later editions to 20,500, to 25,000, and to 29,000. Assyrian casualties are hardly ever mentioned.

A vivid pictorial representation of the battle is found on the famous bronze* Balawat Gates. Found by H. Rassam in 1878 at a site 24 km. (15 mi.) SE of Nineveh,* these bronze bands, 2.4 m. (8 ft.) long and 28 cm. (11 in.) wide, covered a gate* which was about 8 m. (26 ft.) high. The figures in repoussé depict the city* being assaulted and spoil being brought before the seated Shalmaneser.

II. *The Assyrian Strategy.* It was with Shalmaneser III that Assyrian campaigns became more than raids for plunder. In 858 Shalmaneser was checked in his drive to the NW by a coalition of N Syrians including Sam'al and Carchemish.* During 857–855 he succeeded in capturing Bit-Adini (the Beth Eden of Amos 1:5), an area by the bend of the Euphrates ruled from Til Barsip.* As the Assyrian army, which numbered about 120,000, advanced W again in 853 it was opposed by a grand coalition of about a dozen states.

III. *The Anti-Assyrian Forces.* All told the anti-Assyrian coalition was able to muster a force of 62,900 infantry, 1,900 horses,* and 3,900 chariots.*

A. *Damascus.* Hadad-ezer of Aram* supplied 1,200 chariots, 1,200 cavalry, and 20,000 soldiers. It is from this period that Damascus* emerges as the head of a unified Aramean state. Though it is agreed that Hadad-ezer is another name for the biblical Ben-hadad, considerable controversy exists about the exact identification of the following figures: (1) *Ben-Hadad*, son of Tabrimmon (1 Kings 15:18) to whom Asa appealed c. 885; (2) *Ben-Hadad*, contemporary of Ahab, who fought at the battle of Qarqar in 853 (1 Kings 20); and (3) *Bir-Hadad* of the Melcart Stele,* found near Aleppo,* dating to the mid-ninth century.

On the basis of a conjectural restoration of the Melcart Stele, Albright maintained that all of these references were to a Ben-Hadad I, reigning c. 885–42, a position followed by Unger, Black (*DOTT*, 239f.), and Rosenthal (*ANE*, 655).

The restoration has been questioned by Mazar and others who propose a Ben-Hadad I (c. 900–?) and a Ben-Hadad II (c. 870–842), the Bir-Hadad of the Melcart Stele. The latest proposal by Cross, however, would make Bir-Hadad of the Melcart Stele a Ben-Hadad III (c. 845–842), the son of and coregent with Ben-Hadad II.

B. *Hamath** was the major Syrian city to the S of Qarqar. Its chief Irhuleni (Jarhuleni) supplied seven hundred chariots, seven hundred cavalry, and ten thousand men.

C. *Israel.* A-ha-ab-bu Sir'-i-la-a-a, i.e. Ahab of Israel, though listed third, was actually second in importance, supplying no less than two thousand chariots and ten thousand men. The ascription of the stables* at Megiddo* by Yadin to Ahab comports with this text. It has been suggested that contingents from Judah,* though not named, may also have been included.

D. *Qua* is usually interpreted as Que, i.e., Cilicia* in SW Turkey. Tadmor has argued that it is a misspelling for *Gu-(bal)-a-a*, i.e., Byblos (Gebal*). This region provided five hundred soldiers.

E. *Muṣri*, which provided one thousand soldiers, is usually taken to be Cappadocia, N of Cilicia. Tadmor has argued for the older identification with Egypt.*

F. *Other Allies.* Gandabu the Arab provided one thousand camels*—one of the earliest references to Arabs. Baasha the Ammonite* provided ten thousand foot soldiers. Other contingents were supplied by cities along the Phoenician* coast.

IV. *The Battle.* The battle may have begun badly for the Assyrians as troops of Hamath* are shown pressing over some Assyrian corpses. Shalmaneser III claims a complete victory with enemy dead blocking the Orontes River like a dam. The allies were pursued as far as Gilzau. As in the case of Deborah's battle (Judg 5:20–21), a storm may have mired the enemy chariots, for the king boasts: "like the god Hadad, I caused a deluge to overwhelm them."

V. *The Consequences.* That the Assyrian victory was far from complete is shown by the failure of the Assyrians to proceed to Hamath and by the fact that Shalmaneser III had to face the same coalition (without Israel) in his tenth, eleventh, and fourteenth years. Finally in 841 he invaded Israel itself (cf. Hos. 10:14–15).

Though the battle is not mentioned in the OT, the events before and after it may be better understood in relation to Qarqar. After initial hostilities between Ben-Hadad and Ahab (1 Kings 20), the two combatants were forced to join together in the face of the Assyrian threat (1 Kings 20:34; 22:1). After stopping the Assyrians at Qarqar, probably in July or August of 853, Ahab sought to recover Ramoth-Gilead from Damascus and perished in the attempt (that same year, according to Thiele's chronology; 1 Kings 22:3, 34–35).

VI. *Sargon II's Battle.* In 720 Sargon suppressed a coalition led by Ilubi'di of Hamath and joined by Arpad, Damascus, and Samaria* at Qarqar. His commemorative stele was found at Asharne (ancient Gilzau?) in 1924.

BIBLIOGRAPHY: L. W. King, ed., *Bronze Reliefs from the Gates of Shalmaneser . . .* (1915); A. T. Olmstead, "Shalmaneser III and the Establishment of the Assyrian Power," *JAOS*, 41 (1921), 345–82; D. Luckenbill, *ARAB*, 1 (1926), 200–252; F. Thureau-Dangin, "La Stèle d'Asharné," *Revue d'assyriologie*, 30 (1933), 53–56; G. Cameron, "The Annals of Shalmaneser III King of Assyria," *Sumer*, 6 (1950), 6–26; C. Whitley, "The Deuteronomic Presentation of the House of Omri," *VT*, 2 (1952), 137–52; E. Michel, "Die Assur-Texte Salmanassars III (858–824)," *WO*, 2.1 (1954), 27–45; ibid., 2.2 (1955), 137–57; ibid., 2.3 (1956), 221–33; ibid., 2.5–6 (1959), 408–15; M. Unger, *Israel and the Aramaeans of Damascus* (1957); J. Laessøe, "A Statue of Shalmaneser III from Nimrud," *Iraq*, 21 (1959), 147–57; W. Hallo, "From Qarqar to Carchemish . . . ," *BA*, 23 (1960), 34–61; H. Tadmor, "Que and Muṣri," *IEJ*, 11 (1961), 143–48; B. Mazar, "The Aramean Empire and Its Relations with Israel," *BA*, 25 (1962), 98–120; P. Hulin, "The Inscriptions on the Carved Throne-Base of Shalmaneser III," *Iraq*, 25 (1963), 48–69; E. Thiele, *The Mysterious Numbers of the Hebrew Kings*, 2d ed. (1965); M. Astour, "841 B.C.: The First Assyrian Invasion of Israel," *JAOS*, 91 (1971), 383–89; F. Cross, "The Stele Dedicated to Melcarth by Ben-Hadad of Damascus," *BASOR*, 205 (1972), 36–42; R. D. Barnett, "More Balawat Gates," *Symbolae Biblicae et Mesopotamicae*, ed. M. A. Beek et al. (1973); J. Brinkman, "Additional Texts from the Reigns of Shalmaneser III and Shamshi-Adad V," *JNES*, 32 (1973), 40–46; M. Elat, "The Campaigns of Shalmaneser III against Aram and Israel," *IEJ*, 25 (1975), 25–35; N. Na'aman, "Two Notes on the Monolith Inscription of Shalmaneser III from Kurkh," *Tel Aviv*, 3 (1976), 89–106; C. C. Smith, "Jehu and the Black Obelisk of Shalmaneser III," *Scripture in History and Theology*, ed. A. Merrill and T. Overholt (1977), 71–105; A. R. Green, "Sua and Jehu: The Boundaries of Shalmaneser's Conquest," *PEQ*, 111 (1979), 35–39; W. Shea, "The Kings of the Melqart Stela," *Maarav*, 1 (1979), 159–76.

EY

QASILE. See TELL QASILE.

QATNA (qät′nä). Identified with modern Mishrefeh, a tell* in central Syria about 21 km. (13 mi.) NE of Homs. An important city* from c. 2100 B.C. through the end of the Bronze Age,* with Hyksos* fortifications that rival those of Hazor* and Tell el-Yehudiyeh.

Mishrefeh was identified through excavations carried on from 1924 to 1929 by Count du Mesnil du Buisson and the French Archaeological Expedition. The ancient name was known through references from as early as the Sumerian Ur III period (when Qatna may have become something of a Sumerian* colony and pilgrimage center for worship of the goddess Nin-Egal) (cf. M. C. Astour, *Hellenosemitica* [1967], 160), and later from the Mari* correspondence, the Amarna Letters,* and even a reference in the annals of the Hittite* king Suppiluliumas* (c. 1360 B.C.). That the mound of Mishrefeh is actually to be identified with Qatna is considered certain, both through discovery of tablets within the city and through identification of the great temple to the goddess Belitekallim (Akkadian for Nin-Egal, a lesser goddess in the Sumerian pantheon).

Although there is some evidence of prehistoric occupation, Qatna first became prominent through its contacts with Ur,* and it has been suggested that Qatna, like Mari, was a Sumerian colony. Its original importance may have related to its situation on the shorter trade route across the desert from Mari on the Euphrates River, through Tadmor* (Palmyra*) and into central Syria (roughly the route of the railroad across Syria today). Pottery,* jewelry, and architecture indicate influence from Mesopotamia* in the early period, evidence which, taken with the treasures of the great temple, seems clearly to show its Mesopotamian dependence.

Qatna was in the area destined to be contested by Egypt,* Mesopotamia, and Hatti throughout the second millennium, and the rise of the Twelfth Dynasty (c. 1991 B.C.) with its sphere of influence extending to Syria, introduced a new element in the life of the city. Together with Sumerian or Akkadian* elements, there appear items of Egyptian manufacture, notably two sphinxes. From what is known of the times, it is probable that a loose Egyptian hegemony was exercised in the entire region until the rise of Hyksos power in the eighteenth century. It was also during this period that a dynasty of kings with Amorite* names was installed at Qatna, and relations with the Amorite dynasty in Mari are shown in some detail through the extensive correspondence discovered in the latter city.

In the Hyksos period, however, Qatna was destined for a new and more important role. Though temple and palace continue from the earlier times, and pottery styles are not radically different, a new element is added with a vast enclosure 1.2 km. (¾ mi.) square, making the city into what is thought to have been a mammoth military camp or cavalry center. Apparently this method of defense came S with the Hyksos rulers (whose origin is still unclear), and examples have been found as far N as Carchemish* and as far S as Tell el Yehudiyeh in the Egyptian Delta.

From c. 1550 until the Hittite* conquest in 1360, Qatna's fortunes varied. A restored text of Thutmose III points to that monarch's having taken the area (ANET, 239) in the mid-fifteenth century, and the name appears again in lists of cities made by the successors of Thutmose in the Eighteenth, Nineteenth, and Twentieth dynasties (ANET, 242-43). During this period Egyptian influence was on the decline, replaced to a large extent in Syria by the expanding Hurrian* state of Mitanni* with its capital at Washshuganni, probably near the Upper Khabur River. Egypt was, for a time, allied with Mitanni, and certainly the dominant cultural influence in Qatna, as in other cities of Syria in the period, was Hurrian. In the latter part of the period, known as the Amarna* Age, neither the Egyptian pharaohs, who were the nominal rulers of the area, nor the Mitannian princes, who controlled much of the trade and military movement in the region, were able to withstand the incursions of the growing Hittite Empire. A series of letters from Akizzi, prince of Qatna, addressed to the heretic Pharaoh Akhen-aton* (c. 1370–1353), poignantly appeal for help, not only against the rising power of the Hittites but against lesser but more immediate threats like his rapacious neighbor, Aziru of Amurru. The entire episode is brought to an end by the intervention of the great Hittite king, Suppiluliumas (1375–1340 B.C.), who lists Qatna as one of the cities deported in his campaign against Mitanni (ANET, 318; the entire period is discussed in detail in K. A. Kitchen, Suppiluliuma and the Amarna Pharaohs [1962]). Excavation of Mishrefeh confirms the completeness with which Suppiluliumas did his work, and the site was reduced to a state of second-rate importance, from which it never recovered.

Short reoccupations are recorded in the reigns of Seti I and Ramses II* and the city was finally taken from Hittite control when that empire and indeed the entire Levant was overrun by the Sea Peoples* in the early twelfth century B.C. The site was then abandoned and only briefly reoccupied in the sixth century.

BIBLIOGRAPHY: Preliminary reports in Syria, 7–11 (1926–30); Count du Mesnil de Buisson, Le Site Archéologique de Mishrife-Qatna (1935); W. Hallo, BW, 467–70.

CEA

QATRA. See EKRON.

QELT, WADI. See ACHOR, VALLEY OF.

QILA, KHIRBET. See KEILAH.

QIZZA. See KADESH KAH.

QSAR EL-ABD. See ARAQ EL-EMIR.

QUADRANT METHOD. A system of trench excavation designed particularly for exploring circular sites. When opposite quadrants have been exposed it is possible to observe the stratigraphy* of the area by studying the character of the major axes.

HWP

QUARRY. Limestone for the pyramids* of Egypt* was obtained from the Moktan hills just eastward across the Nile from Giza,* while grey and red sandstone, alabaster,* and diorite were brought from the Aswan* quarries* about 805 km. (500 mi.) upstream. In Palestine there are numerous sites which furnish evidence of quarrying. The place from which stones were obtained for Solomon's temple* (cf. 1 Kings 6:7) was most probably located E of the Damascus* Gate. Excavations at the site have uncovered partly-hewn blocks of stone and have thrown some light on ancient methods of quarrying. The quarries here, at Lachish,* Samaria,* and elsewhere indicate that the blocks of stone were outlined by means of narrow channels dug with iron picks on the four sides, and then pried loose or split along the grain of the rock by means of wooden wedges soaked in water. If the stone was not dressed immediately at the quarry, it was finished at the location of the building, as the stone chips from various sites suggest. Considerable engineering skill was involved in moving enormous blocks of stone, whether of Hittite* statuary, the limestone blocks of the Great Pyramid, some of which weighed an estimated 54,430 kg. (60 tons), or the more modest menhirs,* obelisks,* and monuments such as the Moabite Stone.*

RKH

Stone quern from Late Bronze Age (1550-1200 B.C.) and muller from Israelite Period (1200-586 B.C.), both found at Hazor. Courtesy Dagon Collection—Archaeological Museum of Grain Handling in Israel.

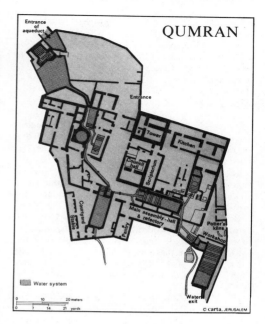

QUDEIRAT, AIN EL. *See* AIN EL QUDEIRAT.

QUERN (kwûrn). A device consisting of two hard stones used for grinding flour. The primitive saddle quern had a smaller upper stone with a raised thicker end like a saddle, providing an easy handgrip for the required backward and forward movement. This type has been recovered in Palestine from Megiddo,* while from Egypt* comes a Fifth-Dynasty statue* of a woman from Gizeh using a quern. The more elaborate type consisted of two round stones powered by a capstan or by water, and these querns were in general use during the post-Roman period. Matt 18:6 and Mark 9:42 seem to describe a mill whose power was supplied by a donkey.   HWP

QUIRINIUS (CYRENIUS) (kwī ri′ni us). This is not the place to discuss or recount the career of this distinguished Roman nobleman, nor the controversy over his period of authority at the time of the Herodian census. Two facts need to be borne in mind—first, that Luke, in these vital chapters, is obviously going out of his way to integrate the story of the Nativity with world history; and secondly, that details relevant to the issue are lamentably fragmentary. Archaeology has no certain evidence to offer, though it is a matter for which some as yet undiscovered epigraphical* evidence could easily provide the vital clue. In *Buried History*, the journal of the Australian Institute of Archaeology (vol. 10 [1974], 16–31), D. J. Hayles shows the indecisive nature of the Quirinius inscriptions used by W. M. Ramsay, and the famous Lapis Tiburtinus similarly falls short of providing decisive evidence.

BIBLIOGRAPHY: E. M. Blaiklock, *ZPEB*, 5 (1975), 5–6; id., *The Century of the NT* (1962), Appendix 1; R. Syme, *The Roman Revolution* (1939), index; W. M. Ramsay, *The Bearing of Recent Discovery of the Trustworthiness of the NT* (1915), 284ff.

EMB

QUJUNYIK. *See* NINEVEH.

QUMRAN (kūm rän′). A locality about 13 km. (8 mi.) S of Jericho,* where the Wadi Qumran emerges from the Judean hills on its way to the Dead Sea,* perhaps the City of Salt of Josh 15:62. On a rocky shelf N of the wadi,* about 1.2 km. (¾ mi.) W of the Dead Sea, lie the ruins called Khirbet Qumran. A cemetery

between the ruins and the sea was partially excavated by C. S. Clermont-Ganneau in 1873. Between 1947 and 1956 many manuscript scrolls (*see* DEAD SEA SCROLLS) and fragments were discovered in eleven caves* in the neighborhood. These manuscripts, which were written between c. 200 B.C. and A.D. 50, and include several copies of Hebrew scripture, apparently belonged to the library of a religious Jewish community, probably related to the Essenes.* Khirbet Qumran was thoroughly excavated between 1953 and 1956 and proved to have been occupied from c. 130 B.C. onward by a well-organized community, almost certainly the same community that owned the manuscripts. A break in the occupation coincided roughly with Herod the Great's reign (37–4 B.C.). The second phase of occupation was violently terminated c. A.D. 68; for the next twenty years the site was occupied by a Roman garrison. It was again briefly occupied by insurgents in the Second Jewish Revolt against Rome (A.D. 132–135).

See also QUMRAN NT FRAGMENTS.

BIBLIOGRAPHY: G. Vermés, *The Dead Sea Scrolls: Qumran in Perspective* (1977).

FFB

QUMRAN NT FRAGMENTS. Greek papyrus* fragments from Qumran* were identified by José O'Callaghan in 1972 as portions of the NT, dated to the first century A.D. If the identifications are correct, these portions would be our earliest NT MSS.

The Cave 7 Fragments. Cave 7, explored in 1955, is unique among the Qumran caves* as a site which yielded only Greek MSS (*see* DEAD SEA SCROLLS). The twenty-one tiny fragments inscribed in Greek uncial letters were originally published by M. Baillet in 1962. At that time the only fragments which were identified were 7Q1.1–2 as the LXX Exod 28:4–17 and 7Q.2 as the apocryphal Epistle of Jeremiah 43b–44. Palaeographically* these portions were dated to 100 B.C. In the cave was a large jar inscribed in Hebrew or Aramaic* *RWM'* "Rome." The cache of MSS may possibly have been deposited at the time of the Bar Kochba* Revolt c. A.D. 132–35.

O'Callaghan's Identifications. José O'Callaghan startled the scholarly world in 1972 by identifying ten of the Qumran 7 fragments as texts of the NT, dated between A.D. 50 and 100—four fragments from Mark, two from 1 Tim, and one each from Acts, Rom, James, and 2 Peter. O'Callaghan is the founder of *Studia Papyrologica*, head of the department of papyrology* at the Theological Seminary of San Cugat in Barcelona, Spain, and also professor of Greek papyrology at the Pontifical Biblical Institute in Rome. In making his identifications, O'Callaghan distinguishes between those which he believes are certain (7Q4, 7Q5, 7Q6.1, 7Q8), those that are probable (7Q6.2, 7Q7, 7Q9), and those that are possible (7Q10, 7Q15).

7Q4.1–2 is identified by O'Callaghan with 1 Tim 3:16–4:1, 3 and is dated c. A.D. 100. One fragment has the ends of five lines of text with seventeen whole and partial letters preserved and another fragment has but one line with three letters.

7Q5, identified with Mark 6:52–53 and dated to A.D. 50, has been the most publicized fragment. It is a fragment about 2.5 cm. (1 in.) wide and 3.8 cm. (1½ in.) long with five lines containing about twenty letters, nine of which are but partially preserved and uncertain. The reconstructed text differs from earlier MS evidence in omitting the phrase "EPI TĒN GĒN" and in spelling one word with an initial "T" instead of an initial "D." Before O'Callaghan's identification, 7Q5 had been dated by C. H. Roberts to 50 B.C.—A.D. 50 because of its "Zierstil" script. If its identification as a copy of a part of Mark's Gospel dated to A.D. 50 can be sustained, we could assume that the gospel was composed shortly after Christ's death.

7Q6.1 is identified with Mark 4:28 and dated to A.D. 50. This has but two lines with but ten letters, including six uncertain ones, inscribed in the Herculaneum script.

7Q8 is identified with James 1:23–24 and is dated to A.D. 70. There are four lines with seven letters in the Herculaneum* script.

7Q6.2 is identified with Acts 27:38 and is dated to A.D. 60. There are two lines with six letters, three of which are uncertain.

7Q7 is identified with Mark 12:17 and is dated to A.D. 50. There are two lines with but four letters.

7Q9 is identified with Rom 5:11–12 and is dated to A.D. 60. One line contains but four letters, two of which are uncertain.

7Q10 is identified with 2 Peter 1:15 and is of an uncertain date. It has but one line with two letters, one of which is uncertain.

7Q15 is identified with Mark 6:48 and is of an uncertain date. It contains one line with four letters.

Criticisms and Rejoinders. The tiny size of the fragments and the paucity of the letters preserved have raised doubts as to any possible identifications. What is an even graver criticism is the fact that other scholars working from the photos and in the case of Benoit firsthand from the papyri themselves in the Rockefeller Museum in Jerusalem differ in their identification of crucial letters in 7Q6.1, 7Q5, etc. from O'Callaghan's readings.

Since his initial studies O'Callaghan has studied the papyri themselves firsthand, and also infrared photos of the papyri and has continued to maintain his identifications. His supporters have argued that the probabilities involved in fitting an identification into the stichometry of several lines favor O'Callaghan's identifications. His critics, however, have suggested LXX passages that may fit some of the fragments. Baillet has suggested that 7Q3 may come from the LXX of Jer 43:28–29.

Inasmuch as O'Callaghan's identifications are based on his readings of a large number of uncertain letters, they cannot be accepted as incontrovertible evidence of NT MSS at Qumran.

BIBLIOGRAPHY: M. Baillet, J. T. Milik, and R. de Vaux, *Les "petites grottes" de Qumrân*, 1 (1962), 146–49; ibid., 2, plate xxx; J. O'Callaghan, "Papiros neotestamentarios en la cueva 7 de Qumrān?" *Bib.*, 53 (1972), 91–100; C. Martini, "Note sui papiri della grotta 7 di Qumrān," *Bib.*, 53 (1972), 101–4 (An English trans. by W. Holladay of the articles by O'Callaghan and Martini was distributed as a supplement of *JBL*, 91 [1972]); M. Baillet, "Les manuscrits de la Grotte 7 de Qumrân et le Nouveau Testament," *Bib.*, 53 (1972), 508–16; P. Benoit, "Note sur les fragments grecs de la grotte 7 de Qumrân," *RB*, 79 (1972), 321–24; D. Estrada, "The Fragments from Cave 7," *Eternity* (1972), 25–26; id., "On the Latest Identification of NT Documents," *WTJ*, 34 (1972), 109–17; J. A. Fitzmyer, "A Qumran Fragment of Mark?" *America* (June 24, 1972), 647–50; C. J. Hemer, "NT Fragments at Qumran?" *Tyndale Bulletin*, 23 (1972), 125–28; J. O'Callaghan, "1 Tim 3, 16; 4, 1.3 en 7Q4?" *Bib.*, 53 (1972), 362–67; id., "Notas sobre 7Q tomadas en el 'Rockefeller Museum' de Jerusalén," *Bib.*, 53 (1972), 517–33; id., "Tres probables papiros neotestamentarios en la cueva 7 de Qumrān," *SPap*, 11 (1972), 83–89; C. H. Roberts, "On Some Presumed Papyrus Fragments of the NT from Qumran," *JTS*, 23 (1972), 446–47; E. J. Vardaman, "The Earliest Fragments of the NT?" *ET*, 83 (1972), 374–76; W. White, Jr., "A Layman's Guide to O'Callaghan's Discovery," *Eternity*, 23 (1972), 27–31; id., "O'Callaghan's Identifications: Confirmation and Its Consequences," *WTJ*, 34 (1972), 15–20; G. E. Wright, "Are NT Manuscripts to be Found among the Dead Sea Scrolls?" *ASOR Newsletter*, 11 (June, 1972), 1–4; M. Baillet, "Les manuscrits de la grotte 7 de Qumrân et le Nouveau Testament," *Bib.*, 54 (1973), 340–50; P. Benoit, "Nouvelle note sur les fragments grecs de la grotte 7 de Qumrân," *RB*, 80 (1973), 5–12; G. D. Fee, "Some Dissenting Notes on 7Q5=Mark 6:52–53," *JBL*, 92 (1973), 109–12; P. Garnet, "O'Callaghan's Fragments: Our Earliest

NT Texts?" *EQ*, 45 (1973), 6–12; C. J. Hemer, "The 7Q Fragments Reconsidered," *Themelios*, 9 (1973), 14–16; A. C. Urbán, "Observaciones sobre ciertos papiros de la cueva 7 de Qumran," *RQ*, 30 (1973), 233–51; E. J. Vardaman, "The Gospel of Mark and 'The Scrolls,'" *ChT*, 17.25 (Sept. 28, 1973), 4–7; W. White, Jr., "Notes on the Papyrus Fragments from Cave 7 at Qumran," *WTJ*, 35 (1973), 221–26; J. O'Callaghan, *Los Papiros Griegos de la Cueva 7 de Qumran* (1974); A. C. Urbán, "La identificación de 7Q4 con Núm 14.23–24 y la restauración de textos antiquos,"*Estudios Biblicos*, 34 (1974); R. Lester, "Does Qumran Cave 7 Contain NT Materials?" *Perspectives in Religious Studies*, 2 (1975), 203–14; D. Estrada and W. White, Jr., *The First New Testament* (1978).

R

RAAMSES. *See* RAMESES, CITY OF.

RABBAH (rab′ə; Heb. רַבָּה, *rabbāh*, great or capital city). Also called Rabbat of the sons of Ammon.* The capital city of Ammon, Rabbah, near the headwaters of the brook Jabbok E of Jordan, was the name given to the capital city* of the Ammonites. The site gives evidence of having had some kind of occupation from Palaeolithic* times down to the present when it is better known as Amman, the capital of Jordan. Excavations in Amman have been extensively carried out, with major efforts mounted by the Museo Nazionale Romano under G. Guidi from 1927–29 and continuously since 1947 by various scholars under the general sponsorship of the Jordan Department of Antiquities. Particularly noteworthy have been discoveries of Iron Age* tombs, a Late Bronze Age* temple (discovered when building the Amman airport), a major new inscription probably dating to the ninth century B.C., and an abundance of Greco-Roman buildings.

From prehistoric times come flint implements (probably Palaeolithic) but of more interest are a series of dolmens* and menhirs* (kinds of crude stone monuments) considered to date from the Neolithic* or Chalcolithic* periods. Much later in time is a putative Early Bronze–Middle Bronze burial, followed by tombs SW of the citadel* dating to the Hyksos* period (MB II, c. 1600 B.C.).

True Ammonite occupation can be traced to the Late Bronze Age when a wall* was built around the Citadel Hill, remains of which may be seen only in the NE corner of the hill. Much fuller documentation for the period came with the discovery of the LB temple at the site of the current airport. It is a small shrine, about 4.3 sq. m. (46 sq. ft.), formed of a shrine within a shrine and a series of outer rooms. Construction is of unhewn stone, and within the rubble were uncovered offerings of various kinds of jewelry, seals,* scarabs,* and pottery.* Most notable is the presence, for the first time in Trans-Jordan, of a horde of Mycenaean* pottery.

While it is not known how extensive the Bronze Age city was (it has been suggested that the temple may have been used for travelers), it is clear in the light of the sedentary nature of the occupation that some modification of Nelson Glueck's strictures against an earlier Exodus may be in order. Nevertheless, it is with the Iron Age that the city referred to in the Conquest narrative (Deut 3:11) as the resting place of the iron* bedstead* of Og is more clearly known. The biblical narrative (2 Sam 11–12, 1 Chron

Figure of man carved in limestone (height: 45 cm.) from ninth to eighth century B.C., found at northern end of citadel in Amman. Courtesy Studium Biblicum Franciscanum, Jerusalem.

20) reflects an Israelite conquest of the city, following a long siege, and accomplished in two parts. After the initial capture by Joab and his men of the "royal city" (probably the Citadel on the hill N of the Wadi Amman), and the "city of waters" (probably related to the water supply for the citadel), David finished the conquest of the entire city.

From the Iron Age has come a series of tombs, fully furnished with a good supply of "Ammonite" pottery (cf. R. Amiran, *Ancient Pottery of the Holy Land*, pl. 101). Unfortunately, most of the tombs come from the later or Iron II period (Amiran dates the pottery from 731–550 B.C.), so there is little evidence for the time of David.

A startling find made in 1961 during excavations on the SW crest of the citadel by R. W. Dajani was a stone inscription of eight lines, dated by F. M. Cross and others to the mid-ninth century B.C. The script and the language closely resemble Hebrew of the period, a fact that is demonstrated even more graphically in the Amman Citadel Inscription (as it has come to be known) than in the eighth-century Moabite Stone.*

Sometime after the death of Solomon,* Ammon again became independent, a condition that continued without a break through both the Assyrian and Babylonian conquests, though destruction of the city was prophesied by Amos (1:14), Jeremiah (49:2–3) and Ezekiel (21:20, 28–32 and 25:2–7). In the latter case it was the gloating of the Ammonites at the destruction of Judah's temple* that called forth the prophetic wrath, and apparently the fulfillment came shortly thereafter in c. 580 B.C.

The city was rebuilt by Ptolemy* Philadelphus (285–247 B.C.), who renamed it Philadelphia.* Conquest by the Seleucids followed in 218 B.C., utilizing a water tunnel, remains of which can be seen, and the city eventually became a member of the league of the Decapolis.* Under the Romans most of the remaining monuments were built, including an impressive amphitheater,* a colonnaded street,* a smaller theater* of Odeum, an aqueduct,* and a bath. The height of this glory came in the second and third centuries A.D. In Byzantine* times Philadelphia was the seat of a Christian bishopric, but the city fell to the Muslim conqueror Yezid in 635 A.D. It has continued as an Arab city to the present time.

BIBLIOGRAPHY: D. MacKenzie, "The Megalithic Monuments of Rabbath Ammon at Amman," *PEFA*, 1 (1911), 1–40; J. B. Hennessy, "Excavation of Late Bronze Age Temple," *PEQ* (1966), 155–62 and plates; S. H. Horn, "The Amman Citadel Inscription," *BASOR*, 193 (1969), 2–12; F. M. Cross, "Epigraphic Notes on the Amman Citadel Inscription," *BASOR*, 193 (1969), 13–18; W. F. Albright, "Some Comments on the Amman Citadel Inscription," *BASOR*, 198 (1970), 4–7; R. Amiran, *Ancient Pottery of the Holy Land* (1970), 294–97; E. K. Vogel, "Amman" in "Bibliography of Holy Land Sites," *HUCA*, 42 (1971), 7–8; M. Avi-Yonah and E. Stern, "Rabbath-Ammon," *EEHL*, 4 (1978), 987–92; J. Kaplan, "Rabah, Wadi," *EEHL* 4 (1978), 994.   CEA

RACHEL, TOMB OF. The traditional site of Rachel's

Rachel's Tomb. Courtesy Israel Government Press Office.

burial place (Gen 48:7), about 1.6 km. (1 mi.) N of Bethlehem,* was marked originally by a pillar which was still in existence in the time of Samuel (1 Sam 10:2). Some scholars have interpreted Gen 35:16; 1 Sam 10:2; and Jer 31:15 as locating the site on the northern border of Benjamin, about 19 km. (12 mi.) N of Jerusalem.* Against this the reference in Gen 35:19 has been held to suggest a place S of Jerusalem in the vicinity of Bethlehem. The topography presents problems, if only because of the difficulty of identifying the location of Benjamin's border. Jer 31:15 can hardly be adduced as evidence since it says nothing about the location of Ramah or that Rachel's tomb was actually there. If the traditional site is rejected as being too far S of the border of Benjamin, some other unidentified Ephrath farther to the N would have to be posited. The traditional site was marked by a small pyramid* about A.D. 350. The present domed structure with its vestibule was constructed by the Crusaders in the twelfth century A.D.

BIBLIOGRAPHY: B. K. Waltke, *ZPEB*, 4 (1975), 25–26.   EMB

RACING. *See* GAMES.

RADDANA (rə dan′ ə). The Arabic name of a hill near the village of Ramallah 16 km. (10 mi.) N of Jerusalem.* Although Raddana is not mentioned in the Bible, Professor Y. Aharoni of Tel Aviv University proposes that it be identified with the biblical Ataroth Adar (Josh 16:5; 18:13), a border town between Benjamin and Ephraim.

Several seasons of excavation were conducted at the site after 1969 by Robert Cooley and Joseph Callaway.

The excavators found evidence of four phases of occupation in the history of the site. Some Early-Bronze* pottery* (3200–2100 B.C.) may indicate some type of early habitation, but the two main phases were Iron I* (1200–900 B.C.). Two extensive resident complexes with five units of rooms gave evidence of an agricultural* settlement. Numerous pits, storage jars, grinding stones, and flint sickle blades were found. Several water collection systems and cisterns* with filtering pits were excavated. The houses* had packed dirt floors and roofs were probably also made with clay.* An interesting example of the use of hewn pillars for building was also connected with this phase; it may illustrate the architecture of the Philistine* house in which Samson* killed 3,000 people by pushing the pillars apart. Byzantine* pottery (A.D. 323–638) may be evidence for a later phase of habitation, but no structures were excavated.

Among the other finds were a large crater bowl, a chalice, a stone bowl, metal chisels, spatula, hoe, and pins, as well as an inscription that provides clear evidence for settlements in the region and for the date of the Israelite conquest. There was evidence of destruction by war and resettlement, which may illustrate the Benjamite civil war (Judg 19–21); hundreds of sling-stones were found.

BCC

RADIOCARBON (CARBON 14) DATING. See DATING, ARCHAEOLOGICAL.

RADIOMETRIC ASSAY. A test which works on the same general principle as that of the fluorine assay. It seeks to measure the amount of uranium in an artifact* such as a bone. Since osseous tissue in deposits absorbs a certain amount of water from the site, a reasonably exact measurement can provide valuable chronological and other information. The test is best employed in conjunction with others. See also DATING.

HWP

RAM. See ARAM, ARAMEANS.

RAMAH. See HIGH PLACE.

RAMESES (RAAMSES), CITY OF (ram'ə sēz; from Egyp. *[pr]-R'mss*, *"Estate of [king] Ramses"*). A famous Delta residence largely built by Ramses II* (thirteenth century B.C.). In that area, at an earlier date, Joseph's* family was settled in the land of Goshen (Gen 47:11). Pithom* and Rameses were store-cities, among the last projects on which the Hebrew slaves* worked on the eve of the Exodus (Exod 1:11), and Rameses was in fact the starting point of their long odyssey (Exod 12:37; Num 33:3, 5).

The location of Rameses (the Per-Ramesses of numerous Egyptian texts) has long been discussed. For many years, it and the Hyksos* city of Avaris were identified with Tanis*/Zoan, mainly because of the sheer quantity of Ramesside stonework—statues,* obelisks,* temple wall-blocks, pillars, stelae*—found there by Montet and earlier excavators. However, three factors now make it almost certain that Tanis is not, in fact, Avaris and Rameses. First, the total geographical data of the Egyptian references do not suit: Tanis is in a salt marsh region that was never the agricultural* paradise of the texts (exaggerations being allowed for), and it is not on "the Water of Re" Nile course. But both geographical aspects are amply fulfilled by a large site at Qantir-Khataana-Tell Daba, in a fertile region and directly adjoining the course of the former "Water of Re." Second, some textual references (Memphis* and onomasticon* lists) distinguish between Per-Ramesses and Tanis as two distinct places. Third, all the mass of Ramesside stonework at Tanis is reused building material,

brought from elsewhere to build Tanite temples cheaply, by the Twenty-first and Twenty-second dynasties. None of it is *in situ*, and there are no Rameside foundations. Meanwhile, at Qantir-Khataana-Tell Daba, original Ramesside foundations and remains *in situ* have now been found, including house* doorways of the chief ministers of state of Ramses II, feet of colossi, etc. The gods of Rameses were Amun, Re, Seth, and various goddesses. Brilliantly colored tiles* from a palace of Ramses II are known, and small stelae dedicated by soldiers to his deified statues.* The glories of Rameses rivaled those of Memphis and Thebes.*

BIBLIOGRAPHY: M. Hamza, *ASAE*, 30 (1930), 31–68; L. Habachi, *ASAE* 52 (1954), 443–559; W. C. Hayes, *Glazed Tiles from the Palace of Ramesses II at Kantir* (1937); J. van Seters, *The Hyksos* (1966), 127–51; E. P. Uphill, *JNES*, 27 (1968), 299–316; id., 28 (1969), 15ff.; M. Bietak, *Tell el-Dab'a II*, (1975).

KAK

RAMET EL-KHALIL. See MAMRE.

RAMET RAHEL. See BETH HACCEREM.

RAMITH, TELL. See RAMOTH GILEAD.

RAMOTH GILEAD (rā'məth gil'i əd; Heb. רָמוֹת גִּלְעָד, *rāmôṯ gil'āḏ*). An important site of uncertain location in former Gileadite territory. It was a city of refuge (Deut 4:43; Josh 20:8) of the Merarite Levites (Josh 21:38). Solomon* established the city* as the chief of his sixth administrative district, but from the time when the kingdom divided, Ramoth Gilead was subjected to attack and occupation by Syria. Ahab* attempted to assert Israel's* claim to the city after the battle of Qarqar* (853 B.C.), but was killed there in an indecisive battle. It was a decade before Ahab's son Joram captured and fortified Ramoth Gilead, but when a follower of Elisha anointed Jehu as king, the new ruler rode immediately to Jezreel and slew Joram, who had been recuperating there from battle wounds (2 Kings 8:28–9:28).

The *Onomasticon* of Eusebius located Ramoth Gilead 24 km. (15 mi.) W of Philadelphia,* modern Amman, while Glueck and Albright preferred Husn Ajlun, somewhat to the N. Excavations by P. Lapp at Tell er-Ramith in 1967 provide the best evidence for locating ancient Ramoth Gilead. The site is 5 km. (3 mi.) S of Ramtha and 24 km. (15 mi.) E of Irbid, an area that preserves part of the ancient name, while the elevated location of the tell* on a hill above the nearby plain would be ideal for a defensive fortress.

BIBLIOGRAPHY: N. Glueck, *AASOR*, 25–28 (1951), 95–100; S. Cohen, *IDB*, 4 (1962), 10; H. Jamieson, *ZPEB*, 5 (1975), 33–35.

RKH

RAMSES (RAMESSES) II (ram'sēz; Egyp. *r'mssw*, "Ra [the sun-god] is the one who begot him"). A pharaoh of the Nineteenth Dynasty noted for his monumental building activity, who ruled c. 1290–1224 B.C.

The reign of Ramses II was the high-water mark of the Nineteenth Dynasty, a fact reflected in the

Ramses II, detail of seated granite statue (height: 1.94 m.). The king wears a blue war crown with the uraeus (raised cobra) on the front. He holds a crook in his right hand, reminiscent of the god Osiris. Courtesy Turin Museum.

long period of peace attendant upon his rule, as well as in the monumental architecture of the time. For the first twenty-one years of his reign foreign affairs commanded much of the monarch's attention, as the growing power of the Hittites* challenged the traditional suzerainty of Egypt* in central and N Syria.

In his fifth year he undertook what was intended to be a showdown battle with the Hittite Muwatallis at Kadesh* on the Orontes River. Although Egyptian records praise the greatness of the victory, it is clear that the result was less than conclusive. By the twenty-first year of Ramses an alliance was created by the signing of a treaty between the king and Hattusilis, the text of which has been preserved both in Egyptian and Hittite records.

Most of the rest of the reign of Ramses II is concerned with building. Although he shamelessly attached his own name to much that was built by his predecessors, he was personally responsible for some of the most massive construction to be seen in Egypt today. His new capital in the Delta, Pi-Ramses, or House of Ramses, was built on the foundation of the old Hyksos* capital at Avaris and may have been the scene of the Hebrew slave* labor noted in Exodus. The more impressive monuments were left in the S. The Hypostyle* Hall at Karnak, the Rameseum at Thebes,* the colossi at Memphis* and especially the massive cliff temple at Abu-Simbel* stand as mute testimony to his power and vision. Although the dominant impression is one of power and might rather than grace and beauty, the total picture is magnificent by any standards and represents the glory of Egypt at its height.

BIBLIOGRAPHY: J. H. Breasted, *A History of Egypt* (1905), chs. 21, 22; J. A. Wilson, *The Burden of Egypt* (1951, also published as *The Culture of Ancient Egypt*), ch. 10; A. Gardiner, *Egypt of the Pharaohs* (1961), ch. 10, plus bibliography (especially pictorial) from sites mentioned above; R. Giveon, "Two Inscriptions of Ramesses II," *IEJ* 25 (1975), 247–49.

CEA

RAS ABU TABAT. *See* TABBATH.

RAS EL-AIN. *See* ANTIPATRIS.

RAS ES-SIYAGHA. *See* NEBO.

RASSAM CYLINDER. This cuneiform* record is dated 660 B.C. and, in typical Assyrian language, describes the revenge taken on the assassins of Sennacherib* (2 Kings 19:37).

"I tore out the tongues of those whose slanderous mouths had uttered blasphemies against my god Ashur and had plotted against me . . . I defeated them. The others I smashed alive with the very same statues of protective deities with which they had smashed my own grandfather Sennacherib. . . . I fed their corpses, cut into small pieces, to dogs, pigs, zibu-birds, vultures, the birds of the sky and to the fish of the ocean."

Sennacherib had died twenty years earlier, as is described in an inscription of Esarhaddon*—the so-called Prism S. It runs:

"In the month Nisan . . . I made my glad entrance into the royal palace, the awesome place in which is the fate of kings. A firm determination fell upon my brothers. They forsook the gods and returned to their deeds of violence. . . . They slew Sennacherib, their father. . . . The gods looked with disfavour upon the deed of the villains, which was committed in defiance of the will of the gods, and did not aid them. But they brought their forces to utter confusion and made them submit themselves to me.

"I rent my garments, and raised a cry. I roared like a lion, my passion was aroused. . . . I did not delay one day nor two. I did not even wait for my armies. I did not look back . . . I made my way to Nineveh [q.v.] painfully but quickly. . . . The people of Assyria . . . kissed my feet.

"As for those villains who instigated revolt . . . they fled to parts unknown."

BIBLIOGRAPHY: *ANET* (1950), 288–89.

EMB

RAS SHAMRA. *See* UGARIT.

RECONSTRUCTION. The restoration of archaeological sites by the use of fallen material, or the reconstruction of buildings and the painting* of fresco copies as they are known to have been originally. Pillars and stones at the Parthenon and Stonehenge have been set back in place, and this procedure has met with general acceptance. At Knossos, however, walls have been rebuilt and the original frescoes removed, while copies have been painted on the restored walls. The synagogue* at Capernaum* and the storehouse* walls and fortifications at Masada* have also been partially restored.

HWP

RED SEA. Together with the two northern branches, the Gulf of Aqaba and the Gulf of Suez, it forms part of the Great Rift Valley which extends from N of the Sea of Galilee* S into Africa. It separates Egypt* from Arabia.*

The term in the OT *"yam suph"* is used particularly of the Bitter Lakes region, between the Gulf of Suez and the Nile Delta. It is generally recognized that *"suph"* is a Hebrew borrowing from the Egyptian word *"th w f"*—papyrus,* attested by many texts. The Egyptian term *"p th w f"* is identified as the papyrus marshes in the NE Delta region, in the same area as the localized meaning of the Hebrew term. *"Yam suph"* also includes more general references. Num 33:10–11 seems to refer to the Gulf of Suez, while Num 14:25; 21:4; Deut 1:40; 2:1; Judg 11:16; 1 Kings 9:26 seem to indicate the Gulf of Aqaba.

The record of the crossing of the sea is found in Exod 14:10–15:22. The Israelites moved out from Rameses* in the NE Delta and went SE to Succoth.* They did not attempt to leave Egypt by the coastal highway known as "the way of the land of the Philistines"—the main military route to Canaan* and well fortified. From Succoth they turned northward, and, finding the way barred, they moved S to cross the sea. This crossing may well have taken place just N of the present-day Bitter Lakes area. The digging of the Suez Canal has now drained this region considerably, resulting in some original marshland disappearing. When the Israelites crossed this area, the marshlands would have been more extensive than the present land would indicate and would have constituted a formidable military barrier. The Lord drove the waters back by a strong E wind so that there was dry land on which the Israelites could cross this area (Exod 14:21).

It has been observed that this area can be affected by an E wind in the same way as in Exod 14. In 1882 Major-General Tulloch was engaged in military investigations relating to the Suez Canal. He noticed that the waters of Lake Menzaleh, about 1.5 to 1.8 m. (5 to 6 ft.) in depth, had been affected by an easterly gale during one day. The water had receded for about 11 km. (7 mi.). A similar phenomenon has been observed later (1945–46).

Therefore, on the evidences from geographical data, natural phenomena, and language, the *"yam suph"* of Exod 14 seems best to be located in the watery marshlands around the Bitter Lakes.

No one knows exactly where the name Red Sea came from; it may have been a mistake of one of the early Greek historians, or there may be some simple explanation like the red color of the light reflecting from the mountains, red corals, the complexion of the people in the vicinity, or, as some classical writers explain, the name of a king, Erythras (i.e., "red"). Whatever the origin of the designation "red," it does not come from the Hebrew Bible.

"Yam suph," as is mentioned above, is also used for the Gulf of Aqaba (1 Kings 9:26) in reference to

Solomon's* commercial fleet at Ezion Geber*—Elath.* The color "red" does not even appear in the Septuagint translation of this reference. In this area, archaeologists have identified several sites as possible large copper and iron* mines and furnaces.*

The discovery of mining* sites in the Arabah N of the Gulf of Aqaba dating from the era of Solomon, together with the exploration of the Nabataean* city of Aila and Tell el-Kheleifeh, have given archaeologists evidence that possibly identifies Ezion Geber on the Red Sea. These discoveries also show that the shoreline of the gulf has remained almost where it was three thousand years ago, contrary to popular belief that it had receded.

BIBLIOGRAPHY: N. Glueck, "Explorations in Eastern Palestine," *AASOR*, 15 (1934, 1935), 1ff.; W. F. Albright, *BASOR*, 109 (1948), 15ff.

DWS and BCC

REFINING. The Hebrews described the general process of melting by the term *zāqaq* (cf. 1 Chron 28:18; Job 28:1 et al.), reserving the more specific word *tsāraph* (Akkad. *ṣarpu*) for the smelting of ores by fire (cf. Isa 1:25; Jer 6:29 et al.). The earliest attempts at refining involved the placing of ore on a fire without the use of a container, but later techniques employed well-baked pottery* crucibles (cf. Prov 17:3) on a hearth or in an oven.* For the refining of iron* ore, which required higher temperatures than copper, gold,* or silver,* a natural forced-draft furnace was developed by the Hittites.* This technique appears to have been employed c. 2500 B.C. by a group which lived to the N and E of Mount Ararat.* In this area Russian archaeologists discovered an astronomical observatory and ancient iron smelters. These archaeologists claim that this center, excavated about 1972, is the oldest known metallurgical* processing plant of its kind.

The remains of a Palestinian copper smelting furnace from the Early Iron Age* were found at Tell Qasile.* Twin* clay crucibles were placed on a tile hearth, and the coals underneath were supplied with air which passed through a channel lined with mud bricks. A conical shaft made of stones covered the hearth, thereby concentrating the heat. When refined, the ore was withdrawn from the bottom of the structure.

At Timnah* in S Israel,* Beno Rothenberg uncovered a network of copper mines in 1971, dating from about 1400 B.C. This was in the general area in which Glueck, thirty years earlier, had found an enormous slag heap which he had associated with "King Solomon's* mines," thought to have been in the locality. The mines discovered by Rothenberg proved to be more complex and sophisticated than most mines constructed a millennium later. He estimated that the refining of copper ore may have begun at the site as early as 4000 B.C. At that period the ore was heated up in a roughly dug hole in the ground. The heat was insufficient to enable the copper to separate, but it did make it possible for the metal to form into pellets which could be chipped off when the mass was sufficiently cool.

Later on the miners used iron oxide as a means of

separating the metal from the ore. Rothenberg maintains that the iron as oxide was mined at the site, as was the case with other copper mines. In a metaphorical sense God was described as the master refiner, ever seeking to recover the pure metal of spirituality from among men (cf. Isa 1:25; Jer 6:29–30; Mal 3:2–3 et al.).

BIBLIOGRAPHY: J. R. Partington, *A Text-book of Inorganic Chemistry* (1950 ed.), 776–80, 786–89; W. A. Phair, *EBr*, 12 (1970), 602–28; F. C. Thompson, *EBr*, 15 (1970), 232–35.

RKH

REGGIO. *See* RHEGIUM.

RELIGION. *See* ABLUTIONS; ALTAR; AMULET; ARK OF THE COVENANT; ARTEMIS; ASHERAH; BAAL; BAPTISM; BASIN; CALF, GOLDEN; CHERUBIM; CHILD SACRIFICE; COVENANT; CREATION EPIC, BABYLONIAN; CRUCIFIXION; DAGON; EPISKOPOS; ESCHATOLOGY; ESSENES; EXORCISM; FOUNDATION SACRIFICE; FUNERARY CUSTOMS, PALESTINIAN; GENIZEH; GILGAMESH EPIC; HEBREW RELIGION; HIGH PLACE; IDOLS; IMMORTALITY; INCANTATION; INCENSE; ISHTAR, DESCENT OF; LACERATION; MARRIAGE; MITHRAS; NABONIDUS, PRAYER OF; OFFERINGS; OSIRIS; PHYLACTERIES; PROSTITUTION, CULTIC; PSEUDEPIGRAPHA; SYNAGOGUE; TEMPLE, JERUSALEM; TERAPHIM; THOMAS, GOSPEL OF; ZEUS.

RESURRECTION. *See* NAZARETH DECREE.

RETABA, TELL ER-. *See* PITHOM.

RHEGIUM (rē'ji um; Gr. Ῥήγιον, *Rhégion*; modern Reggio). The spelling is disputed and is complicated by naive ancient ideas of etymology. The Greeks, thinking of Sicily as "broken" from Italy by the 11.3 km. (7 mi.)–wide Messina strait, derived the word from *rhēgnumi*—"to break." Italians favored the root meaning "royal," hence the "h" or the absence of it. The name is probably pre-Greek, and if one derivation is to be preferred to the other, the Latin (Italian) origin of the word is the more likely.

The town, at any rate, was a Greek colony on the toe of the Italian peninsula opposite Messana and founded in 720 B.C. by Chalcis with a strong infusion of Messenians, whose colony was itself only a few years older.

Rhegium was originally an oligarchy, but little is known of the first two centuries of its history. Anaxilas is named as its "tyrant" (in the Greek sense of that word) in the generation 494 to 476 B.C. and led the city* in a bout of imperialism. Thus involved in Sicilian politics, Rhegium found destruction at Syracuse's hands in 387 B.C. Rebuilt, it is found later in control of Campanian mercenaries (280 to 270 B.C.) and successfully resisted the two conquerors Pyrrhus and Hannibal in the same century.

As the occupant of a strategic watch-point opposite the Sicilian bridgehead into Italy, Rhegium was especially cultivated by Rome* and proved a loyal ally, receiving municipal status in 90 B.C.

The history, pieced together by coinage,* epigraphy,* and literary sources, has so far received scant help from archaeology.

BIBLIOGRAPHY: H. Philipp, "Rhegium," *PWRE*, 2.Reihe (1914), cols. 487–502; E. M. Blaiklock, *ZPEB*, 5 (1975), 100–101.

EMB

RHODES (rōdz; Gr. Ῥόδος, *Rhódos*). An island 69 km. (43 mi.) by approximately 16 km. (10 mi.), off the SW coast of Asia Minor,* with its main city* (on the N) bearing the same name. In the Bible, Rhodes is mentioned only in Acts 21:1.

The island's earliest civilization starts with the Bronze Age.* Later, Minoans* and Dorians made their influence felt on the cities of Ialysos, Lindos, and Camirus. In the city of Rhodes, founded in 408 B.C. by the great city-planner, Hippodamos of Miletus* (Strabo, 14.2.9, 654), was established the greatest of all Rhodian festivals, the Halieia, dedicated to the great Rhodian god, Helios; games were celebrated every four years as inscriptions of the fourth century B.C. testify.

After successful resistance to the siege of Demetrius (305–304 B.C.), an immense Colossus, a bronze* statue* of Helios 32 m. (105 ft.) high, was erected at the entrance to the harbor of Rhodes. It was broken off in an earthquake of about 227 B.C. In Roman times the city of Rhodes was famous for its monuments and art.

Archaeological work has been difficult to do at ancient Rhodes because of the extensive rebuilding of the city. The ancient remains of the cities of Lindos and Camirus and the cemeteries (*see* NECROPOLIS) of Ialysos are better preserved.

Excavations conducted in 1930–32 in Rhodes and the islands under the direction of Professor Giulio Jacopi have produced from Camirus tomb groups, acropolis* remains, archaic votive offerings,* inscriptions, pottery* dating from late Minoan to Hellenistic times (including some Eastern Greek seventh-century jugs, Attic black-and-red-figured ware), two sixth-century sculptured archaic male torsos, and statuettes with Egyptian and orientalizing motif. Also, excavation of the cemetery of Rhodes was conducted, and excavations at Nisyros produced some Eastern Greek vases and part of a seated woman of a late fifth-century Attic stele.* Work at Scarpanto showed mosaics* in the early Christian basilicas* of Arcassa.

BIBLIOGRAPHY: *Clara Rhodos*, 6–7 (1932–33), Instituto Storico-Archaeologico di Rodi, in "Reviews and Notes," *PEQ*, 65 (1933), 212–13; I. R. Arnold, "Festivals of Rhodes," *AJA*, 40 (1936), 432–36; E. G. Kraeling, *Bible Atlas* (1956), 452; E. M. Blaiklock, *ZPEB*, 5 (1975), 101–3; *PECS*, 755–75.   WHM

RHYTON (rī'ton). An elongated oval jar, sometimes made of precious metal, with a shaped base for easy insertion into the ground. Occasionally some specimens had a hole at the lower extremity by which the flow of the liquid, usually a libation to a deity, could be controlled. Rhytons were a product of the Minoan* civilization and were common among the earlier Greeks. They also appeared in Persia during the Achaemenid regime.   HWP

ROADS, ROMAN. The Roman world of the first century A.D. had an excellent system of communications. Major roads radiated out from Rome* to all areas of the empire. Lengthy sections of these roads are still traceable today throughout the empire; sometimes portions have been incorporated into existing highways. The course of others has been revealed by aerial photography.* Many milestones have been discovered.

Construction. The classic formula for building a major Roman highway was to lay a foundation of large stones (or of wooden piles in marshy ground). On this was laid a layer of smaller stones cemented with lime.* Next came another layer of even smaller stones and rubble or gravel and concrete. The paving consisted of flat blocks of flint stones of irregular shape. The whole construction was .6 to .9 m. (2 to 3 ft.) in depth. The surface was cambered, and gutters on the sides helped to carry off excess rainwater. Naturally, construction methods varied from area to area, and there were lesser roads of less solid form. There were milestones at regular intervals and resting places or posthouses (*mansiones* in Latin;* cf. John 14:2) for relays for the imperial post.

Names. Roman roads generally bore the names of distinguished Romans connected with their original construction, hence such names as the Appian Way,* the "queen of roads" that ran S from Rome. The Appii Forum and Tres Tabernae (the Three Taverns of Acts 28:15 were situated on it. When Romans traveled E they sailed from Brundisium to the Adriatic Coast opposite and used the great Egnatian Way* through Macedonia.* There were many local provincial roads, such as those used by Paul in Asia Minor.* When traveling from Perga* to Iconium* (Acts 13:13ff.), he is most likely to have used the road in the area built by the emperor Augustus* and called the Via Sebaste in an inscription (*ILS* 5828). Sebaste is Greek for Augusta.

BIBLIOGRAPHY: W. M. Ramsay, "Roads," *HDB* (1904, rev. 1963); F. J. Foakes-Jackson and K. Lake, eds., *The Beginnings of Christianity*, 5 (1932, rep. 1966), 224ff.; J. E. Forbes, *Notes on the History of Ancient Roads* (1934). For photographs, see V. W. von Hagen, *The Roads That Led to Rome* (1967) and R. Chevallier, *Roman Roads*, 1976; for an exhaustive treatment of the Roman roads in Britain, see I. D. Margary, *Roman Roads in Britain* (1957).

DBS

ROMAN GOVERNMENT, ADMINISTRATION OF CITIES. The Roman Empire was far less centralized than other empires and had a remarkably small bureaucracy for administrative purposes. This meant that much devolved upon local initiative in the provinces. The provinces themselves were not homogeneous geographical units from the juridical angle. The inhabitants differed widely from each other in status, even apart from the basic distinction between slave* and free. A person's status depended upon the city* or community of which he was a legal member. The Roman Empire has in fact been described as a collection of cities, and this condition is faithfully reflected in the NT. The basic distinction was between colonies and other cities enjoying varying degrees of "freedom," i.e., autonomy.

I. *Colonies.* A colony, in Roman terminology, was not a country as in the modern phrase "a colonial territory." It was a town whose inhabitants were Roman citizens of the same status as those of Rome* itself. (Note the use of the phrase "us . . . being Romans" by citizens of Philippi* in Acts 16:21.) They enjoyed full local self-government and generally modeled their administrative system on that of Rome itself. Every year annual "magistrates" or executive officials were elected. The two most important were usually simply called "the two men" (*duouiri*), to avoid the title of "consul" used in Rome. Their attendants were called lictors, the "officers" of Acts 16:35. The magistrates were members of the permanent town council, called the *ordo* to distinguish it from the senate at Rome. By the first century A.D. the ordinary citizen played a subordinate role, as at Rome.

A. *Corinth.* The Romans had destroyed Corinth* when they conquered Greece, but in 45 B.C. they founded a colony on the ruined site and made the new city the seat of the governor of Achaea. If the Erastus called *oikonomos tēs poleōs* ("treasurer of the city") in Rom 16:23 was a Corinthian, there may be a link with the municipal archaeology of Corinth. *Oikonomos* is found on inscriptions with the meaning of "city treasurer" (*SIG* 4, index, s.v.). An inscription of the first century A.D. from Corinth records an Erastus concerned with municipal functions: *Erastus pro aedilitate s(ua) p(ecunia) strauit*—"Erastus had this paved at his own expense for his aedileship" (*AE* 1930, 118). One of the functions of aediles was the administration and maintenance of public amenities, which would provide the background to this inscription. As *oikonomos*, however, the Erastus of Romans was concerned with finance, the Latin magistracy for which was the quaestorship, not the aedileship. Too much, however, must not be built on this inscription, as the link with Erastus is tenuous in the extreme.

B. *Philippi.* (In Macedonia*) Philippi* is actually called a colony in Acts (16:12). The authorities in the city are called *archontes* ("authorities") and *stratēgoi* ("magistrates"; 16:19ff.). The first word is a regular Greek term of general application. Some, however, have assigned special significance to the use of the second word, since this represents *praetores* in technical Greek (cf. *SIG* 4, index, s.v. IIy) and would correspond to the use of *praetores* instead of *duoviri* in certain early Italian colonies. But, as Sherwin-White (*Roman Society and Roman Law in the NT* [1963], 92) has pointed out, the use of *praetores* in this sense at Philippi would have been anachronistic. The Greek must be nontechnical, in the general sense of "magistrate" (cf. *SIG* 4, index, s.v. I d).

C. *The "free" cities.* In the late Republican period the Romans regularly made treaties with important cities—treaties that guaranteed them varying degrees of autonomy in spite of their being situated in provinces. In a sense, these cities were the urban counterparts of client kingdoms. The most favored of these cities were technically known as *civitates foederatae*, "federated cities" or "cities with a treaty"; others were *civitates liberae*, "free cities," or *stipendiariae*, "cities paying taxes to the Romans." These distinctions were becoming of merely historical interest in the Early Imperial period. Using the term "free" to designate all these types of cities, we may note that they were technically independent of the authority of the governor of the province in which they were situated (but cf. Acts 19:38ff., for the governor very much in the background), and governed themselves under their own constitution. This latter was generally one that had been in force before Roman times but was often voluntarily adapted to the Roman model provided by the colonies. Most of the big cities in the Greek-speaking areas of the Roman provinces mentioned in the NT fell into this category.

D. *Athens*. Roman Athens* was far less democratic in its constitution than the Athens of Pericles or Demosthenes. The Areopagus* became a prominent organ of the government of the city. It was known officially as "the council of the Areopagus" (i.e., of the Hill of Ares, the Greek Mars) or of "the Areopagites" (*SIG* 4, index, s.vv.). The council met on the Areopagus, or the "Hill of Mars," a small hill connected to the Acropolis* by a low saddle, or in the Stoa Basileos or Royal Portico in the agora,* or marketplace, of Athens. It had wide legal powers and supervised the introduction of new divinities into the city. Paul is recorded as being taken "to the Areopagus" and as speaking "in the middle of the Areopagus" (Acts 17:19, 22), where the council, rather than the actual hill, is probably meant (cf. v. 34 for one of the councilors).

E. *Ephesus*. Ephesus* was a famous Greek city whose Greek institutions are shown to have been very much alive by the riot inspired by Demetrius the silversmith (Acts 19:23ff.). The crowd that was aroused rushed into the theater* and held an assembly there. The assembly of citizens, the *ekklēsia*, was the sovereign authority in Greek-type constitutions, and its meeting in the theater at Ephesus is recorded on inscriptions (e.g., "the assembly in the theater," *OGIS* 480, 9). The angry crowd was made quiet by the town clerk. The *grammateus*, to give him his Greek title, was one of the chief executive officials at Ephesus, and he appears on inscriptions (*OGIS* 493, 10, e.g.). There may even be an epigraphical* mention of Demetrius himself. An inscription, dated to the first century A.D., mentions a Demetrius who was a *neōpoios* (*Inscr. Br. Mus.* 578), which would be especially appropriate since the *neōpoioi* (cf., e.g., *SIG* 364, 20), or Board of Wardens (lit., "temple-builders"), were officials charged with the maintenance of the temple of Artemis* (Diana's original Greek title) and responsible for introducing temple business to the city council. Finally it may be noted that Ephesus is called *neōkoron* "temple-warden" of the great Diana. In the second century A.D. *neōkoros* was a technical term meaning that a city had a temple for the imperial cult (cf., e.g., *OGIS* 481, 3), but

the other usage found here is reflected in an inscription of the fourth century B.C. mentioning an Ephesian who was "temple-warden of Artemis (Diana) in Ephesus" (*SIG* 282). The theater itself, of course, is one of the great archaeological sights of Ephesus.

F. *Thessalonica*. Thessalonica* was a free city of Macedonia. Acts 17:6 calls its executive officials *politarchs* (*politarchai*, "city officials"). Though it is a rare term, it appears on inscriptions (E. Gabba, *Iscrizioni . . . per lo studio della Bibbia* [1958], no. 20).

II. *Cities in the Judean Area*. A. *Caesarea*. Judea* had no colonies until Emperor Vespasian* raised Caesarea* to that status in the 70s A.D. Caesarea* was a typical Greco-Roman city founded by Herod the Great to serve as a port for Judea. It had a dis-

Fragment of Greek inscription found in 1935 near St. Stephen's Gate in Jerusalem, from Herodian period. The full text reads: "No Gentile shall enter within the partition and barrier surrounding the temple, and whoever is caught shall be responsible to himself for his subsequent death." Courtesy Israel Dept. of Antiquities and Museums.

tinctly pagan atmosphere, and its government would have approximated to that of the cities discussed above. When Judea became a Roman province the governor took up his residence in Caesarea, and most of the armed forces* in the province were stationed there.

B. *Jerusalem.* By contrast, Jerusalem* remained intensely Jewish, both under the Herods and under the Roman governors. Because of its old associations and the presence of the temple* there, it was to a large extent identified administratively with the whole of Judea and in a sense even with the Jews* of the Diaspora. In this it paralleled the relationship of Rome to Italy and the Roman Empire. The high priest and the Sanhedrin or Council of the city exercised wide powers under the Romans. An archaeological reflection of this is an inscription (*OGIS* 598) threatening any non-Jew who entered the sacred precincts of the temple with death. After the Jewish Revolt of A.D. 66–70, Jerusalem, like the rest of Judea, became part of the private estates of Emperor Vespasian and served as the headquarters of a legion, the Tenth Fretensis.

C. *Damascus.* Damascus* is of interest in view of Paul's escape from the city. It was annexed by the Romans under Emperor Augustus.* Whether it was a member of the Decapolis* is uncertain. During the principate of Emperor Gaius (A.D. 38–41) it appears to have been assigned to the Nabataean* Arab king, Aretas IV. This appears to find confirmation in the archaeological record in that its issue of coins* ceases from A.D. 38 to A.D. 62/3 under Emperor Nero (*BMC*, Galatia, etc., 283). Nero presumably reannexed the city to the province of Syria.

BIBLIOGRAPHY: J. S. Reid, *The Municipalities of the Roman Empire* (1913); F. F. Abbott and A. C. Johnson, *Municipal Administration in the Roman Empire*, (1926, rep. 1968); A. H. M. Jones, *Cities of the Eastern Roman Provinces* (1937, rep. 1971); id., *The Greek City* (1940, rev. 1966); C. Schuler, "The Macedonian Politarchs," *Classical Philology*, 55 (1960), 90ff.; D. J. Geagan, *The Athenian Constitution after Sulla* (1967).

DBS

ROMAN GOVERNMENT, ADMINISTRATION OF PROVINCES.

A large amount of the basic information in this area is archaeological in origin and confirmation.

In the first century A.D. the Roman Empire embraced most of the lands around the Mediterranean. Italy, with Rome* supreme, stood apart. Other areas were either directly administered as *provinciae* (Gr. *eparcheiai*) or were more loosely linked to Rome as "client kingdoms." Provinces were either "imperial" or "senatorial," depending on whether they came under the authority of the emperor or of the senate.

1. *Imperial Provinces.* In theory these were governed directly by the emperor himself. They tended to consist of the more warlike areas of the Empire or of those recently added to it. The larger were governed by a representative of the emperor usually styled *legatus Augusti pro praetore*—"the deputy of

the emperor with the status of an ex-praetor" (the praetors being the second highest officials in Rome after the consuls). *Legatus Caesaris* is a variant of the title found on the inscription (*ILS* 2683) to P. Sulpicius Quirinius,* the governor of Syria named in Luke 2:2, where the verb *hēgemoneuein* is used to designate Quirinius's position. The other provinces in this category named in the NT are Galatia* and the double province of Pamphylia and Lycia, both in what is today Turkey; Illyricum* and Dalmatia, its southern section, later an independent province, now Yugoslavia.

Less important imperial provinces, such as Judea,* were governed by an official called a *praefectus*, as the inscription (*AE* 1963, 104) to Pontius Pilate from Caesarea* shows. From the time of Emperor Claudius* (A.D. 41 onward), the official's title became *procurator*. The first means simply "placed in charge," the second "manager" or "administrator." The prefects or procurators of Judea are called *hēgemones* or its equivalent in the NT. Cappadocia is the other province in the NT with the same status as Judea. Egypt* was in a special position, in that its governor was regarded as a viceroy, representing the emperor as the successor of the pharaohs and Ptolemies. His title was *praefectus* in the Imperial period.

2. *Senatorial Provinces.* These tended to be the less warlike provinces that had long been under Roman control. The senate sent ex-consuls (called proconsuls) to govern the most important, and ex-praetors (called propraetors) to the rest. In distinction from the imperial provinces the governor usually remained in office for a year only. The senatorial provinces named in the NT are Achaea (Greece), Asia (Western Turkey), Bithynia* and Pontus (Northern Turkey), Crete and Cyrene (the second element being in N Africa), Cyprus* and Macedonia* (N Greece). Two governors are recorded, Junius Gallio* in Achaea and Sergius Paulus* in Cyprus. They are styled *anthypatoi* in Acts (18:12; 13:7, 8, 12; 19:38), a term regularly found on inscriptions.

3. *Client Kingdoms.* The Romans, as in the case of Judea for two brief periods in the first century A.D., allowed native kings to retain their kingdoms with full internal autonomy provided that they observed Roman foreign policy. The local ruler had to receive official Roman recognition, which was highly prized. Not all were allowed the title "king" or "king and friend of the Roman people" (*rex et amicus populi Romani*). Some were merely tetrarchs, a term meaning originally "ruler of a fourth part" of a kingdom, but then any petty ruler, or ethnarchs, meaning "rulers of a people."

4. *Internal Aspects of the Provinces.* One of the main duties of a Roman governor was the administration of justice. Normally he toured his province holding assizes in districts known as *conventus.* These were *agoraioi*, to which Demetrius of Ephesus* was referred for his complaint against Paul (Acts 19:38; for the term, cf. *IG Rom.* 4.790).

Sometimes ancient divisions and arrangements

were perpetuated in the Imperial period. Macedonia had been divided into four districts at the time of its conquest. These had the name of *merides*, an unusual term, but one mentioned on an inscription of the latter part of the first century A.D.: *Makedonōn . . . synedrion prōtēs meridos*—"of the assembly of the first district of the Macedonians" (*AE* 1900, 130, as emended by J. Larsen in *Classical Philology*, 44 [1949], 89). The wording of *prōtē tēs meridos Makedonias polis kolōnia*—" a city of the first rank in that district of Macedonia" (Acts 16:12), where the term appears in the Bible, is difficult. It would be easier to understand if *prote* ("first") were genitive and referred to *meridos*, giving the meaning "a city of the first *meris* or division of Macedonia, a colony." Whatever the correct. explanation, the term *meris* bears the note of authenticity.

Malta* (the ancient Melita), where Paul was shipwrecked, was administratively part of the province of Sicily. Acts (28:7) refers to Publius, "the chief magistrate of the island." The Greek—*tōi prōtōi tēs nēsou*—is paralleled by inscriptions recording the *prōtos Melitaiōn*, "the first man of the Maltese" (*IG* 14, 601; *ILS*, 5415). The office so described was probably pre-Roman in origin.

The first century A.D. saw the spread of provincial *concilia* (*koina*), or assemblies of notables, charged chiefly with the administration of the worship of the emperor. The priests of the province of Asia were called Asiarchs in the plural. (For the term on inscriptions, cf. Dittenberger on *OGIS* 498, n. 3). Other provinces had a single official with such a title—Lyciarch, Bithyniarch, for example. Acts (19:31) gets the plural for Asia right (*tines tōn Asiarchōn*—"some of the dignitaries of the province").

5. *Terminology.* The boundaries of the provinces and their designations altered from time to time, and the "names" of the provinces were also used to refer to geographical districts that had been in existence before the creation of the Roman provinces. Thus Asia and Galatia can bear a different geographical connotation to their strict provincial definition, and areas such as Libya in Africa or Phrygia* in Turkey were not provincial terms.

6. *Judea and the Surrounding Districts.* Of the Palestinian districts under Herod the Great (*see* HEROD, FAMILY OF) that feature in the NT, Judea formed the nucleus. On his death in 4 B.C. together with Samaria and Idumaea it continued its "client" status under his son Archelaus,* who was, however, given the title of ethnarch, not king. When he was removed in A.D. 6, Judea, including Idumaea and Samaria,* became a Roman province under a *praefectus*. The most famous of its governors was of course Pontius Pilate under Emperor Tiberius.* In A.D. 41, however, Judea reverted to client status under Agrippa I, who received the title of king. On his death, Judea became a Roman province once again under procurators, the most famous being Felix* and Festus. After the Jewish Revolt that was crushed in A.D. 70, the governors had the rank of imperial legates. Galilee,* N of Samaria, and Peraea,* E of the

Drawing of dedicatory Latin inscription in limestone found in Roman theater at Caesarea, A.D. 26-36. The translation of the fragment reads: "Tiberius/[Po]ntius Pilate/[Pref]ect of Judaea." The restored inscription reads: "The prefect of Judaea Pontius Pilate erected the Tiberium in honor of Tiberius Caesar." Courtesy Carta, Jerusalem.

Jordan, were assigned to Herod Antipas as tetrarch in 4 B.C. In A.D. 39 his nephew Agrippa I replaced him. He had the title of king, but it must be remembered that he had other areas under his control. On his death in 44 these northeastern districts came under the province of Syria, but in A.D. 53 parts of them (technically called toparchies) were given to Agrippa II. Further NE lay the area called Ituraea, which had been split at the end of the first century B.C. A small area, Abilene,* formed a tetrarchy under Lysanias.* Trachonitis and other districts in Ituraea went to Philip, a son of Herod the Great, in 4 B.C. as tetrarch. These he retained until A.D. 34. They were then joined to the province of Syria, but in 37 they came to Agrippa I, together with Abilene. On his death these areas were annexed to Syria, but in 53 they were given to Agrippa II.

Two administrative districts that were distinct from this "Herodian" area but were geographically adjacent to it were the Decapolis* and Nabataean* Arabia.* The Decapolis* (meaning the Ten Cities) was a group of cities in roughly the same area E of Jordan that had been declared free cities in the first century B.C., at the time of the Roman intervention in Palestine. The number of the cities, and the membership of the group, fluctuated from time to time. Nabataean Arabia was a client kingdom, one of whose rulers, Aretas IV,* is mentioned in the NT. This was probably the "Arabia" to which Paul withdrew soon after his conversion (Gal 1:17).

In many ways the Herodian kings and tetrarchs modeled their internal administration after that of the Hellenistic kingdoms and Rome. This can be illustrated by the terminology used in their armies, and by such terms as *epitropos*, or "procurator," in the sense of financial administrator of Chuza under Herod Antipas (Luke 8:3). Aretas IV of Nabataean Arabia assigned the supervision of Damascus to an ethnarch of his (2 Cor 11:32). Judea and the surrounding client kingdoms were divided into small administrative localities called toparchies (*topos*, "place"). *Hē oreinē* (Luke 1:39, 65), "the mountain locality," was one such.

As in the case of provincial terminology, so in the Palestinian area, terms like Phoenicia* or Syro-Phoenician will appear that do not correspond to administrative entities but to older geographical names.

BIBLIOGRAPHY: G. E. Stevenson, *Roman Provincial Administration* (1939, rep. 1949).

DBS

ROME. As with Athens,* the rich archaeology of Rome goes back through Medieval, to Imperial and Republican centuries to the proto-Italian days when the tribes of the Latin enclave by the Tiber mouth and ford joined their settlements on the seven spurs cut by the Tiber River through the soft tufa rock in the river valley to federate and begin the city.* Her search for a stable frontier took her conquests from Britain, to the Rhine, Danube, Euphrates, and the Sahara. The city moves into the biblical story only with the coming of the Gospel, and the bulk of Roman archaeology does not relate to NT studies.

BIBLIOGRAPHY: E. M. Blaiklock, *ZPEB*, 5 (1975), 162–68.

EMB

ROPE (CORD). The flax industry assured that rope was available for all common uses from earliest times. Samples survive in the Cairo Museum, and rope is depicted on tomb paintings. Such documentation extends to Mesopotamia.* Ropes used for erecting obelisks,* moving colossi and huge building stones, must have had great strength. To "undergird" a hull (Acts 27:17) must similarly have required cables of reliable strength.

BIBLIOGRAPHY: W. B. Emery, *Ancient Egypt* (1961); L. S. De Camp, *The Ancient Engineers* (1960).

EMB

ROSETTA STONE. This famous stone, now in the British Museum, takes its name from the Egyptian village 48 km. (30 mi.) from Alexandria,* where it was discovered during the Napoleonic campaigns (1799). Its trilingual inscription led to the decipherment of the hieroglyphic* and demotic scripts of the ancient Egyptian language, the third script being in Hellenistic Greek.* The decipherment was confirmed by the discovery of another stele* in 1866, with the text of the "Decree of Canopus."

The stone itself is partly damaged. It is of black basalt, and measures 1.1 m. by .7 m. (3 ft. 9 in. by 2 ft. 4½ in.), and the text is from a decree of 196 B.C., in honor of Ptolemy V Ephiphanes, whose benefactions to the priests at Memphis* are recorded. The stone came into British possession in 1801 after the cession of Egypt* by the French.

BIBLIOGRAPHY: D. Diringer, *The Alphabet*, 1 (1948), 36–37; ibid., 2 (1948), 54–56.

BFH

RUDDER. Acts 27:40 speaks of untying "the ropes that held the rudders" (Gr. *pedalia*). James uses the same word in the singular (3:4; "helm" KJV). The word applies to the steering oars thrust out on each side of the stern a few meters from the end of the hull. The projecting portion above deck and bulwark was joined, each oar to the other, by a rope.* When this was loosed the ship* was no longer capable of a steered course. The double oar device is visible in illustrations of Egyptian ships as early as 2500 B.C. *National Geographic Magazine* of November 1974 shows on pages 622–23 a carefully constructed picture, with cut-away side to show the stepping of the mast, of a small Greek galley of mid-fourth century B.C., recovered and restored from Kyrenia in Cyprus.* The illustration clearly shows the *pedalia*. The single helm was known and had the advantage of protection from the hull of the ship, but the double oar device, though more exposed to damage, was quite efficient.

BIBLIOGRAPHY: S. W. and M. L. Katzev, "Last Harbor for the Oldest Ship," *The National Geographic Magazine*, 146 (1974), 618–25.

EMB

The Rosetta Stone. Reproduced by courtesy of the Trustees of the British Museum.

S

SABEANS (sə bē'ənz; Heb. שְׁבָאִים, *šᵉḇāîm*). A Semitic people living in a kingdom in SW Arabia,* N of Qataban, and roughly equivalent to modern Yemen. The Sabeans lived in a fertile area of Arabia, and excavations at Marib have uncovered the remains of an elaborate irrigation* system. Despite their emphasis on agriculture,* the Sabeans were best known in the OT for their trade in such commodities as incense,* precious stones, gold,* and copper (cf. Job 6:19; Isa 60:6; Jer 6:20 et al.). Some of their economic strength came from the periodic control which they exercised over certain seaports in the general area of modern Aden. Now that excavations in southern Arabia have helped to clarify the history of kingdoms such as Ma'in, Ausan, Saba, Qataban, and Hadhramaut, it is possible to see Sabean civilization in much better perspective. In the ethnographic Table of Nations in Genesis, Seba and Sheba* were regarded as descendants of both Ham and Shem (Gen 10:7, 28), a situation which may have arisen through early intermarriage and doubtless fostered by trade and commerce. Excavations in Qataban have shown that Saba preceded the other S Arabian states chronologically and indicate that at the end of the Middle Bronze Age* the Sabeans and related groups migrated to S Arabia, and by the beginning of the Iron Age* they had expanded their commercial dealing both by sea and land. Cuneiform* inscriptions show that queens ruled large tribal confederations in Northern Arabia from the ninth to the seventh centuries B.C., while the office of priest-king (*mukarrib*) was also a feature of Sabean life between 800 and 400 B.C. The ruins of Mariaba (Mareb) testify to the splendor and virility of the Sabean Empire, which lasted into the seventh century A.D.

Camel* caravans played an important part in the development of the early Sabean economy, and commercial interests most probably prompted a tenth-century B.C. Sabean queen to undertake a 1500-mile journey by camel in order to visit Solomon* of Jerusalem (1 Kings 10:1ff.). While this queen has not as yet been attested in S Arabian inscriptions, there is no reason to question the genuineness of OT stories relating to her. The Sabeans were developing their commercial empire at this period, and its ultimate extent can be judged from the discoveries of imported Italian pottery* and glass* at Timnah* and the bronze* statuette* of an Indian dancing girl. In the areas which the Sabeans controlled, exports from India and the E were traded for the products of the Aegean and E Africa. The Sabeans were not a militaristic people, and because of their valuable function as traders they seem to have been unmolested by the great Near Eastern powers.

BIBLIOGRAPHY: C. W. Van Beek, in G. E. Wright, ed., *The Bible and the Ancient Near East* (1961), 229ff.; E. Ullendorff, *BJRL*, 45, no. 2 (1963), 486ff.

RKH

SAIDON. See SIDON.

SALAMIS (sal'ə mis; Gr. Σαλαμίς, *Salamís*). A large city* on the E coast of the island of Cyprus,* the first place Paul visited on his trip to Cyprus (Acts 13:5). The city seems to have been founded at least by the eleventh century B.C. In Roman times, from which most of the ruins date, Salamis had a large Jewish population.

In 1952, the Cyprus Department of Antiquities investigated the remains called by Munro and Tubbs (1891) "the temenos* of Zeus" and by Jeffery (*The Ruins of Salamis* [1926], 13) "the marble forum.*" This colonnaded court, measuring 70 by 50 m. (230 by 165 ft.), was cleared, as well as the W stoa and parts of those on the E and S. Eight of the marble columns were reerected. The finds included a fragmentary inscription naming a gymnasiarch which aided in identifying this court. Further help came through the excavations of 1953–54 when the identification of this peristyle court as a gymnasium was confirmed by new inscriptions, one of which mentions repairs to it by Trajan. The structure had been built over a Hellenistic gymnasium. In the center of the building was found a stepped podium of masonry faced with reused blocks of grey marble; a displaced block of this marble carries a Hadrianic decree by the linen weavers of Salamis (*hoi kata Salameina lunuphoi*).

In the second century A.D. the gymnasium was embellished with marble statues,* some of the remains of which are as follows: an over life-size Apollo, a large figure of Nemesis, pieces of statues of Asklepios, and a seated Zeus*—the last three of which were headless.

Behind the E portico connected with the Augustan gymnasium was an extensive bathing facility with the walls decorated with mosaics* and frescoes. Not far from the gymnasium was found a fifteen thousand capacity theater* built toward the end of the first century B.C. and destroyed by an earthquake in the fourth century A.D.

Other ruins found include a Greco-Roman agora,* a reservoir, the temple of Zeus Olympios (originally built in the Hellenistic period), part of the city wall,* and tombs dating from the late Geometric to the Greco-Roman periods (including archaic royal tombs). Characteristically, these royal sepulchers had large dromoi (entrances) and reflected Homeric burial customs.

The excavations of the basilica* of St. Epiphanios at Salamis were reexamined, and there was no conclusive evidence to confirm or disprove the accepted dating of the original building to the time of Epiphanios, archbishop of Salamis-Constantia from A.D. 368 to 403.

BIBLIOGRAPHY: E. Oberhummer, "Salamis," *PWRE*, 2d ser. 1.2 (1920), 1826–44; A. H. S. Megaw, "Archaeology in Cyprus, 1952," *JHS*, 73 (1953) 136–37; id., "Archaeology in Cyprus, 1954," *JHS*, 75 (1955) supp., 31–33; V. Karageorgis, *The Ancient Civilization of Cyprus* (1969).

WHM

SALEM. *See* JERUSALEM, OT.

SALINIZATION. The natural pollution of river water, especially when put to work in irrigation* along an extended tract of stream, can have marked effects on human habitation. This is especially true of the enhanced salinity of water due to the dissolving of salts in the soil. The increased salinity of the Colorado River in the U.S.A., for example, is causing agricultural* and other problems along the course of the river system, as is also the case in Egypt* following the construction of the Aswan* Dam. The proposal of Israel's enemies before the 1967 war to divert the chief source of the Jordan at Caesarea Philippi* (modern Banyas) into the Litani River, would have inevitably caused salinity from the underwater springs near Tiberias* to pollute the Galilee* and lower Jordan water to the point at which it would have been useless for irrigation.

The intrusion of salt can destroy agricultural land and so play a part in the decline of civilizations. The ancient peasant knew the menace. Vergil in his *Georgics* lists some rough and ready methods of detecting soil salinity. No wheat will grow if soil contains 1/2 percent salt. Double that and barley will not grow. Raise the figure to 2 percent and the palm yields no fruit. This is of great archaeological significance because it was the growing salinity of the Mesopotamian* rivers, obviously first felt at points nearer to the sea, which occasioned the progressive northward movement of urban civilization up the Euphrates. How early this was observed is not known, but archives from the temple of Baba, wife of the patron god Ningirsin, of Lagash,* contain a report dating from Urukagina's* reign in the twenty-fourth century B.C., in which it is stated that certain temple lands had been made useless for agriculture by salt (cf. Judg 9:45). A boundary stone of the thirteenth century invokes a curse of salinity on any who violate the boundary. A Sumerian agricultural manual of the twenty-second century suggests spacing of crops to allow time for the leaching out of excess salt.

BIBLIOGRAPHY: M. A. Beek, *Atlas of Mesopotamia* (1962), 13, 16; *New York Times*, May 13, July 10,

Aug. 26, 27 (1973), articles dealing with Colorado River salination.

EMB

SALONIKA. *See* THESSALONICA.

SALT. Salt was an important item in the economy of the Romans, as with many other peoples, and may have influenced their occupation of Palestine, since the Israelites shared with the ancient Chinese the technique of extracting and purifying salt. Some archaeological evidence of this technology could come to light amid the vast salt deposits of the Dead Sea* area. Jebel Usdum, the "hill of salt," a 30 sq. km. (15 sq. mi.) elevation SSW of the Dead Sea, was the source of Hebrew supplies. Khirbet Qumran,* site of the Dead Sea Scrolls,* is probably the "City of Salt" of Josh 15:62. The identification seems confirmed by the discovery of an Iron Age* II fort beneath the Qumran settlement ruins. The Valley of Salt (2 Sam 8:13; 2 Kings 14:7; 1 Chron 18:12; 2 Chron 25:11) seems to be the plain below Jebel Usdum, which merges treacherously into salt marsh country.

EMB

SALT SEA. *See* DEAD SEA.

SAMA. *See* SHEBA.

SAM'AL. *See* ZINJERLI.

SAMARIA (sə mâr'i ə; Heb. שֹׁמְרוֹן, *šômᵉrôn*; Akkad. *samerina*; Gk. Σαμαρεία, *samareia*, meaning uncertain. Biblical etymology is from the name of original owner, Shomer). A city,* built as capital of Northern Kingdom by Omri,* c. 880 B.C., and continuing into the Roman period.

Samaria is located on a hill rising 91 m. (300 ft.) above the floor of a basin valley in the N-central hill country of Palestine. Its strategic location commands natural trade routes N to the Esdraelon, E and S to the Shechem plain, and W to the Sharon, making it a natural site for a more centrally-located capital city in the time of Omri.

Although the site was selected and fortified by Omri, much of its luster must have been added by his son Ahab,* whose ivory* palace (1 Kings 22:39) and Baal* temple (1 Kings 16:32) gained for the city both prominence and notoriety. Samaria continued with varying fortunes as the chief city of the northern kingdom until its fall to the Assyrian Sargon II* in 722 B.C. While serving as capital of the Assyrian region called Samerina, the city and indeed the entire region was populated by a mixture of peoples (2 Kings 17:24ff.), reference to whom may also be found in Ezra and Nehemiah. By the late fourth century B.C., a Samaritan center was established in the city, but it was soon taken, first by the Greeks under Alexander (331 B.C.) and then by the Hasmonean king John Hyrcanus (108 B.C.). The Roman Pompey and his successors rebuilt the city after 63 B.C., but the greatest splendor came as a result of Herod's activity (*see* HEROD, BUILDING ACTIVITIES). He renamed

Ivory object found at Samaria. Courtesy Israel Dept. of Antiquities and Museums, photographed and exhibited at the Israel Museum.

the city Sebaste (Gk. for Augustus), a name that continues in the present village on the site. After a short period of destruction resulting from the Jewish Revolt, Samaria grew again to prominence in the time of Septimum Severus (A.D. 193–211), many of whose buildings are still visible. Although the seat of a bishopric in the early Byzantine* period, Samaria was in decline and was eventually reduced to the small village currently on the mound.

Excavations beginning in 1908 and continuing for two years were conducted by Harvard University under D. G. Lyons, G. A. Reisner, and C. S. Fisher. An expedition jointly sponsored by Harvard, the British School of Archaeology in Jerusalem, the Palestine Exploration Fund, and the Hebrew University worked from 1930–35 under the leadership of J. W. Crowfoot. Finally, Paul Lapp excavated for the Jordanian Department of Antiquities in 1965–67, and J. B. Hennessy continued work in 1968 under the auspices of the British School of Archaeology.

During the Israelite period, six occupation levels were discerned, the first two of which relate to the time of Omri and Ahab and reflect the high period of Israelite construction. Two walls, one 1.5 m. (5 ft.) and the other 6 m. (19½ ft.) thick, enclosed the summit, on which several buildings were constructed. These walls, apparently the work of Omri, were of the header-stretcher type. Modifications and an additional casemate* defensive wall were added by Ahab, creating a fortification that proved more than equal to the task. Remains of yet another defensive wall are visible, however, surrounding a lower city. Though in later Roman times there was an impressive lower city, from this period little is known of building activities in that area.

Within the acropolis* itself some of Israel's most significant archaeological discoveries have been made. The royal palace, measuring 27 by 24 m. (89 by 79 ft.), undoubtedly contained two stories (2 Kings 1:2), a courtyard, and a shallow pool (possibly the place where Ahab's chariot* was washed, 1 Kings 22:38). No remains of a temple have yet been found, probably because of massive rebuilding on the site in the Roman period. Of great interest from this period were the remains of more than two hundred fragments of ivory inlay found in a storehouse* near the

palace, probably representing the ivory construction referred to in 1 Kings 22:39. These show Phoenician* influence and preserve some of the finest art work discovered in ancient Israel.*

Level III begins with the revolution under Jehu and involved some destruction and rebuilding but much continuity with the earlier city. It was a time of material decline and little is known about some of its later kings. Levels IV–VI come from the eighth century and represent the period of Jeroboam II, best known from the book of Amos. Although it was a time of great prosperity, less of the elegance of earlier artistry and architecture is evident. Coming from this period, however, are some of the ivories mentioned above, as well as a cache of sixty-three inscribed potsherds (see SHARDS), or ostraca* (ANET, 321). These consist mainly of business or tax* records, but are important for the light they shed on the state of Hebrew writing.* Finally, in the Israelite period, a seventh level is associated with the destruction of Samaria in 722/721 B.C. by the Assyrians.

Levels VII, VIIa, VIII, and IX cover Assyrian, Babylonian, and Persian times. Although it is known that Samaria was occupied during large portions of the period, little more can be said. A large garden in the Babylonian or Persian city may have been attached to a palace, but nothing remains of the building itself.

Little remains from the Hellenistic occupation (332–63 B.C.) except walls and towers.* A series of massive round towers was built on the old Israelite wall at the end of the fourth century, and a totally new wall was constructed with rectangular towers in c. 150 B.C. Coins* and an abundance of pottery,* including Rhodian stamped jar handles, attest to the level of trade and culture.

From the conquest of the city by Pompey in 63 B.C. the city's fortunes were connected with those of

One of three Hellenistic (end of fourth century B.C.) round towers found at Samaria. Courtesy Israel Dept. of Antiquities and Museums.

the Roman power until the dissolution of the empire. Three periods of building activity are associated with Gabinius, provincial governor from 57–55 B.C., Herod the Great (37–34 B.C.), and Septimus Severus, the Roman emperor from A.D. 193–211. Gabinius rebuilt the walls and set the pattern for a new city with both forum and stadium included. Herod, who concentrated much of his attention on the city, raised it to new heights in honor of his emperor Augustus.* It was he who built the new city wall, enclosing a much greater part of the lower city than was previously included, and fortified with towers at regular intervals. But his greatest achievement was the beautiful, multi-faceted temple to Augustus that occupied the crown of the acropolis. The temple was approached by a series of steps, had several levels, and measured 35 by 24 m. (115 by 79 ft.) in its totality. Finally, following a destruction resulting from the Jewish Revolt, the city was rebuilt and expanded in the time of Severus. To the temple on the summit was added a stadium,* a forum* with adjoining basilica,* a lovely little theater,* the long colonnaded street* lower down on the S side, and an aqueduct* over 3.2 km. (2 mi.) in length. The remains of this period, together with a small Byzantine basilica connected with the traditional site of John the Baptist's burial, make up most of the visible ruins on the mound today.

BIBLIOGRAPHY: G. A. Reisner, C. S. Fisher, and D. G. Lyon, *Harvard Excavations at Samaria* (1924); J. W. and G. M. Crowfoot, *Early Ivories from Samaria* (1938); J. W. Crowfoot, K. M. Kenyon, and E. L. Sukenik, *The Buildings at Samaria* (1942); J. W. and G. M. Crowfoot, and K. M. Kenyon, *The Objects from Samaria* (1957); A. Parrot, *Samaria, the Capital of the Kingdom of Israel*, trans. S. H. Hooke (1958); A. F. Rainey, "The Samaria Ostraca in the Light of Fresh Evidence," *PEQ*, 99 (1967), 32–41; P. R. Ackroyd, "Samaria," in D. W. Thomas, ed., *Archaeology and OT Study* (1967), 343–54; J. B. Hennessy, "Samarie-Sabaste," *EB*, 56 (1969), 417–19; J. L. Kelso, *ZPEB*, 5 (1975), 232–40; M. Tadmor, "Fragments of an Achaemenid Throne From Samaria," *IEJ*, 24 (1974), 37–43; W. H. Shea, "Date and Significance of the Samaria Ostraca," *IEJ*, 27 (1977), 16–27; S. Applebaum, S. Dar, and Z. Safrai, "The Towers of Samaria," *PEQ*, 110 (1978), 91–100; N. Avigad, "Samaria," *EEHL*, 4 (1978), 1032–50; A. Demsky, "The Permitted Towns in the Boundaries of Sebaste according to the Rehob Mosaic Inscription," *Qadmoniot*, 11 (1978), 75–78.

CEA

SAMARITAN OSTRACA. Excavators clearing a floor level of the first phase of the second period of the palace of Samaria, discovered sixty-five ostraca* inscribed in the old Hebrew script (*see* EPIGRAPHY, HEBREW). These documents are receipts for oil, wine,* etc., dispatched to Samaria* from towns in the region and credited to specific owners. They are of great significance for the script, spelling, personal names, topography, administrative system, and religion of Israel* in the eighth century B.C. Many of the names contain one of the divine elements Yah or

Samaritan ostracon, eighth century B.C., with inscription in cursive Hebrew script incised on fragment of red-slipped bowl. It reads: "Baruch, Peace!.../Baruch...pay attention and [give...to]/Jimnah [personal name] barley 13 [measures]." Courtesy Israel Dept. of Antiquities and Museums.

Baal* (cf. Elijah and Elibaal). On the ostraca there are seven Baal names to every eleven Yah names, suggesting the popularity of Baal in the region. The ostraca are generally dated to the time of Jeroboam II (c. 786–746 B.C.), although the days of Joash (c. 801–786 B.C.) and Menahem* (c. 745–738 B.C.) also have been suggested.

BIBLIOGRAPHY: G. A. Reisner et al., *Harvard Excavations at Samaria* (1924), 227–46; *ANET* (1955), 320.

JAT

SAMSON. The story of Samson (Judg 13–16), last of the judges, is illustrated at various significant points by archaeological investigations in southern Palestine. At the time of Samson's birth, about 1100 B.C., there was an upsurge of Philistine* power, due, no doubt, to an influx of Aegean refugees. The Philistines had held a bridgehead on the Palestine coast since Abraham's day, and periods of strong activity on their part probably reflect some large intrusion of refugees and the consequent need for "living room." The capture of the ark and the burning of Shiloh* represent one deep penetration from the coastal plain (1 Sam 4).

Samson was a Danite, and prior to the migration northward of the large proportion of that tribe in retreat from their encirclement, the people of Dan* felt the full strength of the Philistine pressure from the W. In Macalister's opinion, the migration of Dan can best be explained by Philistine pressure. Their depleted numbers were unable to prevent a strong Philistine infiltration in the direction of the territory of Judah,* a fact verified by the excavations of 1928–32 conducted by Elihu Grant. Abundance of Philistine pottery* marks the incursion.

Samson was born at Zorah, toward which the Vale of Sorek, home district of Delilah, forms a road. In the same vale lies Timnah.* Ashkelon,* on which town Samson wreaked one of his acts of vengeance, had, it seems, been taken from Dan in the twelfth century, though originally captured by Judah (Judg 1:18). It is clear, therefore, that the point of closest social, cultural, and military contact between Israel and the Philistines lies precisely in the region where Samson's stories take place. The archaeological picture is in complete accord.

The tragic wedding feast at Timnah was one of the drinking bouts of which there is much evidence in Philistine contexts. Beer jugs are found in plenty, often with a strainer spout to enable the drinker to avoid a mouthful of barley husks. This need was, in fact, the origin of the drinking straw, described by Xenophon in his *Anabasis* (4.5.25–27). "It is not difficult to infer," says W. F. Albright, "from the ubiquity of these wine craters and beer jugs, that the Philistines were mighty carousers." Archaeology confirms the biblical tradition of the story of Samson, where drinking bouts are mentioned several times in connection with the Philistines.

The woman of Timnah, and Delilah, the prostitute of the Vale of Sorek, may perhaps be pictured from the Minoan* frescoes of Knossos in Crete, which may be seen to best advantage in the Herakleion Museum in Crete. The elegant fair-skinned ladies must have stood in strong contrast with the Hebrew girls of Samson's own environment. The Philistines, too, whatever be their precise origin, were in the Aegean Minoan-Mycenaean tradition, and were great lovers of sport, as the Cretan frescoes show—cruel sport, such as they enjoyed to Samson's agony, and bull fighting, such as that depicted at Knossos.

Gaza,* scene of Samson's next tragic fall, is just over 3.2 km. (2 mi.) from the coast, perhaps Tell el-'Ajjul, where Flinders Petrie, who examined the site from 1930 to 1934, found much clear evidence of Philistine occupation. It was the southernmost of the Philistine cities, and probably more easy for Samson to visit at night, in one of his reckless moods, than any other city of the Philistine pentapolis. He may have been making a clandestine reconnaissance when he met the woman who tempted him. Such places of immoral resort were often against the walls* of towns, as Rahab's story shows. Samson's liaison was almost fatal.

Then came Delilah, and the defeat which Samson had long risked. Blinded and shorn, he was set to grind grain as a sign of Dagon's* superiority, for the Ugaritic literature has shown that Dagon is not connected with the Hebrew *dag* (a fish) but with *dagan* (grain). He was the father of Baal* and the giver of grain. Samson's humiliation was meant to acknowledge the might of the grain-god, which the Philistines had taken from the Canaanites. The pillared porticoes of the Knossos palace may give some notion

Philistine pottery "beer jug" painted with birds and fish from tomb at Tell 'Eton, SW of Lachish. Courtesy Israel Dept. of Antiquities and Museums. Exhibited and photographed at Israel Museum, Jerusalem.

of the architecture of the temple which he brought down (see RADDANA). Of all Aegean structures these pillars taper downward, not upward. Samson's last feat of strength was to slide two pillars from their stone bases. There are foundations, as at Beth Shan, which seem to illustrate such ground plans.

BIBLIOGRAPHY: W. F. Albright, *The Archaeology of Palestine* (1960), 115, for the Philistine beer mugs; E. Grant, *Haverford Archaeological Expedition* (1929); M. Pearlman and Y. Yannai, *Historical Sites in Israel* (1965), 164–70, for Ashkelon at this time; *BA*, 14 (1951), 44 for the columned Philistine temple; R. A. S. Macalister, *The Philistines* (1914), 38, 44; J. C. Moyer, *ZPEB*, 5 (1975), 249–52.

EMB

SANBALLAT (san bal'ət; Heb. סַנְבַלַּט *sanḇallaṭ*). Nehemiah's determined opponent of 445 B.C. is mentioned in one of the letters of the Elephantine Papyri* in 407 B.C. The letter of Jedoniah, high priest of the troubled Jewish garrison on the Egyptian island, wrote a letter to Bagoas the Persian satrap of Jerusalem.* In an outburst of mob violence, common enough in ancient Egypt,* the temple of the expatriate Jews* had been destroyed. With Persian policy toward monotheistic cults, and Jerusalem's precedent in mind, the priest sought permission to rebuild. Significantly, the applicants thought it wise to propitiate the neighboring satrap of Samaria,* no less a person than Sanballat. There is a hint of bribery in the final paragraph, and perhaps light is shed on Sanballat's much earlier opposition to Nehemiah, who was not the sort of man to bribe.

It is interesting to observe the disarray and lawlessness in the remoter provinces of the Persian Empire in both Nehemiah's story and the Yeb papyri.

BIBLIOGRAPHY: C. C. Torrey, *JBL*, 42 (1928), 384–85; H. H. Rowley, *Men of God* (1963), 246–76; J. S. Wright, *ZPEB*, 5 (1975), 264. EMB

SANDAGANNAH; SANDAHANNAH. *See* MARESHAH.

SANHEDRIN (san hē drən; Gr. συνέδριον, *sunedrion*, "sitting in council"). A Greek term, transliterated into Hebrew and Aramaic* and designating the supreme ecclesiastical court of the Jews.* Rabbinic scholars traced the origin of the Sanhedrin to the council of seventy elders appointed as judicial assistants by Moses (Num 11:16; cf. M. Sanhed. 1:6), and claimed that this council was reconstituted by Ezra in the postexilic period. There is no reliable evidence, however, for the existence of the Sanhedrin prior to the Greek period, and the earliest specific mention of such a council (Jos. *Antiq.* 12.3.3) occurs in connection with the regime of Antiochus the Great (223–187 B.C.). Throughout its existence the Sanhedrin was controlled by a Sadducean priestly aristocracy, with the high priest as president (cf. Mark 14:53; Acts 24:1). In the NT period leading lawyers and scribes of predominantly Pharisaic sympathies were also members of the Sanhedrin, and these persons no doubt challenged many of the proposals put forward by the Sadducean priests.

Little can be said archaeologically about the Sanhedrin except to speculate as to its meeting place in the time of Christ. According to Talmudic tradition the sessions were held on the S side of the temple* court in the "hall of hewn stone" (M. Mid. 5:4). When Jesus was put on trial, the Sanhedrin met in the palace courtyard of the high priest (Mark 14:53-55), but this was an emergency session that did not follow the usual procedures In Josephus (Jos. *Wars* 5.4.2; 6.6.3) two different sites were claimed as the meeting place for the Sanhedrin, but these may have been used subsequent to the time of Christ.

BIBLIOGRAPHY: S. B. Hoenig, *The Great Sanhedrin* (1953); P. Winter, *On the Trial of Jesus* (1960); T. A. Burkill, *IDB*, 4 (1962), 214–18; J. Jeremias, *Jerusalem in the Time of Jesus* (1967), 222–32; D. A. Hagner, *ZPEB*, 5 (1975), 268–73. RKH

SANIRU. *See* HERMON.

SAQQARA. *See* MEMPHIS.

SARAFAND. *See* ZAREPHATH.

SARCOPHAGUS. The name derives from the Greek σαρκοφάγος λίθος, *sarkophagos lithos*, "flesh-eating stone," the adjective becoming a noun. In Latin* it was called *lapis Assius*, or "Assos stone." From Assos* in the Troas* of Asia Minor* came a type of limestone which was said to consume the bodies of the dead and so was used for coffins. The word then was extended to mean any stone coffin. They are found all over the world—beside the road at Tintern

Abbey, made by Cistercian monks who were unhealthily preoccupied with death, and abundantly in the catacombs.* The method of cutting is demonstrated by a sample on the roadside of Magdala* near Tiberias.* An oblong loculus* is cut in a massive stone evidently to form a coffin by the trimming away of the surrounding material. Artistic decoration was not uncommon. Fifty-one examples from the catacombs and elsewhere now in the Lateran Museum in Rome show scenes from the OT and NT. They mostly date from Constantine onward when burial could be more obvious and expensive. They are indicative of the beliefs and preoccupations of early Christians.

An excavation in 1972 at Deir el Balah in the Gaza Strip concentrated on a Late Bronze Age* cemetery (fourteenth/thirteenth century B.C.). The archaeologists concentrated on an untouched area and removed the dunes to study the types of burial. In the area, according to preliminary reports, were traces of plain burials with only a few burial offerings of pottery,* a recurring type being a standing storage jar with an upturned bowl as a lid. There were also more elaborate burials where the dead were in anthropoid (man-shaped) pottery coffins. Two such coffins, one next to the other, were the most important finds.

Top: Thirteenth-century B.C. anthropoid clay coffin being exposed at Deir el-Balah cemetery in Gaza Strip. Bottom: Contents of a coffin revealed skeletons of two persons, one lying on its back and the other face down. Also found in the coffin were a bronze bowl and jar set, cosmetic holder figurine and a silver-coated mirror, pottery flasks, and alabaster goblets. (*See also photo under* LEAD.) Courtesy The Hebrew University of Jerusalem; Photo Z. Radovan.

These two coffins were recovered with their skeletons and offerings only partly intact. The first, though found unbroken, seems to have been robbed in ancient times, only a few remains of the burial gifts being found inside and scattered nearby. The second coffin revealed a striking picture of the burial and its offerings. When the lid with its molded face, wig, and arms was removed and the upper part of the coffin lifted off, two skeletons were revealed—a male and a female, buried together with their burial offerings. The finds from this burial include six pairs of gold* earrings, necklaces, and variously shaped semiprecious stones, many gold beads, and seventeen gold pendants. There is a cat*-shaped pendant and amulets in the form of Bes, Egyptian god of fertility. The coffin also contained near the skulls pottery flasks, a lotus-shaped alabaster* cup, an alabaster cosmetics* bowl held by a figurine of a swimming girl, and a silvered bronze* mirror.* On the legs of one of the skeletons lay a set of two bronze vessels,* a bowl and a jug, with lotus flower decoration incised on their handles. One of the skeletons wore two rings on its fingers, one of gold and the other of red stone. The finds from both coffins, judging by the scarabs* and the pottery, seem to belong to the Ramesside period (thirteenth century B.C.). The style of burial in anthropoid coffins, as well as the burial gifts, are clearly influenced by Egyptian burial customs, and the people who used this cemetery (see NECROPOLIS) were well versed in Egyptian culture and customs, a significant pointer to Egyptian influence and power in Palestine before the Exodus.

Such finds, in fact, date back to C. S. Fisher's excavations at Beth Shan* of half a century ago. They were cylinders of baked clay* with the hands, arms, and head of the deceased formed in high-relief on the molded clay lid, the features curiously reminiscent of the golden death masks of Mycenae* in the Athens Archaeological Museum—an indication, among others, of the European origin of the Philistines,* with whom the anthropoid coffins seem to be consistently linked. C. E. Wright suggests reasonably that "Philistine" was a Hebrew generic term for the Sea People* invaders of more than one origin. J. L. Starkey and others discovered similar coffins at Lachish,* and, Egyptian though the concept may have been, the custom seems to be a marker of Philistine intrusion in Israelite and pre-Israelite times.

BIBLIOGRAPHY: W. F. Albright, *The Archaeology of Palestine* (1960), 115–17; E. E. Hindson, *The Philistines and the OT* (1971), 63–67, 71, 78–79; W. H. Withrow, *The Catacombs of Rome* (1890), 340–43; G. Wilpert, *I Sarcofagi Cristiani Antichi* (1929–36).

EMB

SARDANAPALUS. *See* ASHURBANIPAL.

SARDIS (sär'dis; Gr. Σάρδεις, *Sardeis*). This major city* of Lydia has received much recent attention from archaeologists. As early as 1910, H. C. Butler, with a magnificently equipped expedition, worked on the site which was at the junction of the royal highways linking Ephesus,* Pergamum,* and Smyrna* with the interior of Asia Minor. After the

excavation was abandoned in 1914, Harvard and Cornell Universities continued the work. The temple of Artemis at Sardis has been uncovered. It appears that under the influence of the Cybele cult of Ephesus that goddess was associated with Artemis in joint worship. It was an unfinished building and has no significance in the interpretation of John's apocalyptic letter, save that a cross cut here and there into the stone shows that the pagan shrine was converted to Christian purposes. The remains of a brick chapel are also visible in the ruin. A mortgage deed, dated some three centuries before Christ, gives some idea of the wealth of the temple. One Mnesimachus acknowledges a huge gold* loan and specifies whole villages as security.

Anatolia was a crossroads of Near Eastern and Aegean civilizations, and its archaeological exploration has long since ceased to be a chapter and facet of classical archaeology. It has moved backward into the earlier history of the peninsula, and Sardis has shared in the widening scope of recent discovery. New material from the prehistory of Achaean, Mycenaean,* and Hittite* cultures do not concern the present theme, nor the extremely interesting discoveries in the remains of the gold industry of Sardis. Anatolia was a great land of metallurgy,* and the gold of the Pactolus was the foundation of the legendary wealth of Croesus of Sardis.

Of closer relevance to biblical archaeology and to the difficulties of the "seven churches" in relation to contemporary and local Judaism, is the revelation of the strength of the Jewish colony in Sardis. It is clear from epigraphical* evidence that, during the Persian era (547–334 B.C.), there was an Aramaic*-speaking group in the town. This seems to support the contention that Sepharad, famous in the history of Judaism, was Sardis. Obadiah (v. 20) speaks of "the exiles from Jerusalem* who are in Sepharad" as an important element in a distant dispersion. An enormous synagogue* was discovered in 1962 which presupposes a congregation of several thousand worshipers in the second century A.D. Antiochus III destroyed Sardis in 213 B.C., and Josephus states (Jos. *Antiq.* 12.147–153) that the king transferred large numbers of Jews* from Mesopotamia* and Babylonia to "the most important areas." Did Sardis receive a large accession at the time? Josephus (Jos. *Antiq.* 16.171) quotes a directive of Gaius Norbanus Flaccus, proconsul of Asia from 31 to 27 B.C. to the magistrates and council of Sardis: "Caesar [i.e., Augustus] has written that the Jews shall not be prevented from collecting sums of money, however great they be, in accordance with their ancestral custom, and sending them up to Jerusalem." This is clear enough evidence that the Jews of Sardis, just before the Christian era, were rich enough to send such sums to their holy city as a temple* tax that the local authorities were concerned at the movement of capital out of the area.

There are many gaps to fill in the archaeological documentation of Anatolian Jewry, and the results will probably have considerable biblical relevance. We know of the strength of the Jews of Smyrna who helped in the martyrdom of Polycarp.

The synagogue at Sardis looking from the apse on the right (east) to the forecourt at the left. The synagogue is over 115 m. (130 yds.) long and 18 m. (20 yds.) wide. Built in the late second century A.D., it was renovated around A.D. 400 and destroyed in 616. Courtesy Archaeological Exploration of Sardis.

BIBLIOGRAPHY: E. M. Blaiklock, *The Cities of the NT* (1965), 112–19; G. M. A. Haufmann and J. C. Waldbaum, "New Excavations at Sardis," in *Near Eastern Archaeology of the Twentieth Century* (1970), 306–20. EMB

SAREPTA. See ZAREPHATH.

SARGON (I) OF AKKAD (sär′gôn, äk′äd). A Babylonian ruler of the third millennium B.C., who brought the Semitic inhabitants of the Plain of Shinar into prominence in the twenty-fourth century B.C. by establishing a Semitic dynasty in Babylonia. Almost all extant historical sources dealing with Sargon of Akkad* are later copies recovered from Nippur.* Legendary material has also survived in Sumerian and Akkadian texts. Sargon established Agade (Akkad, or Accad) as his capital, and about 2355 B.C. conquered the powerful Lugalzaggisi of Sumer* and occupied the country. In his inscriptions Sargon claimed to be ruling over territory from the Upper Sea (Persian Gulf) to the Lower Sea (Mediterranean). Archaeological sources point to his activity in Elamite* territory, at Nineveh,* Chagar Bazar, and at Tell Brak. Some historical legends also connected him with Syria and Anatolia. Of humble birth, he ruled with vigor for fifty-six years, according to the Khorsabad king list,* maintaining the stability of his realm by means of a standing army and an effective bureaucracy. His sons Rimush and Man-ishtisu, and his grandson Naram-Sin continued his policies, but ultimately his kingdom fell to Gutian invaders from Iran, c. 2200 B.C. The capital of Agade, which had given its name to its Akkadian inhabitants, was destroyed and never rebuilt, thus terminating a vigorous Semitic dynasty. The site of Agade has yet to be identified with certainty.

BIBLIOGRAPHY: *CAH*, 1, part 2, 113, passim.

RKH

SARGON II. An Assyrian ruler from 722 to 705 B.C., son of Tiglath-pileser III* and father of Sennacherib.* After his brother Shalmaneser V was murdered he succeeded to the throne, probably taking advantage of political conflicts in Assyria. Many details of his reign have survived from inscriptions in his Khorsabad* palace, and also from historical texts recovered from Nineveh* and Nimrud* (*see* CALAH). He is mentioned only once in the OT (Isa 20:1), but despite this his military campaigns in Syria and Palestine formed an important historical and political background to the eighth-century B.C. OT prophecies.

In his first campaign he was defeated near Der by Merodach-baladan with Elamite* help, and after this reverse he moved against Syria, where an anti-Assyrian coalition led by Hamath* and Damascus* challenged his advance. In 720 B.C. Sargon defeated the Syrian allies at Qarqar* on the Orontes River in northern Syria, where Shalmaneser III had battled a similar alliance in 853 B.C. The confederate cities*

King Sargon II, a drawing from relief on palace at Khorsabad. Courtesy Carta, Jerusalem.

were made Assyrian vassals, and an Egyptian contingent was pursued as far as Raphia. In the light of this event Isaiah warned Judah* against relying upon help from Egypt* (Isa 10:9), pointing to the fate of Carchemish,* Hamath, and Damascus.

On returning from the Egyptian border, Sargon reduced Samaria* and transported its inhabitants to Assyria and Media, thus ending the northern kingdom of Israel.* The repopulating of the area with Hamathites, Arabs, Cuthaites, and Babylonians continued into the reign of Esarhaddon* (cf. Ezra 4:2). In 716 B.C. Sargon warred against the Arabs of Sinai,* and also exacted some tribute (*see* BOOTY AND TRIBUTE) from the Egyptians, who were trying to foment rebellion in Palestine. This policy succeeded at Ashdod,* but independence was unfortunately short-lived, being crushed in 711 B.C. (cf. Isa 20:1). The warlike Urartu* peoples fought Sargon II intermittently between 719 and 714 B.C., and as the result of Elamite resurgence an Assyrian campaign against Merodach-baladan in 707 B.C. overthrew that Babylonian ruler, who promptly fled to Elam. Sargon's final years were spent in campaigns leading to the annexation of territory between the Taurus range and the Euphrates. In a minor attack against the Cimmerians Sargon was killed in 705 B.C. His main building activities centered upon his royal city Khorsabad (Dur-Sharruken), which he intended to become the most splendid in the Ancient Near East, but which was never completed and at his death was abandoned.

BIBLIOGRAPHY: H. W. F. Saggs, *Iraq*, 17 (1955), 146–49; H. Tadmor, *JCS*, 12 (1958), 22–40, 77–100; W. W. Hallo, *BA*, 23 (1960), 50–56; G. Roux, *Ancient Iraq* (1965), 257–62; L. L. Walker, *ZPEB*, 5 (1975), 278–80.

RKH

SAW. See TOOLS.

SCARAB. The dung beetle of Egypt,* the scarab became a sacred symbol for the Egyptians through their belief that it had been born without procreation. The female places the eggs in the body of a dead beetle, and a pellet of dung provides food for the hatched beetles. The scarab symbolized resurrection and was associated with the journey of the sun across the sky. Examination of scarabs from the period of Thutmose III at Jericho* led Garstang to assign an early date to the Exodus. Scarabs occur frequently in art forms on Middle Kingdom stamp seals* made of stone or faience,* with inscriptions in hieroglyphics.* The scarab seals were often worn on the neck or on the hands as rings.

HWP

SCIENCE AND TECHNOLOGY, ANCIENT. *See* AGRICULTURE; ASTROLOGY, ASTRONOMY; CALENDAR; CHEMICAL TECHNOLOGY; CLOTH; DYE; ECOLOGY; EMBALMING; ENGINEERING; FERMENTATION; FOOD PROCESSING; GLASS; GLAZE; HEZEKIAH'S TUNNEL; IRRIGATION; KILN; MACHINES, WAR; MEDICINE; METALLURGY; MILL; MINING; MORTAR; MUSICAL INSTRUMENTS; PLASTER; POTTERY; QUARRY; REFINING; TILE; TOOLS; VESSELS; WEIGHTS AND MEASURES; WHEEL; WINE. *See also* cross references under BUILDING MATERIALS; BUILDING METHODS; BUILDINGS.

SCRIBAL TRAINING, EGYPTIAN. The requirements of a highly complex bureaucracy led to the establishing in Egypt* by the middle of the third millennium B.C. of an educational system for training young men for government and the civil service. Diodorus Siculus (*Historicus* 1.52.2–4) describes the system, but there is much archaeological evidence in Egyptian texts. Beginning in the Old Kingdom period, special compositions were used to give the

Limestone scarab seal with hieroglyphic inscription, from Lachish, 18th century B.C. (*See also photo under* TAXES.) Courtesy Israel Dept. of Antiquities and Museums.

scribes practice in copying hieroglyphs.* Some of the texts employed in the scribe's education were written on potsherds (*see* SHARDS), particularly after the close of the Second Intermediate period. The process by which a person became a professional scribe in Egypt was long and exacting. Apart from the difficulties involved in becoming proficient at writing* hieroglyphics, the scribes were confronted with the arduous task of learning other languages such as Babylonian cuneiform,* which was the *lingua franca* of the Amarna* Age, as well as Canaanite and Hittite. So highly respected was the office of the scribe that on becoming professionally qualified in Egypt he was exempted from income tax for the remainder of his life. These standards can be exemplified quite readily from Egyptian sources.

Scribal education seems to have been a sort of apprenticeship. Ptahshepses of the Fifth Dynasty period describes himself as having been "brought up amongst the royal children in the palace of the king and more esteemed by the king than any child." There was an official called "the Chief Teacher of Royal Children."

A reference to a palace school occurs in an inscription on the stele* of Ikhnernofret, an important Twelfth-Dynasty official of Abydos* during a time of wide bureaucratic expansion. The text runs: "My Majesty sends you with my mind certain that you will do everything in accordance with My Majesty's confidence, since you have certainly had recourse to My Majesty's teaching, you have indeed grown up as a foster-son of My Majesty, a unique pupil of my palace."

A great deal of educational material comes from the New Kingdom period, including school texts on ostraca,* wooden tablets, and papyri.* Open-air schools were sometimes attached to temples, such as that of Ramses II* at Thebes* or the temple of Mut at Karnak. Others were located in the royal palaces, where the princes received their education.

Although the scribe occupied a position of great eminence in ancient Egypt, there was sometimes a lighter side to his responsibilities, as indicated by the scribe Khety of the Twelfth Dynasty. In his *Satire on the Trades* Khety created a new literary form. The office of scribe alone is extolled, as all other careers are decried: "I do not see a sculptor on a mission nor a goldsmith who has been despatched. But I have seen the coppersmith at his task beside his furnace. His fingers are like crocodile-skin and he stinks more than fish-roe. . . . The quarryman seeks for excellence in every sort of hard stone. It is with his arms ruined and himself exhausted that he has brought things to completion. He sits down at the setting of the sun with his knees and his back cramped. . . . Look, there is no job free of a boss—except for the scribe: he is the boss!"

BIBLIOGRAPHY: R. J. Williams, "Scribal Training in Ancient Egypt," *JAOS*, 92 (1972), 214–20; H. Brunner, *Altägyptische Erziehun* (1957).

EMB

SCRIP. *See* PURSE.

Aramaic scroll rolled and tied with cord, from Elephantine. Courtesy The Brooklyn Museum, Bequest of Miss Theodora Wilbour.

SCROLL. A scroll is a rolled, written document, on papyrus* or vellum* which varied in length. By uniform Hebrew tradition the Pentateuch was from the beginning written on leather* scrolls. The scribes who copied out the Scriptures were extremely careful and accurate in their work, as the Dead Sea Scrolls* have shown. At Qumran,* excavations uncovered the remains of the scriptorium in which the scrolls had been written. Documents which ran to considerable length were often written in bifid fashion, so that the work actually consisted of two parts, each of which represented the author's thought and could circulate independently. Most probably the Book of Isa was issued originally in this form. Shorter works were contained in one scroll, however.

Sir F. G. Kenyon calculated that a short epistle such as 2 Thessalonians would form a roll about 38 cm. (15 in.) in length, arranged in some five columns, while the longer Epistle to the Romans would run to about 3.4 m. and 15.2 cm. (11 ft. and 6 in.). In the same way the Gospel of Mark would occupy about 5.9 m. (19 ft.) of an average-sized roll, that of John 7.1 m. and 15.2 cm. (23 ft. and 6 in.), Matthew 9.6 m. (31 ft.), the Acts and Luke's gospel about 9.6 or 9.9 m. (31 or 32 ft.). A papyrus* roll could be cut into any number of sections, the slice (*tomos*) giving rise to the word "tome," which originally did not carry the idea of a large and weighty volume. The reader used both hands, unrolling from the stick in one hand on to a similar stick in his other hand, reversing the process when his reading was concluded. The scroll when rolled up was tied with a cord, and in the case of official documents was sealed. Aramaic* contracts from the fifth-century B.C. Elephantine* settlement in Egypt* were often tied up and sealed in this manner. In a second-century papyrus (*O.P.*, G. & H.1, 173f.106) a certain Ptolema acknowledges receipt of a will "under its own seals," i.e., intact, which she had deposited in the archives and now wished to revoke. Rev 5:1 probably refers to some such legal affirmation of a document.

BIBLIOGRAPHY: *Handbook to Textual Criticism of the NT* (1912), 34; R. K. Harrison, *Introduction to the OT* (1969), 786–88.   EMB

SCYTHIANS (sith'i ∂nz; Gr. Σκύθης, *Skythēs*). A nomadic, Indo-Iranian-speaking group who apparently originated in the Caucasus area. In Genesis 10:3 Ashkenaz, an earlier name for the Scythians, is recorded as being a son of Gomer and a grandson of Japheth. The Scythians formed part of a nomadic movement in the eighth century B.C. which first saw the Cimmerians (Akkad. *Gimirrai*) move into the Near East. Then the Scythians (Akkad. *Ashguzai*) entered Assyrian territory under their leader Ishpaka and were opposed by Esarhaddon* (681–669 B.C.) as well as by the Cimmerians.

Subsequently the Scythians allied with Assyria, and may even have tried to prevent the downfall of Nineveh* in 612 B.C. What seems evident is that Scythian raiders traversed Phoenicia* and then attempted to enter Egypt,* where, according to Herodotus, the pharaoh Psammetichus (663–609 B.C.) bribed them not to attack his land. At a later time the Medes* destroyed Scythian power and dispersed the remnants to the N.

The Scythians have been supposed to be the foe from the north (Jer 1:14), although the general sense of the chapter seems to refer instead to Babylon as the nation's enemy. In Jer 51:27 the Scythians were pictured with other horse-riding groups in alliance against Babylon. The savagery of the Scythians seems alluded to in Col 3:11. Beth Shan* was named Scythopolis* in the Greek period, perhaps perpetuating the memory of the seventh-century B.C. invasion.

BIBLIOGRAPHY: T. T. Rice, *The Scythians* (1957); A. L. Oppenheim, *IDB*, 4 (1962), 252; H. A. Hoffner, *ZPEB*, 4 (1975), 315–16.

RKH

SCYTHOPOLIS (si tho′pə lis; Gr. Σκυθόπολις, *Skythopolis*). The name of the Hellenistic and Roman city* on the site of Beth Shan* (No. III Level: A. Rowe, *Beth-Shan Excavations*, I [1930], 44–50). During the period of the Ptolemies' suzerainty over Palestine (third century B.C.) a large temple was built of which the foundations, in basalt, were discovered 37 by 22 m. (121 by 72 ft.). It was probably devoted to Dionysus, whose name was also reflected in the name "Nysa" which preceded Scythopolis and was in use through Roman times. In a reservoir to the S a marble head, perhaps also of Dionysus, was found 42 cm. (16 in.) high. Some tetradrachms of Ptolemy Philadelphus and the traces of tombs also belong to the third century. From the Seleucid period comes an inscription containing a list of priests.

In the first century prior to the Roman conquest, Scythopolis was in Jewish hands, but the remaining finds come after Pompey, who is said to have restored the city (Jos. *Antiq.* 14.4.4), although Gabinius carried out the reconstruction (Jos. *Antiq.* 14.5.3).

In NT times Scythopolis was chief city of the Decapolis* (Mark 7:31) and possessed a fine theater* and hippodrome. The games of Scythopolis are referred to in Asian inscriptions. It provided a natural headquarters for Vespasian* and his two legions in the Jewish War. Coins* of the period refer to Pompey (64 B.C.) and Julius Caesar (47 B.C.); they also illustrate the multiplicity of gods worshiped—Dionysus, Athena, Demeter, Astarte, and the Jordan river-god all appear. Inscriptions also name two of the city "quarters" (the Cornmarket and Demetrius).

The best remains of the Roman period come from the cemetery (*see* NECROPOLIS) to the N; here tombs of the loculus* type (rectangular, with oblong chambers cut in the side) contained many bodies and artifacts.* Most notable is the sarcophagus* of

Antiochus, son of Phallion, perhaps the cousin of Herod the Great (*see* HEROD, FAMILY OF).

BIBLIOGRAPHY: G. M. Fitzgerald, *Beth-Shan Excavations, III 1921–23* (1931); R. W. Hamilton, *IDB*, 1 (1962), 397–401; G. M. Fitzgerald, in D. W. Thomas, ed., *Archaeology and OT Study* (1967), 185–96; J. M. Houston, *ZPEB*, 1 (1975), 543–45.

BFH

SEALS. References to seals or signets* of various sorts go back to the story of Judah and Tamar (Gen 38:18, 25). Judah may have worn a cylinder seal on a cord round his neck. "Your seal and its cord," says Tamar, naming the "pledges" (NEB). According to Herodotus (1.195) every man in Babylon* bore a staff and a seal. Joseph's* investiture with royal authority involved a signet ring (Gen 41:42). Jezebel used Ahab's* seal to authenticate her forged documents (1 Kings 21:8), and this, in all likelihood, was a ring (cf. Esth 3:10, 12; 8:2, 8, 10). Other references are numerous (e.g., Jer 32:10–11, 14, 44; Neh 9:38; 10:1; Dan 6:17; Matt 27:66). Metaphorically the seal was widely used (e.g., Isa 8:16; 29:11; Jer 22:24; Hag 2:23). The figure is common in the NT (Rom 4:11; 1 Cor 9:2; 2 Tim 2:19; and many times in Rev). The verb is frequent (e.g., John 3:33; 6:27; Rom 15:28; and four times in Rev).

Surviving Hebrew seals go back to the eighth or ninth century B.C. and inscribed signets to the fourth century. They are commonly oval and with raised surface ("scarabaeoid") and cut from a large variety of precious, semiprecious, and hard stone. Examples in cheap limestone suggest that their use was not confined to upper and literate sections of society. Some seals have been found in their original rings, others, pierced longitudinally, were obviously meant to be worn on a neckcord. Hebrew prejudice against representational art, did not rule out seal devices such as winged lions,* human heads, sphinxes, and griffins. Egyptian seals are of extreme variety and art. The fact that later seals tend increasingly to omit pictorial representation and bear the inscription only, suggests that the post-Exilic reverence for the law was finding expression here also.

The last century has provided abundant samples from a widespread series of archaeological projects extending from SW Iran (ancient Elam*) to Egypt* and the Aegean. Seals of peculiar biblical relevance may be listed as follows.

1. *The Seal of Shema.* This seal was found at Tell el-Mutesellim, the ancient fortress of Megiddo,* in 1904 and can be traced from the Sultan's treasury to the Istanbul Museum of Antiquities. It has disappeared, but the description speaks of a piece of scarabaeoid jasper, with an engraved face set in an oval. A line separated the lower part of the inscription and served as a platform for the vivid representation of a roaring lion, a favorite motif in early Hebrew and Phoenician* art. Several stone lions were found at Megiddo and no other wild animal is mentioned so frequently in the OT. The consonantal inscription ran, "Shemas's, servant of Jeroboam." Whether this is the first or second Jeroboam is not known, but it is likely to have been Jeroboam II (786–746 B.C.).

Drawing of seal of Shema, servant of Jeroboam (probably Jeroboam II of Israel). Courtesy Carta, Jerusalem.

Seal of Jaazaniah. (*See also photos under* BETHEL; EZION GEBER; SCARAB; TAXES.) Courtesy Israel Dept. of Antiquities and Museums.

2. *The Seal of Jaazaniah.* The description "thy servant" and "servant of the king's" (cf. 2 Kings 16:7; 22:12) appears on a beautiful signet from Tell en-Nasbeh, the ancient Mizpah.* It is a black and white banded onyx, discovered in 1932, scarabaeoid in shape, dated about sixth century B.C. and to be seen in the Palestine Archaeological Museum in Jerusalem. There are three divisions on the engraved surface. The two upper zones bear the inscription in beautifully executed early Hebrew characters, reading "Jaazaniah's, servant of the king." The lower part shows a fighting cock and proves that this bird was known early in Palestine, though it is not mentioned in the OT. The name, Jaazaniah ("God hears"), occurs in 2 Kings 25:23 and Jer 40:8. It is considered likely that the seal belonged to the person mentioned in 2 Kings 25:23 and the passage in Jer (40:8), an army captain of Gedaliah's* time.

Incidentally, a seal impression of the said Gedaliah was found three years later (1935) at Tell ed-Duweir, the ancient Lachish* and is now at the London University Institute of Archaeology. There is no decoration, only an inscription reading "Gedaliah's, master of the household." This functionary, a chief steward, is mentioned in the OT as a senior servant (1 Kings 4:6; 2 Kings 18:18). In the Mizpah* inscription we probably meet Gedaliah, son of Ahikam, son of Shaphan (2 Kings 25:22–25; Jer 39:14; 40:5–41:8; 43:6) whom Nebuchadnezzar* made governor of Judah* after the fall of Jerusalem.* He was stationed at Mizpah. The Gedaliah impression, like four others

from Lachish, show on the reverse side some traces of the papyrus* documents to which they were attached, an indication that papyrus was used in Jeremiah's time in Israel.*

3. *The Seal of Jotham.* A seal from Tell el-Kheleifeh, the ancient Ezion Geber,* discovered in 1940, has been attributed to Jotham, king of Judah (742–735). It is mounted on a copper ring and shows a ram walking with what appears to be a shepherd going ahead. The inscription simply reads "Jotham's." Chronology* and location support the identification with the king (2 Kings 15:33ff.; Isa 1:1; 7:1 et al.). Judah prospered under Azariah, Jotham's father (2 Chron 26) both economically and militarily, but the identification, and even the spelling, of the inscription is not certain.

4. *Seals of Hananiah.* Two finely engraved signets found in Jerusalem, and at present in Berlin, show respectively a decoration of pomegranates and a palm leaf (Deut 8:8; Song of Songs 4:3, 13; 8:2). One reads "Hananiah's, son of Azariah." Both names are in the OT. The second seal, with a seven-leafed palmette design, nearly identical with a synagogue* frieze decoration from Korazin* (Khirbet Kerazeh), is inscribed "Hananiah's, son of Achbor."

BIBLIOGRAPHY: D. Diringer gives a full bibliography in *DOTT* (1958), 218–26.

EMB

SEA OF THE PLAIN. *See* DEAD SEA.

SEA PEOPLES. The modern term is derived from the Egyptian and means "the foreigners of the sea." It is a general designation used by the ancient Egyptians, c. 1230–1170 B.C., and by modern scholars to describe a series of peoples who began to penetrate the Aegean basin and to reach the coastlands of the Near East in the fourteenth and thirteenth centuries B.C., invading Libya in the late thirteenth century and overcoming Cyprus,* N Syria, and then Canaan,* finally attempting to invade Egypt* (under Ramses III*) c. 1200–1180 B.C. The pharaoh repulsed them, and some settled in Palestine, while others sought homes elsewhere.

The Sherden occur in the Amarna letters,* under Ramses II, Merneptah, Ramses III, and after. Migration westward may have given their name to Sardinia. The Luka also occur in Amarna letters and under Merneptah and (as a personal name) under Ramses III—they gave their name to Lycia, famed at times for its pirates. The Danuna occur in the Amarna letters (land N of Ugarit*) and under Ramses III, and may in part be the Danaoi of Greek tradition from W Asia Minor.*

Basically, however, "Danuna" refers to the people of the Plain of Adana* in Cilicia* (see esp. E. Laroche, *Syria*, 35 [1958], 263–75 on this). The Tursha under Merneptah and Ramses III are generally linked with the later Etruscans. The Shakalusha perhaps also went westward, to Sicily (cf. Sherden:Sardinia), and both Merneptah and Ramses III had to fight them. Just once, as opponents of Merneptah, occur the Aqaiwasha. Controversy still rages over whether or not they were in fact Achaiwoi, Achaeans (Greeks).

Next come the Pulisati (Ramses III and later), long since indubitably identified with the Philistines* of the OT. The Tjikaru (same dates) may be Teucrians; the Wasasha remain unknown. After being repulsed by Ramses III, the Philistines settled in SW Palestine, hence the term Philistia. The Tjikaru settled in part further N, around Dor* (S of Carmel*), and in part in Cyprus. The main representations of these peoples are in the war scenes of Ramses III in his W Theban funerary temple at Medinet Habu.* Here several of these peoples (Philistines, Tjikaru, Danuna) dress alike. Furthermore the clay* coffins from Palestinian sites (as at Beth Shan*) should not be attributed exclusively to the Philistines, but also to related Sea People groups. Furthermore, the occurrence or nonoccurrence in texts or art forms of this or that special group (e.g., the Philistines) under Ramses III or earlier or only later is of very limited value for estimating their real date of appearance in the Near Eastern world, since these depend too much on the capricious historical sense of the Egyptians, who often neglected to use new names of peoples except when these were forced upon the scribes' view. The general anonymity of the material evidences found in Palestine of the late thirteenth to early twelfth centuries B.C. also hinders accurate dating.*

BIBLIOGRAPHY: J. H. Breasted, *Ancient Records of Egypt*, III (1906), §§ 569ff.; *ANET*, 262–63; Sir A. H. Gardiner, *Ancient Egyptian Onomastica*, 1 (1947), 194–205; H. W. Helck, *Die Beziehungen Ägyptens zu Vorderasien im 3. und 2. Jahrtausend v. Chr.*, 2d ed. (1962, 1970), chap. 17; A. Malamat, in B. Mazar, ed., *World History of the Jewish People, 1st Series*, 3 (1971), 23–38, 294–300, 347; K. A. Kitchen, in D. J. Wiseman, ed., *Peoples of OT Times* (1972).

KAK

SEBA, TELL ES-. See BEERSHEBA.

SEBASTE. See SAMARIA.

SEILUN. See SHILOH.

SELA; SELAH. See PETRA.

SELEUCIA (sə lū'shi ə; Gr. Σελεύκεια, *Seleukeia*). Seleucia stands on the coast of Syria on the NE corner of the Mediterranean, some 8 km. (5 mi.) N of the mouth of the Orontes River. Antioch,* the capital of Syria and royal seat of the Seleucid kings, was a few miles inland, at the point where the Orontes, after its northern course between the Lebanon ranges, turns sharply W to the sea. The grave deforestation of the Lebanon range, which began thirteen centuries before Christ, when the Phoenician* occupants of the coastal strip became aware that there was an international market for cedar* timber, produced a problem of erosion which has not been adequately solved even today. Hence the heavy burden of eroded soil carried to the sea by the Orontes and the wisdom of constructing Seleucia's artificial harbor somewhat N of the Orontes mouth. It was formed, according to the visible remains, of two stone jetties of which

the southern one takes a wider sweep and overlaps the northern, thus giving an entrance sheltered from the prevailing S wind and blocking the northward drift of the Orontes silt. Even so, the silt deposited along the coast by the outflow of the river ultimately filled and choked Seleucia's outlet to the sea. The site of the harbor today is a damp flat, built of alluvial deposits, in which a few fragments of the harbor masonry can be distinguished. Seleucia, designed to serve as a port for Antioch, was one of nine cities which bore the name of Seleucus, the first ruler of the dynasty which ruled Syria and adjacent territories from the beginning of the third century before Christ, until the Romans assumed control of the eastern Mediterranean, two and a half centuries later.

One of the most astonishing phenomena of history was the transformation of the political pattern of the Eastern Mediterranean, by the rapid conquests of Alexander the Great, and the partition of his subjugated territories by the Successors, as his generals, who carved themselves kingdoms, were called. Seleucus, who took the title Nicator, was one of Alexander's lesser generals and boldly seized control of the northern central satrapies of Alexander's empire. He founded the Seleucid kingdom of Syria in 312 B.C. and in 301, eleven years later, built the port which bore his name. Seleucus and Antiochus were both common Seleucid names. Hence the various Seleucias and Antiochs which are scattered over the map of the Hellenistic kingdom.

The Syrian Seleucia was known as Seleucia Pieria, to distinguish it from the similarly named foundations in Mesopotamia,* and in the neighboring region of Cilicia.* There is no evidence to prove the fact, for serious archaeological investigation has not yet been undertaken on what is likely to prove a richly rewarding site, but the appended adjective Pieria preserves in all probability the name of an existing Phoenician port, overlaid by Seleucus's major foundation. The Syrian monarch intended his port to be a strong fortress guarding one of the chief approaches to his kingdom. For all its strength, natural and engineered, some half-century later, Seleucia was captured by Ptolemy III Euergetes, who launched an attack on Syria, probably from Cyprus as his base (1 Macc 11:8). Lacking the compactness of Ptolemaic Egypt,* Syria found it difficult to control the various territories and tortuous frontiers of her far-flung complex of heterogeneous peoples and provinces and lived in long rivalry with her fellow successor state of Egypt, but she suffered no set-back more serious than this damaging inroad into the heart of her kingdom by the third Ptolemy.* Seleucia remained in Egyptian hands, a menace to the security of nearby Antioch, for over thirty years. It was recaptured by Antiochus the Great in 219 B.C. but again fell briefly into the hands of the Ptolemies in 146 B.C. Polybius's chapters on Antiochus's siege of Seleucia contain a lucid description of the port's military importance and its topography.

Antiochus's recovery of Seleucia from Syria's Egyptian rival, was part of the program of that military king to recapture and consolidate all the varied regions of the Seleucid kingdom, and it was obvious that he would reduce Seleucia first of all. He regarded the port as a symbol of all his soldierly success, and the story is told that, in 205 B.C., he entered Seleucia in triumph, like a second Alexander, with a train of elephants and masses of plunder. It was probably on this festive occasion that the monarch assumed the ancient royal title of the Achaemenid rulers and called himself "the great king." Hence his common appellation "Antiochus the Great." Under his rule Seleucia was greatly beautified and its fortifications strengthened to enable the port more effectively to fulfill its major purpose and provide a bastion of defense for Antioch, the capital.

It was the far campaigning of Antiochus the Great, in his efforts to regain control of all areas once held by Seleucid Syria, which brought him into direct confrontation with the Romans, who, awakened to their international obligations by the Second Punic War, were realizing that their quest for a stable frontier must extend to the Hellenistic kingdoms of the eastern end of the Mediterranean. Antiochus's great political mistake was his failure to recognize the emerging power of Rome and her vital interest in the eastern Mediterranean. He thrust his conquests too far to the W and was decisively defeated by the Romans. By a treaty signed at Apamea on the Orontes in 188 B.C., the Seleucid kingdom of Syria ceased to be a great power in the Mediterranean world but retained her place as a continental power in the Middle East. Seleucia was still a major fortress in Syrian hands. Rome, after all, was not seeking conquests, so much as a stable eastern wall.

It was not till well over a century later that the Romans appeared in power in the heartlands of the Syrian empire. Mithridates of Pontus, and Tigranes of Armenia, looked with hostility and suspicion on the consolidation of Roman power in Asia Minor,* and it was because of a general breakdown of order in the eastern Mediterranean and its associated territories that the Roman Senate invested the great soldier Pompey with special powers in 66 B.C. to deal with the growing chaos of the area and restore peace. Pompey's three years in the E were a remarkable feat of soldiering and administration. When Pompey arrived he found an Armenian and Pontic invasion had reached as far as Jerusalem.* Seleucia, thanks to the strengthened fortifications of a century before, was still intact in the rear of the invading armies. Pompey formed Syria into a Roman province, making Seleucia a "free town" within the provincial borders and an essential port of entry for the distant power which had assumed control. The port was further fortified to act, as Caesarea* did on the same difficult coast, as a harbor, a base, and a bridgehead.

With the coming of Roman domination came the Pax Romana (Roman peace) to an area which had been rent and enfeebled by chaos, weak government, and chronic war. Seleucia began a century of significant development. The maritime activity of the port must have been great. Seleucia was not only a place of exit and entry for an important Roman province, but it was a staging post for ships* in an age when navigation favored coastal sailing. From Seleu-

cia Paul and Barnabas sailed for neighboring Cyprus (Acts 13:4) on their first missionary journey. Half a century later, Ignatius, bishop of Antioch, passed through Seleucia on his way to martyrdom in Rome.

Paul and Barnabas undoubtedly returned that way (Acts 14:26), but it was so taken for granted that Seleucia was the gateway to Antioch, to which the two were proceeding to make report, that no specific reference is made to the port. It is unlikely that they sailed up the lower reach of the Orontes to Antioch itself, although, for smaller ships, this was navigationally possible. It is an odd fact that, in the sea beyond the silt-covered remains of Seleucia's harbor works there are two fragments of the old masonry which are known as Paul and Barnabas. It is also likely that it was from Seleucia, in Paul's second tour abroad, that he and Silas set sail (Acts 15:40–41). Barnabas and Mark no doubt used the same departure point (Acts 15:39). Cyprus* is visible on a clear day. The current on the coast sets in a NE direction, but a good offshore wind would counteract its thrust and land the travelers in Cyprus in less than a day.

Seleucia retained its status as a free city, and this dignity was confirmed by Vespasian* in A.D. 70. All through the first century, Seleucia was the base of Rome's Syrian fleet. There were continual Roman attempts in imperial times to improve a not very satisfactory port, and there are traces of Roman engineering.* Chief among these remains is a vast tunnel some 183 m. (200 yd.) long, designed to direct some of the downflow from the hills away from Seleucia's harborworks. The problem of erosion and silting was evidently a serious concern. The tunnel bears the inscribed names of both Vespasian and his son Titus.* The inference might be that Seleucia had assumed large importance as a base and supply port during the Great Rebellion in Judea.* It had a clear advantage over Caesarea for this purpose because of its relative remoteness from the scene of war and guerrilla harrassment.

The city* in the time of Paul must have been a splendid place with a wealth of temples and an amphitheater* cut out of a cliff side, which is still to be seen. The great road which linked Seleucia with Antioch may also be traced here and there, and the lofty ruin of the market gate* through the city wall* survives. On the steep lower slopes of Mounsa Dagh, there are great man-made caverns which, it is suggested, were warehouses in the days of Seleucia's commercial prosperity and seaborne trade.

Seleucia presents a strong challenge to modern archaeology. Princeton University has been interested in the whole area and from 1932, has conducted extensive excavations at neighboring Antioch. The nearby ruins of Seleucia, spread along the Mediterranean shore and for some distance inland, are as yet hardly touched by the diggers. For two years before the long interruption of World War II, some digging was done at Seleucia. Some houses,* the market gate, and a Doric temple were cleared, as was a fifth-century memorial Christian church, the Martyrion.

BIBLIOGRAPHY: H. V. Morton, In the Steps of St. Paul (1944), 114–17; R. Stillwell, ed., Antioch on-

the-Orontes, III, The Excavations 1937–1939 (1941); *FLAP*, 339, 542–43; N. Turner, "Seleucia in Syria," *IDB*, 4 (1962), 264–66.

EMB

SENJERLI. See ZINJERLI.

SENKEREH. See LARSA.

SENNACHERIB (sə na′ kə rib; Heb. סַנְחֵרִיב, *sanᵉḥērîḇ*). This man was the successor of Sargon II,* and ruled Assyria from 705–681 B.C. He established military control over rebellious Babylonia in 703 B.C., and the following year crushed Elamite* and Chaldean* opposition in battles at Kish* and Cutha. A series of punitive raids against the northern tribes were followed by an expedition to the W, where Cilicia* was invaded and Tarsus* captured. In 701 B.C. he marched against Hezekiah of Jerusalem* (2 Kings 18:13), having first reduced a number of strongholds in Phoenicia* and Philistia for anti-Assyrian activities. The Taylor Prism* gives Sennacherib's own account of the siege of Jerusalem, in which he claimed to have shut up Hezekiah "like a caged bird within his royal capital." For reasons unmentioned in the Assyrian sources, Sennacherib withdrew his armies and the following year launched another attack on Babylonia. Neither the Assyrian nor the Babylonian annals support the theory of a second campaign against Judah,* perhaps between 689 and 686 B.C., as maintained by many modern scholars. During that period Sennacherib was actively involved in conflict with rebellious elements in Babylonia and captured Babylon* itself in 689 B.C. Eight years later Sennacherib was assassinated by his sons while worshiping in the shrine of his god Nisroch (2 Kings 19:36–37). Earlier, with his wife's encouragement, he had rebuilt Nineveh* his capital, making it one of the most splendid of Near Eastern cities. Some of the bas-reliefs* from the royal palace are now in the British Museum.

Sennacherib seated on throne receives prisoners (not seen in this detail) and spoils from Lachish. This detail is from a series of gypsum reliefs at Kuyunjik, showing the storming of Lachish by Sennacherib. Reproduced by courtesy of the Trustees of the British Museum.

BIBLIOGRAPHY: D. D. Luckenbill, *The Annals of Sennacherib* (1924); L. L. Honor, *Sennacherib's Invasion of Palestine* (1926); D. J. Wiseman, *DOTT* (1958), 64–73; id., *ZPEB*, 5 (1975), 338–42.

EMB

SEPHARAD. See SARDIS.

SEPULCHER, CHURCH OF THE HOLY. The church that has marked, since the fourth century, the traditionally accepted site of the tomb of Jesus.

The term "holy sepulcher" nowhere appears in the NT, although there are several Greek terms used for tomb or sepulcher. Even the location of the tomb of Jesus is an enigma. Only John records that "At the place where Jesus was crucified, there was a garden, and in the garden a new tomb . . ." (John 19:41). Beyond that, only the fact that the place of Crucifixion was outside the city wall* is known.

When Jerusalem was destroyed in A.D. 70, with the subsequent dislocation of its inhabitants, a break in tradition occurred. It was not until the fourth century, after the conversion of the Emperor Constantine, that any official attempt was made to mark the place of the tomb of Jesus. At that time the pagan temple of Venus, erected by Hadrian, was accepted as marking the original spot, and the first of a series of churches was constructed. The foundations of the Constantinian church and the general outline of his sanctuary are preserved in the present structure. Destruction of the first structure was effected by the Persians in 614, but the church was restored a few years later. Again in 1010 the church was destroyed, this time by the Caliph Hakim of Egypt,* but it was rebuilt in 1048 and totally reconstructed by the Crusaders in 1144. It was then that the various parts of the sanctuary were brought under a single roof, and since then the history of the church has been one of rebuilding and refurbishing the Crusader structure.

The question of the authenticity of the traditional site of our Lord's burial is still of utmost interest to Christians. The work of Kathleen Kenyon in a small area just S of the present church has proven to her satisfaction that the entire area was outside the city wall until the second century A.D. (K. Kenyon, *Jerusalem* [1967], 146–54). Of course, this does not prove that the site is authentic, but only that it can be authentic. The excavations, however, lowered yet further the probability that the scene of Jesus' crucifixion and burial is accurately preserved in the Garden Tomb and Gordon's Calvary, to the N of the present-day Damascus Gate.

In 1976 excavations at the site of the Church of the Holy Sepulcher uncovered for the first time in 1600 years what is the most probable site of Christ's crucifixion. Dr. Christos Katsimbinis and his associates exposed a cone of grey rock, standing about 10.5 m. (35 ft.) in height and rising sharply from the top of a larger incline up which prisoners were taken for execution. The site of Christ's death was close to a busy thoroughfare leading from the city,* and within a few meters of the wall, which was probably crowded with spectators for the event. Excavation of the hill showed two small caves* in it, which from a distance

Façade of edicule containing marble slab that marks site of the tomb of Jesus. The edicule is located in the rotunda covered by the large dome of the Church of the Holy Sepulcher. *(See also photo under* JERUSALEM, NEW TESTAMENT.) Courtesy Israel Government Press Office.

would give it the appearance of a skull. Subsequent excavations are expected to prove the authenticity of the site beyond reasonable doubt.

BIBLIOGRAPHY: G. Dalman, *Sacred Sites and Ways* (1935), 346–81; J. W. Crowfoot, *Early Churches in Palestine* (1941), 9–21; C. C. McCown, *The Ladder of Progress in Palestine* (1943), 244–53; K. M. Kenyon, *Jerusalem* (1967), 146–54; R. H. Smith, "The Tomb of Jesus," *BA*, 30 (1967), 74–89.

CEA

SEQUENCE DATING. See DATING, ARCHAEOLOGICAL.

SERABIT EL-KHADEM (ser'ə bit el-kä'dēm). A nonbiblical site in the western Sinai* region, where Sir Flinders Petrie discovered eleven unusual inscriptions on stone objects or on rock panels in 1905. The script was not Egyptian but had Egyptian affinities. There were approximately twenty-three signs in all, which are now known to represent the first alphabet* ever used. The language was Canaanite.* Later alphabets developed from this protoalphabetic script, which is provisionally dated to between c. 1500 and c. 1450 B.C.—before the days of the Exodus. Fragmentary inscriptions on pottery* and metal in a similar script come from Lachish,* Shechem,* Gezer,* Tell el-Hesy,* and Tell el-'Ajjul.

BIBLIOGRAPHY: W. F. Albright, "The Early Alphabetic Inscriptions from Sinai and Their Decipherment," *BASOR*, 110 (1948), 6–22; id., *The Proto-Sinaitic Inscriptions and Their Decipherment*, *HTS*, 22 (1966).

JAT

SERA, TELL. See ESH-SHARI.

SERAPEUM. See ALEXANDRIA.

SERGIUS PAULUS. Paul and Barnabas met this proconsul of Cyprus* on their first missionary journey (Acts 13:7–12). Epigraphy* contributes to the identification of this Roman official. Luke reports only the second and third names (the *nomen* and *cognomen*) and neither is uncommon in Roman history and both are of old standing. Nothing like a complete list of the proconsuls of Cyprus exists, and the relevant inscriptions here mentioned are fragmentary. They are as follows. First, from Soli on the N coast of Cyprus a badly executed inscription, which could be dated A.D. 50, contains the phrase *epi Paulou [anthy]patou*—as though one read "under Paulus [proc]onsul." The Gallio Inscription seems to date Paul's first journey between A.D. 46 and 49 so the worth of the Soli inscription must be held lightly. Secondly, an undated Latin* inscription (*CIL*, 6.31545) names one Lucius Sergius Paullus (Latin usually favors a second "l") as one of the "curators of the banks and bed of the Tiber" under Claudius.* The date would fit well, if the official's next appointment was to the proconsulship of Cyprus—as scholars as diverse as K. Lake and F. F. Bruce agree. Round this inscription and others of later date, W. M. Ramsay built an ingenious succession of members of this Roman family following similar careers in office and inheriting a Christian confession. The date of the Latin inscription makes the identification of the member of the Tiber River Authority and the proconsul possible, but there is still a large area of uncertainty. The third inscription, from Kytheria on Cyprus and housed in the Metropolitan Museum of Art in New York, regulates sacrifices and offerings* and is fragmentary. The first syllable of "Sergius" alone is complete, and the *praenomen* seems to be Quintus, not Lucius. Hence, it must be concluded, conclusive proof is thus far lacking. A Polish archaeological team at present engaged in work at New Paphos (*see* PAPHOS) may throw light on the problem.

BIBLIOGRAPHY: B. Van Elderen, *Apostolic History and the Gospel* (1970), 151–55.

EMB

SERIATION. A system of typology,* the analysis of which studies the shape of artifacts.* As a result, it is sometimes possible to explain the development of the relationship between similar types. Where such a process has been established, the rate of change may need to be determined in conjunction with various forms of external dating.*

HWP

SERPENT. Serpents are mentioned often in the Bible. The ancient talking serpent who deceived the woman in the Garden of Eden (Gen 3) is identified as Satan (Rev 20:2). Serpents are used figuratively as a threat of death (Gen 49:17) or of cleverness (Matt 10:16).

Archaeology has provided numerous illustrations of serpent representations in artifacts* from biblical periods. Gods and goddesses are often represented as holding serpents, or with the serpents coiled around them. This may symbolize power over the threat of death (cf. Acts 28:3–6 where Paul's resistance to the viper made him a god in the eyes of the onlookers) or simply the cleverness of the god. A household stela* showing a Canaanite* serpent goddess with a snake around her neck was found at Tell Beit Mirsim (see Debir*). The same representation turned up at Shechem,* Hazor,* Gezer,* and several were discovered in the four Canaanite temples at Beth Shan* in the form of serpent plaques and shrine houses. Another was found at Beth Shemesh* dating from the late Canaanite and early Israelite period. And 2 Kings 18:4 records the destruction of a serpent image by Hezekiah, perhaps reflecting the influence of Canaanite idolatry. In Greek mythology, serpents were connected with healing. The Caduceus symbol of two snakes on a pole appears as a sign of the medical arts in the Hellenistic period at Ashklepion,* Ephesus,* etc. These may reflect the serpent of Moses (Num 21:8). Mycenaean* art, as well, has several representations of snake goddesses.

BIBLIOGRAPHY: W. C. Graham and H. G. May, *Culture and Conscience* (1936), 81–90; *FLAP*, 139–46; Y. Yadin, "Further Light from Biblical Hazor," *BA*, 20 (1957), 43–44.

BCC

SEVENEH. *See* ASWAN.

SHAGAR BAZAR. *See* HABOR RIVER.

SHAKALUSHA. *See* SEA PEOPLES.

SHALMANESER, BLACK OBELISK OF. A four-sided object of black limestone, 2.02 m. (6½ ft.) high, from the reign of Shalmaneser III (858–824 B.C.), king of Assyria. The pillar, which was discovered in Kalhu (biblical Calah,* modern Nimrud) by A. H. Layard in 1846, is composed of five registers or rows of bas-relief* panels, intended to be read around the four sides of the pillar, making twenty individual panels in all. Over each row of panels is a descriptive inscription, in addition to the three small steps at the top of the obelisk,* and about the bottom one-third of the obelisk, supply descriptive material.

The text depicts Shalmaneser's triumphs over several kingdoms of Syria and the West. Of special interest to biblical students is one panel in the second row in which a bearded Semite bows before the king while his servants present gifts. The text refers to the humble suppliant as Jehu, son of Omri* (a name by which all Israelite kings were identified, whether of the Omride dynasty or not) and describes the gifts brought. The event, apparently from the year 841 B.C., gives us the earliest surviving picture of an Israelite and shows how such a person might have appeared to an Assyrian sculptor. There is no evidence,

Drawing of detail from Black Obelisk of Shalmaneser showing the king receiving the tribute of "Jehu, son of Omri," who is prostrating himself. Courtesy Carta, Jerusalem.

however, that the obelisk was actually depicting the Israelite monarch Jehu. The obelisk is now in the British Museum.

BIBLIOGRAPHY: *ANET*, 281; *ANEP*, 351–55; R. D. Barnett, *Illustrations of OT History*, The British Museum (1966), 48–49.

CEA

SHARD (SHERD). A fragment of broken earthenware, also called an ostracon,* of great importance in archaeological dating.*

SHARI, ESH-. *See* ESH-SHARI.

SHARUHEN. *See* TIRZAH.

SHEBA. 1. The name of several OT personages (cf. Gen 10:7; 10:28; 25:3; 2 Sam 20:1–2, 6–7, 10, 21–22; 1 Chron 5:13) and of two places.

2. The Sheba of Josh 19:2 is associated in the MT with Beersheba,* and may be an explanatory gloss furnishing the shorter or more popular designation. The MT of 1 Chron 4:28 omits Sheba from the parallel list, but the LXX reads Sama. Most probably the reference is to an area close to or identical with Beersheba in S Palestine.

3. Sheba, the homeland of the celebrated Arab queen, who visited Solomon* (1 Kings 10:1ff.; 2 Chron 9:1ff.), was located in SW Arabia* and was probably settled by one or more of the persons named under 1 above. Sheba was the home of the Sabeans,* orginally a nomadic group which by the Israelite monarchy period had settled in the E in the area of what is now known as Yemen. They traded in precious metals, jewels, spices, and odoriferous resins (cf. 1 Kings 10:2; Ezek 27:22; Jer 6:20 et al.), and once their commercial activities developed they appear to have founded colonies farther to the N. The original capital of Sheba was Ṣirwaḥ, but this was replaced subsequently by Marib (Mahram Bilqis), where outstanding examples of Sabean architecture have been discovered. Particularly noteworthy are the ruins of a majestic temple dedicated to the moon deity Ilumquh. While priest-kings (*mukarribs*) generally ruled Sheba in the first half of the first millennium B.C., cunei-

form* inscriptions have been recovered which show that, particularly in N Arabia, tribal confederacies were sometimes governed by queens during the period of the ninth to the seventh centuries B.C. Inscriptions from Ṣirwaḥ, Marib, and elsewhere have proved extremely valuable for epigraphy* as well as the study of S Arabian art and architecture. Funerary furnishings utilized by the Sabeans have been illustrated from the mausoleum and S tombs at Marib. The most distinctive style of Sabean masonry was one borrowed during the seventh century B.C. from Assyrian sources. The Sabeans built dams to divert water from flash floods in the wadis* to a complex of channels and sluices. This procedure enabled them to develop their agriculture* to an advanced degree.

BIBLIOGRAPHY: R. L. Bowen and W. F. Albright, *Archaeological Discoveries in S Arabia*, 2 (1958); G. W. Van Beek, "S Arabian History and Archaeology," *The Bible and the Ancient Near East* (1961), 229–49; E. Ullendorff, "The Queen of Sheba," *BJRL*, 45, no. 2 (1963); H. von Wissnamm, *Zur Geschichte und Laundeskunde von Alt-Südarabien* (1964); J. A. Thompson, *ZPEB*, 5 (1975), 379–80.

RKH

SHEBNA. This rich official of Hezekiah's court is variously described by Isaiah (22:15; 36:3), who rebuked him for his pretentious tomb (22:15–19). A rock lintel apparently from this tomb held an inscription which was deciphered by N. Avigad in 1953. It read, with some restoration: "This is the sepulcher of Shebnayahu, who is over the house. There is no silver* or gold* here but only his bones, and the bones of his slave-wife with him. Cursed be the man who breaks this open." The restoration of Shebna's full name is based on his office of palace governor, which occurs on a number of seals.*

BIBLIOGRAPHY: N. Avigad, *IEJ*, 3 (1953), 137–52; D. J. Wiseman, *IBA* (1958), 59; A. E. Cundall, *ZPEB*, 5 (1975), 380–81.

EMB

SHEBNAYAHU. See SHEBNA.

SHECHEM (shek'əm; Heb. שְׁכֶם, *sheḵem*; "shoulder"). It is the modern Tell Balata (Balatah), situated in the center of Palestine (Judg 9:37) at the eastern end of the pass between Mount Ebal and Mount Gerizim.* The town controlled all the roads through the central hill country in ancient times but was not itself well placed for defense. Hence it needed strong defenses at all times.

Several excavations have been carried out this century by E. Sellin in 1913–14, 1934; by G. Welter in 1928 and 1932; and by the Drew-McCormick Expeditions under G. Ernest Wright and others in 1956–57, 1960, 1962.

There is scattered evidence of encampments in the area in the early Chalcolithic* period (c. 4000 B.C.), but there was a long gap in occupation, at least in excavated areas, until c. 1800 B.C., i.e. until the Middle Bronze IIA* period. The Execration Texts* and a battle report by an officer of Sesostris III of Egypt* (1878–1843 B.C.) suggest that the Shechem area was a trouble to Egypt at this early date.

Soon after 1800 B.C., however, the city* became a Hyksos* center. Strong defenses were erected and a palace, which was itself enclosed by a substantial wall,* was built. This palace was reconstructed at least three times during the Hyksos period. A street,* which skirted the temple inside the closed area, was restored nine times. At the height of the Hyksos period, c. 1650–1550 B.C., the palace area was filled over, and the city wall moved to the N. This wall is visible today. It is built of huge stones and is known as the Cyclopean wall. A fine temple was built over the buried palace area. Excavation beneath the temple platform brought to light the remains of structures—temples and palace. The Hyksos period ended with the Egyptian campaigns of c. 1550 B.C. The city recovered only slowly after these troubles. The temple was finally rebuilt but was somewhat smaller and was reoriented. Both temples were in the nature of fortress temples, with substantial walls and a large tower* on each side of the entrance. This was the temple of Baal-Berith (Judg 9:4), which was standing when the Israelites entered the land. Unlike other towns in Palestine, Shechem does not seem to have suffered a general destruction in the thirteenth century. But during the twelfth century Abimelech destroyed the temple and its defenses (Judg 9:46–49).

The fortifications of Shechem during these years were impressive. The first city wall was pre-Hyksos (c. 1750–1725). The early Hyksos built a typical earthen embankment (c. 1725–1700), and then the Cyclopean wall, and an impressive gate* in the NW, with a type of casemate wall* and a triple gateway (c. 1650 B.C.). A little later (c. 1625–1575), a fine gate was built in the E. It was later rebuilt. It was destroyed by the Egyptians c. 1550 B.C., but built again, and continued in use until about 1100 B.C.

There is no biblical reference to Shechem in the days of the monarchy, although Rehoboam was crowned here (1 Kings 12:1). However, during the ninth and eighth centuries, the city was a prosperous one to judge from the remains of fine houses.* Toward the end of the eighth century Shechem suffered severely. Masses of fallen bricks and burned beams were found in excavated buildings. The destruction should be linked to the campaigns of Tiglath-pileser III* (2 Kings 15:29) or Shalmaneser V (2 Kings 17:3–6). Shechem was little more than a village until the fourth century, when it was rebuilt. Between c. 325 and 100 B.C., in the Samaritan period, the city was again prosperous. Coins* found in the excavations range from the fourth century to c. 110 B.C., when they cease. The destruction of the city can be linked with the campaign of John Hyrcanus (Jos. *Antiq.* 13.9.1), possibly in 107 B.C., when he destroyed Samaria.*

The relationship with the Sychar* of the NT (John 4:5) is not clear. Excavated areas do not reveal an occupation in the Roman period.

BIBLIOGRAPHY: G. E. Wright, "The First Campaign at Tell Balatah (Shechem)," *BASOR*, 144 (1956), 9–23; id., "Shechem . . . The Archaeology of the City," *BA*, 20 (1957), 19–32; id., "The Second Campaign at Tell Balatah (Shechem)," *BASOR*, 148 (1957), 11–28; W. Harrelson, "Shechem in Extra-Biblical

References," *BA*, 20 (1957), 2–10; G. E. Wright, *Shechem, The Biography of a Biblical City* (1965).

JAT

SHEDET. See CROCODILOPOLIS.

SHEPHELAH (she'fə lə; Heb. שְׁפֵלָה, *shᵉpēlāh*). Ancient Hebrew term for the lowland area between the Palestinian coastal plain and the uplands of Judah* and Samaria.*

SHEPHERD, GOOD. Shepherding is one of the ancient occupations of the E. Such is the nature of the sheep and the duties that nature imposes on the keeper that "good shepherd" became a metaphor for regal and divine care, and for the relation of God and king to helpless men and women. The theme finds archaeological illustration from Sumer* to the catacombs.* Kudur-Mabug (see MELCHIZEDEK), in a surviving prayer, hopes that he may be a good shepherd of his people, while the extended metaphors of Ps 23, Ezek 34, and John 10, inspired elaborate early Christian art—roughly scratched on funeral slabs, sculptured on sarcophagi,* on lamps,* vases, seals,* rings, and vaulted ceilings. The pictured sheep sometime form a visual parable—some at rest, some feeding nearby, some turning heedlessly away, some disappearing over a hill-crest. The shepherd carries staff or crook and is sometimes weary. In a fresco of the Catacomb of St. Agnes, a hireling roughly lays hold of the leg of a struggling animal, and the same catacomb shows a sheep between two wolves labeled *SENIORES*—an allusion, evidently, to the apocryphal (see PSEUDEPIGRAPHRA) story of Susannah and the "elders." Tertullian, in the second century, speaks of the Good Shepherd theme on chalices, and a fifth-century mosaic* from Ravenna displays it.

SHEPHERD KING. See HYKSOS.

SHERD. See SHARD.

SHERDEN. See SEA PEOPLES.

SHESHONK. See BUBASTIS; EGYPT; SHISHAK.

SHIELD. See ARMS AND WEAPONS.

SHILOH (shī' lō; Heb. שִׁילֹה, *šîlōh*). The modern Seilun, a ruined site on a hill some 14.5 km. (9 mi.) N of Bethel.* It was excavated by Danish expeditions in 1926, 1929, 1932, and 1963. The first three excavations seemed to suggest that the occupation was interrupted during the Iron I* period and resumed in the Hellenistic to Byzantine* periods. This seemed to give special point to Jer 7:12, since it was believed that Shiloh had been destroyed in a Philistine* attack (1 Sam 4), about 1050 B.C. The 1963 campaign shows occupation during the days of the Hebrew kings, so that Jeremiah's reference to its destruction would seem to be an allusion to events closer to his time (cf. Jer 41:5). There were traces of occupation in the Middle Bronze Age* (c. 2000–1550 B.C.), but there was no substantial occupation until the Iron I Age

suggesting that the Israelites built here (Josh 18:1; 1 Sam 1:1–4; 1 Kings 14:2, 4). Further excavation is necessary to clarify the historical questions.

BIBLIOGRAPHY: W. F. Albright, "The Danish Excavation at Shiloh," *BASOR*, 13 (1923), 10–11; H. Kjaer, "The Excavations at Shiloh, 1929," *JPOS*, 10 (1930), 87–174; O. Eissfeldt, *VTSup*, 4 (1957), 138–47; H. G. Andersen, *ZPEB*, 5 (1975), 402–4.

JAT

SHINAR (shī' när; Heb. שִׁנְעָר, *šin'ār*; LXX Σεναάρ, *senaār*). A biblical name for the region of Babylonia. Attempts to derive Shinar from the name of Sumer* are without support. Some have suggested a derivation from W Sem. *Sangar*, Akkad. *Shanhar*, Egypt. *Sangar*; these nonbiblical references seem to denote a region NW of Babylonia. Late Syr. *Sen^car* designated an area around Baghdad. Archaeological research could in the future elucidate this geographical problem.

The general location of Shinar can be determined from the biblical texts themselves. Gen 10:10 indicates that the cities of Nimrod's kingdom—Babel (Babylon*), Erech* (ancient Uruk, modern Warka), Akkad* (Agade), "all of them" (reading the consonantal text *kullānā*, rather than *kalnēh*) (see CALNEH)—were in the land of Shinar. The tower of Babel* (Gen 11:2) was built on a plain of Shinar. Amraphel,* one of the kings of the E (Gen 14:9), was a king of Shinar. Achan coveted a mantle, or robe, of Shinar (Josh 7:21; see NIV f.n.).

Nebuchadnezzar* carried off Jewish captives to Shinar (Dan 1:2), and the Lord promised to recover the remnant from Shinar (Isa 11:11). The ephah of Zechariah's vision was borne to Shinar (Zech 5:11).

BIBLIOGRAPHY: E. A. Speiser, "In Search of Nimrod," *Eretz Israel*, 5 (1958), 32–36; D. J. Wiseman, *ZPEB*, 5 (1975), 407–9; J. A. Thompson, "Samaritan Evidence for 'All of Them in the Land of Shinar' (Gen 10:10)," *JBL*, 90 (1971), 99–102.

EY

SHIPS. In classical archaeology the question of ships, navigation, and naval warfare,* occupies a large place with evidence from art, especially vase paintings,* and coins.* It is not so relevant in biblical archaeology. Two or three contexts may be singled out for comment.

1. The "ark" in which the infant Moses was set adrift on the Nile (Exod 2:3–6) was probably a smaller version of the river and swamp boats built of bound fascines of papyrus* stems, and which may be illustrated from mural scenes of bird hunting among the papyrus fens of the Delta. Similar fresco illustrations from the account of Hatshepsut's mid-fifteenth-century B.C. expedition to open trade contacts with the Somali coast, show sturdier Egyptian ships of seagoing capability.

2. The "ships of Tarshish" (2 Chron 9:21; 20:36–37; Ps 48:7 et al.) were evidently a successful type of Phoenician* merchantman designed for the ore trade. The word Tarshish,* often thought to refer to Tartessos in Spain, where the ships went for silver* ore, as they also fetched tin* from Cornwall, is, ac-

cording to W. F. Albright, a word from the vocabulary of metallurgy* and mining. It is possible, therefore, that the word simply meant "ore ship." Significantly, it was a "Tarshish fleet" based on Aqaba in the maritime partnership of Solomon* and the Tyrians. Solomon's mining activities were located N of the head of the Gulf.

3. On his way to Rome* and shipwreck, Paul traveled on three large freighters, and evidence for these great cargo vessels is mainly literary (Josephus, Lucian, Tatius, for example), to which archaeology has little to add. Some underwater photography, for example of a wreck near the Phare du Titan off the French Riviera coast, provides a few shreds of evidence. Paintings from decorated walls in Herculaneum* and Pompeii* depict freighters contemporary with the ships of Acts 27. In the stern ornament of the ship depicted on the tomb of Naevoleia Tyche at Pompeii the head of Minerva is visible, a device like a figurehead. Castor and Pollux (twin sons of Leda, regarded as protectors of persons at sea) were probably similarly placed in the ship in which Paul reached Puteoli* (Acts 28:13).

See also TRANSPORTATION.

BIBLIOGRAPHY: E. M. Blaiklock, *ZPEB*, 5 (1975), 410–15.

EMB

SHIPWRECKED SAILOR, STORY OF THE. An ancient Egyptian romantic tale of adventure, preserved only on Papyrus Ermitage 1115 (in Leningrad), of Twelfth Dynasty, c. 1900 B.C.

At the start, as a ship* returns safely to Elephantine* from Nubia,* a sailor seeks to cheer up his commander by telling how his adversity has been rectified. He speaks of sailing on the Red Sea,* being shipwrecked, and cast alone upon a magic isle ruled by a great but kindly serpent.* The serpent tells him its tale of sorrow and predicts a safe return in a coming Egyptian ship. This happens and the sailor is given rich products to take back to Egypt.*

Biblically, the story is of interest (1) because, as a literary unit, it combines narrative, dialogue, lists (products), and reflections of religious practice (burnt offerings), and (2) it gives background to early travel on the Red Sea to Punt a millennium before Solomon's* fleets sailed to more distant Ophir.*

BIBLIOGRAPHY: A. Erman and A. M. Blackman, reed. by W. K. Simpson, *The Ancient Egyptians: A Sourcebook of Their Writings*, 23–24 (1966), 29–35; G. Lefebvre, *Romans et contes égyptiens* (1949), 29–40; T. G. H. James, *Myths and Legends of Ancient Egypt* (1969, rep. 1971), 117–24.

KAK

SHISHAK (shī'shak; following the Heb. Qere שִׁישַׁק, *šîšaq*, rather than the Kethib שׁוּשַׁק; LXX Σουσακίμ, *Sousakim*; Egypt. *Ššnḳ*, which in the light of Akkad. *Susinḳu*, is to be vocalized Shoshenḳ, rather than Sheshonḳ). The founder of the Twenty-second Dynasty, and the greatest pharaoh in military prowess during a half millennium of Egyptian weakness (1200–700 B.C.).

I. *Background.* A. *The Libyan Meshwesh.* In Egyptian texts Shishak is called a Great Chief of the Me(shwesh), a Libyan tribe. The Meshwesh attacked Egypt* during the reigns of Merneptah and Ramses III* (c. 1220–1170). After their defeat, the Egyptians used them as mercenaries, settling them in the eastern delta and forcing them to learn Egyptian. Shishak came from a Meshwesh family who had been settled at Heracleopolis for five generations and who occupied high offices there.

Shishak rose to power as a loyal servant of Psusennes II, the last king of the Twenty-first Dynasty, and eventually married the king's daughter. After the death of Psusennes, Shishak established his new dynasty at Bubastis* in the eastern delta and installed his son in the important post of high priest of the chief Egyptian god, Amon of Thebes.* Shishak and his Libyan compatriots were able to dominate Egypt for over two centuries (945–730 B.C.) during the Twenty-second and the Twenty-third Dynasties.

B. *Dates.* Manetho gives Shishak a reign of twenty-one years, which accords with the evidence from contemporary inscriptions. Most Egyptologists would date his reign 945–924 B.C. A lower date of c. 935–914 would have to be adopted by scholars who favor Albright's lower dates for Solomon,* inasmuch as Shishak's invasion of Palestine took place in Rehoboam's fifth year or 918 B.C. by this reckoning.

II. *Biblical Data.* Shishak plays a role in the Bible in two incidents. He received Jeroboam who fled from Solomon (1 Kings 11:40), and maintained him until the latter's death, when Jeroboam returned to lead the ten northern tribes in revolt. Shishak later invaded Palestine during Rehoboam's fifth year (1 Kings 14:25–26), removing treasures from the temple* and the palace in Jerusalem.* According to the fuller account in 2 Chron 12:2–10, Shishak invaded with a force of 1,200 chariots* and 60,000 horsemen, accompanied by *Lubim* (Libyans), "Ethiopians" (*Cushim* or Nubians* from the Sudan), and *Sukkim.* The latter word represents the Egyptian *Tjuku,* scouts of a Libyan origin.

An earlier generation of scholars (Sellin, Breasted, Olmstead) suggested that Shishak was Solomon's Egyptian father-in-law (*see* SOLOMON, sec. V.A.).

III. *Egyptological and Archaeological Data.* A. *The Karnak Inscription.* An important inscription of Shishak describing his invasion of Palestine reveals that his campaign was far more extensive than the biblical texts suggest. The text is on the S wall of an immense court of the temple of Amon at Karnak. The figure of the pharaoh himself was not completed and much of the monument has deteriorated. A gigantic figure of Amon grasps cords attached to ten rows of captives, representing from 156 to 180 separate sites. Of these about half can still be read, but only about a score or so identified with any certainty. The first 65 names included major sites in Central Palestine; names 66 to 150 were of smaller settlements in Judah* and the Negeb.*

Mazar has suggested that the line of march can be reconstructed if the text were read in boustrophedon fashion (lines run alternately from right to left and from left to right). The main force proceeded from Gaza* to Gezer,* Aijalon,* Beth-horon, Gibeon,* Tirzah(?),* down to Adam in the Jordan Valley, to Succoth* and other sites in the Trans-Jordan, back to Beth Shan,* Taanach,* and Megiddo.* At this point Yeivin suggests that the Egyptian army proceeded around the Carmel* headland. Secondary forces proceeded from Gaza eastward to Arad* and southward to Ramat Matred (as proposed by Aharoni).

In view of the biblical text, the omission of Jerusalem is noteworthy. This may have been included in the part of the text which has worn away. Aharoni suggests that the Egyptians received the treasures from Jerusalem when they reached Gibeon as a voluntary bribe from Rehoboam.

In 1914 Wellhausen dismissed Shishak's inscription as worthless, but excavations have provided indisputable evidence of the pharaoh's campaign in a stele* of Shishak found at Megiddo. Though the Solomonic gate* was not destroyed, convincing signs of a great destruction were found in Megiddo level VB. At Gezer recent excavations have yielded evidence of Shishak's raid in the area of the Solomonic gate and in Field III, where the destruction was so thorough that casemates* were never reopened. Destruction levels of the late tenth century at Tell Jerishe (Gath-rimmon?) NE of Joppa* and at Ramat Matred S of Gaza may have resulted from Shishak's campaign. Glueck believed that the Solomonic level at Tell el-Kheleifeh was destroyed by Shishak's forces.

Indeed, a likely purpose of Shishak's invasion may have been the crippling of the trade routes built up by Solomon (see SOLOMON, sec. IV. B–F.)

B. *Other Monuments.* Shishak maintained good relations with Phoenicia,* as evidenced by a statue* of his which was given to Abiba'al, the ruler of Byblos (Gebal*).

An inscription from Gebal Silsileh which describes the quarrying* of stones by Shishak's architect, no doubt for his court at Karnak, is dated to the pharaoh's twenty-first year. Other monuments come from Abydos,* el-Hiba, Dakhla, etc.

C. *The Monuments From Tanis.* Next to the Karnak inscription the most important monuments associated with Shishak and his dynasty have come to light in P. Montet's excavations at Tanis* in the eastern Delta. No statue of Shishak himself has been recovered, but we have some idea of the appearance of his family in the statue of his son Osorkon I from Byblos, and in particular the silver* coffin (see SARCOPHAGUS) of his grandson Shishak II found at Tanis in 1939. On the mummy of the pharaoh were two bracelets originally owned by Shishak I, which Montet speculates were part of the Jerusalem booty.* Though a canopic jar* with Shishak I's name has been found, his mummy, which was probably buried in Tanis, has not yet been recovered.

BIBLIOGRAPHY: J. Wilson, "The Libyans and the End of the Egyptian Empire," *AJSL*, 51 (1934–35), 73–82; J. Breasted, *Ancient Records of Egypt*, 4 (1927), 344–61; A. Blackman, "The Stela of Shoshenk, Great Chief of the Meshwesh," *JEA*, 27 (1941), 83–95; B. Grdseloff, "Édôm, d'après les sources

Fragment of limestone Egyptian stele found at Megiddo, dated tenth century B.C. The names and titles of Shishak I are incised in hieroglyphs. Courtesy Israel Dept. of Antiquities and Museums.

égyptiennes," *Revue de l'histoire juive en Egypte*, 1 (1947), 69–99; P. Elgood, *The Later Dynasties of Egypt* (1951); R. Caminos, "Gebel es-Silsilah no. 100," *JEA*, 38 (1951), 46–49; B. Maisler (Mazar), "The Campaign of Pharaoh Shishak to Palestine," *VTSup*, 4 (1957), 57–66; A. Gardiner, *Egypt of the Pharaohs* (1961); Y. Yeivin, "Topographic and Ethnic Notes III," *JEA*, 48 (1962), 75–80; G. Wainwright, "The Meshwesh," *JEA*, 48 (1962), 89–99; Y. Aharoni, *The Land of the Bible* (1967), 283–90; P. Montet, *Egypt and the Bible* (1968); id., *Lives of the Pharaohs* (1968); K. A. Kitchen, "Late-Egyptian Chronology and the Hebrew Monarchy," *Journal of the Ancient Near East Society of Columbia University*, 5 (1973), 231–33; K. A. Kitchen, *The Third Intermediate Period in Egypt* (1973), 72–76, 287–302, 432–47; A. R. Green, "Israelite Influence at Shishak's Court," *BASOR*, 233 (1979), 59–62.

EY

SHITTIM (shi'təm; Heb. שִׁטָּה, *šiṭṭāh*). A place of this name ("acacia trees") was located NE of the Dead Sea* in the Plains of Moab and was an Israelite encampment prior to the crossing of the Jordan. The full form of the name was probably Abel Shittim (Num 33:49). While the Israelites encamped there, Balak of Moab* secured the services of the Mesopotamian* diviner Balaam in an attempt to thwart Israelite progress (Num 22–24). Subsequently the Israelites were drawn into immoral conduct with Midianite* and Moabite women at Baal-peor. Hence the "doctrine of Balaam" of the NT (Rev 2:14). After Moses died, Joshua sent spies from Shittim to examine the Jericho* area and the land of Canaan* (Josh 2:1). The place has been identified with Tell el-Kefrein, located on an eminence 9.7 km. (6 mi.) N of the Dead Sea E of the Jordan, and commanding an excellent view of the Plains of Moab. Potsherds (see SHARDS) from Iron Ages* I and II (twelfth to sixth centuries B.C.) have been recovered from the site. Alternatively, it is argued by Nelson Glueck that a location about 3.2 km. (2 mi.) further E at Tell el-Hammam has been proposed for Shittim. It occupied a strategic position on the Wadi el-Kefrein, and the remains of Iron Age I and II fortresses, whose outer walls* were nearly 1.2 m. (4 ft.) thick, have been uncovered there. The area of this site was nearly a hundred times bigger than that of Tell el-Kefrein. The place mentioned in Joel 3:18, if an actual valley, could be the Wadi es-Sant, although some have identified it with the Kidron* ravine (Wadi en-Nar).

BIBLIOGRAPHY: N. Glueck, "Some Ancient Towns in the Plains of Moab," *BASOR*, 91 (1943), 13–18; id., "Explorations in Eastern Palestine, IV," *AASOR*, 25–27 (1945–48), 221, 371–82; T. E. McComiskey, *ZPEB*, 5 (1975), 418–19.

RKH

SHOPHAR. *See* MUSIC.

SHOSHENK. *See* SHISHAK.

SHURUPPAK (shū′ru pak). The city is not mentioned in the Bible but is significant in the study of Noah's Flood (Gen 6:8–8:22). Shuruppak, now a mound called Fara, about 193 km. (120 mi.) S of Baghdad, was one of the most important in ancient Sumer.* The Sumerian King List* names Shuruppak as the last ruling city* before the flood and states that its king Ubar-Tutu reigned there for 18,600 years. The Gilgamesh Epic* (which corresponds in part to the Gen account of the great flood) makes Utnapishtim (*see* ZIUSUDRA) the son of Ubar-Tutu the hero of the flood who is commanded by the gods to build a large boat. The site of this divine revelation in the Gilgamesh Epic is the city of Shuruppak.

Shuruppak was excavated for the German Oriental Society by R. Koldewey in 1902–3, with the result that water-laid silt about .6 m. (2 ft.) thick was found and dated in the Jemdet Nasr* period (end of the fourth millennium B.C.). This could not be taken as evidence of a general flood since the dates were different from those at Ur* and other Sumerian sites. Other discoveries included buildings, tablets, seals,* and painted ware typical of the Jemdet Nasr period.

BIBLIOGRAPHY: *CAH*, 1, part 2, 72 passim.

BCC

SHUSHAN. *See* SUSA.

SIALK, TEPE. *See* TEPE SIALK.

SIDON (sīd′ən; Heb. צִידוֹן, *ṣîdôn*). The modern Saidon, on the Lebanese coast about 40 km. (25 mi.) N of Tyre,* was, according to tradition, the first Phoenician* city* to be founded. In Greek and Roman documents it is frequently identified with, or associated closely with, Tyre, a situation no doubt reflecting historical fact. The Amarna letters* indicate that, in the thirteenth century, while Tyre maintained her loyalty to Egypt,* Sidon pursued an independent policy, professing loyalty but cultivating an Amorite* alliance. Egypt was apparently overextended in the area. Trade was, however, still active two centuries later.

The city appears to have resisted pressure both from the Habiru* and the equally vague Sea Peoples.* Assyrian texts show that Sidon paid tribute to Ashurnasirpal II* in 876 B.C., to Shalmaneser III a generation later, to Tiglath-pileser III* a century later still, and in 725 B.C. to Shalmaneser V. All these

monarchs intruded into the Phoenician coastal strip. Sennacherib* crushed a revolt of Tyre in 701 B.C. The king, Luli, who had challenged the Assyrians, escaped to Cyprus,* and Sennacherib inscribed the story of his victory beside the inscription of Ramses II* on the rock near the mouth of the Nahr-el-Kelb River. Sennacherib set up Tubaʿal as king. "And Luli, king of Sidon, fearing to fight me, fled to Cyprus [Iadnana], which is (an island) amid the sea, and sought refuge. In that same year he died infamously through awe inspired by the weapon of the god Ashur, my lord. I sat Tubaʿal on his royal throne and fixed upon him tribute [due] to my overlordship. I laid waste the wide district of Judah [*Iaudi*] and made the overbearing and proud Hezekiah, its king, bow submissively at my feet" (Bull Inscription, *DOTT*, 68). When Tubaʿal's son, Abdimilkutte, also rebelled, Esarhaddon* destroyed the city. The conqueror vainly tried to build another port near the site, but Sidon reasserted itself, fell briefly under Egyptian control, and then under Nebuchadnezzar.* This covers the archaeological record. The historical record of Sidon under the succeeding empires, Persian, Hellenistic, and Roman, is literary.

BIBLIOGRAPHY: G. A. Cooke, *A Text Book of N Semitic Inscriptions* (1903), 26–43; B. Van Elderen, *ZPEB*, 5 (1975), 426–28.

EMB

SIEGECRAFT. *See* MACHINES, WAR.

SIGNET. A ring, consisting either of engraved metal or an inset engraved stone, used for establishing ownership and frequently associated with personal authority. The seal-stone or signet of the Hebrews (*tabbaʿath*; Akkad. *timbuʾu*) was generally of exquisite workmanship (*see* CRAFTS; cf. Exod 28:11–23; 39:6) and was frequently used by the rich as an ornament (cf. Isa 3:21) or for religious purposes (cf. Exod 35:22; Num 31:50). The latter function has been illustrated archaeologically by the discovery of a group of seals* in the Canaanite* shrine at Hazor.* The rings of officials were used for impressing documents by way of signature, so that to receive a ring from a ruler, as Joseph* did from pharaoh (Gen 41:42) and Haman and Mordecai* did from the Persian ruler Xerxes* (Esth 3:10; 8:2) was a particularly significant token of royal favor, indicating the bestowal of unusual powers. Up to the Persian period signet rings normally had a seal-stone inset in the metal face, but from the fifth century B.C. rings engraved in plain gold* became increasingly popular. Metaphorical allusions to the use of the signet ring occur in Jer 22:24; Hag 2:23; John 3:33; 1 Cor 9:2 et al.

BIBLIOGRAPHY: L. E. Toombs, *IDB*, 5 (1962), 347–48; J. B. Scott, *ZPEB*, 5 (1975), 431–32.

RKH

SILOAM; SILOAM INSCRIPTION (sī lō əm; Gr. Σιλώαμ, *Silōam*). A pool to the S of the temple* area at the exit of Hezekiah's tunnel* (cf. John 9:7). In the early days of the monarchy an aqueduct* brought water along the hillside from the Spring of Gihon* to a reservoir. This aqueduct may represent the gently

Siloam inscription in cursive Hebrew script incised on face of rock wall of the tunnel, near exit. It measures 50 cm. in height and 66 cm. in width. It was discovered in 1880, later removed, and is now in the Istanbul Museum. Courtesy Israel Dept. of Antiquities and Museums.

flowing waters of Shiloah (Isa 8:6). Hezekiah's tunnel added yet another feature to a complex of waterways and pools* (2 Kings 18:17; 20:20; 2 Chron. 32:30; Neh 3:15; Isa 7:3; 22:9–11; 36:2). At the southern end of Hezekiah's tunnel, workmen inscribed in the ancient Hebrew script on the walls of the tunnel a vivid description of the completion of the tunnel on the day when workmen cutting from the two sides met. The inscription is now in the Istanbul Museum. The text runs in part: ". . . while there were still three cubits to be cut through, (there was heard) the voice of a man calling to his fellow, for there was *an overlap* in the rock on the right (and on the left). And when the tunnel was driven through, the quarrymen hewed [the rock], each man toward his fellow, axe against axe; and the water flowed from the spring toward the reservoir for 1,200 cubits, and the height of the rock above the head[s] of the quarrymen was one hundred cubits."

BIBLIOGRAPHY: *ANET* (1955), 321; K. M. Kenyon, *Jerusalem, Excavating 3000 Years of History* (1967), 69–77, 96–99; J. B. Payne, *ZPEB*, 5 (1975), 434–37.   JAT

SILOAM TUNNEL. *See* HEZEKIAH'S TUNNEL.

SILVER. This metal is mentioned about three hundred times in the Bible, and it seems to have been known in the Near East as early as gold* and copper. The biblical references establish its use as a standard of wealth (Gen 13:2), as money (Gen 20:16), as jewelry and ornamentation (Song of Songs 1:11), and as the material of cult objects and images.

In spite of the extensive use of silver for all of the above items, archaeologists have turned up relatively few silver artifacts* in excavations. A silver bowl and a ladle in the form of a female figure were found at Shuruppak* and date from the Persian period. From the royal tombs at Ur* came musical instruments,* and statuettes ornamented with silver as well as gold. A small bronze* god from Ugarit* was covered with gold and silver. Several silver dishes were recovered from the ruins of Pompeii* (destroyed in A.D. 79), and the silver chalice of Antioch has been dated as early as the first century A.D., but probably comes from the fourth. Silver and silver-plated coins* have often been found in excavations (e.g., at Shechem* and especially at Caesarea*), but the oldest coins are

from the seventh century B.C. Small shekel symbols found on weights* from Lachish* are believed to indicate the *seror*, or tied bundles in which silver was carried when used as a medium of exchange before coinage. In 1947 a number of silver bowls were found at Tell el-Maskhuta in Egypt;* one of the dedicatory inscriptions in Aramaic* reads: "That which Qaynu, son of Gashmu, king of Qedar, brought in offering to Han-Ilat." Gashmu has been identified as one of the rulers (Geshem) who opposed Nehemiah's rebuilding of the walls of Jerusalem,* and Qedar (Kedar) is also referred to in the Bible.

Silver was first used in coins about 700 B.C., and for a long period the Hittites* seemed to be in control of the silver bullion market—a light perhaps on Abraham's transactions with the sons of Heth (Gen 23:15–16). Economic historians seem able to trace fluctuations in the fortunes of the ancient world to periodic exhaustion of silver supplies. It is significant, for example, that the eclipse of Athens* as a powerful state seems to have coincided with the exhaustion of the silver mines of Laurion in Attica. Augustus* established a financially healthy bimetallism with honest coinage based on gold and silver. It was a silver denarius* of either Augustus or Tiberius* that lay in the hand of Christ when he said his famous words (Matt 22:19–21) concerning tribute money. Nero was the first to debase this currency and to introduce the inflation that accompanied the fall of the Roman world. Relapse and resurgence seem to be linked to the exhaustion or infusion of silver—new mines or loot from eastern conquest being

Silver goblet found in Middle Bronze Age I tomb at Ein Samiya, about 16 km. northwest of Jericho. The goblet is made of silver sheeting, decorated in repoussé. It apparently portrays two scenes of the Mesopotamian Creation Epic. Courtesy Israel Dept. of Antiquities and Museums.

the common sources of relief (as under Aurelian, A.D. 270–275). H. Mattingly discusses the phenomenon in *Roman Imperial Civilization* (1957), 190, 194ff.

Silver is fragile, and hence the small amount discovered. The rolled silver band the woman in the death pit in Ur had in her pocket was only a granulated lump by her thigh bone. The amount of silver recovered from ancient sites must be negligible compared with what has been lost. The loss of silver occurs because coins and jewelry were dropped and lost in the soil or in the ashes of burnt houses,* palaces, and cities;* sunk in shipwrecks; buried in graves;* and hidden in secret hoards. Most of the lost silver, therefore, corroded and dispersed back into the earth as silver salts.

Lead* is obtained as a byproduct of silver mining,* for silver comes from a sulphide ore of lead, and it is calculated that about 362,800 kg. (400 tons) of lead were extracted for each ton of silver (*see* METAL-LURGY). Traces of that ancient lead indicate how much of it was produced and give some indication of the large quantities of silver that was in some form of circulation. However, mined silver had a halflife of about thirty-five years. That is, every thirty-five years half the existing stock disappeared. Alexander the Great, for example, seized an estimated 1,995,400 kg. (2200 tons) of silver bullion in Persia. Within 160 years this great mass would have shrunk to about 81,630 kg. (90 tons), entirely from loss in handling.

BIBLIOGRAPHY: H. H. Read, *Rutley's Elements of Mineralogy* (1970 ed.), 255–62; S. L. Smith, "Silver," *EBr*, 20 (1970), 536–37; D. R. Bowes, *ZPEB*, 5 (1975), 437–38.

BCC and EMB

SILWAN, AIN. *See* SILOAM INSCRIPTION.

SIMBEL, ABU-. *See* ABU-SIMBEL.

SIMEON BEN KOSIBA. *See* BAR KOCHBA.

SIMON BAR KOCHBA. *See* BAR KOCHBA.

SINAI (sī′ nī; Heb. סִינַי, *sînay*; Gr. Σεῖνα, *Seina*). The name given both to the mountain at which the covenant* with Israel* was made and to the peninsula joining Egypt* to Canaan* in which Mount Sinai is located.

Although the Sinai peninsula always occupied an important place in the history of Israel, most of the archaeological remains are concentrated in the habitable portion of the peninsula called the Negev.* Settlements on the coastal areas in the S and E were rare and tended to be small. The mountain of Sinai itself, perhaps as important as any site in biblical history, has been the subject of extensive debate as to location, with no firm agreement possible. Traditions attach the name Sinai to at least three mountains in the peninsula, and some scholars hold to yet a fourth possibility in the mountains of Arabia* E of the Gulf of Aqaba. In any case, there remains nothing of archaeological interest at any of the suggested locations, with the exception of what has accrued to the place as a result of Jewish or Christian venera-

tion. St. Catherine's Monastery, at the foot of the massive Jebal Musa in S Sinai, was built in the early sixth century A.D., and there is little that can be identified as earlier.

The Sinai peninsula was, however, extensively used both as a trading bridge and mining* center from earliest times. In addition to the meager remains reflecting the presence of travelers, notably inscriptions, there is abundant evidence of Egyptian mining activity from the third millennium onward. The most interesting finds have come from Serabit El-Khadem,* a center both for copper and turquoise mining from the days of the Old Kingdom onward. In and around this area were found a series of temples and shrines, together with various inscriptions, including the famed Proto-Sinaitic inscriptions, the earliest evidence of a Semitic alphabetic* script.

BIBLIOGRAPHY: B. Rothenberg, *God's Wilderness* (1961); R. Amiran et al. "Interrelationship Between Arad and Sites in Southern Sinai in the Early Bronze Age II; Preliminary Report," *IEJ*, 23 (4, 1973), 193–97; E. D. Oren, "Overland Route Between Egypt and Canaan in the Early Bronze Age; Preliminary Report," *IEJ*, 23 (4, 1973), 198–205; G. H. Forsyth and K. Weitzmann, *The Monastery of Saint Catherine at Mount Sinai* (1974); Y. Gilead et al., "Northern and Central Sinai," *IEJ*, 25 (2–3, 1975), 161–62; A. F. Rainey, "Notes on Some Proto-Sinaitic Inscriptions," *IEJ*, 25 (2–3, 1975), 106–16. S. Agourides and J. H. Charlesworth, "New Discoveries of Old Manuscripts on Mt. Sinai: A Preliminary Report," *BA*, 41 (Mar 1978), 29–31; J. H. Charlesworth, "St. Catherine's Monastery: Myths and Mysteries," *BA*, 42 (1979), 174–79;

CEA

SINGING. *See* MUSIC.

SINUHE, THE STORY OF. An interesting account of life during the Twelfth Dynasty of Egypt* (c. 1990 B.C.), when the Hebrew patriarchs were associated with such Palestinian sites as Dothan,* Gerar,* Shechem,* and Bethel,* is provided by the story of Sinuhe. The author was a prominent Egyptian official who became involved in the political upheaval which followed the death of Amenhemet I, a vigorous leader who had restored the military and economic strength of Egypt following the social chaos of the Eleventh Dynasty. Fearing for his life, Sinuhe escaped with some difficulty through the fortifications which Amenhemet I had built on the Asiatic border and fled to Canaan* to seek asylum. His story describes the hardships experienced on his way to Kedem (cf. Gen 29:1), where he was befriended by an Amorite* chieftain of the same sort as Abraham, Laban, and Jacob. Sinuhe himself subsequently became chief of an Amorite tribe and was in command of this group during raids. His description of Amorite life corresponds very closely to what the OT has to say about the times of Abraham, Isaac, and Jacob, and his appraisal of the Palestinian uplands resembles that of Deut 8:8.

BIBLIOGRAPHY: *ANET* (1950), 18–22.

RKH

SIPPAR (si'pär). A city* on the middle Euphrates, identified with modern Abu Habba.

Sippar, the northernmost of the old Babylonian city-states, was mentioned in the Sumerian King List* along with Eridu,* Bad-tibira, Larak, and Shurup-pak* as existing before the Flood. Eridu is known to have been founded before 4000 B.C., but Sippar, which comes fourth in the list, may not precede Early Dynastic times (c. 2800–2400 B.C.). Excavation of the site, conducted largely in the days before the establishment of modern methods of stratigraphy,* was limited to tablet mining, so little is known of the earliest levels, and speculation about the age of the city* is based on other sources. That Sippar contin-ued to be an important city after the Flood is clear from various references. The prologue of Hammu-rabi's Code* (*ANET*, 164) credits that king with hav-ing "relaid the foundations of Sippar" and "decked with green the chapels of Aya [consort of Shamash, god of sun and justice, whose temple-shrine was in Sippar], the designer of the temple of Ebabbar, which is like a heavenly dwelling." That same ruler is cred-ited with having provided for Sippar, "the primeval city of the sun-god Utu (Shamash) a wall of piled-up earth" (*ANET*, 270f. and notes 8 and 13). In later years Tukulti-Ninurta II and Sennacherib* of As-syria, Nebuchadnezzar* and Nabonidus* of Baby-lon,* and Cyrus* of Persia are all credited with having campaigned in the city. Of special note from the var-ious records are further references to the temple which was clearly the greatest attraction in the city. In fact, the first archaeological expedition recorded in the history of Sippar was the work of Nabonidus (555–539 B.C.) who, like Hammurabi and Nebu-chadnezzar before him, determined to rebuild the temple. After criticizing Nebuchadnezzar for build-ing the walls without proper attention to the divinely revealed floor plan (with the result that the walls collapsed within forty-five years), Nabonidus wrote: "I sought out its ancient foundation-platform and I went down into the soil (to a depth of) eighteen cu-bits, and the Sun-god, the Great Lord of Ebabbara, the Dwelling of His Heart's-ease, showed me per-sonally the foundation-platform of Naram-Sin son of Sargon,* which for 3200 years no king preceding me had seen" (H. W. F. Saggs, *The Greatness That Was Babylon* [1962], 366). Even with allowance for Nab-onidus's chronological miscalculation (Naram-Sin's dates are approximately 2291–2255 B.C.), it is ap-parent that the history of the sun-temple Ebabbara was a long and glorious one.

More recent archaeological work has, though for different reasons, also concentrated on finding the temple and its remains. Excavations sponsored by the British Museum were undertaken by Hormuzd Rassam in 1881 after it was determined that Abu Habba was the probable site of Sippar. The temple was soon located and yielded over sixty thousand tablets, most of which dealt with the various business aspects of maintaining an important temple. Many of the tablets were unbaked and therefore have not survived, but included among those preserved are some important literary tablets including a bilingual version of the creation story (Enuma Elish*). Con-

tinuing excavations under the auspices of the Otto-man Museum in 1894 were directed by J. Vincent Scheil, while a final campaign was conducted by W. Andrae in 1927.

BIBLIOGRAPHY: T. G. Pinches, "Antiquities Found at Abu-Habba, Sippara," *TSBA*, 8 (1883), 164–71; H. Rassam, "Recent Discoveries of Ancient Babylo-nian Cities," *TSBA*, 8 (1883), 172–97; H. Rassam, *Ashur and the Land of Nimrod* (1897); M. Jastrow, "Nebopolassar and the Temple to the Sun-god at Sip-par," *AJSL*, 15 (1899), 65–86; V. Scheil, *Une saison de fouilles à Sippar* (1907); W. Andrae and J. Jordan, "Abu Habba-Sippar," *Iraq*, 1 (1934), 51–55; A. L. Oppenheim, "A New Look at the Structure of Meso-potamian Society, Based on Texts Found in Sip-par," *JESHO*, 10 (1967), 1–16; *CAH*, 1, part 2, 97 passim.

CEA

SIRION. See HERMON.

SIRQU. See TERQA.

SISITHROS. See ZIUSUDRA.

SIYALK. See TEPE SIALK.

SLAVES. References to slavery in the Bible extend from Joseph* to Onesimus, and in the OT are the theme of a good deal of codified legislation. Much archaeological information illustrates the biblical pro-visions and may be briefly listed as follows: (1) Exod 21:16. The death penalty attached to abduction and kidnapping, the fate of Joseph at his brothers' hands. The Code of Hammurabi,* from the Middle Bronze Age,* also tersely stipulates death for the offense. "If a citizen steals the child of a citizen he shall die" (code 14, *DOTT*, 30). (2) Exod 22:3. The appre-hended thief unable to make restitution was similarly dealt with by the Hammurabi code (code 53, 43). (3) The enslavement of the defaulting debtor's family (2 Kings 4:1; Neh 5:5, 8) is similarly paralleled in the Hammurabi code (code 117, *DOTT*, 30) where a pe-riod of three years' servitude is stipulated. (4) The price of a slave in the Patriarchal period is named in the Hammurabi code (code 116, 214, 252, *DOTT*, 35), paralleled by contemporary Mari* documents, as one-third of a mina, or twenty shekels, the price paid for Joseph (Gen 37:28). By the fifteenth century the average price had risen to thirty shekels in Nuzi* and was between twenty and forty shekels at Ugarit.* The same inflation continued into Assyrian, Baby-lonian, and Persian days. The Israelite aristocrats under Menahem* (2 Kings 15:30) apparently es-caped deportation by paying over their current value as slaves, to wit, fifty shekels (D. J. Wiseman, *Iraq*, 15 [1953], 135). (5) The extradition of escaped slaves was provided for by international agreement (e.g., Hammurabi code 280, *DOTT*, 35). In 1 Kings 2:39–40, it is reported that Shimei thus recovered two escaped slaves from Gath.* Some treaty between Solomon* and Achish must have covered the process of extradition. The Alalakh* Tablets (tablets 2 and 3) mention this type of international agreement. Deut

23:15–16 runs counter to this law and specifies rights of asylum.

The slave society of NT times was not condemned by Christ or the apostles. Slaves who became Christians were urged to obey their masters (Eph 6:5–8; Col 3:22–25; 2 Tim 6:1–2; 1 Peter 2:18–21). Abuses of slavery were denounced, however, and owners were urged to treat their slaves with consideration (Eph 6:9; Col 4:1).

EMB

SLING. The earliest sling seems to have been a throwing device made of stag's antlers carved into the shape of a horse's head. The stone must have been wedged in the horse's jaw and discharged by an overarm jerk. It would be obviously difficult to determine the trajectory, and the answer devised was the sling made from a double strip of leather,* a very formidable weapon in practiced hands. Naturally such fragile material has not survived to form raw material for archaeology, but a Tell Halaf orthostat depicts a slingman vividly. The relief shows the mode of operation. The stone was placed in the leather pouch, and the thongs were pulled taut to turn the pad into a bag. The soldier held the bag in the left hand and the ends of the taut thongs in the right above his head. He then whirled the sling to build momentum and at the proper moment let one string go. The bag opened and the stone was projected. The relief is from the tenth century B.C.

See ARMS AND WEAPONS; GOLIATH, ARMOR OF; WARFARE.

BIBLIOGRAPHY: Y. Yadin, *The Art of Warfare in Biblical Lands* (1963), 364; G. C. Trench, *A History of Marksmanship* (1972), 14.

EMB

SMYRNA (smûr'nə; Gr. Σμύρνα, *Smyrna*). The town, modern Izmir, is mentioned only twice in the Bible (Rev 1:11; 2:8). It was the home of the second of the seven churches to which John was commanded to write. Ancient Smyrna is located on the western coast of Turkey in a natural harbor of the Aegean Sea, a gulf into which the Hermus River flows. It absorbed the trade of the Hermus and Maeander valley routes into Asia Minor,* competing with, and ultimately winning the advantage over Ephesus.* Izmir is today, and has always been, one of the largest and busiest commercial centers in the region.

There is evidence of early habitation along the gulf in the third millennium B.C., and a Greek colony named Smyrna had been established by 1000 B.C. The title on some of its ancient coins* called Smyrna the "first of Asia," and Strabo called it the most beautiful of all the cities. Ancient writers often referred to the "crown of Smyrna," which perhaps referred to a crown of flowers worn by worshipers of the goddess Cybele. W. M. Ramsay suggested that it referred to a "crown" of porticoed buildings that ringed the hilltop. The biblical relevance of the city* lies in its wealth and vigor in the Roman period, its fine buildings and devotion, in the Old Ionian tradition, to science and medicine. Like Ephesus, it was a temple-warden of the imperial cult.

Some remains are visible, but Smyrna shares the difficulties which other heavily occupied sites present to the archaeologist. Most of ancient Smyrna, and much that it may contain of archaeological interest, lies lost under modern Izmir. Excavations, however, in 1948 and 1951, by Ankara University and the British School of Archaeology as well as those of 1966 by the Turkish Historical Society have been successful mainly in pre-Roman discoveries. A seventh-century B.C. temple was positively identified by an inscription as dedicated to Athena. The symbol of Smyrna was a lion's head (one appears on a coin from the sixth century B.C.); in 1967 four stone lion* heads were found in the ruins of the temple.

The Smyrna of Roman times is known mostly from literary sources, but the State Agora is well preserved and was excavated between 1932 and 1941 by the Turkish Historical Society. The courtyard of the agora* is 120 by 80 m. (130 by 88 yd.) and was surrounded by colonnades, those of the N being two stories high. The N side also had basement shops. In A.D. 156, the eighty-six-year-old Bishop, Polycarp, died in the stadium* here as the twelfth martyr of Smyrna, remaining faithful to death, and the place is still pointed out today.

BIBLIOGRAPHY: C. S. Cadoux, *Ancient Smyrna* (1938); W. M. Ramsay, *Letters to the Seven Churches of Asia* (1904), 251–80; E. M. Blaiklock, *Cities of the NT* (1965), 98–103.

BCC and EMB

SNAKE. See SERPENT.

SODALITATES. See TRADE GUILDS.

SODOM (sô'dəm; Heb. סְדֹם, *sᵉḏōm*). This center was one of the "cities of the plain,*" and is mentioned more frequently in Genesis than the others in the area. In the Bible it typified the most sinful of cities and, with Gomorrah,* serves as an example of divine visitation upon sin. While the site has not yet been positively identified, it is thought to be submerged under the waters of the Dead Sea* S of the el-Lisan peninsula in what was originally the Vale of Siddim (Gen 14:3). Jebel Usdum ("Mount of Sodom"), a salt* mountain located on the W side of the Dead Sea at the southern end, seems to preserve the ancient name. Perhaps the citizens of the Vale of Siddim used Bab edh-Dhra', about 8 km. (5 mi.) from the Dead Sea SE of el-Lisan, as a place for religious pilgrimages between c. 2300 and c. 1900 B.C., as suggested by excavations there. The cessation of visits at that time implies the destruction of the cities of the plain, about 1900 B.C., and also furnishes support for the presence of Abram in Canaan* at the end of the twentieth century B.C. God's destruction of Sodom most probably was produced by the combustion of petroleum gases emanating from the bituminous deposits in the area. This doubtlessly was accompanied by seismic disturbances, which caused the plain to sink some 6.1 m. (20 ft.) under the surface of the Dead Sea. In 1953 the first oil well of the State of Israel went into production just N of Jebel Usdum, indicating significant petroleum deposits in the region. The heavy pall of smoke which Abram saw (Gen 19:28) would characterize ignited petroleum products.

BIBLIOGRAPHY: W. F. Albright, *BASOR*, 14 (1924), 5–7; id., *AASOR*, 6 (1924–25), 58–62; M. G. Kyle, *Explorations in Sodom* (1928); F.-M. Abel, *Géographie de la Palestine*, 2 (1938), 467–68; N. Glueck, *AASOR*, 15 (1934–35); ibid., 18–19 (1937–39); J. P. Harland, *BA*, 5 (1942), 17–32; ibid., 6 (1943), 41–54; ibid., *IDB*, 4 (1962), 395–97; R. L. Alden, *ZPEB*, 5 (1975), 466–68.

RKH

SOIL ANALYSIS. *See* PEDOLOGY.

SOLOMON (sol'ə môn; Heb. שְׁלֹמֹה, *shᵉlōmōh*; LXX Σαλωμών, *Salōmōn*). The third and the last king of the United Kingdom of the twelve tribes.

I. *Dates.* Two alternative sets of dates for Solomon's forty-year reign (1 Kings 11:42) are favored by scholars: (1) 971–931, as proposed by Thiele, and (2) 961–922, as proposed by Albright. Solomon began construction on the temple* in his fourth year (1 Kings 6:1), a project which lasted seven years (1 Kings 6:38). He then spent thirteen years building his palace (1 Kings 7:1), after which he began the rebuilding of the structure known as the Millo (1 Kings 11:27). It is apparently after Solomon's twenty-fourth year, and in any case after 945 B.C. (the accession date of Shishak*), that Jeroboam fled into Egypt* (1 Kings 11:40).

II. *The Organization of His Kingdom.* Solomon made a drastic reorganization of his kingdom into twelve administrative districts which were with some exceptions not based upon the old tribal areas (1 Kings 4:1–20). This arrangement seems to have been effected in the second half of his reign after the transfer of towns in the Acco* plain to Hiram* (1 Kings 9:12–13), as these are missing from the list. Each of the districts was to provide food for the court for one month (1 Kings 4:7).

The demands for provisions could have been prodigious. An interesting ninth-century Assyrian parallel to Solomon's fourteen-day feast (1 Kings 8:65) has come to light in the stele* of Ashurnasirpal II* found at Nimrud (Calah*). The king boasted: "The happy people of all the lands together with the people of Kalhu [Calah], for ten days I feasted. . . ." There were 69,574 party guests!

Many scholars believe that Solomon's administration owed much to Egyptian prototypes, as the titles of his various officers seem to be the Hebrew equivalents of Egyptian titles.

Solomon introduced a fundamental change in Israel's military organization—a reliance upon chariotry. His father David had disabled the horses* which he had captured from the king of Zobah in Syria (2 Sam 8:4). We are told that Solomon had 4,000 stalls (*see* STABLES) for horses and 12,000 horses (2 Chron 9:25). If one assumes teams of three horses, including a reserve horse, for each chariot,* the figure of stalls would accord with the number of 1,400 chariots (1 Kings 10:26) which Solomon is said to have had.

III. *Building Activities.* Solomon was the greatest builder in Israel's history before Herod the Great (*see* HEROD, BUILDING ACTIVITIES OF). Some earlier scholars, e.g., G. Leroux in 1913, had dismissed the biblical accounts of Solomon's building activities as late inventions of the sixth century. A considerable number of archaeological discoveries now lend substance to these accounts.

A. *Megiddo.* The famous "Solomon's Stables" at the key site of Megiddo* were demonstrated by Yadin in 1960 to belong to the later city* of Ahab* (ninth century). The excavators estimated that there were about 450 stalls originally. Since these have been left *in situ*, it is possible that Solomonic stables may lie underneath these which are visible.

An indisputable Solomonic structure is the magnificent gate* with three chambers on each side. This has been associated by Yadin with the casemate wall* dated to stratum IVB. The stables, on the other hand, are linked with a later solid wall with alternating salients and recesses. Yadin's reinvestigation of the Megiddo stables was prompted by the discovery that the Solomonic gate at Hazor* was built in conjunction with casemate walls.

Yadin's excavations in 1966–67 have identified two splendid palatial buildings as Solomonic. (Aharoni, however, believes they are Davidic.) These are building 6000 in the N and building 1723 in the S. Both are built of fine ashlar* blocks similar to those used in the Solomonic gate. The northern palace has been compared to Assyrian buildings called *bit hilāni*, which were used as ceremonial palaces. This may have been used by Solomon on his visits to Megiddo. The southern building has been compared to the ninth century palace of Kilamuwa at Zincirli and may have served as the residence of the governor.

Recent investigations have also shown that the approaches to the underground water system, originally dated to the twelfth century, should now be attributed to Solomon's period.

B. *Hazor.* The great Canaanite* mound of Hazor, N of the Sea of Galilee,* abandoned since the time of the conquest under Joshua, was refortified by Solomon as one of his royal cities. Yadin's excavations in 1955–59 revealed that Solomon enclosed just the western part of the acropolis* with a casemate wall furnished with a triple gate identical to that found at Megiddo.

C. *Gezer.* On the basis of 1 Kings 9:15, which linked Hazor, Megiddo, and Gezer,* Yadin suspected that there might be a similar Solomonic gate at Gezer, an important city guarding the road from the coast to Jerusalem.* A reexamination of what Macalister, who excavated Gezer early in the 1900s, had called a Maccabean castle, revealed to Yadin half of such a gateway. Excavations by the Hebrew Union College under W. Dever have confirmed Yadin's hunch. The recent clearing has also revealed that there were low plastered stone benches in all six of the rooms of the triple gateway (cf. Gen 19:1; 2 Sam 15:2–6; 1 Kings 22:10 et al. for the gate as the place for public transactions). In one room there was a large stone trough for drinking water for animals.

D. *Jerusalem.* Excavations in Jerusalem from 1961

to 1967 by K. Kenyon were undertaken to discover the limits of the OT city in the area of Ophel, the SE hill just S of the SE corner of the present walled city. Very little was discovered that could be attributed to the Solomonic period.

1. *The Temple.* In 1966 clearance on the E side of the Haram, the Herodian temple platform, revealed a straight join some 33 m. (109 ft.) from the SE corner between Herodian masonry and stones with heavy bosses to the N. M. Dunand identified the latter as similar to Persian construction of the sixth–fifth centuries. This may then indicate the southern edge of Zerubbabel's* temple, which in turn no doubt continued Solomon's platform.

According to 1 Kings 6:2, the temple was 27.4 m. (60 cubits) long, 9.1 m. (20 cubits) wide, and 13.7 m. (30 cubits) high. Since Solomon employed Phoenician* craftsmen* (1 Kings 7:13ff.), we can be sure that the temple incorporated a number of elements of foreign inspiration. In 1936 a ninth-century temple was discovered at Tell Ta'Yinat* E of Syrian Antioch,* which, though two-thirds the size of Solomon's temple, had a tripartite plan of (1) vestibule, (2) holy place, and (3) holy of holies strikingly similar to Solomon's building. Like the columns Jachin and Boaz (1 Kings 7:21) the Ta'Yinat temple also had two columns in the front of the building. Ussishkin has called attention to another parallel of a ninth–tenth-century royal chapel at Hamath.* A tripartite Late Bronze Canaanite temple at Hazor has sometimes been cited as a possible prototype.

After a thorough examination of all possible prototypes of Solomon's temple, Busink, while acknowledging the Phoenician inspiration of certain elements, stresses the basic originality of Solomon's temple design.

Various features of the temple appurtenances may be illustrated by archaeological finds. The winged cherubim* which served as decorative devices may have been similar to winged figures found on ivories from Megiddo and Nimrud. The bronze* laver (basin*) resting on oxen* (1 Kings 7:23–26) may be compared to a large stone basin from Cyprus* which rests upon bulls' heads. Basins on wheels (eleventh century B.C.) from Cyprus must have been similar to the wheeled stands (NEB "trolleys," 1 Kings 7:27ff.) used in the temple.

2. *The Palace.* We do not know the exact relationship of Solomon's temple to his palace, but from the fact that the temples at Ta'Yinat and Hamath were smaller than the palaces, scholars have been led to describe Solomon's temple as a royal chapel. This should not lead us to underestimate the temple's significance for the nation as Jehovah's first permanent shrine.

Solomon's palace may have been similar to the palaces uncovered at Megiddo (see above). The structure called "the house of the forest of Lebanon" (1 Kings 7:2) was a great hypostyle* hall 45.7 m. (100 cubits) long, 23 m. (50 cubits) wide, and 13.7 m. (30 cubits) high, with three or four rows of cedar* pillars. It was used in part as an armory (Isa 22:8). For his Egyptian wife Solomon built a separate house (1 Kings 7:8; 9:24).

3. *Millo.* Both David and Solomon devoted their attention to the building up of the Millo, "Filling" (2 Sam 5:9; 1 Kings 9:24; 11:27), an enigmatic structure, which has been identified by Kenyon as the precarious terraces on the E side of Ophel which were in constant need of repair.

IV. *Trading Enterprises.* A. *Hiram of Tyre.* King Hiram* of Tyre,* who had been David's ally (1 Kings 5:1–12), actively aided Solomon by supplying him with gold,* timber, and craftsmen, and by cooperating with Solomon in his maritime ventures. In exchange for these favors Solomon ceded to Hiram a district in the area of Acco called Cabul (1 Kings 9:11–14).

The Tarshish* ships* (1 Kings 10:22) which were employed by Solomon in cooperation with Hiram were originally vessels which went to Tarshish, a word which means "smeltery," perhaps to the distant Phoenician colony of Tartessus in S Spain, or to Sardinia (the ninth-century Nora inscription from Sardinia contains the word "Tarshish"). Albright's thesis that Phoenician expansion in the western Mediterranean is to be dated to the era of Solomon and of Hiram and not after the Greek expansion in the eighth century B.C., as held by classical historians, has received added support by the acquisition by the Seville Museum in 1963 of an eighth-century Phoenician inscription. F. M. Cross in 1979 dated a Phoenician fragment from Nora in Sardinia to the eleventh century B.C.

B. *Cilicia.* Though Solomon was content to leave the Mediterranean maritime trade in the hands of Hiram, he controlled the overland trade and in particular the important traffic in horses. The KJV translation of 1 Kings 10:28 has obscured this by translating "linen yarn" for a Hebrew phrase which actually means "from Que," i.e., from Cilicia,* the region in SE Turkey where the best horses were to be obtained. Solomon thus served as the middleman between Egypt* and the Neo-Hittite and Aramaean states (1 Kings 10:29).

C. *The Arabah and Ezion Geber.* The Edomite* threat did not prevent Solomon's great project of establishing a port at Ezion Geber near Elath* (1 Kings 9:26) to give him access to trade in the Red Sea* and beyond. In 1938–40 N. Glueck excavated Tell el-Kheleifeh, a small tell* a short distance from the shore, now located in Jordanian territory, which he identified as Ezion Geber. A building enclosed in an area protected by a casemate wall was originally interpreted by Glueck as a smeltery because of holes in the wall which he thought were flue-holes but has now been reinterpreted as a storehouse* and/or granary.* Rothenberg has recently suggested that the actual port of Ezion Geber may be located at the Jeziret Fara'un (now called the Coral Island by the Israelis) 12.9 km. (8 mi.) SW of Elath.

Glueck attributed the considerable evidence of copper mining in the Arabah, the valley between the Dead Sea* and Elath, to Solomon. Additional sites were discovered in the 1950s and 1960s by Rothenberg, who demonstrated that the copper-bearing ores were smelted in open pits on charcoal* fires fanned by bellows. In 1969 Rothenberg discovered at the base of the so-called "Solomon's Pillars," a favorite tourist site at Timnah N of Elath, an Egyptian temple with inscriptions of the Nineteenth–Twentieth Dynasties from Seti I (1318–1304) down to Ramses V (1160–1156). He now suggests that it was these Egyptian kings, rather than the Judean kings of the tenth–sixth centuries, who were responsible for all the copper mines in the Arabah—a suggestion which Glueck steadfastly rejected.

D. *The Queen of Sheba and Arabia.* Evidence of Solomon's far-flung renown is found in the visit of the Queen of Sheba* (an area in SW Arabia* near Yemen and Aden). According to 1 Kings 10:1–3 the queen came to test Solomon's famed wisdom. It is quite probable that she also made the arduous journey of 2413 km. (1500 mi.) through rugged terrain with commercial interests in mind.

Earlier critics rejected this account as folkloristic, arguing that the Sabeans* were still nomadic at this period. Work by Wendell Phillips and W. F. Albright from 1950–53 has now established that the Sabeans preceded the Minaeans in the early first millennium B.C., and that they had a sedentary and even literate civilization. Albright (1958) has affirmed the possibility of contact between Solomon and S Arabia.

In 1957 J. Kelso discovered an inscribed S Arabian clay* seal* dated to the ninth century at Bethel.* Despite doubts raised by Yadin, G. W. Van Beek, and A. Jamme, authorities on S Arabia stoutly affirm the seal's authenticity.

E. *Ophir.* The joint Red Sea fleet of Solomon and Hiram made voyages every three years (1 Kings 10:22) to a distant port called Ophir* (1 Kings 10:11), from which they brought back a variety of objects including fine gold.* That this was not a legendary land is proven by the discovery of an eighth-century ostracon* with the text "Ophir gold . . ." at Tell Qasile.* Ophir has been variously placed in: (1) S Arabia (J. Montgomery, J. Gray, O. Eissfeldt); (2) the Somali coast of E. Africa (W. Albright, J. Myers); (3) NW India (R. Barnett).

V. *Marriages.* Solomon's great international prestige is demonstrated by the fact that he was given a pharaoh's daughter in marriage. References are made to this Egyptian wife in no less than five passages (1 Kings 3:1; 7:8; 9:16; 9:24 [cf. 2 Chron 8:11]; 11:1). This is the only firmly attested instance in which a king of Egypt deigned to give his daughter in marriage to an alien. In the Amarna* Age a Babylonian king who sought to marry an Egyptian princess was rebuffed by Amenophis III, who wrote: "From of old a daughter of the king of Egypt has not been given to anyone" (cf. Herodotus 3.1).

A. *The Egyptian Pharaoh.* As the Bible does not give us the name of the pharaoh in question, scholars have had to speculate upon the identity of Solomon's Egyptian father-in-law. In view of the weakness of the Twenty-first Dynasty which seemed to make a capture of Gezer,* which was given as a dowry, unlikely, earlier scholars (Alt, Breasted, Olmstead) had suggested Shishak,* the vigorous founder of the Twenty-second Dynasty. More recently, scholars have

favored one of the last two kings of the Twenty-first Dynasty, Siamun or Psusennes II. The approximate dates of these two kings are probably: Siamun (978–960) and Psusennes II (960–945). Evidence in favor of Siamun includes a monument found at Tanis* showing the king smiting an enemy who holds a double axe, an Aegean weapon perhaps of the Philistines, and a scarab* with the pharaoh's name found at Tell el-Far'ah (Sharuhen).

B. *Gezer as a Dowry.* In 1924 Albright, who was troubled by the fact that Macalister, the excavator of Gezer, reported no signs of destruction in the early tenth century B.C., suggested the emendation in 1 Kings 9:16 of Gezer to Gerar,* a less significant city* to the S. This emendation has now been shown to be unjustified, as the recent Hebrew Union College excavations at Gezer yielded dramatic evidence of a destruction in the mid-tenth century which left up to 1.2 m. (4 ft.) of debris and ash. Other sites which may have been destroyed in this campaign include Tell el-Far'ah and Tel Mor, the seaport of Ashdod.*

C. *Other Wives.* According to 1 Kings 11:3, Solomon had seven hundred wives and three hundred concubines, among whom were Moabite,* Ammonite,* Edomite,* Sidonian, and "Hittite*" women (1 Kings 11:1). The mother of Rehoboam, Solomon's successor, was Naamah, an Ammonite princess. Hellenistic sources suggest that Solomon married the daughter of Hiram of Tyre.*

VI. *Religious Devotion.* Solomon began his reign humbly asking for wisdom from Jehovah (1 Kings 3:3–15) and seeking to honor the Lord by building His temple. His prayer of dedication at the completion of the temple (1 Kings 8:12–62) was answered by a second vision from the Lord (1 Kings 9). In later years, however, his foreign wives led him astray in the worship of other deities (1 Kings 11:4–6). Solomon's construction of a high place* for Chemosh on the Mount of Olives* (1 Kings 11:7) is vividly illustrated by a pagan cult center with two pillars discovered by Kenyon on the slopes of Ophel, dated c. 700 B.C.

VII. *Solomon's Reputation.* A. *Literary Renown.* Solomon, of course, was famed for his wisdom, which included his judicial insight (1 Kings 3:16–28) and his literary ability. He was the author of 3,000 proverbs and 1,005 songs (1 Kings 4:32). Specific compositions which are ascribed to Solomon include Proverbs 10:1–22, 16; 25:1–29:27; and Psalms 72 and 127.

In the apocrypha we have the Wisdom of Solomon (after 100 B.C.), in the Pseudepigrapha* the Psalms of Solomon (c. 100 B.C.), and in Syriac literature the Odes of Solomon (c. A.D. 100).

B. *Magic and Legend.* Solomon is one of the most popular figures in magic and legend. By the first century A.D., Solomon's seal on a ring was considered to be a potent magical device by which to exorcise* demons as demonstrated before Vespasian* (Jos. *Antiq.* 8.47). Solomon's reputation continued to expand in later Jewish, Aramaic,* and Arabic literature and magical lore.

The most interesting legend surrounds the visit of the Queen of Sheba to Solomon. This story was developed in the Ethiopian national saga, the *Kebra Nagast*, "Glory of the Kings," written down in the fourteenth century, to include the begetting of a son, Menelik, the presumed ancestor of the modern emperor Haile Selassie.

BIBLIOGRAPHY: I. *General*. D. Hubbard, "Solomon," *NBD* (1962), 1201–4; J. Myers, "Solomon," *IDB*, 4 (1962), 399–408; O. Eissfeldt, *The Hebrew Kingdom* (1965); J. Myers, *II Chronicles* (1965); J. Gray, *I and II Kings*, 2d ed. (1970); J. R. Bartlett, "An Adversary against Solomon, Hadad the Edomite," *ZAW*, 88 (1976), 205–26. II. *The Organization of His Kingdom*. Y. Yadin, *The Art of Warfare in Biblical Lands* (1963); Y. Aharoni, *The Land of the Bible* (1967), 272–80; T. Mettinger, *Solomonic State Officials* (1971); D. B. Redford, "Studies in Relations between Palestine and Egypt . . . The Taxation System of Solomon," *Studies in the Ancient Palestinian World*, ed. J. W. Wevers and D. B. Redford (1972), 141–56; B. Halpern, "Sectionalism and the Schism," *JBL*, 93 (1974), 519–32; E. W. Heaton, *Solomon's New Men* (1974); Y. Aharoni, "The Solomonic Districts," *Tel Aviv*, 3 (1976), 5–15; C. Hauer, "The Economics of National Security in Solomonic Israel," *JSOT*, 18 (1980), 63-73. III. *Building Activities*. Y. Yadin, "Solomon's City Wall and Gate at Gezer," *IEJ*, 8 (1958), 80–86; id., "New Light on Solomon's Megiddo," *BA*, 23 (1960), 62–68; D. Ussishkin, "King Solomon's Palace and Building 1723 in Megiddo," *IEJ*, 16 (1966), 174–86; id., "Building IV in Hamath and the Temples of Solomon and Tell Tayanat," *IEJ*, 16 (1966), 104–10; K. Kenyon, *Jerusalem* (1967); Y. Yadin, "The Fifth Season of Excavations at Hazor, 1968–1969," *BA*, 32 (1969), 49–78; id., "Megiddo of the Kings of Israel," *BA*, 33 (1970), 66–96; T. Busink, *Der Tempel von Salomo bis Herodos* (1970); W. Dever et al., "Further Excavations at Gezer, 1967–71," *BA*, 34 (1971), 94–132; K. Kenyon, *Royal Cities of the OT* (1971), 36–70; H. Schmid, "Der Tempelbau Salomos in religionsgeschichtlicher Sicht," *Archäologie und Altes Testament*, ed. A. Kuschke and E. Kutsch (1970), 241–50; Y. Aharoni, "The Solomonic Temple, the Tabernacle and the Arad Sanctuary," *Orient and Occident*, ed. H. Hoffner (1973), 1–8; D. Ussishkin, "King Solomon's Palaces," *BA*, 36 (1973), 78–105; J.A. Gutmann, ed., *The Temple of Solomon* (1976); C. Davey, "Temples of the Levant and the Buildings of Solomon," *TB*, 31 (1980), 107-46. IV. *Trading Enterprises*. W. Albright, "Was the Age of Solomon without Monumental Art?" *Eretz Israel*, 5 (1958), 1*–9*; id., "The Role of the Canaanite in the History of Civilization," in G. E. Wright, ed., *The Bible and the Ancient Near East* (1961), 328–62; B. Rothenberg, "Ancient Copper Industries in the Western Arabah," *PEQ*, 94 (1962), 5–71; id., "Ecyon-Gébèr," *Bible et Terre Sainte*, 72 (1965), 10–16; R. Barnett, *Illustrations of OT History* (1966); N. Glueck, *Rivers in the Desert*, 2d ed. (1968); B. Rothenberg, "King Solomon's Mines No More," *ILN* (15 November 1969), 32–33; id., "The Egyptian Temple of Timna," *ILN* (29 November 1969), 28–29; G. W. Van Beek and A. Jamme, "The Authenticity of the Bethel Stamp Seal," *BASOR*, 199 (1970), 59–65; N. Glueck, *The Other Side of the Jordan*, 2d ed. (1970); id., "Iron II Kenite and Edomite Pottery," *Perspective*, 12 (1971), 45–56; F. M. Cross, "The Old Phoenician Inscription from Spain Dedicated to Hurrian Astarte," *HTR*, 64 (1971), 189–95; N. Glueck, "Tel el-Kheleifeh," *Near Eastern Studies in Honor of William Foxwell Albright*, ed. H. Goedicke (1971), 225–42; B. Rothenberg, *Timna* (1972); B. Peckham, "Israel and Phoenicia," *Magnalia Dei*, ed. F. M. Cross et al. (1976), 231–44; L. Berkowitz, "Has the U.S. Geological Survey Found King Solomon's Gold Mines?" *BAR*, 3 (1977), 1, 28–33; S. B. Hoenig, "Tarshish," *JQR*, 69 (1978), 181–82; F. M. Cross, "Early Alphabetic Scripts," *Symposia*, ed. F. M. Cross (1979), 103–11. V. *Marriages*. A. Malamat, "The Kingdom of David and Solomon in Its Contact with Egypt and Aram Naharaim," *BA*, 21 (1958), 96–102; id., "Aspects of the Foreign Policies of David and Solomon," *JNES*, 22 (1963); S. Horn, "Who Was Solomon's Egyptian Father-in-Law?" *BR*, 12 (1967), 3–17; P. Montet, *Egypt and the Bible* (1968); K. A. Kitchen, *The Third Intermediate Period in Egypt* (1973), 281–83; H. D. Lance, "Solomon, Siamun, and the Double Ax," in Cross, *Magnalia Dei*, 209–23; A. R. Green, "Solomon and Siamun," *JBL*, 97 (1978), 353–67. VI. *Solomon's Reputation*. L. Ginzberg, *Legends of the Bible* (1956); J. Trachtenberg, *Jewish Magic and Superstition* (1961); E. Ullendorff, "The Queen of Sheba," *BJRL*, 45 (1963), 486–504; J. B. Pritchard, ed., *Solomon and Sheba* (1974); B. Bamberger, "Solomon and Sheba," *JQR*, 66 (1976), 245–46.

EY

SOLOMON, POOLS OF. The so-called pools of Solomon are in the Valley of Urtas, not far from Bethlehem.* The three pools are on separate levels and are connected by conduits. All are roughly rectangular, the largest (lower) measuring c. 61 m. (200 ft.) wide, 183 m. (600 ft.) long, and 15 m. (50 ft.) deep. It is known that they were part of Jerusalem's* water supply in Roman times, a fact attested by the remains of an aqueduct* in the vicinity.

BIBLIOGRAPHY: B. C. Stark, *ZPEB*, 4 (1975), 819.

EMB

SOLOMON'S PORCH. A double colonnade at the E end of the outer court of the Jerusalem* temple,* where Jesus taught and the primitive church met for public witness (John 10:23; Acts 3:11; 5:12). According to Josephus (Jos. *Antiq.* 15.401; Jos. *War* 5.185), Solomon* built up the eastern side of the temple area and erected the colonnade on the platform thus made; it ran the entire length of the eastern enclosing wall. It seems unlikely that it survived intact from Solomon's time to the Roman period, although Josephus implies such in the passages referred to and in his account of the proposal to Agrippa II that he should raise its height (Jos. *Antiq.* 20.220ff.). On the other hand, his statement that Herod (see HEROD, FAMILY OF) reconstructed the colonnades "from the foundation" (Jos. *War* 1.401) would appear to include that on the E. He may have incorporated, in his extensions on this side, an older structure which retained its original name.

Only the platform survives today. Such pre-Herodian platforms as may have existed have been engulfed beneath Herod's, and it would require a major excavation to uncover them. Below the site of Solomon's colonnade, on the outside, a stone foundation wall of pre-Herodian date (perhaps Zerubbabel's) has been brought to light, with the later Herodian wall abutting on it.

BIBLIOGRAPHY: J. B. Payne, *ZPEB*, 4 (1975), 479.

FFB

SOMALILAND. *See* OPHIR.

SOPHER. *See* OPHIR.

SPEAR. *See* ARMS AND WEAPONS.

SPECTROGRAPHIC ANALYSIS. A method of identifying the ingredients of a small-sample compound, based on typical light patterns emitted by elements when rendered volatile. The light is refracted onto a screen, or is photographed for study. Metals, glass,* and pottery* can be analyzed accurately in this manner. HWP

SPELLS. *See* INCANTATION.

SPICES. *See* EMBALMING; INCENSE; OINTMENT.

SPORTS. *See* BOXING; GAMES.

STABLES. Stables or stalls for horses* are alluded to in the Bible especially with reference to the expansion of the kingdom of Solomon.* He built the royal cities of Hazor,* Gezer,* and Megiddo,* which were probably the main "chariot* cities," included with Jerusalem,* in which his forty thousand stalls of horses were kept. Solomon was also an international horse trader (cf. 1 Kings 4:26; 9:15–19; 10:26; 2 Chron 1:14–17; 9:25).

Archaeologists have found many chariots or representations of them, the earliest being a plaque relief found at Ur.* Solomon's royal cities* have been extensively excavated. There are hitching posts and other installations at Hazor which indicate that in the Solomonic era it was one of the chariot cities. A long narrow building at Gezer, called by Macalister "the Semitic Temple," has been identified by others as the stables since the plan of the building is similar to the stables at Megiddo. At Megiddo itself, the approach to Stratum IVb is a stone-paved ramp which leads to the well-guarded main gate.* From the gate a road leads to the "stable units," which are capable of housing perhaps five hundred horses. The plan of each of the four units gave access through double doors to a center passageway paved with lime plaster.* The stalls on the sides were separated by stone pillars to which the horses could be tied, and which probably also supported a mud roof. There were carved stone manger* troughs between the pillars. A large grain-silo pit was located nearby. This "stable" complex is now dated to the time of Ahab,* about one hundred years after the time of Solomon; it perhaps followed the plan of earlier stables of Sol-

Stable complex (building 364 in stratum IV A) at Megiddo. Courtesy The Oriental Institute, University of Chicago.

omon. One archaeologist sees these units as storehouses* where animals were unloaded and fed.

Jesus Christ was born in a small inn stable, which according to early and reliable traditions lies beneath the present Church of the Nativity at Bethlehem.*

BIBLIOGRAPHY: K. Kenyon, *Royal Cities of the OT* (1971), 58, 66, 93, 95–105 (for Megiddo).

BCC

STADIUM (Gr. *stadion*). A running track 183 m. (200 yd.) long and 27 m. (30 yd.) wide, usually with banked seats for spectators, as at Olympia and Delphi.

STAIRWAY. *See* LADDER.

STATUES. The sculpturing of statues was first undertaken by the Sumerians* and constituted one of their accredited art forms. The first example of sculpture in the round appears to have come from Ur,* consisting of a crouching boar executed in soapstone and dated at the end of the fourth millennium B.C. A bas-relief* from Uruk* in the Jemdet Nasr* period depicted two men fighting three lions.* Gods or rulers were more commonly represented by statues, however, the men wearing full beards and long skirts, while the women wore ankle-length dresses fastened over one shoulder. The hands were usually clasped across the chest, and the poses adopted became standard for much of Sumerian statuary. However, the statue of Gudea,* the governor of Lagash* (c. 2000 B.C.), shows this able *ensi* seated upon a throne. Egyptian statues such as that of Queen Hatshepsut, the remarkable daughter of Thutmose I (c. 1525 B.C.), tended to become stylized, depicting the individual concerned wearing a headdress* or other regal ornamentation and seated in a formal pose. By contrast, the statue of Nefrure, daughter of Hatshepsut, showed her wrapped in the protective mantle of Senenmut, the architect of Hatshepsut's mortuary temple at Deir el-Bahri, near Thebes,* and other structures. The most consistent Egyptian attempts at sculpture in the round, however, occurred in the renaissance of culture seen in the New Kingdom period, the celebrated bust of Nefertiti being an outstanding example.

Assyrian statues reflected general Babylonian traditions, that of Ashurnasirpal II* (883–859 B.C.) being characteristic. He was represented as wearing a full beard and a floor-length robe, with his left hand at the center of his chest holding the hilt of a sword. Roman statues of conquerors such as Pompey and Caesar Augustus* followed the traditions of Greek sculpture. Hebrew statuary was precluded by the prohibition of Exod 20:4, although by the Roman period the profile of one or two of the Herodians was appearing on Palestinian coins.*

BIBLIOGRAPHY: *ANEP* (1954), 6 passim; A. Parrot, *The Arts of Mankind: Sumer* (1960); id., *Nineveh and Babylon* (1961).

RKH

STELE (STELA) (stē'lē; ste'lə). A standing stone or vertical slab containing an inscription or design in bas-relief,* such as the Code of Hammurabi,* which was engraved on a black diorite stele in Babylon.*

STOA. A roofed colonnade, especially that at Athens,* where Zeno, the founder of Stoicism, taught.

STONE. *See* BUILDING MATERIALS.

STONE AGE. *See* MESOLITHIC; NEOLITHIC; PALAEOLITHIC.

STOREHOUSES. Such buildings (cf. Deut 28:8; Jer 50:26; Joel 1:17), royal or communal, for storing grain (*see* GRANARY) are first known from Egyptian reliefs—for example, on a twelfth-century tomb at Beni Hasan. Granaries of the kind employed by Joseph (Gen 41:56) appear to have been circular, with ventilation beneath a flat roof. Outside stairways enabled the silo to be filled from the top. Some of the structures were stone built and some were cut into basic rock. Examples are to be seen at Megiddo,* Jericho,* Tell Beit Mirsim (*see* DEBIR), Tell el-Ajjul, Tell Qasile,* Gezer,* Beth Shemesh,* and Beth Shan.* Some still contained recognizable grain. W. F. Albright suggested that the frequency of such storage facilities in early Israelite contexts signifies a high level of insecurity. His argument might be supported by the abundant facilities for household storage of grain in Troy 7a, which was clearly in expectation of the massive Greek assault. A number of large silos were found at Tell Jemmeh by W. F. M. Petrie. They had conical tops after the Assyrian pattern and may have constituted a military supply depot. The excavations at Masada* revealed the oblong storerooms whose abundant capacity made the long resistance by the Zealots possible.

BIBLIOGRAPHY: Y. Yadin, *Masada* (1966), 86, 91–101, 246–47.

EMB

STRATIGRAPHY. An important means of interpreting the character of excavations. It rests on the fact that the lower deposit is earlier than the one above it. Artifacts* in a given layer can, therefore, be earlier than the material in that deposit but cannot be later. Apart from minor disturbances of the soil, the layer, when isolated, is identified primarily by

color, soil, and contents. Subsequently the extent to which the different layers resulted from natural accumulation, man-made deposits, or the deterioration or destruction of buildings can be established. Drawings of a section help to clarify the stratigraphic picture further.

See also DATING; TYPOLOGY.

HWP

STREET. Properly, "street" in the Roman context meant a "paved way" (*strata*, from *sterno*—"to strew or spread"). The "street which is called Straight" (Acts 9:11) and the street of Jerusalem* down which Peter escaped, fall under this heading of paved ways. So does the "street" of the characteristically added phrase in Beza's Codex of Acts 19:18. Inflamed by the speech of the rabble-rouser, Demetrius, says this unorthodox text, no doubt delivered in the guild hall of the silversmiths, the audience "poured into the street" and made for the theater,* sweeping the crowd before them. This is evidently the marble-paved street which is a feature of the ruins of Ephesus,* and leads, in an elegant straight line, to the fine theater of Acts 19:29. Tyre* has the paving, mosaic* in this case, of a similar fine shopping street to show. It appears to be first century and could have been trodden by Christ in his northern journey. The street called "Straight" was undoubtedly paved, but the Greek word (*rhumê*—"alley," or "city communication") need not imply this finish, nor does the Vulgate's Latin *vicum*. "Street" appears to have originated with the KJV. There is papyrological evidence for street names.

In the ancient world the streets were frequently nothing more than narrow passageways between houses.* Generally there was only enough room for a heavily laden animal or a chariot* to proceed in one direction. Domestic refuse was commonly deposited in the streets, and although scavenging animals picked through some of the litter, there was still a great deal left. In the heat of summer infection was rife as a result of the dirt and filth of many Near Eastern cities,* especially in Palestine. An early exception to the use of narrow streets was found in Babylon* in the Old Babylonian period (c. 1830–1550 B.C.), where excavations from the time of Hammurabi* have provided the first definite indications of town planning. The streets were laid out in straight lines, with right-angled intersections. Many centuries later, the Babylon of the Neo-Babylonian period (612–539 B.C.) was still following the same tradition of spacious, well laid-out streets, as indicated by the magnificent processional avenue leading from the massive Ishtar Gate.

The streets of Egyptian cities were generally far more spacious and sanitary than their Palestinian counterparts. In the latter the only open street area was at the city gates,* where business and legal activities were conducted. It was only in the Roman period that streets in Palestinian cities were paved.

BIBLIOGRAPHY: C. C. McCown, *IDB*, 1 (1962), 632–38.

EMB

STRIP METHOD. A form of excavation suited particularly to a large area, but now used infrequently.

A long transverse trench is dug in close proximity to another which is parallel to it. Material from the second is deposited in the first trench, and subsequent trenches are treated in the same manner. No longitudinal section can be available for study when this method is used.

HWP

SUCCOTH (suk′kəth; Heb. סֻכּוֹת, *sukkôṭ*; LXX Σοκχώθ, *sokchōth*). 1. In Egypt,* Succoth was the first stopping place of the Israelites from Rameses,* on their way out of Egypt. Linguistically, it corresponds closely to the Tjeku (*Tkw*) of Egyptian texts, which can be very reasonably located at present-day Tell el-Maskhuta in Wadi Tumilat, as Tjeku is named on numerous monuments found there. Since Tjeku is said to be a day's journey from the palace at Rameses in an Egyptian papyrus* (Anastasi V, 19:3–8), this corresponds well with its being the first Hebrew stopping place after Rameses (Exod 12:37; 13:20; Num 33:5–6). Archaeological discoveries at the site include fragments of a temple of Atum (sun-god) from Pharaoh Ramses II* onward. In Papyrus Anastasi VI, Edomites* are mentioned as visiting Tjeku to go to the pools* there (*ANET*, 259a).

2. In Palestine, a settlement E of the Jordan, commonly located at Tell Deir Alla. Jacob stayed there (Gen 33:17); it was assigned to Gad (Josh 13:27); and Gideon chastised its uncooperative inhabitants (Judg 8:5ff.). Nearby, in clay* ground, bronzework was cast for Solomon* (1 Kings 7:46); the psalmists sang of its district as the Vale of Succoth (Pss 60:6; 108:7). At Deir Alla the most remarkable finds date from c. 1200 B.C., comprising clay tablets inscribed in an unknown script, possibly of the Sea Peoples,* and jar fragments of Queen Tewosret, last ruler of Egypt's Nineteenth Dynasty.

BIBLIOGRAPHY: 1. (Egypt): E. Naville, *The Store City of Pithom and the Route of the Exodus*, 4th ed. (1903); B. Porter and R. L. B. Moss, *Topographical Bibliography of Anc. Egyp. . . . Texts . . .*, 4 (1934), 53–55; R. A. Caminos, *Late-Egyptian Miscellanies* (1954), 253, 269. 2. (Palestine): N. Glueck, *The River Jordan* (1946), 145–55; H. J. Franken, *VT*, 11 (1961), reports up to XIV (1964); id., *PEQ*, 96 (1964), 73ff.; id., *Excavations at Deir 'Alla*, 1 (1970).

KAK

SULTAN, TELL ES-. TELL ES-SULTAN.

SUMER (sū′mər). There are no direct references to Sumer in the Bible, although it corresponds to the "land of Shinar*" mentioned eight times in the OT.

Sumer is the area of Lower Mesopotamia* from Baghdad to the Persian Gulf; the Sumerian culture began about 3500 B.C. and was a major factor in the development of later Mesopotamian cultures. Our knowledge of this culture helps illustrate social and economic elements in the OT.

Archaeology has made vast contributions to our understanding of Sumerian culture from the excavations of such sites as Ur,* Nippur,* Uruk,* Kish,* Lagash,* etc. These indicate that religion was a basic and unifying factor in the culture; each of the great

Queen Shub-ad's headdress with her four gold diadems, nine yards of gold band, gold comb, lunate earrings, and necklace. The head was copied from a Sumerian statuette in the Louvre and the hair restored after the best Sumerian tradition. The headdress and other jewelry were found with the crushed skull of Queen Shub-ad at Ur. The date is about the 25th century B.C. Courtesy The University Museum, University of Pennsylvania.

urban centers was built around a temple or ziggurat* (holy hill or tower). Besides a powerful priesthood, various craftsmen* in wood,* metal, and stone were associated with the temple and were supported from its stores. The Sumerian pantheon included such deities as Enki, Enlil, Nannar, Ninlil, Anu, Inanna, Nanna, and Ningal. Some Sumerian gods and goddesses reappear in later Semitic cultures; Nannar becomes Sin, and Inanna becomes Ishtar (*see* ISHTAR, DESCENT OF). The kings in the city-state units thought of themselves not as gods but as servants of the gods in their city.*

The Sumerian King List (the Weld-Blundell prism) compiled between 2250 and 2000 B.C. gives a chronological list of the Sumerian kings before the Flood in greatly exaggerated lengths and becomes more accurate in listing those after the Flood (cf. P. Carleton, *Buried Empires* [1939], 68 passim).

Thousands of tablets in Sumerian cuneiform* (a form of writing* which began in Sumer by 3000 B.C. and continued until the first century B.C.) illustrate everyday life, accomplishments of kings, and an elaborate Sumerian mythology including accounts of creation and the flood (*see* GILGAMESH EPIC).

Sumerian art was highly developed also; numerous statues* have come to light, several of King Gudea* of Lagash.* The delicate mosaic* Standard of Ur* discovered by Woolley dates hundreds of years before the time of Abraham and depicts scenes of war and peace.

Sumerian culture did not die out after the conquest by the Semites of Akkad* under Sargon* but remained as a dominant strain in the developing Semitic cultures. There are linguistic elements in OT Hebrew which have Sumerian derivation, and the sexagesimal system in mathematics comes from ancient Sumer.

BIBLIOGRAPHY: S. N. Kramer, *History Begins in Sumer* (1958); A. Parrot, *Sumer* (1961); S. N. Kramer, *The Sumerians: Their History, Culture and Character* (1963).

BCC

SUPARA. *See* OPHIR.

SUPPILULIUMA (sup i lū li ū'mə; Hitt., meaning "he of the pure pool"). The name of two Hittite* great-kings. Suppiluliuma I reigned over the Hittite Empire in the mid-fourteenth century B.C. for about forty years. He raised his kingdom from a state of weakness to that of a dominant empire in the Ancient Near East, rivaling Egypt* and N Mesopotamian Mitanni.* He was a persistent and very able warrior and international politician; he probably considerably rebuilt Hattusas his capital (Boghazköy*). He established orderly rule over his vassals, and official relations with other great powers by making treaties with them. These documents (like those of his thir-

teenth-century successors) show clear similarity of form with the covenants* of Moses and Joshua in the books of Exodus through Joshua, confirming the antiquity of the form. The content, of course, is entirely distinct.

Suppiluliuma II was the last-known Hittite emperor, c. 1200 B.C., after whom the realm was destroyed by migrating peoples; his spirited defense failed.

BIBLIOGRAPHY: A. Goetze, *CAH*, 1, part 1 (1965), 206, 215, 229–30; id., *CAH*, 2, part 2 (1975), 117 passim. KAK

SUR. *See* TYRE.

SUSA (sū'sə; Heb. שׁוּשַׁן, *šûšan*; Akkad. *šu-ša-an*; Elamite *šu-šu-un*; LXX Σοῦσα, *Sousa*). The major city of Elam,* the area of SW Iran.

I. *Biblical References.* Daniel (8:2) saw himself in a vision in Susa, and the city* was the locale of the story of Esther in the days of Ahasuerus (Xerxes*). Ezra 4:9–10 refers to the men of Susa (KJV "Susanchites"; KJV transliterates the name of the city as "Shushan") who were deported to Samaria* by Ashurbanipal* (KJV Asnappar). Nehemiah (1:1) was at Susa when he received news of the ruined state of Jerusalem.*

II. *Site.* Susa is situated in a fertile alluvial plain 241 km. (150 mi.) N of the Persian Gulf. It is within easy access of southern Mesopotamia* and its history

Aerial view of mounds at Susa. (*See also photo under* KASSITES.) Courtesy The Oriental Institute, University of Chicago.

was linked with that region. The area of Susa is watered by several rivers: (1) The Kerkha River flows W of Susa. The Greeks called it the Choaspes and knew that Xerxes drank only from its waters, which he carried with him (Herodotus 1.188). (2) To the E of Susa flows the Ab-e-Diz, which has at times been linked to the Kerkha by a channel. (3) Still farther E is the Karun River, into which the Ab-e-Diz flows. (4) Susa itself is located on the E bank of the Sha'ur, an affluent which flows from the Kerkha then back into it. The Greeks called it the Eulaios.

During the winter the area is pleasant and Susa was used as a winter residence by the Achaemenid kings. Rains in January and February create lush pastures for the shepherds.

On the other hand, the area is intolerably hot for six months of the year, particularly in July and August, when temperatures reach 60 degrees centigrade (140 degrees Fahrenneit). Strabo (15.3.10) notes that snakes and lizards crossing the street at noon in the summer heat were roasted to death. The Elamite texts from Persepolis* translated by Hallock record only five references of travel to Susa from June through October, compared to forty-two references for the rest of the year.

III. *The Mounds.* There are four major mounds at Susa, which the French excavators call: Acropolis (Ac), Apadana (Ap), Ville Royale (VR), and Ville des Artisans (VA). The first three form a triangular area with sides about 1,000 m. (1,100 yd.) long.

A. *The Acropolis.* This is the most important of the mounds; it was settled at the earliest date and has been the most extensively excavated. The Ac rises steeply at its highest point c. 38 m. (41 yd.) above the waters of the Sha'ur. The southern part of the Ac averages about 22 m. (24 yd.) above the plain, half of which is made up of debris from settlements. A castle* built by the French excavators now stands on the northern point of the Ac.

B. *Apadana.* N of the Ac is the Apadana, which is so called because the Achaemenids built their audience hall there. They built on earlier Elamite structures.

C. *Ville Royale.* To the E of the Ac and the Ap is the long hill where merchants, artisans, and court functionaries lived. In its SE corner is the area called the *Donjon* or the "Keep."

D. *Ville des Artisans.* To the E of the VR beyond the Tudela Valley is a hill where an Achaemenid village was excavated. This was an area inhabited by tradesmen.

The modern village of Shūsh lies on the Sha'ur below the slopes of the Ac. Susa was occupied continuously from 3500 B.C. to the thirteenth century A.D.

IV. *The Excavations.* The famous Jewish traveler Benjamin of Tudela visited the site in A.D. 1170 and took note of the Jewish community there. W. K. Loftus, who made soundings in 1851–53, confirmed its identification with biblical Shushan. M. Dieulafoy worked on the Ap in 1884–86, securing for the Louvre objects such as the archer frieze.

In 1894 the French secured a monopoly on excavations in Persia from Nassr ed-Din. The French have sponsored excavations at Susa from 1897 to the present, except for the periods of the world wars. The first director from 1897 to 1912 was Jacques de Morgan, a mining engineer. Almost immediately the expedition made one of its most famous discoveries; in the S part of the Ac, Morgan in 1901-02 found the 2.4 m. (8 ft.) high basalt stele* of Hammurabi's Code.* It was promptly published by V. Scheil, who was to contribute over a dozen volumes on the texts from Susa.

Morgan trenched a large area in the SW part of the Ac. He discovered the Stele of Naram-Sin and the Obelisk of Manishtusu. Unfortunately Morgan's purpose was to remove as much earth as possible to discover monuments for the Louvre in Paris. He used 1200 workers at a time and estimated that he could remove a square meter of earth for two gold francs.

R. de Mecquenem, who began his career as an architect in 1903, succeeded Morgan from 1913 to 1939. He uncovered large areas in the VR, including the site of the Donjon, and in the N, S, and central part of the Ac. In the center Mecquenem uncovered the temple of Ninhursag and found the large bronze* statue* of Queen Napirasu.

Since 1946 the expedition has been under R. Ghirshman, who has opened up new areas. He began work in the N part of the VR, where settlements from the Islamic period to the late third millennium B.C. have been uncovered. In the early 1950s Ghirshman uncovered an Achaemenid village in the VA.

In the 1960s, M.-J. Steve and H. Gasche conducted work on the central W area of the Ac and uncovered important structures of the third millennium B.C. J. Perrot has been studying the Achaemenid remains on the Ap. In 1969–70, A. Labrousse excavated a new Achaemenid palace on the plain W of the Sha'ur.

The only exception to the work of the French has been a sondage in the S part of the Ac by the American, R. Dyson, in 1954.

V. *Inscriptions.* From c. 3000 B.C. the Elamites wrote in a pictographic* script known as Proto-Elamite. The latest of these texts dates to the time of Hammurabi.* More than 1400 texts have been recovered from Susa, 19 from Tepe Siyalk,* and 6 from Tepe Yahya, a site in SE Iran. The most important text is a treaty between the Elamite king Khita and Naram-Sin of Agade (2280 B.C.), which gives a list of the Elamite gods. Despite attempts at decipherment by W. Hinz, the Proto-Elamite script is very imperfectly understood (*see* ELAMITE WRITING).

The Elamite language was later written in cuneiform* script. We have numerous inscriptions from the Middle Elamite period (thirteenth–twelfth centuries B.C.). Then there is a four hundred-year blank until the seventh century. From the Neo-Babylonian* period we have three hundred economic texts, twenty-five letters, and one astrological text in Elamite. The Achaemenids regularly used Elamite for their royal inscriptions and for accounting purposes.

VI. *History and Archaeology.* A. *Prehistory.* The earliest pottery* of the area is the Susiana a—e series from Djafferabad and Djowi N of Susa, dating from 5000 B.C. The earliest pottery from Susa comes from a depth of 11 m. (36 ft.) on the Ac from a cemetery with over two thousand burials. It is dated about 3600 B.C. This is a brilliantly designed pottery decorated with the curved horns of an ibex, geometric patterns, etc.

The earliest excavators distinguished only between Susa I and Susa II (from 2800) pottery. LeBreton has developed a chronological series from A to D (A-3600, B-3500, C-3200, and D-2800). The earliest copper appears c. 3000. From this period comes a powerfully musculatured lion* demon in white magnesite only 8 cm. (3¼ in.) high.

B. *Early Dynastic Period.* The history of Susa and the area of Elam* is inextricably connected with that of Sumer* in the third millennium B.C. Elam is first mentioned in Sumerian texts c. 2700. Enmebaragisi of Kish "carried off the arms of the land of Elam as booty." This action was to characterize relations between the areas. Eannatum of Lagash* c. 2400, who erected the famous Stele of Vultures,* attacked Elam.

C. *The Agade Period.* There were numerous contacts between Elam and Mesopotamia during the reigns of the Semitic Sargon* of Agade (Akkad,* or Accad; 2360), and his successors: Manishtusu (2300–), Naram-Sin (2280–), and Shar-kali-sharri (2240–). Sargon conquered Susa. It may be that it was under his influence that Susa became an important city. A copy of the treaty signed between Naram-Sin and Khita of Elam was found in Susa. Excavators have recently uncovered a granary* on the Ac (dated to the reign of Shar-kali-sharri) similar to those of the Indus River civilization.

It was a millennium later, in the Middle Elamite period (see below), that the famous Obelisk of Manishtusu and the Stele of Naram-Sin, now in the Louvre, were carried off to Susa.

Puzur-In-Shushinak, who was the governor of Susa as a vassal under Naram-Sin, showed increasing independence as Shar-kali-sharri was overwhelmed by the Gutian barbarians. His constructions on the Ac and numerous inscriptions in Akkadian and Proto-Elamite have been found.

D. *The Ur III Period.* Shulgi (2095–48), the Sumerian king of Ur,* conquered Susa in his twenty-eighth year and installed a non-Elamite governor. But he placated the Elamites by building a temple for In-Shushinak, "Lord of Susa." The foundations of this building and of a temple he built for Ninhursag have been traced in the center of the Ac. His son, Ibbi-Sin (2039–2006), however, was attacked not only by the Amorites* from the W but by the Elamites who sacked the city of Ur, as we are informed in the plaintive Lamentation over Ur* published by Kramer (see *ANE*, 611–19).

E. *Simash and Eparti Dynasties.* In the early second millennium B.C., Elam was governed by the Simash Dynasty (until 1850), and then by the Eparti

Dynasty. The period from 1850 to 1550 is known as the Epoch of the *Sukkal-makh*, or "Grand Regent," who was succeeded by his brother rather than by his son. The main documents of this period are eight hundred legal and commercial texts in Akkadian, mainly from Susa. The sole historical document from this period is an Elamite text of Siwe-palar-khuppak, who was defeated in 1764 by Hammurabi. From an inscription of Ashurbanipal* (640 B.C.), we learn that Kutir-Nahhunte attacked in the reign of Hammurabi's successor, Shamshu-Iluna, and carried off the goddess Nanai to Elam "a place not befitting her."

For this period the most important remains at Susa come from Ghirshman's work on the VR. From the period of Kutir-Nahhunte the excavators have uncovered the vast dwellings of an Elamite lord, Temti-wartash, who received silver* payments from the island of Bahrein. From the seventeenth century comes a large house* with jars full of exercise tablets, indicating that it was used as a school. The most striking discoveries from the fourteenth century are votive beds depicting nude couples participating in the sacred marriage rite.

The Kassites* not only brought an end to the Old Babylonian dynasty but must have also overrun Elam as well. We know that the Kassite king Kurigalzu II (c. 1330) conquered Susa. There is a blank in Elamite documents from 1500 to 1300.

F. *The Classical Elamite Age.* The apogee of Elamite culture was reached in the Middle Period (1300–1100), with a succession of energetic kings: Untash-Gal (Humban) fl. 1250, Shutruk-Nahhunte fl. 1200, Kutir-Nahhunte fl. 1150, and Shilkhak-In-Shushinak fl. 1130.

Untash-GAL defeated the Kassite Kashtiliash III and carried off his protective deity to Susa. A broken but still massive bronze* statue* of the Elamite queen Napirasu was found in the center of the Ac. The 1.2 m. (4 ft.) high monument weighs almost 1814 kg. (2 tons) and is the largest metal statue found in the Near East. Untash-Gal's greatest monument is the ziggurat* which he erected at Choga-Zanbil, 40 km. (25 mi.) SE of Susa. Excavated by Ghirshman, it is one of the best preserved ziggurats with three of the original five stories intact.

It was Shutruk-Nahhunte and his son Kutir-Nahhunte who c. 1160 brought an end to Kassite rule in Babylonia. Shutruk-Nahhunte removed from Sippar the Stele of Naram-Sin and the Hammurabi Code, and probably from Kish the Obelisk of Manishtusu. He installed his son as ruler over Babylonia. Their worst crime in Babylonian eyes was the removal of the god Marduk from Babylon to Susa.

Shilkhak-In-Shushinak was the most brilliant of these kings. His conquests extended to the island of Bushire and to the interior area of Shiraz. Numerous inscriptions attest to his building activities on the Ac. A unique bronze object from his reign, the *Sit-Shamshi* ("Sunrise"), depicts a ceremony on the Ac of Susa. Two nude figures are performing ablutions between two staged towers.

The collapse of the Elamites coincided with the rise of the energetic Babylonian ruler, Nebuchadnezzar I* (1124–1103), who recovered the statue of

Marduk from Susa. The Elamites disappear from the historical sources until they are mentioned by Shamshi-Adad V, three hundred years later.

G. *The Neo-Elamite Period.* There was but a brief Elamite renaissance from 720 B.C. until Ashurbanipal* brutally destroyed Susa in 640. A small chapel on the SE Ac dates to this period. When a puppet installed by the Assyrians aided rebels in Babylon, Ashurbanipal vented his fury upon the Elamite capital. "His soldiers trod the paths of secret groves into which no stranger had ever been permitted to enter, and set them on fire." They tore up the cemetery and carried off the bones to Assyria. The goddess Nana, whom the Elamites had taken from Uruk, was returned to her home, and In-Shushinak and thirty-two royal statues were borne away to Mesopotamia. So thoroughly did the Assyrians tear down the ziggurat of Susa that it was only recently that excavators have recognized its location in the blank area on the Ac between the temple of In-Shushinak and the temple of Ninhursag.

Silence once again envelopes Elamite history until the Neo-Babylonian period, when we learn that the first recorded act of Nabopolassar* was the restoration of the Elamite gods from Uruk to Susa.

H. *The Achaemenid Period.* When Cyrus* captured Babylon in 539, he returned additional Elamite gods to Susa according to the Cyrus Cylinder.* We have three hundred Elamite texts dealing with revenues from his reign.

Though there had been a Persian settlement on the VA, excavated by Ghirshman, since the end of the seventh century, it was in 521 that Susa regained its importance when Darius made it his administrative capital. Thus it remained throughout the Achaemenid period.

From a detailed inscription we know that from 518 to 512 Darius (*see* DARIUS, sec. V.C) built a palace on the Ap by employing materials and workmen from every part of his realm. He built upon a terrace made with gravel enclosed with brick walls, covering an Elamite graveyard and perhaps even Elamite palaces. In 1969 two perfectly preserved tablets of marble bearing a new inscription of Darius in Akkadian and Elamite were discovered in the W court of the Ap.

Xerxes,* who destroyed Babylon when it revolted, must have made Susa his principal winter residence. It was to Susa that Xerxes retired from Sardis* after his disastrous campaign in Greece (Herodotus 9.108). The drama of the book of Esther must have taken place in the palace of Darius, which was used by Xerxes. Horn has suggested that we may have an attestation of Mordecai in the person of *Marduka*, who was a finance officer at Susa under Xerxes.

Artaxerxes I (464–23) resided at Susa and here received the embassy of Callias in 449 which ended Greek-Persian hostilities. In his reign the palace of Darius burned to the ground. Though no inscription attests his building activities, he may have begun the small palace in the Donjon area of the VR, completed by his successor, Darius II (423–404). From this small hypostyle* hall have come all the fragments of stone bas-relief* from Susa, as we now have ornamentation

for the first time entirely of stone.

The remains of the Ap as we have it today belong to the reconstruction by Artaxerxes II (404–360), who seems to have faithfully reproduced Darius's structure as his Ap is closely similar to Darius's Ap at Persepolis.* It includes a square central hall, 58.5 m. (192 ft.) on a side, with six rows of six columns, and porticoes on three sides. The columns were 20 m. (65 ft.) high, capped by double bull protomes. Colorful decorations in moulded enameled brick covered the walls. Around the area was a wall flanked with projecting towers,* and below the area a moat flooded with the waters of the Sha'ur. Ghirshman believes that the Ac, the Ap, and the VR were entirely surrounded by a wall.

In 1969 bulldozers accidentally uncovered on the plain W of the Sha'ur a new hypostyle hall, which proved to cover 1,650 sq. m. (nearly 1,800 sq. yd.) when fully excavated in 1970. It may have been the provisional palace of Artaxerxes II while he proceeded with the reconstruction on the Ap. From his reign we have the fire sanctuary with two altars* and a stairway, discovered by Dieulafoy a distance NE of the Ac.

As inscriptions inform us, Artaxerxes III (359–38) completed the reconstruction on the Ap.

I. *The Hellenistic and Parthian Periods.* Alexander captured Susa without fighting in 331, and with it enormous treasure. The classical sources (Arrian, Plutarch, Diodorus, Curtius) agree that the sum was between 40–50,000 talents though they disagree as to how much of this was in coins.* Leaving the satrap of Susa in his post, Alexander proceeded to Persepolis. In 324 after his return from campaigns in the E, Alexander celebrated the symbolic marriage of himself and eighty Macedonian officers to native brides at Susa.

Under the Seleucids Susa was renamed Seleucia-on-the-Eulaios. The city suffered destruction perhaps during the revolt of Molon against Antiochus III (223–187 B.C.). Thereafter the area fell under the Parthians, who gave the Greek inhabitants of Susa considerable freedom. Greek inscriptions from this period include the manumission of slaves* in the temple of Artemis* (Nanaia), and poetic compositions.

Ghirshman excavated in the VA a necropolis* of the Partho-Seleucid period (300 B.C.–A.D. 200). About A.D. 100 an interesting change in burial practice takes place: the dead are laid on benches for their flesh to decay—a practice similar to that of the early Magi and the later Zoroastrians.

J. *The Sassanid and Muslim Periods.* From c. A.D. 250 under Ardashir I and Shapur I Susa began to flourish. However a revolt by the Christians was suppressed by the destruction of Susa by Shapur II (A.D. 309–79). Evidence of Christians buried with Nestorian crosses has been recovered from this period. Though rebuilt under the name Eranshahr-Shapur by later Sassanids, Susa never flourished again.

The Arabs captured it in 638. The mosque with its conical tower at the edge of the Sha'ur is venerated as the tomb of Daniel. This tradition was reported by Benjamin of Tudela and may go back to the eighth or even seventh century A.D.

BIBLIOGRAPHY: The official excavation reports have been issued in folio volumes under a variety of names: (A) *Mémoires de la Délégation en Perse* (I–XIII), (B) *Mémoires de la Mission Archéologique de Susiane* (XIV), (C) *Mission Archéologique de Perse* (XV), (D) *Mémoires de la Mission Archéologique de Perse, Mission en Susiane* (XVI–XXVIII), and (E) *Mémoires de la Mission Archéologique en Iran, Mission de Susiane* (XXIX–XLVI). For a detailed listing of the contents up to vol. XXXVI (1954) and other works on Susa, see L. van den Berghe, *Archéologie de l'Iran ancien* (1959), 165–74. Cf. also: A. Poebel, "The Acropolis of Susa in the Elamite Inscriptions," *AJSL*, 49 (1932–33), 125–40; G. Cameron, *History of Early Iran* (1936); G. Richter, "Greeks in Persia," *AJA*, 50 (1946), 15–30; A. Olmstead, *History of the Persian Empire* (1948); R. Kent, *Old Persian* (1953); R. Ghirshman, *Iran* (1954); id., *Village perse-achéménide* (1954); R. North, *Guide to Biblical Iran* (1956), 93–107; L. LeBreton, "The Early Periods at Susa," *Iraq*, 19 (1957), 79–124; A. Parrot; *Le musée du Louvre et la Bible* (1957), 125–35; A. Barucq, "Esther et la cour de Suse," *BTS*, 39 (1961), 3–5; R. Adams, "Agriculture and Urban Life in Early Southwestern Iran," *Science*, 136 (1962), 109–22; W. Brice, "The Writing System of the Proto-Elamite Account Tablets of Susa," *BJRL*, 45 (1962), 15–39; W. Hinz, "Zur Entzifferung der elamischen Strichschrift," *IrAnt*, 2 (1962), 1–21; R. Ghirshman, "L'Apadana de Suse," *IrAnt*, 3 (1963), 148–54; W. Hinz, "Persia c. 2400–1800 B.C.," *CAH*, 2 (2d ed., 1963), chap. 23; S. Kramer, *The Sumerians* (1963); R. Labat, "Elam c. 1600–1200 B.C.," *CAH*, 1 (2d ed., 1963), part 2, chap. 29; R. Ghirshman, *The Art of Ancient Iran* (1964); W. Hinz, "Persia c. 1800–1550 B.C.," *CAH*, 2, (2d ed., 1964), part 2, chap. 7; id., *Das Reich Elam* (1964); S. Horn, "Mordecai, A Historical Problem," *BR*, 9 (1964), 14–25; R. Labat, "Elam and Western Persia c. 1200–1000 B.C.," *CAH*, 2 (2d ed., 1964), part 2, chap. 32; J.-L. Huot, *Persia* (1965); F. W. König, *Die elamischen Königsinschriften* (1965); M. Mallowan, *Early Mesopotamia and Iran* (1965); E. Porada, *The Art of Iran* (1965); P. Amiet, *Elam* (1966); E. Reiner, "The Elamite Language," *Handbuch der Orientalistik* (1969), 54–67; R. Ghirshman, "The Elamite Levels at Susa and Their Chronological Significance," *AJA*, 74 (1970), 223–25; J. Perrot, "Suse," *Iran*, 8 (1970), 190–94; C. Moore, *Esther* (1971); J. Perrot et al., "Recherches archéologiques à Suse et en Susiane," *Syria*, 48 (1971), 21–51; M.-J. Steve and H. Gasche, *L'Acropole de Suse* (1971); J. Hansman, "Elamites, Achaemenians and Anshan," *Iran*, 10 (1972), 101–25; J. Perrot, "Suse et Susiane," *Iran*, 10 (1972), 181–83; P. Amiet, "Sceaux syriens découverts à Suse," *Mélanges de l'Université Saint-Joseph*, 45 (1970–71), 129–35; J. Perrot, "Récents découvertes de l'époche achéménide à Suse," *Archeologia*, 39 (1971), 7–17; P. Amiet, "Elamites et Perses en Susiane," *Archeologia*, 44 (1972), 6–13; id., *Glyptique susienne des origines à l'époque des Perses achéménides* (1972); id., "Les ivoires achéménides de Suse," *Syria*, 49 (1972), 167–91; H. Gasche, *La poterie élamite du deuxième millénaire avant J.-C.* (1973); P. Amiet,

"Quelques observations sur le palais de Darius à Suse," *Syria*, 51 (1974), 65–73; W. White, Jr., *ZPEB*, 5 (1975), 544; S. Pelzel, "Dating the Early Dynastic Plaques from Susa," *JNES*, 36 (1977), 1–16; E. Carter, "The Susa Sequence—3000–2000 B.C.: Susa, Ville Royale I," *AJA*, 83 (1979), 451–54.

EY

SUSITA. See HIPPOS.

SWASTIKA. See MOSAICS.

SWORD. See ARMS AND WEAPONS.

SYCHAR (sī'kär; Gr. Συχάρ, *suchar*). A city* in Samaria* located near Mount Ebal and Mount Gerizim* near where Jesus came to meet the woman at the well (John 4:5). It was near the field that Jacob gave to his son, Joseph* (cf. Gen 48:22, where Jacob gave Joseph "the ridge of land," NIV; Heb. *Shechem**; LXX *síkima*). The question then is whether the Sychar of John 4:5 is the same place as Shechem, or whether it is to be located and identified with the modern Arab village of Askar at the SW foot of Mount Ebal.

The reasons many modern scholars have held that Sychar is not Shechem and is to be identified with Askar include the following. The ancient Greek MS evidence for John 4:5 overwhelmingly favors the reading Συχάρ, "Sychar," with only the Sinaitic and Curetonian Syriac MSS giving the name that would correspond to Greek Συχέμ, i.e. שׁכם (Shechem) in Hebrew. Further, early Christian writers, such as Eusebius (*Onomasticon*, ed. Klosterman, 164), bear testimony to the reading of Sychar.

The *Bordeaux Pilgrim** (*CCSL*, 175, 13–14) clearly distinguishes Shechem from Sychar when he says that a thousand paces from Sichem (i.e., Shechem) is the place called Sechar (i.e., Sychar), from which the Samaritan woman came to Jacob's well.

Archaeologically, the sixth-century A.D. Medeba Mosaic Map* in the floor of the church there has noted at the area of Askar: "[Sy]char, now [S]ychora." Then much later a fourteenth-century A.D. Samaritan Chronicle speaks of a town called Ischar near Shechem, a name which matches with both Sychar and Askar.

Those who hold that Sychar and Shechem are to be identified as the same place argue on the basis of the textual evidence of the Sinaitic and Curetonian Syriac, which alone give the name that would correspond to Shechem. It is noted that excavations at Tell Balatah have shown that Shechem came to an end c. the close of the second century B.C., as witnessed by Josephus (Jos. *Antiq.* 13.9.1; Jos. *War* 1.2.6). G. E. Wright believes that a village of Shechem probably continued to exist where the village of Balatah now is and that the Samaritan woman came from this village. On this view the overwhelming evidence of the Greek MSS would have to be discounted and Sychar assumed to have derived from an ancient textual corruption of Sychem (Shechem).

BIBLIOGRAPHY: M. Avi-Yonah, *The Madaba Mosaic Map* (1964), pl. 6; G. E. Wright, *Shechem* (1965),

183–84, 243–44, n. 6; J. Finegan, *The Archaeology of the NT* (1969), 34–38; J. M. Houston, *ZPEB*, 5 (1975), 549–50.

WHM

SYENE. *See* ASWAN.

SYNAGOGUE. The term *synagogue* comes from a Greek word, *sunagōgē*, meaning "assembly," or "congregation." The origins of the synagogue have been ascribed variously to Moses, to the legal-political structure of Israelite society, to groups such as the fifth-century B.C. Elephantine* Jews* of Egypt,* and to Ezra. Most probably it had its roots in the ministry of Ezekiel to the Babylonian exiles (*see* EXILE) from Judea,* and seems to have arisen from a need for corporate Bible study, prayer, and perhaps theological discussion. During the Persian and Greek periods the synagogue became an important religious and cultural institution among Palestinian and other Jews. Whereas there was only one temple,* there were synagogues in nearly every village and town, controlled not by priests but by teaching rabbis. Quite possibly there were two or three synagogues in Jerusalem* in the time of Jesus, though the extent to which they may have been connected with the temple is unknown.

Epigraphy* attests to the existence of early synagogues in Corinth,* Rome,* and Jerusalem. The Jerusalem synagogue was dated approximately in the middle of the first century A.D.

The remains of a Byzantine* synagogue at Beth Alpha are probably sixth century in date, as with the synagogue mosaic* pavement uncovered at Gaza* in 1965. The mosaic floor of the Beth Alpha synagogue contains a panel which depicts the signs of the zodiac arranged in a circle.

BIBLIOGRAPHY: E. L. Sukenik, *Ancient Synagogues in Palestine and Greece* (1934); S. Klein, *Jewish Settlements in Palestine*, 1 (1939); I. Sonne, *IDB*, 4 (1962), 476–91; *EEHL*, 1 (1975), 187–90; ibid., 2 (1976), 412–17; W. White, Jr., *ZPEB*, 5 (1975), 554–67.

EMB

SYRIA. *See* ARAM.

Theodotos synagogue inscription. An inscription in Greek from the Herodian period, found in excavations of the southern part of the "Ophel" hill in 1914. It reads: "Theodotos [son of (or: of the family of)] Vettenos priest and head of the synagogue, who was also the son of the head of the synagogue, (re)built the synagogue for the reading of the Law and for the study of the precepts, as well as the hospice and the chambers and the bathing establishment, for lodging those who need them, from abroad; it [the synagogue] was founded by his ancestors and the elders and Simonides." (*See also photos under* CAPERNAUM; GAZA; HEBREW RELIGION; KORAZIN; SARDIS.) Courtesy Israel Dept. of Antiquities and Museums.

SYRTIS (sür'təs; Gr. Σύρτις, *Syrtis*). This name was applied to the shallow waters in the great oblong bay on the N African coast between Tunisia, Tripolitania, and Cyrenaica. Fighting westward with a beam wind from Crete, the captain of the Alexandrian grain ship* which carried Paul's party to Rome* feared being driven S into these notoriously shoaling waters (Acts 27:17). *OCD* (p. 874) is of the opinion that the Phoenicians* propagated rumors about the dangers of these waters in an effort to protect their own trade monopolies on the coast. Underwater archaeology,* which pronounces the whole area to be full of ancient wrecks, refutes the allegation. Winds, like that which Paul's ship encountered (Acts 27:14), blowing into the vacuum created by the heat-lifted air of the Sahara, even when the Sahara occupied a smaller area, must have created a great hazard. The wind pressure drove the sea lanes S, and the whole coast is low and shelving.

EMB

T

TAANACH (tä′ ä näk; Heb. תַּעֲנָךְ, ta‛anāk). An important Canaanite* and early Israelite city* guarding one of the strategic passes on the southern edge of the Plain of Esdraelon. The tell* is a large one, covering about 5.6 ha. (14 a.) and is situated on a rise which combines with the occupational debris to reach a height of 49 m. (160 ft.). Its location has never been uncertain. The Arab village at its base still bears the name Ta‛annek. The city does not loom large in biblical history, however, probably because it remained a Canaanite stronghold until the reign of Solomon* and shortly thereafter was destroyed by the Egyptians.

Joshua originally defeated its king (Josh 12:21) but failed to capture the city (Judg 1:27). The tribal allocation to Manasseh* included Taanach (Josh 17:11; 1 Chron 7:29) as a Levitical city (Josh 21:25), but it is likely that this circumstance was not achieved until the early Israelite monarchy. The important victory of Deborah and Barak* took place at Taanach "by the waters of Megiddo*" (Judg 5:19), and Solomon included it in his administrative reorganization (1 Kings 4:12).

Extrabiblical references to Taanach include three Egyptian references and one uncertain reading in the Amarna letters* (No. 248). Pharaoh Thutmose III mentions the city in planning his celebrated campaign prior to the battle of Megiddo* (1479 B.C.) and later lists it as one of his conquests. Sheshonk I also claims to have captured Taanach along with other Palestinian towns in 926 B.C. The *Onomasticon* of Eusebius contains the final reference to the city from an ancient source (157.11).

Archaeological research was instituted at Taanach by the Austrian scholar Ernst Sellin between the years 1902–4. The excavations were fruitful in producing incense stands from a "cultic area" the first season, and several Akkadian* cuneiform* tablets in the second and third seasons. Sellin also found a strongly fortified building dating from the MB IIC period (1650–1550). This W building (or so-called "patrician's house") had walls 1.2 m. (4 ft.) thick founded on the earlier EB city walls* and may have been the official residence of the ruler. Associated with this phase were numerous infant jar burials and a massive plaster* glacis* typical of Hyksos* defensive architecture.

Paul Lapp conducted three campaigns at Taanach in 1963, 1966, and 1968 for the American Schools of Oriental Research. The Americans concentrated on four areas of the SW quadrant of the mound: the W building, the cult area, and the W and S defenses. They were able to check the stratigraphy* and clarify the chronological (*see* CHRONOLOGY) picture as well as expand the knowledge of the Iron Age* city and the Early and Middle Bronze Age* walls.

Taanach was apparently founded c. 2700 B.C. and flourished from late EB II through EB III. At that time the massive walls were built. The wall of the earliest phase measured almost 4.3 m. (14 ft.) thick at the widest point and probably boasted multiple towers,* one of which was uncovered in the trench on the S slope. On the W, a double-ring wall formed the earliest defense. The second phase wall was approximately 3.7 m. (12 ft.) wide, while the third was composed of a stone scree more than 9.1 m. (30 ft.) thick in one area. Impressive earth fills were utilized to level the space inside the walls. A strange underground chamber with rock-cut stairway, interpreted by Sellin as a subterranean sanctuary, was claimed by Albright to be an EB tomb on the model of those known from the Egyptian Third Dynasty.

The Middle Bronze Age saw a second period of prosperity for the city after a long period of abandonment, with a corresponding expansion of building efforts. At first, a "sandwich" type of plastered glacis was constructed over the EB walls to protect the base of the citadel* from access by battering rams, and later two other phases were added, the latter one being almost 1.8 m. (6 ft.) thick with chalk layers on the inner face alternating with earth fill in order to tie the glacis more firmly into the embankment.

Buildings of the Late Bronze I and Iron I periods were found in the 1963–66 excavations, with all except one being dubious in function. A large LB I structure with plaster floor was found under the late Abbasid fortress. Two buildings came from the twelfth

Drainpipe and water system from a 12th-century B.C. building at Taanach. Courtesy Taanach Excavation, Albert E. Glock, director.

Tablet written in Canaanite alphabetic cuneiform script from early 12th century B.C., found at Taanach. The text registers the receipt of a grain shipment. Courtesy Taanach Excavation, Albert E. Glock, director.

century B.C., one with a unique drainpipe and water system, and another which yielded a small but epigraphically* significant tablet written in Canaanite alphabetic* cuneiform script. The "cult area" was apparently a storeroom housing some clearly cultic objects mixed with common secular material. It is not certain that the building was a temple, since only part of it was preserved. The date of its destruction approximates that of Sheshonk's invasion. Thereafter Taanach was sparsely occupied, with only fragmentary remains of later periods.

BIBLIOGRAPHY: E. Sellin, *Tell Ta'anek* (1904); id., *Eine Nachlese auf dem Tell Ta'anek in Palestina* (1905); P. Lapp, "The 1963 Excavations at Tell Ta'annek," *BASOR*, 173 (1964), 4–44; id., "The 1966 Excavations at Tell Ta'annek," *BASOR*, 185 (1967), 2–39; id., "The 1968 Excavations at Tell Ta'annek," *BASOR*, 195 (1969), 2–49; id., "Tell Ta'annak," *RB*, 75 (1968), 93–98; id., "Taanach by the Waters of Megiddo," *BA*, 30 (1967), 1–27; D. R. Hillers, "An Alphabetic Cuneiform Tablet from Taanach (TT433)," *BASOR*, 173 (1964), 45–50; F. M. Cross, Jr., "The Canaanite Cuneiform Tablet from Ta'anach," *BASOR*, 190 (1968), 41–46; C. Graesser, Jr., "Taanach," in C. F. Pfeiffer, ed., *The Biblical World* (1966), 556–63; J. M. Houston, *ZPEB*, 5 (1975), 571–72.   JEJ

TAANNEK, TELL. See TAANACH.

TAANATH-SHILOH (tä'ä nath shī'lō; Heb. תַּאֲנַת שִׁלֹה, ta‘nath šilōh). This village, as is clear from Josh 16:6, lay between Michmethah and Janohah, on the NE border of Ephraim. It has been tentatively located 11.3 km. (7 mi.) SE of Shechem,* where there is evidence of an ancient hill fort (modern Khirbet Ta'nah el-Foqa). The name may mean "approach to Shiloh."

TABAQAT FAHIL. See PELLA.

TABARIYEH. See TIBERIAS.

TABBATH (tab'əth; Heb. טַבָּת, ṭabāt). Tentatively located E of the Jordan River and mentioned in Judg 7:22 as the terminal point of Gideon's pursuit of the Midianites* routed in the Plain of Jezreel. Judges 8:10–13 implies a position near Karkor in Gilead, though Karkor itself is insufficiently identified to serve

as a point of reference. The Gilead hill country would have been a natural rallying point for the defeated host. It is possibly to be identified with Ras Abu Tabat on the slopes of Jebel 'Ajlun.

EMB

TABGHA (tab'gə; Arab. ṭābgha; the Arabized form of the Gr. *Heptapegon*, literally, "seven springs"; Lat. *Septem Fontes*). A valley and beach on the N shore of Galilee* near the site of ancient Capernaum.* On the site is the ancient church of "The Multiplication of the Fishes." Numerous churches were built and rebuilt on this site to commemorate Jesus' miracle (Mark 6:34–46). The present church is erected over magnificent mosaics* remaining from a Byzantine* church which stood on the spot. The German Palestine Society acquired the site in 1888, and it has been carefully excavated. The earliest church is dated about A.D. 350, while several later churches were built over it. The Benedictine Order now tends the site and has built a monastery on either side of the small church. The seven springs from which the site derives its name are much diminished, but the water course leading away from them in Roman times has been excavated.

BIBLIOGRAPHY: *From Kfar-Nachum to Tabigha*, 2d ed. (Heb. 1958); D. Neeman and B. Sapir, *Capernaum* (1967).   WW

TABLE. See FURNITURE.

TABOR (tā'bər; Heb. תָּבוֹר, tābôr). 1. A Levitical settlement on the Zebulun-Issachar border (1 Chron 6:77; cf. Josh 19:22; Judg 8:18), probably located on or near the mountain of that name.

2. A hill situated in the Jezreel Valley some 9.7 km. (6 mi.) SE of Nazareth.* Though smaller than Mount Hermon,* its imposing appearance made it somewhat comparable (cf. Ps 89:12). There was a shrine on its summit in the eighth century B.C. (cf. Hos 5:1), which might have survived from the Middle Bronze Age* (cf. Deut 33:19). In the Hellenistic

Detail from mosaic in northern (left) transept in church at Tabgha, showing cormorant (upper left), and flamingo in combat with water snake. The mosaic is late fourth to early fifth century A.D. Courtesy Israel Government Press Office.

Mount Tabor with Jezreel Valley in background. Courtesy Israel Government Press Office.

period a fortified town was apparently built there by Antiochus III in 218 B.C., and in 53 B.C. the area was the locale of a battle between the Romans and Alexander, son of Aristobulus. Early Christian tradition associated Tabor with the scene of Christ's transfiguration (Matt 17:1–8 et al.), but in view of the fact that in NT times a town was located on the top this identification is unlikely.

BIBLIOGRAPHY: G. W. Van Beek, *IDB*, 4 (1962), 508–9; R. L. Alden, *ZPEB*, 4 (1975), 302.

RKH

TADMOR (tad′mōr; Heb. תַּדְמֹר, *tadmōr*). In 2 Chron 8:4, this was a Solomonic* city* in the deserts NE of Palestine, which may or may not be the Tamar (RSV, NEB) of 1 Kings 9:18, where the Masoretic variant has "Tadmor." If the latter is correct, the reference is to the city in the Syrian desert familiar to the Greeks as Palmyra,* an oasis 193 km. (120 mi.) NE of Damascus.* It was mentioned by name in Assyrian annals from the time of Tiglath-pileser I* (1115–1100 B.C.) onward and reached its peak of prosperity in the middle of the third century A.D., being destroyed shortly thereafter by Aurelian. The remains of tall columns and other indications of its former glory can still be seen at the site, known to the Arabs as Tudmur.

BIBLIOGRAPHY: L. Cottrell, *The Past* (1960), 337–38; S. Cohen, *IDB*, 4 (1962), 509–10; J. D. Douglas, *NBD* (1962), 1235–36; G. F. Owen, *ZPEB*, 5 (1975), 586–88.

RKH

TAE; TAIA. *See* TELL TA′YINAT.

TAFILE. *See* TOPHEL.

TAHPANHES (tä pan′ ēz; Heb. תַּחְפַּנְחֵס, *tahpanhēs*). Known also from Herodotus (2.30,107) as Daphnai, Tahpanhes was organized as a border fortress by Psammetichus I (664–610 B.C.) to guard the E Egyptian Delta, manned by Greek mercenary troops; its site is the modern Tell Defenneh, some 43.5 km. (27 mi.) SSW of Port Said. Jeremiah (2:16; 44:1; 46:14) and Ezekiel (30:18) included it with the main centers of Egypt's power in their prophecies. Thither went the party that bore Jeremiah off to Egypt,* and there he symbolically hid stones in the

brickwork before "Pharaoh's house in Tahpanhes" (cf. Jer 43:7ff.), proclaiming Nebuchadnezzar's* future presence there. This building was probably a royal fort, excavated by Petrie (cf. his *History of Egypt*, 3 [1905], 330, fig. 138); however, clay* cylinders of Nebuchadnezzar II said to have been found there are now known to be counterfeits. A sixth-century B.C. Phoenician* papyrus* also names Tahpanhes.

BIBLIOGRAPHY: W. M. F. Petrie, *Tanis, Part II* (1888); id., *Nebesheh (AM) and Defenneh (Tahpanhes)* (1888); W. Spiegelberg, *Aegyptologische Randglossen zum Alten Testament* (1904), 39; A. Dupont-Sommer, *PEQ*, 81 (1949), 52–57.

KAK

TAHTIM HODSHI (tä′tim hod′shī; Heb. תַּחְתִּים חָדְשִׁי, *tahtîm hodšî*). A district between Gilead and Dan-jaan, mentioned in relation to David's census (2 Sam 24:6). The name is not mentioned elsewhere, and the text is uncertain. The RSV follows Wellhausen's palaeographical* reconstruction and renders "to Kadesh in the land of the Hittites,*" that is, the Kadesh on the Orontes River, to which David's kingdom extended at the height of its power.

EMB

TALPIOTH (tal′ pē ŏth; Heb. תַּלְפִּיוֹת, *talpiôt*). A suburb of Jerusalem,* where, in 1945, a collection of ossuaries* was discovered which could be very early evidence of Christianity. Two of the containers bore the name "Jesus"—a not uncommon name at the time, for it was the Greek form of "Joshua." A second word in each case seemed to read "woe" and "alas," and there was the rough sign of a cross, marked in one case in charcoal,* and in the other deeply cut into the soft stone of the ossuary. Most of such burial places in the near vicinity of Jerusalem must be dated before A.D. 70, after which life was less vigorous, and more poverty stricken in what was left of Jerusalem and its people. They cannot be dated after A.D. 135 and Hadrian's foundation of a non-Jewish Aelia Capitolina.* A coin* of Agrippa I, in the case of the Talpioth burial place, may date the tomb 42/43. The interpretation of "woe" and "alas" has been strongly contested (e.g., J. P. Kane, *PEQ*, 103 [1971], 103–8), but the cross seems to be beyond doubt. Sukenik writes: "With regard to the crosses of our tomb, it would be unwise to insist that the cross had already become a venerated symbol of Christianity; these may be a pictorial expression of the event, tantamount to exclaiming, 'He was crucified.' My suggestion, therefore, is that the crosses and the graffiti* on ossuaries nos. 7 and 8 represent a lamentation for the crucifixion* of Jesus by some of His disciples" (*AJA*, 51.4 [1947], 351–65). This does not suggest in any way a wider use of the symbol. Another ossuary bears the name "Simeon Barsaba" (cf. Acts 1:23). It is not possible to draw firm conclusions and to postulate a Christian family with a name known in NT records, burying its dead with the accompaniment of a Christian symbol a decade from the crucifixion.

EMB

TAMAR. *See* TADMOR.

TANANIR. *See* GERIZIM, MOUNT.

TANIS (ta′nis; Heb. צֹעַן, *zōan*; LXX Τάνις, *Tanis*). The ancient Egyptian city* of Dja′net, Tanis, in the NE Delta. The early history of the town is obscure, apart from the laconic note of Hebron* being seven years older (Num 13:22), especially as it can no longer be identified with Avaris or Rameses.* In the later New Kingdom, the region was known as Sekhet Dja′, Fields of Tan(is), to which the OT "Field of Zoan" corresponds closely (Ps 78:12,43).

By the end of the Twentieth Dynasty, Tanis was a growing satellite town of Rameses to its S and had become an important trading port with Phoenicia.* At the death of Ramses XI, its ruler Smendes founded the Twenty-first Dynasty (c. 1170 B.C.), and Tanis then became joint capital with Memphis,* replacing Rameses as Delta residence of the kings. This status Tanis retained for some five hundred years, throughout the Twenty-second into the Twenty-fifth Dynasty. Even after c. 655 B.C. (when Sais replaced it), Tanis remained important. As Zoan, its place in Ezekiel (30:14) and Isaiah (19:11,13; 30:4) is obviously one of importance.

BIBLIOGRAPHY: P. Montet, *Les Nouvelles Fouilles de Tanis* (1933); id., *Tanis* (1942); H. Kees, *Tanis* (1944); A. H. Gardiner, *Anc. Egyp. Onomastica*, 2 (1947), 199–201; P. Montet, *Nécropole de Tanis*, 1–3 (1947–60).

KAK

TAR. *See* BITUMEN.

TARSHISH (tär shish; Heb. תַּרְשִׁישׁ, *taršîš*). This name seems basically connected with metals and their refining* (i.e., a generic word), but in the OT comes to be associated with two areas which were prominent in this respect. (1) At Ezion Geber* on the Red Sea* at the head of the Elanitic Gulf: thus Solomon's* fleet of "ships* of Tarshish" (1 Kings 10:22), meaning a refinery fleet. (2) The western Mediterranean, in connection with Phoenician* trade in metals and other commodities: thus Jonah's intended voyage to Tarshish (1:3; 4:2).

Most scholars therefore identify the name with Tartessus, the city* in SW Spain mentioned by Herodotus (4.152). The site is uncertain but was in the lower Guadalquivir near the mouth of the Baetis River, in an area rich in silver,* copper,* and lead,* and the Phoenicians and later the Greek Samians and Phocaeans exploited its wealth. Herodotus records that the Samians, after the visit of the seaman Colaeus to Tartessus, dedicated to Hera a bronze* vessel* decorated with griffins' heads, which rested on three huge kneeling figures. A similar vessel, and small "kneeling colossi," have been discovered in France (*CAH*, vol. of pl. I, 352a–b).

BIBLIOGRAPHY: A. Schulten, *Tartessos* (1922); J. M. Blazquez, *Tartessos* (1968); S. Moscati, *The World of the Phoenicians*, trans. A. Hamilton (Eng. ed. 1968), 231–32; B. Rothenberg, "Ancient Copper Industries in the Western Arabah," *PEQ*, 94 (1962), 5–71; R. F. Gribble, *ZPEB*, 5 (1975), 597–98.

BFH

TARSUS (tär′ sas; Gr. Ταρσός, *Tarsos*). The city* Paul mentioned five times in the book of Acts. It is located on the SE coast of Asia Minor,* in the province of Cilicia.* The excavated part of the city, a mound on the SW side called Gozlu Kule, shows habitation from the Neolithic* period and was a fortified town in the third millennium B.C. There was also evidence of architecture and objects of the Hittite* Empire (1400–1200 B.C.) and its destruction by the Sea Peoples* about 1200 B.C. The Black Obelisk of Shalmaneser* (850 B.C.) mentions Tarsus as one of the cities captured. In 333 B.C. Alexander saved the city from destruction by the Persians. Tarsus became capital of the Roman province of Cilicia in 67 B.C., and it was here that Cleopatra met Mark Antony in 41 B.C. The apostle Paul was born and educated here in the Roman city, a fact which he proudly asserts in Acts 21:39. Unfortunately the city of his time lies buried beneath the modern town. A small Roman theater* has been excavated, and there are remains of a huge temple foundation. The digging for the construction of a courthouse in 1947 unearthed a large Roman building decorated with mosaics.* The Cydnus River, which flowed through the Roman city, is now silted up, and its inland harbor-lake is a marsh, but Tarsus is still on the main road from E to W through the Cilician Gates.

BIBLIOGRAPHY: W. M. Ramsay, *The Cities of St. Paul* (1908), 85–224; D. Magie, *Roman Rule in Asia Minor* (1950), 272, 1146–48; H. Goldman, *Excavations at Gözlü Kule, Tarsus*, 1, 2 (1950, 1956); E. M. Blaiklock, *Cities of the NT* (1965), 18–22; id., *ZPEB*, 5 (1975), 598–603.

BCC

TARTESSUS. *See* TARSHISH.

TAVERNS, THREE. *See* THREE TAVERNS.

TAXES. It is difficult in all pre-Roman records of ancient history to distinguish taxes as the modern world knows them (the citizen's contribution to the expenses of a state) from tribute (the sign of submission and the penalty imposed upon the defeated; *see* BOOTY) and from the tithe, which was a feature of Hebrew law. References are many to such exactions and their collection from a perennially unwilling and often oppressed community. They extend from Joseph's corn tax to the burdens of Solomon's* golden age (when forced labor and taxation were a cause of the division that followed his reign) to the taxgatherers of NT times.

Archaeological evidence is scattered and meager. A situation illustrative of the discontent and burdensome taxation which precipitated the revolt of the Ten Tribes under Rehoboam, comes to light from a document from Lagash* of 2500 B.C. Lagash, once self-contained and prosperous, had been led into poverty by its rulers' bellicose ambitions of self-aggrandisement. The historian records the activities of the ubiquitous inspector, seizing the boatman's boat for tax delinquency, appropriating the fisherman's fish, and with age-old inventiveness, imposing taxes on every activity of life, shearing, divorce—

Royal ("lamelekh") two-winged scarab seal impression on pottery jar handle found at Ramat Rahel, from seventh century B.C. It reads: "[Belonging] to the king/Hebron." To the left is a private seal impression: "[Belonging] to Nera/[son of] Shebna." Courtesy Israel Dept. of Antiquities and Museums.

even death itself. Urukagina* appeared, the document declares, and by the mercy of heaven cut death duties in half, abolished the tax on wool, reduced the levies on all private enterprise, and so lifted the burden from the heavy-laden people that the ancient document could conclude: "There was no tax collector."

Archaeological evidence of taxation in Israel* and Judah* is small. Some jar handles from Gibeon* and Lachish* marked "for the king" would appear to be of the same order as the wheat container in the small museum at Chesters, on the Roman wall in Britain—measures for exactions in kind. The silver* denarii of Augustus* and Tiberius,* bearing Caesar's "image and superscription" (Matt 22:20) are common enough. The census (Luke 2:2), of which numerous papyrological records exist, was designed for "taxing"—or for the collection of tribute and met the social resistance that such imposition always provoked (Acts 5:37)—and which was to become a way of life in a much later Rome. The poor of Egypt,* as is known from numerous papyri, were heavily burdened by taxation, rendered the more oppressive by the illegal exactions of the tax collector. This group of hated officials throve on the iniquitous system of tax-farming, whereby the collection of dues from a stated area was auctioned to the highest bidder. "Do not threaten blackmail or slander, but carry on your business according to the law," runs a papyrus* circular of the early first century (cf. Luke 3:13).

Egyptian ostraca* from the first and adjoining centuries throw light upon the conditions of taxation at that time. There are receipts for taxes on baths, olive* oil, land, grain, ferryboats and ferrymen, dikes, salt,* bricks (both royal monopolies), wine,* and cobblers, strangers, and weavers. Many receipts from weavers have been found, and no doubt Paul had to pay some such tax as this.

The tax upon many commodities, such as vegetables, clothes,* cattle, could not be standardized, so that the amount was left to the judgment of the tax collector—leading to constant injustice.

Many of the ostraca are receipts for the poll tax. One of these which was given to Psemmonthes and his wife Tachoulis, July 29, A.D. 68, is dated in the fourteenth year of Nero—which seems to indicate that the people of Thebes* had not heard of Nero's death seven weeks after it had occurred.

The only business which was not taxed in Palestine seems to have been fishing (Delitzsch, *Jewish Artisan Life*, 47).

The tax upon wine shops is almost as much in evidence as the poll tax. Religious organizations were also compelled to pay a tax; indeed, the place of prayer (*proseuchē*) was taxed higher than either manufacturers or taverns. Almost the only business which had to pay a larger tax than these churches or "places of prayer" were the houses of prostitution. Petrie found at Koptos a tax report in which seamen were taxed 5 drachmae, skilled artisans 8, prostitutes 102.

It is a fact that oppressive taxation, amply documented from literary and numismatic sources proved a major reason for the collapse of the Western Roman Empire. The taxpayer was finally exhausted.

EMB

TA'YINAT, TELL. *See* TELL TA'YINAT.

TAYLOR PRISM. This is the name given to a hexagonal cylinder now in the British Museum which bears an account of Sennacherib's* "Wolf on the Fold" raid into Judah.* It is dated 701 B.C. and runs in part: "In my third campaign I went up against Syria. Elulaeus (*Lule*) king of Sidon* . . . I defeated. His strong cities . . . bowed in submission at my feet. Ethbaal (Tuba'lu) I seated on the royal throne over them . . . But Sidka king of Ashkelon* who had not submitted to my yoke . . . I tore away and brought to Assyria.

"As for Hezekiah the Jew, who did not submit to my yoke, 46 of his strong walled cities, as well as the small cities in their neighbourhood which were without number—by escalade and by bringing up siege-engines [*see* ENGINES, WAR], by attacking and storming on foot, by mines, tunnels, and breaches, I besieged and took: 200,150 people great and small, male and female, horses,* mules, asses, camels,* cattle and sheep without number, I brought away from them and counted as spoil.

"Himself [Hezekiah] like a caged bird I shut up in Jerusalem,* his royal city. Earthworks I threw up against him. The one coming out of his city gate I turned back to his misery.

"The cities of his, which I had despoiled, I cut off from his land, and to Mitinti king of Ashdod,* Padi king of Ekron,* and Silli-bel king of Gaza* I gave them. And thus I diminished his land. I added to the former tribute [*see* BOOTY AND TRIBUTE] and laid upon them their yearly payment, a tax* in the form of gifts for my majesty.

"As for Hezekiah, the terrifying splendour of my majesty overcame him, and the Arabs and his picked troops, which he had brought in to strengthen Jerusalem his royal city, deserted him.

"In addition to 30 talents of gold* and 800 talents

The Taylor Prism. Reproduced by courtesy of the Trustees of the British Museum.

of silver,* there were gems, antimony, jewels, large sandu-stones, couches of ivory,* elephants' hides, tusks, maple, boxwood, all kinds of valuable treasures, as well as his daughters, his harem, his male and female musicians (see MUSIC) which he had them bring after me to Nineveh,* my royal city. To pay tribute and to accept servitude, he dispatched his messengers."

It should be noted that Jerusalem's defiance is slurred over but is consistent with the Assyrian account. The tribute is admitted in the OT (2 Kings 18:14). Discrepancies between Sennacherib's claims and the biblical record are not important in the light of the usual royal boasting of the Assyrian records.

BIBLIOGRAPHY: L. L. Honor, *Sennacherib's Invasion of Palestine* (1926); *ANET* (1950), 287–88; *DOTT* (1958), 64–69; D. J. Wiseman, *ZPEB*, 5 (1975), 338–42. EMB

TEIMA. See TEMA.

TEL. The Hebrew equivalent of the more common Arabic tell.*

TEL ASSAR (THELASSAR) (tel'as ər; Heb. תְּלַאשָּׂר, *t^elas̄ār*). The town of the "children of Edom*" listed by Sennacherib* as one of the many overrun and obliterated by the aggressive hosts of Assyria. The name occurs twice in the Bible (2 Kings 19:12; Isa 37:12) and, according to D. J. Wiseman, means "mound of Assur." The first element (tel; see TELL) of the name suggests a site of ancient habitation. No certain identification is possible, and Wiseman disapproves of the emendation of Grollenberg (*Atlas of the Bible*, trans. and ed. by Joyce M. H. Reid [1956], 164) to Tell Bassor. In areas so ravaged by man-made and natural devastation, geographical precision is not always possible. EMB

TEL AVIV. The great, rapidly growing Israeli port, one of the youngest major cities* of the world, covers at least twenty ancient sites of habitation, extending, like every complex of remains on that ancient coast, from Neolithic* to Hellenistic and Roman times. They have come to light during building operations. Two periods are of some interest. The area seems to have been important in the Middle Bronze Age* when Egypt* and the adjacent Palestinian coast was dominated by the Hyksos,* and in the Hasmonean period when, according to Josephus (Jos. *War* 1.99) Alexander Jannaeus flung a system of earthwork defenses from Antipatris* to Joppa* (an extension of modern Tel Aviv) to bar the path of Antiochus Dionysus. Remains have emerged at two points in Tel Aviv, constituting another archaeological vindication of Josephus. They are in the form of two considerable towers,* dated by contemporary pottery* and a coin* of Alexander. EMB

TELEILAT GHASSUL. A Bronze Age* site N of the Dead Sea* whose remains have given a name to the Ghassulian Culture.* The Jesuits Alexis Mallon and Robert Kneppel excavated the site between 1929 and 1938. The village was notable for its well-constructed stone houses* and its advanced fresco painting,* but is of no direct biblical significance. EMB

TELL. The Arabic for "hill," or "mound," equivalent to the Hebrew *tel*, the Persian *Tepe*, and the Turkish *Hüyük*. A tell commonly contains the remains in stratified form of earlier human habitations and is thus of great archaeological value.

TELL ABIL. See ABILA.

TELL ABU HUREIRAH. See GERAR.

TELL AHMAR. See TIL BARSIP.

TELL AL-'UBAID (tel al ū'bid). This small mound, or tell,* representing one of the earliest settled civilizations of Mesopotamia,* is located 7.2 km. (4½ mi.) NW of Ur.* Early ruins were explored in 1919 by H. R. Hall, and serious excavation of the site began

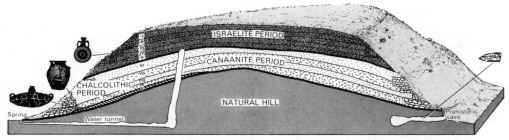

Schematic section of tell. Courtesy Carta, Jerusalem.

in 1923 under C. L. Woolley. The mound gave its name to the fifth millennium B.C. Obeid culture, which is also represented elsewhere in Mesopotamia, and is related to the lowest levels excavated at Susa,* on the island of Bahrain, and at other localities. Earliest Obeid houses* were made of reeds lashed together and coated with mud, and these were followed by sun-dried mud-brick buildings, whose walls were often decorated with patterns of baked clay* cones. One of the oldest temples known to man comes from this period at another site (Tepe Gawra,* level XIX). Obeid pottery* was an attractive greenish ware, much of it being handmade and decorated with painted* geometric designs. Pottery and other objects from this early period were conspicuous in the lowest levels at Ur, the home of Abraham. Early contacts between the Obeid culture and India are seen in the presence in early Mesopotamia of beads made from Indian lapis lazuli* and amazonite. This early culture was subsequently taken over by the Sumerians* at Ur and other sites in the southern Mesopotamian marshes.

BIBLIOGRAPHY: H. R. Hall and C. L. Woolley, *Ur Excavations, I, Al-'Ubaid* (1927); C. L. Woolley, *Ur of the Chaldees* (1929); id., *Excavations at Ur* (1954); *CAH*, 1, part 1, 327 passim. RKH

TELL ARAD. *See* ARAD.

TELL ARPACHIYAH (-är pə kē'yə). A small but important prehistoric mound 6.4 km. (4 mi.) N of Nineveh,* situated in a fertile area. A peaceful community, Arpachiyah must have relied upon Nineveh as a trading mart and as a place of refuge.

Excavations were conducted at the site by M. E. L. Mallowan in 1933 for the British School of Archaeology in Iraq and the British Museum.

Arpachiyah's importance lies in the great wealth of Halaf (fifth millennium B.C.) ware which the tell* produced. In the VIth level from the top the excavators found a craftsman's* shop, which had been razed by fire. Many pieces of the fine, polychrome Halaf-type pottery* were discovered here, along with thousands of flint and obsidian chips.

Of considerable interest are the ten *tholoi*, or circular building foundations, that were found in the various levels. A tholos found in level X is the earliest known example of domical construction in Mesopotamia.* Some of the later tholoi had antechambers and were similar in pattern to the much later My-

cenaean* tholos tombs. The Arpachiyah tholoi were not graves,* however; they may have been shrines.

Level VI was destroyed by newcomers from the S, who brought with them the cruder Ubaidian ware. The Ubaidian community, which was much poorer, no longer kept up the cobbled streets* of the Halaf people. Arpachiyah was abandoned by the beginning of the Uruk period (mid-fourth millennium B.C.).

BIBLIOGRAPHY: M. E. L. Mallowan and J. C. Rose, "The Excavations at Tell Arpachiyah, 1933," *Iraq*, 2 (1935), 1–78 [reprinted separately as *Prehistoric Assyria* (1935)]; M. E. L. Mallowan, "Recovered Skulls from Arpachiyah," *Iraq*, 31 (1969), 49–58; *CAH*, 1, part 1, 276 passim. EY

TELL ASHARA. *See* TERQA.

TELL ASMAR. *See* ESHNUNNA.

TELL ATSHANA. *See* ALALAKH.

TELL BALATA. *See* SHECHEM.

TELL BEITIN. *See* BETHANY.

TELL BEIT MIRSIM. *See* DEBIR.

TELL CHAGAR BAZAR. *See* HABOR RIVER.

TELL DEFENNEH. *See* TAHPANHES.

TELL DEIR ALLA. *See* SUCCOTH.

TELL DOTHA. *See* DOTHAN.

TELL ED-DUWEIR (-ed dū'wir). An ancient mound (tell*) lying 8 km. (5 mi.) SW of the modern village of Beit Jibrin, in the low hills to the W of Hebron.* It has been identified with biblical Lachish* because its topography and archaeological periods provide good correspondence to written records.

BIBLIOGRAPHY: O. Tufnell, C. H. Inge, and L. Harding, *Lachish II (Tell Ed Duweir), The Fosse Temple* (1940); W. F. Albright, *BASOR*, 68 (1937), 23–24; ibid., 74 (1939), 20–22; C. C. McCown, *The Ladder of Progress in Palestine* (1943), 100–117; *CAH*, 1, part 1, 514, 531; ibid., part 2, 210, 213, 218, 225–26, 228, 547, 576–77. JAT

TELL EL-AJJUL. *See* BETH-EGLAIM.

TELL EL-AMARNA. See AMARNA.

TELL EL-AREINI. See TELL SHEIKH AHMED EL-AREINI.

TELL EL-BEDEIWIYEH. See HANNATHON.

TELL EL-FAR'AH. See TIRZAH.

TELL EL FUKKHAR. See ACCO.

TELL EL-FÛL (-el fûl'). The site of ancient Gibeah,* Saul's capital. It lies about 4.8 km. (3 mi.) N of Jerusalem,* on a high point of the central mountain ridge, commanding a good view in all directions. It was excavated in 1922–23 and 1933.

BIBLIOGRAPHY: W. F. Albright, *The Archaeology of Palestine* (1960), 8, 14, 27, 111, 118, 120, 228; P. W. Lapp, "Tell el-Ful," *BA*, 28 (1965), 2–10.

JAT

TELL EL-HAMMAM. See SHITTIM.

TELL EL-HESY (HESI) (-el he'si). This notable tell* lies 11.3 km. (7 mi.) SW of Lachish* (Tell ed-Duweir*), strategically located to cover a valley which opened up the hill country which juts out into the coastal plain of Palestine W of Hebron.* It was an occupied site, of between .8 and 1.2 ha. (2 and 3 a.), from about 2600 to 400 B.C., a period interrupted several times by incidents of destruction. C. R. Conder first identified the stronghold as Lachish—a mistake accepted by the first excavators, Petrie and Bliss. The Wellcome-Marston expeditions of 1932 to 1938, directed by J. L. Starkey, established, however, the correct location of Lachish. It was W. F. Albright who eventually identified the tell with Eglon, an identification generally accepted. Tell el-Hesy has major importance in the history of archaeology in Palestine, for it was here that the stratigraphic* method was first applied in the course of Petrie's six weeks' work on the site in 1890. Petrie's datings* of pottery* were later considerably modified, but he and his successor on the site, F. J. Bliss, had successfully established a principle now universally accepted in archaeology.

The earliest occupation date (2600 B.C.) was established by an ax head in the lowest stratum which was similar to one found in a late Early Bronze Age* tomb at Jericho.* The fortifications later built demonstrated the glacis,* or protective incline, discovered at Taanach,* Shechem,* and Tell Beit Mirsim (see DEBIR).

The fortress, as Petrie and Bliss established, was destroyed about 1200 B.C., about the same time as Lachish, Bethel,* and Debir, in just such a planned campaign against the strong points of the land as the account of Josh 10 suggests. Eglon was one of an Amorite coalition led by Adonizedek of Jerusalem.*

BIBLIOGRAPHY: W. F. Albright, *BASOR*, 17 (1925), 7; id., *The Archaeology of Palestine* (1960), 8, 17–18, 29, 100, 103, 125.

EMB

TELL EL-HUSN. See BETH SHAN.

TELL EL-JEZER. See GEZER.

TELL EL KEFREIN. See SHITTIM.

TELL EL-KHELEIFEH. See ELATH; EZION GEBER.

TELL EL-KHUWEILFEH. See ZIKLAG.

TELL EL-MASKHUTA. See PITHOM; SUCCOTH.

TELL EL MILH. See ARAD.

TELL EL-MUTESELLIM. See MEGIDDO.

TELL EL-QADI. See DAN.

TELL EL-QEDAH. See HAZOR.

TELL EL-QOQA'. See AIJALON.

TELL EL-UKHEIMIR. See KISH.

TELL EL-YAHUDIYA (YEHUDIYEH). See LEONTOPOLIS.

TELL EN-NASBEH. See MIZPAH.

TELL ER-RAMITH. See RAMOTH GILEAD.

TELL ER-RAS. See GERIZIM, MOUNT.

TELL ER-RATABA. See PITHOM.

TELL ER-RUMEILEH. See BETH SHEMESH.

TELL ER-RUWEISI. See BETH SHEMESH.

TELL ESH-SHARIAH. See GATH.

TELL ESH-SHEIKH MADHKUR. See ADULLAM.

TELL ES SAFI. See GATH.

Battered brick corner structure of Persian Period fortification system, from Tell el-Hesi. Photo: T. Rosen (Tell el-Hesi, 1971).

TELL ES-SAIDIYEH. *See* ZARETHAN.

TELL ES-SEBA. *See* BEERSHEBA.

TELL ES-SULTAN (-es sul'tən). This is generally regarded as the mound (tell*) of OT Jericho,* situated about 1.6 km. (1 mi.) NW of the modern city.* The perennial spring there attracted inhabitants by about 8000 B.C., and until its conquest by the Israelites after 1240 B.C. it was inhabited continuously. Kathleen Kenyon's work has shown that much of the mound is sixteenth century B.C. or earlier in date, with the lower levels being Neolithic.* Unfortunately the tell presents a confused archaeological picture due to indifferent excavation by Sellin and Watzinger in 1907–11, and by Garstang from 1929 to 1936, which in turn has aided the already vigorous forces of natural erosion. In particular, it is impossible to say anything with certainty about the nature of Jericho in the time of Joshua. The oldest town was graced with a stone revetment in the seventh millennium B.C., while pottery*-making was introduced there in the fifth and fourth millenniums B.C. By 3200 B.C. Jericho had become a typical Early Bronze Age* walled town, but a millennium later had been conquered and resettled, probably by the Middle Bronze Age Canaanites.* It was overthrown again c. 1600 B.C., presumably by the Egyptians, and later became a Hyksos* fortress. By the period of the Hebrew conquest Jericho served as a fortress to block the approach to Canaan. Since the accounts of Josh 3–8 reflect accurately the topography of the area, there seems little doubt that the city itself corresponded to the general descriptions furnished by the narrative. For centuries after Joshua's curse (Josh 6:26) no attempt was made to rebuild the city, though the oasis was still frequented (Judg 3:13; 2 Sam 10:5). Hiel refounded Jericho in the Iron Age* (cf. 1 Kings 16:34). Remains are fragmentary, but the city survived to postexilic times. NT Jericho was situated S of the great mound.

Jericho, where a human community gathered round a sure water supply, and in the course of time combined to form an organized society, a state, in short, preoccupied with social problems such as fortification and defense, is an obvious alternative to the doctrines propounded by Toynbee, who saw such phenomena as a "response" to the "challenge" of the great rivers.

BIBLIOGRAPHY: J. L. Kelso, *AASOR* (1955), 29–30; K. M. Kenyon, *Digging Up Jericho* (1957); id., *Excavations at Jericho*, 5 (1960), 1–2; H. Jamieson, *ZPEB*, 3 (1975), 451–55.

RKH

TELL EZ-ZAKARIYEH. *See* AZEKAH.

TELL FAKHARIYA. *See* GOZAN.

TELL HALAF. *See* GOZAN.

TELL HAMUDI. *See* HABOR RIVER.

TELL HANNATON. *See* HANNATHON.

TELL HARIRI. *See* MARI.

TELL HASSUNA (-ha sū'nə). This site, immediately S of modern Mosul, was excavated by the Iraq Museum in 1943, 1944, which unearthed the early Neolithic* settlement dated c. 5000 B.C. Flint and obsidian weapons and tools* were recovered, along with coarse Neolithic pottery.* The primitive huts were later followed by crude houses,* marking one of the earliest village settlements in northern Mesopotamia.* It is a striking example of a village culture hinted at in the early chapters of Genesis where small farming provided human needs, and metals were not yet used. Burials (e.g., infant skeletons in pottery jars with containers for food and water at hand) have been thought to suggest belief in immortality.

BIBLIOGRAPHY: S. Lloyd and F. Safar, *JNES*, 4 (1945), 255–89.

RKH

TELL HAUSH. *See* BAAL GAD.

TELL HISN. *See* HELIOPOLIS.

TELL HUM. *See* CAPERNAUM.

TELL IRAQ EL-MENSHIYEH. *See* TELL SHEIKH AHMED EL-AREINI.

TELL JEMMEH. *See* GERAR.

TELL JOKHA. *See* UMMAH.

TELL KHELEIFEH. *See* EZION GEBER.

TELL MARDIKH (-mär'dik). A site in Syria about 48.3 km. (30 mi.) S of Aleppo,* where a team of Italian archaeologists excavating in 1975 made a major discovery when they uncovered the ruins of a Semitic kingdom that was at its height more than 4,300 years ago and lasted for about 800 years. Dr. Paolo Matthiae, Director of the Italian Archaeological Mission to Syria, had been excavating at the site since 1964 under the impression that the ruins were of a much later date. But in 1973 it became apparent that the site was of great antiquity, and the nature of the occupation even more clear in 1975, when a room in the royal palace was excavated which contained thousands of clay* tablets inscribed in a completely strange language. Dr. Giovanni Pettinato found in the ruins a bilingual vocabulary list of about a thousand terms in both Sumerian and the local language.

The list has helped greatly in the deciphering of this tongue, now known as Eblaite, after Ebla, the ancient name of the city-state which the mound represented. At the time of writing only a few tablets have been deciphered, owing to the difficult nature of the language. However, enough is already known to make it apparent that a large Canaanite* empire was flourishing in Syria between the twenty-sixth and the twenty-third centuries B.C. The name Ebla, which does not appear in the Bible, was not completely unknown previously, since it occurred in Hittite,* Egyptian, and Mesopotamian writings. But none of these references gave any indication as to the size and importance of the kingdom.

The 57-ha. (140-a.) site was surrounded in antiquity by reinforced walls,* entered through four gates* of different sizes. The city* was divided into two main sections, consisting of a lower area subdivided into four districts, each with its own leader, or nase (Heb. *nāsî*, "ruler"), and an upper, or acropolis,* section. In the latter were located the royal residences and the administrative offices, and, like the lower city, it was organized in terms of four areas. These contained the royal palace, a city palace which apparently controlled the administration of Ebla, a service palace which was perhaps responsible for supervising the labor forces of the city-state, and a "stables" division which no doubt organized the vast range of commercial activity for which Ebla was famous. At one stage in the history of the city it was inhabited by an estimated 260,000 people.

The period when Ebla was flourishing saw, among other things, the movement into Syria, and subsequently into southern Canaan, of a nomadic group later known as Hebrews. Dr. Pettinato was astonished to observe in photographic copies of the tablets a great many references to names familiar from the OT narratives. They included Abraham (Ab-ra-mu), Esau (E-sa-um), Saul (Sa-u-lum), Israel (Is-ra-ilu), and Eber (Ib-rum). The name David (Da-'u-dum) occurred more than a dozen times and was especially significant because, until the discoveries at Tell Mardikh, there had been no evidence for the use of the name elsewhere than in the OT in the ancient world. For Pettinato, the Ebla tablets established the Hebrew patriarchs and their names as historical realities. He also drew attention to the fact that in Ebla the leaders of conquered cities were described as "judges," which accounts for the Hebrew tradition of the premonarchy period.

Some of the tablets dealt with the history of the kingdom itself, describing a particularly influential dynasty of six kings: Igrish-halam, Irkab-damu, Arennum, Ib-rum, Ibbi-sippish, and Dubuhu-ada—the best known being Ib-rum. Pettinato saw in this name the root of the word "Hebrew," and if this man can be identified with the Eber who was described in Genesis as an ancestor of Abraham, it may be that in some manner he gave his name to the Hebrews. The tablets indicated the nature of ancient bureaucracy by stating that at one point the ruler of Ebla employed no fewer than eleven thousand civil servants and administrators.

The archaeologists have estimated that 80 percent of the texts deal with commercial and business matters. The economic records show that Ebla was an exporting center for timber, textiles, marble, and metals to such biblical sites as Hazor,* Gaza,* Megiddo,* and Jerusalem.* The mention of Jerusalem (U-ru-sa-li-ma) has proved particularly significant because it antedates by almost a thousand years any previous reference to this celebrated city. Sodom* and Gomorrah,* thought by many to have been more legendary than real, were mentioned in a commercial text, and thus were given firm historical status for the first time in an extrabiblical source. Ebla thus

appears not just as a small city-state in Syria, but rather as the hub of a vast commercial empire which engaged in trade with surrounding nations and, with Egypt* and Mesopotamia,* competed for domination of many of the minor kingdoms of Syria and Palestine. Not merely is it emerging as a major Ancient Near Eastern Semitic culture, but also as the possible locale for early Hebrew history.

In addition to the commercial tablets examined up to the time of writing, there are a number of cultic, ritual, and mythological texts, as well as incantations addressed to hundreds of deities. One cosmological tablet recorded that the heavens, earth, sun, and moon were created in that order, which corresponds exactly to the sequence in Genesis. Another tablet (*see* GILGAMESH EPIC) referred to a great flood sent by the god Enlil, well known in Mesopotamia as the deity who controlled the winds and storms. During the flood the angry god poured water down upon the earth for six days, a period of time which has more in common with Sumerian and Babylonian legends than with the account of Noah's flood in Genesis.

The religious and mythological texts are extremely valuable in that they are expected to provide more information about the pagan religions from which the early Hebrews parted company, but which continued to influence them to varying degrees for centuries to come. The Ebla gods appear to have comprised a mixture of Sumerian and Semitic deities, the principal one apparently being Dagon.* This god was perhaps the patron of agriculture,* and in the tablets was depicted as having the hands of a man but the body of a fish. Baal,* Chemosh,* and Ishtar* were mentioned in the religious texts, as also in various OT narratives.

Pettinato reported encountering the biblical name of God as YHWH in the form *Ya* in the Ebla tablets, and assumed that under Ib-rum this name came into general use. There is some doubt, however, about the accuracy of the reading, but even if correct it may only indicate an ending used to construct a hypocoristic, or "pet," name. Clearly more information is necessary before any firm association between a particular Eblaite deity and the God of Israel can be established.

Of the many amazing features of the Ebla tablets, one of the most important has been the discovery that Eblaite and the language of the biblical Hebrews have important affinities. Indeed, Eblaite appears to be of the same W Semitic family as Hebrew, even though it was inscribed on clay* in a combination of Sumerian logograms and the unfamiliar syllabic script of the Eblaite scribes. The affinity between names on the tablets and their counterparts in the OT narratives is particularly striking. Many of the names are identical in form, making it clear that if in fact the Hebrew patriarchs and their descendants did not actually reside in Ebla or the immediate vicinity, they certainly shared the same traditions of culture and moved in a geographical area in which those traditions received respect.

In addition to shedding light on the early traditions of Genesis, some of the tablets may compel a revision of certain traditional ideas. For example, one of the geographic texts described the city of Ur* as being located in Haran,* a site in N Mesopotamia, rather than in the lower Tigris-Euphrates valley, as the description "Ur of the Chaldees" implies (Gen 15:7).

Further clarification of this and similar matters is obviously desirable, but even before the Ebla materials had been discovered, certain scholars had suggested that some of the early Mesopotamian cities, including Ur, had had their names bestowed on other locations by migrant citizens, much in the fashion of more recent times. It must also be noted that at the point of writing there is no absolute proof that all the place-names mentioned in the OT are necessarily the same locations as those occurring in the tablets. No doubt the Ebla sources will have preserved many names of localities which have long since disappeared, since one tablet alone contained more than 250 geographical designations.

There can be no doubt that this material is some of the most important ever discovered as far as OT studies are concerned. The texts will have a far-reaching effect upon the understanding of the cultural and religious origins of the Hebrews and will doubtless help to explain the manner in which their own particular traditions were transmitted. The sources increase the stature of the ancient Hebrews by showing that they were evidently part of a vigorous urban civilization which in some areas rivaled the great Babylonian and Egyptian empires. Hitherto these had been thought to be the only two main cultures in the early history of civilization. Now a third must be added, namely that of the prominent Canaanite city-state of Ebla.

BIBLIOGRAPHY: P. Matthiae, *Orientalia*, N.S. 44 (1975), 337–60; *BA*, 39 (1976), 94–113; G. Pettinato, *Orientalia*, N.S. 44 (1975), 361–74; *BA* 39 (1976), 44–52; K. A. Kitchen, *The Bible in Its World* (1977); C. Bermant and M. Weitzman, *Ebla, A Revelation in Archaeology* (1979); G. Pettinato, *The Archives of Ebla* (1981); P. Matthiae, *Ebla, an Empire Rediscovered* (1981). HWP

TELL MUQDAM. *See* LEONTOPOLIS.

TELL NAGILA (-nə gi'lə). Located 30.5 km. (19 mi.) E of Gaza,* and but 5.6 km. (3½ mi.) SE of Tell el-Hesy,* this mound (tell*) covers about 4 ha. (10 a.) and rises some 6–7 m. (19–21 ft.) above the plain. Since it rests on a hill, the surface deposits are only 3–4 m. (10–13 ft.) deep. Excavations under R. Amiran and A. Eitan were conducted in four areas on top of the mound in 1962–63 and on the S slopes.

Fourteen strata from the Chalcolithic* to the Mameluke (A.D. 1500) period were discovered. The only extensive period of settlement, however, was the Middle Bronze* II B-C (1750–1550 B.C.) period of the Hyksos.* The mound owed its shape to the Hyksos beaten earth (glacis*) fortification. An early Proto-Canaanite inscription came from an uncertain context.

Among the few Late Bronze finds is a bichrome crater with vivid figures of a bull, a bird, and an ibex. There was a gap in settlement during the Iron I* (1200–1000 B.C.) period.

The identification of a large structure, covering 1 ha. (2½ a.), on the top of the mound is disputed. The four casemate walls* range from 83 to 104 m. (85 to 112 yd.) in length. Both Iron II and Arabic pottery* were found in the enclosure. S. Bülow, R. A. Mitchell, and G. E. Wright have interpreted the building as an Iron Age fortress (c. eighth century B.C.). But R. Amiran and A. Eitan believe that it was an Arab caravanserai (thirteenth–fifteenth century A.D.).

After excavations in the 1950s at Tell Sheikh Ahmed el-'Areini* demonstrated that this could not be Gath,* scholars proposed the site of Tell Nagila* for that elusive Philistine* city. A major disappointment of the excavations at Tell Nagila was the lack of Philistine ware and even a settlement in Iron Age I.

Some have proposed an identification of the mound as Eglon, though most scholars would prefer to place Eglon at Tell el-Hesy. Another suggestion is Dilean, mentioned but once in the OT (Josh 15:38).

BIBLIOGRAPHY: S. Bülow and R. A. Mitchell, "An Iron Age II Fortress on Tel Nagila," *IEJ*, 11 (1961), 101–10; R. Amiran and A. Eitan, "Tel Nagila," *IEJ*, 13 (1963), 143–44, 333–34; R. Amiran, "Tell Nagila," *RB*, 70 (1963), 568–69; ibid., 71 (1964), 396–99; R. Amiram and A. Eitan, "A Krater of Bichrome Ware from Tel Nagila," *IEJ*, 14 (1964), 219–31; id., "A Canaanite-Hyksos City at Tell Nagila," *ARC*, 18 (1965), 113–23, reprinted in *Archaeological Discoveries in the Holy Land* (1967), 41–48; G. E. Wright, "A Problem of Ancient Topography: Lachish and Eglon," *HTR*, 64 (1971), 447–48, reprinted in *BA*, 34 (1971), 85. EY

TELL NEBI MEND. *See* KADESH KAH.

TELLO (TELLOH). *See* AL-HIBA; LAGASH.

TELL QASILE (kə sēl'). A small 1.6-ha. (4-a.) but important Philistine* settlement discovered on the outskirts of Tel Aviv.* The tell* is located but a short distance from the mouth of the Yarkon River in an area of Kurkar sandstone, a material used for its buildings. It provides us with the best stratified evidence for Philistine pottery.*

B. Mazar excavated areas in the southern and western part of the tell from 1948 to 1950. In 1972 an area in the northern part of the mound was opened

Philistine temple from Tell Qasile, c. 12th century B.C., with raised platform and steps. Courtesy Israel Government Press Office.

up by T. Dothan and A. Mazar. Evidence of continuous occupation from the twelfth to the eighth centuries B.C. and from the Persian to the Arabic periods was found.

The deepest level, stratum XII, was founded by the Philistines in the mid-twelfth century. The site was fortified in stratum XI (eleventh century). From this same level came furnaces* with crucibles containing smelted copper. In the Philistine religious center of the town, a unique temple some 18 by 14.5 m. (19 by 15 yd.) was uncovered by A. Mazar in 1972. It contained a rich collection of religious and ritual objects and pottery, some of quite unique structure. The building's roof was upheld by two pillars in the middle also reminiscent of Judg 16:29. Stratum X was destroyed, perhaps by David. The final destruction of the site seems to have taken place in the eighth century by the Assyrians.

Tell Qasile continued to prosper under Israel.* Grain pits, stores for wine,* and fruit presses indicate a prosperous agriculture* which supplemented its strategic position for trade. B. Mazar has suggested that the cedars* of Lebanon may have been floated ashore at Tell Qasile (2 Chron 2:16; Ezra 3:7), rather than at Joppa* itself.

Before the excavations two important ostraca,* probably from the eighth century B.C., were discovered. One ostracon is an invoice of oil for export: ". . . of the king, one thousand and one hundred (measures) of oil." The other describes "Ophir gold to Beth Horon, 30 shekels," i.e., a shipment of fine gold* (cf. 1 Chron 29:4; Ps 45:9; Isa 13:12) for a temple of Hauron, a Canaanite* god.

BIBLIOGRAPHY: M. Avnimelech, "The Geological History of the Yarkon Valley and Its Influence on Ancient Settlements," *IEJ*, 1 (1950–51), 77–81; B. Maisler (Mazar), "The Excavations at Tell Qasile," ibid., 67–76, 125–40, 194–218; id., "Two Hebrew Ostraca from Tell Qasile," *JNES*, 10 (1951), 43–49; J. Kaplan, "The Archaeology and History of Tel Aviv-Jaffa," *BA*, 35 (1972), 56–95; A. Mazar, "A Philistine Temple at Tell Qasile," *BA*, 36 (1973), 42–48; A. Mazar, "Excavations at Tell Qasile, 1971–72," *IEJ*, 23 (1973), 65–71.

EY

TELL QERQUR. See QARQAR.

TELL RAS EL-KHARRUBEH. See ANATHOTH.

TELL SANDAHANNAH. See MARESHAH.

TELL SERA. See ESH-SHARI.

TELL SHEIKH AHMED EL-'AREINI (-shāk äh'med el ə re'ni). It is so-called from the tomb on the mound (tell*), and also known as Tell 'Irâq el-Menshîyeh from the deserted village to the S of the mound, and is one of the largest tells in the plain between the Philistine* coast and the Shephelah. Situated 24 km. (15 mi.) ESE from Ashkelon and 8 km. (5 mi.) NW of Lachish,* it lies at the opening of the valley which leads past Mareshah* to Hebron.*

The tell consists of a high mound of about 1.6 ha. (4 a.) rising 30 m. (32 yd.) above the plain, a high terrace of 24.8 ha. (62 a.), and a low terrace which merges into the plain. S. Yeivin conducted excavations primarily on the high mound and the edge of the high terrace from 1956 to 1961. Because of the discontinuity between the acropolis* and the high terrace, strata in these two areas were numbered separately.

Occupation on the high terrace lasted from the Chalcolithic* period until 2600 B.C. An important discovery in stratum V (c. 3100 B.C.) was a shard* with the name Narmer,* the Egyptian pharaoh usually identified with Menes, who was the founder of the First Dynasty.

The site was reoccupied in the Late Bronze Age* and a few Philistine* shards have been found in pits and cisterns.* The Canaanite* and the Philistine settlement, however, was confined to the small citadel* of the high mound. From the Israelite period jar handles "for the king" (of Judah*) from about the seventh century were discovered. The later strata on the acropolis were greatly disturbed by the intrusion of an Arab cemetery.

On the basis of 1 Sam 7:14, which seems to imply that Gath* was to be located in the opposite direction from Ekron* which was in the N, Albright in 1923 suggested that Tell el-'Areini was Gath. His arguments persuaded most scholars and the Israeli government, which renamed the mound Tel Gath and the new industrial city* just W of it Kiriath Gath.

When Yeivin's excavations failed to reveal a major Philistine settlement here, most scholars (except Albright) abandoned the identification. Kassis has tried to argue that Gath was really a Canaanite city under vassalage to the Philistines. The presence of royal Judean seals* also militates against the identification with Gath, as Gath was conquered by Sargon* in 712 B.C.

BIBLIOGRAPHY: W. F. Albright, "Contributions to the Historical Geography of Palestine," *AASOR*, 2–3 (1923), 1–17; B. Mazar, "Gath and Gittaim," *IEJ*, 4 (1954), 227–35; S. Yeivin, *First Preliminary Report on the Excavations at Tel "Gat" [Seasons 1945–1958]* (1961); id., *IEJ*, 9 (1959), 269–71; ibid., 10 (1960), 122–23, 193–203; ibid., 11 (1961), 191; id., "Early Contacts between Canaan and Egypt," *IEJ*, 10 (1960), 193–205; H. E. Kassis, "Gath and the Structure of 'Philistine' Society," *JBL*, 84 (1965), 259–71; W. F. Albright, *The Amarna Letters from Palestine; Syria, the Philistines and Phoenicia* (1966), 26; A. F. Rainey, "Gath of the Philistines," *CNFI*, 17.2–3 (1966), 30–38; ibid., 17.4 (1966), 23–34.

EY

TELL TAANNEK. See TAANACH.

TELL TA'YINAT (-tä'yi nat). An ancient city-mound (tell*) in N Syria, eastward from Antioch-on-Orontes; possibly the ancient Taiâ or Tae in inscriptions 600 and 772 of Luckenbill's ARAB,I. It belonged to the kingdom of Hattina (later, Unqi) of the ninth–eighth centuries B.C. and contained a small palace of the type called hilani and a still smaller temple about

23 m. (25 yd.) long. Fragmentary Hittite* hiero-glyphic* inscriptions mentioned King Halparuntas who paid tribute (see BOOTY AND TRIBUTE) to the Assyrians under Shalmaneser III, c. 857–848 B.C.

Biblically, the main fame of Tell Ta'yinat is the temple, because its ground plan closely resembles that of Solomon's* temple*—a porch, main hall, and holy of holies, with not dissimilar proportions.

BIBLIOGRAPHY: C. W. McEwan, *AJA*, 41 (1937), 8–16; W. F. Albright, *Archaeology and the Religion of Israel* (1953), 143 and n. 45; *ANEP* (1954), 739–40.

KAK

TEL MELAH (-me'lə). *Melaḥ* means salt,* and it is possible that the ruined city,* implied by the word tel (tell*), had been sown with salt (Judg 9:45). It was another locality, mentioned along with Tel Harsha, to which returning Jewish exiles were unable to es-tablish their lineage by genealogical proof. The site is unknown. It could be the Thelma of Ptolemy,* situated near a salty tract of terrain on the Persian Gulf.

EMB

TEMA (tē'mə; Heb. תֵּימָא, *têmā*). All contexts sug-gest a remote oasis, perhaps on one of the Arabian trade routes (Job 6:19; Isa 21:14; Jer 25:23). A sixth-century B.C. Aramaic* stele* discovered at modern Teima probably identifies the place. Tema is over 322 km. (200 mi.) NNE of Medina on an old road to Damascus* and must have been an important cara-van staging post. The reference in Isaiah may refer to a campaign of Tiglath-pileser III* in 738 B.C., which penetrated that part of Arabia.* Tema appears to have offered tribute (see BOOTY AND TRIBUTE) and so escaped assault. Jeremiah's predictions refer to similar military operations by Nebuchadnezzar.* Nabonidus,* last king of Babylonia, made Tema his residence while his son Belshazzar* was regent in Babylon* (*AS*, 8 [1958], 80). The sequence of events is recoverable from the relevant documents.

BIBLIOGRAPHY: C. M. Doughty, *Arabia Deserta*, 1 (1925), 285–300; J. A. Montgomery, *Arabia and the Bible* (1934), 58–68; S. Cohen, *IDB*, 4 (1962), 533; S. Barabas, *ZPEB*, 5 (1975), 621.

EMB

TEMENOS (tem'ə nōs; Gr. Τεμενος, *temenos*). A reserved piece of ground, especially a sacred precinct in which stood a temple or other building or sanc-tuary. The classical word *temenos* seems to have been of Homeric origin (Hom. *Il.* 18) and refers to a piece or parcel of land held by the king (lit. a "cut," or "section"), or one that was set aside for the temple complex, a kind of special landholding. The king was probably held to be divine, or near-divine, because his title (*wanax*) and the name of his special allotment of land (*temenos*) were used in later times in con-nection with the gods, and subsequently came to refer to the temple areas set apart for them.

There is no explicit biblical reference containing this word. In Greek architecture, a city* temenos normally contained a principal temple and perhaps

"Temple Oval" at Khafajah, Iraq; c. 2900 B.C. This is a reconstruction of the temple and its surrounding walls. Courtesy The Oriental Institute, University of Chicago.

one or two subsidiary temples or shrines, together with treasuries in which were stored the offerings* and processional regalia of other cities that held the presiding deity in esteem (as at Delphi). There were also stoas,* or colonnaded shelters, altars,* statues,* and votive columns (cf. Athens,* Ephesus*) which were set up in honor of deities, heroes, benefactors, or visitors in the games.* Also there were exedrae, i.e., semicircular seats or walled recesses for rest and contemplation, and sacred groves of trees (e.g., Olympia, Corinth,* Epidauros, Eleusis, Delos—all famous in Doric Greece, as well as the infamous Grove of Daphne, near Antioch* in Syria).

Roman architecture made lesser use of the teme-nos, in favor of the more openly standing temple and basilica.* A good example of Roman usage is the Temple of Venus in Rome (A.D. 123–25), built by Hadrian. The plan included a large centrally located temple, with a peribolus of columns surrounding the temenos. The temple had Pentelic columns, sculp-tured pediments,* and a roof covered with gold*-plated bronze* tiles,* which were later stripped off by Pope Honorius (A.D. 625) to be used in the con-struction of the church of St. Peter. Little remains of this complex.

No structure from the Neolithic* has been iden-tified as a temple with temenos. In Cyprus* a clay* model from the Early Bronze* period (to be seen in the Archaeological Museum at Nicosia) seems to rep-resent a rounded temenos containing a large seated figure, a woman and child, worshipers, and two bulls near the entrance.

The early development of the temenos is evident in both Mesopotamian* and Egyptian* archaeology. At Khafajah, a most impressive monument of the Early Dynastic II–III period is a sacred enclosure called the "Temple Oval," in the SW part of the city, separating the temple itself from the ordinary houses which surround it. This self-sufficient unit covered more than 3 ha. (7.4 a.), including its enclosure walls, large courtyard, workshops, and storage buildings, plus the sanctuary at one end and priest's house at the other. An inner perimeter wall separated the sanctuary from the priest's house. It may be noted that these temenos walls present very early evidence of the fortification concept in town-building—surrounding the temple and residence of the ruler, who is also the high priest.

In the earliest towns the temenos provided a focus toward the northern end, and its setting was either a natural hill or an artificial platform. This N location was selected because of the prevailing winds, which brought coolness and carried away the odors of the lower town. Examples are Kish, Tell Asmar, Ashur,* Dur-Kurigalzan, Khorsabad,* and Babylon.* At the latter city the temples were grouped within a temenos near the bank of the Euphrates River, and the palace was located at the N end of the city, surrounded by a double wall.*

In Egypt* the Temple of Karnak at Thebes* is enclosed with a temenos of trapezoidal shape, measuring 470–560 m. (514–612 yd.) by 470 m. (514 yd.) which was connected to an artificial lake. The earliest towns in the Near East were usually oval shaped, with an internal arrangement functionally related to the temenos or sacred enclosure surrounding the temple, as a kind of nucleus. The second enclosure, surrounding the palace was frequently rectangular, oriented by its corners to the cardinal compass directions and was in reality a citadel.* As time went on, the functions and designs of the temple and palace both diverged and coalesced.

BIBLIOGRAPHY: F. Banister, *A History of Architecture on the Comparative Method* (17th ed., 1963), 102, 188; A. Badawy, *Architecture in Ancient Egypt and the Near East* (1966), see index; W. A. McDonald, *Progress Into the Past: The Rediscovery of Mycenaean Civilization* (1967), 322–23.   MHH

TEMPLE. There are more than 250 biblical references to "temple," and they allude mainly to the temple of the Lord in Jerusalem* in its three phases of existence. The first temple (Solomon's*) was begun in 957 B.C. (1 Kings 6:1–7) and completed in seven years (1 Kings 6:38). In many passages this temple is called the "house" of the Lord (1 Kings

6:1). The first temple was very elaborate, constructed of white limestone (tradition points to the quarries in Jerusalem as the source). The interior was wainscoted with imported cedar* inlaid with gold.* The plan of Solomon's temple included an outer court with a large bronze* altar* for sacrifices and a brass laver (basin*) on the backs of twelve bulls for the ceremonial washings of the priests. In front of the temple was a porch, and inside, a long narrow nave called the Holy Place. It was not intended for congregations but housed symbolic, holy furniture: ten golden lampstands (*see* MENORAH), a gold-plated table for the Bread of the Presence, and a portable incense altar. A veil separated the Holy Place from the Most Holy Place (Holy of Holies) at the very back of the temple; behind the veil were the ark,* guarded by two cherubim,* and the mercy seat. The only facts from "dirt" archaeology that relate directly to Solomon's temple are the plans of pagan temples found in Egypt,* Mesopotamia,* Syria, Lebanon, and Palestine. Archaeologists have compared these various plans in search of parallels to the plan of Solomon's temple. A closer parallel exists between the temple and the tent, or tabernacle, the first "house of the Lord." The Solomonic temple was destroyed by the Babylonians in 587 B.C.

The second temple, that of Zerubbabel, who had been appointed governor when the Jews* were allowed to return to Palestine, was completed in 515 B.C. It was the least impressive, but longest lasting temple structure. It was built on the same site as Solomon's, but there are no details of its plan. It continued in sacred use and esteem until it was taken down for the building of Herod's temple. There is no archaeological evidence for the second temple.

The third temple (Herod's) is the one usually referred to in the NT. The Jews* include the Herodian phase with that of the second temple, in spite of the fact that it was a completely new and distinct edifice. Herod (*see* HEROD, BUILDING ACTIVITIES) began

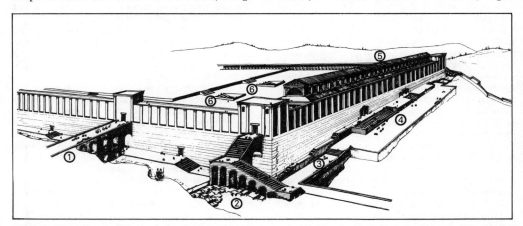

Restoration of western and southern wall of Temple Mount, Herodian Period: (1) "Wilson's Arch": bridge across Tyropoean Valley, joining upper city with Temple Mount; (2) "Robinson's Arch," previously believed to have been a bridge and now ascertained to be a span supporting stairs leading down from the Mount; (3) street leading to Hulda Gates; (4) stairs leading to Hulda Gates; (5) Royal stoa; (6) Tunnel openings leading under Temple Mount. Courtesy The Institute of Archaeology, Hebrew University, Jerusalem.

the work in the eighteenth year of his reign (20 B.C.), according to Josephus, in order to restore the temple to its former glory. Herod provided a thousand wagons, ten thousand workmen, and trained a thousand priests to work in the most sacred area. The basic structure was completed in about a year and a half, but the sanctuary was not completely finished for forty-six years (John 2:20), and the work in the outer courts may still have been going on when the temple was destroyed by Titus* in A.D. 70.

The plan was similar to Solomon's temple, but was larger and included more adjoining courts. Outside the main building where the Holy of Holies and the Holy Place were located was a porch; outside that was the Court of the Priests; and surrounding that on three sides was the Court of Israel. There were seven double gates leading up to the Court of Israel; one of these was on the E side, and opened into the Court of Women. Both the Court of Women and the Court of Israel were completely surrounded by a stone fence or partition; Gentiles were not permitted inside this fence. The rest of the temple mound was known as the Court of Gentiles;* it included colonnaded walkways on all four sides. The walkways on the E were called Solomon's Porch,* and are referred to in John 10:23; Acts 3:11; 5:12. The colonnades to the S of the Court of Gentiles were under the Royal Mansion and were called the Royal Portico. Just outside the NW corner of the Court of Gentiles was the fortified palace that Herod rebuilt and named Antonia, after his friend Antony.

The Dome of the Rock Mosque now stands over the site of the temple itself, and Muslim sanctity has shrouded the spot for centuries so that it has not been possible to conduct archaeological investigations. From time to time work has been done around the outside walls of the temple platform, and some interesting finds have come to light. Charles Warren was able to do some important work in 1867–70. By digging shafts and tunnels outside the supporting walls of the temple area, he found that Herod, in enlarging the area, had built the wall right on the bedrock. The characteristic Herodian drafted masonry can be seen at a number of places in the wall today. In 1864 Charles Wilson investigated an arch* (now called Wilson's Arch) that stretches W from the western wall of the temple platform; W. F. Stinespring has established (1963, 1965, and 1966) that the arch is an integral part of the Herodian wall and dates from the same period. The Arch of Titus* in Rome* (A.D. 81) depicts among the spoils carried off from Jerusalem in the destruction of A.D. 70, both the table and the lampstand (Menorah) from Herod's temple. Two of the stone slabs from the stone fence around the temple courts have been found; one (published in 1871) has the complete text of the warning that Gentiles must not enter.

In February 1968 new excavations began under Benjamin Mazar at the SW corner of the wall of the temple area. Beneath several strata of later remains extensive ruins from the Herodian period and the destruction of A.D. 70 were found. Evidence indicated that there was a massive stairway at this corner supported in part by Robinson's Arch and coming

down on a Herodian street* with shops and a public square. Thousands of coins* and mounds of pottery,* some of which may have been used in the temple sacrifices, also appeared. In front of the Double Gate, on the Herodian street,* was found a fragment of a stone utensil inscribed with the Hebrew word *corban*, meaning "dedicated"; it may have been an instrument actually used in the temple. A large aqueduct* uncovered here was also from the Herodian period. Other finds here included stoneware, weights,* and two sundials. These excavations have made possible a more precise conception of this corner as one of the main entrances of the temple in the time of Herod.

BIBLIOGRAPHY: A. Parrot, *The Temple of Jerusalem* (1957) has a comprehensive bibliography; L.-H. Vincent, *Jérusalem de l'Ancien Testament*, 1 and 2 (1954). There is much recent material in Hebrew University periodical publications.   BCC

TENTYRA. *See* DENDERA.

TEPE (te´pē). The Persian equivalent of tell.*

TEPE GAWRA (-gä´rə). A tall and narrow mound (tepe, or tell*) 22.5 km. (14 mi.) ENE of Nineveh* and but 3.2 km. (2 mi.) E of Khorsabad.*

Excavations at the site were conducted under E. A. Speiser and Charles Bache from 1931–38 for the American Schools of Oriental Research, the University of Pennsylvania Museum, and Dropsie College.

Some twenty-six building levels were found; all but the top six were prehistoric. The lowest level belonged to the beginning of the Ubaid period (early fifth millennium B.C.), and the latest level to the end of the fifteenth century B.C.

In level XIII of the late Ubaid period, the acropolis* featured three brilliantly colored temples. These were similar to temples of Eridu* in southern Mesopotamia.* The buildings were destroyed in a conflagration, marking the end of the Ubaid period. It seems that the wealthy of Gawra XII had sought refuge in the acropolis, but in vain.

A magnificent circular building 18–19 m. (59–62 ft.) in diameter stood on level XIA of the Uruk period. Gawra in later Uruk and Jemdet Nasr* periods was prosperous but was marked by a conservative lag in its continuing use of stamp seals.*

Gawra is the primary archaeological source for studying prehistoric Assyria and provides abundant finds which illustrate the development of metallurgy,* trade, and religion. Some of our earliest metal objects are from Gawra XIII. Thousands of beads were found in the burials; 750 cowry shells had their ultimate origin in the Indian Ocean. Lapis lazuli* had been imported from Afghanistan.

A stone model of a phallus in a Proto-literate level is a rare piece of evidence for circumcision, otherwise unknown from Mesopotamian sources.

BIBLIOGRAPHY: E. A. Speiser, *Excavations at Tepe Gawra I* (1935); A. J. Tobler, *Excavations at Tepe Gawra II* (1950); E. A. Speiser, "Mesopotamia—Evolution of an Integrated Civilization," in *At the Dawn of Civilization*, E. A. Speiser, ed. (1964), 178–92; M. E. L. Mallowan, "The Development of Cities from al-'Ubaid to the End of Uruk 5," *CAH*, 1, part 1, 377–98.

EY

TEPE SIALK (-si'älk). Midway between Tehran and Isfahan, Tepe Sialk is the most important prehistoric settlement which has been excavated in Iran. It is located 4 km. (2½ mi.) SW of the oasis of Kashan, bounded on the W by the Zagros Mountains and on the E by the great Dasht-i-Kavir Desert.

Two habitation mounds and two cemeteries (*see* NECROPOLIS) were excavated by Roman Ghirshman for the Louvre in three seasons during 1933–34, and 1937–38.

The earliest habitation of Sialk I (5500–4200 B.C.) was on the northern mound (tepe, or tell*) and was characterized by a late Neolithic* culture. The first settlers used reed and brushwood huts, which were eventually replaced by pisé (pounded earth) buildings. The dead were buried under the floors of the houses*—a practice which was maintained through the fourth millennium B.C. Pestles (*see* MORTAR) indicate the use of cosmetic paints,* and hammered copper objects represent the oldest metal work in Iran.

During Sialk II (4200–4000 B.C.) houses were made of hand-molded brick and were decorated with red paint. The handmade pottery* features vivid animal figures.

The people of Sialk III (4000–3200 B.C.) abandoned the northern mound and moved to the southern mound. Although many of the buildings were built on a grand scale, some of the doors were but 1 m. (3 ft.) high. The use of cast copper was an innovation, as was the use of the potter's wheel, which was probably introduced from Mesopotamia.* The settlement was apparently sacked.

The most important feature of Sialk IV (3200–c. 2700 B.C.) is the presence of tablets inscribed in Proto-Elamite, a script found also at Susa* and at Tepe Yahya (in SE Iran). The increased use of lapis lazuli* from Baluchistan indicates more intensive contacts with the E.

After a gap of about 1500 years Sialk was settled once more in Iron Age I.* Sialk V (1300–1000 B.C.) is represented by finds made in Cemetery A. The pottery is almost entirely grey-black ware, which is similar to that found at a number of sites in northwestern Iran.

Evidence for Sialk VI (1000–c. 750 B.C.) comes from Cemetery B. The graves* are covered by gabled roofs, which indicate links with the N. Most distinctive are highly decorated jars with long spouts. Warriors and horses* are favorite subjects of the artists. On the mound itself a massive terrace was constructed for the ruler's citadel.* There seems to have been a sharp distinction between the rich and the poor both in the city of the living and of the dead. The settlement was finally destroyed by the Assyrians.

Ghirshman had argued that the people of Sialk VI must be the first Iranians; the Medes* and the Persians are first mentioned in Assyrian sources in the ninth century B.C. T. Cuyler Young, Jr., however, has suggested that the widespread culture represented by Sialk V should be considered our first evidence for the Iranians. By 1977 Girshman agreed that the evidence from Cemetery A was to be associated with the earliest Iranians.

BIBLIOGRAPHY: R. Ghirshman, *Fouilles de Sialk près de Kashan* (1938–39); id., *Iran* (1954), 29–37, 42–50, 73–88; id., *The Art of Ancient Iran* (1964), 1–23; E. Porada, *The Art of Ancient Iran* (1965), 23–28, 105–6; T. C. Young, Jr., "The Iranian Migration into the Zagros," *Iran*, 5 (1967), 11–34; *CAH*, 1, part 1, 447–56; R. Girshman, *L'Iran et la migration des Indo-Aryens et des Iraniens* (1977).

EY

TERAPHIM (ter'ə fim; Heb. תְּרָפִים, *t*e*rāpîm*). Although its root meaning is unknown, the word in Scripture always signifies small and portable idols,* such as those Rachel stole (Gen 31:19, 34) which were Laban's household gods (31:30), or man-sized image (the word can be used for one idol, although in form it is always plural), such as that which appears to have been available to Michal, David's wife (1 Sam 19:13, 16). The use of teraphim in Israelite worship was, significantly, a practice in the darker days of the Judges (Judg 17:5; 18:14, 20; 2 Kings 23:24; Hos 3:4–5). Such images are archaeologically attested, and the Nuzi* documents make it clear that Laban's sons, not Rachel, had the right to hold the household teraphim as a guarantee of title and succession.

See NUZI.

BIBLIOGRAPHY: C. H. Gordon, *BA*, 3 [1940], 1–12; M. Greenberg, *JBL*, 81 (1962), 239–48; C. LaBuschagne, *VT*, 16 (1966), 115–17; A. E. Cundall, *Judges* (1968), 183–85; J. Oswalt, *ZPEB*, 5 (1975), 677–78.

EMB

TERQA (tür'kə). A city* on the middle Euphrates, 15 mi. (24 km.) below the confluence of the Euphrates and the Habor rivers. Probably one of several sites so named. Called Sirqu by Assyrian sources and Tell 'Ashara in modern times.

While little specific information about the earliest periods of the city is known, it was apparently, from Sumerian* times, a center of the worship of the Amorite* god Dagan (biblical Dagon*). The extension of Sumerian power into the "upper country," attested as early as 2450 B.C. in Mari,* provided probably the first contact between the Sumerians and the grain-god Dagan (*see* SAMSON). This development, continued and heightened by Sargon of Akkad* and all those following him, surely made Terqa an important cult center for Mesopotamians* from that time on.

The great Shamshi-Adad I of Assyria (c. 1814–1782 B.C.) came, according to the Assyrian King List (cf. A. Ungnad, "Datenlisten," *Reallexikon der Assyriologie*, vol. 2, 187ff.), from Terqa, whose temple he built (possibly rebuilt) after becoming established as ruler in Babylon.* Following the death of that king, the nearby city of Mari regained its prominence under Zimri-Lim and it is from this period and from Mari rather than from Terqa that we have the most extensive historical records of the latter place.

Hundreds of letters to and from Terqa attest to the political and religious situation of the city, including an intriguing reference to Banu-yamina, or Benjamites in the district (*ANET*, 482), and a dream story connected with the Dagan temple (*ANET*, 623f.).

Terqa, like Mari, fell within the kingdom of Hammurabi* for a brief period, following which it became the chief city of an independent kingdom called Hana. The early Amorite names of the rulers give way eventually to the Kassite* Kashtili-ashu, marking possibly the beginnings of Kassite rule in Mesopotamia. Later Kassite rulers were to sit in Babylon rather than Terqa, and by neo-Assyrian times Terqa is called Sirqu, and even the exact location of the city referred to may have changed. An important stele* of Tukulti-Ninurta II (890–884 B.C.), found in the ruins of Terqa in 1948, records the conquest of the city by that ruler. Subsequent Assyrian kings mention the city, which was probably a part of the empire until its dissolution. There is no reference to Terqa following the Assyrian period, and its fate in later times is not known.

Tell 'Ashara was identified as Terqa by Ernst Herzfeld in 1910 from an inscription found there, and the site was briefly excavated by Edouard Dhorme and Francois Thureau-Dangin in 1923, but most of the information above comes from the more extensive records found downstream at Mari. The stele mentioned above was discovered in 1948 and published by R. J. Tournay and Soubhi Saouaf.

In 1975 an American excavation began under the sponsorship of the Johns Hopkins University. This American expedition was expanded in the Fall 1976 with Giorgio Buccellati and Marilyn Kelly-Buccellati directing the work. Two further seasons of excavations followed in Spring 1976 and Fall 1977.

The three seasons of excavations have greatly supplemented the information obtained from Mari. Terqa is one of the few sites where it is possible to obtain an unbroken stratigraphic* record stretching from the Old Babylonian through the Middle Babylonian Periods. Manufacturing and storage facilities such as pottery* kilns* and bins have been found, in addition to numerous ceramic vessels,* stone tools,* human figures and other artifacts.* Of special importance is a cuneiform* tablet found in the second season that has striking similarities to the Mari tablets. Dated as belonging to the period following the end of Ur* III, it is significant evidence of a common scribal tradition at an early period. In the 1977 excavation, five more tablets, or fragments of tablets were found. Three of these are identified as contracts from the Hana Period, and with other artifacts, add valuable information concerning this major, but little known, cultural period. The excavation of Terqa's burial complexes (*see* NECROPOLIS) has also been significant.

BIBLIOGRAPHY: E. E. Herzfeld, "Hana et Mari," *RA*, 11 (1914), 131–39; F. Thureau-Dangin and E. Dhorme, "Cinq jours de fouilles a 'Asharah," *Syria*, 5 (1924), 265–93; R. J. Tournay and S. Saouaf, "Stele de Tukulti-Ninurta II," *AASy*, 2 (1952), 169–90; G. Buccellati and M. Kelly-Buccellati, "Terqa Preliminary Reports, No. 1: General Introduction and the Stratigraphic Record of the First Two Seasons," *SMS*, 1 (1977), 73–133; G. Buccellati, "Terqa Preliminary Reports, No. 2: A Cuneiform Tablet of the Early Second Millennium B.C.," ibid., 135–42; M. Kelly-Buccellati and L. M. Williams, "Terqa Preliminary Reports, No. 3: Object Typology of the Second Season: The Third and Second Millennia," ibid., 143–69; M. Kelly-Buccellati and W. R. Shelby, "Terqa Preliminary Reports, No. 4: A Typology of Ceramic Vessels of the Third and Second Millennia from the First Two Seasons," ibid., 171–236; A. Mahmoud, "Terqa Preliminary Reports, No. 5: Die Industrie der islamischen Keramik aus der zweiten Season," *SMS*, 2 (1978), 95–114; G. Buccellati and M. Kelly-Buccellati, "Terqa Preliminary Reports, No. 6: The Third Season: Introduction and the Stratigraphic Record," ibid., 115–64; O. Rouault, "Terqa Preliminary Reports, No. 7: Les documents epigraphiques de la troisieme saison," *SMS*, 2 (1979), 165–80.　　　　　　　　　　　　　　　　　　CEA

TETRARCH. *See* ROMAN GOVERNMENT, ADMINISTRATION. OF PROVINCES.

TEYASIR. *See* TIRZAH.

THAPSACUS. *See* TIPHSAH.

THEATER. A place for viewing, but also a convenient assembly point for a mass meeting of citizens, as in the Ephesian riot (Acts 19:29,31). It is used once in the NT literally (as just mentioned) and once figuratively (1 Cor 4:9). It is to be distinguished from the amphitheater,* which was a full circle or oval of seats (e.g., the Colosseum* at Rome*), whereas the theater was a semicircle, usually set into a hillside and achieving remarkable acoustic efficiency by the slope and angle of its seating, aided perhaps by the concave formation of the lower part of the seats. Notable examples are the fourth-century B.C. theater in the Peloponnesian town of Epidaurus (the best preserved theater of all, and a remarkable structure which seated something near ten thousand spectators), the theater of Dionysius in Athens,* set into the S side of the Acropolis,* and the theater spectacularly surmounting the temple of the oracle at Delphi. In biblical lands there are theaters in many areas where Hellenistic culture was dominant for any length of time—for example, the theater above the unique

Aerial view of Herodian theater at Caesarea. (*See also photo under* BETH SHAN.) Courtesy Israel Government Press Office.

oval forum of Jerash (ancient Gerasa*), and the solid little theater of Beth Shan,* as remarkable for its acoustic properties as the larger structures. The Herodian theater at Caesarea* has been restored and is now in use. The theater at Ephesus,* which may have held twenty thousand people, is at the head of the great axial street* of the city* and strikingly illustrates Acts 19.

BIBLIOGRAPHY: D. G. Robinson, *Greek and Roman Architecture* (1943), 164, 171; M. Bieber, *The History of the Greek and Roman Theater* (1961); F. B. Huey, Jr., *ZPEB*, 5 (1975), 714.

EMB

THEBES (thēbz; Heb. אָמוֹן נֹא, נֹא, *no, no-'amôn*; LXX Διόσπολις, *Diospolis*, Heb. from Egyp. for *"city"* [par excellence], *"city of [god] Amun"*). Thebes, now represented by spectacular ruins at modern Luxor* (some 528 km., or 330 mi., S of Cairo), was once Egypt's* most splendid city,* straddling the Nile. On the E bank was the town proper, with the vast temple-precinct (Karnak) of the god Amun and his "Southern Harim" at Luxor Temple. On the W bank was a line of funerary temples of the great New Empire kings just beyond the cultivated plain. The cliffs and sandy hills behind were pierced by the tomb-chapels of the nobles and curtained-off the desolate Valley of the Kings and Valley of the Queens, with the long tunnel-tombs of the kings, queens, and royal offspring.

Thebes existed already in the third millennium B.C. (Pyramid* Age) but only achieved prominence when her princes reunited Egypt c. 2040 B.C. (Eleventh Dynasty) and ushered in the prosperous Middle Kingdom era (Twelfth–Thirteenth dynasties). Hyksos* rule brought eclipse, but a new line of Thebans eventually ejected the alien line, again reuniting Egypt and ushering in the brilliant age of the New Kingdom or Empire (Eighteenth–Twentieth dynasties, c. 1550–1070 B.C.). At this time, the administrative capital was soon moved back to Memphis* as being more practical, but Thebes remained the southern capital and became the sacred city of Amun, a status it held for a further one thousand years. Unimaginable must have been the plunder carried off to Assyria at the sack of Thebes by Ashurbanipal* in 663 B.C. The echoes of that event were drawn upon by the prophet Nahum (3:8ff.) when he sought to proclaim the fall of Nineveh* in her turn—so resounding would her ruin be. After 663, the Thebans labored to repair and restore the damage; under the Saite kings, Thebes gradually lost political influence but retained her sacred fame for some centuries more. In their turn, Jeremiah (46:25) and Ezekiel (30:15–16) proclaimed again judgment on Thebes and other Egyptian centers. Persians, Ptolemies,* Romans, all both adorned and ravaged the sometimes rebellious city. In modern times, the wealth of scenes and inscriptions on the walls of temples and tombs and the mass of archaeological finds have yielded rich material for OT background studies.

BIBLIOGRAPHY: B. Porter, R. L. B. Moss, E. W. Burney, *Topographical Bibliography of Anc. Egypt . . . Texts . . .*, 2d ed., 1.1 (1960); ibid., 1.2 (1964); ibid., 2 (1971); C. F. Nims, *Thebes of the Pharaohs* (1965); K. A. Kitchen, *ZPEB*, 5 (1975), 714–17.

KAK

THELASSAR. See TEL ASSAR.

THELMA. See TEL MELAH.

THERIOMACHY. The reference to fighting with beasts (theriomachy) in 1 Cor. 15:32 is figurative, although many of the older commentators took it literally. Though he was a Roman citizen like Paul, the consul Acilius Glabrio was forced by Domitian* to fight with beasts, as a *bestarius*. *Christianos ad leonem* ("Christians to the lion") was, none the less, a cry of the cruel Roman proletariat, and, as archaeological evidence shows, Corinth* was the most Roman of imperial cities* outside Italy. Paul's metaphor was readily understood, and many Roman mobs saw Christians actually thrown to lions* and other beasts. Some archaeological evidence of theriomachy was discovered in 1973. The severed head of a bear and the bones of other animals, including panthers, were found under the Colosseum* in Rome,* where gladiators (and perhaps Christians) once fought with such wild beasts. Archaeologists found the material during an excavation into a rubbish heap under the arena.

EMB

THERMOLUMINESCENCE. See DATING, ARCHAEOLOGICAL.

THESSALONICA. The chief city* of ancient Macedonia,* situated on the Via Egnatia (see EGNATIAN WAY) at the northernmost part of the Thermaic Gulf. It also served as an outlet to the Aegean from the Danube area. The city (modern Salonika) was founded c. 316 B.C. and had a continuous history from which there are considerable Greek, Roman, and Byzantine* remains. The account of Paul's visit in Acts 17:1–10 refers to *politarchai* ("city officials," v. 6) and an inscription on the Vardar Gate at the W wall (destroyed in 1876) lists seven holders of this office in Thessalonica. Other inscriptions of the period attest the title for this and other Macedonian cities.

At the E end of the city is the arch* of Emperor Galerius, adjacent to which are the ruins of a Christian church apparently built over an earlier foundation. The sites of the agora* and hippodrome (see CIRCUS) have also been found.

BIBLIOGRAPHY: C. Diehl, M. Le Tourneau, and H. Saladin, *Les Monuments Chrétiens de Salonique*, 2 vols. (1918); O. Trafali, *Thessalonique des origines aux XIVe siècle* (1919); A. Rupprecht, *ZPEB*, 5 (1975), 727–29.

BFH

THOMAS, GOSPEL OF. Among the Nag Hammadi papyri* is a collection of 114 alleged sayings of Christ (see AGRAPHA), inaccurately called a gospel. Narrative is omitted, and the collection is of very unequal value. Some of the sayings are patently absurd and contrary to the NT record of Christ's teaching. For example: "They said to Him: Shall we then, being children, enter the Kingdom? Jesus said to them: When you make the two one, and when you make the inner as the outer and the outer as the inner and the above as the below, and when you make the male and the female into a single one, so that the male will not be male and the female not be female, when you make eyes in the place of an eye, and a hand in the place of a hand, and a foot in the place of a foot, and an image in the place of an image, then shall you enter the Kingdom."

These words refer to Mary, for they recur as the collection ends. "Simon Peter said to them: Let Mary go out from among us, because women are not worthy of the Life. Jesus said: See, I shall lead her, so that I will make her male, that she too may become a living spirit, resembling you males. For every woman who makes herself male will enter the Kingdom of Heaven."

And again: "Blessed is the lion which the man eats and the lion will become man; and cursed is the man whom the lion eats and the lion will become man."

Others repeat or distort known sayings. Others are clearly influenced by some form of mystical belief or deviant practice. Still others are new but contain shrewd wisdom and even a touch of authenticity. For example: "Be passers by . . ." and "the Kingdom of the Father is like a woman who was carrying a jar full of meal. While she was walking on a distant road, the handle of the jar broke. The meal streamed out behind her on the road. She did not know it; she had noticed no accident. After she came into her house, she put the jar down, she found it empty."

R. K. Harrison, who comments perceptively on the documents (*Archaeology of the NT*, chap. 7, 94), concludes: "While the *Gospel According to Thomas* cannot in any sense be considered as a 'fifth gospel,' it is of very great importance for quite a different reason. Along with the other writings from the monastic community at Nag Hammadi, it is an invaluable witness to the nature of a religious movement with which early Christianity came into contact. So far from undermining the Christian faith, the recently-discovered Coptic *Gospel* has actually rendered it an indirect service by demonstrating quite convincingly that there is no valid reason for questioning the genuine nature of the sayings of Jesus as recorded in the Four Gospels. Above everything else they have shown that behind the literary tradition of the Evangelists stands a Person whose words have been transmitted in substantially unchanged form by responsible New Testament authors."

Archaeology, we might say, reveals the struggle, which has not yet ended, between the simplicities of the Christian revelation and its Christ and the complicated philosophies of men, perennially eager to distort the straight, and darken the clear. The meal so easily pours from the cracked jar.

BIBLIOGRAPHY: J. Jeremias, *Unknown Sayings of Jesus* (1957); J. Doressé, *Les Livres secrets des gnostiques d'Égypte* (1958); id., *L'Évangile selon Thomas* (1959); A. Guillaumont, H-Ch. Puech, G. Quispel, W. Till, and T. 'Abd Al Mash, trans., *The Gospel According to Thomas* (1959); W. C. van Unnik, *Newly Discovered Gnostic Writings* (1960); B. Gärtner, *The*

Theology of the Gospel According to Thomas (1961); R. K. Harrison, *Archaeology of the NT* (1964); D. M. Scholer, *Nag Hammadi Bibliography, 1948–1969* (1971), 136–65; R. McL. Wilson, *ZPEB*, 5 (1975), 735–36.

EMB

THREE TAVERNS. The name is a translation of the Latin* designation (*Tres Tabernae*) of a staging-post 53 km. (33 mi.) S of Rome.* It should possibly be rendered Three Shops. The place is epigraphically* attested (*CIL* 10.685). It stands at the junction of the Appian Way* and the side road to Antium, near the modern town of Cisterna, 16 km. (10 mi.) nearer Rome than Forum Appii. It owed its importance to the fact that it was one day's journey from Rome* for fast travelers proceeding S from the city to Brundisium, the port for Greece and intermediate places (cf. Acts 28:15; Cicero *Att.* 2:12). Hence it was that representatives of the Roman Christian community met Paul's party here.

BIBLIOGRAPHY: *PWRE*, 2.4.2 (1932), col. 1875.

EMB

THRONE. See FURNITURE.

THYATIRA (thi ə tī rə). Inscriptions are a major source of archaeological material, and from Thyatira, the fourth city* of the Apocalypse, they are numerous. Thyatira's valley was a broad and ancient highway of trade, and in the days of the Roman peace (*pax Romana*) the city became, like Laodicea,* a center of busy commerce. More trade guilds, those ubiquitous ancient associations of businessmen and craftsmen,* have been identified in Thyatira than in any other Asian city. Inscriptions mention workers in wool, linen,* leather,* and bronze,* as well as dyers,* tanners, potters,* and bakers.

The people of the Thyatira church were thus drawn from a commercial community, alive to salesmanship, keen to do business, and alert to capture trade. Lydia,* it will be remembered, when she met Paul in distant Macedonia,* was a Thyatiran abroad with purple cloth* to sell. The trade guilds must have been an anxious problem to the Christian craftsman. He hardly could have attended the formal meetings and banquets without witnessing licentiousness and implicitly condoning pagan rites. It was the old Corinthian problem of "sitting at meat in the idol's temple" which confronted the struggling church. Archaeology, with its revelation of the scope of the city's trade organization, sets the moral dilemma in high relief. But as with Philadelphia* and Laodicea, little more than preliminary surveys have been carried out for the excavation of Thyatira. Systematic archaeological investigation will surely have much more to say on John's seven churches.

BIBLIOGRAPHY: E. M. Blaiklock, *The Cities of the NT* (1975), 107–11; id., *ZPEB*, 5 (1975), 743–46.

EMB

TIBERIAS. A town (modern Tabariyeh) on the W side of Lake Galilee,* about 24 km. (15 mi.) NE of Nazareth* and mentioned only in John 6:23. Named

Enlarged drawing of reverse side of bronze coin, 18 mm. The legend reads: "TIBE/PIAC" (Tiberias), where the coin was minted. The legend on the obverse side identifies the coin with Herod Antipas, A.D.29/30, who ruled Galilee from Tiberias. Courtesy Carta, Jerusalem.

in honor of Emperor Tiberius,* it was built by Herod Antipas (see HEROD, FAMILY OF) as the center of his tetrarchy and was laid out on the Greek model around a natural acropolis.* Josephus (Jos. Antiq. 17.2.3) says that many of its foreign and Galilean inhabitants remained under the patronage of Herod after he settled them there. Hadrian built a temple there, but the only remains today are of the wall, which appears once to have been 4.8 km. (3 mi.) in length, a synagogue* of Roman type, and a castle* (prob. Herod's). The place was a spa and remnants of the architectural accoutrements of the hot springs are visible.

Josephus states that the town was founded in A.D. 26, but numismatic evidence seems to contradict this. A coin* of Tiberias of Claudius's* principate, is dated the thirty-third year of the city, and Claudius died in A.D. 54. This would appear to thrust the date back to A.D. 21. Two coins of Trajan offer congruent evidence. Trajan's principate began in A.D. 98 and ended in A.D. 117, but the title "Dacicus" was conferred in A.D. 103. One of the coins omits this title while retaining the honorary designation "Germanicus." The coins are dated the eightieth and eighty-first years of the city's founding. If they date between A.D. 98 and A.D. 103, the evidence suggests again that Josephus's dating is several years too late.

BIBLIOGRAPHY: G. A. Smith, Historical Geography of the Holy Land (1973), 447–51; E. M. Blaiklock, ZPEB, 5 (1975), 745–46.

BFH and EMB

TIBERIAS, SEA OF. See GALILEE.

TIBERIEUM. The Latin* word is not noted by Lewis and Short's Latin Dictionary, probably because it is a recent discovery. The suffix is a Latinization of a Greek* ending meaning "the shrine of," and Tiberieum means "the shrine or temple of Tiberius.*" Its significance lies in the fact that the word occurs in a fragmentary dedication inscription from Caesarea,* which mentions Pilate (VS PILATVS) in the next line along with the customary abbreviations of date and dedication. Pontius Pilate evidently set up a shrine of the imperial cult, dedicated to the prince at the

Roman garrison town. In light of Pilate's clumsy and repeated attempts to conciliate Tiberius, the word and the inscription are of some importance.   EMB

TIBERIUS. This Roman emperor is mentioned in Luke 3:1. References to "Caesar" in Matt 22:17–21; Mark 12:14–17; Luke 20:22–25; 23:2; John 19:12–15 are also to him, whose full title was Tiberius Claudius Caesar Augustus. This second emperor of Rome held power for twenty-three years, covering the whole period of Christ's ministry and much of his earlier life. Tiberius's character, the fruit of his long rejection by Augustus,* and the events of his principate, his posthumous suffering in reputation at the hands of the mordant historian Tacitus, and the contributions of epigraphy* to the considerable rehabilitation accorded him by modern historical research, are matters of classical rather than biblical interest. The "Pilate stone" of Caesarea* attests the presence of a shrine to Tiberius (a Tiberieum*) in the Roman garrison town.

Coinage* has something to say about his appearance. The gold* and silver* coinage of Tiberius was struck at Lugdunum, but the aes coinage, struck in Rome,* shows several fine portraits. The Ara Pacis (Altar of Peace), set up in honor of Augustus by a senatorial decree of 4 July 13 B.C. (and to be seen today in the Museo delle Terme), shows Tiberius in procession, along with his father-in-law Augustus. The altar,* a fine work of art, commemorates the Augustan Peace, the emperor's finest gift to the world. It has been pieced together from fragments in widely scattered collections and some brilliant archaeological engineering, which included freezing the ground to check the springs which hampered the recovery of the buried ruins of the altar. Some of the foundations of Tiberius's palace are visible in the gardens of the Villa Fornese but inaccessible to excavation by that very fact. Portrait busts and statuary (see STATUES) representing Tiberius are as rare as those of Augustus are plentiful.

BIBLIOGRAPHY: F. B. Marsh, The Reign of Tiberius (1931); E. M. Blaiklock, ZPEB, 5 (1975), 746–47.

EMB

TIBERIUS CLAUDIUS NERO GERMANICUS. See CLAUDIUS.

TIGLATH-PILESER   (TIGLATH-PILNESER) (tig'lath pī lē'zər; Heb. תִּגְלַת פְּלְאֶסֶר, tiglaṯ pilʾeser [2 Kings 15:29]; tiglaṯ pᵉleser [2 Kings 16:7]; tilgaṯ pilnᵉʾeser [1 Chron 5:6]; tilgaṯ pilneser [1 Chron 5:26]; LXX, thalgathphellasar [2 Kings 15:29], and many variants; derived from Akkad. Tukultī-apil-Ešarra, "My trust is [in] the son of Esharra, i.e., in Ashur." The king is also known as Pul [2 Kings 15:19; 1 Chron 5:26] after the Akkad. Pūlu, the name under which he ruled as king in Babylon).

Tiglath-pileser III (745–727 B.C.) was one of the greatest of all the Assyrian kings. Coming to the throne after nearly a century of Assyrian weakness, he laid the foundations for the empire by confederating his power over the provinces, reforming the army, and conducting far-reaching campaigns.

Tiglath-pileser III portrayed on fragment of gypsum slab from central palace at Nimrud. Reproduced by courtesy of the Trustees of the British Museum.

He seems to have been an usurper, as the eponym* canon for 746 speaks of "rebellion in Calah.*" A copy of the king list (*see* KHORSABAD KING LIST), however, calls him the son of the preceding king. Instead of postdating his first regnal year to the first new year after his accession, Tiglath-pileser began dating his reign from the year of his accession, 745.

I. *Sources.* A. *Annals and Reliefs.* Almost all of the evidence for Tiglath-pileser comes from Nimrud (ancient Calah). Stone slabs bearing reliefs and inscriptions were discovered by A. Layard from the first days of his excavations in 1845. These came from the king's central palace and also from the southwestern palace of Esarhaddon* (c. 672 B.C.). The annals which were engraved toward the end of the king's reign, are fragmentary; we have perhaps 30–40 percent of the texts. We are moreover uncertain of the exact order of the texts.

Some of the texts are "display inscriptions" which describe the king's conquests in a geographical rather than a chronological sequence. To this category belong the Nimrud Slab, 3 by 2.6 m. (10 by 8½ ft.), discovered in 1851, and a number of tablets found in more recent excavations at Nimrud conducted by M. Mallowan from 1949 to 1963. As the king's central palace was in such a badly damaged state, Mallowan concentrated his efforts elsewhere.

B. *Letters.* The recent excavations uncovered about two hundred letters from the Nimrud chancery. Many of these date from the reign of Tiglath-pileser and shed interesting light on developments such as the Chaldean* revolt.

C. *Provincial Palaces.* Excavations by F. Thureau-Dangin at two sites in the area of the western bend of the Euphrates have uncovered provincial Assyrian palaces from the king's reign. Tell Ahmar (Til Barsip*), S of Carchemish,* has yielded magnificently colored frescoes. Arslan-Tash (Hadatu*), E of Carchemish, has provided us with important ivory* objects.

II. *Campaigns.* A. *North and Northeast.* In his second, third, seventh, ninth, and tenth years, Tiglath-pileser was occupied with the threats of the Urartians* and of the Medes.* In 743 he defeated the Urartian king Sarduri II and his allies at Arpad in N Syria. Then in 735 he attacked the Urartian capital of Tushpa on the eastern shore of Lake Van.

B. *Northwest and West.* 1. *North Syria.* The campaigns of the third through the sixth year were directed against Arpad, whose king Matti'el had renounced his treaty with the Assyrians (cf. *ANE*, 532–33). It was this same king who signed the Sfire treaties with a king of KTK (cf. *ANE*, 659–61). With the fall of Kullani (biblical Calneh;* cf. Isa 10:9; Amos 6:2) in 738, the way was opened for the Assyrian advance southward. A stele* set up c. 730 by Barrakab (cf. *ANE*, 655) and found by the Germans in 1891 at Zinjerli* (ancient Sam'al) in N Syria acknowledges that Barrakab owed his throne to Tiglath-pileser.

2. *Phoenicia.* Interesting light is shed on Assyrian government in Tyre* c. 736 by a letter from Nimrud published by Saggs in 1955. After a futile effort at leniency, the Assyrians sent in an armed contingent who "made the people jump around!" They nationalized the important timber industry and forbade the Phoenicians from selling to the Egyptians or Palestinians.

3. *Philistia.* A text from Nimrud published by Wiseman in 1951 gives us details on the king's campaign of 734 in Philistia. Hanunu, the king of Gaza,* fled, leaving his wife and treasures behind. After making submission, he was later reinstated by the Assyrians over Gaza. Tiglath-pileser boasts that he set up a monument at the Brook of Egypt* (near modern el-Arish).

4. *Damascus.* The campaigns of 733 and 732 were directed against Rezin of Damascus, who had originally paid tribute (*see* BOOTY AND TRIBUTE) to Assyria. The Bible (2 Kings 16:5ff.; 2 Chron 28:5ff.) describes how Rezin and Pekah of Israel* fought against Ahaz of Judah* in the so-called Syro-Ephraimite war. Ahaz appealed to Tiglath-pileser (2 Kings 16:7–9), who needed no encouragement to attack Damascus.

5. *Israel.* Menahem* of Israel paid tribute to the Assyrians (2 Kings 15:19–20), a fact confirmed by the Assyrian annals (cf. *ANET*, 283). This may have been paid as early as c. 741, or, as a new text published by Levine seems to indicate, as late as 738. In conjunction with his campaigns against Damascus in 733–32, Tiglath-pileser ravaged Gilead and Galilee,* and destroyed Hazor* and Megiddo* (cf. 2 Kings 15:29). Excavations at the latter sites have produced debris and ash layers from the Assyrian attacks. A relief from Nimrud depicts the capture of Astartu (i.e., Ashteroth—Karnaim in Gilead).

Tiglath-pileser boasts that he placed Hoshea on the throne of Israel (*ANET*, 284), after the assassination of Pekah. The latter's name was found on a jar from the level at Hazor destroyed by the Assyrians.

6. *Judah.* The annals speak of a revolt early in the king's reign of N Syrian cities led by an *Azriau* of *Ia-ú-da-a-a* (*ANET*, 282). After H. Winckler's proposal

in 1893, many scholars placed this country in N Syria in the region of Sam'al. The more recent consensus of scholars is that this king is none other than Azariah (i.e., Uzziah) of Judah, who died in 740. Under his successors, Jotham and then Ahaz, Judah escaped attack by dutifully paying tribute to the Assyrians (*ANET*, 282).

The city of Gezer,* according to one of the reliefs, was captured probably in the course of the Philistine campaign of 734. Some signs of burning uncovered by the recent Hebrew Union College excavations at Gezer may be attributed to Tiglath-pileser's time.

C. *The South.* After Tiglath-pileser's first regnal year, when he had to aid the king of Babylon,* Nabonassar, against revolts by the Chaldeans and Arameans,* the area to the S of Assyria remained quiescent until 732. Then a Chaldean chieftain named Mukin-zeri seized Babylon. A Nimrud letter published by Saggs in 1955, describing the Assyrian attempts to get the city of Babylon to surrender, is a perfect commentary on 2 Kings 18–19. When Tiglath-pileser had himself installed as king over Babylon in 731, he became the first Assyrian king in five centuries to rule directly over Babylonia.

BIBLIOGRAPHY: A. Anspacher, *Tiglath Pileser III* (1912); A. T. Olmstead, *History of Assyria* (1923), 175–205; W. Chapman, "Palestinian Chronological Data, 750–700 B.C. . . . ," *HUCA*, 8–9 (1931–32), 151–68; D. J. Wiseman, "Two Historical Inscriptions from Nimrud," *Iraq*, 13 (1951), 21–26; W. F. Albright, "The Son of Tabeel (Isaiah 7:6)," *BASOR*, 140 (1955), 34–35; H. W. F. Saggs, "The Nimrud Letters . . . ," *Iraq*, 17 (1955), 21–50, 126–54; D. J. Wiseman, "A Fragmentary Inscription of Tiglath-pileser III from Nimrud," *Iraq*, 18 (1956), 117–31; A. Parrot, *The Arts of Assyria* (1961); H. Tadmor, "Azriyau of Yaudi," *Scripta Hierosolymitana*, 8 (1961), 232–71; R. Barnett and M. Falkner, *The Sculptures of . . . Tiglath-pileser . . .* (1962); E. Thiele, *The Mysterious Numbers of the Hebrew Kings*, (2d ed., 1965); H. Tadmor, *Introductory Remarks to . . . the Annals of Tiglath-pileser III* (1967); J. Brinkman, *A Political History of Post-Kassite Babylonia 1158–722* (1968); J. Reade, "The Palace of Tiglath-pileser III," *Iraq*, 30 (1968), 69–73; B. Obed, "Observations on Methods of Assyrian Rule in Transjordania after the Palestinian Campaign of Tiglath-Pileser III," *JNES*, 29 (1970), 177–86; id., "The Historical Background of the Syro-Ephraimite War Reconsidered," *CBQ*, 34 (1972), 153–65; L. D. Levine, "Menahem and Tiglath-Pileser: A New Synchronism," *BASOR*, 206 (1972), 40–42; M. Cogan, "Tyre and Tiglath-Pileser III," *JCS*, 25 (1973), 96–99; J. N. Postgate, "The Inscription of Tiglath-Pileser III at Mila Mergi," *Sumer*, 29 (1973), 47–59; H. Tadmor, "The Inscriptions of Tiglath-Pileser III, King of Assyria," *AJA*, 77 (1973), 290–91; B. Obed, "The Phoenician Cities and the Assyrian Empire in the Time of Tiglath-pileser III," *ZDPV*, 90 (1974), 38–49; D. J. Wiseman, *ZPEB*, 5 (1975), 748–50; W. H. Shea, "Menahem and Tiglath-pileser III," *JNES*, 37 (1978), 43–50; M. C. Astour, *The Arena of Tiglath-Pileser III's Campaign* (1979); H. Tadmor and M. Cogan, "Ahaz and Tiglath-pileser in the Book of Kings," *Biblica*, 60 (1979), 491–508.

EY

TIL-BARSIP (til bär'sip). An ancient city* on the left (E) bank of the Euphrates, some 19.2 km. (12 mi.) S of Carchemish,* now represented by the mound (tell*) of Tell Aḥmar.

Early settlements existed here in the second and third millennia B.C. and even before; but the main known historical period of Til-Barsip begins from c. 1000 B.C. with a line of Neo-Hittite and Aramean* kings who there ruled the state of Bit-Adini. In 855 B.C., Shalmaneser III of Assyria vanquished the last king, Ahinas II ("Ahuni"), turning the state into an Assyrian province. Excavations have produced Hittite* hieroglyphic* inscriptions of the kings Hametas and his father, Assyrian stelae* and painted palace, and Aramean occupation-traces.

Bit-Adini appears in the OT as Beth Eden in Amos 1:5, where the prophet (who ministered c. 780–750 B.C.) proclaims the fall of "the one who holds the scepter in Beth Eden." At that time, Til-Barsip and Bit-Adini were ruled by the powerful governor of Haran,* Shamshi-ilu, whose unwonted local supremacy was later ended under Tiglath-pileser III* (c. 745–727 B.C.). Cf. also 2 Kings 19:12.

BIBLIOGRAPHY: F. Thureau-Dangin et al., *Til-Barsib* (1939); A. Malamat, *BASOR*, 129 (1953), 25–26; K. A. Kitchen, *Hittite Hieroglyphs, Aramaeans and Heb. Traditions* (forthcoming), Table IX; *CAH*, 1, part 1, 413; ibid., part 2, 333–34, 691.

KAK

TILE. Baked clay* slabs often used in making roofs, walls,* or floors. Glazed* tiles were prominent in the decoration of the Ishtar Gate and the Processional Street in ancient Babylon.* Pieces of unglazed tile were sometimes used as writing* materials.

EMB

TIMNAH (TIMNATH) (tim'nə). A valley N of the Gulf of Aqaba enclosed by the range known as Zuqe Timnah. J. Petherick, the region's first explorer (1860) noted the traces of metalworking in the archaeological debris. F. Frank in 1934 marked seven copper-smelting sites dating from the tenth to the sixth century (see N. Glueck, *King Solomon's Mines* [1940]). The Tel Aviv University Arabah Expedition of 1959 discovered large ancient copper workings at the foot of the range. Rich copper ore was mined during the years of transition between the Late Bronze* and Early Iron Age* on several sites. The earliest copper smelting (*see* REFINING) installation in any area is a stone built furnace* 549 m. (500 yd.) E of the modern Timnah Copper Mines, and it was possible to trace the process of production. A work camp was associated with the site. An early Iron Age camp W of Mount Timnah, and dated by pottery* remains to the twelfth century, was rich in the antiquities of metallurgy.* A full reconstruction of the processes used was possible. A Semitic sanctuary was associated with this site, together with a "high place.*"

In the center of Timnah's copper industrial area,

Hathor sanctuary at Timnah from c. end of 14th to middle of 12th centuries B.C. Courtesy Institute of Mining and Metals, Tel Aviv.

close by a feature known as Solomon's Pillars, a modern tourist resort, a temple of the Egyptian goddess Hathor was discovered by B. Rothenberg in 1969. The niche for the image was identifiable, while the standing stones known as "masseboth*" and the masses of offerings* reveal the nature of the copper-miners' cult. Of immense historical usefulness were hieroglyphic* inscriptions from the first two strata of the temple ruins which relate to the Nineteenth and Twentieth dynasties. Inscriptions run from Seti I (1318–1304) down to Ramses* V (1160–1156). There were large pottery finds characteristic of the region (Negev*-type pottery) and a beautiful copper serpent* with a gilded head was found in the last and fourth stratum of the temple.

The temple was significant in that it took the beginnings of copper mining in the area back four centuries before the activities of Solomon* and the kings of Israel* and Judah.* The Egyptians themselves took up the metallurgical operations of indigenous tribes—the Midianites,* Kenites, and Amalekites, whose activities were prehistoric (see Gen 4:22). Perhaps the reference in a papyrus* of Ramses III (1198–1167 B.C.) to mines in "Antika" refer to this locality. Perhaps further discovery and knowledge will throw light on Exodus—e.g., the three-day journey into the desert (Exod 5:3) and Moses' contact with Jethro (Exod. 18:1–27).

BIBLIOGRAPHY: E. Yamauchi, *The Stones and the Scriptures* (1973), 63–64, for remarks on the smelting processes, and Rothenberg's reidentification of Glueck's "furnace." A footnote on 64 lists an accessible bibliography of the most recent findings.

EMB

TIN. Tin is mentioned in the Bible only in lists of metals. According to Num 31:22, it and other metals could be purified. Its use as an alloy was known, and the technique was used figuratively in Ezek 22:18, 20.

Tin was an import (Ezek 27:12) and was necessary for making bronze* vessels* and implements (*see* TOOLS), but there is no archaeological evidence of its mining* or use except in bronze artifacts.* Analyses of bronze objects found in Egypt* have established the tin content as being between 2 and 16 percent.

BIBLIOGRAPHY: R. J. Forbes, *Metals in Antiquity* (1950), 231–54; C. Singer et al., eds., *A History of Technology*, 1 (1954), 563–92.

BCC

TIPHSAH (tif'sə; Heb. תִּפְסַח, *tipsah*). The word means a "ford," and the place was probably Thapsacus, the Amphipolis* of Seleucid times, modern Dibseh, an important crossing on the middle Euphrates River. It is claimed in 1 Kings 4:24 that Solomon's* kingdom, in Israel's golden age, reached to this strategic caravan town.

There is no means of knowing how strongly the remote frontier was held. A great EW trade route, moving round the Fertile Crescent,* had a staging post here. Xenophon mentions the place (*An.* 1.4.11). The Tiphsah mentioned in 2 Kings 15:16 as having been attacked by Menahem* of Israel,* could be the same place. Others, without lower critical justification, amend to Tippnah (e.g., RSV mg.).

EMB

TIRZAH (tür'zə; Heb. תִּרְצָה, *tirzah*). A Canaanite* city* famed for its beauty (S of Songs 6:4) whose king was defeated by Joshua (Josh 12:24). It became the capital of the northern kingdom in the days of Jeroboam I (931–909 B.C.), displacing Shechem* (cf. 1 Kings 14:17), perhaps as the result of increasing political and economic relationships with Syria. Tirzah was the capital of Israel* during the time of Baasha (1 Kings 15:21,33) and Elah (1 Kings 16:8–9). The seven-day reign of Zimri ended when he burned the palace over himself as Tirzah was being besieged by Omri* (1 Kings 16:17–18). After ruling from Tirzah for six years, Omri moved the capital of Israel to Samaria* (1 Kings 16:23–24), probably because of his

Corner of unfinished house from time of Omri, c. 882-871 B.C., at Tirzah (Tell el-Far'ah, north). Courtesy École Biblique et Archeologique Française, Jerusalem. Photo Israel Dept. of Antiquities and Museums.

economic and political alignment with Phoenicia.*
Menahem,* a resident of Tirzah, was able to overthrow Shallum (752 B.C.) toward the close of the
northern kingdom's existence and to usurp the throne,
ruling for almost eleven years.

The OT evidence does not furnish an exact location
for Tirzah. If it was in the general vicinity of Samaria,
it might be identified with Tullaza, N of Mount Ebal,
or with the ruined fortress Teyasir, further to the N.
De Vaux has identified Tirzah with Tell el-Far'ah,
11.3 km. (7 mi.) NE of Nablus, where the stratigraphic* and pottery* data correspond to the chronology* of Tirzah. The remains of a palace complex
also support the record of Omri's reign at Tirzah. A
less probable identification is with Jemma'in, 11.3 km.
(7 mi.) S of Shechem.

BIBLIOGRAPHY: W. F. Albright, *JPOS*, 11 (1930),
241–51; G. E. Wright, *BA*, 12 (1949), 66–68;
R. de Vaux and A. M. Steve, *RB*, 54–62 (1947–55);
J. M. Houston, *ZPEB*, 5 (1975), 754.

RKH

TITUS. Titus Flavius Vespasianus, son of Vespasian,* and second ruler of the Flavian dynasty, succeeded his father in A.D. 79 and died, universally
adored for his generosity, in 81. His lavish expen-
ditures, had he lived, would have produced a financial
crisis. As it was, coming after the necessary restor-
ative measures of Vespasian, and the tyranny of
Domitian,* Titus won universal popularity, shad-
owed only by his much resented liaison with Bernice, sister of Herod Agrippa II (*see* HEROD, FAMILY
OF; Acts 15:23). The eruption of Vesuvius and the
destruction of Herculaneum* and Pompeii* fell in
his reign (24 August 79). He concluded the Jewish
War with the burning of Jerusalem* and finished
construction of the Colosseum.*

Titus was only forty-two years of age when he died.
The strong realism of the coinage* of Titus, as of
Vespasian, does nothing to support Titus's reputation
for good looks. Pompeii and Herculaneum form an
archaeological treasure house of relics indicative of
life as it was lived in a provincial town in the time
of the Flavians. The newly located Oplonti, on the
slopes of Vesuvius, may prove as illuminating. It is
certain that a Christian group was established in the
area.

BIBLIOGRAPHY: R. C. Stone, *ZPEB*, 5 (1975), 759–
61.

EMB

TITUS, ARCH OF. Titus* Flavius Vespasianus (emperor A.D. 79–81) was the elder son of emperor Vespasian,* and served under him as a legionary
commander in the Jewish War. He commanded the
Roman forces at the siege and capture of Jerusalem*
in A.D. 70. The arch* erected in his honor by his
brother Domitian* stood before the Flavian Palace
at the top of the Via Sacra and remains one of Rome's*
impressive monuments. It marked a new advance
both in architecture and art, particularly the interior
reliefs which depict Titus's triumph celebrated in
A.D. 71. In one, officials are bearing on two biers the
most prized Jewish spoils—first the golden* table for
the shewbread and the pair of long silver* trumpets,

Drawing of detail from relief on Arch of Titus depicting
Jerusalem temple vessels being carried as spoils in
triumphal procession. Courtesy Carta, Jerusalem.

then the golden candlestick (menorah*) with its seven
branches. Near them are heralds with placards (*tituli*) identifying these objects for the crowds. In the
second relief Titus himself appears in his chariot,*
drawn by four white horses,* on his way to deposit
in the temple of Jupiter on the Capitol the symbols
of his victory.

The reliefs provide a dramatic portrayal of the fulfillment of Christ's prophecy about Jerusalem (Luke
13:34–35; 21:20–24).

BIBLIOGRAPHY: *CAH*, *The Imperial Peace*, 11
(1936); *CAH* (11), vol. of pl. V (1939), 78–79;
H. Kahler, *Rome and Her Empire* (Art of the World),
J. R. Foster, trans. (Br. ed., 1963), 120–26, with
plates.

BFH

TITUS FLAVIUS VESPASIANUS. *See* TITUS;
VESPASIAN.

TJEKU. *See* SUCCOTH.

TJIKARU. *See* SEA PEOPLES.

TOB (tōb). A town and district of S Hauran mentioned as Jepthah's place of refuge (Judg 11:3–5), and
in connection with the Ammonite-Syrian war (2 Sam
10:6). It is possibly the Dubu of the Amarna letters,*
an Aramean* state E of the Jordan River, but N of
the Galilean* hill-country. This makes a suggested
identification with Hippos* of the Decapolis* reasonable. The present Al-Tabiya, 16 km. (10 mi.) S of
Gadara,* has also been suggested, and the name does
appear to conserve the Hebrew word (tōb, "good").
There was a post-Exilic settlement of Jews* there,
and this occasioned an intrusion into the area of Judas
Maccabaeus (1 Macc 5:13; 2 Macc 12:17), if indeed
Tubias and the Tubieni are to be identified with Tob
and the inhabitants of the place.

EMB

TOBIAH. *See* ARAQ EL-EMIR.

TOMB. *See* CATACOMBS; GRAVE; NECROPOLIS;
SARCOPHAGUS.

TOOLS. The earliest hand implements were of a
very rough variety, and in Palestine dated from pre-

historic times. Worked flints in the form of knives* and primitive agricultural* implements occur in Near Eastern sites at Neolithic* levels. Even when metallurgy* made more efficient tools possible, flint and stone continued to be used for various purposes. Wooden implements, stone pestles and mortars,* and stone hammers were used prior to 4000 B.C. With the development of copper and bronze,* from the Chalcolithic* period onward, drills, saws, and chisels came into increasing use.

In 1973, Russian archaeologists working at the foot of Mount Ararat* discovered a large number of kilns* used for smelting ores, including those of copper and iron.* These were dated c. 2500 B.C., thus showing the antiquity of the manufacture of iron implements (cf. Gen 4:22).

When Hittite* technology introduced the Iron Age* proper, about 1200 B.C., metal tools increased in number significantly. The Hebrew ḥereb ("sword") included knives and other sharp cutting instruments. Adzes, hoes, iron ax-heads (cf. 2 Kings 6:5), chisels, nails* (Jer 10:3–4), plumblines (Amos 7:7–8), and other tools have left their marks on artifacts* recovered from Near Eastern sites. The potter's* rotary wheel, used in Palestine from 3000 B.C. onward, has been found at Megiddo,* Lachish,* Hazor,* and elsewhere.

The ancient craft* of carpentry, followed by both Joseph (Matt 13:55) and Jesus (Mark 6:3), found its expression, among other areas, in the exquisite furniture* possessed by the wealthy in Babylonia, Egypt,* and Palestine in the Bronze Age* and later periods. Copper was commonly used for saws and chisels, while for a drill the carpenter employed a copper bit attached to a wooden handle which was turned by means of a box and a leather* thong. Files, wooden mallets, and hammers (Jer 10:4; Judg 5:26; Isa 44:12) also formed part of the carpenter's tool kit. The stonemason used implements similar to those of the carpenter, including a saw for cutting the soft limestone (1 Kings 7:9), metal hammers (Jer 23:29), chisels, and wooden wedges used in quarrying* large blocks of stone. The use of hammers for flattening metal and making it into sheets is referred to in Isa 41:7. Such smiths fashioned tools for domestic and agricultural* use and were equally in demand in war or peace (Joel 3:10; Mic 4:3). In Isa 28:17 the plumbline was employed as a symbol of righteousness, while

Flint hand-axe found at Holon (near Tel Aviv) belonging to Lower Paleolithic Period (c. 700,000 B.C.). Courtesy Israel Dept. of Antiquities and Museums. Photo Israel Museum.

in Rev 11:1; 21:15, the measuring rod was used to delineate the boundaries of the Temple* and the holy city. One sample of a pruning hook seems to have survived from Tell Jemmeh, dated around 800 B.C. It has a curved iron head, almost complete, attached to a handle. To forge and reshape a spear into such an implement of arboriculture or viticulture, would have involved no great difficulty (Isa 2:4 et al.).

BIBLIOGRAPHY: R. J. Forbes, *Studies in Ancient Technology*, 1-4 (1955–58); C. Singer et al., eds., *A History of Technology*, 1-4 (1964).

RKH

TOPHEL (tō'fəl; Heb. תֹּפֶל, *tōpel*) is mentioned only in Deut (1:1), locating, among associated localities, the place of Moses' speech. Tophel has been identified as Tafile, a village 24 km. (15 mi.) from Kerak on the road to Petra.* Otherwise nothing is known of the place.

EMB

TOPHETH. *See* HINNOM VALLEY.

TOWERS. Towers or turrets in a wall* were to increase protection. Because they protruded not only above the wall but also beyond its outer face, they exposed the attackers to flanking fire while they were attacking, even if they managed to gain a foothold on the wall itself. Gates,* being weak points, were normally flanked by towers. Walls and towers are often linked in the OT (as in 2 Chron 14:7, and in the prayer for the peace of Jerusalem in Ps 122:7). Towers formed an integral part of wall structures from Babylon* to the "mile castles" of Hadrian's Wall and were incorporated into the defenses of gates.

Some of the towers in the wall of Jerusalem* are named in Nehemiah's account of its construction (Neh 3) and are referred to elsewhere (e.g., 2 Chron 26:9), but their identification is uncertain. Some scholars regard the Millo built by Solomon* as a tower (1 Kings 9:15), but this is debated. In the OT the word "tower" (Heb. *migdāl*) may also refer to a citadel* or strong point within the city* and to a small fortress like a castle* in the desert. The former meaning is clear in passages such as Judg 9:51ff., and the latter in e.g., 2 Chron 26:10.

See also ANTONIA, TOWER OF; WARFARE.

BIBLIOGRAPHY: Y. Yadin, *The Art of Warfare in Bible Lands* (1963). WFR

TRADE GUILDS. The evidence for these clubs or societies (*collegia, sodalitates*) is mainly epigraphical* and so falls firmly within the province of archaeology. Such organizations, which existed in every country of the ancient world, were of varied types, and a major section of them related to tradesmen and craftsmen* of all sorts. Records exist of producers of linen*-goods, wool, leather* and bronze* workers, dyers,* tanners, potters,* bakers, pastry cooks, embalmers,* and carters. There were also professional groups such as bankers, doctors, and architects. Guilds often grew up where the raw materials for their trades were to be found—as with the manufacture of woolen cloth* in the Tell Beit Mirsim (*see*

DEBIR) sheep-raising area, or the mining* industry in ore-rich Edom.*

There are also records of convivial or fellowship groups, as of veterans or sportsmen, and the "Late Sleepers" and "Late Drinkers" who left their record, perhaps in jest, on the walls of Pompeii.* "There was a craving," says S. Dill, "for some form of social life greater than the family and narrower than the state" which in some way "satisfied the need of the humble for the pleasures of social intercourse and the dignity of self-expression." Wages or conditions of work do not seem to have been priorities with ancient trade guilds. In large Near Eastern cities, tradesmen often pursued their activities in separate quarters. Jerusalem* had a street* for bakers (Jer 37:21) and an area in which goldsmiths worked (Neh 3:32).

The pagan guilds had a patron deity in whose temple it is probable periodic meetings of fellow craftsmen met—hence the moral problem for Christians who scrupled to eat "in an idol's temple" (1 Cor 8:10) or to eat "food sacrificed to idols" (Acts 15:29).

The trade guilds in adroit hands could be a dangerous political force, as the riot of the Ephesian silversmith (Acts 19:23–41) and associated craftsmen demonstrates. The guild of butchers was probably anxious about the fall-off in the trade for temple meat, which precipitated the trouble in Bithynia;* and the repression of the Christian church by Pliny, as described by the governor himself in surviving letters to Emperor Trajan (Pliny Ep. 10.96–97), may well have been guild related.

The authorities were sensitive over the potential strength of the trade guilds and all similar groupings liable to form a coherent pressure force within the state. Hence Trajan's prohibition, contained in the same illuminating volume of Pliny's Bithynian letters, on the forming of a needed fire brigade in Nicomedia (Pliny Ep. 10.34).

Official anxiety was more pointed when a trade group was religious, that is, met formally for worship, as distinct from merely acknowledging a patron deity. The scandal of the Baachanalian groups in southern Italy (c. 186 B.C.) which led to a senatorial decree of suppression (Liv. 39.8–15ff.; and S. C. de Bacch. and C. G. Bruns, ed., Fontes iuris romani antiqui [1969], 7.36) was an early reflection of this attitude and provided archaeology with a major linguistic and historical find. It is relevant to mention this cause célèbre, because there is tenuous epigraphical evidence that certain Christians were organized under the name cultores Verbi ("worshipers of the Word"). A. De Marchi presents the evidence (Il Culto Privato di Roma Antica, part 2 [1903], 75).

BIBLIOGRAPHY: On the general theme, epigraphical evidence is massive. See ILS (1892–1916), 2.2, chap. 15 and 3.2, 710–25; CIL, 8.9409, 14.2112. Also, S. Dill, Roman Society from Nero to Marcus Aurelius (1905), 251ff.; E. G. Hardy, Studies in Roman History (1906), 125–50; E. M. Blaiklock, The Christian in Pagan Society, Tyndale NT Lecture (1951); J. L. Kelso, ZPEB, 5 (1975), 792.

EMB

TRANSFIGURATION, MOUNT OF. See HERMON.

TRANS-JORDAN. See PEREA.

TRANSPORTATION. The earliest major cultures of the Ancient Near East were associated with rivers, so that water transport was an important consideration in trading. Egyptian paintings and clay* models from c. 3500 B.C. depicted ships* with a forked stern and a square sail, as well as the more familiar papyrus* Nile boats. A Mesopotamian* cylinder seal* dated about 3200 B.C. depicts a flat-bottomed barge loaded with goods and an animal. From almost a millennium later an elegant model of an eight-oared canoe, fashioned in silver,* was recovered from Ur.* The familiar Amarna Age seagoing vessels of the Egyptians had large sails as well as oarsmen, and some even boasted a keel. The earlier Middle Kingdom (c. 2000–1780 B.C.) ships which traded with Byblos (Gebal*; cf. Deut 28:68) were most probably Phoenician* in origin.

Overland travel was done on foot, on donkeys,* or by means of a camel* caravan. The domestication of the camel as a beast of burden has been evidenced by deposits of camel bones at Mari* (c. 2400 B.C.), and by reliefs from Tell Halaf, Byblos, and other locations. In patriarchal times (c. 1900–1700 B.C.) camels formed part of the livestock of Abraham and Jacob (Gen 12:16; 32:7 et al.), though the donkey was still the most common beast of burden at that time. The horse,* by contrast, was associated with warfare,* aggression, and power (cf. Pss 76:6; 147:10 et al.) and was employed at first in chariot* formations. Later it also became a beast of burden. A Babylonian text from the time of Hammurabi* (c. 1750 B.C.) describes the horse as the "ass from the east," presumably a reference to its supposed Mongolian origin.

In addition to the presence of navigable rivers, transportation was facilitated by established caravan trading routes such as those between northern India, Sumer,* and Egypt,* or the ones which connected the principal cities of Sumer, Akkad,* Syria, and Palestine, and also by roads of the kind known as the King's Highway* (Num 20:17) and the "way of the sea" (Isa 9:1). According to the Egyptian writer of the Satirical Letter, Palestinian roads were boulder-strewn, rutted, and difficult for chariots to negotiate. Among other hazards to travel and transportation were bands of marauding thieves (cf. Luke 10:30).

BIBLIOGRAPHY: R. J. Forbes, Studies in Ancient Technology, 2 (1955), 126–83; M. Avi-Yonah, A Geographical and Historical Atlas of Israel (1956); I. Mendelsohn, IDB, 5 (1962), 688–90; J. L. Kelso, ZPEB, 5 (1975), 799–807.

RKH

TREATY. See COVENANT.

TREPANNING (TREPHINING) (trē'pan ing; trē'fin ing). The ancient practice of cutting a disc of bone from the living skull tissue. The technique may have been used to relieve a skull fracture or the incidence of tumors or headaches in ancient times. Evidence from Neolithic* and other skulls indicates that the bone healed quite well and that the patient survived the operation in most instances. The technique had the advantage of being able to be repeated if unsuccessful at first. One female skull exhibits six different apertures as the result of trepanning.

HWP

TRIBUTE. See BOOTY AND TRIBUTE.

TRIGLYPH (trig′lif). A tablet of stone in Doric architecture with three vertical grooves or glyphs repeated along a frieze, usually one over each column and between the columns.

TROAS. A city* founded in 300 B.C. in the spate of city building which followed Alexander's conquest of Asia Minor.* Alexandria Troas, an ancient name, was a port of some consequence, marked by very considerable ruins and romantically described by early travelers (William Lithgow, 1096, and Thomas Coryat, 1612. See Rose Macaulay's *Pleasure of Ruins* [1953], 40–48). The port had once, according to Suetonius (*Iul.*, 79; cf. Hor., *Odes* 3.3) stirred Julius Caesar to the thought of moving his capital "to Illum or Alexandria." Early travelers confused Troas with ancient Troy* (Illium, which is 16 km. [10 mi.] from Troas) of Homeric legend, the discovery of which on the escarpment of Hissarlik in 1870, was the initiation of classical archaeology. Gibbon wondered "how anyone could confuse Illium with Alexandria Troas" (E. Gibbon, *Decline and Fall of the Roman Empire*, 2 [Everyman's ed., 1954], 75), but the first ruingazers were romanticists rather than historians or scientists.

Paul visited the city at least three times (Acts 16:8–11; 20:1–3; 2 Cor 2:12).

BIBLIOGRAPHY: E. M. Blaiklock, *Cities of the NT* (1965), 27–38; id., *ZPEB*, 5 (1975), 825–26.

EMB

TROGYLLIUM (trō jil′i um; Gr. τρογύλλιον, *Trogyllion*). A cape 32 km. (20 mi.) S of Ephesus,* where a high headland N of the mouth of the Maeander forms a sharply pointed promontory protruding westward. It makes a narrow channel between the mainland and Samos, a protected passage in which a coastal vessel might naturally sail before running across the open gulf to Miletus.* The pause in the anchorage is mentioned in Acts 20:15 (KJV), but the verse is subject to some textual difficulties, summarized in the critical note in *EGT*, vol 2, 428. The disputed phrase occasions no difficulty geographically or historically. There is archaeological evidence of a town on the promontory, and an anchorage there is traditionally known as Paul's Port.

BIBLIOGRAPHY: W. M. Ramsay, *The Church in the Roman Empire* (1893), 155; id., *Saint Paul the Traveller and the Roman Citizen* (1896), 293–94.

EMB

TROY. The notable mound of Hissarlik, 12.8 km. (8 mi.) inland from the mouth of the Dardanelles, where the stratified remains of three thousand years of occupation of a strategic site have been uncovered by a succession of archaeologists, has no biblical relevance, save as a landmark in the history of archaeology. Heinrich Schliemann, the rich German businessman, who discovered ancient Troy in 1869, taught the world of archaeology the need to take tradition seriously and to use ancient documents, as Nelson Glueck taught the next century, as prime sources of information.

See also TROAS.

BIBLIOGRAPHY: *CAH*, 1, part 1, 170; *CAH*, 1, part 2, 368, passim.

EMB

TUBAL. See MESHECH AND TUBAL.

TULLAZA. See TIRZAH.

TUNNELS. See ENGINEERING; GEZER; HEZEKIAH'S TUNNEL; SILOAM.

TURRET. See TOWERS.

TURSHA. See SEA PEOPLES.

TUTANKHAMEN (tūt ən kä′mən). This pharaoh was originally known as Tutankhaton and was married to the third daughter of Ikhnaton, a prominent Amarna* Age pharaoh who ruled Egypt* in the New Kingdom period (c. 1570–1150 B.C.). Ikhnaton had instituted a far-reaching reformation of Egyptian religious life in which he made Re the supreme deity and suppressed the cult of Amen (Amun). A reaction after his death restored the suppressed priesthood, a situation which was probably aided by a period of political and social weakness in Egypt. At this juncture Tutankhaton came to power and moved his capital to Thebes.* He restored the Amen priesthood, and in order to remove any trace of the Aton religion favored by his predecessor on the throne he also changed his name to Tutankhamen ("beautiful in life is [the god] Amen").

His reign was short, however, and when he died at about eighteen years of age he was given a splendid burial by the Amen priesthood. His resting-place in the Valley of the Kings near Luxor* had been identified c. 1910, with the stairway leading to the tomb coming to light a decade later. In 1922 Lord Carnarvon and Howard Carter opened several anterooms and were astonished at the magnificence and opulence of the artifacts* found there. These included many articles of richly made clothing,* elaborate furnishings of various kinds which had belonged to the deceased king, weapons, articles made from precious metals, and food for the pharaoh's needs in the afterlife.

In 1923 the burial shrine was excavated and the chamber in which the body of Tutankhamen lay was entered. His yellow quartzite sarcophagus* was covered with an enormous cracked and cemented rose granite lid, beneath which were the three coffins enclosing the pharaoh's mummified remains. Following the tradition of royal burials, the mummy was decorated with a great many precious objects, which can now be seen in the Cairo Museum. Part of Tutankhamen's tomb proper had been undisturbed by robbers, and thus afforded some true indication of the

One of two identical wooden statues of King Tutankhamen. They "guarded" the sealed entrance to the sepulchral chamber of the king. Photo: Egyptian Expedition, The Metropolitan Museum of Art.

wealth of an otherwise comparatively insignificant Amarna Age pharaoh. To the biblical student the interest lies in the picture which was presented of the wealth and glory of Egypt—the land and culture which Moses abandoned for God and for his people's destiny. If the tomb of a boy king could produce the beauty, wealth, and art which has so astounded the world, what must the palace of really great pharaohs such as Ramses II* have been like?

BIBLIOGRAPHY: H. Carter, *The Tomb of King Tutankhamen*, 3 vols. (1933); W. MacQuitty, *Tutankhamun: The Last Journey* (1978). EMB

TUTANKHATON. See TUTANKHAMEN.

TWO BROTHERS, STORY OF THE. This ancient Egyptian tale is a curious mixture of folklore, mythology, and ancient humor and has survived in a beautifully written hieratic* manuscript now in the British Museum. Although this document was written c. 1200 B.C., the story itself goes back at least a millennium earlier.

The narrative is given a village setting and describes the lives of two brothers, one of which is married, as they follow their agricultural* pursuits. The wife of the married brother attempts to seduce her brother-in-law, Bata, but his virtuous resistance of her advances causes the frustrated wife to hate him and to accuse him falsely to her husband. The animals in the stable warn Bata that his brother intends to kill him, whereupon he flees for safety, though not with complete impunity. Ultimately the lecherous wife is killed by her husband.

While there are certain similarities to the narrative of Joseph* (Gen 39), the divergence in matters of detail is so great as to preclude the Egyptian version from being the origin of that narrative. Eastern Mediterranean texts of the Amarna*-Mycenaean* age contain parallel material, showing the general currency of the basic theme. Whereas the story of the brothers is pure fantasy, the Joseph narrative is biography which is in contact with historical reality at every point.

BIBLIOGRAPHY: *ANET* (1950), 23–25; J. H. Breasted, *History of Egypt* (1945), 455. RKH

TYPOLOGY. An adjunct to stratigraphy* as a means of dating* and identification by comparison of shape, material, manufacture, and ornamentation of artifacts.*

TYRE. The rise in the level of the Mediterranean since ancient times has covered many of the earlier remains of the great port of the Phoenicians,* 40 km. (25 mi.) S of Sidon.* The harbor constructed on the S side of the island in the tenth century before Christ by Hiram,* Solomon's* associate, may be traced, its huge foundations now submerged by 15 m. (50 ft.) of water.

A very considerable area has been excavated including a unique oblong Greek theater,* and a mosaic*-floored first-century pavement between what appears to have been a double row of shops with pillared porticoes. Christ could have walked here on his visit to the area—his furthest journey N (Matt 15:21–28; Mark 7:24–30). Remains of the Phoenician harbor works lie deep beneath Greek and Roman superstructures, so the stratification itself defeats full periodic study. The large area of remains, only partially uncovered, with some lying beneath the dwellings of the modern town, give a great impression of the wealth and importance of the place. It abundantly confirms Ezekiel's account of the magnificence of the Phoenician port in the sixth century before Christ (Ezek 26–28; KJV "Tyrus").

Tyre's greatness as a port continued until Roman days, for there is evidence of Tyrian port facilities maintained at Puteoli.* Alexander built a causeway from the mainland to the island when besieging Tyre in 333 B.C. This .8 km. (½ mi.) of filling became a breakwater which held the sand, and now it forms the core of the thick neck of land which makes the former island a peninsula.

BIBLIOGRAPHY: W. B. Fleming, *The History of Tyre* (1915); D. de Lasseur, *Syria*, 3 (1922), 1–26, 116–33; P. K. Hitti, *History of Syria* (1957), 39 passim; E. M. Blaiklock, *ZPEB*, 5 (1975), 832–35. EMB

TYRUS. See TYRE.

U

UBAID (UBEID). *See* Tell Al-'Ubaid.

UGARIT (ū′gə rit). This large mound, at Ras Shamra
on the Syrian coast, about 40 km. (25 mi.) S of the
mouth of the Orontes River, was an important Canaanite* cultural center during the Amarna* Age.
An accidental discovery in 1928 at the neighboring
mound of Minet el-Beida, led to twenty-two seasons
of excavation in the area by Schaeffer between 1929
and 1960. Administrative buildings, temples, and
palaces dating from the early fourteenth century B.C.
were unearthed, along with a great many splendid
ivories,* stelae,* weapons (*see* Arms and Weapons),
and other artifacts.* Particularly valuable were the
voluminous cuneiform* texts in Akkadian* and the
new Canaanite alphabetic* script now known as
Ugaritic, as well as numerous inscriptions in Hittite*
and Egyptian hieroglyphs.* This literary deposit is
unquestionably the most significant archaeological
discovery of the century as far as the elucidation of
the OT is concerned, if only because of the strategic
geographical location and cultural significance of Ras
Shamra.

The site was apparently settled in Neolithic* times,
and excavations at the Chalcolithic* level (stratum IV)
uncovered some painted* pottery* similar to that
found at Tell Halaf. The Early Bronze-Age* levels
(stratum III) showed obvious cultural contacts with
Mesopotamia,* reflecting the period of westward
Amorite* movement at the end of the First Babylonian Dynasty. In the Middle Bronze Age (stratum
II) Ugarit was a very important commercial center,
having political and commercial contacts with Mesopotamia, Anatolia, and Egypt.* In the Late Bronze
Age, Ugarit was garrisoned by the Egyptians to offset
Mitanni* and Hittite* influence, but in the fourteenth century B.C. the port and city* were virtually
demolished by an earthquake. A century later Ugarit
took advantage of a Hittite-Egyptian peace treaty to
enlarge its trading activities. In the twelfth century
B.C., however, it was destroyed by the Aegean Sea
Peoples and was never rebuilt. The many royal letters,* treaties, contracts, and other administrative
documents recovered from Ugarit are extremely
valuable in reconstructing the history of Syria in the
Bronze Age.

With the decipherment of Ugaritic, a close linguistic relative of biblical Hebrew, some 350 texts
were shown to be highly important for OT studies.
Religious epics have disclosed the beliefs and cultic
practices of the Canaanites, and the emphasis upon
gross sexuality, prostitution, and general moral de-

Baal (god) of lightning. This limestone relief was found in
the sanctuary to the west of the great temple at Ras
Shamra, dated by the excavator from 1900-1750 B.C.; by
Albright, from 1650-1500 B.C. Courtesy Réunion des Musées Nationaux, Paris.

pravity. OT condemnations of Baal,* a Canaanite "high god," and Asherah,* his savage consort, are placed in an entirely new historical perspective. Studies in Ugaritic grammar have shed unexpected light on the Hebrew text, particularly on poetic sections, and have shown that many earlier proposed emendations of the Hebrew were entirely unwarranted. Linguistic similarities also extend to parallels between Canaanite and Hebrew sacrificial* terminology. Thus Ugaritic texts mention the whole burnt-offering (*kll*), burnt-offering (*šrp*), peace-offering (*šlmn*), trespass-offering (*'asm*), and gift-offerings (*mtn*), though the use is different in nature from OT rituals.

Many phrases in OT poetry occur in characteristic fashion in Ugaritic texts and have had their meaning illumined by these archaeological sources. Social institutions of the Pentateuch have also been paralleled in Ugaritic material, such as that of slavery* for debt (Exod 21:7 et al.) and the ritual seclusion of the mother at childbirth (Lev 12:1–8). Intrafamily adoptions of a kind known to the Hebrew patriarchs (cf. Gen 48:5; 50:23) were also practiced at Ugarit.

BIBLIOGRAPHY: C.F.A. Schaeffer, *The Cuneiform Texts of Ras Shamra-Ugarit* (1939); C. H. Gordon, *Ugaritic Handbook* (1947); J. Gray, *The Legacy of Canaan* (1957); A. S. Kapelrud, *The Ras Shamra Discoveries and the OT* (1962); id., *IDB*, 5 (1962), 724–32; C. F. Pfeiffer, *ZPEB*, 5 (1975), 836–42.

RKH

ULAI (ū'lī). The name of a stream (KJV "river") or, more probably, an irrigation* canal near Susa* in SW Persia where Daniel had a strange vision (Dan 8:2–16). In an alluvial plain, which has been subject to varied forms of erosion and collapse of organization, topographical change has been catastrophic, but D. J. Wiseman has suggested a possible identification (*NBD*, 1304). He thinks that the present upper Kherbah and Lower Karun rivers may once have been a single stream running through the delta at the head of the Persian Gulf. It is visible in reliefs of Ashurbanipal's* attack on Susa in 640 B.C., where, typically, the king claims to have made the Ulai "red with blood."

EMB

UMMAH (UMMA) (um'ə). A Sumerian city* which flourished in the last half of the third millennium B.C., Ummah has been identified with Tell Jokha, an unexcavated mound (tell*) which rises about 15 m. (50 ft.) above the plain, located 24 km. (15 mi.) NW of Telloh (once identified as Lagash,* but now considered to be Girsu) and 48 km. (30 mi.) NW of al-Ḥiba (Lagash).

Early in this century W. Andrae surveyed Tell Jokha and observed traces of a large building 70 m. (75 yd.) square. Texts record that in the time of Shu-Sin of the Ur* III dynasty the Ummaites spent seven years building a temple for their patron deity Shara, using some twenty-six million bricks in the process.

Unauthorized digging by Arabs has uncovered thousands of economic texts of the Ur III period (twenty-first century B.C.), of which about six thousand have been published.

We are informed about Ummah's history primarily from the accounts of its bitter rival, Lagash. For three centuries the two cities fought over the Gu-Edena, a fertile plain which lay between them.

Mesilim (twenty-sixth century B.C.), king of Kish,* arbitrated between the cities and set up a boundary. When this treaty was disregarded by the Ummaites c. 2400 B.C., Eannatum, a great military king of Lagash defeated Ummah, a feat which he commemorated in the famous Stele of Vultures.* Two generations later, Eannatum's nephew, Entemena, again defeated Umma.

It was only c. 2350 B.C. that the Ummaites gained revenge, when their king, Lugalzaggesi, sacked Lagash in the course of his conquest of Sumer.* His rise to power was short-lived, however, as an even greater conqueror, Sargon of Akkad* (Agade) defeated Lugalzaggesi. Thereafter Ummah's fortunes declined as it was subjected to conquest by one power after another.

BIBLIOGRAPHY: L. King, *History of Sumer and Akkad* (1923), 21–23; G. A. Barton, *The Royal Inscriptions of Sumer and Akkad* (1929), 22–33, 56–65, 96–113; S. N. Kramer, *History Begins at Sumer* (1959), 35–44; T. Jones and J. Snyder, *Sumerian Economic Texts from the Third Ur Dynasty* (1961); S. N. Kramer, *The Sumerians* (1963), 34–38, 53–68, 322–24; M. Lambert, "La vie économique à Umma," *RA*, 59 (1965), 61-72, 115-26; id., "L'occupation du Girsu par Urlumma roi d'Umma," *RA*, 59 (1965), 81-84; H. Sauren, *Topographie der Provinz Umma* . . . (1966); T. Jacobsen, "A Survey of the Girsu (Telloh) Region," *Sumer*, 25 (1969), 103–9; *CAH*, 1, part 1, 224–25, 373; ibid., part 2, 104 passim.

EY

UM QUEIS. See GADARA.

UMM EL-AMAD. See BOZRAH.

UMM EL-AWAMID. See HAMMON.

UNCIAL SCRIPT. See PALAEOGRAPHY, GENERAL.

UNICORN. See OX, WILD.

UNKNOWN GOD, ALTAR TO THE. Paul says in Acts 17:23, "I even found an altar with this inscription: TO AN UNKNOWN GOD." In the Greek there is noun and adjective only, without either a definite or indefinite article. One or two examples of such inscriptions survive, but always in the plural—to unknown gods. In the plural, English can avoid a choice. In the singular, however, choice must be made between the definite and indefinite articles. The definite seems better, provided the reference and context of the inscription are realized. The inscription in each case refers to the unknown deity concerned with the altar's* foundation, not generally or transcendentally to a god vaguely realized and sought. Paul adapted the inscription for homiletic ends. He was not deceived about its meaning, but like any perceptive preacher sought an illustration and a point of contact in a known environment. The device captured attention and anchored the theme in experience.

Plato preserves a tradition that Epimenides, the Cretan religious teacher and miracle-worker, was in Athens* about 500 B.C. Some said it was 600 B.C., but dates are not important in a half-legendary situation. The story was that, to combat an epidemic, Epimenides directed the Athenians to loose sheep from the Areopagus* and, wherever they lay down, to build an altar "to the unknown god" of the place, and to make sacrifice. Perhaps the story is an etiological myth, a tale invented to explain a visible phenomenon. Perhaps the altars merely represented a scrupulosity which, in a city full of deities from all the Eastern Mediterranean, sought to avoid offense to any in this slightly naïve fashion. It is impossible to say more.

BIBLIOGRAPHY: K. Lake, *BC*, part 1, 5 (1933), 240–46; B. Gärtner, *The Areopagus Speech and Natural Revelation* (1955), 242–47; W. L. Leifeld, *ZPEB*, 5 (1975), 844.

EMB

UPHAZ (ū'faz; Heb. אוּפָז, 'ûpāz). This name is mentioned twice in the OT as a location (Jer 10:9; Dan 10:5). Fine gold,* certainly alluvial in origin, is associated with the term. Professor D. J. Wiseman, probing the etymology, has suggested that the term may not be geographical at all, but rather a technical word for refined gold (*NBD*, 1304). Another suggestion is that the word is a confusion with Ophir,* a paleographically* likely situation. The Syrian Hexapla actually reads "Ophir" in the first of the two references.

EMB

UR (ûr; Heb. אוּר, 'ûr). The city* of Ur is mentioned four times in the Bible. It is the place where Haran, the brother of Abraham, died (Gen 11:28). Terah, Abraham's father, moved his family out of Ur in the plan of God (Gen 11:31), so that the Lord later reminded Abraham that He had brought Abraham out of Ur (Gen 15:7). God's selection of Abraham and bringing him to Canaan* was the historical point of reference for the beginning of Israel as the people of God. Ezra mentions the city of Ur with this significance in his prayer in Neh 9:7.

The traditional location of Ur is about 322 km. (200 mi.) SE of Baghdad and about 16 km. (10 mi.) W of the Euphrates River. There is debate as to whether Abraham came from this southern Mesopotamian* city or a northern one with similar name, but the southern city is most significant archaeologically and helps define the culture from which Abraham came.

Ur was excavated by J. E. Taylor for the British Museum after 1854, by R. C. Thompson in 1918, and by H. R. Hall in 1919. Charles Woolley systematically excavated the site from 1922–34 for the British Museum and the University of Pennsylvania.

Woolley found that Ur had been inhabited from 4000 to 300 B.C. and illustrated the development of Sumerian* culture. The earliest level of habitation was named the Ubaid period by comparison with the same level at a nearby tell* of that name. It was in

Gold helmet (15-carat) of Mes-Kalam-Dug (not the king) from tomb at Ur; 25th century B.C. Courtesy The University Museum, University of Pennsylvania.

this earliest period that Woolley found water-laid soil, which he interpreted as evidence of the Genesis flood. Scholars have since explained this as being laid by the river, which has now considerably changed its course.

The next period of culture at Ur was designated as the Warka period, after another contemporary city. Among the more significant finds were mosaics* made from baked clay* pegs, a potter's wheel, and cylinder seals.* The Proto-literate period was so called because it gives evidence of very early Sumerian writing.*

The Early Dynastic period is richly illustrated by finds from the royal cemetery (*see* NECROPOLIS). The gold* helmet of Mes-Kalam-Dug from this period is carved to resemble locks of hair. Gold daggers and cups witness the wealth of the culture.

Although not much was learned of the Second Dynasty at Ur, the Third Dynasty royal tombs revealed the striking fact that the kings were followed into the grave by an entire retinue. Servants willingly lay down and died (perhaps by drinking poison) in order to continue to be with their master in death. The architecture of the tombs was quite varied, displaying the main types known today.

Other artifacts* from Ur, including numerous cuneiform* tablets, cylinder seals, the elaborate headdress and jewelry of Queen Shubad, the gold and silver* statue* of a goat* standing by a tree, the gold lyre with a bull's head, indicate that the city had one of the most advanced cultures in the world.

Perhaps the most outstanding archaeological item at Ur is its ziggurat,* or holy tower. It is typical of others in that part of the world and is the best preserved of all. It is a solid tower with a mud-brick core and fired-brick shell about 21 m. (70 ft.) high and served as a religious center of the moon god.

BIBLIOGRAPHY: C. S. Gadd, *The History and Monuments of Ur* (1929); C. L. Woolley, *Ur of the Chaldees* (1929); id., *Excavations at Ur* (1954); C. J.

Gadd, in *Archaeology and OT Study*, D. W. Thomas, ed. (1967), 87–101; D. J. Wiseman, *ZPEB*, 5 (1975), 846–48.

BCC

URARTU (ū rär'tū). A mountainous region N of Mesopotamia* which proved to be a formidable rival to the Assyrians in the ninth and eighth centuries B.C. The name first occurs in the form Uruaṭri but is later spelled Urarṭu. Another term used by the Assyrians to describe the general area is Nairi. The Urartians themselves called their kingdom Biaini(li). The same general area became the home of the Armenians.

I. *Biblical References*. Urartu is cognate with the Heb. word transliterated Ararat* by the KJV in Gen 8:4 and in Jer 51:27, but is rendered Armenia, following the LXX, in 2 Kings 19:37 and its parallel, Isa 37:38.

Gen 8:4 describes the resting of Noah's ark after the Flood upon the "mountains of Ararat." The 2 Kings and Isa passages describe the escape of Sennacherib's* sons into the "land of Ararat" after they had murdered their father (cf. Tobit 1:21). Jeremiah associates the kingdom of Urartu with the Minni (i.e., the Mannai S of Lake Urmia) and the Ashkenaz (the Scythians*).

II. *Geography and Resources*. Beginning from an area around Lake Van, the kingdom of Urartu expanded to incorporate the regions around Lake Urmia to the E and Lake Sevan to the NE and the headwaters of the Euphrates to the W. Today the NE section around Lake Sevan is in Soviet Armenia, the SE section around Lake Urmia is in NW Iran, and the central section around Lake Van is in eastern Turkey.

Only Lake Sevan is a fresh water lake; Van and Urmia are filled with concentrations of salts and soda. The plateaus around the lakes are about 1.6 km. (1 mi.) above sea level, surrounded by even higher mountains. The most spectacular mountain is the extinct volcano in eastern Turkey—the so-called Mount Ararat, known as Massis to the Armenians and Agridagh to the Turks—which towers nearly 5,200 m. (17,000 ft.) high.

Though the lakes exert a moderating influence, winters are severe and summers short. The Urartians were famed for the raising of horses* and for viticulture (cf. Gen 9:20–21). The region is also rich in copper, iron,* and lead.*

III. *Sources*. A. *Urartian*. The Urartian language is an agglutinative tongue which is akin to the language of the earlier Hurrians* who hailed originally from the area. We possess about five hundred Urartian inscriptions written in the cuneiform* script borrowed from the Assyrians. These include a few annals and religious texts but are for the most part prosaic royal documents listing conquests and buildings. In addition there are some short texts in an as yet undeciphered system of native pictographs.

B. *Assyrian*. The Akkadian annals describing the conquests of the Assyrian kings—particularly of Shalmaneser III, Tiglath-pileser III,* and Sargon II*—provide us with the greatest information on Urartian history and topography.

C. *Other Sources*. Greek writers such as Herodotus describe the post-Urartian period. Xenophon's *Anabasis* gives a firsthand account of the area c. 400 B.C. Berossus (third century B.C.) gives us an account of the traditional resting place of the ark. It appears that Moses of Chorene (fifth century A.D.) has preserved some ancient traditions of the area.

IV. *History*. The history of Urartu may be divided into four periods: (1) thirteenth–ninth centuries—a period of tribal units which have not yet united; (2) ninth to mid-eighth centuries—a period marked by the formation of the kingdom of Urartu; (3) mid-eighth century to 714—the period of bitter conflict with Assyria; (4) 714–590—the final days of Urartu.

A. *The Earliest Periods*. The first reference to Uruatri appears in the texts of Shalmaneser I (1273–44). Our first substantial accounts come from Shalmaneser III (858–24). His campaigns against Aramu and Sarduri I are reported not only in his annals but in a unique poetic document from Sultantepe and in his famous bronze* gates* from Balawat.

Sarduri I has given us texts, written in Akkadian,* at the base of the Citadel of Van on the eastern shore of Lake Van. The next king, Ishpuini (830–810), has left us the oldest Urartian texts in the capital city* of Tushpa (modern Van) below the citadel.*

Menua (810–786) was one of the greatest of Urartian builders, leaving about one hundred inscriptions. His 76 km. (47 mi.) canal to Tushpa is still in use today. He extended his kingdom to the Araxes River in the N, and to Malatya on the Euphrates in the W. In 1961 Menua's annals were discovered at Aznavur N of Lake Van.

Argishti I (786–64) established the city of Argishtihinili in the Araxes plain and subjugated the area to the N up to Lake Sevan. In the foothills N of Mount Ararat with the labor of 6,600 deported N Syrians he established the town of Erebuni, whose name is preserved in modern Yerevan, the capital of Soviet Armenia. His annals, which are the longest of the Urartian inscriptions, are carved beside his tomb on the Citadel of Van.

B. *Conflict With Assyria*. Until the rise of the great Assyrian king Tiglath-pileser III in 745, Urartu's influence overshadowed that of Assyria in N Syria. Tiglath-pileser, however, defeated Sarduri II in 743 at Arpad and then in 735 besieged the Urartian king in the Citadel of Van. Though he was not able to take the citadel itself, Tiglath-pileser devastated the town and set up his statue* in its ruins.

Rusa I (735–14) attempted to reestablish the Urartian kingdom. In 714, however, his northern borders were overrun by Cimmerians invading over the Caucasus, as we learn from the intelligence reports gathered by the Assyrian crown prince, Sennacherib. We have a detailed account of Sargon II's invasion of Urartu in 714 in the form of a letter* addressed to the god Ashur. Sargon defeated the Urartians at Mount Uaush E of Lake Urmia. If we can believe the report, the Assyrian army marched some 2,415 km. (1500 mi.), proceeding N of Lake Urmia, then

N and W around Lake Van. (Many scholars do not believe that Sargon reached Lake Van.) Sargon then attacked by surprise Musasir, the holy city of the Urartians located between the two lakes. He carted off several tons of gold,* silver,* and bronze* objects.

Urartu was weakened by a second Cimmerian raid in 707. For its part Assyria under Esar-haddon* (680–69) was alarmed at the threat of the Cimmerians and Scythians, as we learn from the questions addressed by the king to his oracles. Urartu survived Assyria's downfall in 612 by only a few years. By 590 Urartu had been conquered by the Medes.*

C. *Armenia.* Classical texts inform us that the Urartians survived as Alarodians. From the sixth century B.C. the dominant group in the area are the Thraco-Phrygian Armenians. Barnett suggests that the name of the last Urartian king Rusa III (605–590) means Rusa "the Armenian" and not the son of Erimena. The name *Armina* appears in the famous Behistun inscription* of Darius,* under whom the area of Van formed the thirteenth satrapy. The Alarodians were to be found in the eighteenth satrapy in the Araxes Valley.

Xenophon led the remnants of ten thousand Greek mercenaries through Armenia to the Black Sea c. 400 B.C. Armenians fought for the Persians against Alexander the Great at Arbela in 331. In the second century B.C. the Artashesid dynasty established the new capital of Armavir in the Araxes Valley with the help of the exiled Hannibal. The dynasty flourished under Tigranes II (95–55 B.C.), who assisted his father-in-law Mithradates against Rome. After Pompey's conquest in 66 B.C. Armenia served as a buffer state between Rome and the Parthians.

In A.D. 66 Tiridates traveled all the way to Rome* to receive the crown of Armenia from the hand of Nero. Trajan in his campaign against Parthia in A.D. 113 captured Armenia. In 1967 an inscription of the Fourth Scythian Legion was discovered at the capital of Artaxata.

V. *Archaeology and Culture.* A. *History of Archaeology.* Urartian studies began with the efforts of travelers such as F. Schulz, who copied inscriptions from the Citadel of Van in the 1820s. The first attempts at excavations were the efforts of H. Rassam in 1879–80 at Toprak-Kale, N of Tushpa; his reports, however, were not made public until the 1950s. C. Lehmann-Haupt conducted more careful excavations at the same site in 1898.

It is only since 1939 that truly scientific excavations have been carried out at Urartian sites by Turkish and Soviet scholars.

B. *Turkish Sites.* 1. *Altintepe.* The "Golden Hill" 19 km. (12 mi.) E of Erzinjan in eastern Turkey is an important Urartian site which has been excavated since 1959 by T. Özgüç. The Urartian settlement, which flourished in the seventh century, includes the best preserved of all Urartian temples and a columned reception hall, which may be the prototype of the later Persian *apadana.* The tombs of Altintepe yielded more gold and silver objects than had ever been found in Urartu.

2. *Lake Van.* Numerous sites around Lake Van

have been explored. A. Erzen continued work at Toprak-Kale between 1959 and 1963. Erzen discovered a fortress of Sarduri II (645–635) at Çavuştepe, E of Lake Van. At Kayalidere, NW of Van, C. Burney in 1965 uncovered a fortress of either Sarduri II or Rusa I which had been destroyed by the Cimmerians. The remains of the Urartian capital of Tushpa still lie under the ruins of the old Turkish city of Van, destroyed by the Russians in 1916.

C. *Russian Sites.* 1. *Karmir-Blur,* or ancient Teishebaini on the outskirts of Yerevan, was a great administrative center founded by Rusa II in the mid-seventh century. It has been subject to excavations for some twenty years from 1939–41 and since 1949 under B. Piotrovsky. The Russians have excavated the main citadel, wine* stores which could hold 100,000 gallons, and granaries* which could hold 750 tons. Bronze shields and helmets inscribed with the names of eighth-century kings had apparently been transferred from nearby Erebuni (see below). Socketed arrowheads in the walls, horse* skeletons, and signs of a devastating fire are evidences of the Scythian attack which destroyed Karmir-Blur c. 600 B.C.

2. *Erebuni,* also in the area of Yerevan, was an Urartian city founded in 783 B.C. It has been subject to excavations under K. Oganesyan since 1951. The well-preserved buildings are decorated with multicolored paintings in the Assyrian style. The site seems to have been voluntarily abandoned when Teishebaini was founded.

3. *Argishtihinili,* another foundation of Artishti I, was identified with the Hill of David in Armavir by B. Arakelian in 1964.

D. *Material Culture.* Though the Urartians were indebted to the Assyrians for their frescoes, they were innovators in other respects. The columned hall at Altintepe may have been the prototype of the Persian *apadana.* Their thick-walled square temples have been compared with the later Persian "tower temples." The temple at Musasir, which is known to us from a relief from Khorsabad,* has a triangular pediment which is strikingly like the later Greek temples. The Urartians were superb metallurgists.* Their bronze cauldrons were imported or imitated in Phrygia,* Greece,* Crete, and even distant Etruria.

E. *Religion.* The head of the Urartian pantheon was the god of heaven and war, Haldi. Some of the earlier German scholars called the Urartians Haldians or Chaldians, a nomenclature which has been abandoned. Haldi's temple was adorned with all manner of weapons.

The second god was the storm god *Teisheba* (cf. Hurrian Teshub), whose wife was Huba (cf. Hurrian Heba). The third god was the sun-god Shivini (cf. Hurrian Shimigi). A long ninth-century text from Mher-Kapusi near Van lists the tariff of offerings* to be presented to the various gods.

It is possible that the Urartians practiced human sacrifice. Lehmann-Haupt found some decapitated skeletons at Toprak-Kale, and an Urartian seal* depicts a beheaded body by an altar.*

VI. *Noah's Ark and Mount Ararat.* In recent times interest has been aroused by widely publicized attempts to identify wooden beams embedded in a glacier slightly below the 4,267 m. (14,000 ft.) level on Mount Ararat as the remains of Noah's ark. The object was sighted by a Russian aviator in 1916. A French industrialist, F. Navarra, has made a number of trips to Mount Ararat and has brought back samples of the wood.* It is reported that the Forestry Institute at Madrid has estimated that the wood is about five thousand years old. Radiocarbon dates, however, have not confirmed such an antiquity.

There are a number of difficulties with the facile identification of the modern Mount Ararat with the mountain of Noah's ark. Gen 8:4 speaks of the "mountains" of Ararat. It is true that Berossus (third century B.C.) quoted by Polyhistor (first century B.C.) relates: "A part of the boat, which came to rest in the Gordyaean mountains of Armenia, still remains, and some people scrape pitch off the boat and use it as charms." Nicolaus of Damascus (cited in Jos. Antiq. 1. 94–95) also located the ark on Baris in Armenia, i.e., Mount Ararat.

On the other hand, there is reason to believe that Noah's ark rested on a mountain in southern rather than northern Urartu. The rendering of Ararat by Qardu, i.e., Kurdistan in southeastern Urartu, is maintained by the Samaritan Pentateuch, Targum Onkelos, and the Peshitta. According to the flood story in the Gilgamesh Epic* (11.140f.), Utnapishtim's boat landed on Mount Nisir. This was identified in the reign of Ashurnasirpal II (ninth century B.C.) with Mount Kinipa, perhaps Pir Omar Gudrun, a peak 2,743 m. (9,000 ft.) high S of the Lower Zab, i.e., in Kurdistan. The original home of the Urartians seems to have been the area of the Upper Zab. It was not until the reign of Menua (810–786 B.C.) that the area of Mount Ararat became a part of Urartu.

BIBLIOGRAPHY: A. T. Olmstead, History of Assyria (1923); R. H. Pfeiffer, State Letters of Assyria (1935); H. Rigg, "Sargon's Eighth Military Campaign," JAOS, 62 (1942), 130–38; E. Wright, "The Eighth Campaign of Sargon II," JNES, 2 (1943), 173–86; K. Maxwell-Hyslop, "Urartian Bronzes in Etruscan Tombs," Iraq, 18 (1956), 150–66; C. Burney, "Urartian Fortresses and Towns in the Van Region," AnSt, 7 (1957), 37–53; R. Follet, " 'Deuxième Bureau' et information diplomatique dans l'Assyrie des Sargonides," RSO, 32 (1957), 61–81; H. W. F. Saggs, "The Nimrud Letters . . . The Urartian Frontier," Iraq, 20 (1958), 182–212; W. Benedict, "Urartians and Hurrians," JAOS, 80 (1960), 100–104; W. G. Lambert, ". . . Shalmaneser in Ararat," AnSt, 11 (1961), 143–58; H. W. F. Saggs, "Assyrian Warfare in the Sargonid Period," Iraq, 25 (1963), 145–54; C. Burney, "A First Season . . . at the Urartian Citadel of Kayalidere," AnSt, 16 (1966), 55–111; M. N. Van Loon, Urartian Art (1966); T. Özgüç, Altintepe (1966); id., "Ancient Ararat," Scientific American, 216 (1967), 37–46; B. Piotrovskii (Piotrovsky), Urartu: The Kingdom of Van and Its Art (1967); M. Salvini, Nairi e Ur(u)aṭri (1967); D. Stronach, "Urartian and Achaemenian Tower Temples," JNES, 26 (1967), 278–88; G. Huxley, ". . . Nikolaos of Damascus on Urartu," Greek, Roman and Byzantine Studies, 9 (1968),

319–20; V. Alekseev et al., Contributions to the Archaeology of Armenia (1968); G. Azarpay, Urartian Art and Artifacts (1968); T. Özgüç, "Urartu and Altintepe," ARC, 22 (1969), 256–63; B. Piotrovsky, The Ancient Civilization of Urartu (1969); D. Lang, Armenia: Cradle of Civilization (1970); Bible et Terre Sainte, no. 131 (1971), 6–15; G. Melikishvili, Die urartäische Sprache (1971); J. W. Montgomery, "Ark Fever," ChT, 15 (2 July 1971), 38–39; id., "Arkeology," ChT, 16 (7 January 1972), 50–51; C. Burney and D. Lang, The Peoples of the Hills: Ancient Ararat and Caucasus (1972); J. W. Montgomery, The Quest for Noah's Ark (1972); O. Muscarella, "Qalatgah: An Urartian Site in Northwestern Iran," Expedition, 13 (1971), 44–49; C. Burney, "Urartian Irrigation Works," AnSt, 22 (1972), 179–86; F. Navarra, Noah's Ark, I Touched It (1974); M. Van Loon, "The Inscription of Ishpuini and Meinua at Qalatgah, Iran," JNES, 34 (1975), 201–8; W. H. Stiebing, "A Futile Quest: The Search for Noah's Ark," BAR, 2 (1976), 1, 13–20; L. R. Bailey, "Wood from 'Mount Ararat': Noah's Ark?" BA, 40 (1977), 137–46; A. J. Hoerth, "In Search of Noah's Ark," Near East Archaeological Society Bulletin, 9 (1977), 5–24; M. Van Loon, "The Place of Urartu in First-Millennium B.C.," Iraq, 39 (1977), 229–32; E. Yamauchi, "Critical Comments on the Search for Noah's Ark," Near East Archaeological Society Bulletin, 10 (1977), 5–27; O. Muscarella, "Urartian Bells and Samos," Journal of the Ancient Near East Society of Columbia University, 10 (1978), 61–72; M. Salini and C. Saporetti, A Dedicatory Inscription of the Urartian King Išpuini . . . (1979); W. Kleiss, "Bastam, an Urartian Citadel Complex of the Seventh Century B.C.," AJA, 84 (1980), 299–304; E. Yamauchi, Foes From the Northern Frontiers (1982). EY

URFA (ûr'fə). An important city* from the second century B.C. located 32 km. (20 mi.) NW of Haran* on the upper reaches of the Balik River in SE Turkey.

An old tradition identified Urfa with Ur* of the Chaldees,* but there seems to be no foundation for considering the city to be much older than the time of the Seleucid monarchs. The Greeks called the city Edessa, after the first capital of the conquering Macedonians, and by c. 137 B.C. it had become the capital of the Kingdom of Osroene. The Romans took Edessa, together with all of the area, keeping it until the Persian king Shapur I captured the city (along with the Roman Emperor Valerian) in 260 A.D.

Syrian Christianity became dominant in the third century, and although the city was again controlled by Christians in the eleventh and twelfth centuries (first by Byzantium, then by the Armenians Vahram and Thoros, with a brief interregnum by the Turks, and finally by the Frankish knight Baldwin of Boulogne and his successors), the city was predominantly Muslim from the time of the Arab conquest in 639 A.D. The great fortress of the Byzantine* and Crusader city testifies to the importance of Edessa as a border town and regional capital.

Recent Turkish excavations in the region have focused on prehistoric remains.

BIBLIOGRAPHY: H. Alkim, "Explorations and Excavations in Turkey, 1963," *Jaarbericht . . . Ex Oriente Lux*, 18 (1964), sec. 1, 345–82; H. Alkim, "Explorations and Excavations in Turkey, 1964," *Anatolica*, 1 (1967), sec. 8, 1–43.

CEA

UR, LAMENTATION OVER THE DESTRUCTION OF. A Sumerian* text recovered from twenty-two tablets excavated at Nippur* and Ur.* The composition is in the form of eleven epic poems describing the overthrow of Ur, the desecration of the temple Ekishnugal, and the capture of the last king of the Third Dynasty, Ibbi-Sin. This conquest by the Elamites* and their allies is also attested by archaeological remains. The gods are portrayed as declaring the city's destruction over the protests of Ningal, the patron goddess. The text is the earliest formal lament yet discovered. Jeremiah's Lamentations are a distant example of the same literary tradition. Apart from this the composition is of biblical interest only as a final page in the history of Abraham's city.

BIBLIOGRAPHY: S. N. Kramer, "The Lamentation Over the Destruction of Ur," *AS*, 12 (1940); id., *The Sumerians, Their History, Culture and Character* (1963), 38, 89, 142–43, 200, 259.   WW

UR-NAMMU (ûr nä'mü). The first king of the great Third Dynasty of Ur,* which ushered in the Neo-Sumerian period (c. 2070–1960 B.C.). His outstanding constructional achievement was the great ziggurat* at Ur, and bricks stamped with his name have been recovered from the site, which was excavated by Woolley in 1922–23. The ziggurat design was unusual in that the walls were built on curves to give a delicate structural effect, a concept later revived by the Greeks. A fragmentary stele* of Ur-Nammu in white limestone furnished a contemporary record of the building of the ziggurat and contains among other things the earliest known artistic representation of an angel.

Ur-Nammu was also a social reformer, and the author of a legal code which has been recovered in an unfortunately late and fragmentary form. The social changes which he instituted regulated weights and measures (cf. Lev 19:35), forbade the exploitation of the widow and orphan (cf. Exod 22:22; Deut 14:29 et al.), and strove to promote the aims of justice in the land. Restitution rather than a strict *lex talionis* emphasized the distinctively humanitarian approach of his code, which in other respects has much in common with the spirit of Mosaic legislation.

BIBLIOGRAPHY: S. N. Kramer, *The Sumerians* (1963); *CAH*, 1, part 1, 200, 331; ibid., part 2, 289 passim.   RKH

UR, STANDARD OF. This is a wood-enclosed mosaic* in lapis lazuli,* recovered by Sir Leonard Woolley from the royal graves* at Ur.* When restored it proved to have comprised a wooden panel 56 cm. (22 in.) long and 23 cm. (9 in.) wide, inlaid with mosaic scenes. It was apparently carried in procession by a standard-bearer, and the two sides depicted the themes of war and peace, i.e., representative of Sumerian* life as a whole. The standard is particularly interesting for the way in which it depicted weapons (*see* ARMS) of warfare* and especially the nature and deployment of Sumerian chariotry.* It also testifies to the wealth and prosperity of the Early Dynastic III period (c. 2500 B.C.).

In his *Ur of the Chaldees*, C. Leonard Woolley describes the discovery of this amazing piece of Sumerian art: "In the largest of all the stone-built royal tombs, which had been entered by robbers and most thoroughly plundered, there remained only one corner of the last chamber to be cleared, and we had given up expectation of any 'finds' when suddenly a loose bit of shell inlay turned up, and the next minute the foreman's hand . . . laid bare the corner of a mosaic in lapis lazuli and shell. This was the famous 'Standard' of Ur, but at the time we had very little idea of what it might be. . . . So delicate was the

"War panel" from standard found at Ur, depicting triumph of the king over his enemies. Mosaic panel in shell, lapis lazuli and red limestone, 25th century B.C. Reproduced by courtesy of the Trustees of the British Museum.

task of removing the dirt without further disturbing the mosaic that only about a square inch could be dealt with at a time—each section was waxed as soon as cleared, but so much of the surrounding dirt mingled with the hot wax that the face of the panel became invisible. When at last it could be lifted from the earth, I knew that we had found a very fine thing, but should have been hard put to it to say exactly what it was."

Woolley goes on (81–87) to describe the careful restoration which brought to life this panel. The royal family is shown feasting, sitting in chairs, clad with their sheepskin kilts. A musician accompanies on a harp a woman singing with her hands on her bosom. In a lower band of mosaic, attendants bring in food captured from the enemy—a goat,* two large fish, a corded bale. The king, in another part stands by his chariot,* reviewing bound lines of prisoners. Then a royal regiment with copper helmets and long cloaks* parades with battle axes, together with lighter-armed auxiliaries, armed with spears, and without cloaks. The chariotry forms an impressive scene, moving over the battlefield with driver and archer in each.

Woolley concludes: "The 'Standard' is a remarkable work of art, but it has yet greater value as an historical document, for here we have figured the earliest detailed picture of that army which carried the civilization of the Sumerians from their early settlements on the fringe of the Persian Gulf to the mountains of Anatolia and to the shores of the Mediterranean Sea. We know from actual examples found in their graves* that their weapons were, both in design and in manufacture, far superior to anything that their contemporaries possessed or any other nation was to adopt for two thousand years; from this representation we can learn enough about the organization of the army to know that it must have been more than a match for anything that could be brought against it at that time."

BIBLIOGRAPHY: C. L. Woolley, *Ur of the Chal-*

dees (1929), 81–87; H. W. F. Saggs, *Iraq*, 22 (1960), 200–209; C. J. Gadd, *Archaeology and OT Study* (1967), 87–101; D. J. Wiseman, *ZPEB*, 5 (1975), 846–48.

EMB

URUK. *See* ERECH.

URUKAGINA (û rū kə gē'nə). A king of Lagash* who ruled in the early dynastic period. He fell heir to a corrupt and oppressive social system which seems to have resulted from the aggressive policies of the dynasty founded at Lagash about 2500 B.C. by Ur-Nanshe. Eventually the imperialistic drive of the latter was halted, and by the time that Urukagina came to power the state had become vulnerable militarily and weak in structure and economy. All the evidence is, of course, archaeological.

Inspired by Ningirsu, the patron deity of Lagash, Urukagina promulgated an enlightened series of social reforms which restored freedom and justice to Lagash, protected helpless members of the community (cf. Deut 16:11; 24:17 et al.), and reduced bureaucracy. He terminated the fiscal interests which previous *ensis* had had in commercial and legal transactions, redistributed property which had been wrongly accumulated by palace authorities, and terminated the activities of oppressive tax* collectors. The exploitation of the poor by the rich (cf. Amos 2:6–7) was prohibited, and in general his reforms demonstrated much the same social concerns as those evident in the Mosaic legislation.

BIBLIOGRAPHY: *CAH*, 1, part 1, 220–21; ibid., part 2, 105 passim.

RKH

UTENSILS AND IMPLEMENTS. *See* AMPHORA; BASIN; CANOPIC JAR; KEY; KNIFE; LADDER; LAMP; MIRROR; MORTAR; NEEDLE; OVEN; PADDLE; POTTERY; QUERN; VESSELS.

V

VALLEY, CITIES OF THE. *See* PLAIN, CITIES OF THE.

VALLEY OF SALT. *See* SALT.

VALLUM. An entrenchment and earthen rampart topped by a palisade.

VEGETABLES. *See* FOOD.

VELLUM. *See* PARCHMENT.

VESPASIAN. Titus Flavius Vespasianus, founder of the Flavian dynasty of emperors (Vespasian, Titus,* Domitian*—A.D. 69–96), was born A.D. 9 and died A.D. 79. He was commander in Britain under Claudius,* was proconsul of Asia, and was commander of the legions which took in hand the suppression of the great Jewish rebellion (A.D. 66–80). Vespasian was the architect of recovery after the "year of the four emperors" (A.D. 69), when he proved the survivor after a multilateral civil war between the legionary commanders over the principate. Ironically, Nero had chosen Vespasian for the eastern command because, in Harold Mattingly's phrase, "he combined the necessary military requirements with the lack of social distinction which ensured his harmlessness." These qualities proved the Empire's salvation. Vespasian, said Tacitus, was the one man whom supreme authority improved.

Statues* and coins* show Vespasian for what he was, a tough soldier, earthy, able, solid, shrewd. He built the Colosseum,* employing thousands of Jewish captives, and the name of this vast monument (*theatrum Flavianum*) commemorates him. A stele* from Jerusalem* contains Vespasian's name together with

Bronze coin, 35 mm., minted in Rome. Obverse: laureate head of Vespasian. Reverse: captive Jewess weeping, seated on armor. In center, tall palm tree. On left, Titus(?). Legend: IVDAEA CAPTA; S(enatus) C(onsulto). Courtesy Israel Museum, Jerusalem.

that of Titus, who carried on the siege when Vespasian left for Rome,* and the half obliterated name of the Tenth Legion's commander.

BIBLIOGRAPHY: H. Mattingly, *Roman Imperial Civilization* (1957), passim; H. C. Newton, "The Epigraphical Evidence for the Reigns of Vespasian and Titus, Cornell Studies in Classical Philology (1901); H. Mattingly and E. Sydenham, *The Roman Imperial Coinage*, 4, part 2 (1923), 1–213; *CAH*, 11 (1936), 1–45.   EMB

VESSELS. Vessels of many sorts were used for storage of food* or valuables (e.g., the Dead Sea Scrolls*; cf. Paul's figure in 2 Cor 4:7). Materials were varied, from the ubiquitous pottery* of ancient civilizations to precious metals, glass,* and ornamental stone such as alabaster* (Mark 14:3). Survival depends upon the durability of the material, but there is much illustration of all forms of containers in art.

The earliest Near Eastern village settlements of the Neolithic Age* employed coarse pottery containers, and in Palestine in the biblical period ceramic ware comprised the commonest form in which vessels appeared. Nomadic peoples had a natural preference for skin bags or bottles, as well as for containers made of woven fibers—baskets of wicker, for example. Cloth* bags were almost certainly in use from the beginning of the Chalcolithic* period but have not survived in recognizable form. Stone utensils such as mortars* or querns,* used for pulverizing or grinding, dated from the Neolithic period in both Mesopotamia* and Egypt.*

From 3000 B.C. the goldsmiths and silversmiths of Sumer* were making elegant vessels from precious metals, and by the beginning of the Iron Age* a full complement of materials for the manufacture of containers was available. Metal gradually displaced stone for most vessels, although substances such as alabaster continued in use, especially for expensive ointments* (Matt 26:7). Bowls of bronze* (Exod 27:3), silver* (Num 7:13), and gold* (2 Chron 4:8) were used in the Hebrew sacrificial system of the pre-Exilic period, matched after the Exile* by smaller ones in silver and gold (cf. Ezra 1:10; 8:27). Glass* containers were still only a novelty in the NT period.

Size varied from small flasks for cosmetics* (Mark 14:3) to huge jars, which may be seen, fitted with multiple handles for ropes, in the storerooms of Minos's palace at Knossos in Crete. Baskets varied from those that could be carried on head or shoulder (Gen 40:16; Exod 29:3), made to hold fruit (Jer 24:1–2) or

Khirbet Kerak ware Early Bronze Age III pot found at Afula. Courtesy Israel Dept. of Antiquities and Museums.

to serve as a brickmaker's hod (Ps 81:6), to containers large enough to hold up a person (Acts 9:25; 2 Cor 11:33). The following alphabetical* survey is representative but not exhaustive.

Baskets. Add to above the baskets mentioned in connection with the feeding of the five thousand and the four thousand. The former instance (Matt 14:20) has the word *kophinos*, a rush or wicker basket used by Jews* to contain food free from alien pollution. Juvenal mentions the word in a reference to the Jews in the slum ghetto outside Rome's Capena Gate (Juv. *Sat.* 3.14). Curiously the second instance (Matt 15:37) has a word which appears to describe the large bottle-shaped Gentile basket. The incident took place in the predominantly Gentile territory of the Decapolis.* Plaited baskets of rush have survived from Egypt's second millennium B.C.—the so-called New Kingdom (1580–1085). Roman wicker baskets, like a modern wastepaper basket, also survive from the early centuries of the Christian era in Egypt.

Bottles. Animal skins for keeping water (Gen 21:14–15, 19), milk (Judg 4:19), wine* (Josh 9:4, 13; 1 Sam 1:24; 10:3; 2 Sam 16:1). Figuratively used at Job 32:19.

Buckets. Perhaps pitchers were used for drawing water from wells.* They could be lowered by a rope* through the handles, and it is not known whether there were buckets of leather* or wood* (Gen 24:14–19; John 4:11). A Theban tomb shows a man lifting water for a garden in a bucket.

Baths and Bushels. They are both measures of capacity and containers (cf. 1 Kings 7:26, 38; 2 Chron 2:10; Matt 5:15). From estimates of the contents of two eighth-century B.C. jars, which, in archaic Hebrew characters, were labeled "bt," or "bath," a capacity of 22 liters (5½ gal.) is estimated.

Basins (or bowls). Mainly for libation and mentioned frequently in connection with the ritual utensils of tabernacle and temple* (e.g., 1 Kings 7:42, 50), but also in domestic contexts (2 Sam 17:28; John 13:5). Bowls and cups, in ceramic ware or metal, were frequently works of art.

Cups. Nomenclature is wide and distinctions uncertain. Size and shape were varied in all contexts.

The "dishes" and "bowls" of several references may well be cups in modern terminology.

Dishes. Usually for food on the table, a large deep container commonly of bronze, still used for the common meal of the Bedouin. Some such dish was used at the Last Supper as at all Passover feasts. See Judg 5:25; Prov 19:24, 26; Matt 26:23.

Pitchers. Commonly with two handles, jugs large and small, flat, rounded or pointed bottoms for insertion in a perforated board, like the wine* jars in the taverns of Pompeii* and in the hold of the sunken Roman ship* near Marseilles. Normally they were carried by women fetching water (Gen 24:14–19), rarely by men (Luke 22:10). People often slept with a pitcher of water near at hand (1 Sam 26:7–11).

BIBLIOGRAPHY: R. B. K. Amiran, "The Story of Pottery in Palestine," *Antiquity and Survival*, II, 2, 3 (1957), 187–207; J. L. Kelso, *IDB*, 3 (1962), 846–53; P. W. Lapp in J. Sanders, ed., *Near Eastern Archaeology in the Twentieth Century* (1970), 101–31; H. Jamieson, *ZPEB*, 4 (1975), 824–29.

RKH and EMB

VIA APPIA. *See* APPIAN WAY.

VIA EGNATIA. *See* EGNATIAN WAY.

VICTORY STELE OF EANNATUM. *See* VULTURES, STELE OF.

VIPER. *See* SERPENT.

VIZIER OF PHARAOH. J. H. Breasted, in a long and amply documented chapter in his *A History of Egypt* discusses the high position and responsibility of Pharaoh's chief executive officer at the period of Egyptian history relevant to Joseph's* story.

The viziers of Egypt's Eighteenth Dynasty were officials of great power. Breasted says: ". . . no higher praise could be proffered to [the god] Amon when addressed by a worshiper than to call him 'the poor man's vizier who does not accept the bribe of the guilty.' His appointment was a matter of such importance that it was conducted by the king [Pharaoh] himself, and the instructions given him by the monarch on that occasion were not such as we should expect from the lips of an oriental conqueror three thousand five hundred years ago. They display a spirit of kindness and humanity and exhibit an appreciation of state craft surprising in an age so remote."

An official of the Eighteenth Dynasty mentions his exaltation in youth from humility to the high and trusted station of vizier and the rewards which attended his efficient administration.

For comments on Joseph's position, as to whether he was vizier or Overseer of the Granaries, see D. Kidner, *Genesis* (1967), 196 and f.n.

BIBLIOGRAPHY: J. H. Breasted, *A History of Egypt* (1945), 233–45; J. Vergote, *Joseph en Égypt* (1959); K. A. Kitchen, *NBD* (1962), 656–60.

EMB

VULTURES, STELE OF. Also called the Victory Stele of Eannatum, this limestone monument is both a masterpiece of Sumerian art and an important historical document of Eannatum of Lagash* (c. 2400 B.C.).

The stele,* which was originally 1.88 m. (c. 5 ft.) high, 1.3 m. (just over 4 ft.) wide, and 11 cm. (almost 4 in.) thick, was found in fragments in the excavations at Telloh conducted by Ernest de Sarzac at the end of the nineteenth century. It is now one of the prize possessions of the Louvre.

The Stele of Vultures commemorates Eannatum's victory over the forces of Ummah,* depicting the human agents of the triumph on one side and the divine intervention on the other side.

The monument received its name from the presence of vultures who are devouring the enemy corpses. In the top register Eannatum and his phalanx of heavy infantry march over the prostrate enemy. In the next register the king in a war chariot* leads his light infantry. In the third register the Lagashites are providing a decent burial for their own dead. All that survives of the fourth register is a spear striking the forehead of a captive.

The large figure of Ningirsu, tutelary god of Lagash, dominates the other side of the stele. The god holds the bodies of the enemy in a net in his left hand and a stone mace in his right hand.

The accompanying inscription justifies Eannatum's campaign on the basis of Ummah's failure to observe the provisions of an earlier settlement. Some 3,600 casualties were inflicted.

BIBLIOGRAPHY: G. A. Barton, *The Royal Inscriptions of Sumer and Akkad* (1929), 22–33; *ANEP* (1954), figs. 298–302; A. Parrot, *Sumer* (1960), 134–37; A. Moortgat, *The Art of Ancient Mesopotamia* (1969), 42–43.

EY

W

WADI (wä'di). An Arabic term for a seasonal water-course that is usually dry, but is also a valley for perennial springs.

WADI MURABBAAT. *See* DEAD SEA SCROLLS.

WAILING WALL. Part of the western wall* of Je-rusalem* which was rebuilt by Herod (*see* HEROD, BUILDING ACTIVITIES) during his reconstruction of the temple* and the general enlargement of its pre-cincts. The presence of valleys precluded any exten-sion of the temple area to the E or W, hence the emphasis there upon the rebuilding of the walls. The celebrated Wailing Wall, now known in Israel as the West Wall, was supposedly erected upon Solomonic foundations. However, no traces of what can be re-garded confidently as Solomon's* walls have been recovered to date. The most that can be said is that the two lowest courses of stone comprising the pres-ent West Wall may perhaps go back to the period of Nehemiah. The association of the wall with wailing arose from the tradition among the Jews* of going to that area to lament the fate which had overtaken the Herodian temple.   RKH

WALLS, CITY. City walls were for defense, and in an area as prone to invasion as Palestine the defense of the city* was of prime importance. Some of the city walls of which archaeology has uncovered traces are of very great antiquity. Excavations at Jericho* showed that the city was already defended by a stone wall and ditch in the Neolithic* period (c. 7000 B.C.). In the OT it is taken for granted that every town and city will have its wall; only small and insignificant villages could feel secure without one (Ezek 38:11; Zech 2:4).

Defense walls had of necessity to be very large; that of Mizpah,* not a big city, was some 10.7 m. (35 ft.) high and 4.6–6 m. (15–20 ft.) thick. Their height explains David's metaphor at 2 Sam 22:30 (Ps 18:29), "by my God I can leap over a wall"—i.e., this superhuman feat could be accomplished only by the power of God. On top they were wide enough to walk upon. Here watchmen were stationed (Isa 62:6); here the king of Israel walked as he worried about the famine in Samaria* (2 Kings 6:26–30); and here the king of Moab* sacrificed his eldest son (2 Kings 3:27). They were built of stone (Hab 2:11); those at Mizpah, for instance, were built of limestone rocks set in clay* mortar.* Walls of bronze* and iron* appear in the OT as metaphors of impregnable strength (bronze, Jer 1:18; iron, Ezek 4:3).

Western Wall on Jerusalem Day, 1971. To the left is the Dome of the Rock and to the right the Al-Aqsa Mosque. In the background is Mount Scopus and the Mount of Olives. Courtesy Israel Government Press Office.

Archaeology has revealed two characteristic types of Israelite defense wall. One of these is the case-mated wall.* The other is that furnished with redans, or angled projections breaking the straight line of the walls; these appear, e.g., at Megiddo.* Sometimes the outside of the wall was given a smooth coating to make it more difficult to scale; sometimes there was the additional protection of a glacis.* A wall on a hill might be protected by a parallel wall some distance below but within weapon range; together these are the "rampart and wall" of, e.g., Lam 2:8. Defense walls were usually strengthened by means of towers.* It is not known for certain whether the Israelites topped their walls with battlements.

The role of the city walls in time of war has been illustrated graphically by bas-reliefs* on Assyrian monuments, depicting such scenes as the capture of Lachish,* and can be readily exemplified from the OT. The defending soldiers were stationed on them (Ezek 27:11), from where they could shoot their ar-rows down on the attackers (2 Sam 11:20, 24), or from where, as a last resort, citizens could hurl down pieces of masonry (2 Sam 11:21). Men stationed on the walls could overhear a conversation going on be-low; and the Rabshakeh took advantage of this to convey a propagandist message to the inhabitants of Jerusalem* (2 Kings 18:26ff.).

Mounting an attack on such a wall involved two different operations: an onslaught with battering rams in an effort to make a breach in it, and the building of a mound to raise some of the attackers to the level of the defenders. These two operations are men-

Israelite northern city gate at Mizpah (Tell en-Nasbeh), ninth century B.C. Courtesy Israel Dept. of Antiquities and Museums.

tioned in 2 Sam 20:15 and Ezek 26:8–9. If the attack was successful the defenders would be dislodged from the wall and the attackers would stream over it into the city; the process is very vividly portrayed in Joel 2:7–9. The battering ram might also create a breach in the wall; and this process is described in a graphic poetic picture in Isa 30:13.

The metaphorical use of walls in Hebrew poetry should not be allowed to pass unnoticed; some instances have already been given. As symbols of defense and protection they appear in Isa 26:1 and 60:18 (where they are linked with the idea of salvation) and at Prov 18:11. Particularly interesting is Prov 25:28 where a man without self-control is said to be as defenseless as a city without walls. The image of destruction when the walls of a city yield to the battering rams and collapse is used by Isa to suggest the destruction on the Day of Yahweh (Isa 2:15; 22:5; cf. Ezek 38:20). But his finest use of this image is that already mentioned (Isa 30:13), where he likens the Israelites' sin to the break in the wall which precedes its collapse. The building of walls is a metaphor for reestablishment in Mic 7:11; and the astonishing reversal of role whereby foreigners built up Jerusalem's walls (Isa 60:10) instead of trying to break them down is a vivid poetic picture of peace among the nations.

BIBLIOGRAPHY: Y. Yadin, *The Art of Warfare in Biblical Lands* (1963); illustrations are given on the following pages: 115 (Jericho); 178, 9 (Hazor—also 370, 1, 8, 9); 228 (Ashkelon); 372, 3 (Megiddo); 430–37 (Lachish), etc.   WFR

WARFARE. The organized violence by which one nation, by military force, endeavors to impose its desires upon another, is as old as man himself (cf. Gen 4:8). Warfare has been refined progressively from antiquity to today and linked with technology to produce increasingly effective and sophisticated weaponry (*see* ARMS AND WEAPONS). Even early third-millennium B.C. Mesopotamian* warriors were surprisingly well equipped, as the mosaic* panel known as the Standard of Ur* (c. 2600 B.C.) shows. They used the chariot* as a weapon, and fought with bows and arrows, maces of various styles, narrow-bladed axes, spears, daggers, javelins, and such de-

fensive devices as helmets,* shields, and coats of mail.

These basic weapons were improved by various nations over the centuries, as, for example, by the introduction of the compound Asiatic bow, which had several times the range of the ordinary variety. Evidence from archaeological sources is abundant. When iron* began to be manufactured by the Hittites,* the sword was one of the first weapons to be made of the new metal. Ancient art and surviving remnants give a comprehensive picture of the tools of war.

For warfare in open terrain the deep phalanx, devised by the Sumerians,* was a popular method of frontal attack. The infantry moved forward under the shelter of rectangular shields, their spears at the ready, integrating their tactics with those of the chariotry.* Once enemy forces had been halted, hand-to-hand combat with spears and axes generally decided the outcome. Egyptian wall paintings provide some striking illustrations.

Warfare, of course, was not always of the offensive variety, and excavations at the prepottery Neolithic* levels of Jericho* showed the presence there of defensive fortifications. Major Near Eastern cities* had defense walls* of various thicknesses, and consequently were able to withstand sieges reasonably well (cf. Samaria,* 1 Kings 20; 2 Kings 6:24). Penetrating such walls involved using battering rams (cf. Ezek 4:2; 21:22), burning the gates,* or scaling (cf. 2 Sam 5:8). Assyrian siege tactics are vividly shown in their realistic mural art. At times attempts were made to undermine the walls, usually a hazardous undertaking. Water supplies were sometimes located outside the city walls, making it necessary on occasions for tunnels such as the Siloam* conduit (2 Kings 20:20) to be constructed.

Warfare was generally conducted along well-recognized lines. Fortified cities were given an opportunity of surrendering to a besieging enemy (cf. 2 Kings 18:28–37). If they did, the people and the buildings were spared, though booty* would be taken. If they resisted, they could usually expect to be annihilated if the siege was successful (cf. Josh 6:21, etc.). The sanguinary Assyrian inscriptions and frescoes are eloquent in this regard.

Occasionally an army would march through the night and launch a surprise attack at dawn (cf. Josh 10:9 et al.). The ambush was sometimes used effectively by small forces (cf. Josh 8:12 et al.), but the hazards of such an attack are described vividly in the Anastasi Papyrus.

BIBLIOGRAPHY: Y. Yadin, *The Art of Warfare in Biblical Lands* (1963). RKH

WARKA. *See* ERECH.

WASHERMAN. *See* FULLER.

WATERWORKS. *See* AQUEDUCT; CISTERN; DRAIN; IRRIGATION; POOLS.

WEAPONS. *See* ARMS AND WEAPONS.

WEAVING. *See* CRAFTS.

WEDDINGS. *See* MARRIAGE.

WEIGHTS AND MEASURES. The references in the bibliography below give adequate information on the terminology of weights and measures relevant to the accurate understanding of the Bible. In accordance with the purpose of this volume, only the archaeological contributions will be listed—extrabiblical references, literal and metaphorical, and the relevant tools* and implements which have survived.

Ur Nammu,* the first ruler and founder of the Third Dynasty of Ur* (c. 2050 B.C.), first established standard weights and measures in an attempt to regularize the practice of the marketplace. His regulations are found in one of the earliest legal codes. In a surviving hymn to the goddess Nanshe there are words of denunciation against evildoers who substitute a small for a large weight, and a small for a large measure (cf. Deut 24:13–14 et al.). The Code of Hammurabi* contains similar references.

Balances. The balance was basically a beam suspended in equilibrium or supported in such equilibrium on an upright support. A papyrus* from the twenty-first-century Egyptian Book of the Dead,* the so-called Millbank Papyrus, shows such a balance—a high and substantial structure, on which the heart of the deceased is weighed (cf. Dan 5:27 and elsewhere). A feather representing truth is weighed against the heart, or else the full figure of the deity of Ma'at. A relief from the temple of the princess Hatshepsut (1486–1469 B.C.) shows a similar implement with weights in a pan balanced against rings of metal. This was part of the cargo from the famous voyage to Punt. A descending arm is at right angles to the beam. Ramses III* (1198–1167) boasts of the enormous quantities of precious metal used in building the temple balances which weighed the tribute (*see* BOOTY AND TRIBUTE) brought in (J. H. Breasted, *A History of Egypt* [1945], 491). The Black Obelisk of Shalmaneser* from the time of Ashurbanipal II* (880 B.C.) shows Assyrian scribes weighing tribute.

Weights. Balances require use of known and somewhat standardized weights, and the existing pieces of stone, metal, and glass* which were so used leave room for much conjecture. Some are inscribed, some not, and D. J. Wiseman (*NBD*, 1320) remarks on the difficulty of establishing any uniformity regarding the weights which survive. Weights were sometimes ornamental. A fifteenth-century tomb painting from Thebes* shows a tall ornamental scale some 1.8 m. (6 ft.) high with a weight in the pan the shape of a bull's head, another ready in a container on the floor, and a third in the shape of a cat* couchant (lying on its stomach with its hind legs and forelegs pointed forward), and probably of smaller value, beside it. Egyptian weights exhibit many animal, bird, and geometrical forms. A bronze* weight from the palace of Shalmaneser, inscribed as his property (845 B.C.) is shaped like a roaring, couchant lion* and is fitted with a handle to lift it. Babylon* provides from the eighteenth century a series of five cylindrical polished hematite weights. Bronze weights inlaid with gold,* of uncertain date and decorated with the figure of a beetle, come from Nimrud.* Flinders Petrie, in fact, from Egypt* and Palestine, collected 5,400 weights, and diligently assigned Egyptian, Hebrew, and Greek names to them. Again, the difficulty of

1. Bronze lion-weight found at Nimrud. The cuneiform inscription reads: "Palace of Shalmaneser [V] king of Ashur, two-thirds mina of the king." The Aramaic inscription reads: "Two-thirds [mina] of the land." 2. Bronze weights inlaid in gold with figures of beetles, found at Nimrud but probably of Egyptian origin. Reproduced by courtesy of the Trustees of the British Museum.

establishing anything like a standard is obvious. An early Babylonian oval stone is inscribed "one half mina true weight," but the ancient world was as non-uniform as the world of today in fixing ratios and standards.

Inscribed weights from Israelite areas—Lachish,* Zahariyeh, Samaria,* Tell en-Nasbeh, Beth Zur,* Gezer,* Silwan, and Salah—bear archaic Hebrew characters (see EPIGRAPHY, HEBREW), and large numbers date from the seventh century B.C. Some of them have provided unknown words. A weight found in Nablus, for example, in 1890, was marked "netseph." The term does not occur in the Bible, and its meaning can only be conjectured.

Pîm is another weight term previously unknown, which clears up previous mistranslation of 1 Sam 13:21 (see RSV, "The charge was a pim," about two-thirds of a shekel; cf. NIV v. and f.n.).

The half shekel was a *beqa'*, a word found in Gen 24:22, though again the surviving samples give no accurate confirmation of this estimate. They seem to be overweight.

Capacity. Turning to measures of capacity, there is some evidence (of no direct biblical significance) in the Rhind Mathematical Papyrus, and abundant terms are in existence from the northern cultures—Sumerian,* Assyrian, Babylonian, and Nuzian* texts. Hebrew terms for capacities are, of course, part of the OT vocabulary. But the evidence which archaeology can provide for these is naturally scarcer than that for weights. Containers are often only implied in the text and are generally more fragile than the implements of weight. There is a broken jar top from Lachish,* marked "royal bath." A similar amphora fragment comes from Tell Beit Mirsim (see DEBIR). A guess based on an extrapolated reconstruction of these fragments suggests that a bath was between 19 and 22.7 liters (5 and 6 gal.). This seems the total of the evidence.

Length. The most common measure of length was the cubit, and it is significant that this unit was represented by the hieroglyph* of a horizontal forearm with the thumb down. A cubit rule with markings and overlaid with gold* comes from the treasures of Amenhotep II and bears his name. Graduated scales discovered by archaeologists are notable for their variation. Graduated rules on statues* of Gudea* show slight variation between the cubits of Lagash.* A Sumerian ideogram* for a span implies the distance between the tip of the thumb and the tip of the little finger in the extended palm. This was half a cubit. No cubit measures have come from Palestine. The Siloam Inscription,* which gives the length of Hezekiah's Tunnel* as 1,200 cubits, suggests a length of 44.5 cm. (17½ in.) for the cubit; but the 1,200 is no doubt only a round number.

BIBLIOGRAPHY: O. R. Sellars, "Weights and Measures," *IDB*, 4 (1962), 828–39; D. J. Wiseman and D. H. Wheaton, "Weights and Measures," *NBD* (1962), 1319–25; F. N. Pryce and M. Lang, "Measures," *OCD* (1970 ed.), 659; id., "Weights," ibid., 1138; J. B. Graybill, "Weights and Measures," *ZPBD* (1971), 890–92; F. B. Huey, Jr., *ZPEB*, 5 (1975), 913–22.

EMB

WELL. A well is any kind of opening dug into the ground for the purpose of collecting water, whether for tapping a subterranean spring or for furnishing a small reservoir in which water can collect (see CISTERN). The scarcity of rainfall in Near Eastern lands such as Palestine made wells extremely important, hence the celebrations associated with the finding of water in Num 21:17–18. The well of Rachel (Gen 24:11) was evidently a shaft dug to tap an underground stream (cf. John 4:6). Wells of this kind were valuable possessions over which people often quarreled (cf. Gen 21:25) and were located in such widely-differing places as the wilderness (Gen 16:14), in courtyards (2 Sam 17:18), in fields (Gen 29:2), and outside cities* (Gen 24:11). Early wells were frequently little more than muddy watering holes, but by the Iron Age* it had become customary to build a low circular retaining wall around the well to avoid contamination of the valuable water and also to prevent accidents to people and animals. Typical wells outside villages and towns had walls of three or four courses of stone, which were generally surmounted by a crossbar and pulley system so that the heavy containers of stone or pottery* could be raised and lowered quite readily by women, who normally discharged this kind of task. Plastered* cisterns of various sizes were also used for collecting and storing rain water, the well at Bethlehem* (1 Chron 11:17) being a probable example. The structures at Qumran* were typical storage cisterns rather than wells.

BIBLIOGRAPHY: W. L. Reed, *IDB*, 4 (1962), 839; H. Jamieson, *ZPEB*, 5 (1975), 925.

RKH

WENAMON. See CEDAR.

WHEEL. The invention of the wheel was one of the great technological advances of man. Fourth-millennium B.C. clay* representations of chariot* wheels and fragments of a potter's wheel recovered from Ur* of the Chaldees form the earliest definite evidence to date for the antiquity of the wheel. The first wheels were probably suggested to some inventive mind by a rolling log and were simply slabs cut from a log. The evidence for the device is from works of art, especially from Egypt* and Assyria, and actual examples, e.g., from Tutankhamen's* tomb. The more primitive of these devices was apparently of solid wood,* being made from three short planks pegged together on both sides and given a circular shape. They were usually fitted with some sort of rim, and because they were solid they gave the vehicle a cumbersome appearance. When the spoked wheel was developed about 2000 B.C. it made for lighter and firmer construction, and by 1500 B.C. the horse*-drawn vehicles had become much more maneuverable. Pharaoh's chariot wheels, bogged in the mire of the Red Sea,* were probably of this light and more efficient variety (Exod 14:25).

The wheel formed a necessary part of chariots (Isa 5:28; Jer 47:3), carts (Isa 28:27–28), and the working equipment of the potter* (Jer 18:3). Wheels having axles, spokes, rims, and hubs were fitted to the ten stands which held the lavers (basins*) in the court of

Solomon's* temple* (1 Kings 7:30–33). Probably the model was the heavy Assyrian chariot wheel, rather than the lighter Egyptian model. The northern war chariots were heavily wheeled and rolled noisily (Jer 47:3; Nah 3:2). For Jeremiah and Nahum the noise of the chariot wheels signaled the near approach of an enemy. Both Daniel (7:9) and Ezekiel (1:15–17) had apocalyptic visions in which wheels were an image of strength, speed, and rapid movement from place to place. In Ezek 23:24 and 26:10 "wheels" are a synecdoche for the whole war chariot, which depended upon their speed and sturdiness. In Eccl 12:6, death is described metaphorically in terms of a broken pulley wheel at a well.*

BIBLIOGRAPHY: ANEP (1954), 167–68, 183–84; C. L. Woolley, Ur Excavations IV (1956), 28, pl. 24; Y. Yadin, The Art of Warfare in Biblical Times (1963), illustrations passim.

RKH and EMB

WIMPLE. See CLOAK.

WINE. The Hebrew words yayin and tirôs were commonly employed to describe the pressed juice of the common grape, which probably had the Ararat* region as its original habitat (cf. Gen 9:20). Tomb reliefs and paintings such as those in the Sixth Dynasty tomb of Mereruka (c. 2250 B.C.) at Saqqarah (Memphis*), or the decorations from the tomb of Nakht at Thebes* (c. 1400 B.C.), depict the various stages in the preparation of wine. The Hebrew shekhar "strong drink" (Akkad. shikru) probably included beer, as well as other intoxicants.

Palestine was notable in antiquity for its vineyards in the Valley of Eshcol (cf. Num 13:23–24) and the Sorek Valley (Judg 14:5), as well as at Sibmah (Jer 48:32) and En Gedi (Song of Songs 1:14). When the grapes were ripe they were harvested in baskets and taken to wine presses (Hos 9:2), which were usually hewn out of solid rock. The grapes were trodden out (Amos 9:13) by jubilant workers (cf. Jer 25:30) and the juice allowed to flow into a lower, deeper reservoir in the vat. Fermenting began within a few hours after the pressing had begun, and subsequently the wine was stored either in new wineskins made from goats'* hides (Matt 9:17) or in large ceramic containers (Jer 13:12).

As well as being a popular drink, wine featured as an item in Hebrew commercial dealings (2 Chron 2:8–10, 15). It was also used as a rejuvenating medicine* (cf. 2 Sam 16:2), a carminative (1 Tim 5:23), and as an antiseptic dressing for wounds (Luke 10:34). Wine accompanied meat or cereal offerings in the Pentateuchal sacrificial legislation (Exod 29:40; Lev 23:13 et al.), and this "blood of the grape" was given deep sacramental significance by Christ at the Last Supper (Matt 26:27–28 et al.).

BIBLIOGRAPHY: C. Seltman, Wine in the Ancient World (1957); A. C. Schultz, ZPEB, 5 (1975), 935–38.

RKH

WOOD. The vulnerability of wood to fire, wetness, and dry rot has prevented much of its survival as archaeological evidence. However, enough wooden objects, especially furniture,* have survived from Egyptian tombs (see TUTANKHAMEN) to give some idea of the fine craftsmanship* of the Egyptian workmen. A funeral barge, recently discovered, with the scent of the cedar* still heavy in the burial trench, casts some light on the cedar trade with Lebanon, mentioned in the accounts of Solomon's* building activities. This was also the subject of the vivid report of Wenamon, dating from the eleventh century before Christ (J. H. Breasted, A History of Egypt [1948], 513–18; J. Baikie, Egyptian Papyri and Papyrus Hunting [1925], 117–39). It recounts the misadventures of his trade mission to Byblos (Gebal*) in quest of cedar wood. There are other unusual survivals. For example, Roman wooden reinforcing has survived in the ramp laboriously built by Silva up the cliffs of Masada.* Viking ships exquisitely built in wood have been excavated from tumulus burials.

Scientific technology has enabled archaeology in recent years to use the remains of wooden materials for several significant purposes. It was found possible so to reinforce chemically some Neolithic* wooden paddles* found in N England in a Yorkshire swamp. Although they had been reduced almost to the consistency of the mud in which they were discovered, the chemical treatment allowed them to be lifted and studied. In the redwood areas of America a dendrochronological* record based on interlocking timber and charcoal* has proved of immense value in the study of climatic influence on migration. This technique is not usable in biblical lands, since there are no surviving traces of the considerable forests implied in the OT in areas that have been long barren until the days of modern reforestation (cf. Deut 19:5; Josh 17:15, 18; 1 Sam 14:25–26; 2 Sam 18:6; 2 Kings 2:24; Ezek 34:25 et al.).

Even completely decayed wood can indicate the position of posts and trees. The bridge over the vallum* around the garrison camp in Roman London, discovered in the bomb ruins S of Cripplegate in 1950, was indicated by the brown remains of wood. Israeli students of dry farming discovered that they were not the first in this field when they found brown dust of olive* wood that revealed symmetrical arrangements of stone in the southern arid regions. These were used as stone-mulching for trees and were designed to collect dew, which is heavy in the area.

EMB

WOOL. See CLOTH, CLOTHING.

WRESTLING. Artistic representation of wrestling goes back to third millennium figurines from Mesopotamia* and Egypt* which seem to indicate a contest in which the belt played a significant part. The belt mentioned in Isa 11:5 possibly refers to a wrestling belt. A mosaic* from Pompeii* (in the Stabian Thermae) shows two muscular wrestlers sparring for a grip. On an Athenian statue* pedestal a relief shows two wrestlers who had come to grips with hands on forearms. An elegant young man judges a wrestling bout on a vase from Etruria, and a wrestling pair in a sculpture from Herculaneum* shows the influence of Lycippus. Such, no doubt, was the wrestling Paul had in mind (cf. Col 4:12; Eph 6:12). It was taught to young boys in the palestra* as a feature of Greek physical education. Identifiable palestras are found in Pompeii and Olympia.

BIBLIOGRAPHY: H. Wilsdorf, *Ringkampf im Alten Ägypten* (1939); C. H. Gordon, *HUCA*, 23 (1950–51), 131–36, pls. I–V.

EMB

WRITING. All available archaeological evidence seems to indicate that the earliest scripts were devised in Mesopotamia* after the middle of the fourth millennium B.C. The oldest extant deciphered inscriptions are probably in the Sumerian language, since writing, if it was not actually the creation of the Sumerians,* was certainly utilized by them for administrative and general economic purposes very early in the third millennium B.C. Writing evidently developed from a pictographic* phase, in which pictures of objects were used to convey ideas. Probably the oldest example of pictographic script occurs on a small limestone tablet from Uruk,* dated about 3000 B.C.

The popularity of this new means of communication soon spread, and other peoples borrowed it, adapted it to the particular needs of their own languages, and made it current throughout the Near East by the second millennium B.C. The process and progress of the art of writing may be traced in the great mass of surviving records. Early Sumerian scripts were impressed on soft clay* tablets by means of a stylus, the writing beginning at the top right-hand corner of the tablet. When the angle at which the material was held was altered subsequently, the result was a horizontal line of script which quite soon became rather stylized and in the end developed into wedge-shaped representations of the pictographs known as cuneiform.*

This development brought about the use of a great many new syllabic signs which the Sumerians endeavored to simplify and reduce in number, only to have them enlarged again as the use of written language by other peoples widened and was enriched by the presence of loan words. In the third millennium B.C. the Sumerian* writing system was adopted by the Akkadians* and Elamites,* and by the Hurrians, Hittites,* and Urartians (*see* URARTU) in the following millennium. The requirements of Semitic speech were somewhat different from those of Sumerian, and even after further attempts at simplification the linguistic forms were still cumbersome and complicated.

By the first millennium B.C. cuneiform was the medium of expression for half a dozen unrelated Near Eastern languages and was also influential in the development of Old Persian, Ugaritic, and hieroglyphic* scripts. Although the Egyptians were influenced by Mesopotamian writing systems, they proceeded independently from a pictographic phase to produce their characteristic hieroglyphic writings, which, unlike the highly stylized cuneiform, changed very little over the centuries of usage. As an art form,

hieroglyphic writing was generally restricted to stone inscriptions, and when it was committed to papyrus* a modified cursive script emerged, described as hieratic.*

Another style of Egyptian writing known as demotic lasted well into the Christian era, while the final phase of writing in that land, known as Coptic, used the Greek alphabet* for Egyptian words and flourished from the third century A.D. until about the sixteenth century.

In the Amarna* Age (fifteenth and fourteenth centuries B.C.), when Egypt* was the dominant Near Eastern power, international diplomacy was conducted in Akkadian cuneiform, as indicated by the Amarna letters.* By the Persian period, however, Aramaic* had become the dominant literary medium, followed later on by Greek.* The previously unknown script in which Ugaritic, a language closely related to biblical Hebrew, was written, was found to be alphabetic, like Egyptian, rather than syllabic, as were the Mesopotamian languages. Aramaic, a language which had a prehistory reaching back to the third millennium B.C., was also alphabetic rather than syllabic.

As far as Palestinian writing is concerned, probably the first alphabetic script came from the turquoise mines of Serabit el-Khadem* in the Sinai* Peninsula, where about twenty-five inscriptions dated approximately 1500 B.C. have been recovered. The same alphabet occurred also in some brief inscriptions found at Shechem,* Gezer,* and Lachish,* which may be even earlier than 1500 B.C. Another very early example of writing in Palestine was found at Balu'ah, a site in ancient Moab.* Unfortunately, the linear script was badly worn, and to date it has not been possible to decipher it with any certainty. Some scholars, however, have dated it as early as the third millennium B.C. and have suggested that it might have been native to the area.

The script of the Proto-Canaanite texts (thirteenth to twelfth centuries B.C.) recovered from Lachish, Beth Shemesh,* and elsewhere, bridges the gap between that of the Proto-Sinaitic inscriptions and the tenth-century B.C. Canaanite*-Phoenician* materials from Byblos (Gebal*). About 1000 B.C. Aramean inscriptions appeared in the later Canaanite form of writing and were accompanied by certain phonetic modifications.

It was only about seven centuries later that Aramaic was written in the "square" character found in modern Hebrew Bibles, and this represented a significant change from the traditional Phoenician style. About 800 B.C. the Phoenician consonantal script was used for writing in Greek and was later supplemented by written vowels and diphthongs. The inclusion of vowels as part of the written form of a word was a novelty, for most Semitic alphabetic scripts were only consonantal.

Under the Romans, the Greek alphabet was modified further and became the basis for European usage. Many examples of the development of writing are available from Near Eastern sites, and there are some inscriptions which still remain to be deciphered and identified. Although there are fewer early writings from Palestine and Syria than from other Near Eastern nations, there is no question as to the importance which Palestinian culture exerted over the development of writing, not least in connection with the emergence of a genuine alphabet.

Many kinds of material were used for writing, with stone being favored for inscriptions. An edict such as the Code of Hammurabi* was carved on the prepared surface of a stele,* whereas the massive Behistun Inscription* was chiseled high on a rocky cliff-face. Stone tablets measuring about 30.48 by 45.72 cm. (12 by 18 in.) were often used for royal proclamations, religious texts (cf. Exod 32:16), and secular laws. Where the surface was unsuitable, the Egyptian practice of applying a plaster* coating upon which the writing was subsequently inscribed was very often followed (cf. Josh 8:32).

Clay tablets and bricks were widely used for writing in Mesopotamia and elsewhere and have been unearthed in great quantities. The Egyptians devised papyrus* as a writing material, and after the eleventh century B.C. it appeared also in Phoenicia, Assyria, and Babylonia. Outside the dry Egyptian climate, however, papyrus soon deteriorated, and frequently its use elsewhere can only be attested indirectly, as with the marks on the reverse side of Gedaliah's seal.*

Potsherds (or shards,* ostraca*) were also popular as writing material in the Near East, being particularly suitable for writing with brush or pen and ink.* From Samaria* in the time of Jeroboam II (782–753 B.C.) have been excavated potsherds recording commercial and other dealings and are representative of the use to which pottery* fragments were put on occasions. Parchment* was used in Egypt from the thirteenth century B.C. for writing and in Mesopotamia for some centuries earlier. The use of leather* scrolls* by the Dead Sea sect (see QUMRAN) points to the way in which ancient Jewish scribes traditionally wrote the Law upon leather or parchment for sheer durability of the product. Parchment was used by Paul as a writing material (cf. 2 Tim 4:13). Boards made of wood or some other substance and having a specially prepared wax surface (cf. Isa 30:8; Hab 2:2) were also used for writing and were occasionally joined by means of a hinge. An eighth-century B.C. Assyrian writing board* contained a lengthy composition of about six thousand lines and was recovered from Nimrud (ancient Calah*).

Writing implements included chisels and other engraving tools* (as used for cuneiform) which were generally made of iron,* copper, or bronze.* Although many pointed implements have been excavated from various sites, it is not yet possible to be certain about the nature of the instrument used for writing linear scripts in Mesopotamia. The stylus with an iron point may have been employed in writing on a hard surface, though it could have served equally well for making deep impressions in rather softer material. The pens of scribes (cf. Jer 8:8) were actually more like brushes and were meant for writing with ink on potsherds, papyrus, and possibly parchment. Ancient Egyptian scribes (see SCRIBAL TRAINING, EGYPTIAN) cut such pens from reeds and

fashioned one end so that it was wedge-shaped, thereby enabling thick and thin strokes to be made in the same manner as the modern sign-writing pen does. In the Roman period the reed was cut much like a quill pen. The ink used on papyrus was a mixture of charcoal* (cf. 2 Cor 3:3; 2 John 12), a resinous gum or oil, and some metallic component, usually a compound of iron. A similar but nonmetallic ink was used on parchment. Both kinds were represented on the scrolls found in the Qumran caves.

When scribes were depicted in Near Eastern art they were generally shown carrying a board containing a slot for the pens and circular depressions for the dried cakes of red and black ink, as well as a penknife (cf. Jer 36:23) used for erasing, for trimming reeds, and for cutting scrolls. As with scrolls, clay documents varied in shape and size. While some were as large as 30.48 by 45.72 cm. (12 by 18 in.), many were much smaller, depending upon content. Historical material was sometimes written down on prisms or cylinders of clay, while contracts inscribed on clay tablets were often placed in a clay envelope and sealed by witnesses. In OT times the scroll was the normal form of a book, the codex* most probably being a Christian invention.

OT references to writing include the compiling of the Decalogue (Exod 24:12; 34:27), the writing of the divine words (Exod 24:4), and the composition of the Torah (Josh 8:31) by Moses, as well as the recording of statutes (Deut 30:10), judgments (Exod 34:27), and other material (e.g., Num 33:2; Deut 24:1 et al.). Scribes of the royal court were employed in compiling lists of names (1 Chron 4:41; 24:6 et al.) and in preserving historical records and annals. Isaiah himself wrote (Isa 8:1) and also dictated to a scribe (Isa 30:8), while Jeremiah seems to have been the only prophet to have had continuous secretarial help (Jer 30:2 et al.).

The NT epistles provide ample evidence of the use of written communications. Writing was used metaphorically to describe the Spirit's impression upon the mind and heart (cf. 2 Cor 3:2f.; Heb 8:10; 10:16).

BIBLIOGRAPHY: G. R. Driver, Semitic Writing (1948); I. J. Gelb, A Study of Writing (1952); N. M. Davies, Picture Writing in Ancient Egypt (1958); D. Diringer, Writing (1962); H. Hornung, Lexikon der Alten Welt (1965), 2726–34; CAH, 1, part 1, 122–55; W. White, Jr., ZPEB, 5 (1975), 995–1015 and bibliography.

RKH

WRITING BOARD. The scribe of the OT world appears to have used a writing board of clay* with insets for ink (a mixture of carbon black and yellow sulphide of arsenic). Such implements (see INK AND PEN) have been recovered from a well* at Calah.* Egyptian sculpture seems to show scribes cross-legged with some such device across the taut linen* of their kilts from knee to knee (see SCRIBAL TRAINING, EGYPTIAN). There is a fine example in the Louvre, the scribe's face square-jawed and eager, and singularly alive with its inlaid eyes of alabaster,* black stone, and silver* rock crystal. It dates from about 2650 B.C. Three similarly postured scribes, with what appear to be writing boards, are in the Rijksmuseum of Oudhedon (from 2800 B.C.), the Berlin Museum (from 2750 B.C.)—both from Giza—and a third from Saqqara (Memphis*) in the Cairo Museum (from 2700 B.C.). The Librairie Orientaliste Paul Geunther (Paris) has a fresco of Assyrian scribes who appear to be writing on clay and papyrus.* It is difficult to see what supports the material. The Oriental Institute of the University of Chicago has a complete scribal outfit. There is no board, but the set does include, along with pen case and water-well, a double palette for ink.

BIBLIOGRAPHY: Hermann Rauke's *The Art of Ancient Egypt*, pl. 63 to 67 (1936); D. J. Wiseman, "The Literary Involvement of the O.T.," *Tyndale Paper*, 15.3 (1970).

EMB

WRITING, PICTORIAL. The origin of writing* may be traced back to early Sumerian* times where, for example, at Uruk (Erech*) lists on tablets from the temple of Inanna have signs, presumed to be numbers, followed in each case by an object—such as heads of animals, fish, plants, utensils, or parts of the human body. Thus writing appears to have begun with pictures and was associated with the economic structure of society, as in the need for records of payments.

In 1979 a new suggestion was made by Denise Schmandt-Besserat. She has shown that different shaped tokens (over ten known), plus additional incised markings in later times, could well be the real origin of writing. These tokens, found especially in Iran, Tepe Asiab, and Susa,* for example, were in use from about 8000 B.C. to 2000 B.C., reaching a peak about 3500, when writing on clay* tablets first appeared.

The tokens were obviously used as counters or numbers. Cones represented one (small) or sixty (large) and circles represented tens. But the different shapes and markings suggest they represented products as well. Thus, a circle with incised cross meant sheep, a semicircle with vertical strokes, metal.

As the pictographs* or picture signs on the earliest clay tablets bear the same shapes and markings as the tokens, Schmandt-Besserat has drawn the logical conclusion that the tokens are the forerunners of the pictographic writing system. After cuneiform* was established as an efficient writing system, developing

from the early symbols, the tokens reverted to their original purpose as counters (cf. the abacus).

With the contemporaneous use of both tokens and simple writing tablets, employing the same symbols, it seems that the first pictographs were not pictures of objects so much as pictures of the clay tokens. Thus a pool of existing symbols was available to the inventors of the writing tablet. No doubt additional pictures were then added to enlarge the writing system.

Picture writing includes both pictographic and ideographic forms (pictograms and ideograms*). In such writing the graphic image has no phonetic value. Thus, a drawing of the sun simply represents the sun and gives no indication of pronunciation for the spoken word for sun. Originally each image represented a single definite thing, and not an abstract idea or relationship.

Pictography is picture writing in the more restricted sense: the image represents nothing more than the physical object portrays. For example, represented only the sun.

Ideography is an advance in which ideas also are conveyed by the graphic image. For example, the sun symbol now represents warmth, light, or day, as well as the sun itself.

Other developments included the attempt to express verbal actions or notions by compound images. Thus eating would be expressed by a head with a mouth, plus a picture of food.

When the Sumerians and Egyptians discovered how to make the pictures represent sounds as well as objects, true writing had begun (e.g., the sun in Sumerian was represented by UTU or ud). Some early possible attempts to express names, contemporary with the use of the compounds referred to above, could well represent this beginning. Certainly in both civilizations homonyms (words with the same sounds but with different meanings) were employed to represent concepts otherwise difficult of graphic expression. So "Enlil + arrow" read "Enlil causes to live," because *Ti*, the term for arrow, also meant life. This development shows that writing in the Ancient Near East had progressed beyond the pictographic stage before 3000 B.C., over a thousand years before Abraham.

BIBLIOGRAPHY: D. Schmandt-Besserat, *ARC*, 32, no. 3 (1979), 22ff.

GGG

X

XERXES (zûrk'sēz). The Greek* form of the Old Persian name *Xšayāršan*, used by two Persian kings. 1. Xerxes I (485–465 B.C.), the son of Darius* the Great, was the heir apparent before succeeding his father in 485 B.C. (cf. Hdt. VII, 1–4). On his accession he had to crush a series of rebellions that broke out in the empire. He was not an impressive military leader and only suppressed the initial revolts successfully by employing considerable violence. After quelling trouble in Egypt,* he turned his attention to Greece. Crossing the Hellespont, he conquered Athens* in 480 and trapped the Greek fleet in the Bay of Salamis.* The Greeks fought desperately and turned near disaster into victory. The Persian fleet was routed, and the army failed to conquer the valient Greeks at Plataea in 479. Xerxes then withdrew to Persepolis* and Susa,* where he spent his time enlarging and beautifying his palaces. Inscriptions from Persepolis show that he was intolerant of any other deity than Ahuramazda, and accordingly sought to destroy other religions wherever he encountered them. Xerxes I has been identified with King Ahasuerus, mentioned in the book of Esther.

2. A minor Persian ruler, Xerxes II, who reigned for 45 days in 424 B.C.

BIBLIOGRAPHY: A. T. Olmstead, *History of the Persian Empire* (1959 ed.), 214–71; *ANET*, 316–17.

RKH

XISUTHROS. *See* ZIUSUDRA.

X-RAY FLUORESCENCE. The use of X-rays to irradiate a quantity of material with the aim of producing fluorescence. The refracted light can be examined by spectrographic* techniques to determine the nature of the elements in the sample.

HWP

X-RAYS AND ARCHAEOLOGY. Only occasionally have medical studies been carried out on the mummified bodies of pharaohs and nobles of Egypt.* G. Maspero (1889) and G. E. Smith (1912) conducted investigations at the Egyptian Museum. Some years later Dr. Derry dissected part of Tutankhamen's* mummy. In 1966, however, the School of Dentistry at the University of Michigan began a study for orthodontal purposes on a large number of bodies, naturally preserved, at Gebal Adda in Nubia,* ranging from 6 B.C. to the eighteenth century A.D. It was then decided to extend this research by X-raying the bodies of the pharaohs at the museum in Cairo.

This latter program, published in *Roentgenographic Atlas of the Pharaohs* by J. E. Harris and K. R. Weeks, has provided information on both dental and medical afflictions suffered by nobles and pharaohs.

In the dental studies, evidence has been found of impacted molars, abscesses, malocclusion and, on occasion, extreme dental wear. Ramses II,* possibly the pharaoh of the Exodus, suffered from heavy dental wear and painful alveolar abscesses.

Medical studies demonstrate that Ramses also must have been plagued with cold feet because of arteriosclerosis of all major arteries of the lower extremities of his body; he also suffered from severe degenerative arthritis of the hip joints. His successor, Merneptah, whose records provide the first written reference to Israel,* also suffered from very poor dentition as well as from arteriosclerosis of the thigh and severe degenerative arthritis of the vertebral column. There are also signs of fractures in the heads of the femurs.

In general, many of the pharaohs were afflicted by arthritis of the back, knees, or vertebrae. Also evident in some instances were a fractured pelvis (Thutmoses/Thutmosis I), an inguinal hernia (Ramses V), and, more in the wives of the early Eighteenth Dynasty rulers, scoliosis (abnormal curvature of the spine). Siptah's body (Nineteenth Dynasty) revealed severe deformity of the left foot, possibly through poliomyelitis, which could prove significant, since only one tentative case has been identified before.

Although circumcision was normal for the upper classes, there are some instances where the practice was not observed. Ahmose/Ahmosis I, who expelled the Hyksos* from Egypt and may have been "the pharaoh who knew not Joseph," was uncircumcised, as probably was Amenhotep/Amenophis I. This raises the question as to whether the lack of circumcision was for medical reason (they may have been hemophiliacs) or because they were of foreign origin.

A number of general observations have also been made. First, the homogeneity of the nobles of the Old Kingdom is in direct contrast to that of the New Kingdom period, where there is considerable variation—perhaps in part due to foreigners being incorporated into society, such as Joseph* in the preceding era. Secondly, with some exceptions, such as the dentition and large nose structure which link Ramses II, Seti/Sethos, and Merneptah as close relatives, the pharaohs are an extremely heterogenous group, who would not normally be recognized as having any relationship.

Marked similarities between Tutankhamen and Smenkhkare, sons of Amenhotep/Amenophis III, have been established in other X-ray studies by Professor Harrison of Liverpool University. The two skulls, of virtually identical diameter, reveal almost complete conformity with one another.

Some kings' reigns may have to be adjusted as to length if the bodies X-rayed are those of the kings they are supposed to be, since the new evidence is against a long life (e.g., Thutmoses/Thutmosis I and Thutmose/Thutmosis III). That problems occur in identification may be seen in the case of Makare, probably the wife of the high priest of Amun in the Twenty-first Dynasty, who presumably died during or soon after childbirth. X-rays of the small wrapped body buried with her established it was a baboon, not a baby! The reason for this practice is obscure, but it demonstrates that one cannot assume the correct identity of a mummified body.

Thus X-rays provide a picture of the medical and dental problems of the past, and may also be helpful in providing some keys to the social structure of different eras.

X-rays are used in other ways to assist the archaeologist and conservator. Comparative dating* of bones, to establish whether finds come from the same age, is possible through X-ray absorption and defraction techniques. Part of the thermoluminescent dating of pottery* uses X-rays to determine the potassium 40 content of the sample.

The chemical content and proportions in any artifact* can also be established by X-raying, although spectrographic analysis* is more common for this purpose. Work is progressing in identifying the different flows of obsidian (volcanic glass*), often used in the ancient world, by their chemical composition. If more complete X-ray analysis is able to establish the origin of the obsidian used for the artifacts, it will provide useful data for interpreting trade and travel in the past.

Corroded metal objects, often unidentifiable under heavy crusts of rust, may be identified and drawn from X-ray plates. Since the depth and distribution of oxidization is also revealed, especially with iron,* cleaning and restoration work is made easier. Even ivories* from Nimrud (Calah*) were studied by X-ray before final cleaning and treatment.

See also BLOOD GROUPING; X-RAY FLUORESCENCE.
GGG

Y

YALO. *See* AIJALON.

YAUDI. *See* ZINJERLI.

YAUKIN. *See* JEHOIACHIN.

YEHUDIYEH (YAHUDIYA), TELL EL. *See* LEONTOPOLIS.

YEMEN. *See* SABEANS.

YORGHAN TEPE. *See* NUZI.

Z

ZADOKITE FRAGMENTS (zā'də kīt). The fragments from two MSS (tenth to twelfth century A.D.) of a sectarian manual in Hebrew found in a genizah* (a repository for sacred MSS no longer in use) in one of the buildings of the ancient Qaraite synagogue* in Cairo.

These MSS, found in 1896–97, were first published by S. Schechter in 1910 as *Fragments of a Zadokite Work*. The fragments, called texts A and B, are now to be found in the Cambridge University Library. Rabin, in his edition of the material, has distinguished two treatises in the MSS; one he calls the *Admonition* and the other the *Laws*. In both these parts, the Zadokite Fragments show belief in a salvation to be found in following the teachings of the Teacher of Righteousness.

Following upon the discovery of the Dead Sea Scrolls* material in the vicinity of Qumran* from 1947 on, there was noted a close affinity between some of the scrolls'* material and the Zadokite Fragments. Further excavation continued in the Qumran area, and subsequently fragments of the Zadokite work were found there. By way of comparison, it is to be noted that the Qumran community itself also had much to say about following the Teacher of Righteousness, and the Essene* communities described by Josephus (Jos. *Antiq.* 18.1,5; Jos. *War* 2.2–13) exhibit, in a similar way to that set forth in the Zadokite Fragments, some of the same strict teachings and ascetic tendencies. The conclusion has been drawn that the Zadokite Fragments belonged to a document originally composed and used in an Essene-type community.

The manuscript of the Zadokite Fragments is defective in places, with pages 13–16 being greatly mutilated and the MS torn in some places. Many of the words have the vowel points according to the Palestinian method, and others according to the Babylonian.

Because the document contains the name Damascus,* it is sometimes called the Damascus Document. Actually text A speaks of "the sons of Zadok . . . the chosen of Israel" who lived in the land of Damascus—possibly a symbolic reference to this name.

BIBLIOGRAPHY: L. Rost, *Die Damaskusschrift* (1933); S. Zeitlin, *Zadokite Documents* (1952); C. Rabin, *The Zadokite Documents* (1954); H. H. Rowley, *The Zadokite Fragments and the Dead Sea Scrolls* (1955); F. F. Bruce, *The Teacher of Righteousness in the Qumran Texts* (1956); H. E. Del Medico, *The Riddle of the Scrolls* (1959), 98–111, 385–425; *FLAP* (1959), 282–88; O. Betz, "Zadokite Fragments," *IDB*, 4 (1962), 929–33; G. R. Driver, *The Annals of Leeds University Oriental Society* (1969), 23–48; W. White, Jr., *ZPEB*, 4 (1975), 1029–33; T. H. Gaster, *The Dead Sea Scriptures*, 3rd ed. (1976), 10, 66,–91.

WHM

ZAHARIYEH. See DEBIR.

ZAKARIYEH (ZAKARIYA), TELL EL-. See AZEKAH.

ZAKIR STELE (za'kər stē'lē). A monument found in 1904, some 40.3 km. (25 mi.) SE of Aleppo,* which

Stele of Zakir, king of Hamath, found at Afis, northern Syria. Dated to the eighth century B.C., it is one of the oldest Aramaic inscriptions yet discovered. Courtesy Encyclopaedia Judaica, Photo Archive, Jerusalem.

records the conflict between Zakir, king of Hamath,* and Ben Hadad of Damascus* and ten allies, early in the eighth century B.C. At a time when the Assyrians were fighting the Urartu* people to their N, the Aramean* (Syrian) people were fighting one another. Thus military pressure was taken off Israel* and Judah,* enabling them to prosper and to exploit trade.

BIBLIOGRAPHY: *ANET* (1955), 501–2.

JAT

ZAREPHATH (zâr'ə fath; Heb. צָרְפַת, *ṣārepaṭ*; LXX Σαρεπτά, *Sarepta*). A Phoenician* coastal city* located between Tyre* and Sidon,* 12.8 km. (8 mi.) by road from the latter city. The name of the town occurs in Egyptian as *D-r-p-t*, vocalized *ṣa-r-pu-'u-ta*, and in Akkadian as *Ṣa-ri-ip-tu*, and is derived from the root *ṣarāpu*, "to dye red." The ancient name has been preserved in the Arabic name of the modern village, Sarafand.

I. *Biblical References.* The town is most famous as the place where Elijah aided a widow by providing food in the time of famine and by raising her child to life (1 Kings 17:8–24). This was a noteworthy manifestation of Jehovah's power in the territory of Baal.* The area of Zarephath is promised to the children of Israel* in Obad 20. The story of Elijah at Zarephath is used by Jesus (Luke 4:25–26) as an illustration of the maxim, "No prophet is accepted in his own country."

II. *Non-biblical References.* The earliest known reference to Zarephath is in the Egyptian satirical Letter of Hori (*ANET*, 477). When Sennacherib* invaded the area in 701, the town belonged to Sidon. His successor, Esarhaddon,* gave it to Tyre. The city is known in classical sources, such as Pliny the Elder, for its wine* and other products. A Greek inscription discovered at Puteoli* in Italy in 1901 makes reference to "the holy god of Sarepta." This text, which is dated to A.D. 79, reveals that the town was important enough to have a tutelary deity independent of Tyre and Sidon.

It is the association of Elijah's miracles with the town that attracted numerous pilgrims there, beginning with the Bordeaux Pilgrim* in A.D. 333. Later, in the fourth century, Paula, Jerome's disciple, noted that a small turret had been erected at the site as a shrine to Elijah.

III. *Excavations.* Since Ernest Renan took notice of the site in 1861, there have been some sporadic investigations of tombs. In 1929 rain exposed a burial cave* with Mycenaean* objects. In 1968 officials examined forty tombs, mainly from the sixth–fifth centuries B.C., but found that most had been robbed by ancient and modern looters.

A five-year program of excavations sponsored by the University of Pennsylvania under the direction of J. B. Pritchard began in 1969. The first season uncovered a Roman quay (landing place), built in the first century A.D. and used until Byzantine* times. The second season exposed strata from the Hellenis-

tic, the Iron Age,* and the Late Bronze Age.* From the ninth–sixth centuries B.C. came important objects which are similar to those known from the western Phoenician* colonies: clay* lamps* with two spouts, mushroom-lip jugs, buildings with the so-called "rib" construction, and a symbol of Tanit, the chief goddess of Carthage.

Since the Iron Age deposits of the more famous Phoenician cities—Tyre, Sidon, Beirut*—lie inaccessible under modern cities, Zarephath has now given to us the most extensive and best stratified documentation from the Phoenician homeland ever recovered.

BIBLIOGRAPHY: D. C. Baramki, "A Late Bronze Age Tomb at Sarafend, Ancient Sarepta," *Ber.*, 12 (1958), 129–42; R. Saidah, "Archaeology in the Lebanon 1968–1969," *Ber.*, 18 (1969), 134–37; J. B. Pritchard, "The Phoenician City of Sarepta," *ARC*, 24 (1971), 61–63; id., "The Phoenicians in Their Homeland," *Exped.*, 14 (1971), 14–23; id., "Sarepta in History and Tradition," in J. Reumann, ed., *Understanding the Sacred Text* (1972), 101–14; J. A. Thompson, *ZPEB*, 5 (1975), 1034; J. B. Pritchard, *Sarepta: A Preliminary Report on the Iron Age* (1975); id., *Recovering Sarepta, a Phoenician City: Excavations at Sarafand, Lebanon, 1969–1974* (1978).

EY

ZARETHAN (za'rə than). Pritchard and Glueck identified Zarethan (Josh 3:16; 1 Kings 7:45–46) as Tell es-Sa'idiyeh E of Jordan, where copper and bronze* working activities of pre-Solomonic days were discovered. The identification is not certain and is complicated by the variant "Zaredatha" in the parallel reference in 2 Chron 4:17 (see NIV f.n.).

BIBLIOGRAPHY: J. B. Pritchard, *BA*, 28 (1965), 16–17; J. A. Thompson, *ZPEB*, 5 (1975), 1035–36.

EMB

ZENO PAPYRI. Archives, comprising c. 1,200 papyrus* documents, discovered in the Fayûm in 1915, belonging to Zeno, an official on the staff of Apollonius, finance minister (*dioikētēs*) of Ptolemy II* (Philadelphus), king of Egypt* 285–246 B.C. About 40 of the documents relate to a year-long mission which Zeno undertook in 259 B.C. to Palestine (which was then part of the Ptolemaic Empire), from which he brought back records, and to the correspondence which he thereafter maintained with Palestine. These papyri supplement and correct the scanty data provided by Josephus and others regarding Palestine in the third century B.C. They enable us to plot the frontiers of the Ptolemaic dominions in Syria and Trans-Jordan. Much of the land was the king's property and the tenants paid taxes directly to him. Apollonius had a private estate at Beth-Anath, which probably bestowed on him by the king; it may have been a royal estate (*pardēs*) under the Persians.

The papyri reflect attempts to superimpose on the local traditional administrative pattern the whole system of Egyptian bureaucracy. All departments of life were under scrutiny; trade in slaves,* foodstuffs, and other merchandise was supervised in detail; property (including sheep and cattle) had to be registered annually. Since Palestine was the Ptolemies' first line of defense against the Seleucids, its military organization was carefully planned. Military settlements (klērouchiai) were established, and garrisons were stationed in cities* of strategic importance. Garrison troops intermarried with local women. An important military settlement in Trans-Jordan, around 'Araq el-Emir,* guarded the king's territory against Bedouin attacks. The head of this settlement was a native prince named Tobiah, apparently father of Joseph the Tobiad, whose career as a tax collector is described by Josephus (Jos. Antiq. 12.160–79), and related to Tobiah the Ammonite* of Nehemiah's day, c. 445 B.C. (Neh 2:10 et al.).

In general, the Zeno papyri throw valued light on the progressive and thorough Hellenization of Palestine and neighboring territories under the Ptolemies.

BIBLIOGRAPHY: M. Rostovtzeff, *A Large Estate in Egypt in the Third Century* B.C. (1922); R. A. Bowman, *IB*, 3 (1954), 676–77, 804–8; C. C. McCown, *BA*, 20 (1957), 63–64.

FFB

ZERUBBABEL LISTS (zə ru′bə bel). Minor variations in the lists of Zerubbabel describing the returning exiles (*see* EXILE), as reported by Ezra (ch. 2) and Nehemiah (ch. 7), probably reflect scribal variants from an original copy. The system of notation used by both Nabataean* and Palmyrene* scribes was open to such error and some of the Samaritan ostraca* suggest that similar systems were current among the Jews.* As H. L. Allrik remarks (*BASOR*, 136 [1954], 27), such numerical variations enhance the value of the lists by the very fact that they imply their nature and antiquity.

BIBLIOGRAPHY: J. A. Thompson, *The Bible and Archaeology* (1962), 185–88, assembles some archaeological details on the second temple and the fortunes of the shadowy Zerubbabel. See also W. F. Albright, *The Biblical Period* (1952), 50; J. S. Wright, *The Building of the Second Temple* (1958); R. K. Harrison, *ZPEB*, 5 (1975), 1056–58.

EMB

ZEUS, OLYMPIAN. The name of the chief deity of the Greek pantheon, incorrectly rendered Jupiter by the Latin*-dominated KJV. At Lystra* there was a temple of Zeus-before-the-city, whose priest, superstitiously prompted by the myth of Philemon and Baucis, was preparing to sacrifice to Paul and Barnabas (Acts 14:13). An inscription from Isauria, not far from Lystra, speaks of "Zeus-before-the-gate." The sacred precinct and its cult probably antedated Greek infiltration in the area and represented some Anatolian high god equated with Zeus by the first immigrants. Ramsay also reports an inscription from the same area linking Zeus and Hermes.*

BIBLIOGRAPHY: E. M. Blaiklock, *The Acts of the Apostles, An Historical Commentary* (1959), 107–8; W. M. Ramsay, *The Church in the Roman Empire* (1893), 51.

EMB

ZIGGURAT (zig′u rat). The Babylonian term *zigguratu* meant "something lifted high," or "temple tower," and described structures found in the Euphrates Valley which were usually erected in cube form. The ziggurat was intended to be an artificial mountain which concentrated the life forces of nature and provided a suitable locus for the activities and the worship of specific Mesopotamian deities.

This type of architecture was a distinctive feature of Mesopotamia,* and originated in the third millennium B.C. What is probably the earliest ziggurat known to date was discovered at Erech* (cf. Gen 10:10) and comprised a small shrine on a raised base or platform of clay,* reinforced with unburnt bricks. The structure measured about 42.6 by 45.8 m. (140 by 150 ft.), and was about 9.1 m. (30 ft.) high. The corners of the ziggurat were oriented in terms of the cardinal points of the compass.

When the Sumerian* designers developed the technique of recessed-niche construction, the foundation level was then able to bear the weight of several stories. This construction principle also made possible the building of the Egyptian pyramids,* with their enormous weights and internal stresses. The tower known as Etemenanki in Babylon* was seven stories high, and the various levels were reached by means of ramps or stairways. On the uppermost story was a shrine dedicated to the local deity, which he was supposed to visit on certain ceremonial occasions. The ziggurat of Ur* was about 61 m. (200 ft.) long, 45.8 m. (150 ft.) wide, and 21.3 m. (70 ft.) high. It was built of unbaked brick with an outside of baked brick set in bitumen.* The tower of Babel* was evidently an early Mesopotamian ziggurat (Gen 11: 1–5).

BIBLIOGRAPHY: C. L. Woolley, *Excavations at Ur* (1954), 125–35; A. Parrot, *The Tower of Babel* (1954); D. J. Wiseman, *ZPEB*, 5 (1975), 1059–61.

EMB

ZIKLAG (zik′lag; Heb. צִיקְלַג, ṣîqlag). A city* which in the settlement period was assigned to the tribe of Simeon (Josh 19:5; 1 Chron 4:30), and was listed with twenty-nine other towns in the Negev* in Joshua 15:31. After the Philistines* settled in the S coastal area of Judah* in the twelfth century B.C., they moved into Simeonite territory and controlled Ziklag (1 Sam 27:6) among other places. David received Ziklag as a gift from Achish, the Philistine ruler of Gath* (1 Sam 27:5–7; 1 Chron 12:1, 20), and used it as his base of operations against marauding groups. At the time of the final battle between Saul and the Philistines, Ziklag was raided by Amalekites and its citizens taken captive. David soon caught and destroyed the invaders and rescued the people, including his two wives. From Ziklag David expressed gratitude to the people of the Negev for assisting him in his activities (1 Chron 12:1–20). After Saul's death at Gilboa David went to Ziklag (2 Sam 1:1), and in subsequent days the city became part of David's kingdom. The sedentary occupation of the city was mentioned once only subsequently in the OT, in connection with the return of exiled Jews* from Babylonia (Neh 11:28).

The site has been identified with Tell el-Khuweilfeh,

about 8 km. (5 mi.) SW of Tell Beit Mirsim (formerly identified with Debir*), and some 16 km. (10 mi.) E of Tell esh-Sheri'a.

BIBLIOGRAPHY: V. R. Gold, *IDB*, 4, 955–56; J. A. Thompson, *ZPEB*, 5, 1061.   RKH

ZIMBABWE. See OPHIR.

ZINJERLI (zin'jer lē). The capital city* of a West-Semitic (OT, "Hittite*") principality in N Syria, called *Sm'l* and *Y'dy* in its own records, and Sam'al, Yaudi, and Bit Gabbar by the Assyrians. Zinjerli or Sam'al lay to the NE of the later Antioch,* across the Amanus range from Karatepe,* capital of ancient Danuna.

Because of the suggestion that passages like 2 Kings 14:28 have confused Judah* with the northern Yaudi (cf. NIV f.n.), the history of this kingdom has special interest for biblical studies (cf. C. H. Gordon, *The Ancient Near East* [1965], 219, where the alternate translation is given, ". . . he restored Dan and Hamath from Yehuda into Israel," thus making the verse refer to a battle between Jeroboam II and this northern power). At any rate, it is known that Sam'al was one of the independent principalities of N Syria that flourished from the time of Thutmose II (early fifteenth century B.C.) to the close of the Assyrian Empire (late seventh century B.C.). The site of Zinjerli was excavated by F. von Luschan and others from 1888 to 1891, in a campaign that produced monumental inscriptions in both Phoenician and Aramaic,* together with extensive remains of ninth- and eighth-century Phoenician* palaces (the *bît hilani* type) that have proved helpful in reconstructing the buildings of Solomon.* Extensive studies of the symbolism reflected in the various orthostats (stone slabs) of kings from the late ninth century B.C. onward have shed light on the gods of the area. A pantheon including Ba'al-Hammam, Hadad, Rekub-el, and Ba'al Semed, each with his own symbolic representation, shows that the basic culture of the area was Semitic, though some of the sculptures show Hittite or Anatolian influence. Since also some Hittite hieroglyphics* were used in the ninth-century inscriptions, and the Anatolian kingdom of Asitawandas (Karatepe) was a scant 40 km. (25 mi.) across the mountains, it is probably correct to assume a somewhat mixed population.

Among the many sculptures and stelae* uncovered, none is of more interest than a stele depicting the Assyrian Esarhaddon* standing before two defeated enemies, one of whom is identified in the accompanying cuneiform* text as Tirhakah of Egypt* and Ethiopia* (2 Kings 19:2) (cf. *ANEP*, 447, 154 and *ANET*, 293).

BIBLIOGRAPHY: For the texts and extensive coverage of the monuments, consult *ANET*, *ANEP*, and H. Donner and W. Roellig, *Kanaanaïsche und Aramaïsche Inschriften* (1964), texts 24–25 and 214–21. General: F. von Luschan et al., *Ausgrabungen in Sendschirli*, 1–4 (1893–1913); B. Landsberger, *Sam'al* (1948); H. Donner, "Ein Orthostatenfragment des Koenigs Barrakab von Sam'al," *MIOr*, 3 (1955), 73ff.; R. D. Barnett, "The Gods of Zinjirli," *RAI*, 11 (1964), 59–87; D. Ussishkin, "King Solomon's Palace and

Building 1723 in Megiddo (Compared with the bît-hilani and Palace of Kilamuwa and Barrekub in Zincirli)," *IEJ*, 16 (1966), 174–86; Y. Yadin, "Symbols of Deities at Zinjerli, Carthage and Hazor," in J. A. Sanders, *Near Eastern Archaeology in the Twentieth Century* (1970), 199–231; P. Dion, "The Language Spoken in Ancient Sam'al," *JNES*, 37 (1978), 115–18.

CEA

ZIUSUDRA (zē ə sū'drə). A king of Shuruppak* (modern Fara), who is the hero of the Sumerian flood story. He corresponds to Utnapishtim and Atrahasis of the Akkadian flood traditions.

Excavations at Shuruppak have yielded a flood deposit c. 2850 B.C., which Mallowan suggests as the historical basis of the Mesopotamian* stories of the flood.

The Sumerian story of the Flood is known from a unique six-column fragment from Nippur,* of which only the lower third has been preserved. The text which dates to the seventeenth century B.C. was first published by Arno Poebel in 1914.

After narrating the creation of man and the animals, the text describes the founding of the five antediluvian cities. Shuruppak was the last of the cities before the Flood. We are not told in this text why the Flood was decreed (*see* ATRA-HASIS EPIC). A god, probably Enki, warns the pious Ziusudra of the impending disaster. The latter survives the deluge, which sweeps over the land for seven days and seven nights, in a huge boat. After the flood Ziusudra offers thanks to the sun-god Utu. The gods reward Ziusudra's piety with immortality, transporting him to Dilmun.*

In a Sumerian wisdom text (c. 2500 B.C.), one of our oldest literary texts, Ziusudra is given some sage advice by his father, Shuruppak.

His fame is still recalled over two thousand years later in the Greek work of the Babylonian priest, Berossus (third century B.C.), in the form Xisuthros (as cited in Polyhistor) or Sisithros (as cited in Abydenus).

BIBLIOGRAPHY: S. N. Kramer, *Sumerian Mythology* (1944), 97–99; id., *ANET* (1955), 42–44; id., *History Begins at Sumer* (1959), 150–54; A. Heidel, *The Gilgamesh Epic and OT Parallels* (1963), 102–5; J. J. Finkelstein, "The Antediluvian Kings," *JCS*, 17 (1963), 39–51; M. E. L. Mallowan, "Noah's Flood Reconsidered," *Iraq*, 26 (1964), 62–82; S. N. Kramer, "Reflections on the Mesopotamian Flood," *Exped.*, 9 (1967), 12–18; D. Hämmerly-Dupuy, "Some Observations on the Assyro-Babylonian and Sumerian Flood Stories," *AUSS*, 6 (1968), 1–19; M. Civil, "The Sumerian Flood Story," in W. G. Lambert and A. R. Millard, *Atrahasis: The Babylonian Story of the Flood* (1969), 138–45, 167–72; *ANE* (1969), 594–95; R. Raikes, "The Physical Evidence for Noah's Flood," *Iraq*, 28 (1969), 52–63; W. W. Hallo, "Antediluvian Cities," *JCS*, 23 (1973), 57–67; S. Burstein, *The Babyloniaca of Berossus* (1978).   EY

ZOAN. See RAMESES, CITY OF; TANIS.

Maps

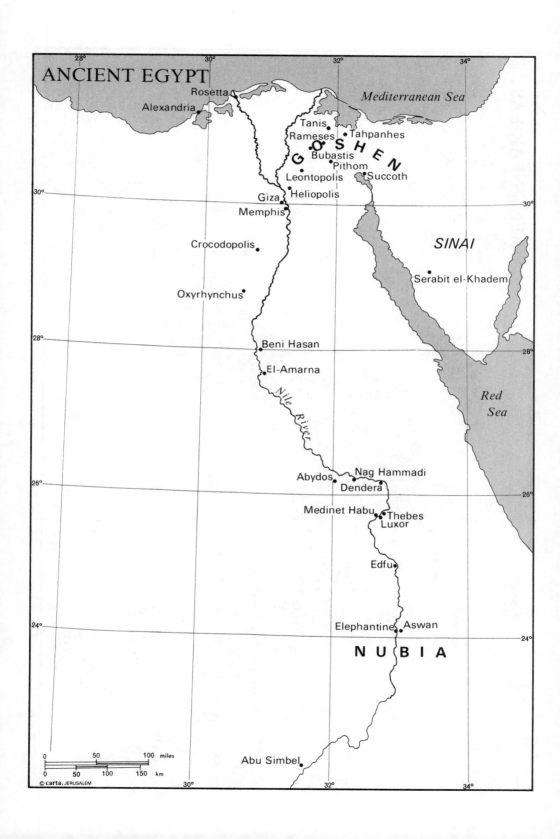

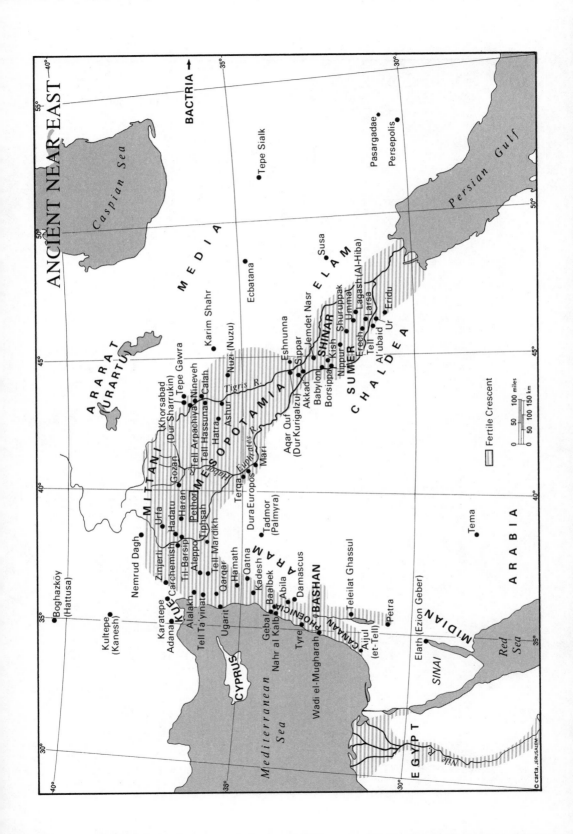

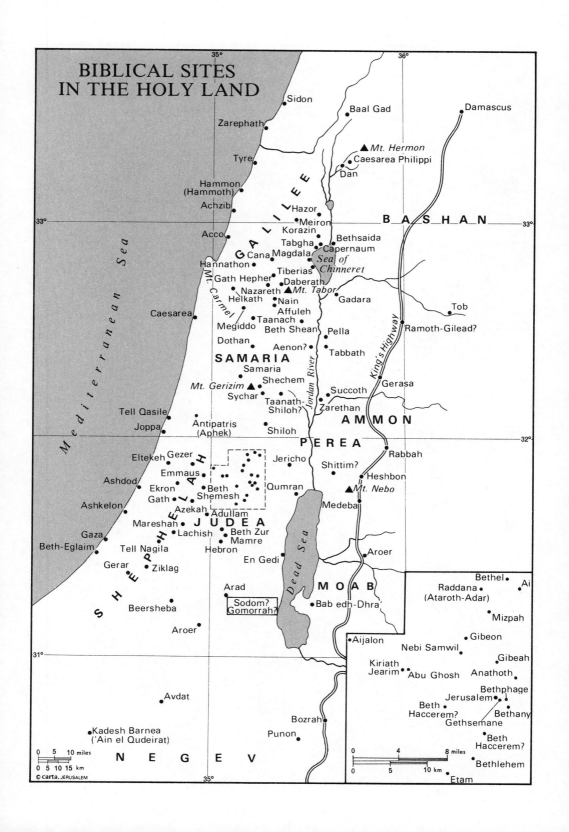

BIBLICAL SITES
IN THE HOLY LAND

Sidon

Baal Gad

Damascus

Zarephath

▲ *Mt. Hermon*

Tyre

Caesarea Philippi

Dan

Hammon
(Hammoth)

Achzib

Hazor

B A S H A N

Meiron

Acco

Korazin

Bethsaida

Tabgha

Capernaum

Cana

Magdala

Sea of
Chinneret

Hannathon

Tiberias

Gath Hepher

Daberath

Nazareth ▲ *Mt. Tabor*

Helkath

Gadara

Nain

Tob

Caesarea

Affuleh

Ramoth-Gilead?

Taanach

Megiddo

Beth Shean

Pella

Dothan

Aenon?

Tabbath

S A M A R I A

Samaria

Mt. Gerizim ▲

Shechem

Gerasa

Sychar

Succoth

Taanath-
Shiloh?

Zarethan

A M M O N

Tell Qasile

Antipatris
(Aphek)

Shiloh

P E R E A

Joppa

Eltekeh

Gezer

Jericho

Rabbah

Emmaus

Shittim?

Ashdod

Ekron

Beth
Shemesh

Qumran

Heshbon

Gath

▲ *Mt. Nebo*

Azekah

Adullam

Medeba

Mareshah

J U D E A

Lachish

Beth Zur

Mamre

Gaza

Hebron

Beth-Eglaim

Tell Nagila

En Gedi

Aroer

Gerar

Ziklag

Arad

M O A B

Sodom?
Gomorrah?

Bab edh-Dhra

Beersheba

Aroer

Avdat

Bozrah

Punon

Kadesh Barnea
('Ain el Qudeirat)

N E G E V

S H E P H E L A H

Mt. Carmel

G A L I L E E

Jordan River

King's Highway

Mediterranean Sea

Dead Sea

0   5   10 miles
0 5 10 15 km
© carta, JERUSALEM

35°

36°

33°

33°

32°

31°

35°

Bethel

Ai

Raddana
(Ataroth-Adar)

Mizpah

Gibeon

Aijalon

Nebi Samwil

Gibeah

Kiriath
Jearim

Abu Ghosh

Anathoth

Bethphage

Jerusalem

Beth
Haccerem?

Bethany

Gethsemane

Beth
Haccerem?

Bethlehem

Etam

0   4   8 miles
0   5   10 km

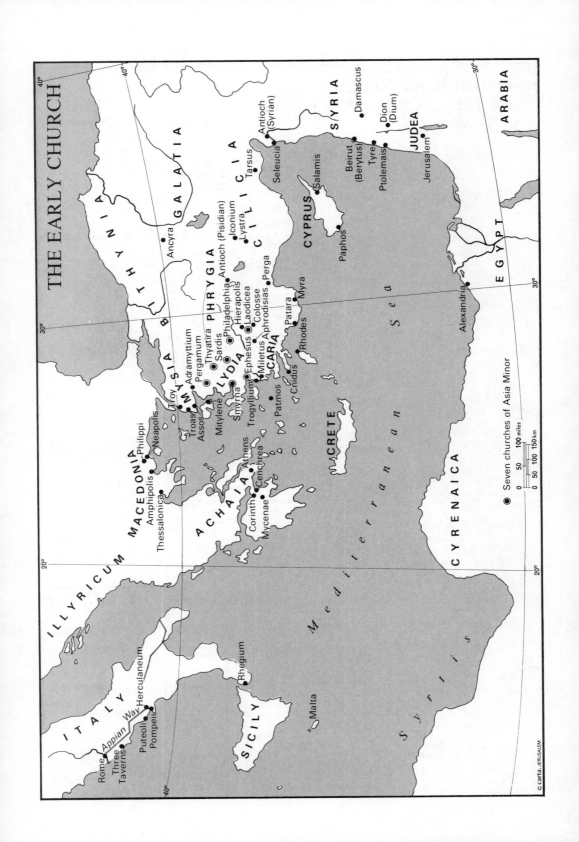

THE EARLY CHURCH

● Seven churches of Asia Minor

```
0    50   100 miles
0  50 100 150 km
```

© Carta, JERUSALEM

Index to Full-color Maps

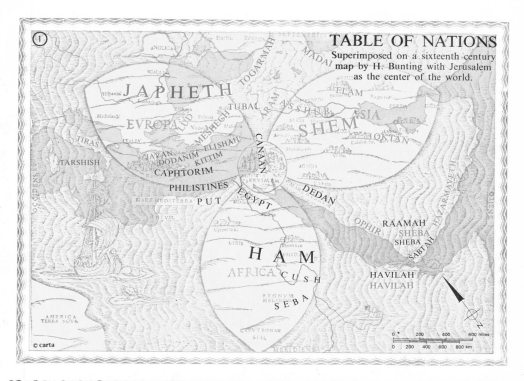

TABLE OF NATIONS

Superimposed on a sixteenth-century map by H. Bunting with Jerusalem as the center of the world.

JAPHETH

EVROPA

SHEM

ASIA

CANAAN

HAM

AFRICA   CUSH

SEBA

TARSHISH

TIRAS

JAVAN DODANIM ELISHAH
KITTIM
CAPHTORIM

PHILISTINES
PUT

EGYPT

DEDAN

OPHIR   RAAMAH
SHEBA
SHEBA
SABTAH

HAVILAH
HAVILAH

© carta

| 0 | 200 | 400 | 600 miles |
| 0 | 200 | 400 | 600 | 800 km |

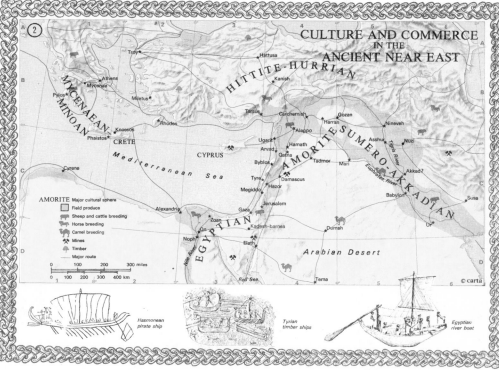

CULTURE AND COMMERCE IN THE ANCIENT NEAR EAST

HITTITE-HURRIAN

MYCENAEAN-
MINOAN

SUMERO-AKKADIAN

AMORITE

EGYPTIAN

Mediterranean Sea

CRETE

CYPRUS

Arabian Desert

Troy
Hattusa
Athens
Mycenae
Miletus
Kanish
Tarsus
Carchemish
Gozan
Nineveh
Rhodes
Aleppo
Harran
Asshur
Nuzi
Knossos
Ugarit
Hamath
Phaistos
Arvad
Byblos
Tadmor
Mari
Cyrene
Tyre
Damascus
Megiddo
Hazor
Babylon
Susa
Alexandria
Jerusalem
Ur
Gaza
Zoan
Kadesh-barnea
Dumah
On
Noph
Elath
Tema

Nile River
Tigris River
Euphrates River
Red Sea

AMORITE Major cultural sphere
- 🟩 Field produce
- Sheep and cattle breeding
- Horse breeding
- Camel breeding
- Mines
- Timber
- Major route

| 0 | 100 | 200 | 300 miles |
| 0 | 100 | 200 | 300 | 400 km |

© carta

Hasmonean pirate ship

Tyrian timber ships

Egyptian river boat

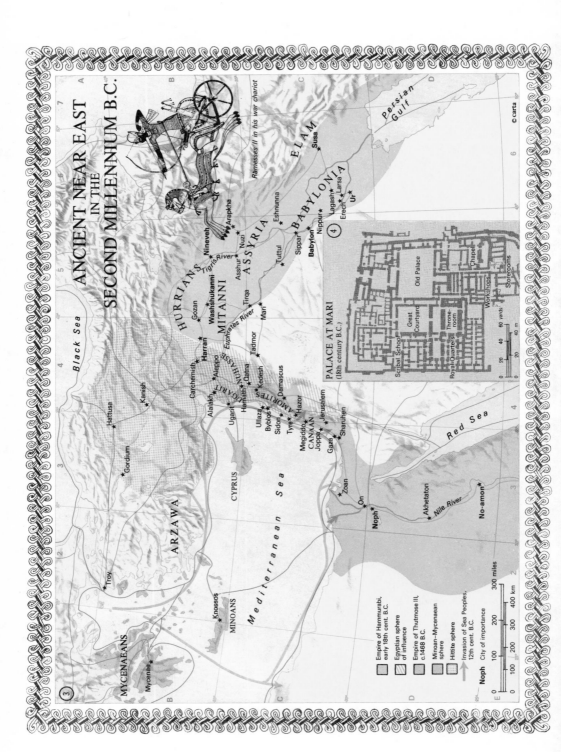

ANCIENT NEAR EAST
IN THE
SECOND MILLENNIUM B.C.

Black Sea

MYCENAEANS
Mycenae
Knossos
MINOANS
Troy
Gordium
ARZAWA
CYPRUS
Hattusa
Kanish
Carchemish
Harran
HURRIANS
Gozan
Washshukanni
Nineveh
Arapkha
Tigris River
Asshur
Nuzi
MITANNI
ASSYRIA
ELAM
Susa
Tirqa
Mari
Tuttul
Eshnunna
Sippar
Babylon
Nippur
BABYLONIA
Lagash
Larsa
Erech
Ur
Persian Gulf
Euphrates River
Tadmor
Alalakh
Aleppo
Hamath
UGARIT
Ullaza
Byblos
Sidon
Tyre
AMORITES
Kedesh
Qatna
Damascus
Hazor
Megiddo
Jerusalem
CANAAN
Joppa
Gaza
Sharuhen
Zoan
On
Noph
Akhetaton
Nile River
No-amon
Red Sea
Mediterranean Sea
Ramesses II in his war chariot

© carta

PALACE AT MARI
(18th century B.C.)

Scribal School
Great Courtyard
Old Palace
Chapel
Throne-room
Royal Quarters
Workshops
Storerooms
0   20   40   60 yards
0   20   40 m

Empire of Hammurabi,
early 18th cent. B.C.
Egyptian sphere
of influence
Empire of Thutmose III,
c.1468 B.C.
Minoan–Mycenaean
sphere
Hittite sphere
Invasion of Sea Peoples,
12th cent. B.C.
Noph   City of importance

0   100   200   300 miles
0 100 200 300 400 km

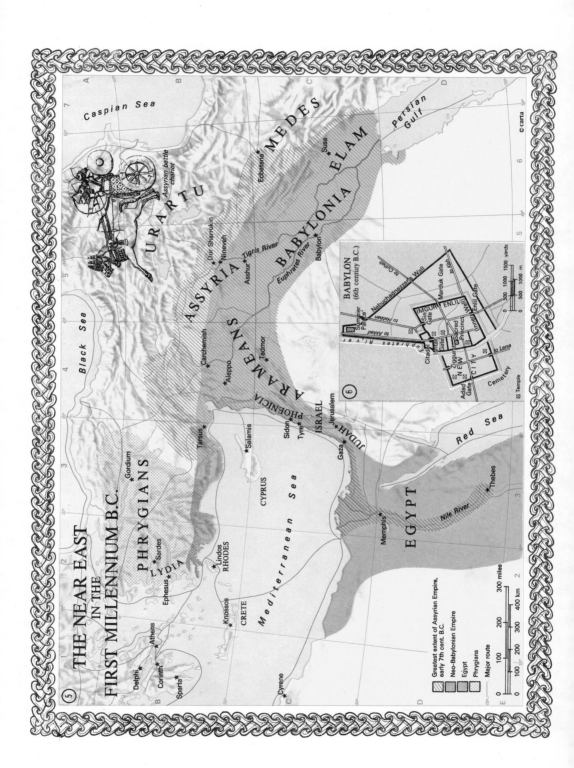

THE NEAR EAST IN THE FIRST MILLENNIUM B.C.

Caspian Sea

Black Sea

URARTU

MEDES

ELAM

Susa

Ecbatana

ASSYRIA

Dur Sharrukin
Nineveh
Asshur
Tigris River

BABYLONIA

Euphrates River
Babylon

Persian Gulf

© carta

Assyrian battle chariot

ARAMEANS

Carchemish

Aleppo

Tadmor

PHOENICIA

Tarsus

Salamis

Sidon
Tyre
ISRAEL
Jerusalem
JUDAH
Gaza

CYPRUS

Mediterranean Sea

Red Sea

Memphis

EGYPT

Nile River

Thebes

PHRYGIANS

Gordium

Sardes
LYDIA
Ephesus

Lindos
RHODES

Knossos
CRETE

Delphi
Athens
Corinth
Sparta

Cyrene

BABYLON
(6th century B.C.)

to Kutha

Nebuchadnezzar's Wall

Sumer
Palace
Citadel
Sin Gate
Marduk Gate
to Habban
to AKKAD
Ishtar Gate
Adad Gate
Sacred Precinct
Ziggurat
Enlil Gate
(Inner Wall)
IMGUR ENLIL
N E W CITY
Euphrates River
to Larsa
Cemetery

0   500   1000   1500 yards
0   500   1000 m

⊠ Temple

Greatest extent of Assyrian Empire, early 7th cent. B.C.

Neo-Babylonian Empire

Egypt

Phrygians

Major route

0   100   200   300 miles
0   100   200   300   400 km

THE LAND OF CANAAN

7

Arvad
Sumur
Arqa
Kedesh
1286 B.C.
Ullaza
Ardata
Zedad
Ziphron
Batruna
Mt. Hor
Hazar-enan
Byblos
Lebo
Khashabu
Hazi
Sidon
Migdal
Litani River
Damascus
Mt. Hermon
Ijon
Tyre
Abel
Usu
Laish
Kadesh
Hazor
Acco
Ashtaroth
Mishal
Hannathon
Sea of Chinnereth
Kenath
Achshaph
Mt. Carmel
Shimon
Mt. Tabor
En-anab
Dor
Yanoam
Yarmuk River
Megiddo
Shunem
Bezer
Salecah
1468 B.C.
Taanach
Beth-shean
Migdal
Jordan River
Pehel
Ramoth-gilead
Gath-padalla
Zaphon
Shechem
Zarethan
Jabbok River
Joppa
Aphek
Lod
Rabbah
Gezer
Beth-horon
Ashdod
Aijalon
Gibeon
Jericho
Beth-haram
Heshbon
Ashkelon
Gath
Jerusalem
Mt. Nebo
Gaza
Eglon
Keilah
Lachish
Hebron
Dibon
Yurza
Arnon River
Sharuhen
c. 1570 B.C.
Arad
Beersheba
Hormah
Kir-moab
Zoar
Negeb
Zered River
Mt. Seir
Tamar
Bozrah
Kadesh-barnea
Punon

Mediterranean Sea

Dead Sea

□ Mentioned in the Execration Texts, 20th-19th cent. B.C.
■ Mentioned in the el-Amarna Letters, 15th-14th cent. B.C.
○ Egyptian garrison city
⚔ Battle

0   20   40   60 miles
0 20 40 60 80 km

© carta

Canaanite priest

THE WALLS OF JERICHO
(7th to late 2nd millennia B.C.)

8

Cemetery area

Later Canaanite walls

Early Canaanite walls

Neolithic tower

Spring

Middle Canaanite buildings

Modern road

0   20 40 60 yards
0   20 40 m

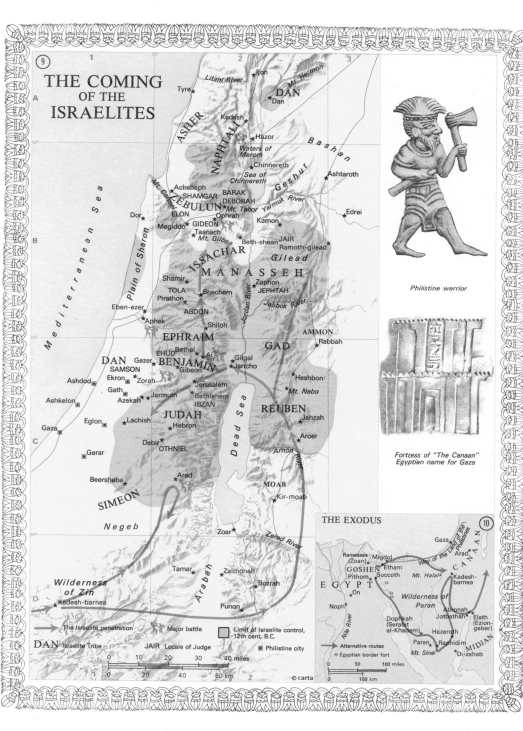

THE COMING OF THE ISRAELITES

⑨

Litani River · Ijon · Mt. Hermon

DAN

Tyre · Kedesh · Dan

ASHER · Hazor

NAPHTALI · Waters of Merom

Bashan

Achshaph · Chinnereth · Sea of Chinnereth · Ashtaroth

Mt. Carmel · SHAMGAR · BARAK · Geshur

ZEBULUN · DEBORAH · Yarmuk River

ELON · Mt. Tabor · Edrei

Dor · GIDEON · Ophrah · Kamon

Megiddo · Taanach

Mt. Gilboa · Beth-shean · **JAIR**

ISSACHAR · Ramoth-gilead

Gilead

Shamir · **MANASSEH** · Zaphon

TOLA · Shechem · **JEPHTAH**

Pirathon · *Jabbok River*

Eben-ezer · ABDON

Aphek · Shiloh

EPHRAIM · **AMMON**

Bethel · Ai · Rabbah

EHUD · Gilgal

DAN · Gezer · **BENJAMIN** · Jericho

SAMSON · Gibeon

Ashdod · Ekron · Zorah · Jerusalem · Heshbon

Gath · Azekah · Bethlehem · Mt. Nebo

Ashkelon · Jarmuth · **IBZAN**

Gaza · Eglon · **JUDAH** · **REUBEN**

Lachish · Hebron · Jahzah

Gerar · Debir · **OTHNIEL** · Aroer

Arnon River

Beersheba · Arad

MOAB

SIMEON · Kir-moab

Negeb

Zoar · Zered River

Wilderness of Zin · *Arabah*

Kadesh-barnea · Tamar · Zalmonah · Bozrah

Punon

Mediterranean Sea · Plain of Sharon · Jordan River · Dead Sea

→ The Israelite penetration ⚔ Major battle ▢ Limit of Israelite control, 12th cent. B.C.

DAN Israelite Tribe **JAIR** Locale of Judge ◼ Philistine city

0 10 20 30 40 miles
0 20 40 60 km

© carta

Philistine warrior

Fortress of "The Canaan" Egyptian name for Gaza

THE EXODUS ⑩

Gaza · Arad

Ramesses (Zoan) · Migdol · *Way of the Land of the Philistines*

GOSHEN · Etham · **CANAAN**

Pithom · Succoth · Mt. Halal · Kadesh-barnea

On · *Wilderness of Paran*

EGYPT

Noph

Abronah

Dophkah (Serabit el-Khadem) · Jotbathah · Elath (Ezion-geber)

Nile River · Hazeroth

Paran · Rephidim · **MIDIAN**

Mt. Sinai · Di-zahab

→ Alternative routes ⊕ Egyptian border fort

0 50 100 miles
0 100 km

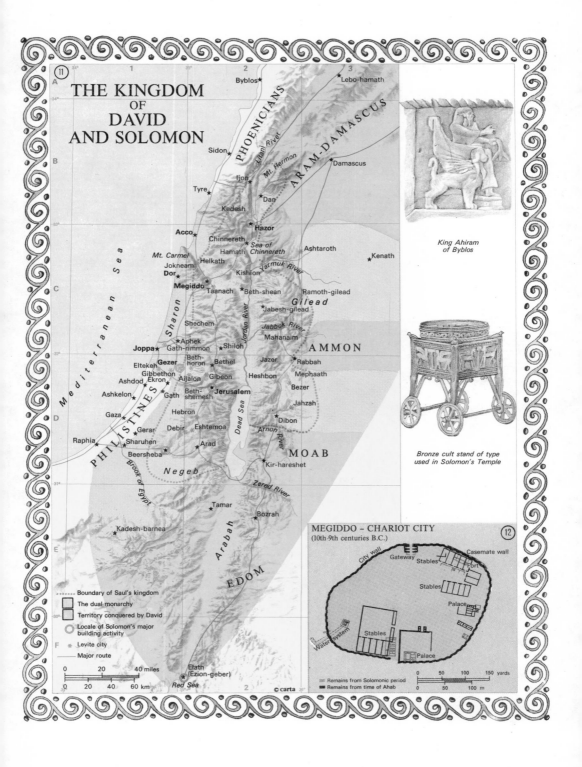

THE KINGDOM OF DAVID AND SOLOMON

11

Byblos ★

Lebo-hamath ★

PHOENICIANS

ARAM-DAMASCUS

Sidon ★

Damascus ★

Litani River

Mt. Hermon

Ijon ★

Tyre ★

Dan ★

Kedesh ★

Acco ★

Chinnereth ★

Hazor ★

Hamath

Sea of Chinnereth

Ashtaroth ★

Mt. Carmel

Helkath ★

Kenath ★

Jokneam ★

Kishion

Yarmuk River

Dor ★

Megiddo ★

Taanach ★

Beth-shean ★

Ramoth-gilead ★

Gilead

Jabesh-gilead ★

Mediterranean Sea

Sharon

Shechem ★

Jabbok River

Mahanaim ★

Jordan River

AMMON

Joppa ★

Aphek ★

Gath-rimmon ★

Shiloh ★

Jazer ★

Rabbah ★

Eltekeh ★

Gezer ★

Beth-horon ★

Bethel ★

Gibbethon ★

Ashdod ★

Ekron ★

Aijalon ★

Gibeon ★

Heshbon ★

Mephaath ★

Ashkelon ★

Gath ★

Beth-shemesh ★

Jerusalem ★

Bezer ★

Jahzah ★

Gaza ★

Hebron ★

Dead Sea

Dibon ★

Gerar ★

Debir ★

Eshtemoa ★

Arnon River

Raphia ★

Sharuhen ★

Arad ★

MOAB

Beersheba ★

Kir-haresheth ★

Negeb

Zered River

Tamar ★

Bozrah ★

Kadesh-barnea ★

Arabah

EDOM

.... Boundary of Saul's kingdom

▢ The dual monarchy

▢ Territory conquered by David

◯ Locale of Solomon's major building activity

★ Levite city

— Major route

0   20   40 miles
0   20   40   60 km

Elath (Ezion-geber) ★

Red Sea

© carta

King Ahiram of Byblos

Bronze cult stand of type used in Solomon's Temple

MEGIDDO – CHARIOT CITY
(10th-9th centuries B.C.)

12

City wall

Gateway

Stables

Casemate wall

Fort

Stables

Palace

Water system

Stables

Palace

▢ Remains from Solomonic period
▢ Remains from time of Ahab

0   50   100   150 yards
0   50   100 m

13

THE KINGDOMS
OF
JUDAH
AND ISRAEL

Byblos
★Lebo-hamath

Zarephath★

PHOENICIANS

Litani River

Sidon

Mt. Hermon

★Damascus

ARAM-DAMASCUS

Tyre★

Dan★

Kedesh★

Bashan

Hazor★

Mediterranean Sea

ISRAEL

Karnaim★
★Ashtaroth

Rumah★
Jezreel Valley
Mt. Carmel
Sea of Chinnereth

Dor★
Megiddo★
Jezreel★

Yarmuk River

Taanach★

Jordan River

★Ramoth-gilead

Samaria★
Tirzah★

Shechem★
Succoth★
Penuel★

Plain of Sharon

Joppa★
Aphek★

AMMON

Gedor★

Rabbah★

Bethel★
Gezer★
Jericho★

PHILISTINES
Ashdod★
Ekron
Jerusalem
Heshbon★

Ashkelon★
Gath★
Lachish★

JUDAH
Hebron★

Gaza★
En-gedi★

Dead Sea

★Dibon

Arnon River

MOAB

Beersheba★
Arad★

Kir-haresheth★

Negeb

Zered River

Tamar★

Bozrah★

Kadesh-barnea★

EDOM

Arabah

Teman★

Divided Kingdom
10th cent. B.C.

Jeroboam II and Uzziah,
mid 8th cent. B.C.

Israel at the time of
Tiglath-Pileser III, 732 B.C.

Josiah,
639 B.C.

Border between
Israel and Judah

★Copper Mines

| 0 | 20 | 40 miles |

| 0 | 20 | 40 | 60 km |

Elath★

*Seal of a high
Judean official*

*Royal Judean
seal-stamp*

14

JERUSALEM
OF THE OLD TESTAMENT
(early 6th century B.C.)

Hananel
Tower
"The
Corner"

Fish Gate
Sheep
Gate

Markets
Temple
Muster
Gate

Old Gate
East Gate

Palace

Ephraim Gate
Horse Gate

Prison
Water
Gate

MISHNEH
Ophel
Wall

Broad Wall

Tower of
Ovens
"Angle"

Valley Gate
Gihon
Spring

CITY OF DAVID
OPHEL

MAKHTESH

Royal
Tombs

Dung Gate

Siloam Pool
Fountain Gate

"Gate between the
Two Walls"

© carta

| 0 | 100 | 200 | 300 yards |

| 0 | 100 | 200 m |

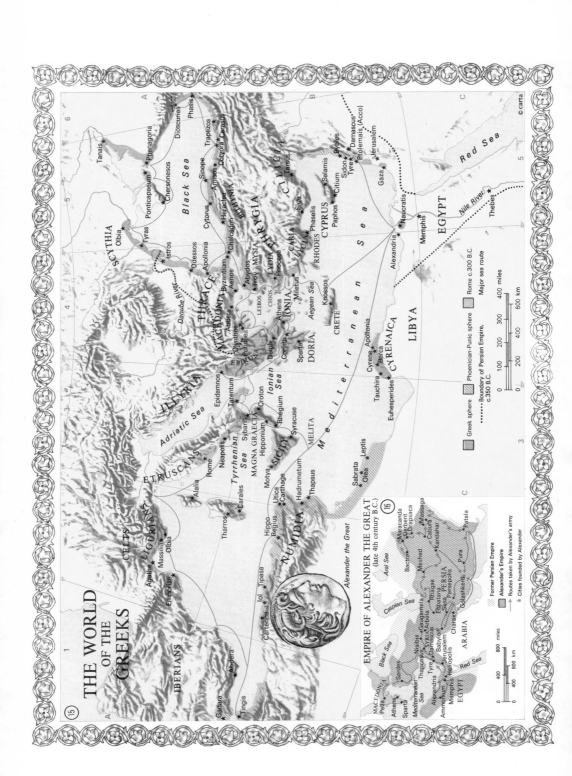

THE WORLD
OF THE
GREEKS

15

IBERIANS

Gadara
Tingis
Abdera
Cartenna
Iol Tipasa
Emporiae
Olbia
Massilia
Agathe
CELTS
LIGURIANS

Tharros
Tingis
Hippo Regius
Carales
Alalia
Rome
Neapolis
ETRUSCANS
Tyrrhenian Sea

Utica
Carthage
Hadrumetum
Thapsus

Motya
Hipponium
Rhegium
Syracuse
Croton
Sybaris
Tarentum
Epidamnos

MAGNA GRAECIA
SICILIA
MELITA
Ionian Sea
Adriatic Sea

ILLYRIA

NUMIDIA

Sabrata
Olea
Leptis

LIBYA

Tauchira
Barca
Euhesperides
Cyrene
Apollonia
CYRENAICA

Alexander the Great

SCYTHIA

Tanais
Phenagoria
Chersonesos
Ponticapaeum
Olbia
Tyras
Istros

Danube River

THRACE

Odessos
Apollonia
Byzantium
Aenos
Abdera
Chalcedon
Abydos

MACEDONIA
Olynthos
Potidaea

EPIRUS
Delphi
Corcyra
Athens
Sparta

LESBOS
CHIOS
Troy
MYSIA
PHRYGIA
LYDIA
IONIA
Phocaea
Miletus
CARIA
LYCIA

Aegean Sea

DORIA

CRETE
Knossos

Mediterranean Sea

RHODES

Black Sea

Dioscurias
Phasis
Trapezos
Cerasus
Cotyora
Amisos
Sinope
Heraclea
Cytorus
BITHYNIA

CILICIA
Tarsus
Side
Byblos
Damascus (Acco)
Sidon
Tyre
Ptolemais (Acco)
Jerusalem
Salamis
Citium
Paphos
Phaselis
CYPRUS
Gaza

Red Sea

Naucratis
Memphis
EGYPT
Nile River
Thebes

Alexandria

Greek sphere
Phoenician-Punic sphere
Rome c.300 B.C.
Boundary of Persian Empire, c.350 B.C.
Major sea route

0 100 200 300 400 miles
0 200 400 600 km

© carta

EMPIRE OF ALEXANDER THE GREAT
(late 4th century B.C.)

16

MACEDONIA
Pella
Athens
Sparta

Black Sea

Sardes
Thapsacus
Nisibis
Gaugamela
Arbela
SYRIA
Tyre
Babylon
Jerusalem
Charax

EGYPT
Ammonium
Memphis
Heliopolis

ARABIA

Red Sea

Mediterranean Sea
Alexandria

Caspian Sea
Aral Sea

Rhagae
Ecbatana
Susa
PERSIA
Persepolis
Pura
Gedrosia
Patala

Meshed
Bactra
Maracanda
Drapsaca
Herent
Caburn
Massaga
Kandahar

Former Persian Empire
Alexander's Empire
Routes taken by Alexander's army
Cities founded by Alexander

0 400 800 miles
0 400 800 km

THE ROMAN EMPIRE

Roman infantry officers

⑰

Atlantic Ocean

North Sea

HIBERNIA

BRITANNIA
Eburacum
Lindum
Londinium
Aquae Sulis

GALLIA
Lutetia
Burdigala
Narbo
Massilia
Nemausus

HISPANIA
Gades
Corduba
Toletum
Valentia
Tarraco

MAURETANIA

AFRICA
Carthage
Hippo Regius
Leptis Magna

GERMANIA
Regina Castra
Vindobona
Colonia Agrippina
Mogontiacum
Augusta
Genava

Mediolanum
Aquileia

RAETIA
NORICUM
PANNONIA
ILLYRICUM
DACIA
MOESIA
THRACE

ITALIA
Rome
Ancona
Neapolis
Brundisium

Rhine River
Danube River

SARMATIA

Black Sea

MACEDONIA
ACHAIA
Thessalonica
Athens
Corinth
Byzantium
Olbia
Ponticapaeum

CRETE

Mediterranean Sea

CYRENE
Cyrene

EGYPT
Memphis
Alexandria
Nile River

BITHYNIA
PAPHLAGONIA
Pergamum
Ephesus
Ancyra
PHRYGIA
GALATIA
CAPPADOCIA
PONTUS
Tarsus
CILICIA

CYPRUS

SYRIA
Antioch
Tyre
Damascus
JUDEA
Jerusalem

ARMENIA
Artaxata
ASSYRIA
MESOPOTAMIA
Palmyra
Tigris River
Euphrates River
PARTHIA
Ctesiphon

ARABIA

Roman Empire, A.D.14
Roman Empire at its greatest extent, A.D. 117
Major route

0   200   400   600 miles
0   200   400   600   800 km

© carta 2

ROME (1st–3rd centuries A.D.)

⑱

Circus of Nero
VATICAN HILL
Circus of Hadrian
Tomb of Augustus
Mausoleum of Hadrian
Theater of Pompey
Circus of Pompey
Pantheon
CAPITOLINE HILL
Capitol
Roman Forum
PALATINE HILL
Circus Maximus
AVENTINE HILL
CAELIAN HILL
Divi Claudii
Baths of Caracalla
Colosseum
Imperial Fora
Baths of Trajan
ESQUILINE HILL
VIMINAL HILL
Baths of Diocletian
QUIRINAL HILL
PINCIAN HILL
Castra Praetoria

+ Earliest Christian sites

0   500   1000   1500 yards
0   500   1000 m

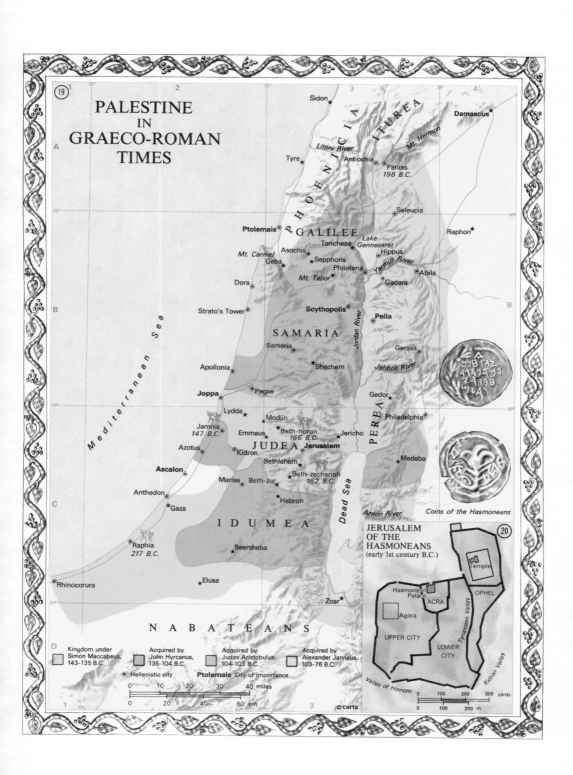

PALESTINE
IN
GRAECO-ROMAN
TIMES

⑲

A

Sidon ★

Damascus ★

Litani River

PHOENICIA ITUREA

Mt. Hermon

Tyre ★

Antiochia ★

Panias
198 B.C.

Seleucia

Raphon ★

Ptolemais ●

GALILEE

Taricheae ●

Lake
Gennesaret

Hippus ●

Mt. Carmel

Asochis ●

Sepphoris ●

Geba ★

Philoteria ●

Yarmuk River

Abila ●

Dora ●

Mt. Tabor ★

Gadara ●

Scythopolis ●

Pella ●

B

Strato's Tower ●

SAMARIA

Jordan River

Gerasa ●

Samaria ●

Jabbok River

Apollonia ●

Shechem ●

Joppa ●

Pegae ●

Gedor ★

Lydda ★

Philadelphia ●

Jamnia
147 B.C.

Modiin ★

PEREA

Emmaus ★

Beth-horon
166 B.C.

Jericho ★

Azotus ★

JUDEA Jerusalem

Kidron ●

Ascalon ●

Bethlehem ●

Medeba ●

Marisa ★

Beth-zur ★

Beth-zechariah
162 B.C.

Anthedon ●

Hebron ★

C

Gaza ★

Arnon River

Coins of the Hasmoneans

IDUMEA

Dead Sea

Raphia
217 B.C.

Beersheba ★

Rhinocorura ●

Elusa ★

Zoar ★

NABATEANS

JERUSALEM
OF THE
HASMONEANS
(early 1st century B.C.)

⑳

Temple

Hasmonean
Palace

OPHEL

ACRA

Tyropoeon Valley

Agora

Kidron Valley

UPPER CITY

LOWER
CITY

Valley of Hinnom

0   100   200   300 yards

0   100   200 m

D

Kingdom under
Simon Maccabeus,
143-135 B.C.

Acquired by
John Hyrcanus,
135-104 B.C.

Acquired by
Judas Aristobulus,
104-103 B.C.

Acquired by
Alexander Janneus,
103-76 B.C.

● Hellenistic city   **Ptolemais** City of importance

0   10   20   30   40 miles

0   20   40   60 km

© carta

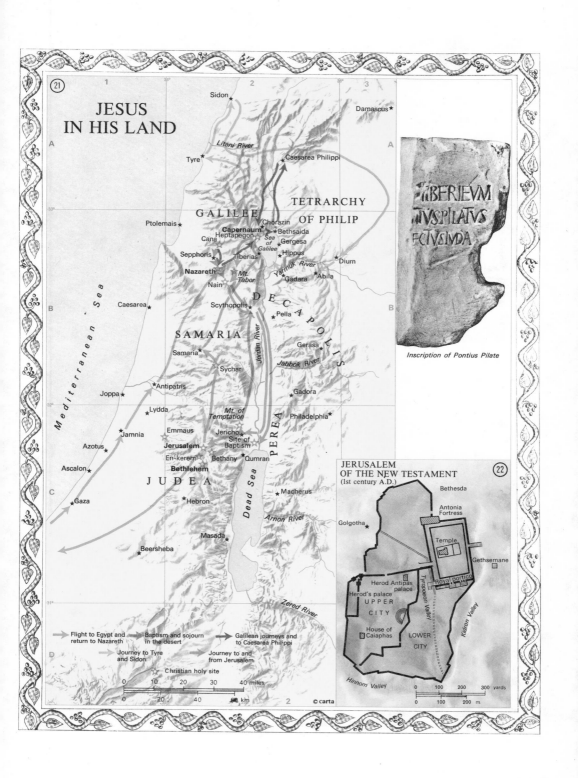

21

JESUS
IN HIS LAND

1   2   3

Sidon★

Damascus★

Litani River

A

Tyre★

★Caesarea Philippi

TETRARCHY

GALILEE   **OF PHILIP**

Ptolemais★

Chorazin★

Capernaum★ ★Bethsaida
Heptapegon

Cana★ *Sea of Galilee*

Gergesa

Sepphoris★

Tiberias★

Hippus

Nazareth★

Mt. Tabor

Yarmuk River

Dium★

Nain★

Gadara★ ★Abila

B

Caesarea★

Scythopolis★

Pella★

DECAPOLIS

Mediterranean Sea

SAMARIA

Samaria★

Gerasa★

Sychar★

Jordan River

Jabbok River

★Antipatris

Gadora★

Joppa★

Lydda★

Mt. of Temptation

Philadelphia★

Emmaus★

Jericho★

Jerusalem

Site of Baptism

Jamnia★

Azotus★

En-kerem★ Bethany★ ★Qumran

P E R E A

Ascalon★

Bethlehem

C

J U D E A

Dead Sea

★Gaza

Hebron★

Macherus★

Arnon River

Masada★

Beersheba★

Zered River

→ Flight to Egypt and
    return to Nazareth

→ Baptism and sojourn
    in the desert

→ Galilean journeys and
    to Caesarea Philippi

→ Journey to Tyre
    and Sidon

→ Journey to and
    from Jerusalem

D

★ Christian holy site

0   10   20   30   40 miles

0   20   40 km

© carta

Inscription of Pontius Pilate

22

JERUSALEM
OF THE NEW TESTAMENT
(1st century A.D.)

Bethesda

Golgotha★

Antonia
Fortress

Temple

Gethsemane

Herod Antipas
palace

Royal portico

Herod's palace

Tyropoeon Valley

Kidron Valley

**UPPER
CITY**

House of
Caiaphas

**LOWER
CITY**

Hinnom Valley

0 100 200 300 yards

0 100 200 m

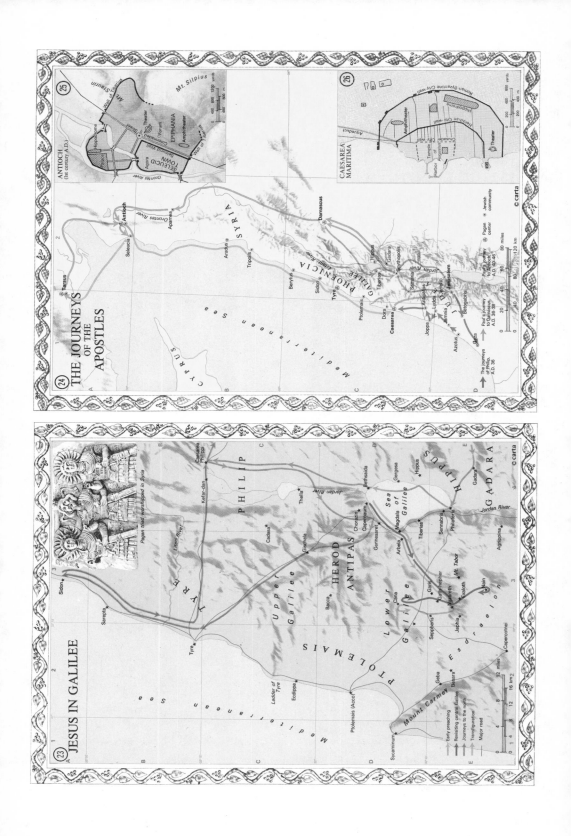

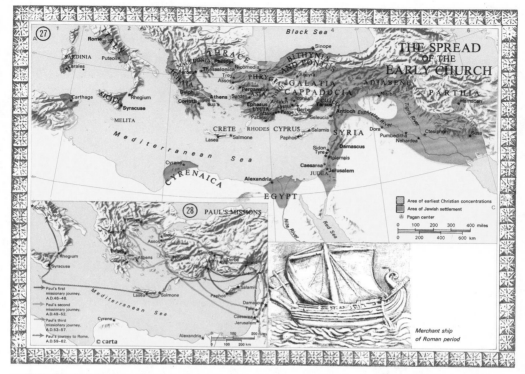

Black Sea

SARDINIA
Rome
Puteoli
Carales

THRACE
MACEDONIA
Philippi
Thessalonica
Troy
Assos
Delphi
Corinth
Athens
Pergamum
Ephesus
Attalia
Perge
Patara

Sinope

BITHYNIA AND PONTUS
Nicomedia
Ancyra
PHRYGIA
GALATIA
CAPPADOCIA
ASIA
LYCIA
Iconium
Lystra
Derbe
Sardes
Antioch
Tarsus
Seleucia

ADIABENE

PARTHIA

Hamadan

Carthage
Rhegium
Syracuse

MELITA

CRETE
Lasea
Salmone

RHODES

CYPRUS
Salamis
Paphos

Antioch
Euphrates River
SYRIA
Dora
Pumbeditha
Nehardea
Nisibis
Ctesiphon
Susa
Tigris River

THE SPREAD
OF THE
EARLY CHURCH

Mediterranean Sea

Cyrene

CYRENAICA

Alexandria

EGYPT

Sidon
Tyre
Ptolemais
Caesarea
JUDEA
Jerusalem
Damascus

Nile River
Red Sea

Area of earliest Christian concentrations
Area of Jewish settlement
Pagan center

0   100   200   300   400 miles
0   200   400   600 km

(28) PAUL'S MISSIONS

Rome
Puteoli

Rhegium
Syracuse

Philippi
Troy
Assos
Delphi
Corinth
Athens
Ephesus
Miletus

Antioch
Tarsus
Derbe
Lystra
Antioch
Seleucia

Mediterranean Sea

Lasea   Salmone

Salamis
Paphos

Damascus
Tyre
Caesarea
Jerusalem

Alexandria

Cyrene

Paul's first
missionary journey,
A.D. 46–48.

Paul's second
missionary journey,
A.D. 49–52.

Paul's third
missionary journey,
A.D. 53–57.

Paul's journey to Rome,
A.D. 59–62.

C carta

0   100   200 miles
0   100   200 km

Merchant ship
of Roman period

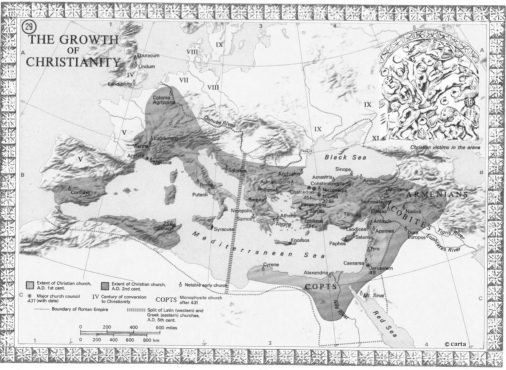

THE GROWTH
OF
CHRISTIANITY

VIII   IX

Eburacum
Lindum
Londinium
IV

VII

VIII

Colonia
Agrippina

Danube River

IX

IX

XI

Christian victims in the arena

V

Lugdunum
Vienna
Arelate
Massilia

V

V

Salonae

Black Sea

Sinope
Anchialus
Amastris
Amisos
Adrianopolis
Constantinople
Nicomedia
Nicaea   325
Chalcedon   451
Pergamum
Melitene
ARMENIANS

Corduba

Rome
Puteoli

Beroea
Philippi
Nicopolis
Samos
Athens
Aegina

Ephesus   431

Tarsus
Samosata
Edessa
Nisibis
JACOBITES
Antioch
Laodicea
Apamea
Dura
Europos

Tigris River
Euphrates River

256
Carthage

Syracuse

Knossos
Paphos

Mediterranean Sea

Cyrene

Alexandria

Caesarea
Tyre
Jerusalem   49

COPTS

Mt. Sinai

Nile River
Red Sea

Extent of Christian church, A.D. 1st cent.
Extent of Christian church, A.D. 2nd cent.
Major church council *431* (with date)
IV Century of conversion to Christianity
Boundary of Roman Empire

Notable early church
COPTS Monophysite church after 431
Split of Latin (western) and Greek (eastern) churches, A.D. 5th cent.

0   200   400   600 miles
0   200   400   600   800 km

© carta

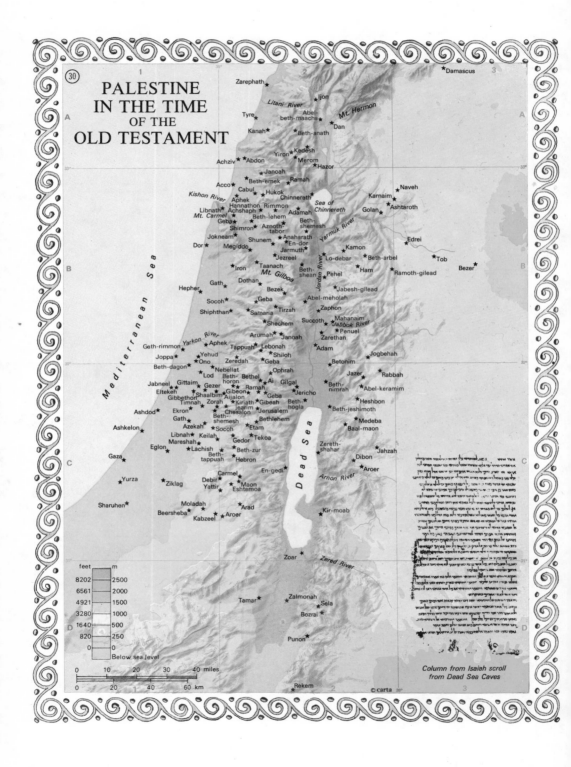

PALESTINE IN THE TIME OF THE OLD TESTAMENT

30

★ Damascus

Zarephath ★

Litani River

Ijon ★

Tyre ★   Abel-beth-maacha ★   Mt. Hermon

Kanah ★   Beth-anath ★   Dan ★

Yiron ★ Kedesh ★

Achziv ★ Abdon ★   Merom ★   Hazor ★

Janoah ★

Acco ★   Beth-emek ★ Ramah ★

Cabul ★   Hukok ★   Karnaim ★   Naveh ★

Kishon River   Aphek ★   Chinnereth ★

Hannathon ★ Rimmon ★   Sea of Chinnereth   Golan ★ Ashtaroth ★

Libnath ★ Achshaph ★   Adamah ★

Mt. Carmel   Beth-lehem ★   Beth-shemesh ★

Geba ★   Aznoth-tabor ★   Yarmuk River

Shimron ★   Anaharath ★   Edrei ★

Jokneam ★   Shunem ★ En-dor ★   Kamon ★   Tob ★

Dor ★ Megiddo ★   Jarmuth ★   Lo-debar ★ Beth-arbel ★   Bezer ★

Jezreel ★   Beth-shean ★ Pehel ★   Ham ★

Iron ★ Taanach ★   Ramoth-gilead ★

Hepher ★   Dothan ★ Mt. Gilboa   Jabesh-gilead ★

Gath ★   Bezek ★   Abel-meholah ★

Socoh ★ Geba ★   Zaphon ★

Shiphthan ★ Samaria ★ Tirzah ★   Succoth ★ Mahanaim

Shechem ★   Jabbok River   Penuel ★

Arumah ★ Janoah ★   Zarethan ★

Geth-rimmon ★   Aphek ★ Lebonah ★   Adam ★

Yarkon River   Tappuah ★ Shiloh ★

Joppa ★   Yehud ★   Zeredah ★ Geba ★   Betonim ★   Jogbehah ★

Beth-dagon ★   Ono ★   Ophrah ★

Nebellat ★   Beth-horon ★ Bethel ★   Jazer ★ Rabbah ★

Lod ★   Ai ★ Gilgal ★

Jabneel ★ Gittaim ★   Gezer ★ Ramah ★   Jericho ★   Beth-nimrah ★ Abel-keramim ★

Eltekeh ★   Gibeon ★ Geba ★

Gibbethon ★ Shaalbim ★ Aijalon ★   Gibeah ★   Heshbon ★

Timnah ★ Zorah ★   Kiriath-jearim ★ Jerusalem ★ Beth-hogla ★

Ekron ★   Chesalon ★   Beth-jeshimoth ★

Ashdod ★   Gath ★ Azekah ★   Beth-shemesh ★ Bethlehem ★   Medeba ★

Socoh ★ Etam ★   Baal-maon ★

Ashkelon ★   Libnah ★ Keilah ★   Tekoa ★

Mareshah ★   Gedor ★   Zereth-shahar ★ Jahzah ★

Eglon ★ Lachish ★ Beth-zur ★   Dibon ★

Gaza ★   Beth-tappuah ★ Hebron ★   Aroer ★

En-gedi ★   Arnon River

Yurza ★   Carmel ★

Ziklag ★   Debir ★ Maon ★   Kir-moab ★

Yattir ★ Eshtemoa ★

Sharuhen ★   Arad ★

Moladah ★

Beersheba ★ Kabzeel ★ Aroer ★

Mediterranean Sea

Jordan River

Dead Sea

Zoar ★   Zered River

Tamar ★   Zalmonah ★ Sela ★

Bozrah ★

Punon ★

Rekem ★

© carta

feet / m
feet	m
8202	2500
6561	2000
4921	1500
3280	1000
1640	500
820	250
0	0

Below sea level

0 10 20 30 40 miles
0 20 40 60 km

Column from Isaiah scroll from Dead Sea Caves

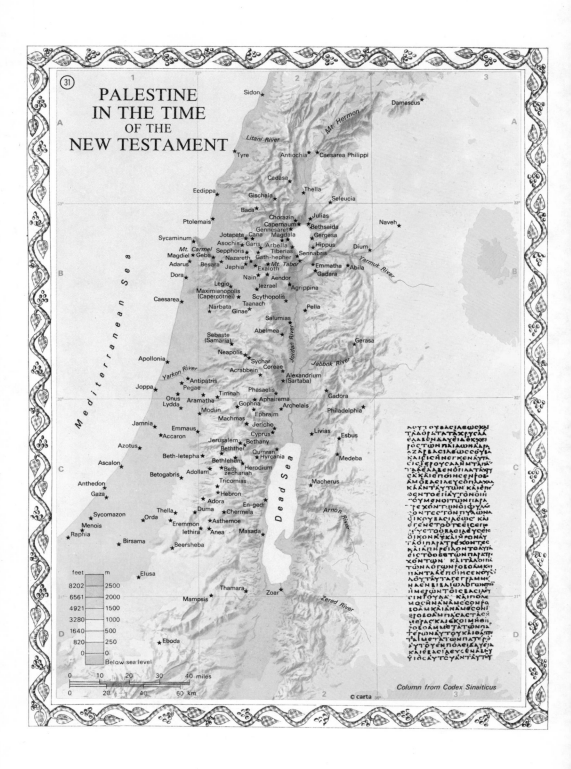

31

PALESTINE
IN THE TIME
OF THE
NEW TESTAMENT

Sidon

Damascus

Mt. Hermon

Litani River

Tyre

Antiochia   Caesarea Philippi

Cadasa

Ecdippa   Gischala   Thella

Baca   Seleucia

Ptolemais   Chorazin   Julias

Capernaum   Bethsaida

Sycaminum   Gennesaret   Naveh

Jotapata Cana   Magdala

Asochis Garis   Gergesa

Mt. Carmel Sepphoris Arbella   Hippus   Dium

Magdiel Geba   Nazareth Tiberias   Sennabris   Yarmuk River

Adarus   Besara Japhia Gath-hepher Sarnabris

Dora   Nain   Exaloth Mt. Tabor   Emmatha Abila

Aendor   Gadara

Legio   Jezreel Agrippina

Maximianopolis   Scythopolis

Caesarea   (Capercotnei)

Narbata Ginae   Taanach   Pella

Salumias

Abelmea

Sebaste   Gerasa

(Samaria)

Apollonia   Neapolis

Sychar   Jabbok River

Yarkon River   Acrabbein Coreae

Joppa   Antipatris   Alexandrium

Pegae   Phasaelis   (Sartaba)

Onus Aramatha Timnah   Gadora

Lydda   Gophna Aphairema   Philadelphia

Jamnia   Modin   Archelais

Emmaus   Machmas Ephraim

Accaron   Jericho   Livias

Jerusalem Cyprus   Esbus

Azotus   Bethany

Bethther   Qumran   Medeba

Ascalon   Beth-letepha Bethlehem Hyrcania

Betogabris Adollam Beth-   Herodium   Macherus

zechariah

Anthedon   Tricornias

Gaza   Hebron

Adora   En-gedi   Arnon River

Sycomazon   Thella Duma Chermela

Menois Orda Eremmon Asthemoe

Raphia   Iethira Anea Masada

Birsama

Beersheba

Elusa

Thamara

Mampsis   Zoar   Zered River

Eboda

Mediterranean Sea

Jordan River

Dead Sea

feet	m
8202	2500
6561	2000
4921	1500
3280	1000
1640	500
820	250
0	0
	Below sea level

0   10   20   30   40 miles

0   20   40   60 km

© carta

Column from Codex Sinaiticus

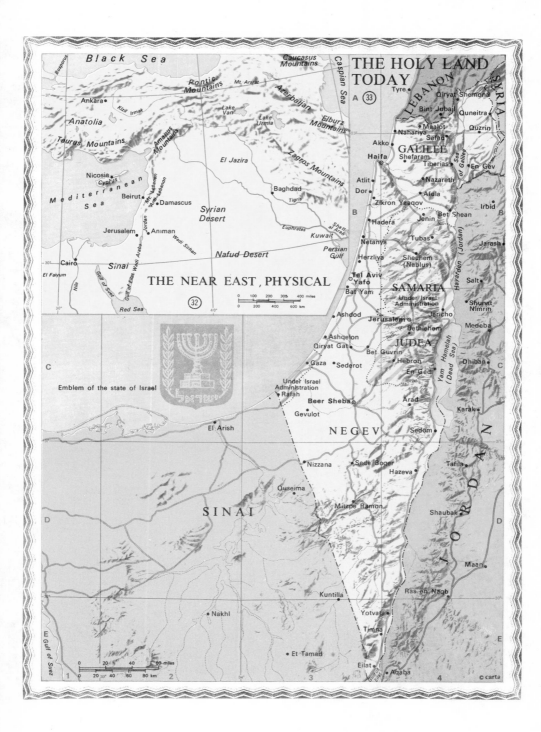

THE HOLY LAND TODAY

A ③③

Black Sea

Caucasus Mountains

Caspian Sea

LEBANON

SYRIA

Pontic Mountains

Mt. Ararat

Tyre

Qiryat Shemona

Ankara

Kizil Irmak

Lake Van

Azerbaijan

Bint Jubail

Quneitra

Anatolia

Lake Urmia

Elburz Mountains

Maalot

Quzrin

Nahariya

Taurus Mountains

Amanus Mountains

El Jazira

Zagros Mountains

Akko

Safad

En Gev

Nicosia

Cyprus

Baghdad

Haifa

GALILEE

Shefaram

Tiberias

Sea of Galilee

Mediterranean

Mt. Lebanon

Anti-Lebanon

Beirut

Damascus

Tigris

Atlit

Nazareth

Sea

Dor

Afula

Irbid

Syrian Desert

Zikron Yaaqov

Bet Shean

B

Jerusalem

Anman

Euphrates

Shatt al Arab

Hadera

Jenin

Jarash

Jordan

Wadi Sirhan

Kuwait

Netanya

Tubas

Cairo

Nafud Desert

Persian Gulf

Herzliya

Shechem (Nablus)

Salt

El Faiyum

Sinai

Tel Aviv Yafo

SAMARIA

Havarden (Jordan)

THE NEAR EAST, PHYSICAL

Bat Yam

Under Israel Administration

Shunat Nimrin

③②

Nile

Gulf of Elat, Wadi Araba

Gulf of Suez

Red Sea

0 100 200 300 400 miles
0 200 400 600 km

Ashdod

Jericho

Medeba

Jerusalem

Bethlehem

Yam Hamelah (Dead Sea)

Dhiban

30°

Ashqelon

JUDEA

Qiryat Gat

Bet Guvrin

Hebron

En Gedi

C

Gaza

Sederot

Karak

Emblem of the state of Israel

Under Israel Administration

Rafah

Beer Sheba

Arad

Gevulot

NEGEV

Sedom

JORDAN

El Arish

Nizzana

Sede Boqer

Hazeva

Tafila

Quseima

Mitzpe Ramon

Shaubak

SINAI

D

Maan

Kuntilla

Ras en Naqb

Nakhl

Yotvata

Timna

Gulf of Suez

Et Tamad

Eilat

Aqaba

E

0 20 40 60 miles
0 20 40 60 80 km

1   2   3   4

© carta